A D A

MINNESOTA
Duluth
Minneapolis ★ St. Paul
Sioux City
IOWA
Des Moines
Omaha Cedar Rapids Iowa City
CENTRAL LOWLAND
Topeka Kansas City
Jefferson City
MISSOURI St. Louis
OZARK
Tulsa PLATEAU
Little Rock
ARKANSAS
Memphis
llas Shreveport
LOUISIANA Jackson
MISSISSIPPI
Baton Rouge Mobile
Lake Charles New Orleans Pensacola
Houston

Lake Superior

WISCONSIN
Madison ★
Milwaukee
Grand Rapids Flint
Detroit
Lansing
Chicago
Peoria
ILLINOIS INDIANA
Springfield ★ Muncie
Indianapolis ★

MICHIGAN
Lake Michigan
Lake Huron

Lake Erie
Toledo Cleveland
OHIO
Columbus
Cincinnati
Wheeling
Louisville Frankfort
KENTUCKY Lexington
Bowling Green
Nashville Knoxville
TENNESSEE
Chattanooga
Birmingham
ALABAMA
Montgomery
GEORGIA
Macon
Atlanta
Columbia
SOUTH CAROLINA
Savannah
Charleston
Tallahassee Jacksonville

Wabash R.
Ohio R.
Missouri R.
Mississippi R.
Tennessee R.
Alabama R.

Lake Ontario
St. Lawrence
VERMONT MAINE
Augusta
Montpelier ★ Portland
Concord NEW HAMPSHIRE
Manchester
Boston
Springfield MASSACHUSETTS
Rochester Albany Providence
Buffalo Hartford RHODE ISLAND
NEW YORK CONNECTICUT
Newark New York City
PENNSYLVANIA Trenton
Harrisburg NEW JERSEY
Pittsburgh Philadelphia
Baltimore Dover
Annapolis DELAWARE
Washington, D.C. MARYLAND
WEST Charleston Richmond
VIRGINIA
VIRGINIA Norfolk
Winston- Raleigh
Salem
NORTH CAROLINA
Charlotte

Hudson R.
James R.
APPALACHIAN MTS.
ATLANTIC COASTAL PLAIN

ATLANTIC OCEAN

Orlando
Tampa
St. Petersburg FLORIDA
Miami
Key West

GULF OF MEXICO

Elevation

Feet		Meters
10,000		3,050
5,000		1,525
2,000		610
1,000		305
500		153
Sea level		Sea level
Below sea level		Below sea level

⊛ National capital
★ State capital
• Other city

0   100   200   300   400   500 miles
0   200   400   600   800 kilometers

A PEOPLE AND A NATION

A People and A Nation

A HISTORY OF THE UNITED STATES

Fourth Edition

Mary Beth Norton
Cornell University

David M. Katzman
University of Kansas

Paul D. Escott
Wake Forest University

Howard P. Chudacoff
Brown University

Thomas G. Paterson
University of Connecticut

William M. Tuttle, Jr.
University of Kansas

HOUGHTON MIFFLIN COMPANY

Boston   Toronto
Geneva, Illinois   Palo Alto   Princeton, New Jersey

Mary Beth Norton

Born in Ann Arbor, Michigan, Mary Beth Norton received her B.A. from the University of Michigan (1964) and her Ph.D. from Harvard University (1969). Her dissertation won the Allan Nevins Prize. She is now Mary Donlon Alger Professor of American History at Cornell University. She has written *The British-Americans* (1972) and *Liberty's Daughters* (1980), and she has edited *To Toil the Livelong Day: America's Women at Work, 1790–1980* (with Carol Groneman, 1987), *Women of America* (with Carol Berkin, 1979) and *Major Problems in American Women's History* (1989). Her many articles have appeared in such journals as the *William and Mary Quarterly*, *Signs*, and the *American Historical Review*. Mary Beth has served on the National Council on the Humanities, as president of the Berkshire Conference of Women Historians, as vice president for research of the American Historical Association, and as general editor of the *AHA Guide to Historical Literature* (3rd edition). She has advised many colleges on curriculum development in women's history and gender studies. She also helped to organize the International Federation for Research in Women's History. Her scholarship has received assistance from the Shelby Cullom Davis Center, Charles Warren Center, National Endowment for the Humanities, Rockefeller Foundation, and Guggenheim Foundation. Siena College, Marymount Manhattan College, DePauw University, and Illinois Wesleyan University have recognized her with honorary degrees.

David M. Katzman

Born in New York City and a graduate of Queens College (B.A., 1963) and the University of Michigan (Ph.D., 1969), David M. Katzman is now professor of history at the University of Kansas. He has written *Before the Ghetto: Black Detroit in the Nineteenth Century* (1973) and *Seven Days a Week: Women and Domestic Service in Industrializing America* (1978), which won the Philip Taft Labor History Prize. With William M. Tuttle, Jr., he has edited *Plain Folk* (1982). He has contributed to *Three Generations in Twentieth-Century America* (1982) and has written articles for the *Dictionary of American Biography*. The Guggenheim Foundation, National Endowment for the Humanities, and Ford Foundation have awarded him research assistance. David has been a visiting professor at University College, Dublin, Ireland, and at the University of Birmingham, England. He has also directed National Endowment for the Humanities Summer Seminars for College Teachers. Active in the profession, David has served on committees of the American Historical Association, Organization of American Historians, Southern Historical Association, and Immigration History Association. He has sat on the Board of Directors of the National Commission on Social Studies and has been Editor of *American Studies*. At the University of Kansas, where he has directed the College Honors Program, he has been recognized for his teaching excellence.

Paul D. Escott

Born and raised in the Midwest (St. Louis, Missouri), Paul D. Escott studied in New England (Harvard College, B.A., 1969) and the South (Duke University, Ph.D., 1974). Paul is now Reynolds Professor of History at Wake Forest University. He has written *After Secession: Jefferson Davis and the Failure of Confederate Nationalism* (1978), *Slavery Remembered: A Record of Twentieth-Century Slave Narratives* (1979), *Many Excellent People: Power and Privilege in North Carolina, 1850–1900* (1985), and *A History of African Americans in North Carolina* (with Jeffrey J. Crow and Flora J. Hatley, 1992). He has also edited *W.J. Cash and the Minds of the South* (1992) and co-edited *Major Problems in the History of the American South* (with David R. Goldfield, 1990) and *Race, Class, and Politics in Southern History* (with Jeffrey J. Crow and Charles L. Flynn, Jr., 1989). The Rockefeller Foundation has assisted his research. Paul's articles have appeared in *Civil War History*, *The Journal of Southern History*, and *The North Carolina Historical Review*, among others. He has also contributed to W. Buck Yearns, ed., *The Governors of the Confederacy* (1984). Paul is a member of the editorial board of the forthcoming *The Encyclopedia of the Confederacy*.

Howard P. Chudacoff

University Professor and professor of history at Brown University, Howard P. Chudacoff was born in Omaha, Nebraska. He earned his A.B. (1965) and Ph.D. (1969) degrees from the University of Chicago. He has written three books: *Mobile Americans: Residential and Social Mobility in Omaha, 1880–1920* (1972), *The Evolution of American Urban Society* (with Judith Smith, 4th edition, 1993), and *How Old Are You? Age Consciousness in American Culture* (1989). He has also edited *Major Problems in American Urban History* (1993). His many articles have appeared in such journals as the *Journal of Family History, Reviews in American History,* and *Journal of American History*. He contributed "Success and Security: The Meaning of Social Mobility in America" to Stanley I. Kulter and Stanley N. Katz, eds., *The Promise of American History* (1982). The National Endowment for the Humanities, Ford Foundation, and Rockefeller Foundation have given Howard awards to advance his scholarship. In this country and abroad, he has lectured on many topics, among them the American family and social mobility. At Brown University, he has co-chaired the American Civilization Program and chaired the department of history.

Thomas G. Paterson

Born in Oregon City, Oregon, and graduated from the University of New Hampshire (B.A., 1963) and the University of California, Berkeley (Ph.D., 1968), Thomas G. Paterson is now professor of history at the University of Connecticut. He has written *Soviet-American Confrontation* (1973), *Meeting the Communist Threat* (1988), *On Every Front: The Making and Unmaking of the Cold War* (1992), and *American Foreign Relations* (with J. Garry Clifford and Kenneth J. Hagan, 4th edition, 1994). Tom has also edited *Kennedy's Quest for Victory* (1989), *Origins of the Cold War* (with Robert J. McMahon, 3rd edition, 1991), *Explaining the History of American Foreign Relations* (with Michael J. Hogan, 1991), *Imperial Surge* (with Stephen G. Rabe, 1992), and *Major Problems in American Foreign Relations* (with Dennis Merrill, 4th edition, 1994). His articles have appeared in the *American Historical Review, Journal of American History,* and *Diplomatic History*. He has served on the editorial boards of the latter two journals and on committees of the Organization of American Historians and the American Historical Association. He has been president of the Society for Historians of American Foreign Relations, has directed National Endowment for the Humanities Summer Seminars for College Teachers, and has been a member of the Board of Trustees of Stonehill College. A recent award was a fellowship from the Guggenheim Foundation. Tom has lectured and researched widely in the United States, as well as in Canada, China, Cuba, England, New Zealand, Puerto Rico, Russia, and Venezuela.

William M. Tuttle, Jr.

A native of Detroit, Michigan, William M. Tuttle, Jr., received his B.A. from Denison University (1959) and his Ph.D. from the University of Wisconsin (1967). Now a professor of history at the University of Kansas, Bill has written *Race Riot: Chicago in the Red Summer of 1919* (1970) and *"Daddy's Gone to War": The Second World War in the Lives of America's Children* (1993). He has also edited *W.E.B. Du Bois* (1973) and *Plain Folk* (with David Katzman, 1982). His many articles have appeared in such journals as the *Journal of American History, American Studies,* and *Technology and Culture*. He has contributed essays to Glen H. Elder, Jr., et al., eds., *Children in Time and Place* (1993) and to Paula Petrik and Elliot West, eds., *Childhood and Adolescence in America* (1992). Active in the profession, he has frequently delivered papers at the annual meetings of the American Historical Association and the Organization of American Historians. His scholarly work has been assisted by the American Council of Learned Societies, Institute of Southern History at Johns Hopkins University, Charles Warren Center, Guggenheim Foundation, Stanford Humanities Center, and National Endowment for the Humanities. He has been a research associate at the Institute of Human Development at the University of California, Berkeley. As a historical consultant, Bill has helped prepare several public television documentaries and a docudrama, *The Killing Floor,* which appeared on PBS's "American Playhouse."

Sponsoring Editor: Sean W. Wakely
Senior Development Editor: Frances W. Gay
Project Editor: Jean Levitt
Senior Production/Design Coordinator: Pat Mahtani
Cover Designer: Linda Manley Wade
Senior Manufacturing Coordinator: Priscilla Bailey
Marketing Manager: Rebecca Dudley

Cover photograph researched by Rose Corbett Gordon/Corbett Gordon Associates.

Text photographs researched by Pembroke Herbert & Sandi Ruggiel/Picture Research Consultants, Inc.

About the Cover

Chandlery figure, photograph courtesy of Mystic Seaport Museum, Inc.

Chapter Opening Photo Credits

Page 2: Illustration from the *Codex Florentino* by Fray Bernadino de Sahagen. Biblioteca Medicea Laurenziana, Florence. Photo by Alberto Scardigli.

Page 34: Detail of *America* by Theodor de Bry. Photo courtesy of the John Carter Brown Library at Brown University.

Page 62: Detail of *The Mason Children* attributed to the painter Freake-Gibbs, 1670. The Fine Arts Museum of San Francisco, gift of Mr. and Mrs. John D. Rockefeller 3rd.

Page 92: Detail of Needlepoint by Mary Woodhull, 1700. Courtesy of Colonial Williamsburg Foundation.

Page 122: Detail of *Landing of the British Troops in Boston* by Paul Revere, 1768. American Antiquarian Society.

Page 150: Detail of *The Surrender of Lord Cornwallis at Yorktown* by John Trumbull, 1787. Copyright Yale University Art Gallery.

Page 178: Detail of *William Smith and Grandson* by Charles Willson Peale, 1788. Virginia Museum of Fine Arts.

Page 208: Detail of *Arch Street* by Thomas Birch, 1799. Free Library of Philadelphia.

Page 236: Detail of *Liberty in the Form of the Goddess of Youth Giving Support to the Bald Eagle* by Abijah Canfield, 1800. Henry Ford Museum and Greenfield Village.

Printed in the U.S.A.

Library of Congress Catalog Card Number: 93-78644

ISBN: 0-395-63455-5

23456789-VH-98 97 96 95 94

(Credits continue after index.)

Brief Contents

Contents

Charts

Maps

Preface

When the authors of *A People and a Nation* began work on this fourth edition, we set several goals for ourselves. We wanted to preserve those features of the third edition that students and faculty have found attractive: our basic approach to American history as the story of all the people, our spirited narrative based upon letters, diaries, oral histories, and other sources that reveal the pulse of human experience, and our effort to challenge readers to think about the meaning of American history, not just to memorize it. We have appreciated hearing, too, that we have presented our interpretations openly and fairly and with a welcoming style that invites debate.

The authors set out to write a thorough revision. We reexamined every paragraph, interpretation, map, illustration, chart, caption, bibliography, and each part of the appendix. We scrutinized the form of each chapter—opening vignette, introduction, chronology, conclusion, suggested readings. We rewrote throughout, condensing wherever possible. One-half of the opening vignettes are new. The concluding paragraphs of each chapter have been revised to become more explicit summaries. We reorganized chapters, and we added new ones at the beginning and end to account for advances in scholarship and for momentous changes in international relations. Finally, we have added a new critical thinking feature to the fourth edition. These many revisions are described in detail later.

The Authors' Goals

Given the urgency of issues surrounding the natural environment and technology and the increasing availability of outstanding scholarship on these topics, the authors determined to expand coverage of these subjects. We immersed ourselves in the literature and sought expert advice from historians who have researched and explored these subjects. Throughout the book, then, readers will discover a greater integration of environmental and technological questions and their intersection with the experiences of the American people.

Eager to help students understand how historians go about using evidence to arrive at conclusions, the authors have introduced a new feature in each chapter: *How Do Historians Know?* A brief highlighted paragraph, coupled with an illustration, explains how historians have drawn generalizations from particular kinds of sources—census data, political cartoons, letters, maps, autobiographies, artifacts, labor records, government documents. This feature also helps us to understand how scholars can claim knowledge about particular historical events or trends.

Certain that one of the strengths of the book has been its incorporation of the very latest scholarship, the authors have drawn upon their own recent scholarly research and activities (see the biographical sketches of the authors) and the innovative work of other scholars. Changes in emphasis and interpretation mark every chapter. The Suggestions for Further Reading have been revised to present the new literature.

Determined to improve every aspect of the book, the authors and the Houghton Mifflin editors also developed a new design to make *A People and a Nation* more accessible. The graphs and charts have been redrawn, captions have been added to them and to the maps, the link between illustrative material and text has been defined more sharply, and a contemporary new look throughout reflects the freshness of this thoroughly revised edition.

In preparing this new edition, the authors maintained their tradition of enviable cooperation: They met in frank and friendly planning sessions, wrote critiques of each other's chapters, responded to many reports from instructors, and worked closely with Houghton Mifflin's talented staff to consider and reconsider every detail. We strove to give this multiauthored text a seamless quality.

As teachers and students we are always recreating our past, restructuring our memory, rediscovering the personalities and events that have shaped us, inspired us, and bedeviled us. This book is our rediscovery of America's past—its people and the nation they founded and have sustained. This history is sometimes comforting, sometimes disturbing. As with our own personal experiences, it is both triumphant and tragic, filled with both injury and healing. As memory, history is the way we identify ourselves. As this book reveals, there are many different Americans and many competing memories. We have sought to present all of them, in both triumph and tragedy.

Our View of American History

A People and a Nation is a comprehensive book in its treatment of major subject areas—social, political, diplomatic, economic, military, environmental, intellectual, and more. Issues of gender, class, religion, race, work, sexual orientation, medicine, ecology, region, and ethnicity appear throughout, as does the friction that often arises from such a diverse people.

We emphasize the everyday life of the American people, from the ordinary to the exceptional—the factory worker, the slave, the immigrant, the sales clerk, the baseball player, the small-town merchant, the urban entrepreneur, the small farmer, the film celebrity, the scientist, the army general, the senator, the president. We pay particular attention to lifestyles, diet and dress, family life and structure, gender roles, workplace conditions, and childbearing and childrearing. We ask how Americans have entertained themselves through sports, music, the graphic arts, reading, theater, film, radio, and television. We account for demographic change, geographic and social mobility, and peoples' adaptation to new environments.

Because the private sphere of everyday life intersects with public policies of government and the influential trends of a world economy, we explore the interactions of these different spheres. We also delve into Americans' expectations of their governments and the practices and impact of local, state, and federal institutions. We study not only politics, but also the culture of politics. We identify the mood and mentality of an era, searching for what Americans thought about themselves and others. We seek to understand why and how America goes to war and why diplomacy often fails. The sources of American expansion and empire abroad are plumbed throughout the book.

One of the major changes in *A People and a Nation* is the addition of considerable new material at the beginning of the book. Mary Beth Norton, who had primary responsibility for Chapters 1–8, wrote the new first chapter with expanded treatment of American peoples before Columbus, voyages of exploration and discovery, colonization of the Atlantic islands, the origins of slavery, and the development of fishing in the New World. The recast second chapter more fully covers the Caribbean islands and the sugar industry, New France, and New Netherland. This chapter also includes a revised discussion of the introduction of slavery into the mainland English colonies. Her other chapters reflect recent scholarly works.

Major Changes in This Edition

David M. Katzman, who had primary responsibility for Chapters 9–11 and 13, integrated new literature on western expansion and the impact of settlement and manufacturing on the environment, wrote a new and more focused assessment of the War of 1812, gave greater emphasis to population changes, social diversity, and education and the spread of literacy, and added a fuller explanation of the banking system.

Paul D. Escott, who had primary responsibility for Chapters 12, 14, and 15–16, expanded coverage of Supreme Court cases. He also explored in greater detail aspects of military history—strategy, tactics, technology, and the experience of soldiers.

Howard P. Chudacoff, who had primary responsibility for Chapters 17–21 and 24, like others introduced new material on the environment, especially water issues. He has redistributed the material of the previous edition's Chapter 19 (Everyday Life and Culture, 1877–1920) to two other chapters, Chapter 18 on the Machine Age and the dawn of consumerism and the current Chapter 19 on cities in the late nineteenth and early twentieth centuries. This change provides a greater chronological flow in these chapters. Also, the discussion of bosses and reformers in Chapter 19 has been substantially revised and reorganized to take into account new perspectives on urban politics.

Thomas G. Paterson, who served as the coordinating author for this book and who prepared the Appendix, had primary responsibility for Chapters 22–23, 26, 29, 31, and the new Chapter 34 on the Bush-Clinton years. With the end of the Cold War came the opportunity to rethink post-1945 foreign-relations history and to reorganize it into two chapters that address the two most prominent characteristics of the period—the Soviet-American confrontation of the Cold War and the rise of the Third World through decolonization, revolution, and war. The declassification of documents—such as those on the Cuban missile crisis—has permitted the recasting of many events. He also expanded discussion of cultural relations, military events, and U.S.-Puerto Rican affairs.

William M. Tuttle, Jr., who had primary responsibility for Chapters 25, 27, 28, 30, and 32–33, expanded treatment of the impact of government policies and economic growth on the environment, the domestic impact of war, the baby boom, child care issues, women's employment, the rise of the sunbelt, technological change (including home computers), the Watergate scandal, and immigration. He also reorganized post-1945 domestic history to coordinate it with the new foreign-relations chapters.

Many instructors and students who have used this book in their courses have found its many learning and teaching aids very useful.

Study and Teaching Aids

The *Study Guide*, prepared by George Warren and Cynthia Ricketson of Central Piedmont Community College, includes an introductory chapter on studying history that focuses on interpreting historical facts, test-taking hints, and critical analysis. The guide also includes learning objectives, a thematic guide, lists of terms, multiple-choice and essay questions for each chapter, as well as map exercises and sections on organizing information for some chapters. An answer key alerts students to the correct response and also explains why the other choices are wrong.

A *Computerized Study Guide* is also available for students. It provides approximately 15 multiple-choice questions for each chapter and functions as a tutorial that gives students information on incor-

rect as well as correct answers. The computerized guide is available in Macintosh, IBM, and IBM-compatible formats.

"Places in Time" Map Software, an animated map program, consists of four computer sessions, each focusing on a specific time period (1763, 1860, 1920, and 1980), in which the themes of population, territory, and economic development are explored.

"Places in Time" Map Workbook, a printed version of the computer program, is available for students in workbook format and can be used independently of the computer program.

A new *Instructor's Resource Manual*, prepared by Donald Frazier, Marvin Schultz, and Bruce Winders of Texas Christian University and Robert Pace of Longwood College, contains ten chronological resource units in addition to teaching ideas for each chapter of the text. Each chronological resource unit includes sections on geography, technology, physical and material culture (artifacts), historical sites, documentary films, popular films, and music. The manual also includes for each text chapter an overview of material in the chapter, a brief list of learning objectives, a comprehensive chapter outline, ideas for classroom activities, discussion questions, and ideas for paper topics.

A *Test Items* file, also prepared by George Warren, provides approximately 1,700 new multiple-choice questions, more than 1,000 identification terms, and approximately 500 essay questions.

A *Computerized Test Item File* is available to adopters for IBM and Macintosh computers. This computerized version of the printed *Test Items* file allows professors to create customized tests by editing and adding questions.

There is also a set of 95 full-color *Map Transparencies* available on adoption. All of these maps appear in *A People and a Nation*.

A variety of *videos*, documentaries and docudramas by major film producers, are available for use with *A People and a Nation*, including "The American Revolution: The Cause of Liberty," "Views of a Vanishing Frontier," "The Civil War: 1861: The Cause," "The Indomitable Teddy Roosevelt," "The Home Front," and "Awakenings" (from *Eyes on the Prize*).

At each stage of this project, historians read drafts of our chapters. Their suggestions, corrections, and pleas helped guide us through our revi-

Acknowledg-ments ────

sions. We could not include all of their recommendations, but the book is better for our having heeded most of their advice. We heartily thank:

Harriett Alonso, *Fitchburg State College*
Michael Bellesiles, *Emory University*
John D. Buenker, *University of Wisconsin, Parkside*
Ruth Schwartz Cowan, *State University of New York, Stony Brook*
Linda Ford, *Keene State College*
Duane Gage, *Tarrant County Junior College*
Roger Grant, *University of Akron*
Deborah E. Gray, *Worcester State College*
Barbara Green, *Wright State University*
David Hamilton, *University of Kentucky*
Theresa McGinley, *North Harris College*
Peter C. Mancall, *Kansas State University*
Martin Melosi, *University of Houston*
Eric Monkkonen, *University of California, Los Angeles*
Margaret Newell, *Ohio State University*

Stephen Norwood, *University of Oklahoma*
Magne Olson, *Chicago State University*
Barbara Posadas, *Northern Illinois University*
Louis Potts, *University of Missouri, Kansas City*
Henry Sage, *Northern Virginia Community College*
Richard Stott, *George Washington University*
Robert M. Weir, *University of South Carolina*
Marie Wiener, *University of Maine, Orono*

We are also pleased to thank others who helped us in various ways: Jan D. Emerson, Kathryn Nemeth Kretschmer, Brian Murphy, Gary Y. Okihiro, Noah Schwartz, Glenn Sheffield, and Samuel Watkins Tuttle. Finally, the fourth edition of this book received careful handling from several Houghton Mifflin people who have always set high standards and thrived on excellence: Jean Woy, Editor-in-Chief; Sean Wakely, Sponsoring Editor; Ann Goodsell, Development Editor; Charleen Akullian, Project Editor; and Pat Mahtani, Art Editor. We thank them very much.

For the Authors, THOMAS G. PATERSON

A PEOPLE AND A NATION

1

The Meeting of Old World and New, 1492–1600

AT BIRTH, SHE WAS CALLED Malinalli. The Spaniards christened her Doña Marina. History knows her as Malinche, a name formed by adding the Aztec suffix *che*, a term of respect, to her original name. She has been both celebrated as the symbolic mother of the modern Mexican people and maligned as a traitor to that nation's ancient residents.

Born near the Gulf Coast of Mexico sometime between 1502 and 1505, Malinalli was the daughter of a cacique, or village chief, within the Aztec empire. Her father died while she was young, and her mother soon remarried. To protect the inheritance of the son born to that second marriage, the mother sold her daughter into slavery. Eventually, Malinalli came to live with Mayan-speaking people in the province of Tabasco.

Along with nineteen other enslaved women, she was presented as a gift to the Spanish conquistador, Hernán Cortés, when he marched through Tabasco in 1519. Cortés, who first arrived in the Spanish West Indies in 1504, embarked for the mainland in search of wealthy cities rumored to exist there. Little did he know that the young woman whom the Spaniards baptized as a Christian and renamed Doña Marina would be one of the keys to his conquest of Mexico.

Doña Marina, who spoke both Nahuatl (the language of her birth and of the Aztecs) and Mayan (the language of her masters), and who soon learned Spanish, became Cortés's translator and mistress. She bore him a son, Martín—the first *mestizo*, or mixed-blood Mexican. Accompanying Cortés throughout his travels in Mexico, she did more than simply interpret words for him: she explained the meanings that lay behind the language, opening the Aztec world to the Spaniards.

Bernal Díaz del Castillo, one of Cortés's lieutenants, greatly admired Doña Marina. In his *History of the Conquest of New Spain*, he observed that she was "a valuable instrument to us. . . . It was, through her only, under the protection of the Almighty, that many things were accomplished by us: without her we never should have understood the Mexican language, and, upon the whole, have been unable to surmount many difficulties." The Aztecs even called Cortés "El Malinche," or "the captain of Marina," Bernal Díaz explained, because she "was always in his company, especially when ambassadors arrived and during talks with chiefs."

On one occasion Doña Marina saved the Spaniards from an ambush. The European invaders had halted in a village en route to Tenochtitlan, the Aztec capital. Doña Marina learned from an old woman that the villagers—friends of the Aztecs—intended to attack the invaders as they departed. Forewarned, Cortés ordered all the local chiefs killed. The Aztecs and subsequent Mexican historians blamed Malinche for betraying her own people. But who were her people? The Aztecs, in whose empire she had been born and who had sold her as a slave? The Mayas, among whom she was raised? Or the Europeans, who relied on her translations?

Malinche's life history, and her dual image as betrayer of ancient Mexico and symbolic mother of the modern mixed-race nation, encapsulate many of the ambiguities of the initial encounter between Europeans and Americans. Sold into slavery by her Aztec-connected family, she owed that people little loyalty, whereas the Spaniards gave her respect. Yet she did not become Spanish: Cortés never married her, although she was the mother of his son. She did eventually marry one of Cortés's subordinates, but it is unclear whether she had any choice in the matter. Malinche may simply have been passed from one conquistador to another, much as her family had sold her to slave traders or the Tabascans had given her to the Europeans.

Until she died around 1540, Malinche was caught between two worlds, part of both and of neither, alternately praised and blamed for her actions. Many people from both sides of the Atlantic were to meet the same fate as they attempted to cope with the rapidly changing world of the fifteenth and sixteenth centuries.

For thousands of years before 1492, human societies in the Americas had developed in isolation from the rest of the world. The era that began in the Christian fifteenth century brought that longstanding isolation to an end. As European explorers and colonizers sought to exploit the resources of the rest of the globe, peoples from different races and cultural traditions came into regular contact for the first time. All were profoundly changed by the resulting interaction. By the time Spanish troops invaded Mexico in 1519, the age of European expansion and colonization was already well under way. Over the next 350 years, Europeans would spread their influence across the globe. The history of the tiny colonies in North America that became the first members of the United States must be seen in this broad context of European exploration and exploitation.

The continents that European sailors reached in the late fifteenth century had their own history, one the invaders largely ignored. The residents of the Americas were the world's most skillful plant-breeders; they had developed vegetable crops more nutritious and productive than those grown in Europe, Asia, or Africa. They had invented systems of writing and mathematics and had created calendars fully as accurate as those used on the other side of the Atlantic. In the Americas, as in Europe, states rose and fell as leaders succeeded or failed at the goal of expanding their political and economic power. The Europeans' arrival in their world immeasurably altered the Americans' struggles with each other.

After 1400, European nations tried to improve their positions relative to neighboring countries not only by waging wars on their own continent but also by acquiring valuable colonies and trading posts elsewhere in the world. In response, nations in Asia, Africa, and the Americas attempted to use the alien intruders to their own advantage or, failing that, to adapt successfully to the Europeans' presence in their midst. All the participants in the resulting interaction of divergent cultures were indelibly affected by the process. The contest among Europeans for control of the Americas and Africa changed the course of history on four continents. Strategies selected by American and African leaders influenced the outcome of the Europeans' competition and determined the fates of their own societies. Although in the end the Europeans emerged politically dominant, they by no means controlled all aspects of the interaction among the divergent cultures of the Americas and Africa.

AMERICAN SOCIETIES

Human beings probably originated on the continent of Africa, where humanlike remains about 3 million years old have been found in what is now Ethiopia. Over many millennia, the growing human population slowly dispersed to the other continents. Because the climate was then far colder than it is now, much of the earth's water was con-

• *Important Events* •

c. 1000 B.C.E.	Olmec civilization appears	**1513**	Ponce de León explores Florida
c. 300–600 C.E.	Height of influence of Teotihuacan	**1518–1530**	Smallpox epidemic devastates Indian population of West Indies, Central and South America
c. 600–900 C.E.	Classic Mayan civilization	**1519**	Hernán Cortés invades Mexico
1001	Norse establish settlement in "Vineland" (Newfoundland)	**1521**	Tenochtitlan surrenders to Cortés; Aztec empire falls to Spaniards
1050–1250	Height of influence of Cahokia; prevalence of Mississippian culture, midwestern and southeastern United States	**1534–1535**	Jacques Cartier explores St. Lawrence River
14th century	Aztec rise to power	**1539–1542**	Hernando de Soto explores southeastern United States
1450s–1480s	Portuguese explore and colonize islands in the Mediterranean Atlantic and São Tomé in Gulf of Guinea	**1540–1542**	Francisco Vásquez de Coronado explores southwestern United States
1477	Publication of Marco Polo's *Travels*, describing China	**1565**	Spanish establish St. Augustine, first permanent European settlement within boundaries of present United States
1492	Christopher Columbus reaches Bahama Islands		
1494	Treaty of Tordesillas divides land claims between Spain and Portugal in Africa, India, and South America	**1587–1590**	Sir Walter Raleigh's Roanoke colony vanishes
1496	Last of the Canary Islands falls to Spanish attack	**1588**	Thomas Harriot publishes *A Briefe and True Report of the New Found Land of Virginia*
1497	John Cabot reaches North American coast		

centrated in huge rivers of ice called glaciers. Sea levels were accordingly lower, and land masses covered a larger proportion of the earth's surface than they do today. About 30,000 years ago, a land bridge that scholars have called Beringia linked the Asian and North American continents at the site of the Bering Strait. Some of the peoples participating in the vast worldwide migration crossed this land bridge. When the climate warmed, the glaciers receded, and the sea levels rose about 10,000 years ago, those migrants were irrevocably separated from their fellow human beings who had remained in the connected continents of Asia, Africa, and Europe.

These forerunners of the American population are known as Paleo-Indians. The earliest confirmed

Paleo-Indians

evidence of their presence in the Americas dates to approximately 28,000 years ago. The Paleo-Indians were nomadic hunters of game and gatherers of wild plants. They spread throughout North and South America, probably moving as extended families or *bands*. (*Tribes* were composed of allied bands.) By about 11,500 years ago the Paleo-Indians were making fine stone projectile points, which they attached to wooden spears and used to kill and butcher bison (buffalo), woolly mammoths, and other large mammals then living in the Americas. But as the Ice Age ended and the human population increased, all the large American mammals except the bison disappeared. Scholars cannot agree whether their

Leonhard Fuchs drew the earliest known European depiction of maize, the most important North American crop. It appeared in a book published in Basel, Switzerland, in 1542. By permission of the Houghton Library, Harvard University.

demise was caused by overhunting or by the change in climate. In either case, deprived of their primary source of meat, the Paleo-Indians had to find new ways of survival.

The most significant innovation was the development of agricultural innovation in the Americas. By approximately 7,000 years ago, the residents of what is now central Mexico began to cultivate food crops, especially maize (corn), squash, beans, and peppers. Centuries before that, people living in the Andes mountains of South America had started to grow potatoes. As knowledge of agricultural techniques improved and spread through the Americas, vegetables and maize proved a more reliable source of food than hunting and gathering. Except for those living in the harshest climates, most Americans started to adopt a more sedentary style of life so they could tend fields regularly. Some established permanent settlements; others moved several times a year among fixed sites. They became adept at clearing forests through the use of controlled burning. All the Native American cultures emphasized producing sufficient food to support them-

selves. Although they traded goods, no tribe ever became wholly dependent on another group for items vital to its survival.

Wherever agriculture dominated the economy, more complex civilizations flourished. Such societies, assured of steady supplies of grains and vegetables, no longer had to devote all their energies to subsistence. Instead, they were able to accumulate wealth, produce ornamental objects, and create elaborate rituals and ceremonies. In North America, the successful cultivation of such nutritious crops as maize, beans, and squash seems to have led to the growth and development of all the major civilizations: first the large city-states of Mesoamerica (modern Mexico and Guatemala), then the urban clusters known collectively as the Mississippian culture and located in the present-day United States. Each of these societies, many historians and archaeologists now believe, reached its height of population and influence only after achieving success in agriculture, and each declined and collapsed after reaching the limits of its food supply, with dire political and military consequences. Even the powerful Aztec empire that the Spaniards encountered in 1519 is thought to have been approaching the point at which it could no longer sustain its population.

The Aztecs were the heirs of a series of Mesoamerican civilizations, the history of which stretched back for thousands of years. The first

Olmecs and Mayas

great civilization in the region was that of the Olmecs, whose culture mysteriously appeared in the swampy lowlands near the Gulf of Mexico more than three thousand years ago and just as mysteriously disappeared about one thousand years later. The Olmecs created urban centers with ceremonial plazas flanked by temple pyramids, a construction style that would be adopted by all the later Mesoamerican societies. Their chief deity was a jaguar god, whose image would also reappear in the pantheons of later civilizations. The Olmec civilization, like its successors, was a highly stratified society ruled by an elite priestly caste that claimed the exclusive ability to communicate with the gods.

After the decline of the Olmec cities, the Mayan civilization developed in the Yucatan peninsula, to the east of the major Olmec sites. The Mayas also built large cities containing tall pyramids and constructed temples with brightly painted stuccoed and carved façades. They studied astronomy, created the first writing system in the Americas, and developed a richly symbolic religious life in which rituals of bloodletting played a major role. The kings of the great Mayan city-states vied with each other for power. By the fifth century C.E. (Common Era), or about 1,500 years ago, they had begun to engage in open warfare, attempting conquest on a grand scale. But no king or city could win total victory. Eventually, the constant fighting combined with overpopulation and resulting environmental stress to cause the collapse of the most powerful cities. By the time the Spaniards arrived, only a few remnants of the once-mighty Mayan civilization remained intact.

The largest Mesoamerican metropolis was contemporary with, and a major trading partner of, the Mayas. Teotihuacan, founded about 300 B.C.E.

The City of Teotihuacan

(Before Common Era)—some 2,300 years ago—in the Valley of Mexico, was one of the largest cities in the world in the fifth century C.E., with an estimated population of up to 200,000. The rulers of Teotihuacan gained their position through commerce rather than warfare, and their trading network extended hundreds of miles in all directions. Thousands of craftspeople lived in the city, and many were especially skilled in working the green glass called obsidian, which was found nearby and was valued throughout the region as a source of fine knives and mirrors. Teotihuacan also served as a religious center; pilgrims must have come long distances to visit the impressive Pyramids of the Sun and Moon and the great temple of Quetzalcoatl—the feathered serpent, the primary god of central Mexico.

Teotihuacan's influence was felt so widely in Mesoamerica before its decline in the eighth century C.E. that some scholars have argued that this great Mexican city-state also influenced societies farther north, in what is now the United States. The Moundbuilders of the Ohio River region, who flourished about two thousand years ago, just as Teotihuacan rose to prominence, constructed earthen mounds that bear some resemblance to structures in Mesoamerica. But the Ohioan mounds were used exclusively as burial places for the dead, not as bases for temple pyramids. Also, the Moundbuilders' economy, which was based on hunting and gathering, bore little resemblance to

that of Mesoamerica. Trade goods from as far away as the Great Lakes and the Gulf of Mexico have been found in the mounds, but direct evidence of contact with Teotihuacan is lacking.

More likely, but still unproved, is the possibility that Teotihuacan and later Mesoamerican empires like that of the Aztecs had some impact on the development of the Mississippian culture, which flourished around 1000 C.E. in what is now the midwestern and southeastern United States. This civilization, like those to the south, was based on the cultivation of maize, beans, and squash. Not until about 700 to 900 C.E. were these crops grown successfully in the present-day United States; soon after their introduction, large cities with plazas and earthen pyramids first appeared in the region. The largest of the cities was Cahokia, near modern St. Louis. At its peak (before 1250 C.E.), Cahokia covered more than five square miles and had a population of about 10,000—small by Mesoamerican standards but far larger than any other northern community. Like Teotihuacan, Cahokia seems to have been a center for religion and trade. Its main pyramid, today called the Monk's Mound, was the largest earthwork built in North America and stood about half as high as the Pyramid of the Sun. Other Mississippian sites were located in present-day Alabama and Georgia. Traces of this civilization still remained when Spaniards first visited the area in the sixteenth century.

Aztec histories tell of the long migration of their people (who called themselves Mexica) into the Valley of Mexico during the twelfth century.

Aztecs

The uninhabited ruins of Teotihuacan, which by then had been deserted for at least two hundred years, awed and mystified the migrants. The Aztecs' primary god, Huitzilopochtli, was a god of war, represented by an eagle. Aztec chronicles record that Huitzilopochtli directed them to establish their capital at the spot on an island where they saw an eagle eating a serpent (thus symbolizing Huitzilopochtli's triumph over the traditional deity, Quetzalcoatl). That island city became Tenochtitlan, the center of a rigidly stratified society composed of hereditary classes of warriors, merchants, priests, common folk, and slaves. The Aztecs conquered their neighbors and forced them to pay tribute in luxury items, raw materials, and human beings who could be sacrificed to Huitzilopochtli. They also engaged

How do historians know

that the great civilizations of Mesoamerica influenced the Mississippian culture, which flourished nearly simultaneously in North America? In addition to the similarity of the ritual structures produced by the societies—that is, the large mounds topped with temples described in the text—artifacts like the one shown here lead many to suspect that the cultures must have been in contact. Common to both the Mississippians and the Mesoamerican civilizations (especially the Mayas and the Aztecs) was a reliance on symbols combining birds, animals, and humans. This warrior wearing a feathered costume on a shell gorget, or necklace, was found at Etowah Mound, Georgia, one of the most important Mississippian sites. It bears a striking resemblance to the ceramic statue of an eagle warrior unearthed in recent excavations in Mexico City at the site of the Templo Mayor, the main Aztec temple, which stood at the heart of Tenochtitlan (see page 9). A belief that such comparable motifs could not have developed independently has led some historians and archaeologists to conclude that contact must have occurred, even in the absence of definitive proof.   Photo: Etowah Mounds National Historic Site.

in ritual combat, known as "flowery wars," to obtain further sacrificial victims. The war god's taste for blood was not easily quenched. In the Aztec year Ten Rabbit (1502) at the coronation of Motecuhzoma II (whose name the Spaniards could not pronounce correctly, so they called him "Montezuma"), five thousand people were said to have been sacrificed by having their still-beating hearts torn from their bodies.

The Aztecs believed that they lived in the age of the Fifth Sun. Four times previously, they wrote, the earth and all the people who lived on it had been destroyed: first by wild beasts, then by wind, by fire, and finally by water. They predicted that their own world would end in earthquakes and hunger. In the Aztec year Thirteen Flint, volcanoes erupted; sickness and hunger spread; wild beasts attacked their children; and an eclipse of the sun darkened the sky. Did some priest wonder if the Fifth Sun was approaching its end? But nothing ominous happened, at least not immediately. Eventually, the Aztecs learned that their year Thirteen Flint was called 1492 by the Europeans.

NORTH AMERICA IN 1492

Over the centuries, the Americans who lived north of Mexico adapted their once-similar ways of life to very different geographical settings, thus creating the diverse cultures that the Europeans encountered when they first arrived (see map). Bands that lived in environments not well suited to agriculture—because of inadequate rainfall or poor soil, for example—followed a nomadic lifestyle similar to that of the Paleo-Indians. Within the area of the present-day United States, these tribes included the Paiutes and Shoshones, who inhabited the Great Basin (now Nevada and Utah). Because of the difficulty of finding sufficient food for more than a few people, such hunter-gatherer bands were small. They were usually composed of one or more related families, with men hunting small animals and women gathering seeds and berries. Where large game was more plentiful and food supplies therefore more certain, as in present-day Canada and the Great Plains, bands of hunters were somewhat larger.

In more favorable environments, larger groups combined agriculture with gathering, hunting, and fishing. Tribes that lived near the seacoasts, like the Chinooks of present-day Washington and Oregon, consumed fish and shellfish in addition to growing crops and gathering seeds and berries. Tribes of the interior (for example, the Arikaras of the Missouri River valley) hunted large animals while also cultivating maize, squash, and beans. The Algonkian tribes of what is now eastern Canada and the northeastern United States also combined hunting and agriculture. The Algonkians typically moved four or five times a year. Once crops were well established, villages broke into small mobile bands to engage in gathering, hunting, and fishing. Villages reassembled for harvest, then dispersed again for the fall hunting season. Finally, the people would spend the harsh winter months together in a protected location before returning to their fields in the spring. Every few years they would employ controlled burning tech-

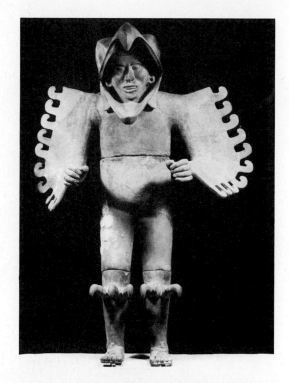

For centuries it was believed that the Spaniards had built their cathedral on the exact site of the Aztecs' Templo Mayor, but in the 1970s construction workers in Mexico City discovered the remains of the great temple about a block away from the cathedral. Now fully excavated, the ruins have yielded many important finds, none more dramatic than several life-size "eagle warrior" statues (located in 1982), which guarded the temple's entrances.   Museo del Templo Mayor. Photo José Naranjo

niques to clear new fields and ensure continuing fertility.

Societies that relied primarily on hunting large animals like deer and buffalo assigned that task to men, allotting food-processing, clothing-production, and child-rearing chores to women. Before such nomadic bands acquired horses from the Spaniards, women—occasionally assisted by dogs—also carried the family's belongings whenever the band relocated. Such a sexual division of labor was universal among hunting tribes, regardless of their location. Agricultural societies, by contrast, differed in how they assigned cultivating crops to the sexes. In what is now the southwestern United States, the Pueblo peoples, who lived in sixty or seventy autonomous

Sexual Division of Labor in America

Bering Strait

ARCTIC

SUB-ARCTIC

ARCTIC

NORTHWEST COAST

SUB-ARCTIC

PLATEAU

PACIFIC
OCEAN

GREAT
PLAINS

NORTHEAST

GREAT
BASIN

PRAIRIES

ATLANTIC
OCEAN

CALIFORNIA

SOUTHEAST

SOUTHWEST

NORTHEAST
MEXICO

CARIBBEAN

MESO-AMERICA

Primary mode of subsistence:

Agriculture

Hunting

Hunting-gathering

Fishing

Native Cultures of North America   *The natives of the North American continent effectively used the resources of the regions in which they lived. As this map shows, coastal tribes relied on fishing, residents of fertile areas engaged in agriculture, and other tribes employed hunting (often combined with gathering) as a primary mode of subsistence.*

Jacques Le Moyne, an artist accompanying the French settlement in Florida in the 1560s (see below), produced some of the first European images of North American peoples. His depiction of native agricultural practices shows the sexual division of labor, with men breaking up the ground with fish-bone hoes before women drop seeds into the holes. But his version of the scene cannot be accepted uncritically: unable to abandon a European view of proper farming methods, he erroneously drew plowed furrows in the soil. Courtesy of the John Carter Brown Library at Brown University.

villages and spoke five different languages, began raising squash and beans about five thousand years ago. All of them defined agricultural labor as men's work. In the East, though, Algonkian, Iroquoian, and Muskogean peoples allocated agricultural chores to women, whereas men hunted and cleared the land—a sexual division of labor illustrated in the accompanying drawing by French artist Jacques Le Moyne. In all the farming societies, women gathered wild foods, prepared food for consumption or storage, and cared for children.

The southwestern and eastern agricultural peoples had similar social organizations. They lived in villages, sometimes sizable ones with a thousand or more inhabitants. Pueblo villages were large, multistory buildings, constructed on terraces along the sides of cliffs or other easily defended sites in what is now New Mexico and Arizona. Northern Iroquois villages (in modern New York

State) were composed of large, rectangular, bark-covered structures, or long houses; the name *Iroquois* means "People of the Long House." In the present-day southeastern United States, Muskogeans and southern Algonkians lived in large houses made of thatch. Most of the eastern villages were surrounded by wood palisades and ditches to aid in fending off attackers. The defensive design of such villages and of the western pueblos suggests the significance of warfare in pre-Columbian America. Long before the Europeans arrived, the residents of North America fought with each other for control of the best hunting and fishing territories, the most fertile agricultural lands, or the sources of essential items like salt (for preserving meat) and flint, used for making knives and arrowheads.

In all these agricultural societies, each dwelling housed an extended family defined matrilineally (through a female line of descent). Mothers, their married daughters, and their daughters' husbands and children all lived together. Matrilineal descent did not imply matriarchy, or the wielding of power by women, but rather served as a means of reckoning kinship. Extended families were linked into clans, also defined by matrilineal ties. The nomadic bands of the Great Plains, on the other hand, were most often related patrilineally, through the male line. They lacked settled villages and defended themselves from attack primarily through their ability to move to safer locations when necessary.

The authority of American leaders rested ultimately on the consent of their fellow tribesmen, but political structures in the various tribes differed considerably. Among

Native American Politics and Religion

Pueblo and Muskogean peoples, the village council, composed of ten to thirty men, was the highest political authority; there was no government at the tribal level. Nomadic hunters also lacked formal structures linking the separate bands. The Iroquois, by contrast, had an elaborate political hierarchy incorporating villages into tribes and tribes into a widespread confederation. (The Iroquois Confederacy is discussed in detail in Chapter 3.) In all the North American cultures, political power was divided between civil and war leaders, who wielded authority only so long as they retained the confidence of the people. Consensus rather than autocratic rule characterized these political systems.

The political position of women varied from tribe to tribe. Women were more likely to assume leadership roles among agricultural peoples (especially those in which females were the chief cultivators) than among nomadic hunters. For example, women led certain Algonkian villages, but they were never chosen to lead hunting bands of the Great Plains. Iroquois women did not become chiefs, yet tribal matrons exercised political power (see page 170). Probably the most powerful female chiefs were found in what is now the southeastern United States. In the mid-sixteenth century a female ruler known as the Lady of Cofitachequi governed a large group of villages in present-day western South Carolina. Early English settlers in New England also noted in nearby villages the presence of female chiefs, most of them the wives, sisters, or widows of male leaders.

Americans' religious beliefs varied even more than did their political systems, but all the peoples were polytheistic, worshipping a multitude of gods. One common thread was their integration with nature. Thus each tribe's most important beliefs and rituals were closely tied to its economy. The major deities of agricultural peoples like the Pueblos and Muskogeans were associated with cultivation, and their chief festivals centered on planting and harvest. The most important gods of hunting tribes (like those living on the Great Plains) were associated with animals, and their major festivals were related to hunting. A tribe's economy and women's role in it helped to determine women's potential as religious leaders. Women held the most prominent positions in those agricultural societies (like the Iroquois) in which they were also the chief food producers.

A wide variety of cultures, comprising perhaps 4 to 6 million people, inhabited mainland North America when the Europeans arrived. In modern Mexico, hereditary rulers presided over vast agricultural empires. Along the Atlantic coast of the present-day United States, Americans likewise cultivated crops, but their political systems differed greatly from those of Mesoamerica. To the north and west, in what is now Canada and the Great Plains, lived nomadic and seminomadic societies primarily dependent on hunting large animals. Still farther west were the hunter-gatherer bands of the Great Basin and the agricultural villages of the Southwest. Finally, on the Pacific coast lived tribes that based their subsistence chiefly on fish. All told, these diverse groups spoke well over one thousand different languages. For obvious reasons, they did not consider themselves one people, nor did they—for the most part—think of uniting to repel the European invaders. Instead, each tribe or band continued to try to better its circumstances relative to its neighbors, regardless of who those neighbors were.

AFRICAN SOCIETIES

Fifteenth-century Africa, like fifteenth-century America, housed a variety of cultures adapted to different geographical settings (see map). Many of these cultures were of great antiquity. In the north, along the Mediterranean Sea, lived the Berbers, a Muslim people. (Muslims are adherents of Islam,

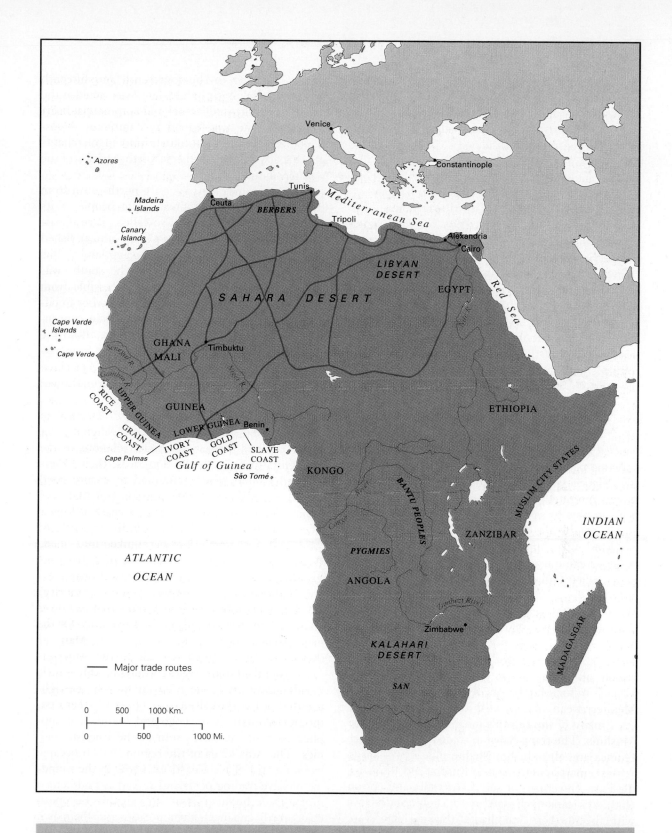

Venice

Constantinople

Azores

Madeira
Islands

Tunis

Ceuta

BERBERS

Tripoli

Mediterranean Sea

Alexandria
Cairo

Canary
Islands

*LIBYAN
DESERT*

EGYPT

Red Sea

Nile R.

S A H A R A   D E S E R T

Cape Verde
Islands

Cape Verde

Senegal R.

GHANA
MALI

Timbuktu

Gambia R.

Niger R.

RICE
COAST

UPPER GUINEA

GUINEA

ETHIOPIA

GRAIN
COAST

LOWER GUINEA

Benin

Cape Palmas

IVORY
COAST

GOLD
COAST

SLAVE
COAST

Gulf of Guinea

São Tomé

KONGO

BANTU PEOPLES

MUSLIM CITY STATES

INDIAN
OCEAN

Congo River

PYGMIES

ZANZIBAR

ATLANTIC

OCEAN

ANGOLA

Zambezi River

MADAGASCAR

Zimbabwe

*KALAHARI
DESERT*

—— Major trade routes

SAN

| 0 | 500 | 1000 Km. |
| 0 | 500 | 1000 Mi. |

Africa and Its Peoples, ca. 1400 *On the African continent resided many different peoples in a variety
of ecological settings and political units. Even before Europeans began to explore its coastlines, Africa's northern
regions were linked to the Mediterranean (and thus to Europe) via a network of trade routes.*

founded by the prophet Mohammed in the seventh century C.E.) On the east coast of Africa, Muslim city-states engaged in extensive trade with India, the Moluccas (part of modern Indonesia), and China. In these ports, sustained contact and intermarriage among Arabs and Africans created the Swahili language and culture. Through the East African city-states passed a considerable share of the trade between the eastern Mediterranean and the Far East; the rest followed the long land route across Central Asia known as the Silk Road.

In the African interior, south of the Mediterranean coast, lie the great Sahara and Libyan deserts, vast expanses of nearly waterless terrain that served as a barrier to certain types of travel yet also acted as a great highway for transmitting religious and cultural ideas throughout the region. Below the deserts, much of the continent is divided between tropical rain forests (along the coasts) and grassy plains (in the interior). People speaking a variety of languages and adopting quite different economies lived in a wide belt south of the deserts. Below the Gulf of Guinea (see map, page 12), the grassy landscape came to be dominated by Bantu-speaking peoples, who left their homeland in modern Nigeria about two thousand years ago and slowly migrated south and east across the continent, gradually assimilating and conquering other ethnic groups like the Pygmies and the San.

Most of the unwilling black migrants to North America came from West Africa, which the Europeans called Guinea, a land of tropical forests and small-scale agriculture that had

West Africa (Guinea)

been inhabited for at least ten thousand years before Europeans set foot there in the fifteenth century. The northern region of West Africa, or Upper Guinea, was heavily influenced by the Islamic culture of the Mediterranean. As early as the eleventh century C.E., many of the region's inhabitants had become Muslims. The trans-Saharan trade between Upper Guinea and the Muslim Mediterranean was black Africa's major connection to Europe and the Middle East. In return for salt, dates, silk, and cotton cloth, Africans exchanged ivory, gold, and slaves with the northern merchants. (Slaves, who were mostly criminals and wartime captives, were in great demand as household servants in the homes of the Muslim Mediterranean elite.) This commerce was controlled by the great interior kingdoms of Ghana (ca. 900–1100 C.E.) and later, Mali,

which flourished in the fourteenth and fifteenth centuries. Black Africa and Islam intersected at the city that was the intellectual and commercial heart of the trade, the near-legendary Timbuktu. A cosmopolitan center, Timbuktu attracted merchants and scholars from all parts of North Africa and the Mediterranean.

Upper Guinea runs roughly north-south from Cape Verde to Cape Palmas. The people of its northernmost region, the so-called Rice Coast (present-day Gambia, Senegal, and Guinea), fished and cultivated rice in coastal swamplands. The Grain Coast, the next region to the south, was thinly populated and not readily accessible from the sea because it had only one good harbor (modern Freetown, Sierra Leone). Its people concentrated on farming and raising livestock. Both the Rice and Grain Coasts—especially the former—supplied slaves destined for sale in the Americas, but even more enslaved migrants came from Lower Guinea, to the east of Cape Palmas.

In the fifteenth century, most Africans in Lower Guinea practiced traditional religions, not the precepts of Islam. As in the religions of the agricultural peoples of the Americas, their beliefs revolved around rituals intended to ensure good harvests. The vast interior kingdoms of Mali and Ghana had no counterparts on the coast of Lower Guinea. Throughout the region, individual villages composed of groups of kin were linked into small, hierarchical kingdoms. At the time of initial contact with the Europeans, the region was characterized by decentralized political and social authority.

The Ivory Coast and the Gold Coast in Lower Guinea were each named by the Europeans for the major trade goods they obtained there. Many of the first slaves destined for sale in the Americas came from the Gold Coast, comprising thirty little kingdoms known as the Akan States. By the eighteenth century, though, it was the area farther east, the modern nations of Togo and Benin, that supplied most of the slaves sold in the English colonies. The Adja kings of the region, which became known as the Slave Coast, encouraged the founding of slave-trading posts and served as middlemen in the trade because access to valuable European trade goods enhanced their positions in their own societies and improved the kingdoms' standing relative to their neighbors. Initially, enslaved people sent to the Americas fell into the same categories as those previously traded to the Mediterranean: criminals, enemy captives, and individuals sold into slavery to repay debts. By the mid-eighteenth century, after the demand for enslaved labor in the American colonies had increased dramatically, raiding parties from the coast often attacked interior villages to acquire captives for the trade.

The societies of West Africa, like those of the Americas, assigned different tasks to men and women. In general, the sexes shared agricultural duties. Men also hunted, managed livestock, and did most of the fishing. Women were responsible for childcare, food preparation, and cloth manufacture. Everywhere in West Africa women were the primary local traders. They managed the extensive local and regional networks through which goods were exchanged among the various families, villages, and small kingdoms.

Sexual Division of Labor in West Africa

Despite their different economies and the rivalries among states, the peoples of Lower Guinea had similar social systems organized on the basis of what anthropologists have called the *dual-sex principle.* In Lower Guinea, each sex handled its own affairs: just as male political and religious leaders governed the men, so females ruled the women. In the Dahomean kingdom, for example, every male official had his female counterpart; in the Akan States, chiefs inherited their status through the female line, and each male chief had a female assistant who supervised the other women. Many West African societies practiced polygyny (one man having several wives, each of whom lived separately with her children). Thus few adults lived permanently in marital households, but the dual-sex system ensured that their actions were subject to scrutiny by members of their own sex, if not by a spouse.

Throughout Lower Guinea religious beliefs likewise stressed the complementary nature of male and female roles. Both women and men served as heads of the cults and secret societies that directed the spiritual life of the villages. Young women were initiated into the Sandé cult, young men into Poro. Neither cult was allowed to reveal its secrets to the opposite sex. Although West African women (unlike some of their Native American contemporaries) rarely held formal power over men, female religious leaders did govern other members of their sex within the Sandé cult, enforcing conformity to accepted norms of behavior and overseeing their spiritual well-being.

This decorative brass weight, created by the Asante peoples of Lower Guinea, was used for measuring gold dust. It depicts a family pounding fu-fu, a food made by mashing together plantains (a kind of banana), yams, and cassava. The paste was then shaped into balls to be eaten with soup. Thus a weight probably employed in trading with Europeans showed a scene combining foods of African origin (plantains and yams) with an import from the Americas (cassava), bringing the three continents together in ways both symbolic and real. Courtesy of the Trustees of the British Museum. Photo by Michael Holford.

The West Africans who were brought to the Americas, then, were agricultural peoples, skilled at tending livestock, hunting, fishing, and manufacturing cloth from plant fibers and animal skins. Both men and women were accustomed to working communally, alongside other members of their own sex. They were also accustomed to a relatively egalitarian relationship between the sexes, especially within the context of religion. In the New World, they entered societies that used their labor but had little respect for their cultural traditions. Of the three peoples whose experience intersected in the Americas, their lives were the most disrupted.

EUROPEAN SOCIETIES

In the fifteenth century, Europeans, too, were agricultural peoples. The daily lives of Europe's rural people had changed little for several hundred years. Split into numerous small, warring countries, that continent was divided linguistically, politically, and economically, yet in social terms Europeans' lives were more similar than different. European societies were hierarchical, with a few families wielding arbitrary power over the majority of the people. Europe's kingdoms accordingly resembled those of Africa or Mesoamerica but differed greatly from the more egalitarian, consensus-based societies then established in America north of Mexico.

Most Europeans, like most Africans and Native Americans, lived in small villages. Only a few cities dotted the landscape, most of them po-

Sexual Division of Labor in Europe

litical capitals. European farmers, who were called peasants, owned or leased separate landholdings, but they worked the fields communally. Because fields had to lie fallow every second or third year to regain their fertility, a family could not have ensured itself a regular food supply had not the work and the crop been shared annually by all the villagers. Men did most of the field work; women helped out chiefly at planting and harvest. In some areas men concentrated on herding livestock. Women's duties consisted primarily of childcare and household tasks, including preserving food, milking cows, and caring for poultry. If a woman's husband was an artisan or a storekeeper in a city, she might assist him in business. Since Europeans kept domesticated animals (pigs, goats, sheep, and cattle) for meat, hunting had little economic importance in their cultures. Instead, hunting was a sport engaged in by male aristocrats.

Unlike African and Native American societies, in which women often played prominent roles in politics and religion, men dominated all areas of life in Europe. A few women from noble families—notably Queen Elizabeth I of England—achieved status or power, but the vast majority of European women were excluded from positions of political authority. In the Roman Catholic church, leadership roles were reserved for men, who alone could become priests and bishops. At the familial level, husbands and fathers expected to control the lives of their wives, children, and servants (a *patriarchal* system of family governance). In short, European women held inferior positions in both public and private realms.

When the fifteenth century began, the European nations were slowly beginning to recover from the devastating epidemic of plague known as the Black Death, which had first struck them in 1346. The bubonic plague, spread by rats and fleas as well as by human contact, arrived in Europe from China (where it was recorded in 1331), traveling with long-distance traders along the Silk Road. The disease then recurred with particular severity in the 1360s and 1370s. Although no precise figures are available and the impact of the Black Death varied from region to region, the best estimate is that fully one third of the continent's people died during those terrible years. That led to a precipitous economic decline—in some regions more than half the workers were lost—and to severe social, political, and religious disruption because of the deaths of clergymen and other leading figures.

As the plague ravaged the population, England and France were waging the Hundred Years' War (1337–1453), initiated because the English monarchy claimed the French throne. The war interrupted overland trade routes through France that connected northern Europe to the Italian city-states and thence to Central Asia. The merchants of the eastern Mediterranean sought new ways of reaching their markets in Belgium and Holland, eventually solving that dilemma by forging a regular maritime link with the north to replace the overland route. Adding a triangular, or lateen, sail created by Arab mariners to the square-rigged mainsail developed by Europeans created more maneuverable ships that could sail out of the Mediterranean and into the North Sea. Also of key importance was the perfection of navigational instruments like the astrolabe and the quadrant, which allowed oceanic sailors to estimate their position (latitude) by measuring the relationship of sun, moon, or stars to the horizon.

In the aftermath of the Hundred Years' War, ruthless European monarchs relied on nationalistic feelings fostered by the conflict to consolidate

Political and Technological Changes

their previously diffuse political power and to raise new revenues through increased taxation of an already hard-pressed peasantry. The long military struggle led to new pride in national identity (regional loyalties had previously held sway) and to heightened hostility toward foreigners. In England, Henry VII in 1485 founded the Tudor dynasty and began uniting a previously divided land. In France, the successors of Charles

VII unified the kingdom and levied new taxes. Most successful of all, at least in the short run, were Ferdinand of Aragon and Isabella of Castile. In 1469 they married and combined their kingdoms, thus creating the foundation of a strongly Catholic Spain. In 1492, they defeated the Muslims, who had lived in Spain and Portugal for centuries, and expelled all Jews and Muslims from their domain.

The fifteenth century also brought technological change to Europe. Movable type and the printing press, invented in Germany in the 1450s, made information more accessible than ever before. Printing stimulated the Europeans' curiosity about fabled lands across the seas, lands they could now read about in books. The most important such work was Marco Polo's *Travels*, which recounted a Venetian merchant's adventures in thirteenth-century China, describing that nation as being bordered on the east by an ocean. Polo's account circulated widely among Europe's educated elites after it was printed in 1477. The book led many Europeans to believe that they could trade directly with China via ocean-going vessels instead of relying on the Silk Road or the trade route through East Africa. That would allow them to circumvent the Muslim and Mediterranean merchants who had hitherto controlled their access to Asian goods.

The European explorations of the fifteenth and sixteenth centuries were therefore made possible by technological advances and by the growing strength of newly powerful national rulers. The

Motives for Exploration
——

primary motivation for exploratory voyages was each country's craving for easy access to desirable African and Asian goods—spices like pepper, cloves, cinnamon, and nutmeg (needed to season the bland European diet), silk, dyes, perfumes, jewels, and gold. Avoiding middlemen and acquiring such valuable products directly would improve a nation's income and its standing relative to its neighbors. The economic motive was supported by a secondary concern about spreading Christianity around the world. The linking of materialist and spiritual goals might seem contradictory today, but fifteenth-century Europeans saw no necessary conflict between the two. Explorers and colonizers could honestly want to convert "heathen" peoples to Christianity. At the same time they could hope to increase their nation's

The increased taxation levied on European populations to support overseas expansion and wars at home in the fifteenth, sixteenth, and seventeenth centuries gave rise to many complaints, some of which were presented in pictorial terms. A French artist's conception of a peasant paying his taxes to a rich nobleman is headed, "The more one has, the more one wants." Bibliothèque Nationale.

wealth by establishing direct trade with Africa, China, India, and the Moluccas (also known as the Spice Islands).

EARLY EUROPEAN EXPLORATIONS AND THE COLUMBUS VOYAGES

Before European mariners could discover new lands, they had to discover the oceans. Until 1291, when Genoese sailors defeated the Moroccans who had closed the Straits of Gibraltar to other nations' shipping, southern Europeans had sailed only in the Mediterranean. To reach Asia, seafarers needed not merely the maneuverable vessels and navigational aids increasingly used in the fourteenth century, but also knowledge of the sea, its currents, and especially its winds. Wind would power their ships: but how did the winds run? Where would Atlantic breezes carry their square-

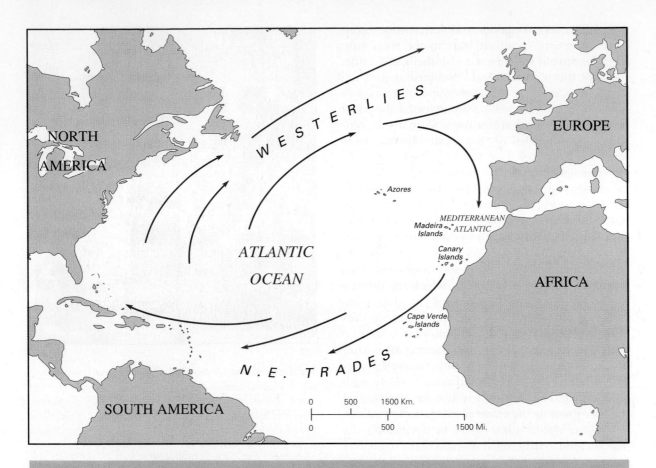

Atlantic Winds and Islands   *European mariners had to explore the oceans before they could find new lands. The first realm they discovered was that of Atlantic winds and islands.*

rigged ships, which, even with the addition of a triangular sail, needed to run before the wind (that is, to have the wind directly behind the vessel)?

Europeans learned the answers to these questions in the region that has been called the "Mediterranean Atlantic," the expanse of ocean that is south and west of Spain and is bounded by the island groups of the Azores (on the west) and the Canaries (on the south), with the Madeiras in their midst (see map). Europeans reached all three sets of islands during the fourteenth century. The Canaries proved a popular destination for mariners from Iberia (the peninsula that includes Spain and Portugal). Sailing to the Canaries from Europe was easy, because strong winds known as the Northeast Trades blow southward along the Iberian and African coastlines. The voyage took about a week, and the volcanic peaks on the islands made them impossible to miss, even with navigational instruments that were less than precise.

The problem was getting back. The Iberian sailor attempting to return home faced a major obstacle: the very winds that had brought him so quickly to the Canaries now blew directly at him. Early travelers to the islands sometimes used galleys powered by oarsmen as well as by sails, but even oarsmen had a difficult time fighting the contrary winds and currents. Another alternative was similarly tedious: tacking back and forth to the east and west, attempting each time to make a little more headway north. The problem seemed intractable, and in earlier eras European sailors had been unable to solve it. When confronted with contrary winds, they simply waited for the wind to change. But for the most part, the Northeast Trades did not change. They blew steadily, never reversing course, though shifting slightly with the seasons.

What could be done? Some unknown seafarer figured out the answer. It was to sail "around the wind." If he could not sail against the trade winds, a mariner had to sail as close as possible to the direction from which the wind was coming without being forced to tack. In the Mediterranean Atlantic, that meant pointing his vessel northwest into the open ocean, away from land, until—weeks later—he reached the winds that would carry him home, the so-called "Westerlies." Those winds blow (we now know, though the mariners at first did not) northward along the coast of North America before heading east toward Europe.

This solution must at first have seemed to defy common sense, but it proved to be the key to successful exploration of both the Atlantic and Pacific oceans. Once a sailor understood the winds and their allied currents, he no longer feared leaving Europe without being able to return. Faced with a contrary wind, all he had to do was sail around it—along its periphery without tacking—until he found a wind to carry him in the proper direction. This strategy might seem to take him hundreds of miles out of the way, but in the long run it was safer and surer than attempting the monumental task of tacking against the wind.

During the fifteenth century, armed with knowledge of the winds and currents of the Mediterranean Atlantic, Iberian seamen regularly visited its islands, all of which could be reached in two weeks or less from Gibraltar. The uninhabited Azores were soon settled by Portuguese migrants who raised wheat for sale in Europe and sold livestock to passing sailors. The Madeiras also had no native peoples, and by the 1450s Portuguese colonists were employing slaves (probably Jews and Muslims brought from Iberia) to grow large quantities of sugar for export to the mainland. The Madeiras thus developed by the 1470s into the world's first colonial plantation economy.

The first islands the Europeans had found—arriving as early as the 1330s—were the Canaries, inhabited by the Guanche people, who began trading animal skins and dyes

Canary Islands with their European visitors. In 1402 the French attacked one of the islands; thereafter, Portuguese and Spanish expeditions continued the sporadic assaults. The Guanches resisted vigorously, but one by one the seven islands came under European control. The resident Guanches were then carried off as slaves to the Madeiras or the Iberian peninsula. The last island fell to the Spanish in 1496, and the last known Guanche died in the middle of the next century. The Spanish con-

One of the few surviving contemporary illustrations of a fifteenth-century European vessel, or caravel, is this engraving by the well-known Flemish artist Peter Breughel. Note the combination of square-rigged and lateen sails, the former for moving as efficiently as possible with a following breeze, the latter for maneuvering in unfavorable winds. Private Collection.

querors then devoted the land of the Canary Islands to sugar cultivation. Collectively, the Canaries and Madeira became known as the Wine Islands because much of their sugar production eventually was employed to make sweet wines.

While some Europeans concentrated on exploiting the islands of the Mediterranean Atlantic, others used them as steppingstones to Africa. In 1415, Portugal seized control of Ceuta, a Muslim city in North Africa (see map, page 13). Prince Henry the Navigator, son of King John I of Portugal, knew that vast wealth awaited the first European nation to tap the riches of Africa and Asia directly. Each year he dispatched ships southward along the African coast, attempting to discover an oceanic route to Asia. But not until after Prince Henry's death did Bartholomew Dias round the southern tip of Africa (1488) and Vasco da Gama finally reach India (1498).

Long before that, though, Portugal reaped the benefits of its seafarers' voyages. Although West African states successfully resisted European penetration of the interior, they allowed the Portuguese to establish trading posts along their coasts. Charging the traders rent and levying duties on the goods they imported, the African chiefdoms set the terms of exchange and benefited considerably from their new, easier access to European manufactures. The Portuguese gained too, for they no longer had to rely on the long trans-Saharan trade route. They earned immense profits by swiftly transporting African gold to Europe. Another valuable cargo was slaves. When they carried African Muslim prisoners of war back to the Iberian peninsula, the Portuguese introduced black slavery into Europe.

Two groups of islands off the African coast, both previously uninhabited, proved critical to Portuguese success. The first, São Tomé, in the Gulf of Guinea (see map, page 13) was colonized in the 1480s. By that time Madeira had already reached the limit of its capacity to produce sugar. The soil of São Tomé proved ideal for raising that valuable crop, and plantation agriculture there expanded rapidly. Large numbers of slaves were imported from the mainland to work in the cane fields, thus creating the first economy based primarily on the bondage of black Africans.

African Islands

The second group, the Cape Verde Islands, served a different function for the Portuguese. Three hundred miles off the coast and too dry for sugar cultivation, the Cape Verdes became an important resupply station for ships in the Africa trade. Isolated from the diseases of the African continent—which devastated Europeans—the islands played host to a racially mixed population, the offspring of various African and European groups. The Cape Verdes and their inhabitants were to play an important role in the colonization of the Americas. There the products and peoples of four continents mingled, and the islands became one of the primary staging areas for the African slave trade.

By the 1490s, even before Christopher Columbus set sail to the west, Europeans had learned three key lessons of colonization from their experiences in the islands of the Mediterranean Atlantic and the African coast. First, they knew that they could transplant their crops and livestock successfully to exotic locations. Second, they had learned that the native peoples of unknown lands could be either conquered (the Guanches) or exploited to European advantage (the Africans). Finally, they had successfully developed a model of plantation slavery—an exploitative economy based on the labor of large numbers of people held in perpetual bondage—and a system for supplying nearly unlimited quantities of such workers. The stage was set for a critical moment in world history, and the man of the hour was a sailor named Christopher Columbus.

Columbus was well-schooled in the lessons of the Mediterranean Atlantic. Born in 1451 in the Italian city-state of Genoa, Columbus, the largely self-educated son of a wool merchant, was by the 1490s an experienced sailor and mapmaker. Like many mariners of the day, he was drawn to Portugal and its islands, especially the Madeiras, where he lived for several years, commanding a merchant vessel sailing in nearby waters. At least once he voyaged to the Portuguese colony on the Gold Coast. There he acquired an obsession with gold that never left him; and there he came to understand the economic potential of the slave trade.

Christopher Columbus

Like all accomplished seafarers, Columbus knew the world was round. (So, indeed, did most people: the idea that his contemporaries believed the world to be flat is a myth dating from the nineteenth century.) But he differed from other cartographers in his estimate of the earth's size: he thought that Japan lay only three thousand miles from the southern European coast. Thus, he argued, it would be easier to reach Asia by sailing west than by making the difficult voyage around the southern tip of Africa. Experts scoffed at this crackpot notion, accurately predicting that the two continents lay twelve thousand miles apart. When Columbus in 1484 asked the Portuguese authorities to back his plan to sail west to Asia, they rejected the proposal. After all, why should they adopt such a crazy scheme, just as their efforts to round the Cape of Good Hope promised success?

Ferdinand and Isabella of Spain, ruling a newly united kingdom and jealous of the profits Portugal was earning in Africa, were more receptive to Columbus's ideas. Urged on by some Spanish noblemen and a group of Italian merchants resident in Castile, the monarchs agreed to finance the risky voyage. And so, on August 3, 1492, in command of three ships—the *Pinta*, the *Niña*, and the *Santa Maria*—Columbus set sail from the southern Spanish port of Palos.

The first part of the journey must have been very familiar, for the ships steered down the Northeast Trades to the Canary Islands, where the crew repaired, refitted, and resupplied the vessels. On September 6 they weighed anchor and headed out into the unknown ocean. Just over a month later, pushed by the favorable trade winds, the ships found land approximately where Columbus had predicted (see map, page 24). On October 12, he and his men landed on an island in the Bahamas, which its inhabitants called Guanahaní, but which he renamed San Salvador. (Because Columbus's sketchy description of his landfall can be variously interpreted, two different places—Watling Island and Samana Cay—are today proposed as possible contenders for Columbus's landing site.) Later he went on to explore the islands now known as Cuba and Hispaniola, which their residents, the Taíno people, called Colba and Bohío. Because he thought he had reached the Indies, Columbus referred to the inhabitants of the region as *Indians*.

Three themes predominate in Columbus's log, the only source of information on this first encounter. First, he insistently asked the Taínos where he could find gold, pearls, and valuable spices. Each time, his informants replied (largely via signs) that such products could be obtained on other islands, or on the mainland, or in cities in the interior. Eventually he came to mistrust such answers, noting, "I am beginning to believe . . . they will tell me anything I want to hear."

Second, Columbus wrote repeatedly of the strange and beautiful plants and animals he was seeing. "Here the fishes are so unlike ours that it is amazing. . . . The colors are so bright that anyone would marvel," he noted, and again, "The song of the little birds might make a man wish never to leave here. I never tire from looking at such luxurious vegetation," he wrote. Yet Columbus's interest was not merely aesthetic. "I believe that there are many plants and trees here that could be worth a lot in Spain for use as dyes, spices, and medicines," he observed, adding that he was carrying home to Europe "a sample of everything I can," so that experts could examine them.

Third, Columbus also described the islands' human residents, and he seized some to take back to Spain. The Taínos were, he said, very handsome, gentle, and friendly, though they told him of fierce people who raided their villages and lived on other nearby islands. Those Caniba (today called Caribs), from whose name the word *cannibal* is derived, were reported to eat their captives, though today scholars disagree about whether the tales were true. By contrast, Columbus believed the Taínos to be likely converts to Catholicism, remarking that "if devout religious persons knew the Indian language well, all these people would soon become Christians." But he had more in mind than conversion. The islanders "ought to make good and skilled servants," Columbus declared. It would be easy, he asserted, to "subject everyone and make them do what you wished."

The Taíno People

Thus the very first encounter between Europeans and America and its residents revealed a theme that would be of enormous significance for centuries to come: the Europeans' desire to extract profits from the continent by exploiting its natural resources, including plants, animals, and peoples alike.

Christopher Columbus made three more voyages to the west, exploring most of the major Caribbean islands and sailing along the coasts of Central and South America. Until the day he died in 1506 at the age of 55, Columbus believed that he had reached Asia, as shown in the map produced in 1489 (see page 22). Even before his death, others knew better. Because the Florentine Amerigo Vespucci, who explored the South American coast in 1499, was the first to publish the idea that a new continent had been discovered, Martin Waldseemüller in 1507 labeled the land *America*, as is evident in the photo of his map (see page 23). By then, Spain, Portugal, and Pope Alexander VI had signed the Treaty of Tordesillas (1494), confirming Portugal's dominance in Africa and Brazil in exchange for Spanish preeminence in the rest of the New World.

The first mariners to explore the region of North America that was to become the United States and Canada followed a very different route. Some historians argue that European sailors probably found the rich Newfoundland fishing grounds in the 1480s, even before Columbus's first voyage, but that such men would have kept their discoveries a secret so that they alone could exploit the sea's

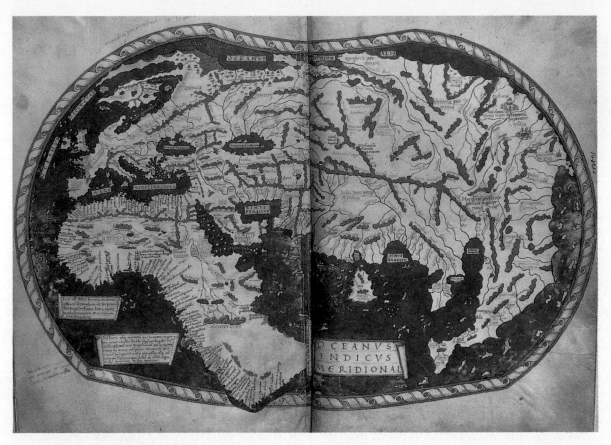

The map produced in 1489 by Henricus Marcellus represented the world as it was known to Christopher Columbus, for it incorporated information obtained after Bartholomew Dias, a Portuguese sailor, rounded the Cape of Good Hope at the southern tip of Africa in 1488. Yet Marcellus did not try to estimate the extent of the ocean separating the west coast of Europe from the east coast of Asia.   Courtesy of the Trustees of The British Library.

bounty. Whether or not fishermen had crossed the entire width of the Atlantic, they had thoroughly explored its northern reaches. In the same way the Portuguese traveled regularly in the Mediterranean Atlantic, fifteenth-century English seafarers and others voyaged among the European continent, England, Ireland, and Iceland.

The winds these seafarers confronted posed problems on their outbound rather than homeward journeys. The same westerlies that carried Columbus and other southern voyagers back to Europe blew in the faces of northerners looking west. But sailors soon learned that the strongest winds shifted southward during the winter, and that, by departing from northern ports in the spring, they could make adequate headway if they steered

northward to catch sporadic easterly breezes. Thus, whereas the first landfall of most sailors to the south was somewhere in the Caribbean, those taking the northern route usually reached America along the coast of what is now Maine or the Canadian maritime provinces.

Five hundred years before Columbus, in the year 1001, Leif Ericsson and other explorers from Greenland briefly established a settlement at a western site they named Vineland. (In the 1960s, archaeologists determined that this encampment was located at what is now L'anse aux Meadows, Newfoundland.) Attacks by local residents forced them to depart hurriedly, the tale of their exploits subsequently being preserved in oral-history sagas. Therefore, the European generally credited with

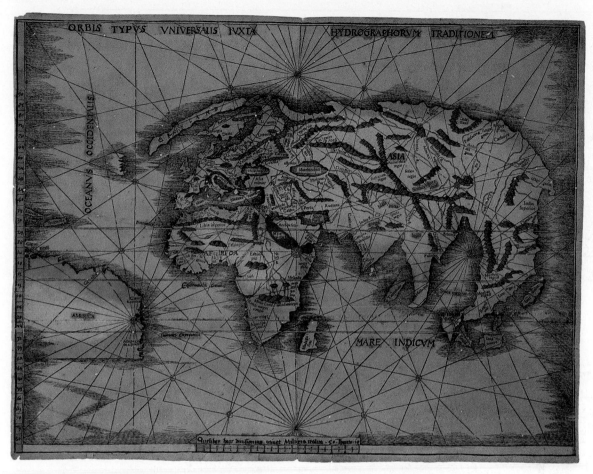

In 1507 Martin Waldseemüller, a German mapmaker, was the first person to designate the newly discovered southern con-tinent as "America." He named the continent after Amerigo Vespucci, the Italian explorer who realized that he had reached a "new world" rather than islands off the coast of Asia.   Courtesy of the John Carter Brown Library at Brown University.

"discovering" North America is John Cabot. More precisely, it might be said that Cabot brought to Europe the first formal knowledge of the northern coastline of the continent.

Like Columbus, Cabot was a master mariner from the Italian city-state of Genoa. He is known to have been in Spain when Columbus returned from his first trip to America.

John Cabot's Northern Explorations

Calculating that England—which traded with Asia only through a long series of middlemen stretching from Belgium to Venice to the Muslim world—would be eager to sponsor exploratory voyages, Cabot sought and won the support of King Henry VII. He set sail from Bristol in late

May 1497 in a little ship named the *Mathew*, reaching his destination on June 24. Scholars disagree as to the location of his landfall (some say it was Cape Breton Island, others that it was Newfoundland), but all recognize the importance of his month-long exploration of the coast. Having achieved his goal, Cabot rode the westerlies back to England, arriving just fifteen days after he left North America.

The voyages of Columbus, Cabot, and their successors finally brought the Eastern and Western Hemispheres together. The Portuguese explorer Pedro Alvares Cabral reached Brazil in 1500; John Cabot's son Sebastian followed his father to North America in 1507; France financed Giovanni da Verrazzano in 1524 and Jacques Cartier in 1534; and in 1609 and 1610 Henry Hudson explored the

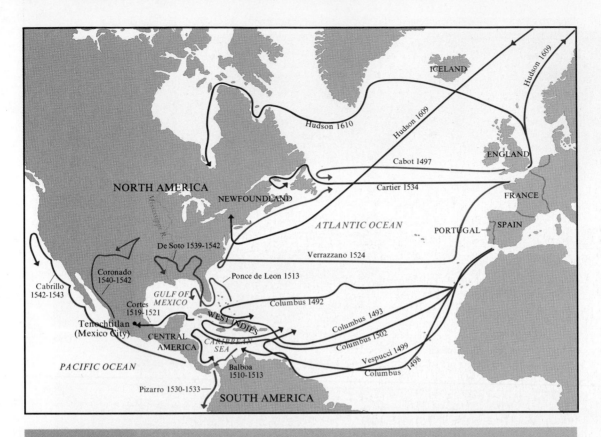

European Explorations in America   *In the century following Columbus's voyages, European adventurers explored the coasts and parts of the interior of North and South America.*

North American coast for the Dutch West India Company (see map). All these men were primarily searching for the legendary, nonexistent "Northwest Passage" through the Americas, hoping to find an easy route to the riches of Asia. Although they did not attempt to plant colonies in the Western Hemisphere, their discoveries interested European nations in exploring the New World for its own sake.

SPANISH COLONIZATION AND THE EXCHANGE OF DISEASES, PLANTS, AND ANIMALS

The Europeans' greatest impact on the Americas was unintended. Diseases carried from the Old World to the New by the alien invaders killed millions of Native Americans, who had no immunity to germs that had infested Europe, Asia, and Africa for centuries. The statistics are staggering. When Columbus landed on Hispaniola in 1492, more than one million people probably resided there. Fifty years later, only five hundred were still alive. Within thirty years of the first landfall at Guanahaní, not one Taíno survived in the Bahamas. The lethal combination of diseases and slave-raiding parties had wiped them out.

Although measles, influenza, and other illnesses severely afflicted the Native Americans, the greatest killer was smallpox, which was spread by direct human contact. A Spanish priest recorded the words of an old Aztec man who survived the first smallpox epidemic in Tenochtitlan, the Aztec capital. That epidemic began in Hispaniola in 1518 and was carried to the mainland by Cortés and his army of invaders. Even though the Spaniards failed in their first attempt to take Tenochtitlan in 1520, they left behind the germs that would ensure their eventual triumph. Four months after their departure, in the Aztec month of Tepeilhuitl, the

Theodore de Bry, an engraver who collected and published views of America in the sixteenth century, here depicted Brazilian Indians mourning relatives dead from alien European diseases.   Courtesy of the John Carter Brown Library at Brown University.

epidemic peaked. "It spread over the people as great destruction," the elderly Aztec remembered. "Some it quite covered [with pustules] on all parts—their faces, their heads, their breasts. . . . There was great havoc. Very many died of it. . . . Great was its destruction. . . . And very many starved; there was death from hunger, [for] none could take care of [the sick]; nothing could be done for them."

By the time the invaders returned in the month of Izcalli, the epidemic had fatally weakened Tenochtitlan's defenders. Even so, the city held out for more than two months. But in the Aztec year Three House, on the day One Serpent (August 1521), Tenochtitlan finally surrendered. The Spaniards had conquered Mexico, and on the site of the Aztec capital they built what is now Mexico City.

Far to the north, where smaller American populations encountered only a few European explorers, missionaries, traders, and fishermen, disease also ravaged the countryside. A great epidemic, most likely chicken pox, swept through the villages along the coast north of Cape Cod in 1616 to 1618. The mortality rate may have been as high as 90 percent. An English traveler several years later commented that the people had "died on heapes, as they lay in their houses," and that bones and skulls covered the remains of their villages. Because of this dramatic depopulation of the area, just a few years later English colonists were able to establish settlements virtually unopposed by Native Americans. As the historian Francis Jennings has observed, North America was more a widowed land than a virgin one when the English arrived there.

The Americans, though, took a revenge of sorts. They gave the Europeans syphilis, a virulent venereal disease. The first recorded case of the new disease in Europe occurred in Barcelona, Spain, in 1493, shortly after Columbus's return from the Caribbean. Although less likely than smallpox to cause immediate death, syphilis was extremely dangerous and debilitating. Carried by soldiers, sailors, and prostitutes, it spread quickly through Europe and Asia, reaching as far as China by 1505.

The exchange of diseases was only part of a broader mutual transfer of plants and animals that resulted directly from European voyages. The two hemispheres had evolved separately for millions of years, developing widely different forms of life. Many large mammals like cattle and horses were native to the connected continents of Europe, Asia, and Africa, but the Americas contained no domesticated beasts larger than dogs and llamas. On the other hand, the vegetable crops of the New World—particularly corn, beans, squash, cassava, and potatoes—were more nutritious and produced higher yields than those of the Old, like wheat and rye. In time, the Native Americans learned to raise and consume European livestock, and the Europeans and Africans became accustomed to planting and eating American crops. As a result, the diets of all three peoples were vastly enriched. One consequence was the doubling of the world's population over the next three hundred years.

Exchange of Plants and Animals

The exchange of two other commodities significantly influenced European and American civilizations. In America, Europeans encountered tobacco (see the sixteenth-century woodcut showing an example of its use), which was at first believed to have beneficial medicinal effects. Smoking and chewing the "Indian weed" became a fad in the Old World after it began to be grown in Turkey in the sixteenth century. Despite the efforts of such skeptics as King James I of England, who in 1604 pronounced smoking "loathsome to the eye, hatefull to the Nose, harmfull to the brain, [and] dangerous to the Lungs," tobacco's popularity climbed. Its contribution to another disease, lung cancer, was discovered only in the twentieth century.

More immediately important was the impact of the horse on some Indian cultures. Horses brought to America by the Spaniards inevitably fell into the hands of Native Americans. Traded northward among the tribes, they eventually became essential to the life of the nomadic buffalo hunters of the Great Plains. Apaches, Comanches, and Blackfeet, among others, used horses for transportation and hunting, calculated their wealth in the number of horses owned, and waged wars primarily from horseback. Women no longer had to carry the bands' belongings on their backs. Some tribes that previously had cultivated crops abandoned agriculture altogether. Through the acquisition of horses, then, a mode of subsistence that had been based on hunting several different animals, combined with gathering and agriculture, became one focused almost wholly on hunting buffalo.

The historian Alfred W. Crosby has coined the useful term *portmanteau biota* to describe the biological aspect of the European and African invasion of the Americas. That is, the invaders carried with them—in effect, in their luggage (or portmanteaus)—the plant and animal life with which they were familiar. Some creatures, such as livestock, they brought deliberately. Others, including rats, weeds, and diseases, arrived unexpectedly. And the same process occurred in reverse. When the Europeans packed their suitcases to return home—to extend the metaphor—they deliberately took back such crops as corn, potatoes, and tobacco, along with that unanticipated hitchhiker, syphilis.

All the residents of the Americas would eventually feel the effects of the Europeans' portmanteau biota, but only in the areas explored and claimed by Spain did formal colonization begin immediately. On his second voyage in 1493, Columbus brought to Hispaniola seventeen ships loaded with 1,200 men, seeds, plants, livestock, chickens, and dogs—along with germs and weeds. The settlement named Isabela (in the modern Dominican Republic) and its successors became the staging area for the Spanish invasion of America. On the islands of Cuba and Hispaniola the Europeans learned to adapt to the new environment, as did the horses, cattle, and hogs they imported. When the Spaniards explored the mainland, they rode island-bred horses and ate island-bred cattle and hogs. Everywhere they carried with them what Crosby has termed their "invasion team": European diseases and hooved animals. Those germs and livestock ensured the Spaniards' success.

At first, Spanish explorers fanned out around the Caribbean basin. In 1513, Juan Ponce de León reached Florida and Vasco Núñez de Balboa crossed the Isthmus of Panama to the Pacific Ocean. Eight years later, the Spaniards' dreams of wealth were realized when Cortés conquered the Aztec empire,

Conquistadores

The first Europeans to visit the Americas recorded seeing the inhabitants smoke and chew tobacco on both northern and southern continents and in the Caribbean islands. A sixteenth-century French woodcut shows a Brazilian native smoking a roll of tobacco leaves resembling a modern cigar, while a man and a boy nearby start a fire by using friction. By permission of the Houghton Library, Harvard University.

seizing a fabulous treasure of gold and silver. Venturing northward, conquistadores like Juan Rodriguez Cabrillo (who sailed along the California coast), Hernando de Soto (who journeyed to the Mississippi River), and Francisco Vásquez de Coronado (who explored the southwestern portion of what is now the United States) found few of the products the Spanish coveted. By contrast, Francisco Pizarro, who explored the western coast of South America, acquired the richest silver mines in the world by conquering and enslaving the Incas in 1535. Pizarro easily defeated the Incas, partly because their leaders had largely been wiped out by a smallpox epidemic shortly before his arrival. Just half a century after Columbus's first voyage, the Spanish monarchs—who treated the American territories as their personal possessions—controlled the richest, most extensive empire Europe had known since ancient Rome.

Spain established the model of colonization that other countries later attempted to imitate, a model with three major elements. First, the crown maintained tight control over the colonies, establishing a hierarchical government that allowed little autonomy to New World jurisdictions. That control included, for example, limiting the number of persons permitted to emigrate to America and insisting that the colonies import all their manufactured goods from Spain. Roman Catholic priests were dispatched to ensure the colonists' conformity with orthodox religious views. Second, most of the colonists sent from Spain were male. They married Indian—and later black—women, thereby creating the racially mixed population that characterizes much of Latin America to the present day.

Third, the colonies' wealth was based on the exploitation of both the native population and slaves imported from Africa. The Mesoamerican peoples, many of whom lived in urban areas, were accustomed to autocratic rule. Spaniards simply took over roles once assumed by native leaders, who had also exacted labor and tribute from their

In this early view of a Spanish gold mine in South America, enslaved Africans process gold—mining, washing, and drying the nuggets before giving them to a Spanish overseer.   Pierpont Morgan Library.

subjects. The *encomienda* system, which granted tribute from Indian villages to individual conquistadores as a reward for their services to the crown, in effect legalized Indian slavery. Laws adopted in 1542 later reformed the system, forbidding Spaniards from enslaving Indians while still allowing them to collect money and goods from their tributary villages. In response, the conquerors, familiar with slavery in Spain, began to import Africans in order to increase the labor force under their direct control. Indian and African workers were primarily employed on huge ranches, where horses, cat-

tle, and sheep were raised; in gold and silver mines; and on sugar plantations.

The New World's gold and silver, initially a boon, ultimately brought about the decline of Spain as a major power. The influx of unprece-

Spain's Economy Crumbles
——

dented wealth led to rapid inflation, which (among other adverse effects) caused Spanish products to be overpriced in international markets and imported goods to become cheaper in Spain. The once-profitable Spanish textile-manufacturing industry collapsed, as did scores of other businesses. The seemingly endless income from New World colonies emboldened successive Spanish monarchs to spend lavishly on wars against the Dutch and the English. Several times in the late sixteenth and early seventeenth centuries the monarchs repudiated the state debt, thus wreaking havoc on the nation's finances. When the South American gold and silver mines started to give out in the mid-seventeenth century, Spain's economy crumbled and the nation lost its international importance.

Spanish wealth derived from American suffering. The Spaniards deliberately leveled American cities, building cathedrals and monasteries on sites once occupied by Aztec, Incan, and Mayan temples. Some conquistadores sought to erase all vestiges of the great Indian cultures by burning the written records they found. With traditional ways of life in disarray, devastated by disease, and compelled to labor for their conquerors, many demoralized residents of Mesoamerica accepted the Christian religion brought to New Spain by Franciscan and Dominican friars.

At first the friars devoted their energies to persuading the Native Americans to move into new towns and to build Roman Catholic churches. In

Christianity in New Spain

such towns, they were exposed to European customs and to religious rituals newly elaborated in an attempt to assimilate Christianity and pagan beliefs. For example, the friars deliberately juxtaposed the cult of the Virgin Mary with that of the corn goddess. These conversion efforts met with remarkable success. Thousands of Native Americans residing in Spanish territory embraced Catholicism, at least partly because it was the religion of their new rulers and they were accustomed to obedience.

The Spanish missionaries who ventured farther north, into the territory of the present-day eastern United States, were less able to win converts, for villages there resisted the invaders. After several failed Spanish attempts to colonize the Atlantic coast, in 1565 a group of people led by Pedro Menendez de Avilés destroyed a feeble and short-lived French settlement in what is now northern Florida. Near its site they established St. Augustine, the first permanent European settlement in the modern United States. Efforts to Christian-

ize the local Indians succeeded only after the Franciscans, with the assistance of soldiers, forcibly moved them to mission towns; even then, many resisted the friars' message. Still, by the end of the sixteenth century a chain of Spanish missions stretched across northern Florida.

EUROPEAN TRADERS, FISHERMEN, AND EARLY SETTLEMENTS

Unlike the Spanish, other European nations did not start at once to colonize the coasts their sailors had explored. The Portuguese finally turned their attention away from Africa and India to Brazil, founding a small colony there in 1532. Not until after the middle of the century, though, did Brazil begin to develop a booming economy based on large-scale sugar production for the European market. By 1600, Portuguese ships were annually carrying thousands of enslaved Africans from Lower Guinea to labor on Brazilian sugar plantations.

Other Europeans were more interested in exploiting natural wealth than in conquering territories or introducing alien crops. The first important natural resource of North America was fish. John Cabot had reported that fish were so plentiful they could be caught merely by lowering baskets over the side of a vessel. Europeans rushed to take advantage of the abundance of fish, a product in great demand in their homelands as an inexpensive source of protein. By the 1570s, more than 350 ships were exploiting the bounty of the Newfoundland Banks each year.

Fishermen adopted different modes of working that were to have significant consequences for the history of the region. Mariners from Spain, Portugal, and southern France had abundant supplies of salt, produced in their home countries by evaporating sea water. Thus they employed "wet" fishery techniques: the sailors filled cask after cask with salted, gutted fish until the ship could hold no more. Such vessels commonly made two round trips from Europe each year, and the sailors rarely if ever went on shore.

In contrast, English seafarers, lacking ready access to salt, were forced to use "dry" fishing. They set up camps on shore, where half the fishermen stayed to process and dry the fish their fellow crew members caught. Because dried fish did not need to be carried quickly to Europe, English sailors made just one voyage a year to North America, and sometimes remained even through the winter. And because they needed more reliable sunshine to dry their catch than the foggy Newfoundland coast provided, they tended to fish in the more southerly waters off what is now Maine. As a result, when European nations moved to colonize what is now eastern Canada and the far northeastern United States, England had the best claim to the land, long though sporadically inhabited by its fishermen.

European fishermen soon learned that they could supplement their profits by exchanging cloth and metal goods like pots and knives for the Native Americans' beaver pelts, which Europeans used to make fashionable hats. At first the Europeans conducted their trading from ships sailing along the coast, but later they established permanent outposts on the mainland to centralize and control the traffic in furs. All were inhabited primarily by male adventurers, whose chief aim was to send as many pelts as possible home to Europe. (See Chapter 2 on the European trading posts.)

Northern Traders

The Europeans' insatiable demand for furs, especially beaver, was matched by the Native Americans' desire for European goods that could make their lives easier and establish their superiority over neighboring tribes. Some tribes began to concentrate so completely on trapping for the European market that they abandoned their traditional economies. The Abenakis of Maine, for example, became partially dependent on food supplied by their neighbors to the south, the Massachusett tribe, because they devoted most of their energies to catching beaver to sell to French traders. The Massachusetts, in turn, intensified their production of foodstuffs, which they traded to the Abenakis in exchange for the European metal tools they preferred to their own handmade stone implements. The intensive trade in pelts also had serious ecological consequences. In some regions, beavers were completely wiped out. The disappearance of their dams led to soil erosion, especially when combined with the extensive clearing of forests by later European settlers.

Though their nation was profiting handsomely from the fisheries and the fur trade, English merchants and political leaders watched enviously as Spain's American possessions enriched that country immeasurably. In the mid-sixteenth century, English "sea dogs" like John Hawkins and Sir Francis Drake began to raid Spanish treasure fleets sailing home from the West Indies. Their actions caused friction between the two countries and helped to foment a war that culminated in the defeat of a huge invasion force—the Spanish Armada—off the English coast in 1588. As a part of their contest with Spain, English people started to think about planting colonies in the Western Hemisphere, thereby preventing their enemy from completely dominating the New World and simultaneously gaining better access to valuable American commodities.

The first English colonial planners took Spain's possessions in the New World as both a model and a challenge. They hoped to reproduce Spanish successes by dispatching to America men who would similarly exploit the native peoples for their own and their nation's benefit. In the 1580s, a group that included Sir Humphrey Gilbert and his younger half-brother Sir Walter Raleigh promoted a scheme to establish outposts that could trade with the Indians and provide bases for attacks on New Spain. Approving the idea, Queen Elizabeth I authorized Raleigh and Gilbert to colonize North America. Gilbert failed to plant a colony in Newfoundland, dying in the attempt, and Raleigh was only briefly more successful. After two preliminary expeditions, in 1587 he sent 117 colonists to the territory he named Virginia (for Elizabeth, the "Virgin Queen"). They established a settlement on Roanoke Island, in what is now North Carolina, but in 1590 a resupply ship could not find them. The colonists had vanished, leaving only the word *Croatoan* (the name of a nearby island) carved on a tree.

Raleigh's Roanoke Colony

Thus England's first attempt to plant a permanent settlement on the North American coast failed, as had earlier efforts by Portugal on Cape Breton Island (early 1520s) and France in northern Florida (mid-1560s). All three enterprises collapsed for the same two reasons: inability to be self-sustaining with respect to food; and the hostility of neighboring groups, both American and European. The Spanish attack wiped out the French colony in 1565, and neither the Portuguese nor the English were able to maintain friendly relations with local Indians for very long.

The explanation for such failings becomes clear in Thomas Harriot's *A Briefe and True Report of the New Found Land of Virginia*, published in 1588 to publicize Raleigh's colony. Harriot was a noted English scientist who sailed with the second of the preliminary voyages to Roanoke and who was charged with describing the animals, plants, and people of the region for an English readership. His account revealed that though the explorers had been almost wholly dependent on nearby villagers for food, they had needlessly antagonized their neighbors by killing some of them for what Harriot himself admitted were unjustifiable reasons.

The scientist concluded by advising later colonizers to deal with the native peoples of America more humanely than his comrades had. But the content of his book suggested why that advice would rarely be followed. *A Briefe and True Report* essentially examined the possibilities for economic development in America. Harriot stressed three points: the availability of commodities familiar to Europeans, like grapes, iron, copper, and fur-bearing animals; the potential profitability of exotic American products such as maize, cassava, and to-bacco; and the relative ease of manipulating the native population to the Europeans' advantage. Should the Americans attempt to resist the English by force, Harriot asserted, the latter's advantages of disciplined soldiers and superior weaponry would quickly deliver victory.

"In respect of us they are a people poore, and for want of skill and judgement in the knowledge and use of our things, doe esteeme our trifles before thinges of greater value," he declared, though simultaneously acknowledging that "they seeme very ingenious" in their adaptation to the environment. The Americans, he thought, would come to recognize the superiority of English technology and would want to share in that knowledge as well as in the "true religion," Protestant Christianity. And they would be further encouraged in a desire "for pleasing and obeying us" by what Harriot termed a "rare and strange accident." In towns that had angered the English, he recorded, "the people began to die very fast, and many in short space. . . . The disease [was] also so strange, that they neither knew what it was, nor how to cure it." Some of the villagers concluded that "it was the worke of our God through our meanes, and that wee by

John White, an artist with Raleigh's 1585 expedition (and later the governor of the ill-fated 1587 colony), illustrated three different fishing techniques used by Carolina Indians: to the left, the construction of weirs and traps; in the background, spearfishing in shallow water; and, in the foreground, fishing from dugout canoes. The fish are accurately drawn and can be identified by species today. Courtesy of the Trustees of the British Museum.

him might kil and slai whom wee would without weapons," others that the English were themselves gods, "since there was no man of ours knowne to die, or that was specially sicke."

Harriot's *Briefe and True Report* thus depicted for his English readers a bountiful land open to easy exploitation, full of opportunities for profit. The people already resident there would, he thought, "in a short time be brought to civilitie" through conversion to Christianity, admiration of European superiority, conquest, or, quite simply, death from disease. Thomas Harriot understood the key elements of the story, but his prediction was far off the mark. European dominance of North America was to be difficult to achieve. Indeed, some historians today argue that it never was fully achieved, in the sense Harriot and his compatriots intended, and that the societies that subsequently developed in North America owed as much to their native origins as to their immigrant ones.

The process of initial contact between Europeans and Americans that ended with Thomas Harriot near the close of the sixteenth century had begun approximately 250 years earlier when Portuguese sailors first set out to explore the Mediterranean Atlantic and to settle on its islands. That region of the Atlantic so close to European and African shores nurtured the mariners who, like Christopher Columbus, ventured into previously unknown waters, those who sailed to India and Brazil as well as to the Caribbean and the North American coast. When he first reached the Americas, Columbus thought he had found his intended destination, Asia. Later explorers knew better but, except for the Spanish, regarded the Americas primarily as a barrier that prevented them from reaching their long-sought goal of an oceanic route to the riches of China and the Moluccas. Ordinary European fishermen were the first to realize that the northern coasts had valuable products to offer: fish and furs, both much in demand in their homelands.

Of course, the wealth of the north could not compare to that of Mesoamerica. The Aztec empire, heir to the trading networks of Teotihuacan as well as to the intellectual sophistication of the Mayas, dazzled the conquistadores with the magnificence of its buildings and its seemingly unlimited wealth. As an old man, Bernal Díaz del Castillo recalled his first sight of Tenochtitlan, situated in the midst of Lake Texcoco: "We were amazed and said that it was like the enchantments . . . on account of the great towers and cues [temples] and buildings rising from the water, and all built of masonry." Some soldiers asked, he remembered, "whether the things that we saw were not a dream?"

The Aztecs had predicted that their Fifth Sun would end in earthquakes and hunger. Hunger they surely experienced after Cortés's invasion; and, if there were no earthquakes, the great temples tumbled to the ground nevertheless, as the Spaniards used their stones (and Indian laborers)

to construct cathedrals honoring their God and his son Jesus rather than Huitzilopochtli. The conquerors employed first American and later enslaved African workers to till the fields, mine the precious metals, and herd the livestock that earned immense profits for themselves and their mother country.

The initial impact of Europeans on the Americas proved devastating. Flourishing civilizations were, if not entirely destroyed, markedly altered in just a few short decades. The Europeans' "invasion team" of diseases and livestock, along with a wide range of other imported plants and animals, irrevocably changed the American environment, affecting the lives of the Western Hemisphere's inhabitants. By the end of the sixteenth century, many fewer people resided on the continent than had lived there before Columbus's arrival, even taking European immigration into account. And the people who did live there—Indian, African, and European—resided in a world that was literally new—a world engaged in the unprecedented process of combining foods, religions, economies, styles of life, and political systems that had developed separately for millennia. Understandably enough, conflict and dissension were to permeate that process.

SUGGESTIONS FOR FURTHER READING

General

Alfred W. Crosby, *The Columbian Exchange: Biological and Cultural Consequences of 1492* (1972); Alfred W. Crosby, *Ecological Imperialism: The Biological Expansion of Europe, 800–1900* (1986); Jay A. Levenson, ed., *Circa 1492: Art in the Age of Exploration* (1991); William H. McNeill, *Plagues and Peoples* (1976); D. W. Meinig, *Atlantic America, 1492–1800* (1986); Zvi Dor Ner and William Scheller, *Columbus and the Age of Discovery* (1991); Ann Ramenofsky, *Vectors of Death* (1987); Kirkpatrick Sale, *The Conquest of Paradise: Christopher Columbus and the Columbus Legacy* (1990); Tzvetan Todorov, *The Conquest of America* (1984); Herman Viola and Carolyn Margolis, eds., *Seeds of Change: Five Hundred Years Since Columbus* (1991); Eric Wolf, *Europe and the People Without History* (1982).

Mesoamerican Civilizations

Inga Clendinnen, *Aztecs* (1991); Michael Coe, *Mexico*, 3rd. ed. (1984); Nigel Davies, *The Aztecs: A History* (1973); Brian Fagan, *Kingdoms of Gold, Kingdoms of Jade: The Americas Before Columbus* (1991); Charles Gallenkamp, *Maya: The Riddle and Rediscovery of a Lost Civilization*, 3rd. ed. (1985); Linda Schele and David Friedel, *A Forest of Kings* (1990); Linda Schele and Mary Ann Miller, *The Blood of Kings* (1986); Smithsonian Institution, *Handbook of Middle American Indians*, 16 vols. (1964–1976); Jacques Soustelle, *The Olmecs: The Oldest Civilization in Mexico* (1984).

North American Indians

Harold E. Driver, *Indians of North America*, 2nd ed. (1969); Brian Fagan, *The Great Journey: The Peopling of Ancient America* (1987); Melvin Fowler, *Cahokia: Ancient Capital of the Midwest* (1974); Alvin Josephy, Jr., ed., *America in 1492* (1992); Alice B. Kehoe, *North American Indians* (1981); Robert Silverberg, *The Moundbuilders of Ancient America: The Archaeology of a Myth* (1968); Smithsonian Institution, *Handbook of North American Indians*, 8 vols. (1978–1990); Colin F. Taylor, ed., *The Native Americans: The Indigenous People of North America* (1992).

Africa

Philip Curtin et al., *African History* (1978); Robert July, *Precolonial Africa* (1975); Richard Olaniyan, *African History and Culture* (1982); Roland Oliver, ed., *The Cambridge History of Africa, vol. 3: c. 1050–c. 1600* (1977); Roland Oliver and J. D. Fage, *A Short History of Africa* (1988).

Exploration and Discovery

Fredi Chiappelli et al., eds., *First Images of America: The Impact of the New World on the Old*, 2 vols. (1976); Sandra Cypess, *La Malinché in Mexican Literature* (1991); J. H. Elliott, *The Old World and the New, 1492–1650* (1970); Felipe Fernández-Armesto, *Before Columbus: Exploration and Colonization from the Mediterranean to the Atlantic, 1229–1492* (1987); Felipe Fernández-Armesto, *Columbus* (1991); Jerald T. Milanich and Susan Milbrath, eds., *First Encounters: Spanish Explorations in the Caribbean and the United States, 1492–1570* (1989); Samuel Eliot Morison, *The European Discovery of America: The Southern Voyages*, A.D. *1492–1616* (1974); Samuel Eliot Morison, *The European Discovery of America: The Northern Voyages*, A.D. *1500–1600* (1971); J. H. Parry, *The Age of Reconnaissance* (1963); J. H. Parry, *The Discovery of the Sea* (1974); William and Carla Phillips, *The Worlds of Christopher Columbus* (1992); David B. Quinn, *North America from Earliest Discovery to First Settlements* (1977); Paolo Emilio Taviani, *Columbus: The Great Adventure* (1991); John Noble Wilford, *The Mysterious History of Columbus* (1991).

Early European Settlements

Kenneth Andrews, *Trade, Plunder and Settlement: Maritime Enterprise and the Genesis of the British Empire, 1480–1630* (1984); Leslie Bethel, ed., *The Cambridge History of Latin America, vol. 2: Colonial Latin America* (1984); Nancy Farriss, *The Maya Under Colonial Rule* (1984); Charles Gibson, *The Aztec Under Spanish Rule* (1984); Charles Gibson, *Spain in America* (1966); Karen O. Kupperman, *Roanoke, the Abandoned Colony* (1984); Daniel Reff, *Disease, Depopulation, and Culture Change in Northwest New Spain, 1518–1764* (1991); John Super, *Food, Conquest, and Colonization in Sixteenth-Century Spanish America* (1988); David H. Thomas, ed., *Columbian Consequences*, 3 vols. (1989–1991); David J. Weber, *The Spanish Frontier in North America* (1992).

Europeans Colonize North America, 1600–1640

ROBERT RYCE WAS WORRIED, for he had learned that a good friend was seriously considering emigrating to North America. In August 1629 he took up his pen to convince John Winthrop, a Suffolk justice of the peace, to think twice before embarking for the New World. "Plantations ar for yonge men, that can enduer all paynes and hunger," he advised Winthrop, who was then 41, with eight children born to three wives. "To adventure your wholle famylly vpon so many manifeste vncerteynties standeth not with your wysdome and longe experience. . . . How harde wyll it bee for one browghte up amonge boockes and learned men to lyve in a barbarous place where is no learnynge and lesse cyvillytie."

John Winthrop politely acknowledged Ryce's letter, but he was not dissuaded. Like many of his pious contemporaries, he believed that England had become corrupt—that it was no longer possible, as he put it, for a "good and uprighte man" to live "comfortably" in his homeland. In his opinion, the Church of England, which had split from Roman Catholicism during the sixteenth century, needed to be purified; hence, Winthrop and others like him were called "Puritans." The easi-est way to avoid conflicts with the leaders of the English church and to worship as he pleased, he thought, was to emigrate to America, a remote land beyond the immediate reach of English religious authorities.

Winthrop also believed that Protestants should become as active as Catholics in attempting to convert nonbelievers to Christianity. "It is a scandale to our Religion," he declared, "that we shewe not as muche zeale in seekinge the conversion of the heathen, as the Papistes doe." Puritan colonizers in America could work toward that goal. And why, Winthrop asked, should people continue to live in crowded England, when "whole countrys . . . lye waste without any improvement"? When someone pointed out to him that "other sonnes of Adam" already lived on the land he coveted, he responded confidently that "these salvadge peoples ramble over muche lande without title or propertye."

As John Winthrop made his plans to move to New England in 1629 and 1630, he had the unqualified support of his wife. Margaret Tyndal Winthrop fell in eagerly with the scheme, as certain as her husband that "it is the place whearein god will have us to settle in." Although John left her behind when he sailed to America in the spring of 1630, Margaret followed him the next year, immediately after the birth of the baby that had occasioned the delay. Some of the older Winthrop children surely agreed with their parents' decision, but perhaps not all of them did. John's second son, Henry, drowned shortly after reaching New England—committing suicide, it was rumored, as soon as he saw the wild, uninviting coastline of what was to be his new home.

More than any other European people colonizing the Americas, the English who moved to mainland North America tried to reproduce the society they had left. They did not, of course, want to copy it without any modifications; Winthrop and his fellow Puritans sought to reform English religious practices, and other emigrants were trying to better their economic circumstances. Yet even so,

John Winthrop, the steadfast first governor of the Massachusetts Bay Colony, stares purposefully out from the portrait painted before he left England. His strength of character is evident even from this image. American Antiquarian Society.

the English colonists differed significantly from their Spanish, French, and Dutch counterparts. The American settlements of those nations were composed primarily of male emigrants who hoped to make a quick profit from the New World's lands and peoples and then return to their homelands. That not all of them succeeded in that endeavor did not change their basic motivation or the fact that most of them planned to remain in America only temporarily.

The English, as both John Winthrop and Thomas Harriot made clear, were no less interested in profiting financially from North America. But especially in New England they emigrated as families, sometimes along with friends and relatives from neighboring villages. Most of the English people came to America with the intention of staying, though not all of them did. They recreated European society and family life to an extent not possible in the other, more thinly populated colonies, where migrant men had to find their sexual partners within the Native American or African populations. Among the English colonies, those in the Chesapeake region and on the Caribbean islands most closely resembled colonies founded by other nations. Their economies, like those of New Spain or Brazil, soon came to be based on large-scale production for the international market by a labor force composed of bonded servants and slaves.

Wherever they settled, the English, like other Europeans, failed to prosper until they had learned to adapt to the alien environment. The first permanent English colonies survived only because nearby Indians assisted the newcomers. The settlers had to learn to grow such unfamiliar American crops as maize (corn) and tobacco. They also had to develop extensive trading relationships with Native Americans and with colonies established by other European countries. In need of laborers for their fields, they eventually began to import African slaves, copying the example of the Spanish in the Atlantic islands and New Spain, and the Portuguese in São Tomé and Brazil. Thus the early history of the region that became the United States and the English Caribbean can best be understood as a series of complex interactions among a variety of European, African, and American peoples and environments rather than as the simple story of a triumph by only one of those groups—the English colonists.

• *Important Events* •

1533	Henry VIII divorces Catherine of Aragon; English Reformation begins	**1624**	Dutch settle on Manhattan Island (New Amsterdam)
1558	Elizabeth I becomes queen		English colonize St. Christopher, first island in Lesser Antilles to be settled by Europeans
1603	James I becomes king	**1625**	Charles I becomes king
1607	Jamestown founded; first permanent English settlement in North America	**1630**	Massachusetts Bay colony founded
1608	Quebec founded by the French	**1634**	Maryland founded
1611	First Virginia tobacco crop	**1635**	Roger Williams expelled from Massachusetts Bay; founds Providence, Rhode Island
1614	Fort Orange (Albany) founded by the Dutch	**1636**	Connecticut founded
1619	First Africans arrive in Virginia	**1637**	Pequot War in New England
	Virginia House of Burgesses established, first representative assembly in the English colonies		Anne Hutchinson expelled from Massachusetts Bay colony; goes to Rhode Island
1620	Plymouth colony founded; first permanent English settlement in New England	**c. 1640**	Sugar cultivation begins on Barbados
		1642	Montreal founded
1622	Powhatan Confederacy attacks Virginia colony	**1646**	Treaty ends hostilities between Virginia and Powhatan Confederacy

NEW FRANCE, NEW NETHERLAND, AND THE CARIBBEAN

England was not the only European country to become interested in colonizing North America and its offshore islands in the early seventeenth century. The Netherlands and France also established permanent settlements in the region north of New Spain. Varying by location and economic goals, the French and Dutch colonies also for the most part developed very differently from their English neighbors. The mass migration of English people to mainland North America had no counterpart in other nations' colonies; consequently, population and settlement patterns diverged significantly in the three countries' American possessions.

After Spain's destruction of France's Florida settlement in 1565, the French turned their atten-

New France

tion northward, to the area explored by Jacques Cartier in the 1530s. Several times in the late sixteenth century they tried futilely to establish permanent bases along the coast of what is now Canada. Finally, in 1608 Samuel de Champlain founded a trading post at an interior site the local Iroquois had called Stadacona when Cartier spent the winter there seventy-five years earlier. Champlain renamed it Quebec. He had chosen well: Quebec was the most easily defended spot in the entire St. Lawrence River valley, a stronghold that controlled access to the heartland of the continent. In 1642, the French established a second post, Montreal, at the falls of the St. Lawrence (and thus at the end of navigation by ocean-going vessels), a place the Indians called Hochelaga.

Before the founding of Quebec and Montreal, French fishermen had served as the major conduits through which North American beaver pelts reached France, but the two new posts quickly

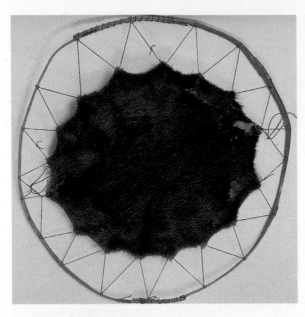

A modern re-creation of a beaver pelt being cured on a frame demonstrates how Native Americans prepared the furs they subsequently traded to the Europeans in exchange for metal goods, guns, and alcohol. Massachusetts Fish & Wildlife Commission. Photo by Mark Sexton of the Peabody and Essex Museum, Salem.

took over control of the lucrative trade in furs, which were prepared by stretching on a wooden frame (see photo). The settlements had only a few European residents, most of them men, some of whom married Native American women. The colony's leaders offered land grants along the river to prospective settlers, including wealthy seigneurs (nobles) who were expected to import tenants to work their farms. A small number of Frenchmen brought their wives and took up agriculture; even so, more than twenty-five years after Quebec's founding, it had just sixty-four resident families, along with traders and soldiers. With respect to territory occupied and farmed, the colony of New France never grew much beyond the confines of the river valley between Quebec and Montreal.

One other important group comprised part of the population of New France: missionaries of the Society of Jesus (Jesuits), a Roman Catholic order

Jesuit Missions in New France

dedicated to converting non-believers to Christianity. The first Jesuits arrived in the colony in 1625, determined to follow the lead of the Franciscans in New Spain. In 1639 they were joined in New

France by two orders of nuns, the most important of which were the Ursulines. The Jesuits, whom the Native Americans called Black Robes, initially tried to persuade the tribal peoples to live near French settlements and to adopt European lifestyles as well as the Europeans' religion. When that effort failed, the Jesuits concluded that they could introduce Roman Catholicism to their new charges without insisting that they alter most of their customary modes of existence. So the Black Robes learned Native American languages and traveled to remote regions in pursuit of their goal. By the early eighteenth century, they were living in present-day Illinois.

In their pursuit of conversions, the Jesuits sought to undermine the authority of village shamans (the traditional religious leaders) and to gain the confidence of leaders who could influence others. The Black Robes used a variety of weapons to attain the desired end. Trained in rhetoric, they won admirers by their eloquence. Seemingly immune to smallpox, they explained epidemics among the Native Americans as God's punishment for sin, their arguments aided by the ineffectiveness of the shamans' traditional remedies for illness against that deadly disease. Drawing on European science, the Jesuits predicted solar and lunar eclipses. Perhaps most important of all, they amazed the villagers by communicating with each other over long distances and periods of time by employing marks on paper. The Native Americans' desire to learn how to harness the extraordinary power of literacy was one of the most critical factors in making them receptive to the Jesuits' message.

Although the process took many years, the Jesuits slowly gained thousands of converts, some of whom moved to reserves set aside for Christian Indians. In those communities they followed Catholic teachings with fervor and piety. The converts replaced their own culture's traditional equal treatment of men and women with notions more congenial to the Europeans' insistence on male dominance and female subordination. Further, they altered their practice of allowing premarital sexual relationships and easy divorce because Catholic doctrine prohibited both customs.

The Jesuit missionaries had no competition from other Europeans for the Native Americans' souls, but French traders confronted a challenge. In 1614, just five years after Henry Hudson sailed

The Founding of Permanent European Colonies in North America, 1565–1640

Colony	Founder(s)	Date	Basis of Economy
Florida	Pedro Menendez de Avilés	1565	farming
New Mexico	Juan de Oñate	1598	livestock
Virginia	Virginia Company	1607	tobacco
New France	France	1608	fur trading
New Netherland	Dutch West India Company	1614	fur trading
Plymouth	Pilgrims	1620	farming, fishing
Maine	Sir Ferdinando Gorges	1622	fishing
St. Kitts, Barbados, et al.	European migrants	1624	sugar
Massachusetts Bay	Massachusetts Bay Company	1630	farming, fishing, fur trading
Maryland	Cecilius Calvert	1634	tobacco
Rhode Island	Roger Williams	1635	farming
Connecticut	Thomas Hooker	1636	farming, fur trading
New Haven	Massachusetts migrants	1638	farming
New Hampshire	Massachusetts migrants	1638	farming, fishing

up the river that now bears his name, his Dutch sponsors established an outpost (Fort Orange) on the site of present-day Albany, New York. Like the French, they sought beaver pelts, and their presence so close to Quebec posed at least a potential threat to French domination of the region. Holland, at the time the world's dominant commercial power, was interested primarily in trade rather than colonization. Thus New Netherland, like New France, remained small, also focused on a river valley—the Hudson. The colony's southern anchor was New Amsterdam, a town founded in 1624 on Manhattan Island, at the mouth of the Hudson.

New Netherland

As the Dutch West India Company's outpost in North America, New Netherland was a relatively unimportant part of a vast commercial empire that included posts in Africa, Brazil, the West Indies, and modern-day Indonesia. Autocratic directors-general ruled the colony for the company; with no elected assembly, settlers felt little loyalty to their nominal leaders. Migration was sparse. Even a company policy of 1629 that offered a large land grant, or patroonship, to anyone who would bring fifty settlers to the province failed to attract takers. (Only one such tract—Rensselaerswyck, near Albany—was ever fully developed.) As late as the mid-1660s, New Netherland had only about five thousand inhabitants.

Despite their geographical proximity, New France and New Netherland did not come into serious conflict with each other. Yet their respective American trading partners did. In the 1640s, the Iroquois, who traded chiefly with the Dutch and lived in modern upstate New York, went to war against their northern neighbors the Hurons, who traded primarily with the French and lived in present-day Ontario. The Iroquois wanted to become the major supplier of pelts to the Europeans and to ensure the security of their hunting territories. They achieved both goals by practically exterminating the Hurons (whose population had already been decimated by a recent epidemic) through the use of guns they obtained from their

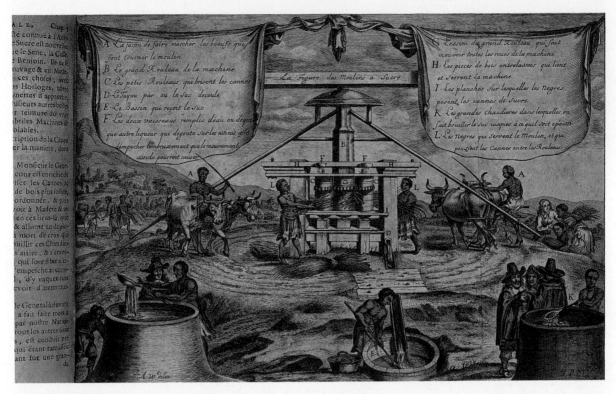

In the 1660s, a French book illustrated the various phases of sugar processing for curious European readers. Teams of oxen (A) turned the mill, the rollers of which crushed the canes (C), producing the sap (D), which was collected in a vat (E), then boiled down into molasses (K). All phases of the process were managed primarily by African slaves, with minimal supervision by a few Europeans (foreground). Library Company of Philadelphia.

Dutch allies. The Iroquois thus established themselves as a major force in the region, one that Europeans could ignore only at their peril.

It was in the Caribbean that France, Holland, and England, the third entrant into the contest for North America, clashed most openly in the first half of the seventeenth century. The Spanish had concentrated their colonization efforts on the larger islands (the Greater Antilles)—Cuba, Hispaniola, Jamaica, and Puerto Rico. They had left many smaller islands alone, partly because of resistance by the Carib inhabitants, partly because the conquistadores were more interested in exploiting the greater wealth of the mainland. But to the other European powers, the tiny islands were attractive targets: not only could they provide bases from which to attack each other and Spanish vessels loaded with American gold and silver, they also could serve as a source of valuable tropical products.

The English were the first of the northern European nations to establish a permanent foothold in the smaller islands of the West Indies (the Lesser Antilles). They founded a settlement on St. Christopher (St. Kitts) in 1624, followed by others on such islands as Barbados (1627). The French and the Dutch sought similar outposts in the early 1630s. The French also moved on to St. Kitts, then to Guadeloupe and Martinique, while the Dutch settled on Curaçao (near the South American coast) in 1634, as well as on St. Eustatius, an islet strategically located close to St. Kitts. Some of these islands had been uninhabited, but Guadeloupe and Martinique in particular were vigorously defended by the Caribs. It took the French many years to secure their control of these two relatively large and fertile islands. In addition to the native inhabitants, the northern European interlopers had to worry about conflicts with the Spanish and each other. Most of the islands were attacked at least once during the course of the century, and some changed hands. For example, the English drove the Spanish out of Jamaica in 1655, and the French soon thereafter took over half of Hispaniola, creating the colony of St. Domingue (modern Haiti).

Why did the European powers devote so much energy to gaining control of these tiny bits of land that Spain had neglected? After 1640 there was one

Supplying Europe's Sweet Tooth
——

primary answer to that question: sugar. Early in the 1640s the English residents of Barbados discovered that their soil and climate were ideally suited for the cultivation of sugar cane, then the major source of sweetness in the human diet. Europeans at the time grew that expensive, desirable luxury food in only a few widely scattered locations: Madeira, the Canaries, São Tomé, and Brazil.

Sugar, along with maize and livestock, was one of the most important components of the post-Columbian exchange of plants and animals. First domesticated in the East Indies, sugar spread to the Asian mainland. By 1000 C.E. it was being grown in North Africa and southern Spain. But neither those regions nor the Atlantic islands settled in the fifteenth century could supply the demands of Europe's insatiable sweet tooth. Canary Island sugar canes were among the plants Columbus carried to Hispaniola on his 1493 voyage; by the 1520s, plantations (probably worked by African slaves) in the Greater Antilles were regularly shipping cargoes of sugar to Spain. The Spanish, though, were chiefly interested in the mainland, so the government did not encourage sugar cultivation in the Caribbean. By the last decades of the sixteenth century, most American sugar was being produced in Brazil.

The Dutch provided the key to the introduction of sugar-cane agriculture to the newly colonized Lesser Antilles. In 1630 they seized control of Brazil from the Portuguese, holding it until 1654. There the Dutch learned how to grow and—more importantly—to process sugar cane, and they taught those skills to the Barbadians. The Dutch were not being altruistic: they expected to sell African slaves to West Indian planters and to carry the barrels of sugar back to Europe. The results must have exceeded their wildest dreams. The Barbados sugar boom in the 1640s was both explosive and lucrative. Planters, slave-traders, and Dutch ship-

ping interests alike earned immense profits. Of course, as other Caribbean planters adopted sugar-cane cultivation, the Barbadians' profits fell. Nevertheless, sugar remained the most valuable American commodity for more than one hundred years. In the eighteenth century, sugar grown in British Jamaica and French St. Domingue dominated the world market. Yet, in the long run, the future economic importance of the Europeans' American colonies lay on the mainland rather than in the Caribbean.

——

ENGLAND COLONIZES MAINLAND NORTH AMERICA

The failure of Raleigh's attempt to colonize Virginia had ended English efforts at settlement in North America for nearly two decades. When the English decided in 1606 to try once more, they again planned colonies that imitated the Spanish model. Success came only when they abandoned that model and founded settlements very different from those of other European powers. Unlike Spain, France, or The Netherlands, England eventually sent large numbers of men and women to set up agriculturally based colonies on the mainland. Two major developments prompted approximately 200,000 ordinary English men and women to move to North America in the seventeenth century and led their government to encourage that migration.

The first development was a significant change in English religious practice, a transformation that eventually led large numbers of English dissenters

English Reformation
——

to leave their homeland. In 1533, Henry VIII, wanting a male heir and infatuated with Anne Boleyn, sought to annul his marriage to his Spanish-born queen, Catherine of Aragon, despite nearly twenty years of marriage. When the pope refused to approve the annulment, Henry left the Roman Catholic church, founded the Church of England, and—with Parliament's concurrence—proclaimed himself its head. The English people welcomed the schism. Many had little respect for the English Catholic church, which at the time was filled with corrupt bishops and ignorant priests. At first the reformed Church of England differed little from

Tudor and Stuart Monarchs of England, 1509–1649

Monarch	Reign	Relation to Predecessor
Henry VIII	1509–1547	Son
Edward VI	1547–1553	Son
Mary I	1553–1558	Half-sister
Elizabeth I	1558–1603	Half-sister
James I	1603–1625	Cousin
Charles I	1625–1649	Son

Catholicism in its practices, but under Henry's daughter Elizabeth I (child of his marriage to Anne Boleyn), new currents of religious belief that had originated on the European continent early in the sixteenth century dramatically affected the English church.

The leaders of the continental Protestant Reformation were Martin Luther, a German monk, and John Calvin, a French cleric and lawyer. Combating the Catholic doctrine that priests must serve as intermediaries between lay people and God, Luther and Calvin insisted that each person could interpret the Bible for himself or herself. One result of that notion was the spread of literacy: to understand and interpret the Bible, people had to learn how to read it for themselves. Both Luther and Calvin rejected Catholic rituals and denied the need for an elaborate church hierarchy. They also asserted that salvation came through faith alone, rather than—as Catholic teaching had it—through a combination of faith and good works. Calvin, though, went further than Luther in stressing God's absolute omnipotence and emphasizing the need for people to submit totally to God's will.

Elizabeth I tolerated religious diversity among her subjects as long as they generally acknowledged her authority as head of the Church of England. Accordingly, during her

Puritans

long reign (1558–1603) Calvin's ideas gained influence within the English church. By the late sixteenth century, many English Calvinists—those who, like John Winthrop, came to be called "Puritans"—believed that the English Refor-

mation had not gone far enough. Henry had simplified the church hierarchy; they wanted to abolish it altogether. Henry had subordinated the church to the interests of the state; they wanted a church free from political interference. And the Church of England, like the Roman Catholic church, continued to include all English people in its membership. The Puritans preferred a more restricted definition; they wanted to confine church membership to persons believed to be "saved."

Elizabeth I's Stuart successors, her cousin James I (1603–1625) and his son Charles I (1625–1649), were less tolerant of Puritans than she. As Scots, they also had little respect for the traditions of representative government that had developed in England under the Tudors and their predecessors. The wealthy, taxpaying landowners who sat in Parliament had grown accustomed to having considerable influence on government policies, especially taxation. But James I, taking a position later endorsed by his son, publicly declared his adherence to the theory of the divine right of kings. The Stuarts insisted that a monarch's power came directly from God and that his subjects had a duty to obey him. A king's authority was absolute, they argued, just like the authority of a father over his children. Both James I and Charles I believed that their authority included the power to enforce religious conformity among their subjects. Because Puritans were challenging many of the most important precepts of the English church, the monarchs authorized the removal of Puritan clergymen from their pulpits. In the 1620s and 1630s a number of English Puritans accordingly decided to move to America, where they hoped to put their religious beliefs into practice unmolested by the Stuarts or the church hierarchy.

The second major development that led English folk to move to North America was the onset of dramatic social and economic change caused by

Social Change in England

the doubling of the English population in the 150-year period after 1530, largely as a result of the introduction of nutritious American crops into Europe. All those additional people needed food, clothing, and other goods. The competition for goods led to high inflation, coupled with a fall in real wages as the number of workers increased. In these new economic and demographic circumstances, some English people—especially those

London in 1616, with London Bridge at center right. Overcrowding in the city led many observers to conclude that American colonization could remove "excess" population and provide new employment for poverty-stricken persons. The rapidly growing community of London merchants also sought to develop new sources of overseas profits.   Courtesy of the Trustees of The British Library.

with sizable landholdings that could produce food and clothing fibers for the growing population— substantially improved their lot. Others, particularly landless laborers and those with very small amounts of land, fell into unremitting poverty. When landowners raised rents or decided to enclose and combine small holdings into large units, they forced tenant farmers off the land. Geographical as well as social mobility increased, and the population of the cities swelled. London, for example, more than tripled in size between 1550 and 1650, by which year 375,000 residents lived on its crowded streets, as shown in the illustration of London in 1616.

Well-to-do English people reacted with alarm to what they saw as the disappearance of traditional ways of life. The streets and highways were filled with steady streams of the landless and the homeless. Officials, obsessed with the problem of maintaining order, came to believe that England was overcrowded. They concluded that colonies established in the New World could siphon off England's "surplus population," thus easing the social strains at home. For similar reasons, many English people decided that they could improve their circumstances by migrating from a small, land-scarce, apparently overpopulated island to a large, land-rich continent. Such economic considerations affected English people's decisions to migrate to the colonies as much as, if not more than, a desire for escape from religious persecution.

The initial impetus for the establishment of what was to become England's first permanent colony in the Western Hemisphere came from a group of merchants and wealthy gentry. In 1606, envisioning the possibility of earning great profits from a New World settlement by finding precious metals and opening new trade routes, they set up a joint-stock company, the Virginia Company, to plant colonies in America.

Joint-stock companies had been developed in England during the sixteenth century as a mechanism for pooling the resources of many small investors. These forerunners

Joint-Stock Companies

of modern corporations were funded through the sale of stock. Until the founding of the Virginia Company, they had been used primarily to finance trading voyages; for that purpose they worked well. No one person risked too much money, and investors usually received quick returns. But joint-stock companies turned out to be a poor way to finance colonies, because the early settlements required enormous amounts of capital and, with rare exceptions, failed to return much immediate profit. The colonies founded by joint-stock companies consequently suffered from a chronic lack of capital—investors did not want to send good money after bad—and from constant tension between stockholders and colonists (who claimed they were not being adequately supported by the joint-stock companies).

The Virginia Company was no exception to this rule. Chartered by James I in 1606, the company tried but failed to start a colony in Maine and barely succeeded in planting

Founding of Virginia

one in Virginia. In 1607 it dispatched 144 men and boys to North America. Ominously, the vessels were ravaged by disease, and only 104 passengers survived the voyage, which followed the well-known route from the Canaries to the Caribbean before heading northward. In May of that year, they reached a region called Tsenacomoco by its native inhabitants. There they established the settlement called Jamestown on a swampy peninsula in a river they also named for their monarch. The colonists were ill-equipped for survival in the unfamiliar environment, and the settlement was afflicted by dissension and disease.

By January 1608, only 38 of the original colonists were still alive. Many of the first migrants were gentlemen unaccustomed to working with their hands and artisans with irrelevant skills like glassmaking. Having come to Virginia expecting to make easy fortunes, most could not adjust to the conditions they encountered. They resisted living "like savages," retaining English dress and casual work habits despite their desperate circumstances. Such attitudes, combined with the effects of chronic malnutrition and epidemic disease, took a terrible toll. Only when Captain John Smith, one of the colony's founders, imposed military discipline on the colonists in 1608 was Jamestown saved from collapse. But after Smith's departure the settlement experienced a severe "starving time" (the winter of 1609–1610), during which some colonists even resorted to cannibalism. Although a few wives and children of early settlers arrived in 1609 and living conditions began to improve, as late as 1624 only 1,300 of approximately 8,000 English migrants to Virginia remained alive.

That the colony survived at all was a tribute not to the English but rather to the Native Americans within whose territories they settled, a group of six Algonkian tribes known

Powhatan Confederacy

as the Powhatan Confederacy (see map, page 46). Powhatan, a shrewd and powerful leader, was aggressively consolidating his authority over some twenty-five other small tribes in the area when the Europeans arrived. Fortunately for the English, Powhatan at first viewed them as potential allies. He found the English colony a reliable source of such items as steel knives and guns, which gave him a technological advantage over his Indian neighbors. In return, Powhatan's tribes traded their excess corn and other foodstuffs to the starving colonists. The initially cordial relationship soon deteriorated, however. The English colonists kidnapped Powhatan's daughter, Pocahontas, holding her as a hostage in retaliation for Powhatan's seizure of several settlers. In captivity, she agreed in 1614 to marry an Englishman, John Rolfe, who expressed the desire to convert her to Christianity.

Thereafter the relationship between the Jamestown colony and the coastal tribes was an uneasy one. English and Algonkian peoples had much in common: deep religious beliefs, a lifestyle oriented around agriculture, clear political and social hierarchies, and sharply defined gender roles. Yet the English and the Powhatans themselves usually focused on their cultural differences, not their similarities. English men thought that Indian men were lazy because they hunted (hunting was a sport in English eyes) and did not work in the fields. Indian men thought English men effeminate because they did "women's work" of cultivation. In the same vein, the English believed that Algonkian women were oppressed since they did heavy field labor.

Other differences between the two cultures caused serious misunderstandings. Although both societies were hierarchical, the nature of the hierarchies differed considerably.

Algonkian and English Cultural Differences ——— Among the East Coast Algonkian tribes, people were not born to positions of leadership, nor were political power and social status necessarily inherited through the male line. The English gentry inherited their position from their fathers, and English political and military leaders tended to rule autocratically. By contrast, the authority of Algonkian leaders rested on consensus among their fellow tribesmen. Accustomed to the European concept of powerful kings, the English sought such figures within the tribes. Often (for example, when negotiating treaties) they willfully overestimated the ability of chiefs to make independent decisions for their people.

Furthermore, the Algonkians and the English had very different notions of property ownership. In most eastern tribes, land was held communally by the entire group. It could not be bought or sold absolutely, although certain rights to use the land (for example, for hunting or fishing) could be transferred. The English, on the other hand, were accustomed to individual farms and to buying and selling land. In addition, the English refused to accept the validity of tribal claims to traditional hunting territories, insisting that only land intensively cultivated could be regarded as owned or occupied by a tribe. Like John Winthrop, they assumed that people who "rambled" over a landscape without farming it could not claim it as their property.

Above all, the English settlers believed unwaveringly in the superiority of their civilization. Although in the early years of colonization they often anticipated living peacefully alongside the Native Americans, they always assumed that they would dictate the terms of such coexistence. Like Thomas Harriot at Roanoke, they expected the Native Americans to adopt English customs and to convert to Christianity. They showed little respect for traditional Indian ways of life, especially when they believed their own interests were at stake. That attitude was clearly revealed in the Virginia col-

Theodor de Bry's America *depicted crucial events in the continents' history. This illustration is de Bry's version of the kidnapping of Pocahontas, Powhatan's daughter, in 1612. In the foreground, Pocahontas is being enticed by other Native Americans to join the English; at right center, she is led onto a ship, while in the background English raiders burn the villages of Powhatan's people.* Library of Congress.

ony's treatment of the Powhatan Confederacy in subsequent years.

What upset the balance between the English and the Indians was the spread of tobacco cultivation. In tobacco—the American crop previously introduced to Europe

Tobacco: The Basis of Virginia's Success ——— by the Spanish—the settlers and the Virginia Company found the salable commodity for which they had been searching. John Rolfe planted the first crop in 1611. In 1620 Virginians exported 40,000 pounds of cured leaves, and by the end of that decade shipments had jumped dramatically to 1.5 million pounds. The great tobacco boom had begun, fueled by high prices and substantial profits for planters. The price later fell almost as sharply as it had risen, and it fluctuated wildly from year to year in response to increasing supply and international competition. Nevertheless, tobacco became the foundation of Virginia's prosperity, and the colony developed from a small outpost peopled exclusively by males

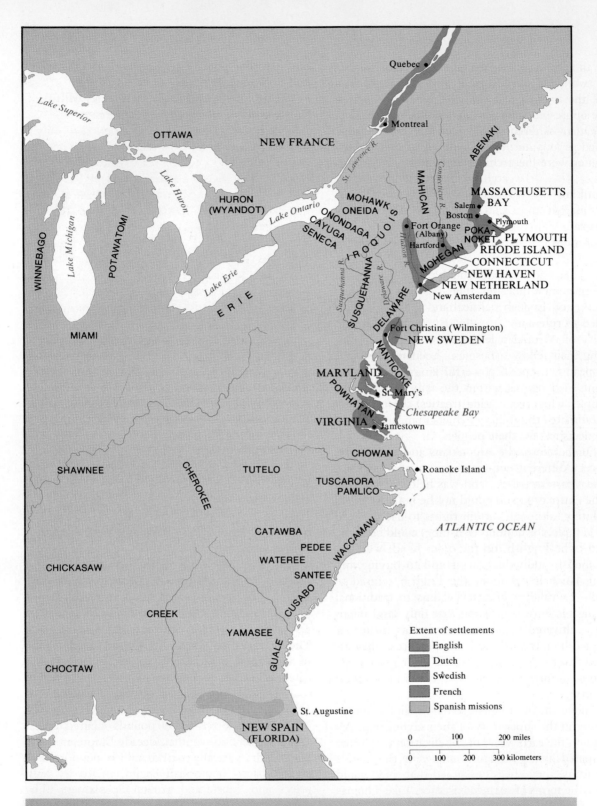

European Settlements and Indian Tribes in Eastern North America, 1650 *The few European settlements established before 1650 were widely scattered, hugging the shores of the Atlantic Ocean and the banks of its major rivers. By contrast, America's native inhabitants controlled the vast interior expanse of the continent.*

into an agricultural settlement inhabited by both men and women.

Successful tobacco cultivation required abundant land, since the crop quickly drained soil of nutrients. Planters soon learned that a field could produce only about three satisfactory crops before it had to lie fallow for several years to regain its fertility. Thus the once-small English settlements began to expand rapidly: eager planters applied to the Virginia Company for large land grants on both sides of the James River and its tributary streams. Lulled into a false sense of security by years of peace, the planters established farms at some distance from one another along the river banks—a settlement pattern convenient for tobacco cultivation but poorly designed for defense.

Opechancanough, Powhatan's brother and successor, watched the English colonists steadily encroaching on the confederacy's lands and attempting to convert its members to Christianity. Recognizing the danger his brother had overlooked, the great war leader launched coordinated attacks all along the river on March 22, 1622. By the end of the day, 347 colonists (about one-quarter of the total) lay dead, and only a timely warning from two Christian converts saved Jamestown itself from destruction.

The Virginia colony reeled from the blow but did not collapse. Reinforced by new shipments of men and arms from England, the settlers attacked Opechancanough's villages. For some years an uneasy peace prevailed, but then in April 1644 Opechancanough tried one last time to repel the invaders. He failed, giving his life in the war that ensued. In 1646, survivors of the Powhatan Confederacy accepted a treaty formally subordinating them to English authority. Although they continued to live in the region, their alliance crumbled and their efforts to resist the spread of European settlement ended.

LIFE IN THE CHESAPEAKE: VIRGINIA AND MARYLAND

The 1622 Powhatan Confederacy uprising that failed to destroy the colony did succeed in killing its parent. The Virginia Company never made any profits from the enterprise, for all its earnings were offset by the heavy cost of supporting the settlers and by internal corruption. In 1624 James I revoked the charter and made Virginia a royal colony, ruled by the king through appointed officials. At the same time, though, he continued an important policy designed to attract settlers, which the company had adopted in 1617. Under the "headright" system, every new arrival paying his or her own way was promised a land grant of fifty acres; those who financed the passage of others received headrights for each. To ordinary English farmers, many of whom had owned little or no land, the headright system offered a powerful incentive to migrate to Virginia. To wealthy gentry, it promised even more: the possibility of establishing vast agricultural enterprises worked by large numbers of laborers.

In 1619, the company had introduced a second policy that James was more reluctant to retain: it had authorized the landowning men of the major Virginia settlements to elect representatives to a legislature called the House of Burgesses. Although England was a monarchy, English landholders had long been accustomed to electing members of Parliament and controlling their own local governments. In accordance with his belief in the absolute power of the monarchy and his distrust of legislative bodies, James at first abolished the Virginia assembly. But the settlers protested so vigorously that by 1629 the House of Burgesses was functioning once again. Only two decades after the first permanent English settlement had been planted in North America, the colonists were insisting on governing themselves at the local level. Thus the political structure of England's American possessions came to differ from that of New Spain, New France, and New Netherland, all of which were ruled autocratically.

By the 1630s, tobacco was firmly established in Virginia as the staple crop and chief source of revenue. It quickly became just as important in the second English colony planted on Chesapeake Bay: Maryland, chartered by Charles I in 1632 and given to the Calvert family as a personal possession (proprietorship). (Because Virginia and Maryland both border Chesapeake Bay—see map, page 46—they are often referred to collectively as "the Chesapeake.") The Calverts intended the colony to serve as a haven for their fellow Roman Catholics, who

Founding of Maryland

were being persecuted in England. Cecilius Calvert, second Lord Baltimore, became the first colonizer to offer freedom of religion to all Christian settlers; he realized that protecting the Protestant majority was the only way to ensure Catholics' rights.

In everything but religion the two Chesapeake colonies resembled each other. In Maryland as in Virginia, tobacco planters spread out along the river banks, establishing isolated farms instead of towns. The region's deep, wide rivers offered dependable water transportation in an age of few and inadequate roads. Each farm or group of farms had its own wharf, where ocean-going vessels could take on or discharge cargo. As a result, Virginia and Maryland had few towns, for these colonies did not need commercial centers in order to buy and sell goods.

The planting, cultivation, and harvesting of tobacco had to be done by hand; these tasks did not take much skill, but they were repetitive, time-consuming, and labor-intensive. Clearing land for new fields, a necessary process every few years, was also a slow, labor-intensive task. Above all else, then, successful Chesapeake tobacco plantations required laborers. But where and how could they be obtained? Nearby tribes could not supply the needed workers because the region was not densely populated. Dutch traders carried a few Africans to the Chesapeake beginning in 1619, but such merchants could more easily and profitably sell slaves in the West Indies, their first American landfall. Moreover, most Virginians and Marylanders did not at first seek to acquire African workers. In the first half of the seventeenth century only a few Africans, not all of them slaves, arrived in the Chesapeake. By 1650, only about three hundred blacks lived in Virginia, comprising just a tiny fraction of the population.

Chesapeake tobacco planters thus looked primarily to England to supply their labor needs. Because of the headright system (which Maryland also adopted in 1640), a prospective tobacco planter anywhere in the Chesapeake could simultaneously obtain both land and labor by importing workers from England. Good management could make the process self-perpetuating: a planter could use his profits to pay for the passage of more workers and thereby gain title to more land.

Since men did the agricultural work in European societies, planters and workers alike assumed that field laborers should be men, preferably young, strong ones. Such male laborers, along with a few women, migrated to America as indentured servants—that is, in return for their passage they contracted to work for planters for periods ranging from four to seven years. Indentured servants accounted for 75 to 85 percent of the approximately 130,000 English migrants to Virginia and Maryland during the seventeenth century; the rest were mostly young couples with one or two children. Roughly three-quarters of the servant migrants were males between the ages of fifteen and twenty-four; only one in five or six was female. Most of the men had been farmers and laborers, and many came from parts of England experiencing severe social disruption. Some had already moved several times within England before migrating to America. They were what their contemporaries called the "common" sort. Judging by their youth, most had probably not yet established themselves in their homeland.

For such people the Chesapeake appeared to offer good prospects. Once they had fulfilled the terms of their indentures, servants were promised "freedom dues" consisting of clothes, tools, livestock, casks of corn and tobacco, and sometimes even land. From a distance at least, America seemed to hold out chances for advancement unavailable in England. Yet the migrants' lives were difficult. Servants typically worked six days a week, ten to fourteen hours a day, in a climate much warmer than they were accustomed to. Their masters could discipline or sell them, and they faced severe penalties for running away. Even so, the laws did offer them some protection. For example, their masters were supposed to supply them with sufficient food, clothing, and shelter, and they were not to be beaten excessively. Servants who were especially cruelly treated turned to the courts for assistance and sometimes won verdicts directing that they be sold to more humane masters or freed from their indentures.

Servants and planters alike had to contend with epidemic disease, but not the same illnesses that continued to kill Native Americans in large numbers. Migrants first had to survive the process the colonists called "seasoning"—a bout with disease (probably malaria) that usually occurred during their first summer in the Chesapeake. They

Migrants to the Chesapeake

Conditions of Servitude

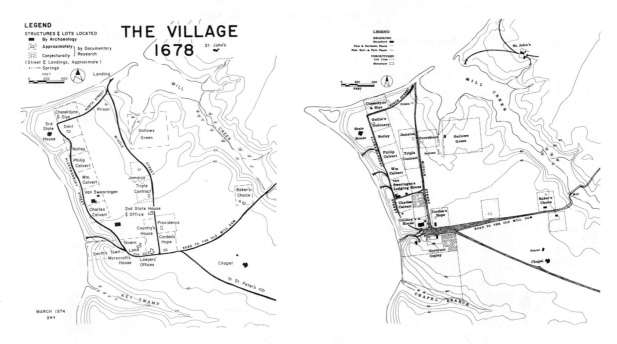

How do historians know

what seventeenth-century settlements looked like? Recent excavations at St. Mary's City, Maryland, founded as the capital of Calvert's colony in 1634, demonstrate the importance of cooperation between historians and archaeologists. St. Mary's City is unique, since it is the only major seventeenth-century English settlement in America not now buried underneath a modern city. (The site was abandoned in 1696 when the capital was moved to Annapolis, and the land was incorporated into a tobacco plantation.) Working only from written documents like deeds and wills, historians

hypothesized that the layout of the town resembled that illustrated in the figure on the left. When archaeologists began digging into the soil, however, they discovered that the documents alone had not told the whole story and that the tentative map had to be refined in several ways (figure on the right). Yet at the same time the archaeologists would have had difficulty interpreting their findings had it not been for the detailed archival research completed by historians prior to the excavations.   Photo: Historic St. Mary's City Commission.

then had to endure recurrences of malaria, along with dysentery, typhoid fever, and other diseases. As a result, approximately 40 percent of male servants did not survive long enough to become freedmen. Even young men of twenty-two who had successfully weathered their seasoning could expect to live only another twenty years at best.

For those who survived the term of their indentures, however, the opportunities for advancement were real. Until the last decades of the century, former servants were usually able to become independent planters ("freeholders") and to live a modest but comfortable existence. Some even assumed such positions of political prominence as

justice of the peace or militia officer. But in the 1670s tobacco prices entered a fifty-year period of stagnation and decline. At the same time, good land grew increasingly scarce and expensive. In 1681 Maryland dropped its legal requirement that servants receive land as part of their freedom dues, forcing large numbers of freed servants to live as wage laborers or tenant farmers instead of acquiring freeholder status. By 1700 the Chesapeake was no longer the land of opportunity it once had been.

Life in the seventeenth-century Chesapeake was hard for everyone, regardless of sex or status. Farmers (and sometimes their wives) toiled in the fields alongside the servants, laboriously clearing

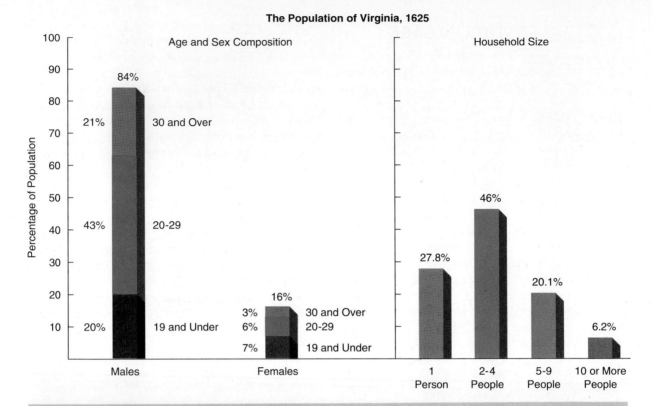

The Population of Virginia, 1625

Age and Sex Composition

Household Size

Population of Virginia, 1625   *The only detailed census taken in the English mainland North American colonies during the seventeenth century was prepared in Virginia in 1625. It listed a total of 1,218 people, comprising 309 "households" and living in 278 dwellings—so some houses contained more than one family. The chart shows, on the left, the proportionate age and gender distribution of the 765 individuals for whom full information was recorded and, on the right, the percentage variation in the sizes of the 309 households. The approximately 42 percent of the residents of the colony who were servants were concentrated in 30 percent of the households, with nearly 70 percent of the households containing no servants at all.*   Source of data: Robert V. Wells, *The Population of the British Colonies in America Before 1776: A Survey of Census Data* (Princeton: Princeton University Press, 1975), tables V-5, V-6, and pp. 165–166.

the land, then planting and harvesting not only tobacco but also corn and wheat. Because hogs could forage for themselves in the forests and needed little tending, Chesapeake households subsisted mainly on pork and corn, which were filling but did not supply all the nutrients necessary for human beings. Planter families supplemented this monotonous fare by occasionally eating fish, clams, oysters, and wildfowl, in addition to such vegetables as lettuce and peas, which they grew in tiny kitchen gardens. The health problems caused by epidemic disease were magnified by the deficiencies of this diet and the near-impossibility of preserving food for safe winter consumption. Salting,

drying, and smoking, the only methods the colonists knew, did not always prevent spoilage.

Few households had many material possessions other than farm implements, beds, and basic cooking and eating utensils. Chairs and tables, knives and forks were luxury items; most people sat on crude benches or storage chests and held their plates or bowls in their hands while eating with spoons. Even the houses were little more than shacks. Planters devoted their income to improving their farms, buying livestock, and purchasing more laborers rather than to improving their standard of living. Instead of making such items as clothing and tools, planter families concentrated their energies solely on growing tobacco, importing necessary manufactured goods from England.

The predominance of males, the incidence of servitude, and the high mortality rates combined to produce unusual patterns of family life. Female

Family Life in the Chesapeake

servants normally were not allowed to marry during their terms of indenture because masters did not want pregnancies to deprive them of workers. Many male ex-servants could not marry at all because there were so few women. On the other hand, nearly every adult free woman in the Chesapeake married, and widows usually remarried within a few months of a husband's death. Yet because their marriages were delayed by servitude or broken by death, Chesapeake women bore only one to three children, in contrast to English women, who normally had at least five.

Thus Chesapeake families were relatively few, small, and short-lived. The migrants could not reproduce the English patriarchal system, even if they wanted to, for they came to America as individuals free of paternal control and tended to die while their own children were still quite young. In one Virginia county, for example, more than three-quarters of the children had lost at least one parent by the time they either married or reached age twenty-one.

As a result of the demographic patterns that led to a low rate of natural increase, migrants made up a majority of the Chesapeake population

Chesapeake Politics

throughout the seventeenth century. That fact had important implications for politics in Maryland and Virginia. Since migrants dominated the population, they also composed the vast majority of the membership of Virginia's House of Burgesses and Maryland's House of Delegates (established in 1635). So, too, in each colony they dominated the governor's council, which was simultaneously the colony's highest court, part of the legislature, and executive adviser to the governor.

English-born colonists naturally tended to look to England for solutions to their problems, and migrants frequently relied on English allies to advance their cause. Because of the low birth rates and high mortality, no cohesive native-born ruling elite could emerge. The immigrant leaders of the Chesapeake colonies engaged in bitter and pro-

longed struggles for power and personal economic advantage; these struggles then crossed the Atlantic, and decisions made in America were laid open to reversal in London. The incessant quarreling and convoluted political tangles thwarted the Virginia and Maryland governments' ability to function effectively.

Representative institutions based on the consent of the governed, it is often argued, are a major source of political stability. In the seventeenth-century Chesapeake, most property-owning white males could vote, and such freeholders chose as their legislators the local elites who seemed to be the natural leaders of their respective areas. But because most such men were migrants without strong ties to each other or to the colonies, the existence of the assemblies did not lead to political stability. Indeed, the contrary may well have been true. Virginia and Maryland paid a high political price for their unusual demographic patterns.

THE FOUNDING OF NEW ENGLAND

The economic motives that prompted English people to move to the Chesapeake colonies also drew men and women to New England, as the area north and east of the Hudson River soon came to be called (see map, page 52). But because Puritans organized the New England colonies, and also because of environmental differences between the two regions, the northern settlements turned out very differently from those in the South. The northern climate was too cold and the soil too infertile to raise tobacco on a large scale or to raise sugar cane at all. Accordingly, diversified small farms at first dominated the landscape. Except for the Catholics who moved to Maryland, migrants to the Chesapeake seem to have been little affected by religious motives. Yet religion was a primary motivating factor in the minds of many, though certainly not all, of the people who colonized New England. The Puritan church quickly became one of the most important institutions in colonial New England; neither the Church of England nor Roman Catholicism had much impact on the settlers or the development of the Chesapeake colonies.

Religion was a constant presence in the lives of pious Puritans. As followers of John Calvin, they believed that an omnipotent God predestined souls to heaven or hell before birth and that Christians could do nothing to change their ultimate fate. One of their primary duties as Christians, though, was to assess the state of their own souls. They thus devoted themselves to self-examination and Bible study, and families prayed together each day under the guidance of the husband and father. Yet even the most pious could never be absolutely certain that they were numbered among the saved. Consequently, devout Puritans were filled with anxiety about their spiritual state. Many kept diaries in which they minutely examined their everyday feelings for signs of their status: Did they regularly feel the assurance of God's presence in their lives? Could they easily obey God's commandments? Did God send them providential signs—of special favor or special affliction? (Both types of signs could be interpreted positively.)

Puritan Beliefs

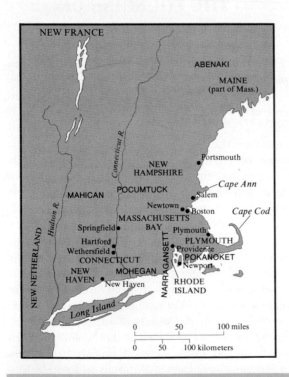

New England Colonies, 1650 *The most densely settled region of the mainland was New England, where English settlements and Indian villages existed side by side.*

Some Puritans (called Congregationalists) wanted to reform the Church of England rather than abandon it. Another group, known as Separatists, believed the Church of England to be so corrupt that it could not be salvaged. The only way to purify it, they believed, was to start anew, establishing their own religious bodies, with membership restricted to the saved, as nearly as they could be identified.

Separatists were the first to move to New England. In 1609 a group of Separatists migrated to Holland, where they found the freedom of worship denied them in Stuart England. But they were nevertheless troubled by The Netherlands' too-tolerant atmosphere; the nation that tolerated them also tolerated religions and behaviors they abhorred. Hoping to isolate themselves and their children from the corrupting influence of worldly temptations, these people, who were to become known as Pilgrims, received permission from a branch of the Virginia Company to colonize the northern part of its territory.

In September 1620, more than one hundred people, only thirty of them Separatists, set sail from Plymouth, England, on the old and crowded *Mayflower*. Two months later they landed in America, but farther north than they had intended. Still, given the lateness of the season—winter was closing in—they decided to stay where they were. They established their colony on a fine harbor previously visited by the French explorer Champlain, whose drawing of it appears in the accompanying photo on page 53. The English named their settlement Plymouth, after the city from which they had sailed; it was located on the site of an Indian village destroyed in the great epidemic of 1616 to 1618.

Founding of Plymouth

Even before they landed, the Pilgrims had to surmount their first challenge—from the "strangers," or non-Puritans, who had sailed with them to America. Because they landed outside the jurisdiction of the Virginia Company, some of the strangers questioned the authority of the colony's leaders. In response, the Mayflower Compact, signed in November 1620 while everyone was still on board the ship, established a "Civil Body Politic" and a rudimentary legal authority for the colony. The settlers elected a governor and at first made all decisions for the colony at town meetings. Later, after more towns had been founded and the population

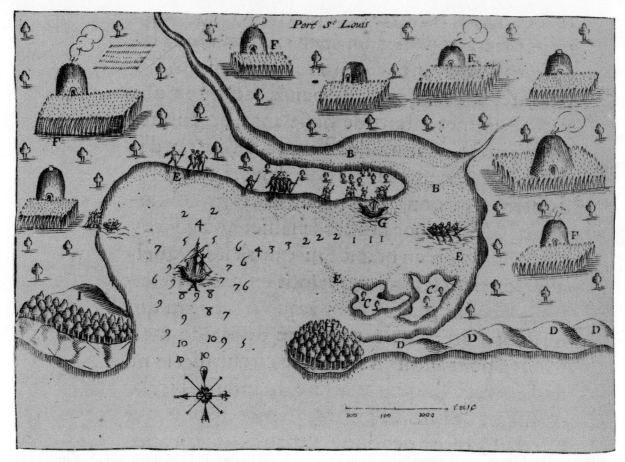

When Samuel de Champlain mapped the New England coast while on the exploratory voyage for France that led him to the St. Lawrence River, he drew the harbor on which the Pilgrims settled about a decade and a half later. Most of the people of the village he depicted, probably the home of Squanto before he was kidnapped and carried to England around 1611, died in the great chicken pox epidemic of 1616–1618.   Courtesy of the John Carter Brown Library at Brown University.

had increased, Plymouth, like Virginia and Maryland, created an assembly to which the landowning male settlers elected representatives.

A second challenge facing the Pilgrims in 1620 and 1621 was, quite simply, survival. Like the Jamestown settlers before them, they were poorly prepared to survive in the new environment. Their difficulties were compounded by the season of their arrival, for they barely had time to build shelters before winter descended on them. Only half of the *Mayflower's* passengers were still alive by spring. But, again like the Virginians, the Pilgrims benefited from the political circumstances of their Native American neighbors.

The Pokanokets (also called Wampanoags) controlled the area in which the Pilgrims had settled, yet their villages had suffered terrible losses in the epidemic of 1616–1618. To protect themselves

from the powerful Narragansetts of the southern New England coast (who had been spared the ravages of the disease), the Pokanokets decided to ally themselves with the newcomers. In the spring of 1621, their leader, Massasoit, signed a treaty with the Pilgrims, and during the colony's first difficult years the Pokanokets supplied the English with essential foodstuffs. The settlers were also assisted by Squanto, who, like Malinché (see Chapter 1), served as a conduit between the Americans and the Europeans. Squanto had been captured by fishermen in the early 1610s and taken to England, where he learned to speak the language. When he returned to North America, he discovered that his village had been wiped out by the epidemic. Squanto became the Pilgrims' interpreter and, like Malinché, a major source of information about the unfamiliar environment.

Before the 1620s had ended, another group of Puritans—this time Congregationalists—launched the colonial enterprise that would come to dominate New England and would absorb Plymouth in 1691. The event that stimulated their interest in the New World was the accession of Charles I to the throne in 1625. Charles was more hostile to Puritan beliefs than his father had been, and for eleven years after 1629 he refused to call Parliament into session because it was dominated by Puritans. In 1633 he named William Laud, a prominent persecutor of Puritans, as archbishop of Canterbury, thus giving him the most important post in the Church of England. Some non-Separatists therefore began to think about settling in America. A group of Congregationalist merchants sent out a body of colonists to Cape Ann, north of Cape Cod, in 1628. The following year the merchants obtained a royal charter, constituting themselves as the Massachusetts Bay Company.

Massachusetts Bay Company

The new company quickly attracted the attention of Puritans of the "middling sort" who were becoming increasingly convinced that they would no longer be able to practice their religion freely in England. They remained committed to the goal of reforming the Church of England but concluded that they should pursue that aim in America rather than at home. In a dramatic move, the Congregationalist merchants boldly decided to transfer the headquarters of the Massachusetts Bay Company to New England. The settlers would then be answerable to no one in the mother country and would be able to handle their affairs, secular and religious, as they pleased.

The most important recruit to the new venture was John Winthrop. In October 1629, the members of the Massachusetts Bay Company elected Winthrop as their governor. With the exception of a few scattered years, he served in that post until his death in 1649. It thus fell to Winthrop to organize the initial segment of the great Puritan migration to America. In 1630 more than one thousand English men and women came to Massachusetts—most of them to Boston, which soon became the largest town in British North America. By 1643 nearly twenty thousand compatriots had followed them. A large proportion of the migrants

Governor John Winthrop

came from East Anglia, a region to the north and east of London; not surprisingly, they gave familiar East Anglian place names to their new towns (like Boston) and counties (for example, Suffolk).

On board the *Arbella*, en route to New England in 1630, John Winthrop preached a sermon, "A Modell of Christian Charity," laying out his expectations for the new colony. Above all, he stressed the communal nature of the endeavor on which he and his fellow settlers had embarked. God, he explained, "hath so disposed of the condition of mankind as in all times some must be rich, some poor, some high and eminent in power and dignity, others mean and in subjection." But differences in status did not imply differences in worth. On the contrary: God had planned the world so that "every man might have need of other, and from hence they might be all knit more nearly together in the bond of brotherly affection." In America, Winthrop asserted, "we shall be as a city upon a hill, the eyes of all people are upon us." If the Puritans failed to carry out their "special commission" from God, "the Lord will surely break out in wrath against us."

Winthrop's was a transcendent vision. The society he foresaw in Puritan America was a true commonwealth, a community in which each person put the good of the whole ahead of his or her private concerns. It was, furthermore, to be a society whose members all lived according to the precepts of Christian charity, loving and aiding friends and enemies alike. Of course, such an ideal was beyond human reach. Early New England had its share of bitter quarrels and unchristian behavior. What is remarkable is how long the ideal prevailed as a goal to be sought, though seldom if ever attained.

The Puritans expressed their communal ideal chiefly in the doctrine of the covenant. They believed God had made a covenant—that is, an agreement or contract—with them when they were chosen for the special mission to America. In turn they covenanted with each other, promising to work together toward their goals. The founders of churches and towns in the new land often drafted formal documents setting forth the principles on which such institutions would be based. The same was true of the colonial governments of New England. The Pilgrims' Mayflower Compact was a cov-

Ideal of the Covenant

enant; so too was the Fundamental Orders of Connecticut (1639), which laid down the basic law for the settlements established along the Connecticut River valley in 1636 and thereafter.

The leaders of Massachusetts Bay likewise transformed their original joint-stock company charter into the basis for a covenanted community based on mutual consent. Under pressure from landowning male settlers, they gradually changed the General Court—officially the company's small governing body—into a colonial legislature. They also granted the status of freeman, or voting member of the company, to all property-owning adult male church members residing in Massachusetts. Less than two decades after the first large group of Puritans had arrived in Massachusetts Bay, the colony had a functioning system of self-government composed of a governor and a two-house legislature. The General Court also established a judicial system modeled on England's.

New England Towns

The colony's method of distributing land helped to further the communal ideal. Unlike Virginia and Maryland, where individual applicants sought headrights for themselves and their servants, in Massachusetts groups of families—often from the same region of England—applied together to the General Court for grants of land on which to establish towns. The men who received the original town grant had the sole authority to determine how the land would be distributed. Understandably, they copied the villages from which they had come. First they laid out town lots for houses and a church. Then they gave each family parcels of land scattered around the town center: pasture here, a woodlot there, an arable field elsewhere. They also reserved the best and largest plots for the most distinguished among them (usually including the minister); people who had been low on the social scale in England were given much smaller and less desirable allotments. Even when migrants began to move beyond the territorial limits of the Massachusetts Bay colony into Connecticut (1636), New Haven (1638), and New Hampshire (1638), the same pattern of town land grants was maintained. Only Maine, with coastal regions thinly populated by fishermen and their families, deviated from the standard practice.

Thus New England settlements initially tended to be more compact than those of the Chesapeake. Town centers grew up quickly, developing in three distinctly different ways. Some, chiefly isolated agricultural settlements in the interior, tried to sustain Winthrop's vision of harmonious community life based on diversified family farms. A second group, the coastal towns like Boston and Salem, became bustling seaports, serving as places of entry for thousands of new migrants and as focal points for trade. The third category, commercialized agricultural towns, grew up in the Connecticut River valley, where easy water transportation made it possible for farmers to sell surplus goods readily. In Springfield, Massachusetts, for example, the merchant-entrepreneur William Pynchon and his son John began as fur traders and ended as large landowners with thousands of acres on which tenant farmers produced grain for export. Even in Puritan New England, therefore, the acquisitive, individualistic spirit characteristic of the Chesapeake found some room for expression.

The migration to the Connecticut valley ended the Puritans' relative freedom from clashes with their Native American neighbors. The first English settlers in the valley moved there from Newtown (Cambridge, Massachusetts), under the direction of their minister, Thomas Hooker. Connecticut was

An English beaver felt hat, made by combining American beaver fur with other fibers, including wool. Such fashionable items were worn by men and women in England and on the continent, thus creating the insatiable demand for pelts that fueled the fur trade for many years. Courtesy of The Pilgrim Society, Plymouth, Massachusetts.

Among John Eliot's principal converts to Christianity was a young Native American named Daniel Takawampbartis. Ordained as a minister, he served at the head of the Indian congregation at Natick, Massachusetts, a "Praying Town," until his death in 1716. This desk was made for him by members of his congregation in about 1677, incorporating elements of English design (brass pulls), Native American motifs (incised lines), and uniquely American hooved feet. The top, a hinged box, is intended to hold a Bible.   The Morse Institute, Natick, Massachusetts. Photo by Mark Sexton of the Peabody and Essex Museum, Salem.

fertile, though remote from the other English towns, and the wide river promised ready access to the ocean. The site had just one problem: it fell within the territory controlled by the Pequots.

The Pequots' dominance was based on their role as primary middlemen in the trade between New England tribes and the Dutch in New Netherland. The arrival of English settlers signaled the end of Pequot power over the regional trading networks, for their tributary bands could now trade directly with Europeans. Clashes between the Pequots and the English began even before the Connecticut valley settlements were established, but their founding tipped the balance toward war. The Pequots tried without success to enlist other tribes in resisting

Pequot War
———

English expansion into the interior. After two English traders were killed (probably not by Pequots), the English raided a Pequot village. In retaliation, the Pequots attacked the new town of Wethersfield in April 1637, killing nine and capturing two of the colonists. In retaliation, a Massachusetts Bay expedition the following month attacked and burned the main Pequot town on the Mystic River. The Englishmen and their Narragansett allies slaughtered at least four hundred Pequots, mostly women and children, and captured the few survivors. John Winthrop and other Puritan leaders thereafter employed Pequot women as domestic servants.

Just five years later, the Narragansett leader Miantonomi realized that the Pequots had been correct in assessing the danger posed by the Puritan settlements. He in turn attempted to forge a pan-Indian alliance, telling other bands that "so are we all Indians as the English are . . . so must we be one as they are, otherwise we shall all be gone shortly." But his words fell on deaf ears, and he was killed in 1643 by other tribesmen acting at the English colonists' behest.

For the next thirty years, the New England Indians tried to accommodate themselves to the spread of white settlement. They traded with the whites and sometimes worked for them, but for the most part they resisted acculturation or incorporation into English society. The Native Americans clung to their traditional farming methods, which did not employ plows, fertilizer, or fences; and women rather than men continued to be the chief cultivators. When tribesmen whose hunting territories had been overrun by whites did learn "English" trades in order to survive, they chose those that—like broom making, basket weaving, and shingle splitting—most nearly accorded with their customary occupations and simultaneously ensured both independence and income. The one European practice they did adopt was keeping livestock, for in the absence of game, domesticated animals provided excellent alternative sources of meat.

Although the official seal of the Massachusetts Bay colony showed an Indian crying, "Come over and help us," most colonists showed little interest in converting the New England Algonkians to Christianity. Only a few Massachusetts clerics, most notably John Eliot, seriously undertook missionary activities. Eliot insisted that converts reside in towns, farm the land in English fashion, assume English names, wear European-style clothing and shoes, cut their hair, and stop observing a wide range of their own customs. Since Eliot was demanding a total cultural transformation from his adherents—on the theory that the Indians could not be properly Christianized unless they were also "civilized"—he understandably met with little success. At the peak of Eliot's efforts, only 1,100 Native Americans lived in the fourteen "Praying Towns" he established, and just 10 percent of those town residents had been formally baptized.

The Jesuits' successful missions in New France contrasted sharply with the Puritans' failure to win many converts. Three factors account for the difference. First, the small French **Puritan and Jesuit Missions Compared** outposts along the St. Lawrence did not substantially encroach on tribal lands and therefore did not alienate potential converts. Second, Catholicism had several advantages over Puritanism. It employed attractive rituals, instructed converts that through good works they could help to earn their own salvation, and offered women in particular inspiring role models—the Virgin Mary and the communities of nuns who resided in Montreal and Quebec. Third, and perhaps most important, the Jesuits understood that Christian beliefs were to some extent compatible with Native American culture. Unlike the Puritans, the Jesuits were willing to accept converts who did not wholly adopt European styles of life.

But what attracted Native Americans to these religious ideas? Conversion often alienated new Christians—both Catholic and Puritan—from their relatives and traditions, which must have caused many potential converts to think twice about making such a commitment. Surely one primary motive was a desire to use the Europeans' religion as a means of coping with the dramatic changes the intruders had wrought. The combination of disease, alcohol, new trading patterns, and the loss of territory disrupted customary ways of life to an unprecedented extent. Shamans had little success in restoring traditional ways. Many Native Americans must have concluded that the Europeans' own ideas could provide the key to survival in the new circumstances.

John Winthrop's description of a smallpox epidemic that swept through southern New England in the early 1630s reveals the relationship among smallpox, conversion to Christianity, and English land claims. "A great mortality among the Indians," he noted in his diary in 1633. "Divers of them, in their sickness, confessed that the Englishmen's God was a good God; and that if they recovered, they would serve him." But most did not recover: in January 1634 an English scout reported that smallpox had spread "as far as any Indian plantation was known to the west." By July, Winthrop observed that most of the Indians within a 300-mile radius of Boston had died of the disease. Therefore, he declared with satisfaction, "the Lord hathe cleared our title to what we possess."

LIFE IN NEW ENGLAND

White settlers in New England adopted lifestyles that differed considerably from those of both their Indian neighbors and their European counterparts in the Chesapeake. The agricultural Algonkians usually moved four or five times each year to take full advantage of their environment. In the spring, women planted the fields, but once the crops were established they would not need regular attention for several months. Villages then divided into small groups, the women gathering wild foods and men hunting and fishing. The villagers returned to their fields for harvest, then separated again for fall hunting. Finally, the people spent the winter together in a sheltered spot before returning to the fields to start the cycle anew the following spring.

Unlike the mobile Algonkians, English people lived year-round in the same location. And unlike residents of the Chesapeake, New Englanders constructed sturdy dwellings intended to last. (Indeed, some survive to this day.) They used the same fields again and again, believing it was less arduous to employ fertilizer than to clear new fields every few years. Furthermore, they had to fence their croplands to prevent them from being overrun by the cattle, sheep, and hogs that were their chief sources of meat. When New Englanders began to spread out over the countryside, the reason was not so much human crowding as it was animal crowding. All that livestock constantly needed more pasturage.

Puritans commonly moved to America in family groups, in contrast to the Chesapeake migrants, most of whom came individually. The age range

Both children and older people flourished in the healthy climate of colonial New England. More infants survived their first year of life than in other contemporary societies, and more people lived longer. Thus settlers with numerous children needed high chairs, like the one made in seventeenth-century Massachusetts for the use of the Mather family. American Antiquarian Society. Gift of Hannah Mather Crocker, 1819.

Family Life in New England

of New Englanders was wide, and because many more women went there than to the tobacco colonies, the population could immediately begin to reproduce itself. Moreover, New England's climate was much healthier than the Chesapeake's. Once Puritan settlements had survived the difficult first two or three years and established self-sufficiency in foodstuffs, New England proved to be even healthier than the mother country. Though adult male migrants to the Chesapeake lost about ten years from their English life expectancy of fifty to fifty-five years, their Massachusetts counterparts gained five or more years.

Consequently, while Chesapeake population patterns gave rise to families that were few in number, small in size, and transitory, the demographic characteristics of New England made families there numerous, large, and long-lived. In New England most men were able to marry; migrant women married young (at age twenty, on the average); and marriages lasted longer and produced more children, who were more likely to live to maturity. If seventeenth-century Chesapeake women could expect to rear one to three healthy children, New England women could anticipate raising five to seven.

The nature of the population had other major implications for family life. New England in effect created grandparents like Mary Mirick Davie, since in England people rarely lived long enough to know their children's children. And whereas early southern parents normally died before their children married, northern parents exercised a good deal of control over their adult children. Young men could not marry without acreage to cultivate, and given the communal land-grant system they were dependent on their fathers to supply them with that land. Daughters, too, needed the dowry of household goods that their parents would give them when they married. Yet parents needed their children's labor and often were reluctant to see them marry and start their own households. These needs at times led to considerable conflict between the generations. On the whole, though, children seem to have obeyed their parents' wishes, for they had few alternatives.

Another important difference lay in the influence of religion on New Englanders' lives. The governments of Massachusetts Bay, Plymouth, Connecticut, and the other early northern colonies were all controlled by Puritans. Congregationalism was the only officially recognized religion; except in Rhode Island, members of other sects had no freedom of worship. Some non-Puritans appear to have voted in town meetings, but in Massachusetts Bay and New Haven, church membership was a prerequisite for voting in colony elections. All households were taxed to build meetinghouses and pay ministers' salaries. Massachusetts's first legal codes (1641 and 1648) incorporated regulations drawn from Old Testament scriptures into the laws of the colony; those codes were later copied by New Haven, Plymouth, and Connecticut. Penalties were prescribed for expressing contempt for ministers or their preaching and for failing to attend church services regularly.

In addition, the Puritan colonies attempted to enforce a strict moral code of conduct. Maryland punished only sexually active couples who had

Moral Codes
———

bastard children. In New England, though, couples who had sex during their engagement—as revealed by the birth of a baby less than nine months after their wedding—were fined and humiliated, sometimes by a public whipping. Perhaps as a result, fewer than 10 percent of seventeenth-century New England brides were pregnant when they married, in contrast with more than one-third of Chesapeake brides. More harshly treated in both regions were men—and a handful of women—who engaged in behaviors that today would be called homosexual. (The term did not then exist, nor were some people thought more likely to perform such acts than any others.) Several men who had consenting same-sex relationships were hanged, as were other men suspected of bestiality (sex with animals). One unfortunate resident of New Haven was executed because the colonists believed he had fathered a piglet, now known to be a biological impossibility.

In the New England colonies, church and state were thus intertwined, for Puritans believed they were following Old Testament rules in assigning such penalties to those they believed to be moral miscreants. Puritans objected to secular interference in religious affairs but at the same time expected the church to influence the conduct of politics and the affairs of society. They also believed that the state had an obligation to support and protect the one true church—theirs. As a result, though they came to America seeking freedom to worship as they wished, they saw no contradiction in their refusal to grant that freedom to others. Indeed, the two most significant divisions in early Massachusetts were caused by religious disputes and by Massachusetts Bay's unwillingness to tolerate dissent.

Roger Williams, a Separatist, migrated to Massachusetts Bay in 1631. Williams soon began to express the eccentric ideas that the king of England

Roger Williams
———

had no right to give away land already occupied by Native Americans, that church and state should be kept entirely separate, and that Puritans should not impose their religious beliefs on others. Banished from Massachusetts in 1635, Williams founded the town of Providence on Narragansett Bay. Because of Williams's beliefs, Providence and other towns in what became the colony of Rhode Island adopted a policy of tolerating all religions, including Judaism.

Many New England men and women lived to become grandparents—though few would have equaled the lifespan of Mary Mirick Davie, who died at the age of 117 in 1752. Massachusetts Historical Society.

The other dissenter, and an even greater challenge to Massachusetts Bay orthodoxy, was Anne Marbury Hutchinson. A skilled midwife popular with the women of Boston, she

Anne Hutchinson
———

was a follower of John Cotton, a minister who stressed the covenant of grace, or God's free gift of salvation to unworthy, helpless human beings. By contrast, most Massachusetts clerics emphasized the need for Puritans to engage in good works, study, and reflection in preparation for receiving God's grace. In 1636 Hutchinson began holding women's meetings in her home to discuss Cotton's sermons. Soon men also started to attend. Hutchinson emphasized the covenant of grace more than did Cotton himself, and she even adopted the belief that the elect could communicate directly with God and be assured of salvation. Such ideas had an immense appeal for Puritans. Anne Hutchinson offered them certainty of salvation instead of a state of constant tension. Her approach also made the institutional church and its ministers less important.

Hutchinson's ideas were a dangerous threat to Puritan orthodoxy, so in November 1637 she was brought before the General Court of Massachusetts. For two days she defended herself cleverly against her accusers, matching scriptural references and wits with John Winthrop himself. But Hutchinson then declared that God had spoken to her "by an immediate revelation," telling her that he would curse the Puritans' descendants for generations if they harmed her. That assertion assured her banishment. After she had also been excommunicated from the church, she and her family, along with some faithful followers, were exiled to Rhode Island. Several years later, after she moved to New Netherland, she and most of her children were killed by Indians. John Winthrop, learning of the deaths, pronounced it God's judgment on a heretic.

The authorities in Massachusetts Bay perceived Anne Hutchinson as doubly dangerous to the existing order: she threatened not only religious orthodoxy but also traditional gender roles. Puritans believed in the equality before God of all souls, including those of women, but they considered actual women (as distinct from their spiritual selves) inferior to men. Christians had long followed Saint Paul's dictum that women should keep silent in church and be submissive to their husbands. Anne Hutchinson did neither. The magistrates' comments during her trial reveal that they were almost as outraged by her "masculine" behavior as by her religious beliefs. Winthrop charged her with having set wife against husband, since so many of her followers were women. A minister at her church trial told her bluntly: "You have stept out of your place, you have rather bine a Husband than a Wife and a preacher than a Hearer; and a Magistrate than a Subject."

The New England authorities' reaction to Anne Hutchinson reveals the depth of their adherence to European gender-role concepts. To them, an orderly society required the submission of wives to husbands as well as the obedience of subjects to rulers. English people intended to change many aspects of their lives by colonizing North America, but not the sexual division of labor or the assumption of male superiority.

By the middle of the seventeenth century, Europeans had unquestionably come to North America to stay, a fact that signaled major changes for the peoples of both hemispheres. Europeans had indelibly altered not only their own lives but also those of the Native Americans, on whose lands they settled. Europeans killed Indians with their weapons and diseases and had but limited success in converting them to European religions and styles of life. Contacts with the Native Americans taught Europeans to eat new foods, speak new languages, and recognize—however reluctantly—the persistence of other cultural patterns. The prosperity and even survival of many of the European colonies depended heavily on the cultivation of American crops (maize and tobacco) and an Asian one (sugar), thus attesting to the importance of post-Columbian ecological change.

European political rivalries, once confined to Europe, now spread around the globe, as the competing nations of England, Spain, Portugal, France, and The Netherlands vied for control of the peoples and resources of Asia, Africa, and the Americas. In America, France earned its primary profits from Indian trade and the cultivation of sugar cane. Sugar also enriched the Portuguese. The Netherlands concentrated on commerce— trading in furs and sugar as well as carrying human cargoes of African slaves to South America and the Caribbean. None of these nations imitated the Spanish example and engaged in wars of conquest.

Although they, too, at first sought to rely on trade, the English colonies quickly took another form altogether when so many English people of the "middling sort" decided to migrate to North America. To a greater extent than their European counterparts, the English transferred the society and politics of their homeland to a new environment. Their sheer numbers, and their need for vast quantities of land on which to grow their crops and raise their livestock, inevitably brought them into conflict with their Native American neighbors. New England and the Chesapeake differed in the sex ratio and age range of their migrant populations, in the nature of their developing economies, in their settlement patterns, and in the impact of religious beliefs on their settlers' lives. Yet both were English in origin, and in the years to come both regions would be drawn into the increasingly fierce rivalries besetting the European powers. Those rivalries would continue to affect Americans of all races until after France and England fought the greatest war yet known in the mid-eighteenth century and the Anglo-American colonies had won their independence.

SUGGESTIONS FOR FURTHER READING

General

Charles M. Andrews, *The Colonial Period of American History: The Settlements*, 3 vols. (1934–1937); David Hackett Fischer, *Albion's Seed: Four British Folkways in America* (1989); D. W. Meinig, *Atlantic America, 1492–1800* (1986); Gary B. Nash, *Red, White, and Black: The Peoples of Early America*, 2nd ed. (1982); John E. Pomfret, *Founding the American Colonies, 1583–1660* (1970); Helena Wall, *Fierce Communion: Family and Community in Early America* (1990).

New Netherland, New France, and the Caribbean

Karen Anderson, *Chain Her by One Foot: The Subjugation of Women in Seventeenth-Century New France* (1991); Charles R. Boxer, *The Dutch Seaborne Empire, 1600–1800* (1965); Carl and Roberta Bridenbaugh, *No Peace Beyond the Line: The English in the Caribbean, 1624–1690* (1972); Richard S. Dunn, *Sugar and Slaves: The Rise of the Planter Class in the English West Indies, 1624–1713* (1972); William J. Eccles, *France in America*, rev. ed. (1990); Jonathan Israel, *Dutch Primacy in World Trade, 1585–1740* (1989); Donna Merwick, *Possessing Albany, 1630–1710* (1990); Sidney Mintz, *Sweetness and Power: The Place of Sugar in Modern History* (1985); Simon Schama, *The Embarrassment of Riches: An Interpretation of Dutch Culture in the Golden Age* (1988).

England

Susan Dwyer Amussen, *An Ordered Society: Gender and Class in Early Modern England* (1988); Carl Bridenbaugh, *Vexed and Troubled Englishmen, 1590–1642*, rev. ed. (1976); Mildred Campbell, *The English Yeoman Under Elizabeth and the Early Stuarts* (1942); Nicholas Canny, *Kingdom and Colony: Ireland in the Atlantic World, 1560–1800* (1988); Peter Laslett, *The World We Have Lost*, 3rd ed. (1984); Wallace Notestein, *The English People on the Eve of Colonization, 1603–1630* (1954); Michael Walzer, *The Revolution of the Saints* (1965); Keith Wrightson, *English Society, 1580–1680* (1982).

Early Contact Between Europeans and Indians

James Axtell, *After Columbus* (1988); James Axtell, *The Invasion Within: The Contest of Cultures in Colonial North America* (1985); James Axtell, *The European and the Indian* (1981); Philip Barbour, *Pocahontas and Her World* (1970); James Bradley, *Evolution of the Onondaga Iroquois* (1987); William Cronon, *Changes in the Land: Indians, Colonists, and the Ecology of New England* (1983); Francis Jennings, *The Invasion of America: Indians, Colonialism, and the Cant of Conquest* (1975); Karen O. Kupperman, *Settling with the Indians: The Meeting of English and Indian Cultures in America, 1580–1640* (1980); Patrick Malone, *The Skulking Way of War: Technology and Tactics among the Indians of New England* (1991); Kenneth Morrison, *The Embattled Northeast: The Elusive Ideal of Alliance in Abenaki-Euroamerican Relations* (1984); Helen C. Rountree, *Pocahontas's People: The Powhatan Indians of Virginia Through Four Centuries* (1990); Neal Salisbury, *Manitou and Providence: Indians, Europeans, and the Making of New England, 1500–1643* (1982); Bernard Sheehan, *Savagism and Civility: Indians and Englishmen in Colonial Virginia* (1980); Timothy Silver, *A New Face on the Countryside: Indians, Colonists, and Slaves in South Atlantic Forests, 1500–1800* (1990); Alden T. Vaughan, *The New England Frontier: Puritans and Indians 1620–1675*, rev. ed. (1979); Peter Wood, et al., eds., *Powhatan's Mantle: Indians in the Colonial Southeast* (1989).

Chesapeake Society and Politics

Lois Green Carr, et al., *Robert Cole's World: Agriculture and Society in Early Maryland* (1991); Lois Green Carr, et al., eds., *Colonial Chesapeake Society* (1988); Wesley Frank Craven, *The Southern Colonies in the Seventeenth Century, 1607–1689* (1949); David Galenson, *White Servitude in Colonial America: An Economic Analysis* (1981); Ivor Noël Hume, *Martin's Hundred: The Discovery of a Lost Colonial Virginia Settlement* (1979); A. J. Leo Lemay, *The American Dream of Captain John Smith* (1991); Gloria L. Main, *Tobacco Colony: Life in Early Maryland, 1650–1720* (1983); Edmund S. Morgan, *American Slavery, American Freedom: The Ordeal of Colonial Virginia* (1975); James Perry, *The Formation of a Society on Virginia's Eastern Shore, 1615–1655* (1990); Darrett Rutman and Anita Rutman, *A Place in Time: Middlesex County, Virginia, 1650–1750* (1984); Thad W. Tate and David L. Ammerman, eds., *The Chesapeake in the Seventeenth Century* (1979); John Van der Zee, *Bound Over: Indentured Servitude and American Conscience* (1985); Alden T. Vaughan, *American Genesis: Captain John Smith and the Founding of Virginia* (1975).

New England Communities, Politics, and Religion

David Grayson Allen, *In English Ways: The Movement of Societies and the Transferral of English Law and Custom to Massachusetts Bay in the 17th Century* (1981); Virginia DeJohn Anderson, *New England's Generation: The Great Migration and the Formation of Society and Culture in the 17th Century* (1991); Charles Cohen, *God's Caress: The Psychology of Puritan Religious Experience* (1986); Stephen Foster, *The Long Argument: English Puritans and the Shaping of New England Culture, 1570–1700* (1991); Philip Gura, *A Glimpse of Sion's Glory: Puritan Radicalism in New England, 1620–1660* (1984); David D. Hall, *Worlds of Wonder, Days of Judgment: Popular Religious Belief in Early New England* (1989); Stephen Innes, *Labor in a New Land: Economy and Society in 17th-Century Springfield* (1983); Sydney V. James, *Colonial Rhode Island* (1975); George Langdon, *Pilgrim Colony: A History of New Plymouth, 1620–1691* (1966); Kenneth A. Lockridge, *A New England Town: The First Hundred Years (Dedham, Massachusetts, 1636–1736)* (1970); John Frederick Martin, *Profits in the Wilderness: Entrepreneurship and the Founding of New England Towns in the 17th Century* (1991); Edmund S. Morgan, *The Puritan Dilemma: The Story of John Winthrop* (1958); Sumner Chilton Powell, *Puritan Village* (1963); Darrett Rutman, *Winthrop's Boston* (1965).

New England Women and Family Life

David Cressy, *Coming Over: Migration and Communication Between England and New England in the Seventeenth Century* (1987); John Demos, *A Little Commonwealth: Family Life in Plymouth Colony* (1970); Philip J. Greven, Jr., *Four Generations: Population, Land, and Family in Colonial Andover, Massachusetts* (1970); Lyle Koehler, *A Search for Power: The "Weaker Sex" in Seventeenth-Century New England* (1980); Edmund S. Morgan, *The Puritan Family*, rev. ed. (1966); Roger Thompson, *Sex in Middlesex: Popular Mores in a Massachusetts County, 1649–1699* (1986).

3

American Society Takes Shape, 1640–1720

STANDING ON A LADDER with the condemned man, the hangman tightened the noose around the neck of the notorious pirate Captain William Kidd— and pushed him off. The rope broke. Kidd lay on the ground, dazed. The hangman repeated the procedure with a new rope. This time it held, and Kidd died violently, as he had lived. It was May 23, 1701; the site was Wapping, near the London docks. Kidd's body, shrouded in chains, was then left dangling from a gibbet on the bank of the Thames as a warning to all who saw it.

William Kidd, born in Scotland, had made his home in New York, the port once known as New Amsterdam. Merchants there were none too choosy about how they earned their profits— and at the end of the seventeenth century the vast expansion of worldwide trading networks had opened practically unlimited opportunities for buccaneers who preyed on ships carrying valuable commodities long distances by sea. The merchants of Manhattan eagerly provisioned pirates' ships and purchased their loot. In the 1690s, the economy of the town depended on this illegal trade. For years Kidd and other pirates could even count on the complicity of New York's governors, who

ignored their activities in exchange for shares of the bounty.

Then why was Captain Kidd condemned to die? His fatal enterprise began in London in early 1696, when he gained financial backing for a voyage to the Indian Ocean from several powerful and prominent English investors. He cleverly planned to attack other pirates and to seize the booty they had already stolen. After recruiting a crew in New York, Kidd sailed for Madagascar, the main pirate haven in the Indian Ocean. But he found no easy prey and began to take whatever vessels he came across—a ship from Bombay flying the English flag, a Dutch merchantman, a Portuguese vessel. His most valuable prize, the *Quedah Merchant*, carried a large cargo of cloth, sugar, opium, and iron.

After more than a year of buccaneering, Kidd returned to New York via the Caribbean, hoping to avoid prosecution for piracy by claiming he had taken only legal prizes and by paying off his investors in full (in addition to bribing the relevant officials). Unfortunately for Kidd, one of his financial backers, the Earl of Bellomont, had become the governor of New York. Bellomont had been waging a vigorous campaign against piracy and

Only children of the wealthiest Americans wore the elaborate garb donned by the Mason daughters in 1670.

could not afford to protect Kidd. In addition, as governor he could claim one-third of any confiscated illegal cargo for his personal use, whereas as a backer he was entitled to less than one-fifth of the partnership's proceeds. Kidd's fate was sealed when Bellomont ordered his arrest and shipped him back to England for trial.

The saga of William Kidd illustrates above all the involvement of the English mainland colonies in a growing network of trade and international contacts, not all of them legal. North America, like England itself, was becoming increasingly embedded in a worldwide matrix of exchange and warfare. The web woven by oceangoing vessels—once composed of only a few strands spun by Christopher Columbus, John Cabot, and their successors—now crisscrossed the globe, carrying West Indian sugar to Europe, Africans to America, cloth and spices from the East Indies to Africa, and New England fish and wood products to the Caribbean. Formerly tiny outposts, the North American colonies expanded their territorial claims and embarked on a deliberate course of economic development. In response, the English government for the first time began to adopt policies to systematize colonial administration.

Three developments shaped life in the mainland colonies between 1640 and 1720: the introduction of a system of chattel slavery, especially in the south Atlantic coastal regions; changes in the colonies' relationship with their mother country; and increasing conflicts with their North American neighbors, both European and Native American. All these developments were intimately connected with the historical processes that produced Captain Kidd and others like him.

The explosive growth of the slave trade was of critical significance in the colonial economy. Carrying human cargoes paid off handsomely, as many slave traders learned; planters who could afford to buy slaves also reaped huge profits. The arrival of large numbers of West African peoples dramatically reshaped colonial society and fueled the international trading system. The burgeoning North American economy, invigorated by the arrival of so many laborers, attracted new attention from colonial administrators. Especially after the Stuarts had been restored to the throne (having lost it for a time as a result of the Civil War in the 1640s), the rulers and bureaucrats in London attempted to

supervise the American settlements more effectively and to ensure that the mother country benefited from their economic growth.

Neither English colonists nor London administrators could ignore the other peoples living on the North American continent. As the English settlements expanded, they came into violent conflict not only with the powerful tribes of the interior but also with the Dutch, the Spanish, and especially the French. By 1720, war—between Europeans and Indians, among Europeans, and among Indians allied with different colonial powers—had become an all-too-frequent feature of American life. No longer isolated from each other or from Europe, the people and products of the North American colonies were now integral to the world trading system and inextricably enmeshed in its conflicts.

THE ENGLISH CIVIL WAR, THE STUART RESTORATION, AND THE AMERICAN COLONIES

In 1640, Charles I, who had ruled England arbitrarily for the previous eleven years, called Parliament into session because he needed money and wanted to propose new taxes. But Parliament instead passed laws limiting his authority, and tensions heightened. In 1642, civil war broke out between royalists and the supporters of Parliament. Four years later, Parliament triumphed, and Charles I was executed in 1649. Oliver Cromwell,

Stuart Monarchs of England, 1660–1714

Monarch	Reign	Relation to Predecessor
Charles II	1660–1685	Son
James II	1685–1688	Brother
Mary	1688–1694	Daughter
William	1688–1702	Son-in-law
Anne	1702–1714	Sister, sister-in-law

• Important Events •

1642–46	English Civil War; end of first New England economic system based on furs and migrants		**1685**	James II becomes king
1649	Charles I executed		**1686–89**	Dominion of New England established, superceding all charters of colonies from Maine to New Jersey
1651	First Navigation Act passed to regulate colonial trade		**1688–89**	James II deposed in Glorious Revolution; William and Mary ascend throne
1660	Stuarts restored to throne; Charles II becomes king		**1689–97**	King William's War fought on northern New England frontier
1662	Halfway Covenant drafted in New England, creating category of partial membership in Congregational churches		**1692**	Witchcraft outbreak in Salem Village; nineteen executions result
1663	Carolina chartered		**1696**	Board of Trade and Plantations established to coordinate English colonial administration
1664	English conquer New Netherland; New York founded New Jersey established		**1701**	Iroquois adopt neutrality policy toward France and England
1670s	Jacques Marquette, Louis Jolliet, and Robert Cavelier de la Salle explore the Great Lakes and Mississippi Valley for France		**1702–13**	Queen Anne's War fought by French and English
1675–76	King Philip's (Metacomet's) War devastates New England		**1711–13**	Tuscarora War (North Carolina) leads to capture or migration of most Tuscaroras
1676	Bacon's Rebellion disrupts Virginia government; Jamestown destroyed		**1715**	Yamasee War nearly destroys South Carolina
1680–92	Pueblo revolt temporarily drives Spaniards from New Mexico		**1718**	New Orleans founded in French Louisiana
1681	Pennsylvania chartered		**1732**	Georgia chartered

the leader of the parliamentary army, then assumed control of the government, taking the title of Lord Protector in 1653. After Cromwell's death five years later, Parliament decided to restore the monarchy if Charles I's son and heir would agree to certain restrictions on his authority. In 1660, Charles II ascended the throne, having promised to seek Parliament's consent for any new taxes and to support the Church of England. Thus ended the tumultuous chapter in English history known as the Interregnum (Latin for "between reigns") or the Commonwealth period.

The Civil War, the Interregnum, and the reign of Charles II (1660–1685) had far-reaching significance for the English colonies in the Americas. During the Civil War and the Commonwealth pe-

riod, Puritans dominated the English government. Therefore the migration to New England largely ceased, and some colonists packed up to return home. During the subsequent reign of Charles II, six of the thirteen colonies that would eventually form the American nation were either founded or came under English rule: New York, New Jersey, Pennsylvania (including Delaware), and North and South Carolina (see map, page 66). All were proprietorships; like Maryland they were granted in their entirety to one man or a group of men who held title to the soil and controlled the government. Charles II gave these vast American holdings as rewards to men who had supported him during his years of exile. Several of his favorites even shared in more than one grant. Collectively, these became

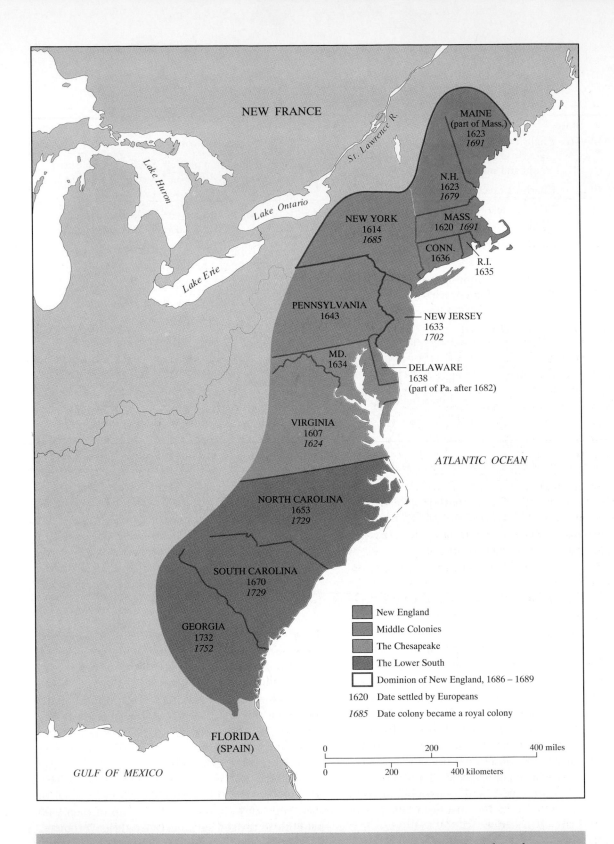

NEW FRANCE

St. Lawrence R.

Lake Huron

Lake Ontario

Lake Erie

MAINE
(part of Mass.)
1623
1691

N.H.
1623
1679

NEW YORK
1614
1685

MASS.
1620 *1691*

CONN.
1636

R.I.
1635

PENNSYLVANIA
1643

NEW JERSEY
1633
1702

MD.
1634

DELAWARE
1638
(part of Pa. after 1682)

VIRGINIA
1607
1624

ATLANTIC OCEAN

NORTH CAROLINA
1653
1729

SOUTH CAROLINA
1670
1729

GEORGIA
1732
1752

FLORIDA
(SPAIN)

GULF OF MEXICO

New England

Middle Colonies

The Chesapeake

The Lower South

Dominion of New England, 1686 – 1689

1620   Date settled by Europeans

1685   Date colony became a royal colony

| 0 | 200 | 400 miles |

| 0 | 200 | 400 kilometers |

The American Colonies in the Early Eighteenth Century   *By the early eighteenth century, the English colonies nominally dominated the Atlantic coastline of North America. But the colonies' formal boundary lines are deceiving, both because the western reaches of each colony were still largely unfamiliar to Europeans and because much of the land was still inhabited by Native Americans.*

The Founding of English Colonies in North America, 1664–1732

Colony	Founder(s)	Date	Basis of Economy
New York (formerly New Netherland)	James, Duke of York	1664	farming, fur trading
New Jersey	Sir George Carteret, John Lord Berkeley	1664	farming
North Carolina	Carolina Proprietors	1665	tobacco, forest products
South Carolina	Carolina Proprietors	1670	rice, indigo
Pennsylvania	William Penn	1681	farming
Georgia	James Oglethorpe	1732	rice, forest products

known as the Restoration colonies, because they were created by the restored Stuart monarchy.

One of the first to benefit was Charles's younger brother James, the duke of York. In 1664, acting as though the Dutch colony of New Netherland did not exist, Charles II gave James the region between the Connecticut and Delaware rivers, including the Hudson valley and Long Island. James immediately organized an invasion fleet. In late August the vessels anchored off Manhattan Island and demanded New Netherland's surrender. The colony's director-general, Peter Stuyvesant, complied without offering resistance. Although The Netherlands briefly regained control of the colony in 1672, the Dutch permanently ceded the province in 1674.

Thus England acquired a tiny but heterogeneous possession. In 1664, an appreciable minority of English people (mostly Puritan New Englanders

New Netherland Becomes New York

who had moved to Long Island) already lived in the colony. New York, as it was now called, also included sizable numbers of Native Americans, Germans, French-speaking Walloons (from the southern part of modern Belgium), Scandinavians, and Africans, as well as a smattering of other European peoples. The Dutch West India Company, the world's greatest slave-trading power at midcentury (see page 73), had actively imported slaves into the colony, intending some of them for resale in the Chesapeake. Many, though, remained in New Netherland as laborers; at the time of the English conquest, almost one-fifth of Manhattan's approximately 1,500 inhabitants were of African descent.

Slaves constituted a higher proportion of New York's urban population than of the Chesapeake's at the same time.

Recognizing the diversity of the population, the duke of York's representatives moved cautiously in their efforts to establish English authority. The Duke's Laws, a legal code proclaimed in 1665, at first applied only to the Puritan settlements on Long Island; they were later extended to the rest of the colony. Dutch forms of local government were maintained and Dutch land titles confirmed. Religious toleration was guaranteed through a multiple establishment: each town was permitted to decide which church to support with its tax revenues. And the Dutch were allowed to maintain their customary legal practices. Until the 1690s, many Dutch couples wrote joint wills, which were enforced in New York courts even though under English law married women could not draft wills. Much to the chagrin of English residents of the colony, the Duke's Laws made no provision for a representative assembly. Like other Stuarts, James was suspicious of legislative bodies, and not until 1683 did he agree to the colonists' requests for an elected legislature. Before then, New York was ruled by an autocratic governor as it had been under the Dutch.

The English takeover thus had little immediate effect on the colony. Its population grew slowly, barely reaching eighteen thousand by the time of the first English census in 1698. Until the second decade of the eighteenth century, New York City remained a commercial backwater within the orbit of Boston.

One of the chief reasons the English conquest brought so little change to New York was that the

In 1679 a traveler drew this picture of the Stadt Huys (State House) on Manhattan Island, in the colony of New York. But the government building and its adjoining houses, built under Dutch rule while the settlement was still called New Amsterdam, made the scene look more like Holland than England.   The Brooklyn Historical Society.

Founding of New Jersey

duke of York quickly regranted the land between the Hudson and Delaware rivers—East and West Jersey—to his friends Sir George Carteret and John Lord Berkeley. That left his own colony confined between Connecticut to the east and the Jerseys to the west and south, depriving it of much fertile land and hindering its economic growth. He also failed to promote migration. Meanwhile the Jersey proprietors acted rapidly to attract settlers, promising generous land grants, limited freedom of religion, and—without authorization from the Crown—a representative assembly. In response, large numbers of Puritan New Englanders migrated southward to the Jerseys, along with some

Dutch New Yorkers and a contingent of families from Barbados. New Jersey grew quickly; at the time of its first census as a united colony in 1726, it had 32,500 inhabitants, only 8,000 fewer than New York.

Within twenty years, Berkeley and Carteret sold their interests in the Jerseys to separate groups of investors. The purchasers of all of Carteret's share (West Jersey) and portions of Berkeley's (East Jersey) were members of the Society of Friends, seeking a refuge from persecution in England. The Society of Friends, also called the Quakers, denied the need for an intermediary between the individual and God. They believed anyone could receive the "inner light" and be saved, and all were equal in God's sight. They had no formally trained clergy; any Quaker, male or female, who felt the call could become a "public Friend" and travel from meeting to meeting to discuss God's word. Moreover, any member of the society could speak in meetings if he or she desired. The Quaker message of radical egalitarianism was not welcome in the hierarchical society of seventeenth-century England, or, for that matter, in Puritan New England. For example, Mary Dyer—who had followed Anne Hutchinson into exile—became a Quaker, returned to Boston as a missionary, and was hanged for preaching Quaker doctrines.

The Quakers obtained their own colony in 1681, when Charles II granted the region between Maryland and New York to William Penn, one of the sect's most prominent members (see portrait). Penn was then thirty-seven years old. His father, Admiral William Penn, had originally served Oliver Cromwell; later, however, he joined forces with Charles II and loaned the monarch a substantial sum of money. The younger Penn became a Quaker in the mid-1660s, much to his father's dismay. But despite the younger Penn's radical political and religious beliefs, he and Charles II were close personal friends. Because of that friendship (and the desire of Charles's advisers to rid England of religious dissenters), Charles gave a huge tract of land to Penn, nominally as a repayment for the loan from his father.

Pennsylvania: A Quaker Haven

William Penn held the colony as a personal proprietorship, and the vast property holdings earned profits for his descendants until the American Revolution. Even so, Penn, like the Roman Catholic Calverts of Maryland before him, saw the province not merely as a source of revenue but also as a haven for his persecuted coreligionists. Penn offered land to all comers on liberal terms, promised toleration of all religions (though only Christians were given the right to vote), guaranteed such English liberties as the right to bail and trial by jury, and pledged to establish a representative assembly. He also publicized the ready availability of land in Pennsylvania through promotional tracts printed in German, French, and Dutch and distributed widely throughout Europe.

Penn's activities and the natural attraction of his lands for Quakers gave rise to a migration whose magnitude was equaled only by the Puritan

William Penn, the proprietor of Pennsylvania, as drawn by the artist Francis Place.   Historical Society of Pennsylvania.

exodus to New England in the 1630s. By mid-1683, over three thousand people—among them Welsh, Irish, Dutch, and Germans—had already moved to Pennsylvania, and within five years the population reached twelve thousand. (By contrast, it took Virginia more than thirty years to achieve a comparable population.) Philadelphia, carefully planned to be the major city in the province, drew merchants and artisans from throughout the English-speaking world. From mainland and West Indian colonies alike came Quakers seeking religious freedom; they brought with them years of experience on American soil and well-established trading connections. Pennsylvania's lands were both plentiful and fertile, and the colony soon began exporting flour and other foodstuffs to the West Indies. Practically overnight Philadelphia acquired more than two thousand citizens and began to challenge Boston's commercial dominance.

A pacifist with egalitarian principles, Penn was determined to treat the Native Americans fairly. He purchased tracts of land from the Delawares (or Lenapes), the dominant tribe in the region, in order to sell them to settlers. Penn also established strict regulations for trade and forbade the sale of alcohol to the tribal people. In 1682 he visited a number of Lenape villages, after taking pains to learn the language. "I must say," Penn commented, "that I know not a language spoken in Europe that hath words of more sweetness in Accent and Emphasis, than theirs."

Penn's Indian policy illustrates the complexity of the interaction among Euroamericans and Amerindians. Indians from western Maryland, Virginia, and North Carolina moved to Pennsylvania near the end of the seventeenth century to escape repeated clashes with white settlers. Most important were the Tuscaroras, whose experiences are described later in this chapter. Likewise, Shawnees and Miamis chose to move eastward from the Ohio valley. By a supreme irony, however, the same toleration that attracted Native Americans to Penn's domains also brought non-Quaker Europeans who showed little respect for Indian claims to the soil. In effect, Penn's policy was so successful that it caused its own downfall. The Scotch-Irish, Palatine Germans, and Swiss who settled in Pennsylvania in the first half of the eighteenth century clashed repeatedly over land with tribes that had also recently migrated to the colony.

The other proprietary colony, granted by Charles II in 1663, encompassed a huge tract of land stretching from the southern boundary of Virginia to Spanish Florida. The

Founding of Carolina

area had great strategic importance; a successful English settlement there would prevent the Spanish from pushing farther north. The semitropical land was also extremely fertile, holding forth the promise of producing such exotic and valuable commodities as figs, olives, wines, and silk. The proprietors named their new province Carolina in honor of Charles, whose Latin name was *Carolus*. The "Fundamental Constitutions of Carolina," which they asked the political philosopher John Locke to draft for them, set forth an elaborate plan for a colony governed by a hierarchy of landholding aristocrats and characterized by a carefully structured distribution of political and economic power. But Carolina failed to follow the course the proprietors laid out. Instead, it quickly developed two distinct population centers, which in 1729 permanently split into two separate colonies.

The Albemarle region that became North Carolina was settled by Virginia planters. They established a society much like their own, with an econ-omy based on tobacco cultivation and the export of such forest products as pitch, tar, and timber. Because North Carolina lacked a satisfactory harbor, its planters continued to rely on Virginia's ports and merchants to conduct their trade, and the two colonies remained tightly linked. Although North Carolina planters held some slaves, they never became as dependent on slave labor as did the other population center in Carolina.

Charleston, South Carolina, was founded in 1670 by a group of settlers from the island of Barbados, which was already overcrowded less than fifty years after English people had first moved there. The white Barbadians brought with them the slaves who had worked on their sugar plantations and the legal codes that had governed those laborers, thereby irrevocably shaping the future of South Carolina and the subsequent history of the United States.

THE FORCED MIGRATION OF AFRICANS

Since England had no tradition of slavery, why did English settlers in North America and the Caribbean islands begin to enslave Africans around the middle of the seventeenth century? The answer to that question lies in a combination of their need for labor and the customs of other Europeans.

Although the English had not previously practiced slavery, other Europeans had. As has already been pointed out, the Spanish and Portuguese imported enslaved Africans as laborers into the islands of the Mediterranean Atlantic during the fifteenth century. They then extended that practice to their American possessions, New Spain and Brazil, especially after the Catholic church began actively discouraging enslavement of Native Americans. No free people were willing to toil for wages in the difficult and dangerous conditions of South American mines or Caribbean sugar plantations. To produce the profitable goods they had come to America to seek, the Europeans needed bound laborers—people who, by law or contract, could be forced to work at jobs that no person would do voluntarily.

Such a large proportion of the native inhabitants of North America and the Caribbean had

Slavery Established

died from imported diseases that they could not supply the labor needs of English settlers. English tobacco planters in the Chesapeake at first relied on indentured servants from their homeland (see Chapter 2). But by the mid-1660s, population pressures in England had eased; in addition, the founding of the Restoration colonies meant that prospective migrants could choose to move elsewhere in Anglo-America. Accordingly, the supply of English servants began to dry up, and mainland planters had to find a new source of laborers.

They found their workers in the French, Dutch, and Spanish Caribbean islands, among the ranks of already enslaved Africans. Early in the history of the mainland English settlements, the few residents of African descent varied in status—some were free, some indentured, and some enslaved. Before the 1660s, none of the English colonies systematically categorized Africans as slaves. But the beginnings of large-scale importation of Af-

ricans to the mainland in the 1670s, first from the Caribbean islands and then directly from Africa, changed that situation decisively. As increasing numbers of enslaved Africans arrived each year, laws governing them were more comprehensively and tightly drawn, and fewer and fewer of them were allowed to live free of European supervision. Most of the English colonies, even those without many slaves, adopted codes to govern blacks' behavior. By the end of the century, African slavery was firmly established as the basis of the economy in the Chesapeake as well as in the Caribbean.

One of the most remarkable aspects of the adoption of the slave system was the English enslavers' evident lack of moral qualms. No one at the time seems to have questioned—or even felt the need to justify with racist rationalizations—the decision to hold Africans and their descendants in perpetual bondage. That fact suggests the importance both of prior Spanish and Portuguese practice and of economic motives in leading to this momentous development. Certainly the latter was the

At forts along the African coast, Europeans purchased slaves from local rulers. This contemporary illustration of such a transaction is taken from a book published in 1729. Library of Congress.

theme of one New Englander's argument for declaring war on the Narragansetts in 1645. If they captured Narragansett men, women, and children in a "Just warre," he contended, the prisoners could be exchanged for "Moores [Africans], which will be more gayneful pilladge for us then wee conceive." The problem with indentured servants, he pointed out, was that they would become free "and not stay but for verie great wages." Further, "wee shall maynteyne 20 Moores cheaper then one Englishe servant." He concluded, "I doe not see how wee can thrive untill we gett into a stock of slaves suffitient to doe all our buisnes." To this Puritan, profits were the only concern. He arrogantly disregarded the humanity of Native Americans and Africans but did not develop an elaborate, explicitly racist justification for his proposal.

Between 1492 and 1770 more Africans than Europeans were carried to the New World, the vast majority of them to Brazil or the Caribbean. Of at least 10 million enslaved people brought to the Americas, a minimum of about 120,000 by 1740, or 260,000 by 1775, were imported into the region that later became the United States. The magnitude of this trade raises three related questions. First, what was its impact on West Africa and Europe? Second, how was the trade organized and conducted? Third, what was its effect on the people it carried and on the region to which they were taken?

The West African coast was one of the most fertile and densely inhabited regions of the continent. Despite the extent of forced migration to the Western Hemisphere, the area was not seriously depopulated by the trade in human beings.

West Africa and the Slave Trade

Even so, because American planters preferred to purchase male slaves, the sex ratio of the remaining population was significantly affected by the trade. The relative lack of men increased the work demands on women and simultaneously encouraged polygyny (the practice of one man having several wives). In Guinea, the primary consequences of the trade were political and economic. Coastal rulers—like the one pictured on the previous page—served as middlemen in the trade, using it as a vehicle to consolidate their power and extend their rule over larger territories. They controlled European traders' access to slaves and at the same time controlled inland peoples' access to

desirable European trade goods like cloth, beads, alcohol, tobacco, firearms, and iron bars that could be made into knives and other tools. The centralizing tendencies of the trade thus helped in the formation of such powerful eighteenth-century kingdoms as Dahomey and Asante (created from the Akan States; see page 14). At the same time, smaller polities were destroyed and traditional economic patterns disrupted, as trade once sent north toward the Mediterranean was redirected to the coast, and as local manufactures declined in the face of European competition.

West African kings played a crucial role in the functioning of the slave trade. Europeans set up permanent slave-trading posts in Lower Guinea under the protection of local rulers, who then supplied the resident Europeans with slaves to fill the ships that stopped regularly at the coastal forts. In Upper Guinea, the lack of good harbors promoted a somewhat different trading pattern: Europeans would sail along the coast, stopping when signaled from the shore. Prisoners of war, criminals, debtors, and kidnap victims comprised the cargoes of the slave-trading vessels.

Europeans were the chief beneficiaries of this traffic in slaves, despite its importance to some African kings. The expanding network of trade between Europe and its colonies in the seventeenth and eighteenth centuries was fueled by the sale and transportation of slaves, the exchange of commodities produced by slave labor, and the need to feed and clothe so many bound laborers. The sugar planters of the Caribbean and Brazil, along with the tobacco and rice planters of North America, eagerly purchased slaves from Africa, dispatched shiploads of valuable staple crops to Europe, and bought large quantities of cheap food, much of it from elsewhere in the Americas. By the 1720s, more than 80 percent of English cotton textile exports were traded to Africa or slaveholding American colonies. The European economy, previously oriented toward the Mediterranean and Asia, shifted its emphasis to the Atlantic Ocean. Whereas European merchants' profits had once come primarily from trade with North Africa, the Eastern Mediterranean, and China, by the late seventeenth century commerce in slaves and the products of slave labor constituted the basis of the European economic system. The irony of Columbus's discoveries was thus complete: seeking the wealth of Asia, Columbus had found instead the lands that

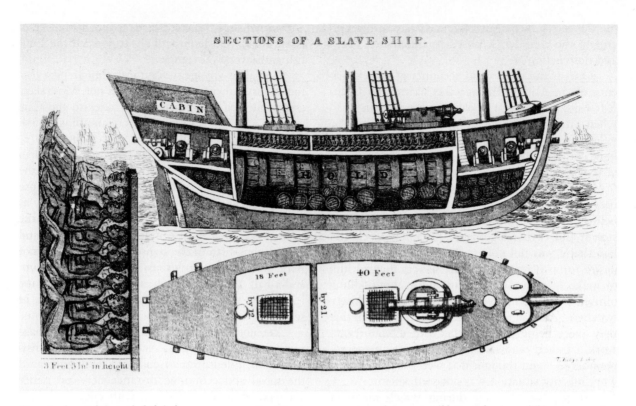

SECTIONS OF A SLAVE SHIP.

Slave traders tightly packed their human cargoes, attempting to carry as many slaves as possible on each voyage. This cutaway view of a typical vessel gives the ship's dimensions and shows the way slaves were transported in cramped quarters, with only small openings providing light and air.   Courtesy of the Trustees of The British Library.

ultimately replaced Asia as the source of European prosperity.

Given the economic importance of the slave trade, it is hardly surprising that European nations fought bitterly to control it. The Portuguese, who initially dominated the trade, were supplanted by the Dutch in the 1630s. The Dutch in turn lost out to the English, who controlled the trade through the Royal African Company, a joint-stock company chartered by Charles II in 1672. Holding a monopoly on all English trade with black Africa, the company built and maintained eight forts, dispatched to West Africa hundreds of ships carrying English manufactured goods, and transported more than 120,000 slaves to England's colonies in the Caribbean and on the North American mainland. Yet even before the company's monopoly expired in 1712, many individual English traders illegally entered the market for slaves. By the early eighteenth century, such independent traders were carrying most of the Africans imported into the colonies and earning huge profits from successful voyages.

The experience of the Middle Passage (thus named because it was the middle section of the so-called triangular trade among England, Africa, and the Americas; see pages 84–85) was always traumatic and sometimes fatal for the Africans who made up a ship's cargo. An average of 10 to 20 percent of the slaves died en route. On voyages that were unusually long or plagued by epidemic diseases, the mortality rates were much higher. In addition, some slaves died either before the ships left Africa or shortly after their arrival in the New World. Their white captors died at the same, if not higher, rates, chiefly through exposure to diseases endemic to Africa. Just 10 percent of the men sent to run the Royal African Company's forts in Lower Guinea lived to return home to England, and one in every four or five white sailors died on the Mid-

The Middle Passage

dle Passage. Once again, the exchange of diseases among the continents caused unanticipated death and destruction.

One of the most vivid accounts of the experience of the Middle Passage was written by Olaudah Equiano, who was eleven years old in 1756 when African raiders kidnaped him from his Ibo village in what is now Nigeria. Terrified by the light complexions, long hair, and strange language of the sailors on the slave ship, he was afraid that "I had gotten into a world of bad spirits and that they were going to kill me." Equiano was placed below decks, where "with the loathsomeness of the stench and crying together, I became so sick and low that I was not able to eat, nor had I the least desire to taste anything." The slavers flogged him to make him eat. Equiano thought about killing himself by jumping overboard but was too closely watched. At last some other Ibos told him that they were being taken to the whites' country to work. "I then was a little revived," Equiano remembered, "and thought if it were no worse than working, my situation was not so desperate."

After a long voyage during which many of the Africans died of disease brought on by the cramped, unsanitary conditions and poor food, the ship arrived at Barbados. Equiano and his shipmates feared that "these ugly men" were cannibals, but experienced slaves were brought on board to assure them that they would not be eaten and that many blacks like themselves lived on the islands. "This report eased us much," Equiano recalled, "and sure enough soon after we landed there came to us Africans of all languages." Everything in Barbados was new and surprising, but Equiano later remarked particularly on two-story buildings and horses, neither of which he had ever seen.

Equiano was not purchased in the West Indies, where planters preferred older, stronger slaves. Instead, he was carried to Virginia along with the other less-valuable Africans. There, on the plantation of his new owner, he was separated from the other Africans and put to work weeding and clearing rocks from the fields. "I was now exceedingly miserable and thought myself worse off than any of the rest of my companions," Equiano reported, "for they could talk to each other, but I had no person to speak to that I could understand." But Equiano did not remain in Virginia for long. Bought by a sea captain, Olaudah Equiano became an experienced sailor. He learned to read and write English, purchased his freedom at the age of twenty-one, and later actively supported the English antislavery movement.

Equiano's voyage was typical, though his eventual ability to win his freedom was not. Most slave ships followed the Northeast Trades to the Caribbean before heading north to Virginia. After about 1675, when the shortage of English indentured servants became acute, imports of Africans into the Chesapeake increased dramatically. As early as 1690, the Chesapeake colonies contained more black slaves than white indentured servants, and by 1710 one-fifth of the region's population was of African descent. Slaves usually cost about two-and-a-half times as much as servants, but they repaid the greater investment with a lifetime of service.

Slavery in the Chesapeake

Yet not all planters could afford to purchase such expensive workers. Accordingly, the transition from indentured to enslaved labor increased the social and economic distance between richer and poorer planters. Whites with enough money could acquire slaves and accumulate greater wealth, whereas the less affluent could not even buy indentured servants, whose price had been driven up by scarcity. As time passed, white Chesapeake society became more and more stratified—that is, the gap between rich and poor steadily widened. The introduction of large numbers of Africans into the Chesapeake thus had a significant impact on white society, in addition to reshaping the population as a whole.

That impact involved cultural values as well as demographic and economic change. Without realizing it, Chesapeake whites adopted African modes of thought about the use of time and the nature of work. Africans were more accustomed than European migrants to life in a hot climate, and whites soon learned the benefits of African patterns of time usage—working early and late, taking a long rest in the midday heat. They also assimilated African attitudes toward work, which were far more casual than those of New England. There, Puritans emphasized the necessity of "improving" every moment and scorned all leisure-time activities. In the Chesapeake, whites, like blacks, came to recognize the importance of recreation and to understand that work could be performed at a leisurely pace on most occasions.

How do historians know

that enslaved Africans were able to preserve at least some aspects of their cultural heritage in colonial North America? Although most enslaved people were illiterate and therefore did not leave written records of their cultural beliefs or practices, African-Americans did create objects that showed their connections to their homeland even more vividly than could words on a page. Many such objects have been found in the United States. The drum on the left was constructed on the Gold Coast of Africa in the nineteenth century, that on the right in Virginia sometime before the middle of the eighteenth century. The similarities of style and decoration suggest strong cultural affinities between the two drum builders, though they were separated by three thousand miles of ocean and at least one hundred years. Photo: Trustees of The British Museum; Smithsonian Institution, Washington, D.C.

In South Carolina, Africans were among the first colonists to come from Barbados. Indeed, one-quarter to one-third of South Carolina's early population was black. The Barbadian slaveowners quickly discovered that Africans had a variety of skills well suited to the semitropical environment of South Carolina. African-style dugout canoes became the chief means of transportation in the colony, which was crisscrossed by rivers. Fishing nets copied from African models proved more efficient than those of English origin. The baskets enslaved laborers wove and the gourds they hollowed out came into general use as containers for food and drink. Africans' skill at killing crocodiles equipped them to handle alligators

African-Americans in South Carolina

as well. And, finally, Africans adapted their traditional techniques of cattle-herding for use in the American context. Since meat and hides—not the exotic products originally envisioned—were the colony's chief exports in its earliest years, blacks contributed significantly to South Carolina's prosperity by drawing upon their African heritage.

The similarity of South Carolina's environment to West Africa's, coupled with the large number of blacks in the population, ensured that more aspects of West African culture survived in that colony than elsewhere on the mainland of North America. Only in South Carolina did black parents continue to give their children African names; only there did a dialect develop that combined English words with African terms. (Known as Gullah, it has survived to the present day in isolated areas.)

African skills remained useful, and so techniques that in other regions were lost when the migrant generation died were instead passed down to their children. And in South Carolina, as in West Africa, black women were the primary traders, dominating the markets of Charleston as they did those of Guinea. One observer commented that "these women have such a connection with and influence on the country negroes who come to that market, that they generally find means to obtain whatever they choose, in preference to any white person; thus they forestall and engross many articles, which some hours afterwards you must buy back from them at 100 or 150 per cent advance."

Significantly, the importation of large numbers of Africans near the end of the seventeenth century coincided with the successful introduction of rice as a staple crop in South Carolina. English people knew little about the techniques of growing and processing rice, and their first attempts to raise it were unsuccessful. But the former residents of Africa's Rice Coast (see page 14) had spent their lives working with the crop. Although the evidence is circumstantial, it seems likely that the Africans' expertise enabled their English masters to cultivate the crop profitably. After rice had become South Carolina's major export, 43 percent of the Africans imported into the colony came from rice-producing regions, and blacks' central position in the colony's economy was unchallenged. A South Carolina merchant commented in the mid-eighteenth century that "the Slaves from the River Gambia are preferred to all others with us save the Gold Coast."

South Carolina later developed a second staple crop, and it too made use of slaves' special skills. The crop was indigo, much prized in Europe as a blue dye for clothing. In the early 1740s, Eliza Lucas, a young white West Indian woman who was managing her father's South Carolina plantations, began to experiment with indigo cultivation. Drawing on the knowledge of white and black West Indians, she developed the planting and processing techniques later adopted throughout the colony. Indigo was grown on high ground, and rice was planted in low-lying swampy areas; rice and indigo also had different growing seasons. Thus the two crops complemented each other perfectly. Although South Carolina indigo never matched the quality of that raised in the West Indies, the indigo industry flourished because Parliament offered Carolinians a bounty on every pound they exported to Great Britain.

After 1700, therefore, white southerners were irrevocably committed to black slavery as their chief source of labor. The same was not true of white northerners. Only a small proportion of the blacks brought to the English colonies in America went to the northern mainland provinces, and most of those who did worked as enslaved domestic servants. Lacking large-scale agricultural enterprises, the rural North did not demand many bound laborers. In northern urban areas, though, white domestic servants were hard to find and harder to keep because higher wages were paid for other jobs in the labor-scarce economy. Thus blacks there filled an identifiable need. In some northern colonial cities (notably Newport, Rhode Island, and New York City), black slaves accounted for more than 10 percent of the population.

Slavery in the North

The introduction of large-scale slavery in the South, coupled with its near-absence in the rural North, accentuated regional differences that had already begun to develop in England's American colonies. To the distinction between diversified agriculture and staple-crop production was now added a difference in the status of most laborers. That difference was one of degree, for slavery was legal everywhere in the colonies, but it was nonetheless crucial. In the latter years of the seventeenth century, white Southern planters chose a course of action that nearly two centuries later took the future United States into civil war.

RELATIONS BETWEEN EUROPEANS AND INDIANS

Everywhere in North America, European colonizers depended heavily on the labor of native peoples, but their reliance took varying forms in different parts of the continent. In the Northeast, France, England, and The Netherlands competed for the pelts supplied by Indian trappers. In the Southeast, England, Spain, and later France each tried to control a thriving trade with the tribes in deerskins and Indian slaves. In the Southwest, meanwhile, Spain attempted to exploit the agricultural and artisan skills of the Pueblo peoples.

In 1598, drawn northward by accounts that rich cities lay in the region, Juan de Oñate, a Mexican-born adventurer, led a group of about five hundred soldiers and settlers to New Mexico (see map). When residents of Acoma pueblo resisted the Spaniards' demands for food and water, the invaders responded ferociously, killing more than eight hundred people and capturing the remainder. All the captives above the age of twelve were ordered enslaved for twenty years, and men older than twenty-five had one foot amputated. Not surprisingly, the other Pueblo villages surrendered. But when it became apparent that New Mexico held little wealth and offered only a hard life, many of the Spaniards returned to Mexico. In 1609, Spanish authorities decided to maintain only a small military outpost and a few Christian missions in the area, with the capital at Santa Fe (founded 1610).

Thereafter, Franciscan friars worked energetically to convert the residents of the pueblos, with mixed success. The Pueblo peoples were willing to add Christianity to their own religious beliefs but not to give up their indigenous rituals. Friars and secular colonists who held *encomiendas* (grants of labor) also placed heavy demands on the Indians. As the decades passed, the Franciscans adopted brutal and violent tactics in an effort to wipe out

Popé and the Pueblo Revolt

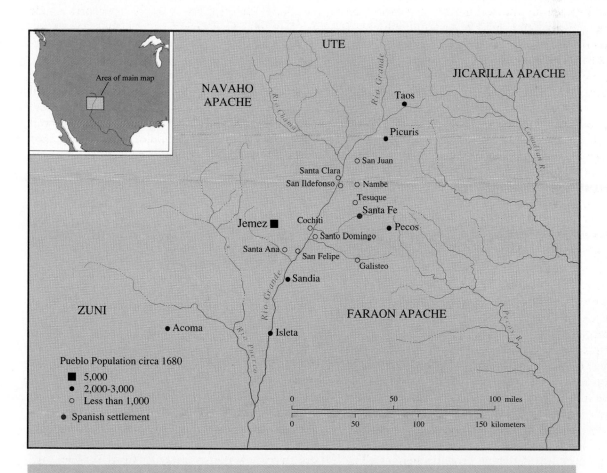

New Mexico, ca. 1680 *In 1680, the lone Spanish settlement at Santa Fe was surrounded and vastly outnumbered by the many Pueblo villages nearby.* Source: Adapted from *Apache, Navaho, and Spaniard,* by Jack D. Forbes. Copyright © 1960 by the University of Oklahoma Press. Used by permission.

all vestiges of the native religion. Finally, in 1680 the Pueblos revolted under the leadership of Popé, a respected shaman, and successfully drove the Spaniards out of New Mexico. Although Spanish authority was restored in 1692, Spain had learned its lesson. From that time on, Spanish governors stressed cooperation with the Pueblos, rather than confrontation, and no longer attempted to reduce them to bondage or to violate their cultural integrity. The Pueblo revolt was the most successful and longest-sustained Indian resistance movement in colonial North America.

When the Spanish expanded their territorial claims to the east and the north, they followed the same strategy they had used in New Mexico, establishing their presence through widely scattered military outposts and Franciscan missions. The army's role was to maintain order among the subject Indians—with the dual aims of protecting them from attack by other tribes and ensuring the availability of their labor—and to guard the boundaries of the Spanish empire from possible incursions, especially by the French. The friars continued to concentrate on conversion efforts. By the late eighteenth century, Spain claimed a vast territory that stretched from California (initially colonized in 1769 to prevent Russian sea-otter trappers from taking over the region) through Texas (settled after 1700) to the Gulf Coast. Throughout that region, the Spanish presence consisted of a mixture of missions and forts dotting the countryside at considerable distances from each other.

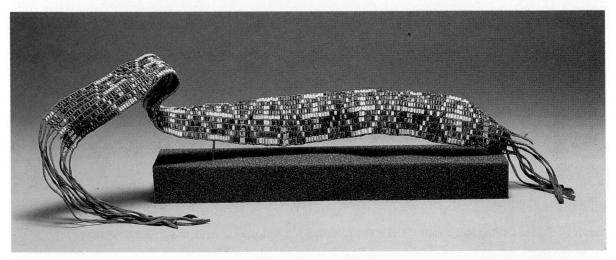

Trade between Europeans and Indians provided both societies with essential items. The Europeans manufactured tomahawks specifically for the Native American market. Likewise, the Indians of Long Island increased their production of wampum (made from clam shells) when English and Dutch colonists adopted the purple and white beads as a medium of exchange. Wampum served as a substitute for European coins, which were scarce in the remote colonial outposts. Peabody & Essex Museum, Peabody Museum Collections. Photos by Mark Sexton.

Europeans along the eastern seaboard valued the Indians as hunters and traders rather than as agricultural workers, but they were no less dependent on Indian labor than were the Spanish. South Carolina provides a case in point. The Barbadians who colonized the region moved quickly to establish a vigorous trade in deerskins with nearby tribes. During the first decade of the eighteenth century, South Carolina exported to Europe an average of 54,000 skins annually, a number that later climbed to a peak of 160,000. The trade gave rise to other exchanges that reveal the complexity of the economic relationships among Native Americans and Europeans. For example, white Carolinians carried the deerskins on horses they obtained from the Creeks, who had in turn acquired them from Spaniards in Florida through trade and capture.

Another important component of the Carolina trade was traffic in Indian slaves. The warring tribes of South Carolina (especially the Creeks)

Indian Slave Trade
_____

profited from selling their captive enemies to the whites, who either kept them as slaves or exported them to other mainland settlements or to the West Indies. There are no reliable statistics on the extent of the trade in Indian slaves, but in 1708 they made up 14 percent of the population of South Carolina. Many were Christians converted by the Spanish missions in northern Florida, then captured by Englishmen and their tribal allies.

A bitter conflict between white Carolinians and neighboring tribes added to the supply of Indian slaves. In 1711 the Tuscaroras, an Iroquoian people, attacked a Swiss-German settlement at New Bern, which had expropriated their lands without payment. The Tuscaroras had been avid slavers and had sold to the whites many captives from weaker Algonkian tribes. Those tribes seized the opportunity to settle old scores, joining with the English colonists to defeat their enemy in a bloody two-year war. In the end, more than a thousand Tuscaroras were themselves sold into slavery, and the remnants of the tribe drifted northward, where they joined the Five Nations Iroquois in New York.

The abuses of the slave trade led to the most destructive Indian war in Carolina. Colonial traders regularly engaged in corrupt, brutal, and fraudulent practices. They were notorious for cheating the Native Americans, physically abusing them

(including raping the women), and selling friendly tribal peoples into slavery when no enemy captives came readily to hand. In the spring of 1715, the Yamasees, aided by Creeks and a number of other tribes, retaliated by attacking English settlements. As the raids continued through the summer, refugees by the hundreds streamed into Charleston. Often guided by information from enslaved Indians held by the colonists, the Creek-Yamasee offensive at times came close to driving the intruders from the mainland altogether. But colonial reinforcements arrived from the north, and the Cherokees joined the English settlers against their ancient enemies the Creeks. The war pointed up both the difficulty of achieving unity among the tribes and the Indians' now-critical dependence on European weapons. When the tribal allies ran out of ammunition and could not repair their broken guns, their cause was lost. The Yamasees moved south to seek Spanish protection, and the Creeks retreated to villages in the west. It was years before South Carolina fully recovered from the effects of the Yamasee War, though the existence of the colony was never again seriously threatened.

That the Yamasees could escape by migrating southward exposed the one remaining gap in the line of English coastal settlements, the area between the southern border of

Founding of Georgia
_____

South Carolina and Spanish Florida. The gap was plugged in 1732 with the chartering of Georgia, the last of the colonies that would become part of the United States. Intended as a haven for English debtors by its founder James Oglethorpe, Georgia was specifically designed as a garrison province. Since all its landholders were expected to serve as militiamen to defend English settlements, the charter prohibited women from inheriting or purchasing land in the colony. The charter also prohibited the use of alcoholic beverages and forbade the introduction of slavery. Such provisions reveal the founders' intention that Georgia should be peopled by sturdy, sober yeoman farmers who could take up their weapons at a moment's notice against the Native Americans or Spaniards. None of the original conditions of the charter were enforced, however, and all of them had been abandoned by 1752, when Georgia became a royal colony.

In the Northeast, relationships were complicated by the number of European nations and Indian tribes involved in the fur trade. The key play-

Philip Georg Friedrich von Reck, an artist who visited Georgia in the early years of English settlement there, recorded a festival celebrated by the local Yuchi Indians in 1736. European guns hang from the rafters of the open shelter, showing that extensive trade connections already existed between the two peoples.   The Royal Library, Copenhagen.

Iroquois Confederacy
_____

ers were the Iroquois, not one tribe but five—the Mohawks, Oneidas, Onondagas, Cayugas, and Senecas. (In 1722, the Tuscaroras became the sixth.) Under the terms of a defensive alliance forged early in the sixteenth century, decisions of war and peace for the entire Iroquois Confederacy were made by a council composed of tribal representatives. Each tribe retained some autonomy and could not be forced to comply with a council directive against its will. The Iroquois were unique among Native Americans, not only because of the strength and persistence of their alliance but also because of the role played by their tribal matrons. The older women of each village chose its chief and could either start wars (by calling for the capture of prisoners to replace dead relatives) or stop them (by refusing to supply warriors with necessary foodstuffs).

Before the arrival of the Europeans, the Iroquois had waged wars primarily for the purpose of acquiring captives to replenish their population. Contact with white traders brought ravaging disease as early as 1633 and thus intensified the need for captives. At the same time, the arrival of Europeans created an economic motive for warfare: the desire to control the fur trade and gain unimpeded access to European goods. The war with the Hurons in the 1640s (see page 37) was but the first of a series of conflicts with other tribes known as the Beaver Wars, in which the Iroquois fought desperately to maintain a dominant position in the trade. In the mid-1670s, just when it appeared they would be successful, the French stepped in; an Iroquois triumph would have destroyed France's plans to trade directly with the Indians of the Great Lakes and Mississippi valley regions. Over the next twenty years the French launched repeated attacks on Iroquois villages. The English offered little assistance other than weapons to their trading partners and nominal allies. Their people and resources depleted by constant warfare, the Iroquois in 1701 negotiated neutrality treaties with France, England, and their tribal neighbors. For the next half-century they maintained their power through trade and skillful diplomacy.

The wars against the Iroquois Confederacy were crucial components of French Canada's plan to penetrate the heartland of North America. In

French Expansion
━━━

the 1670s, Louis de Buade de Frontenac, the governor general of Canada, encouraged the explorations of Father Jacques Marquette, Louis Jolliet, and Robert Cavelier de La Salle in the Great Lakes and Mississippi valley regions. Officials at home in France approved the expeditions because they wanted to find a route to Mexico. La Salle and Frontenac, by contrast, hoped to profit personally, monopolizing the fur trade by establishing trading posts along the Mississippi River.

Unlike the Spanish, the French adventurers did not attempt to subjugate the Native American peoples they encountered. Nor, at first, did they even claim the territory formally for France. Still, when France decided to strengthen its presence near the Gulf of Mexico by founding New Orleans in the early eighteenth century—to counter both the westward thrust of the English colonies and the eastward moves of the Spanish—the Mississippi posts became the glue of empire. *Coureurs de bois* (literally, "forest runners") used the rivers and lakes of the American interior to travel regularly between Quebec and Louisiana, carrying French goods to such outposts as Michilimackinac (at the junction of Lakes Superior and Huron), Cahokia and Kaskaskia (in present-day Illinois), and Fort Rosalie (Natchez), on the lower Mississippi River (see map).

Most of the posts consisted of a small military garrison and a priest, surrounded by powerful nations such as the Choctaws, Chickasaws, Osages, and Illinois. The tribes permitted the French to remain among them because the traders gave them ready access to precious European goods. The French, for their part, sought political as well as economic ends, attempting to prevent the English from encroaching too far into the interior. Their goals were limited; they did not engage in systematic efforts to convert the nearby tribal peoples to Christianity. Given their geographical isolation, such efforts could well have been suicidal. Along the Mississippi just south of modern St. Louis and north of Fort Chartres (see map), migrants from

Quebec and Montreal established six small villages (known collectively as *le pays de Illinois*) that produced wheat for export to New Orleans. But a shortage of manpower—the population never rose much above three thousand—meant that the French could not significantly expand the amount

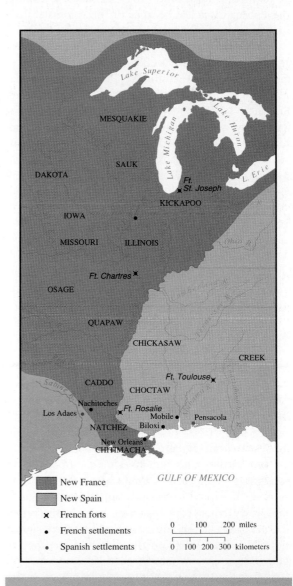

Louisiana, ca. 1720 *By 1720, French forts and settlements dotted the Mississippi River and its tributaries in the interior of North America. Two isolated Spanish outposts were situated near the Gulf of Mexico.*   Source: Adapted from *France in America*, by William J. Eccles. Copyright © 1972 by William J. Eccles. Reprinted by permission of Harper & Row, Publishers, Inc.

of land under cultivation. And the lack of French women led to interracial unions between French men and Native American women, along with the creation of mixed-race people known as *metís*.

Matters were very different in the English colonies, where white colonists had an avid interest in acquiring more land. In Virginia, the conflict was especially acute because of the colonists' insatiable hunger for tobacco acreage.

By the early 1670s, some Virginians were eagerly eyeing the rich lands north of the York River that had been reserved for Native Americans under earlier treaties. Using as a pretext the July 1675 killing of a white servant by some members of the Doeg tribe, they attacked not only the Doegs but also the Susquehannocks, a powerful tribe that had recently occupied the area. In retaliation, Susquehannock bands began to raid frontier plantations in the winter of 1676. The land-hungry whites rallied behind the leadership of Nathaniel Bacon, a recently arrived planter, who, like many of his followers, had immigrated too late to acquire fertile lands in the already settled tidewater region. Bacon and his followers wanted, in his words, "to ruine and extirpate all Indians in general." Governor William Berkeley, however, hoped to avoid setting off a major war, which would have the potential to devastate the colony.

Bacon's Rebellion

Berkeley and Bacon soon clashed. After Bacon forced the House of Burgesses to authorize him to attack the tribes, Berkeley declared Bacon and his men to be in rebellion. As the chaotic summer of 1676 wore on, Bacon alternately pursued Indians and battled with the governor's supporters. In September he marched on Jamestown itself and burned the capital to the ground. But when Bacon died of dysentery the following month, the rebellion collapsed. Even so, a new Indian treaty signed in 1677 opened much of the disputed territory to whites.

More than coincidentally, New England—also settled more than fifty years earlier—was wracked by conflict with Native Americans at precisely the same time. In both areas, the colonists' original accommodation with the tribes, reached after the defeat of the Pequots in the North and the Powhatan Confederacy in the South, no longer satisfied both parties. In New England, though, it was the tribal peoples, rather than the colonists, who felt aggrieved.

In the half-century since the founding of New England, colonial settlement had spread far into the interior of Massachusetts and Connecticut. In the process, the colonists had completely surrounded the ancestral lands of the Pokanokets (Wampanoags) on Narragansett Bay. Their chief, Metacomet (known to the English as King Philip), was the son of Massasoit, who had signed the treaty with the Pilgrims in 1621. Troubled by the encroachments on Pokanoket lands and equally concerned about the impact European culture and Christianity were having on his people, Metacomet led his warriors in attacks on nearby communities in June 1675.

King Philip's War

Two more tribes, the Nipmucks and the Narragansetts, soon joined Metacomet's forces. In the fall, the three tribes jointly attacked settlements in the northern Connecticut River valley. In early 1676, they devastated well-established villages and even attacked Plymouth and Providence. Altogether, the alliance totally destroyed twelve of the ninety Puritan towns and attacked forty others. One-tenth of the able-bodied adult white males in Massachusetts were captured or killed. Proportional to population, it was the most costly war in American history. New England's very survival seemed to be at stake.

But the tide turned in the summer of 1676. The Indian coalition ran short of food and ammunition, and whites began to use Christian Indians as guides and scouts. After Metacomet was killed in an ambush in August, the alliance crumbled. Many surviving Pokanokets, Nipmucks, and Narragansetts, including Metacomet's wife and son, were captured and sold into slavery in the West Indies. The power of New England's coastal tribes was broken. Thereafter they lived in small clusters, subordinated to the colonists and often working as servants or sailors. Only on the isolated island of Martha's Vineyard were some surviving Pokanokets able to preserve their tribal identity intact.

NEW ENGLAND AND THE WEB OF IMPERIAL TRADE

From the early years of colonization to the close of the seventeenth century, the New England settlements had changed in three major ways. The population had grown dramatically; the residents' relationship to the Puritan church had altered; and the economy had developed in unanticipated ways.

The expansion of the population was the result not of continued migration from England (for that had largely ceased after the outbreak of civil war in 1642), but rather of natural increase. The original settlers'

Population Pressures
——

many children also produced many children, and subsequent generations followed suit. By 1700, New England's population had quadrupled to reach approximately 100,000. Such an increase placed great pressure on the available land, and many members of the third and fourth generations of New Englanders had to migrate—north to New Hampshire or Maine, south to New York, west beyond the Connecticut River—to find sufficient farm land for themselves and their children. Others abandoned agriculture and learned skills like blacksmithing or carpentry so that they could support themselves in the growing number of towns that dotted the countryside.

In addition, many second-generation Puritans seemed less willing to become church members than their parents had been. Historians disagree about the causes of the relative decline in church membership; some postulate that American-born Puritans were less fervent than their ancestors, others that such people were simply less willing to declare publicly that they had experienced the gift of God's grace, or "saving faith," a ritual required for full membership in the church. These New Englanders had been baptized as children, attended church services regularly, and wanted their own infants baptized, even though the sacrament of baptism was supposed to be available only to the children of church members. At the same time, many clergymen grew concerned about the increasing numbers of unchurched adults, who were not formally subject to religious supervision.

A synod of Massachusetts ministers, convened in 1662 to consider these problems, responded by establishing a category of "halfway" membership in the church. In a statement

Halfway Covenant
——

that has become known as the Halfway Covenant, the clergymen declared that adults who had been baptized as children but were not full church members could acknowledge the authority of the church in a ceremony called "owning the covenant," which obliged them to live according to moral precepts. If married,

they could then have their children baptized. Halfway members, however, were not allowed to vote in church affairs or to take communion.

Most of the second-generation New Englanders who joined the churches as full members were female; as early as 1660, women comprised a majority of every congregation for which records still survive. Women also were more likely than men to become halfway members, thus submitting themselves and their children to church governance. Searching for the cause of this phenomenon, Cotton Mather, the most prominent member of a family of distinguished ministers, speculated that the fear of dying in childbirth made women especially sensitive to their spiritual state. Modern historians have argued that women were attracted to religion because the church offered them spiritual equality that offset their secular inferiority. Whatever the explanation, the increasingly female composition of his audiences prompted Mather to deliver sermons outlining women's proper role in church and society—the first formal examination of that theme in American history. Mather was the first of many men to publish sermons urging American women to be submissive to their husbands, watchful of their children, and attentive to religious duty.

If Mather thought to ask the parallel question—why had New England's men become so reluctant to acknowledge the church's authority over them?—he did not propose an answer, though scholars have done so. One historian hypothesizes that the connection between church membership and political obligation was critical, since in Massachusetts only male church members could vote in colony elections and hold office. Today voting and officeholding are viewed as desirable, but in the seventeenth century, many farmers sought to avoid the burden of holding one of the numerous public offices of New England's villages. They did not want to have to arrest their acquaintances, assess the quality of fences, round up stray cattle or hogs, or serve as militia officers. Such duties could take them away from their farms and families and cause dissension in their neighborhoods. Thus Massachusetts men may have decided not to seek church membership, since unchurched men were unlikely to be elected to office.

Another hypothesis focuses on the male residents of such seaport towns as Boston and Salem. Men in these urban areas, some historians argue, became more worldly and less interested in religion as the economy of the New England colonies changed after the outbreak of the English Civil War.

New England's first commercial system had been based on two foundations: the fur trade and the constant flow of migrants. Together, those had allowed New Englanders to acquire the manufactured goods they needed: the fur trade gave them valuable pelts to sell in England, and the migrants were always willing to exchange clothing and other items for the earlier settlers' surplus seed, grains, and livestock. But New England's supply of furs was quickly exhausted by excessive trapping, and the migrants stopped coming after the English Civil War began. Thus in the early 1640s that first economic system collapsed.

The Changing Economic System

The Puritans then began a search for new salable crops and markets. They found such crops in the waters off the coast—fish—and on their own land—grain and wood products. By 1643 they had also found the necessary markets: first the Wine Islands and then the English colonies in the Caribbean. All these islands lacked precisely the goods that New England could produce in abundance: cheap food (corn and salted fish) to feed to slaves and wood for barrels to hold wine and molasses (the form in which sugar was shipped).

Thus developed the series of transactions that has become known, inaccurately, as the triangular

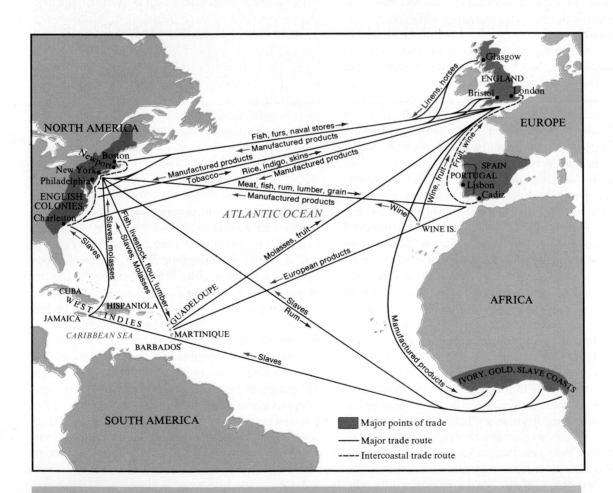

Atlantic Trade Routes *By the late seventeenth century, the countries and colonies bordering the Atlantic Ocean were linked by an elaborate trade network. The most valuable commodities exchanged were enslaved people and the products of slave labor.*

trade. The northern colonists sold their goods in the West Indies and elsewhere to earn the money with which to purchase English imports. There soon grew up in New England's ports a cadre of merchants who acquired—usually through barter—cargoes of timber and foodstuffs, which they then dispatched to the West Indies for sale. In the Caribbean, the ships sailed from island to island, exchanging fish, barrel staves, and grains for molasses, fruit, spices, and slaves. Once they had a full load, the ships returned to Boston, Newport, or New Haven to dispose of their cargoes. New Englanders traded the items they did not use to other colonies or to England. Most important, they distilled West Indian molasses into rum, a widely used alcoholic beverage. Rum was a key component of the only part of the trade that could be termed triangular: Rhode Islanders took rum to Africa and traded it for slaves, whom they carried to the West Indies to exchange for more molasses to produce still more rum. With that exception, the trading pattern was not a triangle but a shifting set of two-way voyages (see map). Its sole constant was uncertainty, due to the weather, rapid shifts in supply and demand in the small island markets, and the delicate system of credit on which the entire structure depended.

The New Englanders who ventured into commerce were soon differentiated from their rural counterparts by their ties to a wider transatlantic

Puritans and Anglicans

world and their preoccupation with material endeavors. As time passed, increasing numbers of Puritans became involved in trade. Small investors who owned shares of voyages soon dominated the field numerically if not monetarily. The gulf between commercial and farming interests widened after 1660, when, with the restoration of the Stuarts to the English throne, Anglican merchants began to migrate to New England to participate directly in the booming trade in slaves and staple crops produced by enslaved laborers. Such men had little stake in the survival of Massachusetts Bay and Connecticut in their original form, and some were openly antagonistic to Puritan traditions. As non-Congregationalists they were denied the vote, but they were still taxed to support the church. Further, Anglicans were forbidden to practice their own religion freely. They resented their exclusion from the governing elite, believing that their

Captain Thomas Smith, a Boston ship captain, painted this self-portrait in the late seventeenth century. The seafaring scene in the background disclosed his occupation, while the skull and religious verse portrayed under his right hand symbolized his piety. Probably few individuals succeeded as well as Smith did in this portrait in simultaneously reflecting the values of the two worlds. Worcester Art Museum, Worcester, Massachusetts.

wealth and social status entitled them to political power. Congregationalist clergymen returned their hostility in full measure and preached sermons called jeremiads lamenting New England's new commercial orientation. The Reverend Increase Mather (Cotton Mather's father) reminded his congregation in 1676 that "Religion and not the World was that which our Fathers came hither for."

But Mather spoke for the past, not for the future or even for many of his own contemporaries. By the 1670s, New England and the other American colonies were deeply enmeshed in an intricate international trading network. The seventeenth-century colonies should not be seen as primitive, isolated, self-sufficient communities. Indeed, if anything, the early colonies were more dependent on overseas markets and imported goods than was eighteenth-century America. During the 1600s the colonies lacked sufficient population to support manufacturing. For example, all attempts to establish ironworks or glass factories in the first decades of settlement failed because there simply were not enough colonial consumers. Furthermore, the colonies' economic fortunes depended on the sale of their exports in foreign markets: furs, deerskins, sugar, tobacco, rice, fish, and timber products together formed the basis for Anglo-America's prosperity.

English officials seeking a new source of revenue after the disruptions of the Civil War realized that the colonies could make important contributions to England's economic well-being. Tobacco from the Chesapeake and sugar from the West Indies had obvious value, but other colonial products also had profitable potential. Additional tax revenues could put the nation back on a sound financial footing, and English merchants wanted to ensure that they—not their Dutch rivals—reaped the benefits of trading with the English colonies. Parliament and the restored Stuart monarchs accordingly began to draft a system of laws designed to confine the profits of colonial trade primarily to the mother country.

Like other European nations, they based their commercial policy on a series of assumptions about the operations of the world's economic system. Collectively, these assumptions are usually called *mercantilism*, though neither the term itself nor a unified mercantilist theory was formulated until a century later. The economic world was seen as a collection of national states, each government actively competing for shares of a finite amount of wealth. What one nation gained was automatically another nation's loss. Each nation's goal was to become as economically self-sufficient as possible while maintaining a favorable balance of trade with other countries (that is, exporting more than it imported). Colonies had an important role to play in such a scheme. They could supply the mother country with valuable raw materials to be consumed at home or sent abroad, and they could serve as a market for the mother country's manufactured goods.

Parliament applied mercantilist thinking to the American colonies in a series of laws known as the Navigation Acts. The major acts—passed between 1651 and 1673—established **Navigation Acts** three main principles. First, only English or colonial merchants and ships could engage in trade in the colonies. Second, certain valuable American products could be sold only in the mother country. At first, these "enumerated" goods were wool, sugar, tobacco, indigo, ginger, and dyes; later acts added rice, naval stores (masts, spars, pitch, tar, and turpentine), copper, and furs to the list. Third, all foreign goods destined for sale in the colonies had to be shipped via England and were subject to English import duties. Some years later, a new series of laws established a fourth principle: the colonies could not make or export items (such as wool clothing, hats, or iron) that competed with English products.

The intention of the Navigation Acts was clear: American trade was to center on England. The mother country was to benefit from colonial imports and exports both. England had first claim on the most valuable colonial exports, and all foreign imports into the colonies had to pass through England first, enriching its customs revenues in the process. Some colonies, like those in the West Indies and the Chesapeake, were adversely affected by the laws because they could not seek new markets for their staple crops. In others, the impact was less severe. Shipbuilders and owners benefited from the monopoly on American trade given to English and colonial merchants. And the northern and middle colonies in particular produced many goods that were not enumerated—for example, fish, flour, and barrel staves. These products could be traded directly to foreign purchasers as long as they were carried in English or American ships.

The English authorities soon learned that it was easier to write mercantilist legislation than to enforce it. The many harbors of the American coast provided ready havens for smugglers, and colonial officials often looked the other way when illegally imported goods were offered for sale. In ports such as Curaçao in the Dutch West Indies, American merchants could easily dispose of enumerated goods and purchase foreign items on which duty had not been paid. Consequently, Parliament in 1696 enacted another Navigation Act designed to strengthen enforcement of the first four. This law established in America a number of vice-admiralty courts, which operated without juries. In England such courts dealt only with cases involving piracy, vessels taken as wartime prizes, and the like. But since American juries had already demonstrated a tendency to favor local smugglers over customs officers (a colonial customs service had been instituted in 1671), Parliament decided to remove Navigation Act cases from the regular colonial courts.

England took another major step in colonial administration in 1696 by creating the fifteen-member Board of Trade and Plantations, which thereafter served as the chief organ of government concerned with the American colonies. (Previously, no single body had that responsibility.) It gathered information, reviewed Crown appointments in America, scrutinized legislation passed by colonial assemblies, supervised trade policies, and advised successive ministries on colonial issues. Still, the Board of Trade did not have any direct powers of enforcement. It also shared jurisdiction over American affairs not only with the customs service and the navy but also with the secretary of state for the southern department, the member of the ministry responsible for the colonies. In short, although the Stuart monarchs' reforms considerably improved the quality of colonial administration, supervision of the American provinces remained decentralized and haphazard.

COLONIAL POLITICAL DEVELOPMENT AND IMPERIAL REORGANIZATION

English officials in the 1670s and 1680s were confronted not only by resistance to the Navigation Acts but also by a bewildering array of colonial governments. Massachusetts Bay and Plymouth functioned under their original charters, and neighboring Connecticut (including the formerly independent New Haven) and Rhode Island had been granted charters by Charles II in 1662 and 1663, respectively. Virginia was a royal colony, and New York also became one when its proprietor ascended the throne in 1685 as James II. All the other mainland settlements were proprietorships, whose royal charters gave proprietors a great deal of leeway in governing their possessions.

Still, in political structure the colonies shared certain characteristics. Most were ruled by a governor and a two-house legislature. In New England,

Colonial Political Structures

the governors were elected by property-holding men or by the legislature; in the Chesapeake and the middle colonies, they were appointed by the king or the proprietor. A council, either elected or appointed, advised the governor on matters of policy and sometimes served as

the colony's highest court. The councils also served as the upper house of the colonial legislatures. At first, councilors and elected representatives met jointly to debate and adopt laws affecting the colony. But as time passed, the fundamental differences between the two legislative groups' purposes and constituencies led them to separate. In Virginia that important event occurred in 1663; in Massachusetts Bay it happened earlier, in 1644. Thus developed the two-house legislature still used in almost all of the states.

Meanwhile, local political institutions were taking shape. In New England, elected selectmen initially governed the towns, but by the end of the century the town meeting—held at least annually and attended by most free adult male residents, regardless of church membership—handled matters of local concern. In the Chesapeake the same function was performed by the judges of the county court and by the parish vestry, a group of laymen charged with overseeing church affairs, whose power also encompassed secular concerns.

By late in the seventeenth century, therefore, the American colonists were accustomed to exercising a considerable degree of local political autonomy. The tradition of consent was especially firmly established in New England. Massachusetts, Plymouth, Connecticut, and Rhode Island were, in effect, independent entities, subject neither to the direct authority of the king nor to a proprietor. Everywhere in the English colonies, free adult men who owned more than a stated minimum of property (which varied from province to province) expected to have an influential voice in how they were governed, and especially in how they were taxed.

After James II became king, these expectations clashed with those of the monarch. The new king and his successors sought to bring order to the apparently chaotic state of colonial administration by tightening the reins of government and reducing the colonies' political autonomy. (Simultaneously, they used the Navigation Acts to reduce the colonies' economic autonomy.) They began to chip away at the privileges granted in colonial charters and to reclaim proprietorships for the Crown. New Hampshire (1679), its parent colony Massachusetts (1691), New Jersey (1702), and the Carolinas (1729) all became royal colonies. The charters of Rhode Island, Connecticut, Maryland, and Pennsylvania were temporarily suspended but were ultimately restored to their original status.

James II's charter for the Dominion of New England, issued in 1686, inscribed a portrait of the monarch within his decorative first initial.   Massachusetts State Archives.

Dominion of New England

The most drastic reordering of colonial administration targeted Puritan New England. Reports from America convinced English officials that New England was a hotbed of smuggling. Moreover, the Puritans refused to allow freedom of religion to non-Congregationalists and insisted on maintaining laws that ran counter to English practice. New England thus seemed an appropriate place to exert English authority with greater vigor. The charters of all the colonies from New Jersey to Maine (then part of Massachusetts) were revoked, and a Dominion of New England was established in 1686 with the issuance of the charter reproduced in the accompanying photo. (For the boundaries of the dominion, see map on page 66.) Sir Edmund Andros, the governor, was given immense power: all the assemblies were dissolved, and he needed only the consent of an appointed council to make laws and levy taxes.

New Englanders endured Andros's autocratic rule for more than two years. Then came the dramatic news that James II had been overthrown in a bloodless coup known as the Glorious Revolution and had been replaced on the throne by his daughter Mary and her husband, the Dutch prince William of Orange. James II, like his father Charles I, had levied taxes without parliamentary approval. He had also announced his conversion to Roman Catholicism. When Parliament offered the throne to the Protestants William and Mary, the Glorious Revolution affirmed the supremacy of both Parliament and Protestantism.

Glorious Revolution in America

Seizing the opportunity to rid themselves of the hated Dominion, New Englanders jailed Andros and his associates, proclaimed their loyalty to William and Mary, and wrote to England for instructions about the form of government they should adopt. Most of Massachusetts Bay's political leaders hoped that the new monarchs would renew their original charter, revoked in 1684 prior to establishment of the Dominion. In other American colonies, too, the Glorious Revolution was a signal for revolt. In Maryland the Protestant Association overturned the government of the Catholic proprietor, and in New York a militia officer of German origin, Jacob Leisler, assumed control of the government. Like the New Englanders, the Maryland and New York rebels allied themselves with the supporters of William and Mary. They saw themselves as carrying out the colonial phase of the English revolt against Stuart absolutism. But William and Mary, like James II, believed that England should exercise tighter control over its unruly American possessions.

Consequently, the only American rebellion that received royal sanction was that in Maryland, primarily because of its anti-Catholic thrust. In New York, Jacob Leisler was hanged for treason, and Massachusetts (including the formerly independent jurisdiction of Plymouth) became a royal colony with an appointed governor. The province was allowed to retain its town meeting system of local government and to elect its council, but the new charter issued in 1691 eliminated the traditional religious test for voting. An Anglican parish was set up in the heart of Boston. The "city upon a hill" as John Winthrop had envisioned it was no more.

Compounding New England's difficulties in a time of political upheaval and economic uncertainty was a war with the French and their Native American allies. King Louis XIV of France allied himself with the deposed James II, and England declared war on France in 1689. The conflict, which lasted until 1697, was known in Europe as the War of the League of Augsburg, but the colonists called it King William's War. The American war was fought chiefly on the northern frontiers of New England and New York; among the English settlements devastated by enemy attacks in 1690 were Schenectady, New York, and Casco (Falmouth), Maine. Expeditions organized by the colonies against Montreal and Quebec that same year both failed miserably, and throughout the rest of the war New England found itself on the defensive.

In this period of extreme stress occurred an outbreak of witchcraft accusations in Salem Village (now Danvers), Massachusetts, a rural community adjoining the bustling port of

Witchcraft in Salem Village
——

Salem. Like their contemporaries elsewhere, seventeenth-century New Englanders believed in the existence of witches, whose evil powers came from the Devil. If people could not find other explanations for their troubles, they tended to suspect they were bewitched. Before 1689, 103 New Englanders, most of them middle-aged women, had been accused of practicing witchcraft, chiefly by neighbors who attributed their misfortunes to the suspected witch, with whom they usually had an ongoing dispute. Only a few of the accused were convicted, and fewer still were executed. Although most accusations were isolated incidents, a witchcraft panic occasionally resulted when one charge set off a chain reaction. But nothing else in New England's history ever came close to matching the Salem Village cataclysm.

The crisis began in early 1692 when a group of adolescent girls accused some older women of having bewitched them. Before the hysteria spent itself ten months later, nineteen people (including several men, most of them related to accused female witches) had been hanged, another pressed to death with heavy stones, and more than one hundred persons jailed. Historians have proposed various explanations for this puzzling episode, but to be understood it must be seen in the context of political and legal disorder, Indian war, and religious and economic crises. Puritan New Englanders must have felt as though their entire world was collapsing. At the very least they could have had no sense of security about their future.

Nowhere was that more true than in Salem Village, a farming town torn between old and new

styles of life because of its position on the edge of a commercial center. And no residents of the village had more reason to feel insecure than the girls who issued the initial accusations. Many of them had been orphaned in the recent Indian attacks on Maine; they were living in Salem Village as domestic servants. Their involvement with witchcraft began as an experiment with fortunetelling as a means of foreseeing their futures, in particular the identities of their eventual husbands. As the most powerless people in a town apparently powerless to direct its fate, they offered their fellow New Englanders a compelling explanation for the seemingly endless chain of troubles afflicting them: their province was under direct attack from the Devil and his legion of witches. Accordingly, it is not so much the number of witchcraft prosecutions that seems surprising but rather their abrupt cessation in the fall of 1692.

There were two reasons for the rapid end to the crisis. First, the accusers grew too bold. When they began to accuse some of the colony's most distinguished and respected residents of being in league with the Devil, members of the ruling elite began to doubt their veracity. Second, the new royal charter was fully implemented in late 1692, ending the worst period of political uncertainty and eliminating a major source of psychological stress. King William's War continued and, although the Puritans were not entirely pleased with the charter, at least order had formally been restored.

Over the course of the next three decades, Massachusetts and the rest of the English colonies

No seventeenth-century New Englander ever drew a picture of a witchcraft trial or execution, but an artist did record the hanging of several witches in England, ca. 1650. The multiple executions of Salem witches in the summer of 1692 probably resembled this gallows scene.   Folger Shakespeare Library.

in America accommodated themselves to the new imperial order. Most colonists resented alien officials who arrived in America determined to implement the policies of king and Parliament, but they adjusted to their demands and to the trade restrictions imposed by the Navigation Acts. They fought another imperial war—the War of the Spanish Succession, or Queen Anne's War—from 1702 to 1713, without enduring the psychological stress of the first, despite the heavy economic burdens the conflict imposed. Colonists who allied themselves with royal government received patronage in the form of offices and land grants and composed "court parties" that supported English officials. Others, who were either less fortunate in their friends or more principled in defense of colonial autonomy (opinions differ), made up the opposition, or "country" interest. By the end of the first quarter of the eighteenth century, most men in both groups had been born in America and were members of elite families whose wealth derived from staple-crop production in the South and commerce in the North.

The eighty years from 1640 to 1720, then, established the basic economic and political patterns that were to structure all subsequent changes in colonial society. In 1640 there were just two isolated centers of English population, New England and the Chesapeake. In 1720, nearly the entire east coast of mainland North America was in English hands, and Indian power east of the Appalachian Mountains had been broken. What had been a migrant population was now mostly American-born; economies originally based on the fur trade had become far more complex and more closely linked with the mother country; and a wide variety of political structures had been reshaped into a more uniform pattern. Yet at the same time the introduction of large-scale slavery into the Chesapeake and the Carolinas irrevocably differentiated their societies from those of the colonies to the north. Staple-crop production for the market was not the key distinguishing feature of the southern regional economies; rather, their uniqueness lay in their reliance on a system of perpetual servitude.

Meanwhile, from a small outpost in Santa Fe, New Mexico, the Spanish had expanded their influence throughout the region as far east as Texas and, by just after midcentury, as far north as California. The French had moved from a few settlements along the St. Lawrence to dominate the length of the Mississippi River and the entire Great Lakes region. Both groups of colonists lived near Indian nations and were dependent on the tribes' labor and goodwill. The French and Spanish could not fully control their Native American allies—and the French did not even try to. The extensive Spanish and French presence to the south and west of the English settlements meant that future conflicts among the European powers in North America were nearly inevitable.

By 1720, the essential elements of the imperial administrative structure that would govern the English colonies until 1775 were firmly in place. The regional economic systems originating in the late seventeenth and early eighteenth centuries also continued to dominate North American life for another century—until after independence had been won. And Anglo-Americans had developed the commitment to autonomous local government that would later lead them into conflict with Parliament and the king.

SUGGESTIONS FOR FURTHER READING

General

Charles M. Andrews, *The Colonial Period of American History*, vol. 4 (1938); Carl Bridenbaugh, *Cities in the Wilderness: The First Century of Urban Life in America, 1625–1742* (1938); Wesley Frank Craven, *The Colonies in Transition, 1660–1713* (1968); W. J. Eccles, *France in America*, rev. ed. (1990); W. J. Eccles, *The Canadian Frontier, 1534–1760*, rev. ed. (1983); Jack P. Greene and J. R. Pole, eds., *Colonial British America* (1984); John J. McCusker and Russell R. Menard, *The Economy of British America, 1607–1789* (1985); Gary Walton and James Shepherd, *The Economic Rise of Early America* (1979).

New Netherland and the Restoration Colonies

Edwin Bronner, *William Penn's "Holy Experiment": The Founding of Pennsylvania, 1681–1701* (1962); Wesley Frank Craven, *New Jersey and the English Colonization of North America* (1964); Mary Maples Dunn, *William Penn: Politics and Conscience* (1967); Joyce Goodfriend, *Before the Melting Pot: Society and Culture in Colonial New York City, 1664–1730* (1992); Ronald Hutton, *Charles II: King of England, Scotland, and Ireland* (1990); Michael Kammen, *Colonial New York: A History* (1975); Oliver Rink, *Holland on the Hudson: An Economic and Social History of Dutch New York* (1986); Robert C. Ritchie, *The Duke's Province: A Study of Politics and Society in Colonial New York, 1660–1691* (1977); Robert M. Weir, *Colonial South Carolina: A History* (1983).

Africa and the Slave Trade

Jay Coughtry, *The Notorious Triangle: Rhode Island and the African Slave Trade, 1700–1807* (1981); Philip D. Curtin, *The Atlantic*

Slave Trade: A Census (1969); David Brion Davis, The Problem of Slavery in Western Culture (1966); David W. Galenson, Traders, Planters, and Slaves: Market Behavior in Early English America (1986); Joseph Inikori and Stanley Engerman, eds., The Atlantic Slave Trade (1992); Herbert Klein, The Middle Passage (1978); Robin Law, The Slave Coast of West Africa, 1550–1750: The Impact of the Atlantic Slave Trade on an African Society (1991); Daniel C. Littlefield, Rice and Slaves: Ethnicity and the Slave Trade in Colonial South Carolina (1981); Paul Lovejoy, ed., Africans in Bondage: Studies in Slavery and the Slave Trade (1986); James Rawley, The Transatlantic Slave Trade: A History (1981).

Africans in Anglo-America

T. H. Breen and Stephen Innes, "Myne Owne Ground": Race and Freedom on Virginia's Eastern Shore, 1640–1676 (1980); Allan Kulikoff, Tobacco and Slaves: The Development of Southern Cultures in the Chesapeake, 1680–1800 (1986); Edgar J. McManus, Black Bondage in the North (1973); Edmund S. Morgan, American Slavery, American Freedom: The Ordeal of Colonial Virginia (1975); Peter H. Wood, Black Majority: Negroes in Colonial South Carolina from 1670 Through the Stono Rebellion (1974).

European-Native American Relations

Russell Bourne, The Red King's Rebellion: Racial Politics in New England 1675–1678 (1991); Henry Bowden, American Indians and Christian Missions: Studies in Cultural Conflict (1981); David H. Corkran, The Creek Frontier, 1540–1783 (1967); Verner W. Crane, The Southern Frontier, 1660–1732 (1929); Ramón Gutiérrez, When Jesus Came, the Corn Mothers Went Away: Marriage, Sexuality, and Power in New Mexico, 1500–1846 (1991); Francis Jennings, The Ambiguous Iroquois Empire (1984); Elizabeth A. H. John, Storms Brewed in Other Men's Worlds: The Confrontation of Indians, Spanish, and French in the Southwest, 1540–1795 (1975); Douglas Leach, Flintlock and Tomahawk: New England in King Philip's War (1958); James Merrell, The Indians' New World: Catawbas and Their Neighbors from European Contact through the Era of Removal (1989); Michael Puglisi, Puritans Beseiged: The Legacies of King Philip's War in the Massachusetts Bay Colony (1991); Daniel Richter and James Merrell, eds., Beyond the Covenant Chain: The Iroquois and Their Neighbors in Indian America, 1600–1800 (1987); Roberto M. Salmon, Indian Revolts in Northern New Spain (1990); Marc Simmons, The Last Conquistador: Juan de Oñate and the Settling of the Far Southwest (1991); Dean Snow, The Iroquois (1992); Daniel H. Usner, Jr., Indians, Settlers, and Slaves in a Frontier Exchange Economy: The Lower Mississippi Valley before 1783 (1992); Richard White, The Middle Ground: Indians, Empires, and Republics in the Great Lakes Region, 1650–1815 (1991); J. Leitch Wright, Jr., The Only Land They Knew: The Tragic Story of the American Indians in the Old South (1981).

New England

Bernard Bailyn, The New England Merchants in the Seventeenth Century (1955); Paul Boyer and Stephen Nissenbaum, Salem Possessed: The Social Origins of Witchcraft (1974); Richard Bushman, From Puritan to Yankee: Character and the Social Order in Connecticut, 1690–1765 (1967); John Demos, Entertaining Satan: Witchcraft and the Culture of Early New England (1982); Richard Godbeer, The Devil's Dominion: Magic and Religion in Early New England (1992); Christine Heyrman, Commerce and Culture: The Maritime Communities of Colonial Massachusetts, 1690–1750 (1984); Carol Karlsen, The Devil in the Shape of a Woman: Witchcraft

The Mason Children, attributed to painter Freake-Gibbs, 1670. A detail of this painting appears at the beginning of Chapter 3, on page 62. The Fine Arts Museum of San Francisco. Gift of Mr. and Mrs. John D. Rockefeller III, 1979.7.3.

in Early New England (1987); Richard I. Melvoin, New England Outpost: War and Society in Colonial Deerfield (1990); Robert Pope, The Half-Way Covenant (1969); Amanda Porterfield, Female Piety in Puritan New England (1991); Laurel Thatcher Ulrich, Good Wives: Image and Reality in the Lives of Women in Northern New England, 1650–1750 (1982).

Colonial Politics

Lois Green Carr and David W. Jordan, Maryland's Revolution of Government, 1689–1692 (1974); Richard P. Johnson, Adjustment to Empire: The New England Colonies, 1675–1715 (1981); David W. Jordan, Foundations of Representative Government in Maryland, 1632–1715 (1987); David S. Lovejoy, The Glorious Revolution in America (1972); Jack M. Sosin, English America and Imperial Inconstancy: The Rise of Provincial Autonomy, 1696–1715 (1985); Jack M. Sosin, English America and the Revolution of 1688 (1982); Jack M. Sosin, English America and the Restoration Monarchy of Charles II (1980); Stephen Saunders Webb, 1676: The End of American Independence (1984).

Imperial Trade and Administration

Robert M. Bliss, Revolution and Empire: English Politics and the American Colonies in the Seventeenth Century (1991); Lawrence W. Harper, The English Navigation Laws: A Seventeenth-Century Experiment in Social Engineering (1939); Michael Kammen, Empire and Interest: The American Colonies and the Politics of Mercantilism (1970); Marcus Rediker, Between the Devil and the Deep Blue Sea: Merchant Seamen, Pirates, and the Anglo-American Maritime World, 1700–1750 (1987); Robert C. Ritchie, Captain Kidd and the War Against the Pirates (1986); I. K. Steele, Politics of Colonial Policy: The Board of Trade in Colonial Administration (1968); Stephen Saunders Webb, The Governors-General: The English Army and the Definition of the Empire, 1569–1681 (1979).

Growth and Diversity, 1720–1770

IN JUNE 1744, Dr. Alexander Hamilton, a thirty-four-year-old Scottish-born physician living in Annapolis, Maryland, paid his first visit to Philadelphia. There he encountered two quite different worlds. One consisted of men of his own status, the merchants and professionals he called "the better sort." Hamilton mingled with them at the Governor's Club, "a society of gentlemen that [meet] at a tavern every night and converse on various subjects." The night Hamilton attended, the "entertaining" discussion focused on Cervantes and some English poets.

Hamilton reacted differently to the other world of Philadelphia, composed of people he variously termed "rabble" or "a strange medley." Most spoke, he thought, "ignorantly," regardless of the subject. One evening he dined at a tavern with "a very mixed company" of twenty-five men. "There were Scots, English, Dutch, Germans, and Irish; there were Roman Catholics, Church men, Presbyterians, Quakers, Newlightmen, Methodists, Seventh day men, Moravians, Anabaptists and one Jew." Some discussed business, and a few argued about religion, but the "prevailing topick" was politics and the threat of war with France. Hamilton refused to be drawn

into any of the conversations. As a gentleman, he consciously set himself apart from ordinary folk, commenting on their behavior but not participating in their exchanges.

And what of the women in Philadelphia? Hamilton met few of them, other than his landlady and one of her friends. "The ladies," he explained, "for the most part, keep at home and seldom appear in the streets, never in publick assemblies except at the churches or meetings." Hamilton was referring to women of "the better sort." He could hardly have walked the streets of the city without seeing many female domestic servants, market women, and wives of ordinary laborers going about their daily chores.

Despite his obvious biases, Dr. Hamilton was an astute observer. The Philadelphians' chief employment, he wrote, "is traffick and mercantile business," and the richest merchants of all were the Quakers. Members of that sect also controlled the colony's government, but, Hamilton noted, "the standing or falling of the Quakers in the House of Assembly depends upon their making sure the interest of the Palatines [Germans] in this province, who of late have turned so numerous that they can sway the votes which

Mary Woodhull, a colonial needleworker, stitched this idyllic pastoral vision of a young man harvesting grain with the assistance of his wife.

way they please." And Hamilton deplored the impact on the city of the Great Awakening, a religious revival then sweeping the colonies. "I never was in a place so populous where the gout [taste] for publick gay diversions prevailed so little," he remarked. "There is no such thing as assemblys of the gentry among them, either for dancing or musick; these they have an utter aversion to ever since Whitefield preached among them."

Hamilton's comments provide an excellent introduction to mid-eighteenth-century American life, for the patterns he observed in Philadelphia were not unique to that city. Although ethnic diversity was especially pronounced in urban areas, by midcentury non-English migrants were settling in many regions of the mainland colonies. Their arrival not only swelled the total population, but also altered political balances and affected the religious climate by introducing new sects. The diverse group of men Hamilton encountered in that

Dr. Alexander Hamilton's self-portrait, drawn in 1750—six years after the journey described in this chapter—shows a well-dressed, haughty gentleman. The book in his hand is his manuscript record of the Tuesday Club, an Annapolis men's social club of which he was a co-founder.   Maryland Historical Society Library, Manuscript Division.

tavern could have been duplicated in other cities and even in some rural areas.

Hamilton correctly recognized that the Quakers maintained control of Pennsylvania politics because they had managed to win the support of recent German immigrants. The ruling elites in other provinces were not always such astute politicians. Instead of consulting the newcomers, they often refused to allow them adequate representation and government services. A series of violent clashes ensued after midcentury. By that time, native-born elites dominated each of the colonies and contended with English-born governors and councilors for control of the governmental machinery. Sometimes they won, and those victories were to serve them well when they began battling for independence later in the century.

Hamilton also accurately assessed the importance of commerce in Americans' lives. The web of imperial trade woven before 1720 became even more complex and all-encompassing during the next fifty years. Americans of all descriptions were tied to an international commercial system that fluctuated wildly for reasons having little to do with the colonies but inescapable in their effects. As the colonies would learn when they attempted to break their trade ties with Great Britain at the time of the Revolution, they were heavily dependent on England for both imported manufactured goods and markets for their exports.

Well-educated Americans like Dr. Hamilton were heavily influenced by the Enlightenment, the prevailing European intellectual movement of the day. The Enlightenment stressed reason and empirical knowledge, deliberately discarding superstition and instinct as guides to human behavior. Like other enlightened thinkers, Hamilton believed above all in rationality. To him, God was a distant presence who had ordered the world, setting forth natural laws that humans could discover through careful investigation and logical thought. From this perspective came Hamilton's distaste for the Great Awakening, since that revival drew primarily on the Calvinistic concept of a God that people could never fully comprehend. Moreover, the hallmark of the Great Awakening was emotion, expressed in a conversion experience. To a believer in the primacy of reason, the passions of the newly converted were incomprehensible.

The Enlightenment also helped to create the elite world of which Hamilton was a part, a world

• *Important Events* •

1690	Locke's *Essay Concerning Human Understanding* published; key example of Enlightenment thought	**1760s**	Baptist congregations take root in Virginia
1720–40	Black population of Chesapeake begins to grow by natural increase, contributing to rise of large plantations	**1760–75**	Peak of eighteenth-century European and African migration to English colonies
1739	Stono Rebellion (South Carolina) leads to increased white fears of slave revolts	**1765–66**	Hudson River land riots pit tenants and squatters against large landlords
	George Whitefield arrives in America; Great Awakening broadens	**1767–69**	Regulator movement (South Carolina) tries to establish order in backcountry
1739–48	King George's War disrupts American economy	**1771**	North Carolina Regulators defeated by eastern militia at Battle of Alamance
1741	New York City "conspiracy" reflects whites' continuing fears of slave revolts		

quite different from that of ordinary folk. Wealthy, well-read Americans participated in a transatlantic intellectual community, whereas many colonists of "the lesser sort" could neither read nor write. Hamilton and his peers lived in comfortable houses and entertained at lavish parties; most colonists struggled just to make ends meet. Hamilton could take a leisurely four-month journey for his health (his visit to Philadelphia was only one stop on a long trip), but most Americans had to work daily from dawn to dark. The eighteenth century, then, brought an increasing gap between rich and poor. The colonies had always been composed of people of different ranks, but by the last half of the century the social and economic distance between those ranks had widened noticeably.

After 1720 the population of the English colonies increased dramatically, and the area settled by whites and blacks expanded until it filled almost all of the region between the Appalachian Mountains and the Atlantic Ocean, displacing the Native Americans who had previously lived there. At the same time, the colonies became more diverse; the two original regional economies (the Chesapeake and New England) became four (those two plus the middle colonies and the Lower South). Before 1720, the colonies were still inhabited mainly by

English, African, and Indian peoples; just half a century later, a large proportion of the white population was of non-English origin. Many of the colonies were home to a variety of ethnic groups and religious sects. The urban population, though still tiny by today's standards, grew considerably after 1720, and the cities harbored the greatest extremes of wealth and poverty. Such changes transformed the character of England's North American possessions. The colonies that revolted in unison against British rule after 1765 were very different from the colonies that revolted separately against Stuart absolutism in 1689.

POPULATION GROWTH AND ETHNIC DIVERSITY

One of the most striking characteristics of the mainland colonies in the eighteenth century was their rapid population growth. Only about 250,000 European- and African-Americans resided in the colonies in 1700. Thirty years later, that number had more than doubled, and by 1775 it had become 2.5 million. Although migration accounted for a considerable share of the growth, most of

"Rachel Weeping" by Charles Willson Peale conveys as few other colonial portraits can the affection of eighteenth-century parents for their children, and the grief they consequently felt when those children died (as was so often the case) at an early age. Peale movingly revealed his wife's sorrow at the death of their daughter; thus his painting helps to refute the interpretation—advanced by some historians—that high levels of infant mortality led colonists to avoid becoming too attached to their young children. Philadelphia Museum of Art, The Barra Foundation.

it resulted from natural increase. Once the difficult early decades of settlement had passed, the American population doubled approximately every twenty-five years. Such a rate of growth was unparalleled in human history until very recent times. It had a variety of causes, chief among them women's youthful age at marriage (early twenties for whites, late teens for blacks). Since married women became pregnant every two or three years, women normally bore five to ten children. Because the colonies were healthful places to live (especially north of Virginia), a large proportion of children reached maturity and began families of their own. As a result, about half the American population, white and black, was under sixteen years old in 1775. (By contrast, only about one-third of the American population was under sixteen in 1990.)

Newcomers from Africa and Europe

Africans (about 278,000 of them) constituted the largest racial or ethnic group that came to the mainland English colonies during the eighteenth century. In the slaveholding societies of South America and the Caribbean, a surplus of males over females and the appallingly high mortality rates meant that only a large, continuing flow of enslaved Africans could maintain the captive work force at constant levels. South Carolina, where rice cultivation was difficult and unhealthy (chiefly because malaria-carrying mosquitoes bred in the rice swamps), and where planters preferred to purchase men, bore some resemblance to such colonies in that it too required an influx of Africans to sustain as well as expand its labor force. But in the Chesapeake the number of black residents grew especially rapidly, because the new African workers were added to a population that began to sustain itself through natural increase after 1740.

The offspring of slaves were also slaves, whereas the children of servants were free. The consequences of this important difference between enslaved and indentured labor were not clear until after 1720. It then became evident that a planter who owned adult female slaves could watch the size of his labor force increase steadily—through the births of their children—without making additional major investments in workers. Not coincidentally, the first truly large Chesapeake plantations appeared in the 1740s. Some years later, the slaveholder Thomas Jefferson indicated that he fully understood the connections when he declared, "I consider a woman who brings a child every two years more profitable than the best man of the farm. What she produces is an addition to the capital, while his labors disappear in mere consumption."

In addition to the new group of Africans, about 585,000 Europeans moved to North America during the eighteenth century, most of them after 1730 (see maps). Because some of the whites (for example, convicts sentenced to exile by English courts) and all the blacks did not freely choose to come to the colonies, approximately one-third of the migrants moved to America against their will. That contrasts sharply with the voluntary migration from Europe and Asia discussed later in this text.

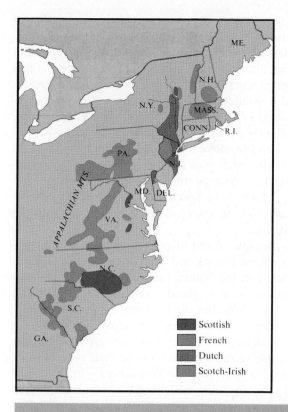 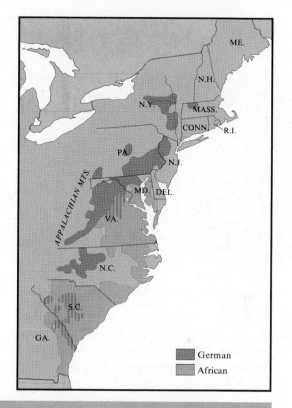

Non-English Ethnic Groups in the British Colonies, ca. 1775 *Non-African immigrants arriving in the years after 1720 were pushed to the peripheries of settlement, as is shown by this map. Scottish, Scotch-Irish, French, and German newcomers had to move to the frontiers, whereas the Dutch remained where they had originally settled in the seventeenth century. Africans were concentrated in coastal plantation regions.*

The largest group of white non-English immigrants to America—over 100,000—came from Ireland. About 66,000 were Scotch-Irish, descended

Scotch-Irish, Germans, and Scots

from Presbyterian Scots who had settled in the north of Ireland during the seventeenth century. Another 43,000 (both Protestants and Catholics) migrated from southern Ireland. Fleeing economic distress and religious discrimination—Irish law favored Anglicans over Presbyterians and Catholics—they were also lured by hopes of obtaining land. Irish immigrants often arrived in Philadelphia and other ports along the Delaware River. They moved west and south, settling chiefly in the western portions of Pennsylvania, Maryland, Virginia, and the Carolinas. Frequently unable to afford any acreage, they squatted on land

belonging to Indian tribes, land speculators, or colonial governments.

Migrants from Germany numbered about 85,000. Most emigrated from the Rhineland between 1730 and 1755, also usually arriving in Philadelphia. They became known locally as Pennsylvania Dutch (a corruption of *Deutsch*, as the Germans called themselves); late in the century they and their descendants accounted for one-third of Pennsylvania's residents. But many other Germans moved west and then south along the eastern slope of the Appalachian Mountains, eventually finding homes in western Maryland and Virginia. Others sailed first to Charleston or Savannah and settled in the interior of South Carolina or Georgia, often initially living under very difficult conditions, as is evident in contemporary drawings. The Germans belonged to a wide variety of Protestant sects—

The first German immigrants in Georgia had to live in crude shelters they erected in the wilderness at the settlement they named New Ebenezer. Note the similarity to the structures inhabited by the Indians of the region, illustrated in a painting by the same artist, Philip Georg Friedrich von Reck, on page 80.   The Royal Library, Copenhagen.

primarily Lutheran, German Reformed, and Moravian—and therefore added to the already substantial religious diversity of the middle colonies.

The 35,000 or more Scots who came directly to America from Scotland should not be confused with the Scotch-Irish. Many early Scottish immigrants were supporters of Stuart claimants to the throne of England (called Jacobites, for the Latin version of James Stuart's name). After the death of William and Mary's successor Queen Anne in 1714, the British throne passed to the German house of Hanover, in the person of King George I. In 1715 and again in 1745, Jacobite rebels attempted unsuccessfully to capture the crown for the Stuart pretender, and many were exiled to America as punishment. Most of the Jacobites settled in North Carolina. Ironically, they tended to become loyalists during the Revolutionary War because of their strong commitment to monarchy.

The most concentrated period of immigration to the colonies fell between 1760 and 1775. Tough times in Europe led many to decide to seek a better life in America. In those fifteen years alone arrived more than 220,000 persons—or 10 percent of the entire population of British North America. At least 90,000 migrants came from the British Isles:

34,000 Irish (over 1 percent of the population of Ireland), 25,000 Scots (about 2 percent of the population of Scotland), perhaps 11,000 Welsh, and about 20,000 English people. To them were added approximately 20,000 Germans, 100,000 Africans, and a smattering of people from other places, including a few from the West Indies. Late-arriving free immigrants had little choice but to remain in the cities or move to the peripheries of settlement; land elsewhere was fully occupied. In the borderlands they became the tenants of, or bought property from, land speculators who had purchased giant tracts in the (usually vain) hope of making a fortune.

Because of the migration patterns of the various ethnic groups and the concentration of slaveholding in the South, half the colonial population south of New England was of non-English origin by 1775. Whether the migrants assimilated readily into Anglo-American culture depended on patterns of settlement, the size of the group, and the strength of the migrants' ties to their common culture. For example, the Huguenots—French Protestants who fled religious persecution in their homeland after 1685—settled in tiny enclaves in American cities like Charleston and New York. They were unable to sustain either their language or their religious practices, and within two generations they were almost wholly absorbed into Anglo-American culture. By contrast, the equally small group of colonial Jews maintained a distinct identity. Most Jews in early America were Sephardic; that is, they were descended from the group of Jews who had escaped persecution in Spain and Portugal by migrating to The Netherlands and later to Dutch colonies in the New World. In a few cities—notably New York and Newport, Rhode Island—they established synagogues and worked actively to preserve their culture (for example, by opposing intermarriage with Christians).

Members of the larger groups of migrants (the Germans, Irish, and Scots) found it easier to sustain Old World ways. Countless localities were settled almost exclusively by one group or another. Near Frederick, Maryland, a visitor would have heard more German than English; in Anson and Cumberland counties, North Carolina, the same visitor might have thought she was in Scotland. Where migrants from different countries settled in the same region, ethnic antagonisms often surfaced. One German clergyman, for example, ex-

Who Moved to America and Scotland in the Early 1770s, and Why?

	English Emigrants	Scottish Emigrants	Free American Population
Destination			
13 Colonies	81.1%	92.7%	—
Canada	12.1%	4.2%	—
West Indies	6.8%	3.1%	—
Age Distribution			
Under 21	26.8%	45.3%	56.8%
21-25	37.1%	19.9%	9.7%
26-44	33.3%	29.5%	20.4%
45 and over	2.7%	5.3%	13.1%
Sex Distribution			
Male	83.8%	59.9%	—
Female	16.2%	40.1%	—
Unknown	4.2%	13.5%	—
Traveling Alone or with Families			
In families	20.0%	48.0%	—
Alone	80.0%	52.0%	—
Known Occupation or Status			
Gentry	2.5%	1.2%	—
Merchandising	5.2%	5.2%	—
Agriculture	17.8%	24.0%	—
Artisanry	54.2%	37.7%	—
Laborer	20.3%	31.9%	—
Why They Left			
Positive Reasons (e.g., desire to better one's position)	90.0%	36.0%	—
Negative Reasons (e.g., poverty, unemployment)	10.0%	64.0%	—

Between December 1773 and March 1776, the British government questioned individuals and families leaving ports in Scotland and England for the American colonies to learn who they were, where they were going, and why they were leaving. This table summarizes just a few of the findings of the official inquiries, which revealed a number of significant differences between the Scottish and English emigrants. Source of data: Bernard Bailyn, *Voyagers to the West* (New York: Knopf, 1986), Tables 4.1, 5.2, 5.4, 5.7, 5.23, and 6.1.

plained his efforts to prevent German youths from marrying people of different ethnic origins by asserting that the Scotch-Irish were "lazy, dissipated and poor" and that "it is very seldom that German and English blood is happily united in wedlock."

Recognizing the benefits of keeping other racial and ethnic groups divided, the white elites on occasion deliberately fostered such antagonisms. When the targets of their policies were European migrants, the goal was the maintenance of political and economic power. When the targets were Indians and blacks, as they were in South Carolina, the stakes were considerably higher. In 1758 one official reported, "It has been allways the policy of this government to create an aversion in them [Indians] to Negroes." South Carolina whites, a minority of the population, wanted to prevent Indians and blacks from making common cause against them. To keep slaves from running away to join the Indians, whites hired Indians as slave catchers. To keep Indians from trusting blacks, whites used blacks as soldiers in Indian wars.

The elites would probably have preferred to ignore the colonies' growing racial and ethnic diversity, but they could not do so for long and still maintain their power. When such men decided to lead a revolution in the 1770s, they recognized that they needed the support of non-English Americans. Quite deliberately, they then began to speak of "the rights of man," rather than "English liberties," when they sought recruits for their cause.

ECONOMIC GROWTH AND DEVELOPMENT

The eighteenth-century American economy was characterized by sharp fluctuations rather than by a consistent long-term trend. Those fluctuations had two primary causes: the impact of European wars and variations in overseas demand for American products. The only source of stability in the shifting economic climate was the dramatic increase in the colonial population.

Each year the rising population generated ever-greater demands for goods and services, which led to the development of small-scale colonial manufacturing and a complex network of internal trade. As the area of settlement expanded, roads, bridges, mills, and stores were built to serve the new communities. A lively coastal trade developed; by the late 1760s, 54 percent of the vessels leaving Boston harbor were sailing to other mainland colonies rather than to foreign ports. Such ships not only collected goods for export and distributed imports but also sold items made in America. The colonies thus began to move away from their earlier pattern of near-total dependence on Europe for manufactured goods. For the first time, the American population was generating sufficient demand to encourage manufacturing enterprises. The largest indigenous industry was iron making; by 1775, 82 American furnaces and 175 forges were producing more iron than was England itself. Almost all of that iron was for domestic consumption.

The major energizing, yet destabilizing, influence on the colonial economy was foreign trade. Colonial prosperity still depended heavily on overseas demand for American products like tobacco, rice, indigo, fish, and barrel staves; the sale of such items earned the colonists the credit they needed to purchase English and European imports. If demand for American exports slowed, as it did at different times during the century, the colonists' income dropped and so did their ability to buy imported goods. Merchants were particularly vulnerable to economic downswings, and bankruptcies were quite common.

Despite fluctuations, the economy grew slowly during the eighteenth century. That growth, which resulted in part from Americans' higher earnings from their exports, in turn produced better standards of living for all property-owning Americans. In the first two decades of the century, as the price of British manufactures fell in relation to Americans' incomes, households began to acquire such amenities as chairs, knives and forks, and earthenware dishes. Diet also improved as trading networks brought access to more varied foodstuffs. After 1750, luxury items like silver plate could be found in the homes of the wealthy, and "the middling sort" started to purchase imported English ceramics and teapots. Even the poorest property owners had more and better household possessions.

Yet the benefits of economic growth were not evenly distributed: wealthy Americans improved their position relative to other colonists. The native-born elite families who dominated American

Rising Standard of Living

How do historians know

that wealthier Americans were starting to acquire more luxury goods in the eighteenth century? One way to learn what the colonists possessed is to examine documents called probate inventories, which listed the belongings of recently deceased individuals before estates were distributed to heirs. Another way is to study material culture—that is, to find objects that were used in colonial homes and to determine their origins, chronology, and possible uses. The silver coffee pot pictured here, for example, was manufactured about 1755 in Charleston, South Carolina, by a silversmith named Alexander Petrie. It is important for two reasons.

First, it provides evidence that by midcentury at least some well-to-do colonists had started to drink coffee, an exotic, expensive drink made from imported beans. Second, its elegant form revealed the refined taste of both its owner and its maker. Artisans like Petrie, with skills much in demand by wealthy colonial customers, could earn large sums of money by practicing their trades. By the time Petrie died in 1768, he had achieved the status of "gentleman," one of the highest rungs on the ladder of colonial status.   Photo: Museum of Early Southern Decorative Arts, Winston-Salem, N.C.

political, economic, and social life by 1750 were those who had begun the century with sufficient capital to take advantage of the changes caused by population growth. They were the urban merchants who exported raw materials and imported luxury goods, the large landowners who rented small farms to immigrant tenants, the slave traders who supplied white planters with their bondspeople, and the owners of rum distilleries. The rise of this group of monied families helped to make the social and economic structure of mid-eighteenth-century America more stratified than before.

New immigrants accordingly did not have the opportunities for advancement that had greeted their predecessors. Even so, there seems to have been relatively little severe poverty among whites in rural areas, where 90 percent of the colonists lived. But in the cities, the story was different. Families of urban laborers lived on the edge of destitution. In Philadelphia, for instance, a male laborer's average annual earnings fell short of the amount needed to supply his family with the bare necessities. Even in a good year, his wife or children had to do wage

Urban Poverty

work; in a bad year, the family could be reduced to beggary. By the 1760s public urban poor-relief systems were overwhelmed with applicants for assistance, and some cities began to build workhouses or almshouses to shelter the growing number of poor people. Among them were recent immigrants, the elderly and infirm, and widows, especially those with small children.

Within this overall picture, it is important to distinguish among the various regions: New England, the middle colonies, the Chesapeake, and the Lower South (the Carolinas and Georgia). Each region of the colonies had its own economic rhythm derived from the nature of its export trade.

In New England, three elements combined to influence economic development: the nature of the landscape, New England's leadership in colonial shipping, and the impact of the imperial wars. New England's soil was rocky and thin, and farmers did not normally produce large agricultural surpluses to sell abroad, although they did find an overseas market for wood products. Farms were worked primarily by family members; the region had relatively few hired laborers. It also had the lowest average wealth per freeholder in the colonies. But New England had its share of wealthy men; they were the merchants and professionals whose income was drawn from trade in such items as fish and livestock, primarily with the West Indies.

Boston's central position in the New England economy and its role as a shipbuilding center ensured that it would be directly affected by any resumption of warfare. In 1739, English vessels began clashing with Spanish ships in the Caribbean, setting off a conflict that became known in America as King George's War. Nominally the war was fought to determine who would

New England and King George's War

New England

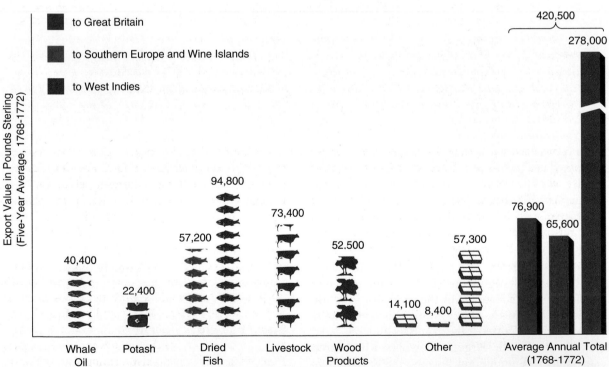

Regional Trading Patterns: New England *New England's major exports—dried fish, livestock, and wood products—were sold primarily in the West Indies.*   Source: James F. Shepherd and Gary M. Walton, *Shipping, Maritime Trade, and the Economic Development of Colonial North America* (Cambridge: Cambridge University Press, 1972). Copyright 1972. Used by permission of Cambridge University Press.

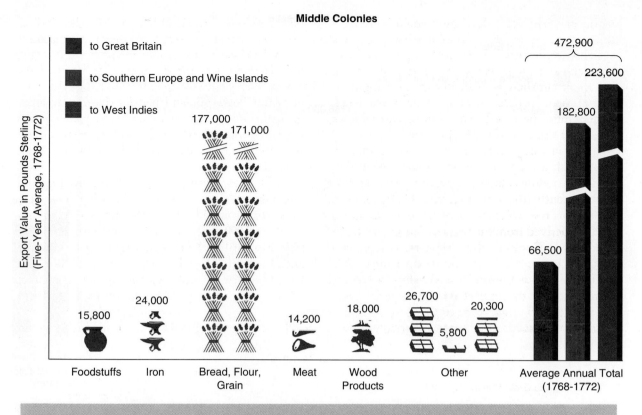

Middle Colonies

- to Great Britain
- to Southern Europe and Wine Islands
- to West Indies

Export Value in Pounds Sterling (Five-Year Average, 1768-1772)

Foodstuffs: 15,800

Iron: 24,000

Bread, Flour, Grain: 177,000 / 171,000

Meat: 14,200

Wood Products: 18,000

Other: 26,700 / 5,800 / 20,300

Average Annual Total (1768-1772): 472,900 / 223,600 / 182,800 / 66,500

Regional Trading Patterns: Middle Colonies   The middle colonies' major trading partners were the West Indies, the Wine Islands, and Southern Europe; bread, flour, and grains were the region's most valuable exports. Source: James F. Shepard and Gary M. Walton, *Shipping, Maritime Trade, and the Economic Development of Colonial North America* (Cambridge: Cambridge University Press, 1972). Copyright 1972. Used by permission of Cambridge University Press.

sit on the Austrian throne (in Europe it was called the War of the Austrian Succession), but one of its causes was European commercial rivalries in the Americas, as nations jockeyed for position in the lucrative West Indian trade. The war's first impact on Boston's economy was positive. Ships—and sailors—were in great demand to serve as privateers (privately owned vessels authorized by the British to capture the enemy's commercial shipping). Wealthy merchants like Thomas Hancock became even wealthier by profiting from contracts to supply military expeditions.

But Boston suffered heavy losses of manpower in several Caribbean battles and in forays against the French in Canada after 1744, when France became Spain's ally. The most successful expedition was also the most costly. In 1745 a Massachusetts force captured the French fortress of Louisbourg (in modern Nova Scotia), which guarded the sea lanes leading to New France. Afterwards, though,

the colony had to levy heavy taxes on its residents to pay for the expensive effort. For decades Boston's economy felt the continuing effects of King George's War. The city was left with unprecedented numbers of widows and children on its relief rolls. The boom in shipbuilding ended when the war did, and taxes remained high. As a final blow to the colonies, Britain gave Louisbourg back to France in the Treaty of Aix-la-Chapelle (1748).

The middle colonies were more positively affected by King George's War and its aftermath because of the greater fertility of the soil in New York

Prosperity of the Middle Colonies

and Pennsylvania, where commercial farming was the norm. An average Pennsylvania farm family consumed only 40 percent of what it produced, selling the rest. New York and New Jersey both had many tenant farmers, who rented acreage from large landowners and often

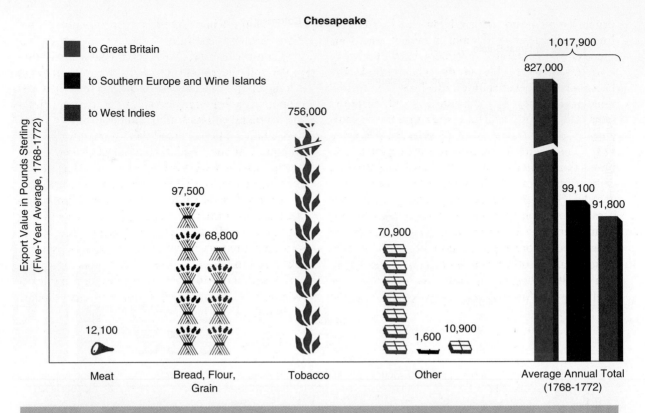

Chesapeake

- to Great Britain
- to Southern Europe and Wine Islands
- to West Indies

Export Value in Pounds Sterling (Five-Year Average, 1768-1772)

Meat — 12,100

Bread, Flour, Grain — 97,500 / 68,800

Tobacco — 756,000

Other — 70,900 / 1,600 / 10,900

Average Annual Total (1768-1772) — 1,017,900 / 827,000 / 99,100 / 91,800

Regional Trading Patterns: The Chesapeake Tobacco—*legally exported only to Great Britain under the terms of the Navigation Acts—was the Chesapeake's dominant product, with grain making up an increasing proportion of the crops it sold to other destinations.* Source: James F. Shepherd and Gary M. Walton, *Shipping, Maritime Trade, and the Economic Development of Colonial North America* (Cambridge: Cambridge University Press, 1972). Copyright 1972. Used by permission of Cambridge University Press.

paid their rental fees by sharing crops with their landlords. Prosperous landlords and farmers were thus in an ideal position to profit from the wartime demand for grain and meat, especially in the West Indies. After the war a series of poor grain harvests in Europe caused flour prices to rise even more rapidly. Philadelphia and New York, which could draw on large fertile grain- and livestock-producing areas, took the lead in the foodstuffs trade. Meanwhile Boston, which had no such fertile hinterland, found its economy stagnating.

Increased European demand for grain had a significant impact on the Chesapeake as well. After 1745, when the price of grain began rising faster than that of tobacco, some Chesapeake planters began to convert tobacco fields to wheat and corn. By diversifying their crops, they could avoid dependency on just one product for their income.

Tobacco still ruled the region and remained the largest single export from the mainland colonies. (The value of tobacco exports was nearly double that of grain products, the next contender.) Yet the conversion to grain cultivation brought about the first significant change in Chesapeake settlement patterns by encouraging the development of port towns (like Baltimore) to house the merchants who marketed the new products.

Like the Chesapeake, the Lower South depended on staple crops and an enslaved labor force, but its pattern of economic growth was distinctive.

Chesapeake and the Lower South

In contrast to tobacco prices, which rose slowly through the middle decades of the century, rice prices climbed steeply, doubling by the late 1730s. The sharp rise was caused primarily by heavy demand for rice in southern Europe. Because Parliament removed rice from the list of enumerated products in 1730, South Carolinians were able to do what colonial tobacco planters never could: trade directly with continental Europe. But dependence on European sales had its drawbacks, as rice growers discovered at the outbreak of King George's War in 1739. Trade with the continent was disrupted, rice prices plummeted, and South Carolina entered a depression from which it did not emerge for a decade. Still, prosperity returned by the 1760s because of rapidly rising European demand for South Carolina's exports; indeed, the Lower South experienced more rapid economic growth in that period than the other regions of the colonies. Partly as a result, it had the highest average wealth per freeholder in Anglo-America by the time of the Revolution.

Though King George's War initially helped New England and hurt the Lower South, in the long run those effects were reversed. In the Chesapeake and the middle colonies, the war initiated a long period of prosperity. The variety of these economic experiences points up a crucial fact about the mainland colonies: they did not compose a unified whole. They were linked economically into regions, but they had few political or social ties beyond or even within those regions. Despite the growing coastal trade, the individual colonies' economic fortunes depended not on their neighbors in America but rather on the shifting markets of Europe and the West Indies. Had it not been for an unprecedented crisis in the British imperial system (discussed in Chapter 5), it is hard to see how they could have been persuaded to join in a common endeavor. Even with that impetus, they found unity difficult to maintain.

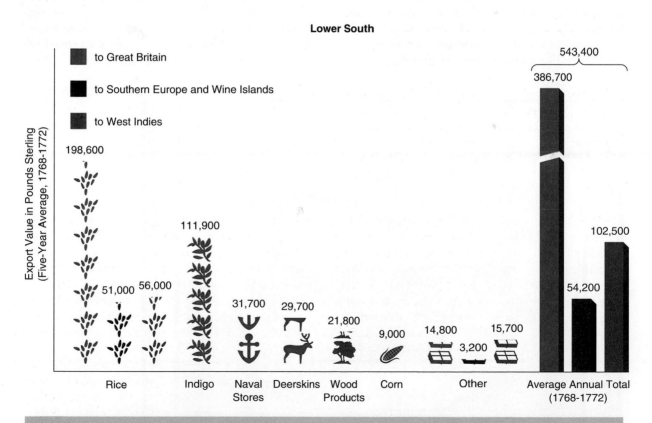

Lower South

Regional Trading Patterns: The Lower South   *Rice and indigo, sold primarily in the mother country, dominated the exports of the Lower South.*   Source: James F. Shepherd and Gary M. Walton, *Shipping, Maritime Trade, and the Economic Development of Colonial North America* (Cambridge: Cambridge University Press, 1972). Copyright 1972. Used by permission of Cambridge University Press.

THE DAILY LIVES OF EUROPEAN-AMERICANS

The basic unit of colonial society was the household. Headed by a white male (or his widow), the household was the chief mechanism of production and consumption. Its members—bound by ties of blood or servitude—worked together to produce goods for consumption or sale. The white male head of the household represented it to the outside world, serving in the militia or political posts, casting the household's sole vote in elections. He managed the finances and held legal authority over the rest of the family—his wife, his children, and his servants or slaves. (Eighteenth-century Americans used the word *family* for people who occupied one house, whether or not they were blood kin.) Such households were considerably larger than American families today; in 1790, the average home housed 5.7 whites. Most of those large families were nuclear—that is, they did not include extended kin like aunts, uncles, or grandparents.

The vast majority of colonial families lived in rural areas. As a result, nearly all adult white men were farmers, and nearly all adult white women farm wives. Though rural men might work as millers, blacksmiths, or carpenters, and women might sell surplus farm produce to neighbors, they typically did so in addition to their primary agricultural tasks. In colonial America, as in the European, African, and Native American societies discussed in Chapter 1, household tasks were allocated by sex. The master, his sons, and his male servants or slaves performed one set of chores; the mistress, her daughters, and her female servants or slaves, an entirely different set. So rigid were these gender classifications that in households without a master or mistress the corresponding jobs were not done. A foreign traveler visiting a Pennsylvania farm remarked that its owner, a bachelor, did not keep poultry or make cheese or clothing because "these domestic farm industries . . . can be carried on well only by women." Only in emergencies and for

Sexual Division of Labor Among White Americans

Farmer Abraham's Almanac, *published in Philadelphia in 1759, contained this crude woodcut showing women engaged in chores associated with dairying: at right, milking a cow; at left, churning butter.*   American Antiquarian Society.

brief periods of time would women do men's work or men do women's.

The mistress of the rural household was responsible for what were termed "indoor affairs." She and her female helpers prepared food, cleaned the house, did laundry, and often made clothing. In eighteenth-century America, these basic chores were complex and time-consuming. Preparing food involved planting and cultivating a garden, harvesting and preserving vegetables, salting and smoking meat, drying apples and pressing cider, milking cows and making butter and cheese, not to mention cooking and baking. Making clothes (the chief job of daughters) meant processing raw wool and flax fibers, spinning thread, weaving cloth, dyeing and softening the cloth, and finally cutting out and sewing garments by hand. No wonder one harried Long Island housewife filled her diary in 1768 and 1769 with such entries as these: "It has been a tiresome day it is now Bedtime and I have not had won minutts rest"; "full of fretting discontent dirty and miserabel both yesterday and today."

The head of the household and his male helpers, responsible for "outdoor affairs," also had heavy workloads. They had to plant and cultivate the fields, build fences, chop wood for the fireplace, harvest and market crops, care for livestock, and butcher cattle and hogs to provide the household with meat. Only on southern plantations and in northern cities could a few adult white males lead lives free from arduous physical labor. Indeed, so extensive was the work involved in maintaining a farm household that a married couple could not do it alone. They had to have help—if they had no children, they then turned to servants or slaves.

Farm households were governed by the seasons and the hours of daylight. (Candles, too, had to be manufactured at home; because they were too precious to be wasted, most people rose and went to bed with the sun.) Men and boys had the most leisure in winter, when there were no crops that needed care. Women and girls were freest in the summer, before embarking on autumn food preservation and winter spinning and weaving. Other activities, including education, had to be subordinated to seasonal work. Thus farm boys studied in the winter, and their sisters did so in the summer. The seasons also affected travel plans. Because the roads were muddy in the spring and fall, most vis-

Rhythms of Rural Life

iting took place in the summer and, in the North, winter, when sleighs could be used.

Because of the isolation and heavy workloads of farm households, rural folk took advantage of every possible opportunity for socializing. Men taking grain to a mill would stop at a crossroads tavern for a drink and conversation with friends. Women gathering to assist at childbirth would drink tea and exchange news. Barbecues and week-long house parties were popular among southern planter families. The Reverend Charles Woodmason, an English missionary, found to his consternation that residents of the Carolina backcountry regarded his church services as social events. "No making of them sit still during Service—but they will be in and out—forward and backward the whole Time (Women especially) as Bees to and fro to their Hives," he wrote of one congregation in 1768. And work itself provided opportunities for visiting. Harvest frolics, corn-husking bees, and other communal endeavors drew neighbors from miles around, often for several days of work followed by feasting, dancing, and singing.

The few colonial cities were nothing but large towns by today's standards. In 1750 the largest, Boston and Philadelphia, had just seventeen thousand and thirteen thousand inhabitants respectively. Still, city life differed considerably from rural life. City dwellers' lives were likely to be governed by clocks instead of the sun, and by work schedules that did not depend so wholly on the seasons. A city wife might preserve a ham in the fall, and a merchant's business might vary with the weather (which determined sailing schedules), but city people were not inextricably tied to the seasons. Year-round, they could purchase foodstuffs and wood at city markets and cloth at dry-goods stores. They could see friends any time they wished. Wealthy urbanites had leisure time to visit taverns (like the men in the illustration on page 108), and to read, take walks around town or rides in the countryside, play cards, or attend dances, plays, and concerts—by midcentury, most colonial cities had theaters and assembly halls.

Rhythms of Urban Life

City people also had much more contact with the world beyond their own homes than did their rural compatriots. By the 1750s, every major city had at least one weekly newspaper, and most had two or three. Newspapers printed the latest "ad-

This trade card (advertisement) issued by a Philadelphia tobacco dealer in 1770 showed a convivial group of men at a tavern, discussing the quality of the tobacco they were smoking. Library Company of Philadelphia.

vices from London" (usually two to three months old) and news from other English colonies, as well as local reports. Newspapers were available at taverns and inns, so people who could not afford to buy them could catch up on the news. Even illiterates could do so, since the papers often were read aloud by literate customers. However, contact with the outside world also had drawbacks. Sailors sometimes brought exotic and deadly diseases into port with them. Cities like Boston, New York, and Philadelphia endured terrible epidemics of smallpox and yellow fever, which the countryside largely escaped.

Cities attracted migrants from rural areas. Young men came to learn a skill through apprenticeship, for cities housed the artisans who printed books and newspapers, crafted fine furniture, and made shoes or other items. Ordinary laborers came seeking work, and widows came looking for a means of supporting their families. Without an adult man in the household, a woman had a difficult time running a farm. Consequently, widows tended to congregate in port cities, where they could sell their services as nurses, teachers, laundresses, seamstresses, servants, or prostitutes; if they had some capital, they might open shops, inns, or boardinghouses.

Only widows and the very few never-married women could legally run independent businesses.

Status of Women

An unmarried colonial woman had the same legal rights as a man (with the exception of voting), but a wife was subordinate to her husband in law as well as custom. Under the common-law doctrine of coverture, a married woman became one person with her husband. She could not independently sue or be sued, make contracts, buy or sell property, or draft a will. Any property she owned prior to marriage became her husband's after the wedding; any wages she earned were legally his; and all children of the marriage fell under his control. Moreover, since divorces were practically impossible to obtain, men and women had little chance to escape from bad marriages, other than through desertion or the early death of a spouse.

The man's legal and customary authority extended to his children as well. Indeed, child rearing was the one task regularly undertaken by both sexes in colonial America. Women cared for infants and toddlers, but thereafter both parents disciplined the children. The father set the general standards by which they were raised and usually had the final word on such matters as education and vocational training. White parents normally insisted on unquestioning obedience from their offspring, and many freely used physical punishment to break a child's will. In the homes of elite fami-

Images of ordinary colonists are rare, and pictures of servants are even rarer. But in 1748 the Boston artist John Greenwood engraved and sold this portrait of Ann Arnold, a wet nurse known as "Jersey Nanny," probably a native of the English Isle of Jersey. Museum of Fine Arts, Boston. Gift of Henry Lee Shattuck.

lies, though, more nurturant child-rearing practices prevailed. In such households, the most burdensome chores were performed by servants, freeing parents to spend more time with their offspring and reducing the need for strict disciplinary measures to keep children out from underfoot. The relaxed upbringing of these wealthy youngsters foreshadowed nineteenth-century Americans' greater indulgence of their children.

THE DAILY LIVES OF AFRICAN-AMERICANS

A white man's authority could include black families as well as his own kin. More than 95 percent of colonial blacks were held in perpetual bondage. The trend toward consolidation of slaveownership after 1740 had a profound effect on the lives of African-Americans. In areas with high proportions of blacks in the population, most slaves resided on plantations with at least nine other bondspeople.

Although many southern blacks lived on farms with only one or two other slaves, the majority had the experience of living and working in a largely black setting. In South Carolina, a majority of the population was of African origin; in Georgia, about half; and in the Chesapeake, 40 percent. In some parts of the southern backcountry less than one-fifth of the population was black, but portions of the Carolina low country were nearly 90 percent African-American by 1790.

The concentration of the slave population also had a profound effect on whites. One Virginia woman recalled that in her childhood "I believed the world one vast plantation bounded by negro quarters." Whites may have controlled their bondspeople in a formal sense, but living surrounded by blacks affected them in ways they rarely acknowledged. Plantation housing styles, for example, were more African than English in origin, with clusters of small buildings—serving as kitchens, dairies, storage sheds, spinning rooms, and so forth—taking the place of one large structure encompassing all those functions. Just as blacks mimicked the whites' dances in their evening frolics, so too it became customary for whites to perform "Negro jigs" at the end of their cotillions. And words of African origin were incorporated into American English.

Large plantations allowed for the specialization of labor. Some African-American men and women became highly skilled at tasks whites believed appropriate to their sex. Each large plantation had its own male blacksmiths (whose skill is evidenced in the brass buckle shown on page 110), carpenters, valets, shoemakers, and gardeners, and its female dairymaids, seamstresses, cooks, and at least one midwife, who attended white and black women alike. These skilled slaves— between 10 and 20 percent of the black population—were essential to the smooth functioning of the plantation. But most slaves, male or female, worked in the fields. Since West African women were accustomed to agricultural labor, that task must have coincided with their own cultural expectations. To whites, however, black women's work in the fields connoted inferior status.

Sexual Division of Labor Among African-Americans

The typical Chesapeake tobacco plantation was divided into small "quarters" located at some distance from one another. White overseers super-

A skilled slave blacksmith at George Washington's Mount Vernon plantation crafted this brass harness buckle, depicting part of the Washington family crest.   Mount Vernon Ladies' Association of the Union.

vised work on the distant quarters, whereas the planter personally took charge of the "home" quarter, which included the planter's house. In the Carolina low country, where planters usually spent months in Charleston to avoid the malaria and yellow-fever seasons, blacks often supervised their fellow slaves. Planters commonly assigned "outlandish" (African-born) slaves to do field labor in order to accustom them to plantation work routines and to enable them to learn some English. Artisans, on the other hand, were usually drawn from among the plantation's American-born blacks. Skills like carpentry and midwifery were typically passed down from father to son and mother to daughter; such knowledge often constituted a slave family's most valuable possession.

Because all the English colonies legally permitted slavery, discontented blacks had few potential refuges from bondage. Some recently arrived Africans stole boats to try to return home or ran off in groups to the frontier, where they joined the Indians or attempted to establish traditional West African villages. Occasionally slaves from South Carolina tried to reach Spanish Florida. But most slave runaways merely wanted to visit friends or rela-

tives or to avoid their normal work routines for a few days or months. In a society in which blackness automatically connoted perpetual servitude, no black person anywhere could claim free status without being challenged. Violent resistance had even less to recommend it than running away. Whites may have been in the minority in some areas, but they controlled the guns and ammunition. Even if a revolt succeeded for a time, whites could easily muster the armed force necessary to put it down. Only in very unusual circumstances did colonial slaves attempt to rebel against their white oppressors (see page 117).

African-Americans did try to improve the conditions of their bondage. Their chief vehicle for gaining some measure of control over their lives was the family. Planters' records reveal how members of extended-kin groups provided support, assistance, and comfort to each other. They protested excessive punishment of relatives, asked to live on the same quarters, and often requested special treatment for children or siblings. On one Virginia plantation, for instance, a mother arranged for her daughter to be treated by a particular black doctor, and a father successfully convinced his master that his daughter should be allowed to live with her stepmother. The extended-kin ties that developed among African-American families who had lived on the same plantation for several generations served as insurance against the uncertainties of existence under slavery. If a nuclear family was broken up by sale, other relatives could help with child rearing and similar tasks. Among colonial blacks, the extended family served a more important function than it did among whites.

African-American Families

Most black families managed to carve out a small measure of autonomy by a variety of means. On many plantations, slaves were allowed or required to plant their own gardens, hunt, or fish in order to supplement the standard diet of corn and salt pork. Some Chesapeake mistresses permitted their female slaves to raise chickens, which they then sold or exchanged for such items as extra clothing or blankets. In South Carolina, where most rice and indigo plantations operated on a task system, slaves were often able to accumulate personal property. Once they had completed their assigned tasks for the day, they were free to work for themselves. Occasionally they could even cultivate rice or indigo crops of their own. In Maryland and Virginia, where by the end of the century planters and especially their widows began to hire out slaves to others because of a surplus of bound laborers, blacks were sometimes allowed to keep a small part of the wages they earned. Some tobacco planters began to adopt a tasking system in the same era, thus allowing Chesapeake slaves more freedom from direct supervision by whites. Such advances were slight, but against the bleak backdrop of slavery they deserve to be highlighted.

Yet even the most autonomous enslaved African-Americans were always subject to white intrusions into their lives. In some households, masters

Master–Slave Relations

and mistresses enforced their will chiefly through physical coercion. Thus one woman's diary noted matter-of-factly: "December 1: Lucy whippt for getting key of Celler door & stealing apples. December 2: Plato Anthoney & Abraham Pegg's housband whipt for Hog stealing." Other masters and mistresses were more lenient and respectful of slaves' property and their desire to live with their families. But even in households where whites and blacks displayed genuine affection for one another, there were inescapable tensions. Such tensions were caused by the dynamics of day-to-day relationships in which a small number of whites wielded arbitrary power over the lives of many African-Americans.

Thomas Jefferson was deeply concerned about this issue. In 1780 he observed, "The whole commerce between master and slave is a perpetual exercise of the most boisterous passions, the most unremitting despotism on the one part, and degrading submission on the other. Our children see this, and learn to imitate it. . . . The man must be a prodigy who can retain his manners and morals undepraved by such circumstances." What troubled Jefferson most was the impact of the system on whites, not on the people they held in bondage. Before the Revolution, only a tiny number of Quakers (most notably John Woolman in his *Some Considerations on the Keeping of Negroes*, published in 1754) criticized slavery out of sympathy for blacks. The other white colonists who questioned slavery took Jefferson's approach, stressing the institution's adverse effect on whites. Even they were extremely few in number. A labor system so essential to the func-

tioning of the colonial economy met with little open challenge.

If the routines of daily life in the American colonies seemed fixed and unchanging, the wider context in which those routines unfolded did not. In both Europe and America, the eighteenth century was a time of great cultural and intellectual ferment. The movement known as the Enlightenment first influenced the educated elites; ordinary people seemed little touched by it. But enlightened thinking was to play a central role in the ideology of the American Revolution and thus eventually had a profound impact on the lives of all Americans.

COLONIAL CULTURE

Traditional colonial culture was oral, communal, and—at least through the first half of the eighteenth century—intensely local. The culture of the elite was increasingly print-oriented, individualized, and self-consciously cosmopolitan. Although discussed separately here, the two cultures mingled in a variety of ways, for people of both descriptions lived side by side in small villages and cities.

A majority of the residents of British America (almost all blacks, half the white women, and at least one-fifth of white men) could neither read nor write. That had important consequences for the transmission and development of American culture. In the absence of literacy, the primary means of communication was face-to-face conversation. Information tended to travel slowly and within relatively confined regions. Different locales developed divergent cultural traditions, and those differences were heightened by racial and ethnic variations. Public rituals served as the means through which the colonists forged their cultural identities.

Attendance at church was perhaps the most important such ritual. In Congregational (Puritan) churches, seating was assigned by church leaders

Religious Rituals

to reflect standing in the community. In early New England, men and women sat on opposite sides of a central aisle, arranged in ranks according to age, wealth, and church membership. By the middle of the eighteenth century, wealthy men and their wives sat in privately owned pews; their children, servants, and the less fortunate were still seated in sex-segregated fashion at the rear or sides of the church. In eighteenth-century Virginia, seating in Anglican parishes also conformed to the local status hierarchy. Planter families purchased their own pews, and in some parishes the landed gentlemen customarily strode into church as a group just before the service, deliberately drawing attention to their exalted position. Quite a different message emanated from the egalitarian but sex-segregated seating system used in Quaker meeting-houses. Where one sat in colonial churches, in other words, symbolized one's place in society and the values of the surrounding community.

Communal culture also centered on the civic sphere. Particularly in New England, colonial governments proclaimed official days of thanksgiving (for good harvests, victories in war, and so forth) and days of fasting and prayer (when the colony was experiencing difficulties such as droughts or epidemics of disease). Everyone was expected to participate in the public rituals held in churches on such occasions. Monthly militia musters (known as training days) brought the community together, since all able-bodied men between the ages of sixteen and sixty were members of the militia.

Civic Rituals

In the Chesapeake, important cultural rituals occurred on court and election days. When the county court was in session, men would come from miles around to file suits, appear as witnesses, serve as jurors, or simply observe the goings-on. Attendance at court functioned as a method of civic education; from watching the proceedings men learned what behavior their neighbors expected of them. Elections served the same purpose, for freeholders voted in public. An election official, often flanked by the candidates for the office in question, would call each man forward to declare his preference. The voter would then be thanked politely by the gentleman for whom he had cast his oral ballot. Traditionally, the candidates treated their supporters to rum at nearby taverns.

In such settings as church and courthouse, then, elite and ordinary folk alike participated in the oral culture that served as the cement holding their communities together. But the genteel residents of the colonies also took part in a newer kind of culture, one organized through the world of print. Its messages were conveyed by reading as well as by observing one's neighbors.

Literacy was far less essential in eighteenth-century America than it is today. People, especially women, could live their entire lives without ever being called on to read a book or write a letter. Moreover, teaching slaves to read or write was forbidden as too subversive of the social order.

Attitudes Toward Education

Thus education beyond the bare rudiments of reading, writing, and "figuring" was usually regarded as a frill for either sex. Free men might have to know how to read a contract or keep rough accounts, and women might need or want to read the Bible. Beyond that, little learning appeared necessary, for books were scarce and expensive. Thus public schools supported by taxes were few and far between. Children who learned to read usually did so in their own homes, taught by their parents or older siblings. A few months at a private "dame school" run by a literate local widow might complete their education by teaching them the basics of writing and simple arithmetic.

Accordingly, advanced education was primarily a sign of status. Only parents who wanted to distinguish their children from less-fortunate peers (perhaps for reasons of piety or a desire for upward mobility or maintenance of status) were willing to forgo their children's valuable labor to allow them to attend the few private schools, many of them located in cities. Even at such institutions, girls ordinarily received little intellectual training beyond the rudiments, though they might learn music, dancing, or fancy needlework (skills that connoted genteel status). Elite boys, on the other hand, studied with tutors or attended schools run by college graduates that prepared them to enter college at age fourteen or fifteen.

The colonial system of higher education for males was more fully developed than was basic instruction for either sex. The first American colleges were designed to train young men for the ministry. Following the earlier examples of Harvard (1636), William and Mary (chartered 1693, but not operational until 1726), and Yale (1701), the colleges founded in the mid-eighteenth century—those now known as Princeton (1747), Columbia (1754), Brown (1764), and Rutgers (1766)—were intended to supply clergymen to fill the pulpits of Presbyterian, Anglican, Baptist, and Dutch Reformed churches respectively. (Dartmouth College, founded in 1769, though not explicitly committed to educating clerics, also had a religious purpose, that of Christianizing the Native Americans.) But during the eighteenth century the curriculum and character of all these colleges changed considerably. Their students, the sons of the colonial elite, were now interested in careers in medicine, law, and business instead of the ministry. And the learned men who headed the colleges, though ministers themselves, were deeply affected by the Enlightenment's stress on reason.

In the seventeenth century, some European thinkers began to analyze nature in an effort to determine the laws that govern the universe. They employed experimentation and abstract reasoning to discover the general principles behind such phenomena as the motions of the planets and stars, the behavior of falling objects, and the characteristics of light and sound. Above all, Enlightenment philosophers emphasized the acquisition of knowledge through reason, taking particular delight in challenging previously unquestioned assumptions. John Locke's *Essay Concerning Human Understanding* (1690), for example, disputed the notion that human beings are born already imprinted with innate ideas. All knowledge, Locke asserted, derives from one's observations of the external world.

The Enlightenment

The Enlightenment had an enormous impact on educated, well-to-do people in Europe and America. It supplied them with a common vocabulary and a unified view of the world, one that insisted that the enlightened eighteenth century was better than all previous ages. It joined them in a common endeavor, the effort to make sense of God's orderly creation. Thus American naturalists like John and William Bartram supplied European scientists with information about New World plants and animals so that they could be included in newly formulated universal classification systems. So, too, Americans interested in astronomy took part in an international effort to learn about the workings of the solar system by studying a rare occurrence, the transit of Venus across the face of the sun in 1769.

Enlightenment rationalism affected politics as well as science. Locke's *Two Treatises of Civil Government* (1691) and other works by French and Scottish philosophers challenged previous concepts of a divinely sanctioned political order. Governments, declared Locke, were created by men and so could be altered by them. If a ruler broke his contract with the people and did not protect their

Nabby Martin, an eighteenth-century girl living in Providence, depicted in her needlework sampler buildings representing higher education (University Hall at Brown University) and politics (the Rhode Island State House). Ironically, she was excluded from participating in both on account of her sex. Museum of Art, Rhode Island School of Design, Providence, R.I.

rights, he could legitimately be ousted from power by peaceful—or even violent—means. The aim of government was the good of the people, Enlightenment theorists proclaimed. A proper political order could prevent the rise of tyrants, and even the power of monarchs was subject to God's natural laws.

These intellectual currents had a dramatic effect on the curriculum of the colonial colleges. In the seventeenth century Harvard courses had focused on ancient languages and theology. After the 1720s, however, colleges began to introduce courses in mathematics (including algebra, geometry, and calculus), the natural sciences, law, and medicine (including anatomy and physiology). The young men educated in such colleges—and their sisters at home, with whom they occasionally shared their books and ideas—developed a rational outlook on life that differentiated them from their fellow colonists. This was the world of Dr. Alexander Hamilton and his associates. When he left Annapolis in 1744, he carried letters of introduction to "the better sort" in all the places he intended to visit. Such people had learned the value of reading, of regular correspondence with like-minded friends, of convivial gatherings at which conversation focused on books imported from Europe, and of attendance at plays performed by touring companies of English actors.

Well-to-do graduates of American colleges, along with others educated in Great Britain, formed the core of genteel culture in the colonies.

Elite Culture
——

Men and women from these families wanted to set themselves apart from ordinary folk. Beginning in the 1720s they constructed grandiose residences furnished with imported carpets, silver plate, and furniture. They entertained their friends at elaborate dinner parties and balls at which all present dressed in the height of European fashion. They cultivated polite manners and saw themselves as part of a transatlantic and intercolonial network.

Benjamin Franklin, ca. 1746, by Robert Feke. The forty-year-old Franklin, a mature man at the height of his career as a printer, already exudes in this portrait the self-confidence that would mark his later years.   Harvard University Portrait Collection. Bequest, Dr. John C. Warren, 1856.

How did this genteel, enlightened culture affect the lives of the majority of colonists? Certainly no resident of the colonies could have avoided some contact with members of the elite. Ordinary folk were expected to doff their hats and behave deferentially when conversing with their "betters." Many others besides employees and tenants were economically dependent on the gentry; for example, the elite's demand for consumer goods of all kinds led to the growth of artisan industries like silversmithing and fine furniture-making. And, of course, elite men controlled the colonial governments, in which men of the "lesser" sort and women of all ranks played no role.

If the lives of genteel and ordinary folk in the eighteenth-century colonies seemed to follow different patterns, one man appeared to combine their traits; appropriately enough,

Benjamin Franklin, the Symbolic American
——

he later became for Europeans the symbolic American. That man was Benjamin Franklin. Born in Boston in 1706, he was the perfect example of a self-made, self-educated man. Apprenticed at an early age to his older brother James, a Boston printer and newspaper publisher, Franklin ran away to Philadelphia in 1723. There he worked as a printer and eventually started his own publishing business, printing books, a newspaper, and *Poor Richard's Almanack*. The business was so successful that Franklin was able to retire from active control in 1748 at age forty-two—soon after his portrait (*opposite*) was painted. He thereafter devoted himself to intellectual endeavors and public service, as deputy postmaster general for the colonies, as an agent representing colonial interests in London, and finally as a diplomat during the Revolution. Franklin's *Experiments and Observations on Electricity* (1751) was the most important scientific work by a colonial American; it established the terminology and basic theory of electricity still in use today. He also invented a number of practical devices (like a more efficient stove) designed to make life easier for his contemporaries.

In 1749 and 1751 Franklin published pamphlets proposing the establishment of a new educational institution in Pennsylvania. The purpose of Franklin's "English School" was not to produce clerics or scholars but to prepare young men "for learning any business, calling or profession." He wanted to enable them "to pass through and execute the several offices of civil life, with advantage and reputation to themselves and country." The College of Philadelphia (now the University of Pennsylvania), founded in 1755, was intended to graduate youths who would resemble Franklin himself—talented, practical men of affairs competent in a number of different fields.

Franklin and the student he envisioned thus fused the conflicting tendencies of colonial culture. Free of the Old World's restrictive traditions, the ideal American would achieve distinction through hard work and the application of common-sense principles. Like Franklin he would rise from an ordinary family into the ranks of the genteel, thereby transcending the cultural boundaries that divided the colonists. He would be unpretentious but not unlearned, simple but not ignorant, virtuous but not priggish. The American would be a true child of the Enlightenment, knowledgeable about European culture yet not bound by its fetters, advancing through reason and talent alone. To him all things would be possible, all doors open.

The contrast with the original communal ideals of the early New England settlements could not have been sharper. John Winthrop's American, outlined in his "Modell of Christian Charity," had been a component of a greater whole that required his unquestioning submission. Franklin's American was an individual, free to make choices about his future, able to contemplate a variety of possible careers. But the two visions did have one point in common: both described only white males. Blacks, Indians, and females played no part in them. Not until many years later would America formally recognize what had been true all along: that women and nonwhites had participated in the creation of the nation's cultural tradition.

POLITICS AND RELIGION: STABILITY AND CRISIS AT MIDCENTURY

In the first decades of the eighteenth century, colonial political life exhibited a new stability. Despite the substantial migration from overseas, most residents of the mainland colonies had been born in America. Men from genteel families dominated the political structures in each province, for voters (property-holding white men) tended to defer to their well-educated "betters" on election days.

Throughout the colonies, political leaders sought to increase the powers of the elected assemblies relative to those of the governors and other appointed officials. Assemblies began to claim privileges associated with the British House of Commons, such as the rights to initiate all tax legislation and to control the militia. The assemblies also developed effective ways of influencing British appointees, especially by threatening to withhold their salaries. In some colonies (Virginia and South Carolina, for example), the elite members of the assemblies usually presented a united front to royal officials, but in others (like New York), they fought with each other long and bitterly. The latter province took the first steps on the road to modern American democracy. In their attempts to win hotly contested elections, New York's genteel leaders began to appeal to "the people," competing openly for the votes of ordinary freeholders. Yet in 1733 that same New York government imprisoned a newspaper editor, John Peter Zenger, who had too vigorously criticized its actions. Defending Zenger against the charge of "seditious libel," his lawyer argued that the truth could not be defamatory, thus helping to establish a free-press principle now found in American law.

Rise of the Assemblies

Eighteenth-century assemblies bore little resemblance to twentieth-century state legislatures. Much of their business would today be termed administrative; only on rare occasions did they formulate new policies or pass laws of real importance. Members of the assemblies also saw their roles differently than do modern legislators. Instead of believing that they should act positively to improve the lives of their constituents, eighteenth-century assemblymen saw themselves as acting defensively to prevent encroachments on the people's rights. In their minds, their primary function was, for example, to stop the governors or councils from enacting oppressive taxes, rather than to pass laws that would actively benefit their constituents.

By the middle of the century, politically aware colonists commonly drew analogies between their own governments and Great Britain's balance of king, lords, and commons—a combination that had been thought to produce a stable polity since

In 1713, the colony of Massachusetts constructed its impressive State House in Boston. Here met the Assembly and the Council. The solidity and imposing nature of the building must have symbolized for its users the increasing consolidation of power in the hands of the Massachusetts legislature. The Bostonian Society.

the days of ancient Greece and Rome. Although the analogy was not exact, political leaders equated their governors with the monarch, their councils with the aristocracy, and their assemblies with the House of Commons. All three were thought essential to good government, but Americans did not regard them with the same degree of approval. They saw the governors and appointed councils as aliens who posed a potential threat to colonial freedoms and customary ways of life. As representatives of England rather than America, the governors and councils were to be feared rather than trusted. Colonists saw the assemblies, on the other hand, as the people's protectors. And in turn the assemblies regarded themselves as representatives of the people.

Again, though, such beliefs should not be equated with modern practice. The assemblies, firmly controlled by dominant families whose members were re-elected year after year, rarely responded to the concerns of their poorer constituents. Although settlement continually spread

westward, assemblies failed to reapportion themselves to provide adequate representation for newer communities—a lack of action that led to serious grievances among frontier dwellers, especially those from non-English ethnic groups. Thus it is important to distinguish between the colonial ideal, which placed the assembly at the forefront in the protection of people's liberties, and the reality that those protected tended chiefly to be the wealthy and the assembly members themselves.

At midcentury, the political structures that had stabilized in a period of relative calm were confronted with a series of crises. None affected all the mainland provinces, but no colony escaped wholly untouched by at least one. The crises were of various sorts—ethnic, racial, economic, religious. They exposed the internal tensions building in the pluralistic American society, foreshadowing the greater disorder of the revolutionary era. Most important, they demonstrated that the political accommodations arrived at in the aftermath of the Glorious Revolution were no longer adequate to govern Britain's American empire. Once again, changes appeared necessary.

One of the first and greatest of the crises occurred in South Carolina. Early one morning in September 1739, about twenty South Carolina slaves gathered near the Stono River south of Charleston. Seizing guns and ammunition from a store, they killed the storekeepers and some nearby planter families. Then, joined by other local slaves, they headed south toward Florida in hopes of finding refuge in that Spanish colony. By midday, however, the alarm had been sounded among whites in the district. That afternoon a troop of militia attacked the fugitives, who then numbered about a hundred, killing some and dispersing the rest. More than a week later, most of the remaining conspirators were captured. Those not killed on the spot were later executed, but for over two years renegades were rumored to be still at large.

Stono Rebellion

The Stono Rebellion shocked white South Carolinians and residents of other colonies as well. Throughout British America, laws governing the behavior of African-Americans were stiffened. But the most immediate response came in New York City, which had itself suffered a slave revolt in 1712. There the news from the South, coupled with fears of Spain generated by the outbreak of **King George's War**, set off a reign of terror in the summer of 1741. Hysterical whites interpreted a biracial gang of thieves and arsonists as malevolent conspirators who wanted to foment a slave uprising under the guidance of a supposed priest in the pay of Spain. By summer's end, thirty-one blacks and four whites had been executed for participating in the "plot." The Stono Rebellion and the New York conspiracy not only exposed and confirmed whites' deepest fears about the dangers of slaveholding but also revealed the assemblies' inability to prevent serious internal disorder. Events of the next two decades confirmed that pattern.

By midcentury, most of the fertile land east of the Appalachians had been purchased or occupied. As a result, conflicts over land titles and conditions of landholding grew in number and frequency as colonists competed for control of land good for farming. In 1746, for example, New Jersey farmers holding land under grants from the governor of New York (dating from the brief period when both provinces were

Land Riots

owned by the duke of York) clashed violently with agents of the East Jersey proprietors. The proprietors claimed the land as theirs and demanded annual payments, called quitrents, for the use of the property. Similar violence occurred in the 1760s in the region that later became Vermont. There, farmers (many of them migrants from eastern New England) holding land grants issued by New Hampshire battled with speculators claiming title to the area through grants from New York authorities.

The most serious land riots of the period took place along the Hudson River in 1765 and 1766. Late in the seventeenth century, Governor Benjamin Fletcher of New York had granted several huge tracts in the lower Hudson valley to prominent colonial families. The proprietors in turn divided these estates into small farms, which they rented chiefly to poor Dutch and German migrants who regarded tenancy as a step on the road to independent freeholder status. By the 1750s some proprietors were earning large sums annually from quitrents and other fees.

After 1740, though, increasing migration from New England brought conflict to the great New York estates. The mobile New Englanders, who had moved in search of land, did not want to become tenants. Many squatted on vacant portions of the manors and resisted all attempts at eviction. In the mid-1760s the Philipse family brought suit against the New Englanders, some of whom had lived on Philipse land for twenty or thirty years. New York courts upheld the Philipse claim and ordered the squatters to make way for tenants with valid leases. Instead of complying, the farmers organized a rebellion against the proprietors. For nearly a year the insurgent farmers controlled much of the Hudson valley. They terrorized proprietors and loyal tenants, freed their friends from jail, and on one occasion battled a county sheriff and his posse. The rebellion was put down only after British troops dispatched from New York City captured its leaders.

Violent conflicts of a different sort erupted just a few years later in the Carolinas. The Regulator movements of the late 1760s (South Carolina) and early 1770s (North Carolina) pitted backcountry farmers against the wealthy eastern planters who controlled the provincial governments. The frontier dwellers, most of whom were Scotch-Irish, protested their

The Regulators

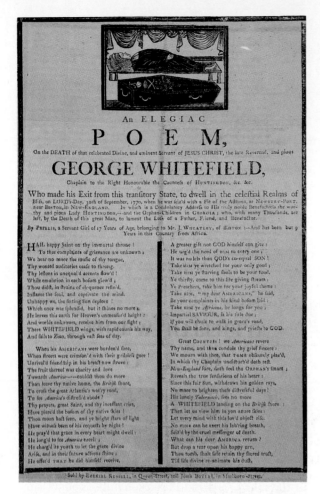

Phillis Wheatley, an African-born slave living in Massachusetts, was so moved by the death of George Whitefield in 1770 that she wrote "an elegiac poem" about the great evangelist, who had shown as much concern for black Americans as for their white compatriots. Although he did not condemn slavery as an institution, Whitefield urged slaveholders to encourage the conversion of their slaves, and blacks, both slave and free, often attended his sermons. Historians credit Whitefield with bringing Christianity to the enslaved populations of South Carolina and Georgia. Library Company of Philadelphia.

lack of an adequate voice in colonial political affairs. The South Carolinians for months policed the countryside in vigilante bands, contending that law enforcement in the region was too lax and biased against them. The North Carolinians, whose prime grievance was heavy taxation, fought and lost a battle with eastern militiamen at Alamance in 1771. Regional, ethnic, and economic tensions thus combined to create these disturbances, which ultimately arose from frontier people's dissatisfaction with the Carolina governments.

The most widespread crisis, however, was religious. From the late 1730s through the 1760s, waves of religious revivalism—today known collectively as the Great Awakening—swept over various parts of the colonies, primarily New England (1735–1745) and Virginia (1750s and 1760s). Orthodox Calvinists were eager to combat Enlightenment rationalism, which denied innate human depravity. At the same time, the economic and political uncertainty accompanying King George's War made colonists receptive to the spiritual certainty offered by evangelical religion. In addition, many recent immigrants and residents of the backcountry had no prior religious affiliation, thus presenting evangelists with a potential source of converts.

First Great Awakening

The first signs of what was to become the Great Awakening appeared in western Massachusetts, in the Northampton Congregational Church led by the Reverend Jonathan Edwards, a noted preacher and theologian. During 1734 and 1735, Edwards noticed a remarkable response among the youthful members of his flock to a message based squarely on Calvinist principles. Individuals could attain salvation, Edwards argued, only through recognition of their own depraved natures and the need to surrender completely to God's will. Such surrender brought to members of his congregation an intensely emotional release from sin and came to be seen as a single identifiable moment of conversion.

The effects of such conversions remained isolated until 1739, when an English Methodist named George Whitefield arrived in America. For fifteen months he toured the colonies, preaching to large audiences from Georgia to New England and concentrating his efforts in the major cities: Boston, New York, Philadelphia, and Charleston. A gripping orator, Whitefield was the chief generating force behind the Great Awakening. Everywhere he traveled, his fame preceded him. Thousands turned out to listen—and to experience conversion. At first, regular clerics welcomed Whitefield and the American-born itinerant evangelist preachers who sprang up to imitate him.

George Whitefield

Soon, however, many clergymen began to realize that "revived" religion, though it filled their churches, ran counter to their own approach to doctrine and matters of faith. They disliked the emotional style of the revivalists, whose itinerancy also disrupted normal patterns of church attendance because it took churchgoers away from the services they usually attended.

Opposition to the Awakening heightened rapidly, and large numbers of congregations splintered in its wake. "Old Lights"—traditional clerics and their followers—engaged in bitter disputes with the "New Light" evangelicals. American Protestantism, already characterized by numerous sects, became further divided as the major denominations split into Old Light and New Light factions and as new evangelical sects—Methodists and Baptists—gained adherents. Paradoxically, the angry fights and the rapid rise in the number of distinct denominations eventually led to an American willingness to tolerate religious diversity. No single sect could make an unequivocal claim to orthodoxy, so they all had to coexist if they were to exist at all.

The most important effect of the Awakening was its impact on American modes of thought. The revivalists' message directly challenged the colonial tradition of deference. Itinerant preachers, only a few of whom were ordained clergymen, claimed they understood the will of God better than did the orthodox clerics. The Awakening's emphasis on emotion rather than learning undermined the validity of received wisdom, and New Lights questioned not only religious but also social and political orthodoxy. For example, New Lights began to defend the rights of groups and individuals to dissent from a community consensus, thereby challenging one of the most fundamental tenets of colonial political life.

Impact of the Awakening

Nowhere was this trend more evident than in Virginia, where the plantation gentry and their ostentatious lifestyle dominated society. By the 1760s Baptists had gained a secure foothold in Virginia; their beliefs and behavior were openly at odds with the way most genteel families lived. They rejected as sinful the horse racing, gambling, and dancing that occupied much of the gentry's leisure time. Like the Quakers before them, they dressed plainly, in contrast to the fashionable opulence of the gentry. They addressed each other as "brother" and "sister" regardless of social status, and they elected the leaders of their congregations—more than ninety of them by 1776. Their monthly "great meetings," which attracted hundreds of people, introduced new public rituals that rivaled the more conventional weekly Anglican services.

Strikingly, almost all the Virginia Baptist congregations included both black and white members. When the Dan River Baptist Church was founded in 1760, for example, eleven of its original seventy-four members were black, and other congregations had black majorities. Church rules governed the behavior of both blacks and whites; interracial sexual relationships, divorce, and adultery were forbidden to all. In addition, masters were directed not to break up slave marriages through sale. Complaints about church members' misbehavior were investigated by biracial committees. Churches excommunicated slaves for stealing from their masters, but they also excommunicated whites for physically abusing their slaves. One such slaveowner excommunicated in 1772 experienced a true conversion. Penalized for "burning" one of his slaves, Charles Cook apologized to the congregation and became a preacher in a largely black church. Other white Baptists decided slaveowning was "unrighteous" and freed their bondspeople; Robert Carter manumitted more than nine hundred slaves.

The Great Awakening thus injected an egalitarian strain into American life at midcentury and further disrupted traditional structures of existence. Although primarily a religious movement, the Awakening also had important social and political consequences, calling into question habitual modes of behavior in the secular as well as the religious realm. In short, the Great Awakening helped to break Americans' ties to their limited seventeenth-century origins. So, too, did the newcomers from Germany, Scotland, Ireland, and Africa, who brought their languages, customs, and religions to North America. The European immigrants settled throughout the English colonies, but were concentrated in the growing cities and in the backcountry. By contrast, enslaved migrants from Africa lived and worked primarily within one hundred miles of the Atlantic coast. In many areas of the colonial South, 50 to 90 percent of the population was of African origin.

The economic life of the colonies proceeded simultaneously on two levels. On the farms on which most Americans resided, the daily, weekly, monthly, and yearly rounds of chores for men, women, and children alike dominated people's lives, while providing the goods consumed by households and sold in the marketplace. At the same time, the colonies were increasingly enmeshed in an international network of trade that affected their local economic circumstances. The bitter wars fought by Britain, France, Spain, and other European nations during the eighteenth century inevitably involved the American colonists by creating new opportunities for overseas sales or by disrupting their traditional markets. Above all, the colonial economy was volatile, fluctuating for reasons beyond the Americans' control. Those fortunate few who—through skill, control of essential resources, or luck—reaped the profits of international trade made up the wealthy class of merchants and landowners who dominated colonial political and social life.

A century and a half after English people had first settled in North America, the colonies were no longer exclusively English. Rather, they mixed diverse European, American, and African traditions into a novel cultural blend that owed much to the Old World but just as much, if not more, to the New. In the 1760s Americans began to recognize that fact. Their interests, they realized, were not necessarily identical to those of Great Britain or its monarch. For the first time, they offered a frontal challenge to British authority.

SUGGESTIONS FOR FURTHER READING

General

Wayne Craven, *Colonial American Portraiture* (1986); Jack P. Greene, *Pursuits of Happiness: The Social Development of the Early Modern British Colonies and the Formation of American Culture* (1988); Jack P. Greene and J. R. Pole, eds., *Colonial British America* (1984); David F. Hawke, *Everyday Life in Early America* (1988); Richard Hofstadter, *America at 1750: A Social Portrait* (1971); Stephen Innes, ed., *Work and Labor in Early America* (1988); D. W. Meinig, *Atlantic America, 1492–1800* (1986).

Rural Society

T. H. Breen, *Tobacco Culture* (1985); Lois Green Carr et al., eds., *Colonial Chesapeake Society* (1988); Rhys Isaac, *The Transfor-*

mation of Virginia, 1740–1790 (1982); Christopher Jedrey, *The World of John Cleaveland: Family and Community in Eighteenth-Century New England* (1979); Sung Bok Kim, *Landlord and Tenant in Colonial New York: Manorial Society, 1664–1775* (1978); James T. Lemon, *The Best Poor Man's Country: A Geographical Study of Early Southeastern Pennsylvania* (1972); Jackson Turner Main, *Society and Economy in Colonial Connecticut* (1985); Peter Mancall, *Valley of Opportunity: Economic Culture Along the Upper Susquehanna, 1700–1800* (1991); Michael Zuckerman, *Peaceable Kingdoms: New England Towns in the Eighteenth Century* (1970).

Urban Society

Carl Bridenbaugh, *Cities in Revolt: Urban Life in America, 1743–1776* (1955); Gary B. Nash, *The Urban Crucible: Social Change, Political Consciousness, and the Origins of the American Revolution* (1979); Frederick B. Tolles, *Meeting House and Counting House: The Quaker Merchants of Colonial Philadelphia, 1682–1763* (1948); Stephanie G. Wolf, *Urban Village: Population, Community, and Family Structure in Germantown, Pennsylvania, 1683–1800* (1976).

Economic Development

Paul Clemens, *The Atlantic Economy and Colonial Maryland's Eastern Shore: From Tobacco to Grain* (1980); Alice Hanson Jones, *Wealth of a Nation to Be: The American Colonies on the Eve of the Revolution* (1980); John J. McCusker and Russell R. Menard, *The Economy of British America, 1607–1789* (1985); Edwin J. Perkins, *The Economy of Colonial America* (1980); James F. Shepherd and Gary M. Walton, *Shipping, Maritime Trade and the Economic Development of Colonial North America* (1972); Gary M. Walton and James F. Shepherd, *The Economic Rise of Early America* (1979).

Politics

Bernard Bailyn, *The Origins of American Politics* (1968); Patricia U. Bonomi, *A Factious People: Politics and Society in Colonial New York* (1971); Richard Bushman, *King and People in Provincial Massachusetts* (1985); Edward M. Cook, Jr., *The Fathers of the Towns: Leadership and Community Structure in Eighteenth-Century New England* (1976); Jack P. Greene, *The Quest for Power: The Lower Houses of Assembly in the Southern Royal Colonies, 1689–1776* (1963).

Immigration

Bernard Bailyn, *The Peopling of British North America* (1986); Bernard Bailyn, *Voyagers to the West* (1986); Bernard Bailyn and Philip Morgan, eds., *Strangers Within the Realm* (1991); Jon Butler, *The Huguenots in America* (1983); R. J. Dickson, *Ulster Immigration to Colonial America, 1718–1775* (1966); A. Roger Ekirch, *Bound for America: The Transportation of British Convicts to the Colonies, 1718-1775* (1987); Ned Landsman, *Scotland and Its First American Colony* (1985); James G. Leyburn, *The Scotch-Irish* (1962); Sharon Salinger, *To Serve Well and Faithfully: Labor and Indentured Servants in Pennsylvania, 1682–1800* (1988).

African-Americans

Thomas J. Davis, *A Rumor of Revolt: The "Great Negro Plot" in Colonial New York* (1985); Herbert Gutman, *The Black Family in Slavery and Freedom, 1750–1925* (1976); Allan Kulikoff, *Tobacco* and Slaves: The Development of Southern Cultures in the Chesapeake, 1680–1800 (1986); Gerald W. Mullin, Flight and Rebellion: Slave Resistance in Eighteenth-Century Virginia (1972); William Pierson, Black Yankees: The Development of an Afro-American Subculture in Eighteenth-Century New England (1988); Mechal Sobel, The World They Made Together: Black and White Values in Eighteenth-Century Virginia (1987).

Women and Family

Jane Donegan, Women and Men Midwives: Medicine, Morality, and Misogyny in Early America (1978); Philip J. Greven, The Protestant Temperament: Patterns of Child-rearing, Religious Experience, and the Self in Early America (1977); Barry J. Levy, Quakers and the American Family (1988); Mary Beth Norton, Liberty's Daughters: The Revolutionary Experience of American Women, 1750–1800 (1980); Marylynn Salmon, Women and the Law of Property in Early America (1986); Daniel Blake Smith, Inside the Great House: Planter Family Life in Eighteenth-Century Chesapeake Society (1980).

Colonial Culture, Science, and the Enlightenment

Richard Bushman, The Refinement of America (1992); Richard Beale Davis, Intellectual Life in the Colonial South, 1585–1763, 2 vols. (1978); Brooke Hindle, The Pursuit of Science in Revolutionary America (1956); Howard Mumford Jones, O Strange New World. American Culture: The Formative Years (1964); Henry F. May, The Enlightenment in America (1976); Raymond P. Stearns, Science in the British Colonies of America (1970); Louis B. Wright, The Cultural Life of the American Colonies, 1607–1763 (1957).

Education

James Axtell, The School upon a Hill: Education and Society in Colonial New England (1974); Bernard Bailyn, Education in the Forming of American Society (1960); Patricia Cline Cohen, A Calculating People: The Spread of Numeracy in Early America (1982); Lawrence A. Cremin, American Education: The Colonial Experience, 1607–1783 (1970); Kenneth A. Lockridge, Literacy in Colonial New England (1974).

Religion and the Great Awakening

Patricia U. Bonomi, Under the Cope of Heaven: Religion, Society, and Politics in Colonial America (1986); Carl Bridenbaugh, Mitre and Sceptre: Transatlantic Faiths, Ideas, Personalities, and Politics, 1689–1775 (1962); J. M. Bumstead and John E. Van de Wetering, What Must I Do to Be Saved? The Great Awakening in Colonial America (1976); Jon Butler, Awash in a Sea of Faith (1990); Michael Crawford, Seasons of Grace: Colonial New England's Revival Tradition in its British Context (1991); Alan E. Heimert, Religion and the American Mind: From the Great Awakening to the Revolution (1966); David S. Lovejoy, Religious Enthusiasm in the New World (1985); Harry S. Stout, The Divine Dramatist: George Whitefield and the Rise of Modern Evangelicalism (1991); Harry S. Stout, The New England Soul: Preaching and Religious Culture in Colonial New England (1986); Patricia Tracy, Jonathan Edwards, Pastor (1980).

OF THE TOWN OF BOSTON IN NEW ENGLAND AND B...

5

Severing the Bonds of Empire, 1754–1774

I N LATE OCTOBER 1769, the young Boston shopkeeper Betsy Cumming was visiting a sick friend when she heard "a voilint Skreeming Kill him Kill him." Betsy ran to the window and saw John Mein, a bookseller and newspaper publisher, being chased by "a larg Croud of those who Call themselves Gentleman but in reality they ware no other then Murderers for there disigne was certainly on his life." Later that evening a crowd of at least a thousand men and boys passed the door, "& on a Kart a Man was Exibited as we thought in a Gore of blood." Betsy concluded that the mob had caught Mein, but she was mistaken. The victim was a customs informer seized by the crowd after Mein had taken shelter in a British army guardhouse. That same night, Mein fled to a vessel anchored in the harbor. He later sailed to England and never returned to Boston.

What had John Mein done to arouse the antagonism of the "gentlemen" of Boston? He published a newspaper, the *Boston Chronicle*, which generally supported the British side in disputes with the colonies. The offense that led to the mobbing, though, was more specific: he had printed several lists of local merchants who had recently cleared imports through the Boston customs house. The Mein incident thus involved one of the first recorded examples in American history of a carefully orchestrated political "leak" from official sources. Some administrator had given Mein access to the supposedly private customs records. But why was the information Mein revealed so explosive? In the fall of 1769 many merchants had signed an agreement not to import goods from Great Britain; Mein's lists indicated that some of the most vocal supporters of nonimportation (including the patriot leader John Hancock) had been violating the agreement. That was why the "gentlemen" of Boston had to silence the outspoken publisher.

John Mein was not the first—and he would be far from the last—resident of the colonies who found his life wholly disrupted by the growing political antagonism between England and its American possessions. Indeed, even Betsy Cumming was eventually forced into exile in Nova Scotia because she opposed the trend of American resistance to Great Britain. Long afterward, John Adams identified the years between 1760 and 1775 as the period when the true American Revolution had occurred. The Revolution, Adams declared, was completed before the fighting started, for it was "in the Minds of the people," involving not

Paul Revere commemorated the arrival of British troops in Boston in October 1768 in this dramatic engraving.

the actual winning of independence but a shift of fundamental allegiance from England to America. Today, not all historians would agree with Adams's assertion that that shift constituted the Revolution. But none would deny the importance of the events of those crucial years, which led to the division of the American population along political lines and set the colonies on the road to independence.

The story of the 1760s and early 1770s describes an ever-widening split between England and America, and among their respective support-

A LIST of the Names of *those* who AUDACIOUSLY continue to counteract the UNITED SENTIMENTS of the BODY of Merchants thro'out NORTH-AMERICA ; by importing British Goods contrary to the Agreement.

John Bernard,
(In King-Street, almost opposite Vernon's Head.

James McMasters,
(On Treat's Wharf.

Patrick McMasters,
(Opposite the Sign of the Lamb.

John Mein,
(Opposite the White-Horse, and in King-Street.

Nathaniel Rogers,
(Opposite Mr. Henderson Inches Store lower End King-Street.

William Jackson,
At the Brazen Head, Cornhill, near the Town-House.

Theophilus Lillie,
(Near Mr. Pemberton's Meeting-House, North-End.

John Taylor,
(Nearly opposite the Heart and Crown in Cornhill.

Ame & Elizabeth Cummings,
(Opposite the Old Brick Meeting House, all of Boston.

Israel Williams, Esq; & Son,
(Traders in the Town of Hatfield.

And, *Henry Barnes*,
(Trader in the Town of Marlboro'.

The following Names should have been inserted in the List of Justices.

County of Middlesex.	County of Lincoln.
Samuel Hendley	
John Borland	John Kingsbury
Henry Barnes	
Richard Cary	County of Berkshire.
County of Bristol.	Mark Hopkins
George Brightman	Elijah Dwight
County of Worcester.	Israel Stoddard
Daniel Bliss	

A blacklist printed in the North American Almanac *for 1770 identified those Boston merchants who had ignored the nonimportation agreement. Among their number were both John Mein, the object of the mob's wrath the previous October, and Betsy (Elizabeth) Cumming, the narrator of the story, who—with her sister Anne—ran a small dry-goods store.* Library of Congress.

ers in the colonies. In the long history of British settlement in the Western Hemisphere, considerable tension had at times marred the relationship between individual provinces and mother country. Still, that tension had rarely been sustained for long, nor had it been widespread, except during the crisis following the Glorious Revolution in 1689. The primary divisions affecting the colonies had been internal rather than external. In the 1750s, however, a series of events began to draw the colonists' attention from domestic matters to their relations with Great Britain. It all started with the Seven Years' War.

Britain's overwhelming victory in that war, confirmed by treaty in 1763, forever altered the balance of power in North America. France was ousted from the continent, an event with major consequences for both the Indian tribes of the interior and the residents of the British colonies. Northern tribes could no longer play off European powers against one another and so lost one of their major diplomatic tools. Anglo-Americans, for their part, no longer had to fear a French threat on their borders. Some historians have argued that if the colonies had had to worry about the continuing presence of France on the North American mainland, the Revolution could never have occurred. The British colonies would never have dared to break with their mother country, it is said, if an enemy nation and its Indian allies had controlled the interior of the continent.

The British victory in 1763, then, constituted a major turning point in American history because of its direct effect on white and Indian residents of North America. It also had a significant impact on Great Britain, one that soon affected the colonies as well. To win the war, Britain had gone heavily into debt. To reduce the debt, Parliament for the first time imposed revenue-raising taxes on the colonies in addition to the customs duties that had long regulated trade. That decision exposed differences in the political thinking of Americans and Britons—differences that until then had been obscured by a shared political vocabulary.

During the 1760s and early 1770s a broad coalition of white Americans, men and women alike, resisted new tax levies and attempts by British officials to tighten controls over the provincial governments. America's elected leaders became ever more suspicious of Britain's motives as the years passed. They laid aside intercolonial antagonisms to coordinate their response to the new measures,

• *Important Events* •

1754	Albany Congress meets to try to forge colonial unity Fighting breaks out with Washington's defeat at Fort Necessity	**1766**	Stamp Act repealed Declaratory Act insists that Parliament can tax the colonies
1756	Britain declares war on France; Seven Years' War officially begins	**1767**	Townshend Acts lay duties on trade within the empire, send new officials and judges to America
1759	British forces take Quebec	**1770**	Lord North becomes prime minister Townshend duties repealed, except for tea tax Boston Massacre kills five colonial rioters
1760	American phase of war ends with fall of Montreal to British troops George III becomes king	**1772**	Boston Committee of Correspondence formed
1763	Treaty of Paris ends Seven Years' War Pontiac's allies attack British forts in West Proclamation of 1763 attempts to close land west of Appalachians to English settlement	**1773**	Tea Act aids East India Company Boston Tea Party protests the Tea Act
1764	Sugar Act lays new duties on molasses, tightens customs regulations Currency Act outlaws colonial paper money issues	**1774**	Coercive Acts punish Boston and the colony of Massachusetts Quebec Act reforms government of that province
1765	Stamp Act requires stamps on all printed materials in colonies Sons of Liberty formed		

and they slowly began to reorient their political thinking. As late as the summer of 1774, though, most were still seeking a solution within the framework of the empire; few harbored thoughts of independence. When independence rather than loyal resistance became the issue, the coalition broke down. That, however, happened only after the battles of Lexington and Concord in April 1775. Before then, just a few Americans closely connected to colonial administration or the Church of England opposed the trend of resistance.

RENEWED WARFARE AMONG EUROPEANS AND INDIANS

The English colonies along the Atlantic seaboard were surrounded by hostile, or potentially hostile, neighbors: Indians everywhere, the Spanish in Florida and along the coast of the Gulf of Mexico, the French along the great inland system of rivers and lakes that stretched from the St. Lawrence to the Mississippi. The Spanish outposts posed little threat to the English, for Spain's days as a major power had passed. The French were another matter. Their long chain of forts and settlements dominated the North American interior, facilitating trading partnerships and alliances with the tribes of the region. In none of the three wars fought between 1689 and 1748 was England able to shake France's hold on the American frontier. Under the Peace of Utrecht, which ended Queen Anne's War in 1713, the English won control of such peripheral northern areas as Newfoundland, Hudson's Bay, and Nova Scotia (Acadia). But Britain made no territorial gains in King George's War (see map, page 130).

During both Queen Anne's War and King George's War, the Iroquois Confederacy adhered to the policy of neutrality it first developed in 1701.

Iroquois Neutrality

While English and French forces fought for nominal control of the North American continent, the confederacy—which actually dominated a large portion of that continent—skillfully played the Europeans off against each other, refusing to

Lake Superior

NEW FRANCE

Quebec

CHIPPEWA

Montreal

Ft. Western
(Augusta)

MAINE
(Part of Mass.)

Falmouth
(Portland)

Lake Huron

Lake Michigan

CHIPPEWA

OTTAWA

MIAMI

POTAWATOMI

WYANDOT

Ft. Detroit

Lake Erie

Lake Ontario

Ft. Niagara

SENECA

Allegheny R.

St. Lawrence R.

MOHAWK

ONEIDA
TUSCARORA
ONONDAGA
CAYUGA

Ft. Stanwix

Albany

NEW YORK

Hartford

CONN.

N.H.

Boston

MASS.

Portsmouth

Providence

R.I.

ILLINOIS CONFEDERATION

WEA

OHIO COUNTRY

SHAWNEE

PENNSYLVANIA

DELAWARE

Ft. Duquesne
(Pitt)

Ft.
Necessity

Monongahela R.

Ohio R.

Mississippi R.

1720–1760

Tuscarora Migration

New York

Philadelphia

N.J.

New Castle

Baltimore

MD.

DEL.

Richmond

VIRGINIA

Williamsburg

ATLANTIC OCEAN

Proclamation Line of 1763

CHEROKEE

Salem

Hillsboro

NORTH CAROLINA

New Bern

CATAWBA

Camden

SOUTH CAROLINA

Wilmington

CHICKASAW

Ft. Augusta
(Augusta)

Charleston

GEORGIA

CREEK

Savannah

CHOCTAW

NEW SPAIN

St. Augustine

Total population of
English colonies: c.1.5 million

Extent of settlement

European Settlements and Native American Tribes, 1750 *By 1750, Europeans had expanded the limits of the English colonies to the eastern slopes of the Appalachian Mountains. Few independent Indian nations still existed in the East, but beyond the mountains they controlled the countryside. Only a few widely scattered English and French forts maintained the Europeans' presence there.*

commit its warriors fully to either side despite being showered with gifts by both. Instead, the Iroquois fought only their traditional southern enemies, the Catawbas. Since France repeatedly urged them to attack the Catawbas, who were allied with England, the Iroquois achieved three desirable goals. They kept the French happy and simultaneously consolidated their control over the entire interior region north of Virginia. The campaign against a common enemy also enabled the confederacy to cement its alliance with its weaker tributaries, the Shawnees and Delawares, and to ensure the continued subordination of those tribes.

But even the careful Iroquois diplomats could not prevent the region inhabited by the Shawnees and Delawares (now western Pennsylvania and eastern Ohio) from providing the spark that set off a major war. That conflict spread from America to Europe (a significant reversal of previous patterns) and proved decisive in the contest for North America. Trouble began in 1752 when English fur traders ventured into the area known as the Ohio country. The French could not permit their English rivals to gain a foothold in the region, for it contained the source of the Ohio River, which offered direct access by water to their posts on the Mississippi. A permanent English presence in the Ohio country could challenge France's control of the western fur trade and even threaten its prominence in the Mississippi Valley. Accordingly, in

1753 the French pushed southward from Lake Erie, building fortified outposts at strategic points along the rivers of the Ohio country.

In response to the French threat to their western frontiers, delegates from seven northern and middle colonies gathered in Albany, New York, in June 1754. With the backing of administrators in London, they sought two goals: to persuade the Iroquois to abandon their traditional neutrality and to coordinate the defenses of the colonies. In neither aim were they successful. The Iroquois listened politely to the colonists' arguments but saw no reason to change a policy that had served them well for half a century. And although the Albany Congress delegates adopted a Plan of Union (which would have established an elected intercolonial legislature with the power to tax), the plan was uniformly rejected by their provincial governments—primarily because those governments feared a loss of autonomy.

Albany Congress

While the delegates to the Albany Congress deliberated, the war they sought to prepare for was already beginning. Governor Robert Dinwiddie of Virginia had sent a small militia force westward to counter the French moves. Virginia claimed ownership of the Ohio country, and Dinwiddie was eager to prevent the French from establishing a permanent post there. But the Virginia militiamen

The Colonial Wars, 1689–1763

American Name	European Name	Dates	Participants	American Sites	Dispute
King William's War	War of League of Augsburg	1689–97	England, Holland versus France, Spain	New England, New York, Canada	French power
Queen Anne's War	War of Spanish Succession	1702–13	England, Holland, Austria versus France, Spain	Florida, New England	Throne of Spain
King George's War	War of Austrian Succession	1739–48	England, Holland, Austria versus France, Spain, Prussia	West Indies, New England, Canada	Throne of Austria
French and Indian War	Seven Years' War	1756–63	England versus France, Spain	Ohio Country, Canada	Possession of Ohio Country

A colonial soldier in 1758 etched onto his powder horn images of Indians and English troops fighting in the Seven Years' War. New York Historical Society.

arrived too late. The French had already taken possession of the strategic point—now Pittsburgh—where the Allegheny and Monongahela rivers meet to form the Ohio, and they were busily engaged in constructing Fort Duquesne. The foolhardy and inexperienced young colonel who commanded the Virginians attacked a French detachment and then allowed himself to be trapped in his crudely built Fort Necessity at Great Meadows, Pennsylvania. After a day-long battle (on July 3, 1754), during which more than one-third of his men were killed or wounded, twenty-two-year-old George Washington surrendered. He and his men were allowed to return to Virginia.

Washington had blundered grievously. He had started a war that eventually would encompass nearly the entire world. He had also ensured that

Seven Years' War

the tribes of the Ohio valley, many of whom had moved west to escape Iroquois domination and to trade with the French, would for the most part support France in the coming conflict. The Indians took Washington's mistakes as an indication of Britain's inability to win the war, and nothing that occurred in the next four years made them change their minds. In July 1755, a few miles south of Fort Duquesne, a combined force of French and Indians ambushed British and colonial troops led by General Edward Braddock. Braddock was killed and his men were demoralized by their complete defeat. After news of the debacle reached

London, Britain declared war on France in 1756, thus formally beginning the conflict known as the Seven Years' War.

For three more years one disaster followed another for Great Britain. The war went so badly that Britain began to fear France would attempt to retake Newfoundland and Nova Scotia. In an effort to solidify their hold on that area, the British administrators of Nova Scotia forced its French residents to leave the homes they had occupied for generations—the first modern deportation of an entire people. After years of wandering, many of these Acadian exiles made their way to Louisiana, where they became known as Cajuns.

At last, under the leadership of William Pitt, who was named secretary of state in 1757, the British mounted the effort that won them the war in North America. Pitt encouraged cooperation between the colonists and Great Britain, agreeing to reimburse the colonies for their military expenditures and placing troop recruitment wholly in local hands. He thereby gained wholehearted American support for the war effort. Earlier in the war—the years of England's many defeats—British officers had usually tried to coerce the colonies into supplying men and materiel to the army.

In July 1758, British forces recaptured the fortress at Louisbourg, winning control of the entrance to the St. Lawrence and breaking the major French supply route. Then, in a surprise night attack in September 1759 (depicted in a contemporary engraving reproduced here), General James

Wolfe's soldiers defeated the French on the Plains of Abraham and took Quebec. Sensing a British victory, the Iroquois abandoned their policy of neutrality and allied themselves with the British, hoping to gain some diplomatic leverage. A year later the British captured Montreal, the last French stronghold on the continent, and the American phase of the war ended.

When the Treaty of Paris was signed in 1763, France ceded its major North American holdings to Britain. Spain, an ally of France toward the end of the war, gave Florida to the victorious English. Britain, fearing the presence of France on its western borders, also forced the French to cede the region west of the Mississippi (Louisiana) to Spain. The British thus gained control of the fur trade of the entire continent. And no longer would the English seacoast colonies have to worry about the threat to their existence posed by France's extensive North American territories (see maps on page 130).

Because most of the fighting had occurred in the Northeast, the war had especially pronounced effects on New Englanders. As many as one-third of all Massachusetts men between the ages of sixteen and twenty-nine served for a time in the provincial army. Wartime service left a lasting impression on these soldiers. For the first time, ordinary Americans came into extended contact with Britons—and they did not like what they saw. The provincials regarded the redcoats as haughty, profane Sabbath-breakers who arbitrarily imposed overly harsh punishments on anyone who broke the rules. Nearly sixty years later a veteran still vividly recalled an incident in 1762 when hundreds of lashes were inflicted on three men for "some trifling offense. . . . I felt at the time as though I could have taken summary vengeance on those who were the authors of it," he wrote in his memoirs.

American Soldiers

The New England soldiers also learned that British regulars did not share their adherence to principles of contract and consensus—the values that had governed their lives at home. Colonial regiments mutinied or rebelled en masse if they be-

On the night of September 13, 1759, British forces under General James Wolfe scaled the heights of Quebec and defeated the French army led by General Louis Joseph Montcalm. Both generals died on the battlefield.   Library of Congress.

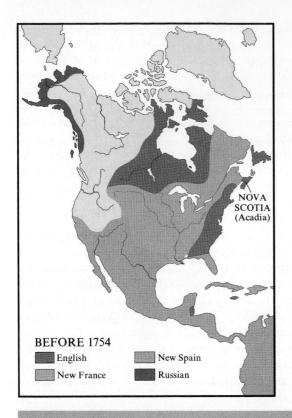

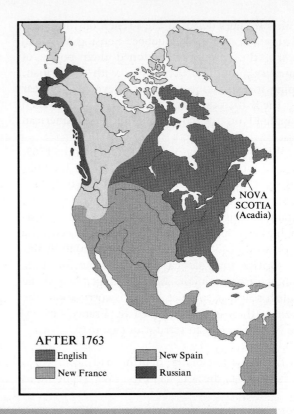

European Claims in North America   *The dramatic results of the British victory in the Seven Years'
(French and Indian) War are vividly demonstrated in these maps, which depict the abandonment of French
claims to the mainland after the Treaty of Paris in 1763.*

lieved they were being treated unfairly, as happened, for example, when they were not allowed
to leave at the end of their formal enlistments. One
private in these circumstances grumbled in his
journal in 1759, "Although we be Englishmen
born, we are debarred Englishmen's liberty. . . .
[The British soldiers] are but little better than
slaves to their officers. And when I get out of their
[power] I shall take care how I get in again." Such
men would later recall their personal experience
of British "tyranny" when they were deciding to
support the Revolution.

The overwhelming British triumph stimulated
some Americans to think expansively about the colonies' future. People like Benjamin Franklin, who
had long touted the colonies' wealth and potential,
predicted a glorious new future for British North
America—a future that included not just geographical expansion but also economic develop-

ment and population growth. Such men were to
lead the resistance to British measures in the years
after 1763. They uniformly opposed any laws that
would retard America's growth and persistently
supported steps to increase Americans' control over
their own destiny.

1763: A TURNING POINT

The great victory over France had an irreversible
impact on North America, felt first by the interior
tribes. With France excluded from the continent
altogether and Spanish territory now confined to
the area west of the Mississippi, the diplomatic
strategy that had served the tribes well for so long
could no longer be employed. The consequences
were immediate and devastating.

Even before the Treaty of Paris, southern Indians had to adjust to the new circumstances. After the British gained the upper hand in the American war in 1758, the Creeks and Cherokees lost their ability to force concessions by threatening to turn instead to the French or the Spanish. In desperation, and in retaliation for British atrocities, the Cherokees attacked the Carolina and Virginia frontiers in 1760. Although initially victorious, the tribes were defeated the following year by a force of British regulars and colonial militia. Late in 1761 the two sides concluded a treaty under which the Cherokees allowed the construction of English forts in tribal territories and opened a large tract of land to white settlement.

The fate of the Cherokees in the South was a portent of things to come in the Ohio country. There, the Ottawas, Chippewas, and Potawatomis reacted angrily when Great Britain, no longer facing French competition, raised the price of trade goods and ended the practice of paying rent for forts. The British also allowed settlers to move into the Monongahela and Susquehanna valleys, onto Delaware and Iroquois lands.

Pontiac, the war chief of an Ottawa village near Detroit, understood the implications of such British actions. Only unity among the western tribes, he realized, could prevent total dependence on and subordination to the victorious British. Using his considerable powers of persuasion, in the spring of 1763 he forged an unprecedented alliance among Hurons, Chippewas, Potawatomis, Delawares, Shawnees, and even some Mingoes (Pennsylvania Iroquois). Pontiac then laid seige to the fort at Detroit while his war parties attacked other British outposts in the Great Lakes region. Detroit withstood the siege, but by the end of June all the other forts west of Niagara and north of Fort Pitt (old Fort Duquesne) had fallen to the Indian alliance.

Pontiac's Uprising

That was the high point of the uprising. The tribes raided the Virginia and Pennsylvania frontiers at will throughout the summer, killing at least two thousand English settlers. But they could not take the strongholds of Niagara, Fort Pitt, or Detroit. In early August, a combined force of Delawares, Shawnees, Hurons, and Mingoes was soundly defeated at Bushy Run, Pennsylvania, by troops sent from the coast. Conflict ceased when Pontiac broke off the siege of Detroit in late October. A treaty ending the war was finally negotiated three years later.

Pontiac's uprising showed Great Britain that the huge territory it had just acquired from France would not be easy to govern. The central administration in London had had no prior experience in managing such a vast tract of land, particularly one inhabited by two hostile peoples—the remaining French settlers along the St. Lawrence and the many different tribes. In October, in a futile attempt to assert control over the interior, the ministry issued the Proclamation of 1763, which declared the headwaters of rivers flowing into the Atlantic from the Appalachian Mountains to be the temporary western boundary for colonial settlement. The proclamation was intended to prevent clashes between Indians and colonists by forbidding whites to move onto Indian lands until the tribes had given up their land by treaty. But many whites had already established farms or purchased property west of the proclamation line, and the policy was doomed to failure from the outset.

Proclamation of 1763

Other decisions made in London in 1763 and thereafter had a wider impact in British North America. The victory in the Seven Years' War created both problems and opportunities for the British government. The most pressing problem was Britain's immense war debt. The men who had to solve that problem were King George III and his new prime minister, George Grenville.

George III succeeded his grandfather, George II, on the English throne in 1760. The twenty-two-year-old king, a man of mediocre intellect and even more mediocre education, was unfortunately also an erratic judge of character. During the crucial years between 1763 and 1770, when the rift with the colonies was growing ever wider, he replaced ministries with bewildering rapidity. Though determined to assert the power of the monarchy, the king was immature and unsure of himself. He often substituted stubbornness for intelligence, and he regarded adherence to the status quo as the hallmark of patriotism.

George III

The man he selected as prime minister in 1763, George Grenville, believed that the American colonies should be more tightly administered than in the past. Grenville confronted a financial crisis:

Benjamin West, the first well-known American artist, engraved this picture of a prisoner exchange at the end of Pontiac's uprising, with Colonel Henry Bouquet supervising the return of whites captured during the war. In the foreground, a white child resists leaving the Indian parents he had grown to love. Many whites were fascinated by the phenomenon West depicted—the reluctance of captives to abandon their adoptive Indian families.   Miriam and Ira D. Wallach Division of Art, Prints and Photographs, The New York Public Library.

England's burden of indebtedness had nearly doubled since 1754, from £73 million to £137 million. Annual expenditures before the war had amounted to no more than £8 million; now the yearly interest on the debt alone came to £5 million. Obviously, Grenville's ministry had to find new sources of funds, and the English people themselves were already heavily taxed. Since the colonists had been major beneficiaries of the wartime expenditures, Grenville concluded that the Americans should be asked to pay a greater share of the cost of running the empire.

It did not occur to Grenville to question Great Britain's right to levy taxes on the colonies. Like all his countrymen, he believed that the government's legitimacy derived ultimately from the consent of the people, but he defined consent far more loosely than did the colonists. Americans had come to believe that they could be represented only by men for whom they or their property-holding neighbors actually voted; otherwise, they could not count on legislators to protect them from oppression.

Theories of Representation

To Grenville and his English contemporaries, Parliament—king, lords, and commons acting together—by definition represented all English subjects, wherever they resided (even overseas) and whether or not they could vote. According to this theory of government, called *virtual representation*, the colonists were seen as virtually, if not actually, represented in Parliament. Thus their consent to acts of Parliament could be presumed.

The Americans and the English began at the same theoretical starting point but arrived at different conclusions in practice. In England, members of Parliament saw themselves as *collectively* representing the entire nation, composed of nobility and common folk. Only members of the House of Commons were elected, and the particular constituency that chose a member had no special claim on his vote. By contrast, in the colonies members of the lower houses of the assemblies were viewed as *individually* representing the voters who had elected them. Before Grenville proposed to tax the colonists, the two notions existed side by side without apparent contradiction. But the events of the 1760s pointed up the difference between the English and colonial definitions of representation.

The same events threw into sharp relief Americans' attitudes toward political power. The colonists had become accustomed to a government that wielded only limited authority over them and affected their daily lives very little. In consequence, they believed that a good government was one that largely left them alone, a view in keeping with the theories of a group of British writers known as the Real Whigs. Drawing on a tradition of English dissenting thought that reached back to John Locke and even the Civil War, the Real Whigs stressed the dangers inherent in a powerful government, particularly one headed by a monarch. Some of them even favored republicanism, which proposed to eliminate monarchs altogether and rest political power more directly on the will of the people. Real Whigs warned the people to guard constantly against government's attempts to encroach on their liberty and to seize their property. Political power was always to be feared, wrote John Trenchard and Thomas Gordon in their essay series *Cato's Letters* (originally published in England in 1720–1723 and reprinted many times thereafter in the colonies). Rulers would try to corrupt and oppress the people. Only the perpetual vigilance of the people and their elected representatives could preserve their fragile yet precious liberty, which was closely linked to their right to hold private property.

Britain's attempts to tighten the reins of government and raise revenues from the colonies in the 1760s and early 1770s convinced many Americans that the Real Whigs' reasoning applied to their circumstances, especially because of the link between liberty and property rights. Excessive and unjust taxation, they believed, could destroy their freedoms. They began to interpret British measures in light of the Real Whigs' warnings and to see oppressive designs behind the actions of Grenville and his successors. Historians disagree over the extent to which those perceptions were correct, but by 1775 a large number of colonists unquestionably believed they were. In the mid-1760s, however, colonial leaders did not immediately accuse Grenville of an intent to oppress them. They at first simply questioned the wisdom of the laws Grenville proposed.

The first such measures, the Sugar and Currency Acts, were passed by Parliament in 1764. The Sugar Act (also known as the Revenue Act)

Sugar and Currency Acts

revised the existing system of customs regulations and laid new duties on certain foreign imports into the colonies. It also established a vice-admiralty court at Halifax, Nova Scotia, and included provisions aimed at stopping the widespread smuggling of molasses, one of the chief commodities in American trade. Although the Sugar Act appeared to resemble the Navigation Acts, which the colonies had long accepted as legitimate, it broke with tradition because it was explicitly designed to raise revenue, not to channel American trade through Britain. The Currency Act effectively outlawed colonial issues of paper money, because British merchants complained that Americans were paying their debts in inflated local currencies. Americans could accumulate little sterling, since they imported more than they exported; thus the act seemed to the colonists to deprive them of a useful medium of exchange.

The Sugar and Currency Acts were imposed on an economy already in the midst of depression. A business boom had accompanied the Seven Years' War, but the brief spell of prosperity ended abruptly in 1760 when the war shifted overseas. Urban merchants could not sell all their imported goods to colonial customers alone, and without the military's demand for foodstuffs, American farmers found fewer buyers for their products. The bottom dropped out of the European tobacco market, threatening the livelihood of Chesapeake planters. Sailors were thrown out of work, and artisans found few employers to hire them. In such circumstances, the prospect of increased customs duties and inadequate supplies of currency aroused merchants' hostility.

Not surprisingly, both individual colonists and colonial governments decided to protest the new policies. But, lacking any precedent for a united campaign against acts of Parliament, Americans in 1764 took only hesitant and uncoordinated steps. Eight colonial legislatures sent separate petitions to Parliament requesting repeal of the Sugar Act. They argued that the act placed severe restrictions on their commerce (and would therefore hurt Britain as well) and that they had not consented to its passage. The protests had no effect. The law remained in force, and Grenville proceeded with another revenue plan.

THE STAMP ACT CRISIS

The Stamp Act, Grenville's most important proposal, was modeled on a law that had been in effect in England for almost a century. It touched nearly every colonist by requiring tax stamps on most printed materials, but it placed the heaviest burden on merchants and other members of the colonial elite, who used printed matter more frequently than ordinary folk. Anyone who purchased a newspaper or pamphlet, made a will, transferred land, bought dice or playing cards, needed a liquor license, accepted a government appointment, or borrowed money would have to pay the tax. Never before had a revenue measure of such scope been proposed for the colonies. The act also required that tax stamps be paid for with sterling, which was scarce, and that violators be tried in vice-admiralty courts, which operated without juries. (Previously the judges of such courts had only heard cases involving violations of maritime law.) Americans feared the loss of their right to trial by a jury of their peers. Finally, such a law would

break decisively with the colonial tradition of self-imposed taxation.

The most important colonial pamphlet protesting the Sugar Act and the proposed Stamp Act was *The Rights of the British Colonies Asserted and Proved*, by James Otis, Jr., a brilliant young Massachusetts attorney. Otis starkly exposed the ideological dilemma that was to confound the colonists for the next decade. How could they justify their opposition to certain acts of Parliament without questioning Parliament's authority over them? On the one hand, Otis asserted that Americans were "entitled to all the natural, essential, inherent, and inseparable rights" of Britons, including the right not to be taxed without their consent. "No man or body of men, not excepting the parliament . . . can take [those rights] away," he declared. On the other hand, Otis was forced to admit that, under the British system established after the Glorious Revolution, "the power of parliament is uncontrollable but by themselves, and we must obey. . . . Let the parliament lay what burthens they please on us, we must, it is our duty to submit and patiently bear them, till they will be pleased to relieve us."

Otis's *Rights of the British Colonies*

Otis's first contention, drawing on colonial notions of representation, implied that Parliament could not constitutionally tax the colonies because Americans were not represented in its ranks. Yet his second point both acknowledged political reality and accepted the prevailing theory of British government—that Parliament was the sole, supreme authority in the empire. Even unconstitutional laws enacted by Parliament had to be obeyed until Parliament decided to repeal them. According to orthodox British political theory, there could be no middle ground between absolute submission to Parliament and a frontal challenge to its authority. Otis tried to find such a middle ground by proposing colonial representation in Parliament, but his idea was never taken seriously on either side of the Atlantic. The British believed that the colonists were already virtually represented in Parliament, and the Americans quickly realized that a handful of colonial delegates to London would simply be outvoted.

Otis published his pamphlet before the Stamp Act was passed. When Americans first learned of its adoption in the spring of 1765, they were uncertain how to react. Few colonists—even appointed government officials—publicly favored the law. But colonial petitions had already failed to prevent its adoption, and further lobbying appeared futile. Perhaps Otis was right that the only course open to Americans was to pay the stamp tax, reluctantly but loyally. Acting on that assumption, colonial agents in London sought the appointment of their American friends as stamp distributors so that the law would at least be enforced equitably.

Not all the colonists were resigned to paying the new tax. Among them was a twenty-nine-year-old lawyer serving his first term in the Virginia House of Burgesses. Patrick

Patrick Henry and the Virginia Stamp Act Resolves

Henry later recalled that he was "young, inexperienced, unacquainted with the forms of the house and the members that composed it"—and appalled by his fellow legislators' unwillingness to oppose the Stamp Act. Henry decided to act. "Alone, unadvised, and unassisted, on a blank leaf of an old law book," he wrote the Virginia Stamp Act Resolves.

Little in Henry's earlier life foreshadowed his success in the political arena he entered so dramatically. The son of a prosperous Scottish immigrant to western Virginia, Henry had had little formal education. After marrying at eighteen, he failed at both farming and storekeeping before turning to the law as a means of supporting his wife and their six children. Henry lacked legal training, but his oratorical skills made him an effective advocate, first for his clients and later for his political beliefs. A prominent Virginia lawyer observed, "He is by far the most powerful speaker I ever heard. Every word he says not only engages, but commands the attention; and your passions are no longer your own when he addresses them."

Patrick Henry introduced his seven proposals near the end of the legislative session, when many members of the House of Burgesses had already departed for home. Henry's fiery speech led the Speaker of the House to accuse him of treason. (Henry denied the charge, contrary to the nineteenth-century myth that he exclaimed, "If this be treason, make the most of it!") The few burgesses remaining in Williamsburg adopted five of Henry's resolutions by a bare majority. Although they repealed the most radical of the five the next day, their action had far-reaching effects. Some colonial newspapers printed Henry's seven original resolutions as if they had been uniformly passed by the House, even though one had been rescinded and two others were evidently never debated or voted on at all.

The four propositions adopted by the burgesses repeated Otis's arguments, asserting that the colonists had never forfeited the rights of British subjects, among which was consent to taxation. The other three resolutions went much further. The one that was repealed claimed for the burgesses "the only exclusive right" to tax Virginians, and the final two asserted that residents of the colony need not obey tax laws passed by other legislative bodies (namely Parliament), terming any opponent of that opinion "an Enemy to this his Majesty's Colony."

The burgesses' decision to accept only the first four of Henry's resolutions anticipated the position most Americans would adopt throughout the following decade. Though willing to contend for their rights, the colonists did not seek independ-

In 1795 the artist Lawrence Sully painted the only known life portrait of Patrick Henry. The old man's fierce gaze reflects the same intensity that marked his actions thirty years earlier, when he introduced the Virginia Stamp Act Resolves in the House of Burgesses. Mead Art Museum, Amherst College. Bequest of Herbert L. Pratt, Class of 1985.

Paul Revere produced this engraving, showing the hanging in effigy of John Huske, an American-born member of Parliament who allegedly supported the Stamp Act. Note the sign, which symbolically designates "Liberty Tree" and includes the date August 14, 1765—the time of the first major anti-Stamp Act demonstration in Boston. American Antiquarian Society.

iel Dulany, whose *Considerations on the Propriety of Imposing Taxes on the British Colonies* was the most widely read pamphlet of 1765, "The colonies are dependent upon Great Britain, and the supreme authority vested in the king, lords, and commons, may justly be exercised to secure, or preserve their dependence." But, warned Dulany, a superior did not have the right "to seize the property of his inferior when he pleases"; there was a crucial distinction between a condition of "dependence and *inferiority*" and one of "absolute *vassalage* and slavery."

Over the next ten years, America's political leaders searched for a formula that would enable them to control their internal affairs, especially taxation, but remain within the British Empire. The chief difficulty lay in British officials' inability to compromise on the issue of parliamentary power. The notion that Parliament could exercise absolute authority over all colonial possessions was basic to the British theory of government. Even the harshest British critics of the ministries of the 1760s and 1770s questioned only the wisdom of specific policies, not the principles on which they were based. In effect, the Americans wanted British leaders to revise their fundamental understanding of the workings of their government. That was simply too much to expect.

The ultimate effectiveness of Americans' opposition to the Stamp Act rested on more than ideological arguments over parliamentary power. What gave the resistance its primary force were the decisive and inventive actions of some colonists during the late summer and fall of 1765.

In August the Loyal Nine, a Boston social club of printers, distillers, and other artisans, organized a demonstration against the Stamp Act. Hoping to show that people of all ranks opposed the act, they approached the leaders of the city's rival laborers' associations, based in the North End and South End. The two gangs, composed of unskilled workers and poor tradesmen, often battled each other, but the Loyal Nine convinced them to lay aside their differences to participate in the demonstration. After all, the stamp taxes would have to be paid by all colonists, not just by affluent ones.

Loyal Nine

Early on August 14, the demonstrators hung an effigy of Andrew Oliver, the province's stamp distributor, from a tree on Boston Common. That

ence. They merely wanted some measure of self-government. Accordingly, they backed away from the assertions that they owed Parliament no obedience and that only their own assemblies could tax them. Indeed, declared the Maryland lawyer Dan-

night a large crowd led by a group of about fifty well-dressed tradesmen paraded the effigy around the city. The crowd tore down a small building they thought was intended as the stamp office and built a bonfire near Oliver's house with the wood from the destroyed building. They then beheaded the effigy and added it to the flames. Members of the crowd broke most of Oliver's windows and threw stones at officials who tried to disperse them. In the midst of the melée, the North End and South End leaders drank a toast to their successful union. The Loyal Nine's demonstration achieved its objective when Oliver publicly promised not to fulfill the duties of his office. One Bostonian jubilantly wrote to a relative, "I believe people never was more Universally pleased not so much one could I hear say he was sorry, but a smile sat on almost every ones countinance."

But another crowd action twelve days later, aimed this time at Oliver's brother-in-law, Lieutenant Governor Thomas Hutchinson, drew no praise from the respectable citizens of Boston. On the night of August 26, a mob reportedly led by the South End leader Ebenezer MacIntosh attacked the homes of several customs officers. The crowd then completely destroyed Hutchinson's elaborately furnished townhouse in one of Boston's most fashionable districts. The lieutenant governor reported that by the next morning "one of the best finished houses in the Province had nothing remaining but the bare walls and floors." His trees and garden were ruined, his valuable library lost, and the mob had "emptied the house of every thing whatsoever except a part of the kitchen furniture." But Hutchinson took some comfort in the fact that "the encouragers of the first mob never intended matters should go this length and the people in general express the utmost detestation of this unparalleled outrage."

The differences between the two Boston mobs of August 1765 exposed divisions that would continue to characterize subsequent colonial protests.

Americans' Divergent Interests

Few residents of the colonies sided with Great Britain during these early years of protest, but the various colonial groups often had divergent goals. The skilled craftsmen who composed the Loyal Nine, and merchants, lawyers, and other members of the educated elite preferred orderly demonstrations confined to political issues.

For the city's laborers, by contrast, economic grievances may have been paramount. Certainly, their "hellish Fury" as they wrecked Hutchinson's house suggests a resentment against his ostentatious display of wealth.

Colonists, like Britons, had a long tradition of crowd action in which disfranchised people took to the streets to redress deeply felt local grievances. But the Stamp Act controversy drew ordinary urban folk into the vortex of imperial politics for the first time. Matters that had previously been of concern only to the gentry or to members of colonial legislatures were now discussed on every street corner. Sally Franklin observed as much when she wrote to her father, Benjamin, then serving as a colonial agent in London, that "nothing else is talked of, the Dutch [Germans] talk of the stompt act the Negroes of the tamp, in short every body has something to say."

The entry of lower-class whites, blacks, and women into the realm of imperial politics both threatened and afforded an opportunity to the elite white men who wanted to mount effective opposition to British measures. On the one hand, crowd action could have a stunning impact. Anti-Stamp Act demonstrations occurred in cities and towns stretching from Halifax, Nova Scotia, in the North, to the Caribbean island of Antigua in the South (see maps, page 138). They were so successful that by November 1, when the law was scheduled to take effect, not one stamp distributor was willing to carry out the duties of his office. Thus the act could not be enforced. But at the same time, wealthy men recognized that mobs composed of the formerly powerless—whose goals were not always identical to theirs (as the Boston experience showed)—could endanger their own dominance of the society. What would happen, they wondered, if the "hellish Fury" of the crowd were turned against them?

They therefore attempted to channel resistance into acceptable forms by creating an intercolonial association, the Sons of Liberty. The first

Sons of Liberty

such group was created in New York in early November, and branches spread rapidly through the coastal cities. Composed of merchants, lawyers, prosperous tradesmen, and others, the Sons of Liberty linked protest leaders from Charleston, South Carolina, to Portsmouth, New Hampshire, by early 1766.

Sites of Major Demonstrations Against the Stamp Act *The Stamp Act of 1765 aroused opposition throughout the British colonies in America, not just in the future United States.* Source: From Lester J. Cappon et al., eds., *Atlas of Early American History: The Revolutionary Era, 1760–1790.* Copyright © 1976 by Princeton University Press. Reprinted by permission of Princeton University Press.

The Sons of Liberty could influence events but not control them. In Charleston in October 1765, an informally organized crowd shouting "Liberty Liberty and stamp'd paper" forced the resignation of the South Carolina stamp distributor. The victory celebration a few days later, the largest demonstration the city had ever known, featured a British flag with the word "LIBERTY" emblazoned on it. But the new Charleston chapter of the Sons of Liberty was horrified when in January 1766 local slaves paraded through the streets similarly crying "Liberty." The local militia was mustered and messengers were sent to outlying areas with warnings of a possible plot. One African-American was banished from the colony.

In Philadelphia, resistance leaders were dismayed when an angry mob threatened to attack Benjamin Franklin's house. The city's laborers believed Franklin to be partly responsible for the Stamp Act, since he had obtained the post of stamp distributor for a close friend. But Philadelphia's artisans—the backbone of the opposition move-

ment there and elsewhere—were fiercely loyal to Franklin, one of their own who had made good. They gathered to protect his home and family from the crowd. The house was saved, but the resulting split between the better-off tradesmen and the common laborers prevented the establishment of a successful workingmen's alliance like that of Boston.

During the fall and winter of 1765–1766, opposition to the Stamp Act proceeded on three separate fronts. Colonial legislatures petitioned Parliament to repeal the hated law and in October sent delegates to an intercolonial congress, the first since the Albany Congress of 1754. The Stamp Act Congress met in New York to draft a unified but conservative statement of protest. At the same time, the Sons of Liberty held mass meetings in an effort to win public support for the resistance movement. Finally, American merchants organized nonimportation associations to pressure British exporters. By the 1760s, one-quarter of all British exports were being sent to the colonies, and American merchants reasoned that London merchants whose sales suffered severely would lobby for repeal. Since times were bad and American merchants were finding few customers for imported goods anyway, a general moratorium on future purchases would also help to reduce their bloated inventories.

In March 1766, Parliament repealed the Stamp Act. The nonimportation agreements had the anticipated effect, creating allies for the colonies among wealthy London merchants. But boycotts, formal protests, and crowd actions were less important in winning repeal than was the appointment of a new prime minister, chosen by George III for reasons unrelated to colonial politics. Lord Rockingham, who replaced Grenville in summer 1765, had opposed the Stamp Act, not because he believed Parliament lacked power to tax the colonies but because he thought the law unwise and divisive. Thus, although Rockingham proposed repeal, he linked it to passage of the Declaratory Act, which asserted Parliament's ability to tax and legislate for Britain's American possessions "in all cases whatsoever."

Repeal of the Stamp Act

News of the repeal arrived in Newport, Rhode Island, in May, and the Sons of Liberty quickly transmitted the welcome tidings throughout the colonies. They also organized many celebrations commemorating the glorious event, all of which stressed the Americans' unwavering loyalty to Great Britain. Their goal achieved, the Sons of Liberty dissolved. Few colonists saw the ominous implications of the Declaratory Act.

RESISTANCE TO THE TOWNSHEND ACTS

The colonists had accomplished their immediate aim, but the long-term prospects were unclear. Another change in the ministry, in the summer of 1766, revealed how fragile their victory had been. The new prime minister, William Pitt, was ill much of the time, and the chancellor of the exchequer, Charles Townshend, became the dominant force in the ministry. Townshend, an ally of Grenville and a supporter of colonial taxation, decided to renew the attempt to obtain additional funds from Britain's American possessions.

The taxes proposed by Townshend in 1767 were to be levied on trade goods like paper, glass, and tea, and thus seemed to be nothing more than extensions of the existing Navigation Acts. But the Townshend duties differed from previous customs taxes in two ways. First, they were levied on items imported into the colonies from Britain, not from foreign countries. Thus they were at odds with mercantilist theory. Second, they were designed to raise money to pay the salaries of certain royal officials in the colonies. That posed a direct challenge to the colonial assemblies, which derived considerable power from threatening to withhold officials' salaries. In addition, Townshend's scheme provided for the creation of an American Board of Customs Commissioners and of vice-admiralty courts at Boston, Philadelphia, and Charleston. Both moves angered merchants, whose profits

British Ministries and Their American Policies

Head of Ministry	Major Acts
George Grenville	Sugar Act (1764) Currency Act (1764) Stamp Act (1765)
Lord Rockingham	Stamp Act repealed (1766) Declaratory Act (1766)
William Pitt/Charles Townshend	Townshend Acts (1767)
Lord North	Townshend duties repealed (all but tea tax) (1770) Coercive Acts (1774) Quebec Act (1774)

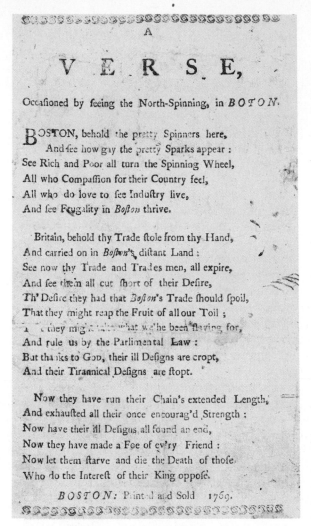

A
VERSE,

Occafioned by feeing the North-Spinning, in *BOTON*.

BOSTON, behold the pretty Spinners here,
    And fee how gay the pretty Sparks appear :
See Rich and Poor all turn the Spinning Wheel,
All who Compaffion for their Country feel,
All who do love to fee Induftry live,
And fee Frugality in *Bofton* thrive.

    Britain, behold thy Trade ftole from thy Hand,
And carried on in *Bofton's* diftant Land :
See now thy Trade and Tradefmen, all expire,
And fee them all cut fhort of their Defire,
Th' Defire they had that *Bofton's* Trade fhould fpoil,
That they might reap the Fruit of all our Toil ;
    they might   what we've been flaving for,
And rule us by the Parlimental **Law** :
But thanks to God, their ill Defigns are cropt,
And their Tirannical Defigns are ftopt.

    Now they have run their Chain's extended Length,
And exhaufted all their once encourag'd Strength :
Now have their ill Defigns all found an end,
Now they have made a Foe of ev'ry Friend :
Now let them ftarve and die the Death of thofe
Who do the Intereft of their King oppofe.

BOSTON: Printed and Sold 1769.

A 1769 Boston broadside commended the spinners, "Rich and Poor," who had "Compassion for their Country" and promoted "Frugality" during the Townshend Act crisis. The poet put into verse precisely the message the spinners intended to convey. Massachusetts Historical Society.

would be threatened by more vigorous enforcement of the Navigation Acts. Last, Townshend proposed the appointment of a secretary of state for American affairs and the suspension of the New York legislature for refusal to comply with the Quartering Act of 1765, which required colonial governments to supply certain items (such as firewood and candles) to British troops stationed permanently in America.

Unlike 1765, when months had passed before the colonists began to protest the Stamp Act, the passage of the Townshend Acts drew a quick re-

sponse. One series of essays in particular, *Letters from a Farmer in Pennsylvania* by the prominent lawyer John Dickinson, expressed a broad consensus. Eventually all but four colonial newspapers printed Dickinson's essays; in pamphlet form they went through seven American editions. Dickinson contended that Parliament could regulate colonial trade but could not exercise that power for the purpose of raising revenues. By drawing a distinction between the regulation of trade and unacceptable commercial taxation, Dickinson avoided the sticky issue of consent and how it affected the extent of colonial subordination to Parliament. But his argument created a different, and equally knotty, problem. In effect it obligated the colonies to assess Parliament's motives in passing any law pertaining to imperial trade before deciding whether to obey it. That was in the long run an unworkable position.

The Massachusetts assembly responded to the Townshend Acts by drafting a circular letter to the other colonial legislatures, calling for unity and suggesting a joint petition of protest. Not the letter itself but the ministry's reaction to it united the colonies. When Lord Hillsborough, the first secretary of state for America, learned of the circular letter, he ordered Governor Francis Bernard of Massachusetts to insist that the assembly recall it. He also directed other governors to prevent their assemblies from discussing the letter. Hillsborough's order gave the colonial assemblies the incentive they needed to forget their differences and join forces to oppose the new threat to their prerogatives. In late 1768 the Massachusetts legislature met, debated, and resoundingly rejected recall by a vote of 92 to 17. Bernard immediately dissolved the assembly, and other governors followed suit when their legislatures debated the circular letter.

Massachusetts Assembly Dissolved

The number of votes cast against recalling the circular letter—92—assumed ritual significance for the supporters of resistance to Great Britain. The figure 45 already had symbolic meaning because John Wilkes, a radical Englishman sympathetic to the American cause, had been jailed for libel early in the decade for publishing an essay entitled *The North Briton No. 45*. In Boston, the silversmith Paul

Rituals of Resistance

Revere made a punchbowl weighing 45 ounces that held 45 gills (half-cups) and was engraved with the names of the 92 legislators; James Otis, John Adams, and others publicly drank 45 toasts from it. In Charleston, the city's tradesmen decorated a tree with 45 lights and set off 45 rockets. Carrying 45 candles, they adjourned to a tavern, where 45 tables were set with 45 bowls of wine, 45 bowls of punch, and 92 glasses.

Such public rituals served important educational functions. Just as the pamphlets by Otis, Dulany, Dickinson, and others acquainted literate colonists with the issues raised by British actions, so the public rituals taught illiterate Americans about the reasons for resistance and familiarized them with the terms of the argument. When Boston's revived Sons of Liberty invited hundreds of the city's residents to dine with them each August 14 to commemorate the first Stamp Act uprising, and the Charleston Sons of Liberty held their meetings in public, crowds gathered to watch and listen. Likewise, the public singing of songs supporting the American cause helped to spread the word. The participants in such events were openly expressing their commitment to the cause of resistance and encouraging others to join them.

During the two-year campaign against the Townshend duties, the Sons of Liberty and other American leaders made a deliberate effort to involve ordinary folk in the formal resistance movement, not just in occasional crowd actions. The signers of a June 1769 Maryland nonimportation agreement, for instance, were identified as "Merchants, Tradesmen, Freeholders, Mechanics [artisans], and other Inhabitants"; all agreed not to import or consume items of British origin. Such tactics helped to increase the number of colonists who were publicly aligned with the protest movement.

Women, previously excluded from political activity, now played a part in resisting British policy. In towns throughout America, young women calling themselves Daughters of

Daughters of Liberty
———

Liberty met to spin in public in an effort to spur other women to make homespun and end the colonies' dependence on English cloth. These symbolic displays of patriotism—commemorated in broadsides—served the same purpose as the male rituals involving the numbers 45 and 92. When young ladies from well-to-do families sat publicly at spinning wheels all day, eating only American food and drinking local herbal tea, and later listening to patriotic sermons, they were serving as political instructors. Many women took great satisfaction in their new-found role. When a New England satirist hinted that women discussed only "such triffling subjects as Dress, Scandal and Detraction" during their spinning bees, three Boston women replied angrily: "Inferior in abusive sarcasm, in personal invective, in low wit, we glory to be, but inferior in veracity, sincerity, love of virtue, of liberty and of our country, we would not willingly be to any."

Women also took the lead in promoting nonconsumption of tea. In Boston more than three hundred matrons publicly promised not to drink tea, "Sickness excepted." The women of Wilmington, North Carolina, burned their tea after walking through town in a solemn procession. Housewives throughout the colonies exchanged recipes for tea substitutes or drank coffee instead. The best known of the protests (because it was satirized in the British cartoon reproduced on page 142), the so-called Edenton Ladies Tea Party, actually had little to do with tea. It was a meeting of prominent North Carolina women who pledged formally to work for the public good and to support resistance to British measures.

But the colonists were by no means united in support of nonimportation. If the Stamp Act protests had occasionally (as in Boston and Philadel-

Divided Opinion over Boycotts
———

phia) revealed a division between artisans and merchants on the one side and common laborers on the other, resistance to the Townshend Acts exposed new splits in the American ranks. The most significant divided the urban artisans and merchants, the former allies of 1765–1766, and it arose from a change in economic circumstances. The Stamp Act boycotts had helped to revive a depressed economy by creating a demand for local products and reducing merchants' inventories. But in 1768 and 1769, merchants were enjoying boom times and had no financial incentive to support a boycott. As a result, merchants signed the agreements only reluctantly. And, as John Mein revealed, they often secretly violated those agreements. In contrast, artisans supported nonimportation enthusiastically, recognizing that the absence of British goods would create a ready market

A Society of Patriotic Ladies, *1775, attributed to Philip Dawes, an English printmaker. This grotesque caricature of female patriots shows the women emptying their tea into a chamber pot (at left) and flirting with their male counterparts (at center), while a neglected child sits below the table. The cartoon bears no resemblance to the actual event, the signing of an anti-British petition by female residents of Edenton, North Carolina.* Library of Congress.

for their own manufactures. Thus tradesmen formed the core of the crowds that coerced both importers and their customers by picketing stores, publicizing offenders' names, and sometimes destroying property.

Such tactics were effective: colonial imports from England dropped dramatically in 1769, especially in New York, New England, and Pennsylvania. But they also aroused heated opposition, creating a second major division among the colonists. Some Americans who supported resistance to British measures began to question the use of violence to force others to join the boycott. In addition, wealthier and more conservative colonists were frightened by the threat to private property inherent in the campaign. Political activism by ordinary colonists challenged the ruling elite's domination,

just as they had feared in 1765. Thus a Charleston essayist who obviously wanted to protect his own position warned in 1769 that "the industrious mechanic [is] a useful and essential part of society . . . in his own sphere," but "when he steps out of it, and sets up for a statesman! believe me he is in a fair way to expose himself to ridicule, and his family to distress, by neglecting his private business."

John Mein's widely circulated disclosure that leading patriots were violating the nonimportation agreement caused dissension in the ranks of the boycotters, so Americans were relieved when news arrived in April 1770 that the Townshend duties had been repealed, with the exception of the tea tax. A new prime minister, Lord North, had persuaded Parliament that duties on trade within the empire were bad policy. Although some political leaders argued that nonimportation should continue until the tea tax was repealed, merchants quickly resumed importing. The rest of the Townshend Acts remained in force, but repeal of the taxes made the other laws appear less objectionable.

Repeal of the Townshend Duties

GROWING RIFTS

At first the new ministry did nothing to antagonize the colonists. Yet on the very day Lord North proposed repeal of the Townshend duties, a clash between civilians and soldiers in Boston led to the death of five Americans. The origins of the event that patriots called the Boston Massacre lay in repeated clashes between customs officers and the people of Massachusetts. The decision to base in Boston the American Board of Customs Commissioners (created by a Townshend Act) was the source of the problem.

From the day of their arrival in November 1767, the customs commissioners were frequent targets of mob action. In June 1768 their seizure of the patriot leader John Hancock's sloop *Liberty* on suspicion of smuggling caused a riot in which prominent customs officers' property was destroyed. The riot in turn helped to convince the ministry in London that troops were needed to maintain order in the unruly port. The assignment of two regiments of regulars to their city confirmed Bostonians' worst fears; the redcoats were a constant reminder of the oppressive potential of British power.

Accustomed to leading their lives with a minimum of interference from government, Bostonians now found themselves hemmed in at every turn. Guards on Boston Neck, the entrance to the city, checked all travelers and their goods. Redcoat patrols roamed the city day and night, questioning and sometimes harassing passers-by. Military parades were held on Boston Common, accompanied by martial music and often the public whipping of deserters and other violators of army rules. Parents began to fear for the safety of their daughters, who were subjected to the soldiers' sexual insults when they ventured out on the streets. But the greatest potential for violence lay in the uneasy relationship between the soldiers and Boston laborers. Many redcoats sought employment in their off-duty hours, competing for unskilled jobs with the city's ordinary workingmen. Members of the two groups brawled repeatedly in taverns and on the streets.

Early on the evening of March 5, 1770, a crowd of laborers began throwing hardpacked snowballs at soldiers guarding the Customs House.

Boston Massacre

Goaded beyond endurance, the sentries acted against express orders to the contrary and fired on the crowd, killing four and wounding eight, one of whom died a few days later. Resistance leaders idealized the dead rioters as martyrs for the cause of liberty, holding a solemn funeral and later commemorating March 5 annually with patriotic orations. Paul Revere's engraving of the massacre (reproduced on page 144) was part of the propaganda campaign.

The leading patriots wanted to make certain the soldiers did not become martyrs as well. Despite the political benefits the patriots derived from the massacre, it is unlikely that they approved of the crowd action that provoked it. Ever since the destruction of Hutchinson's house in August 1765, the men allied with the Sons of Liberty had supported orderly demonstrations and expressed distaste for uncontrolled riots, of which the Boston Massacre was a prime example. Thus when the soldiers were tried for the killings in November, they were defended by John Adams and Josiah Quincy, Jr., both unwavering patriots. All but two of the accused men were acquitted, and those convicted were released after being branded on the thumb. Undoubtedly the favorable outcome of the trials prevented London officials from taking further steps against the city.

For more than two years after the Boston Massacre and the repeal of the Townshend duties, a superficial calm descended on the colonies. The most outspoken colonial newspapers, such as the *Boston Gazette*, the *Pennsylvania Journal*, and the *South Carolina Gazette*, published essays drawing on Real Whig ideology and accusing Great Britain of a deliberate plan to oppress the colonies. After repeal of the Stamp Act, the patriots had praised Parliament; following repeal of the Townshend duties, they warned of impending tyranny. What had seemed to be an isolated mistake, a single ill-chosen stamp tax, now appeared to be part of a plot against American liberties. Essayists pointed to Parliament's persecution of the English radical John Wilkes, the stationing of troops in Boston, and the growing number of vice-admiralty courts as evidence of plans to enslave the colonists. Indeed, patriot writers played repeatedly on the word *enslavement*. Most white colonists had direct knowledge of slavery (either as slaveholders themselves or as neighbors of slaveowners), and the threat of enslavement by Britain must have hit them with peculiar force.

Still, no one yet advocated complete independence from the mother country. Though the patriots were becoming increasingly convinced that they should seek freedom from parliamentary authority, they continued to acknowledge their British identity and to pledge their allegiance to George III. They began, therefore, to try to envision a system that would enable them to be ruled by their own elected legislatures while remaining loyal to the king. But any such scheme was alien to Britons' conception of the nature of their government, which was that Parliament held sole undivided sovereignty over the empire. Furthermore, in the British mind, Parliament encompassed the king as well as lords and commons, and so separating the monarch from the legislature was impossible.

Then, in the fall of 1772, the North ministry began to implement the portion of the Townshend Acts that provided for governors and judges to be paid from customs revenues.

Committees of Correspondence

In early November, voters at a Boston town meeting established a Committee of Correspondence to publicize the

How do historians know

whether ordinary people were familiar with the ideas propounded by the leaders of the American Revolution? This is a difficult question to answer, because most of the evidence about the patriots' ideology comes from pamphlets and newspapers aimed at a well-educated public. Even people who could read at a basic level might not have been able to understand the sophisticated criticisms of British policies advanced in such writings. Because the engraver made his point visually rather than verbally, anyone, even illiterate folk, could inter- *pret an image like Paul Revere's masterful portrayal of the Boston Massacre. The label "Butcher's Hall" on the customs house merely reinforces a patriot's view of the incident on March 5, 1770. The British soldiers are shown firing on an unresisting crowd (not the aggressive, angry mob described at the soldiers' trial), and a gun with smoke drifting up from its barrel emerges from a window above the redcoats, suggesting the complicity of civilian officials in what the patriots interpreted as an outrageous act.*   Photo: Library of Congress.

decision by exchanging letters with other Massachusetts towns. Heading the committee was the man who had proposed its formation, Samuel Adams.

Samuel Adams was fifty-one in 1772, thirteen years older than his distant cousin John and a decade the senior of most other leaders of American resistance. He had been a Boston tax collector, a member and clerk of the Massachusetts assembly, an ally of the Loyal Nine, and a member of the Sons of Liberty. His primary forum was the Boston town meeting. Unswerving in his devotion to the American cause, Adams drew a sharp contrast between a corrupt, vice-ridden Britain and the colonies, peopled by simple, liberty-loving folk. An experienced political organizer, Adams continually stressed the necessity of prudent collective action. His Committee of Correspondence thus undertook the task of creating an informed consensus among all the citizens of Massachusetts.

Such committees, which were eventually established throughout the colonies, represented the next logical step in the organization of American resistance. Until 1772, the protest movement was largely confined to the seacoast and primarily to major cities and towns (see maps, page 138). Adams realized that the time had come to widen the movement's geographic scope, to attempt to involve the residents of the interior in the struggle. Accordingly, the Boston town meeting directed the Committee of Correspondence "to state the Rights of the Colonists and of this Province in particular," to list "the Infringements and Violations thereof that have been, or from time to time may be made," and to send copies to the other towns in the province. In return, Boston requested "a free communication of their Sentiments on this Subject."

Samuel Adams, James Otis, Jr., and Josiah Quincy, Jr., prepared the statement of the colonists' rights. Declaring that Americans had absolute rights to life, liberty, and property, the committee asserted that the idea that "a British house of commons, should have a right, at pleasure, to give and grant the property of the colonists" was "irreconcileable" with "the first principles of natural law and Justice . . . and of the British Constitution in particular." The list of grievances, drafted by another group of prominent patriots, was similarly sweeping. It complained of taxation without representation, the presence of unnecessary troops and customs officers on American soil, the use of imperial revenues to pay colonial officials, the expanded jurisdiction of vice-admiralty courts, and even the nature of the instructions given to American governors by their superiors in London.

The entire document, which was printed as a pamphlet for distribution to the towns, exhibited none of the hesitation that had characterized colonial claims against Parliament in the 1760s. No longer were patriots—at least in Boston—preoccupied with defining the precise limits of parliamentary authority. No longer did they mention the necessity of obedience to Parliament. They were committed to a course that placed American rights first, loyalty to Great Britain a distant second.

The response of the Massachusetts towns to the committee's pamphlet must have caused Samuel Adams to rejoice. Some towns disagreed with Boston's assessment of the state of affairs, but most aligned themselves with the city. From Braintree came the assertion that "all civil officers are or ought to be Servants to the people and dependent upon them for their official Support, and every instance to the Contrary from the Governor downwards tends to crush and destroy civil liberty." The town of Holden declared that "the People of New England have never given the People of Britain any Right of Jurisdiction over us." The citizens of Petersham commented that resistance to tyranny was "the first and highest social Duty of this people." And Pownallborough warned, "Allegiance is a relative Term and like Kingdoms and commonwealths is local and has its bounds." It was beliefs like these that made the next crisis in Anglo-American affairs the final one.

THE BOSTON TEA PARTY

The only one of the Townshend duties still in effect by 1773 was the tax on tea. In the years since 1770 some Americans had continued to boycott English tea, while others had resumed drinking it either openly or in secret. Tea had long been an important component of the Anglo-American diet, and the possession of teapots and matched sets of cups indicated high status. Well-to-do Americans, women and men alike, socialized frequently at private tea parties, so that observing the tea boycott required colonial elites not only to change the beverage they habitually drank but also to alter their lifestyles. Tea thus retained an explosively symbolic character even though the boycott was less than fully effective after 1770.

In May 1773, Parliament passed an act designed to save the East India Company from bankruptcy. The company, which held a legal monopoly on British trade with the

Tea Act

———

East Indies, was of critical importance to the British economy (and to the financial well-being of many prominent British politicians who had invested in its stock). Under the Tea Act, certain duties paid on tea were to be returned to the company. Tea was to be sold only by designated agents, which would enable the East India Company to avoid colonial middlemen and undersell any competitors, even smugglers. The net result would be cheaper tea for American consumers. But resistance leaders interpreted the new measure as a pernicious device to make them admit Parliament's right to tax them, since the less-expensive tea would still be taxed under the Townshend law. Others saw the Tea Act as the first step in the establishment of an East India Company monopoly of all colonial trade. Residents of the four cities designated to receive the first shipments of tea accordingly prepared to respond to what they perceived as a new threat to their freedom.

In New York City, the tea ships failed to arrive on schedule. In Philadelphia, the captain was persuaded to turn around and sail back to England. In Charleston, the tea was unloaded, stored under the direction of local tradesmen, and later destroyed. The only confrontation occurred in Boston, where both sides—the town meeting, joined by participants from nearby towns, and Governor Thomas Hutchinson, two of whose sons were tea agents—rejected compromise.

The first of three tea ships, the *Dartmouth*, entered Boston harbor on November 28. Under the customs laws, a cargo had to be landed and the appropriate duty paid by its owners within twenty days of a ship's arrival. Otherwise, the cargo would be seized by customs officers and sold at auction. After a series of mass meetings, Bostonians voted to prevent the tea from being unloaded and to post guards on the wharf. Hutchinson, for his part, refused to permit the vessels to leave the harbor.

On December 16, one day before the cargo would have to be confiscated, more than five thousand people (nearly a third of the city's population) crowded into Old South Church. The meeting, chaired by Samuel Adams, made a final attempt to persuade Hutchinson to send the tea back to England. But Hutchinson remained adamant. At about 6 P.M. Adams reportedly announced "that he

could think of nothing further to be done—that they had now done all they could for the Salvation of their Country." As if his statement were a planned signal, cries rang out from the back of the crowd: "Boston harbor a tea-pot tonight! The Mohawks are come!" Small groups pushed their way out of the meeting. Within a few minutes, about sixty men crudely disguised as Indians assembled at the wharf, boarded the three ships, and dumped the cargo into the harbor. By 9 P.M. their work was done: 342 chests of tea worth approximately £10,000 floated in splinters on the water.

Among the "Indians" were many representatives of Boston's artisans. Five masons, eleven carpenters and builders, three leatherworkers, a blacksmith, a hatter, three coopers, two barbers, a coachmaker, a silversmith, and twelve apprentices have been identified as participants. That their ranks also included four farmers from outside Boston, ten merchants, two doctors, a teacher, and a bookseller illustrated the widespread support for the resistance movement. The next day John Adams exulted in his diary that the Tea Party was "so bold, so daring, so firm, intrepid and inflexible" that "I can't but consider it as an epoch in history."

The North administration reacted with considerably less enthusiasm when it learned of the Tea Party. In March 1774, the ministry proposed the

Coercive and Quebec Acts

———

first of four laws that became known as the Coercive, or Intolerable, Acts. It called for closing the port of Boston until the tea was paid for and prohibiting all but coastal trade in food and firewood. Colonial sympathizers in Parliament were easily outvoted by those who wished to punish the city that had been the center of opposition to British policies. Later in the spring, Parliament passed three other punitive measures. The Massachusetts Government Act altered the province's charter, substituting an appointed council for the elected one, increasing the powers of the governor, and forbidding special town meetings. The Justice Act provided that a person accused of committing murder in the course of suppressing a riot or enforcing the laws could be tried outside the colony where the incident had occurred. Finally, a new Quartering Act gave broad authority to military commanders seeking to house their troops in private dwellings. Thus the Coercive Acts punished not only

Boston but Massachusetts as a whole, and alerted other colonies to the possibility that their residents, too, could be subject to retaliation if they opposed British authority.

After passing the last of the Coercive Acts in early June, Parliament turned its attention to much-needed reforms in the government of Quebec. The Quebec Act, though unrelated to the Coercive Acts, thereby became linked with them in the minds of the patriots. Intended to ease the strains that had arisen since the British conquest of the formerly French colony, the Quebec Act granted greater religious freedom to Catholics—alarming the Protestant colonists, who equated Roman Catholicism with religious and political despotism. It also reinstated French civil law, which operated without juries and had been replaced by British procedures in 1763, and it established an appointed council (rather than an elected legislature) as the governing body of the colony. Finally, in an attempt to provide the northern Indian tribes some protection against white settlement, the act annexed to Quebec the area east of the Mississippi River and north of the Ohio River. That region, parts of which were claimed by individual seacoast colonies, was thus removed from their jurisdiction.

Members of Parliament who voted for the punitive legislation believed that the acts would be obeyed and that at long last they had solved the problem posed by the troublesome Americans. But the patriots showed little inclination to bow to the wishes of Parliament. In their eyes, the Coercive Acts and the Quebec Act proved what they had feared since 1768: that Great Britain had embarked on a deliberate plan to oppress them. If the port of Boston could be closed, why not those of Philadelphia or New York? If the royal charter of Massachusetts could be changed, why not that of South Carolina? If certain people could be removed from their home colonies for trial, why not all violators of all laws? If troops could be forcibly quartered in private houses, did not that pave the way for the occupation of all of America? If the Roman Catholic church could receive favored status in Quebec, why not everywhere? It seemed as though the full dimensions of the plot against American rights and liberties had at last been revealed.

The Boston Committee of Correspondence urged all the colonies to join in an immediate boycott of British goods. But the other provinces were not yet ready to take such a drastic step. They

Thomas Hutchinson, the governor of Massachusetts who helped to incite the Boston Tea Party by refusing to allow the tea ships to leave the harbor, a solution adopted in Pennsylvania by a governor less intent on seeking a confrontation with colonial resistance leaders. John Singleton Copley's portrait of the haughty Hutchinson reveals the governor's uncompromising character.   Massachusetts Historical Society.

suggested that another intercolonial congress be convened to consider an appropriate response. Few people wanted to take hasty action; even the most ardent patriots remained loyal to Britain and hoped for reconciliation with its leaders. Despite their objections to British policy, they continued to see themselves as part of the empire. Americans were approaching the brink of confrontation, but they had not committed themselves to an irrevocable break. And so the colonies agreed to send delegates to Philadelphia in September.

During the preceding decade, momentous changes had occurred in the ways colonists thought about themselves and their allegiance. The number of colonists who defined themselves as political actors had increased substantially. Once linked unquestioningly to Great Britain, they had begun to develop a sense of their own identity as Americans, including a recognition of the cultural and social gulf that separated them from Britons. They had started to realize that their concept of the political process differed from that held by people in the mother country. They had also come to understand that their economic interests did not necessarily coincide with those of Great Britain. Colonial political leaders reached such conclusions only after a long train of events, some of them violent, had altered their understanding of the nature of their relationship with the mother country. Parliamentary acts such as the Stamp Act and the Townshend Acts had elicited colonial responses—both ideological and practical—that produced further responses from Britain. Tensions escalated until they climaxed in the Tea Party. From that point on, there was to be no turning back.

In the late summer of 1774, the Americans were committed to resistance but not to independence. Even so, they had started to sever the bonds of empire. During the next decade, they would forge the bonds of a new American nationality to replace those rejected Anglo-American ties.

SUGGESTIONS FOR FURTHER READING

General

Ian R. Christie, *Crisis of Empire: Great Britain and the American Colonies, 1754–1783* (1966); Ian R. Christie and Benjamin W. Labaree, *Empire or Independence, 1760–1776: A British-American Dialogue on the Coming of the American Revolution* (1976); Edward Countryman, *The American Revolution* (1985); Marc Egnal, *A Mighty Empire: The Origins of the American Revolution* (1988); Merrill Jensen, *The Founding of a Nation: A History of the American Revolution, 1763–1776* (1968); Edmund S. Morgan, *The Birth of the Republic, 1763–1789* (1956); Robert W. Tucker and David C. Hendrickson, *The Fall of the First British Empire: Origin of the War of American Independence* (1982).

Colonial Warfare and the British Empire

Fred Anderson, *A People's Army: Massachusetts Soldiers and Society in the Seven Years' War* (1984); Lawrence Henry Gipson, *The British Empire Before the American Revolution*, 15 vols. (1936–1970); Douglas Leach, *Roots of Conflict: British Armed Forces and Colonial Americans, 1677–1763* (1986); Robert C. Newbold, *The Albany Congress and Plan of Union of 1754* (1955); Howard H.

Peckham, *The Colonial Wars, 1689–1762* (1963); William Pencak, *War, Politics, and Revolution in Provincial Massachusetts* (1981); Alan Rogers, *Empire and Liberty: American Resistance to British Authority, 1755–1763* (1974); John Shy, *Toward Lexington: The Role of the British Army in the Coming of the American Revolution* (1965); James Titus, *The Old Dominion at War: Society, Politics, and Warfare in Late Colonial Virginia* (1991).

British Politics and Policy

Colin Bonwick, *English Radicals and the American Revolution* (1977); John Brewer, *Party Ideology and Popular Politics at the Accession of George III* (1976); John Brooke, *King George III* (1972); John L. Bullion, *A Great and Necessary Measure: George Grenville and the Genesis of the Stamp Act, 1763–1765* (1981); Bernard Donoughue, *British Politics and the American Revolution: The Path to War, 1773–1775* (1965); Michael Kammen, *A Rope of Sand: The Colonial Agents, British Politics, and the American Revolution* (1968); P.D.G. Thomas, *The Townshend Duties Crisis* (1987); P.D.G. Thomas, *British Politics and the Stamp Act Crisis* (1975); Carl Ubbelohde, *The Vice-Admiralty Courts and the American Revolution* (1960).

Native Americans and the West

John R. Alden, *John Stuart and the Southern Colonial Frontier* (1944); Richard Aquila, *The Iroquois Restoration: Iroquois Diplomacy on the Colonial Frontier, 1701–1754* (1983); David H. Corkran, *The Cherokee Frontier: Conflict and Survival, 1740–1762* (1962); Gregory Dowd, *A Spirited Resistance: The North American Indian Struggle for Unity, 1745–1815* (1992); Francis Jennings, *Empire of Fortune: Crowns, Colonies and Tribes in the Seven Years' War in America* (1988); Georgiana C. Nammack, *Fraud, Politics, and the Dispossession of the Indians: The Iroquois Land Frontier in the Colonial Period* (1969); Howard H. Peckham, *Pontiac and the Indian Uprising* (1947); Jack M. Sosin, *Whitehall and the Wilderness: The Middle West in British Colonial Policy, 1760–1775* (1961); Richard White, *The Middle Ground: Indians, Empires and Republics in the Great Lakes Region, 1650–1815* (1991).

Political and Economic Thought

Bernard Bailyn, *The Ideological Origins of the American Revolution* (1967); J. E. Crowley, *This Sheba, Self: The Conceptualization of Economic Life in Eighteenth-Century America* (1974); Jay Fliegelman, *Prodigals and Pilgrims: The American Revolution Against Patriarchal Authority, 1750–1800* (1982); J.G.A. Pocock, *The Machiavellian Moment: Florentine Political Thought and the Atlantic Republican Tradition* (1975); Caroline Robbins, *The Eighteenth-Century Commonwealthman* (1959); Clinton Rossiter, *Seedtime of the Republic: The Origin of the American Tradition of Political Liberty* (1953).

American Resistance

David Ammerman, *In the Common Cause: American Response to the Coercive Acts of 1774* (1974); Richard Beeman, *Patrick Henry: A Biography* (1974); Richard D. Brown, *Revolutionary Politics in Massachusetts: The Boston Committee of Correspondence and the Towns, 1772–1774* (1970); Joseph Albert Ernst, *Money and Poli-*

tics in America, 1755–1775: A Study in the Currency Act of 1764 and the Political Economy of Revolution (1973); Paul Gilje, The Road to Mobocracy: Popular Disorder in New York City, 1763–1834 (1987); Dirk Hoerder, Crowd Action in Revolutionary Massachusetts, 1765-1780 (1977); Rhys Isaac, The Transformation of Virginia, 1740–1790 (1982); Benjamin W. Labaree, The Boston Tea Party (1964); Pauline R. Maier, The Old Revolutionaries: Political Lives in the Age of Samuel Adams (1980); Pauline R. Maier, From Resistance to Revolution: Colonial Radicals and the Development of American Opposition to Britain, 1765–1776 (1972); Edmund S. Morgan and Helen M. Morgan, The Stamp Act Crisis: Prologue to Revolution (1953); Gary B. Nash, The Urban Crucible: Social Change, Political Consciousness, and the Origins of the American Revolution (1979); Richard Ryerson, The Revolution Has Now Begun: The Radical Committees of Philadelphia, 1765–1776 (1978); Peter Shaw, American Patriots and the Rituals of Revolution (1981); John W. Tyler, Smugglers and Patriots: Boston Merchants and the Advent of the American Revolution (1986); Richard Walsh, Charleston's Sons of Liberty: A Study of the Artisans, 1763-1789 (1959); Alfred F. Young, ed., The American Revolution: Explorations in the History of American Radicalism (1976); Hiller B. Zobel, The Boston Massacre (1970).

6

A Revolution, Indeed, 1775–1783

W HEN JOHN PROVEY AND Richard Weaver appeared before the loyalist claims commissioners in London at the end of the Revolution, the commissioners were not impressed with their descriptions of losses and loyal service to the king. Such men had "no right to ask or expect any thing from Government," the commissioners declared. Their applications "hardly deserve[d] a serious Investigation or a serious Answer." So Provey and Weaver, along with most of the forty-five other men in the same circumstances, were denied any assistance from the funds allocated by Parliament to compensate loyalists for the damages they had incurred by opposing the Revolution. Why were Weaver and Provey treated thus? They were, quite simply, African-Americans.

John Provey, a North Carolinian, had been the slave of a lawyer; Richard Weaver, a Philadelphian, claimed to be freeborn. Provey had served in a black corps of the British army during the war, whereas Weaver had left Philadelphia with the British troops when they evacuated that city in 1778 and had made his way to London the following year. Both had wives and children at the time they requested government assistance. Because they were denied the help they sought, they and their families, along with hundreds of other

African-Americans, became dependent on charity disbursed by a group of civic-minded London merchants, the Committee to Aid the Black Poor, which was formed in 1786.

Seeing no future for themselves in London, they both agreed to emigrate to West Africa, to the new colony of Sierra Leone, which was being sponsored by the Black Poor Committee. John Provey did not make it to his destination; he died on shipboard before the vessels even left London. But Richard Weaver went to Sierra Leone and was elected the first governor of the tiny colony, composed largely of exiled African-American loyalists. Conflicts with a nearby tribal chief and with slavers who established a post near the settlement almost destroyed it. But in 1792 the future of the colony was assured when an additional twelve hundred African-American refugees arrived from Nova Scotia, where they had fled immediately after the war.

The little-known tale of the black loyalists who returned to the homeland of their ancestors is but one dramatic example of the disruptive effects of the American Revolution. The Revolution was more than just a series of clashes between British and patriot armies. It uprooted thousands of families, disrupted the economy, reshaped society

John Trumbull painted Washington and his officers participating in "The Surrender of Lord Cornwallis at Yorktown" six years after the event.

"The Wise Men of Gotham and Their Goose," published in 1776, was a British satirist's look at his nation's American policy. The cartoonist showed British politicians in the process of killing the colonial goose that laid the golden eggs (displayed in a basket in the background) while the British lion slumbers overhead and the king watches unemotionally. As in the cartoon of the "Patriotic Ladies" on page 142, a urinating dog symbolizes the artist's disgust with the proceedings.   Courtesy of the John Carter Brown Library at Brown University.

To enforce the Continental Association, Congress recommended the election of committees of observation and inspection in every county, city,

Committees of Observation

and town in America. By specifying that committee members be chosen by all persons qualified to vote for members of the lower house of the colonial legislatures, Congress guaranteed the committees a broad popular base. In some places the committeemen were former local officeholders; in other towns they were obscure men who had never before held office. Everywhere, these committeemen— perhaps seven to eight thousand of them in the colonies as a whole—became the local leaders of American resistance.

Such committees were officially charged only with overseeing implementation of the boycott, but over the next six months they became de facto governments. They examined merchants' records and published the names of those who continued to import British goods. They also promoted home manufactures and encouraged Americans to adopt simple modes of dress and behavior to symbolize their commitment to liberty and virtuous behavior. Since expensive leisure-time activities were believed to reflect vice and corruption, Congress urged Americans to forgo dancing, gambling, horse racing, cock fighting, and other forms of "extravagance and dissipation." Some committees accordingly forbade dancing, extracted apologies from people caught gambling or racing, prohibited the slaughter of lambs (because of the need for wool), and offered prizes for the best locally made cloth.

Thus the committees gradually extended their authority over many aspects of American life. In particular, they attempted to identify opponents of American resistance, developing elaborate spy networks, circulating copies of the Continental Association for signatures, and investigating reports of dissident remarks and activities. Suspected dissenters were first urged to convert to the colonial cause; if they failed to do so, the committees had them watched, restricted their movements, or tried to force them to leave the area. People engaging in casual political exchanges with friends one day could find themselves charged with "treasonable conversation" the next. One Massachusetts man, for example, was called before his local committee for maligning the Congress as "a Pack or Parcell of Fools" that was "as tyrannical as Lord North and ought to be opposed & resisted." When he refused to recant, the committee ordered him watched.

Those who dissented more openly received harsher treatment, as the experiences of the Reverend John Agnew of Virginia demonstrate. Agnew, an Anglican, insisted on warning his congregation of "the danger and sin of rebellion." He rejected the committee's summons and was thereafter ostracized by its order. Millers would not grind his corn, and doctors would not treat his sick wife and children. The committee tried to intimidate him by sending armed men to his church to beat drums and drill during services. When that failed, the patriots nailed shut the church's doors and windows. Finally Agnew and his oldest son fled, but the persecution of his wife and younger children continued. She was, she later recalled, "daily insulted and robbed . . . [and] searched under various pretense."

While the committees of observation were expanding their power during the winter and early spring of 1775, the established governments of the colonies were collapsing. Only in Connecticut, Rhode Island, Delaware, and Pennsylvania did colonial legislatures continue to meet without encountering patriot challenges to their authority. In every other colony, popularly elected provincial conventions took over the task of running the government, sometimes entirely replacing the legislatures and at other times holding concurrent sessions. In late 1774 and early 1775, these conventions approved the Continental Association, elected delegates to the Second Continental Congress (scheduled for May), organized militia units, and gathered arms and ammunition. Unable to stem the tide of resistance, the British-appointed governors and councils watched helplessly as their authority crumbled.

Provincial Conventions

The frustrating experience of Governor Josiah Martin of North Carolina is a case in point. When a provincial convention was called to meet at New Bern on April 4, 1775—the same day the legislature was to convene—Martin proclaimed that "the Assembly of this province duly elected is the only true and lawful representation of the people." He asked all citizens to "renounce disclaim and discourage all such meetings cabals and illegal proceedings . . . which can only tend to introduce disorder and anarchy." Martin's proclamation had no visible effect, and when the convention met at New Bern its membership proved to be virtually identical to that of the colonial legislature. The delegates proceeded to act alternately in both capacities and even passed some joint resolves. Continuing the farce, the exasperated Martin delivered a speech to the assembly denouncing the election of the convention. On April 7, Martin admitted to Lord Dartmouth, secretary of state for America in North's ministry, that his government was "absolutely prostrate, impotent, and that nothing but the shadow of it is left."

Royal officials in the other colonies suffered the same frustrations. Courts were prevented from holding sessions; taxes were paid to agents of the conventions rather than to provincial tax collectors; sheriffs' powers were questioned; and militiamen refused to muster except by order of the local committees. In short, during the six months preceding the battles at Lexington and Concord, independence was being won at the local level, but without formal acknowledgment and for the most part without bloodshed. Not many Americans fully realized what was happening. The vast majority still proclaimed their loyalty to Great Britain and denied that they sought to leave the empire. Among the few who most clearly recognized the trend toward independence were those who opposed it.

CHOOSING SIDES: LOYALISTS, AFRICAN-AMERICANS, AND INDIANS

The first protests against British measures, in the mid-1760s, had won the support of most colonists. Only in the late 1760s and early 1770s did a significant number of Americans begin to question both the aims and the tactics of the resistance movement. By 1774 and 1775 such people found themselves in a difficult position. Like their more radical counterparts, most of them objected to parliamentary policies and wanted some kind of constitutional reform. Joseph Galloway, for instance, was a conservative by American standards, but his plan for restructuring the empire was too novel for Britain to accept. Nevertheless, if forced to a choice, these colonists sympathized with Great Britain rather than with an independent America. The events of the crucial year between the passage of the Coercive Acts and the outbreak of fighting in Massachusetts crystallized their thinking. Their objections to violent protest, their desire to uphold the legally constituted colonial governments, and their fears of anarchy combined to make them especially sensitive to the dangers of resistance.

Some conservatives began in 1774 and 1775 to publish essays and pamphlets critical of the Congress and its allied committees. In New York City, a group of Anglican clergymen jointly wrote pamphlets and essays arguing the importance of maintaining a cordial connection between England and America. In Pennsylvania, Joseph Galloway published *A Candid Examination of the Mutual Claims of*

Great Britain and the Colonies, attacking the Continental Congress for rejecting his plan of union. In Massachusetts, the young attorney Daniel Leonard, writing under the pseudonym Massachusettensis, engaged in a prolonged newspaper debate with Novanglus (John Adams). Leonard and the others realized that what had begun as a dispute over the extent of American subordination within the empire had now raised the question of whether the colonies would remain linked to Great Britain at all. "Rouse up at last from your slumber!" the Reverend Thomas Bradbury Chandler of New Jersey cried out to Americans. "There is a set of people among us . . . who have formed a scheme for establishing an independent government or empire in America."

Some colonists heeded the conservative pamphleteers' warnings. About one-fifth of the white American population remained loyal to Great Britain, actively opposing independence and remaining true to the colonial self-conception once held by most eighteenth-century white Americans. In other words, it was the patriots who changed their allegiance, not the loyalists. What is surprising is that there were so few active loyalists, not that there were so many.

Loyalists, Patriots, and Neutrals

With notable exceptions, most people of the following descriptions remained loyal to the Crown: British-appointed government officials; merchants whose trade depended on imperial connections; Anglican clergy everywhere and lay Anglicans in the North, where their denomination was in the minority (since the king was the head of their church as well as head of state); former officers and enlisted men from the British army, many of whom had settled in America after 1763; non-English ethnic minorities, especially Scots; tenant farmers, particularly those whose landlords sided with the patriots; members of persecuted religious sects; and many of the backcountry southerners who had rebelled against eastern rule in the 1760s and early 1770s. All these people had one thing in common: the patriot leaders were their long-standing opponents, though for varying reasons. Ethnic minorities in particular had long felt excluded from the colonial political process. Local and provincial disputes thus helped to determine which side people chose in the imperial conflict.

The active patriots, who accounted for about two-fifths of the population, came chiefly from the groups that had dominated colonial society, either numerically or politically. Among them were yeoman farmers, members of dominant Protestant sects (both Old and New Lights), Chesapeake gentry, merchants dealing mainly in American commodities, city artisans, elected officeholders, and people of English descent. Wives usually but not always adopted their husbands' political beliefs. Although all these patriots supported the Revolution, they pursued divergent goals within the broader coalition, as they had in the 1760s. Some sought limited political reform, others extensive political change, and still others social and economic reforms. (The ways in which their concerns interacted are discussed in Chapter 7.)

There remained in the middle perhaps two-fifths of the white population. Some of those who tried to avoid taking sides were sincere pacifists, such as Pennsylvania Quakers. Others opportunistically shifted their allegiance depending on which side happened to be winning at the time. Still others simply wanted to be left alone to lead their lives; they cared little about politics and normally obeyed whichever side controlled their area. But such colonists also resisted the British and the Americans alike when the demands on them seemed too heavy—when taxes became too high, for example, or when calls for militia service came too often. Their attitude might best be summed up in the phrase "a plague on both your houses." Such persons made up an especially large proportion of the population in the southern backcountry, where Scotch-Irish settlers had little love for either the patriot gentry or the English authorities.

To American patriots, that sort of apathy or neutrality was a crime as heinous as loyalism. Those who were not for them were against them; in their minds, there could be no conscientious objectors. By the winter of 1775–1776, less than a year after the battles of Lexington and Concord, the Second Continental Congress was recommending to the states that all "disaffected" persons be disarmed and arrested. The state legislatures quickly passed laws prescribing severe penalties for suspected loyalists. Many began to require all voters (or, in some cases, all free adult males) to take oaths of allegiance; the punishment for refusal was usually banishment or extra taxes. After 1777,

John Singleton Copley, the American artist, married into a loyalist family—his father-in-law, Richard Clarke, was one of the Boston tea agents in 1773. Copley was in Italy studying art when the war began but joined his exiled wife and father-in-law in London in 1776. His sentimental portrait of the family (with himself in the background) commemorated their reunion. The only person in the painting who ever returned to America was his daughter Elizabeth (center), who grew up to marry a Bostonian. Andrew W. Mellon Fund © National Gallery of Art, Washington, D.C.

many states confiscated the property of banished loyalists and used the proceeds for the war effort.

During the war, loyalists tended to congregate in cities held by the British army. When those posts were evacuated at the end of the war, the loyalists scattered to different parts of the British Empire—England, the West Indies, and especially Canada. In the provinces of Nova Scotia, New Brunswick, and Ontario they re-created their lives as colonists, laying the foundations of British Canada. All told, perhaps as many as 100,000 white Americans preferred to leave their homeland rather than live in a nation independent of British rule.

That preference attests to the depth of their loyalty to the monarchy and to an Anglo-American definition of their identity.

The patriots' policies helped to ensure that the weak, scattered, and persecuted loyalists could not band together to threaten the revolutionary cause. But loyalists were not the patriots' only worry. They had reason to believe that Indians and slaves might join the forces arrayed against them. Early in the war, free blacks from New England enlisted in local patriot militias, but the revolutionaries could not assume that enslaved African-Americans would also support the struggle for independence.

Slaves faced a dilemma at the beginning of the Revolution: how could they best pursue their goal of escaping perpetual servitude? Should they fight with or against their white masters? With no correct choice immediately apparent, African-Americans made different decisions. Some indeed joined the revolutionaries, but to most an alliance with the British appeared more promising. Thus news of slave conspiracies surfaced in different parts of the colonies in late 1774 and early 1775. All shared a common element: a plan to assist the British in return for freedom. One group of slaves futilely petitioned General Thomas Gage, the commander-in-chief of the British army in Boston, promising to fight for the redcoats if he would liberate them. The most serious incident occurred in 1775 in Charleston, where Thomas Jeremiah, a free black harbor pilot, was brutally executed after being convicted of attempting to foment a slave revolt.

African-Americans' Dilemma

A fear of such acts made white residents of the British West Indian colonies far more cautious in their opposition to parliamentary policies than their counterparts on the mainland. On most of the Caribbean islands, blacks outnumbered whites by six or seven to one. With the ever-present threat of slave revolt or foreign attack hanging over their heads, the planters could not afford to risk opposing Britain, their chief protector. The Jamaica assembly agreed with the mainland colonial legislatures that citizens should not be bound by laws to which they had not consented. Nevertheless, its members assured the king in 1774 that "it cannot be supposed, that we now intend, or ever could have intended Resistance to Great Britain." They cited as reasons Jamaica's "weak and feeble" condition, "its very small number of white inhabitants, and . . . the incumbrance of more than Two hundred thousand Slaves."

Racial Composition and Patriotic Fervor

Racial composition affected politics in the continental colonies as well. In the North, where whites greatly outnumbered blacks, revolutionary fervor was at its height. In Virginia and Maryland, where whites constituted a safe majority of the population, there was occasional alarm over potential slave revolts but no disabling fear. But in South Carolina, which was over 60 percent black, and in Georgia, where the racial balance was nearly even, whites were noticeably less enthusiastic about resistance. Georgia sent no delegates to the First Continental Congress and reminded its representatives at the Second Continental Congress to consider its circumstances, "with our blacks and tories within us," when voting on the question of independence.

The whites' worst fears were realized in November 1775, when Lord Dunmore, the governor of Virginia, offered to free any slaves and indentured servants who would leave their patriot masters to join the British forces. Dunmore hoped to use African-Americans in his fight against the revolutionaries and to disrupt the economy by depriving white Americans of their labor force. But the African-Americans who rallied to the British standard in 1775 and 1776 were fewer than expected (at most two thousand), and many of them perished in a smallpox epidemic. Even so, Dunmore's proclamation led Congress in January 1776 to modify an earlier policy that had prohibited the enlistment of blacks in the Continental Army.

Although African-Americans did not pose a serious threat to the revolutionary cause in its early years, the patriots turned rumors of slave uprisings to their own advantage. In South Carolina, they won adherents by promoting white unity under the revolutionary banner. The Continental Association was needed, they argued, to protect whites from blacks at a time when the royal government was unable to muster adequate defense forces. Undoubtedly many wavering Carolinians were drawn into the revolutionary camp by fear that an overt division among the colony's whites would encourage a slave revolt.

Similarly, the threat of Indian attacks helped persuade some reluctant westerners to support the struggle against Great Britain. In the years since the Proclamation of 1763, British officials had won the trust of the interior tribes by attempting to protect them from land-hungry whites. The British-appointed superintendents of Indian affairs, John Stuart in the South and Sir William Johnson in the North, lived among and understood the Indians. In 1768, Stuart and Johnson negotiated separate agreements modifying the proclamation line and attempting to draw realistic, defensible boundaries between tribal holdings and white settlements. The two treaties—signed at Hard Labor

Creek, South Carolina, and at Fort Stanwix, New York—supposedly established permanent western borders for the colonies. But just a few years later, in the treaties of Lochaber (1770) and Augusta (1773), the British pushed the southern boundary even farther west to accommodate the demands of whites in western Georgia and Kentucky.

By the time of the Revolution, the tribes were impatient with white Americans' aggressive pressure on their lands. The relationship of the Indians and frontier whites was **Indians' Grievances** filled with bitterness, misunderstanding, and occasional bloody encounters. In combination with the tribes' confidence in Stuart and Johnson, such grievances predisposed most Indians toward an alliance with the British. Even so, the latter hesitated to make full and immediate use of these potential allies. The superintendents were aware that neither tribal war aims nor the Indians' style of fighting were necessarily compatible with those of the British. Accordingly, Stuart and Guy Johnson (who became northern superintendent following his uncle's death) sought from the tribes nothing more than a promise of neutrality. The superintendents even helped to prevent a general Indian uprising in the summer of 1774. Through clever maneuvering, they ensured that the Shawnees attracted few tribal allies for an attack on frontier villages in Kentucky. Lord Dunmore's War, between the Shawnees and the Virginia militia, ended with Kentucky being opened to white settlement but with hunting and fishing rights still reserved to the Shawnees.

Recognizing that their standing with the tribes was poor, the patriots also sought the Indians' neutrality. In 1775 the Second Continental Congress sent a general message to the tribes describing the war as "a family quarrel between us and Old England" and requesting that they "not join on either side" since "you Indians are not concerned in it." A branch of the Cherokee tribe, led by Chief Dragging Canoe, nevertheless decided that the whites' family quarrel would allow them to settle some old scores. They attacked white settlements along the western borders of the Carolinas and Virginia in the summer of 1776. But a coordinated campaign by Carolina and Virginia militia destroyed many Cherokee towns, along with crops and large quantities of supplies. Dragging Canoe and his diehard followers fled west to the Tennessee River, where

In 1776 Benjamin West painted this portrait of Colonel Guy Johnson, the superintendent for Indian affairs in the northern district of America, while he was in London for consultations with British officials. In the background is a man thought to be the Mohawk Chief Joseph Brant (see page 170). Andrew Mellon Fund © National Gallery of Art, Washington, D.C.

they established new outposts; the rest of the Cherokees agreed to a treaty that ceded more of their land to the whites.

The fate of the Shawnees and Cherokees—each failing to enlist other Indian allies, and both more easily defeated as a result—foreshadowed the history of tribal involvement **Lack of Unity Among Native Americans** in the American Revolution. During the eighteenth century the Iroquois had forcefully established their dominance over neighboring tribes. But the basis of their power started to disintegrate with the British victory over France in 1763, and their subsequent friendship with Sir William Johnson could not prevent the erosion of their position. Tribes long resentful of Iroquois power (or of the similar status of the Cherokees in the South) saw little reason to ally themselves with those whose dominance they had just escaped, even to prevent white encroachment on their lands. Consequently, during the Revolution most tribes pursued a course that aligned them with neither side and (as the American leaders wanted) kept them out of active involvement in the war.

Thus, although the patriots could never completely ignore the threats posed by loyalists, neutrals, slaves, and Indians, only rarely did fear of these groups seriously hamper the revolutionary movement. Occasionally militia on the frontier refused to turn out for duty on the seaboard because they feared Indians would attack in their absence. Sometimes southern troops refused to serve in the North because they (and their political leaders) were unwilling to leave the South unprotected against a slave insurrection. But the practical impossibility of a large-scale slave revolt, coupled with tribal feuds and the patriots' successful campaign to disarm and neutralize loyalists, ensured that the revolutionaries would remain firmly in control as they fought for independence.

WAR BEGINS

On January 27, 1775, Lord Dartmouth, secretary of state for America, addressed a fateful letter to General Thomas Gage in Boston. Expressing his belief that American resistance was nothing more than the response of a "rude rabble without plan," Dartmouth ordered Gage to arrest "the principal actors and abettors in the provincial congress." If such a step were taken swiftly and silently, Dartmouth observed, no bloodshed need occur. Opposition could not be "very formidable," Dartmouth wrote, and even if it were, "it will surely be better that the Conflict should be brought on, upon such ground, than in a riper state of Rebellion."

Because of poor sailing weather, Dartmouth's letter did not reach Gage until April 14. The main patriot leaders had by then left Boston, and Gage did not believe that arresting them would serve a useful purpose anyway. The order nevertheless spurred him to action: he decided to send an expedition to confiscate provincial military supplies stockpiled at Concord. Bosto-

Battles of Lexington and Concord

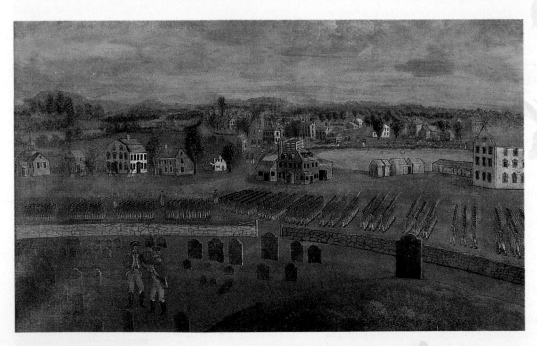

In 1775, Ralph Earle, an American artist and militiaman, painted the redcoat troops entering Concord. The fighting at North Bridge, which occurred just a few hours after this triumphal entry, signaled the start of open warfare between Britain and the colonies. Concord Antiquarian Society.

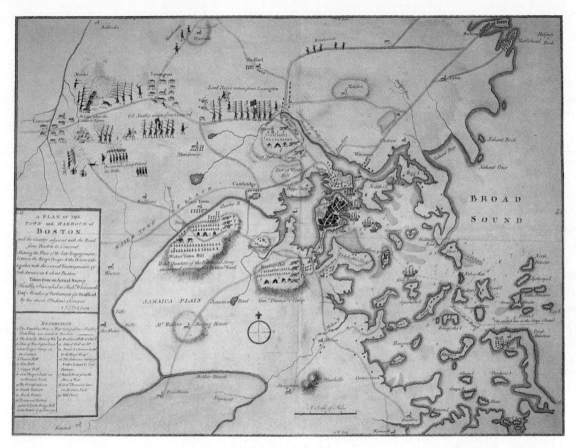

The British mapmaker who prepared this visual account of the events of April 19, 1775, showed the colonial dead at Lexington, the shooting at North Bridge in Concord, and the retreat of British troops into Boston under fire from minutemen. He also depicted the American militia encampments that soon surrounded and besieged the city. Courtesy of the John Carter Brown Library at Brown University.

nians dispatched two messengers, William Dawes and Paul Revere (later joined by Dr. Samuel Prescott), to rouse the countryside. Thus when the British vanguard of several hundred men approached Lexington at dawn on April 19, they found a ragtag group of seventy militiamen—about half the adult male population of the town—drawn up before them on the town common. The Americans' commander, Captain John Parker, ordered his men to withdraw, realizing they could not halt the redcoat advance. But as they began to disperse, a shot rang out; the British soldiers then fired several volleys. When they stopped, eight Americans lay dead and another ten had been wounded. The British moved on to Concord, five miles away.

There the contingents of militia were larger; the men of Concord had been joined by groups from Lincoln, Acton, and other nearby towns. The Americans allowed the British to enter Concord

unopposed, but later in the morning they attacked the British infantry companies guarding the North Bridge. The brief exchange of gunfire there spilled the first British blood of the Revolution: three men were killed and nine (including four officers) were wounded. On their retreat to Boston, the British were attacked by thousands of militiamen, firing from behind trees, bushes, and houses along the road. By the end of the day, the redcoats had suffered 272 casualties, including 70 deaths. Only the arrival of reinforcements from Boston and the militia's lack of coordination prevented much heavier British losses. The patriots suffered just 93 casualties. A British cartographer recorded the day's events on a schematic map.

By the evening of April 20, perhaps as many as 20,000 American militiamen had gathered around Boston, summoned by local committees that had spread the alarm across the New England countryside. Many did not stay long, since they were needed at home for spring planting, but those who remained dug in along siege lines encircling the city. For nearly a year the two armies sat and stared at each other across those lines. The redcoats attacked their besiegers only once, on June 17, when they drove the Americans from trenches atop Breed's Hill in Charlestown. In that misnamed Battle of Bunker Hill, the British incurred their greatest losses of the entire war: over 800 wounded and 228 killed. The Americans, though forced to abandon their position, lost less than half that number. During the same eleven-month period, the patriots captured Fort Ticonderoga, a British fort on Lake Champlain, acquiring much-needed cannon. In the hope of bringing Canada into the war on the American side, they also mounted an uncoordinated northern campaign that ended in disaster at Quebec in early 1776. But the chief significance of the first year of the war lay in the long lull in fighting between the main armies at Boston. The delay gave both sides a chance to regroup, organize, and plan their strategies.

Lord North and his new American secretary, Lord George Germain, made three central assumptions about the war they faced. First, they concluded that patriot forces could

British Strategy   not withstand the assaults of trained British regulars. They and their generals were convinced that the campaign of 1776 would be the first and last of the war. Accordingly, they dispatched to America the largest force Great Britain had ever assembled anywhere: 370 transport ships carrying 32,000 troops and tons of supplies, accompanied by 73 naval vessels and 13,000 sailors. Such an extraordinary effort would, they thought, ensure a quick victory. Among the troops were thousands of Hessian mercenaries (from the German state of Hesse); eighteenth-century armies were often composed of such professional soldiers who hired out to the highest bidder.

Second, British officials and army officers treated this war as comparable to wars they had fought successfully in Europe. They adopted a conventional strategy of capturing major American cities and defeating the rebel army decisively without suffering serious casualties themselves. Third, they assumed that a clear-cut military victory would automatically bring about their goal of retaining the colonies' allegiance.

All these assumptions proved false. North and Germain, like Lord Dartmouth before them, vastly underestimated the Americans' commitment to armed resistance. Defeats on the battlefield did not lead the patriots to abandon their political aims and sue for peace. The ministers also failed to recognize the significance of the American population's dispersal over an area fifteen hundred miles long and more than one hundred miles wide. Although the British would control each of the most important American ports at one time or another during the war, less than 5 percent of the population lived in those cities. Furthermore, the coast offered so many excellent harbors that essential commerce was easily rerouted. In other words, the loss of cities did little to damage the American cause, whereas the desire for such ports repeatedly led redcoat generals astray.

Most of all, the British did not at first understand that a military victory would not necessarily bring about a political victory. Securing the colonies permanently would require hundreds of thousands of Americans to return to their original allegiance. The conquest of America was thus a far more complicated task than the defeat of France twelve years earlier. The British needed not only to overpower the patriots but also to convert them. After 1778, they adopted a strategy designed to achieve that goal through the expanded use of loyalist forces and the restoration of civilian authority in occupied areas. But the new policy came too late. The British never fully realized that they were not fighting a conventional European war but rather an entirely new kind of conflict: the first modern war of national liberation.

The British at least had a bureaucracy ready to supervise the war effort. The Americans had only the Second Continental Congress, originally intended merely as a brief

Second Continental Congress   gathering of colonial representatives to consider the British response to the Continental Association. Instead, the delegates who convened in Philadelphia on May 10, 1775, found that they had to assume the mantle of intercolonial government. "Such a vast Multitude of objects, civil, political, commercial and military, press and crowd upon us so fast, that we know not what to do first," John Adams wrote a close friend early in the session. Yet as the summer passed, Congress slowly organized the colonies for war. It authorized the printing of money with which to purchase necessary goods, established a committee to supervise relations with foreign countries, and took steps to strengthen the militia. Most important, it created the Continental Army and appointed its generals.

Until Congress met, the Massachusetts provincial congress had taken responsibility for organizing the massive army of militia encamped at Boston. But that army, composed of men from all the New England states, was a heavy drain on limited local resources. Consequently, Massachusetts asked the Continental Congress to assume the task of directing the army. First, the Congress had to choose a commander-in-chief. Since the war had thus far been a wholly northern affair, many delegates recognized the importance of naming someone who was not a New Englander. There seemed only one obvious candidate: they unanimously selected their fellow delegate, the Virginian George Washington.

Washington was no fiery radical, nor was he a reflective political thinker. He had not played a prominent role in the prerevolutionary agitation, but his devotion to the American cause was unquestioned. He was dignified, conservative, and respectable—a man of unimpeachable integrity. The younger son of a Virginia planter, Washington had not expected to inherit substantial property and had planned to make his living as a surveyor. But the early death of his older brother and his marriage to the wealthy widow Martha Custis had made George Washington a rich man. Though unmistakably an aristocrat, he was unswervingly committed to representative government, and he had other desirable traits as well. His stamina was remarkable: in more than eight years of war, Washington never had a serious illness and took only one brief leave of absence. Moreover, he both looked and acted like a leader. Six feet tall in an era when most men were five inches shorter, his presence was stately and commanding. Other patriots praised his judgment, steadiness, and discretion, and even a loyalist admitted that Washington could "atone for many demerits by the extraordinary coolness and caution which distinguish his character."

Washington needed all the coolness and caution he could muster when he took command of

George Washington: A Portrait of Leadership

the army outside Boston in July 1775. It took him months to impose hierarchy and discipline on the unruly troops and to bring order to the supply system. But by March 1776, when the arrival of cannon from Ticonderoga finally enabled him to put direct pressure on the redcoats in the city, the army was prepared to act. As it happened, an assault on Boston proved unnecessary. Sir William Howe, who had replaced Gage, had for some time been considering an evacuation; he wanted to transfer his troops to New York City. The patriots' bombardment of Boston early in the month decided the matter. On March 17, the British and more than a thousand of their loyalist allies abandoned Boston forever.

That spring of 1776, as the British fleet left Boston for the temporary haven of Halifax, Nova Scotia, the colonies were moving inexorably toward the act the Massachusetts loyalists on board the ships feared most: a declaration of independence. Even months after fighting had begun, American leaders still denied seeking a break with the empire. But in January 1776 there appeared a pamphlet by a man who both thought the unthinkable and advocated it.

Thomas Paine's *Common Sense* exploded on the American scene like a bombshell. Within three months of publication, it sold 120,000 copies. The author, a radical English printer who had lived in America only since 1774, called stridently and stirringly for independence. More than that: Paine challenged many common American assumptions about government and the colonies' relationship to England. Rejecting the notion that a balance of monarchy, aristocracy, and democracy was necessary to preserve freedom, he advocated the establishment of a republic, a government by the people with no king or nobility. Instead of acknowledging the benefits of a connection with the mother country, Paine insisted that Britain had exploited the colonies unmercifully. In place of the frequently heard assertion that an independent America would be weak and divided, he substituted an unlimited confidence in America's strength when freed from European control.

Thomas Paine's Common Sense

These striking statements were clothed in equally striking prose. Scorning the polite, rational style of his classically educated predecessors, Paine adopted a furious, raging tone. The king, he de-

Thomas Paine, the English radical who wrote Common Sense. *James Watson prepared this 1783 engraving from a portrait by Charles Willson Peale, who depicted his subject accompanied by the tools of the writer's trade—several sheets of paper and a quill pen.*   National Portrait Gallery, Smithsonian Institution, Washington, D.C.

clared, was a "royal brute," a "wretch" who only pretended concern for the welfare of the colonists. Though a printed work, the pamphlet reflected the oral culture of ordinary folk. It was couched in everyday language and relied heavily on the Bible—the only book familiar to most Americans—as a primary source of authority. No wonder the pamphlet had a wider distribution than any other political publication of its day.

There is no way of knowing how many people were converted to the cause of independence by reading *Common Sense*. But by late spring 1776 independence had clearly become inevitable. On May 10, the Second Continental Congress formally recommended that individual colonies "adopt such governments as shall, in the opinion of the representatives of the people, best conduce to the happiness and safety of their constituents in particular, and America in general." From that source grew the first state constitutions. Perceiving the trend of events, the few loyalists still connected with Congress severed their ties to that body.

Then on June 7 came confirmation of the movement toward independence. Richard Henry Lee of Virginia, seconded by John Adams of Mas-

sachusetts, introduced the crucial resolution: "that these United Colonies are, and of right ought to be, free and independent States, that they are absolved of all allegiance to the British Crown, and that all political connection between them and the State of Great Britain is, and ought to be, totally dissolved." Congress debated but did not immediately adopt Lee's resolution. Instead, it postponed a vote until early July, to allow time for consultation and public reaction. In the meantime, a committee composed of Thomas Jefferson, John Adams, Benjamin Franklin, Robert R. Livingston of New York, and Roger Sherman of Connecticut was directed to draft a declaration of independence.

The committee in turn assigned primary responsibility for writing the declaration to Jefferson, who was well known for his apt and eloquent style. Years later John Adams recalled that Jefferson had modestly protested his selection, suggesting that Adams prepare the initial draft. The Massachusetts revolutionary recorded his frank response: "You can write ten times better than I can."

Thomas Jefferson was at the time thirty-four years old, a Virginia lawyer educated at the College of William and Mary and in the law offices of the prominent attorney George Wythe. He had read widely in history and political theory and had been a member of the House of Burgesses. His broad knowledge was evident not only in the declaration but also in his draft of the Virginia state constitution, completed just a few days before his appointment to the committee. Jefferson, an intensely private man, loved his home and family deeply. This early stage of his political career was marked by his beloved wife Martha's repeated difficulties in childbearing. While he wrote and debated in Philadelphia, she suffered a miscarriage at their home, Monticello. Not until after her death in 1782, from complications following the birth of their sixth (but only third surviving) child in ten years of marriage, did Jefferson fully commit himself to public service.

The draft of the declaration was laid before Congress on June 28. The delegates officially voted for independence four days later, then debated the wording of the declaration for two more days, adopting it with some changes on July 4. Since Americans had long ago ceased to see themselves as legitimate subjects of Parliament, the Declaration of

Declaration of Independence

Independence concentrated on George III (see the Appendix). That focus also provided an identifiable villain. The document accused the king of attempting to destroy representative government in the colonies and of oppressing Americans through the unjustified use of excessive force.

The declaration's chief long-term importance, however, did not lie in its lengthy catalogue of grievances against George III (including, in a section omitted by Congress, Jefferson's charge that the British monarchy had introduced slavery into America). It lay instead in the ringing statements of principle that have served ever since as the ideal to which Americans aspire. "We hold these truths to be self-evident: That all men are created equal; that they are endowed by their Creator with certain unalienable rights; that among these are life, liberty and the pursuit of happiness; that, to secure these rights, governments are instituted among men, deriving their just powers from the consent of the governed; that whenever any form of government becomes destructive of these ends, it is the right of the people to alter or to abolish it, and to institute new government." These phrases have echoed down through American history like no others.

The delegates in Philadelphia who voted to accept the Declaration of Independence did not have the advantage of our two hundred years of hindsight. When they adopted the declaration, they risked their necks: they were committing treason. Thus when they concluded the declaration with the assertion that they "mutually pledge[d] to each other our lives, our fortunes, and our sacred honor," they spoke no less than the truth. The real struggle still lay before them, and few of them had Thomas Paine's boundless confidence in success.

THE LONG STRUGGLE IN THE NORTH

In late June 1776, the first of the ships carrying Sir William Howe's troops from Halifax appeared off the coast of New York. On July 2, the day Congress voted for independence, the redcoats landed on Staten Island. But Howe waited until mid-August, after the arrival of more troops from England, to begin his attack on the city. The delay gave Washington sufficient time to march his army south to meet the threat. To defend New York,

Washington had approximately seventeen thousand soldiers: ten thousand Continentals who had promised to serve until the end of the year, and seven thousand militiamen who had enlisted for shorter terms. Neither he nor most of his men had ever fought a major battle against the British, and their lack of experience led to disastrous mistakes. The difficulty of defending New York City only compounded the errors.

Washington's problem was as simple as the geography of the region was complex (see map). To protect the city adequately, he would have to divide his forces among Long Island, Manhattan Island, and the mainland. But the British fleet under Admiral Lord Richard Howe, Sir William's brother, controlled the harbors and rivers that divided the American forces. The patriots thus constantly courted catastrophe, for swift action by the British navy could cut off the possibility of retreat and perhaps even communication. But despite these dangers, Washington could not afford to surrender New York to the Howes without a fight.

Battle for New York City

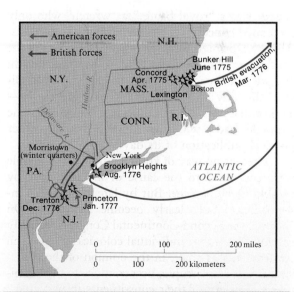

The War in the North, 1775–1777 *The early phase of the Revolutionary War, as shown in this map, was dominated by British troop movements in the Boston area, the redcoats' evacuation to Nova Scotia in the spring of 1776, and the subsequent British invasion of New York and New Jersey.*

Not only did the city occupy a strategic location, but the region that surrounded it was known to contain many loyalist sympathizers. A show of force was essential if the revolutionaries were to retain any hope of persuading waverers to join them.

On August 27, Sir William Howe's forces attacked the American positions on Brooklyn Heights, pushing the untried rebel troops back into their defensive entrenchments. But Sir William failed to press his advantage, even neglecting to send his brother's ships into the East River to cut off a retreat. Consequently, the Americans were able to escape. A troop of fishermen from Marblehead, Massachusetts, ferried nine thousand men to the southern tip of Manhattan Island in less than twelve hours on the night of August 29. Washington moved north on the island, retreating onto the mainland but leaving behind nearly three thousand men in supposedly impregnable Fort Washington on the west shore of Manhattan. Howe slowly followed him into Westchester County, then turned back to attack the fort. Its defenses collapsed, and the large garrison surrendered in early November. Only when Charleston fell to the British in May 1780 did the Americans lose more men on a single occasion.

George Washington had defended New York, but badly. He had repeatedly broken a basic rule of military tactics: never divide your force in the face of a superior enemy. In the end, though, the Howe brothers' failure to move quickly prevented a decisive defeat of the Americans. Although Washington's army had been seriously reduced by casualties, by the surrender of Fort Washington, and by the loss of most of the militiamen (who had returned home for the harvest), its core remained. Through November and December, Washington led his men in a retreat across New Jersey. Howe followed at a leisurely pace, setting up a string of outposts manned mostly by Hessian mercenaries. After Washington crossed the Delaware River into Pennsylvania, the British commander turned back and settled into comfortable winter quarters in New York City.

The British controlled most of New Jersey, and hundreds of Americans there accepted the pardons offered by the Howes. Among them were Joseph Galloway, the conservative Pennsylvanian, and Richard Stockton, who had signed the Decla-

At the battle of Princeton in early 1777, American forces under George Washington cemented the victory they had won a few days earlier at Trenton. This view was painted in 1787 by James Peale, who fought in the battle.   Princeton University Library.

ration of Independence. Occupying troops met little opposition, and the Revolutionary cause appeared to be in disarray. "These are the times that try men's souls," wrote Thomas Paine in his pamphlet *The Crisis*. "The summer soldier and the sunshine patriot will, in this crisis, shrink from the service of his country; . . . yet we have this consolation with us, that the harder the conflict, the more glorious the triumph."

In the aftermath of battle, as at its height, the British generals again let their advantage slip away. The redcoats stationed in New Jersey went on a rampage of rape and plunder. Because loyalists and patriots were indistinguishable to the British and Hessian troops, families on both sides suffered nearly equally. Livestock, crops, and firewood were seized for use by the army. Houses were looted and burned, churches and public buildings desecrated. But nothing was better calculated to rally doubtful Americans to the cause than the wanton murder of innocent civilians and the rape of women.

The soldiers' marauding alienated potentially loyal New Jerseyites and Pennsylvanians whose allegiance the British could ill afford to lose. It also spurred Washington's determination to strike back. The enlistments of most of the Continental troops were to expire on December 31, and Washington also wanted to take advantage of short-term Pennsylvania militiamen who had recently joined him. Moving quickly, he attacked the Hessian encampment at Trenton early in the morning of December 26, while the redcoats were still reeling from their Christmas celebration. The patriots captured more than nine hundred Hessians and killed another thirty; only three Americans were wounded. A few days later, after persuading many of his men to stay on beyond the term of their enlistments, Washington attacked again at Princeton. (This was one of the few battles of the Revolution painted by a participant; see the accompanying illustration.) Having gained command of the field and buoyed American spirits with the two swift victories, Washington set up winter quarters at Morristown, New Jersey.

The campaign of 1776 established patterns that were to persist throughout much of the war, despite changes in British leadership and strategy. The British forces were usually more numerous

Battle of Trenton

and often better led than the Americans. But their ponderous style of maneuvering, lack of familiarity with the terrain, and inability to live off the land without antagonizing the populace partially offset those advantages. Furthermore, although Washington always seemed to lack regular troops—the Continental Army never numbered more than 18,500 men—he could usually count on the militia to join him at crucial times. American militiamen did not like to sign up for long terms of service or to fight far from home, but when their homes were threatened they rallied to the cause. Washington and his officers complained about the militia's habit of disappearing during planting or harvesting. But time and again their presence, however brief, enabled the Americans to launch an attack or counter an important British thrust.

As the war dragged on, the Continental Army and the militia took on decidedly different characters. State governments, responsible for filling military quotas, discovered that most men willing to enlist for long periods in the regular army were young, single, and footloose. Farmers with fami-

The American Army

"Keep up courage, my boys, we will soon bring those villains to terms."

"These damned Extortioners are the worst enemies to the country."

"I serve my country for sixteen pence a day, pinched with cold."

A patriot woodcut portrayed the sufferings and complaints of American soldiers in the field. While the first soldier urges his comrades to keep up their courage, the second complains of war profiteers and the third of low pay and poor living conditions. Private collection.

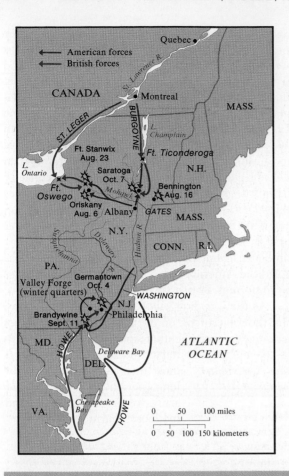

Campaign of 1777 *The crucial campaign of 1777 was fought on two fronts: along the upper Hudson and Mohawk river valleys, and in the vicinity of Philadelphia. The rebels won in the north, the British triumphed—at least nominally—in the south, but the capture of Philadelphia did the redcoats little good.*

lowers worked as cooks, nurses, and launderers, in return for rations and low wages. The presence of women, as well as militiamen who floated in and out of the American camp at irregular intervals, made for an unwieldy army that officers found difficult to manage. Yet the army's shapelessness also reflected its greatest strength: an almost unlimited reservoir of manpower and womanpower.

The officers of the Continental Army—those who enlisted for long periods or for the war's duration—developed an intense sense of pride and commitment to the revolutionary cause. The hardships they endured, the battles they fought, the difficulties they overcame all helped to forge an esprit de corps that was to outlast the war. The realities of warfare were often dirty, messy, and corrupt, but the officers drew strength from a developing image of themselves as professionals who sacrificed personal gain for the good of the entire nation. When Benedict Arnold—an officer who had fought heroically for the patriot cause early in the war—violated that virtuous self-image by defecting to the British in exchange for a promise of £20,000, they made his name a metaphor for villainy. "How black, how despised, loved by none, and hated by all," wrote one patriot.

In 1777, the chief British effort was planned by the flashy "Gentleman Johnny" Burgoyne, a playboy general as much at home at the gaming tables of London as on the battlefield. A subordinate of Howe, Burgoyne spent the winter of 1776–1777 in London, where he gained the ear of Lord George Germain. Burgoyne convinced Germain that he could lead an invading force of redcoats and Indians down the Hudson River from Canada, cutting off New England from the rest of the states. He proposed to rendezvous near Albany with a similar force that would move east from Niagara along the Mohawk River valley. The combined forces would then presumably link up with Sir William Howe's troops in New York City.

That Burgoyne's scheme would give "Gentleman Johnny" all the glory and relegate Howe to a supporting role did not escape Sir William's notice. While Burgoyne was plotting in London, Howe was laying his own plans in New York City. Joseph Galloway and other Pennsylvania loyalists persuaded Howe that Philadelphia could be taken easily and that his troops would be welcomed by many residents of the region. Just as Burgoyne left Howe out of his plans, Howe left Burgoyne out of his. Thus the two major British armies in America

lies tended to prefer short-term militia duty. As the supply of whites willing to sign up with the Continentals diminished, recruiters in the northern states turned increasingly to African-Americans, both slave and free. Perhaps as many as five thousand blacks eventually served in the Revolutionary army, and most of them won their freedom as a result. They commonly served in racially integrated units but were assigned tasks that whites shunned, such as cooking, foraging for food, and driving wagons. Also attached to the American forces were a number of women, who were the wives and widows of poor soldiers. Such camp fol-

would operate independently in 1777, and the result would be a disaster (see map).

Howe accomplished his objective: he captured Philadelphia. But he did so in an inexplicable way, delaying for months before beginning the campaign, then taking six weeks to transport his troops by sea to the head of Chesapeake Bay instead of marching them overland. That maneuver cost him at least a month, debilitated his men, and depleted his supplies. Incredibly, at the end of the lengthy voyage, he was only forty miles closer to Philadelphia than when he started. By the time Howe was ready to move on Philadelphia, Washington had had time to prepare its defenses. Twice, at Brandywine Creek and again at Germantown, the two armies clashed near the patriot capital. Although the British won both engagements, the Americans handled themselves well. The redcoats took Philadelphia in late September, but to little effect. The campaign season was nearly over; the Revolutionary army had gained confidence in itself and its leaders; few welcoming loyalists had materialized; and, far to the north, Burgoyne was going down to defeat.

Howe Takes Philadelphia

Burgoyne and his men set out from Montreal in mid-June 1777, floating down Lake Champlain into New York in canoes and flat-bottom boats. They easily took Fort Ticonderoga from its outnumbered and outgunned patriot defenders, who abandoned the fort without a fight. Trouble began, however, as Burgoyne began his overland march. His clumsy artillery carriages and baggage wagons foundered in the heavy forests and ravines. Patriot militia felled giant trees across the army's path. As a result, Burgoyne's troops took twenty-four days to travel the twenty-three miles to Fort Edward, on the Hudson River. Short of supplies, the general dispatched eight hundred German mercenaries to forage the countryside. On August 16, American militia companies nearly wiped out the Germans near Bennington. Yet Burgoyne failed to recognize the seriousness of his predicament and continued to dawdle, giving the Americans more than enough time to prepare for his coming. By the time he finally crossed the Hudson in mid-September, bound for Albany, Burgoyne's fate was sealed. After several bloody clashes with the American

Burgoyne's Campaign in New York

Anne Catherine Green, the widow of Jonas Green, an Annapolis printer, took over his business after his death in 1767. With the assistance of her two sons, she continued to publish the local newspaper, the Maryland Gazette. *Renowned for her patriotism, she was named official printer to the state. Charles Willson Peale painted this portrait about 1770.* National Portrait Gallery, Smithsonian Institution, Washington, D.C. Art Resource, N.Y.

force commanded by General Horatio Gates, Burgoyne was surrounded near Saratoga, New York. On October 17, 1777, he surrendered his entire force of more than six thousand men.

Two months before, the fourteen hundred redcoats and Indians marching along the Mohawk River from Niagara toward Albany had also been turned back. After they had laid siege to the isolated American outpost at Fort Stanwix in early August, they learned that a patriot relief column was en route to the fort. Leaving only a small detachment at Fort Stanwix, the British under Colonel Barry St. Leger ambushed the Americans at Oriskany on August 6. The British claimed victory in the ensuing battle, one of the bloodiest of the war. But they and their tribal allies abandoned the siege of Fort Stanwix in late August and returned to Niagara after the Americans tricked them into believing that another large patriot force was on the way.

The Battle of Oriskany revealed a split in the Iroquois Confederacy (see page 80). In 1776 the Six Nations had formally pledged to remain neutral in the Anglo-American struggle. But two influential Mohawk leaders, Joseph Brant and Mary Brant, worked tirelessly to persuade their fellow Iroquois to join the British. Mary Brant, a powerful tribal matron, was also the widow of the Indian superintendent Sir William Johnson. Her younger brother Joseph, a renowned warrior, was convinced that the Six Nations should ally themselves with the British in order to prevent American encroachment on their lands. As an observer said of Mary, "One word from her goes farther with them [the Iroquois] than a thousand from any white man without exception." The Brants won over to the British the Senecas, Cayugas, and Mohawks, all of whom contributed warriors to St. Leger's expedition. But the Oneidas—who had

Split of the Iroquois Confederacy

Joseph Brant, the Iroquois leader who helped to persuade the Mohawks, Senecas, and Cayugas to support the British in the latter stages of the Revolution, as painted by Charles Willson Peale in 1797. Independence National Historic Park Collection.

been converted to Christianity by Protestant missionaries—preferred the American side, bringing the Tuscaroras with them. The Onondagas split into three factions, one on each side and one supporting neutrality. At Oriskany, some Oneidas and Tuscaroras joined the patriot militia to fight their Iroquois brethren; thus a league of friendship that had survived over three hundred years was torn apart by the whites' family quarrel.

The collapse of Iroquois unity and the confederacy's abandonment of neutrality had important consequences. In 1778, Iroquois warriors allied with the British raided the frontier villages of Wyoming, Pennsylvania, and Cherry Valley, New York. To retaliate, the Americans dispatched an expedition under General John Sullivan the following summer to burn Iroquois crops, orchards, and settlements. The destruction was so thorough that many bands had to leave their ancestral homeland to seek food and shelter with the British north of the Great Lakes during the winter of 1779–1780. A large number of Iroquois people never returned to New York but settled permanently in British Canada.

The news of Burgoyne's surrender at Saratoga brought joy to patriots, discouragement to loyalists and Britons. In exile in London, Thomas Hutchinson wrote of "universal dejection" among loyalists there. "Everybody in a gloom," he commented; "most of us expect to lay our bones here." The disaster prompted Lord North to authorize a peace commission to offer the Americans everything they had requested in 1774—in effect, a return to the imperial system of 1763. It was, of course, far too late for that: the patriots rejected the overture, and the peace commission sailed back to England empty-handed in mid-1778.

Most important of all, the American victory at Saratoga drew France formally into the conflict. Ever since 1763, the French had sought to avenge their defeat in the Seven Years' War, and the American Revolution gave them that opportunity. Even before Benjamin Franklin arrived in Paris in late 1776, France was covertly supplying the revolutionaries with military necessities. Indeed, 90 percent of the gunpowder that was used by the Americans during the first two years of the war came from France.

Franklin worked tirelessly to strengthen ties between the two nations. Although not a Quaker, he deliberately assumed a plain style of dress that

Franco-American Alliance of 1778

made him stand out amid the luxury of the court of King Louis XVI. Presenting himself as a representative of American simplicity, he played on the French image of Americans as virtuous yeomen. Franklin's effort culminated in 1778 when the countries signed two treaties. In the Treaty of Amity and Commerce, France recognized American independence and established trade ties with the new nation; the second treaty instituted a formal alliance between the two nations. In this Treaty of Alliance, France and the United States promised—assuming that France would go to war with Britain, which it soon did—that neither would negotiate peace with the enemy without consulting the other. France also abandoned all its claims to Canada and to North American territory east of the Mississippi River. The most visible symbol of Franco-American cooperation in the years that followed was the Marquis de Lafayette, a young nobleman who volunteered for service with George Washington in 1777 and fought with the American forces until the conflict ended.

The French alliance had two major benefits for the patriot cause. First, France began to aid the Americans openly, sending troops and naval vessels in addition to arms, ammunition, clothing, and blankets. Second, the British could no longer concentrate their attention on the American mainland alone, for they had to fight the French in the West Indies and elsewhere. Spain's entry into the war in 1779 as an ally of France (but not of the United States) further magnified Britain's problems, for the Revolution then became a global war. French assistance was important to the Americans throughout the conflict, but in its last years the aid was especially vital.

THE LONG STRUGGLE IN THE SOUTH

In the aftermath of the Saratoga disaster, Lord George Germain and the military officials in London reassessed their strategy. Maneuvering in the North had done them little good; perhaps shifting the field of battle southward would bring success. The many loyalist exiles in England encouraged

James Armistead LaFayette, a Virginia slave, was first a spy and later a courier for General LaFayette during the Revolution. After the war, he adopted LaFayette's surname as his own and was freed by a special act of the state legislature.   Valentine Museum, Gift of Mr. Louis E. Franck, Jr.

this line of thinking. They argued that loyal southerners would welcome the redcoat army as liberators, and that once the region had been pacified and returned to civilian control it could serve as a base for attacking the North.

In early 1778 Sir William Howe was replaced by Sir Henry Clinton. As commander-in-chief, Clinton too was afflicted with sluggishness and lack of resolution. Still, he oversaw the regrouping of British forces in America, ordering the evacuation of Philadelphia in June 1778 and dispatching a small expedition to Georgia at the end of the year. When Savannah and then Augusta fell easily into British hands, Clinton became convinced that a southern strategy would work. In late 1779 he sailed down the coast from New York with 8,500 troops to attack Charleston, the most important city in the South (see map, page 172).

The Americans worked hard to bolster Charleston's defenses, but the city fell to the British on May 12, 1780. General Benjamin Lincoln

Fall of Charleston

surrendered the entire southern army—5,500 men—to the invaders. In the weeks that followed, the redcoats spread through South Carolina, establishing garrisons at key points in the interior. As

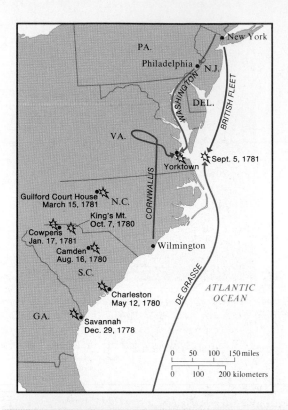

The War in the South *The southern war—after the British invasion of Georgia in late 1778—was characterized by a series of British thrusts into the interior, leading to battles with American defenders in both North and South Carolina. Finally, after promising beginnings, Cornwallis's foray into Virginia ended with disaster at Yorktown in October 1781.*

in New Jersey in 1776, hundreds of South Carolinians renounced allegiance to the United States and proclaimed their loyalty to the Crown. Clinton organized loyalist regiments, and the process of pacification began.

Yet the British triumph was less complete than it appeared. The success of the southern campaign depended on British control of the seas, for only by sea could the widely dispersed British armies remain in communication with one another. For the moment, the Royal Navy safely dominated the American coastline, but French naval power posed a threat to the entire southern enterprise. Moreover, the redcoats never managed to establish full control of the areas they seized. Patriot bands oper-

ated freely throughout the state, and loyalists could not be guaranteed protection against their enemies. Last but not least, the fall of Charleston did not dishearten the patriots; instead, it spurred them to greater exertions. As one Marylander declared confidently, "The Fate of America is not to be decided by the Loss of a Town or Two." Patriot women in four states formed the Ladies Association, which collected money to purchase shirts for needy soldiers. Recruiting efforts were stepped up.

Nevertheless, the war in South Carolina went badly for the patriots throughout most of 1780. In August, a reorganized southern army under Horatio Gates was crushingly defeated at Camden by the forces of Lord Cornwallis, the new commander of British forces in the South. The redcoats were joined wherever they went by hundreds, even thousands, of enslaved African-Americans seeking freedom on the basis of Lord Dunmore's proclamation. They had run away from their patriot masters individually and as families in such numbers that they seriously disrupted planting and harvesting in 1780 and 1781. More than fifty-five thousand slaves were lost to their owners as a result of the war. Not all of them joined the British or won their freedom if they did, but their flight had exactly the effect Dunmore wanted. Many served the British well as scouts, guides, and laborers.

After the defeat at Camden, Washington (who had to remain in the North to oppose the British army occupying New York) appointed General Nathanael Greene of Rhode Island to command the southern campaign. Greene was appalled by what he found in South Carolina. "The word difficulty when applied to the state of things here . . . is almost without meaning, it falls so far short" of reality, he wrote to a friend. His troops needed clothing, blankets, and food, but "a great part of this country is already laid waste and in the utmost danger of becoming a desert." The constant guerrilla warfare had, he commented, "so corrupted the principles of the people that they think of nothing but plundering one another." In such circumstances, Greene had to move cautiously. He adopted a conciliatory policy toward loyalists and neutrals, persuading the governor of South Carolina to offer complete pardons to those who had fought for the British if they would join the patriot militia. He also ordered his troops not to loot loyal-

Greene Rallies South Carolina

A British cartoon of 1780. Even after Spain and The Netherlands had joined France in supporting the Americans' quest for independence, this artist at least had confidence in Britain's ability to outweigh the alliance in "The Balance of Power."   Miriam and Ira D. Wallach Division of Art, Prints and Photographs, The New York Public Library.

ist property and to treat captives fairly. Greene recognized that the patriots could win only by convincing the populace that they could bring stability to the region. He thus helped the shattered provincial congresses of Georgia and South Carolina to begin re-establishing civilian authority in the interior—a goal the British were never able to accomplish, even along the coast.

Greene also took a conciliatory approach to the southern tribes. With his desperate need for soldiers, he could not afford to have frontier militia companies occupied in defending their homes against Indian attacks. Since he had so few regulars (only sixteen hundred when he took command), Greene had to rely on western volunteers. Therefore, he negotiated with the tribes.

His policy eventually met with success, although at first royal officials cooperating with the British invasion forces won allies among a number of southern tribes, especially Dragging Canoe's

Cherokee band. But recalling the disastrous defeat the Cherokees had suffered in 1776, the southern Indians never committed themselves wholeheartedly to the British. In 1781 the Cherokees began negotiations with the patriots, and the next year the other tribes also sued for peace. By the end of the war only the Creeks remained British allies. A group of Chickasaw chiefs explained their reasoning to American agents in 1782, after Greene's battlefield successes had forced the redcoats to withdraw into Savannah and Charleston: "The English put the Bloody Tomahawk into our hands, telling us that we should have no Goods if we did not Exert ourselves to the greatest point of Resentment against you, but now we find our mistake and Distresses. The English have done their utmost and left us in our adversity. We find them full of Deceit and Dissimulation."

Even before Greene took command of the southern army in December 1780, the tide had begun to turn. In October, at King's Mountain, near the border between the Carolinas, a force from the settlements west of the Appalachians defeated a large party of redcoats and loyalists. Then in January 1781 Greene's trusted aide Brigadier General Daniel Morgan brilliantly defeated the crack British regiment Tarleton's Legion at Cowpens, not far from King's Mountain. Greene himself confronted the main body of British troops under Lord Cornwallis at Guilford Court House, North Carolina, in March. Though Cornwallis controlled the field at the end of the day, most of his army had been destroyed. He had to retreat to Wilmington, on the coast, to receive supplies and fresh troops from New York by sea. Meanwhile, Greene returned to South Carolina, where, in a series of swift strikes, he forced the redcoats to abandon their posts in the interior and quickly retire to Charleston.

Cornwallis had already ignored explicit orders not to leave South Carolina unless the state was safely in British hands. Evidently bent on his own destruction, he headed north

Surrender at Yorktown

into Virginia, where he joined forces with a detachment of redcoats commanded by the American traitor Benedict Arnold. Instead of acting decisively with his new army of 7,200 men, Cornwallis withdrew to the edge of the peninsula between the York and James rivers, where he fortified Yorktown and in effect waited for the end. Seizing the opportunity, Washington quickly moved more than 7,000 troops south from New York City. When a French fleet under the Comte de Grasse arrived from the West Indies in time to defeat the Royal Navy vessels sent to rescue Cornwallis, the British general was trapped (see map, page 172). On October 19, 1781, four years and two days after Burgoyne's defeat at Saratoga, Cornwallis surrendered to the combined American and French forces.

When news of the surrender reached England, Lord North's ministry fell. Parliament voted to cease offensive operations in America and authorized peace negotiations. But guerrilla warfare between patriots and loyalists continued to ravage the Carolinas and Georgia for more than a year, and in the North vicious retaliatory raids by Indians and whites kept the frontier aflame. Indeed, the most brutal massacre of the war occurred in March 1782, at Gnadenhuetten in the Ohio country. A group of militiamen, seeking the Indians who had killed a frontier family, encountered a peaceful band of Delawares who had been converted to both Christianity and pacifism by Moravian missionaries. All members of the band were slaughtered. Ninety-six men, women, and children died that day, some burned at the stake, others tomahawked. Two months later, hostile Delawares captured three militiamen and subjected them to gruesome tortures in reprisal. The persistence of conflict between frontier militia and Indians after the Battle of Yorktown, all too often overlooked in accounts of the Revolution, serves to underline the degree to which the Native Americans were the real losers in the war initiated by the colonists.

The fighting finally ended when Americans and Britons learned of the signing of a preliminary peace treaty at Paris in November 1782. The

Treaty of Paris

American diplomats—Benjamin Franklin, John Jay, and John Adams—ignored their instructions from Congress to be guided by France and instead negotiated directly with Great Britain. Their instincts were sound: the French government was more an enemy to Britain than a friend to the United States. In fact, French ministers worked secretly behind the scenes to try to prevent the establishment of a strong and unified government in America. Spain's desire to lay claim to the region between the Appalachian Mountains and the Mississippi River further complicated the issues. But the American delegates proved adept at playing the game of power politics and achieved their main goal: independence as a united nation. The new British ministry, headed by Lord Shelburne (formerly a critic of Lord North's harsh American policies), was weary of war and made numerous concessions—so many, in fact, that Parliament ousted the ministry shortly after the peace terms were approved.

Under the treaty, signed formally on September 3, 1783, the Americans were granted unconditional independence. The boundaries of the new nation were generous: to the north, approximately the present-day boundary with Canada; to the south, the 31st parallel (about the modern northern border of Florida); to the west, the Mississippi River. Florida, which the British had acquired in 1763, was returned to Spain. The Americans also gained unlimited fishing rights off Newfoundland.

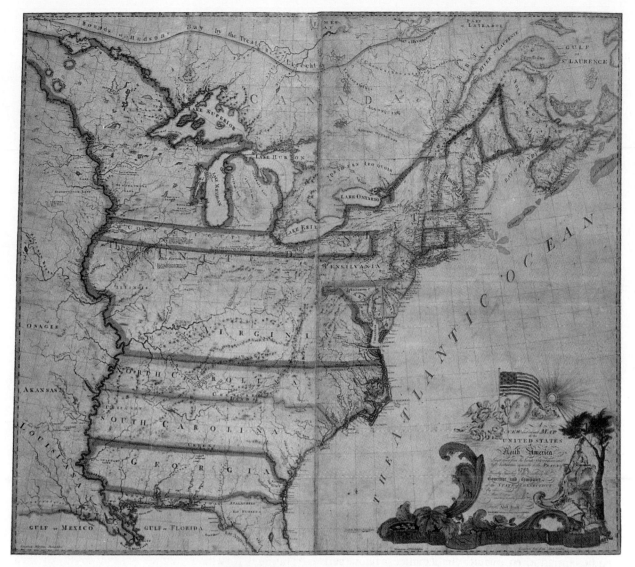

How do historians know

that Americans had only incomplete knowledge of the boundaries of their new nation? One way is to consult their written documents, another is to look at their early maps, like this one, "A New and Correct Map of the United States of North America," produced in 1784. New it certainly was, but correct it was not. A comparison with a standard map of the United States and Canada today shows many errors of scale, proportion, and placement of natural features. To point out just a few: the Ohio River is shown much too far south;

the northern part of the Mississippi River is misplaced to the west; Lake Superior is too small and its islands too large; and the Nova Scotia peninsula is misshapen. What links all these features is that they were on the periphery of the new nation and thus on the margins of Americans' knowledge. But even so well known a waterway as Chesapeake Bay is inaccurately drawn, suggesting that residents of the United States still had much to learn about the geography of their country.
Photo: New Jersey Historical Society.

In ceding so much land to the United States, the British entirely ignored the territorial rights of their tribal allies. Once again, the tribes' interests were sacrificed to the demands of European power politics. Loyalists and British merchants were also poorly served by the British negotiators. The treaty's ambiguously worded clauses pertaining to the payment of prewar debts and the postwar treatment of loyalists caused trouble for years to come and proved impossible to enforce.

The long war finally over, the victorious Americans could look back on their achievement with satisfaction and awe. In 1775, with an inexperienced ragtag army, they had taken on the greatest military power in the world—and eight years later they had won. They had accomplished their goal more through persistence and commitment than through brilliance on the battlefield. Actual victories had been few, but their army had always survived defeats and stand-offs to fight again. Ultimately, the Americans had simply worn their enemy down.

In the course of winning the war, the Americans had reshaped the landscapes in which they lived, both physically and mentally. They had abandoned the British identity that once had been important to them, excluding from their new nation all those unwilling to make a break with the mother country. In the Continental Army in particular, they had begun the process of creating loyalty to an entity that had not previously existed— a nation they named "the United States of America"—composed of the former colonies that had claimed their primary allegiance. They had also established a claim to most of the territory east of the Mississippi River and south of the Great Lakes, thereby greatly expanding the land potentially open to their settlements.

In achieving independence Americans had surmounted formidable challenges. But in the future they faced perhaps even greater ones: establishing stable republican governments at the state and national levels to replace the monarchy they had rejected, and ensuring their governments' continued existence in a world of bitter rivalries among the major powers—England, France, and Spain. Those European rivalries had worked to the Americans' advantage during the war, but in the decades to come they would pose significant threats to the survival of the new nation.

SUGGESTIONS FOR FURTHER READING

General

Colin Bonwick, *The American Revolution* (1991); Edward Countryman, *The American Revolution* (1985); Larry Gerlach, ed., *Legacies of the American Revolution* (1978); Stephen G. Kurtz and James H. Hutson, eds., *Essays on the American Revolution* (1973); Library of Congress, *Symposia on the American Revolution*, 5 vols. (1972–1976); Robert Middlekauff, *The Glorious Cause: The American Revolution, 1763–1783* (1982); Edmund S. Morgan, *The Challenge of the American Revolution* (1976); Alfred F. Young, ed., *The American Revolution: Explorations in the History of American Radicalism* (1976).

Military

John Richard Alden, *The American Revolution, 1775–1783* (1964); Jeremy Black, *War for America: The Fight for Independence, 1775–1783* (1991); E. Wayne Carp, *To Starve the Army at Pleasure: Continental Army Administration and American Political Culture, 1775–1783* (1984); John C. Dann, ed., *The Revolution Remembered: Eyewitness Accounts of the War for Independence* (1980); Don Higginbotham, *The War of American Independence: Military Attitudes, Policies, and Practice, 1763–1789* (1971); Ronald Hoffman and Peter Albert, eds., *Arms and Independence: The Military Character of the American Revolution* (1984); Piers Mackesy, *The War for America, 1775–1783* (1964); James K. Martin and Mark Lender, *"A Respectable Army": The Military Origins of the Republic, 1763–1789* (1982); Charles Royster, *A Revolutionary People at War: The Continental Army and American Character, 1775–1783* (1980); John Shy, *A People Numerous and Armed: Reflections on the Military Struggle for American Independence* (1976).

Local and Regional

Richard Buel, *Dear Liberty: Connecticut's Mobilization for the Revolutionary War* (1980); Edward Countryman, *A People in Revolution: The American Revolution and Political Society in New York, 1760–1790* (1981); Elaine F. Crane, *A Dependent People: Newport, R.I., in the Revolutionary Era* (1985); Jeffrey Crow and Larry Tise, eds., *The Southern Experience in the American Revolution* (1978); Thomas Doerflinger, *A Vigorous Spirit of Enterprise: Merchants and Economic Development in Revolutionary Philadelphia* (1986); Robert A. Gross, *The Minutemen and Their World* (1976); Ronald Hoffman, *A Spirit of Dissension: Economics, Politics, and the Revolution in Maryland* (1973); Ronald Hoffman, Thad W. Tate, and Peter Albert, eds., *An Uncivil War: The Southern Backcountry During the American Revolution* (1985); Stephen Rosswurm, *Arms, Country, and Class: The Philadelphia Militia and the "Lower Sort" During the American Revolution* (1988); John Selby, *The Revolution in Virginia, 1775–1783* (1988).

Indians and African-Americans

Sylvia Frey, *Water from the Rock: Black Resistance in a Revolutionary Age* (1991); Barbara Graymont, *The Iroquois in the American Revolution* (1972); Isabel T. Kelsey, *Joseph Brant, 1743–1807: Man of Two Worlds* (1984); Duncan J. MacLeod, *Slavery, Race, and the American Revolution* (1974); James H. O'Donnell III, *Southern Indians in the American Revolution* (1973); Benjamin Quarles, *The Negro in the American Revolution* (1961); Daniel K. Richter, *The Ordeal of the Longhouse* (1992); Anthony F. C. Wallace, *The Death and Rebirth of the Seneca* (1969); Richard White, *The Middle Ground: Indians, Empires, and Republics in the Great Lakes Region, 1650–1815* (1991).

Loyalists

Bernard Bailyn, *The Ordeal of Thomas Hutchinson* (1974); Robert McCluer Calhoon, *The Loyalists in Revolutionary America, 1760–1781* (1973); William H. Nelson, *The American Tory* (1961); Mary Beth Norton, *The British-Americans: The Loyalist Exiles in England, 1774–1789* (1972); Janice Potter, *The Liberty We Seek: Loyalist Ideology in Colonial New York and Massachusetts* (1983); Paul H. Smith, *Loyalists and Redcoats: A Study in British Revolutionary Policy* (1964); James W. St. G. Walker, *The Black Loyalists: The Search for a Promised Land in Nova Scotia and Sierra Leone, 1783–1870* (1976).

Women

Richard Buel and Joy Buel, *The Way of Duty: A Woman and Her Family in Revolutionary America* (1984); Ronald Hoffman and Peter Albert, eds., *Women in the Age of the American Revolution* (1989); Linda K. Kerber, *Women of the Republic: Intellect and Ideology in Revolutionary America* (1980); Mary Beth Norton, *Liberty's Daughters: The Revolutionary Experience of American Women, 1750–1800* (1980).

Foreign Policy

Jonathan Dull, *A Diplomatic History of the American Revolution* (1985); Felix Gilbert, *To the Farewell Address* (1961); Ronald Hoffman and Peter Albert, eds., *Peace and the Peacemakers: The Treaty of 1783* (1986); Ronald Hoffman and Peter Albert, eds., *Diplomacy and Revolution: The Franco-American Alliance of 1778* (1981); Lawrence Kaplan, ed., *The American Revolution and a "Candid World"* (1977); Richard B. Morris, *The Peacemakers: The Great Powers and American Independence* (1965); Jan Willem Schulte Nordholt, *The Dutch Republic and American Independence* (1982); Richard W. Van Alstyne, *Empire and Independence: The International History of the American Revolution* (1965).

Patriot Leaders

Fawn M. Brodie, *Thomas Jefferson: An Intimate History* (1974); Verner W. Crane, *Benjamin Franklin and a Rising People* (1954); Marcus Cunliffe, *George Washington: Man and Monument* (1958); Noble Cunningham, *In Pursuit of Reason: The Life of Thomas Jefferson* (1987); James T. Flexner, *George Washington*, 4 vols. (1965–1972); Eric Foner, *Tom Paine and Revolutionary America* (1976); Claude A. Lopez and Eugenia Herbert, *The Private Franklin: The Man and His Family* (1975); Dumas Malone, *Jefferson and His Time*, 6 vols. (1948–1981).

Chapter

7

Forging a National Republic, 1776–1789

O N JANUARY 25, 1787, an army of fifteen hundred farmers from the hills and valleys of western Massachusetts advanced on the federal armory at Springfield, which housed 450 tons of military supplies, including seven thousand muskets and thirteen hundred barrels of gunpowder. Inside the arsenal, General William Shepard prepared his group of one thousand militiamen to resist the assault. First, though, he dispatched two aides to warn the farmers that they would soon "inevitably" draw the fire of men who had been their officers during the Revolutionary War. "That is all we want, by God!" replied one of the rebels. The farmers moved toward the armory, urged on by the commands of Daniel Shays, one of their leaders. "March, God Damn you, March!" he shouted. Shepard fired two cannons over the heads of the farmers, and then—when that did not frighten them—ordered his men to shoot directly at the straggling ranks. Four men died, twenty were wounded, and the rebels withdrew from the field.

What caused this violent clash between former comrades in arms, just six short years after the victory at Yorktown? The Massachusetts farmers were angered by high taxes and the

scarcity of money. Since the preceding summer, they had organized committees and crowd actions—the tactics used so successfully in the 1760s and early 1770s—to halt state efforts to seize property for nonpayment of taxes. Many of the insurgents were respected war veterans, described as "gentlemen" in contemporary accounts of the riots. Daniel Shays, their nominal leader (he disclaimed the title, declaring that decisions were made collectively), had been a captain in the Continental Army. Clearly the episode could not be dismissed as the work of an unruly rabble. What did the uprising mean for the future of the republic? Was it a sign of impending anarchy?

The protesters explained their position in an address to the governor and council of Massachusetts. They proclaimed their loyalty to the nation but objected to the state's fiscal policies, which, they said, prevented them from providing adequately for their families. Referring to their experience as revolutionary soldiers, they asserted that they "esteem[ed] one moment of Liberty to be worth an eternity of Bondage." One rebel sympathizer explained, "Whenever any encroachments are made either upon the liberties or properties of the people, if re-

William Smith, painted with his grandson in 1788 by Charles Willson Peale, presented the public image appropriate to a dignified citizen of the new republic.

A woodcut of Daniel Shays and one of his chief officers, Job Shattuck, in 1787.   National Portrait Gallery, Smithsonian Institution, Washington, D.C.

dress cannot be had without, it is virtue in them to disturb government." The Massachusetts government was "tyrannical," Shays asserted, and, like that of Great Britain, deserved to be overthrown.

To the state's elected leaders, the most ominous aspect of the uprising was the rebels' attempt to forge direct links with the earlier struggle for independence. The state legislature issued an address to the people asserting that "in a republican government the majority must govern. If the minor part governs it becomes aristocracy; if every one opposed at his pleasure, it is no government, it is anarchy and confusion." Thus Massachusetts officials insisted that the crowd actions that had once been a justifiable response to British tyranny were no longer legitimate. In a republic, reform had to come about through the ballot box rather than by force. If the nation's citizens refused to submit to legitimate authority, the result would be chaos and the collapse of the government.

The confrontation at the Springfield armory symbolized for many Americans the trials facing the new nation. That the rebels were dispersed easily, that their leaders (including Shays) had to flee to neighboring states for asylum, that two of the insurgents were hanged, and that a newly elected Massachusetts legislature adopted concilia-

tory measures—none of these outcomes altered American political leaders' interpretation of the events in western Massachusetts. In Shays' Rebellion they thought they discerned the first signs of disintegration of the republic they had worked so hard to establish.

Republicanism—the idea that governments should be based wholly on the consent of the people—originated with political theorists in ancient Greece and Rome. Republics, such writers declared, were desirable yet fragile forms of government. Unless their citizens were especially virtuous—that is, sober, moral, and industrious—and largely in agreement on key issues, republics were doomed to failure. When Americans left the British Empire, they abandoned the idea that the best system of government balanced monarchy, aristocracy, and democracy—or, to put it another way, that a stable polity required participation by a king, the nobility, and the people. They substituted a belief in the superiority of republicanism, in which the people, not Parliament, were sovereign. Now Americans had to deal with the potentially unwelcome consequences of that decision. How could they best ensure political stability? How could they foster consensus among the populace? How could they create a virtuous republic?

• Important Events •

1776	Second Continental Congress directs states to draft constitutions			Constitutional Convention drafts new form of government
1777	Articles of Confederation sent to states for ratification		**1788**	Hamilton, Jay, and Madison write *The Federalist* to urge ratification of the Constitution
1781	Articles of Confederation ratified			Constitution ratified
1786	Annapolis Convention meets, discusses reforming government		**1794**	Defeat of Miami Confederacy at Fallen Timbers
1786–87	Shays' Rebellion in western Massachusetts raises questions about future of the republic		**1795**	Treaty of Greenville opens Ohio to white settlement
1787	Northwest Ordinance organizes territory north of Ohio River and east of Mississippi River		**1800**	Mason Locke Weems publishes his *Life of Washington*

America's political and intellectual leaders worked hard to inculcate virtue in their fellow countrymen and countrywomen. After 1776, American literature, theater, art, architecture, and education all pursued explicitly moral goals. The education of women was considered particularly important, for as the mothers of the republic's children, they were primarily responsible for ensuring the nation's future. On such matters Americans could agree, but they disagreed on many other critical issues. Almost all white men concurred that women, Indians, and African-Americans should be excluded from formal participation in politics, but they found it very difficult to reach a consensus on how many of their own number should be included. And when should men's consent be sought: semiannually? annually? at intervals of two or more years? Further, how should governments be structured so as to reflect the people's consent most accurately? Americans replied to these questions in a variety of ways.

Republican citizens had to answer many other questions as well. Should a republic conduct its dealings with Indian tribes and foreign countries any differently than other types of governments did? Were republics, in other words, obliged to negotiate fairly and honestly at all times? And then there were Thomas Jefferson's words in the Declaration of Independence: "all men are created equal." Given that bold statement of principle,

how could white republicans justify holding African-Americans in perpetual bondage? Some answered that question by freeing their slaves or by voting for state laws that abolished slavery. Others responded by denying that blacks were "men" in the same sense as whites.

The most important task facing Americans in these years was the construction of a genuinely national government. Before 1765, the English mainland colonies had rarely cooperated on common endeavors. Many circumstances separated them: their diverse economies, varying religious traditions and ethnic compositions, competing land claims (especially in the West), and different political systems. But fighting the Revolutionary War brought them together and created a new nationalistic spirit, especially among those who served in the Continental Army or the diplomatic corps. Wartime experiences broke down at least some of the boundaries that had previously divided Americans, replacing loyalties to state and region with loyalties to the nation.

Still, forging a national republic (as opposed to a set of loosely connected state republics) was neither easy nor simple. America's first such government, the Articles of Confederation, proved to be inadequate. But some of the nation's political leaders learned from their experiences and tried another approach when they drafted the Constitution in 1787. Some historians have argued that the Articles of Confederation and the Constitution reflect opposing political philosophies, the Constitution representing an "aristocratic" counterrevolution against the "democratic" Articles. The two documents are more accurately viewed as successive attempts to solve the same problems. Both applied theories of republicanism to practical problems of governance; neither was entirely successful in resolving those difficulties.

CREATING A VIRTUOUS REPUBLIC

When the colonies declared their independence from Great Britain, John Dickinson recalled many years later, "there was no question concerning forms of Government, no enquiry whether a Republic or a limited Monarchy was best. . . . We knew that the people of this country must unite themselves under some form of Government and that this could be no other than the republican form." But how should that goal be implemented?

Three different definitions of *republicanism* emerged in the new United States. The first, held chiefly by members of the educated elite (such as the Adamses of Massachu-

Varieties of Republicanism

setts), was based directly on ancient history and political theory. The histories of popular governments in Greece and Rome seemed to prove that republics could succeed only if they were small in size and homogeneous in population. Unless the citizens of a republic were willing to sacrifice their own private interests for the good of the whole, the government would inevitably collapse. A truly virtuous man, classical republican theory insisted, had to forgo personal profit and work solely for the best interests of the nation. In return for sacrifices, though, a republic offered its citizens equality of opportunity. Under such a government, rank would be based on merit rather than inherited wealth and status. Society would be governed by members of a "natural aristocracy," men whose talent had elevated them from what might have been humble beginnings to positions of power and privilege. Rank would not be abolished but instead founded on merit.

A second definition, advanced by other members of the elite but also by some skilled craftsmen, drew more on economic theory than political thought. Instead of perceiving the nation as an organic whole composed of people nobly sacrificing for the common good, this version of republicanism followed the English theorist Adam Smith in emphasizing individuals' pursuit of rational self-interest. The applicability of this approach was underscored by the huge profits some men reaped from their patriotic participation in the war effort by selling supplies to the army. The nation could only benefit from aggressive economic expansion, argued such men as Alexander Hamilton (see page 215). When republican men sought to improve their own economic and social circumstances, the entire nation would benefit. Republican virtue would be achieved through the pursuit of private interests, rather than through their subordination to some communal ideal.

The third notion of republicanism was more egalitarian than the other two, which both contained considerable potential for inequality. This view was less influential because many of its proponents were illiterate or barely literate, and thus wrote little to promote their beliefs. Americans who advanced this version of republicanism, the most prominent of whom was Thomas Paine, called for widening men's participation in the political process. They also wanted government to respond directly to the needs of ordinary folk and openly rejected any notion that "the lesser sort" should automatically defer to their "betters." They were, in fact, democrats in more or less the modern sense. For them, republican virtue was embodied in the untutored wisdom of the people as a whole, rather than in the special insights of a natural aristocracy or the pronouncements of wealthy individuals.

Despite the differences, it is important to recognize that the three strands of republicanism were part of a unified whole and shared many of the same assumptions. For example, all three contrasted a virtuous, industrious America to the corruption of England and Europe. In the first version, that virtue manifested itself in frugality and self-sacrifice; in the second, it would prevent self-interest from becoming vice; in the third, it was the justification for including even propertyless white men in the ranks of voters. "Virtue, Virtue alone . . . is the basis of a republic," asserted Dr. Benjamin Rush of Philadelphia, an ardent patriot, in 1778. His fellow Americans concurred, even if they defined virtue in divergent ways. Most agreed that a virtuous country would be composed of

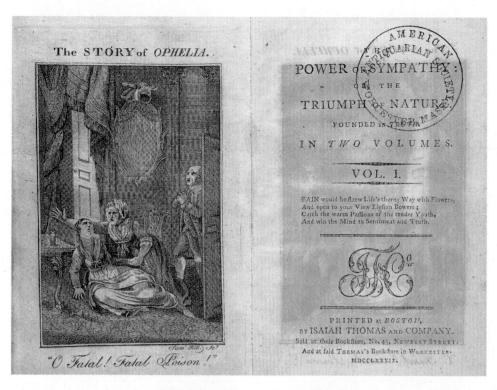

How do historians know

that American women were reading novels after the American Revolution? Modern best-seller lists and readers' surveys did not exist in late eighteenth-century America, so historians have to look to other sources to find the answer to this question. Many types of evidence suggest the popularity of novels among a wide audience of females in the 1780s and 1790s. Women who kept diaries often took note of the titles of books they were reading; others mentioned novels in their letters to friends. Ministers preached sermons decrying young women's addiction to reading novels, and authors of advice books urged readers to turn their attention to more uplifting forms of literature. Perhaps most important is the evidence of the books themselves, like The Power of Sympathy, the first novel written in the United States. After the Revolution the new nation's printers published a myriad of British and American novels, finding in them a ready source of profit. Historians studying the phenomenon of novel-reading have linked it to women's increasing literacy and the availability of leisure time for reading, as well as to the useful messages about life's pitfalls and prospects the novels conveyed to their young readers.   Photo: American Antiquarian Society.

hard-working citizens who would dress simply and live plainly, elect wise leaders to public office, and forgo the conspicuous consumption of luxury goods.

As the citizens of the United States set out to construct their republic, they believed they were embarking on an unprecedented enterprise. With great pride in their new nation, they expected to replace the vices of monarchical Europe—immorality, selfishness, and lack of public-spiritedness—

Virtue and the Arts

with the sober virtues of republican America. They wanted to embody republican principles not only in their governments but also in their society and their culture. They looked to painting, literature, drama, and architecture to convey messages of nationalism and virtue to the public.

Americans faced a crucial contradiction at the very outset of their efforts. To some republicans, the fine arts themselves were manifestations of vice. Their existence in a virtuous society, many contended, signaled the arrival of luxury and corruption. What need did a frugal yeoman have for

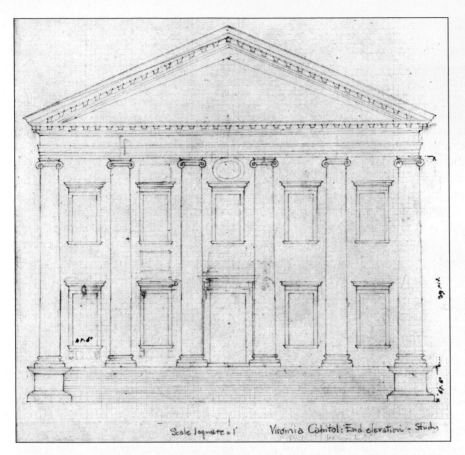

Thomas Jefferson's design for the front of the Virginia State Capitol, c. 1785, epitomized the architectural ideals of the republic.   Massachusetts Historical Society.

a painting—or, worse yet, a novel? Why should anyone spend hard-earned wages to see a play in a lavishly decorated theater? The first American artists, playwrights, and authors thus confronted an impossible dilemma. They wanted to produce works embodying virtue, but those very works, regardless of their content, were viewed by many as corrupting.

Still, they tried. William Hill Brown's *The Power of Sympathy* (1789), the first novel written in the United States, was a lurid tale of seduction intended as a warning to young women, who made up a large proportion of America's fiction readers. In Royall Tyler's *The Contrast* (1787), the first successful American play, the virtuous conduct of Colonel Manly was contrasted (hence the title) with the reprehensible behavior of the fop Billy Dimple. The most popular book of the era, Mason Locke Weems's *Life of Washington*, published in 1800 shortly after George Washington's death, was in-

tended by its author to "hold up his great Virtues . . . to the imitation of Our Youth." Weems could hardly be accused of subtlety. The famous tale he invented—six-year-old George bravely admitting cutting down his father's favorite cherry tree—ended with George's father exclaiming, "Run to my arms, you dearest boy. . . . Such an act of heroism in my son, is worth more than a thousand trees, though blossomed with silver, and their fruit of purest gold."

Painting and architecture, too, were expected to embody high moral standards. Two of the most prominent artists of the period, Gilbert Stuart and Charles Willson Peale, painted innumerable portraits of upstanding republican citizens. John Trumbull's vast canvases depicted such milestones of American history as the Battle of Bunker Hill, Burgoyne's surrender at Saratoga, and Cornwallis's capitulation at Yorktown. Both portraits and historical scenes were intended to instill patriotic sentiments in their viewers. Architects likewise hoped to convey in their buildings a sense of the young republic's ideals. When the Virginia government asked Thomas Jefferson, then ambassador to France, for advice on the design of the state capitol in Richmond, Jefferson unhesitatingly recommended copying a Roman building, the Maison Carrée at Nîmes. "It is very simple," he explained, "but it is noble beyond expression"; his drawing, reprinted here, illustrated his words. Jefferson set forth ideals that would guide American architecture for a generation to come: simplicity of line, harmonious proportions, a feeling of grandeur. Nowhere were these rational goals of republican art manifested more clearly than in Benjamin H. Latrobe's plans for the majestic domed United States Capitol in Washington, D.C., built shortly after the turn of the century.

Despite the artists' efforts (or, some would have said, because of them), some Americans were beginning to detect signs of luxury and corruption by the mid-1780s. The end of the war and resumption of European trade brought a return to fashionable clothing for both men and women and abandonment of the simpler homespun garments patriots had once worn with pride. Elite families again attended balls and concerts. Parties no longer seemed complete without gambling and card playing. Social clubs for young people multiplied; Samuel Adams worried in print about the opportunities for corruption lurking behind innocent plans for tea drinking and genteel conversation among Boston youths. Especially alarming to fervent republicans was the establishment in 1783 of the Society of the Cincinnati, a hereditary organization of Revolutionary War officers and their descendants. Many feared that the group would become the nucleus of a native-born aristocracy. All these developments directly challenged the United States's self-image as a virtuous republic.

Their deep-seated concern for the future of the infant republic focused Americans' attention on their children, the "rising generation." Throughout the history of the colonies, education had been seen chiefly as a private means to personal advancement, of concern only to individual families. Now, though, education would serve a public purpose. If young people were to resist the temptations of vice, they would have to learn the lessons of virtue

Educational Reform

_____

at home and at school. In fact, the very survival of the nation depended on it. The early republican period was thus a time of major educational reform.

The 1780s and 1790s brought two significant changes in American educational practice. First, in contrast to the colonies, where nearly all education had been privately financed, some northern states began to be willing to use tax money to support public elementary schools. In 1789, Massachusetts became one of the first states to require towns to offer their citizens free public elementary education.

Second, schooling for girls was improved. Americans' recognition of the importance of the rising generation led to the realization that mothers would have to be properly educated if they were to instruct their children adequately. Therefore Massachusetts insisted in its 1789 law that town elementary schools be open to girls as well as boys. Throughout the United States, private academies were founded to give teenage girls from well-to-do families an opportunity for advanced schooling. No one yet proposed opening colleges to women, but a few fortunate girls could study history, geography, rhetoric, and mathematics. The academies also trained female students in fancy needlework—the only artistic endeavor considered appropriate for genteel women.

The chief theorist of women's education in the early republic was Judith Sargent Murray of Gloucester, Massachusetts. In a series of essays published in the 1780s and 1790s, Murray argued that women and men had equal intellectual capacities, though women's inadequate education might make them seem less intelligent. "We can only reason from what we know," she declared, "and if an opportunity of acquiring knowledge hath been denied us, the inferiority of our sex cannot fairly be deduced from thence." Therefore, concluded Murray, boys and girls should be offered equivalent scholastic training. She further contended that girls should be taught to support themselves by their own efforts: "Independence should be placed within their grasp."

Judith Sargent Murray on Education

_____

Murray's direct challenge to the traditional colonial belief that, as one man put it, girls "knew quite enough if they could make a shirt and a pud-

Judith Sargent (1751–1820), later Mrs. John Murray, painted by John Singleton Copley when she was in her late teens. Although her steady gaze suggests clear-headed intelligence, there is little in the stylized portrait—typical of Copley's work at the time—to suggest her later emergence as the first notable American feminist theorist. Frick Art Reference Library.

ding" was part of a general rethinking of women's position that occurred as a result of the Revolution. Male patriots who enlisted in the army or served in Congress were away from home for long periods of time. In their absence their wives, who had previously handled only the "indoor affairs" of the household, shouldered the responsibility for "outdoor affairs" as well. As the wife of a Connecticut militiaman later recalled, her husband "was out more or less during the remainder of the war [after 1777], so much so as to be unable to do anything on our farm. What was done, was done by myself." Similarly, John and Abigail Adams took great pride in Abigail's developing skills as a "farmer-

ess." Like her female contemporaries, Abigail Adams stopped calling the farm "yours" in letters to her husband and began referring to it as "ours"— a revealing change of pronoun. Both men and women realized that female patriots had made a vital contribution to winning the war through their work at home and that their notions of proper gender roles had to be rethought. Americans began to develop new ideas about the role women should play in a republican society.

The best-known example of those new ideas is a letter Abigail Adams addressed to her husband in March 1776. "In the new Code of Laws which I suppose it will be necessary for you to make I desire you would Remember the Ladies," she wrote. "Remember all Men would be tyrants if they could. . . . If perticuliar care and attention is not paid to the Laidies we are determined to foment a Rebelion, and will not hold ourselves bound by any Laws in which we have no voice, or Representation." With these words, Abigail Adams took a step that was soon to be duplicated by other disfranchised Americans. She deliberately applied the ideology developed to combat parliamentary supremacy to purposes white male leaders had never intended. Since men were "Naturally Tyrannical," she argued, America's new legal code should "put it out of the power of the vicious and the Lawless to use us with cruelty and indignity." Accordingly, she called for reformation of the American law of marriage, which made wives subordinate to their husbands.

Abigail Adams: "Remember the Ladies"

Abigail Adams did not ask that women be allowed to vote. But other women wanted to claim that right, as events in New Jersey proved. The men who drafted the state constitution in 1776 defined voters carelessly as "all free inhabitants" who met certain property qualifications. They thereby unintentionally gave the vote to property-holding white spinsters and widows, as well as to free blacks. Qualified women and African-Americans regularly voted in New Jersey's local and congressional elections until 1807, when they were disfranchised by the state legislature, which spuriously claimed that their votes could be manipulated too easily. Yet the fact that they had voted at all was evidence of their altered perception of their place in political life.

Such dramatic episodes were unusual. After the war, Americans still viewed women's role in traditional terms. Most eighteenth-century

Women's Role in the Republic

white Americans assumed that women's place was in the home and that their primary function was to be good wives and mothers. They perceived significant differences between male and female characters; that distinction eventually enabled Americans to resolve the conflict between the two most influential strands of republican thought. Because married women could not own property or participate directly in economic life, women in general came to be seen as the embodiment of self-sacrificing, disinterested republicanism. Through female-run charitable and other social-welfare groups, they assumed responsibility for the welfare of the community as a whole. Yet because such public-spirited women worked chiefly with mothers and children in familial settings, women continued to be seen as private beings. Thus men were freed from the naggings of conscience as they pursued their economic self-interest (that other republican virtue), secure in the knowledge that their wives and daughters were fulfilling the family's obligation to the common good. The ideal republican man, therefore, was an individualist, seeking advancement for himself and his family; the ideal republican woman, by contrast, always put the well-being of others ahead of her own.

Together white men and women established the context for the creation of a virtuous republic. But nearly 20 percent of the American population was black. How did approximately 700,000 African-Americans fit into the developing national plan?

EMANCIPATION AND THE GROWTH OF RACISM

Revolutionary ideology exposed one of the primary contradictions in American society. Both blacks and whites saw the irony in slaveholding Americans' claims that one of their aims in taking up arms was to prevent Britain from "enslaving" them. The theme was voiced by many revolutionary leaders. In 1773 the Philadelphia doctor Benjamin Rush

called slavery "a vice which degrades human nature," warning ominously that "the plant of liberty is of so tender a nature that it cannot thrive long in the neighborhood of slavery." Common folk also saw the contradiction. When Josiah Atkins, a Connecticut soldier marching south, saw Washington's plantation, he observed in his journal: "Alas! That persons who pretend to stand for the rights of mankind for the liberties of society, can delight in oppression, & that even of the worst kind!"

African-Americans were quick to recognize the implications of revolutionary ideology. In 1779 a group of slaves from Portsmouth, New Hampshire, asked the state legislature "from what authority [our masters] assume to dispose of our lives, freedom and property," and pleaded "that the name of slave may not more be heard in a land gloriously contending for the sweets of freedom." The same year several black residents of Fairfield, Connecticut, petitioned the legislature for their freedom, characterizing slavery as a "dreadful Evil" and "flagrant Injustice." How could men who were "nobly contending in the Cause of Liberty," they asked, continue "this detestable Practice"?

Both legislatures responded negatively. But the postwar years did witness the gradual abolition of slavery in the North. Vermont abolished slavery

Gradual Emancipation

in its 1777 constitution. Massachusetts courts decided in the 1780s that the clause in the state constitution declaring that "all men are born free and equal, and have certain natural, essential, and unalienable rights" prohibited slavery in the state. Pennsylvania passed an abolition law in 1780; four years later Rhode Island and Connecticut provided for gradual emancipation, followed by New York (1799) and New Jersey (1804). Although New Hampshire did not formally abolish slavery, only eight slaves were reported on the 1800 census and none remained a decade later.

No southern state adopted similar general emancipation laws, but the legislatures of Virginia (1782), Delaware (1787), and Maryland (1790 and 1796) altered laws that had previously restricted slaveowners' ability to free their slaves. South Carolina and Georgia never considered adopting such acts, and North Carolina insisted that all manumissions (emancipations of individual slaves) be approved by county courts.

Revolutionary ideology thus had limited impact on the well-entrenched economic interests of large slaveholders. Only in the North, where slaves were relatively rare and where little money was invested in human capital, could state legislatures vote to abolish slavery with relative ease. Even there, legislators' concern for property rights—the Revolution, after all, was fought for property as well as life and liberty—led them to favor gradual emancipation over immediate abolition. Most states provided only for the freeing of children born after passage of the law, not for the emancipation of adults. And even those children were to remain slaves until reaching adulthood. Still, by 1840 in only one northern state—New Jersey—were African-Americans legally held in bondage.

Despite the slow progress of abolition, the number of free people of African descent in the United States grew dramatically in the first years after the Revolution. Before

Growth of the Free Black Population

the war there had been few free blacks in America. According to a 1755 Maryland census, for example, only 4 percent of the African-Americans in the colony were free. Most blacks who had been freed before the war were mulattos, born of unions between white masters and enslaved black women and specifically granted freedom by their fathers. But wartime disruptions radically changed the size and composition of the freed population. Slaves who had escaped from plantations during the war, others who had served in the American army, and still others emancipated by their owners or by state laws were now free. Because most were not mulattos, dark skin was no longer an automatic sign of slave status. By 1790 there were nearly 60,000 free people of color in the United States; ten years later they numbered more than 108,000, nearly 11 percent of the total African-American population.

The effects of postwar manumissions were felt most sharply in the Chesapeake, where they were fostered by such economic changes as declining soil fertility and the shift from tobacco to grain production. Since grain cultivation was less labor-intensive than tobacco growing, planters began to complain about "excess" slaves. They often solved that problem by freeing the most favored or least productive of their bondspeople. The free black population of Virginia more than doubled between 1790 and 1810, and by the latter year nearly one-

quarter of Maryland's African-American population was no longer in legal bondage.

In the 1780s and thereafter, freed people often made their way, as had landless colonists decades earlier, to the port cities of the North. Boston and Philadelphia, where slavery was abolished sooner than in New York City, were particularly popular destinations. Women outnumbered men among the migrants by a margin of three to two. Like white females, black women found more opportunities for employment, particularly as domestic servants, in the cities than in the countryside. Some freedmen also worked in domestic service, but larger numbers were employed as unskilled laborers and seamen. A few of the women and a sizable proportion of men (nearly one-third of those in Philadelphia in 1795) were skilled workers or retailers. These people chose new names for themselves, exchanging the surnames of former masters for names like Newman or Brown, and as soon as possible they established independent two-parent nuclear families instead of continuing to live in white households. They also began to occupy distinct neighborhoods, probably as a result of both discrimination by whites and a desire for black solidarity.

Emancipation, however, did not bring equality. Even whites who recognized African-Americans' right to freedom were unwilling to accept them as equals. Laws discrimi-

Discrimination Against African-Americans

nated against emancipated blacks as they had against slaves—South Carolina, for example, did not permit free blacks to testify against whites in court. Public schools often refused to educate their children. Freedmen found it difficult to purchase property and find good jobs. And though in many areas African-Americans were accepted as members—even ministers—of evangelical churches, whites rarely allowed them an equal voice in church affairs.

Gradually free African-Americans developed their own separate institutions, often based in the neighborhoods in which they lived. In Charleston, mulattos formed the Brown Fellowship Society, which provided insurance coverage for its members, financed a school for free children, and helped to support black orphans. In 1794, blacks in Philadelphia and Baltimore founded societies that eventually became the African Methodist Episcopal (AME) denomination. AME churches later sponsored schools in a number of cities and, along with African Baptist, African Episcopal, and African Presbyterian churches, became cultural centers of the free black community. Freed people quickly learned that, to survive and prosper, they had to rely on their own collective efforts rather than on the benevolence or goodwill of their white compatriots.

Their endeavors were all the more necessary because the postrevolutionary years witnessed the development of a coherent racist theory in the United States. Whites had long

Development of Racist Theory

regarded their slaves as inferior, but the most influential writers on race had attributed that inferiority to environmental factors. They argued that blacks' seemingly debased character derived from their enslavement, rather than enslavement being the consequence of inherited inferiority. In the aftermath of the Revolution, white southerners needed to defend their enslavement of other human beings against the notion that "all men are created equal." As a result, they began to argue that blacks were less than fully human, and that the principles of republican equality applied only to whites. In other words, to avoid having to confront the contradiction between their practice and the egalitarian implications of revolutionary theory, they redefined the theory so that it would not apply to African-Americans.

This racism had several intertwined elements. First was the asssertion that, as Thomas Jefferson suggested in 1781, blacks were "inferior to the whites in the endowments both of body and mind." Then came the belief that blacks were congenitally lazy, dishonest, and uncivilized (or uncivilizable). Third, and of crucial importance, was the notion that all blacks were sexually promiscuous and that black men lusted after white women. The specter of interracial sexual intercourse involving black men and white women haunted early American racist thought. The reverse situation, which occurred with far greater frequency (as white masters sexually exploited their female slaves), aroused little comment.

African-Americans did not allow these developing racist notions to go unchallenged. Benjamin Banneker, a free black surveyor, astronomer, and mathematical genius, directly disputed Thomas

After Virginia altered its manumission laws and he had become a Baptist, Robert Carter, one of the largest slaveholders in the state, decided to free all his bondspeople. He worked out a plan of gradual emancipation, freeing some slaves each year for several years. Hannah, one of his weavers, wrote to him in April 1792, requesting that she be allowed to buy her loom when she was emancipated the following January. This is one of only a handful of documents known to be written by literate slave women during the eighteenth century. Chicago Historical Society.

Jefferson's belief in blacks' intellectual inferiority. In 1791 Banneker sent Jefferson a copy of his latest almanac (which included his astronomical calculations) as an example of blacks' mental powers. Jefferson's response admitted Banneker's capability but implied that he regarded Banneker as an exception. The future president insisted that he needed more evidence before he would change his mind.

At its birth, then, the republic was defined by whites as an exclusively white enterprise. Indeed, some historians have argued that the subjection

A Republic for Whites Only

of blacks was a necessary precondition for equality among whites. They have pointed out that identifying a common racial antagonist helped to create white solidarity and to lessen the threat to gentry power posed by the enfranchisement of poorer whites. It was, some have asserted, less dangerous to allow whites with little property to participate formally in politics than to open the possibility that they might join with freed blacks to question the rule of "the better sort." That was perhaps one reason why, in the postrevolutionary years, the division of American society between slave and free was transformed into a division between blacks—some of whom were free—and whites. The white male wielders of power ensured their continued dominance in part by substituting race for enslavement as the primary determinant of African-Americans' status.

DESIGNING REPUBLICAN GOVERNMENTS

In May 1776, even before adoption of the Declaration of Independence, the Second Continental Congress directed the states to devise new republican governments to replace the provincial congresses and committees that had met since 1774. Thus Americans initially concentrated on drafting state constitutions and devoted little attention to their national government—an oversight they were later forced to remedy.

At the state level, they immediately faced the problem of defining just what a constitution was. The British Constitution could not serve as a model

Drafting of State Constitutions

because it was an unwritten mixture of law and custom; Americans wanted tangible documents specifying the fundamental structures of government. Several years passed before the states concluded that their constitutions, unlike ordinary laws, could not be drafted by regular legislative bodies. Following the lead established by Vermont in 1777 and Massachusetts in 1780, they began to call conventions for the sole purpose of drafting constitutions. Thus the states sought direct authorization from the people—the

theoretical sovereigns in a republic—before establishing new governments. After drawing up the new constitutions, delegates submitted them to the voters for ratification.

The framers of state constitutions concerned themselves primarily with outlining the distribution of and limitations on government power. Both questions were crucial to the survival of republics. If authority was improperly distributed among the branches of government, or not confined within reasonable limits, the states might become tyrannical, as Britain had. Americans' experience with British rule permeated every provision of their new constitutions. States experimented with different solutions to the problems the framers perceived, and the constitutions they produced varied considerably in specifics while remaining broadly comparable in overall outline.

Under their colonial charters, Americans had learned to fear the power of the governor—usually, the appointed agent of the king or the proprietor—and to see the legislature as their defender. Accordingly, the first state constitutions typically provided for the governor to be elected annually (commonly by the legislature), limited the number of terms any one governor could serve, and gave him little independent authority. At the same time, the constitutions expanded the powers of the legislature. Every state except Pennsylvania and Vermont retained a two-house structure and provided that members of the upper house would have longer terms and be required to meet higher standards of property-holding. But they also redrew the lines of electoral districts to reflect population patterns more accurately, and they increased the numbers of members in both houses. Finally, most states lowered property qualifications for voting. As a result the legislatures came to include some members who before the war would not have been eligible to vote. Thus the revolutionary era witnessed the first deliberate attempt to broaden the base of American government, a process that has continued into our own day.

But the authors of the state constitutions knew that governments designed to be responsive to the people would not necessarily provide sufficient protection if tyrants were elected to office. They consequently included explicit limitations on government authority in the documents they composed. Seven of the constitutions contained formal bills of rights, and the others had similar clauses. Most specifically guaranteed citizens freedom of the press and of religion, the right to a fair trial, the right of consent to taxation, and protection against general search warrants. An independent judiciary was charged with upholding such rights.

In sum, the constitution makers put far greater emphasis on preventing state governments from becoming tyrannical than on making them effective wielders of political authority. Their approach to the process of shaping governments was understandable, given the American experience with Great Britain. But establishing such weak political units, especially in wartime, practically ensured that the constitutions would soon need revision. As early as the 1780s some states began to rewrite the constitutions they had drafted in 1776 and 1777. Invariably, the revised versions increased the powers of the governor and reduced the scope of the legislature's authority. Only then, a decade after the Declaration of Independence, did Americans start to develop a formal theory of checks and balances as the primary means of controlling government power. Once they realized that legislative supremacy did not in itself guarantee good government, Americans attempted to achieve that goal by balancing the powers of the legislative, executive, and judicial branches against one another. The national constitution they drafted in 1787 embodied that principle.

The constitutional theories that Americans applied at the state level did not at first influence their conception of national government. Since American political leaders had little time to devote to legitimizing their de facto government while organizing the military struggle against Britain, the powers and structure of the Continental Congress evolved by default early in the war. Not until late 1777, after Burgoyne's defeat at Saratoga, did Congress send the Articles of Confederation to the states for ratification.

The Articles by and large wrote into law the arrangements that had developed, unplanned and largely unheeded, in the Continental Congress.

Articles of Confederation

_____

The chief organ of national government was a unicameral (one-house) legislature in which each state had one vote. Its powers included the conduct of foreign relations, the settlement of disputes between states, control over maritime affairs, the regulation of Indian trade, and the valuation of state and national coinage. The Articles did not give the national government the ability to tax effectively or to enforce a uniform commercial policy. The United States of America was described as "a firm league of friendship" in which each state "retains its sovereignty, freedom and independence, and every Power, Jurisdiction and right, which is not by this confederation expressly delegated to the United States, in Congress assembled." (See the Appendix for the text of the Articles.)

The Articles required the unanimous consent of the state legislatures for ratification or amendment, and a clause concerning western lands turned out to be troublesome. The draft accepted by Congress allowed the states to retain all land claims derived from their original colonial charters. But states with definite western boundaries in their charters (like Maryland, Delaware, and New Jersey) wanted the other states to cede their lands west of the Appalachian Mountains to the national government. Otherwise, they feared, states with large claims could expand and overpower their smaller neighbors. Maryland absolutely refused to accept the Articles until 1781, when Virginia finally promised to surrender its western holdings to national jurisdiction (see map, page 192). Other states followed suit, establishing the principle that western lands would be held by the nation as a whole.

The capacity of a single state to delay ratification for three years was a portent of the fate of American government under the Articles of Confederation. The unicameral legislature, whether it was called the Second Continental Congress (until 1781) or the Confederation Congress (thereafter), was too inefficient and unwieldy to govern effectively. The authors of the Articles had not given adequate thought to the distribution of power within the national government or to the relationship between the Confederation and the states. The Congress they created was simultaneously a legislative body and a collective executive, but it had no independent income and no authority to compel the states to accept its rulings. What is surprising is not how poorly the Confederation functioned, but rather how much the government was able to accomplish.

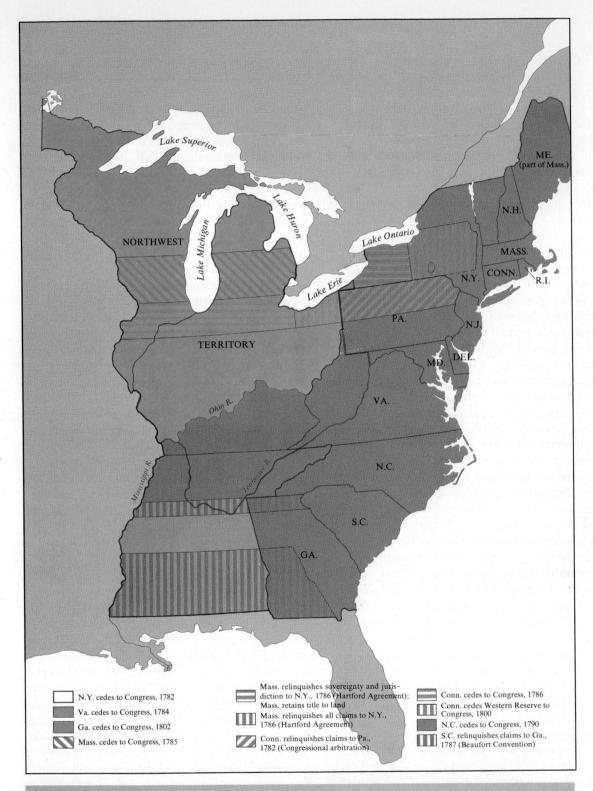

Legend:

- N.Y. cedes to Congress, 1782
- Va. cedes to Congress, 1784
- Ga. cedes to Congress, 1802
- Mass. cedes to Congress, 1785
- Mass. relinquishes sovereignty and jurisdiction to N.Y., 1786 (Hartford Agreement); Mass. retains title to land
- Mass. relinquishes all claims to N.Y., 1786 (Hartford Agreement)
- Conn. relinquishes claims to Pa., 1782 (Congressional arbitration)
- Conn. cedes to Congress, 1786
- Conn. cedes Western Reserve to Congress, 1800
- N.C. cedes to Congress, 1790
- S.C. relinquishes claims to Ga., 1787 (Beaufort Convention)

Map labels: Lake Superior, Lake Michigan, Lake Huron, Lake Ontario, Lake Erie, NORTHWEST, TERRITORY, Ohio R., Mississippi R., Tennessee R., ME. (part of Mass.), N.H., MASS., CONN., R.I., N.Y., PA., N.J., MD., DEL., VA., N.C., S.C., GA.

Western Land Claims and Cessions, 1782–1802 *The colonies' original charters often overlapped or had indeterminate western boundaries. After the United States achieved its independence, states competed with each other for control of valuable lands to which they had possible claims under their charters. That led to a series of compromises among the states or between individual states and the new nation, which are indicated on this map.*

TRIALS OF THE CONFEDERATION

The most persistent problem faced by the American governments, state and national, was finance. Because legislators at all levels were reluctant to

Financial Problems

levy taxes on their fellow countrymen, both Congress and the states tried to finance the war by printing currency. Even though the money was backed by nothing but good faith, it circulated freely and without excessive depreciation during 1775 and most of 1776. Demand for military supplies and civilian goods was high, stimulating trade (especially with France) and local production. Indeed, the amount of money issued in those years was probably no more than what a healthy economy required as a medium of exchange.

But in late 1776, as the American army suffered major reverses in New York and New Jersey, prices began to rise and inflation set in. The value of the currency rested on Americans' faith in their government, a faith that was sorely tested in the years that followed, especially during the dark days of the early British triumphs in the South (1779

and 1780). Some state governments fought inflation by controlling wages and prices, requiring acceptance of paper currency on an equal footing with hard money, borrowing, and even levying taxes. Their efforts were futile. So too was Congress's attempt to stop printing currency altogether and to rely solely on state contributions. By early 1780 it took forty paper dollars to purchase one silver dollar. Soon, Continental currency was worthless.

In 1781, faced with the total collapse of the monetary system, the delegates undertook ambitious reforms. After establishing a department of finance under the wealthy Philadelphia merchant Robert Morris, they asked the states to amend the Articles of Confederation to allow Congress to levy a duty of 5 percent on imported goods. Morris put national finances on a solid footing, but the customs duty was never adopted. First Rhode Island and then New York refused to agree to the tax. The states' resistance reflected genuine fear of a too-powerful central government. As one worried citizen wrote in 1783, "If permanent Funds are given to Congress, the aristocratical Influence, which predominates in more than a major part of the United States, will fully establish an arbitrary Government."

Congress also faced major diplomatic problems at the close of the war. Chief among them were

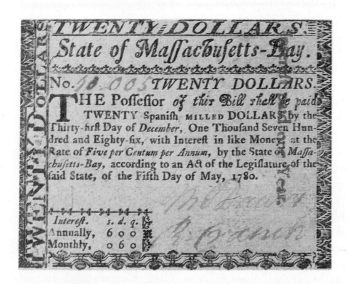

Examples of pieces of paper money issued by the state of Massachusetts and by the United States in the 1780s.   Massachusetts Historical Society.

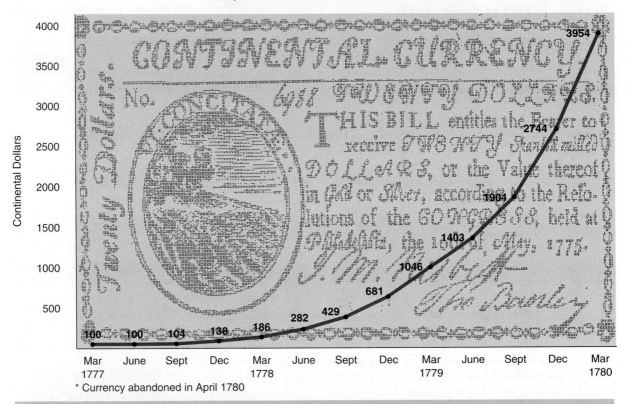

Depreciation of Continental Currency, 1777–1780

Depreciation of Continental Currency, 1777–1780 The depreciation of Continental currency accelerated in 1778, as is shown in this graph measuring its value against one hundred silver dollars. Thereafter, its value dropped almost daily. Source: Data from John J. McCusker, "How Much Is That in Real Money? A Historical Price Index for Use as a Deflator of Money Values in the Economy of the United States," *Proceedings of the American Antiquarian Society*, Vol. 101, Pt. 2 (1991), Table C-1.

Weakness in Foreign Affairs and Commerce

issues involving the peace treaty itself. Article 4, which promised the repayment of prewar debts (most of them owed by Americans to British merchants), and Article 5, which recommended that states allow loyalists to recover their confiscated property, aroused considerable opposition. States passed laws denying British subjects the right to sue for recovery of debts or property in American courts, and town meetings decried the loyalists' return. As residents of Norwalk, Connecticut, put it, few Americans wanted to permit the "Tory Villains" to return "while filial Tears are fresh upon our Cheeks and our Murdered Brethren scarcely cold in their Graves." The state

governments also had reason to oppose enforcement of the treaty. Sales of loyalists' land, houses, and other possessions had helped to finance the later stages of the war; since most of the purchasers were prominent patriots, the states had no desire to raise questions about the legitimacy of their property titles.

The refusal of state and local governments to comply with Articles 4 and 5 gave Britain an excuse to maintain military posts on the Great Lakes long after its troops were supposed to have withdrawn. Furthermore, Congress's inability to convince the states to implement the treaty pointed up its lack of power, even in an area—foreign affairs—in which it had been granted specific authority by the Articles of Confederation. Concerned nationalists argued publicly that enforcement of the treaty, however unpopular, was a crucial test for the republic. "Will foreign nations be willing to undertake anything with us or for us," asked Alexander Hamilton, "when they find that the nature of our governments will allow no dependence to be placed on our engagements?"

Congress's weakness was especially evident in the realm of trade because the Articles of Confederation specifically denied it the power to establish a national commercial policy. Immediately following the war, Britain, France, and Spain all restricted American trade with their colonies. Americans, who had hoped independence would bring about free trade with all nations, were outraged but could do little to change matters. Members of Congress watched helplessly as British manufactured goods flooded the United States while American produce could no longer be sold in the British West Indies, once its prime market. The South Carolina indigo industry, deprived of the British bounty that had supported it, suffered a setback. Although Americans reopened trade with northern European countries like The Netherlands and started a profitable trade with China in 1784, neither substituted for access to closer and larger markets.

Congress also had difficulty dealing with the threat posed by Spain's presence on the southern and western borders of the United States. Determined to prevent the new nation's expansion, Spain in 1784 closed the Mississippi River to American navigation. It thus deprived the growing settlements west of the Appalachians of their major access route to the rest of the nation and the world. If Spain's policy were not reversed, westerners might have to accept Spanish sovereignty as the necessary price for survival. Congress opened negotiations with Spain in 1785, but even John Jay, one of the nation's most experienced diplomats, could not win the necessary concessions on navigation. The talks collapsed the following year after Congress divided sharply on the question of whether agreement should be sought on other issues. Southerners, voting as a bloc, insisted on navigation rights on the Mississippi; northerners were willing to abandon that claim in order to win commercial concessions. The impasse raised doubts about the possibility of a national consensus on foreign affairs.

Diplomatic problems of another sort confronted congressmen when they considered the status of the land on the nation's western borders.

Encroachment on Tribal Lands

Although tribal claims were not discussed by British and American diplomats at the end of the war, the United States assumed that the Treaty of Paris (1783) cleared its title to

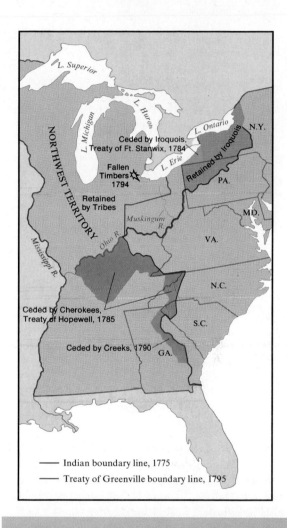

Cession of Tribal Lands to the United States, 1775–1790 The land claims of the United States meant little as long as Indian nations still controlled vast territories within the new country's formal boundaries. A series of treaties in the 1780s and 1790s opened some lands to white settlement. Source: From Lester J. Cappon et al., eds., *Atlas of Early American History: The Revolutionary Era, 1760–1790.* Copyright © 1976 by Princeton University Press. Reprinted by permission of Princeton University Press.

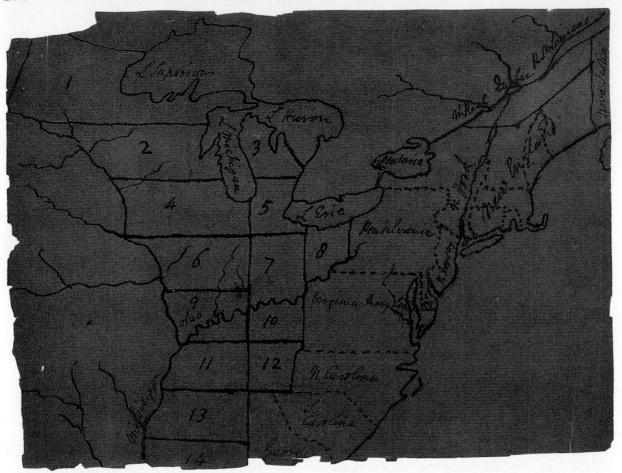

In 1784, Thomas Jefferson proposed a scheme for organizing the new nation's western lands that would have divided the region on a grid pattern, with fourteen new states (given such names as "Metropotamia" and "Pelisipia") composed of 10-mile-square "hundreds." After a year of debate, his plan was replaced by that adopted in the Land Ordinance of 1785, which is described in the text. Note that Jefferson's outline map contains some of the same errors evident in "A New and Correct Map" on page 175.   William L. Clements Library.

all land east of the Mississippi except the areas still held by Spain. But recognizing that some sort of land cession should be obtained from the most powerful tribes, Congress initiated negotiations with both northern and southern Indians. At Fort Stanwix, New York, in 1784, and at Hopewell, South Carolina, in late 1785 and early 1786, American diplomats signed separate treaties with chiefs purporting to represent the Iroquois and with emissaries from the Choctaw, Chickasaw, and Cherokee nations. Later, both groups of Indians denied that the men who agreed to the treaties had been authorized to speak for them. But the United States still took the treaties as final confirmation of its sovereignty over the tribal territories and authorized settlers to move onto the land. Whites

soon poured over the southern Appalachians, provoking the Creeks—who had not agreed to the Hopewell treaties—to defend their territory by declaring war. Only in 1790, when the Creek chief Alexander McGillivray traveled to New York to negotiate a treaty, did the Creeks finally come to terms with the United States.

In the North, meanwhile, the Iroquois Confederacy was in disarray. The members of the Six Nations who had not fled to Canada in 1779 soon found that they had little bargaining power left. In 1786 they formally repudiated the Fort Stanwix treaty and threatened new attacks on frontier settlements, but both whites and Indians knew the threat was an empty one. The flawed treaty was permitted to stand by default. At intervals until the end of the decade the state of New York purchased large tracts of land from individual Iroquois tribes. By 1790 the once-proud Iroquois Confederacy was confined to a few scattered reservations.

Western tribes like the Shawnees, Chippewas, Ottawas, and Potawatomis had once allowed the Iroquois to speak for them. After the collapse of Iroquois power, they formed their own confederacy and demanded direct negotiations with the United States. Their aim was to present a united front, so as to avoid the piecemeal surrender of land by individual tribes.

At first the national government ignored the western tribes' confederacy. Shortly after the state land cessions were completed, Congress began to organize the Northwest Territory, bounded by the Mississippi River, the Great Lakes, and the Ohio River. Ordinances passed in 1784, 1785, and 1787 outlined the process through which the land could be sold to settlers and formal governments organized. To ensure orderly development, Congress in 1785 directed that the land be surveyed into townships six miles square, each divided into thirty-six sections of 640 acres (one square mile). Revenue from the sale of the sixteenth section of each township was to be reserved for the support of public schools—the first instance of federal aid to education in American history. The minimum price per acre was set at one dollar, and the minimum sale was to be one section. Congress was not especially concerned about helping the small farmer: the minimum outlay of $640 was beyond the reach of ordinary Americans (except those veterans who had received part of their army pay in land warrants). The proceeds from the land sales were the first independent revenues available to the national government.

Northwest Ordinances

The most important ordinance was the third, passed in 1787. The Northwest Ordinance contained a bill of rights guaranteeing settlers in the territory freedom of religion and the right to a jury trial, prohibiting cruel and unusual punishments, and forbidding the future importation of slaves. It also specified the process by which residents of the territory could eventually organize state governments and seek admission to the Union "on an equal footing with the original States." Early in the nation's history, therefore, Congress laid down a policy of admitting new states on the same basis as the old and assuring residents of the territories the same rights held by citizens of the original states. Having suffered under the rule of a colonial power, congressmen understood the importance of preparing the new nation's first "colony" for eventual self-government. Nineteenth- and twentieth-century Americans were to be less generous in their attitudes toward residents of later territories, many of whom were nonwhite or non-Protestant. But the nation never fully lost sight of the egalitarian principles of the Northwest Ordinance.

In a sense, though, the ordinance was purely theoretical at the time it was passed. The Miamis, Shawnees, and Delawares refused to acknowledge American sovereignty and insisted on their right to the land. They opposed white settlement violently, attacking unwary pioneers who ventured too far north of the Ohio River. In 1788 the Ohio Company, to which Congress had sold a large tract of land at reduced rates, established the town of Marietta at the juncture of the Ohio and Muskingum rivers. But the Indians prevented the company from extending settlement very far into the interior. After General Arthur St. Clair, the first governor of the Northwest Territory, failed to negotiate a meaningful treaty with the tribes in early 1789, it was apparent that the United States could not avoid a clash with a western confederacy composed of eight tribes and led by the Miamis.

Little Turtle, the able war chief of the Miami Confederacy, defeated first General Josiah Harmar (1790) and then St. Clair himself (1791) in major battles near the present border between Indiana and Ohio. More than six hundred of St. Clair's men were killed and scores more wounded; it was the whites' worst defeat in the entire history of the American frontier. In 1793 the Miami Confederacy declared that peace could be achieved only if the United States recognized the Ohio River as the boundary between white and Indian lands. But the national government refused to relinquish its claim to the Northwest Territory. A new army under the command of General Anthony Wayne, a Revolutionary War hero, attacked and defeated the tribesmen in August 1794 at the Battle of Fallen Timbers (near Toledo, Ohio). Peace negotiations began after the victory.

War in the Northwest

By the summer of 1795, Wayne had reached agreement with the Miami Confederacy. The

After the Battle of Fallen Timbers in August 1794, General Anthony Wayne accepted the surrender of the war chief Little Turtle (above). The following summer, the United States and the Miami Confederacy signed the Treaty of Greenville (right), bringing an end to open conflict after several years of warfare. Above: Chicago Historical Society; right: The National Archives.

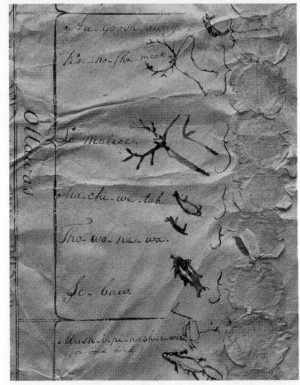

Treaty of Greenville gave each side a portion of what it wanted. The United States gained the right to settle much of what was to become the state of Ohio, the tribes retaining only the northwest corner of the region. The Indians received the acknowledgment they had long sought: American recognition of their rights to the soil. At Greenville, the United States formally accepted the principle of Indian sovereignty, by virtue of residence, over all lands the tribes had not ceded. Never again would the United States government claim that it had acquired Indian territory solely through negotiation with a European or North American country.

The problems the United States encountered in ensuring safe settlement of the Northwest Territory pointed up, once again, the basic weakness of the Confederation government. Not until after the Articles of Confederation were replaced with a new constitution could the United States muster sufficient force to implement all the provisions of the Northwest Ordinance. Thus, although the ordinance is often viewed as one of the few lasting accomplishments of the Confederation Congress, it must be seen within a context of political impotence.

FROM CRISIS TO THE CONSTITUTION

The Americans most deeply concerned about the inadequacies of the Articles of Confederation were those involved in overseas trade and foreign affairs. In those areas the Articles were obviously deficient: Congress could not impose its will on the states to establish a uniform commercial policy or to ensure the enforcement of treaties. The problems involving trade were particularly serious. Less than a year after the end of the war, the American economy slid into a depression. Exporters of staple crops (especially tobacco and rice) and importers of manufactured goods were harmed by the postwar restrictions European powers imposed on American commerce. Although some of the restrictions were eased and recovery began by 1786, the war's effects proved impossible to erase entirely, particularly in the Lower South. Some estimates suggest that between 1775 and 1790 America's per capita gross national product declined by nearly 50 percent.

The war, indeed, had wrought permanent change in the American economy. The near-total cessation of foreign commerce in nonmilitary items

Economic Change

during the war years stimulated domestic manufacturing. Consequently, despite the influx of European goods after 1783, the postwar period witnessed the stirrings of American industrial development—for example, the first American textile mill began production in Pawtucket, Rhode Island,

in 1793. Because of continuing population growth, the domestic market assumed greater relative importance in the overall economy. Moreover, foreign trade patterns shifted from Europe and toward the West Indies, continuing a trend that had begun before the war. Foodstuffs shipped to the French and Dutch Caribbean islands became America's largest single export, replacing tobacco (and thus accelerating the Chesapeake's conversion from tobacco to grain production).

Recognizing the Confederation Congress's inability to deal with commercial matters, Virginia invited the other states to a convention at Annapolis, Maryland, to discuss trade policy. Although eight states named representatives to the meeting in September 1786, only five delegations attended. Those present realized that they were too few in number to have any real impact on the political system. They issued a call for another convention, to be held in Philadelphia nine months later, "to devise such further provisions as shall . . . appear necessary to render the constitution of the federal government adequate to the exigencies of the Union."

The other states did not respond immediately. But then Shays' Rebellion convinced many political leaders that the nation's problems extended far beyond trade policy. Of the major American political thinkers, only Thomas Jefferson could view the incidents in western Massachusetts without alarm. "What country can preserve its liberties, if its rulers are not warned from time to time that their people preserve the spirit of resistance?" Jefferson wrote from Paris, where he was serving as American ambassador. "What signify a few lives lost in a century or two? The tree of liberty must be refreshed from time to time, with the blood of patriots and tyrants. It is its natural manure."

Jefferson was exceptional. The reaction to Shays' Rebellion hastened the movement toward comprehensive revision of the Articles of Confederation. After most of the states had already appointed delegates, the Confederation Congress belatedly endorsed the convention. In mid-May 1787, fifty-five men, representing all the states but Rhode Island, assembled in Philadelphia to begin their deliberations.

The vast majority of the delegates to the Constitutional Convention were men of property and substance, and they all favored reform; otherwise

The Constitutional Convention met in the state capitol of Pennsylvania, now known as Independence Hall. This view dates from 1778.   Miriam and Ira D. Wallach Division of Art, Prints and Photographs, The New York Public Library.

Constitutional Convention
————

they would not have come to Philadelphia. Most wanted to invigorate the national government, to give it new authority to solve the problems besetting the United States. Many had been members of state legislatures, and some had helped to draft state constitutions; all were influenced in their Philadelphia deliberations by their understanding of the success or failure of those constitutions' provisions. Among their number were merchants, planters, physicians, generals, governors, and especially lawyers—twenty-three had studied the law. Most had been born in America, and many came from families that had arrived in the seventeenth century. In an era when only a tiny proportion of the population had any advanced education, more than half of the delegates had attended college. A few had been educated in Britain, but most were graduates of American institutions: Princeton (ten), William and Mary (four), Yale (three), and Harvard and Columbia (two each). The youngest delegate was twenty-six, the oldest—Benjamin Franklin—eighty-one. Like George Washington, whom they

elected chairman, most were in their vigorous middle years. A dozen men did the bulk of the convention's work. Of these, James Madison of Virginia was by far the most important; he truly deserves the title Father of the Constitution.

The frail, shy James Madison—whose slight build is evident in his portrait—was thirty-six years old in 1787. Raised in the Piedmont country of Virginia, he had attended Princeton, served on the local Committee of Safety, and been elected successively to the Virginia provincial convention, the state's lower and upper houses, and the Continental Congress (1780–1783). Although Madison returned to Virginia to serve in the state legislature in 1784, he remained in touch with national politics, partly through his continuing correspondence with his close friend Thomas Jefferson. A promoter of the Annapolis Convention, he strongly supported its call for further reform.

James Madison
————

Madison was unique among the delegates in his systematic preparation for the Philadelphia meeting. Through Jefferson in Paris he bought more than two hundred books on history and government and carefully analyzed their accounts of past confederacies and republics. A month before the Constitutional Convention began, he summed up the results of his research in a lengthy paper entitled "Vices of the Political System of the United States." After listing the flaws he perceived in the current structure of the government (among them "encroachments by the states on the federal authority" and "want of concert in matters where common interest requires it"), Madison revealed the conclusion that would guide his actions over the next few months. What the government most needed, he declared, was "such a modification of the sovereignty as will render it sufficiently neutral between the different interests and factions, to controul one part of the society from invading the rights of another, and at the same time sufficiently controuled itself, from setting up an interest adverse to that of the whole Society."

Thus Madison set forth the principle of checks and balances. The government, he believed, had to be constructed in such a way that it could not become tyrannical or fall wholly under the influence of a particular interest group. He regarded the large size of a potential national republic as an advantage in that respect. Rejecting the common assertion that republics had to be small to survive, Madison argued that a large, diverse republic was in fact to be preferred. Because the nation would include many different interest groups, no one of them would be able to control the government. Political stability would result from compromises among the contending parties.

Madison's conception of national government was embodied in the so-called Virginia Plan, introduced on May 29 by his fellow Virginian Edmund Randolph. The plan provided **Virginia and** for a two-house legislature, the **New Jersey** lower house elected directly by **Plans** the people and the upper house selected by the lower, with proportional representation in both houses, an executive elected by Congress, a national judiciary, and congressional veto over state laws. The Virginia Plan gave Congress the broad power to legislate "in all cases to which the separate states are incompetent." Had it been adopted intact, it would have created a government in which national authority reigned unchallenged and state power was greatly diminished. Propor-

James Madison (1751–1836), the youthful scholar and skilled politician who earned the title Father of the Constitution. Library of Congress.

tional representation in both houses would also have given large states a dominant voice in the national government.

The convention included many delegates who recognized the need for change but believed the Virginians had gone too far in the direction of national consolidation. After two weeks of debate on Randolph's proposal, the disaffected delegates united under the leadership of William Paterson of New Jersey. On June 15 Paterson presented an alternative scheme, the New Jersey Plan, calling for modifications in the Articles of Confederation rather than a complete overhaul of the government. Paterson proposed retaining the unicameral Confederation Congress but giving it new powers of taxation and trade regulation. Even before introducing his proposals, Paterson had made his position clear in debate. Asserting that the Articles were "the proper basis of all the proceedings of the convention," he warned that if the delegates did not confine themselves to amending the Articles

THE FEDERAL
ALMANACK.

FEDERAL HALL·

LET Trumpets found, and fwift wing'd Fame,
Thefe glorious tidings far proclaim ;
On Virtue's bafe, by Wifdom plann'd ;
And rear'd by Union's facred hand ;
The FEDERAL DOME, is rais'd fublime :
Its PILLARS folid, ftrong as time ;
Rife ! Commerce ! rife ! unfurl the fail,
Rich Golden harvefts blefs the vale :
Arts ! Science ! Genius ! fpring to light ;
And Freedom burft on realms of Night

The Federal Almanack for 1789 trumpeted the virtues of the new Constitution. Not all Americans were so certain that the national government, here symbolized as an edifice supported by thirteen pillars, was as "solid, strong as time" as the printer proclaimed. American Antiquarian Society.

they would be charged with "usurpation" by their constituents. All that was needed, Paterson contended, was "to mark the orbits of the states with due precision and provide for the use of coercion" by the national government. Although the delegates rejected Paterson's narrow interpretation of their task, he and his allies won a number of victories in the months that followed.

The delegates began their work by discussing the structure and functions of Congress. They readily agreed that the new national government should have a two-house (bicameral) legislature. But they then discovered that they differed widely in their answers to three key questions: Should representation in both houses of Congress be proportional to population? How was representation in either or both houses to be apportioned among the states? And, finally, how were the members of the two houses to be elected?

The last issue was the easiest to resolve. To quote John Dickinson, the delegates thought it "essential" that members of the lower branch of Congress be elected directly by the people and "expedient" that members of the upper house be chosen by the state legislatures. Since the legislatures had selected delegates to the Confederation Congress, they would expect a similar privilege in the new government. If the convention had not agreed to allow state legislatures to elect senators, the Constitution would have aroused significant opposition among state political leaders.

Considerably more difficult was the matter of proportional representation in the Senate. The delegates accepted without much debate the principle of proportional representation in the lower house. But the smaller states, through their spokesman Luther Martin of Maryland, argued for equal representation in the Senate, while large states supported a proportional plan for the upper house. Martin argued that "an equal vote in each state was essential to the federal idea," but James Wilson of Pennsylvania responded by asking whether they were forming a government "for *men*, or for the imaginary beings called *states*?" For weeks the convention was deadlocked on the issue, neither side able to obtain a majority. A committee appointed to work out a compromise recommended equal representation in the Senate, coupled with a proviso that all appropriation bills originate in the lower house. But not until the convention accepted a suggestion that a state's two senators vote as individuals rather than as a unit was a breakdown averted.

The remaining critical question divided the nation along sectional lines rather than by size of state: how was representation in the lower house to be apportioned among the states? Delegates from states with large numbers of slaves wanted black and white inhabitants to be counted equally; delegates from states with few slaves wanted only free people to be counted. So the role of slavery in

Slavery and the Constitution

the nation became inextricably bound up in the fundamental foundation of the new government. The issue was resolved by using a formula developed by the Confederation Congress in 1783 to allocate financial assessments among the states: three-fifths of the slaves would be included in the population totals. (The formula reflected the delegates' judgment that slaves were less efficient producers of wealth than free people, not that they were 60 percent human and 40 percent property.) The three-fifths compromise was unanimously accepted by the convention. Only two delegates, Gouverneur Morris of New York and George Mason of Virginia, spoke out against the institution of slavery.

Although the words *slave* and *slavery* do not appear in the Constitution (the framers used euphemisms like *other persons*), direct and indirect protections for slavery were deeply embedded in the document. The three-fifths clause, for example, assured white southern voters not only congressional representation out of proportion to their numbers but also a disproportionate influence on the selection of the president, since the number of each state's electoral votes was determined by the size of its congressional delegation. Congress was prevented from outlawing the slave trade for at least twenty years, and the fugitive slave clause required all states to return runaways to their masters. By guaranteeing that the national government would aid any states threatened with "domestic violence," the Constitution promised aid in putting down future slave revolts, as well as incidents like Shays' Rebellion.

Once agreement was reached on the knotty, conjoined problems of slavery and representation, the delegates readily achieved consensus on the other issues confronting them. Instead of giving Congress the nearly unlimited scope proposed in the Virginia Plan, the delegates enumerated congressional powers and then provided for flexibility by granting all authority "necessary and proper" to carry out those powers. Discarding the legislative veto contained in the Virginia Plan, the convention implied a judicial veto instead. The Constitution plus national laws and treaties would constitute "the supreme law of the land; and the judges in every state shall be bound thereby." As another means of circumscribing state powers, the delegates drafted a long list of actions forbidden to the states—such as "impair[ing] the obligation of contracts."

The convention placed primary responsibility for the conduct of foreign affairs in the hands of the president, who was designated commander-in-chief of the armed forces. He could also appoint judges and other federal officers. To select the president, the delegates established an elaborate mechanism, the electoral college, whose members would be chosen in each state by legislatures or qualified voters. This, they hoped, would ensure that the executive would be independent of the national legislature—and of the people. They also agreed that the chief executive should serve a four-year term but be eligible for re-election.

The final document still showed signs of its origins in the Virginia Plan, but compromises had created a system of government less powerful at the national level than Madison

Separation of Powers

and Randolph had originally envisioned. Madison realized during the convention that, properly curbed, the states could be contributors to, not opponents of, effective government, but he was disappointed that a congressional veto of state legislation had been dropped. The key to the Constitution was the distribution of political authority—separation of powers among the executive, legislative, and judicial branches of the national government, and division of powers between the states and the nation. The agreement of two-thirds of both Congress and the states, for example, was required for the adoption of amendments. The branches were balanced against one another, their powers deliberately entwined to prevent them from acting independently. The president was given a veto over congressional legislation, but his treaties and major appointments required the consent of the Senate. Congress could impeach the president and federal judges, but the courts appeared to have the final say on the interpretation of the Constitution. The system of checks and balances would make it difficult for the government to become tyrannical. At the same time, though, the elaborate system would sometimes prevent the government from acting quickly and decisively. Furthermore, the line between state and national powers was so ambiguously and vaguely drawn that the United States had to fight a civil war in the next century before the issue was fully resolved.

The convention held its last session on September 17, 1787. Of the forty-two delegates present, only three refused to sign the Constitution.

(Two of the three declined in part because of the lack of a bill of rights.) Benjamin Franklin had written a speech calling for unity; because his voice was too weak to be heard, James Wilson read it for him. "I confess that there are several parts of this constitution which I do not at present approve," Franklin admitted. Yet he urged its acceptance "because I expect no better, and because I am not sure, that it is not the best." Only then was the Constitution made public. The convention's proceedings had been entirely secret—and remained so until the delegates' private notes were published in the nineteenth century. (See the Appendix for the full text of the Constitution.)

OPPOSITION AND RATIFICATION

Later the same month, the Confederation Congress submitted the Constitution to the states but did not formally recommend approval. The ratification clause of the Constitution provided for the new system to take effect once it was approved by special conventions in at least nine states. The delegates to each state convention were to be elected by the qualified voters. Thus the national Constitution, unlike the Articles of Confederation, would rest directly on popular authority (and the presumably hostile state legislatures would be circumvented).

As the states began to elect delegates to the special conventions, discussion of the proposed government grew more heated. Federalists—supporters of the Constitution—and Antifederalists, its opponents, published newspaper essays and pamphlets vigorously defending or attacking the convention's decisions. The extent of the debate was unprecedented. Every newspaper in the country printed the full text of the Constitution, and most newspapers supported its adoption. Even so, it quickly became apparent that the disputes within the Constitutional Convention had been mild compared with the divisions of opinion within the populace as a whole. After all, the delegates at Philadelphia had agreed on the need for basic reforms in the American political system. Many citizens not only rejected that conclusion but also believed that the proposed government, despite its built-in safeguards, held the potential for tyranny.

Federalists built on the notions of classical republicanism, holding forth a vision of a virtuous, self-sacrificing republic, vigorously led by an aristocracy of talent. They claimed that the nation did not need to fear centralized authority when good men were in charge, and that the carefully structured government would preclude the possibility of tyranny. A republic could be large, they declared, if the government was designed to prevent any one group from controlling it absolutely. The separation of powers among legislative, executive, and judicial branches, and the division of powers between states and nation, would accomplish that goal. Thus the people did not need to be protected from the powers of the new government in a formal way.

Federalists

Antifederalists fell into two main groups: those who emphasized the threat to the states embodied in the new national government and those who stressed the dangers to individuals posed by the lack of a bill of rights. Ultimately, however, the two positions were one. The Antifederalists saw the states as the chief protectors of individual rights and their weakening as the onset of arbitrary power. Unlike the document's supporters, Antifederalists did not fear such democratic "excesses" as state laws protecting debtors or providing for the issuance of paper currency, both of which were prohibited by the proposed Constitution.

Antifederalists

Fundamentally, Antifederalists feared a too-powerful central government. They rejected the Federalists' emphasis on the need for national leadership by a disinterested elite, instead trusting rough-and-tumble politics at the state level to protect their interests. Their arguments against the Constitution often consisted of lists of potential abuses of the national government's authority. They were the heirs of the Real Whig ideology of the late 1760s and early 1770s, which stressed the need for constant popular vigilance to avert oppression (see page 133). Indeed, some of the Antifederalists were the very men who had originally promulgated those ideas—Samuel Adams and Richard Henry Lee were both leaders of the opposition to the Constitution. The Antifederalist ranks were heavily peopled by such older Americans, whose political opinions had been shaped prior to the centralizing, nationalistic Revolution. Joining them were small farmers, who were preoccupied with guarding their property against excessive taxation, and ambitious, upwardly mobile men who would gain more from an economic and political system less tightly controlled than the one the Constitution promised to establish.

As the months passed and public debate continued, the Antifederalists focused more sharply on the Constitution's lack of a bill of rights. Even if the states were weakened by the new system, they believed, the people could still be protected from tyranny if their rights were specifically guaranteed. The Constitution did contain some prohibitions on congressional power. For example, the writ of habeas corpus, which prevented arbitrary imprisonment, could not be suspended except in dire emergencies. But the Antifederalists found such provisions inadequate. Nor were they reassured by the Federalists' assertion that, since the new government was one of limited powers, it could not violate the people's rights. *Letters of a Federal Farmer*, perhaps the most widely read Antifederalist pamphlet, listed the rights that should be protected: freedom of the press and of religion, the right to trial by jury, and guarantees against unreasonable search warrants. From Paris, Thomas Jefferson added his voice to the chorus. Replying to Madison's letter conveying a copy of the Constitution, Jefferson declared, "I like much the general idea," but not "the omission of a bill of rights. . . . A bill of rights is what the people are entitled to against every government on earth, general or particular, and what no just government should refuse, or rest on inference."

As the state conventions met to consider ratification, the lack of a bill of rights loomed larger and larger as a flaw in the proposed government.

Ratification of the Constitution

Four of the first five states to ratify did so unanimously, but serious disagreement then began to surface. Massachusetts, in which Antifederalist forces had been bolstered by a backlash against the state government's heavy-handed treatment of the Shays rebels, ratified by a majority of only 19 votes out of 355 cast. In New Hampshire the Federalists won by a majority of 57 to 47. When New Hampshire ratified, in June 1788, the requirement of nine states had been satisfied. But

New York and Virginia had not yet voted, and everyone realized the new Constitution could not succeed unless those key states accepted it.

In Virginia, despite a valiant effort by the Antifederalist Patrick Henry, the pro-Constitution forces won 89 to 79. In New York, James Madison, John Jay, and Alexander Hamilton campaigned for ratification by publishing *The Federalist*, a political tract that explained the theory behind the Constitution and masterfully answered its critics. Their reasoned arguments, coupled with the Federalists' reluctant promise that a bill of rights would be added to the Constitution, helped win the battle. On July 26, 1788, New York ratified the Constitution by the slim margin of 3 votes. Though the last state (Rhode Island, which had not participated in the convention) did not formally join the Union until 1790, the new government was a reality.

During the 1770s and 1780s the nation took shape as a political union. It began to develop an economy independent of the British Empire and a foreign policy that attempted to chart its own course in the world, focusing primarily on the new nation's best interests. Some Americans started to prescribe rules for the cultural and intellectual life they thought appropriate for a republic, outlining artistic and educational goals for a properly virtuous people. An integral part of the formation of the union was the systematic formulation of American racist thought. Emphasizing race (rather than status as slave or free) as a determinant of African-Americans' standing in the nation allowed white men to define republicanism to exclude all people but themselves and to ensure that they would dominate the country for the foreseeable future.

The experience of fighting a war and of struggling for survival as an independent nation in the 1780s had altered the political context of American life. At the outset of the war, most politically aware Americans believed that "that government which governs best governs least," but by the late 1780s many had changed their minds. These were the drafters and supporters of the Constitution, who had concluded from the republic's vicissitudes under the Articles of Confederation that the United States needed a more powerful central government. They contended during the ratification debates that their proposed solution to the nation's problems was just as "republican" in conception (if not more so) as the Articles. Both sides concurred in a general adherence to republican principles, but they emphasized different views of republicanism. The Federalists advanced a position based on the principles of classical republicanism, whereas the Antifederalists, fearing that elected leaders would not subordinate personal gain to the good of the whole, wanted a weak central government, formal protection of individual rights, and a loosely regulated economy.

The Federalists won their point when the Constitution was adopted, however narrowly. The process of consolidating the states into a national whole was thereby formalized. The 1790s, the first decade of government under the Constitution, would witness hesitant steps toward the creation of a true nation, the *United* States of America.

SUGGESTIONS FOR FURTHER READING

General

Richard Beeman et al., eds., *Beyond Confederation: Origins of the Constitution and American National Identity* (1987); Ronald Hoffman et al., eds., *The Economy of Early America: The Revolutionary Period, 1763–1790* (1988); Staughton Lynd, *Class Conflict, Slavery, and the United States Constitution: Ten Essays* (1967); Forrest McDonald, *Novus Ordo Seclorum: The Intellectual Origins of the Constitution* (1985); Forrest McDonald, *E Pluribus Unum: The Formation of the American Republic, 1776–1790* (1965); Edmund S. Morgan, *Inventing the People: The Rise of Popular Sovereignty in England and America* (1988); Robert R. Palmer, *The Age of the Democratic Revolution: A Political History of Europe and America, 1760–1800*, 2 vols. (1959, 1964); Gordon S. Wood, *The Radicalism of the American Revolution* (1992); Gordon S. Wood, *The Creation of the American Republic, 1776–1787* (1969); Rosemary Zagarri, *The Politics of Size: Representation in the United States, 1776–1850* (1988).

Continental Congress and Articles of Confederation

E. James Ferguson, *The Power of the Purse: A History of American Public Finance, 1776–1790* (1961); H. James Henderson, *Party Politics in the Continental Congress* (1974); Merrill Jensen, *The Articles of Confederation*, 2nd ed. (1959); Merrill Jensen, *The New Nation: A History of the United States During the Confederation, 1781–1789* (1950); Jerrilyn G. Marston, *King and Congress: The Transfer of Political Legitimacy, 1774–1776* (1987); Peter S. Onuf, *The Origins of the Federal Republic: Jurisdictional Controversies in the United States, 1775–1787* (1983); Jack N. Rakove, *The Beginnings of National Politics: An Interpretive History of the Continental Congress* (1979).

State Politics

Willi Paul Adams, *The First American Constitutions: Republican Ideology and the Making of the State Constitutions in the Revolutionary Era* (1980); Robert Gross, ed., *In Debt to Shays* (1992); Ronald Hoffman and Peter Albert, eds., *Sovereign States in an Age of Uncertainty* (1981); Donald Lutz, *Popular Consent and Popular Control: Whig Political Theory in the Early State Constitutions* (1980); Jackson Turner Main, *Political Parties Before the Constitution* (1973); Jackson Turner Main, *The Sovereign States, 1775–1783* (1973); J. R. Pole, *Political Representation in England and the Origins of the American Republic* (1966); David P. Szatmary, *Shays' Rebellion: The Making of an Agrarian Insurrection* (1980); Ann Withington, *Toward a More Perfect Union: Virtue and the Formation of American Republics* (1992).

The Constitution

Douglass Adair, *Fame and the Founding Fathers* (1974); Charles A. Beard, *An Economic Interpretation of the Constitution of the United States* (1913); Jackson Turner Main, *The Anti-Federalists: Critics of the Constitution, 1781–1788* (1961); Frederick W. Marks III, *Independence on Trial: Foreign Affairs and the Making of the Constitution* (1973); Clinton Rossiter, *1787: The Grand Convention* (1973); Robert A. Rutland, *The Ordeal of the Constitution: The Antifederalists and the Ratification Struggle of 1787–88* (1966); Abraham Sofaer, *War, Foreign Affairs, and Constitutional Power*, vol. 1: *The Origins* (1976).

Education and Culture

Lawrence A. Cremin, *American Education: The National Experience, 1783–1876* (1981); Joseph M. Ellis, *After the Revolution: Profiles of Early American Culture* (1979); Carl F. Kaestle, *Pillars of the Republic: Common Schools and American Society, 1780–1860* (1983); Russell B. Nye, *The Cultural Life of the New Nation: 1776–1803* (1960); Kenneth Silverman, *A Cultural History of the American Revolution* (1976).

Women

Charles Akers, *Abigail Adams: An American Woman* (1980); Edith Gelles, *Portia: The World of Abigail Adams* (1992); Ronald Hoffman and Peter Albert, eds., *Women in the Age of the American Revolution* (1989); Joan Jensen, *Loosening the Bonds: Mid-Atlantic Farm Women, 1750–1850* (1984); Linda K. Kerber, *Women of the Republic: Intellect and Ideology in Revolutionary America* (1980); Mary Beth Norton, *Liberty's Daughters: The Revolutionary Experience of American Women, 1750–1800* (1980).

Blacks and Slavery

Ira Berlin, *Slaves Without Masters: The Free Negro in the Antebellum South* (1974); Ira Berlin and Ronald Hoffman, eds., *Slavery and Freedom in the Age of the American Revolution* (1983); David Brion

Davis, *The Problem of Slavery in the Age of Revolution, 1770–1823* (1975); Carol V. R. George, *Segregated Sabbaths: Richard Allen and the Emergence of Independent Black Churches, 1760–1840* (1973); Winthrop Jordan, *White over Black: American Attitudes Toward the Negro, 1550–1812* (1968); Duncan J. Macleod, *Slavery, Race, and the American Revolution* (1974); Gary Nash, *Forging Freedom: The Formation of Philadelphia's Black Community, 1720–1840* (1988); Donald L. Robinson, *Slavery in the Structure of American Politics, 1765–1820* (1971); Shane White, *Somewhat More Independent: The End of Slavery in New York City, 1770–1810* (1991); Arthur Zilversmit, *The First Emancipation: The Abolition of Slavery in the North* (1967).

Indians

Harvey L. Carter, *The Life and Times of Little Turtle* (1987); Dorothy Jones, *License for Empire: Colonialism by Treaty in Early America* (1982); Francis Paul Prucha, *American Indian Policy in the Formative Years: The Indian Trade and Intercourse Acts, 1790–1834* (1962); Bernard Sheehan, *Seeds of Extinction: Jeffersonian Philanthropy and the American Indian* (1973); Anthony F. C. Wallace, *The Death and Rebirth of the Seneca* (1969); Richard White, *The Middle Ground: Indians, Empires, and Republics in the Great Lakes Region, 1650–1815* (1991).

8

Politics and Society in the Early Republic, 1789–1800

T HE FIRST LADY OF the United States, Abigail Adams, was furious. "I am at a loss to know how the people who were formerly so much alive to the usurpation of one Nation can crouch so tamely to a much more dangerous and dareing one," she wrote to her sister Mary Cranch in January 1798. France, she asserted, "aims not only at our independance and libe[r]ty, but a total annihilation of the Christian Religion." Yet every state except one—Connecticut—had inexplicably elected French sympathizers to Congress. "Virginia has but two Federilists, North Carolina but one," she lamented. "Can we expect such measures to be adopted as the safety and security of the Country require?"

Abigail Adams's anger stemmed from a deep division in American public opinion over the French Revolution, which had begun in 1789. Along with many others, she and her husband John—elected president in 1796—viewed the violent tactics of the French revolutionaries with deep alarm and saw the republic's former ally as the major threat to freedom in the world, even though other Americans continued to sympathize with the French. "There is no end to their audaciousness," she wrote her sister in the spring

of 1798. "French emissaries are in every corner of the union sowing and spreading their Sedition. We have renewed information that their System is, to calumniate the President, his family, his administration, untill they oblige him to resign." Her husband's critics were "vile liars," spreading "malice & falshood" in their newspapers. Ultimately, though, she had faith that the people's good sense would prevail. "They cannot suppose that their President can have any object in view for himself or Family, from the whole course & tennor of his Life, incompatable with the honour, dignity and independance of his Country," she concluded.

Opinionated and fiercely loyal to her husband, Abigail Adams found herself in the middle of an unprecedented phenomenon: the first truly heated partisan battle in the new republic. No wonder she was both angry and concerned. She knew her husband had devoted his life to the nation's welfare. What then could explain the bitter invective directed at him by his opponents, the political faction now called Republicans? For her and her husband there was only one answer: the criticism must have been instigated by France, whose revolutionary gov-

Arch Street, Philadelphia, 1799: a typical city street in the new republic.

Abigail Adams, painted by Mather Brown about a decade before her husband was elected president of the United States. Her serious face and sharp features reflect her strength of character.   New York State Historical Association.

ernment saw the Adams administration as its enemy. Indeed, she told her sister, her husband's opponents were "so Criminal they ought to be Presented [indicted] by the grand jurors."

The failure of Americans' quest for unity and unqualified independence during the 1790s was nowhere more evident than in the political battles that absorbed Abigail Adams's attention. The fight over the Constitution had been only the precursor of an even wider division over the major political, economic, and diplomatic questions confronting the young republic. To make matters worse, Americans had not anticipated the political disagreements that characterized the decade. Believing that the Constitution would resolve the problems that had arisen during the Confederation period, they expected the new government to rule largely by consensus. Accordingly, many Americans found it difficult to understand the partisan tensions that accompanied disputes over such fundamental issues as the extent to which authority (especially

fiscal authority) should be centralized in the national government, the formulation of foreign policy in an era of continual warfare in Europe, and the limits of dissent. They could not understand or fully accept the division of America's political leaders into two factions—not yet political parties—known as Federalists and Republicans, because factions were believed to be legitimate only in monarchies. In republics, it was thought, the rise of factions was a sign of decay and corruption. As the decade closed, then, Americans still had not come to terms with the implications of partisan politics.

Nor were prosperity and expansion easily attained. The United States economy still depended on the export trade, as it had throughout the colonial era. When warfare between England and France resumed in 1793, Americans found commerce disrupted once again, with consequent fluctuations in their income and profits. Moreover, the strength of the Miami Confederacy blocked the westward expansion of white settlement north of the Ohio River until after the Treaty of Greenville in 1795. South of the Ohio, settlements were established west of the mountains as early as the 1770s, but the geographical barrier of the Appalachians tended to isolate them from the eastern seaboard. Not until the first years of the nineteenth century did those settlements become more fully integrated into American life through the vehicle of the Second Great Awakening, a religious revival that swept both East and West.

BUILDING A WORKABLE GOVERNMENT

Americans in many cities celebrated the ratification of the Constitution with a series of parades on July 4, 1788. The processions were carefully planned to symbolize the unity of the new nation and to recall its history to the minds of the watching throngs. Like prerevolutionary protest meetings, the parades served as political lessons for literate and illiterate Americans alike. Men and women who could not read were thereby educated about the significance of the new Constitution in the life of the nation. They were also instructed about political leaders' hopes for industry and frugality on the part of a virtuous American public.

• *Important Events* •

1789	George Washington inaugurated as first president
	Judiciary Act of 1789 organizes federal court system
	French Revolution begins
1790	Alexander Hamilton's *Report on Public Credit* proposes assumption of state debts
1791	First ten amendments (Bill of Rights) ratified
1793	France declares war on Britain, Spain, and Holland
	Washington's Neutrality Proclamation keeps the United States out of the war
	Democratic-Republican societies founded; first grassroots political organization
1794	Whiskey Rebellion in western Pennsylvania protests taxation
1795	Jay Treaty with England
1796	First contested presidential election: John Adams elected president, Thomas Jefferson vice president
1798	XYZ affair arouses American opinion against France
	Alien and Sedition Acts punish political dissenters
	Virginia and Kentucky resolutions protest suppression of dissent
1798–99	Quasi-War with France
1800	Franco-American Convention ends the Quasi-War
	Jefferson elected president, Aaron Burr vice president
	Gabriel's Rebellion threatens Virginia whites
1801	Second Great Awakening sweeps through Kentucky

The Philadelphia parade, planned by the artist Charles Willson Peale, was filled with symbols that expressed those goals. About five thousand people took part in the procession, which stretched for a mile and a half and lasted three hours. The parade featured floats portraying such themes as "The Grand Federal Edifice." Marchers representing the first pioneers and revolutionary war troops were joined by groups of farmers and artisans dramatizing their work. More than forty groups of tradesmen, including barbers, hatters, printers, cloth manufacturers, and clockmakers, sponsored floats. The artisans were followed by lawyers, doctors, clergymen of all denominations, and congressmen. Bringing up the rear was a symbol of the nation's future, students from the University of Pennsylvania and other city schools, bearing a flag labeled "The Rising Generation." After the parade, the marchers imbibed beer and cider, the "Federal liquors" celebrated in the broadside circulated at that time (see photo).

The nationalistic spirit expressed in the ratification processions carried over to the first session of Congress. Only a few Antifederalists ran for

Drinking beer and cider (instead of imported spirits like brandy) took on patriotic meaning in the celebrations of the Constitution's ratification. Other forms of alcohol, this broadside proclaimed, were "Anti-federal" and thus inappropriate for the nation's citizens. Rare Book and Manuscript Division, New York Public Library.

First Congress office in the congressional elections held late in 1788, and even fewer were elected. Thus the First Congress consisted chiefly of men who supported a strong national government. The Constitution had deliberately left many key issues undecided, so the nationalists' domination of Congress meant that their views on those points quickly prevailed.

Congress faced four immediate tasks when it convened in April 1789: raising revenue to support the new government, responding to the state ratification conventions' call for a bill of rights, setting up executive departments, and organizing the federal judiciary. The last task was especially important. The Constitution established a Supreme Court but left it to Congress to decide whether to have other federal courts as well.

James Madison, who had been elected to the House of Representatives, soon became as influential in Congress as he had been at the Constitutional Convention. A few months into the first session, he persuaded Congress to impose a 5 percent tariff on certain imports. Thus the First Congress quickly achieved what the Confederation Congress never had: an effective national tax law. The new government would have problems, but lack of revenue in its first years was not one of them.

Madison also took the lead on the issue of constitutional amendments. At the convention and thereafter, he had consistently opposed additional limitations on the national government. He believed it unnecessary to guarantee the people's rights explicitly when the government was one of delegated powers. But Madison recognized that public opinion, as expressed by the state ratifying conventions, was against him. Accordingly, he placed nineteen proposed amendments before the House. Eventually, ten amendments were ratified by the states, officially becoming part of the Constitution on December 15, 1791. Not for many years did they become known collectively as the Bill of Rights (see the Appendix for the Constitution and all amendments).

The First Amendment specifically prohibited Congress from passing any law restricting the people's right to freedom of religion, speech, press, peaceable assembly, or petition. The next two arose directly from the former colonists' fear of standing armies as a threat to freedom. The Second Amendment guaranteed the people's right "to keep and bear arms" because of the need for a "well-regulated Militia." Thus the constitutional right to bear arms was based on the expectation that most able-bodied men would serve the nation as citizen soldiers; there would be little need for a standing army. The Third Amendment defined the circumstances in which troops could be quartered in private homes. The next five pertained to judicial procedures. The Fourth Amendment prohibited "unreasonable searches and seizures"; the Fifth and Sixth established the rights of accused persons; the Seventh specified the conditions for jury trials in civil (as opposed to criminal) cases; and the Eighth forbade "cruel and unusual punishments." Finally, the Ninth and Tenth Amendments reserved to the people and the states other unspecified rights and powers. In short, the authors of the amendments made clear that, in listing some rights explicitly, they did not mean to preclude the exercise of others.

While debating the proposed amendments, Congress also considered the organization of the executive branch. It readily agreed to continue the three administrative departments established under the Articles of Confederation: War, Foreign Affairs (renamed State), and Treasury. Congress also instituted two lesser posts: the attorney general—the nation's official lawyer—and the postmaster general. Controversy arose over whether the president alone could dismiss officials whom he originally had appointed with the consent of the Senate. After some debate, the House and Senate agreed that he had such authority. Thus was established the important principle that the heads of the executive departments are responsible to the president. Though unforeseen at the time, that precedent paved the way for the development of the president's cabinet.

Aside from the constitutional amendments, the most far-reaching piece of legislation enacted by the First Congress was the Judiciary Act of 1789.

Judiciary Act of 1789 That act was largely the work of Senator Oliver Ellsworth of Connecticut, a veteran of the Constitutional Convention who would become the third chief justice of the United States in 1796. The Judiciary Act provided for the Supreme Court to have six members: a chief justice and five associate justices. It also defined the jurisdiction of the federal judiciary and established thirteen district courts and three circuit courts of appeal.

The act's most important provision was its Section 25, which allowed appeals from state courts to the federal court system when certain types of constitutional issues were raised. This section was intended to implement Article VI of the Constitution, which stated that federal laws and treaties were to be considered "the supreme Law of the Land." For Article VI to be enforced uniformly, the national judiciary clearly had to be able to overturn state court decisions in cases involving the Constitution, federal laws, or treaties. Yet nowhere did the Constitution explicitly permit such action by federal courts. The nationalistic First Congress accepted Ellsworth's argument that the right of appeal from state to federal courts was implied in the wording of Article VI. In the nineteenth century, however, judges and legislators committed to states' rights were to challenge that interpretation.

During the first decade of its existence, the Supreme Court handled few cases of any importance, and there was considerable turnover in its membership. (John Jay, the first chief justice, served only six years.) But in a significant 1796 decision, *Ware* v. *Hylton*, the Court for the first time declared a state law unconstitutional. The same year it also reviewed the constitutionality of an act of Congress, upholding its validity in the case of *Hylton* v. *U.S.* The most important case of the decade, *Chisholm* v. *Georgia* (1793), established that states could be sued in federal courts by citizens of other states. This decision, unpopular with the state governments, was overruled five years later by the Eleventh Amendment to the Constitution.

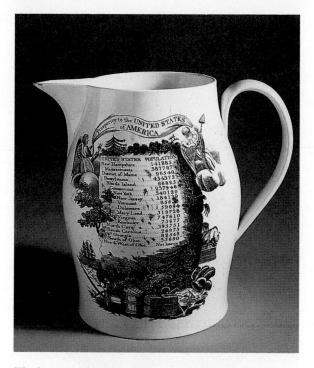

The first census in 1790, demonstrating that the United States had nearly four million residents, was a source of pride to the young republic. A jug of Liverpool ware commemorated the count by reproducing the figures surrounded by symbols of the nation's prosperity—agricultural produce, buildings, a ship, and other items. Division of Political History, Smithsonian Institution, Washington, D.C.

DOMESTIC POLICY UNDER WASHINGTON AND HAMILTON

George Washington did not seek the presidency. When in 1783 he returned to Mount Vernon, his plantation on the Potomac River, he was eager for the peaceful life of a Virginia planter. Yet his fellow countrymen never regarded Washington as just another private citizen. He was unanimously elected the presiding officer of the Constitutional Convention. As such, he did not participate in debates, but he consistently voted for a strong national government. Once the proposed structure of the government was presented to the public, Americans agreed that only George Washington had sufficient stature to serve as the republic's first president. The unanimous vote of the electoral college was just a formality.

Election of the First President

Washington was reluctant to return to public life but knew he could not ignore his country's call. Awaiting the summons to New York City, the nation's capital, he wrote to an old friend, "My movements to the chair of Government will be accompanied by feelings not unlike those of a culprit who is going to the place of his execution. . . . I am sensible, that I am embarking the voice of my Countrymen and a good name of my own, on this voyage, but what returns will be made for them, Heaven alone can foretell."

Washington acted cautiously during his first months in office, knowing that whatever he did would set precedents for the future. He held

John Trumbull, primarily noted for his larger-than-life portraits of patriot leaders, painted this miniature of George Washington, who posed for it during his presidency (ca. 1792–1794).   Division of Political History, Smithsonian Institution, Washington, D.C.

weekly receptions at which callers could pay their respects, and he toured different areas of the country. When the title by which he should be addressed aroused a good deal of controversy (Vice President John Adams favored "His Highness, the President of the United States of America, and Protector of their Liberties"), Washington said nothing; the accepted title soon became a plain "Mr. President." By using the heads of the executive departments collectively as his chief advisers, he created the cabinet. As the Constitution required, he sent Congress an annual State of the Union message. Washington also concluded that he should exercise his veto power over congressional legislation very sparingly—only, indeed, if he was convinced a bill was unconstitutional.

Washington's first major task as president was to choose the men who would head the executive departments. For the War Department he selected an old comrade-in-arms, Henry Knox, who had been his reliable general of artillery during much of the Revolution. His choice for the State Department was his fellow Virginian Thomas Jefferson, who had just returned to the United States from his post as minister to France. And for the crucial position of secretary of the treasury, the president chose the brilliant, intensely ambitious Alexander Hamilton.

The illegitimate son of a Scottish aristocrat and a woman whose husband had divorced her for adultery and desertion, Hamilton was born in the British West Indies in 1757. His early years were spent in poverty; after his mother's death when he was eleven, he worked as a clerk for a mercantile firm. In 1773 Hamilton enrolled in King's College (later Columbia University) in New York City; only eighteen months later, the precocious seventeen-year-old contributed a major pamphlet to the prerevolutionary publication wars of late 1774. Devoted to the patriot cause, Hamilton volunteered for service in the American army, where he came to the attention of George Washington. In 1777 Washington appointed the young man as one of his aides, and the two developed great affection for one another. Indeed, in some respects Hamilton became the son Washington never had.

Alexander Hamilton

The general's patronage helped the poor youth of dubious background to marry well. At twenty-three he took as his wife Elizabeth Schuyler, the daughter of a wealthy New York family. About the time of their wedding, he gave her the portrait of himself reproduced here. After the war, Hamilton practiced law in New York City and served as a delegate first to the Annapolis Convention and then to the Constitutional Convention. Though he exerted little influence at either meeting, his contributions to *The Federalist* in 1788 revealed him to be one of the chief political thinkers in the republic.

In his dual role as secretary of the treasury and one of Washington's major advisers, two traits distinguished Hamilton from most of his contemporaries. First, he displayed an undivided, unquestioning loyalty to the nation as a whole. As a West Indian who had lived on the mainland only briefly before the war, Hamilton had no ties to a particular state. He showed little sympathy for, or understanding of, demands for local autonomy. Thus the aim of his fiscal policies was always the consolidation of power at the national level. Further, he never feared the exercise of centralized executive authority, as did older counterparts who had clashed repeatedly with colonial governors, nor was he afraid of maintaining close political and economic ties with Britain.

Second, he regarded his fellow human beings with unvarnished cynicism. Perhaps because of his difficult early life and his own overriding ambition, Hamilton believed people to be motivated primarily, if not entirely, by self-interest—particularly economic self-interest. He placed absolutely no reliance on people's capacity for virtuous and self-sacrificing behavior. This outlook set him apart from those Americans who foresaw a rosy future in which public-spirited citizens would pursue the common good rather than their own private advantage. Although other Americans (like Madison) also stressed the role of private interests in a republic, Hamilton went beyond them in his emphasis on self-interest as the major motivator of human behavior. And those beliefs significantly influenced the way in which he tackled the monumental task before him: straightening out the new nation's tangled finances.

In 1789, Congress ordered the new secretary of the treasury to assess the public debt and to submit recommendations for supporting the government's credit. Hamilton

National Debt found that the country's remaining war debts fell into three categories: those owed by the national government to foreign governments and investors, mostly to France (about $11 million); those owed by the national government to merchants, former soldiers, holders of revolutionary bonds, and the like (about $27 million); and, finally, similar debts owed by state governments (roughly $25 million). With respect to the national debt, there was little disagreement: politically aware Americans recognized that if their new government was to succeed it would have to repay at full face value the financial obligations the nation had incurred while winning independence.

The state debts were quite another matter. Some states—notably Virginia, Maryland, North Carolina, and Georgia—had already paid off most of their war debts. They would oppose the national government's assumption of responsibility for other states' debts, since their citizens would be taxed to pay such obligations. Massachusetts, Con-

Alexander Hamilton sat for this miniature by Charles Willson Peale in 1780. The future Secretary of the Treasury's determination and purposefulness are reflected even in this early portrait.   Columbiana Collection, Columbia University.

necticut, and South Carolina, on the other hand, still had sizable unpaid debts and would welcome a system of national assumption. The possible assumption of state debts also had political implications. Consolidation of the debt in the hands of the national government would help to concentrate economic and political power at the national level. A contrary policy would reserve greater independence of action for the states.

Hamilton's first *Report on Public Credit*, sent to Congress in January 1790, reflected both his national loyalty and his cynicism. He proposed that

Hamilton's Congress assume outstanding
First *Report on* state debts, combine them with
Public Credit national obligations, and issue
new securities covering both
the principal and accumulated
unpaid interest. Current holders of state or national debt certificates would have the option of taking a portion of their payment in western lands. Hamilton's aims were clear: he

wanted to expand the financial reach of the United States government and reduce the economic power of the states. He also wanted to ensure that the holders of public securities—many of them wealthy merchants and speculators—would have a significant financial stake in the survival of the national government.

Hamilton's plan stimulated lively debate in Congress. The opposition coalesced around his former ally James Madison, who opposed the assumption of state debts since his own state of Virginia had already paid off most of its obligations. As a congressman tied to agrarian rather than moneyed interests, Madison also criticized the proposal to pay off only the current holders of public securities. Well aware that speculators had purchased large quantities of debt certificates at a small fraction of their face value, Madison proposed that the original holders of the debt also be compensated by the government. Madison's plan, though fairer than Hamilton's, would have been difficult, if not impossible, to administer. The House of Representatives rejected it.

At first, the House also rejected the assumption of state debts. The Senate, however, adopted Hamilton's plan largely intact, and a series of compromises followed. Hamilton agreed to changes in the assumption plan that would benefit Virginia in particular. The assumption bill also became linked in a complex way to the other highly controversial issue of that congressional session: the location of the permanent national capital. Both northerners and southerners wanted the capital in their region. The legend that Hamilton and Madison agreed over Jefferson's dinner table to exchange assumption of state debts for a southern site is not supported by the surviving evidence, but a political deal was undoubtedly struck. The Potomac River was designated as the site for the capital, and the first part of Hamilton's financial program became law in August 1790.

Four months later Hamilton submitted to Congress a second report on public credit, recommending the chartering of a national bank. This proposal too aroused considerable opposition. Unlike the earlier debate, which involved matters of policy, this one focused on constitutional issues. It arose primarily after Congress had passed the bill establishing the bank but before Washington had agreed to sign it.

First Bank of the United States

Hamilton modeled his bank on the Bank of England. The Bank of the United States was to be capitalized at $10 million, of which only $2 million would come from public funds. Private investors would supply the rest. The bank's charter was to run for twenty years, and one-fifth of its directors were to be named by the government. Its bank notes would circulate as the nation's currency; it would also act as the collecting and disbursing agent for the Treasury and would lend money to the government. Most political leaders recognized that such an institution would benefit the country, especially because it would solve the problem of America's perpetual shortage of an acceptable medium of exchange. But there was another issue: did the Constitution give Congress the power to establish such a bank?

James Madison, for one, answered that question with a resounding no. He pointed out that the delegates at the Constitutional Convention had specifically rejected a clause authorizing Congress to issue corporate charters. Consequently, he argued, that power could not be inferred from other parts of the Constitution.

Washington was sufficiently disturbed by Madison's contention that he decided to request other opinions before signing the bill. Edmund Randolph, the attorney general, and Thomas Jefferson, the secretary of state, agreed with Madison that the bank was unconstitutional. Jefferson referred to Article I, Section 8, of the Constitution, which gave Congress the power "to make all Laws which shall be necessary and proper for carrying into Execution the foregoing Powers." The key word, Jefferson argued, was *necessary*: Congress could do what was needed, but it could not do what was merely desirable without specific constitutional authorization. Thus Jefferson formulated the strict-constructionist interpretation of the Constitution.

Washington asked Hamilton to reply to these negative assessments of his proposal. Hamilton's *Defense of the Constitutionality of the Bank*, presented to the president in February 1791, was a brilliant exposition of what has become known as the broad-constructionist view of the Constitution. Hamilton argued forcefully that Congress could choose any means not specifically prohibited by the Constitution to achieve a constitutional end. In short, if the end was constitutional and the means was not unconstitutional, then the means was also constitutional.

Washington was convinced. The bill became law; the bank proved successful. So did the scheme for funding the national debt and assuming the states' debts: the new nation's securities became desirable investments for its own citizens and for wealthy foreigners. But two other aspects of Alexander Hamilton's wide-ranging financial scheme did not fare so well.

In December 1791, Hamilton presented to Congress his *Report on Manufactures*, the third and last of his prescriptions for the American economy. In it he outlined an ambitious plan for encouraging and protecting the United States's infant industries, like shoemaking and textile manufacturing. Hamilton argued that the nation could never be truly independent as long as it relied heavily on Europe for manufactured goods. He thus urged Congress to promote the immigration of technicians and laborers, to enact protective tariffs, and to support industrial development. Many of Hamilton's ideas were implemented in later decades, but few congressmen in 1791 could see much merit in his proposals. They firmly believed that America's future lay in agriculture and the carrying trade. The mainstay of the republic was the virtuous yeoman farmer. Therefore, Congress rejected the report.

That same year Congress did accept another feature of Hamilton's financial program, an excise tax on whiskey. Congressmen both recognized the

Whiskey Rebellion

——

need for additional government revenues and hoped to reduce the national consumption of distilled spirits. (Eighteenth-century Americans were notorious for their heavy drinking; annual per-capita consumption of alcohol was about double today's rate.) Import duties adopted in 1789 had raised the price of rum (which was made from imported molasses); the excise tax increased the price of domestically produced whiskey. The new tax most directly affected western farmers, who sold their grain crops in the form of distilled spirits as a means of avoiding the high cost of transporting wagonloads of bulky corn over the mountains.

News of the excise law set off protests in frontier areas of Pennsylvania, where residents were already dissatisfied with the army's as yet unsuccessful attempts to defeat the Miami Confederacy (see pages 197–198). To their minds, the same government that was protecting them inadequately was now proposing to tax them disproportionately. Matters did not come to a head until July 1794, when western Pennsylvania farmers resisted a fed-

If Congress did not react positively to the arguments in Hamilton's Report on Manufactures, *the owners of America's burgeoning industries recognized the importance of the policy he advocated. Ebenezer Clough, a Boston maker of wallpaper, incorporated into his letterhead the exhortation, "Americans, Encourage the Manufactories of your Country, if you wish for its prosperity."* American Antiquarian Society.

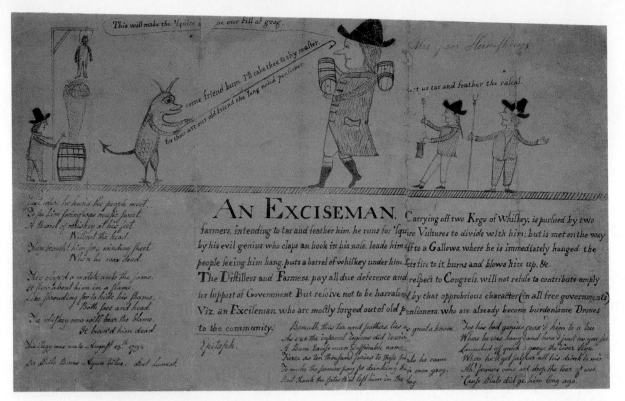

A cartoon from the mid-1790s showed the fate of an exciseman who confiscated two kegs of whiskey: pursued by two farmers, he allies himself with a devil and is hanged from a gallows.   Atwater Kent Museum.

eral marshal and a tax collector trying to enforce the law. Three rioters were killed and several militiamen wounded. About seven thousand rebels convened on August 1 to plot the destruction of Pittsburgh but decided not to face the heavy guns of the fort guarding the town. Unrest nevertheless continued for months on the frontiers of Pennsylvania, Maryland, and Virginia. Crowds of men drafted petitions protesting the excise, raised liberty poles (in deliberate imitation of the 1760s), and occasionally harassed tax collectors. But the Whiskey Rebellion remained largely leaderless and unorganized.

President Washington took decisive action to prevent a crisis reminiscent of Shays' Rebellion. On August 7, he called on the insurgents to disperse by September 1 and summoned nearly thirteen thousand militia from Pennsylvania and neighboring states. By the time the federal forces marched westward in October and November (occasionally led by Washington himself), the disturbances had long since ended. The troops met little

resistance and arrested only twenty suspects. Two, neither of them prominent leaders of the rioters, were convicted of treason, but Washington pardoned both. The rebellion, such as it was, ended almost without bloodshed.

The chief importance of the Whiskey Rebellion was not military victory over the rebels—for there was none—but the forceful message it conveyed to the American public. The national government, Washington had demonstrated, would not allow violent organized resistance to its laws. In the new republic, change would be effected peacefully, by legal means. Those who were dissatisfied with the law should try to amend or repeal it, not take extralegal action.

By 1794, a group of Americans were already beginning to seek change systematically within the confines of electoral politics, even though traditional political theory regarded organized opposition—especially in a republic—as illegitimate. In a monarchy, opposition groups were to be expected, even encouraged. In a government of the people, by contrast, serious and sustained disagreement was taken as a sign of corruption and subversion. Yet the opposition leaders Thomas Jefferson and James Madison became convinced as early as 1792 that Hamilton's policies of favoring wealthy commercial interests at the expense of agriculture aimed at imposing a corrupt, aristocratic government on the United States. They contended that they were the true heirs of the Revolution and that Hamilton was plotting to subvert republican principles. To dramatize their point, Jefferson, Madison, and their followers in Congress began calling themselves *Republicans*.

Hamilton in turn accused Jefferson and Madison of the same crime: attempting to destroy the republic. To legitimize their claims and link themselves with the Constitution, Hamilton and his supporters called themselves *Federalists*. In short, each group accused the other of being an illicit faction working to destroy the republican principles of the Revolution. (In the traditional sense of the term, a *faction* was by definition dangerous and opposed to the public good.)

At first, President Washington tried to remain aloof from the political dispute that divided Hamilton and Jefferson, his chief advisers. Even so, the controversy helped persuade him to seek a second term of office in 1792 in hopes of promoting political unity. But in 1793 and thereafter, a series of developments in foreign affairs magnified the disagreements.

PARTISAN POLITICS AND FOREIGN POLICY

The first years under the Constitution were blessed by international peace. Eventually, however, the French Revolution, which began in 1789, brought about the resumption of hostilities between France, America's wartime ally, and Great Britain, America's most important trading partner.

At first Americans welcomed the news that France was turning toward republicanism. The French people's success in limiting, then overthrowing, an oppressive monarchy seemed to vindicate America's own revolution. Americans saw themselves as the vanguard of an inevitable historical trend that would reshape the world for the bet-

ter. But by the early 1790s the reports from France were disquieting. Outbreaks of violence continued; ministries succeeded each other with bewildering rapidity; executions were commonplace. The king himself was beheaded in early 1793. Although many Americans, including Jefferson and Madison, retained their sympathy for the French revolutionaries, others began to view France as a prime example of the perversion of republicanism. As might be expected, Alexander Hamilton fell into the latter group.

When France declared war on Britain, Spain, and Holland in 1793, the Americans faced a dilemma. The 1778 Treaty of Alliance with France bound them to that nation "forever," and a mutual commitment to republicanism created ideological bonds. Yet the United States was connected to Great Britain as well. Aside from their shared history and language, America and England were economic partners. Americans still purchased most of their manufactured goods from Great Britain. Indeed, since the financial system of the United States depended heavily on import tariffs as a source of revenue, the nation's economic health in effect required uninterrupted trade with the former mother country.

The political and diplomatic climate was further complicated in April 1793, when Citizen Edmond Genêt, a representative of the French government, landed in Charleston. As Genêt made his way northward to New York City, he recruited Americans for expeditions against British and Spanish possessions in the Western Hemisphere and distributed privateering commissions with a generous hand. Genêt's arrival raised a series of troubling questions for President Washington. Should he receive Genêt, thus officially recognizing the French revolutionary government? Should he acknowledge an obligation to aid France under the terms of the 1778 Treaty of Alliance? Or should he proclaim American neutrality in the conflict?

Citizen Genêt

For once, Hamilton and Jefferson saw eye to eye. Both told Washington that the United States could not afford to ally itself firmly with either side. Washington agreed. He received Genêt but also issued a proclamation informing the world that the United States would adopt "a conduct friendly and impartial toward the belligerent powers." In deference to Jefferson's continued support for

Citizen Edmond Genêt, whose visit caused the first major diplomatic crisis in the new nation. His attempts to enlist Americans in support of the French Revolution raised troubling questions about the United States's role in the world. Collection of the Albany Institute of History and Art. Bequest of George Genêt.

France, the word *neutrality* did not appear in the declaration, but its meaning was clear.

Genêt himself was removed from politics when his faction fell from power in Paris. (Instead of returning to face almost-certain execution, he sought political asylum in the United States.) But his disappearance from the diplomatic scene did not lessen the impact of the French Revolution in America. The domestic divisions Genêt helped to widen were perpetuated by clubs called Democratic-Republican societies, formed by Americans sympathetic to the French Revolution and worried about the policies of the Washington administration. These societies thus expressed a growing grassroots concern about the same developments that were troubling Jefferson and Madison.

More than forty Democratic-Republican societies were organized in both rural and urban areas between 1793 and 1800. Their members saw them-

Democratic-Republican Societies

selves as heirs of the Sons of Liberty, seeking the same goal as their predecessors: protection of the people's liberties against encroachments by corrupt and self-serving rulers. To that end, they publicly protested government fiscal and foreign policy and repeatedly proclaimed their belief in "the equal rights of man," particularly the rights to free speech, free press, and assembly. Like the Sons of Liberty, the Democratic-Republican societies were composed chiefly of artisans and craftsmen, although professionals, farmers, and merchants also joined.

The rapid growth of such groups, outspoken in their criticism of the Washington administration for its failure to come to the aid of France and for its domestic economic policies, deeply disturbed Hamilton and eventually Washington himself. Newspapers sympathetic to the Federalists charged that the societies were subversive agents of a foreign power. Their "real design," one asserted, was "to involve the country in war, to assume the reins of government and tyrannize over the people." The climax of the counterattack came in the fall of 1794, when Washington accused the societies of having fomented the Whiskey Rebellion.

In retrospect, the reaction of Washington and Hamilton to the Democratic-Republican societies seems disproportionate to the threat they posed to the administration. But it must be recalled that factional disputes were believed to be dangerous to the survival of a republic. The Democratic-Republican societies were the first formally organized political dissenters in the United States. As such, they alarmed elected officials who had not yet accepted the idea that one component of a free government was an organized loyal opposition.

That same year George Washington decided to send Chief Justice John Jay to England to try to reach agreement on four unresolved questions affecting Anglo-American affairs. Jay's diplomatic mission had important domestic consequences. The first point at issue was recent British seizures of American merchant ships trading in the French West Indies. The United States wanted to establish the principle of freedom of the seas and to assert its right, as a neutral nation, to trade freely with both sides. Sec-

Jay Treaty

ond, Great Britain had not yet carried out its promise in the 1783 Treaty of Paris to evacuate its posts in the American Northwest. Western settlers believed that the British were responsible for the renewed warfare in the region (see pages 193–199), and they wanted that threat removed. The Americans also hoped for a commercial treaty and sought compensation for the slaves who had left with the British army at the end of the war.

The negotiations in London proved difficult, since Jay had little to offer in exchange for the concessions he wanted. In the end, Britain did agree to evacuate the western forts and ease the restrictions on American trade to England and the West Indies. (Some limitations were retained, however, violating the Americans' stated commitment to open commerce.) No compensation for slaves was agreed to, but Jay accepted a provision establishing an arbitration commission to deal with prewar debts owed to British creditors. A similar commission was to handle compensation for the seizures of American merchant ships. Under the circumstances, Jay did remarkably well: the treaty averted war with England at a time when the United States, which lacked an effective navy, could not have hoped to win such a conflict. Nevertheless, most Americans, including the president, were dissatisfied with at least some parts of the treaty.

At first, potential opposition was blunted because the Senate debated and ratified the treaty in secret. Not until after it was formally approved by a vote of 20 to 10 in June 1795 was the public informed of its provisions. The Democratic-Republican societies led protests against the treaty, which were especially intense in the South. Planters criticized Jay's failure to obtain compensation for runaway slaves, as well as the commitment to repay prewar debts. Once President Washington had reluctantly signed the treaty, though, there seemed to be little the Republicans could do to prevent it from taking effect. Just one opportunity remained: Congress had to appropriate funds to carry out the treaty provisions and, according to the Constitution, appropriation bills had to originate in the House of Representatives.

When the House took up the issue in March 1796, members opposing the treaty tried to prevent approval of the appropriations. To that end, they called on Washington to submit to the House all documents pertinent to the negotiations. In suc-

cessfully resisting the House's request, Washington established the doctrine of executive privilege—the power of the president to withhold information from Congress if he believes circumstances warrant doing so. The treaty's opponents initially appeared to be in the majority, but pressure for approval built as time passed. Frontier residents were eager for evacuation of the British posts, fearing a new outbreak of Indian war despite the signing of the Treaty of Greenville. Merchants wanted to reap the benefits of widened trade with the British Empire. Furthermore, Thomas Pinckney of South Carolina had negotiated a treaty with Spain giving the United States navigation privileges on the Mississippi, which would be an economic boost to the West and South. Its popularity (the Senate ratified Pinckney's Treaty unanimously) helped to overcome opposition to the Jay Treaty. For all these reasons, the House voted the necessary funds by the narrow margin of 51 to 48.

Analysis of the vote reveals both the regional nature of the division and the growing cohesion of the Republican and Federalist factions in Congress.

Republicans and Federalists Voting in favor of the appropriations were 44 Federalists and 7 Republicans; voting against were 45 Republicans and 3 Federalists. The final tally was also split by region. The vast majority of votes against the bill were cast by southerners (including the three Federalists, who were Virginians). The bill's supporters were from New England and the middle states, with the exception of two South Carolina Federalists. The seven Republicans who voted for the appropriations were from commercial areas in New York, Pennsylvania, and Maryland.

The small number of defectors on both sides reveals a new force at work in American politics: partisanship. Voting statistics from the first four Congresses show the ever-increasing tendency of members of the House of Representatives to vote as cohesive groups, rather than as individuals. If factional loyalty is defined as voting together at least two-thirds of the time on national issues, the percentage of nonaligned congressmen dropped from 42 percent in 1790 to just 7 percent in 1796. Significantly, this trend toward party cohesion occurred even though Congress experienced extremely heavy turnover. Most congressmen served only one or two terms in office, and fewer than

10 percent were re-elected more than three times. During the 1790s the majority slowly shifted from Federalist to Republican. Federalists controlled the first three Congresses, through spring 1795. Republicans gained the ascendancy in the Fourth Congress. Federalists returned to power with slight majorities in the Fifth and Sixth Congresses, and the Republicans took over—more or less for good—in the Seventh Congress in 1801.

To describe these shifts is easier than to explain them. The growing division cannot be accurately explained in the terms used by Jefferson and Madison (aristocrats versus the people) or by Hamilton and Washington (true patriots versus subversive rabble). Simple economic differences between agrarian and commercial interests do not provide the answer either, since more than 90 percent of Americans in the 1790s lived in rural areas. Moreover, Jefferson's vision of a prosperous agrarian America was based on commercial farming, not rural self-sufficiency. Nor did the Federalist-Republican division simply repeat the Federalist-Antifederalist debate of 1787–1788. Even though most Antifederalists became Republicans, the party's leaders, Madison and Jefferson, had supported the adoption of the Constitution.

Yet certain distinctions can be made. Republicans, who were especially prominent in the southern and middle states, tended to be self-assured, confident, and optimistic about both politics and the economy. Southern planters, firmly in control of their region and of a class of enslaved laborers, did not fear instability, at least among the white population. They foresaw a prosperous future based partly on continued westward expansion, which they expected to dominate. Republicans employed democratic rhetoric to win the allegiance of small farmers south of New England. Members of non-English ethnic groups, especially Irish, Scots, and Germans, found their words attractive. Also included in the Republican coalition were artisans, who saw themselves as the urban equivalent of yeoman farmers and valued their independence from domineering bosses. Republicans of all descriptions emphasized developing America's own resources and were less concerned about the nation's position in the world. Republicans also remained sympathetic to France in international affairs.

By contrast, Federalists, concentrated in New England, came mostly from English stock. They drew considerable support from commercial interests and were insecure, uncertain of the future. They stressed the need for order, authority, and regularity in the political world. Unlike Republicans, Federalists had no grassroots political organization and put little emphasis on involving ordinary people in government. Not all Federalists were wealthy merchants; many were farmers who, prevented from expanding agricultural production because of New England's poor soil, gravitated toward the more conservative party. Federalists, like Republicans, assumed that southern interests would dominate the lands west of the mountains, so they had little incentive to work actively to develop that potentially rich territory. In Federalist eyes, the nation was perpetually threatened by potential enemies, both internal and external, and was best protected by a continuing alliance with Great Britain. Their vision of international affairs may have been more accurate than that of the Republicans, given the warfare in Europe, but it was also narrow and unattractive. Since the Federalist view held out little hope of a better future to the voters of any region, it is not surprising that the Republicans eventually prevailed.

The presence of the two organized groups—not yet parties in the modern sense but active contenders for office nonetheless—made the presidential election of 1796 the first that was seriously contested. Tired of the criticism to which he had been subjected, George Washington decided to retire from office. (Presidents had not yet been limited to two terms by constitutional amendment.) In September Washington published his famous Farewell Address, most of which was written by Hamilton. In it Washington outlined two principles that guided American foreign policy at least until the late 1940s: to maintain commercial but not political ties to other nations and to enter no permanent alliances. He also drew a sharp distinction between the United States and Europe, stressing America's uniqueness and the need for unilateralism (independent action in foreign affairs).

Washington's Farewell Address

Domestically, Washington lamented the existence of factional divisions among his countrymen. His call for an end to partisan strife has often been interpreted by historians as the statement of a man who could see beyond political affiliations to the good of the whole. But it is more accurately read in the context of its day as an attack on the legitimacy of the Republican opposition. What Washington wanted was unity behind the Federalist banner, which he saw as the only proper political stance. The Federalists (like the Republicans) continued to see themselves as the sole guardians of the truth and the only true heirs of the Revolution; they perceived their opponents as misguided, unpatriotic troublemakers who were undermining the ideals of the Revolution.

To succeed Washington, the Federalists in Congress put forward Vice President John Adams, with the diplomat Thomas Pinckney of South Carolina as his vice-presidential running mate. Congressional Republicans caucused and chose Thomas Jefferson as their presidential candidate; the lawyer, Revolutionary War veteran, and active Republican politician Aaron Burr of New York agreed to run for vice president.

Election of 1796

That the election was contested did not mean that its outcome was decided by the people. Voters could cast their ballots only for electors, not for the candidates themselves, and not all electors publicly declared their preferences. More than 40 percent of the members of the electoral college were chosen by state legislatures rather than by popular vote, and some were picked even before the presidential candidates had been named by the congressional caucuses. Moreover, the method of voting in the electoral college did not take into account the possibility of party slates. The authors of the Constitution had not foreseen the development of competing national political organizations, and the Constitution provided no way to express explicit support for one person for president and another for vice president. The electors simply voted for two people. The man with the highest total became president; the second highest, vice president.

This procedure proved to be the Federalists' undoing. Adams won the presidency with 71 votes, but a number of Federalist electors (especially those from New England) did not cast ballots for Pinckney. Thomas Jefferson won 68 votes, 9 more than Pinckney, and became vice president. The incoming administration was thus politically divided. The next four years were to see the new

president and vice president, once allies and close friends, become bitter enemies.

JOHN ADAMS AND POLITICAL DISSENT

John Adams took over the presidency peculiarly blind to the partisan developments of the previous four years. As president he never abandoned an outdated notion discarded by George Washington as early as 1794: that the president should be above politics, an independent and dignified figure who did not seek petty factional advantage. Thus Adams kept Washington's cabinet intact, despite its key members' allegiance to his chief rival, Alexander Hamilton. Adams often adopted a passive posture, letting others (usually Hamilton) take the lead when he should have acted decisively. As a result, his administration gained a reputation for inconsistency. When Adams's term ended, the Federalists were severely divided and the Republicans had won the presidency. But Adams's detachment from Hamilton's maneuverings did enable him to weather the greatest international crisis the republic had yet faced: the so-called Quasi-War with France.

The Jay Treaty improved America's relationship with England, but it provoked retaliation by France. Angry that the United States had reached agreement with its enemy, the Directory (the coalition then in power in Paris) ordered French vessels to seize American ships carrying British goods. In response, Adams appointed three special commissioners to try to reach a settlement with France: Elbridge Gerry, an old friend from Massachusetts; John Marshall, a Virginia Federalist; and Charles Cotesworth Pinckney of South Carolina, Thomas Pinckney's older brother. At the same time, Congress increased military spending, authorizing the building of ships and the stockpiling of weapons and ammunition.

For months, the American commissioners futilely sought negotiations with Talleyrand, the French foreign minister. Talleyrand's agents demanded a bribe of $250,000 before talks could begin. The Americans retorted, "No, no; not a sixpence," and reported the incident in dispatches that President Adams

XYZ Affair

received in early March 1798. Adams informed Congress of the impasse and recommended increased appropriations for defense.

Convinced that Adams had deliberately sabotaged the negotiations, congressional Republicans insisted that the dispatches be turned over to Congress. Adams complied, aware that releasing the reports would work to his advantage. He withheld only the names of the French agents, referring to them as *X*, *Y*, and *Z*. The revelation that the Americans had been treated with utter contempt by the Directory stimulated a wave of anti-French sentiment in the United States. A journalist's version of the commissioners' reply, "Millions for defense, but not a cent for tribute," became the national slogan. Cries for war filled the air. Congress formally abrogated the Treaty of Alliance and authorized American ships to seize French vessels.

Thus began an undeclared war with France. The so-called Quasi-War was fought in the West Indies, between warships of the United States Navy and French privateers seeking to capture American merchant vessels. Although initial American losses of merchant shipping were heavy, by early 1799 the navy had established its superiority in Caribbean waters. Its ships captured eight French privateers and naval vessels, easing the threat to America's vital West Indian trade.

The Republicans, who opposed war and continued to sympathize with France, could do little to stem the tide of anti-French feelings. Since Agent Y had boasted of the existence of a "French party in America," Federalists flatly accused the Republicans of traitorous designs. A New York newspaper declared that anyone who remained "lukewarm" after reading the XYZ dispatches was a "criminal—and the man who does not warmly reprobate the conduct of the French must have a soul black enough to be *fit* for *treason Strategems* and *spoils*." John Adams wavered between calling the Republicans traitors and acknowledging their right to oppose administration measures. His wife was less tolerant. "Those whom the French boast of as their Partizans," Abigail Adams wrote Mary Cranch, deserved to be "adjudged traitors to their country." If Jefferson had been president, she added, "we should all have been sold to the French."

The Federalists saw this climate of opinion as an opportunity to deal a death blow to their Republican opponents. Now that the country seemed to

Alien and Sedition Acts

see the truth of what they had been saying ever since the Whiskey Rebellion in 1794—that the Republicans were subversive foreign agents—the Federalists sought to codify that belief into law. In 1798, the Federalist-controlled Congress adopted a set of four laws known as the Alien and Sedition Acts, intended to suppress dissent and prevent further growth of the Republican party.

Three of the acts were aimed at immigrants, whom the Federalists accurately suspected of being Republican in their sympathies. The Naturalization Act lengthened the residency period required for citizenship and ordered all resident aliens to register with the federal government. The Alien Enemies Act provided for the detention of enemy aliens in time of war. The Alien Friends Act, to be in effect for two years, gave the president almost unlimited authority to deport any alien he deemed dangerous to the nation's security. (Adams never used that authority. The Alien Enemies Act was not implemented either, since war was never formally declared.)

The fourth law, the Sedition Act, sought to control both citizens and aliens. It outlawed conspiracies to prevent the enforcement of federal laws and set the maximum punishment for such offenses at five years in prison and a $5,000 fine. The act also tried to control speech. Writing, printing, or uttering "false, scandalous and malicious" statements against the government or the president "with intent to defame . . . or to bring them or either of them, into contempt or disrepute" became a crime punishable by as much as two years' imprisonment and a fine of $2,000. Today any such law punishing speech alone would be considered unconstitutional. But in the eighteenth century, when organized political opposition was regarded with suspicion, the restrictions that the Sedition Act placed on free speech were acceptable to many.

In all, there were fifteen indictments and ten convictions under the Sedition Act. Most of the accused were outspoken Republican newspaper editors who failed to mute their criticism of the administration in response to the law. But the first victim—whose story may serve as an example of the rest—was a hot-tempered Republican congressman from Vermont, Matthew Lyon. The Irish-born Lyon, a former indentured servant who had purchased his freedom and fought in the Revo-

A cartoon drawn during the XYZ affair depicted the United States as a maiden being victimized by the five leaders of the French government's directorate. In the background, John Bull (England) watches from on high, while other European nations discuss the situation.   The Lilly Library, Indiana University, Bloomington, Indiana.

lution, was indicted for declaring in print that John Adams had displayed "a continual grasp for power" and "an unbounded thirst for ridiculous pomp, foolish adulation, and selfish avarice." Though convicted, fined $1,000, and sent to prison for four months, Lyon was not silenced. He conducted his re-election campaign from jail, winning an overwhelming majority. The fine was ceremoniously paid for him by contributions from leading Republicans around the country.

Faced with the prosecutions of their major supporters, Jefferson and Madison sought an effective means of combating the Alien and Sedition Acts. Petitioning the Federalist-controlled Congress to repeal the laws would clearly do no good. Furthermore, Federalist judges refused to allow accused individuals to question the Sedition Act's constitutionality. Accordingly, the Republican leaders turned to the only other forum

Virginia and Kentucky Resolutions

available for protest: the state legislatures. Carefully concealing their own role—it would hardly have been desirable for the vice president to be indicted for sedition—Jefferson and Madison each drafted a set of resolutions. Introduced into the Kentucky and Virginia legislatures, respectively, in the fall of 1798, the resolutions differed somewhat, but their import was the same. Since the Constitution was created by a compact among the states, they contended, the people speaking through their states had a legitimate right to judge the constitutionality of actions taken by the federal government. Both sets of resolutions pronounced the Alien and Sedition Acts null and void and asked other states to join in the protest.

Although no other state endorsed them, the Virginia and Kentucky resolutions were nevertheless influential. First, they were superb political propaganda, rallying Republican opinion throughout the country. They placed the opposition party squarely in the revolutionary tradition of resis-

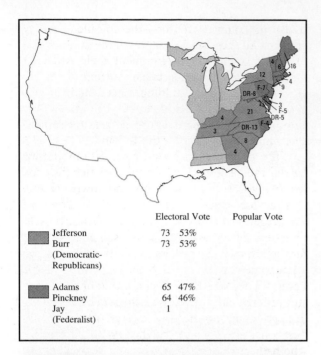

	Electoral Vote	Popular Vote
Jefferson	73	53%
Burr	73	53%
(Democratic-Republicans)		
Adams	65	47%
Pinckney	64	46%
Jay	1	
(Federalist)		

Presidential Election, 1800   The Democratic-Republicans, with their candidates Thomas Jefferson and Aaron Burr, won the votes of the southern states, while the Federalists, the party of John Adams and Charles Cotesworth Pinckney, received votes primarily in New England. The parties split the middle-states' votes, but the Democratic-Republicans dominated the vote-count there and won the election.

legitimizing the undeclared naval war. But Adams received a number of private signals that the Directory regretted its treatment of the three American commissioners. Acting on these assurances, he dispatched the envoy William Vans Murray to Paris. The United States asked two things of France: nearly $20 million in compensation for ships the French had seized since 1793, and abrogation of the treaty of 1778. The Convention of 1800, which ended the Quasi-War, provided for the latter but not the former. Still, it freed the United States from its only permanent alliance, thus allowing it to follow the independent diplomatic course George Washington outlined in his Farewell Address.

The results of the negotiations were not known in the United States until after the presidential election of 1800. Even so, Adams's decision to seek a peaceful settlement probably cost him re-election because of the divisions it caused in Federalist ranks, since Hamilton and many of his followers wanted to widen, rather than end, the Quasi-War.

In sharp contrast, the Republicans entered the 1800 presidential race firmly united behind Jefferson and Burr. Although they won the election, their lack of foresight almost cost them dearly. The problem was the system of voting in the electoral college, which the Federalists understood more clearly than the Republicans. The Federalists arranged in advance for one of their electors to fail to vote for Charles Cotesworth Pinckney, their vice-presidential candidate. John Adams thus received the higher number of Federalist votes (65 to Pinckney's 64). The Republicans failed to make the same distinction between their candidates, and all 73 of them cast ballots for both Jefferson and Burr (see map). Because neither Republican had a plurality, the Constitution required that the contest be decided in the House of Representatives, with each state's congressmen voting as a unit. Since the new House, dominated by Republicans, would not take office for some months, Federalist congressmen decided the election. It took them thirty-five ballots to decide that Jefferson would be a lesser evil than Burr. In response to the tangle, the Twelfth Amendment to the Constitution (1804) changed the method of voting in the electoral college to allow for a party ticket.

Election of 1800

tance to tyrannical authority. Second, the theory of union they proposed inspired southern states'-rights advocates in the 1830s and thereafter. Jefferson and Madison had identified a key constitutional issue: how far could the states go in opposing the national government? How could a conflict between the two be resolved? These questions were not to be definitively answered until the Civil War.

Ironically, just as the Sedition Act was being implemented and northern state legislatures were rejecting the Virginia and Kentucky resolutions, the Federalists split over the course of action the United States should take toward France. Hamilton and his supporters still called for a declaration

WESTWARD EXPANSION, SOCIAL CHANGE, AND RELIGIOUS FERMENT

The United States experienced a dramatic increase in internal migration in the postrevolutionary years. As much as 5 to 10 percent of the population moved each year, approximately half relocating to another state. Young white men were the most mobile segment of the populace, but all groups moved with similar frequency. The major population shifts were from east to west (see map, page 228): from New England to upstate New York and Ohio, from New Jersey to western Pennsylvania, from the Chesapeake to the new states of Kentucky and Tennessee, which entered the union in 1792 and 1796 respectively. Very few people moved north or south, but some southerners (perhaps yeoman farmers escaping the expansion of slavery) did seek new homes farther north.

Some of these migrants moved west of the Appalachian Mountains. The first permanent white settlements beyond the mountains were established in western North Carolina in 1771. But not until after the defeat of the Shawnees in 1774 and the Cherokees in 1776 (see pages 159–160) was the way cleared for a more general migration. Small groups of families filtered through the Cumberland Gap into Kentucky, following the Wilderness Road carved out by Daniel Boone in 1775. Once the war had ended, Americans streamed over the mountains in considerably larger numbers. In 1783, only about twelve thousand whites and blacks lived west of the mountains and south of the Ohio River; less than a decade later, the 1790 census counted more than one hundred thousand residents of the future states of Kentucky and Tennessee.

White Settlement in the West

White settlements grew more slowly north of the Ohio River because of the strength of the Miami Confederacy. But once the Treaty of Greenville was signed in 1795, the Ohio country also grew rapidly. Many whites traveled by land to Pittsburgh, then floated down the Ohio River on flatboats and rafts to Marietta. Others settled along Lake Erie, on land Connecticut had once claimed under its colonial charter—the so-called western reserve. All these settlers repeated the same process of transforming the environment their American forebears had also undertaken: cutting down forests, clearing fields, building fences, and, in general, imposing patterns of land usage derived from European practice on a landscape previously managed quite differently by the Indians.

The transplanted New Englanders in particular did their best to recreate the societies they had left behind, laying out farms and towns in neat checkerboard patterns and founding libraries and Congregational churches. Early arrivals' enthusiastic letters describing Ohio's rich soil and potential for growth recruited others to join them, setting off a phenomenon known in New England as "Ohio Fever." The New Englanders, proud of their literate, orderly culture, viewed their neighbors with disdain. Ohioans, said one, were "intelligent, industrious, and thriving," whereas the Virginians who had settled across the river in Kentucky were "ignorant, lazy, and poor." He continued the contrast: "Here the buildings are neat, . . . there the habitations are miserable cabins. Here the grounds are laid out in a regular manner . . . ; there the fields are surrounded by a rough zigzag log fence."

The westward migration of slaveholding whites, first to Kentucky and Tennessee and then later into the rich lands of western Georgia and eventually the Gulf Coast, had an adverse impact on African-Americans. The web of family connections built up over several generations of residence in the Chesapeake was torn apart by the population movement. Even those few large planters who moved their entire slave force west rarely owned all the members of every family on their plantations. Most commonly the white migrants were either younger sons of eastern slaveholders, whose inheritance included only a portion of the family's slaves, or small farmers with just one or two slaves. In the early years of American settlement in the West, the population was widely dispersed; accordingly, African-Americans raised among large numbers of kin in the Chesapeake had to adapt to lonely lives on isolated farms, far from their parents, siblings, or even spouses and children. The approximately one hundred thousand African-Americans forcibly moved west by 1810

African-Americans in the West

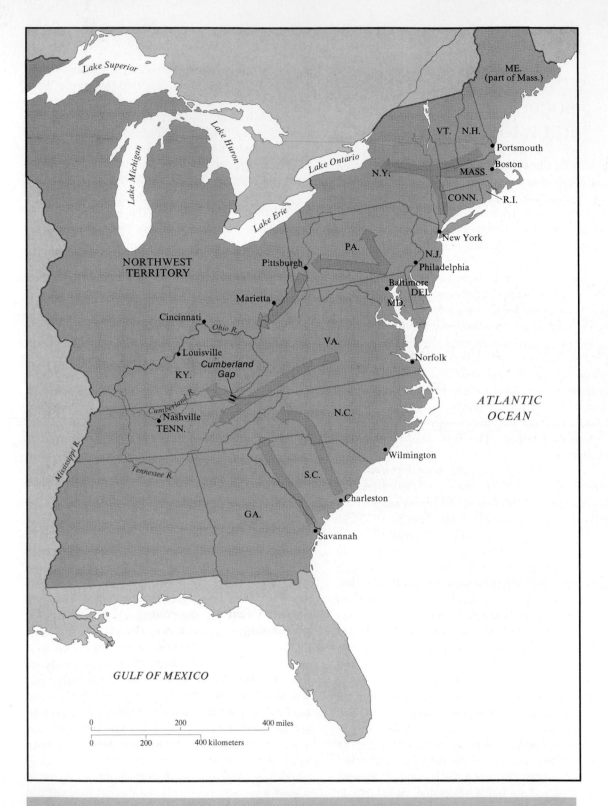

Western Expansion, 1785–1805 *After the Revolutionary War, large numbers of white and black Americans ventured west of the Appalachian Mountains for the first time. Following certain distinct routes, they moved along rivers like the Mohawk (in New York) and the Ohio, or through passes like the Cumberland Gap.*

In 1805, an unidentified artist painted Benjamin Hawkins, a trader and U.S. agent to the Indians of the southeast, at the Creek agency near Macon, Georgia. Hawkins introduced European-style agriculture to the Creeks, who are depicted with vegetables from their fields. Throughout the eastern United States, Indian nations had to make similar adaptations of their traditional life-styles in order to maintain their group identity.   Courtesy of Sumter Priddy and the Greenville County Art Museum, South Carolina.

had to begin to build new families there to replace those unwillingly left behind in the East. They succeeded well, as Chapter 11 will show.

The mobility of both blacks and whites created a volatile population mix in southern frontier areas. Everyone was new to the region and few had relatives nearby. Since most of the migrants were young single men just starting to lead independent lives, western society was at first unstable. Like the seventeenth-century Chesapeake, the late eighteenth-century American West was a society in which single women married quickly. The other side of the same coin was that the few women among the migrants lamented their lack of congenial female friends. Isolated, far from familiar surroundings, women and men strove to create new communities to replace those they had left behind.

Perhaps the most meaningful of the new communities was the affiliation supplied by evangelical religion. Among the migrants to Kentucky and Tennessee were clergymen and committed lay members of the evangelical sects that arose in America after the First Great Awakening: Baptists, Presbyterians, and Methodists. The Awakening had flourished in the southern backcountry well into the 1760s, and therefore the Second Great Awakening, which began around 1800 in the West and continued into the 1840s (see page 370), can in one sense be seen as an extension of the earlier revival. Laymen and clerics alike spread the doctrine of evangelical Christianity through the countryside, carrying the message of salvation to the rootless and mostly uneducated frontier folk.

At camp meetings, sometimes attended by thousands of people and usually lasting from three days to a week, clergymen exhorted their audiences

Second Great Awakening

to repent their sins and become genuine Christians. They declared that salvation was open to all, rejecting the doctrine of predestination that had characterized Calvinism. The emotional nature of the conversion experience was stressed far more than the need for careful study and preparation. Such preachers thus brought the message of religion to the people in more ways than one. They were in effect democratizing American religion, making it available to all rather than to a preselected and educated elite.

The most famous camp meeting took place at Cane Ridge, Kentucky, in 1801. At a time when the largest settlement in the state had no more than two thousand inhabitants, attendance at Cane Ridge was estimated at over ten thousand. One witness, a Presbyterian cleric, marveled that "no sex nor color, class nor description, were exempted from the pervading influence of the spirit; even from the age of eight months to sixty years." He went on to recount how people responded to the preaching with "loud ejaculations of prayer, . . . some struck with terror, . . . others, trembling, weeping and crying out . . . fainting and swooning away, . . . others surrounding them with melodious songs, or fervent prayers for their happy resurrection, in the love of Christ." Such scenes were to be repeated many times in the decades that followed. Revivals swept across different regions of the country until nearly the middle of the century, leaving an indelible legacy of evangelism to many American Protestant churches.

The established churches of the colonial era—supported, like the Congregationalists in Massachusetts or the Anglicans in Virginia, by tax revenues—came under vigorous attack from dissenters who used revolutionary ideology to great advantage. Isaac Backus, a New England Baptist, pointed out forcefully that "many, who are filling the nation with the cry of LIBERTY and against *oppressors* are at the same time themselves violating that dearest of all rights, LIBERTY OF CONSCIENCE." Legislators found it impossible to resist the logic of such arguments. Many states dissolved their ties to churches during or immediately after the war, and others vastly reduced state support for established denominations.

Attacks on Established Churches

These changes meant that congregations could no longer rely on public funds and that all churches were placed on the same footing with respect to the government. Church membership became entirely voluntary, as did monetary contributions from members. If congregations were to survive, they had to generate new sources of support and increase the size of their membership. Revivals proved a convenient means of doing so. The revivals represented genuine outpourings of religious sentiment, but their more mundane function must not be overlooked.

An analysis of secular society can help to explain the conversion patterns of the Second Awakening. Unlike the First Great Awakening, when converts were evenly divided by sex, more women than men—particularly young women—answered the call of Christianity during the Second Awakening. The increase in female converts seems to have been directly related to fundamental changes in women's circumstances at the end of the eighteenth century. In some areas of the country, especially New England (where the revival movement flourished), women outnumbered men after 1790, for many young men had migrated westward (see map). Thus eastern girls could no longer count on finding marital partners. The uncertainty of their social and familial position seems to have led them to seek spiritual certainty in the church.

Women and the Second Awakening

Young women's domestic roles changed dramatically at the same time, as cloth production began to move from the household to the factory (see page 370). Deprived of their chief household role as spinners and weavers, New England daughters found in the church a realm where they could continue to make useful contributions to society. Church missionary societies and charitable associations provided an acceptable outlet for their talents. One of the most striking developments of the early nineteenth century was the creation of hundreds of female associations to aid widows and orphans, collect money for foreign missions, and improve the quality of maternal care. Thus American women collectively assumed the role of keepers of the nation's conscience, taking the lead in charitable enterprises and freeing their husbands from concern for such moral issues.

The religious ferment among blacks and whites in frontier regions of the Upper South contributed to racial ferment as well. People of

African-Americans and the Second Awakening

both races attended the camp meetings to hear both black and white preachers. When revivals spread eastward into more heavily slaveholding areas, white planters became fearful of the egalitarianism implied in the evangelical message of universal salvation and harmony. At the same time, revivals created a group of respected African-American leaders—preachers—and provided them a ready audience for a potentially revolutionary doctrine.

Events in the West Indies gave whites ample reason for apprehension. In 1793, mulattos and blacks in the French colony of Saint Domingue (Haiti) overthrew European rule under the leadership of a mulatto, Toussaint L'Ouverture. The revolt was bloody, vicious, prolonged, and characterized by numerous atrocities on both sides. In an attempt to prevent the spread of such unrest to their own enslaved workers, southern state legislators passed laws forbidding white Haitian refugees from bringing their slaves with them. But North American blacks learned about the revolt anyway. And the preconditions for racial upheaval did not have to be imported into the South from the West Indies: they already existed on the spot.

The Revolution had caused immense destruction in the South, especially in the states south of Virginia. Heavy losses of slaves and constant guerrilla warfare, not to mention the changes in American trading patterns brought about by withdrawal from the British Empire, wreaked havoc on the southern economy. The expansion of cotton production after the invention of the cotton gin in 1793 and the beginnings of large-scale westward migration increased the demand for slaves. Thus after the war Lower South planters rushed to purchase new enslaved laborers; the postwar decades therefore witnessed the single most massive influx of Africans into North America since the beginnings of the slave trade. Before the legal trade was halted in 1808, more than ninety thousand new Africans had been imported into the United States (see map, page 232).

The postwar increase in the number of free blacks severely challenged the slave system that had evolved during the eighteenth century. Like their white compatriots, African-Americans (both slave and free) had become familiar with notions of liberty and equality. They had also witnessed the

benefits of fighting collectively for freedom, rather than resisting individually or running away. The circumstances were ripe for an explosion, and the Second Awakening was the match that lit the fuse in both Virginia and North Carolina.

The Virginia revolt was planned by Gabriel Prosser, a blacksmith who argued that blacks should fight to obtain the same rights as whites and who explicitly placed himself in the tradition of the French and Haitian revolutions. At revival meetings led by his brother Martin, a preacher, Gabriel recruited other African-Americans like

Gabriel's Rebellion

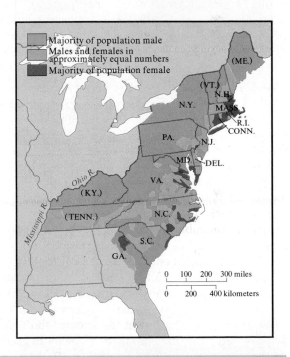

Sex Ratio of White Population, 1790 *The first census revealed that the sex ratio varied dramatically in different parts of the country. In many older, coastal areas, women predominated; on the frontier, men were in the majority. The variations had important implications for life in those regions, as is pointed out in the text.* Source: From Lester J. Cappon et al., eds., *Atlas of Early American History: The Revolutionary Era, 1760–1790.* Copyright © 1976 by Princeton University Press. Reprinted by permission of Princeton University Press.

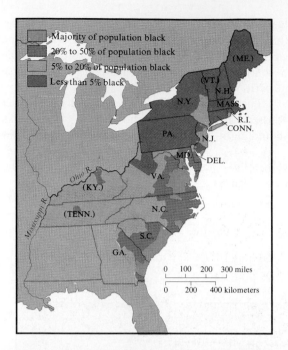

Majority of population black
20% to 50% of population black
5% to 20% of population black
Less than 5% black

African-American Population, 1790: Proportion of Total Population *The first census clearly indicated that the African-American population was heavily concentrated in just a few areas of the United States, most notably in coastal regions of South Carolina, Georgia, and Virginia. Although there were growing numbers of blacks in the backcountry—presumably taken there by migrating slaveowners—most parts of the North and East, with the exception of the immediate vicinity of New York City, had few African-American residents.* Source: From Lester J. Cappon et al., eds., *Atlas of Early American History: The Revolutionary Era, 1760–1790.* Copyright © 1976 by Princeton University Press. Reprinted by permission of Princeton University Press.

carry out on schedule. Several whites then learned of the plan from their slaves and spread the alarm. Gabriel avoided capture for some weeks, but most of the other leaders of the rebellion were quickly arrested and interrogated. The main conspirators, including Prosser himself, were hanged, but in the months that followed other insurrectionary scares continued to frighten Virginia slaveowners.

Two years later a similar wave of fear swept North Carolina and the bordering counties of Virginia. A slave conspiracy to attack planters' homes, kill all whites except small children, and seize the land was uncovered in Bertie County. Similar plots were rumored elsewhere. Again, slave artisans and evangelical preachers played prominent roles in the planned uprisings. Nearly fifty African-Americans were executed as a result of the whites' investigations of the rumors. Some were certainly innocent victims of the planters' hysteria, but there can be no doubt about the existence of most of the plots. In the wake of these disturbances, southern state legislatures increased the severity of slave codes. Before long, all talk of emancipation (gradual or otherwise) ceased, and slavery became even more firmly entrenched as an economic institution and way of life.

The Iroquois, too, experienced a religious revival in the early nineteenth century. Led by their prophet Handsome Lake, the remaining American Iroquois, who were scattered on small reservations, embraced the traditional values of their culture and renounced such destructive white customs as drinking alcohol and gambling. At the same time, though, they began abandoning their ancient way of life. With Handsome Lake's approval, Quaker missionaries taught the Iroquois Anglo-American styles of agricultural subsistence; men were now to be cultivators rather than hunters, and women housekeepers rather than cultivators. Since the tribes had lost their hunting territories to white farmers, Iroquois men accepted the changes readily. But many women, especially the powerful tribal matrons, resisted the shift in the gender division of labor. By surrendering control over food production, they realized, they would jeopardize their status in the tribe. But Handsome Lake branded as "witches" women who opposed the changes too vigorously, and eventually he tri-

Handsome Lake

himself—urban artisans who moved easily in both black and white circles and who lived in semifreedom under minimal white supervision. The artisan leaders then enlisted rural blacks in the cause. The conspirators planned to attack Richmond on the night of August 30, 1800, setting fire to the city, seizing the state capitol, and capturing the governor. Their plan showed considerable political sophistication, but heavy rain made it impossible to

The Destrehan plantation house in St. Charles Parish, Louisiana, was originally constructed between 1787 and 1790 (and remodeled in 1840). Its primary builder was Charles, a "free Mulatto" who was described as "carpenter, wood worker and mason" in the construction contract. In Virginia, skilled blacks like Charles, both slave and free, formed the core of the support for Gabriel's Rebellion.   Gene Cizek.

umphed. A division of work by sex continued to characterize Iroquois economic organization, but the specific tasks assigned changed completely.

To ensure the cultural survival of their people, the Iroquois had to adopt an economic system resembling that of the dominant whites. The plight of the Iroquois may be taken as representative of the plight of tribes located west of the Appalachians, for they, too, would have to find ways of accommodating themselves to the dominant Anglo-American culture. Although most had yet to feel the full force of the whites' westward thrust, the weapon that had served the Iroquois and other interior tribes so well—the countervailing presence of England, France, and Spain—was no longer available to them. Since the United States had established its independence, western tribes had no alternative but to confront directly the problems posed by land-hungry whites. They would delay but not halt the expansion of the United States.

As the new century began, the inhabitants of the United States were moving toward an accommodation to their new lives in the republic. Native American peoples east of the Mississippi found that they had to give up some parts of their traditional culture to preserve others. Blacks and whites tried to create new lives in the West and to adjust to changed economic circumstances in the East. Building on successful negotiations with both Britain (the Jay Treaty) and France (the Convention of 1800), the United States developed its diplomatic independence, striving to avoid entanglement with the European powers. The 1790s spawned vigorous debates over foreign and domestic policy and saw the beginnings of a system of political parties. Dissent was discouraged but not successfully suppressed. Religious revivals swept portions of the countryside, and again those revivals contributed to social unrest.

At the end of the decade, after years of struggle, the Jeffersonian interpretation of republican-

How *do* historians know

that Americans were intensely patriotic in the early years of the republic? One piece of evidence is supplied by the many items incorporating patriotic decorative motifs that were produced for use in the homes of middling and well-to-do American citizens. The artisans of the new nation quickly recognized that "patriotism sold," and so they created a wide variety of objects to satisfy the demand—furniture, wallpaper, curtains,

and pottery goods all drew on such themes. The owner of this four-foot-long parlor wall mirror, for example, would have seen Revolutionary War cannons and swords, a symbolic eagle, and George Washington himself, along with whatever household furnishings it reflected, each time she looked into it. Such reminders of national pride helped to confirm the new republic's identity. Photo: Henry Francis du Pont Winterthur Museum.

ism finally prevailed over Hamilton's approach. As a result, the country would be characterized in the years to come by a decentralized economy, minimal government (especially at the national level), and maximum freedom of action and mobility for individual white men. Jeffersonian Republicans, like white male Americans before them, failed to extend to white women, tribal people, and African-Americans the freedom and individuality they recognized as essential for themselves.

SUGGESTIONS FOR FURTHER READING

National Government and Administration

Kenneth Bowling, *The Creation of Washington, D.C.* (1991); Ralph Adams Brown, *The Presidency of John Adams* (1975); Morton Frisch, *Alexander Hamilton and the Political Order* (1991); Richard H. Kohn, *Eagle and Sword: The Federalists and the Creation of the Military Establishment in America, 1783–1802* (1975); Forrest McDonald, *Alexander Hamilton* (1979); Forrest McDonald, *The Presidency of George Washington* (1974); John C. Miller, *The Federalist Era, 1789–1801* (1960); John R. Nelson, Jr., *Liberty and Property: Political Economy and Policymaking in the New Nation, 1789–1812* (1987); Merrill D. Peterson, *Thomas Jefferson and the New Nation* (1970); Garry Wills, *Cincinnatus: George Washington and the Enlightenment* (1984).

Partisan Politics

Lance Banning, *The Jeffersonian Persuasion: Evolution of a Party Ideology* (1978); Richard Buel, *Securing the Revolution: Ideology in American Politics, 1789–1815* (1972); William Nisbet Chambers, *Political Parties in a New Nation: The American Experience, 1776–1809* (1963); Joseph Charles, *The Origins of the American Party System* (1956); Noble E. Cunningham, *The Jeffersonian Republicans: The Formation of Party Organization, 1789–1801* (1957); Manning J. Dauer, *The Adams Federalists* (1953); Ronald Formisano, *The Transformation of Political Culture: Massachusetts Parties, 1790s–1840s* (1983); Richard Hofstadter, *The Idea of a Party System: The Rise of Legitimate Opposition in the United States, 1780–1840* (1970); Adrienne Koch, *Jefferson and Madison: The Great Collaboration* (1950); Eugene P. Link, *Democratic-Republican Societies, 1790–1800* (1942); Norman K. Risjord, *Chesapeake Politics, 1781–1800* (1978); John Zvesper, *Political Philosophy and Rhetoric: A Study of the Origins of American Party Politics* (1977).

Foreign Policy

Harry Ammon, *The Genêt Mission* (1973); Samuel F. Bemis, *Jay's Treaty*, 2nd ed. (1962); Samuel F. Bemis, *Pinckney's Treaty*, 2nd ed. (1960); Jerald A. Combs, *The Jay Treaty* (1970); Alexander DeConde, *The Quasi-War: Politics and Diplomacy of the Undeclared War with France, 1797–1801* (1966); Alexander DeConde, *Entangling Alliance: Politics and Diplomacy Under George Washington* (1958); Felix Gilbert, *To the Farewell Address: Ideas of Early American Foreign Policy* (1961); Reginald Horsman, *The Diplomacy of the New Republic, 1776–1815* (1985); Lawrence Kaplan, *"Entangling Alliances with None": American Foreign Policy in the Age of Jefferson* (1987); Bradford Perkins, *The First Rapprochement: England and the United States, 1795–1805* (1967); William Stinchcombe, *The XYZ Affair* (1981); Paul A. Varg, *Foreign Policies of the Founding Fathers* (1963).

Civil Liberties

Leonard W. Levy, *Emergence of a Free Press* (1985); Leonard W. Levy, *Origins of the Fifth Amendment* (1968); Robert A. Rutland, *The Birth of the Bill of Rights, 1776–1791*, rev. ed. (1983); James Morton Smith, *Freedom's Fetters: The Alien and Sedition Laws and American Civil Liberties* (1956).

Women, African-Americans, and the Family

Ira Berlin and Ronald Hoffman, eds., *Slavery and Freedom in the Age of the American Revolution* (1983); Nancy F. Cott, *The Bonds of Womanhood: "Woman's Sphere" in New England, 1780–1835* (1977); Toby Ditz, *Property and Kinship: Inheritance in Early Connecticut, 1750–1820* (1986); Gerald W. Mullin, *Flight and Rebellion: Slave Resistance in Eighteenth-Century Virginia* (1972); Christine Stansell, *City of Women: Sex and Class in New York, 1789–1860* (1986); Laurel Thatcher Ulrich, *A Midwife's Tale* (1990).

Social Change and Westward Expansion

Andrew Cayton, *The Frontier Republic: Ideology and Politics in the Ohio Country, 1789–1812* (1986); Reginald Horsman, *The Frontier in the Formative Years, 1783–1815* (1970); Howard Rock, *Artisans of the New Republic: The Tradesmen of New York City in the Age of Thomas Jefferson* (1979); Malcolm Rohrbough, *The Trans-Appalachian Frontier: Peoples, Societies, and Institutions, 1775–1850* (1979); W. J. Rorabaugh, *The Alcoholic Republic: An American Tradition* (1979); Thomas Slaughter, *The Whiskey Rebellion* (1986); Charles G. Steffen, *The Mechanics of Baltimore: Workers and Politics in the Age of Revolution, 1763–1812* (1984); Sean Wilentz, *Chants Democratic: New York City and the Rise of the American Working Class, 1788–1850* (1984).

Religion

Sydney Ahlstrom, *A Religious History of the American People* (1972); Catharine Albanese, *Sons of the Fathers: The Civil Religion of the American Revolution* (1976); Ruth Bloch, *Visionary Republic: Millennial Themes in American Thought* (1985); Jon Butler, *Awash in a Sea of Faith: Christianizing the American People* (1990); Paul Conkin, *Cane Ridge: America's Pentecost* (1990); Nathan O. Hatch, *The Democratization of American Christianity* (1990); Fred J. Hood, *Reformed America, 1783–1837* (1980); William McLoughlin, *Revivals, Awakenings, and Reform* (1978).

The Empire of Liberty, 1801–1824

ANDREW MERRY, THE BRITISH minister to the United States, stormed out of the executive mansion, certain that President Thomas Jefferson had insulted the British government and monarch. "I, in my official costume, found myself at the hour of reception he had himself appointed, introduced to a man as president of the United States, not merely in an undress, but *actually standing in slippers down at the heels*, and both pantaloons, coat, and underclothes indicative of utter slovenliness and indifference to appearances, and in a state of negligence actually studied." Jefferson's predecessors, Washington and Adams, had appeared in public in wigs and breeches (knee-length trousers); Jefferson wore ordinary clothes. No insult had been intended, but Jefferson was making a statement. With the election of 1800 a revolution had swept the United States; aristocratic airs were a thing of the past.

The bitterness of the election of 1800 and the newness of the republic had generated some anxiety about whether a peaceful transfer of power from the Federalists to the Republicans would take place. Amid that uncertainty, Thomas Jefferson had strolled from his New Jersey Avenue boarding house in the new federal capital of Washington, D.C., to take the oath as president at the Capitol. Jefferson walked unguarded, in plain dress, a citizen about to become a president. Though unaware that they were doing so, Republicans and Federalists were establishing the precedent of an orderly and peaceful change of government.

Jefferson was inaugurated at the beginning of a period when Americans were struggling to assert and define their nationalism amid challenges, both foreign and domestic. Monarchial traditions inherited from Great Britain confronted the republican virtues of independence, self-reliance, and equality that arose from the American Revolution and the new traditions pioneered by a younger generation of leaders and politicians. In contrast to the formality of the Federalist presidencies of Washington and Adams, Republicans favored simplicity. Though personally wealthier and with more luxurious tastes than Adams, Jefferson rejected the aristocratic pretensions he associated with the Federalists. He preferred simplicity to pomp, equality to social distinctions. Republican virtue would be restored.

Ordinary folk who came to celebrate Jefferson's inaugural overran Washington, causing Federalists to

In this painting, c. 1800, the image of Liberty celebrates the growing strength of the United States (the eagle) and its divine inspiration.

shudder at the seeming collapse of authority and order. For two weeks following the inauguration, Jefferson ran the government from his modest lodgings a few blocks from the Capitol, and he continued to eat at the communal dining table. His first cabinet meetings were held at Conrad and McMunn's rooming house. Not until March 19 did he move to the president's mansion.

The new city suited the less pretentious Republicans. The government had moved to Washington from Philadelphia in November 1800, and its unfinished federal buildings symbolized the unfinished nation. Augustus John Foster, a British diplomat, lamented the move "to what was then scarce any better than a mere swamp," and Abigail Adams found it "the very dirtyest Hole," its streets "a quagmire after every rain." On the other hand, Washington offered amusements unlike those of any other Atlantic capital. "Excellent snipe shooting and even partridge shooting was to be had on each side of the main [Pennsylvania] avenue and even close under the wall of the capitol," Foster recalled. Chosen for its central location, the District of Columbia had been carved out of Maryland and Virginia. Washington was thus beholden neither to the colonial past nor to any single state.

Few buildings were needed to house a government with functions limited essentially to collecting tariffs, delivering mail, negotiating with foreign governments, and defending the nation's borders. The small government suited the republic: even the Federalists lacked confidence in a strong central government. In an age when it took some congressmen more than a week to travel from home to the capital, most Americans favored government closer to home. Though President Jefferson, after his inauguration in 1801, cut the federal budget and operations, he and his Republican successors (James Madison and James Monroe) invigorated the federal government over the next two decades. Foreign crises, in particular, strengthened federal institutions.

The transfer of power to the Republicans from the Federalists intensified political conflict and voter interest. In the tradition of the Revolution, Republican presidents sought limited government, believing it would further republican virtue and encourage Americans to place obligations of citizenship and the public interest above private ambitions. The Federalists focused more on the market economy and economic individualism. Thus they prized a stronger national government with more centralized authority to promote economic development. With both factions competing for popular support, the basis was laid for the evolution of democratic politics. But factionalism, personal animosities, and partisanship within each group prevented the development of cohesive political parties, and the Federalists, unable to build a popular base, slowly faded away.

Events abroad and on the frontier encouraged and threatened the expansionism Americans had practiced from colonial times. Seizing one opportunity, the United States purchased the Louisiana Territory, pushing the frontier farther west. But then from the high seas came war. Caught between the warring British and French, the United States found its shipping rights as a neutral, independent nation ignored and violated. When the humiliation and threat to U. S. interests became too great, Americans took up arms in the War of 1812, both to defend their rights as a nation and to expand farther to the west and north. Although unprepared for combat, the United States fought Great Britain to a standstill. The Americans also routed tribal resistance and shattered Native American unity. Though the peace treaty restored the prewar status quo, the war and the treaty reaffirmed American independence and strengthened American determination to steer clear of European conflicts.

The War of 1812 unleashed a wave of nationalism and self-confidence. War needs promoted the development of domestic manufacturing and internal transportation. With peace, the federal government championed business and construction of roads and canals. The new spirit encouraged economic growth and western expansion at home, trade abroad, and assertiveness throughout the Western Hemisphere. By the 1820s, the United States was no longer an experiment; a new nation had emerged. Free of its colonial past, the country began energetically shaping its own identity.

Economic growth and territorial expansion, however, generated new problems. In 1819 a financial panic brought hardship and conflict that sowed the seeds for the Jacksonian movement in the 1820s and 1830s. More ominously, sectional differences and the presence of slavery created divisions that would widen in the wake of further westward expansion during the 1840s and 1850s.

• *Important Events* •

1801	John Marshall becomes chief justice Jefferson inaugurated as first Republican president	**1814–15**	Hartford Convention undermines Federalists
1801–05	United States defeats Barbary pirates in Tripoli War	**1815**	Battle of New Orleans makes Andrew Jackson a hero
1803	*Marbury* v. *Madison* establishes judicial review U.S. purchases Louisiana Territory	**1816**	Monroe elected president Second Bank of the United States chartered
1804	Jefferson re-elected	**1817**	Rush-Bagot Treaty limits naval forces on Lakes Ontario and Champlain
1804–06	Lewis and Clark expedition reaches the Pacific Ocean	**1819**	*McCulloch* v. *Maryland* establishes supremacy of federal over state law Adams-Onís Treaty gives Florida to United States and defines Louisiana territorial border
1805	Prophet emerges as Shawnee leader		
1807	*Chesapeake* affair almost leads to war Embargo Act halts foreign trade		
1808	Madison elected president	**1819–23**	Financial panic and depression: hard times for Americans
1808–13	Prophet and Tecumseh organize Native American tribal resistance	**1820**	Missouri Compromise creates a formula for admitting slave/free states Monroe re-elected
1812–15	War of 1812 is fought		
1813	Death of Tecumseh ends effective pan-Indian resistance	**1823**	Monroe Doctrine closes Western Hemisphere to European intervention
1814	Treaty of Ghent ends the War of 1812		

JEFFERSON IN POWER

Jefferson delivered his inaugural address in the Senate chamber, the only part of the Capitol that had been completed by 1801. Nearly a thousand people strained to hear his barely audible voice. In an appeal for unity, he told the assembly that "we are all Republicans, we are all Federalists." Addressing those with little faith in the people's ability to govern themselves, he called America's republican government "the world's best hope." The new president went on to outline his goals:

Jefferson's Inaugural Address

> A wise and frugal government, which shall restrain men from injuring one another, which shall leave them otherwise free to regulate their own pursuits. . . . Equal and exact justice to all men, of whatever state or persuasion, religious or political. . . . The support of the state governments in all their rights, as the most competent administrators for our domestic concerns and the surest bulwarks against antirepublican tendencies.

At the same time, he assured Federalists that he shared their concerns for an active central government and a commercial-minded nation:

> The preservation of the general government in its whole constitutional vigor. . . . The honest payment of our debts and sacred preservation of the public faith. . . . Encouragement of agriculture and of commerce as its handmaid.

Still, the Federalists and Republicans distrusted each other. The outgoing president, John Adams, left Washington before dawn on inaugural day to avoid witnessing the Republican takeover. Republicans considered Federalists antidemocratic and antirepublican at heart and accused them of imitating the court society of England. Federalists accused Republicans of undermining social deference and favoring egalitarianism, which they be-

This portrait of President Thomas Jefferson was painted by Rembrandt Peale in 1805. Charles Willson Peale and his five sons helped establish the reputation of American art in the new nation. Rembrandt Peale was most famous for his presidential portraits; here he captures Jefferson in a noble pose without the usual symbols of office or power, befitting the Republican age. New York Historical Society.

lieved had recently led to anarchy in France. (Indeed, the pantaloons that Jefferson wore when he received the British minister were in the French style.) To Jefferson, the goal was to restore the simplicity and civic virtue that had fueled the American Revolution and that Federalist social pomp and excessive government threatened.

One of Jefferson's first acts as president was to extend the Republicans' grasp over the federal government. Virtually all of the six hundred or so officials appointed under Washington and Adams were loyal Federalists: only six were known Republicans. To restore government to those who shared his visions of an agrarian republic and individual liberty, Jefferson refused to recognize Adams's last-minute "midnight appointments" to local offices in the District of Columbia. He also dismissed Federalist customs collectors from New England ports and awarded vacant treasury and

judicial offices to Republicans. By July 1803 only 130 of 316 presidentially controlled offices were still held by Federalists. Jefferson adroitly used patronage to build a party organization, compete with the Federalists, and restore political balance in government.

The Republican Congress proceeded to affirm its belief in limited government as a check on authoritarianism and deference to elites. Albert Gallatin, secretary of the Treasury, and John Randolph of Virginia, Jefferson's ally in the House, translated ideology into policy, putting the federal government on a diet. Congress repealed all internal taxes, including the whiskey tax. Gallatin cut the army budget in half, to just under $2 million, and reduced the 1802 navy budget from $3.5 to $1 million. Gallatin planned to reduce the national debt—which Alexander Hamilton viewed as the engine of economic growth—from $83 million to $57 million, as part of a plan to retire it altogether by 1817. Jefferson even closed two of the nation's five diplomatic missions abroad—at The Hague and Berlin—to save money.

More than frugality, however, distinguished Republicans from Federalists. Before Jefferson's election, opposition to the Alien and Sedition Acts of 1798 had helped unite Republicans (see pages 224–225). Jefferson now declined to use the acts against his opponents, as President Adams had done in suppressing Republican editors, and pardoned those convicted earlier. Congress let the Sedition Act expire in 1801 and the Alien Act in 1802. Congress also repealed the Naturalization Act of 1798, which had required fourteen years of residency for citizenship. The 1802 act that replaced it required only five years of residency, acceptance of the Constitution, and the forsaking of foreign allegiance and titles. It also, however, continued provisions for the registration of aliens. The new act, which made it easier to become a citizen, would remain the basis of naturalized American citizenship into the twentieth century.

The Republicans turned next to the judiciary, the last stronghold of unchecked Federalist power. During the 1790s not a single Republican had been appointed to the federal bench. The Judiciary Act of 1801, passed in the final days of the Adams administration, had created fifteen new judgeships, which Adams filled by signing midnight appoint-

Attacks on the Judiciary

ments until his term was just hours away from expiring. The act would also reduce by attrition the number of justices on the Supreme Court from six to five. Since that reduction would have denied Jefferson a Supreme Court appointment until two vacancies had occurred, the new Republican-dominated Congress repealed the 1801 act.

The Republicans also targeted opposition judges for removal. Federalist judges had refused to review the Sedition Act under which Federalists had prosecuted critics of the Adams administration. At Jefferson's prompting, the House impeached (indicted) Federal District Judge John Pickering of New Hampshire, an emotionally disturbed alcoholic, and in 1804 the Senate removed him from office. The Republicans were moving against the partisan Federalist judiciary.

The day Pickering was convicted, the House impeached Supreme Court Justice Samuel Chase for judicial misconduct. Chase, an arch-Federalist and leader in pressing for convictions under the Sedition Act, had repeatedly denounced Jefferson's administration from the bench. The Republicans, however, failed to muster the two-thirds majority of senators necessary to convict him. Their failure to remove Chase preserved the Court's independence: it established the precedent that criminal actions, not political disagreements, were the only proper grounds for impeachment. Time soon cured the Republicans' grievances; in his tenure as president, Jefferson appointed three new Supreme Court justices. Nonetheless, the Court remained a Federalist stronghold under Chief Justice John Marshall.

A Virginia Federalist who had served under George Washington in the Revolutionary War, Marshall was an astute lawyer with keen political sense. He had served as minister to France and then secretary of state under Adams before being named chief justice. Jefferson considered Marshall a midnight appointment, believing that any appointment made after Adams learned of his defeat in the electoral college in December 1800 was immoral, if not illegal. But Congress had approved the appointment in January 1801 before Jefferson was sworn in as president.

John Marshall

Although an autocrat by nature, Marshall possessed a grace and openness of manner that complemented the new Republican political style. Saint-Memim's contemporary portrait of Marshall in 1801 captures both his autocratic bearing and his direct manner. Under Marshall's domination, however, the Supreme Court retained a Federalist outlook even after Republican justices achieved a majority in 1811. Throughout his tenure (from 1801 until 1835), the Court consistently upheld federal supremacy over the states and protected the interests of commerce and capital.

Marshall also made the Court an equal branch of government in practice as well as theory. First, by his presence he made service on the Court a coveted honor for ambitious and talented men. Prior to Marshall, during the Court's first twelve years of existence, fifteen justices served on the six-member bench; after Marshall's appointment,

John Marshall (1755–1835) was chief justice of the Supreme Court from 1801 to 1835. Marshall posed for this portrait by the French artist Charles Balthazar Julien Fevret de Saint-Memin in 1801, the year he joined the Court. The artist has captured the power and strength with which Marshall would dominate the Supreme Court. Crayon on paper portrait, Duke University Archives.

it took forty years for fifteen new members to be appointed. Second, he unified the Court, influencing the justices to issue joint majority opinions rather than a host of individual concurring judgments. Marshall himself became the voice of the majority: from 1801 through 1805 he wrote twenty-four of the Court's twenty-six decisions; through 1810 he wrote 85 percent of the Court's opinions, including every important decision.

Marshall also increased the Court's power, notably in the landmark case *Marbury* v. *Madison* (1803). William Marbury had been named a justice of the peace in the District of

Marbury v. Madison
——

Columbia as one of Adams's midnight appointments. The new secretary of state, James Madison, declined to certify his appointment so that Jefferson could appoint a Republican. Marbury then sued, requesting a writ of mandamus (a court order forcing Madison to appoint him). The case presented a political dilemma. If the Supreme Court ruled in favor of Marbury and issued a writ of mandamus, the president might not comply. After all, why should the president, sworn to uphold the Constitution, allow the Court to decide for him what was constitutional? However, if the Federalist-dominated Court refused to issue the writ, it would be handing the Republicans a victory. Marshall avoided both pitfalls. Speaking for the Court, he ruled that Marbury had a right to his appointment but that the Court could not compel Madison to honor it because the Constitution did not grant the Court power to issue a writ of mandamus. Marshall thus declared unconstitutional a section of the Judiciary Act of 1789, which authorized the Court to issue such writs. In *Marbury* v. *Madison*, the Supreme Court denied itself the power to issue writs of mandamus but established its great power to judge the constitutionality of laws passed by Congress.

In succeeding years Marshall fashioned the theory of judicial review, the power of the Court to decide the constitutionality of legislation. Since the Constitution was the supreme law, he reasoned, any federal or state act contrary to the Constitution must be null and void. The Supreme Court, whose duty it was to uphold the law, thus had the responsibility to decide whether a legislative act contradicted the Constitution. If a conflict existed, the Court would declare the act unconstitutional. *Marbury* v. *Madison* ended criticism of the

Court as a partisan instrument, and the power of judicial review permanently enhanced the independence of the judiciary.

While Marshall was enlarging the power of the Court, President Jefferson was keeping an eye on the Louisiana Territory to the west in hopes of enlarging the borders of the na-

Louisiana Purchase
——

tion. Jefferson shared with other Americans the belief that the United States was destined to expand its "empire of liberty." Since the first days of American independence, Louisiana had held a special place in the young nation's expansionist dreams. Louisiana defined the U.S. western border along the Mississippi from the Gulf of Mexico to present-day Minnesota. France had been forced to cede Louisiana to Spain in 1763 at the end of the Seven Years' War (see page 125). By 1800 hundreds of thousands of Americans in search of land had trekked into the rich Mississippi and Ohio valleys to settle, intruding on tribal lands. The settlers then floated their farm goods down the Mississippi and Ohio rivers to New Orleans for export. Whoever controlled the port of New Orleans thus had a hand on the throat of the American economy. Americans feared a Spanish-owned Louisiana less than one controlled by France.

Rumors of the transfer of Louisiana back to France proved true in 1802. France had acquired the territory under secret pacts with Spain in 1800 and 1801, but the United States did not learn of the transfer until 1802, when the expansionist-minded Napoleon threatened to rebuild a French empire in the New World. The acquisition, Jefferson wrote to the American minister in Paris, Robert R. Livingston, "works most sorely" on the United States. "Every eye in the United States is now focused on the affairs of Louisiana." American fears intensified in October 1802 when Spanish officials, on the eve of ceding control to the French, violated Pinckney's Treaty (see page 221) by denying Americans the privilege of storing their products at New Orleans prior to transshipment to foreign markets. Western farmers and eastern merchants alike thought a devious Napoleon had closed the port; they grumbled and talked war. "The Mississippi," Secretary of State James Madison wrote, "is to them everything. It is the Hudson, the Delaware, the Potomac and all navigable rivers of the Atlantic States formed into one stream."

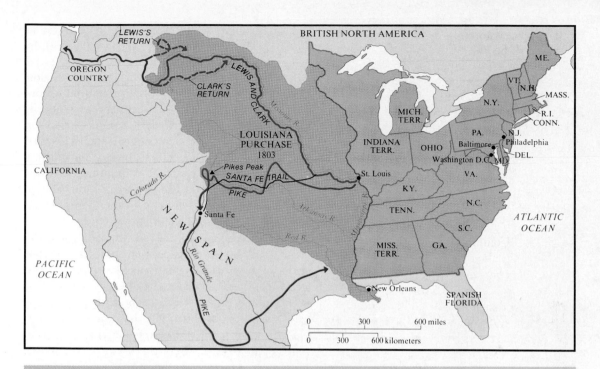

Louisiana Purchase *The Louisiana Purchase (1803) doubled the area of the United States and opened the trans-Mississippi West for American settlement.*

To relieve the pressure for war and to prevent westerners from joining Federalists in opposition to his administration, Jefferson simultaneously prepared for war and sent James Monroe to France to join Robert Livingston in negotiating to buy the port of New Orleans. Meanwhile, Congress authorized the call-up of eighty thousand militia should war become necessary. Arriving in Paris in April, Monroe was astonished to learn that France had already offered to sell all 827,000 square miles of Louisiana to the United States for a mere $15 million. Napoleon had lost interest in the New World. (Although the French had captured Touissant L'Ouverture, the leader of a slave revolt against the French on Santo Domingo, they could not suppress the rebellion. France's dreams of reviving a Caribbean empire ended with its failure to control Santo Domingo.) On April 30 Monroe and Livingston signed a treaty to purchase the vast territory, whose borders were undefined and whose land was uncharted (see map).

At one stroke of the pen, the Louisiana Purchase doubled the size of the nation and opened the way for westward expansion across the continent. It was also the most popular achievement of Jefferson's presidency. Yet for Jefferson, the purchase presented a dilemma. It promised fulfillment of his dream of a continental nation reaching to the Pacific coast, "with room enough for our descendants to the hundredth and thousandth generation." It provided an opportunity to resolve Indian-settler conflict on the frontier by making available land to which eastern tribes could be forcibly removed. But its legality was questionable. The Constitution gave Jefferson no clear authority to acquire new territory and incorporate it into the nation. Although Jefferson considered requesting a constitutional amendment to allow the purchase, he finally justified it on the grounds that he was exercising the president's implied powers to protect the nation. The people, he knew, would accept or reject the purchase on election day in 1804.

The buffalo-skin shirt and compass of William Clark, used on the Lewis and Clark expedition in 1804–1806, were preserved as relics. With courage, daring, and the assistance of Native Americans, Lewis and Clark's fifty-strong "Corps of Discovery" traversed the newly acquired Louisiana Territory, mapping its terrain and recording the people, fauna, and flora. Hunting shirt: Peabody Museum of Archeology and Ethnology, Harvard University; compass: Division of Political History, Smithsonian Institution, Wasnington. D.C.

The president had a long-standing interest in Louisiana and the West. As early as 1782, as an American envoy in France, Jefferson had suggested sending an exploratory mission across the continent to California. As secretary of state in 1793, he commissioned a French emigré botanist, André Michaux, "to find the shortest & most convenient route of communications between the U.S. & the Pacific Ocean." But allegations of Michaux's complicity in the Genêt Affair (see page 219) aborted the mission.

Lewis and Clark Expedition

In 1803 Jefferson renewed Michaux's instructions when he sent an expedition headed by Meriwether Lewis and William Clark to the Pacific Ocean via the Missouri and Columbia rivers. The twenty-nine-year-old Lewis, who had been a regular army officer in the 1790s, had exchanged rugged army life for a position as Jefferson's private secretary. Clark, a thirty-three-year-old explorer and former soldier, had fought and negotiated with Native Americans. Aware of the risks as well as the political importance of their mission, both itched to explore the West.

The first crossing of the continent had been made in Canada by Alexander MacKenzie in the 1790s. The publication of his journal, *Voyages from Montreal* (1801), raised fears that the British would dominate the Far West. Thus the Lewis and Clark expedition from 1804 to 1806 was both political and scientific. Jefferson, an amateur naturalist, had charged the expedition with collecting specimens on its travels. The nearly fifty-strong "Corps of Discovery" was aided along the way by trappers and Native Americans, including a French-Canadian trader, Toussaint Charbonneau, and his young Shoshoni wife, Sacagawea, who joined the expedition. Sacagawea helped negotiate safe passage in the Far West, and she interpreted the terrain and the languages of the West for the explorers. Lewis and Clark knew that this wilderness was a crowded one. They carried twenty-one bags of gifts for Native American leaders, both to establish goodwill and to stimulate interest in trading for American manufactured goods.

Lewis and Clark, and later expeditions, explored and publicized the lands west of the Mississippi unknown to those living in the East. The "Corps of Discovery" brought back stories of fauna and flora unknown to the western scientific community; they encountered the grizzly bear, bighorn sheep, and mountain goats. Their expedition became legendary, and many of the artifacts, like Clark's compass and buffalo-skin shirt were preserved as relics. Jefferson's scientific interests stimulated his curiosity about the natural environment of the West, but his interest in commercial exploration and free land for farm families prompted development that would alter that environment irreversibly.

The changes triggered by the exploration and publicity of the West were gradual. Lieutenant Zebulon Pike followed Lewis and Clark in 1805 and 1806 in search of the source of the Mississippi and a navigable water route to the Far West. Pike and his men wandered into Spanish territory to the south, where the Spanish held them captive for several months in Santa Fe. After his release, Pike wrote an account of his experiences that set commercial minds spinning. He described a potential commercial market in southwestern Spanish cities, as well as bountiful furs and precious minerals. Over the next few decades, as Americans avidly read published accounts of western exploration, expansion seized their imagination. The vision of a road to the Southwest became a reality with the opening of the Santa Fe Trail in the 1820s, and settlement followed the trail.

REPUBLICANS VERSUS FEDERALISTS

Election of 1804

Campaigning for re-election in 1804, Jefferson claimed credit for western expansion and the restoration of republican values. Jefferson considered Louisiana and the opening of the West among his greatest presidential accomplishments. Acquisition of Louisiana had provided millions of acres, which Republicans believed would enable families to buy and work their own land, thus nourishing and sustaining economic independence and civic virtues. Jefferson and the Republicans also bragged of more immediate results. They had ended the Federalist threat to liberty by repealing the Alien and Sedition and Judiciary Acts. They had reduced the size and cost of government by cutting spending. Despite his opponents' charges, Jefferson had demonstrated that Republicans supported commerce and promoted free trade. He had eliminated obstacles to American commercial growth by purchasing the Louisiana Territory, including the port of New Orleans, and by prompting Congress to repeal Federalist excise and property taxes. American trade with Europe was flourishing. Unwisely, Federalists who earlier had criticized Jefferson for not seizing Louisiana now attacked the president for paying too much for it and for exceeding his powers.

Jefferson's opponent was Charles Cotesworth Pinckney, a wealthy South Carolina lawyer and former Revolutionary War aide to George Washington. As Adams's vice-presidential candidate in 1800, Pinckney had inherited the Federalist leadership. Jefferson dumped the disloyal and unreliable Aaron Burr from the 1804 ticket, and he and his running mate, George Clinton of New York, swamped Pinckney and New Yorker Rufus King in the electoral college by 162 votes to 14, carrying fifteen of the seventeen states.

Jefferson's re-election was both a personal and an organizational triumph. The political dissenters of the 1790s had fashioned the Democratic-Republican societies into successful political organizations. More than anything else, opposition to the Federalists had given them cohesion. Indeed, in areas where the Federalists were strongest—in commercial New York and Pennsylvania in the 1790s and in New England in the 1800s—the Republicans had organized most effectively.

Until the Republican victory in 1800, most Federalists had disdained popular campaigning. They believed in government by the "best" people—those whose education, wealth, and experience qualified them to be leaders. For candidates to debate their merits in front of their inferiors—the voters—was demeaning. The Republicans' direct appeals struck the Federalists as a subversion of the natural political order.

Younger Federalists

After the resounding Federalist defeat in 1800, however, a younger generation of Federalists began to imitate the Republicans. Led by men like Josiah Quincy, a young congressman from Massachusetts, they organized statewide and campaigned for popular support. Quincy cleverly presented the Federalists as the people's party, attacking Republicans as autocratic planters. "Jeffersonian Democracy," Quincy gibed in 1804, was "an Indian word, signifying *a great tobacco planter who had herds of black slaves.*" In attacking frugal government, the self-styled Younger Federalists played, with some success, on fears of a weakened army and navy. Eastern merchants depended on a strong navy to protect ocean trade, whereas westerners looked for support from the army as they encroached on Native American tribes.

In states where both factions organized and ran candidates, people became more interested in politics generally, especially at the local level. In some states about 90 percent of the eligible voters—nearly all of whom were white males—cast ballots between 1804 and 1816. As popular interest and participation in elections increased, the states expanded suffrage. But the popular base remained restricted: property qualifications for voting and holding office persisted, and in six states the legislatures still selected presidential electors in 1804. Even Republicans restrained their organizational efforts; fearing the divisiveness of partisanship, most leaders shied away from cohesive political movements.

Yet political competition and a vigorous press that saw its primary role as partisan advocacy prompted grass-roots campaigning. Political barbecues symbolized the new style of campaigns. In New York they roasted oxen, on the New England coast they baked clams, in Maryland they served oysters. Guests washed down their meals with beer and punch and sometimes competed in corn shuckings or horse pulls. Oratory was a popular form of entertainment, and during the barbecues candidates and party leaders delivered lengthy and uninhibited speeches. They often made wild accusations, which—given the slow speed of communications—might go unanswered until after the election. In 1808, for example, a New England Republican accused the Federalists of causing the Boston Massacre. Federalists in turn accused the Republicans of slavishly supporting French interests.

Both factions adopted the political barbecue, but the Federalist party never fully mastered the art of wooing voters. Older Federalists still opposed blatant campaigning. And, though the Federalists were strong in a few states—Connecticut and Delaware, for example—they never offered the Republicans sustained competition. Divisions between Older and Younger Federalists often hindered the party, and the extremism of some Older Federalists tended to discredit the organization. A case in point was Timothy Pickering, a Massachu-

setts congressman and former secretary of state. Pickering opposed the Louisiana Purchase, feared Jefferson's re-election, and urged the secession of New England in 1803 and 1804. He won some support among the few Federalists in Congress, but most opposed his plan for secession. Ever the opportunist, Vice President Aaron Burr flirted with Pickering—Burr fantasized leading New York into secession, with other states following. When Burr lost his bid to become governor of New York in 1804, however, the dream evaporated.

Both Republicans and Federalists suffered from divisions and personal animosities. Aaron Burr and Alexander Hamilton, for instance, had long despised each other. Burr **Hamilton-Burr** had an affinity for conspiracies, **Duel** and Hamilton always seemed to block his path. Hamilton had thwarted Burr's attempt to steal the election of 1800 from Jefferson (see page 226), and in the 1804 New York gubernatorial race Burr lost to a rival Republican faction backed by the Federalist Hamilton. Burr turned his resentment on Hamilton and challenged him to a duel. Hamilton had been so outspoken in denouncing Burr as too dangerous to hold office that there were ample insults to choose from. His honor at stake, Hamilton accepted Burr's challenge though he found dueling repugnant. Because New York had outlawed dueling, they met across the Hudson River at Weehawken, New Jersey. Hamilton deliberately fired astray and paid for that decision with his life. Burr was indicted for murder in New York and New Jersey and faced immediate arrest if he returned to either state.

His political career in ruins, Burr plotted to create a new empire in the Southwest, using the Louisiana Territory as a base. With the collusion of General James Wilkinson, the U.S. army commander in the Mississippi Valley, Burr planned to raise a private army to grab land from the United States or from Spain (his exact plans remain uncertain). Wilkinson switched sides and informed President Jefferson of Burr's ambitions. Jefferson personally assisted the prosecution in Burr's 1807 trial for treason, over which Chief Justice Marshall presided. The jury acquitted Burr, who fled to Europe to avoid further prosecution.

The controversies surrounding Burr highlight some of the shortcomings of the emerging political system. Personal animosities were as strong a force

How do historians know

that popular interest in elections was increasing early in the nineteenth century? Election data are not available, but paintings like John Lewis Krimmel's Election Day in Philadelphia (1815) convey that popularity. Voting was limited to men at the time, and the crowd is composed mostly of white males, although at least one African-American and some women and children are present. The life of the street depicts a festive, holiday air that defines election day. Citizens on a float in the background carry their own flag; they have created a parade. A festive spirit seems to prevail as men cluster in groups talking, arguing, sharing jokes, and generally appearing to have a good time. There is a hint of excessive joy as well. The man sitting on a broken chair (left foreground), with his hat on the ground, seems to have fallen, perhaps from too much drink—a common affliction in the party atmosphere of election day. Among the spectators are the women (center foreground), who suggest a restraining force on the raucous scene. Dressed in white, the prominent woman and her child and caped friend offer a common female image of the time: the woman as emblem of republican virtue. The space between the women and male figures suggests that they stand apart not only as nonvoters but also as symbols of virtue and a seriousness absent in the male world. Over all, the painting depicts a popular event, mixing a party atmosphere with civic duty. From a sober exercise of democratic responsibility, voting had become a popular, festive occasion.   Photo: Henry Francis du Pont Winterthur Museum.

as ideology, and temporary factions flourished. Moreover, although politicians courted voters, and participation in politics broadened, the electoral base remained narrow. As the election of 1804 revealed, the Federalists could offer only weak competition at the national level. And where Federalists were too weak to pose a threat, Republicans fought among themselves.

Thus, although this period is commonly called the era of the first party system, parties as such were not fully developed. Competition at the polls encouraged rudimentary party organization, but personal ambition, personality clashes, and local, state, and regional loyalties undermined it. Increasingly, too, external events would overpower party ties.

PRESERVING AMERICAN NEUTRALITY IN A WORLD AT WAR

"Peace, commerce, and honest friendship with all nations, entangling alliance with none," President Jefferson had proclaimed in his first inaugural address. Jefferson's efforts to stand aloof from European conflict were successful until 1805. Thereafter, though the pursuit of peace and undisturbed commerce occupied nearly his entire second administration, they proved elusive goals.

After the Senate ratified Jay's Treaty in 1795 (see pages 218–219), the United States and Great Britain appeared to reconcile their differences. Britain withdrew from its western forts and interfered less in American trade with France. More importantly, trade between the United States and Britain increased: the republic became Britain's best customer, and the British Empire in turn bought the bulk of American exports.

But in May 1803—two weeks after Napoleon sold Louisiana to the United States—renewal of the Napoleonic wars between France and Britain (and its continental allies, Prussia, Austria, and Russia) again trapped the United States between Britain and France on the high seas. For two years American commerce benefited from the conflict. As the world's largest neutral carrier, the United States became the chief supplier of food to Europe. American merchants also gained control of most of the West Indian trade, which was often transshipped though American ports to Europe.

Meanwhile, the U.S. victory in the Tripoli War on the north coast of Africa (the Barbary states) provided Jefferson his one clear success in protecting American trading rights. In 1801 the sultan of Tripoli had demanded payment to exempt American vessels and sailors in the Mediterranean from being taken hostage by his roving pirate ships. Jefferson refused and instead sent a naval squadron to protect American merchant

ships. In 1803–1804, under Lieutenant Stephen Decatur, the navy blockaded Tripoli harbor while marines marched overland from Egypt to seize the port of Derna. The United States ransomed its hostages and signed a peace treaty with Tripoli in 1805 but continued to pay tribute to other Barbary states until 1815. That year the navy, again under Decatur, forced Algiers and Tunis to renounce attacks against Americans. The Tripoli War and its aftermath made clear that the United States would protect its commerce anywhere, and it helped make the Mediterranean safe for commerce again.

American merchants grew more concerned about Anglo-French interference with trade. In October 1805 Britain tightened its control of the high seas by defeating the French and Spanish fleets at the Battle of Trafalgar. Two months later Napoleon defeated the Russian and Austrian armies at Austerlitz. Stalemated, France and Britain launched a commercial war, blockading each other's trade. As a trading partner of both countries, the United States paid a high price.

Britain, whose navy was the world's largest, was suffering a severe shortage of sailors. Few men enlisted, and those already in service frequently deserted, demoralized by poor food and living conditions and brutal discipline. Meanwhile, some British subjects took jobs on U.S. merchant ships, where conditions were better. The Royal Navy resorted to stopping American ships and forcibly removing British deserters, British-born naturalized American seamen, and other unlucky sailors suspected of being British. Perhaps six to eight thousand Americans were impressed (forcibly drafted) in this manner between 1803 and 1812. Americans saw impressment as a direct assault on the independence of their new republic. The principle of "once a British subject, always a British subject" ignored U.S. citizenship and sovereignty as alleged deserters—in reality American citizens—faced British court martial.

Impressment of American Sailors

In February 1806 the Senate denounced British impressment as aggression and a violation of America's neutral rights. To protest the insult, Congress passed the Non-Importation Act, prohibiting importation from Great Britain of a long list of cloth and metal articles. In November Jefferson suspended the act temporarily while William Pinckney, a Baltimore lawyer, joined James Monroe in London in an attempt to negotiate a settlement. But the treaty Monroe and Pinckney carried home violated their instructions—it did not mention impressment—and Jefferson never submitted it to the Senate for ratification.

Less than a year later, the *Chesapeake* affair exposed American military weakness and intensified the emotional impact of impressment on the public. In June 1807 the forty-gun frigate U.S.S. *Chesapeake* left Norfolk, Virginia, on a mission to protect American ships trading in the Mediterranean. About ten miles out, still inside American territorial waters, it met the fifty-gun British frigate *Leopard*. When the *Chesapeake* refused to be searched for deserters, the *Leopard* repeatedly emptied its guns broadside into the American ship. Three Americans were killed and eighteen wounded, including the ship's captain. The British impressed four deserters from the Royal Navy—three of them American citizens; one of them, Jenkin Ratford, was hanged. Damaged and humiliated, the *Chesapeake* crept back into port.

Chesapeake Affair

Had the United States been better prepared militarily, the ensuing howl of public indignation might have brought about a declaration of war. But the United States was ill-equipped to defend its neutral rights with force; it was no match for the British navy. With Congress in recess, Jefferson was able to avoid hostilities. In July, the president closed American waters to British warships to prevent similar incidents, and soon thereafter he increased military and naval expenditures. In December Jefferson again put economic pressure on Great Britain by invoking the Non-Importation Act, followed eight days later by a new restriction, the Embargo Act.

Intended as a short-term measure to avoid confrontation between American merchant vessels and British and French warships, the Embargo Act forbade virtually all exports from the United States to any country. Imports came to a halt as well, since foreign ships delivering goods left American ports with empty holds. Smuggling blossomed overnight.

Embargo Act

Few American policies were as well intentioned or as unpopular and unsuccessful as Jefferson's embargo. Although "peaceable coercion" was an enlightened concept in the arena of international

American sailors were depicted in art, verse, and song. They symbolized adventure and a new nation with trade extending to the far reaches of the globe. But the impressment of American seamen by the British navy was both a major point of friction between the United States and Britain and eventually a cause of the War of 1812. This Portrait of a Sailor *was painted by an unknown artist around 1825, a decade after that war ended.* Whitney Museum of American Art, Gift of Edgar William and Bernice Chrysler Garbisch.

affairs, some Republicans felt uneasy about using coercive federal power against merchants. The Federalists, commercially minded and generally pro-British, opposed the embargo vociferously. Some feared its impact abroad. "If England [were to] sink," Federalist vice-presidential candidate Rufus King said in 1808, "her fall will prove the grave of our liberties." Mercantile New England, the heart of Federalist opposition to Jefferson, felt the brunt of the resulting depression. Shipping collapsed as exports fell by 80 percent between 1807 and 1808. In the winter of 1808–1809, talk of secession spread through New England port cities.

Although general unemployment soared, some individuals benefited from the embargo. Merchants with ships abroad (thus not idled by the embargo) and those willing to risk the lax enforcement to trade illegally could garner enormous profits. U.S. manufacturers—textile mills, for instance—also received a boost, since the domestic market was theirs exclusively.

Great Britain, meanwhile, was only mildly affected by the embargo. The British citizens most severely hurt—West Indians and English factory workers—had no voice in policy. English merchants actually gained because they took over the Atlantic carrying trade from the stalled American merchant marine. And, because a British blockade of Europe had already ended most trade with France, the embargo had little practical effect on the French. Indeed, it gave France an excuse to set privateers against American ships that had managed to escape the embargo by avoiding American ports. The French argued that such ships must be British vessels in disguise, since the embargo barred American ships from the seas.

In the election of 1808, the Republicans found themselves facing not only the Federalists but also the embargo and factional dissent. Although nine state legislatures passed resolutions urging Jefferson to run again, the president followed Washington's example in renouncing a third term and supported James Madison, his secretary of state, as the Republican standard-bearer. Madison won the endorsement of the congressional caucus, but Virginia Republicans put forth James Monroe (who later withdrew), and some eastern Republicans supported Vice President George Clinton. For the first time, the Republican nomination was contested.

Charles Cotesworth Pinckney and Rufus King again headed the Federalist ticket, but with new vigor. The Younger Federalists, led by Harrison Gray Otis and other Bostonians, made the most of the widespread disaffection with Republican policy, especially the embargo. Although Pinckney received only 47 electoral votes to Madison's 122, the Federalists did manage to make the election a race. Pinckney carried all of New England except Vermont, and he won Delaware and some electoral votes in two other states. Federalists also gained seats in Congress and captured the New York state legislature. For the Younger Federalists, the future looked promising.

The embargo eventually collapsed under the pressure of domestic opposition. Jefferson felt the weight of his failure: "never did a prisoner, released from his chains," he wrote on leaving office, "feel such relief as I in shaking off the shackles of power." In his last days in office Jefferson had tried to lighten the burden by replacing the embargo with the Non-Intercourse Act of 1809. This act reopened trade with all nations except Britain and France, and it authorized the president to resume trade with either country if it ceased to violate neutral rights. But the new act solved only the problems created by the embargo; it did not prevent further British and French interference with American commerce. For one brief moment it appeared to work; President Madison reopened trade with England in June 1809 after the British minister to the United States assured him that Britain would repeal restrictions on American commerce. His Majesty's government in London, however, repudiated the minister's assurances, and Madison reverted to nonintercourse (a ban on trade).

Non-Intercourse Act

When the Non-Intercourse Act expired in 1810, Congress substituted a variant, known as Macon's Bill Number 2, that exchanged the proverbial stick for a carrot. The bill reopened trade with both Great Britain and France but provided that when either nation stopped violating American commercial rights, the president could suspend American commerce with the other. Madison, eager to use the bill rather than go to war, was tricked at his own game. When Napoleon accepted the offer, Madison declared nonintercourse with Great Britain in 1811. Napoleon, however, did not keep his word. The French continued to seize American ships, and nonintercourse failed a second time. But because the Royal Navy dominated the seas, Britain, not France, became the main target of American hostility.

Angry American leaders tended to blame even tribal resistance in the West solely on British agitation, ignoring the Native Americans' legitimate protests against white encroachment and treaty violations. In the opening decade of the 1800s, the Shawnee brothers Prophet and Tecumseh had attempted to build a pan-Indian federation, taking advantage of Anglo-American friction. Prophet's

Shawnee Resistance

The Shawnee Chiefs Prophet (left) and Tecumseh (right). The two brothers led a revival of traditional Shawnee culture and preached Native American federation against white encroachment. In the War of 1812 they allied themselves with the British, but Tecumseh's death at the battle of the Thames (1813) and British indifference thereafter caused the tribal peoples' resistance and unity to collapse. Prophet: National Museum of American Art, Smithsonian Institution; Tecumseh: Field Museum of Natural History, FMNH Neg. #A93851.

early experiences mirrored the fate of many frontier tribes. Born in 1775, a few months after his father's death in battle, Prophet—called Lalawethika (Noisemaker) as a young man—was expelled to Ohio along with other Shawnees under the 1795 Treaty of Greenville (see page 198), and he later moved to Indiana. Within the shrunken territory granted to the Shawnees under the treaty, game soon became scarce. Encroachment by whites and the periodic ravages of disease brought further misery and, like many other Native Americans, Lalawethika turned to whiskey. He also turned to traditional folk knowledge and remedies, and in 1804 he became a tribal medicine man. His medicine, however, could not stop the white man's virulent diseases from ravaging his village.

Lalawethika emerged from his own battle with illness in 1805 as a new man, called Prophet. Claiming to have died and been resurrected, Prophet traveled widely in the Northwest as a religious leader, attacking the decline of moral values among Native Americans, warning of damnation

for those who drank whiskey, condemning intertribal battles, and stressing harmony and respect for elders. He urged the tribal peoples to return to the old ways and abandon white customs, advising them to hunt with bows and arrows, not guns; to release domestic animals and discard the wearing of hats; and to refrain from eating bread and return to cultivating corn and beans.

Prophet's message reassured the Shawnees, Potawatomis, and other peoples of the Old Northwest (Ohio, Indiana, Illinois, Michigan, and Wisconsin) who felt unsettled and threatened by whites. Prophet won converts by performing miracles—he darkened the sun by timing his invocations to coincide with a solar eclipse—and used opposition to federal Indian policy to draw others into his camp. His message spread to southern tribes as well, and the government and white settlers were alarmed.

By 1808, Prophet and his older brother Tecumseh talked less about spiritual renewal and more about resistance to American aggression.

Prophet and Tecumseh

Their refusal to leave lands claimed by the government was encouraged by the British, who looked to alliances with Native American tribes after renewed Anglo-American hostilities followed the *Chesapeake* affair of 1807. In repudiating land cessions to the government under the Treaty of Fort Wayne (1809), Tecumseh told Indiana's governor William Henry Harrison at Vincennes in 1810 that "the only way to check and stop this evil is, for all the red men to unite in claiming a common and equal right in the land, as it was at first, and should be yet; for it never was divided, but belongs to all, for the use of each. . . . No part has a right to sell, even to each other, much less to strangers."

Tecumseh, a towering six-foot warrior and magnetic orator, replaced his brother Prophet as Shawnee leader. Young warriors found Tecumseh's political visions more relevant than Prophet's spirituality in protecting themselves against the United States. Convinced that only a federation of tribes could stop the advance of white settlement, Tecumseh sought to unify northern and southern Indians. He warned Harrison that the tribes would resist white occupation of the 2.5 million acres on the Wabash that they had ceded in the Treaty of Fort Wayne.

THE WAR OF 1812

Conflict over Native American loyalties in the West and over impressment on the seas divided Britain and the United States. Frustrated and having exhausted all efforts to alter British policy, the United States in 1811 and 1812 drifted into war with Great Britain. (Meanwhile, in June 1812, Britain opened the seas to American shipping. Hard times had hit the British Isles: the Anglo-French conflict had blocked much of British commerce with the European continent, and exports to the United States had fallen 80 percent. But two days later, before word had crossed the Atlantic, Congress declared war.)

The War of 1812, the new nation's first general war, was the logical outcome of U.S. policy after the renewal of war in Europe in 1803. The grievances President Madison enumerated in his message to Congress on June 1, 1812, were old ones: impressment, interference with neutral commerce, and British alliances with the western tribes. Unmentioned was the resolve to defend American independence and honor—and the thirst of American expansionists for British Canada.

Yet Congress and the country were divided. Much of the sentiment for war came from the War Hawks, land-hungry southerners and westerners led by Henry Clay of Kentucky and John C. Calhoun of South Carolina. Westerners had increased their numbers in Congress following reapportionment after the 1810 census, and the enlarged delegation was concerned equally with national honor and expansion. Most representatives from the coastal states (including all the Federalists) opposed war, since armed conflict with the great naval power threatened to interrupt American shipping. The vote for war—79 to 49 in the House, 19 to 13 in the Senate—reflected these sharp regional differences. The same split would be reflected in the way Americans fought the war.

War was a foolish adventure for the United States in 1812. The events that led to war were muddled, American goals were unclear, the military campaign was poorly carried out, and the peace treaty was inconclusive. The war was a series of scuffles and skirmishes; full-scale battles were rare. Nonetheless, its outcome ensured the freedom won in the Revolutionary War and dealt a serious blow to tribal resistance to American expansion. It also stimulated American nationalism and self-confidence.

Recruiting an Army

Despite six months of preparation, American forces were unprepared for war. The navy had a corps of well-trained and experienced officers who had proved their mettle in protecting American merchantmen from Mediterranean pirates. But next to the Royal Navy, the ruler of the seas, the U.S. Navy was minuscule. Jefferson's warning that "our constitution is a peace establishment—it is not calculated for war" proved true. The army had neither an able staff nor an adequate force of enlisted men. The U.S. Military Academy at West Point, founded during Jefferson's administration in 1802, had produced only eighty-nine regular officers by 1812. The army thus turned to political leaders and state militia to organize volunteer companies, and not all states cooperated. Much of the

Population, 1810, by States and Territories

State or Territory	Population 1810	State or Territory	Population 1810
Arkansas	1,000	Ohio	231,000
Michigan	5,000	New Jersey	246,000
Alabama	9,000	Georgia	252,000
Illinois	12,000	Connecticut	262,000
District of Columbia	15,000	Tennessee	262,000
Missouri	20,000	Maryland	381,000
Indiana	25,000	Kentucky	407,000
Mississippi	31,000	South Carolina	415,000
Delaware	73,000	Massachusetts	472,000
Louisiana	77,000	North Carolina	556,000
Rhode Island	77,000	Pennsylvania	810,000
New Hampshire	214,000	New York	959,000
Vermont	218,000	Virginia	983,000
Maine	229,000		

New lands to the west attracted settlers and changed the pattern of where Americans lived. Source: U.S. Bureau of the Census, *Historical Statistics of the United States, Colonial Times to 1970*, Bicentennial Edition, 2 parts. (Washington, D.C., 1975), Part I, pp. 24–37.

war effort, including planning, was decentralized. The government offered enlistees a $16 sign-up bonus, $5 monthly pay, a full set of clothes, and a promise of three months' pay and 160 acres of western land upon discharge. Recruiting officers received a $2 premium for each enlistee. Among those who joined, 42 percent were illiterate.

On the frontier, recruitment went well at first. Civic spirit and strong anti-Indian sentiment stimulated thousands of enlistments from the Old Northwest, Kentucky, Tennessee, and the southern frontier. The army made itself more acceptable to new recruits by abolishing flogging in 1812. Within a year, however, frontier enlistments declined. Word spread that the War Department was often slow in meeting its payroll and supplying clothing.

In New England, raising an army proved even more difficult. Many viewed the conflict as a Republican war—"Mr. Madison's War"—and Federalists discouraged enlistments. Some Republican officials in New England declined invitations to raise volunteer companies. Those who accepted promised their men that they would serve only a defensive role, as in Maine where they guarded the coastline. Indeed, the inability of the United States to mount a successful invasion of Canada was due in part to the army's failure to assemble an effective force. State militias in New England and New York often declined to fight outside the borders of their own state.

Invasion of Canada

Canada offered the United States the only readily available battlefront on which to confront Great Britain, as well as land to conquer. The mighty Royal Navy was useless on the Great Lakes separating the United States and Canada, since there was no river access from the Atlantic. Thousands of miles from British supply sources, Canada was vulnerable. And England, preoccupied with fighting Napoleon on the European continent, was unlikely to reinforce its small garrisons in Canada.

Major Campaigns of the War of 1812   *The land war centered on the American-Canadian border, the Chesapeake Bay, and the Louisiana and Mississippi territories.*

Begun with high hopes, the invasion of Canada ended in disaster. The American strategy concentrated on the West, hoping to split Canadian forces and isolate the Shawnees, Potawatomis, and other tribes who supported the British. Tecumseh had joined the British when the war began in return for the promise of an Indian nation in the Great Lakes region. General William Hull, governor of the Michigan Territory, marched his troops into Upper Canada, near Detroit. A more experienced politician than soldier, Hull surrounded himself with newly minted colonels who were as politically astute and militarily ignorant as he was. The British anticipated the invasion: they mobilized their Indian allies, moved troops into the area, and demanded Hull's surrender. When a pro-British,

In the first year of the War of 1812, only the U.S. Navy proved equal to British forces. In August 1812, the U.S.S. Constitution *defeated and sank the H.M.S.* Guerriere *in the Atlantic, 750 miles east of Boston. The* Guerriere *had long plagued American ships, and the victory was widely cheered in the states. Thomas Birch's* Constitution and the Guerriere *recreates the fury of the encounter.* U.S. Naval Academy Museum.

mostly Potawatomi, contingent captured Fort Dearborn near present-day Chicago (see map), Hull capitulated. Farther to the west, other American forts surrendered to superior forces. By the winter of 1812–1813, the British controlled about half of the Old Northwest.

The United States had no greater success on the Niagara front, where New York borders Canada. At the Battle of Queenstown, north of Niagara, the U.S. regular army met defeat because the New York militia refused to leave the state. This scene was repeated near Lake Champlain, where American plans to attack Montreal were foiled when the militia declined to cross the border. The American offensives in the North were probably doomed to fail anyway; the United States lacked the means to hold any part of Canada permanently.

The navy provided the only bright ray in the first year of the war: the U.S.S. *Constitution*, the U.S.S. *Wasp,* and the U.S.S. *United States* all bested British warships on the Atlantic. The defeat

of the H.M.S. *Guerriere* by the *Constitution* in the Atlantic emboldened the U.S. Navy and earned the American ship the title "Old Ironsides." In art and ship models, such as the painting by Thomas Birch, the *Constitution* earned immortality. In defeat, however, the British lost just 1 percent of their strength; in victory, the Americans lost 20 percent of their ships. The British admiralty simply shifted its fleet away from the American ships, and by 1813 the Royal Navy again commanded the seas.

The Royal Navy blockaded the Chesapeake and Delaware bays in December 1812, and by 1814 the blockade covered nearly all U.S. ports along the Atlantic coast. American trade had declined nearly 90 percent since 1811, and the decline in revenues from customs duties threatened to bankrupt the federal government.

The contest for control of the Great Lakes, the key to the war in the Northwest, was largely a shipbuilding race. Under Master Commandant

Great Lakes Campaign

Oliver Hazard Perry and shipbuilder Noah Brown, the United States outbuilt the British on Lake Erie and defeated them at the bloody Battle of Put-in-Bay on September 10, 1813. With this costly victory, the Americans gained control of Lake Erie.

General William Henry Harrison then began the march that proved to be the United States's most successful moment in the war. The volunteers who constituted the majority of Harrison's command were a ragtag group. Recruited as volunteers in the Kentucky militia, they were drafted into the regular army and sent to fight in Lower Canada; they marched twenty to thirty miles a day to join Harrison's forces in Ohio, receiving no training and carrying only swords and knives on the march.

Harrison's force of forty-five hundred men crossed Lake Erie and pursued the British, Shawnee, and Chippewa forces into Canada, defeating them on October 5 at the Battle of the Thames. With this victory the United States retained control of the Old Northwest. And when Tecumseh died in the Battle of the Thames, Native American unity also collapsed—as did the most significant resistance to the federal government's treaty-making tactics. Following the Battle of the Thames, the Americans razed York (now Toronto), the Canadian capital. They looted and burned the Parliament building before withdrawing; they did not have enough troops to hold the city.

After defeating Napoleon in April 1814, the British stepped up the land campaign against the United States, concentrating their efforts in the Chesapeake Bay region. In retaliation for the burning of York—and to divert American troops from Lake Champlain, where the British planned a new offensive—royal troops occupied Washington, D.C., in August and set it ablaze, leaving the presidential mansion scarred by fire. The attack on the capital, however, was only a diversion. The major battle occurred at Baltimore, where the Americans held firm. Francis Scott Key, witnessing the British fleet's bombardment of Fort McHenry in Baltimore harbor, was inspired to write the verses of "The Star-Spangled Banner" (which became the national anthem in 1931). Although the British inflicted heavy damage both materially and psychologically, they achieved little militarily. Equally unsuccessful was their offensive at Lake Champlain, where an American fleet forced a British flotilla to turn back at Plattsburgh. The offensive was discontinued, and the war was essentially stalemated.

The last campaign of the war was waged in the South, along the Gulf of Mexico. Andrew Jackson, a Tennessee militia general, had raised his militia in December 1812 with the promise that they would serve one year. By late fall of 1813 his anti-Creek campaign was stalled by lack of supplies, and his men were talking about disbanding and going home. Jackson refused to discharge them; they could not, he claimed, leave their posts on enemy ground. The officers repeatedly threatened to shoot any man who sought to leave. In March 1814 Jackson executed John Woods, a militiaman, for disobedience and mutiny. This broke the opposition in the ranks, and his men defeated the Creek nation at the Battle of Horseshoe Bend in March 1814. The battle ended the year-long Creek War, which had begun following Tecumseh's visit in late 1811. Creek prophets and their followers—known as the Red Sticks—sparked Indian resistance in the South. President Madison, lacking the regular troops to fight them, left suppression of Creeks to the southern states and territories. Andrew Jackson's defeat of the Creek nation began his rise to political prominence. The Creeks had to cede two-thirds of their land and withdraw to southern and western Alabama; Jackson became a major general in the regular army and continued south toward the Gulf. To forestall a British invasion at Pensacola Bay, which guarded an overland route to New Orleans, Jackson seized Pensacola—in Spanish Florida—in November 1814. After securing Mobile, he marched on to New Orleans and prepared for a British attempt to capture the city.

The Battle of New Orleans was the final military engagement. Early in December the British fleet landed fifteen hundred men east of the city,

Battle of New Orleans

hoping to gain control of the Mississippi River and strangle the lifeline of the American West. They faced American regular army troops, a larger contingent of Tennessee and Kentucky frontiersmen, and two companies of free African-American volunteers from New Orleans. For three weeks the British under Sir Edward Pakenham and the Americans led by Jackson played cat-and-mouse, each trying to gain a major strategic position. Finally, on January 8, 1815, the two forces met head-on. In fortified positions, Jackson and his mostly untrained army held their ground against two suicidal frontal assaults from a reinforced British contingent of six thousand. At day's end, more than two thousand British soldiers lay dead or wounded. The Americans suffered only twenty-one casualties. Andrew Jackson emerged a national hero, and the battle was memorialized in song and paintings. Ironically, the Battle of New Orleans was fought two weeks after the end of the war; unknown to the participants, a treaty had been signed in Ghent, Belgium, on December 24, 1814.

The U.S. government had gone to war reluctantly and throughout the conflict had continued to probe for a diplomatic end to hostilities. In 1813, President Madison had eagerly accepted a Russian offer to mediate, but Great Britain had balked. Three months later, British Foreign Minister Lord Castlereagh suggested opening peace talks. It took over ten months to arrange meetings, but in August 1814 a team of American negotiators, including John Quincy Adams and Henry Clay, began talks with the British in Ghent.

The Ghent treaty made no mention of the issues that had led to war: the United States received no satisfaction on impressment, blockades, or other maritime rights for neutrals.

Treaty of Ghent
——

Likewise, British demands for an independent Indian nation in the Northwest and territorial cessions from Maine to Minnesota were not satisfied. Essentially, the Treaty of Ghent restored the prewar status quo. It provided for an end to hostilities with the British and with Native American tribes, release of prisoners, restoration of conquered territory, and arbitration of boundary disputes.

Why did the negotiators settle for so little? Events in Europe had made peace and the status quo acceptable at the end of 1814, as they had not been in 1812. Napoleon's fall from power allowed the United States to abandon its demands, since peace in Europe made impressment and interference with American commerce moot questions. Similarly, war-weary Britain—its treasury nearly depleted—stopped pressing for a military victory.

The War of 1812 reaffirmed the independence of the young American republic. Nearly three hundred thousand troops had taken up arms to main-

General Andrew Jackson and his forces were widely celebrated for the victory over the British in the Battle of New Orleans in 1815, fought two weeks after the Treaty of Ghent had officially ended the war but before word could reach the armies. For nearly two centuries Americans have sung about the battle and Jackson, illustrated by this sheet music from the 1830s. Historic New Orleans Collection.

Results of the War of 1812
——

tain independence; almost two thousand died and four thousand were wounded. Although conflict with Great Britain continued, it never again led to war. The experience strengthened America's resolve to steer clear of European politics, for it had been the British-French conflict that had drawn the United States into war. For the rest of the century the United States would shun involvement in European political issues and wars.

The war had disastrous results for most Native American tribes. Although they were not a party to the Treaty of Ghent, the ninth article pledged the United States to end hostilities and to restore "all the possessions, rights, and privileges" the tribes had enjoyed before the war. More than a dozen treaties were signed with midwestern tribal leaders in 1815, but they had little meaning. With the death of Tecumseh, the Indians had lost their most powerful political and military leader; with the withdrawal of the British, they had lost their strongest ally. The Shawnees, Potawatomis, Chippewas, and other midwestern tribes had lost the resources with which they could have resisted American expansion.

Domestically, the war exposed weaknesses in defense and transportation. American generals had found American roads inadequate to move an army and its supplies among widely scattered fronts. In the Northwest, General Harrison's troops had had to depend on homemade cartridges and gifts of clothing from Ohio residents, and in Maine troops had melted down spoons to make bullets. Improved transportation and a well-equipped army became national priorities; both were vital for westward expansion. In 1815, President Madison responded by centralizing control of the military and building a line of forts for coastal defense, and Congress voted a standing army of ten thousand men, one-third of the army's wartime strength but three times the size of the army during Jefferson's administration. After the war, improved transportation and weakened tribal leadership would facilitate western settlement.

Possibly most important of all, the war stimulated economic growth. The embargo, the Non-Importation and Non-Intercourse Acts, and the war itself spurred the production of manufactured goods—cloth and metal—to replace banned imports. Unable to invest in embargoed cargoes or manufacturing abroad, New England capitalists began to invest in home manufactures. The effects of these changes were to be far-reaching (see Chapter 10).

And, finally, the war sealed the fate of the Federalist party. Realizing that their chances of winning a presidential election in wartime were slight, the Federalists joined renegade Republicans in supporting DeWitt Clinton of New York in 1812. This was the high point of Federalist organization at the state level, and the Younger Federalists campaigned hard. Clinton nevertheless lost to President Madison by 128 to 89 electoral votes; areas that favored the war (the South and West) voted solidly Republican. The Federalists gained some congressional seats and carried many local elections, but once again extremism undermined the Federalists.

During the war Older Federalists had revived talk of secession, and Federalist delegates from

Hartford Convention

New England met in Hartford, Connecticut, for three weeks in the winter of 1814–1815. With the war stalemated and trade in ruins, they plotted to revise the national compact or pull out of the republic. Moderates prevented a resolution of secession, but convention members condemned the war and the embargo and endorsed radical changes in the Constitution. In particular, they wanted constitutional amendments restricting the presidency to one term and requiring a two-thirds congressional vote to admit new states. They also hoped to abolish the three-fifths compromise, whereby slaves were counted in the apportionment of congressional representatives (see page 203), and to forbid naturalized citizens from holding office. These proposals were aimed at preserving New England Federalist political power by checking the growing strength of the West and South—the heart of Republican electoral strength—and that of Irish immigrants.

The timing of the Hartford Convention proved lethal. The victory at New Orleans and news of the peace treaty made the convention, with its talk of secession and proposed constitutional amendments, look ridiculous if not treasonous. Rather than harassing a beleaguered wartime administration, the Federalists found themselves in retreat before a rising tide of nationalism. Though Federalism survived in a handful of states until the 1820s, the Federalist party began to dissolve. The War of 1812, at first a source of revival as opponents of war flocked to the Federalist banner, helped kill the faction.

POSTWAR NATIONALISM AND DIPLOMACY

With peace came a new surge of American nationalism. Self-confidently, the nation asserted itself at home and abroad as Republicans aped Federalists in encouraging commerce and economic development. In his message to Congress in December 1815, President Madison embraced Federalist doctrine by recommending expansion of the military and a program to stimulate economic growth. Wartime experiences, he said, had demonstrated the need for a national bank (the charter of the first

Bank of the United States had expired) and for better transportation. To raise government revenues and perpetuate the wartime growth of manufacturing, Madison called for a protective tariff—a tax on imported goods designed to protect American manufactures. Though he strayed from Jeffersonian Republicanism, Madison did so within limits. Only a constitutional amendment, he argued, could give the federal government the authority to build roads and canals that were less than national in scope.

The congressional leadership pushed Madison's nationalist program energetically in the belief that it would unify the country. Republican Congressman John C. Calhoun of

American System

South Carolina and Speaker of the House Henry Clay of Kentucky, who named the program the American System, looked to the tariff on imported goods to stimulate industry. New mills would purchase raw materials; new millworkers would buy food from the agricultural South and West. New roads would make possible the flow of produce and goods, and tariff revenues would provide the money to build them. A national bank would facilitate all these transactions.

The new Republican policy revived Hamilton's original plan for the Bank of the United States (see page 216). Fearing the concentration of economic power in a central bank, the Republicans had allowed the charter of the privately owned but federally chartered Bank of the United States to expire in 1811. State banks, however, could not meet the nation's needs; their resources had proved insufficient to assist the government in financing the War of 1812. Moreover, Americans distrusted currency issued by distant banks. Because many banks issued notes without gold to back them up, and because counterfeit notes were common, merchants hesitated to accept unfamiliar currency. Republicans therefore came to favor a bank that could operate nationally. In 1816 Congress chartered the Second Bank of the United States for twenty years. Its headquarters, like those of the first Bank of the United States, were in Philadelphia. The government provided $7 million of the initial $35 million capital and appointed one-fifth of the directors. The bank opened its doors in 1817.

Congress did not share Madison's scruples about the constitutionality of using federal funds to build local roads. "Let us, then, bind the republic together," Calhoun declared, "with a perfect system of roads and canals." But Madison vetoed Calhoun's internal-improvements bill, which provided for the construction of roads of mostly local benefit, declaring it unconstitutional. Internal improvements, Madison insisted, were the province of the states and of private enterprise. (He did, however, approve funds for the further extension of the National Road in Ohio, on the grounds that it was a military necessity.)

Protective tariffs completed Madison's nationalist program. Such tariffs were generally favored by domestic producers who competed with importers, but they were opposed by purchasers of imported goods, who paid higher prices when the tax was passed on to consumers. The embargo and the war had stimulated domestic industry—especially the manufacture of cloth and iron—but resumption of trade after the war revived competition from abroad. Americans accused British firms of dumping goods below cost on the American market to stifle American manufacturing. To aid young industries, Madison recommended and Congress passed the Tariff of 1816, the first substantial protective tariff in American history. The act levied taxes on imported woolens and cottons (especially inexpensive ones) and on iron, leather, hats, paper, and sugar, in effect raising their cost. Some New England congressmen viewed the tariff as interference in free trade, and southern congressmen (except Calhoun and a few others) opposed it because it raised the cost of imported goods to southern families. But the western and Middle Atlantic states backed it, and the tariff passed.

James Monroe, Madison's successor as president, continued Madison's domestic program, supporting the national bank and tariffs and vetoing internal improvements on constitutional grounds. Monroe was the third Virginian president between 1801 and 1825. A former senator, twice governor of Virginia, and an experienced diplomat, he had served under Madison as secretary of state and secretary of war. Monroe fulfilled his ambition to be president largely through perseverance and close association with Jefferson and Madison. Even his admirers admitted that, among the nation's founders, he was an ordinary and colorless man who rarely had an original idea. He rode into office on Republican coattails, easily defeating the last Federalist nominee, Rufus King, and sweeping all the states except the Federalist strongholds of Massachusetts, Connecticut, and Delaware. It was the Federalists' last gasp. "Discord does not belong to our system," Monroe optimistically declared, calling the American people "one great family with a common interest." A Boston newspaper dubbed the one-party period the "Era of Good Feelings." And throughout Monroe's first term that label seemed appropriate.

Under the Federalist Chief Justice Marshall, the Supreme Court in this period became the bulwark of a nationalist point of view. In *McCulloch* v.

McCulloch v. Maryland

Maryland (1819), the Court struck down a Maryland law taxing a branch of the federally chartered Second Bank of the United States. Maryland had imposed the tax in an effort to destroy the bank's Baltimore branch. The issue was thus one of state versus federal jurisdiction. Speaking for a unanimous Court, Marshall asserted the supremacy of the federal government over the states. "The Constitution and the laws thereof are supreme," he declared. "They control the constitution and laws of the respective states and cannot be controlled by them."

The Court went on to consider whether Congress could issue a bank charter; the Constitution did not spell out such power. But Marshall noted that Congress had the authority to pass "all laws which shall be necessary and proper for carrying into execution" the enumerated powers of the government. Echoing Alexander Hamilton's notion of implied powers, Marshall ruled that Congress could legally exercise "those great powers on which the welfare of the nation essentially depends." If the ends were legitimate and the means were not prohibited, Marshall ruled, a law was constitutional. The Constitution was, in Marshall's words, "intended to endure for ages to come, and consequently, to be adapted to the various causes of human affairs." The bank charter was declared legal.

McCulloch v. *Maryland* thus combined Federalist nationalism with Federalist economic views. By asserting federal supremacy, Marshall was protecting the commercial and industrial interests that favored a national bank; this was federalism in the tradition of Alexander Hamilton. The decision was only one in a series. In *Fletcher* v. *Peck* (1810), the Court voided a Georgia law that violated individuals' rights to make contracts. Similarly, in *Dart-*

mouth College v. *Woodward* (1819), the Court nullified a New Hampshire act altering the charter of Dartmouth College. Marshall ruled that the charter was a contract, and in protecting such contracts he thwarted state interference in commerce and business. *Gibbons* v. *Ogden* confirmed federal supremacy in interstate commerce (see page 277).

Monroe's secretary of state, John Quincy Adams, matched the self-confident Marshall Court in assertiveness and nationalist sentiments. A small, austere man once described by

John Quincy Adams as Secretary of State

a British official as a "bulldog among spaniels," Adams was the son of John and Abigail Adams and a superb diplomat who spoke six languages. From 1817 to 1825 he brilliantly managed the nation's foreign policy, stubbornly pushing for expansion, fishing rights for Americans in Atlantic waters, political distance from the Old World, and peace. An ardent expansionist, he nonetheless placed conditions on expansion, believing that it must come about through negotiations, not war, and that newly acquired territories must not permit slavery.

An Anglophobe, Adams nonetheless worked to strengthen the peace with Great Britain. In 1817 the two nations agreed in the Rush-Bagot Treaty to limit their Great Lakes naval forces to one ship each on Lakes Ontario and Champlain and to two vessels each on the other lakes. This first disarmament treaty of modern times led to the demilitarization of the U.S.-Canadian border.

Adams then pushed for the Convention of 1818, which fixed the U.S.-Canadian border from Lake of the Woods in Minnesota westward to the Rockies along the 49th parallel. When agreement could not be reached on the territory west of the Rockies, Britain and the United States settled on joint occupation of Oregon for ten years (renewed indefinitely in 1827). Adams wanted to fix the border along the 49th parallel all the way to the Pacific Ocean, thereby gaining the important inland waterways of Juan de Fuca Strait and Puget Sound, and he hoped for a better negotiating position when the treaty lapsed.

Adams's next move was to settle long-term disputes with Spain. Although the 1803 Louisiana Treaty had omitted reference to Spanish-ruled West Florida, the United States claimed the territory as far east as the Perdido River (the present-day Florida-Alabama border) but occupied only a small finger of the area. During the War of 1812 the United States had seized Mobile and the remainder of West Florida. After the war Adams took advantage of Spain's preoccupation with domestic and colonial troubles to negotiate for the purchase of East Florida. During the talks, which took place in 1818, General Andrew Jackson took it on himself to occupy much of present-day Florida on the pretext of suppressing Seminole raids against American settlements across the border. Adams was furious with Jackson but defended his brazen act.

The following year, Don Luís de Onís, the Spanish minister to the United States, agreed to cede Florida to the United States without payment. The Adams-Onís, or

Adams-Onís Treaty

Transcontinental, Treaty also defined the southwestern boundary of the Louisiana Purchase, a zigzag across the West from Texas to the Pacific Ocean (see map, page 243). (Spain retained Texas, New Mexico, and California.) In return, the United States government assumed $5 million worth of claims by American citizens against Spain and gave up its dubious claim to Texas. Expansion was thus achieved at little cost and without war, and American territorial claims now stretched from the Atlantic to the Pacific.

Conflict between the United States and European nations was temporarily resolved by the Rush-Bagot Treaty, the Convention of 1818, and the Adams-Onís Treaty, but events to the south still threatened U.S. interests. It was John Quincy Adams's desire to insulate the United States and the Western Hemisphere from European conflict that brought about his greatest achievement: the Monroe Doctrine.

The immediate issue was the recognition of new governments in Latin America. Between 1808 and 1822, the United Provinces of the Río de la Plata (present-day northern Argentina, Paraguay, and Uruguay), Chile, Peru, Colombia, and Mexico had all broken free from Spain. Many Americans wanted to recognize the independence of these former colonies, which seemed to be following in the United States's revolutionary tradition. Monroe and Adams moved cautiously. They sought to avoid conflict with Spain and its allies and to assure themselves of the stability of the revolutionary re-

John Quincy Adams (1767–1848), architect of the Monroe Doctrine, was secretary of state from 1817 to 1825, the year Thomas Scully painted this portrait. Begun just before the House of Representatives elected Adams president, Scully's oil portrait captured his determination and stubbornness. New York State, Office of Parks, Recreation, and Historic Preservation, Philipse Manor Hall State Historic Site.

gimes. But in 1822, shortly after the Adams-Onís Treaty was signed and ratified, the United States became the first nation outside Latin America to recognize the new states.

Soon events in Europe again threatened the stability of the New World. Spain suffered a domestic revolt and, in an attempt to bolster the weak Spanish monarchy against the rebels, France occupied Spain. The United States feared that France would seek to restore the new Latin American states to Spanish rule. Great Britain, similarly distrustful of France, proposed a joint U.S.-British declaration against European intervention in the hemisphere and a joint disavowal of territorial ambitions in the region. Adams rejected the British overture; in accordance with Washington's admonition to avoid foreign entanglements, he insisted that the United States act independently.

Determined to avoid joint action with Great Britain, the unbending Adams tenaciously outargued other cabinet members. Those who favored joint action (supported by former president Jefferson in retirement at Monticello) believed the United States needed British naval power to prevent French or Russian expansion in the New World. But Adams won. "It would be more candid, as well as more dignified," he argued, "to avow our principles explicitly to Russia and France, than to come in as a cockboat in the wake of the British man-of-war." Adams interpreted the British proposal to disavow territorial ambitions as a deliberate attempt by London to prevent further American expansion.

President Monroe presented the American position—the Monroe Doctrine—to Congress in December 1823. His message called for, first, *noncolonization* of the Western Hemi-

Monroe Doctrine

sphere by European nations, a principle that addressed American anxiety not only about Latin America but also about Russian expansion on the West Coast. (Russia held Alaska and had built a chain of settlements and forts as far south as California.) Second, he demanded *nonintervention* by Europe in the affairs of independent New World nations. Finally, Monroe pledged *noninterference* by the United States in European affairs, including those of Europe's existing New World colonies.

The Monroe Doctrine proved popular at home as an anti-British, anti-European assertion of American nationalism, and it eventually became the foundation of American policy in the Western Hemisphere. Monroe's words, however, carried no force. Indeed, the policy could not have succeeded without the support of the British, who were already committed to keeping other European nations out of the hemisphere to protect their dominance in the Atlantic trade. Europeans ignored the doctrine; it was the Royal Navy they respected, not American policy.

THE PANIC OF 1819 AND RENEWED SECTIONALISM

Monroe's domestic record did not match the diplomatic successes of his administration. In 1819, financial panic subverted postwar confidence and revived sectional loyalties. Neither panic nor the resurgence of sectionalism hurt Monroe politically; without a rival political party to rally opposition, he won a second term in 1820 unopposed.

But hard economic times spread. The postwar expansion was built on loose money and widespread speculation. State banks extended credit

Hard Times

and printed notes too freely, fueling speculative buying of western land. (Men bought acreage hoping to sell at a profit rather than to settle on and farm the land.) When economic expansion slowed, the manufacturing downturn that began in 1818 deepened and prices spiraled downward. To protect its assets, the Second Bank of the United States cut back on loans, thus accelerating the contraction of the economy. Distressed urban workers lobbied for easy credit and internal improvements and began to take a more active role in politics. Farmers clamored for lower tariffs on manufactured goods to reduce general price levels. Hurt by a sharp decline in the price of cotton, southern planters railed at the protective Tariff of 1816, which had raised prices on all imported goods while their incomes fell sharply. The Virginia Agricultural Society of Fredericksburg, for example, argued that the tariff violated the very principles on which the nation had been founded. In a protest to Congress in 1820, the society called the tariff an unequal tax that awarded exclusive privileges to manufacturers—"oppressive monopolies, which are ultimately to grind both us and our children after us 'into dust and ashes.'" Manufacturers, on the other hand, demanded greater tariff protection—and eventually got it in the Tariff of 1824.

Western farmers suffered, too. Those who had purchased public land on credit lacked sufficient income to repay their loans. To avoid mass bankruptcy, Congress delayed the deadlines for repayment, and western state legislatures passed "stay laws" restricting mortgage foreclosures. Many westerners blamed the panic on the Second Bank of the United States for tightening the money supply. In debt to the national bank, several state banks folded, and westerners bitterly accused the Second Bank of saving itself while the nation went to ruin. Although the economy recovered in the mid-1820s, resentment of the bank contributed to the rise of the Jacksonian movement (see pages 379–383).

Far more divisive was the question of slavery. Ever since the drafting of the Constitution, political leaders had avoided the issue. The one exception was an act closing the foreign slave trade after January 1, 1808, which passed without much opposition. Both supporters and opponents of slavery assumed that Congress would act when the constitutional ban (Article I, Section 9) on closing the slave trade expired in 1808. In 1819, however, slavery finally crept onto the political agenda when Missouri residents petitioned Congress for admission to the Union as a slave state. For the next two-and-a-half years the issue dominated all congressional action. "This momentous question," wrote Thomas Jefferson, in fear for the life of the Union, "like a fire bell in the night, awakened and filled me with terror."

Slavery Question

The debate transcended slavery in Missouri. At stake was the undoing of the compromises that had kept the issue quarantined since the Constitutional Convention. Five new states had joined the Union since 1812: Louisiana (1812), Indiana (1816), Mississippi (1817), Illinois (1818), and Alabama (1819). Of these, Louisiana, Mississippi, and Alabama permitted slavery. Because Missouri was on the same latitude as free Illinois, Indiana, and Ohio (a state since 1803), its admission as a slave state would thrust slavery farther northward. It would also tilt the uneasy political balance in the Senate toward the states committed to slavery. In 1819 the Union consisted of eleven slave and eleven free states. If Missouri entered as a slave state, the slave states would have a two-vote edge in the Senate.

What made the issue so highly charged was not the politics of admission to statehood but the debate over the morality of slavery. The settlers of Missouri were mostly Kentuckians and Tennesseeans who had grown up with slavery. But in the North slavery was slowly dying out with gradual emancipation, and many northerners had concluded that it was evil. When Representative James Tallmadge, Jr., of New York introduced an amendment providing for gradual emancipation in Missouri, a passionate and sometimes violent debate ensued. Southerners accused the North of threatening to destroy the Union. "If you persist, the Union will be dissolved," Thomas W. Cobb of Georgia shouted at Tallmadge. "Seas of blood can only extinguish" the fire Tallmadge was starting, Cobb warned. "Let it come," retorted Tallmadge. The House, which had a northern majority, passed the Tallmadge amendment, but the Senate rejected it. The two sides were deadlocked.

A compromise emerged in 1820 under pressure from House Speaker Henry Clay: the admission of free Maine, carved out of Massachusetts, was linked with that of slave Missouri. In the rest of the Louisiana Territory north of 36°30' (Missouri's southern boundary), slavery was prohibited forever (see map, page 264). The compromise carried, but the agreement almost came apart in November when Missouri submitted a constitution that barred free blacks from settling in the state. Opponents contended that the proposed state constitution violated the federal Constitution's provision that "the citizens of each State shall be entitled to all privileges and immunities of citizens in the several States." Advocates argued that restrictions on free blacks were common in state law in both North and South. In 1821, Clay produced a second compromise: Missouri guaranteed that none of its laws would discriminate against citizens of other states. (Once admitted to the Union, however, Missouri twice adopted laws banning free blacks.)

Missouri Compromise

Although political leaders had succeeded in removing slavery from the congressional agenda, sectional issues would undermine Republican unity and end the reign of the Virginia dynasty. The Republican party would come apart in 1824 as presidential candidates from different sections of the country scrambled for support.

Sectionalism and the question of slavery would ultimately threaten the Union itself. Still, the first decades of the nineteenth century were a time of self-definition and growth for the young republic. Political parties broadened white male involvement in politics and quieted partisan divisions. A tradition of peaceful transition of power through presidential elections was established.

The revolution still cast a shadow over the new nation. Federalists harked back to British precedents; Republicans sought to maintain the ideals and virtues associated with the Revolution and the founding of a new republic in which citizens would place civic virtue above individual gain. A second

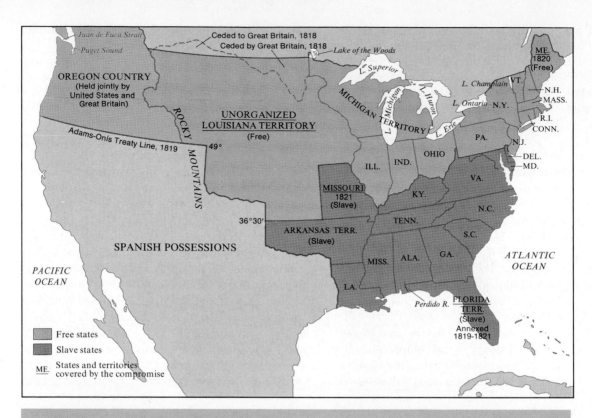

Missouri Compromise and the State of the Union, 1820   *Under House Speaker Henry Clay, the compromise established a formula that avoided debate over whether new states would allow or prohibit slavery. In the process, it divided the United States into northern and southern regions.*

war with Britain—the War of 1812—had to be fought to reaffirm American independence and to thwart the Native American tribes' opposition to U.S. expansion; thereafter the nation was able to settle many disputes at the bargaining table.

The foreign policy problems confronting the infant republic from the turn of the century through the mid-1820s bear a striking resemblance to those that newly established nations of the Third World have faced in the twentieth century. Mother countries often treat their former colonies as if they had not won their independence. Like Third World nations, the young United States shunned alliances with the great powers, preferring neutrality and unilateralism. The War of 1812 and diplomatic assertiveness brought into being a sense of national identity, security, and self-confidence.

After the war, all branches of the government, responding to the popular mood, pursued a vigor-

ous national policy. The Supreme Court promoted national unity by extending federal power over the states and encouraging commerce and economic growth. In spite of Jefferson's vision of an agrarian society of independent farmers and artisans, the country was gradually shifting to a market economy in which people produced goods not just for their own use but to sell to others (see Chapter 10). Disruption of trade during the war had promoted the manufacturing of goods in the United States, lessening dependence on imports from Europe. Developments in transportation further stimulated the economy.

Nationalism and geographic expansion were accompanied by the problem of sectionalism. War, tariffs, economic hard times, and slavery prompted secessionist threats, highlighting sectional discord. While manufacturers and merchants in the North and agricultural producers in the West became linked through transportation and trade, the South was developing its own economy and culture based on cotton, export markets, a plantation system, and slavery (see Chapter 11). Politicians kept the question of slavery off the national agenda as long as possible and worked out the Missouri Compromise as a stopgap measure. But territorial acquisitions and further westward expansion in the 1840s and 1850s collided with a rising tide of reform to make the question of slavery unavoidable (see Chapters 13 and 14).

At the same time, over the next two decades, the way Americans lived and worked changed at a quickening pace. The colonial and revolutionary generations were fading away. The deaths of John Adams and Thomas Jefferson within a few hours of each other on July 4, 1826—the fiftieth anniversary of the signing of the Declaration of Independence—symbolized that passing. As citizens mourned those political giants, they recognized that the future would be far different. Economic development, rising population, the spread of settlement, and the rise of cities were transforming people and their communities. In the face of religious revival, recognition of the imperfections in the new society, broad-based attempts to improve people and institutions, and conflict among groups, people turned to politics as an arena in which they could control, direct, or resist change.

SUGGESTIONS FOR FURTHER READING

General

Henry Adams, *History of the United States of America During the Administration of Thomas Jefferson and of James Madison*, 9 vols. (1889–1891); Noble E. Cunningham, Jr., *The United States in 1800: Henry Adams Revisited* (1988); George Dangerfield, *The Awakening of American Nationalism, 1815–1828* (1965); George Dangerfield, *The Era of Good Feelings* (1952); Jean V. Matthews, *Toward a New Society: American Thought and Culture, 1800–1830* (1991); John Mayfield, *The New Nation, 1800–1845* (1981); Glover Moore, *The Missouri Compromise, 1819–1821* (1953); Murray N. Rothbard, *The Panic of 1819* (1962); Marshall Smelser, *The Democratic Republic, 1801–1815* (1968).

Party Politics

Joyce Appleby, *Capitalism and a New Social Order: The Republican Vision of the 1790s* (1984); James M. Banner, *To the Hartford Convention: The Federalists and the Origins of Party Politics in the Early Republic, 1789–1815* (1967); James Broussard, *The Southern Federalists, 1800–1816* (1978); Noble E. Cunningham, Jr., *The Jeffersonian Republicans in Power: Party Operations, 1801–1809* (1963); David Hackett Fischer, *The Revolution of American Conservatism: The Federalist Party in the Era of Jeffersonian Democracy* (1965); Linda K. Kerber, *Federalists in Dissent* (1970); Shaw Livermore, *Twilight of Federalism: The Disintegration of the Federalist Party, 1815–1830* (1962); Milton Lomask, *Aaron Burr*, 2 vols. (1979, 1983); Richard P. McCormick, *The Presidential Game: The Origins of American Presidential Politics* (1982); Drew McCoy, *The Elusive Republic* (1980); Robert V. Remini, *Henry Clay: Statesman for the Union* (1991); James Sterling Young, *The Washington Community, 1800–1828* (1966).

The Virginia Presidents

Harry Ammon, *James Monroe: The Quest for National Identity* (1971); Noble E. Cunningham, Jr., *In Pursuit of Reason: The Life of Thomas Jefferson* (1987); Noble E. Cunningham, Jr., *The Process of Government Under Jefferson* (1978); Ralph Ketcham, *Presidents Above Party: The First American Presidency, 1789–1829* (1984); Dumas Malone, *Jefferson and His Time*, 6 vols. (1948–1981); Drew R. McCoy, *The Last of the Fathers: James Madison and the Republican Legacy* (1989); Forrest McDonald, *The Presidency of Thomas Jefferson* (1976); Merrill D. Peterson, *Thomas Jefferson and the New Nation* (1970); Merrill D. Peterson, *The Jefferson Image in the American Mind* (1960); Robert Allen Rutland, *The Presidency of James Madison* (1990); Robert Allen Rutland, *James Madison: The Founding Father* (1987); Robert W. Tucker and David C. Hendrickson, *Empire of Liberty: The Statecraft of Thomas Jefferson* (1990).

The Supreme Court and the Law

Leonard Baker, *John Marshall: A Life in Law* (1974); Albert Beveridge, *The Life of John Marshall*, 4 vols. (1916–1919); Robert Lowry Clinton, *Marbury v. Madison and Judicial Review* (1989); Richard E. Ellis, *The Jeffersonian Crisis: Courts and Politics in the Young Republic* (1971); Morton J. Horowitz, *The Transformation of American Law, 1780–1860* (1977); R. Kent Newmyer, *The Supreme Court Under Marshall and Taney* (1968); Francis N. Stites, *John Marshall: Defender of the Constitution* (1981).

Expansionism and the War of 1812

Roger H. Brown, *The Republic in Peril: 1812* (1964); Harry L. Coles, *The War of 1812* (1965); Alexander De Conde, *This Affair of Louisiana* (1976); R. David Edmunds, *Tecumseh and the Quest for Indian Leadership* (1984); R. David Edmunds, *The Shawnee Prophet* (1983); Clifford L. Egan, *Neither Peace nor War: Franco-American Relations, 1803–1812* (1983); Donald R. Hickey, *The War of 1812: A Forgotten Conflict* (1989); Reginald Horsman, *The War of 1812* (1969); Bradford Perkins, *Prologue to War: England and the United States, 1805–1812* (1961); Julius W. Pratt, *Expansionists of 1812* (1925); James P. Ronda, *Lewis and Clark Among the Indians* (1984); J.C.A. Stagg, *Mr. Madison's War: Politics, Diplomacy, and Warfare in the Early Republic, 1783–1830* (1983).

The Monroe Doctrine

Samuel F. Bemis, *John Quincy Adams and the Foundations of American Foreign Policy* (1949); Walter LaFeber, ed., *John Quincy Adams and American Continental Empire* (1965); Ernest R. May, *The Making of the Monroe Doctrine* (1976); Dexter Perkins, *Hands Off: A History of the Monroe Doctrine* (1941); Dexter Perkins, *The Monroe Doctrine, 1823–1826* (1927).

Rails, Markets, and Mills:
The North and West,
1800–1860

THE HUTCHINSON FAMILY, ALSO known as the Tribe of Jesse, was the most popular musical group in nineteenth-century America. Abby, Asa, Jesse, John, and Judson Hutchinson, five of a family of sixteen children from rural New Hampshire, performed throughout the United States and across the Atlantic, singing the patriotic, religious, and sentimental songs that had dominated popular music since the Revolution. Twentieth-century commentators have compared them to Woody Guthrie, Chuck Berry, Bruce Springsteen, and even the Beatles for initiating new musical styles, for their popularity and energy as performers, and for writing their own socially aware lyrics.

The family members were accomplished entertainers. Unlike most groups that just sang, the Tribe of Jesse presented well-rehearsed and elaborately produced performances. They used traditional airs that the audiences knew and found comforting, but they wrote new lyrics exploring such controversial topics as social problems and reform, abolitionism, and temperance. For example, "'Get Off the Track!' represented the railroad with all its terrible enginery and speed and danger,"

according to a contemporary editor. When first performed in 1844, the song was too inflammatory for any publisher to print. The Hutchinsons sang it on stage and the abolitionist press carried its lyrics until a publisher finally printed songsheets.

> Ho! the Car Emancipation
> Rides majestic thro' our nation
> Bearing on its Train, the story.
> LIBERTY! a Nation's Glory.
>   Roll it along, thro' the Nation
>   Freedom's Car, Emancipation.

The song became one of the Hutchinsons' trademarks, electrifying antislavery audiences.

The Hutchinson Family was part of a new phenomenon: singers, songwriters, musicians, publishers, and managers who made a business of music and entertainment. Drawing their largest audiences in the growing cities, they entered the commercial world and made a living from writing and performing music. The Hutchinson Family's fee for a single night in the 1840s could be as much as $1,000. Each performance was planned and choreographed, and they had an entourage of managers, agents, publishers, and concert-hall representatives. Hawkers sold

This detail from a lithograph shows two workers attending a press printing a design on a roll of cloth.

The town of Lockport, New York, owed its existence to the Erie Canal, and serving boats, freight, and passengers was its major industry. This view of the town was rendered in 1836, eleven years after the canal was opened.   Library of Congress.

contrast, at only one place—Bowling Green, Kentucky—did a northern railroad connect with a southern one. Although trade still moved southward along the Ohio and Mississippi rivers, the bulk of western trade flowed eastward by 1850. Thus, by the eve of the Civil War, the northern and Middle Atlantic states were closely linked to the former frontier of the Old Northwest.

Canals

Construction of the 363-mile-long Erie Canal was a visionary enterprise. When the state of New York authorized it in 1817, the longest existing American canal was only 28 miles long. Vigorously promoted by Governor DeWitt Clinton, the Erie cost $7 million, much of it in loans from British investors. The canal shortened the journey between Buffalo and New York City from twenty to six days and reduced freight charges from $100 to $5 a ton. By 1835, traffic was so heavy that the canal had to be widened from forty to seventy feet and deepened from four to seven feet. Skeptics who had called the canal "Clinton's big ditch" had long since fallen silent.

The success of the Erie Canal triggered an explosion of canal building. Sensing the advantage New York had gained, other states and cities rushed to follow suit. By 1840, canals crisscrossed the Northeast and Midwest, and total canal mileage reached 3,300—an increase of more than 2,000 miles in a single decade. Unfortunately for investors, none of these canals enjoyed the financial success achieved by the Erie. As the high cost of construction combined with an economic contraction, investment in canals began to slump in the 1830s. By 1850 more miles were being abandoned than built, and the canal era had unmistakably ended.

Railroads

Meanwhile, however, railroad construction boomed. The railroad era in the United States began in 1830 when Peter Cooper's locomotive Tom Thumb first steamed along 13 miles of track constructed by the Baltimore and Ohio Railroad. In 1833 the nation's second railroad ran 136 miles from Charleston to Hamburg in South Carolina. By 1850 the United States had nearly 9,000 miles of railroad; by 1860, roughly 31,000 (see map). Canal fever stimulated this early railroad construction. Promoters of the Baltimore and Ohio believed that railroads would compete successfully with canals. Similarly, the line between Boston and Worcester in Massachusetts was intended as the first link in a line to Albany, at the eastern end of the Erie Canal. In Providence, Rhode Island, and other ports, the railroads extended to the ocean wharfs.

Foreign visitors thought that the country had gone railroad-crazy. The French traveler Chevalier de Gerstier, who sailed from Europe in 1837, recalled constant shipboard conversations about the railroad. In New York he was shown a "marine railroad" for hauling ships in drydock; in Pennsylvania he saw railroads in mines; when he visited a

Philadelphia prison, the overseer exclaimed, "But you have not seen my Railroad." Indeed, if the Chevalier's account is accurate, he scarcely saw anything but railroads.

The earliest railroads connected two cities or a city and its surrounding area; not until the 1850s did railroads offer long-distance service at reasonable rates. The early lines had technical problems to overcome. Locomotives heavy enough to climb steep grades and pull long trains required strong rails and resilient roadbeds. Engineers met those needs by replacing wooden track with iron rails and by supporting the rails with ties embedded in gravel. A new wheel alignment—called the swivel truck—eliminated another serious obstacle by

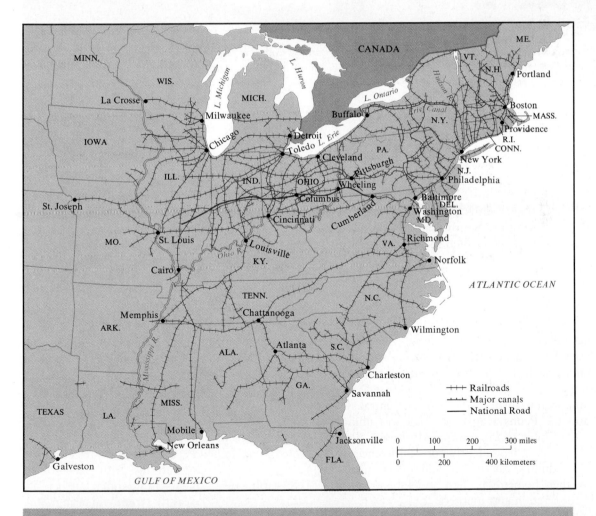

Major Railroads, Canals, and Roads in 1860   *Transportation networks linked port cities to the interior. These links were most dense in the North and the Old Northwest.*

In Providence, Rhode Island, locomotives replaced horses in transporting freight and people. In Atlantic ports the rail lines extended to the water's edge to meet the steamers and sailing ships.   Museum of Art, Rhode Island School of Design.

equipping engines to hold the track on sharp curves. Other problems persisted: the use of hand brakes severely restricted speed, and the lack of a standard gauge for the width of track thwarted development of a national system. Pennsylvania and Ohio railroads, for instance, had no fewer than seven different track widths. A journey from Philadelphia to Charleston, South Carolina, involved eight changes in gauge, which meant that passengers had to change trains seven times.

In the 1850s technological improvements, competition, economic recovery, and a desire for national unity prompted development of regional and, eventually, national rail networks. By 1853 rail lines linked New York to Chicago, and a year later track had reached the Mississippi River. By 1860 rails stretched as far west as St. Joseph, Missouri—the edge of the frontier. In 1853 seven short lines combined to form the New York Central system, and the Pennsylvania Railroad was unified from Philadelphia to Pittsburgh. Most lines, however, were still independently run. Differences in gauge, scheduling, car design, and a commitment to serve their hometowns first and foremost prevented cooperation and mergers.

Railroads did not completely replace water transportation. At midcentury, steamships still carried bulk cargo more cheaply than railroads ex-

cept during freezing weather. **Steamboats** The sealike Great Lakes could accommodate giant ships with propellers in place of paddlewheels; these leviathans carried heavy bulk cargoes like lumber, grain, and ore. On the high seas, steamships gradually replaced sailing vessels, which were dependent on prevailing winds and thus usually could not schedule regular crossings. The biggest breakthrough occurred in 1848, when Samuel Cunard introduced regularly scheduled steamships between Liverpool and New York, reducing travel time across the Atlantic from twenty-five days eastbound and forty-nine days westbound to between ten and fourteen days each way. Sailing ships quickly lost first-class passengers and light cargo to steamships, although they continued to carry immigrants and bulk cargo. By 1860, only the freight trade remained to them.

By far the fastest-spreading technological advance of the era was the magnetic telegraph. Invented by Samuel F. B. Morse, who could not live off his great accomplish-**Telegraph** ments as a painter but became wealthy from tinkering, the telegraph made it possible for long-distance messages to travel faster than any messenger could; instantaneous communication became possible even over long distances. By 1853, only nine years after construction of the first experimental line, 23,000 miles of telegraph wire spread across the United States; by 1860, 50,000 miles were in use. In 1861 the telegraph bridged the continent, connecting the east and west coasts, literally joining the nation together and ending the isolation that westerners felt. Rarely has an innovation had so great an impact so quickly: it revolutionized news-gathering, provided advance information for railroads and steamships, and altered patterns of business and finance.

Time was key to the revolutionary changes in transportation and communications that took place from 1800 to 1860. In 1800 it took four days to travel by coach from New York City to Baltimore, and nearly four weeks to reach Detroit. By 1830 Baltimore was only a day-and-a-half away, and Detroit was only a two-week journey via the Erie Canal. By 1857 Detroit was an overnight train ride from New York City; in a week one could reach Texas, Kansas, or Nebraska. Not only did reduced travel time save money and facilitate commerce, it also brought frontier areas under the control of Chicago and eastern businesses. During the first two decades of the century, wagon transportation cost 30 to 70 cents per ton per mile. By 1860, railroads in New York State carried freight at an average charge of 2.2 cents per ton-mile; wheat moved from Chicago to New York for 1.2 cents per ton-mile. In sum, the transportation revolution transformed the economy.

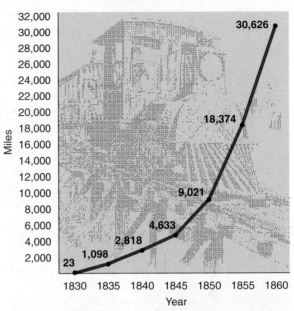

Railroad Mileage, 1830–1860

Miles (y-axis): 2,000 to 32,000
Year (x-axis): 1830, 1835, 1840, 1845, 1850, 1855, 1860

Data points: 23; 1,098; 2,818; 4,633; 9,021; 18,374; 30,626

Railroad Mileage, 1830–1860   *In the 1850s, railroads developed a natural rail network east of the Mississippi River.* Source: U.S. Bureau of the Census. *Historical Statistics of the United States, Colonial Times to 1970.* 2 Parts. (Washington, D.C., 1975), Part 2, p. 731.

THE MARKET ECONOMY

Prior to the transportation revolution, most farmers had geared production to family needs. They lived in interdependent communities and kept detailed accounts of labor and goods exchanged with neighbors. Farm families produced much of what they needed—foodstuffs, clothing, candles, soap, and the like—but they traded for or purchased items they could not produce, such as cooking pots, horseshoes, coffee, tea, and sugar. On most farms, men sold cordwood and women sold eggs and butter to generate the family's only cash.

By the Civil War, however, the United States had an industrializing economy. An increasing number of men and women worked for wages, and most people outside the South—farmers and workers alike—purchased increasing amounts of store-bought goods produced in workshops and factories.

With the advent of a market economy, men and women grew crops and produced goods for sale at home or abroad. The money received in market transactions, whether the sale of goods or of a person's labor, purchased items produced by other people. Such a system encouraged specialization. Formerly self-sufficient farmers began to grow just one or two crops or to raise only cows, pigs, or sheep for market. Farm women gave up spinning and weaving and purchased fabric produced by wage-earning farm girls in Massachusetts textile mills.

Definition of a Market Economy

Improvements in transportation and technology, the division of labor, and new methods of financing all fueled the expansion of the economy—that is, the multiplication of goods and services. This growth, in turn, prompted new improvements and greater opportunities for wage labor. The effect was cumulative; by the 1840s the economy was growing at a faster rate than in the previous four decades. While per capita income doubled between 1800 and 1860, the price of manufactured goods and food fell.

The pace of economic growth, however, was uneven. Prosperity reigned during two long periods, from 1823 to 1835 and from 1843 to 1857.

Boom-and-Bust Cycles

But there were long stretches of economic contraction as well. Between Jefferson's 1807 embargo and the end of the War of 1812, the interruption in trade had contributed to a negative growth rate—that is, fewer goods and services were produced. Contraction and deflation (decline in the general price level) occurred again during the hard times of 1819–1823, 1839–1843, and 1857. During these periods banks collapsed, businesses went bankrupt, and wages and prices declined. Workers faced increasing insecurity as a result of these boom-and-bust cycles; on the down side of such a cycle, they were subject not only to lower incomes but also to unemployment.

As a Baltimore physician noted in 1819, working people felt hard times "a thousand fold more than the merchants." Wage earners could not build up sufficient financial reserves in good times to get them through the next bout of hard times; often they could not even make it through the winter without drawing on charity for food, clothing, and firewood. In the 1820s and 1830s, free laborers in Baltimore typically found steady work from March through October, and unemployment and hunger from November through February.

If even good times were hard on workers and their families, hard times devastated them. In 1839 in Baltimore, when hundreds of small manufacturers for the local market closed their doors, tailors, shoemakers, milliners, and shipyard and construction workers lost their jobs. Ninety miles to the north, Philadelphia took on an eerie aura. "The streets seemed deserted," Sidney George Fisher observed in 1842. "The largest [merchant] houses are shut up and to rent, there is no business . . . no money, no confidence." Only auctions boomed, as sheriffs sold off seized property at a quarter of predepression prices, as the artist E. Didier portrayed in the *Auction in Chatham Street* in nearby New York. In Philadelphia and other cities, soup societies fed the hungry. In New York, bread lines

and beggars crowded the sidewalks. In smaller cities like Lynn, Massachusetts, the poor became scavengers, digging for clams and harvesting dandelions.

Hard times struck again in 1857. The Mercantile Agency—the forerunner of Dun and Bradstreet—recorded 5,123 bankruptcies in 1857, nearly double the number of the previous year. The bankrupt firms owed $300 million, only half of which would be paid off. Contemporary reports estimated that twenty to thirty thousand people were unemployed in Philadelphia, and thirty to forty thousand in New York City. Female benevolent societies expanded their soup kitchens and distributed free firewood to the needy. In Chicago, charities reorganized to meet the needs of the poor; in New York, the city hired the unemployed to repair streets and develop Central Park. And in Fall River, Massachusetts, a citizens' committee disbursed public funds on a weekly basis to nine hundred families. The soup kitchen, the bread line, and public aid had become fixtures in urban America.

What caused the boom-and-bust cycles that brought about such suffering? Generally speaking, they were a direct result of the new market economy.

Cause of Boom-and-Bust Cycles

Prosperity stimulated greater demand for staples and finished goods, such as clothing and furniture. Increased demand in turn led not only to higher prices and still higher production but also, because of business confidence and expectation of higher prices, to speculation in land and to the flow of foreign currency into the country. Eventually production surpassed demand, causing prices and wages to fall; in response, inflated land and stock values collapsed. The inflow of foreign money led first to easy credit and then to collapse when the unhappy investors withdrew their funds.

Some contemporary economists considered this process beneficial—a self-adjusting cycle in which unprofitable economic ventures were eliminated. In theory, people concentrated on the activities they did best, and the economy as a whole became more efficient. Advocates of the system also argued that it enhanced individual freedom, since theoretically each seller, whether of goods or labor, was free to determine the conditions of the sale. But in fact the system tied workers to a perpetual roller-coaster; they became dependent on

E. Didier recorded an Auction in Chatham Street *in 1834. In hard times, auction houses in New York and other cities boomed.*   Museum of the City of New York.

wages—and the availability of jobs—for their very existence. The cycles that governed the market economy dominated every corner of the country as even small localities became tied to regional and national markets.

People experienced the market economy in a variety of ways. Traditional farm women who had contributed to the family as unpaid labor— producing cloth, clothing, and dairy products for family use—found their lives altered in the course of the nineteenth century. They increasingly contributed cash, first from the sale of eggs, butter, cheese, and poultry and then, in New England and the Middle Atlantic states, from industrial work at home, weaving cloth and sewing shoes for contractors who paid them by the piece. By midcentury many women's earnings sustained their families.

Other groups experienced a distinct loss of status in the market economy. For Joseph T. Buckingham, foreman of a Boston printing shop, wage labor represented failure. Buckingham had previously been a master printer, running the shop of

Thomas and Andrews on commission and doing some publishing of his own. In 1814 he purchased the shop but did not get enough work to pay his debts. Lacking the capital to sustain his losses or to compete with larger shops, Buckingham had to sell his presses at auction and become a wage-earner. Although his wages as a foreman were about equal to an ordinary printer's income, Buckingham was unhappy. In his own words, he was "nothing more than a journeyman, except in responsibility."

The market economy also ushered in another type of boom-and-bust cycle: harvest and destruction. Canals and railroads stimulated demand for distant resources, then accelerated the destruction of forests, natural waterways, and any landscape features that represented obstacles. Railroads made possible large-scale lumbering of pinewood forests in northern Michigan, Wisconsin, and Minnesota. During the 1850s, 40 million acres were cleared of lumber, leaving most of that land unfit even for agriculture. Similarly, the extension of railroads to

Kansas and Nebraska brought hunters who slaughtered the great herds of bison for sport. The result was a process that would eventually change the ecology of the United States.

GOVERNMENT PROMOTES ECONOMIC GROWTH

The eighteenth-century political ideas that had captured the imagination of the Revolutionary War generation and found expression in the ideal of republican virtue had economic counterparts in the writings of Adam Smith, a Scottish political economist. Smith's *The Wealth of Nations* first appeared in 1776, the year of the Declaration of Independence. Both works emphasized individual liberty, and both were reactions against forceful government: Jefferson denounced monarchy and distant government; Smith rejected mercantilism, or governmental regulation of the economy to benefit the state (see page 86). Both declared that virtue resided in individual freedom and that the community would benefit most from individuals' pursuit of their own self-interest.

Jefferson, influenced by the economic and egalitarian ideas of republicanism (see pages 180–182), believed that freedom thrived where individuals had scope for independence, creativity, and choice—individuals fettered by government, monopoly, or economic dependence could not be free. Limited government was not an end, according to Jefferson, but a means to greater freedom. Committed to the idea that a republican democracy would flourish best in a nation of independent farmers and artisans and in an atmosphere of widespread political participation, Jefferson recognized that government was a necessary instrument for promoting individual freedom. Beginning with the purchase of Louisiana in 1803, Republican policy, no less than that of the Federalists, endorsed using the federal government to promote economic growth. The result was faith in a market economy in which government also played an active role.

After acquiring Louisiana, the federal government facilitated economic growth and geographic expansion by encouraging westward exploration and settlement and by promoting agriculture. The Lewis and Clark expedition (see page 244) was only the beginning of a continuing federal interest in

geographic and geologic surveying, and the first step in the opening of western lands to exploitation and settlement.

New steps followed quickly. In 1817–1818 Henry Rowe Schoolcraft explored the Missouri and Arkansas region, reporting on its geologic features and mineral resources. In 1819–1820 Major Stephen Long explored the Great Plains, mapping the area between the Platte and Canadian rivers. Between 1827 and 1840 the government surveyed about fifty potential railroad routes. The final door to western settlement was opened in 1843–1844 by John C. Frémont's expedition, which followed the Oregon Trail to the Pacific, turned south to California, and then returned east by way of the Great Salt Lake. Frémont, later a California senator and in 1856 the first Republican presidential candidate, gained fame as a soldier-surveyor of the West. His report of his journey dispelled a long-standing myth that the center of the continent was a desert.

To encourage settlement and cultivation of western lands, the federal government evicted Indian tribes from their traditional lands and offered the land at reasonable prices (see pages 297–298). And because transportation was crucial to the development of the frontier, the government first financed roads and canals and later subsidized railroad construction by means of land grants. Even the State Department aided agriculture: its consular offices overseas collected horticultural information, seeds, and cuttings, and it published technical reports in an effort to improve American farming.

The federal government also played an active role in technological and industrial growth. Federal arsenals pioneered new manufacturing techniques and helped to develop the machine-tool industry. The U.S. Post Office provided a communications link that stimulated interregional trade and briefly played a crucial role in the development of the telegraph. The first telegraph line, from Washington to Baltimore, was constructed in 1844 under a government grant and briefly managed by the Post Office, which employed inventor Samuel F. B. Morse as superintendent. And to create an atmosphere conducive to economic growth and individual creativity, the government protected inventions and domestic industries. Patent laws gave inventors a seventeen-year monopoly on their inventions, and tariffs protected American industry from foreign competition.

The Marshall Court encouraged business competition by ending the state-licensed monopolies on inland waterways. Gibbons v. Ogden *(1824) opened up the New York–New Jersey trade to new lines, and within a short time dozens of steamboats ferried passengers and freight across the Hudson River.*   New-York Historical Society.

The federal judiciary validated government promotion of the economy and encouraged business enterprise. In *Gibbons* v. *Ogden* (1824), the

Legal Foundations of Commerce
———

Supreme Court overturned a New York state law that had given Robert Fulton and Robert Livingston a monopoly on the New York–New Jersey steamboat trade. Aaron Ogden, their successor, lost the monopoly when Chief Justice John Marshall ruled that the congressional prerogative of licensing new enterprises took precedence over New York's grant of monopoly rights to Fulton and Livingston. Marshall declared that Congress's power under the commerce clause of the Constitution extended to "every species of commercial intercourse," including transportation systems. Within a year, forty-three steamboats were plying Ogden's route.

In defining interstate commerce broadly, the Marshall Court expanded federal powers over the economy while restricting the ability of states to control economic activity within their borders. Its action was consistent with the Court's earlier decision in *Dartmouth College* v. *Woodward* (1819),

which protected the sanctity of contracts against interference by the states (see page 260). "If business is to prosper," Marshall wrote, "men must have assurance that contracts will be enforced."

Federal and state courts, in conjunction with state legislatures, also encouraged the proliferation of corporations—groups of investors entitled to hold property and transact business as if they were one person. Investors in corporations, called shareholders, were granted *limited liability*, or freedom from responsibility for the company's debts. An attractive feature to potential investors, limited liability encouraged people to back new business ventures. In 1800 the United States had about three hundred incorporated firms; in 1817 there were about two thousand. By 1830 the New England states alone had issued nineteen hundred charters, one-third to manufacturing and mining firms. At first each firm needed a special legislative act to incorporate, but after the 1830s applications became so numerous that states established routine procedures for firms to incorporate.

Though legislative action created corporations, the courts played a crucial role in defining their status, extending their powers, and protecting them. A particular encouragement to corporate development and free enterprise was the Supreme Court's ruling in *Charles River Bridge* v. *Warren Bridge* (1837) that new enterprises could not be restrained by implied privileges under old charters. The case involved issues of great importance: should a new interest be allowed to compete against existing enterprises, and should the state protect existing privilege or encourage innovation and the growth of commerce through competition?

The Massachusetts legislature had chartered the Charles River Bridge Company in 1785 and six years later extended its charter for seventy years. In return for assuming the risk of building the bridge between Charlestown and Boston, the owners were granted the privilege of collecting tolls. In 1828 the legislature chartered another company to build the Warren Bridge across the Charles nearby; the owner would have the right to collect tolls for six years, after which the bridge would be turned over to the state and be free of tolls. The Charles River Bridge Company sued in 1829, claiming that the new bridge breached the earlier charter and contradicted the principles in *Dartmouth College* v. *Woodward*. Speaking for the Court majority, Marshall's successor Roger Taney declared that the original charter did not confer the privilege of monopoly and that exclusivity could not therefore be implied. Focusing on the question of corporate privilege rather than the law of contracts, Taney ruled that charter grants should be interpreted narrowly and that ambiguities would be decided in favor of the public interest. New enterprises should not be restricted by old charters, and economic growth would best be served by narrowing the application of the Dartmouth College decision. Thus the judiciary supported economic expansion and individual economic opportunity.

In promoting the economy, state governments far surpassed the federal government. From 1815 through 1860, for example, 73 percent of the $135 million invested in canals was government money, most of it from the states. In the 1830s the states started to invest in rail construction. Though the federal government played a larger role in constructing railroads than in building canals, state and local governments provided more than half of the capital for southern rail lines. State governments also invested in corporate and bank stocks, providing those institutions with

State Promotion of the Economy

much-needed capital. In fact, states actually equaled or surpassed private enterprise in their investments. Pennsylvania, probably the most active state in promoting its economy, invested a total of $100 million in canals, railroads, banks, and manufacturing firms; its appointees sat on more than 150 corporate boards of directors. Pennsylvania was the largest state in area, extending from the seaboard to the west beyond the mountains, and thus developed the most extensive program of internal improvements to stimulate settlement and economic growth. But states did more than invest in industry. Through special acts and incorporation laws, they regulated the nature and activities of corporations and banks. They also used their licensing capacity to regulate industry; Georgia, for example, regulated the grading and marketing of tobacco.

Largely as a result of these government efforts, the United States experienced uneven but sustained economic growth from the end of the War of 1812 until 1860. Political controversy raged over questions of state versus federal activity—especially with regard to internal improvements and banking—but all parties agreed on the general goal of economic expansion. Indeed, the major restraint on government action during these years was not philosophical but financial: the public purse was small. As the private sector grew more vigorous, entrepreneurs looked less to government for financial support and the states played less of a role in investment.

THE RISE OF MANUFACTURING AND COMMERCE

The McCormick reaper, invented by Virginia farmer Cyrus McCormick in 1831, was ridiculed in the London *Times* as "a cross between a flying machine, a wheelbarrow, and an Astly chariot." In one continuous motion, a revolving drum on the horse-drawn reaper positioned stalks in front of a blade; the cut grain then fell onto a platform. Put to a competitive test through rain-soaked wheat, only the Chicago-made reaper passed, to the cheers of the skeptical English spectators. The reaper and hundreds of other American products made their international debut at the 1851 London Crystal Palace Exhibition, the first modern world's fair.

There the design and quality of American machines and wares—from familiar farm tools to such exotic devices as the reaper and an ice cream freezer—astonished observers. American manufacturers returned home with dozens of medals, including all three prizes for piano making. Most impressive to the Europeans were three simple machines: Alfred C. Hobb's unpickable padlocks, Samuel Colt's revolvers, and Robbins and Lawrence's rifles with completely interchangeable parts. All were machine-tooled rather than handmade, products of what the British called the American system of manufacturing.

So impressed were the British—whose nation was the leading industrial power of the time—that they sent a parliamentary commission in 1853 to study the American system. A year later a second committee, still skeptical, returned to examine the firearms industry in detail. The committee's report described an astonishing experiment performed at the federal armory in Springfield, Massachusetts. To test the interchangeability of machine-made musket parts, the committee selected rifles made in each of the previous ten years. While the committee watched, the guns were dismantled "and the parts placed in a row of boxes, mixed up together." The Englishmen "then requested the workman, whose duty it is to 'assemble' the arms, to put them together, which he did—the Committee handing him the parts, taken at hazard—with the use of a turnscrew only, and as quickly as though they had been English muskets, whose parts had carefully been kept separate." Britain's Enfield arsenal subsequently converted to American equipment. Other nations quickly followed Great Britain's lead, sending delegations across the Atlantic to bring back American machines.

The American system of manufacturing used precision machinery to produce interchangeable parts that needed no filing or fitting. Eli Whitney, a Yale graduate and inventor,

American System of Manufacturing

had promoted the idea of interchangeable parts in 1798 when he contracted with the federal government to make ten thousand rifles in twenty-eight months. By the 1820s the U.S. Ordnance Department had contracted with private firms to introduce machine-made interchangeable parts for firearms. The American system quickly spread beyond the arsenals, giving birth to the machine-tool industry—the manufacture of machines for the purposes of mass production. One outcome was an explosion in consumer goods: since the time and skill involved in manufacturing had been greatly reduced, the new system permitted mass production at low cost. Waltham watches and Yale locks became household items, inexpensive yet of uniformly high quality.

Interchangeable parts and the machine-tool industry were uniquely American contributions to the industrial revolution. Both paved the way for the swift industrialization that the nation experienced after the Civil War. The process of industrialization began, however, in a simple and traditional way, like that of other nations. In 1800, manufacturing was a relatively unimportant component of the American economy. Most took place in small workshops and homes, where master craftsmen supervised journeymen and taught apprentices, and women worked alone spinning thread and weaving cloth. Tailors, shoemakers, and blacksmiths made articles by hand, to order for specific customers.

The clothing trades illustrate well the changes in manufacturing and distribution and the reliance on the market economy that came into being in the nineteenth century. Previously,

Clothing Trades

most men had worn clothes made by their mothers, wives, or daughters, or occasionally, used clothing. Wealthy men's clothing was made to order by tailors. The nineteenth-century machine-tool industry made textile and clothing production a function of mills and factories, rather than kitchens and home workshops. First in England, then in the United States, cotton-textile mills began processing cotton grown in the slave South. The expanding market economy, fed by the population boom, created demand for the manufactured cotton goods. The first American textile mill, built in Pawtucket, Rhode Island, in 1790, used water-powered spinning machines constructed from British models by the English immigrant Samuel Slater. Slater employed women and children as cheap labor and sold the thread they manufactured from Maine to Maryland. Soon other mills sprang up, stimulated by the embargo on British imports from 1807 through 1815. From 1809 through 1813 alone, 151 cotton and woolen companies incorporated.

These early mills, dependent on water power, were located in rural areas. By erecting dams and water courses, they diverted water from farmers

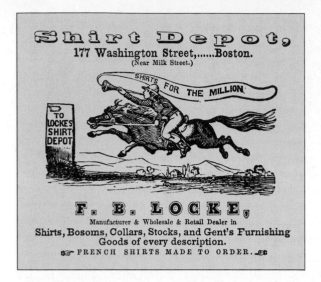

F. B. Locke adapted to the new market for ready-made clothing by becoming a manufacturer, wholesaler, and retailer of men's shirts. Though continuing to make shirts to order, the Shirt Depot's staple was mass-produced shirts, as this advertisement from the Boston Directory, 1848–49 *indicates.*   Warshaw Collection of Business Americana, Smithsonian Institution, Washington, D.C.

and destroyed fishing, an important source of income and protein in rural and village America. Though fishermen and farmers fought the manufacturers in New England state legislatures to protect their customary rights, petitions from hopeful jobseekers in the mill environs supported the manufacturers. The ensuing compromises cleared the way for mill development.

By the 1820s and 1830s, clothing manufacturers had replaced much of the old system. Early mills used the "putting-out" system: typically, a journeyman tailor cut the fabric panels in the factory, and the sewing was put out at piece rates to unskilled or semiskilled labor, often women working in their own homes. Women who traditionally had spun their own yarn and woven it into cloth for their families now received yarn from the mills and returned finished cloth. The change was subtle but significant: although the work itself was familiar, women now operated their looms for piece-rate wages, not to clothe their families.

In 1832, Boston manufacturers employed three hundred journeyman tailors at $2 per day and thirteen hundred women and one hundred boys at 50 cents a day. Apprentices, if used at all, were no longer learning a trade; they were a permanent source of cheap labor. Women learned their sewing skills within a different type of master-apprentice system. Most women worked at home, sewing straight seams by hand; skills were passed down from mother to daughter. By the late 1850s, as many as seventeen different pairs of hands were involved in making a single pair of pants under the putting-out system.

Textile manufacturing was radically transformed by the construction of the first American power loom and the chartering of the Boston Manufacturing Company in 1813. The corporation was capitalized at $400,000—ten times the amount behind the Rhode Island mills—by Francis Cabot Lowell and other Boston merchants. Its goal was to eliminate the problems of timing, shipping, coordination, and quality control inherent in the putting-out system. The owners erected their factories in Waltham, Massachusetts, combining all the manufacturing processes at a single location. They also employed a resident manager to run the mill, thus separating ownership from management. Workers were paid by the piece or by the hour, and the product—first cloth, then both cloth and finished clothing—was sold throughout the United States. The company's cloth was so inexpensive that many women began to purchase it rather than make their own. Nonetheless, spinning and weaving remained women's work in many rural homes. Not until the end of the century would a majority of women purchase ready-made clothing (see pages 550–551).

Waltham (Lowell) System

When not enough hands could be found in rural Waltham to staff the mill, its managers recruited New England farm daughters, accepting responsibility for their living conditions. As inducements, they offered cash wages, company-run boarding houses, and such cultural events as evening lectures—none of which was available on the farm. This paternalistic approach, called the Waltham (or Lowell) system, was adopted in other mills erected alongside New England rivers.

Most of the first mass-produced clothes, crudely made and limited to a few loose-fitting sizes, were produced for men. They were purchased by men who lived in city boarding houses and rooming houses, far from the female kin who would previously have made their clothes. Most women made their own clothes, but those who could afford to do so employed seamstresses.

Improvements in fit and changes in men's fashion made ready-to-wear apparel more acceptable to white-collar and professional men. By the 1850s the short sack coat, without an indentation at the waist, had replaced the embroidered waistcoat. This forerunner of the modern suit jacket fit loosely and needed less hand-tailoring. Now even upper-class men were willing to consider ready-made apparel. The New York City store Henry Sands Brooks opened in 1818, which later became Brooks Brothers, offered tailoring services and ready-made apparel to the carriage trade.

Retail clothing stores with large stocks of ready-made clothes appeared in the 1820s. T. S. Whitmarsh of Boston advertised in 1827 that "he keeps constantly for Sale, from 5 to 10,000 Fashionable ready-made Garments." In 1830, J. T. Jacobs of New York boasted that "Gentlemen can rely upon being as well fitted from the shelves as if their measures were taken—their stock being very extensive and their sizes well assorted." F. B. Locke of Boston made and sold "shirts for the million."

Such merchants often bought goods wholesale, though many manufactured garments in their own factories. Lewis and Hanford of New York City boasted of cutting more than one hundred thousand garments in the winter of 1848–1849. The New York firm sold most of its clothing in the South and owned its own retail outlet in New Orleans. A New Orleans competitor, Paul Tulane, owned a New York factory that made goods for his Louisiana store. In the West, Cincinnati became the center of the new men's clothing industry. By midcentury, Cincinnati's ready-to-wear apparel industry employed fifteen hundred men and ten thousand women. As in Boston, most of the women did outwork.

By 1860 a cotton mill resembled a modern factory. The workforce consisted mainly of immigrant Irish women who lived at home, not in mill-subsidized housing. New England farm women continued to live in the few remaining boarding houses. Technological improvements in the looms and other machinery had made the work less skilled and more routine. The mills could thus pay lower wages, and

Textile Mills

increased immigration meant that mill owners always had a reservoir of unskilled labor to draw on.

Textile manufacturing changed New England, and had its greatest impact on Lowell, Massachusetts. Lowell, "the city of spindles" and the prototype of early American industrialization, grew from twenty-five hundred to thirty-three thousand people between 1826 and 1850. It was the largest of the cotton-mill towns before the Civil War, with the largest workforce, the greatest output, and the most capital invested. It also led in technological change, as an 1836 emblem depicted.

Textiles became the most important industry in the nation before the Civil War, employing 115,000 workers in 1860, more than half of whom were women and immigrants. The key to the success of the textile industry was that the machines, not the women, spun the yarn and wove the cloth. The workers watched the machines and intervened to maintain smooth operation. When a thread broke, the machine stopped automatically; the worker then found the break, pieced the ends together, and restarted the machine. The New England textile mills used increasingly specialized machines, relying heavily on advances in the machine-tool industry. Their application of the American system of manufacturing enabled American firms to compete successfully with British cotton mills.

Outside of New England, as in Pennsylvania's Delaware Valley, the textile industry grew more slowly, combining traditional ways with technol-

This 1836 emblem, a proposed seal for the city of Lowell, linked the arts of manufacturing and technology with bounty and goodness. Private collection.

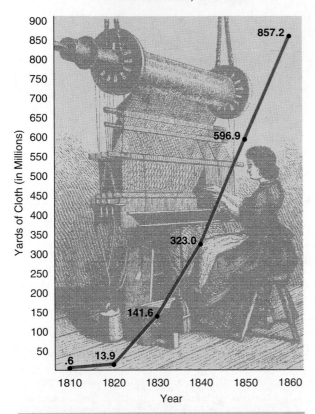

**New England Cotton Industry
Cloth Production, 1810–1860**

New England Cotton Industry Cloth Production, 1805–1860 Textiles was the most important manufacturing industry in the United States in the 1830s, 1840s, and 1850s. The production of cloth increased six-fold during that time. Source: James F. Willis and Martin L. Primack, *An Economic History of the United States.* 2d ed. (Englewood Cliffs, N.J., 1989), p. 171.

ogy. A decade after the Waltham mills first appeared, entrepreneurs in Rockdale, Pennsylvania, converted paper mills to cotton manufacturing. Organized as partnerships rather than corporations, they lacked the large sums available to the Lowell mills, and raised money from friends and relatives. Unlike their counterparts in Waltham and Lowell, the owners lived and worked in the mill villages. Small factories employed entire families, and unmarried workers boarded in other workers' homes. Many Pennsylvania textile workers sought to save

money to buy western land, and a number of them were successful. Growth and change occurred at a modest pace; not until the 1850s would a major manufacturing center arise in once-rural southeastern Pennsylvania.

Though cotton textile mills were the vanguard of industrialization, new manufacturing methods also transformed woolen textiles, farm implements, machine tools, iron, steel, glass, and finished consumer goods into major industries. "White coal"—water power—was widely used to run the machines. By 1860, manufacturing accounted for one-third of the nation's total production, an increase of 200 percent in twenty years.

To a striking extent, industrialization in this period was an outcome rather than an agent of change in American life. Ever since Alexander Hamilton's *Report on Manufactures* (see page 217), national pride had spurred the development of American industry. Contrary to Hamilton's hopes, however, more capital flowed into the merchant marine than into industry between 1789 and 1808. In the early republic, greater profits could be made by transporting British products to the United States than by producing the same items at home. But the embargo and the War of 1812 reversed this situation, and merchants began to shift their capital from shipping to manufacturing (see pages 252–258). It was in this new economic environment that the Waltham system took root.

Other factors also stimulated industry. Population growth, especially in urban areas and the Old Northwest, created a large domestic market for finished goods (see maps). As the rise of commercial agriculture brought farmers more fully into the market economy, they purchased more manufactured goods. Specialty merchants and new modes of transportation hastened the development of these new markets. And the relative scarcity of skilled craftsmen encouraged mechanization: as more workers moved westward than entered the factories, merchants had to find ways to produce more goods with less skilled labor. Finally, beginning with the Tariff of 1816 and culminating in the Tariff of Abominations of 1828, Congress imposed tariffs more to protect the market for domestic manufactures than to increase government revenue.

Commerce expanded in conjunction with manufacturing. Cotton, for instance, had once been traded by plantation agents, who handled all the

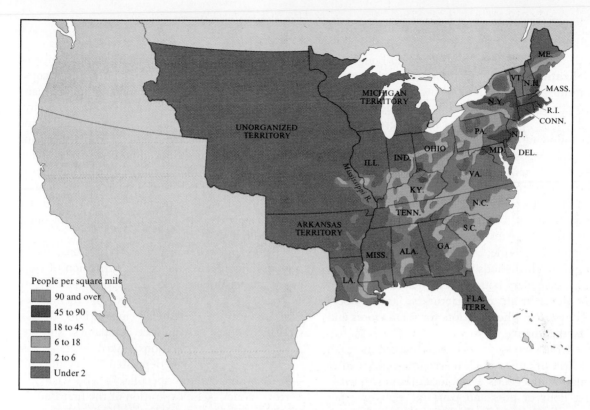

People per square mile
- 90 and over
- 45 to 90
- 18 to 45
- 6 to 18
- 2 to 6
- Under 2

MICHIGAN TERRITORY

UNORGANIZED TERRITORY

ARKANSAS TERRITORY

ILL. IND. OHIO PA. N.J. MD. DEL.

VA. KY. N.C. TENN. S.C.

MISS. ALA. GA.

LA. FLA. TERR.

ME. VT. N.H. MASS. N.Y. R.I. CONN.

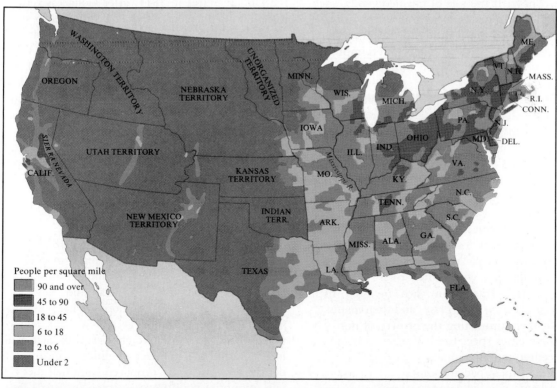

People per square mile
- 90 and over
- 45 to 90
- 18 to 45
- 6 to 18
- 2 to 6
- Under 2

WASHINGTON TERRITORY

OREGON

NEBRASKA TERRITORY

UNORGANIZED TERRITORY

MINN. WIS. MICH.

SIERRA NEVADA

UTAH TERRITORY

CALIF.

KANSAS TERRITORY

IOWA

ILL. IND. OHIO PA. N.J. MD. DEL.

MO. KY. VA. N.C. TENN. S.C.

NEW MEXICO TERRITORY

INDIAN TERR.

ARK. MISS. ALA. GA.

TEXAS LA. FLA.

ME. VT. N.H. MASS. N.Y. R.I. CONN.

United States Population, 1820 and 1860 *Between 1820 and 1860, the United States grew from 9.6 to 31.4 million people, and the density increased significantly in the North and the Old Northwest. Settlement, too, spread farther away from the eastern seaboard.*

Specialization of Commerce

crops produced and bought all the goods purchased by the plantation owners, extending them credit when needed. As cotton became a great staple export following the invention of the cotton gin in 1793, exports rose from half a million pounds in that year to 83 million pounds in 1815. Gradually, some agents came to specialize in finance alone: these were cotton brokers, who for a commission brought together buyers and sellers. Similarly, wheat and hog brokers sprang up in the West—in Cincinnati, Louisville, and St. Louis. The distribution of finished goods also became more specialized as wholesalers bought large quantities of particular items from manufacturers, and jobbers broke down the wholesale lots for retail stores and country merchants.

General merchants persisted longer in small towns than in cities. Such merchants continued to exchange some goods with local farm women—trading flour or pots and pans for eggs or other produce. They left the sale of finished goods, such as shoes and clothing, to local craftsmen. In some rural areas and on the frontier, peddlers acted as general merchants. But as transportation improved and towns grew, even small-town merchants began to specialize.

Commercial specialization transformed some traders in big cities, especially New York, into virtual merchant princes. New York had emerged as the dominant port in the late 1790s, outstripping Philadelphia and Boston. When the Erie Canal opened, New York City became a standard stop on every major trade route from Europe, the southern ports, and the West. New York traders were the middlemen for southern cotton and western grain trading; in fact, New York was the nation's major cotton-exporting city. Merchants in other cities played a similar role within their own regions.

Newly rich traders in turn invested their profits in processing enterprises and then manufacturing, further stimulating the growth of northern cities. Some cities specialized: Rochester became a milling center and Cincinnati—"Porkopolis"—became the first meat-packing center.

Merchants who engaged in complex commercial transactions required large office staffs. Most of the all-male office staff worked on high stools, laboriously copying business forms and correspondence. At the bottom of the office hierarchy were messenger boys, often preteens, who delivered documents. Above them were the ordinary copyists, who hand-copied documents in ink as many times as needed. Clerks handled such assignments as customs-house clearances, shipping papers, and translations. Above them were the bookkeeper and the confidential chief clerk. Those seeking employment in such an office, called a counting house, often took a course from a writing master to acquire a "good hand." All hoped to rise someday to the status of partner, although their chances of doing so were dim.

Banks and other financial institutions, which played a significant role in the expansion of commerce and manufacturing, also represented a leading industry in themselves.

Banking and Credit Systems

Financial institutions (banks, insurance companies, and corporations) linked savers—those who deposited money in banks—with producers and speculators who wished to borrow money. The expiration of the first Bank of the United States in 1811, after Congress refused to renew its charter, acted as a stimulus to state-chartered banks, and over the next five years the number of such banks more than doubled. When state banks proved inadequate to spur national growth, Congress chartered the Second Bank of the United States in 1816 (see page 259). Many farmers, local bankers, and politicians, however, denounced the bank as a monster, claiming that it served national, not local, interests. Western landowners, like Andrew Jackson, had suffered severe losses when the Second Bank reduced loans in the western states during the Panic of 1819. In 1836 critics finally succeeded in killing the bank (see pages 384–385).

The closing of the Second Bank in 1836 caused a nationwide credit shortage, which, in conjunction with the Panic of 1837, stimulated fundamental reforms in banking. Michigan and New York introduced charter laws promoting what was called *free banking*. Previously, every new bank had required a special legislative charter; thus each bank incorporation was in effect a political decision. Under the new laws, any proposed bank that met certain minimum conditions—capital invested, notes issued, and types of loans to be made—would automatically receive a state charter. Banks in Michigan and New York were thus freer to incorporate, but restrictions were placed on their operation in order to reduce the risk of bank failure. Many other states soon followed suit.

Free banking proved to be a significant stimulus to the economy in the late 1840s and 1850s. New banks sprang up everywhere, providing merchants and manufacturers the credit they needed. The free-banking laws also served as a precedent for the general incorporation statutes that allowed manufacturing firms to receive state charters without special acts of the state legislature.

Changes in insurance firms also promoted industrialization by creating a new source of capital. In the course of business, insurance companies accumulated large amounts of money as reserves against future claims. Then as now, their greatest profits derived from investing those reserves. Beginning in the 1840s, insurance companies lent money for longer periods than did banks, and they also bought shares in corporations. They introduced more attractive policies and took advantage of improvements in communications to establish networks of local agencies, thus expanding the number of customers they served and accumulating greater reserves to invest in American businesses.

In the 1850s, with credit and capital both easily obtainable, the pace of industrialization increased. In the North, industry began to rival agriculture and commerce in dollar volume. Meanwhile, commercial farming, financed by the credit boom, was integrating the early frontier into the northern economy. By 1860 six northern states—Massachusetts, New York, Pennsylvania, Connecticut, Rhode Island, and Ohio—were highly industrialized. Their clothing, textile, and shoe industries employed more than one hundred thousand workers each; lumber, seventy-five thousand; iron, sixty-five thousand; and woolens and leather, fifty thousand. Although agriculture still predominated even in these states, industrial employment would soon surpass it.

WORKERS AND THE WORKPLACE

Oh, sing me the song of the Factory Girl!
So merry and glad and free!
The bloom in her cheeks, of health how it speaks,
Oh! a happy creature is she!

She tends the loom, she watches the spindle,
And cheerfully toileth away,
Amid the din of wheels, how her bright eyes
   kindle,
And her bosom is ever gay.

Oh, sing me the song of the Factory Girl!
Whose fabric doth clothe the world.
From the king and his peers to the jolly tars
With our flag o'er all seas unfurled.
From the California's seas, to the tainted breeze
Which sweeps the smokened rooms,
Where "God save the Queen" to cry are seen
The slaves of the British looms.

This idyllic portrait of factory work appeared in the Chicopee, Massachusetts, *Telegraph* in 1850. It was a fitting anthem for the teenage single women who first left the villages and farms of New England to work in the mills. New England mill owners, convinced that the degradation of English factory workers arose from their living conditions and not from the work itself, designed model communities offering airy courtyards and river views, secure dormitories, prepared meals, and cultural activities. Housekeepers enforced strict curfews, banned alcohol, and reported to the corporations on workers' behavior and church attendance.

The promise of steady work, good pay, and kinship ties at first lured eager rural young women into the mills. Many pairs of sisters and cousins worked in the same mill and lived in the same boarding house. They helped each other adjust, and their letters home drew other kin to the mills. Young women then had few opportunities for work outside their own homes and, at the same time, the commercial production of yarn and cloth had reduced their workload in New England farm households. Averaging sixteen and one-half years of age when they entered the mills, the girls usually stayed only about five years—few intended to stay longer. Their earnings brought them independence and the freedom of deciding whether to spend or save their earnings; that satisfaction was not sufficient, however, to change their ambitions to be wives and mothers. Most left the mills to marry and were replaced by other women interested in earning a wage.

Between 1837 and 1842, most mills ran only part-time because of a decline in demand for cloth; subsequently managers applied still greater pressures on workers by means of the speed-up, the stretch-out, and the premium system. The speed-up increased the speed of the machines; the stretch-out increased the number of machines each worker had to operate; and premiums for the overseers whose departments produced the most cloth encouraged them to pressure workers for greater output. The result was that in Lowell the number of spindles and looms increased 150 and 140 percent respectively between 1836 and 1850, while the number of workers increased by only 50 percent. The corporation's goal of building an industrial empire and maximizing profits had taken precedence over its paternalistic concern for workers' living conditions. In the race for profits, owners lengthened hours, cut wages, and tightened discipline, and some millworkers began to think of themselves as slaves.

New England millworkers responded to their deteriorating working conditions by organizing and striking. In 1834, in reaction to a 25 percent wage cut, they un-

Mill Women Protests

successfully "turned out" (struck) against the Lowell mills. Two years later, when boarding house rates were raised, they turned out again.

As conditions continued to worsen, workers adopted new methods of resistance. In the 1840s, strikes gave way to a concerted effort to shorten the workday. Massachusetts mill women joined forces with other workers to press for state legislation mandating a ten-hour day. Eliza R. Hemingway, a three-year veteran of two different Lowell mills, told a Massachusetts House of Representatives committee in 1845 that workers' hours were too long, "her time for meals too limited. In the summer season, the work is commenced at 5 o'clock, a.m., and continued 'til 7 o'clock, p.m., with half an hour for breakfast and three quarters of an hour for dinner."

They also aired their complaints in worker-run newspapers: the *Factory Girl* appeared in New Hampshire, the *Wampanoag and Operatives' Journal* in Massachusetts, in 1842. Two years later the *Factory Girl's Garland* and the *Voice of Industry*, nicknamed "the factory girl's voice," were founded. Even the *Lowell Offering*, the owner-sponsored paper that was the pride of millworkers and managers alike, became embroiled in controversy when workers charged that articles critical of working conditions had been suppressed.

The millworkers' rebellion against paternalism and exploitation took many forms. Their newspa-

pers exposed worsening work conditions, their strikes provoked confrontations, and their songs expressed their resolve and unity, as in "The Factory Girl's Come-All-Ye" (about 1850):

No more I'll take my bobbins out,
No more I'll put them in,
No more the overseer will say
"You're weaving your cloth too thin!"

No more will I eat cold pudding,
No more will I eat hard bread,
No more will I eat those half-baked beans,
For I vow! They're killing me dead!

I'm going back to Boston town
And live on Tremont Street;
And I want all you fact'ry girls
To come to my house and eat!

The women's labor organizations were weakened by the short tenure of most workers. Few of the militant native-born millworkers stayed on to fight the managers and owners, and gradually there were fewer New England daughters to enter the mills. The women who constituted the majority of millworkers by the end of the 1850s were mostly Irish immigrants, driven to the mills by the need to support their families and unable to afford to complain about their working conditions.

A growing gender division in the workplace, especially in the textile, clothing, and shoemaking industries, was one important outcome of indus-

Gender Divisions in Work

trialization. Although women and men tended to perform different tasks in traditional agricultural and artisan households, they worked as a family unit. As wage work spread, however, men's and women's work cultures became increasingly separate. The women and girls who left home to work in textile mills worked and lived in a mostly female world. In the clothing and shoemaking industries, whose male artisans had once worked at home assisted by unpaid family labor, men began working outside the home while women continued to work at home through the putting-out system. Tasks and wages, too became rigidly differentiated: women sewed, whereas men shaped materials and finished products, receiving higher wages in shops employing men only. These new work patterns contributed to social and economic differences between men and women (see pages 346–347).

The market system, wage labor, and the spe-

The young mill women who worked in this New England textile mill stopped work to pose for this early view, ca. 1850. New England farm daughters, and later Irish immigrants, comprised much of the nation's first factory work force.   International Museum of Photography, George Eastman House.

cialization of labor had an impact on unpaid household labor as well. As home and workplace became separate and labor came to be defined in terms of wages (what could be sold in the marketplace) rather than production, the unpaid labor of women was devalued. In a money-based economy in which families increasingly recorded their incomes and expenditures in account books, there was no category in which to enter women's unpaid labor and services. Yet those labors were extensive; indeed, the family depended on women's work within the household. And as the family became more dependent on wage labor, more family members sought outside employment and had less time to do their share of household labor. Thus gender defined household labor and placed a low value on it.

Evolving work patterns also had psychological and social outcomes. The new textile mills, shoe factories, iron mills, insurance companies, whole-

Changes in the Workplace
———

sale stores, and railroads were the antithesis of the old tradition of workshop and household production. Large factories created a workplace in which authority was hierarchically organized. Factory workers lost their sense of autonomy as impersonal market forces seemed to dominate their lives. Stiff competition among mills in the growing textile industry of the 1820s and 1830s led to layoffs and the replacement of operatives with cheaper, less-skilled workers or children. The formal rules of the factory contrasted sharply with the more relaxed pace and atmosphere of artisan shops and farm households. Supervisors represented owners whom workers never saw. The division of labor and the use of machines narrowed the skills required of workers. And the flow of work was governed by the bell, the steam whistle, or the clock. In 1844 the *Factory Girl's Garland* published a poem describing how the ringing of the factory bell controlled when the workers awoke, ate, began and ended work, and went to sleep. The central problem, of course, was the quickening pace of the work between the bells. Since owners and managers no longer shared the workers' tasks, they did not consider the plight of the worker when they increased the speed of the work. Many workers welcomed the new manufacturing methods at first;

TIME TABLE OF THE LOWELL MILLS,

Arranged to make the working time throughout the year average 11 hours per day.

TO TAKE EFFECT SEPTEMBER 21st., 1853,

The Standard time being that of the meridian of Lowell, as shown by the Regulator Clock of AMOS SANBORN, Post Office Corner, Central Street.

From March 20th to September 19th, inclusive.

COMMENCE WORK, at 6.30 A. M.   LEAVE OFF WORK, at 6.30 P. M., except on Saturday Evenings.
BREAKFAST at 6 A. M.   DINNER, at 12 M.   Commence Work, after dinner, 12.45 P. M.

From September 20th to March 19th, inclusive.

COMMENCE WORK at 7.00 A. M.   LEAVE OFF WORK, at 7.00 P. M., except on Saturday Evenings.
BREAKFAST at 6.30 A. M.   DINNER, at 12.30 P.M.   Commence Work, after dinner, 1.15 P. M.

BELLS.

From March 20th to September 19th, inclusive.

Morning Bells.	Dinner Bells.	Evening Bells.
First bell,..........4.30 A. M.	Ring out,.............12.00 M.	Ring out,...........6.30 P. M.
Second, 5.30 A. M. ; Third, 6.20.	Ring in,.........12.35 P. M.	Except on Saturday Evenings.

From September 20th to March 19th, inclusive.

Morning Bells.	Dinner Bells.	Evening Bells.
First bell,..........5.00 A. M.	Ring out,.........12.30 P. M.	Ring out at...........7.00 P. M.
Second, 6.00 A. M. ; Third, 6.50.	Ring in,.............1.05 P. M.	Except on Saturday Evenings.

SATURDAY EVENING BELLS.

During APRIL, MAY, JUNE, JULY, and AUGUST, Ring Out, at 6.00 P. M.
The remain'ng Saturday Evenings in the year, ring out as follows :

SEPTEMBER.	NOVEMBER.	JANUARY.
First Saturday, ring out 6.00 P. M.	Third Saturday ring out 4.00 P. M.	Third Saturday ring out 4.25 P. M.
Second " " 5.45 "	Fourth " " 3.55 "	Fourth " " 4.35 "
Third " " 5.30 "		
Fourth " " 5.20 "	DECEMBER.	FEBRUARY.
	First Saturday, ring out 3.50 P. M.	First Saturday, ring out 4.45 P. M.
OCTOBER.	Second " " 3.55 "	Second " " 4.55 "
First Saturday, ring out 5.05 P. M.	Third " " 3.55 "	Third " " 5.00 "
Second " " 4.55 "	Fourth " " 4.00 "	Fourth " " 5.10 "
Third " " 4.45 "	Fifth " " 4.00 "	
Fourth " " 4.35 "		MARCH.
Fifth " " 4.25 "	JANUARY.	First Saturday, ring out 5.25 P. M.
	First Saturday, ring out 4.10 P. M.	Second " " 5.30 "
NOVEMBER.	Second " " 4.15 "	Third " " 5.35 "
First Saturday, ring out 4.15 P. M.		Fourth " " 5.45 "
Second " " 4.05 "		

YARD GATES will be opened at the first stroke of the bells for entering or leaving the Mills.

⁎ *SPEED GATES commence hoisting three minutes before commencing work.*

How *do* historians know

the nature of the working conditions experienced by New England millworkers? This 1853 timetable from the Lowell Mills is among the rich sources historians consult to reconstruct the workers' experiences in the mills. The textile factories were the first corporations to impose rigid work rules. The size of the labor force, the managerial structure, and the organization of the work made it necessary to print the work rules.

The timetable illustrates the nature of the rules imposed. Exact times were established for beginning and ending work and for meals. Since few workers carried their own timepieces, a system of bells regulated the lives of the factory community. Thus from March 20 to September 19, when work began at 6:30 a.m., bells alerted the workers at 4:30 and 5:50 a.m. and again at 6:20, ten minutes before they had to be at the factory. For their main meal at midday, they had forty-five minutes away from work; the 12:35 bell warned that they had ten minutes to return. For young mill women from the New England countryside, and later for Irish women, such regimentation must have seemed a world apart from the rhythms of rural life.   Photo: Museum of American Textile History.

new jobs and higher wages seemed adequate compensation. But wage reductions, speed-ups, and stretch-outs later changed their minds. Other conditions were trying, too. Mill workers had to tolerate the roar of the looms, and all workers on power machines risked accidents that could kill or maim. Perhaps most demoralizing, opportunities for advancement in the new system were virtually nil.

Changes in the workplace in turn transformed the workers. Initially, mill women drew on kinship, village, and gender ties to build supportive networks in factories. In the 1840s and after, as recent Irish immigrant women came to predominate, more workers were strangers to each other before they entered the mills. Once employed, their only bases for friendship and mutual support were their work experiences. As a sense of distance from their employers took hold, so did deep-seated differences among workers. Nationality, religion, education, and future prospects separated Irish and Yankee millworkers. Many New England women resented the immigrants, and management set one group against the other through selective hiring and promotions. For most Irish women, mill work was not a stage in their lives; it was permanent employment. Unlike their Yankee sisters, they could not risk striking and losing their jobs; they and their families were dependent on their earnings. With legions of unskilled immigrants looking for work, Irish millworkers considered themselves fortunate to hold on to their jobs, even though the mills cut wages three times in the 1850s and continued the speed-ups and stretch-outs. The Irish workers assisted one another as much as possible, but they rarely engaged in formal protest.

As wage work became common and workers sensed a loss of independence, they experienced an erosion of the republican virtues that artisans had shared with the Revolutionary War generation. Thomas Jefferson had hoped to preserve these values with the purchase of the Louisiana Territory and the encouragement of a market economy, but factory work and boom-and-bust cycles did not enhance individual freedom. Those who stayed in the master-journeyman-apprentice system or remained on farms after the 1830s saw themselves as distinct from the new wage workers. So, too, did many of the first generation of Yankee millworkers, for whom factory work was a stage in the life cycle before marriage.

While female textile workers and shoemakers organized and protested, male workers responded to changes in the nature of work by participating actively in reform politics. Labor parties arose in Pennsylvania, New York, and Massachusetts in the 1820s and eventually spread to a dozen states. These parties advocated free public education, abolition of imprisonment for debt, revision of the militia system (in which workers bore the greatest burden), and opposition to banks and monopolies. The interests of workers' reform parties often coincided with those of middle-class benevolent movements. The two groups shared a concern not only for public education but also for public morals: temperance, observance of the Sabbath, and suppression of vice (see Chapter 13). Ironically, however, reform politics tended to divide workers.

Many of the reforms—moral education, temperance, Sabbath closings—served the interests of merchants and industrialists seeking a more disciplined work force. Temperance and Sabbath closings also pitted the native-born against immigrant workers, many of whom were Catholic. Anti-immigrant and anti-Catholic movements further divided workers.

Journeymen recognized that the new system of manufacturing threatened them. When master craftsmen in shoemaking, textiles, and apparel manufacturing attempted to keep up with change by turning their workshops into small factories with themselves as managers, the gap between master and journeymen threatened to become insurmountable. The market economy seemed to free masters and to make journeymen more dependent. Masters stressed individuals' freedom to contract for their labor; journeymen sought out the mutual protection of their fellow workers.

Organized labor's greatest achievement during this period was to gain relief from the threat of conspiracy laws. When journeyman shoemakers organized during the first decade of the century, their employers turned to the courts, charging criminal conspiracy. The cordwainers' (shoemakers') cases, which resulted in six trials between 1806 and 1815, left labor organizations in a tenuous position. Although the journeymen's right to organize was acknowledged, the courts ruled unlawful any coercive action on their part that would harm other businesses or the public. In other words, strikes were ruled illegal. Eventually a Massachusetts case, *Commonwealth* v. *Hunt* (1842), effectively reversed this decision when Chief Justice Lemuel Shaw ruled that Boston journeyman bootmakers could strike "in such manner as best to subserve their own interests." Conspiracy laws no longer thwarted unionization.

Yet permanent labor organizations were difficult to maintain. Most workers outside the crafts were unskilled or semiskilled at best. Moreover, religion, race, ethnicity, and gender divided workers. The first unions arose among urban journeymen in printing, woodworking, shoemaking, and tailoring. These early labor unions tended to be local in nature; the strongest resembled medieval guilds in that they sought to protect themselves against the competition of inferior workmen

Emergence of a Labor Movement

by regulating apprenticeship and establishing minimum wages. They also excluded women and African-Americans. (Massachusetts mill women organized their own unions.)

Umbrella organizations composed of individual craft unions, like the National Trades Union (1834), arose in several cities in the 1820s and 1830s. But the movement fell apart amid wage reductions and unemployment in the hard times of 1839–1843. In the 1850s the deterioration of working conditions strengthened the labor movement again, and affiliated craft unions began to organize into national unions. Workers won a reduction in hours, and the ten-hour day became standard. Though the Panic of 1857 wiped out the umbrella organizations, some of the new national unions in specific trades—notably printers, hat finishers, and stonecutters—survived. By 1860 national unions had also been organized by the painters, cordwainers, cotton spinners, iron molders, and machinists.

The impact of economic and technological change inevitably fell more heavily on individual workers than on their organizations. As a group, workers' share of the national wealth declined after the 1830s. Individual producers—craftsmen, factory workers, and farmers—had less economic power than they had had a generation or two earlier. And workers were increasingly losing control over their own work.

COMMERCIAL FARMING

Beyond the town and city limits, agriculture remained the backbone of the economy. Although urban areas were growing quickly, so too were rural districts. America was still overwhelmingly rural; even in 1860 rural residents far outnumbered city dwellers. Indeed, it was rural population growth that transformed so many farm villages into bustling small cities like Pittsfield in Massachusetts, Rochester in New York, and Springfield in Illinois. And in turn it was the new market orientation of farm families, and their ability to feed the growing town and village populations, that made possible these new concentrations of population.

In 1800 New England and Middle Atlantic farmers worked as their fathers and mothers had. Life centered around a household economy in which the needs of the family and the labor at its disposal determined what was produced and in what amounts. Most implements—wooden plows, rakes, shovels, and yokes—were homemade, with iron parts obtained from the local blacksmith.

Then canals and railroads began transporting grain, especially wheat, eastward from the fertile Old Northwest. And in the same period, northeastern agriculture developed some serious problems. Northeastern farmers had already cultivated all the land they could; expansion was impossible. Moreover, small New England farms with their uneven terrain did not lend themselves to the new labor-saving farm implements introduced in the 1830s—mechanical sowers, reapers, threshers, and balers. Many northeastern farms also suffered from soil exhaustion: the worn-out land produced lower yields while requiring a greater investment in seed.

Northeastern Agriculture

In response to these problems and to competition from the West, many northern farmers either went west or gave up farming for jobs in the merchant houses and factories. For eastern farm sons and daughters, western New York was the first frontier. After the Erie Canal was completed, these Yankees and New Yorkers settled on more fertile and cheaper land in Ohio and Indiana and then in Michigan, Illinois, and Wisconsin. Farm daughters who did not go west flocked to the early textile mills. Still other New Englanders—urban, better-educated, and often experienced in trade—entered the counting houses in New York and other cities. Between 1820 and 1860 the percentage of the population of the North living on farms declined from 71 to 40 percent.

But neither the counting house nor the factory depleted New England agriculture. The farmers who remained proved as adaptable at farming as their children were at copy desks and water-powered looms. By the 1850s New England and Middle Atlantic farm families were adjusting successfully to competition from western agricultural products. Many abandoned the commercial production of wheat and corn and stopped tilling poor land. Instead they improved their livestock, especially cattle, and specialized in vegetable and fruit production and dairy farming, financing these initiatives through land sales and borrowing. In fact, their greatest potential profit was from increasing land values, not from farming itself.

Many women made butter for market in the early nineteenth century. Women's production and earnings in butter, cheese, and other areas were an essential part of farm families' adaptation to the market economy. The Sinclair Hamilton Collection of American Illustrated Books, Princeton University Library.

Farm families everywhere gradually adjusted to market conditions. In 1820 about one-third of all food produced was intended for market; by 1860 the fraction had increased to about two-thirds. Middlemen specializing in the grain and food trades replaced the country storekeepers who had handled transactions for local farmers, acting as both retailers and marketing and purchasing agents.

Women's earning power from wages or market sales was an important factor in the market economy. With increasing commercialization and dependency on cash for both investment and purchases, women's earnings became essential to the survival of the family farm. The "put-out" work women did in New England had its parallel in the Middle Atlantic states and in Ohio—especially near towns and cities—in women's dairy production, which was crucial to family income. Butter and cheese making for local and regional markets replaced spinning and weaving as farm women's major activity, especially since cloth

Women's Paid Labor

could be purchased so cheaply. The work was physically demanding and did not replace regular home and farm chores but was added to them. Yet women took pride in their work; it gave many a sense of independence. Esther Lewis, a widow who sent seventy-five to one hundred pounds of butter monthly to Philadelphia in the 1830s, even hired other women to expand production.

Women's success at butter and cheese making led some farms to specialize in dairy products and some entrepreneurs to seize the opportunity to profit by expanding production. Beginning in 1847 in Ohio, entrepreneurs built cheese factories in rural towns and contracted to buy curd from local dairy farmers. One such factory in Gustavus, Ohio, produced 5,000 pounds of cheese a day from the milk of 2,500 cows in 1852. The cheese was shipped by canal and railroad to cities and eastern ports. In Boston and New York, some merchants began handling cheese and other dairy products exclusively, selling to consumers as far away as California, England, and China. By 1860 Ohio dairies were producing 21.6 million pounds of cheese a year for market.

Most farm families seemed to welcome the opportunities offered by the market economy. While continuing to take pride in self-sufficiency and to value rural serenity, they shifted toward specialization and market-oriented production. The rewards for such flexibility were great; produce sold at market financed land and equipment purchases and made credit arrangements possible. Many farm families flourished.

Meanwhile the economic distance widened between farm owners on the one hand and tenants and hired hands on the other. The rising cost of land and of farming meant that opportunities for hired hands to acquire their own farms were shrinking. By the 1850s it took from ten to twenty years for a rural laborer to save enough money to farm for himself. Thus the number of tenant farmers increased. Previously farmers had relied on the labor of unpaid family members or enslaved workers; now paid farm labor became commonplace. In the North in 1860 there was one hired hand for every 2.3 farms.

Individually and collectively, Americans still valued agrarian life. State governments energetically promoted commercial agriculture in order to spur economic growth and sustain the values of an agrarian-based republic. Massachusetts in 1817 and New York in 1819 subsidized agricultural prizes and county fairs. New York required contestants to submit written descriptions of how they grew their prize crops; the state then published the best essays to encourage the use of new methods and promote specialization. Farm journals also helped familiarize farmers with developments in agriculture. By 1860 nearly sixty journals had a combined circulation of from 250,000 to 300,000.

Even so, the Old Northwest gradually and inevitably replaced the northeastern states as the center of American family agriculture. Farms in the Old Northwest were much larger and better suited to the new mechanized farming implements than were their northeastern counterparts. The farmers of the region bought machines such as the McCormick reaper on credit and paid for them with the profits from their high yields. By 1847 Cyrus McCormick was selling a thousand reapers a year. By introducing interchangeable parts, he expanded production to five thousand a

Mechanization of Agriculture

year, but demand still outstripped supply. Similarly, John Deere's steel plow, invented in 1837, replaced the inadequate iron plow; steel blades kept the soil from sticking and were tough enough to break the roots of prairie grass. By 1856, Deere's sixty-five employees were making 13,500 plows a year.

Mechanized farming was the basis of expanded production. In the 1850s alone wheat production surged 70 percent. By that time the area that had been the western wilderness in 1800 had become one of the world's leading agricultural regions. Midwestern farm families fed an entire nation, including a generation of immigrants—and still had enough food to export.

SETTLING AND CONQUERING THE WEST

Integral to the development of the market economy was the steady expansion of the United States. In 1800 the edge of settlement extended in an arc from western New York through the new states of Kentucky and Tennessee and south to Georgia. By 1820 it had shifted westward to Ohio, Indiana, and Illinois in the North, and Louisiana, Alabama, and Mississippi in the South. By 1860 settlement reached the Southwest and the West Coast; the 1800 backcountry was long settled, and once-unexplored regions were dotted with farms and mines, towns and villages. Unsettled and sporadically settled land remained—mostly the plains and mountain territory between the Mississippi River and the Sierra Nevada—but elsewhere the land and its tribal inhabitants had given way to white settlement (see pages 354–355).

The legal boundaries of the country were also changing rapidly during this period. Between 1803 and 1853 the United States pushed its original boundaries to their present continental limits (except for Alaska). The Louisiana Purchase roughly doubled the nation's size, and the acquisition of Florida from Spain in 1819 secured the Southeast. In the 1840s the United States annexed the Republic of Texas, defined its northern border with Canada, and acquired California, Nevada, Utah, and most of Arizona through war with Mexico (see pages 398–399). Finally, in 1853 the Gadsden Purchase added southern Arizona and New Mexico.

The lore of pioneers on the frontier was already becoming a part of the mythology of America. James Fenimore Cooper's Leatherstocking tales, a series of novels that

Legends of Pioneers
——

began first appearing in 1823, introduced Hawkeye (Natty Bumppo), America's first popular fictional hero. At heart a romantic, Hawkeye preferred the freedom of the virgin forest to domesticated society. Legends, songs, and dime novels also glorified fur trappers, explorers and scouts, and pioneers. The reading public snapped up tales of pioneers crossing the arid plains and snow-covered Rockies by Conestoga wagon to bring civilization to the wilderness; frontiersmen and settlers triumphing over the environment and the Indians to earn their right to make the land productive; Mormons finding Zion in the Great American Desert; and gold seekers sailing on clipper ships to California.

Only recently have Americans come to recognize that there were other sides to these familiar stories. In the colonial period, the backcountry was considered remote and peripheral to most people's lives. After the Revolution, it became a frontier of opportunity—of land to be settled and bounty to be harvested. Yet the frontier was not empty; it was populated by well-established Native American societies. In reality, the frontier was a process in which the people there and the environment were conquered. It was also more inclusive than legends suggest: not just white men, but white women and Indians and African-Americans of both genders were pioneers. Furthermore, explorers and pioneers did not find their way across North America by themselves, nor did the wagon trains fight their way across the plains—Native Americans guided them along traditional paths and led them to food and water. And rather than civilizing the frontier lands, settlers at first brought a rather primitive economy and society, which did not compare favorably with the well-ordered Indian civilizations. In many midwestern settlements tribal peoples introduced pioneers to raising corn, harvesting berries and nuts, and tapping maples for sugar. The frontier was also violent and intolerant; the Mormons who sought a new Jerusalem near the Great Salt Lake, for instance, were fleeing the

gehenna (hell) imposed on them by frontier folk farther east (see page 336). And those who sought to farm the land, dig the gold, trap the furs, and cut the lumber destroyed the natural landscape and ecological balance in the name of progress and development.

The destruction of the environment illustrates the contrast between the idealized version of the frontier and the reality. If pioneers were attracted by the beauty and bounty of the American wilderness and lured by the opportunity to live a simple, rewarding life close to the soil, they were also destroying the land in the process. It was almost as if the vast forests, prairies, and lakes were enemies to be conquered and bent to their will. Settlers felled millions of trees to make way for farms, while lumbermen in Michigan denuded the land. Farther west, miners in search of gold leveled the hills. And even those, like the fur trappers, who sought to escape civilization were forging an economic link between the wilderness and the market economy.

No figure has come to symbolize the frontier more aptly than the footloose and rugged fur trapper who roamed the wilderness in search of

Fur Trade
——

pelts. It was the trapper, with his backpack, rifle, and kegs of whiskey, who spearheaded America's manifest destiny (see page 390), extending the U.S. presence to the Pacific Slope. Fur trading, especially for beaver, had been economically important ever since the early colonial period. Traders were the first link in an elaborate network that reached from beyond the settled frontier to sophisticated European shops, connecting the Far West to the market system and European consumers. After 1800, American investors organized to compete with foreign trading companies such as Hudson's Bay. The German immigrant John Jacob Astor, for instance, became a millionaire through his American Fur Trading Company. In 1825 the St. Louis merchant William Henry Ashley introduced the rendezvous system, an innovation in the method by which furs were acquired. Instead of buying beaver furs from Indians, Ashley sent out non-Indian trappers to roam the Rockies and areas farther west; at season's end the trappers gathered on the Green River in present-day Wyoming to exchange their pelts for goods Ashley had brought in from St. Louis. This annual

Alfred Jacob Miller's 1837 oil painting, "A Bourgeois & His Squaw," depicted mountain man Joseph Reddeford Walker and his Indian wife going to the rendezvous. A "bourgeois" supervised a group of trappers, and Walker was legendary as a bourgeois and scout, having led expeditions to the Great Salt Lake and Yosemite.   Joslyn Art Museum, Omaha, Nebraska.

spring rendezvous was the hallmark of the American fur-trading system until the late 1830s, when silk replaced beaver hats and trapping declined. The legendary Jim Bridger worked the headwaters of the Missouri River for Ashley from 1822 through 1842. He then became a scout and guide for many western expeditions, including that of Yellowstone. In many areas the beaver had been virtually trapped out of existence, and the westward trails and railroads soon overtook the animal's frontier.

Throughout the West, trappers sought the cooperation of the tribes in their territories, and nearly 40 percent wed Indian women. Mountain man and explorer Joseph Reddeford Walker, for instance, married an Indian woman. Usually the trapper or trader conformed to the tribe's custom in negotiating with the bride's parents for the match. When a chief's daughter wed a fur merchant—as when Archibald McDonald of Hudson's Bay Company and Koale-xoa, daughter of a Chinook chief, were married at the mouth of the Columbia River—two cultures convened to celebrate. Many Native American wives of white trappers played important roles in bridging the trapper and tribal cultures. Moreover, an Indian woman shared her husband's special trading privileges as well as family ties and experiences of life on the frontier. Over time Metís, or mixed-bloods (Indian-white offspring), and white women replaced Native American women as trappers' wives. This development not only changed trapper culture but was also a sign of the decline of the fur trade, signaling the arrival of settled agrarian society.

The complex history of trapping illustrates many of the characteristic elements in the conquest of the West. Early fur traders exploited friendly Indian tribes; then mountain trappers monopolized the trade through the systematic organization and financial backing of trading companies, driven by demand in distant markets. Soon settlements and towns sprang up along the trappers' routes. Mining, lumbering, and ranching followed similar patterns as settlement intensified the exploration of the West's natural resources and land. Railroads would later accelerate the process.

Farther west, beyond the trails of the mountain men, it was gold that first stimulated a mass migration to the West Coast. Anglos settled newly acquired California almost over-

California Gold Rush
—

night. In January 1848 James Marshall, a carpenter, spotted a few goldlike particles in the millrace at Sutter's Mill (now Coloma, California, northwest of Sacramento). Word of the discovery spread, and other Californians rushed to scrabble for instant fortunes. When John C. Frémont reached San Francisco five months later, he found that "all, or nearly all, its male inhabitants had gone to the mines." The town, "which a few months before was so busy and thriving, was then almost deserted."

By 1849 the news had spread eastward, and hundreds of thousands of fortune seekers flooded in. Success in the market economy required capital, hard labor, and time; by contrast, gold mining seemed to promise instant riches. Most "forty-niners" never found enough gold to pay their expenses. "The stories you hear frequently in the States," one gold seeker wrote home, "are the most extravagant lies imaginable—the mines are a humbug. . . . The almost universal feeling is to get home." But many stayed, either unable to afford the passage home or tempted by the growing labor shortage in California's cities and agricultural districts. San Francisco, the gateway from the West Coast to the interior, became an instant city, ballooning from one thousand people in 1848 to thirty-five thousand just two years later; the ships that brought the people continuously jammed the harbor, a scene Frank Marryat captured in his 1849 painting. A French visitor in that year wrote, "At San Francisco, where fifteen months ago one found only a half dozen large cabins, one finds today a stock exchange, a theater, churches of all Christian cults, and a large number of quite beautiful

Frank Marryat, a young English artist and writer, painted this scene of San Francisco around 1849. The city was the gateway to the gold fields, and San Francisco became an instant city, growing from one thousand in 1848 to thirty-five thousand in 1850. Ships, which brought people and supplies, jammed the harbor. New York Historical Society.

Women who traveled West with their husbands found their domestic skills in great demand. This watercolor by E. Whitefield, 1856, entitled Laying Out of Karns' City, Minnesota *shows a woman preparing a meal out of her lean-to kitchen for her husband and their guests.*   Chicago Historical Society.

homes." The newcomers came for one reason: instant wealth. In search of gold and silver, they mined the lodes and washed away the surface soil with hydraulic mining, leaving the land unsuitable for anything after they abandoned it.

The forty-niners produced almost nothing, but they had to be fed. Thus began the great California agricultural boom. Wheat was the preferred staple; it required minimal investment, was easily planted, and offered a quick return at the end of a relatively short growing season. California farmers became eager importers of machinery, since labor was scarce (and thus expensive) and the flat treeless plains were well suited to horse-drawn machines. By the mid-1850s, California was exporting wheat. Meanwhile enterprising merchants rushed to supply, feed, and clothe the new settlers. One such merchant was Levi Strauss, a German Jewish immigrant, whose tough mining pants found an enduring and eventually worldwide market as blue jeans.

In the Midwest, family farms were the basic unit of production; in California, by contrast, gold and ore mining, grazing, and large-scale wheat farming were overwhelmingly male occupations. The experiences of women, who constituted about one-seventh of the travelers on the overland trails, differed from those of men moving westward. Most men came alone, drawn by a sense of adventure and personal opportunity. Women most often accompanied their husbands, and they found their lives uprooted. It was a traumatic experience for many, as they left behind networks of friends and kin to journey, often with children, along an unknown path to a strange environment. Yet in the West they found their domestic skills in great demand. They received high fees for cooking, laundering, and sewing. Boarding houses and hotels were run by women, as men shunned domestic work. But not all women were entrepreneurs. Some wives, at their spouses' behest, cooked for and served their husbands' friends; the women did the work while their husbands built reputations as hosts. Abigail Scott Duniway, a leading western

Women Settlers

crusader for women's suffrage and a veteran of the Overland Trail to Oregon, wrote in 1859 that she lived in a "neighborhood composed chiefly of bachelors, who found comfort in mobilizing at meal time at the homes of the few married men of the township, and seemed especially fond of congregating at the hospitable cabin home of my good husband, who was never quite so much in his glory as when entertaining men at this fireside, while I, if not washing, scrubbing, churning, or nursing the baby, was preparing their meals in our lean-to kitchen."

Gold altered the pattern of settlement along the entire Pacific coast. Before 1848 most overland traffic flowed north over the Oregon Trail; few pioneers turned south to California. By 1849 a pioneer observed that the Oregon Trail "bore no evidence of having been much traveled this year." Traffic was flowing south instead, and California was becoming the new population center of the Pacific Slope. One measure of this shift was the overland mail routes. In the 1840s the Oregon Trail had been the main communications link between the Midwest and the Pacific. But the Post Office officials who organized mail routes in the 1850s terminated them in California, not Oregon; there was no route north of Sacramento.

By 1860 farmers and merchants in California, as in the Great Plains and prairies farther east, had become firmly linked to the market economy. Although the experiences of these settlers were less dramatic than those of the trappers and forty-niners, theirs is the story of the overwhelming majority of westerners before 1860. They migrated from the Old Northwest and the Mississippi and Missouri valleys. They cleared the land of trees or prairie grass, hoed in corn and wheat, fenced in animals, and constructed cabins of logs or sod. Success often depended on their access to water, and they sought to divert the streams and rivers of the West to irrigate their land. As settled areas expanded, farmers built roads to carry their stock and produce to market and bring back supplies they could not produce themselves. Growth brought specialization; as western farmers shifted from self-sufficiency to commercial farming, they too tended to concentrate on one crop. As land prices rose, families seeking new land had to go farther west to find cheap land.

Western Farming

Though often thought of as outposts of rugged individualism, many early agricultural settlements depended heavily on family and kinship networks and communal cooperation. Sugar Creek on the Sangamon River in central Illinois exemplified this cooperative spirit. The white settlers who arrived in 1817 named the settlement for its sugar maples, tapped first by the Kickapoos and then by the American settlers. Although the settlement was based on private land ownership, most newcomers over the next decade were members of kin networks who assisted each other in clearing land and turning temporary dwellings into permanent cabins. Whether raising hogs or children, Sugar Creek families depended on kin and friends for support. In crises, too, they rose to the occasion. When someone "would be sick with chills or jaundice, or something else," Sugar Creek farmer James Megredy recalled, "his neighbors would meet and take care of his harvest, get up wood, or repair his cabin, or plant his corn." Neighbors set up a "borrowing system" whereby scarce tools and labor constantly circulated through the neighborhood. Settlers who came without previous ties, if they stayed, did not long remain strangers.

What made possible such settlements as Sugar Creek was the availability of land and credit. Some public lands were granted as a reward for military service: veterans of the War of 1812 received 160 acres; veterans of the Mexican War (see Chapter 14) could purchase land at reduced prices. And until 1820, civilians could buy government land at $2 an acre (a relatively high price) on a liberal four-year payment plan. From 1800 to 1817 the government successively reduced the minimum purchase from 640 to 80 acres, bringing the land within the reach of more Americans. But when the availability of land prompted the flurry of land speculation that ended in the Panic of 1819 (see page 262), the government discontinued credit sales. Instead it reduced the price further, to $1.25 an acre.

Land Grants and Sales

Some eager pioneers settled land before it had been surveyed and offered for sale. Such illegal settlers, or squatters, then had to buy the land at auction and faced the risk of being unable to purchase it. Often neighbors protected squatters; in Sugar Creek, Illinois, they even helped them buy the land. In 1841, to facilitate settlement and end property disputes, Congress passed the Preemption Act, which legalized settlement prior to surveying.

Since most settlers needed to borrow money, private credit systems arose: banks, private investors, country storekeepers, and speculators all extended credit to farmers. Railroads also sold land on credit—land they had received from the government as construction subsidies. (The Illinois Central, for example, received 2.6 million acres in 1850.) Indeed, nearly all economic activity in the West involved credit, from land sales to the shipping of produce to railroad construction. In 1816, 1836, and 1855, easy credit helped boost land prices. As land prices increased beyond farmers' abilities to pay interest or repay their loans, or farm prices or weather conditions reduced farmers' income, farm land values collapsed, ending the speculative bubble. Mortgage bankers and speculators then purchased much land cheaply. As a consequence, many farmers rented instead of owning the land; tenancy became more common in the West than it had been in New England.

The agricultural West was dependent from the start on its links with towns and cities. The cities along the Ohio and Mississippi rivers—Louisville, Cincinnati, and St. Louis—

Frontier Cities
———

predated and promoted the earliest settlement of much of the West. A generation later the lake cities of Cleveland, Detroit, and, especially, Chicago spearheaded settlement farther west. Steamboats connected these cities with eastern markets and ports, carrying grain east and returning with finished goods. As the center of a rail network, Chicago exercised sway over the settling and development of most of the middle United States. As in the Northeast, these western cities eventually developed into manufacturing centers as merchants shifted their investments from commerce to industry. Chicago became a center for the manufacture of farm implements, Louisville of textiles, and Cleveland of iron. Smaller cities specialized in flour mills, and all produced consumer goods for the hinterlands.

Urban growth in the West was so spectacular that by 1860 Cincinnati, St. Louis, and Chicago each had populations exceeding one hundred thousand, and Buffalo, Louisville, San Francisco, Pittsburgh, Detroit, Milwaukee, and Cleveland had surpassed forty thousand. Thus commerce, urban growth, and industrialization overtook the farmers' frontier, wedding the West to the Northeast.

For the North and the West the period from 1800 through 1860 was one of explosive growth. Population increased sixfold. Settlement now extended beyond the Mississippi and was spreading east from the Pacific Ocean by 1860. Agriculture, which had completely dominated the nation at the turn of the century, was by midcentury being challenged by a booming manufacturing sector. And agriculture itself was becoming market-oriented and mechanized.

Economic development changed how people lived. Canals, railroads, steamboats, and telegraph lines linked economic activities hundreds and even thousands of miles apart. The market economy brought sustained growth; it also ushered in cycles of boom and bust. Hard times and unemployment became frequent occurrences. The growing economy also meant larger-scale destruction of the environment: while mills exploited New England waterways as a source of power, Michigan was denuded of its pine forests and the gold rush destroyed land in California.

Commercial and industrial growth also altered traditional patterns of production and consumption. Farmers began to purchase goods formerly produced by their wives and daughters, and farm families geared production to faraway markets. Farm women increasingly contributed income from market sales to the family farm. In New England many young women left the family farm to become the first factory workers in the new textile industry. As workshops and factories replaced household production, and the master-journeyman-apprentice system faded away, workplace relations became more impersonal and working conditions harsher. And men's and women's work became increasingly dissimilar. Industrial jobs began to attract large numbers of immigrants, and some workers organized labor unions.

The American people, too, were changing. Immigration and western expansion made the population more diverse. Urbanization, commerce, and industry were creating significant divisions among Americans, reaching deeply into the home as well as the workshop. The South was not totally insulated from these changes, but its dependence on slave rather than free labor set it apart. Above all else, slavery defined the South.

SUGGESTIONS FOR FURTHER READING

General

Stuart Bruchey, *The Roots of American Economic Growth, 1607–1861: An Essay in Social Causation* (1965); David Klingaman and Richard Vedder, eds., *Essays in Nineteenth-Century History* (1975); Jack Larkin, *The Reshaping of Everyday Life, 1790–1840* (1988); Otto Mayr and Robert C. Post, eds., *Yankee Enterprise: The Rise of the American System of Manufactures* (1981); Douglass C. North, *Economic Growth of the United States, 1790–1860* (1966); Nathan Rosenberg, *Technology and American Economic Growth* (1972).

Transportation

Robert G. Albion, *The Rise of New York Port, 1815–1860* (1939); Albert Fishlow, *American Railroads and the Transformation of the Ante-Bellum Economy* (1965); Carter Goodrich, *Government Promotion of American Canals and Railroads, 1800–1890* (1960); Louis C. Hunter, *Steamboats on the Western Rivers* (1949); Harry N. Scheiber, *Ohio Canal Era: A Case Study of Government and the Economy, 1820–1861* (1969); Ronald E. Shaw, *Canals for a Nation: The Canal Era in the United States, 1790–1860* (1990); George R. Taylor, *The Transportation Revolution, 1815–1860* (1951); James A. Ward, *Railroads and the Character of America, 1820–1887* (1986).

Commerce and Manufacturing

Alfred D. Chandler, Jr., *The Visible Hand: Managerial Revolution in American Business* (1977); Thomas C. Cochran, *Frontiers of Change: Early Industrialization in America* (1981); Robert F. Dalzell, Jr., *Enterprising Elite: The Boston Associates and the World They Made* (1987); Louis Hartz, *Economic Policy and Democratic Thought: Pennsylvania, 1776–1860* (1954); David A. Hounshell, *From the American System to Mass Production, 1800–1932: The Development of Manufacturing Technology in the United States* (1984); David J. Jeremy, *Transatlantic Industrial Revolution: The Diffusion of Textile Technologies Between Britain and America, 1790s–1830s* (1981); Stanley I. Kutler, *Privilege and Creative Destruction: The Charles River Bridge Case* (1971); Merritt Roe Smith, *Harpers Ferry Armory and the New Technology* (1977); Theodore Steinberg, *Nature Incorporated: Industrialization and the Waters of New England* (1991); Barbara M. Tucker, *Samuel Slater and the Origins of the American Textile Industry, 1790–1860* (1984); Anthony F. C. Wallace, *Rockdale: The Growth of an American Village in the Early Industrial Revolution* (1978).

Agriculture

"American Agriculture, 1790–1840, A Symposium," *Agricultural History* 46 (January 1972); Jeremy Atack and Fred Bateman, *To Their Own Soil: Agriculture in the Antebellum North* (1987); Allen G. Bogue, *From Prairie to Corn Belt: Farming on the Illinois and Iowa Prairies in the Nineteenth Century* (1963); Christopher Clark, *The Roots of Rural Capitalism: Western Massachusetts, 1780–1860* (1990); Clarence Danhof, *Change in Agriculture: The Northern United States, 1820–1870* (1969); John Mack Faragher, *Sugar Creek: Life on the Illinois Prairie* (1986); Paul W. Gates, *The Farmer's Age: Agriculture, 1815–1860* (1962); Benjamin H. Hibbard, *A History of Public Land Policies* (1939); Joan M. Jensen, *Loosening the Bonds: Mid-Atlantic Farm Women, 1750–1850* (1986); Robert Leslie Jones, *History of Agriculture in Ohio to 1880* (1983); Edward C. Kendall, *John Deere's Steel Plow* (1959).

The Frontier

Ray A. Billington, *The Far Western Frontier, 1830–1860* (1956); William Cronon, *Nature's Metropolis: Chicago and the Great West* (1991); John Mack Faragher, *Women and Men on the Overland Trail* (1979); William H. Goetzmann, *Exploration and Empire: The Explorer and the Scientist in the Winning of the American West* (1966); Leroy R. Hafen, ed., *The Mountain Men and the Fur Trade of the Far West*, 10 vols. (1965–1972); Julie Roy Jeffrey, *Frontier Women: The Trans-Mississippi West, 1840–1880* (1979); Theodore J. Karamanski, *Fur Trade and Exploration: Opening the Far Northwest, 1821–1852* (1983); Lillian Schlissel, *Women's Diaries of the Westward Journey* (1982); Duane A. Smith, *Mining America: The Industry and the Environment, 1800–1980* (1987); John D. Unruh, Jr., *The Overland Emigrants and the Trans-Mississippi West, 1840–1860* (1979); David J. Wishart, *The Fur Trade of the American West, 1807–1840* (1979).

Workers

Mary H. Blewett, *Men, Women, and Work: Class, Gender, and Protest in the New England Shoe Industry, 1780–1910* (1988); Jeanne Boydston, *Home and Work: Housework, Wages, and the Ideology of Labor in the Early Republic* (1990); Alan Dawley, *Class and Community: The Industrial Revolution in Lynn* (1977); Thomas Dublin, *Women at Work: The Transformation of Work and Community in Lowell, Massachusetts, 1826–1860* (1979); Alice Kessler-Harris, *Out to Work: A History of Wage-earning Women in the United States* (1982); Jonathan Prude, *The Coming of Industrial Order: Town and Factory Life in Rural Massachusetts, 1810–1860* (1983); W. J. Rorabaugh, *The Craft Apprentice: From Franklin to the Machine Age in America* (1986); Steven J. Ross, *Workers on the Edge: Work, Leisure, and Politics in Industrializing Cincinnati, 1788–1890* (1985); Norman Ware, *The Industrial Worker, 1840–1860* (1924); Sean Wilentz, *Chants Democratic: New York City and the Rise of the American Working Class, 1788–1850* (1984); David A. Zonderman, *Aspirations and Anxieties: New England Workers and the Mechanized Factory System, 1815–1850* (1992).

Persac 1861

Slavery and the Growth of the South, 1800–1860

SLAVERY AND RACISM PLAGUED Frederick Bailey from birth. He had no father, for his father was a white man— probably the master. He never knew his mother, for the master separated them before he was a year old. Raised by his grandmother, Frederick later recalled that as a young boy he often saw his aunt stripped to the waist and lashed until "the warm, red blood came dripping to the floor." On many mornings the "heart-rending shrieks" of a slave and the master's "horrid oaths" roused him from sleep. Yet somehow he formed "a deep conviction that slavery would not always be able to hold me within its foul embrace."

Once in his childhood he encountered "a white face beaming with the most kindly emotions." A new mistress, who wanted him as a playmate for her son, treated him warmly and began to teach him to read. But her husband quickly put an end to his instruction, explaining that learning spoiled a slave. Under slavery's influence the tender-hearted mistress changed character. She ceased to treat him as a human being and before long abused him with "tiger-like fierceness."

At about age fifteen, the boy was hired out to a violent man to be "broken"—to learn absolute obedience from a year of constant work and whippings. After six months he thought himself broken "in body, soul, and spirit." Then one day, as the slave breaker began again to beat him, something stirred in the boy. He seized his tormentor by the throat, and they struggled hand-to-hand for nearly two hours. When they parted, one knew his dominance was over, and the other felt "a glorious resurrection, from the tomb of slavery, to the heaven of freedom."

Two years later he escaped from Baltimore, first to New York City and then to New Bedford, Massachusetts, where he took the name Frederick Douglass. In the North he found industrious and prosperous communities, but he also encountered prejudice. A few people treated him decently, but many despised his blackness. Although he knew how to caulk the seams of ships, white caulkers in New Bedford's shipyards refused to work with him, so Douglass had to find dirty and low-paid work shoveling coal, sweeping chimneys, and rolling oil casks.

Frederick Douglass made the most of the freedom to study, to speak, and to agitate that the North offered. He fled from bondage in 1838 and by 1841 had already begun his impressive

Louisiana sugar planters were among the richest of the southern slaveholders.

Frederick Douglass. After escaping from slavery, Frederick Douglass continued to educate himself and became one of the most eloquent voices of black protest in U.S. history. Art Resource/National Portrait Gallery Smithsonian Institution, Washington, D.C.

career as an antislavery orator and editor. But he never escaped the prejudice that had grown so familiar to him in the South. Douglass's career illustrates both the differences that were developing between North and South and their similarities.

Racism was a national phenomenon, but attitudes on slavery were beginning to diverge in the 1820s and 1830s. Many northerners, from ships' caulkers to officeholders, remained undisturbed by the idea of human bondage, but a growing number considered it shocking and backward. In the years after the Revolution, northerners—possessing few slaves and influenced by the revolutionary concept of natural rights—had adopted gradual emancipation laws (see page 187). At the same time they developed a dynamic market economy and embarked on an industrial revolution. These changes rendered forced labor obsolete. An industrializing, free-labor society had no use for slavery.

The years from 1800 to 1860 were a time of growth and prosperity in the South, too; new lands were settled and new states peopled. But as the North grew and changed, economically the South merely grew. Change there only reinforced existing economic patterns. Steadily the South emerged as the world's most extensive and vigorous slave economy. And slavery had a far-reaching influence on the whole society. The South's people were slaves, slaveholders, and nonslaveholders rather than farmers, merchants, mechanics, mill girls, and manufacturers. Its well-being depended on agriculture alone, rather than on agriculture plus commerce and manufacturing. Its population was almost wholly rural rather than rural and urban.

These facts meant that the economic and social lives of southerners were unavoidably distinct from those of northerners. Nonslaveholders operated their family farms in a society dominated by slaveholding planters. A handful of planters developed an aristocratic lifestyle, while slaves—one-third of the South's people—lived without freedom, struggling to develop a culture that sustained hope. The influence of slavery spread throughout the social system, affecting not just southern economics but southern values, customs, and laws.

MIGRATION, GROWTH, AND THE COTTON BOOM

Between 1800 and 1860, small farmers and slave-owning planters migrated westward and brought new territory under cultivation. As human labor, both voluntary and coerced, built a vastly larger slaveholding society, farms and plantations spread across the landscape.

The attraction of rich new lands drew thousands of southerners across the Appalachian Mountains. Early settlers told those back east about "dark, heavy forests, . . . wide, thick canebrakes, [and] clear running river[s], full of fish." These accounts created in many men's minds an irresistible urge to move. Small farmers and ambitious slaveowners poured across the mountains, pushing the Indians off their lands in the Gulf region (see pages 354–355). The floodtide of westward migration reached Alabama and Mississippi in the 1830s, then spilled into Texas in the 1850s.

The earliest settlers in the swelling stream of migration were often yeomen—small farmers, most of whom owned no slaves. Yeomen pioneered the southern wilderness, moving into undeveloped regions and building log cabins. After the War of 1812 they moved in successive waves down the southern Appalachians into new Gulf lands, first as herders of livestock and then as farmers. The herdsmen, who fattened their cattle and pigs on the abundant natural vegetation in the woods, moved on when farmers filled up an area and broke ground for crops. Yeoman farmers forced many herdsmen farther west and eventually across the Mississippi.

Migration became almost a way of life for some yeoman families. Lured by stories of good land beyond the horizon, many men uprooted their wives and children repeatedly. Each new land seemed "like a paradise" to many eager settlers. The Alabama Territory, wrote one new arrival, had "the greatest prospect of corn and cotton I ever saw." Writing to friends in older parts of the South, he asked, "Why will you stay . . . and work them poor stony ridges when one half of the labor and one third of the ground heare will bring you more?" Most migrants agreed that "every young man should emigrate if he is poor," and thousands of poor men did just that. The excitement over new lands alarmed one North Carolinian, who wrote, "The *Alabama Fever* rages here with great violence. . . . I am apprehensive if it continues to spread as it has done, it will almost depopulate the country."

The men worked hard on the frontier to clear fields and establish a farm, while their wives labored in the household economy and patiently re-created the social ties—to relatives, neighbors, fellow churchgoers—that enriched experience. Women seldom shared the men's excitement about moving. They dreaded the isolation and loneliness of the frontier, but few had a voice in the decision. "We have been [moving] all our lives," lamented one woman. "As soon as ever we git comfortably settled, it is time to be off to something new." Maria Lides's father took the family from South Carolina to Alabama, but "his having such a good crop" there, Maria wrote to a relative, "seems to make him more anxious to move." She almost wished that another restless relative, her brother, would decide on California, because "he would be obliged to stop then for he could go no farther."

Some yeomen acquired large tracts of level land and became wealthy planters. Others clung to the beautiful mountainous areas they loved or pressed farther into the wilds because, as one frontiersman told a European visitor, he disliked "seeing the nose of my neighbor sticking out between the trees." Those who moved tended to stick to the climate and soils they knew best. Yeomen could not afford the richest bottomlands, which were swampy and required expensive draining, but they acquired land almost everywhere else.

For slaveholding southerners another powerful motive impelled westward movement: the chance to profit from a spectacular cotton boom. Southern planters were not sentimentalists, holding onto slavery while northerners grew rich from commerce and the industrial revolution. Like other Americans, slaveholding southerners were profit-oriented. But the cotton boom caused nonmechanized, slave-based agriculture to remain highly profitable in the South, sustaining the plantation economy.

Rise of the Cotton South

This had not always seemed likely. At the time of the Revolution, slave-based agriculture was not very profitable in the Upper South, where most southerners then lived. Persistent debt hung heavily over Virginia's extravagant and aristocratic tobacco growers. Farther south, along the coast of the Carolinas and Georgia, slaves grew rice and some indigo. Cotton was a profitable crop only for the sea-island planters of South Carolina and Georgia, who grew the luxurious long-staple variety. The short-staple cotton that grew readily in the interior was unmarketable because its sticky seeds lay tangled in the fibers. Yet, in spite of the limited usefulness of slavery, much wealth was tied up in it. Ingrained social forces and fear of slave revolts prevented its abolition.

Then, late in the eighteenth century, England's burgeoning textile industry demanded more and more cotton. Sea-island cotton became so profitable between 1785 and 1795 that thousands of farmers in the interior tried growing the short-staple variety; by the early 1790s southern farmers were growing 2 to 3 million pounds of it each year, despite their inability to remove the seeds. Some of this cotton was meant for domestic use, but most was grown in the hope that some innovation would make the crop salable to the English. In such circumstances the invention of a cotton gin was almost inevitable, and Eli Whitney, an inventor from

As this 1860 view indicates, New Orleans, the South's largest city and a major port, was a wealthy hub of the cotton trade.   Chicago Historical Society.

Connecticut, responded in 1793 with a simple machine that removed the seeds from the fibers. By 1800 cotton was spreading rapidly westward from the seaboard states.

The voracious appetite of English mills caused a meteoric rise in cotton production (see maps). From 1800 until the Civil War, British demand for cotton multiplied rapidly, and southern planters rushed to increase their acreage. Despite occasional periods of low prices, the demand for cotton surged ahead every decade. Southerners with capital bought more land and more slaves, and planted ever more cotton. Cotton growers boosted production so successfully that by 1825 the South was the world's dominant supplier of cotton; by the 1850s the South was the source of over 70 percent of all the cotton Britain imported.

Thus the antebellum South—the Old South before the Civil War—became primarily a cotton South. Tobacco continued to be grown in Virginia and North Carolina, and rice and sugar were important crops in certain coastal areas, especially in South Carolina, Georgia, and Louisiana. But cotton was the largest and most widespread crop, and it fueled the South's hunger for new territory.

Small slaveowners and wealthier planters (those who owned twenty bondsmen or more) sought out alluvial bottomland and other fertile soils, eager to grasp the opportunity for wealth the cotton boom offered. A Virginian who visited

Vicksburg in 1836 marveled at the atmosphere: "They do business in a kind of frenzy," he wrote. That frenzy produced many brand-new aristocrats. Some old Virginia and South Carolina families were represented among the proud new "cotton snobs," but most of the wealthy were newly rich.

The desire to plant more cotton and buy more slaves often caused men with new wealth to postpone the enjoyment of luxuries. Many first-generation planters lived for decades in their original log cabins, improved only by clapboards or a frame addition. "If you wish to see people worth millions living as [if] they were not worth hundreds," a Mississippi gentleman remarked, "come down here." Yet the planters' wealth put ease and refinement within their grasp, and riches and high social status arrived quickly for some.

A case in point is the family of Jefferson Davis, who later became president of the Confederacy. Like Abraham Lincoln, Davis was born in Kentucky amid humble circumstances. His father was one of

One-Generation Aristocrats

the thousands of American farmers on the western frontier who moved frequently, unwisely buying land when prices were high and selling when they were low. Luckily for Jefferson Davis, his older brother migrated to Mississippi and made good. Settling on rich bottomlands next to the Mississippi River, Joseph Davis profited, ex-

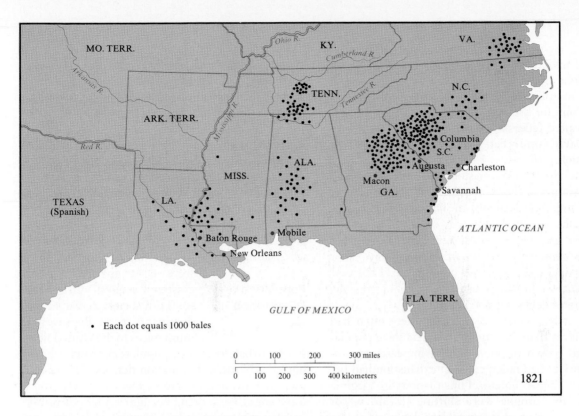

MO. TERR.

Ohio R.

KY.

Cumberland R.

VA.

Arkansas R.

TENN.

Tennessee R.

N.C.

ARK. TERR.

Columbia

S.C.

Red R.

Mississippi R.

ALA.

Augusta

Charleston

MISS.

Macon

GA.

Savannah

TEXAS
(Spanish)

LA.

Baton Rouge

Mobile

ATLANTIC OCEAN

New Orleans

FLA. TERR.

GULF OF MEXICO

• Each dot equals 1000 bales

0   100   200   300 miles

0   100   200   300   400 kilometers

1821

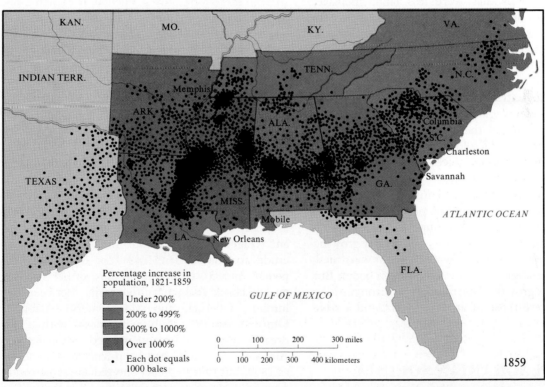

KAN.

MO.

KY.

VA.

INDIAN TERR.

Memphis

TENN.

N.C.

ARK.

ALA.

Columbia

S.C.

Charleston

TEXAS

MISS.

Savannah

GA.

New Orleans

LA.

Mobile

ATLANTIC OCEAN

FLA.

Percentage increase in
population, 1821-1859

GULF OF MEXICO

☐ Under 200%

☐ 200% to 499%

☐ 500% to 1000%

☐ Over 1000%

• Each dot equals
1000 bales

0   100   200   300 miles

0   100   200   300   400 kilometers

1859

Cotton Production in the South.   *These two maps reveal the rapid westward expansion of cotton
production and its importance to the antebellum South.*

panded his holdings of land and slaves, and grew rich. Soon he was an established figure in society, and he used his position to arrange an education at West Point for his younger brother. A large plantation awaited Jefferson's resignation from the army. The Davis family had become aristocrats in one generation.

The rise of new aristocrats in the Gulf and the migration of thousands of aspiring slaveholders across the Appalachians meant another kind of migration—involuntary—for black southerners. Congress had closed the international slave trade in 1808, and, despite some smuggling, slave labor from abroad was essentially unavailable. Thus new slaves for the Lower South had to come from the older states of the Upper South.

As it happened, slaveowners there often had more slaves than they needed. Their slave population had grown through natural increase, but tobacco prices had fallen and soil exhaustion had become a serious problem. Thus planters in Virginia and North Carolina were shifting toward wheat and corn, crops that were less labor-intensive. Slaveowners on worn-out tobacco lands were glad to sell excess slaves to the booming areas of fertile black-belt soil in the cotton South.

Between 1810 and 1820 alone, 137,000 slaves were forced to move from North Carolina and the Chesapeake states to Alabama, Mississippi, and other western regions. Interregional sales and transfers continued thereafter, as an estimated 2 million people were sold between 1820 and 1860 to satisfy the need for slave labor. Thousands of black families were disrupted every year to serve the needs of the cotton economy.

To white southerners the period from 1800 to 1860 was a time of great change and progress, no less than in the North. The South was growing and expanding, driven by excitement over new lands and energies related to the cotton boom. But the South's growth was different: its distinguishing features were those of an agricultural and a slave society.

AN AGRARIAN SOCIETY

The South did exhibit some of the diversity of the bustling, urbanizing, commercial North. There were merchants, artisans, and craftsmen in the larger cities, as well as men of commerce who pro-

moted railways and transportation improvements. Immigrants from Ireland and other parts of Europe arrived in Savannah and other southern ports in dramatically increasing numbers during the 1840s and 1850s. But these developments were only faint shadows of their northern counterparts and had relatively little impact. Southern development was dominated by agriculture and slavery and by the prominence of rural slaves, slaveholders, and yeoman farmers in the population.

Population distribution remained thin. Cotton growers spread out over as large an area as possible to maximize production and income. Farms were set far apart, rather than clustered around villages, and southern society remained predominantly rural. Because most immigrants to the United States sought urban locations, population growth fell behind the North's. Population density, low even in the older plantation states, was extremely low in the frontier areas being brought under cultivation. In 1860 there were only 2.3 people per square mile in vast and largely unsettled Texas, 15.6 in Louisiana, and 18.0 in Georgia. By contrast, population density in the nonslaveholding states east of the Mississippi River was almost three times higher. The Northeast had an average of 65.4 people per square mile. Massachusetts had 153.1 people per square mile, and New York City, where overcrowding reached epic proportions, compressed 86,400 people into each square mile.

Even in the 1850s, much of the South seemed a virtual wilderness. Frederick Law Olmsted, a northerner later renowned as a landscape architect, made several trips through the South in the 1850s as a journalist. Olmsted found that the few trains and stagecoaches available to travelers offered crude accommodations and kept their schedules poorly. Indeed, he had to do most of his traveling on horseback along primitive trails. Between Columbus, Georgia, and Montgomery, Alabama, Olmsted found "a hilly wilderness, with a few dreary villages, and many isolated cotton farms." Alabama, of course, had been frontier as recently as 1800, but Olmsted encountered the same conditions in parts of eastern Virginia: "For hours and hours one has to ride through the unlimited, continual, all-shadowing, all-embracing forest, following roads in the making of which no more labor has been given than was necessary to remove the

Charleston, South Carolina, one of the South's larger cities, remained small compared with many urban centers in the industrializing North. This relaxed scene of the city was painted in 1831 by S. Barnard.   Yale University Art Gallery. Mabel Brady Garvan Collection.

timber which would obstruct the passage of wagons; and even for days and days he may sometimes travel and see never two dwellings of mankind within sight of each other."

Society in such rural areas was characterized by relatively weak institutions outside the family, for it takes a certain concentration of people to create and support organized activity. Where people were scarce, it was difficult to finance and operate schools, churches, libraries, or even inns, restaurants, and other amenities. Southerners were strongly committed to their churches, and some believed in the importance of universities, but all such institutions were far less fully developed than those in the North.

The South's cities were likewise smaller and less developed. Rather than engaging in a broad commerce, they exported little beyond a staple crop, such as cotton or tobacco, and imported only a few necessary supplies and luxuries. Factories—another source of urban growth—were rare because planters invested most of their capital in slaves. A few southerners did invest in iron or tex-

Weak Urban Sector

tiles on a small scale. But the largest southern "industry" was lumbering, and the largest factories made cigars using slave labor.

More decisively, the South was slower than the North to develop a unified market economy and a regional transportation network. Far less money was spent on canals, turnpikes, or railroads. The South had only 26 percent of the nation's railroad mileage in 1850 and, despite concerted efforts, only 35 percent in 1860. As a result, urban growth after 1820 was far less vigorous than in the North, and metropolitan centers were almost nonexistent. In 1860 only 49,000 out of 704,000 South Carolinians lived in towns with 2,500 or more residents. Less than 3 percent of Mississippi's population lived in places of comparable size. The same year the population of Charleston, South Carolina, was only 41,000, that of Richmond, Virginia, 38,000. New Orleans, Louisiana, by far the largest southern city, had only 169,000 residents, and it was being left behind because it was not linked to the national railroad network.

Thus, although the South sold huge amounts of cotton on the international market, its economy at home was semideveloped relative to other sec-

SCHEDULE I.—Free Inhabitants in _Wolf Pitt District_ in the County of _Richmond State_ of _N C_ enumerated by me, on the _5_ day of _Sept_ 1850. _J Dockery_ Ass't Marshal

Dwelling-houses numbered in the order of visitation.	Families numbered in the order of visitation.	The Name of every Person whose usual place of abode on the first day of June, 1850, was in this family.	Age.	Sex.	Color, (white, black, or mulatto.)	Profession, Occupation, or Trade of each Male Person over 15 years of age.	Value of Real Estate owned.	PLACE OF BIRTH. Naming the State, Territory, or Country.	Married within the year.	Attended School within the year.	Persons over 20 y'rs of age who cannot read & write.	Whether deaf and dumb, blind, insane, idiotic, pauper, or convict.
1	2	3	4	5	6	7	8	9	10	11	12	13
		Todd Jackson	2	M	B			N C				1
481	481	Silas Peavy	28	M	M	Farmer		" "				1
		Martha "	26	F				" "				1
		Elizabeth "	3	F	M			" "				
		Frances "	1	F	M			" "				
		Mitchell "	24	M		Farmer		" "				
		Bertha Gates	60	F				Virginia				1
481	482	William Cole	40	M		Farmer	2200	N C				
		Jane "	35	F				N C				
		William "	16	M		Student		" "		1		
		John "	12	M				" "		1		
		Alexander "	10	M				" "		1		
		Elizabeth "	8	F				" "		1		
		Harriet "	6	F				" "				
		Edward "	4	M				" "				
		Frances "	3	F				" "				
		Martha "	1	F				" "				
		William Hicks	28	M		Carpenter		" "				
482	483	John Shortridge	32	M		Superintendant		Rhode Island				
		Mary "	32	F				" "				
		Mary "	10	F				" "		1		
		John "	9	M				" "		1		
		Ann "	4	F				N C				
		Margaret "	2	F				" "				
		Louis "	4	M				" "				
483	484	Duncan McIntyreH	54	M		Schoolteacher	88	" "				
		Emeline "	38	F				S C				
		Mary "	17	F				" "				
		Catherine "	16	F				" "				
		Sarah "	13	F				" "				
		Mary "	10	F				N C				
		Margaret "	8	F				" "				
484	485	Susan Hilliard	45	F				" "				1
		Martha "	22	F				" "				
		Martha Birmingham	21	F				" "				1
		Nancy Ragsdale	21	F				" "				
		Susan "	21	F				" "				
		Miranda Yelverton	17	F	B			" "				
485	486	John Smith	38	M		Shoemaker		" "				
		Nancy "	51	F				" "				
		Judith "	25	F				" "				
		Elizabeth "	18	F				" "				

How do historians know

about the values and ways of life of the South's non-slaveholders? Letters, diaries, and family papers of these people, who generally were not rich or famous, have not been preserved as frequently as the records of the slaveholding elite. Therefore, historians have turned to a wide variety of sources—including travelers' accounts, folklore, and the U.S. Census records—to learn more about them. This page from the manuscript "Population Schedules" of the U. S. census of 1850 supplies information on family structure and a variety of personal characteristics. The manuscript "Census of Agriculture" contains much additional information about the size of each family's farm and the crops grown there.

Photo: North Carolina Division of Archives & History.

tions of the country. Its white people were prospering, but not as rapidly as most residents of the North. There, changes in commerce and industry brought unprecedented advances in productivity, raising the average person's standard of living and widening the range of affordable goods and services. In the South, change was quantitative rather than qualitative. Southern planters continued to use the same farming techniques. They increased their acreage and hoped for continued high demand from foreign customers—but their region remained rural and its internal market undeveloped. Subsistence farmers merely worked harder and hoped to grow a bit more.

FREE SOUTHERNERS: FARMERS, PLANTERS, AND FREE BLACKS

A large majority of white southern families (three-quarters in 1860) owned no slaves. Some lived in towns and ran stores or businesses, but most were yeoman farmers who owned their own land and grew their own food. They were the typical whites, but the social distance between different groups of whites was great. Still greater was the distance between whites and blacks.

Although they were the majority of southern whites, subsistence farmers did not, as a rule, set the direction of the slave society. Normally they occupied a relatively autonomous position within the slavery-based staple-crop economy expanding around them. Independent and motivated by a hearty dose of frontier individualism, they provided for themselves in the traditional way of American farm families, prospering slowly from improvements on their acreage or the settlement of new and better land. This process meant steady progress for thousands of yeomen as the South expanded.

But the lives of most southern yeomen, unlike those of their northern counterparts, had not been transformed by improvements in transportation. Because few railroads penetrated the southern interior, yeomen generally had little contact with the market or the type of progress it could introduce. Families might raise a small surplus to sell for cash

or trade for needed items, but they were remote from large market networks and therefore not particularly concerned about increasing their cash income. Instead, they valued their self-reliance and freedom from others' control. Absorbed in an isolated but demanding rural life, yeomen constituted an important, though often silent, part of southern society. If their rights were threatened, however, they could react strongly.

The yeomen enjoyed a folk culture based on family, church, and community. They spoke with a drawl, and their inflections were reminiscent of their Scottish and Irish backgrounds. Once a year they flocked to religious revivals called protracted meetings or camp meetings, and in between they enjoyed house-raisings, logrollings, quilting bees, and corn-shuckings. Such occasions combined work with fun, offered food in abundance, and usually included liquor. They also provided a fellowship that was especially welcome to isolated rural dwellers.

Folk Culture of the Yeoman

Social conventions imposed more uniformity on women of the yeoman class than on the men. A demanding round of work and family responsibilities shaped their lives in the home. At harvest time yeoman women frequently helped in the fields, and throughout the year the drying, preserving, and preparing of food consumed much of their time. Household tasks continued during frequent pregnancies and the care of small children. Primary nursing and medical care also fell to the mother, who might have a book of remedies to aid her but often relied on family- and folk-wisdom. In some evangelical churches women played respected roles on certain committees, but overwhelmingly the busy life of the yeoman woman was tied to the home.

Among the men there were many who aspired to wealth, eager to join the race for slaves, land, and profits from cotton. Such an individual was a North Carolinian named John F. Flintoff, whose diary reveals that the road to wealth was not always easy. At age eighteen in 1841, Flintoff went to Mississippi to seek his fortune. Like other aspiring yeomen, he worked as an overseer of slaves but often found it impossible to please his employers. At one point he even gave up and returned to North Carolina, where he married and lived in his parents' house, but Flintoff was "impatient to get along in

This illustration from Frederick Law Olmsted's A Journey in the Seaboard Slave States *(1856) suggests the frontier conditions that characterized the lives of many southern yeomen.* North Carolina Farm from *A Journey in the Seaboard States* by Olmsted.

the world," so he tried Louisiana next and then Mississippi again.

For Flintoff, the fertile Gulf region had its disadvantages. "My health has been very bad here," he wrote. "Chills and fever occasionally has hold of me." Routinely, "first rate employment" alternated with "very low wages." Moreover, as a young man working on isolated plantations, Flintoff often felt lonely. Even a revival meeting in 1844 proved "an extremely cold time" with "little warm feeling." His uncle and other employers found fault with his work, and in 1846 Flintoff concluded in despair that "managing negroes and large farms is soul destroying."

A desire to succeed kept him going. At twenty-six, even before he owned any land, Flintoff bought his first slave, "a negro boy 7 years old." Soon he had purchased two more children, the cheapest slaves available. Conscious of his status as a slaveowner, Flintoff resented the low wages he was paid and complained that his uncle offered him "*hand pay*," wages suitable for a day laborer rather than a slaveowner and manager. In 1853, with nine

young slaves and a growing family, Flintoff faced "the most unhappy time of my life." Fired by his uncle, he returned to North Carolina, sold some of his slaves, and purchased 124 acres with help from his in-laws. Flintoff grew corn, wheat, and tobacco and earned extra cash hauling wood in his wagon. By 1860 he owned three horses, twenty-six hogs, ten head of cattle, and several slaves and was paying off his debts. As the Civil War approached, he looked forward to acquiring more land and slaves, freeing his wife from much of the labor of yeoman women, and possibly sending his sons to college. Although Flintoff eventually achieved success, his path had not been easy, and he never became the cotton planter he had aspired to be.

Probably more typical of the southern yeoman was Ferdinand L. Steel, who as a young man moved from North Carolina to Tennessee to work as a hatter and river boatman but eventually took up farming in Mississippi. Steel rose every day at five and worked until sundown. With the help of his family he raised corn, wheat, pork, and vegetables for the family table. Cotton was his cash crop:

like other yeomen he sold five or six bales (about 2,000 pounds) a year to obtain money for sugar, coffee, salt, calico, gunpowder, and a few other store-bought goods.

Steel picked his cotton himself (never exceeding 120 pounds per day, less than many slaves averaged) and complained that cotton cultivation was arduous and time-consuming. The market fluctuated, and if cotton prices fell, a small grower like Steel could be driven into debt and lose his farm. In fact, he wanted to grow less cotton. "We are too weak handed" to manage it, he noted in his diary. "We had better raise small grain and corn and let cotton alone, raise corn and keep out of debt and we will have no necessity of raising cotton."

Steel's life in Mississippi in the 1840s retained much of the flavor of the frontier. He made all the family's shoes; his wife and sister sewed dresses, shirts, and "pantiloons." The Steel women also rendered their own soap and spun and wove cotton into cloth; the men hunted game. House-raisings and corn-shuckings provided entertainment, and Steel doctored his illnesses with boneset tea and other herbs.

The focus of Steel's life was family and religion. The family prayed together every morning and night, and he prayed and studied Scripture for an hour after lunch. Steel joined a temperance society and looked forward to church and camp meetings. "My Faith increases, & I enjoy much of that peace which the world cannot give," he wrote in 1841. Seeking to improve himself and be ready for judgment, Steel borrowed histories, Latin and Greek grammars, and religious books from his church. Eventually he became a traveling Methodist minister. "My life is one of toil," he reflected, "but blessed be God that it is as well with me as it is."

Toil with even less security was the lot of two other groups of free southerners: landless whites and free blacks. A sizable minority of white southern workers—from 25 to 40 percent, depending on the state—were unskilled laborers who owned no land and worked for others in the countryside and towns. Their property consisted of a few household items and some animals—usually pigs—that could feed themselves on the open range. The landless included some immigrants, especially Irish, who did heavy and dangerous work

Landless Whites

such as building railroads and digging ditches. By 1860 immigrants were becoming numerous in a few port cities, such as Savannah and New Orleans.

In the countryside, white farm laborers struggled to become yeomen in the face of low wages or, if they rented, unpredictable market prices for their crops. Some fell into debt and were frequently sued. Others, by scrimping and saving and finding odd jobs, managed to climb into the ranks of yeomen. When James and Nancy Bennitt of North Carolina succeeded in their ten-year struggle to buy land, they decided to avoid the unstable market in cotton; thereafter they raised extra corn and wheat as sources of cash. People like the Bennitts viewed pigs and livestock as a major economic asset; good steady employment was uncertain in a region whose large producers relied on slave labor.

For the nearly quarter-million free blacks in the South in 1860, conditions were generally worse than the yeoman's and often little better than the slave's. The free blacks of the Upper South were usually descendants of men and women emancipated by their owners in the 1780s and 1790s, a period of postrevolutionary idealism that coincided with a decline in tobacco prices. Some made substantial progress in towns or cities, but most lived in rural areas and had few material advantages. They usually did not own land and had to labor in someone else's fields, often beside slaves. By law free blacks could not own a gun, buy liquor, violate curfew, assemble except in church, testify in court, or (throughout the South after 1835) vote. Despite these obstacles, a minority bought land, and others found jobs as artisans, draymen, boatmen, and fishermen. A few prospered and bought slave laborers, but most who owned slaves had purchased their own wives and children (whom they could not free, since laws required newly emancipated blacks to leave their state).

Free Blacks

Farther south, in the cotton and Gulf regions, a large proportion of free blacks were mulattos, the privileged offspring of wealthy planters. Not all planters freed their mixed-race offspring, but those who did often recognized a moral obligation and gave their children good educations and financial backing. In a few cities like New Orleans and Mobile, extensive interracial sex had produced a mulatto population that was recognized as a distinct

The North Carolina planter Duncan Cameron (1776–1853) built this spacious and comfortable farm-house for his bride, Rebecca Bennehan, in 1804. The house, called Fairntosh, is more typical of the average planter's home than the elaborate Greek-revival-style mansions of popular legend.   Library of Congress.

class. These people formed a society of their own and sought a status above slaves and other freedmen, if not equal to that of planters. But outside New Orleans, Mobile, and Charleston, such groups were rare, and most mulattos experienced more disadvantages than benefits from their light skin. (For a more detailed discussion of free blacks during this period, see Chapter 12.)

At the opposite end of the social spectrum from free blacks were slaveholders. As a group they lived well, on incomes that enabled them to enjoy superior housing, food, clothing, and luxuries. But most, like Duncan Cameron, lived in comfortable farmhouses like the one pictured, not on the opulent scale that legend suggests. A few statistics tell the story: 50 percent of southern slaveholders had fewer than five slaves; 72 percent had fewer than ten; 88 percent had fewer than twenty. Thus the average slaveholder was not a wealthy aristocrat but an aspiring farmer, usually a person of humble

Planters

origins, with little formal education and many rough edges to his manner. In fact, he probably had little to distinguish him from a nonslaveholder beyond a degree of wealth and greater ambition.

Consider the Louisiana cotton planter Bennet Barrow, who was neither polished nor unusually coarse. His considerable wealth was new, and he was preoccupied with moneymaking: he worried constantly over his cotton crop, filling his diary with tedious weather reports and gloomy predictions of his yields. Yet Barrow also strove to appear above such worries, and in boom times he grandly cosigned loans for men who later defaulted and left him saddled with debt.

Barrow hunted frequently and had a passion for racing horses and raising hounds. Each year he spent several weeks at the races in New Orleans, where he entered stallions brought from as far away as Tennessee. Barrow could report the loss of a slave without feeling, but emotion broke through his laconic manner when misfortune struck his sporting animals. "Never was a person more unlucky than I am," he mourned. "My favorite pup never lives." His strongest feelings surfaced when his horse Jos Bell—equal to "the best Horse in the South"—"broke down running a mile . . . ruined for Ever." The same day the distraught Barrow gave his field hands a "general Whipping." Barrow was rich, but his wealth had not softened his rough, direct approach to life.

The wealth of the greatest planters gave ambitious men like Barrow something to aspire to. Though most planters lived in spacious, comfortable farmhouses, some did own mansions. Most slaveowners sat down at mealtimes to an abundance of tempting country foods—pork and ham, beef and game, fresh vegetables and fruits, breads and biscuits, cakes and jams—but the sophisticated elite consumed such delights as "gumbo, ducks and olives, *supreme de volaille*, chickens in jelly, oysters, lettuce salad, chocolate cream, jelly cake, claret cup, etc." On formal and business occasions, such as county court days, a traveler in Mississippi would see gentlemen in "black cloth coats, black cravats and satin or embroidered silk waistcoats; all, too, sleek as if just from a barber's hands, and redolent of perfumes." Relations and friends often visited each other for several days or weeks at a time, enjoying good food and good company. Women wore the latest fashions to parties and balls, at which courtship was a major preoccupation. Between social occasions, women and many men kept up their close friendships through constant letter writing.

Slaveholding men dominated society and, especially among the wealthiest and oldest families, justified their dominance through a paternalistic ideology. Instead of stressing

Southern Paternalism

the profitable aspects of commercial agriculture, they focused on *noblesse oblige*, seeing themselves as custodians of the welfare of society as a whole and of the black families who depended on them in particular. The paternalistic planter viewed himself not as an oppressor but as the benevolent guardian of an inferior race. He developed affectionate feelings toward his slaves (as long as they knew their place) and was genuinely shocked at criticism of his behavior.

The letters of Paul Carrington Cameron, North Carolina's largest slaveholder, illustrate this mentality. After a period of sickness among his one thousand North Carolina slaves (he had hundreds more in Alabama and Mississippi), Cameron wrote, "I fear the Negroes have suffered much from the want of proper attention and kindness under this late distemper . . . no love of lucre shall ever induce me to be cruel, or even to make or

These miniatures of Eliza Izard Pinckney and her husband Thomas Pinckney, Jr., were painted in 1801 and 1802. They suggest the comfortable lifestyle and aristocratic manners of the wealthy white slaveholding class.   The Gibbes Museum of Art, Carolina Art Association, Charleston, S.C.

permit to be made any great exposure of their persons at inclement seasons." On another occasion he described to his sister the sense of responsibility he felt: "I cannot better follow the example of our venerated Mother than in doing my duty to her faithful old slaves and their descendants. Do you remember a cold & frosty morning, during her illness, when she said to me 'Paul my son the people ought to be shod' this is ever in my ears, whenever I see any ones shoes in bad order; and in my ears it will be, so long as I am master."

It was comforting to the richest southern planters to see themselves in this way, and slaves—accommodating to the realities of power—encouraged their masters to think their benevolence was appreciated. Paternalism also served as a defense against abolitionist criticism. Still, paternalism affected the manner and not the substance of most planters' behavior. Its softness and warmth were a matter of style, covering harsher assumptions: blacks were inferior, and planters should make money. As talk of paternalistic duties increased, theories about the complete and permanent inferiority of blacks also multiplied.

Even Paul Cameron's benevolence vanished with changed circumstances. After the Civil War, he bristled at African-Americans' efforts to be free and made sweeping economic decisions without regard to their welfare. Writing on Christmas Day 1865, Cameron showed little Christian charity (but a healthy profit motive) when he expressed his desire to get "free . . . of the negro. I am convinced that the people who gets rid of the free negro first will be the first to advance in improved agriculture. Have made no effort to retain any of mine [and] will not attempt a crop beyond the capacity of 30 hands." With that he turned off his land nearly a thousand black agriculturalists, rented his fields to several white farmers, and invested in industry, which he considered more promising economically.

Relations between men and women in the planter class were similarly paternalistic. An upper-class southern woman was typically raised and educated to be the subordinate companion of men. Her proper sphere was home management, not politics or other worldly affairs. In a social system based on the coercion of an entire race, women could not be allowed to challenge society's rules on sexual or racial relations. If she defied or

Elite Women's Role

questioned the status quo, she risked universal condemnation.

Within the domestic circle the husband reigned supreme, and many women were acutely conscious of that authority. "He is master of the house," wrote South Carolina's Mary Boykin Chesnut. "To hear is to obey. . . . All the comfort of my life depends upon his being in a good humor." In a darker mood, Chesnut once observed that "there is no slave . . . like a wife." For the fortunate women whose marriages joined two people of shared tastes and habits, like North Carolina diarist Catherine Devereux Edmondston, the husband's authority weighed lightly or not at all, but many women felt dissatisfaction.

The upper-class southern woman had to clear several barriers in the way of happiness. The right choice of a husband was especially important. With this decision a young woman moved from the rather narrow experience of genteel girlhood into a restrictive lifetime role. After spending her early years within the family circle, a planter's daughter usually attended one of the South's rapidly multiplying academies or boarding schools. There she formed friendships with other girls and received an education that emphasized grammar, composition, penmanship, geography, literature, and languages, but little science and mathematics. As she developed some sense of herself, the young woman typically maintained dutiful and affectionate ties with her parents and entertained suitors whom they approved. But very soon she had to commit herself for life to a man whom she generally had known for only a brief time.

Once married, she ceded to her husband most of her legal rights, became part of his family, and was expected to get along with numerous in-laws during extended visits. Most of the year she was isolated on a large plantation, where she had to learn a host of new duties. Although free from much of the labor of yeoman women, the plantation mistress was not free from care. She had to oversee the cooking and preserving of food, manage the house, supervise care of the children, and attend sick slaves. As a woman, she was forbidden to travel unless accompanied by a man. All these realities were more rigid and confining on the frontier, where isolation was greater and opportunities for social interaction were fewer.

It is not surprising that an intelligent and perceptive young woman sometimes approached marriage with anxiety, for her future depended on the man she chose. Lucy Breckinridge, a wealthy Virginia girl of twenty, sensed how much autonomy she would have to surrender on her wedding day. Thereafter her life would depend on a husband, who, though chivalrous in manner, held the real power and expected to be the center of attention. In her diary she recorded this unvarnished observation on marriage: "If [husbands] care for their wives at all it is only as a sort of servant, a being made to attend to their comforts and to keep the children out of the way. . . . A woman's life after she is married, unless there is an immense amount of love, is nothing but suffering and hard work."

Lucy loved young children but knew that childbearing often involved grief and sorrow. On learning of a relative's death, she wrote, "It is a happy release for her, for her married life has been a long term of suffering. She has been married about seven years and had five children." Such fertility was not too unusual, for in 1840 the birthrate for white southern women in their childbearing years was almost 30 percent higher than the national average. At the beginning of the nineteenth century, the average southern white woman could expect to bear eight children; by 1860 the figure had decreased only to six, and one or more miscarriages were likely among so many pregnancies. For those women who wanted to plan their families, methods of contraception were uncertain. Doctors had few remedies for infection or irritation of the reproductive tract, and the high birthrate took a toll on women's health. Complications of childbirth were a major cause of death, occurring twice as often in the hot, moist South as in the Northeast. Moreover, a mother had to endure the loss of many of the infants she bore. Infant mortality in the first year of life exceeded 10 percent and remained high during early childhood. In the South in 1860 almost five out of ten children died before age five, and in South Carolina more than six in ten failed to reach age twenty.

Slavery was another source of problems that white women had to endure but were not supposed to notice. "Violations of the moral law . . . made mulattoes as common as blackberries," protested a woman in Georgia, but wives had to play "the ostrich game." "A magnate who runs a hideous black harem," wrote Mrs. Chesnut, "under the same roof with his lovely white wife, and his beautiful accomplished daughters . . . poses as the model of all human virtues to these poor women whom God and the laws have given him. From the height of

his awful majesty, he scolds and thunders at them, as if he never did wrong in his life."

In the early 1800s, some southern women, especially Quakers, had spoken out against slavery. Although most white women did not criticize "the peculiar institution," they often viewed it less as a system and more as a series of relationships among individuals. Perhaps sensing this, southern men tolerated no discussion by women of the slavery issue. In the 1840s and 1850s, as northern and international criticism of slavery increased, southern men published a barrage of articles stressing that women should restrict their concerns to the home. A writer in the *Southern Literary Messenger* bemoaned "these days of Women's Rights," and the *Southern Quarterly Review* declared, "The proper place for a woman is at home. One of her highest privileges, to be politically merged in the existence of her husband." Thomas Dew, one of the nineteenth century's first proslavery theorists, advised that "women are precisely what the men make them," and another writer promoted "affection, reverence, and duty" as a woman's proper attitudes.

But southern women were beginning to chafe at their customary exclusion from financial matters. A study of women in Petersburg, Virginia, a large tobacco-manufacturing town, revealed behavior amounting to an implicit criticism of the institution of marriage and the loss of autonomy it entailed. Over several decades before 1860, the proportion of women who never married, or did not remarry after the death of a spouse, grew to exceed 33 percent. Likewise the number of women who worked for wages, controlled their own property, and even ran millinery or dressmaking businesses increased. In managing property, these women benefited from southern legal reforms—beginning with Mississippi's Married Women's Property Act of 1839—that had not been intended to increase female independence. To offset business panics and recessions, the law gave married women some property rights in order to protect families from ruin caused by the husband's indebtedness. But some women seized the resulting opportunity. In the countryside southern women had fewer options, but Petersburg's women were seeking to use the talents they had and the education they had gained.

For a large category of southern men and women, freedom was wholly denied and education in any form was not allowed. Male and female, slaves were expected to accept bondage and ignorance as their condition.

SLAVES AND THE CONDITIONS OF THEIR SERVITUDE

For African-Americans, slavery was a curse that brought no blessings other than the strengths they developed to survive it. Slaves knew a life of poverty, coercion, toil, heartbreak, and resentment. They had few hopes that were not denied; often they had to bear separation from their loved ones; and they were despised as an inferior race. That they endured and found loyalty and strength among themselves is a tribute to their courage, but it could not make up for a life without freedom or opportunity.

Southern slaves enjoyed few material comforts beyond the bare necessities. Although they generally had enough to eat, their diet was plain and

Slaves' Diet, Clothing, and Housing

monotonous. The basic ration was cornmeal, fat pork, molasses, and occasionally coffee. Many masters allowed slaves to tend gardens, which provided the variety and extra nutrition of greens and sweet potatoes, and some could fish and hunt. "It was nothin' fine," recalled one woman, "but it was good plain eatin' what filled you up."* Most slaveowners were innocent of the charge that they starved their slaves, but there is considerable evidence that slaves often suffered the effects of beriberi, pellagra, and other dietary-deficiency diseases.

Clothing too was plain, coarse, and inexpensive. Few slaves received more than one or two changes of clothing for hot and cold seasons and one blanket each winter. Children of both sexes ran naked in hot weather and wore long cotton shirts in winter. When big enough to go to the fields, boys received a work shirt and a pair of

---

*Accounts by ex-slaves are quoted from *The American Slave: A Composite Autobiography*, edited by George P. Rawick (Westport, Conn.: Greenwood Press, First Reprint Edition 1972, Second Reprint Edition 1974), from materials gathered by the Federal Writers' Project and originally published in 1941. The spelling in these accounts has been standardized.

breeches, and girls a simple dress. On many plantations slave women made their own clothing of osnaburg, a coarse cotton fabric that whites called "nigger cloth." The minority who were allowed to earn a little money by doing extra work often bought additional clothing. Many slaves had to go without shoes until December, even as far north as Virginia. The shoes they received were frequent objects of complaint—uncomfortable brass-toed brogans or stiff wraparounds made from leather tanned on the plantation.

Summer and winter, slaves typically lived in small one-room cabins, possibly with a window opening but no glass. Some of the richer plantations provided more substantial houses, some of which survive today, but the average slave lived in crude accommodations. Logs chinked with mud formed the walls; dirt was the only floor; and a wattle-and-daub or stone chimney vented the fireplace, which provided both heat and light. Bedding consisted of heaps of straw, straw mattresses, or wooden bedframes lashed to the walls with rope. A few crude pieces of furniture and cooking utensils completed the furnishings. The gravest drawback of slave cabins, however, was not lack of comfort but their unhealthfulness. Each small cabin housed one or two entire families. Crowding and lack of sanitation fostered the spread of infection and contagious diseases. Many slaves (and whites) carried worms and intestinal parasites picked up from feces or soil. Lice were widespread in both races, and flies and other insects spread such virulent diseases as typhoid fever, malaria, and dysentery.

Hard work was the central fact of the slaves' existence. The long hours and large work gangs that characterized Gulf Coast cotton districts were

Slaves' Work Routines

more reminiscent of factories than of the small-scale isolated work patterns of slaves in the eighteenth-century Chesapeake. Overseers rang the morning bell before dawn, so early that some slaves remembered being "afraid to start work for fear that they would cover the cotton plants with dirt because they couldn't see clearly." And, as one woman recalled when interviewed by workers in the Federal Writers' Project of the 1930s, "it was way after sundown 'fore they could stop that field work. Then they had to hustle to finish their night work [such as watering livestock or cleaning cotton] in time for supper, or go to bed without it."

Coercion was the essence of slavery. To enforce their will, masters relied on whips and instruments like this pronged collar to inflict pain or restrict the slaves' movements. A slave woman in nineteenth-century New Orleans had to wear the collar shown as punishment for running away. The painting suggests that such sights were not unusual on the city's streets.   Painting: Historic New Orleans Collection; slave collar: Massachusetts Historical Society.

Except in urban settings and on some rice plantations, where slaves were assigned daily tasks to complete at their own pace, working "from sun to sun" became universal in the South. Long hours and hard work were at the heart of the advantage that slave labor represented for slaveowners. As one planter put it, slaves were the best labor because "you could command them and *make* them do what was right." White workers, by contrast, couldn't be *driven;* "they wouldn't stand it." Slaves who cultivated tobacco in the Upper South worked long hours picking the sticky, sometimes noxious, tobacco leaves under a harsh discipline that could not be imposed on white labor. The slaves had to "sucker" the plants—pinch off secondary shoots to increase the size of the leaves—and remove tobacco worms by hand. According to many former slaves, workers who overlooked worms were forced to eat them. No white laborers in the South endured such treatment.

Profit also took precedence over paternalistic "protection" of women: slave women did heavy field work, often as much as the men and even during pregnancy. Old people—of whom there were few—were kept busy caring for young children, doing light chores, or carding, ginning, and spinning cotton. Children had to gather kindling, carry water to the fields, or sweep the yard. But slaves had a variety of ways to keep from being worked to death. It was impossible to supervise every slave every minute, and slaves slacked off when they were not being watched. Thus travelers frequently described lackadaisical slaves who seemed "to go through the motions of labor without putting strength into them," and owners complained that slaves "never would lay out their strength freely. . . . It was impossible to make them do it." Stubborn misunderstanding and literal-mindedness were another defense. One exasperated Virginia planter voiced his irritation (and the racism nurtured by slavery) when he said, "You can make a nigger work, *but you cannot make him think.*"

Of course slaves could not slow their pace too much, because the owner enjoyed a monopoly on force and violence. Whites throughout the South

Physical and Mental Abuse of Slaves

believed that Negroes "can't be governed except with the whip." One South Carolinian frankly explained to a northern journalist that he had whipped his slaves occasionally, "say once a fortnight; . . . the Negroes knew they would be whipped if they didn't behave themselves, and the fear of the lash kept them in good order." Evidence suggests that whippings were less frequent on small farms than on large plantations, but the testimony of former slaves indicates that even most small farmers plied the lash. These beatings symbolized authority to the master and tyranny to the slaves, who made them a benchmark for evaluating a master. In the words of former slaves, a good owner was one who did not "whip too much," whereas a bad owner "whipped till he's bloodied you and blistered you."

As these reports suggest, terrible abuses could and did occur. The master wielded virtually absolute authority on his plantation, and courts did not recognize the word of a chattel. Pregnant women were whipped, and there were burnings, mutilations, tortures, and murders. Yet physical cruelty may have been less prevalent in the United States than in other slaveholding parts of the New World. In sugar-growing and mining regions of the Western Hemisphere in the 1800s, slaves were regarded as an expendable resource to be replaced after seven years. Treatment was so poor that death rates were high and the heavily male slave population rapidly shrank in size. In the United States, by contrast, the slave population experienced a steady natural increase as births exceeded deaths and each generation grew larger.

The worst evil of American slavery was not its physical cruelty but the nature of slavery itself: coercion, lack of freedom, belonging to another person, virtually no hope for change. Recalling their days in bondage, some former slaves emphasized the physical abuse—those were "bullwhip days" to one woman. Another woman, asked what she thought of slavery, retorted that the black slave "got [his] back cut in slavery time, didn't he?" But their comments focused on the tyranny of whipping as much as the pain. A woman named Delia Garlic cut to the core when she said, "It's bad to belong to folks that own you soul an' body. I could tell you 'bout it all day, but even then you couldn't

guess the awfulness of it." A man named Thomas Lewis put it this way: "There was no such thing as being good to slaves. Many people were better than others, but a slave belonged to his master and there was no way to get out of it."

As these comments reveal, the great majority of American slaves retained their mental independence and self-respect despite their bondage. They hated their oppression and, contrary to some whites' perceptions, were not grateful to their oppressors. They had to be subservient and speak honeyed words to their masters, but they talked quite differently among themselves. The evidence of their resistant attitudes comes from their actions and their own life stories.

Former slaves reported some warm feelings between masters and slaves, but the prevailing picture was one of antagonism and resistance.

Slaves' Attitudes Toward Whites

Slaves mistrusted kindness from whites and saw the self-interest in it. One woman called her mistress "a mighty good somebody to belong to" but explained that the woman was kind "'cause she was raisin' us to work for her." A man recalled that his owners took good care of their slaves, "and Grandma Maria say, 'Why shouldn't they—it was their money.'" Christmas presents of clothing from the master did not mean anything, observed another, "'cause he was going to [buy] that anyhow."

Slaves also saw their owners as people who used human beings as beasts of burden. One man observed that his master "fed us reg'lar on good, 'stantial food, just like you'd tend to your horse, if you had a real good one." Another recalled his master eyeing the slave children and saying, "'That one will be worth a thousand dollars.' . . . You see, it was just like raisin' young mules."

Slaves were alert to the thousand daily signs of their degraded status. One man recalled the general rule that slaves ate cornbread and owners ate biscuits. If blacks did get biscuits, "the flour that we made the biscuits out of was the third-grade shorts." A woman reported that on her plantation "Old Master hunted a heap, but us never did get none of what he brought in." "Us catch lots of 'possums," said another, but "the white folks ate 'em. Our mouths would water for some of that 'possum, but it wasn't often they let us have none."

If the owner took his slaves' garden produce to town and sold it for them, the slaves suspected him of pocketing part of the profits.

Suspicion and resentment often grew into hatred. According to a former slave from Virginia, white people treated blacks "so mean that all the slaves prayed God to punish their cruel masters." When a yellow-fever epidemic struck in 1852, many slaves saw it as God's retribution. As late as the 1930s an elderly ex-slave named Minnie Fulkes cherished the conviction that God was going to punish white people for their cruelty to blacks. She described the whippings that her mother had had to endure and then exclaimed, "Lord, Lord, I hate white people and the flood waters goin' to drown some more." A young slave girl who had suffered abuse as a house servant admitted that she took vengeance on her mistress when the woman had a stroke. Instead of fanning the mistress to keep flies away, the young slave struck her in the face with the fan whenever they were alone. "I done that woman bad," the slave confessed, but "she was so mean to me."

The bitterness between blacks and whites was vividly expressed by a former slave named Savilla Burrell, who visited her former master on his deathbed long after the Civil War. Sitting beside him, she reflected on the lines that "sorrow had plowed on that old face and I remembered he'd been a captain on horseback in the war. It come into my remembrance the song of Moses: 'the Lord had triumphed glorily and the horse and his rider have been throwed into the sea.'" She felt sympathy for a dying man, but she also felt satisfaction at God's revenge.

On the plantation, of course, slaves had to keep such thoughts to themselves. Often they expressed one feeling to whites, another within their own race and culture.

SLAVE CULTURE AND EVERYDAY LIFE

The resource that enabled slaves to maintain such defiance was their culture: a body of beliefs and values born of their past and their present and of the fellowship of their own community. It was not possible for slaves to change their world, but by drawing strength from their culture they could resist their condition and struggle on against it.

Slave culture changed significantly after the turn of the century. Between 1790 and 1808, when Congress banned further importation of slaves, there was a rush to import more Africans. After that, the proportion of native-born blacks rose steadily, reaching 96 percent in 1840 and almost 100 percent in 1860. (For this reason many blacks can trace their American ancestry back farther than many white Americans can.) Meanwhile, more and more slaves adopted Christianity as pure African culture faded and an African-American culture matured.

Influence of African Culture

African influences remained strong, for African practices and beliefs reminded the slaves that they were and ought to be different from their oppressors and thus encouraged them to resist. The most visible features of African culture were the slaves' appearance and forms of recreation. Some slave men plaited their hair into rows and fancy designs; slave women often wore their hair "in string"—tied in small bunches secured by a string or piece of cloth. A few men and many women wrapped their heads in kerchiefs of the styles and colors of West Africa.

For entertainment slaves made musical instruments with carved motifs that resembled African stringed instruments. Their drumming and dancing clearly followed African patterns; whites marveled at them. One visitor to Georgia in the 1860s described a ritual dance of African origin: "A ring of singers is formed. . . . They then utter a kind of melodious chant, which gradually increases in strength, and in noise, until it fairly shakes the house, and it can be heard for a long distance." This observer also noted the agility of the dancers and the African call-and-response pattern in their chanting.

Many slaves continued to see and believe in spirits. Whites, too, believed in ghosts, but the slaves' belief resembled the African concept of the living dead—the idea that deceased relatives visit the earth for many years until the process of dying is complete. Slaves also practiced conjuration, voodoo, and quasi-magical root medicine. By 1860 the most notable conjurers and root doctors were re-

Percentage of African-Americans Born in the Colonies or the United States

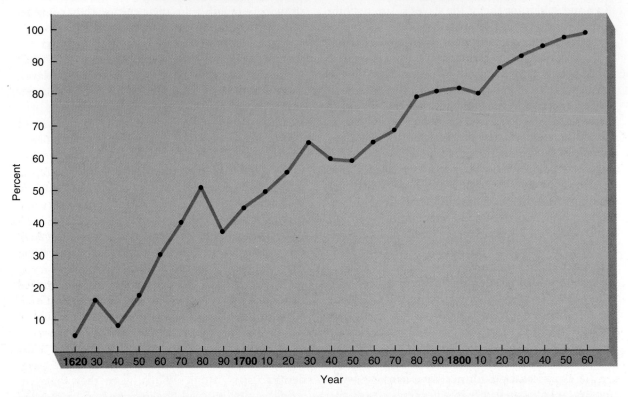

Percentage of Slave Population Native Born.   *The North American slave population increased through natural reproduction. That fact, plus Congress' closing of the international slave trade in 1808, insured that by 1860 virtually all African-Americans had been born in the United States.*

puted to live in South Carolina, Georgia, Louisiana, and other isolated coastal areas of heavy slave importation.

These cultural survivals provided slaves with a sense of their separate past. Black achievement in music and dance was so exceptional that some whites became aware that the slave community was a different world and that they did not "know" their slaves. Conjuration and folklore also directly fed resistance; slaves could cast a spell or direct the power of a hand (a bag of articles belonging to the person to be conjured) against the master. Not all masters felt confident enough to dismiss such a threat.

Slaves fashioned Christianity into an instrument of support and resistance. Theirs was a religion of justice, quite unlike that of the propaganda

Slaves' Religion

their masters pushed at them. "You ought to have heard that preachin'," said one man. "'Obey your master and mistress, don't steal chickens and eggs and meat,' but nary a word about havin' a soul to save." The slaves believed that Jesus cared about their souls and their plight. They rejected the idea that in heaven whites would have "the colored folks . . . there to wait on 'em." Instead, the slaveholders would be "broilin' in hell for their sin" when God's justice came. "These people can't beat up us people and jump up on a bed and close their eyes and die and expect to go to heaven," said one ex-slave. "God is punishin' some of them ol' suckers and their children right now," added a woman, "for the way they used to treat us poor colored folks."

For slaves, Christianity was a religion of personal and group salvation. Devout men and women worshiped and prayed every day, "in the field or by the side of the road," or in special "prayer grounds" such as a "twisted thick-rooted muscadine bush" that afforded privacy. Beyond seeking personal guidance, the slaves prayed for deliverance. Some waited "until the overseer got behind a hill" and then laid down their hoes and called on God to free them. Others held fervent secret prayer meetings that lasted far into the night. Many slaves nurtured an unshakable belief that God would end their bondage. "It was the plans of God to free us," as one man asserted. This faith—and the joy and emotional release that accompanied worship—sustained blacks.

Enslaved African-Americans also developed a sense of racial identity. Their experience taught them that whites despised their race. As one ex-slave put it, white people "have been and are now and always will be against the Negro." Even "the best white woman that ever broke bread wasn't much," said another, " 'cause they all hated [us]." Blacks naturally drew together, helping each other in danger, need, and resistance. "We never told on each other," one woman declared. Although some slaves did betray others, former slaves were virtually unanimous in denouncing those who were disloyal to the group or sought personal advantage through allegiance to whites.

Of course, different jobs, talents, and circumstances created variations in status among slaves. But most slaves did not encounter a class system within the black community. Only one-quarter of all slaves lived on plantations of fifty or more blacks, so few knew a wide chasm between exalted house servants and lowly field hands. Many slaves did both housework and field work, depending on their age and the season, and this arrangement helped create unity rather than division.

The main source of support for individuals was the family. Slave families faced severe dangers. At any moment the master could sell a husband or wife, give a slave child away

Slaves' Family Life

as a wedding present, or die in debt, forcing a division of his property. Many families were broken up in such ways. Others were uprooted in the trans-Appalachian expansion of the South, which caused the forced migration or sale of hundreds of thousands of slaves, often without regard to family ties. When the Union Army registered thousands of black marriages in Mississippi and Louisiana in 1864 and 1865, fully 25 percent of the men over forty reported that they had been forcibly separated from a previous wife. A similar proportion of former slaves later recalled that slavery had destroyed one of their marriages.

But this did not mean that slave families could not exist. American slaves clung tenaciously to the personal relationships that gave meaning to life; some families, like the five-generation group in the photograph from Beaufort, South Carolina, did manage to stay together. Although American law did not protect slave families, masters permitted them; in fact, slaveowners expected slaves to form families and have children. As a result, even along the rapidly expanding edge of the cotton kingdom, where the effects of the slave trade would have been most visible, there was a normal ratio of men to women, young to old.

Following African kinship taboos, African-Americans avoided marriage between cousins (commonplace among aristocratic slaveowners). Adapting the West African custom of polygyny to American circumstances, they did not condemn unwed mothers but did expect a young woman to enter a monogamous relationship after one pregnancy, if not before. By naming their children after relatives of past generations, African-Americans emphasized their family histories. If they chose to bear the surname of a slaveowner, it was often not that of their current master but of the owner under whom their family had begun in America.

Slaves abhorred interference in their family lives. Some of their strongest protests sought to prevent the breakup of a family. Indeed, some individuals refused to accept such separations and struggled for years to maintain or re-establish contact. Rape was a horror for both men and women. Some husbands faced death rather than permit their wives to be sexually abused, and the women sometimes fought back. In other cases slaves seethed with anger at the injustice but could do nothing except soothe each other with human sympathy and understanding. Significantly, they condemned the guilty party, not the victim.

Slave men and women followed sex roles familiar to whites and similar to West African customs. After work in the fields was done, both men

This photograph of five generations of a slave family, taken in Beaufort, South Carolina, in 1862, is silent but powerful testimony to the importance that enslaved African-Americans placed on their ever-threatened family ties. Library of Congress.

Sex Roles in Slavery

and women took part in activities. Men's activities focused on traditional "outdoor" tasks and women did "indoor" work. Men hunted and fished for the family stewpot, fashioned rough furniture, and repaired implements; women cooked, mended, and cleaned house. It is clear, too, that slave families resembled white families in that African-American men held a respected place in their homes. They did not dominate their wives in a manner similar to white husbands, but it would be misleading to say that slave women enjoyed equality in sex roles and family life. The larger truth is that all enslaved people, men and women, were often deprived of the opportunity to provide for or protect their families. Under the pressures of bondage men and women had to share parental and household responsibilities. At any time, each might have to stand in for the other and assume extra duties. Sim-

ilarly, uncles, aunts, and grandparents sometimes raised the children of those who had been sold away.

Work routines frequently promoted among slave women close associations that heightened their sense of sisterhood. On plantations young girls worked together as house servants. Nursing mothers got together to feed and care for their children, and adults worked together at tasks like soap making and stitching quilts like the one prepared for the annual visit of a Texas bishop. Old women gathered to spin thread or supervise a nursery. Female slaves thus spent significant portions of their lives as participants in a group of women, an experience that strengthened their ties to each other.

Slave marriage ceremonies were usually brief, often involving jumping over a broomstick in the master's presence. But partners "stuck lots closer then," in one woman's words. "[When] they marries they stay married," said another. When hus-

In addition to the heavy labor required on southern plantations, slaves also performed work of fine craftsmanship in furniture making, needlework, and other areas. This dining-room corner cupboard is walnut veneer on pine and cedar and was built around 1840. The quilt, emblazoned with chalice cups to celebrate the annual visit of an Anglican bishop, was made around 1860. Both are from Texas. Cupboard: Courtesy of the Witte Museum and the San Antonio Museum Association, San Antonio, Texas; quilt: The American Museum in Britain, photo courtesy of The Museum of the Confederacy.

bands and wives lived on neighboring plantations, visits on Wednesday and Saturday nights included big dinners of welcome and celebration. Christmas was a similarly joyous time "'cause husbands is coming home and families is getting united again."

Slaves brought to their efforts at resistance the same common sense, determination, and practicality that characterized their family lives. American slavery produced some fearless and implacable revolutionaries. Gabriel Prosser's conspiracy was apparently known to more than a thousand slaves when it was discovered in 1800, just before it was put into action (see pages 229–230). A similar conspiracy in Charleston in 1822, led by a free black named Denmark Vesey, involved many of the prominent whites' most trusted slaves. And the most famous rebel of all, Nat Turner, rose in violence in Southampton County, Virginia, in 1831.

Resistance to Slavery

The son of an African woman who passionately hated her enslavement, Nat was a precocious child who learned to read when he was very young. Encouraged by his first owner to study the Bible, he enjoyed certain privileges but also endured hard work and changes of masters. His father, who successfully escaped to freedom, inspired him as an example of defiance. Eventually young Nat became a preacher with a reputation for eloquence among whites as well as blacks. He also developed a tendency toward mysticism and became increasingly withdrawn. After nurturing his plan for several years, Turner led a band of rebels from farm to farm in the predawn darkness of August 22, 1831. The group severed limbs and crushed skulls with axes or killed their victims with guns. Before they were stopped, Nat Turner and his followers had slaughtered sixty whites of both sexes and all ages. Nat and perhaps two hundred African-Americans, including many innocent victims of marauding whites, lost their lives as a result of the rebellion.

But most slave resistance was not violent, for the odds against revolution were especially poor in North America. Whites greatly outnumbered the slaves. Indeed, the South had the highest ratio of whites to blacks in the hemisphere and, because plantations were relatively small, whites could thoroughly supervise the slaves' activities. There was thus literal truth to one slave's remark that "the white man was the slave's jail." Moreover, the South lacked vital geographic and demographic features that had aided revolution in Latin America. The land offered no jungles and few mountain fastnesses to which rebels could flee. Furthermore, compared with those in Latin America, southern slave importations were neither large nor prolonged. The South therefore lacked a preponderance of young male slaves. Nor were its military forces weak and overtaxed like those of many Latin American nations and colonies.

Thus the scales weighed heavily against revolution, and the slaves knew it. Consequently they directed their energies toward creating the means of survival and resistance within slavery. A desperate slave could run away for good, but it was more common for slaves to run off temporarily to hide in the woods. There they were close to friends and allies who could help them escape capture in an area they knew well. Every day that a slave "lay out" in this way, the master lost a day's labor. Most owners chose not to mount an exhaustive search and instead sent word that the slave's grievances would be redressed. The runaway would then return to bargain with the master. Most owners let the matter pass, for, as the owner of a valuable cook put it, they were "glad to get her back."

Other modes of resistance had the same object: to resist but survive under bondage. Appropriating food (stealing, in the master's eyes) was so common that even whites sang humorous songs about it. Blacks were also alert to the attitudes of individual whites and learned to ingratiate themselves and play off one white person against another. Field hands frequently tested a new overseer to intimidate him or win more favorable working conditions. Some blacks fought with patrollers, and others argued with overseers and even resorted to physical violence to deter or resist beatings. The harshest masters were the most strongly resisted. "Good masters had good slaves 'cause they treated 'em good." But "where the old master was mean an' ornery," his slaves were ornery too.

HARMONY AND TENSION IN A SLAVE SOCIETY

As the 1800s advanced, slavery impinged on laws and customs, individual values, and—increasingly—every aspect of southern politics. Legal restrictions on slaves, in effect since the seventeenth century, steadily increased. In all things, from their workaday movements to Sunday worship, slaves fell under the supervision of whites. State courts held that a slave "has no civil right" and could not even hold property "except at the will and pleasure of his master." In response to revolts, legislators tightened the legal straitjacket: after the Nat Turner insurrection of 1831, for example, they prohibited owners from teaching their slaves to read. As the sectional crisis developed, fears of slave revolt grew and restrictions on slaves increased accordingly.

Nonslaveholders were also required by law to help maintain the slave system. All white male citizens were legally obligated to ride in patrols to discourage slave movements at night. Whites in strategic positions, such as ship captains and harbor masters, were required to scrutinize the papers of African-Americans who might be attempting to escape bondage. Urban residents who did not supervise their domestic slaves as closely as planters did were subject to criticism for endangering the community. And the South's few manufacturers, instead of receiving encouragement to expand their enterprises, often felt pressure to substitute slave for free labor.

Slavery had a deep effect on southern values precisely because it was the main determinant of wealth in the South. Ownership of slaves guaranteed the labor to produce cotton and other crops on a large scale—labor otherwise unavailable in rural society. Slaves were therefore vital to the acquisition of a fortune. Beyond that, they were a commodity and an investment, much like gold; people bought them on speculation, hoping for a steady rise in their value. In fact, throughout southern society, slaveholding indicated overall wealth with remarkable precision. Variations in wealth from county to county corresponded very closely to vari-

Slavery as the Basis of Wealth and Social Standing

TO HAVE AND TO HOLD the said *Slave Louisa* unto the said purchaser *his* heirs and assigns forever; the said Vendor —hereby binding *himself* and *his* heirs forever to warrant and defend the *Slave Louisa* herein conveyed, against all legal claims and demands whatever. The said Vendor moreover transfer unto the said purchaser all the rights and actions of warranty to which *she is* entitled, against all the former proprietors of the *Slave Louisa* herein conveyed, hereby subrogating said purchaser to the said rights and actions to be by *him* enjoyed and exercised in the same manner as they might have been by the said Vendor .

ations in slaveholding; important economic enterprises not based on slavery were too rare to have an effect on the pattern.

Slaveholding was the main determinant of a white man's social position, and white women derived high status from their husbands' or fathers' ownership of slaves. Wealth in slaves also translated into political power: a solid majority of political officeholders were slaveholders, and the most powerful were usually large-scale slaveholders. Lawyers and newspaper editors were sometimes influential, but they did not hold independent positions in the economy or society. Dependent on planters for business and support, they served planters' interests and reflected their outlook.

Slavery's influence spread throughout the social system until even the values and mores of nonslaveholders bore its imprint. For one thing, the availability of slave labor tended to devalue free labor. Where strenuous work under another's supervision was reserved for an enslaved race, few free people relished working like a slave. Nonslaveholders preferred to work for themselves, and those who had to sell their labor tended to resent or reject tasks that seemed degrading. This kind of thinking engendered an aristocratic value system ill-suited to a newly established democracy.

The values of the aristocrat—lineage, privilege, pride, and refinement of person and manner—gained a considerable foothold among the masses. Some of those qualities were in short supply, however, in the recently settled portions of the cotton kingdom, where frontier values of courage and self-reliance modified the aristocratic ideal. Independence

Aristocratic Values and Frontier Individualism

A bill of sale documents that this slave woman, Louisa, was owned by the young child whom she holds on her lap. In the future her life would be subject to his wishes and decisions. Missouri Historical Society.

and defense of one's honor became highly valued traits for planter and frontier farmer alike.

Fights and even duels over personal slights were not uncommon in southern communities. Instead of gradually disappearing as it did in the North, the *code duello*, which required men to defend their honor in duels, hung on in the South and gained acceptance throughout the society. In North Carolina in 1851 a wealthy planter named Samuel Fleming responded to a series of disputes with the rising lawyer William Waightstill Avery by "cowhiding" (whipping) him on a public street. According to the code, Avery had two choices: to redeem his honor violently or to brand himself a coward through inaction. Three weeks later Avery shot Fleming dead at point-blank range during a session of Burke County Superior Court, with Judge William Battle and numerous spectators looking on. A jury later took only ten minutes to find Avery not guilty, and the spectators gave him a standing ovation. Some people, including Judge Battle, were troubled by the victory of the unwritten code over the law, but most white males seemed satisfied.

Other aristocratic values of the planter class were less acceptable to the average citizen. Planters believed they were better than other people. In their pride, they expected not only to wield power but to receive special treatment. By the 1850s, some planters openly rejected the democratic creed, vilifying Thomas Jefferson for his statement that all men were equal.

The belief in their own superiority which shaped the outlook of the southern elite for generations was never acceptable to the individualistic members of the yeoman class. Independent and proud, yeomen resisted any infringement of their rights. They believed they were as good as anyone, and many belonged to evangelical faiths that exalted values of simplicity and otherworldliness that were alien to the planters' love of wealth. They were conscious, too, that they lived in a nation in which democratic ideals were gaining strength. Thus occasional conflicts erupted between aristocratic pretensions and democratic zeal. As Mary Boykin Chesnut pointed out, a wealthy planter who sought public office could not announce his status too haughtily. She described the plight of Colonel John S. Preston, a South Carolinian with political ambitions. Preston, a perfect aristocrat, carried his high-flown manners too far; he refused to make the necessary gestures of respect toward

the average voter—mingling with the crowd, exchanging jokes and compliments. His highest aspiration, political leadership, thus eluded him. The voters would not accept him.

Class tensions found significant expression in the western parts of the seaboard states during the 1820s and 1830s. There yeoman farmers and other citizens resented their under-representation in state legislatures, the corruption in government, and the undemocratic control over local government. After vigorous debate, the reformers won most of their battles. Five more recently settled southern states— Alabama, Mississippi, Tennessee, Arkansas, and Texas—adopted white manhood suffrage and other reforms, including popular election of governors, legislative apportionment based on white population only, and locally chosen county government. Kentucky enacted all these measures except for elected county governments. Georgia, Florida, and Louisiana were not far behind, and reformers won significant concessions in Maryland and made some headway in North Carolina. Only South Carolina and Virginia effectively defended property qualifications for office, legislative malapportionment, appointment of county officials, and selection of the governor by lawmakers. The formal structure of government thus became more democratic than many planters wished.

Movements for Electoral Reform

Slaveowners knew that a more open governmental structure could permit troubling issues to arise. In Virginia, nonslaveholding westerners raised a basic challenge to the slave system in 1832, a year after the Nat Turner rebellion. Advocates of gradual abolition forced a two-week legislative debate on slavery, arguing that the institution was injurious to the state and inherently dangerous. When the House of Delegates finally voted, the motion favoring abolition lost by just 73 to 58. This was to be the last public debate on slavery in the antebellum South.

Given such tensions, it was perhaps remarkable that slaveholders and nonslaveholders did not experience more overt conflict. Why were class confrontations among whites so infrequent? Historians who have considered this question have given many answers. One of the most important factors was race. The South's racial ideology stressed whites' superiority to blacks and established race, not class, as the social dividing line. Thus racism inflated the status of all whites and gave them a common interest. In a rural society, furthermore, family bonds and kinship ties are valued, and some of the poor nonslaveholding whites were related to the rich new planters. The experience of frontier living, in which all were starting out together, must also have created a relatively informal, egalitarian atmosphere.

The cotton boom itself had relieved tension by bringing opportunity to thousands of whites. The "Old South" was in fact a new and mobile society, in which many people had risen in status by acquiring land or slaves, and far more were moving about geographically. Even in cotton-rich Alabama in the 1850s, fewer than half the richest families in a typical county belonged to its elite ten years later. Most had not died or lost their wealth; they had merely moved on to some new state. This constant mobility meant that southern society had not settled into a rigid, unchanging pattern.

The place yeoman farmers occupied in society, relative to slaveholders, was also critical. Before the Civil War their social and economic position normally allowed them to pursue unhindered their independent lifestyle. Marginally involved in the market economy, most could maintain their independence free from economic pressure and competition. They lived in a rural and uncrowded region: travel was difficult, and daily life usually took place within the family unit. Consequently, yeomen lived their lives with little reference to, and no interference from, slaveholders. As long as they could follow their values and aspirations, yeomen had no grievance.

Likewise, slaveholders could pursue their goals quite independently of yeomen. Planters farmed for the market but also for themselves. The complementary growing patterns of corn and cotton allowed planters to raise food for their animals and laborers without reducing cotton production: from spring through December, cotton and corn never needed attention at the same time. Thus the planter did not depend on the nonslaveholder as a producer of food crops, and yeomen needed nothing from the planters. In politics, too, national economic issues, such as the tariff, that affected planters rarely had much meaning to yeomen because they were not enmeshed in the market economy.

But suppression of dissent also played a significant and increasing role. After 1830 white southerners who criticized the slave system out of moral conviction or class resentment were intimidated, attacked, or legally prosecuted. (Some, like James Birney, were driven from the South in the 1830s and went north to join the antislavery movement. Two sisters from Charleston, Angelina and Sarah Grimke, became leading advocates of both abolition and women's rights—see pages 378–379.) Southern cities impounded abolitionist literature and sought to bar antislavery influences. Intellectuals developed elaborate justifications for slavery as newspapers railed at northern antislavery agitation. By the 1850s the defense of slavery's interests dominated public discussion, and all groups in society felt pressure to uphold the slave system. Politicians vied with each other to lead an increasingly aggressive defense of the South's peculiar institution. The slavery issue exerted an ever-more-powerful influence on southern politics and society.

Still, there were signs that the relative lack of conflict between slaveholders and nonslaveholders was coming to an end. As cotton lands filled up, nonslaveholders saw their opportunities beginning to narrow; meanwhile, wealthy planters enjoyed expanding profits.

Hardening of Class Lines

The risks of entering cotton production were becoming too great and the cost of slaves too high for many yeomen to rise in society. From 1830 to 1860 the percentage of white southern families holding slaves declined steadily from 36 to 25 percent. At the same time, the monetary gap between the classes was widening. Although nonslaveholders were becoming more prosperous, slaveowners' wealth was increasing much faster. And although slaveowners accounted for a smaller portion of the population in 1860 than in 1830, their share of the South's agricultural wealth remained at between 90 and 95 percent. In fact, the average slaveholder was almost fourteen times as rich as the average nonslaveholder.

Urban artisans and mechanics felt the pinch acutely. Their numbers were few, their place in society was hardly recognized, and in bad times they were often the first to lose work. Moreover, they faced stiff competition from urban slaves, whose masters wanted to hire them out to practice trades. White workers in Charleston, Wilmington, and elsewhere staged protests demanding that economic competition from slaves be forbidden but they were ignored—the powerful slaveowners would not tolerate interference with their property or the income they derived from it. But the angry protests of white workers resulted in harsh restrictions on *free* African-American workers and craftsmen, who had no powerful allies to defend their interests. In Charleston on the eve of the Civil War, many successful free blacks actually felt compelled to leave the city for fear of being re-enslaved.

Pre-Civil War politics reflected these tensions. Anticipating the prospect of a war to defend slavery, slaveowners expressed growing fear about the loyalty of nonslaveholders. Schemes to widen slave ownership were discussed, including reopening the African slave trade. In North Carolina, a prolonged and increasingly bitter controversy over the combination of high taxes on land and low taxes on slaves erupted, and a class-conscious nonslaveholder named Hinton R. Helper denounced the slave system. Convinced that slavery had impoverished many whites and retarded the whole region, Helper attacked the institution in *The Impending Crisis*, published in New York in 1857. Discerning planters knew that such fiery controversies could easily erupt in every southern state.

But for the moment slaveowners stood secure. They occupied from 50 to 85 percent of the seats in state legislatures and a similarly high percentage of the South's congressional seats. In addition to their near-monopoly on political office, they had established their point of view in all the other major social institutions. Professors who criticized slavery had been dismissed from colleges and universities; schoolbooks that contained "unsound" ideas had been replaced. And almost all the Methodist and Baptist clergy, some of whom had criticized slavery in the 1790s, had given up preaching against the institution. In fact, except for a few obscure persons of conscience, southern clergy had become slavery's most vocal defenders.

The South was a diverse society that embraced many contradictions, but the coercive influence of slavery was increasingly pressing it into a single mold. The reality of the region's rapid growth and mobility contrasted with its increasing ideological emphasis on conservatism and stability. Simmering resentments generated by slavery's oppression gave the lie to the benevolent image of bondage put forth in paternalist ideology. Despite the rhetoric of white supremacy, the values of democratic yeomen and aristocratic planters clashed. Yet leading southerners ignored evidence of diversity, preferring to submerge these contradictions in visions of a stable, slaveholding social order.

Slavery's extent and influence in the South had grown markedly since 1800. Powerful groups dependent on slavery worked tirelessly to promote unity and eradicate dissent. The potential for conflict linked to slavery persisted, but few southerners saw it. As the influence of the peculiar institution spread through the region, the evolving South took on the aspect of a conservative and traditional society wedded to slavery. The social order as southerners knew it seemed to be stable, with threats to the status quo under control.

In the nation generally, however, society was anything but stable. As market forces and the rise of industry produced a more diverse population, social and economic change became a central characteristic of the northern economy and society. The American people were changing, and the currents of change would eventually affect the South.

SUGGESTIONS FOR FURTHER READING

Southern Society

Edward L. Ayers, *Vengeance and Justice* (1984); W. J. Cash, *The Mind of the South* (1941); William J. Cooper, *The South and the Politics of Slavery, 1828–1856* (1978); Clement Eaton, *The Growth of Southern Civilization, 1790–1860* (1961); Clement Eaton, *Freedom of Thought in the Old South* (1940); William W. Freehling, *Prelude to Civil War* (1965); Eugene D. Genovese, *The Political Economy of Slavery* (1965); Peter Kolchin, *Unfree Labor: American Slavery and Russian Serfdom* (1987); Donald G. Mathews, *Religion in the Old South* (1977); Robert McColley, *Slavery and Jeffersonian Virginia* (1964); James Hebron Moore, *The Emergence of the Cotton Kingdom in the Old Southwest: Mississippi, 1770–1860* (1987); Frederick Law Olmsted, *The Slave States*, ed. Harvey Wish (1959); Frederick F. Siegel, *The Roots of Southern Distinctiveness: Tobacco and Society in Danville, Virginia, 1780–1865* (1987); Charles S. Sydnor, *The Development of Southern Sectionalism, 1819–1848* (1948); Larry E. Tise, *Proslavery* (1987); Ralph A. Wooster, *Politicians, Planters, and Plain Folk* (1975); Ralph A. Wooster, *The People in Power* (1969); Gavin Wright, *The Political Economy of the Cotton South* (1978); Bertram Wyatt-Brown, *Southern Honor* (1982).

Slaveholders and Nonslaveholders

Edward L. Ayers and John C. Willis, eds., *The Edge of the South* (1991); Bennet H. Barrow, *Plantation Life in the Florida Parishes of Louisiana, as Reflected in the Diary of Bennet H. Barrow*, ed. Edwin Adams Davis (1943); Ira Berlin, *Slaves Without Masters* (1974); Randolph B. Campbell, "Intermittent Slave Ownership:

Texas as a Text Case," *Journal of Southern History* 30, no. 1 (February 1985): 15–30; Joan E. Cashin, *A Family Venture* (1991); Bill Cecil-Fronsman, *The Common Whites* (1992); Everett Dick, *The Dixie Frontier* (1948); Clement Eaton, *The Mind of the Old South* (1967); Drew Faust, *James Henry Hammond and the Old South* (1982); Drew Faust, *A Sacred Circle: The Dilemma of the Intellectual in the Old South* (1977); John Hope Franklin, *The Militant South, 1800–1861* (1956); Eugene D. Genovese, "Yeoman Farmers in a Slaveholders' Democracy," *Agricultural History* 49 (April 1975): 331–342; John Inscoe, *Mountain Masters* (1989); Michael P. Johnson and James L. Roark, *Black Masters* (1984); Robert E. May, *John A. Quitman* (1985); Robert Manson Myers, ed., *The Children of Pride* (1972); James Oakes, *The Ruling Race* (1982); Frank L. Owsley, *Plain Folk of the Old South* (1949); Loren Schweninger, *Black Property Owners in the South, 1790–1915* (1990); J. Mills Thornton III, *Politics and Power in a Slave Society: Alabama, 1800–1860* (1978).

Southern Women

Carol Bleser, *In Joy and in Sorrow* (1990); Carol Bleser, *The Hammonds of Redcliffe* (1981); Jane Turner Censer, *North Carolina Planters and Their Children, 1800–1860* (1984); Catherine Clinton, *The Plantation Mistress* (1982); Elizabeth Fox-Genovese, *Within the Plantation Household* (1988); Jean E. Friedman, *The Enclosed Garden* (1985); Harriet Jacobs, *Incidents in the Life of a Slave Girl*, ed. Jean Fagan Yellin (1987); Jacqueline Jones, *Labor of Love, Labor of Sorrow* (1985); Frances Anne Kemble, *Journal of a Residence on a Georgia Plantation in 1838–1839* (1863); Suzanne Lebsock, *Free Women of Petersburg* (1984); Sally McMillen, *Motherhood in the Old South* (1990); Elisabeth Muhlenfeld, *Mary Boykin Chesnut* (1981); Mary D. Robertson, ed., *Lucy Breckinridge of Grove Hill* (1979); Ann Firor Scott, *The Southern Lady* (1970); Deborah G. White, *Arn'n't I a Woman?* (1985); Virginia Ingraham Burr, ed., *The Secret Eye* (1990).

Conditions of Slavery

Kenneth F. Kiple and Virginia H. Kiple, "Black Tongue and Black Men," *Journal of Southern History* 43 (August 1977): 411–428; Ronald L. Lewis, *Coal, Iron, and Slaves* (1979); Richard G. Lowe and Randolph B. Campbell, "The Slave Breeding Hypothesis," *Journal of Southern History* 42 (August 1976): 400–412; Leslie Howard Owens, *This Species of Property* (1976); Willie Lee Rose, ed., *A Documentary History of Slavery in North America* (1976); Todd L. Savitt, *Medicine and Slavery* (1978); Kenneth M. Stampp, *The Peculiar Institution* (1956); Robert S. Starobin, *Industrial Slavery in the Old South* (1970); Michael Tadman, *Speculators and Slaves* (1989).

Slave Culture and Resistance

Herbert Aptheker, *American Negro Slave Revolts* (1943); John W. Blassingame, *The Slave Community* (1979); Judith Wragg Chase, *Afro-American Art and Craft* (1971); Dena J. Epstein, *Sinful Tunes and Spirituals* (1977); Paul D. Escott, *Slavery Remembered: A Record of Twentieth-Century Slave Narratives* (1979); Eric Foner, ed., *Nat Turner* (1971); Eugene D. Genovese, *From Rebellion to Revolution* (1979); Eugene D. Genovese, *Roll, Jordan, Roll* (1974); Herbert G. Gutman, *The Black Family in Slavery and Freedom, 1750–1925* (1976); Vincent Harding, *There Is a River* (1981); Charles Joyner, *Down by the Riverside* (1984); Lawrence W. Levine, *Black Culture and Black Consciousness* (1977); Stephen B. Oates, *The Fires of Jubilee* (1975); Albert J. Raboteau, *Slave Religion* (1978); Robert S. Starobin, *Denmark Vesey* (1970); Sterling Stuckey, *Slave Culture* (1987).

12

Among Strangers and Friends: People and Communities, 1800–1860

"I HOPE THAT THINGS will get better," Anna Maria Klinger wrote from New York to her family in Wurttemberg, Germany, in March 1849. "For it's always like that, no one really likes it at first, and especially if you are so lonely and forlorn in a foreign land like I am, no friends or relatives around." Twenty-eight-year-old Anna Maria had crossed the Atlantic alone among strangers. Her religious faith kept her going. "The dear Lord is my shield and refuge," she wrote home.

It had taken 105 days to reach America, including seven weeks docked in Plymouth, England, while the ship was fitted. Three other young women who were migrating to America proved unsuitable as traveling companions. They "started behaving so badly" with young men, Anna Maria wrote her parents, that "I got annoyed because I couldn't stand such loose behavior."

Her luck improved in New York. She quickly found a job at $4 a month as a domestic servant with a German family. New York was so large, she wrote her parents, that she could not walk around it in one day. She counted nearly two hundred churches and re-ported that there were "about 4,000 German residents alone." There were actually fifty-six thousand Germans in the city at the time.

Anna Maria Klinger had left Germany during the political and economic crises of 1848. She was the first in her immediate family to emigrate, though two cousins had come to America some years before. Soon after arriving in New York she met her future husband, Franz Schano, a deserter from the Prussian army. Over the next decade she and Schano brought five of her siblings to New York: Babett, Gottlieb, Katharina, Daniel, and finally in 1858 the youngest, Rosina.

Work was not always easy to find—Franz, a stonecutter, was unemployed for a time—but teenagers like Babett and Katharina could always find work as servants. Babett, who now called herself Barbara, came in 1852 and adjusted quickly. "Here you don't go out of the house without a hat or a bonnet," she wrote her parents, "you don't go out on the *Striet* [street] with your head bare, they all look at you and you'd be laughed at. If I were to run into you, none of you would recognize me with my hat on." Barbara found work as a servant, first for an English family then for a French family, and quickly repaid her sister for her fare to America.

Within a year of Barbara's arrival, Franz wrote home that she had taken up with a young man whom "we could see from the start would not be to her advantage." They "tried everything to dissuade her, but to no use." She soon gave birth to a baby son, "for whom she has a father all right but no husband, and when we noticed that she was expecting, we urged him to marry her but then he said he had never promised to marry her and he wouldn't ever marry her." He did provide a cash settlement of $80 to Barbara.

Anna Maria, assisted by Franz, guided the family, seeming to keep them together by sheer force of will. But the siblings' lives eventually diverged. In 1855 Anna Maria and Franz moved to Albany, New York, where Franz opened his own business and they bought a house for $1,000. But in 1860 Franz died of consumption. Thirteen months later Anna Maria married Adam Plantz, a Prussian-born blacksmith; he too died of consumption, only five weeks after the wedding. Anna Maria now had a son and stepson to support. She feared losing her home, but she had been left enough money to prosper in the 1870s. As Anna Maria became more preoccupied with providing for her son and stepson, Gottlieb took over the role of head of the family.

When the Schanos moved to Albany, Barbara went west, leaving her son with Anna Maria and Franz. Within a year she wrote that she was in Indiana, married and living in a log cabin on forty acres of land. She wanted her son, but it was too long a distance to travel; she also complained that living in rural Indiana was boring. In the 1860s, a widow, she remarried and raised seven "Christian children" on her Indiana farm.

Through Gottlieb, the siblings stayed in touch for most of their lives. The brothers settled in Albany near Anna Maria and rode the roller coaster of the economy, prospering in good times, unemployed in hard times. Gottlieb ran a saloon, lost it, then worked in a piano factory and later as a wood carver. Daniel worked as a teamster. Eventually, they lost touch with their other sisters. When Katharina married a prosperous New York grocer after her first husband died, they no longer heard from her. Rosina, too, was lost for a long time; she

had moved to Canada. Years later they heard she was living in New York and had "a whole brood of children" with her tinsmith husband.

The family remained central in the lives of most of the Klingers. Despite jealousies and conflicts, they remained close, helped each other, and regularly sent money back to their parents.

The Klingers represented both the old values of traditional culture and the new values of the market system. Anna Maria worked hard, saved money, and found success in Albany even though widowhood twice threatened her security. Barbara lived a hard-scrabble life and was an unwed mother. She re-established her life amid strangers seven hundred miles from New York, eventually finding peace in a German-American rural community. Katharina worked hard but spent most of her income on herself, saving very little; her siblings complained of her selfishness. Even after years in the United States, the Klinger siblings were only partially Americanized. They always lived in German neighborhoods, and they socialized almost exclusively with family and fellow immigrants from Wurttemberg. Only rarely did they interact with anyone who was not German.

The Klinger family's experiences were similar to those of millions of other Americans. From the 1830s through the 1850s, millions of immigrants arrived on America's shores and hundreds of thousands of native-born Americans moved from farm to town and from town to city. The American population grew so much—largely through natural increase in the first two decades of the century, then through immigration—that most Americans were newcomers in their neighborhoods and on the job. The populations of the largest cities numbered in the hundreds of thousands and were highly diverse ethnically, religiously, and racially. Within large cities and in the countryside, whole districts became enclaves of ethnic groups. In hiring themselves out to build transportation and industry, immigrants reshaped American culture.

As economic opportunity increasingly attracted immigrants and energized the native-born, the American people grew apart. In colonial days, the appearance of strangers in villages had been rare, but in the nineteenth century strangers were commonplace. People were on the move, and one

• *Important Events* •

1810	New York surpasses Philadelphia in population		**1835–42**	Seminoles resist removal in Second Seminole War
1819	Congress passes "civilization act" to assimilate Native Americans		**1837**	Boston employs paid policemen
1823	Catharine and Mary Beecher establish Hartford Female Seminary		**1837–48**	Horace Mann heads the Massachusetts Board of Education
1824	President Monroe proposes removal of Indians		**1841–47**	Brook Farm combines spirituality, work, and play in a utopian rural community
1827	*Freedom's Journal*, first African-American newspaper, appears		**1842**	Knickerbocker baseball club formed
1830	Joseph Smith founds Mormon Church Congress passes Removal Act		**1845**	Start of the Irish potato famine
1830s–50s	Urban riots commonplace		**1846–47**	Mormon trek to the Great Salt Lake
1831	Cherokees turn to courts to defend treaty rights in *Cherokee Nation* v. *Georgia*		**1847–57**	Peak period of immigration before the Civil War
1831–38	Indian tribes resettled in West in Trail of Tears		**1848**	Abortive revolutions in German states

year's frontier became the next year's settled town. Farm families felt a loss of cohesiveness, and some experimented with forming new utopian agrarian communities. The new Mormon church combined spirituality with a strong sense of community, and its members eventually found an agrarian haven in Utah Territory.

The nature of community was changing in the United States. Civic and public institutions had to offer services, like education, that had once been provided by the family. In the nation's cities, opulent mansions rose within sight of notorious slums, and both wealth and poverty reached extremes previously unknown in agrarian America. The private sphere of the family also experienced change. With the growth of commerce and industry, the home began to lose its function as a workplace. Among the middle and upper classes, the home became woman's domain, though working-class women found no such refuge. At the same time, birth control was more widely practiced and families shrank in size.

Free blacks and Native Americans were at a particular disadvantage in a society that considered their very presence disturbing. Free people of color were second-class citizens at best, struggling to better their lot against overwhelming legal and racial barriers. Indians, forced to abandon their lands for resettlement beyond the Mississippi River, fared even worse.

Many Americans were uncomfortable with the new direction of American life. Antipathy toward immigrants was common among native-born Americans, who feared competition for jobs. Riots and violence became commonplace in cities. African-Americans fought unceasingly for equality, and tribal peoples tried unsuccessfully to resist forced removal. In a society growing ever more diverse and complex, conflict became common.

Although the United States remained a predominantly agricultural country, the traditional economic and social arrangements were yielding to the influence of the market economy, urban growth, and immigration. This process would persist throughout the nineteenth century. Though it intensified in the final three decades of the century, the growth of an industrial, urban, and pluralist society had begun before the Civil War.

COUNTRY LIFE

Rural life changed significantly in the first half of the nineteenth century. Within a generation many frontier settlements became sources rather than destinations of migrants. The villages of western New York State had lured the sons and daughters of New England in the first two decades of the century; in the 1820s and 1830s, after the best land was settled and the Erie Canal opened, young people moved from New York villages to the new frontier in the Old Northwest. Later, those Ohio and Michigan towns and farms would watch their young people move farther west. Their counterparts in the Upper South went to Illinois and Ohio, and those farther south settled the Gulf states.

For all the romance of moving westward, many longed for a sense of community. In *Domestic Manners of the Americans* (1832) Frances Trollope, an English writer, described her visit to a farm family near Cincinnati. The family produced all their necessities except coffee, tea, and whiskey, which they acquired by sending butter and chickens to market. But until other settlers moved near them, they lacked the human contact that a community provides. For their inexpensive land and self-sufficiency they paid the price of isolation and loneliness. "'Tis strange to us to see company," observed the mother. "I expect the sun may rise and set a hundred times before I shall see another human that does not belong to the family."

Although most farm families lived in isolation, they did find community in the village. The farm village, with its churches, post office, general store, and tavern, was the center of rural life—the farmers' link with religion, politics, and the outside world. But rural social life was not limited to trips to the village; families gathered on one another's farms to accomplish as a community what they could not manage individually. Barn raisings regularly brought people together. In preparation, the farmer and an itinerant carpenter built a platform and cut beams, posts, and joists. When the neighbors arrived by buggy and wagon on the appointed day, they constructed the walls and raised them into position. After the roof was erected, everyone celebrated with a communal meal and sometimes with singing, dancing, and games. They might

Farm Communities

compete in foot races, wrestling, or marksmanship, and on occasion they raced horses. Similar gatherings took place at harvest time and on special occasions.

Women in particular sought to escape rural isolation. Men had frequent opportunities to meet at general stores, weekly markets, and taverns, and for hunting and fishing. Some women also attended market, but they more typically met at after-church dinners, prayer meetings, bible-study groups, sewing and corn-husking bees, and preparations for marriages and baptisms. These were occasions to exchange experiences, thoughts, and spiritual support, and to swap letters, books, and news.

Irene Hardy, who grew up in rural southwestern Ohio in the 1840s, left a record of the gatherings she attended as a girl. Most vivid in her memory fifty years later were the apple bees, such as the one featured in *Harper's Weekly* in 1859, at which neighbors gathered to make apple butter or preserves. "Usually invitations were sent about by word of mouth," Hardy recalled. "Married folks came and worked all day or afternoon." A dinner feast followed, for which the visiting women made biscuits, vegetables, and coffee. After cleaning up, "the old folks went home to send their young ones for their share of work and fun." The elders gossiped; the youngsters joked and teased each other and flirted. "Then came supper, apple and pumpkin pies, cider, doughnuts, cakes, cold chicken and turkey," Hardy wrote, "after which games, 'Forfeits,' 'Building a Bridge,' 'Snatchability,' even 'Blind Man's Bluff' and 'Pussy Wants a Corner.'"

Traditional country bees had their town counterparts. Fredrika Bremer, a Swedish visitor to the United States, described a sewing bee in Cambridge, Massachusetts, in 1849, at which neighborhood women made clothes for "a family who had lost all their clothing by fire." Yet town bees were not the all-day family affairs typical of the countryside, and when the Hardy family moved to the town of Eaton, Irene missed the country gatherings. Life was changing: the families of Eaton seldom held bees, and they purchased most of their goods at the store. They were wage earners and consumers, and the market economy shaped their daily lives. Many felt a loss of autonomy.

Americans were increasingly conscious of such changes. Some turned to utopian experiments in an effort to find an antidote to the market economy

Harper's Weekly, *November 26, 1859, printed an engraving of an apple bee. As Irene Hardy recalled, men and women and children gathered at such all-day work parties.*   Library of Congress.

and the untamed growth of large urban communities and an opportunity to restore tradition and social cohesion. In the religious ferment of the Second Great Awakening (see pages 229–230), people reacted more favorably to new religious communities, whatever their philosophy. Some turned to utopian experiments in an effort to restore order and regularity in their daily lives and to enjoy a cooperative rather than competitive environment. Virtually all of the utopian experiments offered communal living and nontraditional work, family and gender roles.

The Shakers, named for the way they danced at worship services, undertook one of the earliest utopian experiments. Founder Ann Lee imported this offshoot of the Quakers to America in 1774. While living **Shakers** in England, she had experienced a vision foretelling Jesus's second coming in America and urging her to go there. The Shakers believed that the end of the world was near and that sin entered the world through sexual intercourse. They considered ex-

isting churches too worldly and viewed the Shaker family as the instrument of salvation.

After the death of Mother Ann Lee in 1784, the Shakers turned to communal living to fulfill their mission. In 1787 they "gathered in" at New Lebanon, New York, to live and work communally; other colonies soon followed. At its peak, between 1820 and 1860, the sect had about six thousand members and twenty settlements in eight states; it was the largest and most permanent of the utopian experiments. Shaker communities emphasized agriculture and hand crafts; most managed to become self-sufficient and profitable enterprises. Shaker furniture became famous for its simplicity, excellent construction, and beauty of design.

Though economically conservative, the Shakers were social radicals. They abolished individual families; each colony was one large family. They also gave women new prospects for spiritual leadership. The Shaker ministry was headed by a woman, Lucy Wright, during its period of greatest growth. The sect's practice of celibacy, however, led inevitably to its demise. Unable to perpetuate themselves naturally, the remaining Shaker colonies are dying out in the twentieth century.

By far the most successful communitarian group was the Church of Jesus Christ of Latter-day Saints, known as the Mormons. Joseph Smith, a young farmer in western New York, reported in 1827—a time of religious ferment in northern New England and western New York—that he had been visited by the angel Moroni, who gave him a set of gold plates engraved with divine revelation in an ancient language. The young charismatic Smith and his followers established headquarters in Ohio, but they were persecuted there and in Illinois and Missouri because of their claims of continuous divine revelation and their practice of allowing men to have several wives at once. The Mormons trekked across the continent in 1846 and 1847 to found a New Zion in the Great Salt Lake Valley. There, under Brigham Young, head of the Twelve Apostles (their governing body), they established a cohesive community of Saints—a heaven on earth.

Mormon Community of Saints

Religious conviction fortified the Mormons to withstand persecution and economic hardship. The church offered success and community in this world and the next to anyone who would join them, regardless of background. Indeed, many of their recruits were poor, footloose, and uneducated. They also held out a hand of fellowship to those who rejected existing churches.

In Utah the Mormons distributed agricultural land according to family size. An extensive irrigation system, constructed by men who contributed their labor in proportion to the quantity of land they received and the amount of water they expected to use, transformed the arid valley into a rich oasis. As the colony developed, the church elders came to control water, trade, industry, and even the territorial government of Utah.

Not all utopian communities were founded by religious sects. In 1825 Robert Owen, a wealthy Scottish industrialist, attempted to found a socialist utopia in New Harmony, Indiana. According to his plan, its nine hundred members were to exchange their labor for goods at a communal store. Handicrafts (hat and boot making) flourished at New Harmony, but its textile mill—the economic base of the community—failed after Owen gave it to the community to run. The turnover in membership was too high for the community to develop cohesion, and by 1827 the experiment had ended.

More successful were the New Englanders who lived and worked at the Brook Farm cooperative in West Roxbury, Massachusetts, which was depicted in Josiah Wolcott's idealized painting in 1844. Inspired by transcendentalism—the philosophy that the physical world is secondary to the spiritual realm, which human beings can know only by ignoring custom and received ideas and relying on reason and intuition—Brook Farm's members rejected materialism for a rural communal life combining spirituality, manual labor, intellectual growth, and play. Founded in 1841 by the Unitarian minister George Ripley, a literary critic and friend of Ralph Waldo Emerson, Brook Farm attracted not only farmers and craftsmen but also teachers and writers, among them the novelist Nathaniel Hawthorne. Indeed, the fame of Brook Farm rested on the intellectual achievements of its members. Its school drew students from outside the community, and its residents contributed regularly to the *Dial*, the leading transcendentalist journal. In 1845 Brook Farm's hundred members organized themselves into model phalanxes (working-living units) in keeping with the philosophy of the French utopian Charles Fourier. Rigid regimentation replaced individualism, and membership dropped. After a disastrous fire in 1846, the experiment collapsed in 1847.

Brook Farm

Though short-lived, Brook Farm played a significant role in the flowering of a national literature. During these years Hawthorne, Emerson, and Margaret Fuller, the *Dial*'s editor, joined Henry David Thoreau, James Fenimore Cooper, Herman Melville, and others in creating what is known today as the American Renaissance. In its philosophical intensity and moral idealism, their work was both distinctively American and an outgrowth of the European romantic movement. Their themes were universal, their settings and character American. Cooper, for instance, used the frontier as a backdrop, and Melville wrote of great spiritual quests as seafaring adventures.

The essayist Ralph Waldo Emerson was the prime mover of the American Renaissance and a pillar of the transcendental movement. Emerson had followed his father and grandfather into the ministry but quit his Boston Unitarian pulpit in 1831. After a two-year sojourn in Europe, he returned to lecture and write, preaching individualism and self-reliance. "We live in succession, in division, in parts, in particles," Emerson wrote. "We see the world piece by piece, as the sun, the moon, the animal, the tree; but the whole, of which these are the shining parts, is the soul." Intuitive experience of God is attainable, according to Emerson, because "the Highest dwells" within every individual in the form of the "Over-soul." What gave Emerson's writings force was his simple, direct prose. Beginning with his first book *Nature* (1836) and his noted Phi Beta Kappa talk at Harvard "The American Scholar" (1837), Emerson explored human nature and American culture. Widely admired, he influenced Thoreau, Fuller, Hawthorne, and other members of Brook Farm.

Utopian communities can be seen as attempts to recapture the cohesiveness of traditional agricultural and artisan life in reaction to the competitive pressures of the market economy and urbanization. Utopians resembled Puritan perfectionists; like the Separatists of seventeenth-century New England (see page 52), they sought to begin anew in their own colonies.

CITY LIFE

The transportation revolution and the expansion of commerce and manufacturing caused the populations of American cities to grow geometrically between 1800 and 1860, especially in the North. The nation's population increased during this period from 5 million to 31 million. Meanwhile settlement spread westward, and small rural settlements became towns. In 1800 the nation had only 33 towns with 2,500 or more people and only 3 with more than 25,000. By 1860, 392 towns exceeded 2,500 residents, 35 had more than 25,000, and 9 exceeded 100,000 (see maps, p. 338).

In the Northeast, the percentage of people living in urban areas grew from 9 to 35 percent between 1800 and 1860. Most of this growth occurred in communities located along **Urban Growth** the new transportation routes, where lively commerce created new opportunities. Kingston, New York, located ninety miles north of New York City on the Hudson River, is an example. The Delaware and Hudson Canal, which extended south from the Hudson valley to the coal fields of Pennsylvania, transformed Kingston from a sleepy farm village of 1,000 in the 1820s to an urban center of more than 10,000 in 1850.

Some cities became great metropolitan centers. By 1810, New York City had overtaken Philadelphia as the nation's most populous city and major port and commercial center. Baltimore and New Orleans dominated the South, and San Francisco was the leading West Coast city. In the Midwest, the new lake cities (Chicago, Detroit, and Cleveland) began to overtake the frontier river cities (Cincinnati, Louisville, and Pittsburgh) founded a generation earlier. The largest cities of the North belonged to a nationwide urban network linked by canals, roads, and railroads (see Chapter 10).

New York City became the nation's premier metropolis during these years, growing from 60,500 in 1800 to over 800,000 in 1860. Across the East River, Brooklyn tripled in **New York City** size between 1850 and 1860, becoming the nation's third-largest city with a population of over 260,000. More than 1 million people lived in New York City and Brooklyn. Many were just passing through; the majority would not stay ten years. Although contemporary depictions of New York appear almost pastoral, the city's energy and aromas of sweat, horse dung, and garbage would make twentieth-century cities seem sanitized in comparison. An immigrant port city, mostly Irish and German by the 1850s, New York City teemed with people.

New York City had literally burst its boundaries in the 1820s. Up to that time New Yorkers could still regard the city as a village—not because they knew most of its 150,000 or so inhabitants but because they could walk from one end of the city to the other in an hour. Until the 1820s nearly all New Yorkers had lived within two miles of city hall. In 1825, 14th Street had been the city's northern boundary. By 1860, 400,000 people lived above that divide, and 42nd Street was the city's northern limit. Gone were the cow and horse pastures, kitchen gardens, and orchards of the eighteenth century. George Templeton Strong, a New York lawyer, recorded in his diary in 1856 that he had attended a party at a Judge Hoffman's "in thirty-seventh!!!—it seems but the other day that thirty-seventh Street was an imaginary line running through a rural district and grazed over by cows." It was mass transit that made it possible for cities to expand. Horse-drawn buses appeared in New York in 1827, and the Harlem Railroad, completed

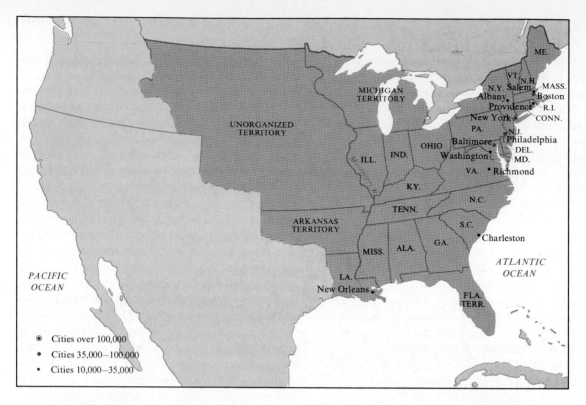

Cities over 100,000
Cities 35,000—100,000
Cities 10,000—35,000

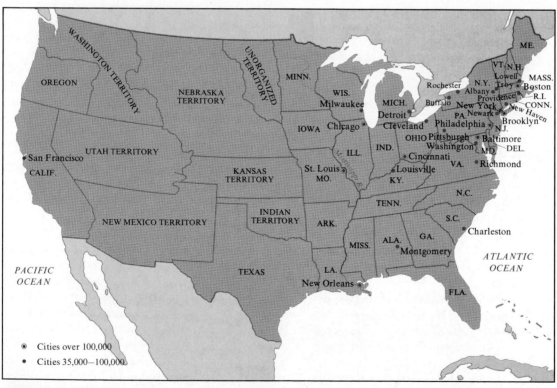

Cities over 100,000
Cities 35,000—100,000

Major American Cities in 1820 and 1860 *The number of Americans who lived in cities increased rapidly between 1820 and 1860, and the number of large cities grew as well. In 1860, each of nine cities had more than one hundred thousand people.*

in 1832, ran the length of Manhattan. By the 1850s all big cities had horse-drawn streetcars.

Strong, like other upper-class New Yorkers, found the density and diversity of the city repugnant. He especially disliked mixing with the masses on the city railroad. In "the choky, hot railroad car," he gagged on the "stale, sickly odors from sweaty Irishmen in their shirt sleeves." He felt repelled by German-Jewish shop clerks and "fat old women, with dirty-nosed babies." Strong's prejudices were conditioned by snobbery and social change, yet by modern standards early nineteenth-century cities were undeniably disorderly, unsafe, and unhealthy. Expansion occurred so rapidly that few cities could handle the problems it brought. For example, migrants from rural areas were accustomed to relieving themselves outside and throwing refuse in any vacant area. In the city, such waste smelled, spread disease, and polluted water. New York City partially solved the problem in the 1840s by abandoning wells in favor of reservoir water piped into buildings and outdoor fountains. In some districts, scavengers and refuse collectors carted away garbage and human waste, but in much of the city it just rotted on the ground. Only one-quarter of New York City's streets had sewers by 1857.

New York and other cities lacked adequate taxing power to provide services for all. The best the city could do was to assess the adjoining property for the cost of sewers, street paving, and water mains. Thus the spread of new services and basic sanitation depended on residents' ability or willingness to pay. As a result, those most in need of services typically got them last. Another solution was to charter private companies to sell basic services. This worked well with gas service. Baltimore first chartered a private gas company in 1816; New York did so in 1842; by midcentury every major city would be lit by a private gas supplier. The private sector, however, failed to supply the water the cities needed. Private firms lacked the capital

The Lackawanna Valley (1855) by George Inness. Hired by the Lackawanna Railroad to paint a railroad scene, Inness blended landscape and machine into an organic whole. American industrialism, Inness seemed to say, belonged to the landscape; it would neither overpower nor obliterate the land. Gift of Mrs. Huttleston Rogers, © National Gallery of Art, Washington, D.C.

to build adequate systems, and they laid pipe only in commercial and well-to-do residential areas, ignoring the poor. As cities grew, water service did not keep pace. Eventually city governments had to take over.

The civic service that had the greatest influence on the nature of American life was the provision of public or common schools. In 1800 there

Horace Mann and Public Schools
___

were no public schools outside New England; by 1860 every state offered some public education. Massachusetts, which had taken the lead in education since Puritan times, again led in expansion of schooling under Horace Mann, secretary of the state board of education from 1837 to 1848. Massachusetts established a minimum school term of six months, formalized the training of teachers, and emphasized secular subjects and applied skills rather than religious training. In the process, common school teaching became a woman's profession. "Females govern with less resort to physical force," Mann asserted, "and exert a more kindly, humanizing and refining influence upon the dispositions and manners of their pupils."

Horace Mann was an evangelist for public education and school reform; his preaching on behalf of free state-sponsored education changed schooling throughout the nation. "If we do not prepare children to become good citizens," Mann argued, "if we do not develop their capacities, . . . imbue their hearts with the love of truth and duty, and a reverence for all things sacred and holy, then our republic must go down to destruction." The abolition of ignorance, according to Mann, would end misery, crime, and suffering. "The only sphere . . . left open for our patriotism," he wrote, "is the improvement of our children—not the few, but the many; not a part of them but all." Mann and others were responding to the changes wrought by the market economy, urbanization, and immigration. The typical city dweller was a newcomer, whether from abroad or from the country. The new public schools would take the children of this nation of strangers and inculcate them with shared values.

In laying the foundation for free public schools, Mann also broadened the scope of education. Schooling had previously focused on literacy, religious training, and discipline. Thus most parents were indifferent about whether their children continued their schooling. Under Mann's leadership, the school curriculum became more secular and more appropriate for future clerks, farmers, and workers. Students studied geography, American history, arithmetic, and science. Moral education was retained, but direct religious indoctrination was dropped.

The basic texts—*McGuffey's Eclectic Readers*—used Protestant scriptures to teach children to accept their position in society. A good child, McGuffey taught, does not envy the rich: "It is God who makes some poor and others rich." In the reader, McGuffey preached that "the rich have troubles which we know nothing of; and . . . the poor, if they are good, may be very happy." Catholics, immigrants, blacks, and working-class people sought to have local control over their communities' schools, but the state legislatures established secular statewide standards under Protestant educators. Catholics in New York responded by building their own educational system over the next half-century. When Los Angeles became a city in 1850, it attempted to establish bilingual Spanish-English instruction. Trained bilingual teachers could not be found, however, and when the schools opened, only English was permitted.

New urban work and living patterns made for different uses of leisure than had been traditional in the countryside or in Europe. Urban Americans

Leisure
___

worked so hard that, as the English visitor Charles Lyell put it, Americans, "whether rich or poor, were labouring from morning till night, without ever indulging in a holiday." Space for recreation was scarce in cities, and the opportunities for games and sport were limited. Neighborly gatherings at the post office, tavern, or general store, or at harvest festivals and fairs, were not part of urban life. Living among strangers, urban dwellers found it difficult to find like-minded people with whom to share recreation.

Nonetheless, urban men engaged in traditional seventeenth-century sports and recreations. Tavern games of skill and strength—arm wrestling, quoits (throwing a two-pound iron or stone ring at a pin), ninepins, and pitching coins—remained popular, and often were accompanied by betting. Though city dwellers had less opportunity than their rural counterparts to ride and hunt, fishing remained popular; some people fished as recreation, others as a livelihood.

Thanks to the expansion of public education, the vast majority of native-born white Americans were literate by the 1850s. Power printing presses and better transportation made possible wide distribution of books and periodicals. The religious press—both traditional sects and dissenters—produced pamphlets, hymnbooks, tracts, bibles, and religious newspapers. But Americans now read secular publications just as religiously. Newspapers and magazines—political organs, literary journals, and the voices of specialized groups like millworkers—abounded in the 1830s and thereafter. In Brookfield, Massachusetts, in 1798, the mails brought one weekly newspaper; fifty years later, in 1848, fifty different newspapers and another fifty-five monthly magazines arrived every week.

Fiction and autobiographies competed with religious tracts as popular literature. Newspapers and magazines printed fiction, and bookstores and stationers in large cities sold book-length novels and autobiographies. Susanna Rowson's 1794 novel *Charlotte Temple*, which offered a critique of women's dependence on men, and the powerful attack on slavery in the *Narrative of the Life of Frederick Douglass, an American Slave, Written by Himself* (1845) were widely read. Many popular novels, written by women, often for women, were set in the home and upheld Christian values. They reflected the growing gender differences in American society in their exploration of the divisions between private and public space, between home and work, between emotion and authority, and between sentimentality and power. Yet in their support of traditional female moral roles, they can also be read as a challenge to prevailing values. Rowson's *Charlotte Temple*, for instance, never depicted the heroine performing domestic chores. And, although Susan Warners' *The Wide, Wide, Wide World* (1850), Nathaniel Hawthorne's *The House of the Seven Gables* (1851), and Fanny Fern's *Ruth Hall* (1855) did not challenge women's traditional domestic roles, they gave women a special moral bearing. In describing in positive terms community and republican virtue, they implicitly criticized the growing market economy.

Hawthorne dismissed women writers for their sentimentality—they sold more books than he did—and literary critics would agree with him for more than a century. Not until the late twentieth century were women's writings of this era to be taken seriously.

Theater was a central institution in American life. A theater was often the second public building constructed in a town. (The first was usually a church.) Large cities boasted two or more theaters that catered to different classes. In New York City the Park Theater enjoyed the patronage of the carriage trade, the Bowery drew the middle class, and the Chatham attracted workers. Yet some theater cut across class lines. Shakespeare was performed so often and appreciated so widely that even illiterate theatergoers knew his blank verse well. In the 1840s, musical and dramatic presentations took on a more professional tone; the Hutchinson Family (see pages 267–268) and their rivals, and the newly popular minstrel shows, offered carefully rehearsed routines.

Sports, like theater, increasingly involved city dwellers as spectators. Horse racing, boxing, pedestrianism (walking races), and, in the 1850s, baseball began to attract large urban male crowds.

Sports

New York State legalized horse racing in 1821, and a large track was built in Queens County across the East River from New York City. "The race of the century" took place there two years later, between American Eclipse representing the North and Sir Henry of Virginia representing the South. Contemporary estimates placed the crowd at over fifty thousand and the newspapers reported a massive traffic jam of carriages leading from the ferry to the Union Park racecourse. American Eclipse won the match. The race became legendary; images of Eclipse's victory were widely collected. Match races typically took three days, and many spectators found the betting as compelling as the sport. Horses and slaves, as well as money, often changed hands. From 1831, sports could be followed in a sports newspaper, *Spirit of the Times*. After 1845, boxing fans could read about their champions in the *National Police Gazette*. In 1849, round-by-round accounts of the Hyer-Sullivan boxing match at Rock Point, Maryland, were telegraphed throughout the East.

Sports and recreation mirrored the growing divisions in American urban society. They had become less spontaneous and relied increasingly on formal rules. Entertainment became a form of specialized commerce: one had to purchase a ticket to go to the theater, the circus, P. T. Barnum's American Museum in New York City, the racetrack, or the ball park. Sports and recreation also frequently depended on exclusive associations and clubs, which advanced the interests of particular

Horse racing was among the well-attended urban leisure activities. Eclipse's defeat of Sir Henry of Virginia in 1823 was widely celebrated, both by the fifty thousand people who attended the race and by those who collected souvenirs, like this cotton handkerchief depicting the match race. National Museum of Racing, Saratoga Springs, N.Y.

groups. The New York [Racing] Association, for instance, sponsored the match race between American Eclipse and Sir Henry of Virginia. In 1829 a group of Ohio merchants organized the Cincinnati Angling Club, which had a formal constitution and bylaws and limited membership to twenty-five. A group of Wall Street office workers formed the Knickerbocker Club in 1842, and in 1845 they drew up rules for the game of baseball. Their rules were widely adopted, and they served as the basis for the game of baseball today.

As cities grew, their populations seemed increasingly fragmented. It required more of a conscious effort to find people similar to oneself;

City Life

groups of all sorts formed clubs and associations to get to know each other and to serve as a bulwark against the cultures of other groups—immigrants, migrants, blacks, and artisans—that spilled onto the city streets. Middle- and upper-class native-born New Yorkers like George Templeton Strong, who felt alienated in the city of their birth, founded societies and clubs designed to be exclusive. Some joined the Masonic order, which offered leisure pursuits and a sense of belonging to middle- and upper-class men. The Masons provided everything the bustling city did

not: an elaborate hierarchy, an orderly code of deference between ranks, harmony, and shared values. Members knew each other. The Masonic order played a public role as well: Masons marched in the parades that were a regular feature of the city's public and political life. Americans of all sorts—native and foreign born, black and white—also formed churches and church-associated clubs. Associations of these kinds brought together similar people, but they also formalized divisions between dissimilar groups.

Other divisions seemed to grow naturally on city streets. A youth culture developed on the Bowery in the 1840s; in the evenings the broad street, dotted with theaters, dance halls, ice-cream shops, and cafes, became an urban midway. Older New Yorkers feared the "Bowery boys and gals," whose ostentatious dress and behavior seemed threatening. The Bowery boy had hair close-cut in back and long in front, greased into a roll. He wore a broad-brimmed black hat, an open shirt collar, a black frock coat that reached below the knee, and as much jewelry as he could afford. His swaggering gait, especially when he had a girlfriend on his arm, frightened many in the middle class. Equally disturbing to old New Yorkers were the young working women who promenaded on the Bowery. They came in groups to enjoy each other's company and to meet Bowery boys. Unlike more genteel ladies who wore modest veils or bonnets, Bowery gals drew attention to themselves with bright, outlandish clothes and ornate hats. Cities offered great diversity and anonymity. People interested in same-sex liaisons, though often publicly ostracized, could find each other in the city and live together in urban boarding houses.

Most working people spent much of their lives outdoors—they worked in the streets as laborers, shopped in open markets, and paraded on special occasions. Young people courted, neighbors argued, and ethnic groups defended their turf on the streets. Increasingly, urban streets served as a political arena as crowds formed to listen to speakers, to parade, and sometimes to form mobs.

Rioting and incidents of violence became frequent. The colonial tradition of disfranchised people taking to the streets (see Chapter 5) had diminished in the first three decades of the nineteenth century, but

Urban Riots

riots again became commonplace in the 1830s as professionals and merchants, skilled craftsmen, and ordinary laborers vented their rage against political and economic rivals. "Gentlemen of property and standing," unnerved by antislavery proponents, sacked abolitionist and antislavery organizations, even murdering newspaper editor Elijah Lovejoy in Alton, Illinois, in 1837. In the 1840s, "respectable" citizens drove the Mormons out of Illinois and Missouri. In Philadelphia native-born workers attacked Irish weavers in 1828, and whites and blacks fought on the docks in 1834 and 1835. Residents of North Philadelphia took to the streets continuously from 1840 to 1842 until the construction of a railroad through their neighborhood was abandoned. These disturbances came to a head in the great Philadelphia riots of 1844, in which mostly Protestant skilled workers attacked Irish Catholics. Smaller cities, too, became battlegrounds as nativist riots peaked in the 1850s; Louisville, for instance, witnessed an anti-German riot in 1855. By 1840 more than 125 people had died in urban riots, and by 1860 fatalities exceeded 1,000.

As public disorder spread, Boston hired uniformed policemen in 1837 to supplement its part-time watchmen and constables, and New York in 1845 established an entirely uniformed force. Nonetheless, middle-class men and women did not venture out alone at night, and even during the day they avoided certain districts. The police increasingly controlled and suppressed street activity, as did local ordinances to license and regulate street vendors and ban their cries, bells, and horns. Local laws against vagrancy and disturbing the peace often were used against free blacks and immigrants. The continuing influx of immigrants to the cities worsened social tensions by pitting people of dissimilar backgrounds against each other in the contest for jobs and housing. Ironically, in the midst of so much dirt, noise, crime, and conflict, the opulent residences of the very rich rose like a deliberate affront to those struggling to survive.

EXTREMES OF WEALTH

Some observers, notably the young French nobleman Alexis de Tocqueville, characterized the United States before the Civil War as primarily a place of equality and opportunity. Tocqueville and his companion Gustave de Beaumont traveled four thousand miles and visited all twenty-four states over a nine-month period in 1831 and 1832. Tocqueville later opened *Democracy in America*, his classic analysis of the American people and nation, with the statement: "No novelty in the United States struck me more vividly during my stay there than the equality of conditions."

Tocqueville attributed American equality— the relative fluidity of the social order in the United States—to Americans' mobility and restlessness. Geographic mobility offered people opportunities to start anew regardless of where they came from or who they were. Wealth and family mattered little; a person could be known by deeds alone. Indeed, Americans seemed driven by restlessness and ambition. "An American will build a house in which to pass his old age," Tocqueville wrote, "and sell it before the roof is on; he will plant a garden and rent it just as the trees are coming into bearing; he will clear a field and leave others to reap the harvest; he will take up a profession and leave it, settle in one place and soon go off elsewhere with his changing desires."

Most Americans believed that talent and hard work reaped rewards, a belief supported by traditional religious values and a deeply rooted work ethic. According to the conventional wisdom, anyone could advance by working hard and saving money. A local legend from Newburyport, Massachusetts, illustrated this theme. Tristram Dalton, a Federalist lawyer, wanted his carriage repaired. Moses Brown, an energetic mechanic, refused to wait for Dalton's servants to tow the carriage to his shop; he sought out the vehicle and fixed it on the spot. After Dalton's death his heirs squandered the family fortune, but Brown's industriousness paid off. Through hard work the humble carriage craftsman became one of Massachusetts's richest men, eventually buying the Dalton homestead and living out his life there. The moral was clear: "Men succeed or fail . . . not from accident or external surroundings," as the *Newburyport Herald* put it in 1856, but from "possessing or wanting the elements of success in themselves."

Others disagreed with this egalitarian view of American life. Among those who traced the rise of a new aristocracy based on wealth and power and the growth of class and ethnic divisions was *New York Sun* publisher Moses Yale Beach. Author of twelve editions of *Wealth and Biography of the*

Differences in Wealth

Wealthy Citizens of New York City, Beach listed 750 New Yorkers with assets of $100,000 or more in 1845. John Jacob Astor led the list of 19 millionaires with a fortune of $25 million. Ten years later, Beach reported more than 1,000 New Yorkers worth $100,000, among them 28 millionaires. Combining gossip-column tidbits with often erroneous guesses at people's wealth, Beach's publications nevertheless suggest the enormous wealth of New York's upper class. Tocqueville himself, ever sensitive to the conflicting trends in American life, had described the growth of an American aristocracy based on industrial wealth. The rich and well educated "come forward to exploit industries," Tocqueville wrote, and become "more and more like the administrators of a huge empire. . . . What is this if not an aristocracy?"

Wealth throughout the United States was becoming concentrated in the hands of a relatively small number of people. In New York City between 1828 and 1845, the wealthiest 4 percent of the city's population increased their holdings from an estimated 63 percent to 80 percent of all individual wealth. Meanwhile the holdings of many ordinary people virtually disappeared; in Brooklyn between 1810 and 1841, the share of wealth held by the bottom two-thirds of families decreased from 10 percent to almost nothing. By 1860 the top 5 percent of American families owned more than half the nation's wealth; the top 10 percent owned more than 70 percent.

Urban Poverty

Meanwhile a cloud of uncertainty hung over working men and women. Many feared unemployment during hard times, and they resented the competition of immigrant and slave labor. They dreaded the insecurities and indignities of poverty, chronic illness, disability, old age, widowhood, and desertion. Women feared having to raise a family without a helpmate. And they had good reason: few women could earn sufficient money to support a family from full-time work in the few fields open to them. Fear of poverty led the Klinger sisters, for instance, to marry again and again.

Poverty and squalor dogged the urban working class. Cities were notorious for the dilapidated districts inhabited by newly arrived immigrants, indigent free blacks, the working poor, and thieves, beggars, and prostitutes. New York City's Five Points, a few blocks from City Hall, was the worst slum in pre-Civil War America. Dominated by the Old Brewery, which had been converted to housing for hundreds of adults and children in 1837, the neighborhood was predominantly Irish and black. Ill-suited to human habitation, lacking such amenities as running water and sewers, Five Points exemplified the worst of urban life, as can be seen in the 1829 painting reproduced here. Contemporaries estimated that more than one thousand people lived in its rooms, cellars, and subcellars. Throughout the city, workers' housing was at a premium. Houses built for two families often held four; tenements built for six families held twelve. Many families took in lodgers to help pay the rent.

New York and other large cities harbored "street rats," children and young men who earned their living on the streets by bootblacking or petty thievery. They slept on boats, in haylofts, or in warehouses. Charles Loring Brace, a founder of the Children's Aid Society (1853), described street rats in *Dangerous Classes of New York* (1872): "Like the rats, they were too quick and cunning to be often caught in their petty plunderings, so they gnawed away at the foundations of society undisturbed." To Brace and others, such rootless people represented a threat to American society more serious than Shays's Rebellion or Burr's conspiracies. "They will vote—they will have the same rights as we ourselves," warned the first report of the Children's Aid Society in 1854, "though they have grown up ignorant of moral principle, as any savage or Indian. . . . They will perhaps be embittered at the wealth and luxuries they never share. Then let society beware, when the vicious, reckless multitude of New York boys, swarming now in every foul alley and low street, come to know their power and use it!"

The Urban Elite

A world apart from Five Points and the people of the streets—though only a short walk away—lived the upper-class elite society of Philip Hone, one-time mayor of New York. Hone's diary, meticulously kept from 1826 until his death in 1851, records the activities of an American aristocrat. On February 28, 1840, for instance, Hone attended a masked ball at the Fifth Avenue mansion of Henry Breevoort, Jr., and Laura Carson Breevoort. The ball began at the fashionable hour of 10 p.m., and the five hundred ladies and gentlemen who filled the mansion wore costumes adorned with ermine and gold. For more than a week, Hone believed, the affair "occupied the minds of people of all sta-

This view of the infamous Five Points section of New York City's Sixth Ward, around 1829, depicts life in what was probably the worst slum in pre–Civil War America. Immodestly dressed prostitutes cruise the streets or gaze from windows, while a pig runs loose in their midst. Courtesy of Mr. & Mrs. Screven Lorillard, photo by Joshua Nefsky.

tions, ranks, and employments." At one time or another similar parties were held in Boston, Philadelphia, Baltimore, and Charleston.

Hone's social calendar was full of elegant dinner parties featuring fine cuisine and imported wines. The New York elite who filled the pages of Hone's diary—the 1 percent of the population who owned 50 percent of the city's wealth—lived in large townhouses and mansions attended by a corps of servants. In the summer, country estates, ocean resorts, mineral spas, and grand tours of Europe offered relief from the strenuous winter and spring social seasons.

Much of this new wealth was inherited. For every John Jacob Astor who made millions in the western fur trade, or George Law who left a farm to become a millionaire contractor and investor, ten others used the money they had inherited or married as a stepping-stone to additional wealth. Andrew H. Mickle, a poor Irish immigrant who became a millionaire and mayor of New York City, derived his fortune from marrying the daughter of his employer. Many of the wealthiest New Yorkers bore the names of the colonial commercial elite—Beekman, Breevoort, Roosevelt, Van Rensselaer, and Whitney. These rich New Yorkers were not idle; they worked at increasing their fortunes and power. Urban capitalists like Philip Hone profited enormously from the transportation, commercial, and manufacturing revolutions; hardly an important canal, railroad, bank, or mill venture lacked the names and investments of the fashionable elite. Wealth begat wealth, and family ties were cemented through marriage.

Meanwhile the hard-working middle class was becoming a distinct part of the urban scene. The growth and specialization of trade had rapidly increased their numbers. The

The Middle Class

men were businessmen or professionals, the women homemakers. Middle-class families enjoyed the fruits of advances in consumption: wool carpeting, fine wallpaper, and rooms full of furniture replaced the bare floors, whitewashed walls, and relative emptiness of eighteenth-century middle-class homes. Houses be-

A world apart from the slums of New York City were the homes of middle-class citizens. This 1828 oil painting (by an unknown artist) of a York, Pennsylvania, home reveals the family's luxurious domestic furnishings and tailored clothing. The Saint Louis Art Museum, Bequest of Edgar William and Bernice Chrysler Garbisch.

came larger, often with four to six rooms, and cheaper. Middle-class children slept one to a bed, and middle-class families used indoor toilets by the 1840s and 1850s. When Philadelphia publishing agent Joseph Engles died in 1861, his estate recorded that his parlor contained two sofas, thirteen chairs, three card tables, a fancy table, a piano, a mirror, and a fine carpet. Other rooms were similarly furnished. Middle-class families also formed the backbone of the rich associational life that Tocqueville had observed in America. They filled the family pews in church on Sundays; their children pursued whatever educational opportunities were available. If they dreamed of entering Philip Hone's world, they were mindful to keep their distance from the working class and the poor.

WOMEN AND THE FAMILY

Distinctions among women grew in the nineteenth century, as a result of changes in work and gender roles. In the eighteenth century, women of different classes, race and ethnicity had had much more in common. Women's and men's work also grew increasingly distinct. As manufacturing left the home, so did wage workers, except those doing putting-out work. On farms, there was still overlap between women's and men's work, but in the new stores and workshops their tasks diverged. Specialization in work tasks was an outcome of specialization in business and production; men acquired narrow new skills that they applied in set ways with purposefully designed tools and systems. Authority within the workplace became formal and impersonal.

Some women shared these experiences for brief periods. The New England farm daughters who were the first textile-mill workers performed new specialized work tasks away from home. In the 1840s the new urban department stores hired young women as clerks and cash runners. Many women worked for a time as teachers, usually for two to five years. Paid employment typically represented a brief stage in their lives before they left their paternal households and entered their marital households.

Working Women

Working-class women—the poor, widows, and free blacks—worked to support themselves and their families. Leaving their parental homes as early as age twelve or thirteen, they earned wages most of their lives, with only short respites for bearing and rearing children. But unlike men and New England farm daughters, most of these women did not work in the new shops and factories. Instead they sold their domestic skills for wages outside of their own households. Unmarried girls and women worked as domestic servants in other women's homes; married and widowed women worked as laundresses, seamstresses, cooks, and boarding-house keepers. Some hawked food and wares on city streets; others did piecework sewing. Few of these occupations enabled them to support themselves or a family at an acceptable level. Widowhood in particular was synonymous with poverty.

Work was increasingly segregated and gender-specific. Most women's work continued to center on the home. As the urban family lost its role in the production of goods, household upkeep and child-rearing claimed women's full-time attention. Devotion to education, religion, morality, domestic arts, and culture began to fill the void left by the decline in the economic functions of the family; these realms came to be known as woman's sphere. For a woman to achieve mastery in these areas was to live up to the middle-class ideal of the cult of domesticity.

Middle-class American women and men idealized the family as a moral institution characterized by selflessness and cooperation. Women were idealized in turn as the embodiment of self-sacrificing republicanism. The role of the mother in this cult of domesticity was to strengthen the nation's future by rearing her children well and creating a spiritual and virtuous environment that contrasted sharply with the world outside the home. The world of work—the market economy—was seen as an arena of conflict increasingly identified with men and dominated by base self-interest. In a rapidly changing world in which young men and women left their parental homes and villages, in which factories and stores replaced traditional means of production and distribution, the family was assigned the role of representing stability and traditional values.

The domestic ideal in turn restricted the range of paying jobs available to middle-class women outside the home. Most paid work was viewed with disapproval, but one occupation came to be recognized as consistent with the genteel female role: teaching. In 1823 the Beecher sisters, Catharine and Mary, established the Hartford Female Seminary and offered philosophy, history, and science in addition to the traditional women's curriculum of domestic arts and religion. A decade later Catharine Beecher successfully campaigned to establish training seminaries for female teachers by presenting such education as an extension of women's nurturing role. By the 1850s schoolteaching was regarded as a woman's vocation, and most urban teachers were women, nearly all unmarried. The employment of female teachers enlarged the scope of work opportunities open to educated women. Outside of the South men shunned common school teaching because it paid very poorly. Even so, women teachers were often paid half what men

Rebecca Lukens pioneered in an unusual role for a woman in early nineteenth-century America as she ran the Lukens Steel Company in eastern Pennsylvania from 1825 until she died in 1854. The deaths of her father in 1823 and of her husband in 1825 left her with the mill and large debts. She revived the steel company and was soon shipping its iron plates as far away as Europe. Lukens Steel Company.

teachers earned. For society, the services of talented, educated women were a bargain, and they remained so as long as women had limited opportunities to use their capacities in other occupations.

Meanwhile family size was shrinking. In 1800 American women bore an average of six to seven children; by 1860 the figure had dropped to five, and by 1900 to four. This decline occurred even while many immigrants with large-family traditions were settling in the United States; thus the birthrate for native-born women declined even more steeply. Although rural families remained larger than their urban counterparts, birthrates in both areas declined comparably.

Decline in the Birthrate

A number of factors reduced family size. For one thing, small families were viewed as increasingly desirable in a market economy, in which the family was a unit of consumption rather than production. Children in smaller families would have greater opportunities; parents could give them more attention, better educations, and more financial help. Also, contemporary marriage manuals stressed that too many births had a harmful effect on a woman's health, weakening her physically and overworking her as a mother.

The evidence suggests that many wives and husbands made deliberate decisions to limit the size of families. In areas where farm land was relatively expensive, for instance, families were smaller than in more affordable agricultural districts. Apparently parents who foresaw difficulty setting up their children as independent farmers chose to have fewer children. In urban areas, children became more of an economic burden than an asset as the family lost its role as a producer of goods. As the length of the period before which children began contributing financially grew, so did their economic costs to parents.

How did men and women limit their families in the early nineteenth century? Average age at marriage rose, thus shortening the period of potential childbearing. Women

Birth Control

also bore their last child at a younger age, dropping from around forty in the mid-eighteenth century to around thirty-five in the mid-nineteenth century. This figure suggests that family planning was becoming more common. Many couples used traditional forms of birth control, such as coitus interruptus (withdrawal of the male before completion of the sexual act) and breast feeding, which makes some women temporarily infertile. Medical devices, however, were beginning to compete with these ancient practices. Although animal-skin condoms imported from France were too expensive for popular use, cheap rubber condoms became available in the 1850s. Some couples used the rhythm method—attempting to confine intercourse to a woman's infertile periods. Awareness of the "safe period," however, was uncertain, even among physicians.

If all else failed, abortion was available, especially after 1830. Ineffective folk methods of self-induced abortion had been around for centuries, but in the 1830s abortionists, mostly women, advertised surgical services in large cities. To protect women from unqualified abortionists, and in response to reformers opposed to abortion, states began to regulate abortions. Between 1821 and 1841, ten states and one territory either restricted late-term abortions or prohibited abortion altogether; by 1860, twenty states had adopted abortion restrictions. Only three of those twenty states punished the woman; the abortionists were the criminals. Such laws, however, were rarely enforced.

Significantly, the birth-control methods women themselves controlled—douching, the rhythm method, abstinence, breast feeding, and abortion—were increasing in popularity. The new emphasis on domesticity encouraged women's autonomy in the home and by extension gave them greater control over their own bodies. According to the cult of domesticity, the refinement and purity of women ruled the household, including the bedroom. As one woman put it, "woman's duty was to subdue male passions, not to kindle them."

Smaller families and fewer births changed the pattern of women's lives. At one time birth and infant care had occupied virtually the entire span of women's adult lives, and few mothers had lived to see their youngest child reach maturity. After the 1830s many women found time for other activities. Smaller families also allowed women to devote more time to their older children, and childhood gradually came to be perceived as a distinct period in the life span. The expansion of public education in the 1830s and the policy of grouping school children by age reinforced this trend.

Sarah Ripley of Greenfield, Massachusetts, who grew up in the eighteenth century and reached adulthood in the nineteenth, traced these changes in her diaries. Daughter of a

Sarah Ripley Stearns

village shopkeeper, Ripley had a privileged childhood. After completing boarding school, she returned home to work as an assistant in her father's store. In 1812, after a five-year courtship, she married Charles Stearns of Shelburn. "I have now acquitted the abode of my youth, left the protection of my parents and given up the name I have always borne," she recorded in her diary. "May the grace of God enable me to fulfill with prudence and piety the great and important duties which now dissolve [fall] on me." Soon she confessed in her diary that she missed the bustle of the shop.

Sarah Ripley Stearns's life was not a settled one; change was a constant. Motherhood occupied her, as she bore three children within four years.

Her brother moved west. She and her family moved three times in six years, and in 1818 she became a widow. In the midst of all this upheaval, Sarah Ripley Stearns found religion an anchor. When a revival visited her village in the 1810s, Stearns declared her faith. Rather than leading to introspection, religion promoted social interaction. With her neighbors she formed a "little band of associated females" and sponsored a school society and juvenile home.

Many Protestant women, like Sarah Ripley Stearns, were moved by religious convictions to enter a new arena. Visits and meetings in parlors and churches led women to extend their domestic concerns into the public realm. Stearns's benevolent-society work not only aided poor children but also provided its female participants with experience in organizing and chairing meetings, raising funds, and cultivating an extended women's network. Thus religion and charity propelled women into public life (see pages 369–371).

Urban life and the market economy offered new roles for some women. Women who made a conscious decision to stay single rejected the cult of domesticity and inten-

Single Women

tionally departed from the centuries-old pattern whereby women moved from their fathers' households to those of their husbands. Louisa May Alcott (1832–1888), the author of *Little Women* (1868) and other novels, sought independence and financial security for herself. Her father, the philosopher Bronson Alcott, had never provided adequately for the family. Not even the family's participation in the utopian cooperative Fruitlands put enough food on the table. Alcott worked as a seamstress, governess, teacher, and housemaid before her writing finally brought her success. "I think I shall come out right, and prove that though an *Alcott*, I *can* support myself," she wrote her father in 1856. "I like the independent feeling; and though not an easy life, it is a free one, and I enjoy it. I can't do much with my hands; so I will make a battering-ram of my head and make a way through this rough-and-tumble world."

Louisa May Alcott had foresworn marriage to risk ridicule as a spinster. She and other like-minded women who chose to pursue their own abilities shared a life defined by female relationships and activities. In large cities, they could establish independent relationships with other single women. Given the difficulty women had finding work that would allow them to be self-supporting, they undertook their independence at great risk. Nonetheless, the proportion of single women in the population increased significantly in the first three-quarters of the nineteenth century. In Massachusetts in 1850, 17 percent of native-born women never married; a far smaller percentage had remained single in colonial days. Independent white women, in sum, were taking advantage of new opportunities offered by the market economy and urban expansion.

IMMIGRANT LIVES IN AMERICA

The 5 million strangers who came to the United States between 1820 and 1860 outnumbered the entire population of the country recorded in the first census in 1790. They came from every continent, though the vast majority were European. During the peak period of pre-Civil War immigration, from 1847 through 1857, 3.3 million immigrants entered the United States; 1.3 million were from Ireland and 1.1 million from the German states. By 1860, 15 percent of the white population was foreign-born.

This massive migration had been set in motion decades earlier. The Napoleonic wars had initiated one of the greatest population shifts in history around the turn of the nineteenth century; it was ultimately to last more than a century. War, revolution, famine, religious persecution, and the lure of industrialization led many Europeans to leave home. The United States beckoned, offering economic opportunity and religious freedom.

Meanwhile both private enterprises and public entities in the United States actively recruited European emigrants. Midwestern and western states lured potential settlers in the

Promotion of Immigration

interest of promoting their economies. Two transplanted New Yorkers, Augustus and Joe Kirby Allen, for instance, set up in Houston in 1836 and advertised in newspapers for settlers. In the 1850s, the state of Wisconsin appointed a commissioner of emigration, who advertised the state's advantages in European newspapers. Wisconsin also opened an office in

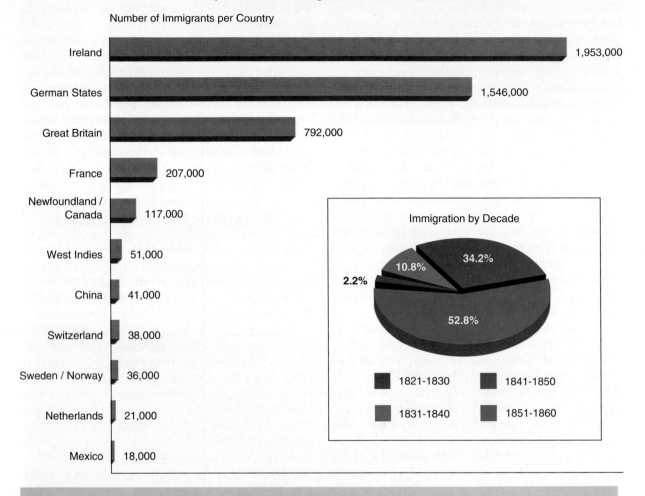

Major Sources of Immigration to the United States, 1821–1860

Number of Immigrants per Country

Country	Number
Ireland	1,953,000
German States	1,546,000
Great Britain	792,000
France	207,000
Newfoundland / Canada	117,000
West Indies	51,000
China	41,000
Switzerland	38,000
Sweden / Norway	36,000
Netherlands	21,000
Mexico	18,000

Immigration by Decade

- 2.2%
- 10.8%
- 34.2%
- 52.8%

- 1821-1830
- 1841-1850
- 1831-1840
- 1851-1860

Major Sources of Immigration to the United States, 1821–1860   *Most immigrants came from western Europe, and the five million immigrants who came to the United States between 1820 and 1860 outnumbered the entire population of the U.S. at the first census in 1790. By 1860, 15 percent of the white population was of foreign birth.*   Source: U.S. Bureau of the Census, *Historical Statistics of the United States, Colonial Times to 1970.* (2 Parts; Washington, D.C., 1975), Part I, pp. 206, 208.

New York and hired European agents to compete with other states and with firms like the Illinois Central Railroad for immigrants' attention.

Large construction projects and mines needed strong young laborers. Textile mills and cities attracted young women workers. Europeans' awareness of the United States grew as employers, states, and shipping companies advertised opportunities across the Atlantic. Often the message was stark: work and prosper in America or starve in Europe. The cost of the regularly scheduled sailing

ships commuting across the ocean after 1848 was within easy reach of millions of Europeans, especially for accommodations on lower decks.

Success in America stimulated further emigration. "I wish, and do often say that we wish you were all in this happy land," wrote shoemaker John West of Germantown, Pennsylvania, to his kin in Corsley, England, in 1831. "A man nor woman need not stay out of employment one hour here." John Down, a weaver from Frome, England, who emigrated to New York without his family, wrote to his wife in 1830 to describe the bountiful meal he had shared with a farmer's family: "They had on the table puddings, pyes, and fruit of all kind that was in season, and preserves, pickles, vegetables, meats, and everything that a person would wish, and the servants [farm hands] set down at the same table with their masters." Though Down sorely missed his family, he wrote, "I do not repent of coming, for you know that there was nothing but poverty before me, and to see you and the dear children want was what I could not bear. *I would rather cross the Atlantic ten times than hear my children cry for victuals once.*" To skeptics who claimed the United States was filling up, he replied, "There is plenty of room yet, and will be for a thousand years to come." Such testimonials to the success of pauper immigrants in America were widely circulated in Europe.

So more immigrants came willingly, enduring the hardships of travel and of settlement in a strange land. The average transatlantic crossing took six weeks; in bad weather it could take three months. Disease spread unchecked among people packed together like cattle in steerage. More than 17,000 immigrants, mostly Irish, died from "ship fever" in 1847. On arrival, immigrants became fair game for the con artists and swindlers who worked the docks. Aggressive agents representing boarding-house owners and employers greeted them and tried to lure them from their chosen destinations. In response, New York State's commissioners of emigration established Castle Garden as an immigrant center in 1855. There, at the tip of Manhattan Island, the major port for European entry, immigrants were somewhat sheltered from fraud. Authorized transportation companies maintained offices in the large rotunda and assisted new arrivals with their travel plans.

Most immigrants gravitated toward cities, since only a minority had farming experience or the means to purchase land and equipment. Many stayed in New York City itself. By 1845, 35 percent of its 371,000 people were of foreign birth. Ten years later, 52 percent of its 623,000 inhabitants were immigrants, 28 percent from Ireland and 16 percent from the German states. Boston, a major entry port for the Irish, took on a European tone; throughout the 1850s the city was about 35 percent foreign-born, of whom more than two-thirds were Irish. The South's largest cities also had sizable immigrant populations. In 1860 New Orleans was 44 percent foreign-born, Savannah 33

percent, and the western city of St. Louis 61 percent. On the West Coast, San Francisco had a foreign-born majority.

Some immigrants did settle in rural areas. German, Dutch, and Scandinavian farmers, in particular, gravitated toward the Midwest. Greater percentages of Scandinavians and Netherlanders took up farming than did other nationalities; both groups came mostly as religious dissenters and migrated in family units. The Dutch who founded colonies in Michigan and Wisconsin, for instance, had seceded from the official Reformed Church of the Netherlands, fleeing persecution in their native land to establish new and more pious communities such as Holland and Zeeland in Michigan.

Not all immigrants found success in the United States; hundreds of thousands returned to their homelands disappointed. Before the potato blight hit Ireland, American

Immigrant Disenchantment

recruiters lured many Irish to swing picks and shovels on American canals and railroads and to work in construction. Among them was Michael Gaugin, who for thirteen years had been an assistant engineer in the construction of a Dublin canal. Gaugin was attracted to the United States by the promise that "he should soon become a wealthy man." The Dublin agent for a New York firm convinced him to quit his job, which included a house and an acre of ground, and emigrate. Gaugin had the misfortune to land in New York City during the financial panic of 1837, and within two months of arriving he became a pauper. Gaugin declared he was "now without means for the support of himself and his family, and has no employment, and has already suffered great deprivation since he arrived in this country; and is now soliciting means to enable him to return with his family home to Ireland." Many of those who had come with the Gaugins had already returned home.

Such experiences did not deter other Irish men and women from coming to the United States. Ireland was the most densely populated country in Europe and among the most

Irish Immigrants

impoverished. From 1815 on, small harvests prompted a steady stream of Irish to emigrate to America. Then in 1845 and 1846 potatoes—Ireland's staple food—rotted in the fields. From 1845 to 1849, death from starvation, malnutrition, and typhus spread. In all, 1 mil-

John McLenan, around 1864, in his pen and ink drawing, Our Foreign Relations, *recorded the diversity of the new immigrants.* Museum of Fine Arts, Boston. M. & M. Karolik Collection.

lion died and about 1.5 million fled, two-thirds of them to the United States. Ireland's major export was its people.

At the peak of Irish immigration, from 1847 to 1854, 1.2 million Irish men and women entered the United States. Every year between 1820 and 1854, with only two exceptions, the Irish constituted the largest single group of immigrants annually. By the end of the century there would be more Irish in the United States than in Ireland.

The new Irish immigrants differed greatly from those who had left Ireland to settle in the American colonies. The Protestant Scotch-Irish who predominated in the eighteenth century (see page 97) had journeyed from one part of the British Empire to another. The nineteenth-century Irish immigrants to America, however, were mostly Roman Catholic, and they were also leaving a colony to settle in an independent republic. The political and religious differences made their cultural adaptation that much more difficult. In comparison with the Scotch-Irish, furthermore, the new immi-

grants from Ireland tended to be younger, increasingly female, and mostly from the rural provinces. Eldest sons stood to inherit family farms and eldest daughters stayed home to care for their parents; thus younger children were expendable in Ireland's declining economy. Farmers' daughters could find work only as domestic servants, and poverty-stricken Ireland could not absorb all of them. In American cities they found work in factories and households. If they wed, they would marry late, as did their sisters in Ireland. They helped support their families still at home, built Catholic churches and schools, and established a network of charitable and social organizations in American cities.

In the urban areas where they clustered in poverty, Irish immigrants met growing anti-immigrant, anti-Catholic sentiment. "No Irish Need Apply" signs were common. During the colonial period, white Protestants had feared "popery" as a system of tyranny and had discriminated against the few

Anti-Catholicism

Catholics in America. After the Revolution anti-Catholicism had receded, but it reappeared in the 1830s wherever the Irish did. Attacks on the papacy and the church circulated widely in the form of libelous texts like *The Awful Disclosures of Maria Monk* (1836), which alleged sexual orgies among priests and nuns. Nowhere was anti-Catholicism more overt and nasty than in Boston, but such sentiments were widespread. Anti-Catholic riots were almost commonplace. In Charlestown, Massachusetts, a mob burned a convent (1834); in Philadelphia a crowd attacked priests and nuns and vandalized churches (1844); and in Lawrence, Massachusetts, a mob leveled the Irish neighborhood (1854).

The native-born who embraced anti-Catholicism were motivated largely by anxiety. They feared that a militant Roman church would subvert American society, that unskilled Irish workers would displace American craftsmen, and that the slums inhabited in part by the Irish were undermining the nation's values. Every social problem from immorality and alcoholism to poverty and economic upheaval was blamed on immigrant Irish Catholics. Americans seemed to have adopted the negative British stereotypes of Irish people. Impoverished native-born workers complained to the Massachusetts legislature in 1845 that the Irish displaced "the honest and respectable laborers of the State . . . and from their manner of living . . . work for much less per day . . . being satisfied with food to support the animal existence alone." American workers, they claimed, "not only labor for the body but for the mind, the soul, and the State." The new public schools, with their Protestant bias, represented another form of attack on Irish Catholics. Friction increased as Irish-American men fought back by entering politics.

In 1854, Germans replaced the Irish as the single largest group of new arrivals. The Klinger family was part of this migration. Potato blight had also prompted emigration from the German states to the United States in the 1840s; other hardships added to the steady stream. Many came from regions of Germany where small landholdings made it hard to eke out a living and to pass on adequate plots of land to their sons. Others were craftsmen displaced by the industrial revolution. These refugees were joined by middle-class Germans—a whole generation of liberals and free-thinkers, some of whom were socialists, communists, and anarchists—who emigrated to the United States after the abortive revolution of 1848.

German Immigrants

Unlike the Irish, who tended to congregate in towns and cities, Germans settled everywhere. Many came on cotton boats, disembarked at New Orleans, and traveled up the Mississippi. In the South they became peddlers and merchants; in the North and West they worked as farmers, urban laborers, and businessmen. They tended more than the Irish to migrate in families and groups; that tendency helped them maintain German culture and institutions in the New World. Many settled in small towns and rural areas where they could preserve their local and regional identities. Many American-born merchants and laborers learned German in order to do business in such settlements in Pennsylvania, Ohio, Illinois, Wisconsin, Missouri, and Texas. In larger cities immigrants from the same German states tended to cluster together. Their presence transformed the tone and culture of cities like Cincinnati and Milwaukee. *Turnvereine*—German physical-culture clubs—sprouted in villages and cities; by 1853 sixty such societies across the nation were hosting exercise groups and German-language lectures.

Native-born Americans treated German immigrants with greater respect than they did the Irish, stereotyping Germans as industrious, hard working, self-reliant, and intelligent. Many believed that Germans would "harmonize" better with American culture. Nevertheless, Germans, too, encountered hostility. A significant number of German immigrants were Jewish, and they experienced anti-Semitism. More than half the German immigrants were Catholic, and their Sabbath traditions differed from those of Protestants. On Sundays urban German families customarily gathered at beer gardens to eat and drink beer, to dance, sing, and listen to band music, and sometimes to play cards. Protestants were outraged by such violations of the Lord's day. In Chicago, riots broke out when Protestants enforced the Sunday prohibition laws. The Germans' persistent use of their native language also set them apart. Even German Protestants—who were mostly Lutherans—founded their own churches and German-language schools.

Not all immigrants came to the United States voluntarily. After the annexation of Texas, the

This painting, ca. 1840, of Saint Isadore of Madrid, patron saint of farmers, is attributed to Rafael Aragon. Hispanic farmers in the Southwest sought the aid of the patron saint of agriculture as they struggled to raise crops and preserve their culture in the region.   Courtesy of Dr. and Mrs. Ward Alan Minge.

Mexican War, and the Gadsden Purchase (see pages 392, 399), many His-

Hispanics

panics—people of Spanish or Mexican origin—found themselves residing in the United States because of boundary changes. The separation of Texas from Mexico after 1836, the discovery of gold in California, and the extension of railroad lines broke the linkage of the Southwest and Mexico and reoriented the Southwest toward the United States.

Hispanic culture persisted in the region, but Anglos and European immigrants seized economic and political power. Hispanics retained their language, Roman Catholic religion, and community affiliations through newspapers, mutual-aid societ-

ies, and the church, but they lost power and status to Anglos. In Nueces County, Texas, at the time of the Texas Revolution (1836), Mexicans held all the land; twenty years later, they had lost it all. Commerce eclipsed their agricultural and ranching economy; rancheros and vaqueros—the cowboys—became obsolete. Although many Hispanics had fought for Texas independence, arriving settlers tended to treat them as inferiors. Within two generations Hispanics became strangers in their own land—second-class citizens on land where they had lived for generations.

Such conflict between immigrants and the society they joined paralleled the inner tensions experienced by individual immigrants. On the one hand they felt impelled to commit themselves wholeheartedly to their new country, to learn its language and adapt themselves to American ways. On the other hand they were rooted in their own cultural traditions—the familiar customs of the society of their birth, the words and ways that came intuitively and required no education.

For immigrants, becoming part of American society involved conflict, but once here they claimed their right to a fair economic and political share. Native Americans, however, like the Hispanics in the Southwest, were defending what they regarded as prior rights. Their land, their religions, and their ways of life came under constant attack because they were viewed as obstacles to expansion and economic growth.

INDIAN RESISTANCE AND REMOVAL

Under the Constitution, the federal government had responsibility for dealing with Native Americans. For better or worse, there had to be a federal Indian policy. From the Indians' point of view, it was usually for the worse. U.S. territorial expansion took place at the tribal peoples' expense. The result was removal of the great Native American nations to lands west of the Mississippi. While the populations of other groups increased by leaps and bounds, the Indian population shrank. Alexis de Tocqueville noticed the contrast. "Not only have these wild tribes receded, but they are destroyed," Tocqueville concluded, after personally observing the tragedy of forced removal, "and as they give way or perish, an immense and increasing people fill their place. There is no instance upon record of so prodigious a growth or so rapid a destruction." War, forced removal, disease—especially small-pox—and malnutrition reduced many tribes by half. More than half of the Pawnees, Omahas, Ottoes, Missouris, and Kansas died in the 1830s alone. Within tribes, the more traditional the family structure, the greater the toll; close contact spread disease.

As had the colonial powers in North America, the United States treated Native American tribes as sovereign nations until Congress ended the practice in 1871. In its relations with tribal leaders, the government followed international protocol. Indian delegations that visited Washington were received with the appropriate pomp and ceremony. Leaders exchanged presents as tokens of friendship, and commemorative flags and silver medals with presidents' likenesses became prized possessions among Indian chiefs. Agreements between a given tribe and the United States were signed, sealed, and ratified like any international pact.

In practice, however, Native American sovereignty was a fiction. Protocol appeared to signify mutual respect and independence, but treaty negotiations exposed the sham. Treaty making was essentially a process used by the American government to acquire Indian land. Instead of bargains struck between two equal nations, such treaties were often coerced agreements between the victor and the vanquished. Old treaties gave way to new ones in which Native Americans ceded their traditional holdings in return for different lands in the West. Beginning with President Jefferson, the government withheld payments due to tribes for previous land cessions to pressure them to sign new treaties.

The War of 1812 snuffed out whatever realistic hopes eastern Indian leaders might have had of resisting American expansion by means of warfare. Armed resistance persisted and blood was shed on both sides, as in the Seminole Wars (see pages 261, 358). Resistance, however, only delayed the inevitable. The Shawnee chiefs Prophet and Tecumseh led the most significant movement against the United States (see pages 228–231), but Prophet failed to sustain the movement after Tecumseh's death.

The experiences of Prophet and other Shawnees were typical of the wanderings of an uprooted people. Until the 1870s only the Delawares and

Indian Resistance

Kickapoos moved more. When the Shawnees gave up 17 million acres in Ohio in the 1795 Treaty of Greenville (see page 198), they scattered to Indiana and eastern Missouri. After the War of 1812, Prophet's Indiana group withdrew to Canada under British protection. In 1822 other Shawnees sought Mexican protection and moved from Missouri to present-day eastern Texas. As the U.S. government began promoting removal to Kansas, Prophet returned from Canada to lead a group to the new Shawnee lands in eastern Kansas in 1825. When Missouri achieved statehood in 1821, the Shawnees there were also forced to move to Kansas, where they were joined in the 1830s by Shawnees removed from Ohio and others expelled from Texas. By 1854 Kansas was open to white settlement, and the Shawnees had to cede back seven-eighths of their land—1.4 million acres.

Removal had a profound impact on all Shawnees. The men had to give up their traditional role as providers; their methods of hunting and knowledge of woodland animals were useless on the prairies of Kansas. As grains became the tribe's dietary staple, Shawnee women played a greater role as providers, supplemented by government aid under treaty provisions. (Typically, treaties required annual distributions of grain, blankets, and cash payments.) Remarkably, the Shawnees preserved their language and culture in the face of these drastic changes. While resistance proved incapable of protecting their lands, it did help maintain their culture.

In the 1820s Native Americans were pressured to cede their lands in Ohio, southern Indiana and Illinois, southwestern Michigan, most of Missouri,

Indian Policy

central Alabama, and southern Mississippi. They gave up nearly 200 million acres for pennies an acre. But white settlers' appetites were insatiable; the expansion of commercial farming in the Midwest and of cotton plantations in the South increased demand for Indian land and for assimilation. The federal Indian agency system, which monopolized trade with Native Americans and paid out the rations, supplies, and annuities they received in exchange for abandoning their land, served both purposes. With time, the tribes became dependent on these government payments—a dependency intended to make them docile in treaty negotiations. It also furthered assimilation by bringing them into the market system.

Ever since the early days of European colonization, assimilation of Native Americans through education and Christianity had been an explicit goal (see page 56). It took on renewed urgency as the United States expanded westward. "Put into the hand of [Indian] children the primer and the hoe," the House Committee on Indian Affairs recommended in 1818, "and they will naturally, in time, take hold of the plough; and, as their minds become enlightened and expand, the Bible will be their book, and they will grow up in habits of morality and industry . . . and become useful members of society." In 1819, in response to missionary lobbying, Congress appropriated $10,000 annually for "civilization of the tribes adjoining the frontier settlements." This "civilization act" was intended to teach Indians to live like white settlers. Protestant missionaries administered the "civilizing fund" and established mission schools. Within five years there were thirty-two such schools in operation. Unlike earlier Christian missions, these new boarding schools substituted English for Native American languages and taught agriculture alongside the Gospel. The emphasis on agriculture was intended to promote interest in private property and hard work and to lay the basis for stable Christian communities.

To settlers eyeing Native American land, assimilation through education seemed too slow a process. At any given time there were never more than fifteen hundred students in all the schools; at that rate it would take centuries to assimilate all the Indians. And Native Americans themselves questioned the instruction. Some tribes found the missionary message repugnant. The Creek nation permitted the schools only after being assured that there would be no preaching. Zealous missionaries, however, violated the agreement, preaching to the Creeks and their black slaves. In response, a band of Creeks sacked the school. Similarly, the Passamaquoddy tribe of New England, many of whose members were Catholics, opposed teachers' efforts to turn them into Episcopalians. Even the vocational education seemed pointless; graduates who returned to their tribal villages had no way to apply the commercial agricultural skills they had acquired.

Wherever Native Americans lived, illegal settlers plagued their lands. The federal government, though obligated to protect the integrity of treaty lands, lacked the resolve to exclude settlers and never committed sufficient troops to keep out aggressive whites. With government support of westward expansion, legitimate Indian claims had to give way to the advance of white civilization.

It became apparent in the 1820s that neither economic dependency nor education nor Christianity could persuade Native Americans to cede much more land to meet the demands of expansionists. Attention focused on southern tribes—Cherokees, Creeks, Choctaws, Chickasaws, and Seminoles—because much of their land remained intact after the War of 1812 and because they aggressively resisted white encroachment. Possessed of more formal political institutions than the northern tribes, they were better organized to resist.

In his last annual message to Congress in late 1824, President James Monroe suggested that all Indians be moved beyond the Mississippi River.

Indian Removal

Three days later he sent a special message to Congress proposing removal. Monroe described his proposal as an "honorable" one that would protect Indians from invasion and provide them with independence for "improvement and civilization." Force would be unnecessary, he believed; the promise of a home free from white encroachment would be sufficient to win Indian acceptance.

The southern tribes at whom the program was aimed—the Cherokee, Creek, Choctaw, and Chickasaw—unanimously rejected Monroe's offer. Between 1789 and 1825 they had negotiated a total of thirty treaties with the United States; they had reached the limits of their tolerance. They wished to remain on what was left of their ancestral land.

Pressure from Georgia had prompted Monroe's policy. Most Cherokees and some Creeks lived in northwestern Georgia, and in the 1820s the state accused the federal government of not fulfilling its 1802 promise to remove the Indians in return for the state's renunciation of its claim to western lands. Georgia sought complete expulsion and was satisfied neither by Monroe's removal messages nor by further Creek cessions. Under federal pressure, the Creek nation ceded all but a small strip of its Georgia acreage in 1826. But Georgia's governor, George M. Troup, wanted all the Creek lands and sent surveyors to the one remaining strip. When President John Quincy Adams threatened to send the army to protect the Indians' claims, Troup countered with his own threats. Only the eventual removal of the Georgia Creeks to the West prevented a clash between the state and the federal government. For the Creeks the outcome was a devastating defeat. In an attempt to hold fast to the remainder of their traditional lands, those in Alabama, they had radically altered their political structure. In 1829, at the expense of traditional village autonomy, they had centralized tribal authority and had forbidden any chief from ceding land. In the end, they lost not only their land but their traditional forms of social and political organization.

Cherokees

If "civilizing" Indians was the goal, no tribe met that test better than the Cherokees. Between 1819 and 1829 the tribe became economically self-sufficient and politically self-governing: during this "Cherokee renaissance" the twelve to fifteen thousand adult Cherokees came to think of themselves as a nation and not a collection of villages. In 1821 and 1822 Sequoyah, a self-educated Cherokee, devised an eighty-six-character phonetic alphabet that made possible a Cherokee-language Bible and bilingual tribal newspaper, *Cherokee Phoenix* (1828). Between 1820 and 1823 the Cherokees created a formal government with a bicameral legislature, a court system, and a salaried bureaucracy. In 1827 they adopted a written constitution, modeled after that of the United States. Cherokee land laws, however, differed from U.S. law. The tribe owned all land, and complex provisions covered land sales (forbidden to outsiders) and proximity of farms (minimum distance apart was one-quarter mile). Nonetheless, the Cherokees assimilated American cultural patterns. By 1833 they held fifteen hundred black slaves whose legal status was the same as that of slaves held by southern whites. Moreover, missionaries had been so successful that the Cherokees could be considered a Christian community.

Although the tribe developed a political system similar to that of an American state, it failed to win respect or acceptance from southerners. Georgia pressed the Cherokees to sell the 7,200 square miles of land they held in the state. Congress appropriated $30,000 in 1822 to buy the Cherokee land in Georgia, but the tribal council refused to negotiate. Most Cherokees preferred to stay where they were and believed that their treaty rights to their land were unquestionable. Impatient with Chero-

kee refusals to negotiate cession, Georgia annulled the Cherokee constitution, extended the state's sovereignty over the tribe, and ordered the tribal lands seized.

Cherokee Nation v. Georgia

Backed by sympathetic whites but not by the new president, Andrew Jackson, the Cherokees under Chief John Ross turned to the federal courts to defend their treaty with the United States and prevent Georgia's seizure of their land. Their legal strategy reflected their maturity as a nation and their political sophistication. In *Cherokee Nation* v. *Georgia* (1831), Chief Justice John Marshall ruled that under the federal Constitution an Indian tribe was neither a foreign nation nor a state and therefore had no standing in federal courts. Nonetheless, said Marshall, the Indians had an unquestionable right to their lands; they could lose title only by voluntarily giving it up. A year later, in *Worcester* v. *Georgia*, Marshall defined the Cherokee position more clearly. The Indian nation was, he declared, a distinct political community in which "the laws of Georgia can have no force" and into which Georgians could not enter without permission or treaty privilege.

But President Andrew Jackson, who as a general had led an expedition against the Seminoles in Spanish Florida in 1818, simply ignored the Supreme Court's ruling since it mandated action by Georgia, not the federal government. It was widely reported that Jackson had said: "John Marshall has made his decision: now let him enforce it." But if Jackson applied any pressure, it was against the Cherokees. Keen to open up new lands for settlement, he was determined to remove the Cherokees at all costs. In the Removal Act of 1830 Congress provided Jackson with the funds he needed to negotiate new treaties and resettle the resistant tribes west of the Mississippi.

Trail of Tears

The infamous Trail of Tears had begun. The Choctaws were the first to go; they made the forced journey from Mississippi and Alabama to the West in the winter of 1831 and 1832 (see map, page 359). Alexis de Tocqueville was visiting Memphis when they arrived: "The wounded, the sick, newborn babies, and the old men on the point of death. . . . I saw them embark to cross the great river," he wrote, "and the sight will never fade from my memory. Neither sob nor complaint rose from that silent assembly. Their afflictions were of long standing, and they felt them to be irremediable."

Other tribes soon joined the forced march. The Creeks in Alabama resisted removal until 1836, when the army pushed them westward. A year later the Chickasaws followed. The Cherokees, having fought removal in the courts, found themselves divided. Some recognized the hopelessness of further resistance and accepted removal as the only chance to preserve their civilization. The leaders of this minority agreed in 1835 to exchange their southern home for western land. Chief Ross and other antitreaty Cherokees lobbied Congress against ratification of the treaty and then against appropriating payment under its provisions. They lost. But when the time for evacuation came in 1838, most Cherokees refused to move. President Martin Van Buren sent federal troops to round up the Native Americans. About twenty thousand Cherokees were evicted, held in detention camps, and marched to present-day Oklahoma under military escort. Nearly one-quarter died of disease and exhaustion on the Trail of Tears. When the forced march to the West ended, the Indians had traded about 100 million acres east of the Mississippi for 32 million acres west of the river plus $68 million. Only a few scattered tribal remnants, among them the Seminoles in Florida and the Cherokees in the southern Appalachian Mountains, remained in the East and South.

The impact of the Trail of Tears on Native American life was drastic and disastrous. In the West they encountered an alien environment: lacking generational ties with the new land, few felt at peace with it. The animals and plants they found there were unfamiliar. Native Americans no longer knew how to live off the land, and many became dependent on government payments for survival. Removal also brought new internal conflicts. The Cherokees in particular struggled over their tribal government. In 1839 followers of Chief John Ross assassinated the leaders who had negotiated the treaty. Violence continued sporadically until a new treaty in 1846 imposed a temporary truce. In 1861 the American Civil War renewed the factionalism, forever shattering Cherokee tribal unity.

Conflict also arose between migrating tribes and western Indians, and among migrants forced to share land and scarce resources. Nearly 100,000 newcomers settled west of the Mississippi, and the existing game could not support them all. The Osages and Pawnees fought the newcomers who were invading their land and homes. The story was repeated among the Apaches and Comanches in the Southwest, as the pressure of white settlement led to treaties, cession, and removal and then to new treaties, further cession, and removal.

In the Southeast a small band of Seminoles successfully resisted removal and remained in Florida. Some Seminole tribal leaders agreed in the

Second Seminole War
———

1832 Treaty of Payne's Landing to relocate to the West within three years. Others opposed the treaty, and some probably did not know it existed. A minority under Osceola, a charismatic leader, refused to vacate their homes and fought the protreaty group. When U.S. troops were sent to suppress the intratribal war and impose removal in 1835, Osceola initiated a fierce guerrilla war against the federal troops.

The Florida Indians were a varied group from all over the South. Though they included many Creeks and mixed Indian–African-Americans (ex-slaves or descendants of runaway slaves), the American army considered them all Seminoles and subject to removal. General Thomas Jesup believed that the runaway-slave population was the key to the war. "This, you may be assured, is a Negro, not an Indian war," he wrote Ben Butler in 1836, "and if it be not speedily put down, the South will feel the effects of it on their slave population before the end of the next season." The army intended to exterminate the Seminoles but did not succeed; nor did Seminole resistance provoke any slave uprisings. Captured under the white flag of truce, Osceola died in an army prison in 1838, but the Seminoles fought on under leaders like Chief Coacoochee (Wild Cat) until 1842, when the United States abandoned the removal effort. Most of Osceola's followers agreed to move west to Indian Territory in 1858, but many Seminoles remained in the Florida Everglades, proud of having resisted conquest.

In the West, Native Americans found themselves pressured to cede land. To facilitate white settlement, Commissioner of Indian Affairs William Medill in 1848 proposed gathering the western Indians into two great reservations, one northern and one southern, separated by a wide corridor for white settlers to use on their way westward. In 1853 and 1854, however, the government took back

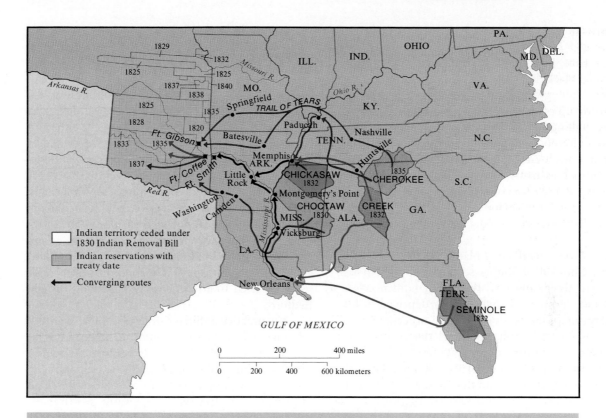

Removal of Native Americans from the South, 1820–1840   *Over a twenty-year period, the federal government and southern states forced Native Americans to exchange their traditional homes for western land. Some tribal groups remained in the South, but most settled in the alien western environment.*   Source: Acknowledgment is due to Martin Gilbert and George Weidenfeld and Nicholson Limited for permission to reproduce this map taken from *American History Atlas.*

most of the northern reservation lands in a new round of treaties, and Kansas and Nebraska were opened to white settlement.

A complex set of attitudes drove whites to inflict removal on Native Americans. Most merely wanted the land and had little or no respect for the rights or culture of the tribes. Others were aware of the injustice but believed that Indians must inevitably give way to white settlement. Some, like John Quincy Adams, believed the only way to preserve Indian civilization was to remove the tribes and establish a buffer zone between them and white settlers. Others, including Thomas Jefferson, doubted that white civilization and Indian "savagery" could coexist. Supported by missionaries and educators, they hoped to "civilize" Indians and assimilate them gradually into American culture. Whatever the source of white attitudes, their

outcome was the devastation of Native American peoples and their cultures. The survival of Indian ways of life in the face of such conditions attests to the resilience of the Native American cultures.

FREE PEOPLE OF COLOR

Free people of color also struggled for recognition and legal rights. Like Native Americans, they were involuntary participants in American society. Unlike Indians, however, they wished to partake fully in American life.

No black person was safe, wrote the abolitionist and former slave Frederick Douglass after the Philadelphia riot of 1849. "His life—his property—and all that he holds dear are in the hands of a mob, which may come upon him at any moment—at midnight or mid-day, and deprive him of his all." Between 1832 and 1849 five major anti-black riots had occurred in Philadelphia. Mobs stormed black dwellings and churches and set them on fire, killing the people inside. Such mobs could be made up of slave hunters seeking runaways but quite willing to kidnap a free black instead. Or they could represent civil authority: Cincinnati city officials, frightened by the growing black population, drove as many as two thousand blacks from the city in 1829 by enforcing a law requiring cash bonds for good behavior. Free blacks faced insecurity daily. They were outsiders in the land of their birth.

Under federal law, blacks' position was unclear. The Bill of Rights seemed to apply to free African-Americans; the Fifth Amendment specified that "no person shall . . . be deprived of life, liberty, or property, without due process of law." But eighteenth-century political theory defined a republic as consisting only of whites (see page 189). This exclusionist thinking was reflected in early federal legislation. Naturalization was limited to white aliens in 1790, and in 1792 the militia was limited to white male citizens. Moreover, Congress approved the admission to the Union of states whose constitutions restricted the rights of African-Americans. After the admission of Missouri in 1821, every new state admitted until the Civil War banned blacks from voting. When the Oregon and New Mexico territories were organized, public land grants were reserved for whites.

In the North, African-Americans faced second-class legal status nearly everywhere; Massachusetts had the fewest restrictions. Many states barred free blacks or required bonds of $500 to $1,000 to guarantee their good behavior, as in Ohio (1804), Illinois (1819), Michigan (1827), and Oregon (1857). Although seldom enforced, these laws clearly signified the second-class status of African-Americans. Only in Massachusetts, New Hampshire, Vermont, and Maine could blacks vote on an equal basis with whites throughout the pre-Civil War period. In 1842 African-Americans gained the right to vote in Rhode Island (where all voters faced restrictive property qualifications), but they had lost it earlier in Pennsylvania and Connecticut. No state but Massachusetts permitted blacks to serve on juries; four midwestern states and California did not allow African-Americans to testify against whites. In Oregon, blacks could not own real estate, make contracts, or sue in court.

Legal status was important, but practice and custom were crucial. Although Ohio repealed its law barring black testimony against whites in 1849, the exclusion persisted as custom in southern Ohio counties. Throughout the North free people of color were either excluded from or segregated in public places. Hotels and restaurants were closed to them, as were most theaters and churches. Abolitionist Frederick Douglass was repeatedly turned away from public facilities during a speaking tour of the North in 1844. A doorkeeper refused him admission to a circus in Boston, explaining "We don't allow niggers in here." He met the same reply when he tried to attend a revival meeting in New Bedford.

Exclusion and Segregation of African-Americans

No practice inflicted greater injury than discrimination in hiring. Counting houses, retail stores, and factories refused to hire black men except as janitors and handymen. New England mills hired only whites. Except for a small professional and skilled elite, free black men in the North found steady work elusive; most toiled as unskilled daily laborers. African-American women found jobs more easily because their domestic skills were in great demand in the cities; they worked as servants, cooks, laundresses, and seamstresses. Unlike their white counterparts, these women did not view paid employment as a temporary phase in their lives; around 40 percent of black women worked for wages during their child-rearing years. Given the low wages received by black workers, few families could survive on one income.

Free people of color faced especially severe legal and social barriers in the southern slave states, where their presence was often viewed as an incentive to insurrection. Indeed, southern states responded to fear of mass rebellion by tightening restrictions on free blacks and forcing them out of small towns and interior counties. After a successful slave rebellion in Haiti in the 1790s and Gabriel Prosser's slave revolt in 1800 (see pages 231–232), southern states barred the entry of free blacks for two decades. In 1806, Virginia required newly freed blacks to leave the state. After the Nat Turner rebellion in 1831, the position of free blacks deteriorated even further. Within five years nearly every southern state prohibited the freeing of slaves

Southern Free Blacks

Black Population of the United States, 1800–1860

Black Population of the United States, 1800–1860   *The free black population rose dramatically between 1800 and 1860. On the eve of the Civil War there were nearly one-half million free people of color.*   Source: U.S. Bureau of the Census, *Negro Population 1790–1915* (Washington, D.C., 1918), p. 25.

without legislative or court approval, and by the 1850s Texas, Mississippi, and Georgia had banned manumission altogether.

To restrict free blacks and encourage them to migrate north, southern states adopted elaborate "black codes." African-Americans, who provided most of the South's skilled labor, encountered licensing requirements and bans restricting work opportunities. Virginia and Georgia banned black river captains and pilots. Some states forbade blacks to assemble without a license; some prohibited them from learning to read and write. In the late 1830s, when these codes were enforced with vigor for the first time, free blacks began to move northward in growing numbers, even though northern states discouraged the migration. In spite of these obstacles, the free black population rose dramatically in the first part of the nineteenth century, from 108,000 in 1800 to almost 500,000 in 1860 (see figure above). Nearly half lived in the

North, some in rural settlements like Hammond County, Indiana, but far more in cities like Philadelphia, New York, and Cincinnati. Baltimore had the largest community, but sizable free black populations also existed in New Orleans, Charleston, and Mobile. Although differences in occupation, wealth, education, religion, and social status divided free people of color, the common necessity of self-defense promoted solidarity.

The ranks of free people of color were constantly increased by ex-slaves. Some, like Frederick Douglass and Harriet Tubman, were fugitives. Douglass had paid his owner $3 a month for the privilege of hiring himself out as a ship caulker in Baltimore. Living among free workers gave him an opportunity to escape slavery. By masquerading as a free black with the help of borrowed seaman's papers, he bluffed his way to Philadelphia and freedom. Tubman, a slave in Maryland, escaped to Philadelphia in 1849 when it was rumored that she

This watercolor of Augustus Jones was painted in 1852 when Jones was forty-nine. A leader in the Philadelphia community of free people of color, he was the grandson of Absalom Jones, a founder of the African Free Society and the African Episcopal Church in Philadelphia. Courtesy of David A. Schorsch.

would be sold out of the state. Within the next two years she returned twice to free her two children, her sister, her mother, and her brother and his family. Other slaves were voluntarily freed by their owners. Some, like a Virginia planter named Sanders who settled his slaves as freedmen in Michigan, sought to cleanse their souls by freeing their slaves in their wills. Others freed elderly slaves after a lifetime of service rather than support them in old age. Whites who inherited the parents of the slave Isabella (Sojourner Truth), for example, freed them to avoid supporting the father, who was too old to work.

Sojourner Truth's experience in New York reveals that the effectiveness of the gradual-emancipation laws of northern states was undermined by the existence of slavery elsewhere. New York State adopted an emancipation plan in 1817 whereby all slaves over forty years old were freed and young slaves would serve ten more years. Owners tried to thwart the law by selling their slaves in other states. Fearing sale to the South,

Sojourner Truth found refuge with a nearby abolitionist couple in 1826. With their help she sued successfully for the freedom of her son Peter, who had been sold unlawfully to an Alabaman. One can only guess how many blacks did not receive such help and were deprived of their freedom.

Free blacks founded strong, independent self-help societies as bulwarks against oppression. In every black community African-Americans organized black churches, fraternal and benevolent associations, literary societies, and schools. More than half the black population in Philadelphia in the 1840s belonged to clubs and societies, and female benevolent societies and schools flourished. The black Masons had more than fifty lodges in seventeen states by 1860. Their leaders believed that these mutual aid societies would encourage thrift, industry, and morality and thus equip their members to improve their lot. But no amount of effort could counteract white prejudice. Blacks remained subordinate in status.

Founding of Black Institutions

The network of voluntary organizations among urban free black men and women did provide a base for African-American protest. From 1830 to 1835, and irregularly thereafter, free blacks held national conventions with delegates drawn from city and state organizations. Under the leadership of the small black middle class, which included the Philadelphia sail manufacturer James Forten and the orator Reverend Henry Highland Garnet, the convention movement served as a forum to attack slavery and agitate for equal rights. Militant new black newspapers joined the struggle. *Freedom's Journal*, the first black weekly, appeared in 1827; in 1837 the *Weekly Advocate* began publication in New York City. Both papers circulated throughout the North, disseminating African-American political analysis and promoting activism.

The mood of free blacks began to shift in the late 1840s and 1850s. Many were frustrated by the failure of the abolitionist movement and angered by the passage of the Fugitive Slave Act of 1850 (see page 406). Some fled to Canada to escape second-class civil rights or to avoid seizure under the Fugitive Slave Act. Others became more militant, and a few joined John Brown in his plans for rebellion (see page 418). Many more were swept up in

Black Nationalism

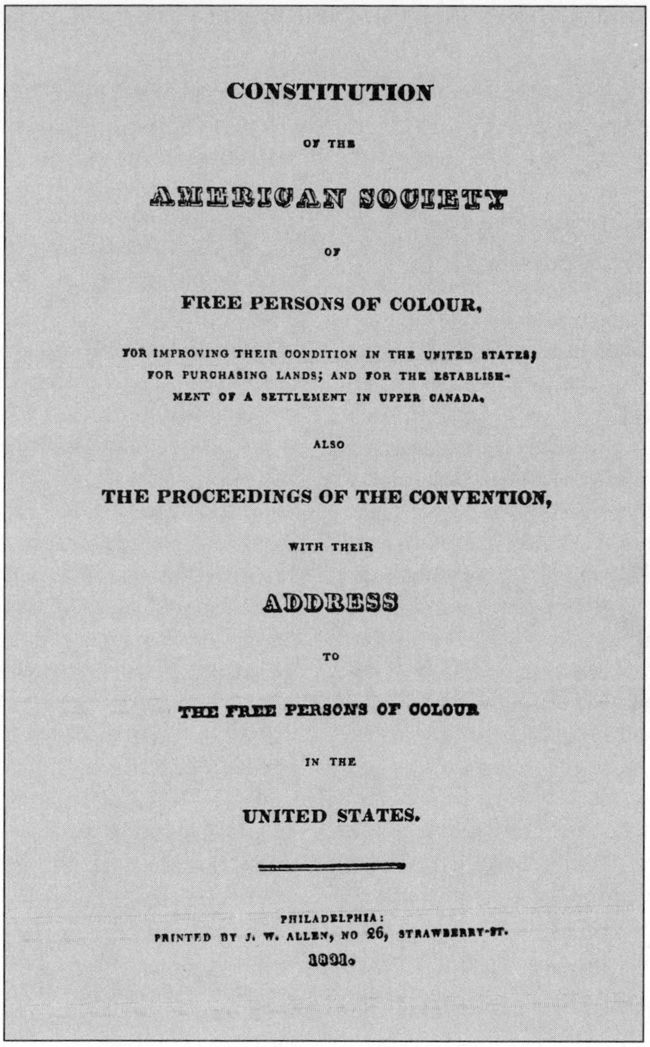

CONSTITUTION

OF THE

AMERICAN SOCIETY

OF

FREE PERSONS OF COLOUR,

FOR IMPROVING THEIR CONDITION IN THE UNITED STATES;
FOR PURCHASING LANDS; AND FOR THE ESTABLISH-
MENT OF A SETTLEMENT IN UPPER CANADA.

ALSO

THE PROCEEDINGS OF THE CONVENTION,

WITH THEIR

ADDRESS

TO

THE FREE PERSONS OF COLOUR

IN THE

UNITED STATES.

PHILADELPHIA:
PRINTED BY J. W. ALLEN, NO 26, STRAWBERRY-ST.
1831.

How do historians know

about African-American political thought and activity in the early nineteenth century? One important source is the published minutes of the black conventions, first held in 1830.

Free people of color held at least eleven national conventions and about forty state conventions prior to the Civil War. The first national convention, a special meeting in Philadelphia in September 1830, presided over by Bishop Richard Allen, founder of the African Methodist Episcopal church, agreed to explore a settlement in Canada as a haven for free people of color and fugitive slaves. It also called for pursuing "all legal means for the speedy elevation of ourselves and brethren to the scale and standing of men."

Less than a year later, the "First Annual Meeting of the People of Colour" condemned the persecution of African-Americans, appealed for funds to support their work, called for the establishment of a college for poor blacks, and stressed the importance of education. The delegates were also self-consciously building a movement of annual conventions. This report, and the subsequent convention minutes and addresses, demonstrate the involvement of African-Americans in the reforms of the times, and the stress they put on education and equality of opportunity. At later conventions in the 1850s nationalism took hold among African-Americans.

The movement was democratic. Most communities elected their delegates to the national conventions at public meetings or at local and state conventions. Though the minutes reveal the wide range of opinion within black communities, they agreed on abolition of slavery, immediate emancipation, and equal rights for free people of color.

a tide of black nationalism that stressed racial solidarity, self-help, and a growing interest in Africa. Before this time, efforts to send African-Americans "back to Africa" had originated with whites seeking to rid the United States of blacks. But blacks held emigrationist conventions of their own in the 1850s under the leadership of abolitionists Henry Bibb and Martin Delany. Delany led an exploration party to the Niger Valley as the emissary of a black convention, there signing a treaty with Yoruba rulers allowing him to settle American blacks in their African kingdom.

Nothing illustrates the position of free blacks in the United States better than the flight of black Americans to Canada and Africa in search of freedom while millions of European migrants were coming to the United States for liberty and opportunity. With the coming of the Civil War, however, the status of blacks would move onto the national political agenda, and African-Americans would focus on their position at home.

The United States was a far more diverse and turbulent society in 1860 than it had been in 1800. The market economy, immigration, and the growth of cities had altered the ways people lived and worked. Economic growth not only created new jobs in towns and cities but also promoted clearer distinctions in wealth and status. Inequality increased everywhere, and competition and insecurity produced resentments and conflict. Cities housed both ostentatious wealth and abject poverty, and disorder became commonplace. Many Americans felt as if they were strangers to each other.

In the midst of these changes, middle-class families sought to insulate their homes from the competition of the market economy. Many women found fulfillment in the domestic ideal, though others found it confining. Middle-class urban women became associated with nurturing roles, first in homes and schools, then in churches and reform societies. Working-class women had more modest goals: escaping poverty and winning respect. Most Americans found some comfort in religion.

Famine and religious and political oppression in Europe propelled millions of people across the Atlantic. They were drawn to the United States by the promise of jobs and tolerance. Yet though conditions were usually better than in their native lands, most found the going rough. In the process of adapting, immigrants changed the profile of the American people; Americans differed from each other more and shared fewer traditions and experiences. Competition and diversity in turn bred intolerance. None suffered more painfully than Native Americans and free African-Americans, who were made to feel like aliens in their own land. Both groups felt powerless. Indians, forced off their traditional lands, found themselves uprooted and deprived of much that had given their lives meaning. African-Americans sought acceptance as citizens, but without much success. A small number even attempted to return to Africa.

Conflict became increasingly commonplace in the public arena. The manifestations of division in America were many: utopian communities, conflicts over public space, backlash against immigrants, urban riots, black protest, and Indian resistance. Conflict also took the form of reform movements, which came to characterize American life from the 1820s through the 1850s. Through reform and political action, many Americans sought to harness and control the forces of change. Spurred on by religious revival and individualism, they turned to politics as a collective means of restoring harmony and order. In the process, divisions became even sharper.

SUGGESTIONS FOR FURTHER READING

Rural and Utopian Communities

Leonard J. Arrington and Davis Bitton, *The Mormon Experience: A History of the Latterday Saints* (1979); Priscilla J. Brewer, *Shaker Communities, Shaker Lives* (1986); R. Carlyle Buley, *The Old Northwest: Pioneer Period, 1815–1840*, 2 vols. (1950); Don H. Doyle, *The Social Order of a Frontier Community: Jacksonville, Illinois, 1825–1870* (1978); John Mack Faragher, *Sugar Creek: Life on the Illinois Prairie* (1986); Laurence Foster, *Religion and Sexuality: Three American Communal Experiments of the Nineteenth Century* (1981); Steven Hahn and Jonathan Prude, eds., *The Countryside in the Age of Capitalist Transformation* (1985); Nathan O. Hatch, *The Democratization of American Christianity* (1989); Joan M. Jensen, *Loosening the Bonds: Mid-Atlantic Farm Women, 1750–1850* (1986); Sally McMurry, *Families and Farmhouses in Nineteenth Century America: Vernacular Design and Social Change* (1988); Wallace Stegner, *The Gathering of Zion: The Story of the Mormon Trail* (1964); Anthony F. C. Wallace, *Rockdale: The Growth of an American Village in the Early Industrial Revolution* (1978); Kenneth H. Winn, *Exiles in a Land of Liberty: Mormons in America, 1830–1846* (1989).

Urban Communities and Inequality

Melvin A. Adelman, *A Sporting Time: New York City and the Rise of Modern Athletics, 1820–1870* (1986); Nelson M. Blake, *Water for the Cities: A History of the Urban Water Supply Problem in the*

United States (1956); Stuart M. Blumin, *The Emergence of the Middle Class: Social Experience in the American City, 1760–1900* (1989); Stuart M. Blumin, *The Urban Threshold: Growth and Change in a Nineteenth-Century American Community* (1976); Lawrence A. Cremin, *American Education: The National Experience, 1783–1876* (1980); Susan G. Davis, *Parades and Power: Street Theater in Nineteenth-Century Philadelphia* (1986); Timothy J. Gilfoyle, *City of Eros: New York City, Prostitution, and the Commercialization of Sex, 1790–1920* (1992); Elliott J. Gorn, *The Manly Art: Bare-Knuckle Prize Fighting in America* (1986); Karen Halttunen, *Confidence Men and Painted Women: A Study of Middle-Class Culture in America, 1830–1870* (1982); Jennie Holliman, *American Sports (1785–1835)* (1931); Carl Kaestle, *Pillars of the Republic: Common Schools and American Society, 1780–1860* (1982); Peter R. Knights, *Yankee Destinies: The Lives of Ordinary Nineteenth-Century Bostonians* (1991); Jack Larkin, *The Reshaping of Everyday Life 1790–1840* (1988); Gary B. Nash, "The Social Evolution of Preindustrial American Cities, 1700–1820: Reflections and New Directions," *Journal of Urban History* 13 (February 1987): 115–145; Edward Pessen, *Riches, Class and Power Before the Civil War* (1973); Christine Stansell, *City of Women: Sex and Class in New York, 1789–1860* (1986); Richard B. Stott, *Workers in the Metropolis: Class, Ethnicity, and Youth in Antebellum New York City* (1990); Stephen Thernstrom, *Poverty and Progress: Social Mobility in a Nineteenth Century City* (1964); Alexis de Tocqueville, *Democracy in America*, 2 vols. (1835, 1840); Richard C. Wade, *The Urban Frontier: 1790–1830* (1957).

Women and the Family

Lee Virginia Chambers-Schiller, *Liberty, A Better Husband: Single Women in America: The Generations of 1780–1840* (1984); Clifford Edward Clark, Jr., *The American Family Home, 1800–1960* (1986); Nancy F. Cott, *The Bonds of Womanhood: "Woman's Sphere" in New England, 1780–1835* (1977); Carl N. Degler, *At Odds: Women and the Family in America from the Revolution to the Present* (1980); Hasia R. Diner, *Erin's Daughters in America: Irish Immigrant Women in the Nineteenth Century* (1983); Linda Gordon, *Woman's Body, Woman's Rights: A Social History of Birth Control in America* (1976); Suzanne Lebsock, *The Free Women of Petersburg: Status and Culture in a Southern Town, 1784–1860* (1984); James C. Mohr, *Abortion in America: The Origins and Evolution of National Policy, 1800–1900* (1978); James Reed, *From Private Vice to Public Virtue: The Birth Control Movement and American Society Since 1830* (1978); Mary P. Ryan, *Women in Public: Between Banners and Ballots, 1825–1880* (1990); Mary P. Ryan, *Cradle of the Middle Class: The Family in Oneida County, New York, 1790–1865* (1981); Kathryn Kish Sklar, *Catharine Beecher: A Study in American Domesticity* (1973); Maris A. Vinovskis, *Fertility in Massachusetts from the Revolution to the Civil War* (1981); Robert V. Wells, *Revolutions in Americans' Lives* (1982); Barbara Welter, "The Cult of True Womanhood, 1820–1860," *American Quarterly* 18 (Summer 1966): 151–174.

Immigrants

Gunther Barth, *Bitter Strength: A History of Chinese in the United States, 1850–1870* (1964); Rowland Berthoff, *British Immigrants in Industrial America* (1953); Kathleen Neils Conzen, *Immigrant Milwaukee: 1836–1860* (1976); Arnoldo De León, *The Tejano Community, 1836–1900* (1982); Jay P. Dolan, *The Immigrant Church: New York's Irish and German Catholics, 1815–1865* (1975); Charlotte Erickson, *Invisible Immigrants* (1972); Robert Ernst,

Immigrant Life in New York City, 1825–1863 (1949); David A. Gerber, *The Making of an American Pluralism: Buffalo, New York, 1825–60* (1989); Jon Gjerde, *From Peasants to Farmers: The Migration from Balestrand, Norway, to the Upper Middle West* (1985); Oscar Handlin, *Boston's Immigrants: A Study in Acculturation*, rev. ed. (1959); Walter D. Kamphoefner, *The Westfalians: From Germany to Missouri* (1987); Dale T. Knobel, *Paddy and the Republic: Ethnicity and Nationality in Antebellum America* (1986); Kerby A. Miller, *Emigrants and Exiles: Ireland and the Irish Exodus to North America* (1985); Stanley Nadel, *Little Germany: Ethnicity, Religion, and Class in New York City, 1845–80* (1990); Harold Runblom and Hans Norman, *From Sweden to America* (1976); Philip Taylor, *The Distant Magnet: European Emigration to the United States of America* (1971); Mark Wyman, *Immigrants in the Valley: Irish, Germans, and Americans in the Upper Mississippi, 1830–1860* (1984).

Native Americans

Robert F. Berkhofer, Jr., *The White Man's Indian* (1978); Grant Foreman, *Indian Removal: The Emigration of the Five Civilized Tribes of Indians*, rev. ed. (1953); Michael D. Green, *The Politics of Indian Removal: Creek Government and Society in Crisis* (1982); Florette Henri, *The Southern Indians and Benjamin Hawkins, 1796–1816* (1986); Charles Hudson, *The Southeastern Indians* (1976); John K. Mahon, *History of the Second Seminole War, 1835–1842* (1967); William G. McLoughlin, *Cherokee Renascence in the New Republic* (1986); William G. McLoughlin, *Cherokees and Missionaries, 1789–1839* (1984); Theda Perdue, *Slavery and the Evolution of Cherokee Society, 1540–1866* (1979); Francis P. Prucha, *The Great Father: The United States Government and the American Indians*, 2 vols. (1984); Francis P. Prucha, *American Indian Policy in the Formative Years* (1967); Ronald N. Satz, *American Indian Policy in the Jacksonian Era* (1975); Bernard Sheehan, *Seeds of Extinction: Jeffersonian Philanthropy and the American Indian* (1973); Herman J. Viola, *Thomas L. McKenney: Architect of America's Early Indian Policy: 1816–1830* (1974); Wilcomb E. Washburn, *The Indian in America* (1975); Richard White, *The Roots of Dependency: Subsistence, Environment, and Social Change Among the Choctaws, Pawnees, and Navajos* (1983); Thurman Wilkin, *Cherokee Tragedy* (1970); J. Leitch Wright, Jr., *Creeks and Seminoles: The Destruction and Regeneration of the Muscogulge People* (1986).

Free People of Color

Ira Berlin, *Slaves Without Masters: The Free Negro in the Antebellum South* (1974); Leonard P. Curry, *The Free Black in Urban America, 1800–1850* (1981); James Horton and Lois Horton, *Black Bostonians: Family Life and Community Struggle in the Antebellum North* (1979); Luther Porter Jackson, *Free Negro Labor and Property Holding in Virginia, 1830–1860* (1942); David M. Katzman, *Before the Ghetto: Black Detroit in the Nineteenth Century* (1973); Rudolph M. Lapp, *Blacks in Gold Rush California* (1977); Leon Litwack, *North of Slavery: The Negro in the Free States, 1790–1860* (1961); Floyd J. Miller, *The Search for a Black Nationality: Black Colonization and Emigration, 1787–1863* (1975); Gary B. Nash, *Forging Freedom: The Formation of Philadelphia's Black Community, 1720–1840* (1988); Emma Lou Thornbrough, *The Negro in Indiana* (1957); Julie Winch, *Philadelphia's Black Elite: Activism, Accommodation, and the Struggle for Autonomy, 1787–1848* (1988); Shirley J. Yee, *Black Women Abolitionists: A Study in Activism, 1828–1860* (1992); Arthur Zilversmit, *The First Emancipation: The Abolition of Slavery in the North* (1967).

Chapter

13

Reform, Politics, and
Expansion, 1824–1844

THE TAPPAN BROTHERS, ARTHUR and Lewis, amassed a fortune in business but lived simple lives. They were not seen at the balls and elaborate dinners of the New York City elite. "A cracker and a tumbler of cold water," Lewis recalled, "sufficed for Arthur's luncheon." The brothers lived by their mother's Calvinist tenet that this world was preparation for the next. When the time came to submit their accounts to God, "luxurious living" and "vain show" would count against them.

Merchants and investors whose businesses included textile mills, an importing house, the *New York Journal of Commerce*, and the Mercantile Agency (the nation's first commercial-credit rating agency), the Tappans prospered with the expansion of the market economy. Although they did not indulge in luxuries, the Tappans nonetheless spent lavishly. Arthur was probably New York City's most generous benefactor. Both brothers contributed unselfishly to evangelical churches and missions, to temperance and antigambling societies, and to Bible printing and distribution. Disturbed by the wasteful habits of rural migrants and Irish Catholic immigrants, they considered education and self-improvement necessary preludes to assimilation.

At one point Lewis Tappan had strayed from the path. Having made his first fortune in his early twenties during the War of 1812, he married and settled in Boston where he joined the Unitarians, the Masons, and an exclusive Federalist club. A financial and personal religious crisis brought Lewis back to the fold at the age of forty. When his business failed, he joined Arthur's New York silk- and feather-importing firm and converted back to Calvinism. Lewis quit the Masons, whom he now viewed as heathen, and threw himself into building a Christian society. Devoting themselves to making money and doing benevolent work, the Tappans lived lives of "silks, feathers and piety."

The lives of the Tappan brothers and many like-minded reformers were changed by one compelling issue: antislavery. Drawn to abolitionism by their religious concerns and William Lloyd Garrison's calls for an immediate end to slavery, Arthur and Lewis Tappan became leaders of the religious antislavery movement. They helped found the National Anti-Slavery Society but eventually broke with the uncompromising Garrison when they supported antislavery political parties in the 1840s. Moved by Christian moral principles, unceasing in their efforts,

In this engraving, George Caleb Bingham captures the festive air of men in elections in rural towns.

Arthur and Lewis Tappan earned their reputations as leading reformers in an age of reform.

The reform fervor from the 1820s to the 1850s was in part a response to the unsettling effect of the enormous transformation that the United States experienced after the War of 1812. Immigration, internal migration, urbanization, the spread of a market economy, growing inequality, loosening family and community ties, the westward advance of settlement, and territorial expansion all contributed to the remaking of the United States. Many Americans felt they were no longer masters of their own fate. People had difficulty keeping up with the rapid pace of change. An apprentice tailor could find his trade obsolete by the time he became a journeyman; a young girl could find her skills no longer needed on her family's farm.

Americans had fought the Revolution to make themselves independent, but poverty and obsolescent trades made them dependent again. And other changes were equally disturbing. Respectable citizens felt threatened by urban mobs and paupers, and the Protestant majority feared the growing Catholic minority, with its mysterious customs and beliefs. Protestants had waged the Revolution to preserve the rights they claimed as Englishmen, not to protect alien cultures and religions. To many, all these changes seemed to undermine their traditional values.

Religious reformers like the Tappans sought to reimpose order on a society in which economic change and discord had reached a crescendo. Prompted by the evangelical ardor of the Second Great Awakening and convinced of their moral rectitude, they crusaded for individual self-improvement. Many renounced alcohol and gambling. Gradually the personal impulse to reform oneself led to the creation of benevolent and reform societies. Religious ardor drew men and women to reform, in time broadening democratic involvement. Reform soon eclipsed benevolent work and became an instrument for restoring discipline and order in a changing society. "Americans love their country not as it is but as it will be," the English visitor Francis Grund observed in the 1830s. Women were prominent in the reform movement, and the role of women in public life became an issue in itself.

Reform organizations eventually turned to government as an instrument of social and economic change. The line between social reform and politics was not always clear. Temperance, institutional reform, and, most notably, Antimasonry and abolition lured new voters into politics. Opponents of reform were no less concerned with social problems. What distinguished them from reformers was their skepticism about human perfectibility and their distrust of institutions and the exercise of power, both public and private. To them, coercion was the greater evil. They sought to reverse, not shape, change.

Two issues in particular served as bridges between reform and politics: the short-lived Antimasonry frenzy and the intense, uncompromising crusade for immediate emancipation. Though Antimasons organized the first third-party movement, abolition eventually overrode all other concerns. No single issue evoked the depth of passion that slavery did. It pitted neighbor against neighbor, settler against settler, section against section. Politicians had recognized that slavery was a political powder keg, and they had adopted the Missouri Compromise of 1820 to avoid igniting it. Territorial expansion in the 1840s and 1850s, however, made slavery politically explosive.

The opponents of religious reform found a champion in Andrew Jackson and a home in the Democratic party in the late 1820s. Yet the Jacksonians, too, saw themselves as reformers; they responded to change by attempting to foster individualism and restore restraint in government. They opposed special privileges and the Second Bank of the United States with the same vigor with which the Tappan brothers opposed sin. President Jackson believed that a strong federal government restricted individual freedom by favoring one group over another. In response, reformers rallied around the new Whig party, which became the vehicle of humanitarian reform. Democrats and Whigs constituted the second party system, which was characterized by strong organizations, intensely loyal followings, energetic religious and ethnic competition, and popular bases among the electorate.

Both Democrats and Whigs eagerly promoted westward expansion to further their goals during the economically prosperous 1840s. Democrats saw the agrarian West as an antidote to urbanization and industrialization; Whigs focused on the new commercial opportunities it offered. Expansion from coast to coast seemed to Americans to be the inevitable manifest destiny of the United States. Texas, California, and Oregon, unknown to most Americans at the turn of the century, had

1790s–1840s	Second Great Awakening spreads religious fervor
1820s	Reformers establish model penitentiaries
1825	House of Representatives elects John Quincy Adams president
1826	American Society for the Promotion of Temperance founded Morgan affair is catalyst for Antimasonry movement
1828	Protectionist Tariff of Abominations stirs nullification Andrew Jackson elected president
1830	Webster-Hayne debate explores nature of the Union
1830s–40s	Democratic-Whig competition gels in second party system
1831	*Liberator* begins publication First national Antimason convention
1832	Jackson vetoes recharter of the Second Bank of the United States Jackson re-elected
1832–33	South Carolina nullifies the Tariff of 1832, prompting nullification crisis
1836	Republic of Texas established
	Specie Circular ends credit purchase of public lands Martin Van Buren elected president
1837	*Caroline* affair sparks U.S.-Canadian hostility Financial panic ends boom of the 1830s
1838–39	United States and Canada mobilize militia over Maine-New Brunswick border dispute
1839–43	Hard times spread unemployment and deflation
1840	Whigs win presidency under William Henry Harrison
1841	Tyler assumes the presidency following death of Harrison Oregon fever attracts settlers to the Northwest and intensifies expansionism
1844	James K. Polk elected president
1845	Texas admitted to the Union
1848	Woman's Rights Convention, Seneca Falls, New York calls for women's suffrage
1851	Maine adopts prohibition

become familiar places by the 1830s and 1840s. Then race was added to the brew as the politics of territorial expansion and the antislavery movement boiled over in the 1850s and 1860s.

FROM REVIVAL TO REFORM

Religion was probably the prime motivating force behind organized benevolence and reform. A tremendous religious revival known as the Second Great Awakening galvanized Protestants, especially women, beginning in the late 1790s (see pages 229–230). The Awakening originated in small villages in the East, intensified after the War of 1812, then spread across western New York and continued to grow through the late 1840s. Under its sway, the role of churches and ministers in community life began to change, and Christians in all parts of the country tried to right the wrongs of the world.

Before the Second Great Awakening, churches found themselves diminishing in influence and having to compete for members with other voluntary societies. A new generation of seminary-trained ministers successfully introduced revivals and advocacy of benevolent works—assistance to the poor, education of the young, and temperance campaigns—to attract new members, especially women. But while churches grew, their authority continued to erode. They stimulated people emotionally, but less and less did they control people's behavior.

Revivals—the lifeblood of evangelical Christianity—won converts to a religion of the heart rather than the head. In 1821 New York lawyer

Second Great Awakening

Charles G. Finney, the acknowledged father of modern revivalism, experienced a soul-shaking conversion that he interpreted as "a retainer from the Lord Jesus Christ to plead his cause." Finney immediately abandoned the law for a career as a converter of souls, traveling from town to town in western New York for "protracted meetings" lasting three to four days. Salvation could be achieved, he preached, through spontaneous conversion or spiritual rebirth like his own. He evoked emotional responses, as Jeremiah Paul depicted in his painting *Revival Meeting*. Using everyday language, Finney told his audiences that "God has made man a moral free agent." In other words, evil was avoidable—Christians were not doomed by original sin, and anyone could achieve salvation. Finney's brand of revivalism transcended sects, class, and race but had a particularly strong base among the middle class. Methodists, Presbyterians, Baptists, and Congregationalists became evangelists. The Second Great Awakening raised people's hopes for the Second Coming of the Christian messiah and establishment of the Kingdom of God on earth. Revivalists resolved to speed the Second Coming by creating a heaven on earth, marshaling the forces of good and light—reform—to combat those of evil and darkness. Some revivalists even believed that the United States had a special mission in God's design and therefore a special role in eliminating evil.

Regardless of theology, all shared a belief in individual self-improvement and self-reliance as forces for good. Thus the Second Great Awakening bred reform, and evangelical Protestants became missionaries for both religious and secular salvation. The stress on individual improvement and conversion also undermined the role of authority in religion. Wherever they preached, evangelists generated new religious groups and voluntary reform societies. New sects like the Mormons and Millerites arose out of this ferment. Evangelical reformers organized an association to address each pressing issue—temperance, education, Sabbath observance, dueling, and later antislavery. Collectively these groups constituted a national web of benevolent and moral-reform societies. Finney's

doctrine of perfectionism demanded an active Christianity that involved working with other people. By converting others and organizing efforts to elevate others, and by renouncing their own personal corruptions and dependency, the converted confirmed their status as Christians. They also moved inevitably toward reform and ultimately toward public action.

Women's involvement in benevolent activities to ameliorate social ills grew remarkably during the Second Great Awakening and invigorated local churches. In Andover, Massachusetts, revivalism gave rise in 1814 to a men's society dedicated to uplifting morals, banishing swearing, observing the Sabbath, and discouraging drunkenness. The next year local women formed the Female Charitable Society, and a year later youth joined the Juvenile Bible Society. During the 1820s, without any revivals in Andover, the benevolent societies brought in new church members, of whom 70 to 80 percent were women.

Women were the earliest converts to evangelism, and they tended to sustain the Second Great Awakening. Pious middle-class women in Rochester, New York, for instance,

Role of Women

responded to Finney's prayer meetings by spreading the word to other women during the day while their husbands were away at work. Gradually women brought their families and husbands into church and under the influence of reform. Churches and reform societies were increasingly influenced and even run by women. Although many businessmen recruited their employees to revivalism and benevolent work, women more than men tended to feel personally responsible for counteracting the increasingly secular orientation of the expanding market economy. Many women felt guilty for neglecting their religious duties, and the emotionally charged conversion experience set them on the right path again.

Revival seemed at first to reinforce the cult of domesticity, because piety and religious values were associated with the domestic sphere (see Chapter 12). In the grip of the

From Revival to Reform

conversion experience, women declared their submissiveness to the will of Providence, vowing to purge themselves and the world of wickedness. But the prayer groups and female missionary societies that characterized the Second Great Awakening gave rise to organized religious and benevolent activity on an unprecedented scale. Thus revival led to new public roles for women as religious and reform leaders, providing a path of certainty and stability in a rapidly changing economy and society.

In the larger cities women responded both to their inner voices and to the growing inequality, turbulence, and wretched conditions around them. The poverty and vice that accompanied urbanization touched the hearts of women, especially those caught up in the fervor of revival. As early as the turn of the nineteenth century, most cities had women's benevolent societies to help needy women and orphans, as did Salem, Massachusetts, with its Female Charitable Society.

Both female and male reformers sometimes acted in defiance of traditional political leaders. An exposé of prostitution in New York City illustrates the gulf between reform-minded men and women on the one hand and the political establishment on the other. John R. McDowall, a divinity student, published a report in 1830 documenting the prevalence of prostitution in New York City. Philip Hone, a prominent civic leader (see pages 344–345), denounced McDowall's report as "a disgraceful document," and he and other New York businessmen and politicians united to defend the city's good name against "those base slanders." In effect, the city had tolerated the presence of prostitution in vice districts in the city. Reform-minded women, on the other hand, moved by the plight of "fallen women" and supported by the Tappan brothers, the now-reverend McDowall, and others, responded by organizing to fight prostitution. Whereas the male societies had made the prostitute the target, the new reform groups focused on the men who victimized young women. The newly organized Female Moral Reform Society, for example, publicized the names of men entering brothels in New York City.

The Female Moral Reform Society led the crusade against prostitution. New York-based, the association expanded its activities and geographical scope during the 1830s as the American Female Moral Reform Society. By 1840 it had 555 affiliated female societies across the nation. They combated prostitution by focusing on men and by assisting poor women, whose economic desperation might lead them to turn to prostitution. They also entered the political sphere. In New York State in the 1840s the movement fostered public morality by successfully crusading for criminal sanctions against men who seduced women into prostitution and against prostitutes.

As the pace of social change quickened in the 1830s and 1840s, so did religious fervor and efforts at reform. In western New York and Ohio, Finney's preaching acted as a catalyst to reform. Western New York experienced such continuous and heated waves of revivalism that it became known as "the burned-over district." The westward migration of New Englanders along the newly opened Erie Canal carried religious ferment as far west as Ohio. There, revivalist institutions—notably Ohio's Lane Seminary and Oberlin College—sent committed graduates out into the world to spread the gospel of reform. Their efforts stirred nonevangelical Protestants, Catholics, and Jews, as well as evangelical Christians. Reform-minded members of all these groups became involved in new grassroots political movements. In the late 1830s and 1840s they rallied around the Whig party in hopes of using government as an instrument of reform.

TEMPERANCE AND ASYLUMS

One of the most successful reform efforts was the campaign against the consumption of alcohol. Drinking was more widespread in the early nineteenth century than it is today. Generally speaking, American men liked to drink—particularly whiskey, rum, and hard cider. They gathered in public houses, saloons, and rural inns to gossip, discuss politics, play cards, escape work and home pressures, and drink. Men drank on all occasions: contracts were sealed, celebrations commemorated, barns raised, and harvests toasted with liquor. Respectable women did not drink in public, but many regularly tippled alcohol-based patent medicines promoted as cure-alls. Moreover, immigration brought to America people for whom drinking was part of everyday life.

Why then did temperance become such a vital issue? And why were women especially active in the movement? Like all nineteenth-century reform, temperance had a strong religious foundation. "The Holy Spirit," a temperance pamphlet proclaimed, "will not visit, much less dwell with him who is under the polluting, debasing effects of intoxicating drink." To evangelicals, the sale of whiskey often involved a Sabbath violation, for workers commonly labored six days a week and spent Sunday at the public house drinking and socializing. Alcohol was seen as a destroyer of families as well, since men who drank heavily often neglected their families and could not adequately support them. Temperance literature was laced with domestic images—abandoned wives, prodigal sons, drunken fathers. Timothy Shay Arthur dramatized all these evils in *Ten Nights in a Barroom* (1853), a classic American melodrama. In the new world of the factory, the habit of drinking could not be tolerated. Employers complained that drinkers took "St. Monday" as a holiday to recover from Sunday. Whatever their attitudes toward other reforms, industrialists typically supported temperance in the interests of promoting the steady work habits needed for factory work.

Demon rum thus became a prime target of reformers. As the movement gained momentum, their goal shifted from temperate use of alcohol to

Temperance Societies

voluntary abstinence and finally to prohibition of the manufacture and sale of spirits. The American Society for the Promotion of Temperance, organized in 1826 to urge drinkers to sign a pledge of abstinence, shortly thereafter became a pressure group for state prohibition legislation. By the mid-1830s there were some five thousand state and local temperance societies, and more than one million people had taken the pledge. Several hundred thousand children, for instance, enlisted in the Cold Water Army. The temperance movement's success was reflected in a sharp decline in alcohol consumption by the 1840s. Between 1800 and 1830, annual per capita consumption of alcohol had risen from three to more than five gallons; by the mid-1840s it had dropped below two gallons. Success bred more victories. Maine prohibited the manufacture and sale of alcohol except for medicinal purposes in 1851, and by 1855 similar laws had been enacted throughout New England and the Old Northwest and in New York and Pennsylvania.

Though consumption of alcohol was declining, opposition to it did not weaken. Many reformers regarded alcohol as an evil introduced and perpetuated by Catholic immigrants. From the 1820s on,

anti-liquor reformers based much of their argument on this prejudice. The Irish and Germans, the *American Protestant Magazine* complained in 1849, "bring the grog shops like the frogs of Egypt upon us." Rum and immigrants defiled the Sabbath; rum and immigrants brought poverty; rum and immigrants supported the feared papacy. Some Catholics did join with nonevangelical Protestant sects like the Lutherans to oppose temperance legislation. But other Catholics took the pledge of abstinence and formed their own temperance organizations, such as the St. Mary's Mutual Benevolent Total Abstinence Society in Boston. Even nondrinking Catholics tended to oppose state regulation of drinking, however; temperance seemed to them a question of individual choice, not state coercion. They favored self-control, not societal control.

Another aspect of the temperance movement was opposition to gambling. People who gathered at taverns to drink also gambled, and reformers believed that both vices undermined independence and self-reliance. Of special concern in the nineteenth century was the spread of lotteries.

Lotteries had been introduced by English colonists at the turn of the eighteenth century. England used lotteries to raise government revenues, and some colonists bought tickets.

Lotteries

In the New World, lotteries were an effective way of selling costly property in an age when few buyers could raise the large purchase price. If hundreds of small investors participated in a lottery for the prize, a merchant could dispose of inventory or a homeowner could sell a valuable house. Local governments used lotteries to ease the tax burden by raising money for capital improvements. The Continental Congress had hoped to raise $1.5 million from a lottery to wage revolutionary war against England, but it failed to raise the anticipated revenue.

Lotteries became a target of reform, and between 1830 and 1860 every state in the Union banned them. Some people compared lotteries to such vices as slavery and alcohol. Others objected to the abuses inherent in the states' practice of delegating their lottery powers to private sponsors. An 1831 Pennsylvania investigation, for instance, revealed that a state-authorized lottery to raise $27,000 a year for internal improvements, specifically for the Union Canal Company, had generated enormous profits for the lottery company. On $5 million annual sales, the state received its $27,000 and the sponsors $800,000. At the urging of Protestant reformers who condemned all forms of gambling, the report led to the prohibition of lotteries in Pennsylvania. (When some states revived lotteries in the twentieth century, they learned from the previous century's experiences and chose to run their own contests.)

The age of reform also brought about the construction of asylums and other institutions to house prisoners, the insane and ill, orphans, delinquent children, and the poor. Such institutions were needed, reformers believed, to shelter victims of society's instability and turbulence and of lack of discipline in families. In an environment of order, stability, and discipline, inmates would have an opportunity to become self-reliant and responsible.

The penitentiary movement exemplified this outlook. In the 1820s New York and Pennsylvania developed competing models for reforming criminals. They rejected incarcera-

Penitentiaries tion simply to punish criminals or remove them from society; instead, disciplined regimens would rehabilitate them. New York's Auburn (1819–1823) and Sing-Sing (1825) prisons isolated prisoners in individual cells but brought them together in common workshops. The Pittsburgh (1826) and Philadelphia (1829) prisons isolated prisoners completely; they ate, slept, and worked in their individual cells and had contact only with guards and visitors. Both systems sought to remove criminals from evil societal and individual influences and to expose them to an ordered, disciplined regimen. It was widely believed that criminals came from unstable families whose lack of discipline and restraint led to vice and drink. Idleness was believed to be both a symptom and a cause of individual corruption and crime; thus the clock governed a prisoner's day, and idleness was banished.

Similar approaches were employed in other kinds of asylums, from insane asylums and hospitals to orphanages and houses of refuge. Doctors attributed mental illness, for instance, to the stress of urban life. Formerly, the prescribed treatment had been to remove disturbed individuals from their families and society and isolate them among strangers; they were often incarcerated with criminals. The new asylums removed them from soci-

ety, but attempted to impose discipline and order in a humane fashion. In response to the appeals of reform societies, states began in the 1830s to erect asylums for the insane in tranquil rural settings, away from the turbulent cities. By 1860, twenty-eight of the thirty-three states had public institutions for the insane.

ANTIMASONRY

Far more intense than the asylum movement, though of shorter duration, was the crusade against Freemasonry, a secret middle- and upper-class fraternity that had come to the United States from England in the eighteenth century. Such sons of the Enlightenment as Benjamin Franklin and George Washington were attracted to Masonry, with its emphasis on individual belief in a deity (as opposed to organized religion) and on brotherhood (as opposed to one church). In the early nineteenth century Freemasonry spread in the growing towns, attracting men prominent in commerce and civic affairs. For ambitious young men, the Masons offered access to and fellowship with the leading lights of the community.

Opponents of Masonry charged that the order's secrecy was antidemocratic and antirepublican, as was its elite membership and its use of regalia and such offices as "knight" and "priest." Publications such as the *Anti Masonic Almanac* attacked Masonic initiation rites. As church leaders took up the moral crusade against Masonry, evangelicals labeled the order satanic. Antimasons argued that Masonry threatened the family because it excluded women and encouraged men to neglect their families for alcohol and ribald entertainments at Masonic lodges.

The Antimasonry movement arose overnight in the burned-over district of western New York in 1826 and virtually disappeared in the 1830s. Foreshadowing abolitionism, it became more of a political than a reform movement. Antimasonry created the first third-party movement and drew new white voters into politics at a time when male suffrage was being extended. As the temperance movement sought to liberate individuals from drink, Antimasons sought to liberate society from the grip of what they considered a powerful and antirepublican secret fraternity. As asylums would restore individual discipline and harmony, the

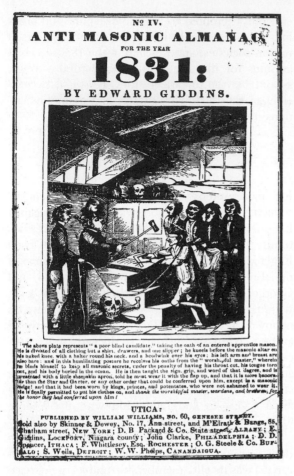

Antimasonic publications, such as this 1831 almanac, made much of the allegedly sinister initiation rites that bound a new member "to keep all Masonic secrets, under the penalty of having his throat cut, his tongue torn out, and his body buried in the ocean." Print collection, Miriam & Ira D. Wallach Division of Art, Prints & Photographs. The New York Public Library.

Antimasons believed, the abolition of Masonry would re-establish communal moral discipline and harmony. The political arena quickly absorbed Antimasonry, and its short life illustrates the close association of politics and reform between the 1820s and the 1840s.

The catalyst for Antimasonry as an organized movement was an incident known as the Morgan affair. In 1826 William Morgan, a disillusioned Mason, published an exposé of

Morgan Affair

——

Masonry, *The Illustration of Masonry, By One of the Fraternity Who Has Devoted Thirty Years to the Subject*, to which his printer David Miller added a scathing attack on the order. Just prior to the

book's appearance, a group of Masons abducted Morgan in Canandaigua, New York. It was widely believed that they murdered Morgan, whose body was never found.

The Antimasonry crusade's characterization of Masonry as a secret conspiracy seemed to be confirmed by events. Many officeholders in western New York, especially prosecutors, were Masons, and they appeared to obstruct the investigation of Morgan's abduction. The public pressed for justice, and the series of notorious trials that ensued from 1827 through 1831 led many to suspect a conspiracy. The cover-up became as much of an issue as distrust of Masonry itself, and the movement spread from the burned-over district to other states.

As a moral crusade, Antimasonry spilled over into the political arena almost immediately. The issue itself was political, because of the perceived obstruction of justice. Furthermore, Antimasonry attracted the lower and middle classes, pitting them against higher-status Masons and exploiting the general public's distrust and envy of local political leaders. And factional leaders, like Governor DeWitt Clinton of New York, were more than willing to join in the public outrage in pursuit of political advantage.

Unwittingly, the Masons stoked the fires of Antimasonry. Their silence seemed to condone the murder of Morgan, and the construction of monumental lodges like the one in Boston signified their affluence and prominence. When newspaper editors who were Masons ignored the crusade against Masonry, the Antimasons founded their own newspapers. The conflict aroused a high level of public interest in politics. Wherever religious fervor flared and wherever families were entering the market economy for the first time, Antimasonry flourished.

As Antimasonry won a wider popular following, it introduced the convention system in place of caucuses for choosing political candidates. Its

Convention System

——

electoral strength lay in New England and New York. In Vermont it became the dominant party for a brief time in 1833; in Massachusetts it replaced the Democrats as the second major party. Like other reforms, however, it found little support in the more traditional southern society. Invoking public morality and republican principles, the Antimasons held conventions in 1827 to oppose

Masons running for public office. The next year the conventions supported the National Republican candidate, John Quincy Adams, and opposed Andrew Jackson because he was a Mason. The Antimasons held the first national political convention in Baltimore in 1831, and a year later nominated William Wirt as their presidential candidate. Thus the Antimasons became a rallying point for those opposed to President Andrew Jackson.

By the mid-1830s, however, Antimasonry had lost momentum as a moral and political movement. The party had a single-issue orientation, and as Freemasonry declined, so did its opposition. Yet the movement left its mark on the politics of the era. As a moral crusade focused on public office-holders, it inspired and welcomed broad participation in the political process.

The revivalist and reform impulses in movements like Antimasonry stimulated conflicts over values and ideology that were in turn reinforced by conflicts over class, religion, and status. These differences helped to polarize politics and to shape political parties as organizations to express those differences. Furthermore, the Antimasons contributed to party development more concretely by pioneering the convention system and stimulating grassroots involvement.

Antimasonry also had much in common with abolitionism. Indeed, as Antimasonry waned, the abolition movement gathered momentum. William Lloyd Garrison, who at first could not fathom the frenzy over the Morgan affair, joined the ranks of Antimasons in 1832. Echoing his stand on emancipation, Garrison wrote: "I go for the immediate, unconditional and total abolition of Freemasonry." In Garrison's eyes, both slavery and Masonry undermined republican values.

ABOLITIONISM AND THE WOMEN'S MOVEMENT

The issue of slavery eventually became so compelling that it consumed all other reforms. Passions would become so heated that they would threaten the nation itself. Those who advocated immediate emancipation saw slavery as, above all, a moral issue—evidence of the sinfulness of the American nation. When territorial expansion forced the issue of slavery to center stage in the 1850s, the abolitionist forces were well prepared (see Chapter 14).

Many groups opposed slavery prior to the 1830s. Quakers had led the way in the eighteenth century, freeing their slaves and preaching that bondage was a sin for Christians. But in the North, where most states had begun to abolish slavery by 1800, whites took little interest in an issue that did not concern them directly. Antislavery sentiment appeared strongest in the Upper South, though northern involvement grew with the expansion of benevolent societies after the War of 1812. The American Colonization Society, founded in 1816 and dedicated to promoting gradual, voluntary emancipation and resettlement of former slaves in Africa, attracted evangelicals, Quakers, some blacks (briefly), and slaveholders who found solace in the society's goal of sending free people of color to Africa. The gradualist antislavery movement remained strong, but in the 1830s the immediatists—those who demanded immediate, complete, and uncompensated emancipation—surpassed the gradualists as propagandists and eventually established themselves as the dominant strand of abolitionism.

At least fifty black abolitionist societies operated in urban African-American communities by 1830. These associations assisted fugitive slaves,

Black Abolitionists
———

lobbied for emancipation, exposed the evils of slavery, and reminded the nation that its mission as defined in the Declaration of Independence remained unfulfilled. A free black press helped to spread the word. Black abolitionists Frederick Douglass, Sojourner Truth, and Harriet Tubman then joined forces in the 1840s with white reformers in the American Anti-Slavery Society. Their militant and unrelenting campaign also won European support. "Brethren, arise, arise, arise!" Henry Highland Garnet commanded the 1843 National Colored Convention. "Strike for your lives and liberties. Now is the day and hour. Let every slave in the land do this and the days of slavery are numbered. Rather die freemen than live to be slaves."

Through the 1820s only African-Americans demanded an immediate end to slavery. In the 1830s, however, a small minority of white reformers resolved to crusade for

William Lloyd Garrison
———

immediate emancipation. The most prominent and uncompromising immediatist, though far from the most representative, was William Lloyd Garrison, who demanded "immediate and complete emancipation." Garrison had begun his career in the late 1820s as editor of the *National Philanthropist*, a weekly newspaper devoted to reform in general and prohibition in particular. In 1828, when Benjamin Lundy, the most outspoken abolitionist of the 1820s, recruited him to another journal, *The Genius of Universal Emancipation*, Garrison entered the ranks of the abolitionists. Lundy supported the American Colonization Society and sought to end slavery through persuasion. While preparing an article, Garrison was shocked to discover that slaveholders supported the American Colonization Society. In 1831 he broke with gradualists like Lundy and, with contributions from the Tappan brothers and others, published the first issue of the *Liberator*, which was to be his major weapon against slavery for thirty-five years. As he declared in the first issue, "I am in earnest—I will not equivocate—I will not excuse—I will not retreat a single inch—*and I will be heard.*"

Garrison's staunch refusal to work with anyone who even indirectly tolerated delay of emancipation isolated him from most people who opposed or disliked slavery. He even forswore political action, on the grounds that it was governments that permitted slavery. (Garrison burned a copy of the Constitution on July 4, 1854, proclaiming, "So perish all compromises with tyranny.") Through sheer rhetorical power, Garrison helped to make antislavery a national issue. His brand of immediatism consisted essentially of a refusal to tolerate delay in ending slavery; he had no specific plan for abolishing it. In essence, what Garrison called for was *conversion*—for those who held slaves or cooperated with institutions that supported slavery to cast off their sins, repent, and do battle against evil.

It is impossible to find consistent differences between those who became immediatists and those who did not. Lewis and Arthur Tappan became **Immediatists** immediatists; three of their brothers supported benevolent and reform activities but not abolition. (The last brother devoted himself to drinking.) But immediatists like Garrison, Elizabeth Chandler, Amos Phelps, Theodore Weld, and Lewis and Arthur Tappan, who resigned from the American Colonization Society and attacked it as sinful in the 1830s, had much in common. They had been young evangelicals active in benevolent societies in the 1820s; many became ordained ministers or flirted with the ministry as a career; and they had personal contact with free blacks and were sympathetic to black rights. They were convinced that slaveholding was a sin. Their immediatism made them more concerned about sin in the United States than about converting "heathens across the seas," and their concern in turn made them more political: to abolish sin they sought to change institutions at home. Finally, they shared great moral intensity. They were unwilling to compromise their beliefs, and their zeal made them activists. Their main organizational vehicle was the American Anti-Slavery Society, founded in 1833.

Most benevolent workers and reformers kept their distance from the immediatists. Many regarded the intensity of the immediatist approach as unchristian behavior. Though they shared the view that slavery was a sin, they believed that it had to be eradicated slowly, in a reasonable and patient manner. If they moved too fast, attacking sinners too harshly or interfering too aggressively in time-honored customs and beliefs, they would destroy the harmony and order they sought to bring about through benevolent and reform work. As for the American Colonization Society, they hoped to cleanse its taint.

Immediatists' greatest recruitment successes came about from defending their own constitutional and natural rights, not those of slaves. Wherever they went, immediatists **Opposition to Abolitionists** found their civil rights at risk, especially their right of free speech. Antislavery speakers often faced hostile crowds, and their presses were under constant threat of attack. Mobs violently defended what they considered to be American traditions. At Utica, New York, merchants and professionals broke up the state Anti-Slavery Convention in 1835. Abolitionist conventions provoked hostility by welcoming both whites and blacks and by allowing women prominent roles. Fear and hatred moved proslavery proponents to take to the streets. In 1837 a mob in Alton, Illinois, murdered the abolitionist editor Elijah P. Lovejoy, who had been driven out of slaveholding Missouri and had re-established his printing plant just across the river in Illinois. Before killing Lovejoy, rioters sacked his office with the cooperation of local authorities. Public outrage at Lovejoy's

How do historians know

about the activities of abolitionists, especially women and black abolitionists?

Abolitionists lived open lives. They used newspapers, pamphlets, speeches, and sermons to expose the evils of slavery, to mount a crusade for emancipation, and to build a network of like-minded people. Most of their speeches and even correspondence were printed in the pages of the abolitionist newspapers.

William Lloyd Garrison's Liberator, which appeared from 1831 to 1866, recorded the weekly activities of immediatist abolitionists. The newspaper printed passionate attacks on slavery, reported meetings of antislavery societies, and published letters, especially from women and African-American abolitionists. Under the banners "No Union with Slaveholders" and "The United States Constitution is a 'covenant with death, and an agreement with hell,'" the Liberator was circulated to abolitionists advocating immediate emancipation. Throughout most of its history, a majority of its subscribers were probably African-Americans. Photo: David M. Katzman.

murder broadened the base of antislavery support in the North.

In the South, mobs blocked distribution of antislavery pamphlets. Using high-speed printing presses, the American Anti-Slavery Society increased its distribution of antislavery propaganda tenfold between 1834 and 1835, when they sent out 1.1 million pieces. But southern mobs seized and destroyed much of the mail, and South Carolina (with the approval of the U.S. postmaster general) intercepted and burned abolitionist literature that entered the state. President Andrew Jackson even proposed a law prohibiting the mailing of antislavery tracts.

The opposition saw danger in abolitionism. Former Federalist Harrison Gray Otis portrayed abolitionists as subversives at a rally in Boston's Faneuil Hall in 1835. He attacked Garrison's American Anti-Slavery Society as a "revolutionary society" that not only recruited all men to its "holy crusade" but also asked women to "turn their sewing parties into abolition clubs." If it prevailed, Otis charged, school primers would teach "that A stands for abolition." The abolitionists, he predicted, would soon turn to politics, causing unforeseeable calamity. "What will become of the nation?" Otis asked. "What will become of the union?" Others believed that the immediatists' opposition to black emigration undermined the best solution. Keeping blacks in America, they believed, would eventually lead to slave rebellions and racial amalgamation. The immediatists' close ties with British abolitionists also provoked charges that the movement was an English plot to subvert American independence.

Another confrontation focused on Congress. Abolitionists, exercising their constitutional right to petition Congress, mounted a campaign to abol-

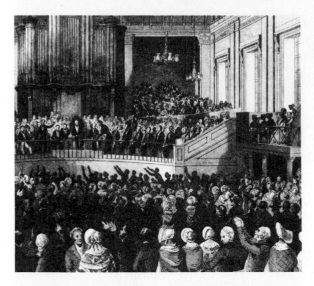

Women played an activist role in reform, especially in abolition-ism. A contemporary engraving shows women at an antislavery rally at Exeter Hall in 1840. Library of Congress.

Gag Rule

ish slavery and the slave trade in the District of Columbia. (Since the district was under federal rule, states'-rights arguments against interfering with slavery did not apply there.) Congress responded in 1836 by adopting the so-called gag rule, which automatically tabled abolitionist petitions, effectively preventing debate on them. Immediatists flooded Congress with nearly seven hundred thousand petitions. In a dramatic defense of the right of petition, former president John Quincy Adams, a Massachusetts representative, took to the floor repeatedly to defy the gag rule and eventually succeeded in getting it repealed in 1844.

Frustration with the federal government also fed northern support for antislavery. Generally speaking, politicians and government officials sought to avoid the question of slavery. The Missouri Compromise of 1820 had been an effort to quarantine the issue by adopting a formula—prohibition of slavery north of 36°30′, Missouri's southern boundary—that would make debate on the slave or free status of new states unnecessary. Censorship of the mails and the gag rule also represented attempts to keep the issue out of the political arena. Yet the more intensely national leaders, especially Democrats, worked to avoid the matter, the more they hardened the resolve of the antislavery forces.

The unlawful, violent, and obstructionist tactics used by opponents of abolition helped unify the movement by forcing the various factions to work together for mutual defense. Antislavery was not at the outset a unified movement. It was splintered and factionalized, and its adherents fought each other as doggedly and as often as they fought the defenders of slavery. They were divided over Garrison's emphasis on "moral suasion" versus the more practical political approach of James G. Birney, the Liberty party's candidate for president in 1844 (see page 393). They were split over support of other reforms, especially the rights of women. And they disagreed about the place of free people of color in American society. Even so, abolitionists eventually managed to unify and make emancipation a major issue in the politics of the 1850s.

Women had less success when it came to their own position in society. At its inception, the American Anti-Slavery Society resembled most other benevolent societies in

Women Abolitionists

its gender structure. Men established and ran the society; women supported it through their own affiliates. The early movement was segregated by gender, with women in a subordinate role. Over time, this pattern changed among the immediatists. By the late 1840s, female abolitionists were breaking free of the domestic sphere—many of them were single women—and becoming genuine colleagues to men in the movement. Men like Garrison came to accept their women colleagues' contributions in providing moral direction. Garrison worked closely with Sarah Grimké after publishing her essays on the equality of the sexes in the *Liberator*. Lydia Maria Child, Maria Chapman, and Lucretia Mott all joined the American Anti-Slavery Society's executive committee; Child edited its official organ, the *National Anti-Slavery Standard*, from 1841 to 1843, and Chapman co-edited it from 1844 until 1848. Many more women joined local female antislavery societies. Based in local churches, these societies were part of the network of benevolent societies created in the wake of the Second Great Awakening. The women who joined acquired organizational experience that many of them would later use on their own behalf.

Negative reaction to the growing involvement of women in reform movements led some women to re-examine their position in society. In 1837 two antislavery lecturers, Angelina and Sarah Grimké, became particular objects of controversy. Natives of Charleston, South Carolina, they moved north in the 1820s to speak out more openly and forcefully against slavery, but they received a hostile reception for speaking before mixed groups of men and women. Some New England Congregationalists and even abolitionists joined in the criticism; as one pastoral letter put it, women should obey, not lecture, men. This reaction turned the Grimkés' attention from slavery to the women's condition. The two attacked the concept of "subordination to man," insisting that men and women had the "same rights and same duties." Sarah Grimké's *Letters on the Condition of Women and the Equality of the Sexes* (1838) and her sister's *Letters to Catharine E. Beecher*, published the same year, were the opening volleys in the long war over the legal and social inequality of women.

In arguing against slavery, some women noticed similarities between their own position and that of slaves. They saw parallels in their legal disa-

Women's Rights

bilities—inability to vote or to control their own property except in widowhood—and their social restrictions—exclusion from advanced schooling and from most occupations. "The investigation of the rights of the slave," Angelina Grimké confessed, "has led me to a better understanding of my own." Some of the women who worked in the Lowell mills came to the same conclusion in the 1840s.

Unlike other reform movements, which succeeded in building a broad base of individual and organizational support, the movement for women's rights was limited. Some men joined the ranks, notably Garrison and ex-slave Frederick Douglass, but most were actively opposed. In the 1840s the question of women's rights split the antislavery movement; the majority declared themselves opposed. The Woman's Rights Convention held at Seneca Falls, New York, in 1848—organized by Elizabeth Cady Stanton and Lucretia Mott, who had met at the 1840 London World Anti-Slavery Convention—issued a much-published indictment of the injustices suffered by women. Echoing the 1776 Declaration of Independence, the Seneca Falls Declaration of Sentiments asserted that "We hold these truths to be self-evident: that all men and women are created equal." The declaration documented the record of male tyranny over women and the inequalities and indignities that women suffered at the hands of government and the law. If women had the vote, these early advocates of women's rights argued, they could protect themselves and realize their potential as moral and spiritual leaders. Their argument won few converts to their cause.

JACKSONIANISM AND THE BEGINNINGS OF MODERN PARTY POLITICS

The distinction between reform and politics began to erode in the 1820s as reform pushed its way into politics. The Antimasons and then the abolitionists appealed directly to voters. No less than reformers, politicians also sought to control the direction of change in the expanding nation. After a brief flirtation with single-party politics following the War of 1812, the United States entered a period of intense and heated political competition. As the age of Virginia presidents came to an end in 1825, the Republican party was split by the Panic of 1819, sectional disputes, the rising tide of abolitionism, and the spread of reform. The 1824 presidential election ignited a political barn fire that would be continuously stoked by reformers, abolitionists, and expansionists. By the 1830s, politics had become the great nineteenth-century American pastime.

The election of 1824, in which John Quincy Adams and Andrew Jackson faced off for the first time, heralded a new, more open political system.

End of the Caucus System

The Federalist party had disappeared after 1816, and James Monroe had run unopposed as the Republican candidate in 1820. From 1800 through 1820 the system whereby a congressional caucus chose Jefferson, Madison, and Monroe as the Republican nominees had worked well. Jefferson and Madison had both hand-picked their secretaries of state as their successors, and the caucuses had in turn nominated them. Such a system limited voter involvement in choosing candidates, but this was not at first an anomaly because in 1800 only five of the sixteen states selected presidential electors by popular vote. (In most cases, state legislatures selected

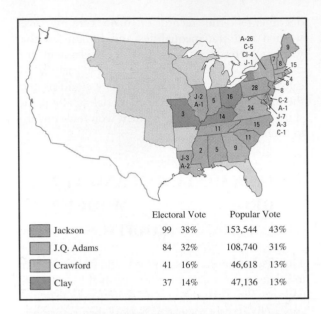

	Electoral Vote		Popular Vote	
Jackson	99	38%	153,544	43%
J.Q. Adams	84	32%	108,740	31%
Crawford	41	16%	46,618	13%
Clay	37	14%	47,136	13%

Presidential Election, 1824 *Although Andrew Jackson led in both the electoral and popular votes, he failed to achieve a majority of electoral college votes, and the House elected John Quincy Adams president.*

the electors who voted for president.) By 1816, however, ten out of nineteen states chose electors by popular vote, and by 1824 eighteen out of twenty-four did so. With the voters choosing electors, Congress could no longer sustain its control over the nomination system.

Outgoing President James Monroe never designated an heir apparent. The Republican caucus in 1824 therefore chose William H. Crawford, secretary of the treasury. But other Republicans, emboldened by the opportunity to appeal directly to voters in most states, put themselves forward as sectional candidates. Secretary of State John Quincy Adams drew support from New England, and westerners backed Speaker of the House Henry Clay of Kentucky. Secretary of War John C. Calhoun looked to the South for support and hoped to win Pennsylvania as well. And Andrew Jackson, a popular military hero whose political views were unknown, was nominated by resolution of the Tennessee legislature. Jackson had the most widespread support, but Crawford, who had declined to oppose Monroe in 1816 and 1820, enjoyed the most support in Washington. Since the choice

of Crawford by the caucus was a foregone conclusion, the other four candidates joined in attacking the caucus system as undemocratic. When their supporters boycotted the deliberations, Crawford's victory by a minority vote became hollow. The role of the congressional caucus in nominating presidents ended.

Andrew Jackson led in both electoral and popular votes in the four-way presidential election of 1824, but no one received a majority in the electoral college (see map). Adams finished second, and Crawford and Clay trailed far behind. (Calhoun had dropped out of the race before the election.) Under the Twelfth Amendment to the Constitution, the House of Representatives—voting by state delegation, one vote to a state—would select the president from among the three leaders in electoral votes. Clay, who had received the fewest votes, was dropped; Crawford, a stroke victim, never received serious consideration. The influential Clay, as Speaker of the House and leader of the Ohio Valley states, backed Adams, who received the votes of thirteen of twenty-four state delegations. Clay became secretary of state in the Adams administration—the traditional stepping-stone to the presidency.

Angry Jacksonians denounced the arrangement as a "corrupt bargain" that had stolen the office from the clear front runner. Congressional intrigue had thwarted the will of the people, Jacksonians believed, and Jackson's bitterness reinforced his opposition to elitism and his later emphasis on the people's will. The Republican party split; the Adams wing emerged as the National Republicans, and the Jacksonians became the Democratic-Republicans (shortened to Democrats). The Jacksonians immediately began laying plans for 1828. After taking the oath as the sixth president, Adams proposed a strong nationalist policy incorporating Henry Clay's American System of protective tariffs, a national bank, and internal improvements (see page 260). Adams believed the federal government should take an activist role not only in the economy but also in education, science, and the arts; he accordingly proposed a national university in Washington, D.C.

Brilliant as a diplomat and secretary of state, Adams was an inept president. The political skills he had demonstrated in winning the office eluded him as chief executive. Adams underestimated the lingering effects of the Panic of 1819 and the resulting bitter opposition to a national bank and protective tariffs. Meanwhile, supporters of Andrew Jackson sabotaged Adams's administration at every opportunity.

The 1828 campaign pitting Adams against Jackson was an intensely personal conflict. Whatever principles the two men stood for were obscured by mudslinging on both sides. Jackson's supporters claimed that the presidency had been stolen from the general in 1824. Adams had a similarly low opinion of General Jackson. In his diary he declared Jackson "incompetent both by his ignorance and by the fury of his passions." The two camps traded charges of adultery and procuring prostitutes. When Rachel Jackson died a month after the election, the president-elect attributed his wife's death to the abuse heaped on him in the campaign. He never forgave her "murderers."

Adams won the same states as in 1824, but this time the opposition was unified, and Jackson swamped him (see map). Jackson polled 56 percent of the popular vote and won in the electoral college by 178 to 83 votes. For him and his supporters, the will of the people had finally been served. Many voters displayed their loyalty to Jackson with badges, medals, pendants, and other campaign paraphernalia, which were being mass-produced for the first time. Through a lavishly financed coalition of state parties, political leaders, and newspaper editors, a popular movement had elected a president. An era had ended, and the Democratic party became the first well-organized national political party in the United States. Tightly organized parties became the hallmark of nineteenth-century American politics.

Andrew Jackson

Nicknamed "Old Hickory" after the toughest of the American hardwoods, Andrew Jackson was a rough-and-tumble ambitious man. Born in South Carolina, he rose from humble beginnings to become a wealthy planter and slave-holder. Jackson was the first American president from the West and the first born in a log cabin; he was a self-made man at ease among both frontiersmen and southern planters. Though vindictive and given to violent displays of temper, he could charm away the suspicions of those opposed to him. A natural leader, Jackson inspired immense loyalty. He had an instinct for politics, and shrewdly picked both issues and supporters.

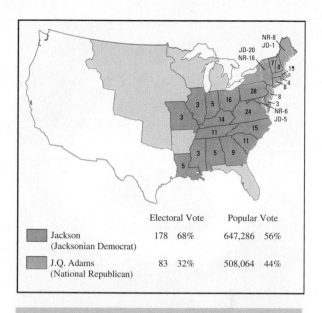

		Electoral Vote		Popular Vote	
▮	Jackson (Jacksonian Democrat)	178	68%	647,286	56%
▮	J.Q. Adams (National Republican)	83	32%	508,064	44%

Presidential Election, 1828 *Andrew Jackson avenged his 1824 loss of the presidency, sweeping the election in 1828.*

Few Americans have been as celebrated in myth and legend as Jackson. Having fought in the Revolution as a boy, he carried scars from a redcoat attack all his life. In the Tennessee militia General Jackson led the campaign to remove Creeks from the Alabama and Georgia frontier. He burst onto the national scene as the great hero of the War of 1812, and in 1818 enhanced his glory in an expedition against Seminoles in Spanish Florida. Jackson also served as a congressman and senator from Tennessee, as a judge in his home state, and as the first territorial governor of Florida (1821) before running for president in 1824.

Democrats

Jackson and his Democratic supporters offered a distinct alternative to the strong federal government advocated by John Quincy Adams. The Democrats represented a wide range of views but shared a fundamental commitment to the Jeffersonian concept of an agrarian society. They harkened back to the belief that a strong central government is the enemy of individual liberty, a tyranny to be feared. Like Jefferson, they favored limited central government. The 1824 "corrupt bargain" had strengthened their suspicion of Washington politics. Jackson himself,

President Andrew Jackson is portrayed here on a pendant and a cameo brooch, campaign paraphernalia from the 1820s that were mass-produced and worn by partisan Jackson supporters. Museum of American Political Life, University of Hartford.

symbol of the backwoodsman and the farmer, affirmed the familiar old values that predated the new party politics and the new market system.

Jacksonians were as fearful of the concentration of economic power as they were of concentrated political power. They saw government intervention in the economy as benefiting special-interest groups and creating corporate monopolies; thus they rejected an activist economic program as favoring the rich. Jacksonians sought to restore the independence of the individual—the artisan and the yeoman farmer—by ending federal support of banks and corporations and restricting the use of paper currency, which they distrusted. Their definition of the proper role of government tended to be negative, and Jackson's political power was largely expressed in negative acts; he exercised the veto more than all previous presidents combined.

Jackson and his supporters were also hostile to reform as a movement and an ideology. Reformers eager to turn their programs into legislation were

calling for a more activist and interventionist government. But Democrats tended to oppose programs like educational reform and the establishment of public education. They believed, for instance, that public schools restricted individual liberty by interfering with parental responsibility and undermined freedom of religion by replacing church schools. Nor did Jackson share reformers' humanitarian concerns. He showed little sympathy for Native Americans, initiating their removal with the Trail of Tears (see page 357).

Jackson and the Jacksonians considered themselves reformers in a different way. By promoting restraint in government and emphasizing individualism, they sought to restore old republican virtues, such as industriousness, prudence, and economy. No less zealously than reformers, Jackson sought to encourage self-discipline and self-reliance and to restore a harmony and unity that he saw as having been disrupted by economic and social change. In doing so, Jackson looked to Jefferson and the generation of founders as models of traditional values. "My political creed," Jackson wrote James K. Polk in 1826, "was formed in the old republican school."

Like Jefferson, Jackson strengthened the executive branch of government even as he weakened the federal role. Given his popularity and the strength of his personality, this concentration of power in the presidency was perhaps inevitable, but his deliberate policy of combining the roles of party leader and chief of state centralized even greater power in the White House. Jackson relied on political friends, his "Kitchen Cabinet," for advice; he rarely consulted his official cabinet. Enamored of power, Jackson never hesitated to confront his opponents with all the weapons at his disposal. He commanded enormous loyalty, and he rewarded his followers handsomely. Invoking the principle that rotating officeholders would make government more responsive to the public will, Jackson used the spoils system to appoint loyal Democrats to office. He removed fewer than one-quarter of the federal officeholders he inherited, but his use of patronage nevertheless strengthened party organization and loyalty.

Jackson himself stressed his rejection of elitism and special favors, rotation of officeholders, and belief in popular government. Time and again he declared that sovereignty resided with the people, not with the states or the courts. Summoning the electorate's support, he confidently claimed to represent the people's will. In this respect Jackson was a reformer; he returned government to majority rule. Yet it is hard to distinguish between Jackson's belief in himself as the instrument of the people and simple egotism and demagogic arrogance. After all, his opponents, too, claimed to represent the people.

Animosity grew year by year among President Jackson's opponents. Daniel Webster feared the men around Jackson; Henry Clay most feared Jackson himself. Rotation in office, they contended, corrupted government. Opponents mocked Jackson as "King Andrew I," charging him with abusing his presidential powers by ignoring the Supreme Court's ruling on Cherokee rights (see page 357), by his use of the spoils system, and by his dependence on the Kitchen Cabinet. Critics challenged his claim of restoring republican virtue and inheriting the mantle of Jefferson. They charged him with recklessly and impulsively destroying the economy.

Jackson injected new vigor into the philosophy of limited government. In 1830 he vetoed the Maysville Road bill—which would have funded construction of a sixty-mile turnpike from Maysville to Lexington, Kentucky—on the grounds that a federally subsidized internal improvement confined to one state was unconstitutional; such projects were properly a state responsibility. The veto undermined Henry Clay's American System and personally embarrassed Clay because the project was in his home district. Such federal-state issues were to loom even larger in the nullification crisis.

THE NULLIFICATION AND BANK CONTROVERSIES

Soon Jackson had to face the question of the proper division of sovereignty between state and central government more directly. The reform crusades, especially the antislavery movement, had made the southern states fearful of federal power—and none was more so than South Carolina, where the planter class was strongest and slavery most concentrated. South Carolinians had seen abolitionist sentiment in Great Britain grow until it resulted in the 1833 emancipation of West Indian slaves, and they were alarmed by the stridency of imme-

diatism in the United States. They feared the same thing would happen at home. Hard-hit by the Panic of 1819, from which they never fully recovered, they also resented the high prices of imported goods due to protectionist tariffs.

To protect their interests, South Carolinian political leaders articulated the doctrine of *nullification*, according to which a state had the right to overrule, or nullify, federal legislation that conflicted with its own. The theoreticians of nullification were expanding on the idea expressed in the Virginia and Kentucky Resolutions of 1798 (see page 225) that the states, representing the people, have a right to judge the constitutionality of federal actions. John C. Calhoun of South Carolina argued in his unsigned *Exposition and Protest* that, in any disagreement between the federal government and a state, a special state convention—like the conventions called to ratify the Constitution—should decide the conflict by either nullifying or affirming the federal law. Only the power of nullification, Calhoun asserted, could protect the minority against the tyranny of the majority.

In public, Calhoun let others take the lead in advancing nullification. As Jackson's running mate in 1828, he avoided publicly endorsing nullification and thus embarrassing the ticket; he hoped to win Jackson's support as the Democratic presidential heir apparent. Thus Calhoun presided silently over the Senate and its packed galleries when Senators Daniel Webster of New Hampshire and Robert Y. Hayne of South Carolina debated nullification in early 1830. The debate explored North-South frictions and the question of the nature of the Union. With Calhoun nodding in agreement, Hayne charged that the North was threatening to bring disunity, as it had before in the Hartford Convention (see page 258). Hayne accused reformers in "the spirit of false philanthropy" of wanting to destroy the South.

Webster-Hayne Debate

For two days Webster eloquently defended the New England states and the republic, keeping nullification on the defensive. Though ostensibly debating Hayne, he aimed his remarks at Calhoun in depicting the nation as a compact of people, not merely of states. Webster, at the climax of his career as a debater, invoked two powerful images. One was the outcome of nullification: "states dissevered, discordant, belligerent; on a land rent with civil feuds, or drenched . . . in fraternal blood!" The other was a patriotic vision of a great nation flourishing under the motto "Liberty *and* Union, now and forever, one and inseparable."

Though sympathetic to states' rights and distrustful of the federal government, Jackson rejected the idea of state sovereignty. It was his strong belief that sovereignty rested with the people. As a committed nationalist and patriot, he was deeply loyal to the Union. Thus he shared Webster's dread and distrust of nullification. Soon after the Webster-Hayne debate, the president made his position clear at a Jefferson Day dinner with the toast "Our Federal Union, it *must* and *shall be* preserved." Calhoun, when his turn came, toasted: "The Federal Union—next to our liberty the most dear." Torn between devotion to the Union and loyalty to his state, Calhoun had revealed his preference for states' rights. Politically and personally, Calhoun and Jackson grew apart, and it soon became apparent that Jackson favored Secretary of State Martin Van Buren, not Calhoun, as his successor.

Nullification Crisis ▬ South Carolina invoked the theory of nullification against the Tariff of 1832, which reduced some duties but retained high taxes on imported iron, cottons, and woolens. Though a majority of southern representatives supported the new tariff, South Carolinians refused to go along. In their eyes, the constitutional right to control their own destiny had been sacrificed to the demands of northern industrialists. More than the tariff, they feared the consequences of accepting such an act; it could set a precedent for congressional legislation on slavery. In November 1832 a South Carolina state convention nullified the tariff, making it unlawful for officials to collect duties in the state. Recruiters immediately began to organize a volunteer army to ensure nonenforcement of the tariff.

"Old Hickory" responded with toughness. Privately he threatened to invade South Carolina and hang Calhoun, his vice president; publicly he sought to avoid the use of force. In December Jackson issued his own proclamation nullifying nullification. He moved troops to federal forts in South Carolina and prepared U.S. marshals to collect the required duties. At Jackson's request, Congress passed the Force Act, which gave Jackson renewed authority to call up troops but also offered a way

to avoid using force by collecting duties before arriving ships reached South Carolina. At the same time, Jackson extended an olive branch by recommending tariff reductions. Calhoun, disturbed by South Carolina's drift toward separatism, resigned as vice president and was soon elected to represent South Carolina in the U.S. Senate. In that body he worked with Henry Clay to draw up the compromise Tariff of 1833. Quickly passed by Congress and signed by the president, the new tariff lengthened the list of duty-free items and reduced duties over the course of nine years. Satisfied, South Carolina's convention repealed its nullification law. In a final salvo, it also nullified Jackson's Force Act. Jackson ignored the gesture.

Although fought over the practical issue of tariffs (and the implicit issue of slavery), the nullification controversy did represent a genuine debate on the true nature and principles of the republic. Each side believed it was upholding the Constitution. Both sides felt they were opposing special privilege and subversion of republican values. South Carolina was fighting the tyranny of the federal government and manufacturers who sought tariff protection. Jackson was fighting the tyranny of South Carolina, whose refusal to bow to federal authority threatened to split the republic. Neither side won a clear victory, though both claimed to have done so. It took another crisis, over a central bank, to define the powers of the federal government more clearly.

At stake was the rechartering of the Second Bank of the United States, whose twenty-year charter expired in 1836. Like its predecessor, the bank served as a depository for **Second Bank of the United States** ▬ federal funds, on which it paid no interest. Its bank notes circulated as currency throughout the country; they could be readily exchanged for gold, and the federal government accepted them as payment in all transactions. Through its twenty-five branch offices, the bank also acted as a clearinghouse for state banks, keeping them honest by refusing to accept their notes if they had insufficient gold in reserve.

Many Americans were suspicious of bank notes, regarding only specie—gold and silver coins—as real money. Coins made from valuable metals had intrinsic value: the worth of the gold or silver contained in the coin. Bank notes, by contrast, represented only a promise to pay specie on demand; the paper itself had no value. As long as people had faith in the issuing institution, the notes circulated freely. But a growing market-oriented society needed more currency than the nation's supply of gold and silver could accommodate. New businesses—manufacturers, wholesalers, retailers—needed capital for investment and cash for transactions.

The enemies of the Second Bank made redemption of bank notes an issue. Most state banks resented the central bank's police role—by presenting state bank notes for redemption all at once, the Second Bank could easily ruin a state bank. Moreover, with less money in reserve, state banks found themselves unable to compete on an equal footing with the Second Bank. Many state governments also regarded the national bank, with its headquarters in Philadelphia, as unresponsive to local needs. Westerners and urban workers remembered with justifiable bitterness the bank's conservative credit policies during the Panic of 1819. Although the Second Bank served some of the functions of a central bank, it was a private profit-making institution, and its policies reflected the self-interest of its owners. Its president, Nicholas Biddle, controlled the bank completely. As an eastern patrician, Biddle symbolized all that westerners found wrong with the bank. Moreover, the bank had great political influence. Many members of Congress and business leaders were beholden to it, and its power could be checked only at rechartering time.

Rechartering was a volatile issue in the 1832 presidential campaign. Although the bank's charter would not expire until 1836, Biddle convinced Congress to approve an early rechartering. This strategy, engineered by Henry Clay, the National Republican presidential candidate, was designed to marshall public pressure either to force Jackson to sign the bill or to override his veto. The plan backfired when the president vetoed the rechartering bill and the Senate failed to override. Jackson's veto message was an emotional attack on the undemocratic nature of the bank. "It is to be regretted," he wrote, "that the rich and powerful too often bend the acts of government to their selfish purposes." Rechartering would grant "exclusive privileges, to make the rich richer and the potent more powerful." Ignoring Chief Justice John Marshall's 1819 ruling in *McCulloch* v. *Maryland* (see page 260),

Jackson's veto message declared the bank unconstitutional.

The bank thus became the prime issue in the presidential campaign of 1832. Jackson led the way by denouncing special privilege and economic power. Operating in a system in which every state but South Carolina now chose electors by popular vote, the Jacksonians used their effective party organization to mobilize voters by advertising the presidential election as the focal point of the political system. When the Antimasons adopted a party platform, the first in the nation's history, the Democrats and the National Republicans quickly followed suit. Jackson and Martin Van Buren, Jackson's first secretary of state and then American minister to Great Britain, were nominated at the Democratic convention, and Clay and John Sergeant at the National Republican convention. South Carolina had its own candidate, John Floyd. Jackson was re-elected easily in a Democratic party triumph.

After his sweeping victory and second inauguration, Jackson moved in 1833 not only to dismantle the Second Bank of the United States but also to ensure that it would not be

Jackson's Second Term

resurrected. He deposited federal funds in favored state-chartered ("pet") banks; without federal money, the Second Bank shriveled. When its federal charter expired in 1836, it became just another Pennsylvania-chartered private bank. Five years later it closed its doors.

In conjunction with this coup de grâce to the Bank of the United States, Congress passed the Deposit Act of 1836 with Jackson's support. Under this act, the secretary of the treasury designated one bank in each state and territory to provide the services formerly performed by the Bank of the United States. The act provided that the federal surplus in excess of $5 million be distributed to the states as interest-free loans beginning in 1837. These loans were never recalled—a fitting Jacksonian restraint on the federal purse.

Jackson was worried about more than just restraining the government. The surplus had derived from wholesale speculation in public lands: purchasers bought public land on credit, used the land as collateral to borrow more for additional acreage, and repeated the cycle. Between 1834 and 1836 federal receipts from land sales rose from $5 million to $25 million. The banks providing the loans issued bank notes. Jackson, an opponent of paper money, feared that the speculative craze threatened the stability of state banks and worked against the interests of settlers, who could not compete with speculators in bidding for the best land.

In keeping with his hard-money instincts and his opposition to paper currency, President Jackson ordered Treasury Secretary Levi Woodbury to issue the Specie Circular. It provided that after August 1836 only specie—gold or silver— or Virginia land scrip would be accepted as payment for federal lands. The circular sought to end "the monopoly of the public lands in the hands of speculators and capitalists" and the "ruinous extension" of bank notes and credit. By ending credit sales, it significantly reduced public-land purchases and the budget surplus. As a result the government suspended its loan payments to the states soon after they began.

Specie Circular

The policy was a disaster on many fronts. Although federal land sales were sharply reduced, speculation continued as available land for sale became scarce. The ensuing increased demand for specie squeezed banks, and many suspended specie payment (the redemption of bank notes for specie). Credit contracted further as banks issued fewer notes and gave less credit. Equally damaging was the way Jackson attacked the problem. He instinctively pursued a tight money policy and remained indifferent to the impact of his policies. More important, the Specie Circular was similar to a bill defeated in the Senate just three months earlier. Jackson's opponents thus saw King Andrew at work. In the waning days of Jackson's administration, Congress voted to repeal the circular, but the president pocket-vetoed the bill. Finally in mid-1838, a joint resolution of Congress overturned the circular. Restrictions on land sales ended, but the speculative fervor was over. The federal government did not revive loans to states.

From George Washington to John Quincy Adams, presidents had vetoed nine bills; Jackson vetoed twelve. Previous presidents believed that vetoes were justified only on constitutional grounds, but Jackson, as in the veto of the Second Bank of the United States, considered policy disagreement legitimate grounds as well. He made the veto an effective weapon for controlling Congress, since representatives and senators had to consider the possibility of a presidential veto in their deliberations on any bill. In effect, Jackson made the executive for the first time a rival branch of government, equal in power to Congress.

THE WHIG CHALLENGE AND THE SECOND PARTY SYSTEM

Historians used to call the 1830s and 1840s the Age of Jackson, and the personalities of leading political figures dominated their accounts of the era. Today, however, most historians view these years as an age of popularly based political parties and reformers. Only when the passionate concerns of reformers and abolitionists spilled over into politics did party differences become paramount and party loyalties solidify. Grassroots political groups, organized from the bottom up, set the tone of political life for the first time in American history.

Opponents of the Democrats, including remnants of the National Republican party, found shelter under a common umbrella, the Whig party, in the 1830s. Resentful of Jackson's domination of Congress, the Whigs borrowed the name of the British party that had opposed the tyranny of Hanoverian monarchs in the eighteenth century. From 1834 through the 1840s, they and the Democrats competed on a nearly equal footing; only a few percentage points separated the two parties in national elections, and both put up candidates at every level—city, county, state, and national. Both parties built strong organizations, commanded the loyalty of legislators, and attracted mass popular followings, achieving a stability previously unknown in American politics. The organized political competition of this period—known as the second party system—resembled that of the first party system of Republicans and Federalists.

The two parties emphasized responsiveness to their supporters, a priority that signified important changes in the electoral process. Only a handful of states significantly restricted adult white male suffrage in nonlocal elections by the 1830s (although many states still permitted only property holders to vote in local elections). Some even allowed immigrants who had taken out their first citizenship papers to vote. Moreover, hotly contested elections stimulated public interest in politics. The net effect of these changes was a sharp increase in the number of votes cast in presidential elections. Between 1824 and 1828 that number increased threefold, from 360,000 to over 1.1 million. In 1840, 2.4 million men cast votes. The proportion of eligible voters who cast ballots also increased, from about 27 percent in 1824 to more than 80 percent in 1840.

The political agenda during these years consisted of numerous constitutional issues. At the national level, politicians questioned the proper constitutional roles of the federal and state governments, national expansion, and Indian policy. Many state conventions drafted new constitutions and deliberated over such basic issues as the rights of individuals and corporations; the rights of labor and capital; government aid to business; currency and sources of revenue; and public education, temperance, and abolition.

Increasingly the parties diverged in their approaches to issues. Whigs favored economic expansion through an activist government, Democrats through limited central government.

Whigs

The Whigs supported corporate charters, a national bank, and paper currency; the Democrats were opposed. The Whigs also favored more humanitarian reforms than did the Democrats, including public schools, abolition of capital punishment, prison and asylum reform, and temperance.

Whigs were more optimistic than Democrats, generally speaking, and more enterprising. They had no objection to helping a specific group if doing so would promote the general welfare. The chartering of corporations, they argued, expanded economic opportunity for everyone by providing work for laborers and thereby increasing demand for food from farmers. The Democrats, meanwhile, distrustful of concentrated economic power and of moral and economic coercion, held fast to their Jeffersonian principle of limited government.

Though extreme, the economic inequality that characterized the era was not the major dividing line between the parties. Nor did the conflicts over the Second Bank and corporate charters divide the haves and have-nots. The Whigs attracted more of the upper and middle class, but both sides drew support from manufacturers, merchants, laborers, and farmers. Instead it was religion and ethnicity that determined party membership. The Whigs' support for energetic government and humanitar-

ian and moral reform won the favor of native-born and British-American evangelical Protestants in the North, especially those involved in religious revival. These Presbyterians, Baptists, and Congregationalists were overwhelmingly Whigs, as were the relatively small number of free black voters. Democrats, on the other hand, tended to be foreign-born Catholics and nonevangelical Protestants, both of whom preferred to keep religious and secular affairs separate.

The Whig party thus became the vehicle of revivalist Protestantism. The membership rolls of reform societies overlapped those of the party in many locales. Indeed, Whigs

Whigs and Reformers

practiced a kind of political revivalism. Their rallies resembled camp meetings; their speeches employed evangelical rhetoric; their programs embodied the perfectionist beliefs of reformers. This potent blend of religion and politics—"intimately united" in America, according to Tocqueville—greatly intensified political loyalties.

In their appeal to evangelicals, the Whigs alienated members of other faiths. The evangelicals' ideal Christian state had no room for Catholics, Mormons, Unitarians, Universalists, or religious free-thinkers. These groups opposed Sabbath laws and temperance legislation in particular and state interference in moral and religious questions in general. As a result, more than 95 percent of Irish Catholics, 90 percent of Reformed Dutch, and 80 percent of German Catholics voted Democratic.

Vice President Martin Van Buren, handpicked by Jackson, headed the Democratic ticket in the presidential election of 1836. Van Buren was a shrewd politician who had built a political machine—the Albany Regency—in New York and had left that state's government to join Jackson's cabinet in 1829. Having helped found the Democratic party, Van Buren belonged to a new generation who made their careers in party politics. The Whigs, who in 1836 had not yet coalesced into a national party, entered three sectional candidates: Daniel Webster of New England, Hugh White of the South, and William Henry Harrison of the West. By splintering the vote, they hoped to throw the election into the House, but Van Buren comfortably captured the electoral college even though he had only a 25,000-vote edge out of a total of 1.5 million votes cast. No vice-presidential candidate received a majority of electoral votes, and for the only time in American history the Senate decided a vice-presidential race, selecting Democratic candidate Richard M. Johnson of Kentucky.

Van Buren took office just weeks before the American credit system collapsed. In response to the impact of the Specie Circular, New York banks stopped redeeming paper currency with gold in mid-1837. Soon all banks suspended payments in hard coin. Thus began a cycle that led to curtailment of bank loans and reduced business confidence. The credit contraction only made things worse; after a brief recovery, hard times persisted from 1839 until 1843.

Martin Van Buren and Hard Times

Economic issues were paramount during these years. Ill-advisedly, Van Buren followed Jackson's hard-money policies. He curtailed federal spending, which caused prices to drop further, and opposed a national bank, which would have expanded credit. Even worse, Van Buren—seeking to prevent further government losses from failing banks—proposed a new regional treasury system for government deposits, replacing banks. The proposed treasury branches would accept and pay out only gold and silver coin; they would not accept paper currency or checks drawn on state banks. Van Buren's independent treasury bill passed in 1840. By creating a constant demand for hard coin, it deprived banks of gold and further accelerated the deflation of prices.

The Whigs and the Democrats faced off at the state level over these issues. The Whigs favored new banks, more paper currency, and more corporations. As the party of hard money, the Democrats favored eliminating paper currency altogether. Increasingly the Democrats became distrustful even of state banks, and by the mid-1840s a majority favored eliminating all bank corporations. The Whigs, riding the wave of economic distress into office, made banking and corporate charters more readily available.

With the nation in the grip of hard times, the Whigs prepared confidently for the election of 1840. Their strategy was simple: keep their loyal supporters and win over independents distressed by hard times. The Democrats renominated President Van Buren at a somber convention. The Whigs rallied behind the military hero General

Election of 1840

William Henry Harrison, conqueror of the Shawnees at Tippecanoe Creek in 1811. Harrison and his running mate, John Tyler of Virginia, ran a "log cabin and hard cider" campaign, a people's crusade against the aristocratic president in "the Palace." Though he presented himself as an ordinary farmer, Harrison was descended from a Virginia plantation family. The Whigs wooed supporters and independents alike with huge rallies, parades, songs, posters, campaign mementoes, and a campaign newspaper, *The Log Cabin*. Harrison took a position above the issues, earning himself the nickname "General Mum," but party hacks bluntly blamed the hard times on the Democrats. In a huge turnout, 80 percent of eligible voters cast ballots—Harrison won the popular vote by a narrow margin but swept the electoral college 234 to 60.

Immediately after taking office in 1841, President Harrison convened a special session of Congress to enact the Whig economic program: repeal of the independent treasury system, a new national bank, and a higher protective tariff. But the sixty-eight-year-old Harrison caught pneumonia and died within a month of his inauguration. Tyler, his successor, was a former Democrat who had left the party to protest Jackson's nullification proclamation, and in office he turned out to be more of a Democrat than a Whig. As critical of the Whigs' economic nationalism as he had been of Jackson's use of executive power, Tyler consistently opposed the Whig congressional program. He repeatedly vetoed Henry Clay's protective tariffs, internal improvements, and bills aimed at reviving the Bank of the United States. The only important measures that became law under his administration were repeal of the independent treasury system and passage of a higher tariff. Two days after Tyler's second veto of a bank bill, the entire cabinet except Secretary of State Daniel Webster resigned; Webster, busy negotiating a new treaty with Great Britain, left shortly thereafter. Tyler thus became a president without a party, and the Whigs lost the presidency without losing an election. Whigs referred to Tyler as "His Accidency."

Hard times in the late 1830s and early 1840s deflected attention from a renewal of Anglo-American tensions that had multiple sources: northern commercial rivalry with Britain, the default of state governments and corporations on British-held debts during the Panic of 1837, rebellion

Anglo-American Tensions

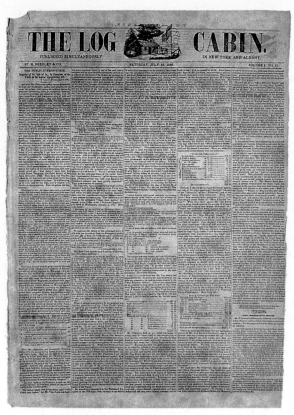

Using many of the techniques of twentieth-century politics, General William Henry Harrison in 1840 ran a "log cabin and hard cider" campaign—a popular crusade—against Jackson's heir, President Martin Van Buren. The campaign handkerchief shows Harrison welcoming two of his comrades to his log cabin, with a barrel of cider outside. The Log Cabin, *a newspaper edited by Horace Greeley, was the voice of the Harrison campaign, and it reached eighty thousand partisans.* Handkerchief: New York Historical Society; Newspaper: Smithsonian Institution, Division of Political History, Washington, D.C.

in Canada, boundary disputes, southern alarm over West Indian emancipation, and American expansionism.

One of the most troublesome disputes arose from the *Caroline* affair, in which a U.S. citizen, Amos Durfee, had been killed when Canadian militia set afire the privately owned steamer *Caroline* in the Niagara River. (The *Caroline* had supported an unsuccessful uprising against Great Britain in 1837.) Britain refused to apologize and American newspapers called for revenge. Fearing that popular support for the Canadian rebels would ignite war, President Van Buren posted troops at the border to discourage border raids. Tensions subsided in late 1840 when Alexander McLeod, a Canadian deputy sheriff, was arrested in New York for the murder of Durfee. McLeod was eventually acquitted; if he had been found guilty and executed, Lord Palmerston, the British foreign minister, might have sought war.

At almost the same time a border dispute disrupted Anglo-American relations. The Treaty of Ghent, which ended the War of 1812, had not resolved the boundary dispute between Maine and New Brunswick. Great Britain had accepted an 1831 arbitration decision fixing a new boundary, but the U.S. Senate had rejected it. Thus when Canadian lumbermen began to fell trees in the disputed region in the winter of 1838–1839, the citizens of Maine attempted to expel them. The lumbermen captured the Maine land agent and posse, both sides mobilized their militia, and Congress authorized a call-up of fifty thousand men. Ultimately, no blood was spilled. General Winfield Scott, who had patrolled the border during the *Caroline* affair, was dispatched to Aroostook, Maine, where he arranged a truce. The two sides compromised on their conflicting claims in the Webster-Ashburton Treaty (1842).

These border disputes with Great Britain prefigured the conflicts that were to erupt in the mid- to late 1840s over the westward expansion of the United States. With Tyler's succession to power in 1841 and a Democratic victory in the presidential election of 1844, federal activism in the domestic sphere ended for the rest of the decade, and attention turned to the debate over territorial expansion. Reform, however, was not dead. Its passions would resurface in the 1850s in the debate over slavery in the territories.

MANIFEST DESTINY AND EXPANSIONISM

The belief that American expansion westward and southward was inevitable, just, and divinely ordained was first called *manifest destiny* by John L. O'Sullivan, editor of the *United States Magazine and Domestic Review*. The annexation of Texas, O'Sullivan wrote in 1845, was "the fulfillment of our manifest destiny to overspread the continent allotted by Providence for the free development of our yearly multiplying millions." Americans had thought similarly for decades, but during the 1840s they used such rhetoric to speed along the process and to justify war and threats of war in the quest for more territory.

Ever since the colonists first turned their eyes westward, Americans had been hungry for new lands with fertile soil, valuable minerals, and the chance for a new beginning. Acquisition of the Louisiana Territory and Florida had set the process in motion (see map). As the proportion of Americans living west of the Appalachians grew from one-quarter to one-half between 1830 and 1860, both national parties were gripped by the popular clamor for expansion. Agrarian Democrats saw the West as an antidote to urbanization and industrialization; enterprising Whigs looked to the new commercial opportunities the West offered. Southerners envisioned the extension of slavery and more slave states.

A fierce national pride also spurred the quest for western land. Subdued during hard times, it reasserted itself during boom times like that of the 1840s. Northern and southern, Whig and Democrat, Americans were convinced that theirs was the greatest country on earth, with a special role to play in the world. "We cannot alter the laws of Providence, as we read them in the experience of the ages," Congressman Richard Wilde of Georgia declared. The "experience of the ages" dictated that the United States expand from coast to coast.

Americans also believed that westward expansion would spread freedom and democracy. The acquisition of new territory, they reasoned, would extend the benefits of America's republican system of government to the less fortunate and the inferior, bringing them the genius of our civilization. Such idealism was self-serving, of course, and it contained an undercurrent of racism as well. Native Americans were perceived as savages best confined to small areas in the West. Mexicans and Central and South Americans were also seen as inferior peoples, fit to be controlled or conquered. Thus the same racism that justified slavery in the South and discrimination in the North supported expansion in the West. Some also looked to expansion to solve the American race problem; free people of color, unwanted in the North and the South, could find refuge in distant territories.

The expansionist fever of the 1840s was also fed by the desire to secure the nation from perceived external threats. The internal enemies of the 1830s—a monster bank, corporations, paper currency, alcohol, Sabbath violation—seemed pale in comparison to threats Americans saw on their borders in the 1840s. Expansion, some believed, was necessary to preserve American independence.

Among the long-standing objectives of expansionists was the Republic of Texas, which in addition to present-day Texas included parts of present-day Oklahoma, Kansas, Colorado, Wyoming, and New Mexico. This territory was originally part of Mexico. After winning its independence from Spain in 1821, the government of Mexico encouraged the development of these rich but remote northern provinces, offering large tracts of land virtually free to settlers called *empresarios*. The settlers in turn agreed to become Mexican citizens, adopt the Catholic religion, and bring two hundred or more families into the area. Americans like Moses and Stephen Austin, who had helped to formulate the policy, responded eagerly.

Republic of Texas

By 1835, thirty-five thousand Americans, including many slaveholders, lived in Texas. These new settlers ignored local laws and oppressed native Mexicans. The dictatorship of General Antonio López de Santa Anna resulted in the tightening of control over the region. In response, Anglos and Tejanos (Mexicans living in Texas) rebelled. At the Alamo mission in San Antonio in 1836, fewer than

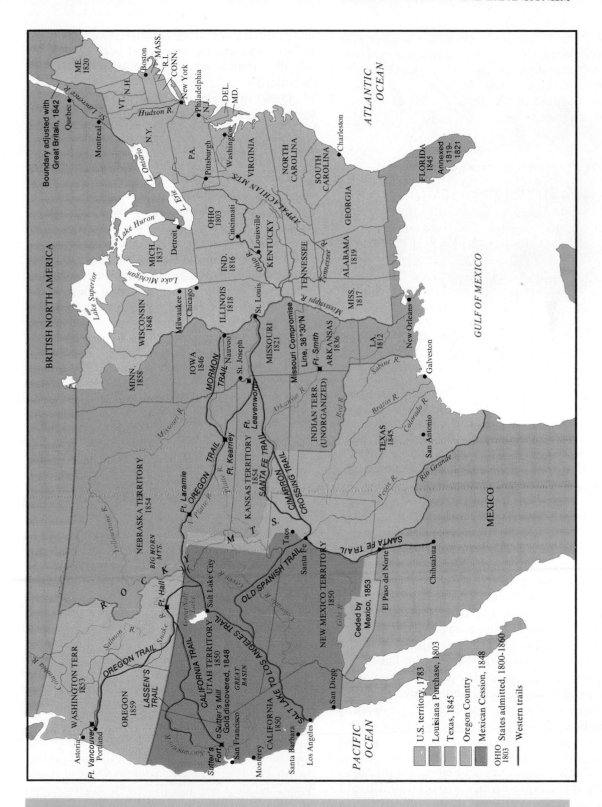

Westward Expansion, 1800–1860 *Through exploration, purchase, war, and treaty, the United States became a continental nation, stretching from the Atlantic to the Pacific oceans.*

To Texans, their War for Independence paralleled the American Revolution. This banner of a lady of liberty, similar to images used during the American Revolution, was carried by Texans in 1836. Archives Division, Texas State Library.

two hundred Texans made a heroic stand against three thousand Mexicans under General Santa Anna. When all the defenders of the mission, including Davy Crockett and Colonel James Bowie, died in the battle, "Remember the Alamo" became the Texans' rallying cry. By the end of the year the Texans had won independence, delighting most Americans. Some saw the victory as a triumph of white Protestantism over Catholic Mexico; others cheered that proslavery Texans had defeated antislavery Mexicans.

Texas established an independent Lone Star republic but soon sought annexation to the United States. Sam Houston, the president of Texas, opened negotiations with Washington, but the issue quickly became politically explosive. Southerners favored annexing proslavery Texas; abolitionists, many northerners, and most Whigs opposed annexation. In recognition of the political dangers, President Jackson refused to recognize Texas and President Van Buren ignored annexation.

Rebuffed by the United States, Texans began to talk about pursuing ties with the British and extending their republic all the way to the Pacific Coast. With British colonies already entrenched in Canada, the prospect of a rival republic to the south caused some Americans to fear encirclement. If Texas reached the ocean and became an English ally, would not American independence be threatened?

President Tyler—committed to expansion, fearful of Texan ties with the British, and eager to build political support in the South—pushed for annexation. Tyler was hoping to build a political base in the South to gain the 1844 Democratic nomination. Southerners also pressed for annexation; they lobbied former president Jackson, who responded that the United States must have Texas, "peacefully if we can, forcibly if we must." But the opposition was too strong, and the Senate rejected annexation in 1844. A letter from Secretary of State Calhoun to the British minister, justifying annexation as a step in protecting slavery, so outraged senators that the treaty was defeated 16 to 35.

Like southerners who sought expansion to the Southwest, northerners looked to the Northwest. "Oregon fever" struck thousands in 1841. Lured

Oregon Fever

by the glowing reports of missionaries, who seemed as enthusiastic about the Northwest's riches and beauty as about conversion of Indians, migrants organized hundreds of wagon trains and followed the Oregon Trail. "Ho for California," Helen Carpenter wrote in her diary, "We are off to the Promised Land." Others' enthusiasm was tempered by apprehension. Lavinia Porter had to face the sober realization that the road would be bumpy: her husband did not know manual labor, "nor had he the training to make a living on the plains of the West or the crossing of the continent in an ox team a successful venture." The two-thousand-mile journey took six months or more, but within a few years five thousand settlers had arrived in the fertile Willamette Valley south of the Columbia River.

Britain and the United States had jointly occupied the disputed Oregon Territory since the Anglo-American Convention of 1818 (see pages 260–261). Beginning with the administration of President John Quincy Adams, the United States had tried to fix the boundary at the 49th parallel, but Britain was determined to maintain access to Puget Sound and the Columbia River. Time only sharpened the American appetite. In 1843 a Cincinnati convention of expansionists demanded the entire Oregon Country for the United States, up to its

An unknown artist depicted, in rich detail, the election of 1844. A team of supporters of James K. Polk offers a campaign handbill to the seated voter. Passions were so high and party organization so extensive that door-to-door politicking became the norm.   Courtesy, Nathan Liverant & Son.

northernmost border of 54°40′. Soon "Fifty-four Forty or Fight" became the rallying cry of American expansionists.

Expansion into Oregon and the rejection of the annexation of Texas, both favored by antislavery forces, worried southern leaders. Anxious about their diminishing ability to control the debate over slavery, they persuaded the 1844 Democratic convention to adopt a rule that the presidential nominee had to receive two-thirds of the convention votes. In effect, the southern states thus acquired a veto, and they used it to block Van Buren as the nominee; most southerners objected to Van Buren's antislavery stance and opposition to Texas annexation. Instead the party chose "Young Hickory," House Speaker James K. Polk, a hard-money Jacksonian, avid expansionist, and slaveholding

Election of 1844
——

cotton planter from Tennessee. The Whig leader Henry Clay, who opposed annexation, won his party's nomination unanimously. The Democratic platform called for occupation of the entire Oregon Territory and annexation of Texas. The Whigs, though they favored expansion, argued that the Democrats' belligerent nationalism would lead the nation into war with Great Britain or Mexico or both. Clay favored expansion through negotiation.

With a well-organized campaign, Polk and the Democrats won the election by 170 electoral votes to 105. (They won the popular vote by just 38,000 out of 2.7 million votes cast.) Polk won New York's 36 electoral votes by just 6,000 votes; abolitionist James G. Birney, the Liberty party candidate, had drawn almost 16,000 votes away from Clay, handing New York and the election to Polk. Abolitionist forces thus unwittingly brought about the choice of a slaveholder as president, but they viewed Polk as more moderate than Clay on slavery and the lesser of two evils.

Interpreting Polk's victory as a mandate for annexation, President Tyler proposed in his final days in office that Texas be admitted by joint resolution of Congress. (The usual method of annexation, by treaty negotiation, required a two-thirds vote in the Senate—which expansionists clearly did not have. Joint resolution required only a simple majority in both houses.) Proslavery and antislavery congressmen debated the extension of slavery into the territory, and the resolution passed the House 120 to 98 and the Senate 27 to 25. Three days before leaving office, Tyler signed the measure. Mexico immediately broke relations with the United States; war was inevitable. In October, the citizens of Texas ratified annexation, and Texas joined the Union in December 1845.

Religion, reform, and expansionism colored politics in the 1830s and 1840s. As the Second Great Awakening spread through villages and towns, the converts—especially women—changed American religion and organized to impose reform on a rapidly changing society. Religion imbued men and women with zeal to right the wrongs of American society and the world. Claiming to personify the republican values that had sparked the American Revolution, reformers pursued perfectionism and republican virtue by doing battle with the evils of the growing cities, seeking to ban alcohol and gambling, and expanding education. Two issues elicited particular intensity: Antimasonry flared only briefly, while abolitionism smoldered over time. The passions both aroused were so potent, and success so elusive, that Antimasons and abolitionists transformed their moral crusades into political movements. But reformers had no monopoly on claims of republican virtue; their opponents laid claim to a heritage of revolutionary values that held individual liberty particularly dear.

Once reform forced itself into politics, it generated a broader-based interest in politics that would remake the political system. The ensuing conflicts, and the highly organized parties that came into being during this era, stimulated even greater interest in campaigns and political issues. The Democrats, rallying around Andrew Jackson, and his opponents who found shelter under the Whig tent competed almost equally for the loyalty of voters. Both built strong organizations that faced off in national and local elections. Both parties favored economic expansion, but their differences reflected fundamentally opposing world views. Whigs were more optimistic and favored greater centralized government initiative. Democrats harbored a deep-seated belief in limited government.

Territorial expansion would provide the kindling for the firestorm that would overtake the United States in 1861. Manifest destiny, the admission of Texas, and debates over territorial expansion awaited a spark. Ultimately, one issue would rivet the attention of nearly all Americans and ignite the fire that would threaten to sever the Union: slavery.

SUGGESTIONS FOR FURTHER READING

Religion, Revivalism, and Reform

Michael Barkun, *Crucible of the Millennium: The Burned-over District of New York in the 1840s* (1986); Terry Bilhartz, *Urban Religion and the Second Great Awakening: Church and Society in Early National Baltimore* (1986); Paul S. Boyer, *Urban Masses and Moral Order in America, 1820–1920* (1978); Anne M. Boylan, *Sunday School: The Formation of an American Institution, 1790–1880* (1988); Whitney R. Cross, *The Burned-over District* (1950); Clifford S. Griffen, *Their Brother's Keepers: Moral Stewardship in the United States, 1800–1865* (1960); Keith J. Hardman, *Charles Grandison Finney, 1792–1875: Revivalist and Reformer* (1987); Nathan O. Hatch, *The Democratization of American Christianity* (1989); Leon A. Jick, *The Americanization of the Synagogue, 1820–1870* (1976); Curtis D. Johnson, *Islands of Holiness: Rural Religion in Upstate New York, 1790–1860* (1989); Paul E. Johnson, *A Shopkeeper's Millennium: Society and Revivals in Rochester, New York, 1815–1837* (1978); William G. McLoughlin, *Revivals, Awakenings, and Reform: An Essay on Religion and Social Change in America, 1607–1977* (1978); Perry Miller, *The Life of the Mind in America: From the Revolution to the Civil War* (1966); Russel B. Nye, *Society and Culture in America, 1830–1860* (1974); Randolph A. Roth, *The Democratic Dilemma: Religion, Reform, and the Social Order in the Connecticut Valley of Vermont, 1791–1850* (1987); Richard D. Shiels, "The Scope of the Second Great Awakening: Andover, Massachusetts, as a Case Study," *Journal of the Early Republic* 5 (Summer 1985): 223–246; Timothy L. Smith, *Revivalism and Social Reform in Mid-Nineteenth Century America* (1957); Alice Felt Tyler, *Freedom's Ferment* (1944); Ronald G. Walters, *American Reformers, 1815–1860* (1978); Kenneth H. Winn, *Exiles in a Land of Liberty: Mormons in America, 1830–1846* (1989).

Temperance, Asylums, and Antimasonry

Paul Goodman, *Towards a Christian Republic: Antimasonry and the Great Transition in New England, 1826–1836* (1988); Gerald N. Grob, *Mental Institutions in America: Social Policy to 1875* (1973); Michael S. Hindus, *Prison and Plantation: Crime, Justice, and Authority in Massachusetts and South Carolina, 1767–1878* (1980);

Kathleen Smith Kutolowski, "Antimasonry Reexamined: Social Bases of the Grass-Roots Party," *Journal of American History* 71 (September 1984): 269–293; W. David Lewis, *From Newgate to Dannemora: The Rise of the Penitentiary in New York, 1796–1948* (1965); W. J. Rorabaugh, *The Alcoholic Republic: An American Tradition* (1979); Charles E. Rosenberg, *The Care of Strangers: The Rise of America's Hospital System* (1987); David J. Rothman, *The Discovery of the Asylum: Social Order and Disorder in the New Republic* (1971); Ian R. Tyrrell, *Sobering Up: From Temperance to Prohibition in Antebellum America, 1800–1860* (1979); William Preston Vaughn, *The Antimasonic Party in the United States, 1826–1843* (1983).

Women and Reform

Barbara J. Berg, *The Remembered Gate: Origins of American Feminism: The Woman and the City, 1800–1860* (1977); Catherine Clinton, *The Other Civil War: American Women in the Nineteenth Century* (1984); Ellen C. Du Bois, *Feminism and Suffrage: The Emergence of an Independent Woman's Movement in America, 1848–1869* (1978); Barbara Leslie Epstein, *The Politics of Domesticity: Women, Evangelism, and Temperance in Nineteenth-Century America* (1981); Lori D. Ginzberg, *Women and the Work of Benevolence: Morality, Politics, and Class in the Nineteenth-Century United States* (1990); Elisabeth Griffith, *In Her Own Right: The Life of Elizabeth Cady Stanton* (1984); Nancy A. Hewitt, *Women's Activism and Social Change: Rochester, New York, 1822–1872* (1984); Gerda Lerner, *The Grimké Sisters of South Carolina* (1967); Mary P. Ryan, *Cradle of the Middle Class: The Family in Oneida County, New York, 1790–1865* (1981); Ian R. Tyrrell, "Women and Temperance in Antebellum America, 1830–1860," *Civil War History* 28 (June 1982): 128–152; Shirley J. Yee, *Black Women Abolitionists: A Study in Activism, 1828–1860* (1992).

Antislavery and Abolitionism

David Brion Davis, *Slavery and Human Progress* (1984); Frederick Douglass, *Life and Times of Frederick Douglass* (1881); George M. Fredrickson, *The Black Image in the White Mind: The Debate on Afro-American Character and Destiny, 1817–1914* (1971); Lawrence J. Friedman, *Gregarious Saints: Self and Community in American Abolitionism, 1830–1870* (1982); Aileen S. Kraditor, *Means and Ends in American Abolitionism: Garrison and His Critics on Strategy and Tactics* (1967); William H. Pease and Jane H. Pease, *They Who Would Be Free: Blacks' Search for Freedom, 1830–1861* (1974); Lewis Perry and Michael Fellman, eds., *Antislavery Reconsidered* (1979); Benjamin Quarles, *Black Abolitionists* (1969); Leonard L. Richards, *The Life and Times of Congressman John Quincy Adams* (1986); Leonard L. Richards, *"Gentlemen of Property and Standing": Anti-Abolition Mobs in Jacksonian America* (1970); James Brewer Stewart, *Holy Warriors: The Abolitionists and American Slavery* (1976); John L. Thomas, *The Liberator: William Lloyd Garrison* (1963); Ronald G. Walters, *The Antislavery Appeal: American Abolitionism After 1830* (1976); Bertram Wyatt-Brown, *Lewis Tappan and the Evangelical War Against Slavery* (1969).

Andrew Jackson and the Jacksonians

Lee Benson, *The Concept of Jacksonian Democracy: New York as a Test Case* (1964); Donald B. Cole, *Martin Van Buren and the American Political System* (1984); Mary W. M. Hargreaves, *The Presidency of John Quincy Adams* (1985); Michael F. Holt, *Political Parties and American Political Development from the Age of Jackson to the Age of Lincoln* (1992); Richard B. Latner, *The Presidency of Andrew Jackson* (1979); Marvin Meyers, *The Jacksonian Persuasion* (1960); John Niven, *Martin Van Buren* (1983); Edward Pessen, *Jacksonian America: Society, Personality, and Politics*, rev. ed. (1979); Robert V. Remini, *The Legacy of Andrew Jackson: Essays on Democracy, Indian Removal, and Slavery* (1988); Robert V. Remini, *The Life of Andrew Jackson* (1988); Robert V. Remini, *Andrew Jackson and the Bank War* (1967); Arthur M. Schlesinger, Jr., *The Age of Jackson* (1945); Charles Sellers, *The Market Revolution: Jacksonian America, 1815–1846* (1991); John William Ward, *Andrew Jackson: Symbol for an Age* (1955); Harry L. Watson, *Jacksonian Politics and Community Conflict: The Emergence of the Second American Party System in Cumberland County, North Carolina* (1981); Major L. Wilson, *The Presidency of Martin Van Buren* (1984).

Democrats and Whigs

William J. Cooper, *The South and the Politics of Slavery, 1828–1856* (1978); Roger A. Fischer, *Tippecanoe and Trinkets Too: The Material Culture of American Presidential Campaigns, 1828–1984* (1988); Ronald P. Formisano, *The Transformation of Political Culture: Massachusetts Parties, 1790s–1840s* (1983); Ronald P. Formisano, *The Birth of Mass Political Parties: Michigan, 1827–1861* (1971); William W. Freehling, *Prelude to Civil War: The Nullification Controversy in South Carolina* (1966); Daniel Walker Howe, *The Political Culture of the American Whigs* (1979); Lawrence Frederick Kohl, *The Politics of Individualism: Parties and the American Character in the Jacksonian Era* (1989); Richard P. McCormick, *The Second American Party System: Party Formation in the Jacksonian Era* (1966); Merrill D. Peterson, *The Great Triumvirate: Webster, Clay, and Calhoun* (1987); Norman Lois Peterson, *The Presidencies of William Henry Harrison and John Tyler* (1989); Robert V. Remini, *Henry Clay: Statesman for the Union* (1991); James Roger Sharp, *The Jacksonians Versus the Banks: Politics in the States After the Panic of 1837* (1970).

Manifest Destiny and Foreign Policy

John M. Belohlavek, *"Let the Eagle Soar!" The Foreign Policy of Andrew Jackson* (1985); Norman B. Graebner, ed., *Manifest Destiny* (1968); Thomas R. Hietala, *Manifest Design: Anxious Aggrandizement in Late Jacksonian America* (1985); Reginald Horsman, *Race and Manifest Destiny* (1981); Michael Hunt, *Ideology and U.S. Foreign Policy* (1987); Frederick Merk, *Manifest Destiny and Mission in American History* (1963); David M. Pletcher, *The Diplomacy of Annexation: Texas, Oregon, and the Mexican War* (1973); Charles G. Sellers, Jr., *James K. Polk: Continentalist, 1843–1846* (1966); Paul A. Varg, *United States Foreign Relations, 1820–1860* (1979); William Earl Weeks, *John Quincy Adams and American Global Empire* (1992); Albert K. Weinberg, *Manifest Destiny* (1935).

14

Slavery and America's Future: The Road to War, 1845–1861

C ELIA WAS ONLY FOURTEEN when Robert Newsom bought her in 1850. He was almost sixty, a widower, and a successful farmer who owned eight hundred acres near Fulton, Missouri. His two adult daughters and four of his grandchildren lived with him, and five male slaves worked the family's land. Celia probably assumed that the white people wanted her as a cook and cleaning girl.

But Robert Newsom had more in mind for Celia. Almost immediately he raped her and made it clear that he would continue to demand her sexual services. Newsom installed Celia in a small house only fifty yards behind his home. Over the next five years he visited her often, fathering two children. Newsom's daughters and the neighbors knew what was happening but said nothing. He was a respected man, and these things happened in slavery.

In 1855, however, something else happened on the Newsom farm. Celia began a relationship with George, another of the Newsom slaves. Moved by her own feelings and by George's insistence, Celia tried to end the relationship with her master. She appealed first to Virginia and Mary, Newsom's daughters. They were troubled by Ce-

lia's story and by her threat to hurt Newsom "if he did not quit forcing her," but they could do nothing to stop their father's behavior. Next Celia begged her master to leave her alone, pleading that she was again pregnant and ill.

One evening in June 1855, Robert Newsom read until his family was asleep and then walked to Celia's door. When he brushed aside her objections to sex, she grabbed a club and struck Robert Newsom on the skull. As he sank to the floor, she struck him again. He never arose. Celia, panicked at having killed her master, proceeded to burn his body all through the night in her large fireplace.

Newsom's disappearance excited great interest, and physical evidence of his murder soon came to light. Celia's trial received only local publicity, but in that district of Missouri it stirred up conflicting passions. While news of the murder made some slaveowners fear for their safety, Celia's attorneys sympathized with her plight enough to argue, unsuccessfully, that laws against rape entitled her to defend herself. After a jury of twelve white men convicted her, Celia went to the gallows four days before Christmas.

U.S. troops land at Vera- cruz in 1847, begin- ning the drive to Mex- ico City that ended the Mexican War.

By the time Celia was hanged, her drama was overshadowed by a larger drama of violence in the territory of Kansas, where warfare had broken out between advocates and foes of slavery. Proslavery men, intent on spreading the peculiar institution and preserving a balance of free and slave states in the U.S. Senate, rode across the border from Missouri, stole elections, and physically attacked those who wanted Kansas to be free soil. Antislavery activists organized the New England Emigrant Aid Company to send opponents of slavery to Kansas.

Before long the New Englanders were arming their settlers with Sharps rifles, called "Beecher's Bibles" after the well-known antislavery minister Henry Ward Beecher of New York. On the proslavery side a U.S. senator, Missouri's David Atchison, publicly advocated violence and pledged his readiness "to shoot, burn and hang." The passions aroused by slavery were influencing national politics as deeply as they had the individuals on the Newsom farm. As the 1850s advanced, slavery pulled Americans deeper and deeper into a maelstrom of conflict.

What brought these issues to center stage was territorial expansion. Between 1845 and 1853 the United States added Texas, the West Coast, and the Southwest to its domain and launched the settlement of the Great Plains. Each time the nation expanded, it confronted a thorny issue—should new territories and states be slave or free? This question spawned disagreements too extreme for compromise. Sensing the danger of conflict, Senator John C. Calhoun of South Carolina called Mexico "the forbidden fruit; the penalty of eating it would be to subject our institutions to political death." A host of political leaders, including Henry Clay, Lewis Cass, Stephen A. Douglas, and Presidents Jackson and Van Buren, tried to postpone or resolve disagreements about slavery in the territories. Repeatedly, though, these disputes injected into national politics the bitterness surrounding slavery. If slavery was the sore spot in the body politic, territorial disputes rubbed salt into the wound.

The United States had always been a diverse, heterogeneous society, not a cohesive unit. Now, however, diverse interests that used to balance each other became linked to one divisive issue. Battles over slavery in the territories broke apart the second party system and then shaped a realigned system that emphasized sectional conflict. Sectional parties replaced nationwide organizations that had promoted compromise.

The ensuing political storms gave rise to a feeling in both North and South that America's future was at stake. The new Republican party charged that southerners were taking over the federal government and planning to make slavery legal throughout the Union. Republicans believed that America's future depended on the free labor of free men, whose rights were protected by a government devoted to liberty. Southern leaders defended slavery and charged the North with lawless behavior in violation of the Constitution. To these southerners enslavement of blacks was the foundation of equality and republicanism among whites, and a government that failed to protect slavery was un-American and unworthy of their loyalty.

Not all citizens were obsessed with these conflicts. In fact, the results of the 1860 presidential election indicated that most voters wanted neither disunion nor civil war. Within six months, however, they had both, for slavery aroused passions that could be neither contained nor resolved. What had begun as a dark cloud over the territories became a storm engulfing the nation. Each section felt threatened by the other, and both believed that the future was at stake. The victorious Republican party and defensive southerners could not agree on desperate last-minute compromise measures, and a vast civil war began.

CONFLICT BEGINS: THE MEXICAN WAR

Territorial expansion surged forward under the leadership of President James K. Polk. The annexation of Texas (see page 394) just before his inauguration did not weaken Polk's determination to acquire California and the Southwest, and he desired Oregon as well. The effective Polk achieved his goals, but he was unaware of the price in domestic harmony that expansion would exact. The expansion of the nation's boundaries had serious repercussions. It divided the Whig party, drove southern Whigs into a full embrace of slavery, and brought into the open an aggressive new southern theory about slavery's position in the territories. Expansion also sparked northern protests and proposals that generated further conflict between the sections.

• *I m p o r t a n t   E v e n t s* •

1846 War with Mexico begins
Oregon Treaty negotiated
Wilmot Proviso inflames sectional divisions

1847 Lewis Cass proposes idea of popular
sovereignty

1848 Treaty of Guadalupe Hidalgo gives U.S.
new territory in southwest
Zachary Taylor elected president
Free-Soil party formed

1849 California applies for admission to Union as
free state

1850 Compromise of 1850 passed in separate bills

1852 Publication of *Uncle Tom's Cabin*, by Harriet
Beecher Stowe
Franklin Pierce elected president

1854 Publication of "Appeal of the Independent
Democrats"
Kansas-Nebraska Act wins approval and
ignites controversy
Republican party formed
Democrats lose ground in congressional
elections

1856 Preston Brooks attacks Charles Sumner in
Senate chamber
"Bleeding Kansas" troubles nation
James Buchanan elected president

1857 *Dred Scott* v. *Sanford* endorses southern views
on race and territories
Lecompton Constitution proposed; president
supports it

1858 Kansas voters reject Lecompton Constitution
Lincoln-Douglas debates attract attention
Douglas proposes Freeport Doctrine

1859 John Brown raids Harpers Ferry

1860 Democratic party splits in two
Lincoln elected president
Crittenden Compromise fails
South Carolina secedes from Union

1861 Six more Deep South states secede
Confederacy established at Montgomery,
Alabama
Attack on Fort Sumter begins Civil War
Four states in the Upper South join the
Confederacy

Although his campaign supporters had threatened war with Great Britain to gain all of the Oregon Territory, Polk as president found that diplomacy had its advantages. The annexation of Texas had outraged Mexican leaders, who severed relations with the United States. Aware that war with Mexico could break out at any time, Polk tried to avoid bloodshed in the Northwest, where America and Britain had jointly occupied disputed territory since 1818. Dropping the demand for a boundary at 54°40′, he pressured the British to accept the 49th parallel. In 1846 Great Britain agreed. In the Oregon Treaty, the United States gained all of present-day Oregon, Washington, and Idaho and parts of Wyoming and Montana (see map, page 401).

Toward Mexico, Polk was much more aggressive. He ordered American troops to defend the border claimed by Texas but contested by Mexico (see map) and attempted to buy from the angry Mexicans a huge tract of land in the Southwest. When purchase failed, Polk resolved to ask Congress for a declaration of war. As he was drawing up a list of grievances, word arrived that Mexican forces had engaged American troops on disputed territory. American blood had been shed. Eagerly, Polk declared that "war exists by the act of Mexico itself" and summoned the nation to arms.

Congress recognized a state of war between Mexico and the United States in May 1846, but controversy soon arose. Although prejudice toward Mexicans was common, public opinion about the wisdom of the war was sharply divided, with southwesterners enthusiastic and New Englanders strenuously opposed. In Congress Whigs charged that Polk, a Democrat, had "literally provoked" an unnecessary war (which they called "Mr. Polk's war") and "usurped the power of Congress by making war upon Mexico." The aged John Quincy Adams denounced the war (he died within minutes of casting a vote against the conflict) and a tall young Illinois Whig named Abraham Lincoln questioned its justification. Moreover, a small minority of antislavery Whigs agreed with abolitionists who charged that the war was no less than a plot to extend slavery. Joshua Giddings of Ohio charged in the House that Polk's purpose was "to render slavery secure in Texas" and to extend slavery's domain to vast expanses of new territory.

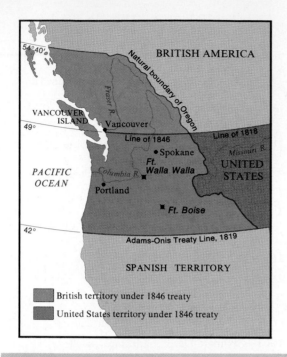

BRITISH AMERICA

54°40'

VANCOUVER
ISLAND

49°

Vancouver

Line of 1846

Line of 1818

Fraser R.

Natural boundary of Oregon

Missouri R.

PACIFIC
OCEAN

Spokane

Ft.
Walla Walla

Columbia R.

Portland

UNITED
STATES

42°

Ft. Boise

Adams-Onis Treaty Line, 1819

SPANISH TERRITORY

☐ British territory under 1846 treaty

☐ United States territory under 1846 treaty

American Expansion in Oregon *Polk's supporters had spoken of "54°40' or fight," but negotiation of a boundary at the 49th parallel avoided the danger of war with Great Britain.*

These charges fed northern fear of the so-called Slave Power. Abolitionists had long warned of a Slave Power—a slaveholding oligarchy that controlled the South and intended to dominate the nation. These dangerous aristocrats had gained power in their region by persecuting critics of slavery and suppressing dissent. The Slave Power's assault on northern liberties, abolitionists argued, had begun in 1836, when Congress passed the gag rule (see page 378). Many white northerners, even those who saw nothing wrong with slavery, had praised John Quincy Adams's fight against the rule as a valiant defense of free speech and the right of petition. It was the battle over free speech that first made the idea of a Slave Power credible.

Idea of a Slave Power

Now the Mexican War fed fears of this sinister power. Antislavery northerners asked why claims to part of Oregon had been abandoned while a questionable war was undertaken for slave terri-

tory. Northern opinion began to shift, but the impact of events on southern opinion and southern leaders was even more dramatic.

At first many southern leaders criticized the war with Mexico. Southern Whigs attacked the Democratic president for causing the war, and few southern congressmen saw defense of slavery as the paramount issue. In 1845 Alexander H. Stephens of Georgia had declared, "I am no defender of slavery in the abstract," and even John C. Calhoun—despite his earlier schemes to annex Texas for slavery—strongly opposed the seizure of large amounts of land from Mexico. A Whig editor in Georgia argued that "we have territory enough, especially if every province, like Texas, is to bring in its train war and debt and death."

But the war proved generally popular with southern voters, and no southern Whig could oppose it once slavery became the central issue. That happened in August 1846, when David Wilmot, a Pennsylvania Democrat, proposed an amendment, or proviso, to a military appropriations bill: that "neither slavery nor involuntary servitude shall ever exist" in any territory gained from Mexico. His proviso did not pass both houses of Congress, but it immediately transformed the debate.

Wilmot Proviso

Alexander H. Stephens, only recently "no defender of slavery," now declared that slavery was based on the Bible and above moral criticism. John C. Calhoun drew up resolutions about the territories that staked out a radical new southern position. According to these resolutions, the territories belonged to all the states, and the federal government could do nothing to limit the spread of slavery there. Southern slaveholders had a constitutional *right*, Calhoun claimed, to take their slaves anywhere in the territories. This position, which quickly became orthodox for every southern politician, was a radical reversal of history. In 1787 the founding fathers, in the Confederation Congress, had excluded slavery from the Northwest Territory (see page 197). Article IV of the federal Constitution authorized Congress to make "all needful rules and regulations" for the territories, and the Missouri Compromise had barred slavery from most of the Louisiana Purchase. Now, however, southern leaders demanded protection for slavery.

In the North, the Wilmot Proviso became a rallying cry for abolitionists. Eventually the legisla-

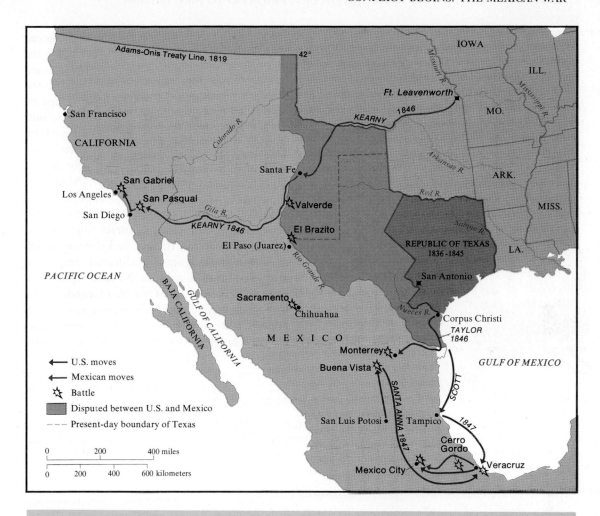

The Mexican War *This map shows the territory disputed between the United States and Mexico. After U.S. gains in northeastern Mexico and in New Mexico and California, General Winfield Scott captured Mexico City in the decisive campaign of the war.*

tures of fourteen northern states endorsed it—and not because all its supporters were abolitionists. David Wilmot, significantly, was neither an abolitionist nor an antislavery Whig. He denied having any "squeamish sensitiveness upon the subject of slavery" or "morbid sympathy for the slave." Instead, his goal was to defend "the rights of white freemen" and to obtain California "for free white labor." Wilmot was fighting for opportunity, in other words, for "the sons of toil, of my own race and own color." His involvement in antislavery controversy is a measure of the remarkable ability of the territorial issue to alarm northerners of many viewpoints.

Like Wilmot, most white northerners were racists, not abolitionists. It was possible, however, to be both racist *and* an opponent of slavery. Fear of the Slave Power was building a potent antislavery movement that united abolitionists and antiblack voters. The latter's concern was to protect themselves, not southern blacks, from the Slave Power. Abolition had few followers, but opposition to slavery's extension and fear of the Slave Power excited growing numbers of voters. And as northerners became increasingly antislavery, southern slaveholders felt deep alarm.

Meanwhile, events on the battlefield went well for American forces. The troops—as in previous

This 1852 lithograph reflects northern hostility to slaveholding, southern expansion, and Texas's role in both. Note that the brutal and depraved Texan is sitting on a slave whose shape and hair call to mind a bale of cotton.   Western Americana Collection, Beinecke Library, Yale University.

wars, mainly volunteers furnished by the states—proved unruly and undisciplined, and their politically ambitious commanders often quarreled. Nevertheless, progress was steady. General Zachary Taylor's forces attacked and occupied Monterrey, securing northeastern Mexico (see map, page 401). Polk then ordered Colonel Stephen Kearny and a small detachment to invade the remote and thinly populated provinces of New Mexico and California. Taking Santa Fe without opposition, Kearny pushed into California, where he joined forces with rebellious American settlers, led by Captain John C. Frémont, and a couple of U.S. naval units. A quick victory was followed by reverses, but American soldiers soon re-established their dominance in distant California.

Because losses on the periphery had not broken Mexican resistance, General Winfield Scott carried the war to the enemy's heartland. From Veracruz on the Gulf of Mexico, he led fourteen thousand men toward Mexico City. This daring invasion was the decisive campaign of the war. Scott's men, outnumbered and threatened by yellow fever, encountered a series of formidable Mexican defenses, but engineers repeatedly discovered flanking routes around the enemy. After a series of hard-fought battles, U.S. troops captured the Mexican capital and brought the war to an end. Representatives of both countries signed the Treaty of Guadalupe Hidalgo in February 1848. The United States gained California and New Mexico (including present-day Nevada, Utah, and Arizona) and recognition of the Rio Grande as the southern boundary of Texas. In return, the American government agreed to settle the claims of its citizens against Mexico and to pay Mexico a mere $15 million.

Treaty of Guadalupe Hidalgo

The costs of the war included the deaths of thirteen thousand Americans (mostly from disease) and fifty thousand Mexicans, plus Mexican-American enmity that endured into the twentieth century. But the domestic cost was even higher. The slavery question divided southern Whigs from antislavery northern Whigs. President Polk tried to unify the Democrats by renouncing a second term and pursuing traditional Jacksonian economic policies, but even these steps did not prevent dissension in his party.

In the presidential election of 1848, slavery in the territories was the overriding issue. Both parties tried to push the question into the background, but it dominated the conventions, the campaign, and the election. Seeking sectional balance, the Democrats nominated Senator Lewis Cass of Michigan for president and General William Butler of Kentucky for vice president. Cass, a party loyalist who had served in Jackson's cabinet, devised the idea of "popular sovereignty" for the territories—letting residents in the territories decide the question of slavery for themselves. His party's platform declared that Congress lacked the power to interfere with slavery and criticized those who pressed the question. The Whigs nominated General Zachary Taylor, a southern slaveholder and the

Election of 1848 and Popular Sovereignty

Enthusiastic publishers vied to furnish the U.S. public with up-to-date news of the Mexican War. Above is one of three lithographs issued by Currier and Ives in 1846 to celebrate the capture by U.S. forces of Mexico's General La Vega during the battle of Resaca, fought near the border of Texas and Mexico. Amon Carter Museum, Fort Worth, Texas.

conqueror of Monterrey, with Congressman Millard Fillmore of New York as his running mate. Their convention similarly refused to assert that Congress had power over slavery in the territories. But the issue would not stay in the background.

Many southern Democrats distrusted Cass and eventually voted for Taylor because he was a slaveholder. Among northerners, concern over slavery led to the formation of a new party. New York Democrats committed to the Wilmot Proviso rebelled against Cass and nominated former president Van Buren. Antislavery Whigs and former supporters of the Liberty party then joined them to organize the Free-Soil Party, with Van Buren as its candidate (see table below). This party, whose slogan was "Free soil, free speech, free labor, and

New Political Parties

Party	Period of Influence	Area of Influence	Outcome
Liberty party	1839–1848	North	Merged with other antislavery groups to form Free-Soil party
Free-Soil party	1848–1854	North	Merged with Republican party
Know-Nothings (American party)	1853–1856	Nationwide	Disappeared, freeing some northern voters to join Republican party
Republican party	1854–present	North (later nationwide)	Became rival of Democratic party in third party system

free men," won almost 300,000 northern votes. Taylor polled 1.4 million votes to Cass's 1.2 million and won the White House, but the results were more ominous than decisive. The North-South division in public opinion was deepening, and sectional issues were dividing both parties.

The conflicts of 1848 would dominate politics throughout the 1850s, as slavery in the territories colored every other national issue. The nation's uncertain attempts to deal with economic and social change gave way to more pressing questions about the nature of the Union itself. Soon the second party system succumbed to the crisis over slavery and the future.

TERRITORIAL PROBLEMS ARE COMPROMISED BUT RE-EMERGE

The first sectional battle of the decade involved the territory of California. More than eighty thousand Americans flooded into California during the gold rush of 1849. With Congress unable to agree on a formula to govern the territories, President Taylor urged these settlers to apply directly for admission to the Union. They promptly did so, submitting a proposed state constitution that did not allow for slavery. Because California's admission as a free state would upset the sectional balance of power in the Senate, southern politicians wanted to postpone admission and make California a slave territory, or at least to extend the Missouri Compromise line west to the Pacific. Representatives from nine southern states, meeting in Nashville, asserted the South's right to part of the territory.

Henry Clay, the venerable Whig leader, sensed that the Union was in peril. Twice before—in 1820 and 1833—Clay, the "Great Pacificator," had taken the lead in shaping sectional compromise; now he struggled one last time to preserve the nation. To hushed Senate galleries Clay presented a series of compromise measures. Over the weeks that followed, he and Senator Stephen A. Douglas of Illinois steered their omnibus bill, or compromise package, through debate and amendment.

The problems to be solved were numerous and difficult. Would California, or part of it, become a free state? How should the territory acquired from

Mexico be organized? Texas, which allowed slavery, claimed large portions of the new land as far west as Santa Fe, so that claim, too, had to be settled. Southerners complained that fugitive slaves were not being returned as the Constitution required, and northerners objected to the sale of human beings in the nation's capital. But most troublesome of all was the status of slavery in the territories.

Clay and Douglas hoped to avoid a specific formula and to preserve the ambiguity inherent in Lewis Cass's notion of popular sovereignty. Cass's idea possessed a vagueness that appealed to practical politicians. Like many others, Cass wanted Congress to stay out of the territorial wrangle. Ultimately Congress would have to approve statehood for a territory, but "in the meantime," he said, it should allow the people living there "to regulate their own concerns in their own way." These few words, apparently clear enough, proved highly ambiguous.

When could settlers prohibit slavery? Southerners claimed that neither Congress nor a territorial legislature could bar slavery. Only when settlers assumed sovereignty under a state constitution could they take that step. Northerners insisted that Americans living in a territory were entitled to local self-government and thus could outlaw slavery at any time. To avoid dissension within their party, northern and southern Democrats had explained Cass's statement to their constituents in these two incompatible ways. Northern and southern Whigs, too, were divided over the issue.

The cause of compromise gained a powerful supporter when Senator Daniel Webster committed his prestige and eloquence to Clay's bill. "I wish to speak today," Webster declaimed, "not as a Massachusetts man, nor as a Northern man, but as an American. I speak today for the preservation of the Union. Hear me for my cause." Abandoning his earlier support for the Wilmot Proviso, Webster urged northerners not to "taunt or reproach" the South with antislavery measures. To southern firebrands he issued a warning that disunion could no more take place "without convulsion" than "the heavenly bodies [could] rush from their spheres, and jostle each other in the realms of space, without causing the wreck of the universe!"

Yet even Webster's influence was not enough. After months of labor, when Clay and Douglas finally brought their legislative package to a vote, they met defeat. But the determined Douglas

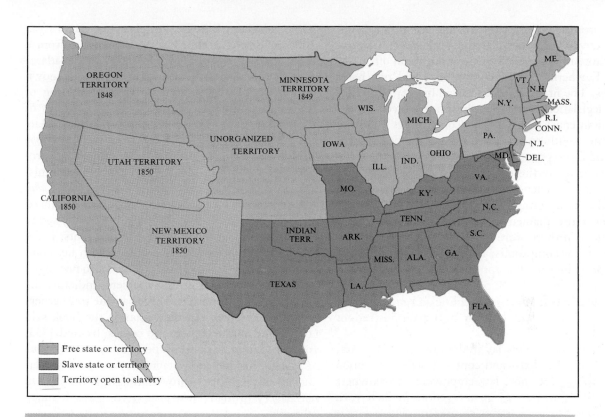

The Compromise of 1850   *The territorial provisions of the Compromise of 1850 made California a free state and set Texas's western boundary. The Utah and New Mexico territories were open to slavery, but northerners and southerners disagreed over when settlers could legally decide to prohibit slavery.*

would not give up. With Clay sick and absent from Washington, Douglas reintroduced the compromise measures one at a time. Though there was no majority for compromise, Douglas shrewdly realized that different majorities might be created for each of the measures. Because southerners favored some measures and northerners the rest, the small bloc for compromise could vote first with one section and then with the other. The strategy worked, and Douglas's resourcefulness salvaged a positive result from more than eight months of congressional effort. The Compromise of 1850, as it was called, became law.

Under its various measures, California became a free state, and the Texas boundary was set at its present limits (see map). The United States paid Texas $10 million in consideration of the boundary agreement. The territories of New Mexico and Utah were organized with power to legislate on

**Compromise
of 1850**
———

"all rightful subjects . . . consistent with the Constitution." A stronger fugitive slave law and an act to suppress the slave trade in the District of Columbia completed the compromise.

Jubilation greeted passage of the Compromise of 1850; in Washington, crowds celebrated the happy news. "On one glorious night," records a modern historian, "the word went abroad that it was the duty of every patriot to get drunk. Before the next morning many a citizen had proved his patriotism," and several prominent senators "were reported stricken with a variety of implausible maladies—headaches, heat prostration, or overindulgence in fruit."

In reality, there was less cause for celebration than people hoped. Fundamentally, the Compromise of 1850 was not a settlement of sectional disputes; at best, it was an artful evasion. Douglas had found a way to pass his proposals without convincing northerners and southerners to agree on them; neither side had given up anything. This compromise bought time for the nation, but it did not create guidelines for the settlement of future territorial questions. It merely put them off.

Furthermore, the compromise had two basic flaws. The first concerned the ambiguity of territorial legislation: what were "rightful subjects of legislation, consistent with the Constitution"? During debate, southerners said these words meant there would be no prohibition of slavery during the territorial stage; northerners declared that settlers could bar slavery whenever they wished. After passage of the compromise, legislators once again went home and explained the act in these two different ways, as if there were two different compromises. In fact, the compromise admitted the disagreement by providing for the appeal of a territorial legislature's action to the Supreme Court, but no such case ever arose. One witty politician remarked that the legislators had enacted a lawsuit instead of a law.

The second flaw lay in the Fugitive Slave Act, which gave added—and controversial—protection to slavery. The new law empowered slaveowners

Fugitive Slave Act

to go into court in their own states to present evidence that a slave who owed them service had escaped. The resulting transcript and a description of the fugitive would then serve as legal proof of a person's slave status, even in free states and territories. Legal authorities would decide only whether the person brought before them was the person described, not whether he or she was indeed a slave. Fees encouraged U.S. marshals to assist in apprehending fugitives, and penalties discouraged citizens from harboring them. (Authorities were paid $10 if the alleged fugitive was turned over to the slaveowner, $5 if not.)

Abolitionist newspapers quickly attacked the Fugitive Slave Act as a violation of fundamental American rights. Why, in a land of freedom, were alleged fugitives denied a trial by jury before being sent into bondage? Why did suspected fugitives have no right to present evidence or cross-examine witnesses? Did not the law give authorities a financial incentive to turn over prisoners to slaveowners? These arguments convinced some northerners that free blacks could be sent into slavery, mistakenly or otherwise, with no means to defend themselves. Protest meetings were held in Massachusetts, New York, Pennsylvania, northern Ohio, northern Illinois, and elsewhere. In 1851 a mob in Boston grabbed a runaway slave from a U.S. marshal and sent him to safety in Canada.

At this point a book by a relatively unknown writer portrayed the humanity and suffering of slaves in a way that captured the sympathies of millions of northerners. Har-

Uncle Tom's Cabin

riet Beecher Stowe, whose New England family had produced many prominent ministers, wrote *Uncle Tom's Cabin* out of deep moral conviction. Her book, serialized in 1851 and published in 1852, conveyed the agony slaves felt as husbands, wives, and parents; it described a mother's dash to freedom with her child across the frozen Ohio River. Stowe also portrayed slavery's evil effects on slaveholders, indicting the institution itself more harshly than the southerners caught in its web. In nine months the book sold over three hundred thousand copies; by mid-1853, over a million. Countless people saw *Uncle Tom's Cabin* performed as a stage play or read similar novels inspired by it. Stowe brought home the evil of slavery to many who had never given it much thought.

The popularity of *Uncle Tom's Cabin* alarmed and appalled sensitive southern whites. In the territorial controversies and now in popular literature, they saw threats to their way of life. Behind the South's aggressive claims about territorial rights lay fear—fear that if nearby areas became free soil, they would be used as bases from which to spread abolitionism into the slave states. Jefferson Davis of Mississippi wrote in 1855 that "abolitionism would gain but little in excluding slavery from the territories, if it were never to disturb that institution in the States." To defend slavery against political threats, southern leaders relied on Calhoun's territorial theories and on the familiar dogmas of states' rights and strict construction.

To protect slavery in the arena of ideas, southerners needed to counter indictments of the institution as a moral wrong. Accordingly, proslavery

Proslavery Theories

theorists elaborated numerous arguments based on partially scientific or pseudoscientific data. They discussed anthropological evidence suggesting separate origins of the races and physicians' views on the inferiority of the black body. Other proslavery spokesmen expounded the new "science" of phrenology, citing data on the external dimensions of human skulls and the volume of the cranial cavity that "proved" blacks were an inferior race.

One southern sociologist, a Virginian named George Fitzhugh, focused on relations between management and labor and declared that slavery was morally superior to free labor. To Fitzhugh, wage labor in northern industry was inhumane because northern employers cared nothing about wage laborers as people. The factory owner, Fitzhugh argued, turned workers out when they grew old or sick, whereas paternalistic slaveowners cared responsibly for their aged slaves. From these points Fitzhugh drew a startling conclusion: slavery ought to be practiced in all societies, whatever their racial composition. His notions, extreme even for the South, reveal how southern defenses often deepened northern fears of the Slave Power.

In private and in their hearts, most southern leaders fell back on two rationales for slavery: the belief that blacks were inferior and biblical accounts of slaveholding. Like many whites, Jefferson Davis believed that whites and blacks could not coexist as equals in freedom; therefore slavery was unavoidable. Among friends Davis ignored the latest racist theories and reverted to the eighteenth-century argument that southerners were doing the best they could with a situation they had inherited. "Is it well to denounce an evil for which there is no cure?" he asked.

Antislavery denunciations troubled Davis, but he was far from despair in 1852. That year's elections gave him and other southerners hope that

Election of 1852
———

slavery would be secure under the administration of a new president. Franklin Pierce, a Democrat from New Hampshire, won an easy victory over the Whig presidential nominee, General Winfield Scott. Pierce had made no secret of his belief that the defense of each section's rights was essential to the nation's unity. Southerners hoped that his firm support for the Compromise of 1850 might end sectional divisions. Because Scott's views on the compromise had been unknown, and the Free-Soil candidate, John P. Hale of New Hampshire, had openly rejected it, Pierce's victory suggested that Americans strongly supported the compromise.

That interpretation of the election was, however, erroneous. Pierce's victory derived less from his strengths than from the Whig party's weakness.

The Webb family toured the North, presenting dramatic readings of Uncle Tom's Cabin. *Performances by the Webbs and others deepened the already powerful impact of Harriet Beecher Stowe's novel.*   Stowe-Day Foundation, Hartford, Conn.

The Whigs were a congressional and state-based party that had never achieved much success in presidential politics. Sectional discord was splitting the party in two, further undermining its national competitiveness, and the deaths of President Taylor, Daniel Webster, and Henry Clay had deprived Whigs of the few dominant personalities they had. In 1852 the Whig party ran on little but its past reputation, and many predicted its demise.

When Pierce as president supported the compromise, the results appalled many northerners. His vigorous enforcement of the fugitive-slave law ignited fears of the Slave Power. In 1854 Pierce learned that a fugitive slave named Anthony Burns was in custody in Boston. Burns had fled from Virginia by stowing away on a ship. In Boston he found a job and began to feel safe in a city well known for its abolitionists. But then Burns wrote to an enslaved relative in Virginia, and his letter was intercepted. Federal marshals placed him under guard in Boston's Federal Courthouse, where abolitionists mounted a violent protest for his freedom.

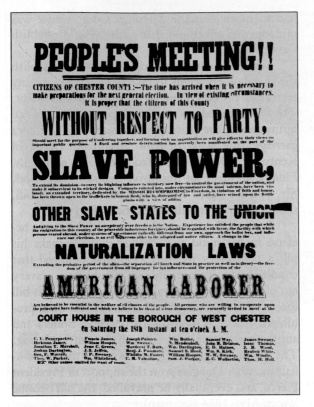

Throughout the North the Kansas-Nebraska Act kindled fires of alarm over the Slave Power's "determination to extend its dominion" and "control the government of the nation." Meetings like this one in West Chester, Pennsylvania, aided the new Republican party.   American Antiquarian Society.

The New Republican Party

on the Kansas-Nebraska bill, six congressmen had published an "Appeal of the Independent Democrats." Joshua Giddings, Salmon Chase, and Charles Sumner—the principal authors of this bitter protest against the Kansas-Nebraska bill—attacked Douglas's legislation as a "gross violation of a sacred pledge" (the Missouri Compromise) and a "criminal betrayal of precious rights" that would make free territory a "dreary region of despotism." Their appeal tapped a reservoir of deep concerns in the North, concerns that Illinois's Abraham Lincoln cogently expressed.

Although Lincoln did not condemn southerners—"They are just what we would be in their situation"—he exposed the moral bankruptcy and real significance of the Kansas-Nebraska Act. De-

nying "that there CAN be MORAL RIGHT in the enslaving of one man by another," Lincoln argued that the founding fathers, from love of liberty, had banned slavery from the Northwest Territory, kept the word *slavery* out of the Constitution, and treated it overall as a "cancer" that must eventually be removed. Rather than encouraging liberty, the Kansas-Nebraska Act put slavery "on the high road to extension and perpetuity," and that constituted a "moral wrong and injustice." America's future, Lincoln warned, was being mortgaged to slavery. The nation should "readopt the Declaration of Independence" and commit itself to freedom.

Thousands agreed. During the summer and fall of 1854, antislavery Whigs and Democrats, Free-Soilers, and other reformers throughout the Northwest met to form the new Republican party, dedicated to keeping slavery out of the territories. The Republicans' influence rapidly spread to the East, and they won a stunning victory in the 1854 elections. In their first appearance on the ballot, Republicans captured a majority of northern House seats. Antislavery sentiment had created a new party and caused roughly a quarter of northern Democrats to desert their party.

For the first time, too, a sectional party had gained significant power in the political system. Previously, every major party was a national organization whose leaders patched up sectional differences to achieve partisan goals. Now the Whigs were gone, and only the Democrats struggled to maintain a national following. The sectional Republican party, which absorbed the weaker Free-Soil party, now grew rapidly in the North by raising moral issues that repelled southern voters.

Nor were Republicans the only new party. An anti-immigrant organization, the American party, briefly seemed likely to replace the Whigs. This party, popularly known as the Know-Nothings (because its members at first kept their purposes secret, answering "I know nothing" to all questions), exploited nativist fear of foreigners. Between 1848 and 1860, nearly 3.5 million immigrants entered the United States—proportionally the heaviest influx of foreigners ever in American history (see pages 349–354). Democrats courted these new citizens and relied on their votes, but many native-born Americans harbored serious misgivings about them. In 1854 anti-immigrant fears gave the Know-

Know-Nothings

Nothings more supporters in some northern states than either Republicans or Free-Soilers. The temperance movement also gained new strength early in the 1850s with its promises to stamp out the evils associated with liquor and immigrants. In this context the Know-Nothings campaigned to reinforce Protestant morality and restrict voting and office holding to the native-born.

By the mid-1850s the American party was powerful and growing; so many new congressmen won office in 1854 with anti-immigrant as well as antislavery support that Know-Nothings claimed to outnumber Republicans. But like the Whigs, the Know-Nothings could not keep their northern and southern wings together, and they melted away after 1856. That left the field to the Republicans, who wooed the nativists and in several states passed temperance ordinances and laws postponing suffrage for naturalized citizens (see table on page 403).

Republicans, Know-Nothings, and Democrats were all scrambling to attract former Whig voters. The demise of that party ensured a major realignment of the political system,

Realignment of Political System

with nearly half the old electorate up for grabs. To woo these homeless Whigs, the remaining parties addressed a variety of issues to appeal to various segments of the electorate. Immigration, temperance, homestead bills, the tariff, internal improvements—all played important roles in attracting voters during the 1850s.

The Republicans appealed strongly to those interested in the economic development of the West. Commercial agriculture was booming in the Ohio–

Republican Appeals

Mississippi–Great Lakes area, but residents of that region needed more canals, roads, and river and harbor improvements to reap the full benefit of their labors. Because credit was scarce, there was also widespread interest in a federal land-grant program: its proponents argued that western land should be made available free to those who would farm it. The Whigs had favored all these measures before their party collapsed, but the Democrats resolutely opposed them. Following long-standing party principles, Democratic presidents vetoed internal-improvements bills and a homestead bill as late as 1859. Seizing their opportunity, the Repub-

licans added internal improvements and land-grant planks to their platform. They also backed higher tariffs as an enticement to industrialists and businessmen, whose interest in tariffs was quickened by a financial panic in 1857.

Partisan ideological appeals, which had a significant impact on the sectional crisis, were another major feature of the realigned political system. In the North, Republicans attracted many voters through effective use of ideology. When they preached "Free Soil, Free Labor, Free Men," they invoked an image that northerners had of themselves and their future. These phrases resonated with traditional ideals of equality, liberty, and opportunity under self-government—the heritage of republicanism. Use of that heritage also undercut charges that the Republican party was radical and unreliable.

"Free Soil, Free Labor, Free Men" seemed an appropriate motto for a northern economy that was energetic, expanding, and prosperous. Untold thousands of farmers had moved west to establish productive farms and growing communities. Midwestern farmers were using new machines, such as disc harrows and mechanical reapers, which multiplied their yields. Railroads were carrying their crops to urban markets. And industry was beginning to perform wonders of production, making available goods that had hitherto been beyond the reach of the average person. As northerners surveyed the general growth and prosperity, they thought they saw a reason for it.

The key to progress appeared, to many people, to be free labor. People believed in the dignity of labor and the incentive of opportunity. Any hardworking and virtuous man, it

Republican Ideology

was thought, could improve his condition and achieve economic independence by applying himself to opportunities that the country had to offer. Republicans pointed out that the South, which relied on slave labor and had little industry, was backward and retrograde compared with the North. Praising both laborers and opportunity, the Republicans captured much of the spirit of the age in the North.

Traditional republicanism hailed the virtuous common man as the backbone of the country. Republicans pointed to Abraham Lincoln, a man of humble origins who had become a successful lawyer and political leader, as a contemporary symbol of that tradition. They portrayed their party as the guardian of economic opportunity, fighting to ensure that individuals had a chance to work, acquire land, and attain success. In the words of an Iowa Republican, the United States was thriving because its "door is thrown open to all, and even the poorest and humblest in the land, may, by industry and application, gain a position which will entitle him to the respect and confidence of his fellow-men."

The Republican party thus attracted support from a variety of sources. Opposition to the extension of slavery had initially brought the party into being, but party members carefully broadened their appeal by adopting the causes of other groups. They were wise to do so. As the New York newspaper editor Horace Greeley wrote in 1856, "It is beaten into my bones that the American people are not yet anti-slavery." Four years later, Greeley again observed that "an Anti-Slavery man *per se* cannot be elected." But, he added, "a Tariff, River-and-Harbor, Pacific Railroad, Free Homestead man, *may* succeed *although* he is Anti-Slavery." As these elements joined the Republican party, they also learned more about the dangers of slavery. Thus the process of party building deepened the sectional conflict.

A similar process was under way in the South. The disintegration of the Whig party had left many southerners at loose ends politically; they included a good number of wealthy planters, smaller slaveholders, and urban businessmen. Some gravitated to the American party, but not for long. In the increasingly tense atmosphere of sectional crisis, these people were highly susceptible to strong states' rights positions, which provided a handy defense for slavery. Democratic leaders emphasized such appeals during the 1850s and managed to convert most of the formerly Whig slaveholders, who responded to their class interests.

Southern Democrats

Most Democrats south of the Mason-Dixon line, however, were not slaveholders. Since Andrew Jackson's day, small farmers had been the heart of the Democratic party. Democratic politicians, though often slaveowners themselves, had lauded the common man and argued that their policies advanced his interests. According to the southern version of republicanism, white citizens in a slave society enjoyed liberty and social equality be-cause the black race was enslaved. Slavery supposedly prevented the evil of aristocracy by making all white men equal. As Jefferson Davis put it in 1851, other societies undermined the status of the common white because in them social distinctions were drawn "by property, between the rich and the poor." In the South, however, slavery elevated every white person's status and allowed the non-slaveholder to *stand upon the broad level of equality with the rich man.* To retain the support of ordinary whites, southern Democrats emphasized this appeal to racism. The issue in the sectional crisis, they warned, was "shall negroes govern white men, or white men govern negroes?"

Southern leaders also portrayed sectional controversies as matters of injustice and insult to the South. The rights of all southern whites were in jeopardy, they argued, because antislavery and Free-Soil forces were destroying constitutional government. By attacking an institution protected in the Constitution, northern agitators were damaging rights precious to southerners. The stable, well-ordered South was the true defender of constitutional principles, but runaway change in the North was threatening to subvert the nation.

These arguments had their effect. Racial fears and traditional political loyalties helped keep the political alliance between yeoman farmers and planters intact through the 1850s. No viable party emerged in the South to replace the Whigs. The result was a one-party system that emphasized sectional issues. No one raised potential conflicts of interest between slaveholders and nonslaveholders. Instead, in the South as in the North, political realignment sharpened sectional divisions.

In both sections political leaders argued that racial change threatened opportunity. The *Montgomery* (Alabama) *Mail* warned southern whites in 1860 that the Republicans intended "to free the negroes and force amalgamation between them and the children of the poor men of the South. The rich will be able to keep out of the way of the contamination." Similarly, Republicans warned northern workers that if slavery entered the territories, the great reservoir of opportunity for decent people without means would be poisoned. Free labor had to be extended to the territories if coming generations were to prosper. Such charges aroused fears and anxieties in both sections.

But events in Kansas, which followed each other like repeated hammer blows, did even more

The Border Ruffians, depicted in this pen-and-ink drawing, were proslavery Missourians who periodically invaded Kansas to vote and help establish slavery there. Conflicts over land claims further complicated the violence in Bleeding Kansas. Yale University Art Gallery, Mabel Brady Garvan Collection.

to deepen the conflict. Put into practice, the Kansas-Nebraska Act spawned hatred and violence; among the settlers in the Kansas territory were both land-hungry claim jumpers and partisans in the sectional struggle. Abolitionists and religious groups sent armed Free-Soil settlers; southerners sent their reinforcements to establish slavery and prevent "northern hordes" from stealing Kansas away. Clashes between the two groups caused bloodshed, and soon the whole nation was talking about "Bleeding Kansas."

Politics in the territory resembled war more than democracy. During elections for a territorial legislature in 1855, thousands of proslavery Missourians invaded the polls and ran up a large but fraudulent majority for slavery candidates. The resulting legislature legalized slavery, and in response Free-Soilers held an unauthorized conven-

Bleeding Kansas

tion at which they created their own government and constitution. A proslavery posse sent to arrest the Free-Soil leaders sacked the town of Lawrence; in revenge John Brown, an antislavery zealot who saw himself as God's instrument to destroy slavery, murdered five proslavery settlers. Soon armed bands of guerrillas roamed the state, battling over land claims as well as slavery.

The passion generated by this conflict erupted in violence in the chamber of the U.S. Senate in May 1856, when Charles Sumner of Massachusetts denounced "the Crime against Kansas." Radical in his antislavery views, Sumner bitterly assailed the president, the South, and Senator Andrew P. Butler of South Carolina. Soon thereafter Butler's cousin, Representative Preston Brooks, approached Sumner at the latter's Senate desk, raised his cane, and began to beat Sumner on the head. Trapped behind his desk, which was bolted to the floor, Sumner tried to rise, eventually wrenching

The earliest known photograph of John Brown, probably taken in 1846 in Massachusetts, shows him pledging his devotion to an unidentified flag, possibly an abolitionist banner. Already Brown was aiding runaway slaves and pondering ways to strike at slavery. Ohio Historical Society.

the desk free before he collapsed, bloodied, on the floor. Shocked northerners recoiled from what they saw as another southern assault on free speech and the South's readiness to use violence to have its way. William Cullen Bryant, editor of the *New York Evening Post*, asked, "Has it come to this, that we must speak with bated breath in the presence of our southern masters?" As if in reply, the *Richmond Enquirer* denounced "vulgar Abolitionists in the Senate" who "have been suffered to run too long without collars. They must be lashed into submission." Popular opinion in Massachusetts strongly supported Sumner; South Carolina voters re-elected Brooks and sent him dozens of new canes. The country was becoming polarized.

The election of 1856 showed how extreme that polarization had become. When Democrats met to select a nominee, they shied away from prominent leaders whose views on the territories were well known. Instead they chose James Buchanan of Pennsylvania, whose chief virtue was that for the past four years he had been ambassador to Britain, uninvolved in territorial controversies. This anonymity and superior party organization helped Bu-

chanan win 1.8 million votes and the election, but he owed his victory to southern support. Eleven of sixteen free states voted against him, and Democrats did not regain ascendancy in those states for decades. The Republican candidate, John C. Frémont, won those eleven free states and 1.3 million votes; Republicans had become the dominant party in the North. The Know-Nothing candidate, Millard Fillmore, won almost 1 million votes, but this election was to be his party's last hurrah. The coming battle would be between a sectional Republican party and an increasingly divided Democratic party.

SLAVERY AND THE NATION'S FUTURE

For years the issue of slavery in the territories had convulsed Congress, and for years Congress had tried to settle the issue with vague formulas. In 1857 a different branch of government stepped onto the scene. The Supreme Court took up this emotionally charged subject and attempted to silence controversy with a definitive verdict in the Dred Scott case.

A Missouri slave named Dred Scott had sued his owner for his freedom. Scott based his claim to freedom on the fact that his former owner, an army surgeon, had taken him for several years into Illinois, a free state, and into the Wisconsin Territory, from which slavery had been barred by the Missouri Compromise. Scott first won and then lost his case as it moved on appeal through the state courts, into the federal system, and finally after eleven years to the Supreme Court.

Dred Scott Case

Normally the Supreme Court justices were reluctant to inject themselves into political battles, and it seemed likely that the Court would stay out of this one. An 1851 decision had declared that state courts had the last word in determining the status of Negroes who lived within their jurisdiction. The Supreme Court had only to follow this precedent to avoid ruling on substantive, and very controversial, issues: Was a black person like Dred Scott a citizen of the United States and thus eligible to sue in federal court? Had residence in a free state or free territory made him free? Did Congress

Dred Scott, a slave who brought suit in Missouri for his freedom, and Chief Justice Roger Taney, a descendant of Maryland's slaveholding elite, were principal figures in the most controversial Supreme Court decision of the century. Roger Taney: Maryland Historical Society; Dred Scott: Missouri Historical Society.

have the power to prohibit slavery in a territory or to delegate that power to a territorial legislature?

Indeed, it appeared initially that the Supreme Court would dispose of *Dred Scott* v. *Sanford* by following the 1851 precedent. The Chief Justice even assigned one justice the task of writing such an opinion. Then, for a number of reasons, the Court decided to rule on the Missouri Compromise after all. Two northern justices indicated that they would dissent from the planned ruling and argue for Scott's freedom and the constitutionality of the Missouri Compromise. Their decision emboldened southerners on the Court, who were growing eager to declare the 1820 compromise unconstitutional. Southern sympathizers in Washington were pressing for a proslavery verdict, and several justices simply felt they should try to resolve an issue whose uncertainties had caused so much strife.

In March 1857, Chief Justice Roger B. Taney of Maryland delivered the majority opinion of a divided Court. Taney declared that Scott was not a citizen of either the United States or Missouri; that residence in free territory did not make Scott free; and that Congress had no power to bar slavery

from a territory, as it had done in the Missouri Compromise. The decision not only overturned a sectional compromise that had been honored for years; it also invalidated the basic ideas of the Wilmot Proviso, and probably popular sovereignty as well.

The Slave Power seemed to have gained vital constitutional ground. African-Americans were especially dismayed, for Taney's decision also declared that at the nation's founding blacks had been regarded "as beings of an inferior order" with "no rights which the white man was bound to respect." The founding fathers, he asserted, had never intended for black people to be citizens. Taney was mistaken; African-Americans had been citizens in several of the original states. Nevertheless, the Dred Scott decision seemed to shut the door permanently on their hopes for justice and equal rights.

Northern whites who rejected the decision's content were suspicious of the circumstances surrounding it. Five of the nine justices were southerners; three of the northern justices actively dissented or refused to concur in crucial parts of the decision. The only northerner who supported Taney's opinion, Justice Robert Grier of Pennsylvania, was known to be susceptible to President Buchanan's influence. In fact, Buchanan had secretly brought to bear improper but effective influence.

A storm of angry reaction broke in the North. The decision alarmed a wide variety of northerners—abolitionists, would-be settlers in the West, and those who scorned black people but feared the influence of the South. Every charge against the aggressive Slave Power seemed now to be confirmed. "There is such a thing as THE SLAVE POWER," warned the *Cincinnati Daily Commercial*. "It has marched over and annihilated the boundaries of the states. We are now one great homogenous slaveholding community." The *Cincinnati Freeman* asked, "What security have the Germans and the Irish that their children will not, within a hundred years, be reduced to slavery in this land of their adoption?" And the *Atlantic Monthly* asked the question, "Where will it end? Is the success of this conspiracy to be final and eternal?" The poet James Russell Lowell expressed and provoked the anxieties of poor northern whites when he had his Yankee character, Ezekiel Biglow, say:

> Wy, it's just ez clear ez figgers,
>   Clear ez one an' one make two,
> Chaps thet make black slaves o' niggers,
>   Want to make wite slaves o' you.

Republican politicians capitalized on these fears to strengthen their coalition of abolitionists and other northerners, including racists who feared that slavery jeopardized their interests. Abraham Lincoln stressed that the territorial question affected every citizen. "The whole nation," he declared as early as 1854, "is interested that the best use shall be made of these Territories. We want them for homes of free white people. This they cannot be, to any considerable extent, if slavery shall be planted within them." The territories must be reserved, he insisted, "as an outlet for *free white people everywhere*" so that immigrants could come to America and "find new homes and better their condition in life."

Abraham Lincoln on the Slave Power

More importantly, Lincoln warned of slavery's increasing control over the nation. In language of biblical majesty, he described chilling prospects that caused northerners to ask what kind of nation America was becoming. The founding fathers had created a government dedicated to freedom, Lincoln insisted. Admittedly they had recognized slavery's existence, but "this Government has endured eighty-two years because," he argued in 1858, "during all that time, until the introduction of the Nebraska Bill, the public mind did rest . . . in the belief that slavery was in course of ultimate extinction." After the Dred Scott decision, he charged, it was clear that slavery's advocates, including highly placed government officials, were trying to "push it forward, till it shall become lawful in *all* the states . . . *North* as well as *South*."

The next step in the unfolding Slave Power conspiracy, Lincoln alleged, would be a Supreme Court decision "declaring that the Constitution does not permit a State to exclude slavery from its limits. . . . We shall lie down pleasantly, dreaming that the people of Missouri are on the verge of making their State free; and we shall awake to the reality instead, that the Supreme Court has made Illinois a slave State." This charge was not mere imagination, for cases soon reached the courts challenging state laws that freed slaves brought within their borders.

Lincoln's most eloquent statement against the Slave Power was his famous "House Divided" speech, in which he declared:

> I do not expect the Union to be dissolved—I do not expect the House to fall—but I do expect it to cease to be divided. It will become all one thing or all the other. Either the opponents of slavery will arrest the further spread of it, and place it where the public mind shall rest in the belief that it is in the course of ultimate extinction; or its advocates will push it forward, till it shall become alike lawful in all the States, old as well as new, North as well as South.

Lincoln warned repeatedly that the latter possibility was real, and events convinced countless northerners that slaveholders were close to their goal of making slavery a national institution.

Politically, these forceful Republican arguments offset the difficulties that the Dred Scott decision posed. By endorsing Calhoun's theories, the Court had in effect declared that the central position of the Republican party—no extension of slavery—was unconstitutional. Republicans could only repudiate the decision, appealing to a "higher law," or hope to change the personnel of the Court.

of suffrage, for a reason of a very different character than the one supposed. The principle of freehold suffrage seems to have been brought over from England with the first colonists, and to have been preserved almost invariably in the colony ever afterwards. In the act of 1743, ch. 1 (Swann's Revisal, 171), it will be seen that a freehold of fifty acres was necessary to entitle the inhabitant of a county to vote, and by the act of 2d Sept. of 1746, ch. 1, *ibid.*, 223, the *freeholders* only of the respective towns of Edenton, Bath, Newbern, and Wilmington were declared entitled to vote for members of the Colonial Legislature. The very Congress which framed our Constitution was chosen by freeholders. That Constitution extended the elective **franchise to every freeman** who had arrived at the age of 21, and paid a public tax, and it is a matter of universal notoriety that under it free persons without regard to color claimed and exercised the franchise until it was taken from free men of color a few years since by our amended Constitution. But surely the possession of political power is not essential to constitute a citizen. If it be, then women, minors, and persons who have not paid public taxes are not citizens—and free white men who have paid public taxes and arrived at full age, but have not a freehold of fifty

How *do historians know*

that African-Americans played a role in government at the nation's founding? In the Dred Scott decision, Chief Justice Roger Taney declared that black people were never considered part of the political community, either in state or nation. Justice Benjamin Curtis, who dissented from the decision, argued that Taney was wrong. Curtis asserted that several of the original states based voting on the ownership of property, and that blacks who qualified did, indeed, vote. This passage, from a decision of the North Carolina Supreme Court in 1838, confirms that black freeholders in North Carolina voted until amendments were made to the state's constitution in 1835. Photo: Martine Sherrill, courtesy Wake Forest University Law Library.

They did both and probably gained politically as fear of the Slave Power grew.

For northern Democrats like Stephen Douglas, the Court's decision posed an awful dilemma. Northern voters were alarmed by the prospect that the territories would be opened to slavery. To retain their support, Douglas had to find some way to reassure them. Yet, given his ambitions to lead the national Democratic party and become president, Douglas could not afford to alienate southern Democrats. His task was problematic at best; given the emotional tenor of the times, it proved impossible.

Douglas chose to stand by his principle of popular sovereignty, which encountered a second test in 1857. In Kansas, after Free-Soil settlers boycotted an election, proslavery forces met at Lecompton and wrote a constitution that permitted slavery. New elections to the territorial legislature, however, returned an antislavery majority, and the legislature called for a popular vote on the new constitution. It was defeated by more than ten thousand votes. The evidence was overwhelming that Kansans did not want slavery, yet President Buchanan tried to force the Lecompton Constitution through Congress.

Debate on the Lecompton Constitution showed that southerners and the Buchanan administration were demanding a proslavery outcome contrary to the desires of the people of Kansas. Never had the Slave Power's influence over the government seemed more blatant. Breaking with the administration, Douglas threw his weight against the Lecompton Constitution. He gauged opinion in Kansas correctly, for in 1858 voters there rejected the constitution a third time. But his action infuriated southern Democrats. After the Dred Scott decision, southerners like Senator Albert G. Brown of Mississippi believed that slavery was *protected* in the territories: "The Constitution as expounded by the Supreme Court awards it. We demand it; we mean to have it."

Douglas further alienated the southern wing of his party in his well-publicized debates with Abraham Lincoln, who challenged him for the Illinois Senate seat in 1858. Speaking at Freeport, Illinois, Douglas attempted to revive the notion of popular sovereignty with some tortured extensions of his old arguments. Asserting that the Supreme Court had ruled only on the powers of Congress, not on the powers of a *territorial* legislature, Douglas claimed that a territorial legislature could bar slavery either by passing a law against it or by doing nothing. Without the patrol laws and police regulations that support slavery, he reasoned, the institution could not exist. This argument, called the Freeport Doctrine, temporarily shored up Douglas's crumbling position in the North. But it gave southern Democrats further evidence that Douglas was unreliable, and many viciously turned against him. Some, like Representative William L. Yancey of Alabama, studied the trend in northern opinion and concluded that southern rights would be safe only in a separate nation.

Stephen Douglas Proposes the Freeport Doctrine

A growing number of slaveholders, in fact, were concluding that slavery could not be safe within the Union. Such concern was not new. As early as 1838, the Louisiana planter Bennet Barrow had written in his diary, "Northern States meddling with slavery . . . openly speaking of the sin of Slavery in the southern states . . . must eventually cause a separation of the Union." And in 1856, a calmer, more polished Georgian named Charles Colcock Jones, Jr., rejoiced at the Democrat James Buchanan's defeat of Republican John C. Frémont for the presidency. The result guaranteed four more years of peace and prosperity, wrote Jones, but "beyond that period . . . we scarce dare expect a continuance of our present relations." Increasingly, slaveowners agreed with Jones and Barrow.

The immediate consequence for politics, however, was the likelihood of formal division in the Democratic party. Northern Democrats could not support the territorial protection for slavery that southern Democrats insisted was theirs as a constitutional right. Thus the issue of slavery in the territories continued to generate wider conflict, even though it had little immediate, practical significance. In territories outside Kansas the number of settlers was small, and everywhere the number of African-Americans was negligible—less than 1 percent of the populations of Kansas and New Mexico. By 1858 even Jefferson Davis had given up on agricultural development in the Southwest and admitted his uncertainty that slavery could succeed in Kansas. Nevertheless, men like Davis and Douglas spent many bitter hours attacking each other on the floor of the Senate. And the general public in both North and South moved from anxiety to anger and alarm. The situation had become explosive.

THE BREAKUP OF THE UNION

One year before the 1860 presidential election, John Brown, who had slain proslavery settlers in Kansas, led a small band of whites and blacks in an attack on Harpers Ferry, Virginia. Hoping to trigger a slave rebellion, Brown failed miserably and was quickly captured, tried, and executed. Yet his attempted insurrection struck fear into the South even before it came to light that Brown had had financial backing from several prominent abolitionists. When northern intellectuals such as Emerson and Thoreau praised Brown as a hero and a martyr, southerners' fears and anger multiplied many times over. The unity of the nation was now in peril.

Many observers feared that the election of 1860 would decide the fate of the Union. Divisions in the Democratic party did nothing to reassure them.

During the 1860 presidential campaign these framed pictures of Abraham Lincoln and Stephen Douglas—widely recognized as rivals since their 1858 debates—were distributed by their supporters.   Museum of American Political Life, University of Hartford.

For several years, the Democratic party had been the only remaining organization that was truly national in scope. Even religious denominations had split into northern and southern wings during the 1840s and 1850s. "One after another," wrote a Mississippi newspaper editor, "the links which have bound the North and South together, have been severed . . . [but] the Democratic party looms gradually up, its nationality intact, and waves the olive branch over the troubled waters of politics." At its 1860 convention, however, the Democratic party broke in two.

Stephen A. Douglas wanted the party's presidential nomination, but he could not afford to alienate northern voters by accepting the southern position on the territories.

Splintering of the Democratic Party

Southern Democrats like William L. Yancey, on the other hand, insisted on recognition of their rights—as Roger Taney had defined them—and they moved to block Douglas's nomination. When Douglas obtained a majority for his version of the platform, delegates from the five Gulf states plus South Carolina, Georgia, and Arkansas walked out of the convention hall in Charleston. After efforts at compromise failed, the Democrats presented two nominees: Douglas for the northern wing, and Vice President John C. Breckinridge of Kentucky

for the southern. The Republicans nominated Abraham Lincoln. A Constitutional Union party, formed to preserve the nation but strong only in the Upper South, nominated John Bell of Tennessee.

Three of the candidates stressed their support for the Union in the ensuing campaign. Bell's only issue was the urgency of preserving the Union intact, and Douglas desperately wanted to hold his northern and southern supporters together. Breckinridge quickly backed away from any appearance of extremism, and his supporters in several states declared that he was not a threat to the Union. Then the *New Orleans Bee* charged that every disunionist in the land applauded Breckinridge, and a Texas paper made an earthy allusion to his association with radicals: "Mr. Breckinridge claims that he isn't a disunionist. An animal not willing to pass for a pig shouldn't stay in the stye." Reacting to such criticism, Breckinridge reversed his decision to do no speaking during the campaign and delivered one address in which he flatly denied that his aim was secession. Thereafter his supporters stressed his loyalty and even ridiculed the possibility of secession in case of a Republican victory. Lincoln and the Republicans denied any intention of interfering with slavery in the states where it existed, but they stood firm against the extension of slavery into the territories.

Presidential Vote in 1860

	Lincoln	Other Candidates
Entire United States	1,866,452	2,815,617
North plus border and southern states that rejected secession prior to war[1]	1,866,452	2,421,752
North plus border states that fought for union[2]	1,864,523	1,960,842

[1]Kentucky, Missouri, Maryland, Delaware, Virginia, North Carolina, Tennessee, Arkansas

[2]Kentucky, Missouri, Maryland, Delaware

Source: From David Potter, *Lincoln and His Party in the Secession Crisis.* Copyright 1942, 1967 by Yale University Press. Reprinted by permission.

The results of the balloting were sectional in character, and though Lincoln won, Douglas, Breckinridge, and Bell together received most of the votes. Douglas had broad-based support but won few states; Breckinridge, whose strength was concentrated in the Deep South, carried nine southern states; Bell won pluralities in Virginia, Kentucky, and Tennessee. Lincoln prevailed in the North, but in the states that ultimately remained loyal to the Union he won only a plurality, not a majority (see table above). Lincoln's victory was won in the electoral college.

Election of 1860

Given the heterogeneous nature of Republican voters, it is likely that many of them did not view the issue of slavery in the territories as paramount. But opposition to slavery's extension was the core issue of the Republican party, and Lincoln's alarm over slavery's growing political power was genuine. The slavery issue would not go away. After the election abolitionists and supporters of free soil in the North worked to keep the Republicans from compromising on their territorial stand. Meanwhile in the South, proslavery advocates and secessionists whipped up public opinion and demanded that state conventions assemble to consider secession.

Lincoln made the crucial decision not to soften his party's position on the territories. He wrote of the necessity of maintaining the bond of faith between voter and candidate and of declining to set "the minority over the majority." Presumably he was referring to the losing parties and the victorious Republicans respectively. But Lincoln's party had not won a majority of votes. His refusal to compromise probably derived both from conviction and from concern for the unity of the Republican party. Although many conservative Republicans—eastern businessmen and former Whigs who did not feel strongly about slavery—hoped for a compromise, the original and most committed Republicans—antislavery voters and "conscience Whigs"—were adamant for free soil. Lincoln chose to preserve party unity by standing firm against slavery's extension.

Southern leaders in the Senate were willing, conditionally, to accept a compromise formula drawn up by Senator John J. Crittenden of Kentucky. Crittenden, hoping to don the mantle of Henry Clay and avert disunion, proposed that the two sections divide the territories between them at 36°30′. But the southerners would agree to this *only* if the Republicans did, too, for they wanted no less and knew that extremists in the South would demand much more. When Lincoln ruled out concessions on the territorial issue, Crittenden's peacemaking effort collapsed. Virginians called for a special convention in Washington, to which several states sent representatives. But this gathering, too, failed to find a solution.

Though political leaders in North and South had communicated clearly with each other about the Crittenden proposal, misjudgment also played a role in the coming of war. As the historian David Potter has shown, Lincoln and other prominent Republicans believed that southerners were bluffing when they threatened secession; Republicans expected a pro-Union majority in the South to assert itself. Therefore Lincoln determined not to yield to threats but to call the southerners' bluff. On their side, moderate southern leaders had become convinced, more accurately, that northern leaders were not taking them seriously and that a posture of strength was necessary to win respect for their position. "To rally the men of the North, who would preserve the government as our fathers found it, we . . . should offer no doubtful or divided front," wrote Jefferson Davis. With such attitudes shaping leaders' actions, confrontation was more likely than compromise.

Meanwhile the Union was being destroyed. On December 20, 1860, South Carolina passed an ordinance of secession amid jubilation and cheering. This step marked the inau-

Secession of South Carolina
———

guration of a strategy favored by secessionists called separate-state secession. Foes of the Union, recognizing the difficulty of persuading all the southern states to challenge the federal government simultaneously, had concentrated their efforts on the most extreme proslavery state. They hoped South Carolina's secession would induce other states to follow, with each decision building momentum for disunion.

The strategy proved effective. By reclaiming its independence, South Carolina raised the stakes in the sectional confrontation. No longer was secession an unthinkable step; the Union was broken. Extremists now argued that other states should secede to support South Carolina and that those who favored compromise could make a better deal outside the Union than in it. Moderates found it difficult to dismiss such arguments, since most of them—even those who felt deep affection for the Union—were committed to defending southern rights and the southern way of life.

Southern extremists soon got their way in the Deep South. Overwhelming their opposition, they quickly called separate state conventions and passed secession ordinances in

Confederate States of America
———

Mississippi, Florida, Alabama, Georgia, Louisiana, and Texas. By February 1861 these states had joined South Carolina to form a new government in Montgomery, Alabama: the Confederate States of America. The delegates at Montgomery chose Jefferson Davis as their president, and the Confederacy began to function independently of the United States.

Yet this apparent unanimity of action was deceiving. Confused and dissatisfied with the alternatives, many southerners who had voted for president in 1860 stayed home a few months later rather than vote for delegates who would decide upon secession. In some state conventions the vote to secede had been close, the balance tipped by overrepresentation of plantation districts. Furthermore, the conventions were noticeably reluctant to seek

ratification of their acts by the people. Four states in the Upper South—Virginia, North Carolina, Tennessee, and Arkansas—flatly rejected secession and did not join the Confederacy until after fighting had begun. In the border states, popular sentiment was too divided for decisive action; minorities in Kentucky and Missouri tried to secede, but these slave states remained under Union control, along with Maryland and Delaware (see map).

Such misgivings were not surprising. Secession posed new and troubling issues for southerners, especially the possibility of war and the question of who would die. Analysis of election returns from 1860 and 1861 indicates that slaveholders and nonslaveholders were beginning to part company politically. Heavily slaveholding counties strongly supported secession. But nonslaveholding areas that had favored Breckinridge in the presidential election proved far less willing to support seces-

On February 18, 1861 in Montgomery, Alabama, Jefferson Davis took an oath as president of the Confederate States of America. Davis later recalled that he foresaw "troubles innumerable," but he committed himself to seek independence as his paramount goal.   Boston Athenaeum.

sion: most counties with few slaves took an antise-cession position or were staunchly Unionist. Large numbers of yeomen also sat out the election. With war on the horizon, nonslaveholders were beginning to consider their class interests and to ask themselves how far they would go to support slavery and slaveowners.

Some opposition to secession was fervently pro-Union, as is apparent in the comment of a northern Alabama delegate after his convention had approved secession: "Here I set & from my window see the nasty little thing flaunting in the breeze which has taken the place of that glorious banner which has been the pride of millions of Americans and the boast of freemen the wide world over." Although such sentiments presented problems for the Confederacy, they were not sufficiently developed to prevent secession.

The dilemma facing President Lincoln on inauguration day in March 1861 was how to maintain the authority of the federal government without provoking war. He decided to proceed cautiously in the states that had left the Union. By holding onto federal fortifications in those states, he reasoned, he could assert federal sovereignty while waiting for a restoration of relations. But Jefferson Davis, who could not claim to lead a sovereign nation if its ports were under foreign control, was unwilling to be so patient. A collision was inevitable.

It arrived in the early morning hours of April 12, 1861, at Fort Sumter in Charleston harbor. A federal garrison there was running low on food, and Lincoln notified the South Carolinians that he was sending a ship to resupply the fort. For the Montgomery government, the alternatives were either to attack the fort or to acquiesce to Lincoln's authority. Accordingly, orders were sent to obtain

Attack of Fort Sumter

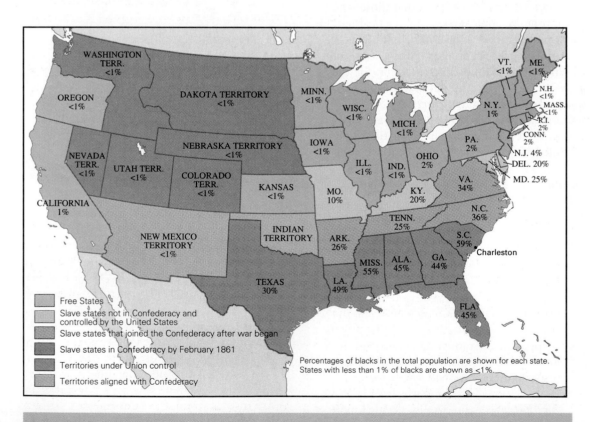

The Divided Nation—Slave and Free Areas, 1861   *After fighting began, the Upper South joined the Deep South in the Confederacy. How does the nation's pattern of division correspond to slavery and the percentage of blacks in the population?*

Voting Returns of Counties with Few Slaveholders, Eight Southern States,1860 and 1861

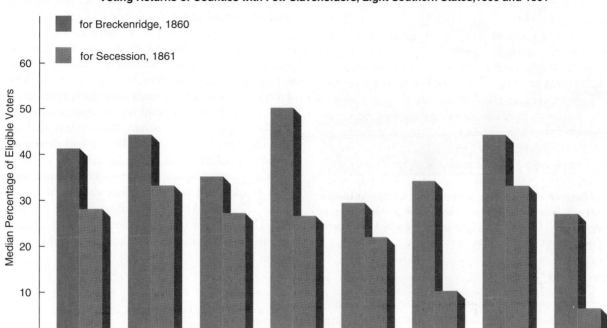

for Breckenridge, 1860

for Secession, 1861

Median Percentage of Eligible Voters

State: Alabama · Georgia · Louisiana · Mississippi · North Carolina · Tennessee · Texas · Virginia

Voting Returns of Counties with Few Slaveholders, Eight Southern States, 1860 and 1861   This chart depicts voting in counties whose percentage of slaveholders ranked them among the lower half of the counties in their state. How does voters' support for secession in 1861 compare with support for John Breckinridge, the southern Democratic candidate in 1860? Why was their support for secession so weak? At this time counties with many slaveholders were giving increased support to secession.

a surrender or attack the fort. After two days of heavy bombardment, the federal garrison finally surrendered. No one died in battle, though an accident during later military ceremonies killed one Union soldier. Confederates permitted the U.S. soldiers to sail away on unarmed vessels while Charlestonians celebrated wildly. The Civil War—the bloodiest war in America's history—had begun.

Throughout the 1840s and 1850s many able leaders had worked diligently to avert this outcome. Most people, North and South, had hoped to keep the nation together. As late as 1858 even Jefferson Davis had declared, "This great country will continue united." He had explained sincerely that the United States "is my country and to the innermost fibers of my heart I love it all, and every

part." Secession dismayed northern editors and voters, but it also plunged some planters into depression. Paul Cameron, the largest slaveowner in North Carolina, confessed that he was "very unhappy. I love the Union." Why, then, had war broken out? Why had all efforts to prevent it failed?

Slavery was an issue on which compromise was impossible. The conflict it generated was fundamental and beyond adjustment. The emotions bound up in attacking and defending it were too powerful, and the motives involved in maintaining or destroying it were too fundamental. It was deeply entwined with almost every major policy question of the present and the foreseeable future. Ultimately each section regarded slavery as too important to put aside.

Landing of the Troops at Veracruz. *Artist unknown. 1848. A detail of the painting appears at the beginning of Chapter 14, on page 396.*   Collection of the Amon Carter Museum, Fort Worth, Texas. AMC 14.80.

Even if one excludes extreme views, the North and the South had fundamentally different attitudes toward the institution. The logic of Republican ideology tended in the direction of abolishing slavery, even though Republicans denied any such intention. Similarly, the logic of southern leaders' arguments led toward establishing slavery everywhere, though southern leaders denied that they sought any such thing. Lincoln put the problem succinctly. Soon after the 1860 election, he assured his old friend Alexander Stephens of Georgia that the Republican party would not attack slavery in the states where it existed. But Lincoln continued, "You think slavery is *right* and ought to be expanded; while we think it is *wrong* and ought to be restricted. That I suppose is the rub."

Fundamental disagreements have not always led to war. A nation may face unresolvable issues yet manage to get past them. New events can capture people's attention; time can alter interests and attitudes, if in the intervening years conflict is contained or restricted. That is precisely what the advocates of compromise sought to achieve. They tried to contain conflict and buy time for the nation, to avoid issues that could not be settled, and to preserve the many areas of consensus among Americans. Their efforts were well-intentioned and patriotic, but they were doomed to failure.

The issue of slavery in the territories made conflict impossible to avoid. Territorial expansion generated disputes so frequently that the nation

never enjoyed a breathing space. As the conflict recurred, its influence on policy and effect on the government deepened. Every southern victory increased fear of the Slave Power, and each new expression of Free-Soil sentiment made alarmed slaveholders more insistent in their demands. The slavery issue cast dark clouds over the future. Even those opposed to war could see no way to avoid it.

In the profoundest sense, slavery was tied up with the war. Concern over slavery had driven all the other conflicts. But as the fighting began, this, the war's central issue, was shrouded in confusion. How would the Civil War affect slavery, its place in the law, and African-Americans' place in society? The answers to those questions, and the degree to which answers were sought, would be of fateful import.

SUGGESTIONS FOR FURTHER READING

Politics: General

Thomas B. Alexander, *Sectional Stress and Party Strength* (1967); Tyler Anbinder, *Nativism and Slavery* (1992); Maurice G. Baxter, *One and Inseparable: Daniel Webster and the Union* (1984); Paul Bergeron, *The Presidency of James K. Polk* (1987); Ray Allen Billington, *The Protestant Crusade, 1800–1860* (1938 and 1964); Frederick J. Blue, *The Free Soilers: Third Party Politics, 1848–1854* (1973); Stanley W. Campbell, *The Slave Catchers* (1968); Don E. Fehrenbacher, *The Dred Scott Case* (1978); George M. Fredrickson, *The Black Image in the White Mind* (1971); Holman Hamilton, *Prologue to Conflict: The Crisis and Compromise of 1850* (1964); Michael F. Holt, *Political Parties and American Political Development* (1992); Michael F. Holt, *The Political Crisis of the 1850s* (1978); Stephen E. Maizlish and John J. Kushma, eds., *Essays on American Antebellum Politics, 1840–1860* (1982); Chaplain W. Morrison, *Democratic Politics and Sectionalism: The Wilmot Proviso Controversy* (1967); Paul D. Nagle, *One Nation Indivisible* (1964); Russell B. Nye, *Fettered Freedom* (1949); Merrill D. Peterson, *The Great Triumvirate: Webster, Clay, and Calhoun* (1987); David M. Potter, *The Impending Crisis, 1848–1861* (1976); James A. Rawley, *Race and Politics* (1969); Leonard L. Richards, *The Life and Times of Congressman John Quincy Adams* (1986); Joel H. Silbey, *The Transformation of American Politics, 1840–1960* (1967); Elbert B. Smith, *The Presidency of James Buchanan* (1975); Kenneth M. Stampp, *America in 1857* (1991); Kenneth M. Stampp, *And the War Came* (1950); Gerald W. Wolff, *The Kansas-Nebraska Bill* (1977).

The South and Slavery

William L. Barney, *The Secessionist Impulse* (1974); Steven A. Channing, *A Crisis of Fear: Secession in South Carolina* (1970); William J. Cooper, Jr., *The South and the Politics of Slavery, 1828–*

1856 (1978); Avery O. Craven, *The Growth of Southern Nationalism, 1848–1861* (1953); Daniel W. Crofts, *Reluctant Confederates: Upper South Unionists in the Secession Crisis* (1989); Merton L. Dillon, *Slavery Attacked* (1991); Drew G. Faust, *The Ideology of Slavery* (1981); Drew G. Faust, *A Sacred Circle: The Dilemma of the Intellectual in the Old South* (1978); Lacy K. Ford, Jr., *Origins of Southern Radicalism* (1988); William W. Freehling, *The Road to Disunion* (1990); Eugene D. Genovese, *The World the Slaveholders Made* (1969); Eugene D. Genovese, *The Political Economy of Slavery* (1967); Michael P. Johnson, *Toward a Patriarchal Republic: The Secession of Georgia* (1977); John Niven, *John C. Calhoun and the Price of Union* (1988); David M. Potter, *The South and the Sectional Conflict* (1968); Thomas E. Schott, *Alexander H. Stephens of Georgia* (1988); William R. Stanton, *The Leopard's Spots* (1960); J. Mills Thornton III, *Politics and Power in a Slave Society* (1978); Larry E. Tise, *Proslavery* (1987); Ralph Wooster, *The Secession Conventions of the South* (1962).

The North and Antislavery

Dale Baum, *The Civil War Party System* (1984); Eugene H. Berwanger, *The Frontier Against Slavery* (1967); Frederick J. Blue, *Salmon P. Chase* (1987); David Donald, *Charles Sumner and the Coming of the Civil War* (1960); Louis Filler, *The Crusade Against Slavery, 1830–1860* (1960); Eric Foner, *Free Soil, Free Labor, Free Men* (1970); Louis S. Gerteis, *Morality and Utility in American Antislavery Reform* (1987); William E. Gienapp, *The Origins of the Republican Party, 1852–1856* (1986); Henry V. Jaffa, *Crisis of the House Divided* (1959); Robert W. Johannsen, *Lincoln, the South, and Slavery* (1991); Robert W. Johannsen, *Stephen A. Douglas* (1973); Aileen S. Kraditor, *Means and Ends in American Abolitionism* (1969); Stephen B. Oates, *To Purge This Land with Blood*, 2nd ed. (1984); Lewis Perry and Michael Fellman, eds., *Antislavery Reconsidered* (1979); Jeffrey Rossbach, *Ambivalent Conspirators* (1982); Richard Sewell, *Ballots for Freedom: Antislavery Politics in the United States, 1837–1860* (1976); Alice Felt Tyler, *Freedom's Ferment* (1944).

The Mexican War and Foreign Policy

K. Jack Bauer, *Zachary Taylor* (1985); Gene M. Brack, *Mexico Views Manifest Destiny, 1821–1846* (1976); Richard Griswold del Castillo, *The Treaty of Guadalupe Hidalgo* (1990); Neal Harlow, *California Conquered* (1982); Reginald Horsman, *Race and Manifest Destiny* (1981); Robert W. Johannsen, *To the Halls of the Montezumas: The Mexican War and the American Imagination* (1985); Ernest M. Lander, Jr., *Reluctant Imperialists: Calhoun, the South Carolinians, and the Mexican War* (1980); Robert E. May, *The Southern Dream of a Caribbean Empire, 1854–1861* (1973); Frederick Merk, *The Monroe Doctrine and American Expansion, 1843–1849* (1966); Frederick Merk, *Manifest Destiny and Mission in American History* (1963); David M. Pletcher, *The Diplomacy of Annexation: Texas, Oregon, and the Mexican War* (1973); John H. Schroeder, *Mr. Polk's War: American Opposition and Dissent* (1973); Otis A. Singletary, *The Mexican War* (1960); David J. Weber, *The Mexican Frontier, 1821–1846* (1982).

15

Transforming Fire: The Civil War, 1861–1865

THEY CAME FROM MANY parts of the nation. They had diverse points of view. Perhaps the only thing they had in common was that they were caught up in a gigantic struggle. Each felt dwarfed by the immense force of the Civil War, a vast and complex event beyond any individual's control.

Moncure Conway, a Virginian who had become an abolitionist and moved to New England, saw the Civil War as a momentous opportunity to promote social justice. But, he warned in a pamphlet, "Slavery, hoary tyrant of the ages," would try to drive justice " 'back! back . . . into the chambers of Night!' " Urging northerners to defeat slavery, Conway lived for the day when "the rays of Freedom and Justice" would shine throughout America.

But Conway's lofty idealism was not what drove most federal soldiers to march grimly to their deaths. Although slaves believed they were witnessing God's "Holy War for the liberation of the poor African slave people," Union troops typically had a different perspective. When a Yankee soldier ransacked a slave family's cabin and stole their best quilts, the mother exclaimed, "Why you nasty, stinkin' rascal. You say you come down here to fight for the niggers, and now you're stealin' from 'em." The soldier replied, "You're a G— D—— liar, I'm fightin' for $14 a month and the Union."

Southerners, too, had limited and pragmatic motives; many fought in self-defense or out of regional loyalty. A Union officer interrogating Confederate prisoners noticed the obvious poverty of one captive. Clearly the man was no slaveholder, so the officer asked him why he was fighting. "Because y'all are down here," was the Confederate's simple reply.

The great suffering and frustration caused by the war were apparent in the bitter words of another southerner. Impoverished by the conflict, this farmer had endured inflation, taxes, and shortages to support the Confederacy. Then an impressment agent arrived to take still more from him— grain and meat, horses and mules, and wagons. In return, the agent offered only a certificate promising repayment sometime in the future. Angry and fed up, the farmer bluntly declared, "The sooner this damned Government falls to pieces, the better it will be for us."

Many northern businessmen, however, viewed the economic effects of the war with optimism and anticipation. The conflict ensured vast government expenditures, a heavy demand

For both sides, the carnage and excitement of battle punctuated much longer periods of drill, preparation, and tedious waiting in camp.

for goods, and lucrative government contracts. *Harper's Monthly* reported that an eminent financier expected a long war, the kind of war that would mean huge purchases, paper money, active speculation, and rising prices. "The battle of Bull Run," predicted the financier, "makes the fortune of every man in Wall Street who is not a natural idiot."

For these people and millions of others, the Civil War was a life-changing event. It obliterated the normal patterns and circumstances of life. Millions of men were swept away into training camps and battle units. Armies numbering in the hundreds of thousands marched over the South, devastating once-peaceful countrysides. Families struggled to survive without their men; businesses tried to cope with the loss of workers. Women in both North and South took on extra responsibilities in the home and moved into new jobs in the work force. No sphere of life was untouched.

Change was most drastic in the South, where the leaders of the secession movement had launched a revolution for the purpose of keeping things unchanged. Never were men more mistaken: their revolutionary means were fundamentally incompatible with their conservative purpose. Southern whites had feared that a peacetime government of Republicans would interfere with slavery and upset the routine of plantation life. Instead their own actions led to a war that turned southern life upside-down and imperiled the very existence of slavery. The leadership of Jefferson Davis, president of the Confederate States of America, resulted in policies more objectionable to the elite than any proposed by President Lincoln. Life in the Confederacy proved to be a shockingly unsouthern experience.

War altered the North as well, but less deeply. Because most of the fighting took place on southern soil, northern farms and factories remained virtually unscathed. The drafting of workers and the changing needs for products slowed the pace of industrialization somewhat, but factories and businesses remained busy. Workers lost ground to inflation, but the economy hummed. A new probusiness atmosphere dominated Congress, where the seats of southern representatives were empty. To the alarm of many, the powers of the federal government and of the president increased during the war.

As shown in Departure of the Seventh Regiment, *flags, bunting, and the spectacle of thousands marching off to war gave a deceptively gay appearance to the beginning of the war, as this scene in New York City shows.*   Museum of Fine Arts, Boston; M. and M. Karolik Collection.

• *Important Events* •

1861	Four more southern states secede from Union
	Battle of Bull Run takes place
	General McClellan organizes Union army
	Union blockade begins
	U.S. Congress passes first confiscation act
1862	Union captures Fort Henry and Fort Donelson
	U.S. Navy captures New Orleans
	Battle of Shiloh shows the war's destructiveness
	Confederacy enacts conscription
	Lee thwarts McClellan's offensive on Richmond
	U.S. Congress passes second confiscation act
	Confederacy mounts offensive
	Battle of Antietam ends Lee's drive into Maryland
1863	Emancipation Proclamation
	U.S. Congress passes National Banking Act
	Union enacts conscription
	African-American soldiers join Union army

	Food riots occur in southern cities
	Battle of Chancellorsville ends in Jackson's death
	Union wins key victories at Gettysburg and Vicksburg
	Draft riots take place in New York City
1864	Battle of Cold Harbor continues carnage in Virginia
	Lincoln requests party plank abolishing slavery
	General Sherman captures Atlanta
	Lincoln wins re-election
	Jefferson Davis proposes Confederate emancipation
	Sherman marches through Georgia
1865	Sherman marches through Carolinas
	Congress approves Thirteenth Amendment
	Hampton Roads Conference
	Lee abandons Petersburg and Richmond
	Lee surrenders at Appomattox
	Lincoln assassinated

The war created social strains in both North and South. Disaffection was strongest in the Confederacy, where poverty and class resentment fed a lower-class antagonism to the war that threatened the Confederacy from within as federal armies assailed it from without. In the North, dissent also flourished, and antiwar sentiment occasionally erupted into violence.

Ultimately, the Civil War forced on the nation new social and racial arrangements. Its greatest effect was to compel leaders and citizens to deal directly with the issue they had tried so hard to avoid: slavery. This issue had, in complex and indirect ways, given rise to the war. Now the scope and demands of the war forced reluctant Americans to confront it.

"FIGHTING MEANS KILLING"

Few Americans understood what they were getting into when the war began. The onset of hostilities sparked patriotic sentiments, optimistic speeches, and gay ceremonies in both regions. Northern communities, large and small, raised companies of volunteers eager to save the Union. In the cities, spectators cheered from flag-draped buildings as men marched off to war (a scene captured in the painting *Departure of the Seventh Regiment*). In the South, confident recruits boasted of whipping the Yankees and returning home in time for dinner. Women sewed dashing uniforms for men who would soon be lucky to wear drab gray or butternut homespun.

Through the spring of 1861 both sides scrambled to organize and train their inexperienced, undisciplined armies. On July 21, 1861, the first battle took place outside Manassas Junction, Virginia, near a stream called Bull Run. General Irvin McDowell and 30,000 federal troops attacked General P.G.T. Beauregard's 22,000 southerners. As soldiers struggled amid the confusion of their first battle, federal forces began to gain ground. Then they ran into a line of Virginia troops under General Thomas Jackson. "There is Jackson standing like a stone wall," shouted one Confederate.

Battle of Bull Run

"Stonewall" Jackson's line held, and the arrival of 9,000 Confederate reinforcements won the day for the South. Union troops fled back to Washington in disarray, and shocked northern congressmen and spectators, who had watched the battle from a point two miles away, suddenly feared their capital would be taken.

The unexpected rout at Bull Run gave northerners their first hint of the nature of the war to come. Victory would not be easy, even though the United States enjoyed an enormous advantage in resources. Pro-Union feeling was growing in western Virginia, and loyalties were divided in the four border slave states—Missouri, Kentucky, Maryland, and Delaware. But the rest of the Upper South had joined the Confederacy. Moved by an outpouring of regional loyalty, half a million southerners volunteered to fight; there were so many would-be soldiers that the Confederate government could not arm them all.

The United States therefore undertook a massive build-up of troops in northern Virginia. Lincoln gave command of the army to General George McClellan, an officer who proved to be better at organization and training than at fighting. McClellan devoted the fall and winter of 1861 to readying a formidable force of a quarter-million men whose mission would be to destroy southern forces guarding Richmond, the new Confederate capital. "The vast preparation of the enemy," wrote one southern soldier, produced a "feeling of despondency" in the South for the first time.

While McClellan prepared, the Union began to implement other parts of its overall strategy, which called for a blockade of southern ports and eventual capture of the Mississippi River (the "Anaconda" plan). At first the Union navy had too few ships to patrol 3,550 miles of coastline and block the Confederacy's avenues of commerce and supply. Gradually, however, the navy increased the blockade's effectiveness, though it never bottled up southern commerce completely.

Confederate strategy was essentially defensive. Not only was a defensive posture consistent with the South's claim that it merely wanted to be left alone, but it also took into account the North's advantage in resources (see figure). Furthermore, communities all across the South demanded to be defended. Jefferson Davis wisely rejected, however, a static or wholly defensive strategy. The South would pursue an "offensive defensive," tak-

ing advantage of opportunities to attack and using its interior lines of transportation to concentrate troops at crucial points.

Strategic thinking on both sides slighted the importance of "the West," that vast expanse of territory between Virginia and the Mississippi River. Both sides were initially unprepared for large-scale and sustained operations in the West, but before the end of the war it would prove to be a crucial theater. North and South also shared a fondness for "turning movements," in which an army marched around its opponent to force a withdrawal or unleashed a flank attack in battle.

The last half of 1861 brought no major land battles, but the North made gains by sea. Late in the summer Union naval forces began to come ashore in the South. Federal squadrons captured Cape Hatteras and then seized Hilton Head, one of the Sea Islands off Port Royal, South Carolina. A few months later, similar operations secured vital coastal points in North Carolina, as well as Fort Pulaski, which defended Savannah. Federal naval operations were biting into the Confederate coastline (see maps on page 432).

Union Naval Campaign

The coastal victories off South Carolina foreshadowed major changes in the slave society. At the gunboats' approach, frightened planters abandoned their lands and fled. Their slaves greeted what they hoped to be freedom with rejoicing and broke the hated cotton gins. Their jubilation and the constantly growing stream of runaways who poured into the Union lines eliminated any doubt about which side slaves would support, given the opportunity. Ironically the federal government, unwilling at first to wage a war against slavery, did not acknowledge the slaves' freedom—though it did find ways to use them in the Union cause.

These coastal incursions worried southerners, but the spring of 1862 brought even stronger evidence of the war's seriousness. In March two ironclad ships—the *Monitor* and the *Merrimack*—fought each other for the first time; their battle, though indecisive, ushered in a new era in naval design. In April ships commanded by Admiral David Farragut smashed through log booms on the Mississippi River and fought their way upstream to capture New Or-

Grant's Campaign in Tennessee

Comparative Resources, Union and Confederate States, 1861

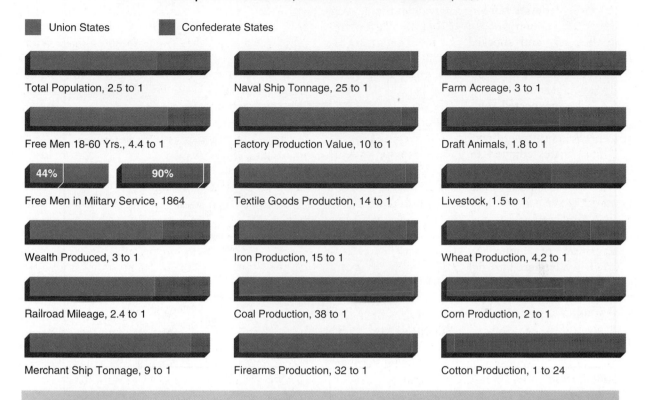

Union States   Confederate States

Total Population, 2.5 to 1

Naval Ship Tonnage, 25 to 1

Farm Acreage, 3 to 1

Free Men 18-60 Yrs., 4.4 to 1

Factory Production Value, 10 to 1

Draft Animals, 1.8 to 1

44%   90%

Free Men in Military Service, 1864

Textile Goods Production, 14 to 1

Livestock, 1.5 to 1

Wealth Produced, 3 to 1

Iron Production, 15 to 1

Wheat Production, 4.2 to 1

Railroad Mileage, 2.4 to 1

Coal Production, 38 to 1

Corn Production, 2 to 1

Merchant Ship Tonnage, 9 to 1

Firearms Production, 32 to 1

Cotton Production, 1 to 24

Comparative Resources, Union and Confederate States, 1861 *The North had vastly superior resources. Although the North's advantages in manpower and industrial capacity proved very important, the South—like the colonies in the American Revolution—could not really be conquered until it chose to give up the fight.* Source: From *Times Atlas of World History*. Time Books, London, 1978. Used with permission.

leans. Meanwhile, in northern Tennessee land and river forces won significant victories for the Union. A hard-drinking, hitherto unsuccessful general named Ulysses S. Grant recognized the strategic importance of Fort Henry and Fort Donelson, the Confederate outposts guarding the Tennessee and Cumberland rivers. If federal troops could capture these forts, Grant realized, two prime routes into the heartland of the Confederacy would lie open. In just ten days he seized the forts, using his forces so well that he was in a position to demand unconditional surrender of Fort Donelson's defenders. A path into Tennessee, Alabama, and Mississippi now lay open before the Union army.

Grant moved on into southern Tennessee and the first of the war's shockingly bloody encounters, the Battle of Shiloh. On April 6, Confederate General Albert Sidney Johnston caught federal troops in an undesirable position on the Tennessee River. With their backs to the water, Grant's men were awaiting reinforcements. The Confederates attacked early in the morning and inflicted heavy damage all day. Close to victory, General Johnston was struck and killed by a ball that severed an artery in his thigh. Southern forces almost achieved a breakthrough, but Union reinforcements arrived that night. The next day the tide of battle turned, and after ten hours of heavy combat, Grant's men forced the Confederates to withdraw. There was no clear victor at Shiloh, but destruction reigned. Northern troops lost 13,000 men (killed, wounded, or captured) out of 63,000; southerners sacrificed 11,000 out of 40,000. Total casualties in this single battle exceeded those in all three of America's previous wars combined. Nearly one of every four soldiers who fought that day had fallen, yet the

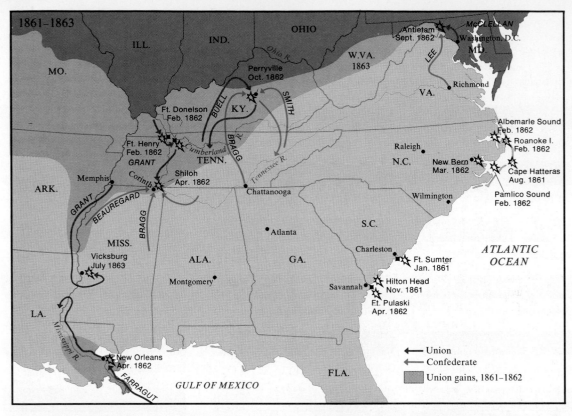

1861–1863

ILL. IND. OHIO

MO.

W.VA. 1863

McCLELLAN
Antietam Sept. 1862
Washington, D.C.
MD.
LEE
Richmond
VA.

Ohio R.
Perryville Oct. 1862
BUELL
KY.
Ft. Donelson Feb. 1862
SMITH
Ft. Henry Feb. 1862
Cumberland R.
GRANT
TENN.
BRAGG
Shiloh Apr. 1862
Corinth
Memphis
GRANT
Tennessee R.
Chattanooga
BEAUREGARD
BRAGG

ARK.

MISS.
Vicksburg July 1863

ALA.
Montgomery
GA.

Raleigh
N.C.
New Bern Mar. 1862

Albemarle Sound Feb. 1862
Roanoke I. Feb. 1862
Cape Hatteras Aug. 1861
Pamlico Sound Feb. 1862

Wilmington

S.C.
Charleston
Ft. Sumter Jan. 1861

ATLANTIC OCEAN

Savannah
Hilton Head Nov. 1861
Ft. Pulaski Apr. 1862

LA.
Mississippi R.
New Orleans Apr. 1862
FARRAGUT

FLA.

GULF OF MEXICO

← Union
← Confederate
▨ Union gains, 1861–1862

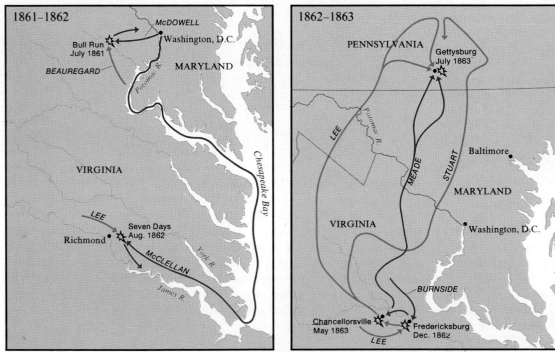

1861–1862

McDOWELL
Bull Run July 1861
Washington, D.C.
MARYLAND
BEAUREGARD
Potomac R.

VIRGINIA

LEE
Seven Days Aug. 1862
Richmond
McCLELLAN
York R.
James R.

Chesapeake Bay

1862–1863

PENNSYLVANIA
Gettysburg July 1863
LEE
Potomac R.
MEADE
STUART
Baltimore
MARYLAND

VIRGINIA
Washington, D.C.

BURNSIDE
Chancellorsville May 1863
Fredericksburg Dec. 1862
LEE

The Civil War, 1861–1863 *(Top) An overview of the Union's "Anaconda" plan and key battles in the West, 1861–1863. (Lower left) The water route chosen by McClellan to threaten Richmond during his unsuccessful peninsular campaign. (Lower right) The engagements at Fredericksburg and Chancellorsville, followed by Lee's march north, which ended at the Battle of Gettysburg.*

battle had settled nothing. Now both sides were beginning to sense the true nature of the war. Shiloh utterly changed Ulysses S. Grant's thinking. He had hoped that southerners would soon be "heartily tired" of the conflict. After Shiloh, he said, "I gave up all idea of saving the Union except by complete conquest."

Meanwhile, on the Virginia front, Abraham Lincoln had a different problem. Conquest was impossible without battles, but he could not get General McClellan to move. Only thirty-six, McClellan had already achieved notable success as an army officer and railroad president. Keenly aware of his historic role, he did not want to fail and insisted on having everything in order before he attacked. Habitually overestimating the size of enemy forces, McClellan called repeatedly for reinforcements and ignored Lincoln's directions to advance.

Finally McClellan chose to move by a roundabout water route, sailing his troops to the York peninsula and advancing on Richmond from the east. By June the sheer size of the federal armies outside the South's capital was highly threatening. But southern leaders foiled McClellan's legions. First, Stonewall Jackson moved north into the Shenandoah Valley behind Union forces and threatened Washington, drawing some of the federals away from Richmond to protect their own capital. Then, in a series of engagements known as the Seven Days' battles, General Robert E. Lee struck at McClellan's army. Lee never managed to close his pincers around the retreating federals, but on August 3 McClellan withdrew to the Potomac. Richmond remained safe for almost two more years.

Buoyed by these results, Jefferson Davis conceived an ambitious plan to turn the tide of the war and compel the United States to recognize the Confederacy. He ordered a general offensive, sending Lee north into Maryland and Generals Kirby Smith and Braxton Bragg into Kentucky. The South would go on the offensive and carry the war north. Davis called on residents of Maryland and Kentucky to make a separate peace with his government and invited the Northwest, which sent much of its trade down the Mississippi to New Orleans, to leave the Union.

Davis Orders an Offensive

The plan was promising, but every part of the offensive failed. In the bloodiest day of the entire war, September 17, 1862, McClellan turned Lee back from Sharpsburg, Maryland. In the Battle of Antietam 5,000 men died (compared with 3,500 at Shiloh), and another 18,000 were wounded. Lee was lucky to escape destruction, for McClellan had obtained a copy of Lee's marching orders. But McClellan moved slowly, failed to attack simultaneously, and allowed Lee's stricken army to retreat to safety across the Potomac. In Kentucky Smith and Bragg had to withdraw just one day after Bragg had attended the inauguration of a provisional Confederate governor. The entire effort collapsed.

Confederate leaders had marshaled all their strength for a breakthrough and had failed. Outnumbered and disadvantaged in resources, the South could not continue its offensive. Profoundly disappointed, Davis admitted to a committee of Confederate representatives that southerners had entered "the darkest and most dangerous period we have yet had." Tenacious defense and stoic endurance now seemed the South's only long-range hope. Perceptive southerners shared their president's despair.

But 1862 did not end without painful lessons for the North as well. First, Confederate General James E. B. (Jeb) Stuart executed a daring cavalry raid into Pennsylvania in October. Then on December 13 Union General Ambrose Burnside unwisely ordered his soldiers to attack Lee's army, which held fortified positions on high ground at Fredericksburg, Virginia. Lee's men performed so coolly and controlled the engagement so thoroughly that Lee, a restrained and humane man, was moved to say, "It is well that war is so terrible. We should grow too fond of it."

The rebellion was far from being suppressed. Although the North had large reserves, it was learning just how high were the costs of the war. Both sides would have to pay a terrible price. As Confederate cavalry leader Nathan Bedford Forrest put it, "War means fighting. And fighting means killing."

WAR TRANSFORMS THE SOUTH

Even more than the fighting itself, disruptions in civilian life robbed southerners of their gaiety and nonchalance. The war altered southern society beyond all expectations and with astonishing speed. One of the first traditions to fall was the southern preference for local government.

The South had been characterized by limited government. States' rights had been its motto, but by modern standards even the state governments were weak and sketchy affairs. The average citizen, on whom the hand of government rested lightly, probably knew his county authorities best. To withstand the massive power of the North, however, the South had to centralize; like the colonial revolutionaries, southerners faced a choice of join or die. No one saw the necessity of centralization more clearly than Jefferson Davis. If the states insisted on fighting separately, said Davis, "we had better make terms as soon as we can."

From the outset, Davis pressed to bring all arms, supplies, and troops under his control. By early 1862 the scope and duration of the conflict required something more. Tens of thousands of Confederate soldiers had volunteered for just one year's service, planning to return home in the spring to plant their crops. To keep southern armies in the field, the War Department encouraged re-enlistments and called for new volunteers. But, as one official admitted, "the spirit of volunteering had died out." Three states threatened or instituted a draft. Finally, faced with a critical shortage of troops, the Confederate government enacted the first national conscription (draft) law in American history. Thus the war forced unprecedented change on states that had seceded out of fear of change.

Confederacy Resorts to a Draft

Though Jefferson Davis was careful to observe the Confederate Constitution, he did not hesitate to be a strong chief executive. Davis adopted a firm leadership role toward the Confederate congress, which raised taxes and later passed a tax-in-kind—a tax paid in farm products. Almost three thousand agents dispersed to collect the tax, assisted by almost fifteen hundred appraisers. Where opposition arose, the government suspended the writ of habeas corpus (which prevented individuals from being held without trial) and imposed martial law. In the face of political opposition that cherished states' rights, Davis proved unyielding.

Centralization of Power in the South

To replace the food that men in uniform would have grown, Davis exhorted farmers to switch from cash crops to food crops; he encouraged the states to require them to do so. But the army was still short of food and labor. In emergencies the War Department resorted to impressing slaves for labor on fortifications, and after 1861 the government relied heavily on impressment of food to feed the troops. Officers swooped down on farms in the line of march and carted away grains, meat, wagons, and draft animals.

Soon the Confederate administration in Richmond was exercising virtually complete control over the southern economy. Because it controlled the supply of labor through conscription, the administration could compel industry to work on government contracts and supply the military's needs. The Confederate congress also gave the central government almost complete control of the railroads; in 1864 shipping, too, came under extensive regulation. New statutes even limited corporate profits and dividends. A large bureaucracy sprang up to administer these operations: over seventy thousand civilians staffed the Confederate administration. By the war's end the southern bureaucracy was larger in proportion to population than its northern counterpart.

Clerks and subordinate officials crowded the towns and cities where Confederate departments had their offices. The sudden population booms that resulted exceeded the existing housing supply and stimulated new construction. The pressure was especially great in Richmond, whose population increased 250 percent. Before the war's end Confederate officials were planning the relocation of entire departments to diminish crowding in Richmond. Mobile's population jumped from 29,000 to 41,000; Atlanta began to grow; and 10,000 people poured into war-related industries in little Selma, Alabama.

Effects of War on Southern Cities and Industry

Another prime cause of urban growth was industrialization. The Union blockade, which disrupted imports of manufactured products, caused the traditionally agricultural South to become interested in industry. Davis exulted that manufacturing was making the South "more and more independent of the rest of the world." Many planters shared his hope that industrialization would bring "deliverance, full and unrestricted, from all commercial dependence" on the North. Indeed, beginning almost from scratch, the Confederacy achieved tremendous feats of industrial development. Chief of Ordnance Josiah Gorgas increased the capacity of Richmond's Tredegar Iron Works and other factories to the point that his Ordnance Bureau was supplying all Confederate small arms and ammunition by 1865. Meanwhile, the government constructed new railroad lines in order to make the South's transportation system much more efficient.

Southerners adopted new ways in response to these changes. Women, restricted to narrow roles in antebellum society, gained substantial new responsibilities. The wives and

Change in the Southern Woman's Role

mothers of soldiers now headed households and performed men's work, adding to their traditional chores the tasks of raising crops and tending animals. Women in nonslaveowning families cultivated fields themselves, while wealthier women suddenly had to manage field hands unaccustomed to female overseers. Only the very rich had enough servants to allow a woman's routine to continue undisturbed. In the cities, white women—who had been virtually excluded from the labor force—found a limited number of respectable new paying jobs. Clerks had always been males, but the war changed that, too. "Government girls" staffed the Confederate bureaucracy, and female schoolteachers became commonplace in the South for the first time. Such experiences undermined the image of the omnipotent male and gave thousands of women new confidence in their own abilities.

One of those women was a young North Carolinian named Janie Smith. Raised in a rural area by prosperous parents, she had faced few challenges or grim realities. Then the war reached her farm, and troops turned her home into a hospital. "It makes me shudder when I think of the awful sights I witnessed that morning," she wrote to a friend. "Ambulance after ambulance drove up with our wounded. . . . Under every shed and tree, the tables were carried for amputating the limbs. . . . The blood lay in puddles in the grove; the groans of the dying and complaints of those undergoing amputation were horrible." But Janie Smith learned to cope with crisis. She ended her account with the proud words, "I can dress amputated

This Confederate soldier, like thousands of his comrades, took advantage of an opportunity to pose with his wife and brother. As the death toll mounted and suffering increased, southern women grew less willing to urge their men into battle. Collection of Larry Williford.

limbs now and do most anything in the way of nursing wounded soldiers."

The Confederate experience introduced and sustained many other new values. Legislative bodies yielded power to the executive branch of government, which could act more decisively in time of war. Aristocratic lineage gave way to achievement and bravery under fire as many men of ordinary background, such as Josiah Gorgas, Stonewall Jackson, and General Nathan Bedford Forrest, distinguished themselves in industry and on the battlefield. Finally, sacrifice for the cause discouraged the pursuit of pleasure; hostesses gave "cold-water parties" (at which water was the only refreshment) to demonstrate their patriotism.

For the elite such sacrifice was symbolic, but for millions of ordinary southerners it was terrifyingly real. Mass poverty descended for the first

Human Suffering in the South

time on a large minority of the white population. Many yeoman families had lost their breadwinners to the army. As a South Carolina newspaper put it, "The duties of war have called away from home the sole supports of many, many families. . . . Help must be given, or the poor will suffer." The poor sought help from relatives, neighbors, friends, anyone. Sometimes they pleaded their cases to the Confederate government, as did an elderly Virginian who wrote, "If you dount send [my son] home I am bound to louse my crop and cum to suffer. I am eaighty one years of adge." One woman begged the government "in the name of humanity to discharge my husband he is not able to do your government much good and he might do his children some good and thare is no use in keeping a man thare to kill and leave widows and poor little orphan children to suffer . . . my poor children have no home nor no Father."

Other factors aggravated the effect of the labor shortage. The South was in many places so sparsely populated that the conscription of one skilled craftsman could work a hardship on the people of an entire county. Often they begged in unison for the exemption or discharge of the local miller or the neighborhood tanner, wheelwright, or potter. Physicians were also in short supply. Most serious, however, was the loss of a blacksmith. As a petition from Alabama explained, "our Section of County [is] left entirely Destitute of any man that is able to keep in order any kind of Farming Tules."

Hoarding and Runaway Inflation in the South

The blockade created shortages of common but important items—salt, sugar, coffee, nails—and speculation and hoarding made the shortages worse. Greedy businessmen cornered the supply of some commodities; prosperous citizens stocked up on food. The *Richmond Enquirer* criticized one man for hoarding seven hundred barrels of flour; another man, a planter, purchased so many wagonloads of supplies that his "lawn and paths looked like a wharf covered with a ship's loads." Some people bought up the entire stock of a store in order to sell later at higher prices. "This disposition to speculate upon the yeomanry of the country," lamented the *Richmond Examiner*, "is the most mortifying feature

of the war." North Carolina's Governor Zebulon Vance asked where it would all stop: "The cry of distress comes up from the poor wives and children of our soldiers. . . . What will become of them?"

Inflation raged out of control, fueled by the Confederate government's heavy borrowing and inadequate taxes, until prices had increased almost 7,000 percent. Inflation particularly imperiled urban dwellers and the many who could no longer provide for themselves. As early as 1861 and 1862, newspapers reported that "the poor of our . . . country will be unable to live at all" and warned that "want and starvation are staring thousands in the face." Troubled officials predicted that "women and children are bound to come to suffering if not starvation."

Some concerned citizens tried to help. "Free markets," which disbursed goods as charity, sprang up in various cities; some families came to the aid of their neighbors. But other people would not cooperate: "It is folly for a poor mother to call on the rich people about here," raged one woman. "Their hearts are of steel they would sooner throw what they have to spare to the dogs than give it to a starving child." The need was so vast that it overwhelmed private charity. A rudimentary relief program organized by the Confederacy offered hope but it was soon curtailed to supply the armies. Thus, Southern yeomen sank into poverty and suffering.

Inequities of the Confederate Draft

As their fortunes declined, people of once-modest means looked around and found abundant evidence that all classes were not sacrificing equally. They saw that the wealthy gave up only their luxuries, while many poor families went without necessities. And they noted that the government contributed to these inequities through policies that favored the upper class. Until the last year of the war, for example, prosperous southerners could avoid military service by hiring substitutes. Prices for substitutes skyrocketed until it cost wealthy men $5,000 or $6,000 to send someone to the front. Well over 50,000 upper-class southerners purchased such substitutes. Mary Boykin Chesnut knew of one young aristocrat who "spent a fortune in substitutes. Two have been taken from him [when *they* were conscripted], and two he paid to

THE NORTHERN ECONOMY COPES WITH WAR

change with him when he was ordered to the front. He is at the end of his row now, for all able-bodied men are ordered to the front. I hear he is going as some general's courier."

As Chesnut's last remark indicates, the rich also traded on their social connections to avoid danger. "It is a notorious fact," complained an angry Georgian, that "if a man has influential friends—or a little money to spare he will never be enrolled." A Confederate senator from Mississippi, James Phelan, informed Jefferson Davis that apparently "nine tenths of the youngsters of the land whose relatives are conspicuous in society, wealthy, or influential obtain some safe perch where they can doze with their heads under their wings."

Anger at such discrimination exploded in October 1862 when the Confederate congress exempted from military duty anyone who was supervising at least twenty slaves. "Never did a law meet with more universal odium," observed one representative. "Its influence upon the poor is most calamitous." Protests poured in from every corner of the Confederacy, and North Carolina's legislators formally condemned the law. Its defenders argued, however, that the exemption preserved order and aided food production, and the statute remained on the books.

Dissension spread as growing numbers of citizens concluded that the struggle was "a rich man's war and a poor man's fight." Alert politicians and newspaper editors warned that class resentment was building to a dangerous level. The bitterness of letters to Confederate officials during this period suggests the depth of the people's anger. "If I and my little children suffer [and] die while there Father is in service," threatened one woman, "I invoke God Almighty that our blood rest upon the South." Another woman swore to the secretary of war that

> an allwise god . . . will send down his fury and judgment in a very grate manar [on] all those our leading men and those that are in power if thare is no more favors shone to . . . the wives and mothers of those who in poverty has with patrootism stood the fence Battles. . . . I tell you that with out some grate and speadly alterating in the conduckting of afares in this our little nation god will frown on it.

Clearly, war was magnifying social tensions in the Confederacy.

THE NORTHERN ECONOMY COPES WITH WAR

With the onset of war, a tidal wave of change rolled over the North as well. Factories and citizens' associations geared up to support the war, and the federal government and its executive branch gained new powers. The energies of an industrializing, capitalist society were harnessed to serve the cause of the Union. Idealism and greed flourished together, and the northern economy proved its awesome productivity.

The war did not destroy the North's prosperity. Northern factories ran overtime, and unemployment was low. Furthermore, northern farms and factories came through the war unharmed, whereas most of the South suffered extensive damage. To Union soldiers on the battlefield, sacrifice was a grim reality, but northern civilians experienced only the bustle and energy of wartime production. (Note the signs of vigorous commerce in the photograph of Hudson Street, New York City, page 438.)

At first the war was a shock to business. With the sudden closing of southern markets, firms could no longer predict the demand for their goods, and many companies had to change their products and find new markets in order to remain open. Southern debts became uncollectible, jeopardizing not only northern merchants but also many western banks. In farming regions, families struggled with an aggravated shortage of labor. Initially, the war caused an economic slump.

Initial Slump in Northern Business

A few enterprises never pulled out of the tailspin: cotton mills lacked cotton; construction declined; shoe manufacturers sold few of the cheap shoes that planters had bought for their slaves. Overall the war slowed industrialization in the North, but its economic impact was not all negative. Certain entrepreneurs, such as wool producers, benefited from shortages of competing products, and soaring demand for war-related goods swept some businesses to new heights of production. To feed the hungry war machine, the federal government pumped unprecedented sums into the economy. The treasury issued $3.2 billion in bonds

Despite initial problems, the task of supplying a vast war machine kept the northern economy humming. This photograph shows the west side of Hudson Street, New York City, in 1865.   New York Historical Society.

and paper money, called greenbacks, while the War Department spent over $360 million in revenues from new taxes (including a broad excise tax and the nation's first income tax). Government contracts soon totaled more than $1 billion.

Secretary of War Edwin M. Stanton's list of the supplies that were needed by the Ordnance Department indicates the scope of government demand: "7,892 cannon, 11,787 artillery carriages, 4,022,130 small-arms, . . . 1,022,176,474 cartridges for small-arms, 1,220,555,435 percussion caps, . . . 26,440,054 pounds of gunpowder, 6,395,152 pounds of niter, and 90,416,295 pounds of lead." Stanton's list covered only weapons; the government also purchased huge quantities of uniforms, boots, food, camp equipment, saddles, ships, and other necessities.

War-related spending revived business in many northern states. In 1863, a merchants' maga-zine examined the effects of the war in Massachusetts: "Seldom, if ever, has the business of Massachusetts been more active or profitable than during the past year. . . . Wealth has flowed into the State in no stinted measure, despite war and heavy taxes. In every department of labor the government has been, directly or indirectly, the chief employer and paymaster." Government contracts had a particularly beneficial impact on the state's wool, metal, and shipbuilding industries, and also saved Massachusetts shoe manufacturers from ruin.

Nothing illustrated the wartime partnership between business and government better than the work of Jay Cooke, a wealthy New York financier. Cooke threw himself into the marketing of government bonds to finance the war effort. With great imagination and energy, Cooke convinced both large investors and ordinary citizens to invest enormous sums in the war effort, in the process earning hefty commissions for himself. But the financier's profit served the Union cause, as the interests of capitalism and government, finance and patriotism, merged.

The booming economy, the Republican alliance with business, and the frantic wartime activity combined to create a new atmosphere in Washington. Attitudes shifted away from wage earners and toward large corporations; the notion spread that government should aid businessmen and not interfere with them. Noting the favorable atmosphere, railroad builders and industrialists—men such as Leland Stanford, Collis P. Huntington, John D. Rockefeller, John M. Forbes, and Jay Gould—took advantage of it. Their enterprises grew with the aid of government loans, grants, and tariffs.

War production also promoted the development of heavy industry in the North. Coal output rose substantially. Iron makers improved the quality of their product while

Effects of War on Northern Industry and Agriculture

boosting the production of pig iron from 920,000 tons in 1860 to 1.1 million tons in 1864. Foundries developed new and less expensive ways to make steel. Although new railroad construction slowed, repairs helped the manufacture of rails to increase. Of considerable significance for the future was the railroad industry's adoption of a standard gauge (width) for track, which eliminated unloading and reloading of boxcars and created a unified transportation system.

Another strength of the northern economy was the complementary relationship between agriculture and industry. Mechanization of agriculture had begun before the war. Wartime recruitment and conscription, however, gave western farmers an added incentive to purchase labor-saving machinery. The shift from human labor to machines created new markets for industry and expanded the food supply for the urban industrial work force.

The boom in the sale of agricultural tools was tremendous. Cyrus and William McCormick built an industrial empire in Chicago from the sale of their reapers. Between 1862 and 1864 the manufacture of mowers and reapers doubled to 70,000 yearly; even so, manufacturers could not satisfy the demand. By the end of the war, 375,000 reapers were in use, triple the number in 1861. Large-scale commercial agriculture had become a reality. As a result, farm families whose breadwinners went to war did not suffer as their counterparts did in the South. "We have seen," one magazine observed, "a stout matron whose sons are in the army, cutting hay with her team . . . and she cut seven acres with ease in a day, riding leisurely upon her cutter."

Northern industrial and urban workers did not fare as well. Jobs were plentiful following the initial slump, but inflation ate up much of a worker's paycheck. By 1863 nine-cent-a-pound beef cost eighteen cents. The price of coffee had tripled; rice and sugar had doubled; and clothing, fuel, and rent had all climbed. Between 1860 and 1864 consumer prices rose at least 76 percent, while daily wages rose only 42 percent. Workers' families consequently suffered a substantial decline in their standard of living.

As their real wages shrank, industrial workers also lost job security. To increase production, some employers were replacing workers with labor-saving machines. Other em-

New Militancy Among Northern Workers

ployers urged the government to liberalize immigration regulations so they could import cheap labor. Workers responded by forming unions and sometimes by striking. Skilled craftsmen organized to combat the loss of their jobs and status to machines; women and unskilled workers, excluded by the craftsmen, formed their own unions. In recognition of the increasingly national scope of business activity, thirteen occupational groups—including tailors, coal miners, and railway engineers—formed national unions during the Civil War. Because of the tight labor market, unions were able to win many of their demands without striking, but the number of strikes also rose steadily.

Employers reacted with hostility to this new spirit among workers—a spirit that William H. Sylvis, leader of the iron molders, called a "feeling of manly independence." Manufacturers viewed labor activism as a threat to their property rights and freedom of action, and accordingly formed statewide or craft-based associations to cooperate and pool information. These employers shared blacklists of union members and required new workers to sign "yellow dog" contracts (promises not to join a union). To put down strikes, they hired strikebreakers from the ranks of the poor and desperate—blacks, immigrants, and women—and sometimes received additional help from federal troops.

Troublesome as unions were, they did not prevent many employers from making a profit. The highest profits were made from profiteering on government contracts. Unscrupulous businessmen took advantage of the sudden immense demand for army supplies by selling clothing and blankets made of "shoddy"—wool fibers reclaimed from rags or worn cloth. Shoddy goods often came apart in the rain; most of the shoes purchased in the early months of the war were worthless, too. Contractors sold inferior guns for double the usual price and passed off tainted meat as good. Corruption was so widespread that it led to a year-long investigation by the House of Representatives. A group of contractors that had demanded $50 million for their products dropped their claims to $17 million as a result of the findings of the investigation.

Legitimate enterprises also made healthy profits. The output of woolen mills increased so dramatically that dividends in the industry nearly tripled. Some cotton mills made record profits on what they sold, even though they reduced their output. Brokerage houses worked until midnight and earned unheard-of commissions. Railroads carried immense quantities of freight and passengers, increasing their business to the point that railroad stocks doubled or even tripled in value. The price of Erie Railroad stock rose from $17 to $126 a share during the war.

Wartime Benefits to Northern Business

Railroads were also a leading beneficiary of government largesse. Congress had failed in the 1850s to resolve the question of a northern versus a southern route for the first transcontinental railroad. With the South absent from Congress, the northern route quickly prevailed. In 1862 and 1864 Congress chartered two corporations, the Union Pacific Railroad and the Central Pacific Railroad, and assisted them financially in connecting Omaha, Nebraska, with Sacramento, California. For each mile of track laid, the railroads received a loan of $16,000 to $48,000 in government bonds plus twenty square miles of land along a free 400-foot-wide right of way. Overall, the two corporations gained approximately 20 million acres of land and nearly $60 million in loans.

Other businessmen also benefited handsomely from the Morrill Land Grant Act (1862). To promote public education in agriculture, engineering, and military science, Congress granted each state 30,000 acres of federal land for each of its congressional districts. The states were free to sell the land as they saw fit, as long as they used the income for the purposes Congress had intended. The law eventually fostered sixty-nine colleges and universities, but one of its immediate effects was to enrich a few prominent speculators. Hard-pressed to meet wartime expenses, some states sold their land cheaply to wealthy entrepreneurs. For example, Ezra Cornell, a leader in the telegraph industry, invested in 500,000 acres in the Midwest.

Higher tariffs also pleased many businessmen. Northern businesses did not uniformly favor high import duties; some manufacturers desired cheap imported raw materials more than they feared foreign competition. But northeastern congressmen traditionally supported higher tariffs, and after southern lawmakers left Washington, they had their way: the Tariff Act of 1864 raised tariffs generously. According to one scholar, manufacturers had only to mention the rate they considered necessary and that rate was declared. Some healthy industries earned artificially high profits by raising their prices to a level just below that of the foreign competition. By the end of the war, tariff increases averaged 47 percent, and rates were more than double those of 1857.

WARTIME SOCIETY IN THE NORTH

The outbreak of war stimulated patriotism in the North, just as it initially had in the South. Northern society, which had suffered the stresses associated with industrialization, immigration, and widespread social change, found a unifying cause in the preservation of the nation and the American form of government. In thousands of towns and communities, northern citizens had a long history of participation in local government; they felt a personal connection to representative government. Secession threatened to destroy their system, and northerners rallied to its defense. Secular and church leaders supported the cause, and even ministers who preferred to separate politics and pulpit denounced "the iniquity of causeless rebellion."

Such enthusiasm proved useful as northerners encountered a multitude of wartime changes. The powers of the federal government and the president grew steadily during the crisis.

Wartime Powers of the U.S. Executive

Abraham Lincoln, like Jefferson Davis, found that war required active presidential leadership. At the beginning of the conflict, Lincoln launched a major shipbuilding program without waiting for Congress to assemble. The lawmakers later approved his decision, and Lincoln continued to act in advance of Congress when he deemed it necessary. In one striking exercise of executive power, Lincoln suspended the writ of habeas corpus (which prevents the government from holding citizens without trial) for everyone living between Washington and Philadelphia. There was scant legal justification for this act, but Lincoln's motive was practical: to ensure the loyalty of Maryland. Later in the war, with congressional approval, Lincoln repeatedly suspended the writ and invoked martial law, mainly in the border states but elsewhere as well. Between fifteen and twenty thousand U.S. citizens were arrested on suspicion of disloyal acts.

On occasion Lincoln used his wartime authority to bolster his own political fortunes. He and his generals proved adept at furloughing soldiers so they could vote in close elections; those whom Lincoln furloughed, of course, usually voted Republican. He also came to the aid of other officeholders in his party. When the Republican governor of Indiana, who was battling pro-peace Democrats in his legislature, ran short of funds, Lincoln had the War Department supply $250,000. This was an unconstitutional procedure, but it furthered the Union cause.

Among the clearest examples of the wartime expansion of federal authority were the National Banking Acts of 1863, 1864, and 1865. Prior to the Civil War the nation lacked a uniform currency, for the federal government had never exercised its authority in this area. Banks operating under state charters issued no fewer than seven thousand different kinds of notes, which were difficult to distinguish from a variety of forgeries. Now, acting on the recommendations of Secretary of the Treasury Salmon Chase, Congress established a national banking system empowered to issue national bank notes. At the close of the war in 1865, Congress imposed a prohibitive tax on state bank notes and forced most major state institutions to join the na-

tional system. This process created a sounder currency and a simpler monetary system—but also inflexibility in the money supply and an eastern-oriented financial structure.

Social attitudes on the home front evolved in directions that would have shocked the soldiers in the field. Amid the excitement of moneymaking, a gaudy culture of vulgar display flourished in the largest cities.

Self-Indulgence versus Sacrifice in the North

A visitor to Chicago commented that "so far as lavish display is concerned, the South Side in some portions has no rival in Chicago, and perhaps not outside New York." Its new residences boasted marble facades and expensive ornamentation that created "a glittering, heartless appearance." As William Cullen Bryant, the distinguished editor of the *New York Evening Post*, observed, "Extravagance, luxury, these are the signs of the times. . . . What business have Americans at any time with such vain show, with such useless magnificence? But especially how can they justify it . . . in this time of war?" The newly rich did not bother to justify it. *Harper's Monthly* reported that "the suddenly enriched contractors, speculators, and stock-jobbers . . . are spending money with a profusion never before witnessed in our country, at no time remarkable for its frugality. . . . The men button their waistcoats with diamonds . . . and the women powder their hair with gold and silver dust." The *New York Herald* summarized that city's atmosphere:

> The richest silks, laces and jewelry are the soonest sold. . . . Not to keep a carriage, not to wear diamonds, . . . is now equivalent to being a nobody. This war has entirely changed the American character. . . . The individual who makes the most money—no matter how—and spends the most—no matter for what—is considered the greatest man. . . .
>
> The world has seen its iron age, its silver age, its golden age, and its brazen age. This is the age of shoddy.

Yet idealism coexisted with ostentation. Many churches endorsed the Union cause as God's cause. One Methodist newspaper described the war as a contest between "equalizing, humanizing Christianity" and "disunion, war, selfishness, [and] slavery." Abolitionists, after initial uncertainty over whether to let the South go, campaigned to turn

Circular No. 8.

WASHINGTON. D. C., *July 14, 1862,*

No candidate for service in the Women's Department for nursing in the Military Hospitals of the United States, will be received below the age of thirty-five years, nor above fifty.

Only women of strong health, not subjects of chronic disease, nor liable to sudden illnesses, need apply. The duties of the station make large and continued demands on strength.

Matronly persons of experience, good conduct, or superior education and serious disposition, will always have preference; habits of neatness, order, sobriety, and industry, are prerequisites.

All applicants must present certificates of qualification and good character from at least two persons of trust, testifying to morality, integrity, seriousness, and capacity for care of the sick.

Obedience to rules of the service, and conformity to special regulations, will be required and enforced.

Compensation, as regulated by act of Congress, forty cents a day and subsistence. Transportation furnished to and from the place of service.

Amount of luggage limited within small compass.

Dress plain, (colors brown, grey, or black,) and while connected with the service without ornaments of any sort.

No applicants accepted for less than three months' service: those for longer periods always have preference.

D. L. DIX.

Approved,
WILLIAM A. HAMMOND,
Surgeon General.

How do historians know

that women had to struggle to serve the nation as nurses? The records of the Surgeon General's Office in the National Archives in Washington, D.C., document the efforts of Dorothea Dix to organize female nurses for the Union cause. A veteran of two decades of reform efforts to provide state hospitals for the mentally ill, Dix went to Washington at age sixty and volunteered to help the cause. Commissioned as the na-tion's first superintendent of women nurses, she sought only serious care-givers who were not trying to be near their husbands and sweethearts. Her Circular Order, pictured here, reflects that intention as well as the need to convince male doctors and superiors that women would be helpful. Although Dix largely succeeded in her efforts, most Civil War nurses were men. Photo: National Archives.

the war into a crusade against slavery. Free black communities and churches both black and white responded to the needs of slaves who flocked to the Union lines, sending clothing, ministers, and teachers in generous measure to aid the runaways.

Northern women, like their southern counterparts, took on new roles. Those who stayed home organized over ten thousand soldiers' aid societies, rolled innumerable bandages, and raised $3 million to aid injured troops. Thousands served as nurses in front-line hospitals, where they pressed for better care of the wounded. Yet women were only a small minority of all nurses, and they had to fight for a chance to serve at all. The professionalization of medicine since the Revolution had created a medical system dominated by men, and many male physicians did not want their aid. Female nurses proved their worth, but only the wounded welcomed them. Even Clara Barton, the most famous female nurse, was ousted from her post in 1863.

The poet Walt Whitman left a record of his experiences as a volunteer nurse in Washington, D.C. As he dressed wounds and tried to comfort suffering and lonely men, **Walt Whitman** Whitman found "the marrow of the tragedy concentrated in those Army Hospitals." But despite "indescribably horrid wounds . . . the groan that could not be repress'd . . . [the] emaciated face and glassy eye," he also found in the hospitals inspiration and a deepening faith in American democracy. Whitman celebrated the "incredible dauntlessness" and sacrifice of the common soldier who fought for the Union. As he had written in the preface to his great work *Leaves of Grass* (1855), "The genius of the United States is not best or most in its executives or legislatures, but always most in the common people." Whitman worked this idealization of the common man into his poetry, which also explored homoerotic themes and rejected the lofty meter and rhyme of European verse to strive for a "genuineness" that would appeal to the masses.

Thus northern society embraced strangely contradictory tendencies. Materialism and greed flourished alongside idealism, religious conviction, and self-sacrifice. While some soldiers risked their lives willingly out of a desire to preserve the Union or extend freedom, efforts to avoid service were widespread and unconcealed. Under the law, a draftee could stay at home by providing a substitute or paying a $300 commutation fee. Many wealthy men chose these options, and in response to popular demand, clubs, cities, and states provided the money for others. In all, 118,000 substitutes were provided and 87,000 commutations paid before Congress ended the commutation system in 1864. It was as if several different wars were under way simultaneously, each serving a different motive.

In June 1861 Harper's Weekly *published this wood engraving of northern women sewing havelocks (cloth covers for hats, each having a flap to protect the back of the neck) for northern soldiers. Such volunteer efforts were just one of the changes that came to women's lives during the war.* Addison Gallery of American Art.

THE STRANGE ADVENT OF EMANCIPATION

At the highest levels of government there was a similar lack of clarity about the purpose of the war. Both Davis and Lincoln studiously avoided references to slavery, the crux of the matter, throughout the first several months of the struggle. Davis realized that emphasis on the issue could increase class conflict in the South. To avoid identifying the Confederacy only with the interests of slaveholders, he articulated a broader, traditional ideology. Davis told southerners they were fighting for constitutional liberty: northerners had betrayed the founding fathers' legacy, and southerners seceded to preserve it. As long as Lincoln also avoided making slavery an issue, Davis's line seemed to work.

Lincoln had his own reasons for not mentioning slavery. It was crucial at first not to antago-

nize the border slave states, whose loyalty to the Union was tenuous. For many months Lincoln also hoped that a pro-Union majority would assert itself in the South. It might be possible, he thought, to coax the South back into the Union and stop the fighting. Raising the slavery issue would severely undermine both goals.

Powerful political considerations also dictated that Lincoln remain silent. The Republican party was a young and unwieldy coalition. Some Republicans burned with moral outrage over slavery; others were frankly racist, dedicated to protecting free whites from the Slave Power and the competition of cheap slave labor; still others saw the tariff or immigration or some other issue as paramount. A forthright stand by Lincoln on the subject of slavery could split the party, gratifying some groups and alienating others. Until a consensus developed or Lincoln found a way to appeal to all the elements of the party, silence was the best approach.

The president's hesitancy ran counter to some of his personal feelings. Lincoln was a sensitive and compassionate man whose humility and moral anguish during the war were evident in his speeches and writings. But as a politician, Lincoln distinguished between his own moral convictions and his official acts. As a result, his political positions were studied and complex, calculated for maximum advantage. Frederick Douglass, the astute and courageous black protest leader, sensed that Lincoln was without prejudice toward black people. Yet Douglass judged him "pre-eminently the white man's president."

Lincoln first broached the subject of slavery in a substantive way in March 1862, when he proposed that the states consider emancipation on their own. He asked Congress **Lincoln's Plan** to pass a resolution promising **for Gradual** aid to any state that decided to **Emancipation** emancipate, and he appealed to border-state representatives to give serious thought to emancipation. What Lincoln proposed was gradual emancipation, with compensation for slaveholders and colonization of the freed slaves outside the United States. To a delegation of free blacks he explained that "it is better for us both . . . to be separated." Until well into 1864 Lincoln steadfastly promoted an unpromising and wholly impractical scheme to colonize blacks in some region like Central America. Despite Secretary of State William H. Seward's care to insert such phrases as "with their consent," the word *deportation* crept into one of Lincoln's speeches in place of *colonization*. Thus his was as conservative a scheme as could be devised. Moreover, since the states would make the decision voluntarily, no responsibility for it would attach to Lincoln.

Others wanted to go much further. A group of Republicans in Congress, known as the Radicals and led by such men as George Julian, Charles Sumner, and Thaddeus Stevens, dedicated themselves to seeing that the war was prosecuted vigorously. They were instrumental in creating a special House-Senate committee on the conduct of the war, which investigated Union reverses, sought to make the war effort more efficient, and prodded

the president to take stronger measures. Early in the war these Radicals, with support from other representatives, turned their attention to slavery.

In August 1861, at the Radicals' instigation, Congress passed its first confiscation act. Designed to punish the Confederate rebels, the law confiscated all property used for "in-**Confiscation** surrectionary purposes"—that **Acts** is, if the South used slaves in a hostile action, those slaves were declared seized and liberated. A second confiscation act (July 1862) was much more drastic: it confiscated the property of all those who supported the rebellion, even those who merely resided in the South and paid Confederate taxes. Their slaves were declared "forever free of their servitude, and not again [to be] held as slaves." The logic behind these acts was that the insurrection—as Lincoln always termed it—was a serious revolution requiring strong measures. Let the government use its full powers, free the slaves, and crush the revolution, urged the Radicals.

Lincoln would not go that far. He stood by his proposal of voluntary gradual emancipation by the states and made no effort to enforce the second confiscation act. His stance provoked a public protest from Horace Greeley, editor of the powerful *New York Tribune*. In an open letter to the president entitled "The Prayer of Twenty Millions," Greeley pleaded with Lincoln to "execute the laws" and declared, "On the face of this wide earth, Mr. President, there is not one disinterested, determined, intelligent champion of the Union cause who does not feel that all attempts to put down the Rebellion and at the same time uphold its inciting cause are preposterous and futile."

Lincoln's letter in reply was an explicit statement of his complex and calculated approach to the question. He disagreed, he said, with all those who would make the maintenance or destruction of slavery the paramount issue of the war. "I would save the Union," announced Lincoln. "If I could save the Union without freeing *any* slave I would do it, and if I could save it by freeing *all* the slaves I would do it; and if I could save it by freeing some and leaving others alone I would also do that. What I do about slavery, and the colored race, I do because I believe it helps to save the Union." Lincoln closed with a personal disclaimer: "I have here stated my purpose according to my view of *official* duty; and I intend no modification of my oft-expressed *personal* wish that all men every where could be free."

When he wrote these words, Lincoln had already decided on a new step: issuance of the Emancipation Proclamation. On the advice of the cabinet, however, he was waiting for a Union victory before announcing the proclamation, so that it would not appear to be an act of desperation. Yet the letter to Greeley was not simply an effort to stall; it was an integral part of Lincoln's approach to the future of slavery, as the text of the Emancipation Proclamation would show.

On September 22, 1862, shortly after the Battle of Antietam, Lincoln issued the first (and often forgotten) part of his two-part proclamation. Invoking his powers as commander-in-chief of the armed forces, he announced that on January 1, 1863, he would emancipate the slaves in states whose people "shall then be in rebellion against the United States." Lincoln made plain that he would judge a state to be in rebellion in January if it lacked bona fide representatives in Congress.

Emancipation Proclamations

Thus, his September proclamation was less a declaration of the right of slaves to be free than a threat to southerners. Unless they stopped fighting and returned to Congress, they would lose their slaves. "Knowing the value that was set on the slaves by the rebels," said Garrison Frazier, a black Georgian, "the President thought that his proclamation would stimulate them to lay down their arms . . . and their not doing so has now made the freedom of the slaves a part of the war." Lincoln may not actually have expected southerners to give up their effort, but he was careful to offer them the option, thus putting the onus of emancipation on them.

When Lincoln designated the areas in rebellion on January 1, he excepted from his list every Confederate county or city that had fallen under Union control. Those areas, he declared, "are, for the present, left precisely as if this proclamation were not issued." Nor did Lincoln liberate slaves in the border slave states that remained in the Union. "The President has purposely made the proclamation inoperative in all places where . . . the slaves [are] accessible," charged the anti-administration *New York World*. "He has proclaimed emancipation only where he has notoriously no power to execute it." The exceptions, said the paper, "render the

proclamation not merely futile, but ridiculous." Partisanship aside, even Secretary of State Seward, a moderate Republican, said sarcastically, "We show our sympathy with slavery by emancipating slaves where we cannot reach them and holding them in bondage where we can set them free." A British official, Lord Russell, commented on the "very strange nature" of the document, noting that it did not declare "a principle adverse to slavery."

By making the liberation of the slaves "a fit and necessary war measure," furthermore, Lincoln raised a variety of legal questions. How long did a war measure remain in force? Did it expire with the suppression of a rebellion? The proclamation did little to clarify the status or citizenship of the freed slaves. And a reference to garrison duty in one of the closing paragraphs suggested that former slaves would have inferior duties and rank in the army. For many months, in fact, their pay and treatment were inferior.

Thus the Emancipation Proclamation was a puzzling and ambiguous document that said less than it seemed to say. It freed no slaves, and serious limitations were embedded in its language. But if as a moral and legal document it was wanting, as a political document it was nearly flawless. Because the proclamation defined the war as a war against slavery, radicals could applaud it, even if the president had not gone as far as Congress. Yet at the same time it protected Lincoln's position with conservatives, leaving him room to retreat if he chose and forcing no immediate changes on the border slave states.

The need for men soon convinced the administration to recruit northern and southern blacks for the army. By spring 1863, African-American troops were proving their value. Lincoln came to see them as "the great *available* and yet *unavailed of* force for restoring the Union." African-American leaders hoped that military service would secure equal rights for their people. Once the black soldier had fought for the Union, wrote Frederick Douglass, "there is no power on earth which can deny that he has earned the right of citizenship in the United States." If black soldiers turned the tide, asked another man, "would the nation refuse us our rights?"

In June 1864, Lincoln gave his support to a constitutional ban on slavery. Reformers such as Elizabeth Cady Stanton and Susan B. Anthony were pressing for an amendment that would write

This wood engraving from Frank Leslie's Illustrated *depicts the various duties performed by African-Americans in the U.S. Army. Confined at first to labor details and supporting roles, black soldiers were especially glad when they received opportunities to prove their courage and manhood in battle.* Archives and Special Collections, Shadek-Fackenthal Library, Franklin and Marshall College.

emancipation into the Constitution. On the eve of the Republican national convention, Lincoln called the party's chairman to the White House and instructed him to have the party "put into the platform as the keystone, the amendment of the Constitution abolishing and prohibiting slavery forever." The party promptly called for a new amendment, the thirteenth. Republican delegates probably would have adopted such a plank without his urging, but Lincoln demonstrated his commitment by lobbying Congress for quick approval of the measure. The proposed amendment passed and was sent to the states for ratification or rejection. Lincoln's strong support for the Thirteenth Amendment—an unequivocal prohibition of slavery—constitutes his best claim to the title Great Emancipator.

Yet Lincoln soon clouded that clear stand, for in 1865 the newly re-elected president considered allowing the defeated southern states to re-enter

Hampton Roads Conference
———

the Union and delay or defeat the amendment. In February he and Secretary of State Seward met with three Confederate commissioners at Hampton Roads, Virginia. The end of the war was clearly in sight, and southern representatives angled vainly for an armistice that would allow the South to remain a separate nation. But Lincoln was doing some political maneuvering of his own, apparently contemplating the creation of a new national party based on a postwar alliance with southern Whigs and moderate and conservative Republicans. The cement for the coalition would be concessions to planter interests.

Pointing out that the Emancipation Proclamation was only a war measure, Lincoln predicted that the courts would decide whether it had granted all, some, or none of the slaves their freedom. Seward observed that the Thirteenth

Amendment, which would be definitive, was not yet ratified; re-entry into the Union would allow the southern states to defeat it. Lincoln did not contradict Seward but spoke in favor of "prospective" ratification: approval with the effective date postponed for five years. He also promised to seek $400 million in compensation for slaveholders and to consider their views on such related questions as confiscation. Such financial aid would provide an economic incentive for planters to rejoin the Union and capital to cushion the economic blow of emancipation.

These were startling propositions from a president on the verge of military victory. Most northerners opposed them, and only the opposition of Jefferson Davis, who set himself against anything short of independence, prevented discussion of the proposals in the South. Even at the end of the war, Lincoln was clearly keeping his options open and maintaining the distinction he had drawn between "*official* duty" and "*personal* wish." Contrary to legend, then, Lincoln did not attempt to mold public opinion on race, as did advocates of equality in one direction and racist Democrats in the other. Instead he moved cautiously, constructing complex and ambiguous positions and avoiding the risks inherent in challenging, educating, or inspiring the nation's conscience.

Before the war was over, the Confederacy, too, addressed the issue of emancipation. Jefferson Davis himself offered a strong proposal in favor of

Davis's Plan for Emancipation

liberation. Though emancipation was far less popular in the South than in the North, Davis did not flinch or conceal his purpose. He was dedicated to independence, and he was willing to sacrifice slavery to achieve that goal. After considering the alternatives for some time, Davis concluded late in 1864 that the military situation of the Confederacy was desperate and that independence with emancipation was preferable to defeat with emancipation. He proposed that the Confederate government purchase 40,000 slaves to work for the army as laborers, with a promise of freedom at the end of their service. Soon Davis upgraded his proposal, calling for the recruitment and arming of slaves as soldiers, who likewise would gain their freedom at the end of the war. The wives and children of these soldiers, he made plain, must also receive freedom from the states. Davis and his advisers did not fa-

vor full equality—they envisioned "an intermediate state of serfage or peonage." Thus they shared with Lincoln and their entire generation racial attitudes that blinded them to the massive changes taking place.

Still, Davis had proposed a radical change for the slaveholding South. Bitter debate resounded through the Confederacy, but Davis stood his ground. When the Confederate congress approved slave enlistments without the promise of freedom, Davis insisted on more. He issued an executive order to guarantee that owners would emancipate slave soldiers, and his allies in the states started to work for emancipation of the soldiers' families. Some black troops had started to drill as the end of the war approached.

Confederate emancipation began too late to revive southern armies or win diplomatic advantages with antislavery Europeans. By contrast, Lincoln's Emancipation Proclamation stimulated a vital infusion of forces into the Union armies. Beginning in 1863 slaves shouldered arms for the North. Before the war was over, 134,000 slaves (and 52,000 free African-Americans) had fought for freedom and the Union. Their participation was crucial to northern victory, and it discouraged recognition of the Confederacy by foreign governments. Lincoln's policy, whatever its limitations and lack of clarity, had profound practical effects.

THE SOLDIER'S WAR

The intricacies of policy making were far from the minds of ordinary soldiers. Military service completely altered their lives. Enlistment took young men from their homes and submerged them in large organizations whose military discipline ignored their individuality. Army life meant tedium, physical hardship, and separation from loved ones even in the best of times. In battle the soldier confronted fear and danger, and the risk of death from wounds or disease was very high. Yet the military experience had powerful attractions as well. It molded men on both sides so thoroughly that they came to resemble each other far more than the civilians back home. Many soldiers found amid war a bond with their fellows and a connection to noble purpose that they cherished for years afterward.

Union soldiers may have sensed most clearly the massive scale of modern war. Most were

After the battle of Chancellorsville began, Union forces momentarily broke through Lee's thin rear guard, which was miles away at Marye's Heights. These dead Mississippi troops fell in the sunken road, behind the stone wall where Lee's army had decimated Union attackers a few months before, in the Battle of Fredericksburg. Library of Congress.

young; eighteen was the most common age, followed by twenty-one. Many went straight from small towns and farms into large armies supplied by extensive bureaucracies. By late 1861 there were 640,000 volunteers in arms, a stupendous increase over the regular army of 20,000 men. The increase occurred so rapidly that it is remarkable the troops were supplied and organized as well as they were. Yet many soldiers' first experiences with a large military organization were unfortunate.

Soldiers benefited from certain new products, such as canned condensed milk, but blankets, clothing, and arms were often of poor quality. Vermin were commonplace. Hospitals were badly managed at first. Rules of hygiene in large camps were badly written or unenforced; latrines were poorly made or carelessly used. One investigation turned up "an area of over three acres, encircling the camp as a broad belt, on which is deposited an almost perfect layer of human excrement." Water supplies were unsafe and typhoid epidemics common. About 57,000 army men died from dysentery and diarrhea.

The situation would have been much worse but for the U.S. Sanitary Commission. A voluntary civilian organization, the commission worked to improve conditions in camps and to aid sick and wounded soldiers. Even so, 224,000 Union troops died from disease or accidents, far more than the 140,000 who died as a result of battle. Confederate troops were less well supplied, especially in the latter part of the war, and they had no sanitary commission. Still, an extensive network of hospitals, aided by many female volunteers, sprang up to aid the sick and wounded.

On both sides troops quickly learned that soldiering was far from glorious. "The dirt of a camp life knocks all its poetry into a cocked hat," wrote a North Carolina volunteer in 1862. One year later he marveled at his earlier innocence. Fighting had taught him "the realities of a soldier's life. We had no tents after the 6th of August, but slept on the ground, in the woods or open fields, without regard to the weather. . . . I learned to eat fat bacon raw, and to like it. . . . Without time to wash our clothes or our persons, and sleeping on the ground all huddled together, the whole army became lousy more or less with body lice." Union troops "skirmished" against lice by boiling their clothes or holding them over a hot fire, but, reported one soldier, "I find some on me in spite of all I can do."

Realities of a Soldier's Life

Few had seen violent death before, but war soon exposed them to the blasted bodies of their friends and comrades. "Any one who goes over a battlefield after a battle," wrote one Confederate, "never cares to go over another . . . . It is a sad sight to see the dead and if possible more sad to see the wounded—shot in every possible way you can imagine." Many men died gallantly; there were innumerable striking displays of courage. But far more often soldiers gave up their lives in the mass, as part of a commonplace sacrifice. "They mowed us down like grass," recalled one survivor of a Union assault. (See the photograph of fallen Mississippi troops.)

Advances in technology made the Civil War particularly deadly. By far the most important were the rifle and the "minie ball." Bullets fired from a smoothbore musket tumbled and wobbled as they flew through the air, and thus were not accurate at distances over eighty yards. Cutting spiraled grooves inside the barrel gave the projectile a spin and much greater accuracy, but rifles remained difficult to load and use until the Frenchman Claude Minie and the American James Burton developed a new kind of bullet. Civil War bullets were sizable lead slugs with a cavity at the bottom that expanded upon firing so that the bullet "took" the rifling and flew accurately. With these bullets, rifles were accurate at four hundred yards and useful up to one thousand yards.

This meant, of course, that soldiers assaulting a position defended by riflemen were in greater peril than ever before. Even though Civil War rifles were cumbersome to load (relatively few of the new untried breechloading and repeating rifles were ordered), the defense gained a significant advantage. While artillery now fired from a safe distance, there was no substitute for the infantry assault or the popular "turning movements" aimed at an enemy's flank. Thus, advancing soldiers had to expose themselves repeatedly to accurate rifle fire. Large lead bullets shattered bones and destroyed flesh and, because medical knowledge was rudimentary, even minor wounds often led to death through infection.

Thus the toll from Civil War battles was very high. Never before in Europe or America had such massive forces pummeled each other with weapons of such destructive power. Yet the armies in the Civil War seemed virtually indestructible. Even in the bloodiest engagements, in which thousands of men died, the losing army was never destroyed. As losses mounted, many citizens wondered at what Union soldier (and future Supreme Court Justice) Oliver Wendell Holmes called "the butcher's bill."

Still, Civil War soldiers developed deep commitments to each other and to their task. As campaigns dragged on, fighting and dying with their comrades became their reality, and most soldiers who did not desert grew determined to see the struggle through. "We now, like true Soldiers go determined not to yield one inch," wrote a New York corporal. When at last the war was over, "it seemed like breaking up a family to separate," one man observed. "We shook hands all around, and laughed and seemed to make merry, while our hearts were heavy and our eyes ready to shed tears," admitted another.

The bonding may have been most dramatic among officers and men in the northern black regiments. Racism in the Union army was strong; one New Yorker objected to fighting beside African-Americans with the words, "We are a too superior race for that." Some white officers volunteered for black units only as a means to gain faster promotion. But black troops had a mission to destroy slavery, and many of their white officers shared,

or came to share, that commitment. After only one month with black troops, a white captain informed his wife, "I have a more elevated opinion of their abilities than I ever had before. I *know* that many of them are vastly the *superiors* of those (many of those) who would condemn them all to a life of brutal degradation." One general reported that his "colored regiments" possessed "remarkable aptitude for military training," and another observer said, "They fight like fiends."

For their part, African-American troops appreciated the dedication and courage of white officers who treated them as men. Just before the 54th Massachusetts launched its famous and costly assault on Fort Wagner, a black soldier called out to abolitionist Colonel Robert Gould Shaw, "Colonel, I will stay by you till I die." "And he kept his word," noted a survivor of the attack. "He has never been seen since."

Such valor emerged despite persistent discrimination. Off-duty black soldiers were sometimes attacked by northern mobs; on duty, they did most of the "fatigue duty," or heavy labor. The government, moreover, paid white privates $13 per month plus a clothing allowance of $3.50, whereas black privates earned only $10 per month less $3 deducted for clothing. Outraged by this injustice, the men of the 54th and 55th Massachusetts (Colored) Infantry refused to accept any pay whatever, and Congress eventually remedied the inequity.

THE TIDE OF BATTLE BEGINS TO TURN

The fighting in the spring and summer of 1863 did not settle the war, but it began to place clear limits on the outcome. The campaigns began in a deceptively positive way for Confederates, as their Army of Northern Virginia performed brilliantly in the battle of Chancellorsville. For once a large Civil War army was not slow and cumbersome but executed tactics with textbook speed and precision. On May 2 and 3, some 130,000 members of the Union Army of the Potomac bore down on fewer than 60,000 Confederates (see map, page 450). Acting as if they enjoyed being outnumbered, Lee and Stonewall Jackson boldly divided their forces, ordering 30,000 men under Jackson

Battle of Chancellorsville

Not only did the Richmond government impose new taxes and a tax-in-kind, but Confederate military authorities also impressed slaves to build fortifications. And when Union forces advanced on plantation areas, Confederate commanders burned stores of cotton that lay in the enemy's path. Such interference with plantation routines and financial interests was not what planters had expected of their government, and they complained bitterly.

Nor were the centralizing policies of the Davis administration popular. Many planters agreed with the *Charleston Mercury* that the southern states had seceded because the federal government had "usurped powers not granted—progressively trenched [infringed] upon State Rights." The increasing size and power of the Richmond administration therefore startled and alarmed them. The Confederate constitution had in fact granted substantial powers to the central government, especially in time of war. But in many planters' minds, states' rights had become virtually synonymous with complete state sovereignty. R. B. Rhett, editor of the *Charleston Mercury*, wishfully (and inaccurately) described the Confederate constitution: "[It] leaves the States untouched in their Sovereignty, and commits to the Confederate Government only a few simple objects, and a few simple powers to enforce them." Governor Joseph E. Brown of Georgia took a similarly inflated view of the importance of the states. During the brief interval between Georgia's secession from the Union and its admission to the Confederacy, Brown sent an ambassador to Europe to seek recognition for the sovereign republic of Georgia from Queen Victoria, Napoleon III, and the king of Belgium. His mentality was more in keeping with the Articles of Confederation than the Constitution of 1789 or the Confederate constitution.

Years of opposition to the federal government within the Union had frozen southerners in a defensive posture. Now they erected the barrier of states' rights as a defense against change, hiding behind it while their capacity for creative statesmanship atrophied. Planters sought, above all, a guarantee that their plantations and their lives would remain untouched; they were deeply committed neither to building a southern nation nor to winning independence. If the Confederacy had been allowed to depart from the Union in peace and continue as a semideveloped cotton-growing region, they would have been content. When secession revolutionized their world, they could not or would not adjust to it.

Confused and embittered planters struck out at Jefferson Davis. Conscription, thundered Governor Brown, was "subversive of [Georgia's] sovereignty, and at war with all the principles for the support of which Georgia entered into this revolution." Searching for ways to frustrate the law, Brown bickered over draft exemptions and ordered local enrollment officials not to cooperate with the Confederacy. The *Charleston Mercury* told readers that "conscription . . . is . . . the very embodiment of Lincolnism, which our gallant armies are today fighting." In a gesture of stubborn selfishness, Robert Toombs of Georgia, a former U.S. senator, refused to switch from cotton to food crops, defying the wishes of the government, the newspapers, and his neighbors' petitions. His action bespoke the inflexibility and frustration of the southern elite at a crucial point in the Confederacy's struggle to survive.

The southern courts ultimately upheld Davis's power to conscript. He continued to provide strong leadership and drove through the legislature measures that gave the Confederacy a fighting chance. Despite his cold formality and inability to disarm critics, Davis possessed two important virtues: iron determination and total dedication to independence. These qualities kept the Confederacy afloat, for he implemented his measures and then enforced them. But his actions earned him the hatred of most influential and elite citizens.

Meanwhile, for ordinary southerners, the dire predictions of hunger and suffering were becoming a reality. Food riots occurred in the spring of 1863 in Atlanta, Macon, Columbus, and Augusta, Georgia, and in Salisbury and High Point, North Carolina. On April 2, a crowd assembled in the Confederate capital of Richmond to demand relief. A passerby, noticing the excitement, asked a young girl, "Is there some celebration?" "There is," replied the girl. "We celebrate our right to live. We are starving. As soon as enough of us get together we are going to the bakeries and each of us will take a loaf of bread." Soon they did just that, sparking a riot that Davis himself had to quell at gunpoint. Later that year, another group of angry rioters looking for food ransacked a street in Mobile, Alabama.

Food Riots in Southern Cities

Throughout the rural South, ordinary people resisted more quietly—by refusing to cooperate with conscription, tax collection, and impressments of food. "In all the States impressments are evaded by every means which ingenuity can suggest, and in some openly resisted," wrote a high-ranking commissary officer. Farmers who did provide food for the army refused to accept certificates of credit or government bonds in lieu of cash, as required by law. Conscription officers increasingly found no one to draft—men of draft age were hiding out in the forests. "The disposition to avoid military service is general," observed one of Georgia's senators in 1864. In some areas tax agents were killed in the line of duty.

Davis was ill equipped to deal with such discontent. Austere and private by nature, he failed to communicate with the masses. For long stretches of time he buried himself in military affairs or administrative details, until a crisis forced him to rush off on a speaking tour to revive the spirit of resistance. His class perspective also distanced him from the sufferings of the common people. While his social circle in Richmond dined on duck and oysters, ordinary southerners leached salt from the smokehouse floor and went hungry. State governors who saw to the common people's needs won the public's loyalty, but Davis failed to reach out to them and thus lost the support of the plain folk.

Such civil discontent was certain to affect the Confederate armies. "What man is there that would stay in the army and no that his family is

Desertions from the Confederate Army

sufring at home?" an angry citizen wrote anonymously to the secretary of war. An upcountry South Carolina newspaper agreed, asking, "What would sooner make our soldiers falter than the cry from their families?" Spurred by concern for their loved ones and resentment of what they increasingly saw as a rich man's war, large numbers of men did indeed leave the armies, supported by their friends and neighbors. Mary Boykin Chesnut observed a man being dragged back to the army as his wife looked on. "Desert agin, Jake!" she cried openly. "You desert agin, quick as you kin. Come back to your wife and children."

Desertion did not become a serious problem for the Confederacy until mid-1862, and stiffer po-

The impoverishment of nonslaveholding white families was a critical problem for the Confederacy. This sheet music was designed not only to boost morale but also to raise money that could be used to aid the hungry and needy. This effort and larger government initiatives, however, failed to solve the problem. Chicago Historical Society.

licing solved the problem that year. But from 1863 on, the number of men on duty fell rapidly as desertions soared. By mid-1863, John A. Campbell, the South's assistant secretary of war, wondered whether "so general a habit" as desertion could be considered a crime. Campbell estimated that 40,000 to 50,000 troops were absent without leave and that 100,000 were evading duty in some way. Liberal furloughs, amnesty proclamations, and appeals to return had little effect; by November 1863, Secretary of War James Seddon admitted that one-third of the army could not be accounted for. The situation was to worsen.

The defeats at Gettysburg and Vicksburg dealt a body blow to Confederate morale. When the news reached Josiah Gorgas, the genius of Confederate ordnance operations, he confided to his diary, "Today absolute ruin seems our portion. The Confederacy totters to its destruction." In desperation President Davis and several state governors resorted to threats and racial scare tactics to drive southern whites to further sacrifice. Defeat, Davis warned, would mean "extermination of yourselves, your wives, and children." Governor Charles Clark of Mississippi predicted "elevation of the black race to a position of equality—aye, of superiority, that will make them your masters and rulers." Abroad, British officials held back the delivery of badly needed warships, and recognition of the Confederate state became even more unlikely.

From this point on, the internal disintegration of the Confederacy quickened. A few newspapers began to call openly for peace. "We are for peace," admitted the *Raleigh* (North Carolina) *Daily Progress*, "because there has been enough of blood and carnage, enough of widows and orphans." A neighboring journal, the *North Carolina Standard*, tacitly admitted that defeat was inevitable and called for negotiations. Similar proposals were made in several state legislatures, though they were presented as plans for independence on honorable terms. Confederate leaders began to realize that they were losing the support of the common people. A prominent Texan noted in his diary that secession had been the work of political leaders operating without the firm support of "the mass of the people without property." Governor Zebulon Vance of North Carolina, who agreed, wrote privately that independence would require more "blood and misery . . . and our people will not pay this price I am satisfied for their independence. . . . The great popular heart is not now & never has been in this war."

In North Carolina a peace movement grew under the leadership of William W. Holden, a popular Democratic politician and editor. Over one **Southern Peace Movements** hundred public meetings took place in the summer of 1863 in support of peace negotiations; many seasoned political observers believed that Holden had the majority of the people behind him. In Georgia early in 1864, Governor Brown and Alexander H. Stephens, vice president of the Confederacy, led a similar effort. Ultimately, however, these movements came to naught. The lack of a two-party system threw into question the legitimacy of any criticism of the government; even Holden and Brown could not entirely escape the taint of dishonor and disloyalty. That the movement existed at all demonstrates deep disaffection.

The results of the 1863 Confederate congressional elections strengthened dissent. Everywhere secessionists and supporters of the Confederate administration lost seats to men who were not identified with the government. Many of the new representatives, who were often former Whigs, openly opposed the administration or publicly favored peace. In the last years of the war, Davis's support in Congress rested heavily on the Union-occupied districts; the people of these districts favored strong measures to expel the North but would share no burdens of the war effort until success was achieved. Having secured the legislation he needed, Davis used the bureaucracy and the army to enforce his unpopular policies. Ironically, as the South's situation grew desperate, former critics such as the *Charleston Mercury* became supporters of the administration. They and a core of courageous, determined soldiers kept the Confederacy alive in spite of disintegrating popular support.

By 1864 much of the opposition to the war had moved entirely outside the political sphere. Southerners were simply giving up the struggle and withdrawing their cooperation from the government. Deserters joined with ordinary citizens who were sick of the war to dominate whole towns and counties. Secret societies dedicated to reaffiliation with the Union, such as the Heroes of America and the Red Strings, sprang up. Active dissent spread throughout the South but was particularly common in upland and mountain regions. "The condition of things in the mountain districts of North Carolina, South Carolina, Georgia, and Alabama," admitted Assistant Secretary of War John A. Campbell, "menaces the existence of the Confederacy as fatally as either of the armies of the United States." Confederate officials tried using the army to round up deserters and compel obedience, but this approach was only temporarily effective. The government was losing the support of its citizens.

ANTIWAR SENTIMENT IN THE NORTH

In the North opposition to the war was similar but less severe. Alarm intensified over the growing centralization of government, and war-weariness was widespread. Resentment of the draft sparked protest, especially among poor citizens, and the Union army struggled with a desertion rate as high as the Confederates'. But the Union was so much richer than the South in human resources that none of these problems ever threatened the stability of the government. Fresh recruits were always available, and there were no shortages of food and other necessities.

Moreover, Lincoln possessed a talent that Davis lacked: he knew how to stay in touch with the ordinary citizen. Through letters to newspapers and to soldiers' families, he reached the common people and demonstrated that he had not forgotten them. Their grief was his also, for the war was his personal tragedy. After scrambling to the pinnacle of political ambition, Lincoln had seen the glory of the presidency turn to horror. The daily carnage, the tortuous political problems, and the ceaseless criticism weighed heavily on him. But this president—a self-educated man of humble origins—was able to communicate his suffering. His moving words helped to contain northern discontent, though they could not remove it.

Much of this wartime protest was political in origin. The Democratic party, though nudged out of its dominant position by the Republican surge of the late 1850s, remained

Peace Democrats

strong. Its leaders fought to regain power by blaming Lincoln for the war's carnage, the expansion of federal powers, inflation and the high tariff, and the emancipation of blacks. Appealing to tradition, they called for an end to the war and reunion on the basis of "the Constitution as it is and the Union as it was." The Democrats denounced conscription and martial law and defended states' rights and the interests of agriculture. They charged repeatedly that Republican policies were designed to flood the North with blacks, depriving white males of their status, their jobs, and their women. These claims appealed to southerners who had settled north of the Ohio River, to conservatives, to many poor people, and to some eastern merchants who had lost profitable southern trade. In the 1862 congressional elections, the Democrats made a strong comeback, and peace Democrats wielded influence in New York State and won majorities in the legislatures of Illinois and Indiana.

Led by outspoken men like Clement L. Vallandigham of Ohio, the peace Democrats made themselves highly visible. Vallandigham criticized Lincoln as a dictator who had suspended the writ of habeas corpus without congressional authority and had arrested thousands of innocent citizens. Like other Democrats, he condemned both conscription and emancipation and urged voters to use their power at the polling place to depose "King Abra-

ham." Vallandigham stayed carefully within legal bounds, but his attacks were so damaging to the war effort that military authorities arrested him for treason after Lincoln suspended habeas corpus. Lincoln wisely decided against punishment—and martyr's status—for Vallandigham and exiled him to the Confederacy. Thus Lincoln rid himself of a troublesome critic and saddled puzzled Confederates with a man who insisted on talking about "our country." (Eventually Vallandigham returned to the North through Canada.)

Lincoln believed that antiwar Democrats were linked to secret organizations that harbored traitorous ideas, such as the Knights of the Golden Circle and the Order of American Knights. These societies, he feared, encouraged draft resistance, discouraged enlistment, sabotaged communications, and plotted to aid the Confederacy. Likening such groups to a poisonous snake, Republicans sometimes branded them—and by extension the peace Democrats—as Copperheads. Though Democrats were connected with these organizations, most engaged in politics rather than treason. And though some saboteurs and Confederate agents were active in the North, they never brought about any major demonstration of support for the Confederacy. Lincoln did not destroy American liberties, but he certainly acted with a heavier hand and with less provocation than Jefferson Davis.

More violent opposition to the government arose from ordinary citizens facing the draft, especially the urban poor and immigrants in strongly Democratic areas. Federal enrolling officers made up the lists of eligibles, a procedure open to personal favoritism and prejudice. Many men, including some of modest means, managed to avoid the army by hiring a substitute or paying commutation, but the poor viewed the commutation fee as discriminatory, and many immigrants suspected (wrongly, on the whole) that they were called in disproportionate numbers. (Approximately 200,000 men born in Germany and 150,000 born in Ireland served in the Union army.)

As a result, there were scores of disturbances and melees. Enrolling officers received rough treatment in many parts of the North, and riots occurred in Ohio, Indiana, Penn-

New York City Draft Riot

sylvania, Illinois, and Wisconsin, and in such cities as Troy, Albany, and Newark. By far the most serious outbreak of violence occurred in New York City in July 1863.

Mobs in the New York City draft riots directed much of their anger at African-Americans. Rioters burned an orphanage for black children and killed scores of blacks. This wood engraving depicted a lynching in Clarkson Street.   Chicago Historical Society.

The war was unpopular in that Democratic stronghold, and racial, ethnic, and class tensions ran high. Shippers had recently broken a longshoremen's strike by hiring black strikebreakers to work under police protection. Working-class New Yorkers feared an influx of black labor from the South and regarded blacks as the cause of the bloody war. Irish workers, often recently arrived and poor themselves, resented being forced to serve in the place of others who could afford to avoid the draft.

Military police offices came under attack first; then mobs crying "Down with the rich" looted wealthy homes and stores. But blacks became the special target. Those who happened to be in the rioters' path were beaten; soon the mob rampaged through African-American neighborhoods, destroying even an orphans' asylum. At least seventy-four people died in the violence, which raged out of control for three days. (Note the contemporary

engraving.) Only the dispatch of army units fresh from Gettysburg ended the episode.

Discouragement and war-weariness reached a peak in the summer of 1864, when the Democratic party nominated the popular General George B. McClellan for president and inserted a qualified peace plank into its platform. The plank, written by Vallandigham, condemned "four years of failure to restore the Union by the experiment of war" and called for an armistice. Lincoln, running with Tennessee's Andrew Johnson on a "National Union" ticket, concluded that it was "exceedingly probable that this Administration will not be reelected."

Then, during a publicized interchange with Confederate officials sent to Canada, Lincoln insisted that the terms for peace include reunion and "the abandonment of slavery." A wave of protest arose in the North from voters who were weary of war and dedicated only to reunion. Lincoln quickly backtracked, denying that his offer meant "that nothing *else* or *less* would be considered, if offered." He would insist on freedom only for those slaves (about 134,000) who had joined the Union army under his promise of emancipation. Lincoln's action showed his political weakness, but the fortunes of war soon changed the electoral situation.

NORTHERN PRESSURE AND SOUTHERN WILL

The success of the North's long-term diplomatic strategy was sealed in 1864. From the outset, the North had pursued one paramount goal: to prevent recognition of the Confederacy by European nations. Foreign recognition would violate the North's claim that it was fighting an illegal rebellion, not a separate nation. More importantly, recognition would open the way to foreign financial and military aid that could ensure Confederate independence.

Northern Diplomatic Strategy

The British elite felt considerable sympathy for southern planters, whose aristocratic values were similar to their own. And in terms of power politics, both England and France stood to benefit from a divided and weakened America. Thus to achieve their goal, Lincoln and Secretary of State Seward needed to avoid both serious military defeats and unnecessary controversies with the European powers. Southerners inadvertently aided them: aware that the textile industry employed one-fifth of the British population directly or indirectly, southern leaders relied overconfidently on "King Cotton diplomacy." They believed that the British government, concerned about obtaining cotton for the country's mills, would have to recognize the Confederacy.

Cotton was a good card to play, but it was not a trump. At the beginning of the war British mills had a 50 percent surplus of cotton on hand. New sources of supply in India, Egypt, and Brazil helped to fill their needs later on, and some southern cotton continued to reach Europe, despite the Confederacy's recommendation that its citizens plant and ship no cotton. The British government, refusing to be stampeded into recognition, kept its eye on the battlefield. France, though sympathetic to the South, was unwilling to act independently of the British. Confederate agents were able to purchase valuable arms and supplies in Europe and obtained some loans from European financiers, but they never achieved a diplomatic breakthrough.

More than once the Union strategy nearly broke down. An acute crisis occurred in 1861 when the overzealous commander of an American frigate stopped the British steamer *Trent* and removed two Confederate ambassadors. The British reacted angrily, but Lincoln and Seward waited until public opinion cooled down enough for them to return the ambassadors. In a series of confrontations with Britain, the United States protested against the sale of warships to the Confederacy. A few ships built in Britain, notably the *Alabama*, reached open water to serve the South. Over twenty-two months, without entering a southern port, the *Alabama* destroyed or captured more than sixty northern ships. But the British government, as a neutral power, soon began to bar delivery of warships such as the Laird rams, formidable vessels whose pointed prows were designed to break the Union blockade.

On the battlefield, the northern victory was far from won in 1864. The course of the war had demonstrated the advantages enjoyed by the defense and the extreme difficulty of destroying an opposing army. General William Tecumseh Sherman now realized that the North had to "keep the war South until they are not only ruined, exhausted, but humbled in pride and spirit." Yet military authorities throughout history have agreed that deep invasion is extremely risky: the farther an army penetrates enemy territory, the more vulnerable its own communications and support become. Moreover, observed the Prussian expert Karl von Clausewitz, if the invader encountered a "truly national" resistance, his troops would be "everywhere exposed to attacks by an insurgent population." Thus, if southerners were determined enough to mount a "truly national" resistance, their defiance and the South's vast size could make a northern victory virtually impossible.

General Grant decided to test these conditions—and southern will—with a strategic innovation of his own: raids on a massive scale. Grant proposed to use whole armies, not just cavalry, to destroy Confederate railroads, thus ruining the enemy's transportation and damaging the South's

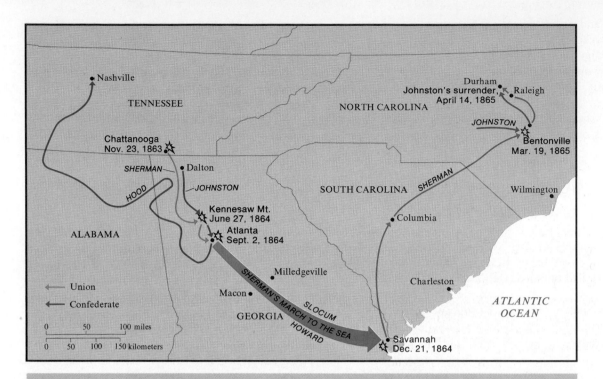

Sherman's March to the Sea   *The West proved a decisive theater at the end of the war. From Chattanooga, Union forces drove into Georgia, capturing Atlanta. Then General Sherman embarked on his march of destruction through Georgia to the sea and then northward through the Carolinas.*

economy. Abandoning their lines of support, federal armies would live off the land while they laid waste all resources useful to the Confederacy. After General George H. Thomas's troops won the Battle of Chattanooga in November 1863 by ignoring orders and charging up Missionary Ridge, the heartland of the South lay open. Moving to Virginia, Grant entrusted General Sherman with 100,000 men for a raid deep into the South, toward Atlanta.

Jefferson Davis countered by positioning the army of General Joseph E. Johnston in Sherman's path. Davis's entire political strategy for 1864 was based on demonstrating Confederate military strength and successfully defending Atlanta. With the federal elections of 1864 approaching, Davis hoped that a display of strength and resolve by the South would defeat Lincoln and elect a president who would sue for peace. When Johnston slowly but steadily fell back toward Atlanta, Davis grew anxious and pressed his commander for information and assurances that Atlanta would be held. From a purely military point of view, Johnston

was conducting the defense skillfully, but Jefferson Davis could not take a purely military point of view. When Johnston remained uninformative and continued to drop back, Davis replaced him with the one-legged General John Hood, who knew his job was to fight. "Our all depends on that army at Atlanta," wrote Mary Boykin Chesnut. "If that fails us, the game is up."

For southern morale, the game was up. Hood attacked but was beaten, and Sherman's army occupied Atlanta on September 2, 1864. The victory buoyed northern spirits and assured Lincoln's re-election. "There is no hope," Mary Chesnut acknowledged, and a government clerk in Richmond wrote, "Our fondly-cherished visions of peace have vanished like a mirage of the desert." Davis exhorted southerners to fight on and win new victories before the federal elections, but he had to admit that "two-thirds of our men are absent . . . most of them absent without leave." Hood's army marched north to cut Sherman's supply lines and force him to retreat, but Sherman began to march sixty thousand of his men straight to the sea, planning to live off the land and destroying Confederate resources as he went (see map).

Sherman's army was an unusually formidable force, composed almost entirely of battle-tested veterans and officers who had risen through the ranks. Before the march began, army doctors weeded out any who were weak or sick. Tanned, bearded, tough, and unkempt, the remaining veterans were determined, as one put it, "to Conquer this Rebelien or Die." They believed "the South are to blame for this war" and were ready to make the South pay. Although many harbored racist attitudes, most had come to support emancipation because, as one put it, "Slavery stands in the way of putting down the rebellion." Confederate General Johnston later commented, "There has been no such army since the days of Julius Caesar."

As Sherman's men moved across Georgia, they cut a path fifty to sixty miles wide and more than two hundred miles long; the totality of the destruction was awesome. A Georgia woman described the "Burnt Country" this way: "The fields were trampled down and the road was lined with carcasses of horses, hogs, and cattle that the invaders, unable either to consume or to carry with them, had wantonly shot down to starve our people and prevent them from making their crops. The stench in some places was unbearable." Such devastation diminished the South's material resources and, more importantly, its faltering will to resist.

After reaching Savannah in December, Sherman marched his armies north into the Carolinas. To his soldiers, South Carolina was "the root of secession." They burned and destroyed as they moved through, encountering little resistance. The opposing army of General Johnston was small, but Sherman's men should have been prime targets for guerrilla raids and harassing attacks by local defense units. The absence of both led South Carolina's James Chesnut, Jr., to write that his state "was shamefully and unnecessarily lost. . . . We had time, opportunity and means to destroy him. But there was wholly wanting the energy and ability required by the occasion." The South put up no "truly national" resistance; its people were near the end of their endurance.

Sherman's march drew additional human resources to the Union cause. In Georgia alone as many as nineteen thousand slaves gladly took the opportunity to escape bondage and join the Union army as it passed through the countryside. Others remained on the plantations to await the end of the

These photographs capture the very different personal styles of Generals Grant (left) and Lee (right). Their bloody battles in 1864 caused northern revulsion to the war but ultimately brought its end in sight. National Archives.

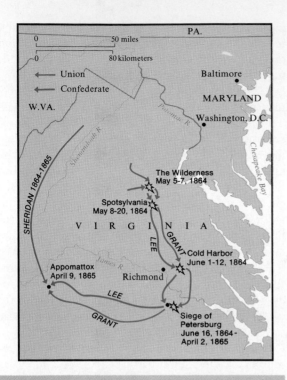

The War in Virginia, 1864–1865 *At great cost, Grant hammered away at Lee's army until the weakened southern forces finally surrendered at Appomattox.*

brutality of Sherman's troops shocked these veterans of the whip. "I've seen them cut the hams off of a live pig or ox and go off leavin' the animal groanin'," recalled one man. "The master had 'em kilt then, but it was awful."

It was awful, too, in Virginia, where the preliminaries to victory proved protracted and ghastly. Throughout the spring and summer of 1864 Grant hurled his troops at Lee's army and suffered appalling losses: almost 18,000 casualties in the Battle of the Wilderness, where skeletons poked out of the shallow graves dug one year before; more than 8,000 at Spotsylvania; and 12,000 in the space of a few hours at Cold Harbor (see map at left). Before the last battle, Union troops pinned scraps of paper bearing their names and addresses to their backs, certain they would be mowed down as they rushed Lee's trenches. In four weeks in May and June, Grant lost as many men as were enrolled in Lee's entire army. Undaunted, Grant kept up the pressure, saying "I propose to fight it out along this line if it takes all summer." The heavy fighting prepared the way for eventual victory: Lee's army shrank until offensive action was no longer possible, while the Union army kept replenishing its forces with new recruits.

The end finally came in the spring of 1865. Grant kept battering Lee, who tried but failed to break through the federal line. With the numerical superiority of Grant's army now greater than two-to-one, Confederate defeat was inevitable. On April 2 Lee abandoned Richmond and Petersburg. On April 9, hemmed in by federal

Heavy Losses Force Lee's Surrender

war, either from an ingrained wariness of whites or negative experiences with the federal soldiers. The destruction of food harmed slaves as well as white rebels, and many blacks lost blankets, shoes, and other valuables to their liberators. In fact, the

At the war's end, the U.S. flag flew over the State House in Richmond, Virginia, which bore many marks of destruction. National Archives.

Lincoln's death caused a vast outpouring of grief in the North. His funeral train stopped at several cities on its way to Illinois to allow local services to be held. Anne S. K. Brown Military Collection, The John Hay Library, Brown University.

troops, short of rations, and with fewer than 30,000 men left, Lee surrendered at Appomattox Courthouse. Grant treated his rival with respect and paroled the defeated troops. Within weeks Jefferson Davis was captured, and the remaining Confederate forces laid down their arms and surrendered. The war was over at last.

With Lee's surrender, Lincoln knew that the Union had been preserved, yet he did not live to see the last southern units lay down their arms. On the evening of Good Friday, April 14, he accompanied his wife to Ford's Theatre in Washington to enjoy a popular comedy. There an embittered southern sympathizer named John Wilkes Booth shot the president in the head at pointblank range. Lincoln died the next day. Twelve days later troops tracked down and killed Booth. The Union had lost its wartime leader, and millions publicly mourned the martyred chief executive along the route of the funeral train that took his body home to Illinois (as shown in the illustration). Relief at the war's end now mingled uncomfortably with a renewed sense of loss and uncertainty about the future.

COSTS AND EFFECTS

The costs of the Civil War were enormous. The total number of military casualties on both sides exceeded 1 million—a frightful toll for a nation of 31 million people. Approximately 364,000 federal soldiers died, 140,000 of them from wounds suffered in battle. Another 275,175 Union soldiers were wounded but survived. On the Confederate side, an estimated 258,000 lost their lives, and almost as many suffered wounds. More men died in the Civil War than in all other American wars combined until Vietnam. Fundamental disagreements that would continue to trouble the Reconstruction era had caused unprecedented loss of life.

Casualties

Although precise figures on enlistments are impossible to obtain, it appears that 700,000 to 800,000 men served in the Confederate armies. Far more, possibly 2.3 million, served in the Union armies. All these men were taken from home, fam-

Civil War Battles

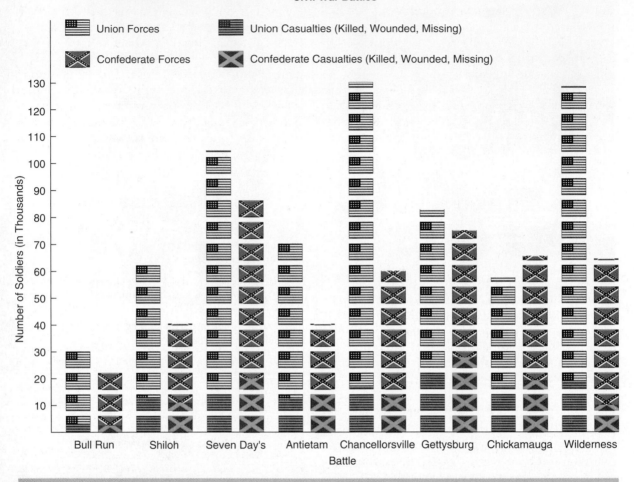

The Unprecedented Losses of the Civil War   *Month after month newspapers in every community pub-lished the names of men who had become casualties. As this figure shows, the newspapers' lists were long.*   Sources: Shelby Foote, *The Civil War, a Narrative*, 3 vols. (1958–1974); Richard B. Morris, *Encyclopedia of American History* (1982); Archer Jones, *Civil War Command and Strategy (1992)*.

ily, and personal goals and had their lives disrupted in ways that were not easily repaired.

Property damage and financial costs were also enormous, though difficult to tally. Federal loans and taxes during the conflict totaled almost $3 bil-lion, and interest on the war debt was $2.8 billion. The Confederacy borrowed over $2 billion but lost far more in the destruction of homes, crops, livestock, and other property. As an example of the wreckage that attended four years of conflict on southern soil, the number of hogs in South Car-

Financial Cost of the War

olina plummeted from 965,000 in 1860 to approxi-mately 150,000 in 1865, leaving many families without their primary source of meat. Scholars have noted that small farmers lost just as much, proportionally, as planters whose slaves were emancipated.

In southern war zones the landscape was deso-lated. Soldiers seeking fuel or shelter had cut down many large stands of trees, and artillery shells had blasted many others. Over wide regions fences and crops were destroyed, houses and bridges burned, and fields abandoned and left to erode. Federal troops had looted factories and put two-thirds of the South's railroad system out of service. Levees and roads had deteriorated. Visitors to the countryside were struck by how empty and impoverished it looked. Nature would repair much of the damage in time, but large investments of human skill and energy were gone.

Estimates of the total cost of the war exceed $20 billion—five times the total expenditures of the federal government from its creation to 1861. The northern government increased its spending by 700 percent in the first full year of the war; by the last year its spending had soared to twenty times the prewar level. By 1865 the federal government accounted for over 26 percent of the gross national product.

Many of these changes were more or less permanent. In the 1880s, interest on the war debt still accounted for approximately 40 percent of the federal budget and Union soldiers' pensions for as much as 20 percent. Thus, although many southerners had hoped to remove government from the economy, the war made such separation an impossibility. Federal expenditures shrank after the war, but they stabilized at twice the prewar level, or at 4 percent of the gross national product.

Did the Civil War bring about fundamental alterations in the life of the nation? Economically, wartime measures had introduced new federal involvement in both the banking and transportation systems. The government had also exercised its power to support manufacturing and business interests by means of tariffs, loans, and subsidies. Industrialization and large economic enterprises clearly had arrived to stay.

Politically, important changes had accompanied the maintenance of national unity. Under Republican leadership, the federal government had expanded its power not only to preserve the Union but also to extend freedom. The government emancipated the slaves, and Lincoln had called for "a new birth of freedom" in America. Did this mean that the nation would now use its power to protect the rights of individuals, even against the states? Extreme forms of states' rights dogma clearly were dead, but would Americans continue to favor a state-centered federalism? How would white southerners, embittered and impoverished by the war, respond to efforts to reconstruct the nation?

Closely related to these issues was a question of central importance: what would be the place of black men and women in American life? The Union victory provided a partial answer: slavery as it had existed before the war could not persist. But what would replace it? About 186,000 African-American soldiers had rallied to the Union cause, infusing it with new strength. Did their sacrifice entitle them to full citizenship? Would the national government become the protector of their rights and the rights of others? Black veterans and former slaves eagerly awaited an answer, which would have to be found during Reconstruction.

SUGGESTIONS FOR FURTHER READING

The War and the South

Thomas B. Alexander and Richard E. Beringer, *The Anatomy of the Confederate Congress* (1972); Richard E. Beringer et al., *Why the South Lost the Civil War* (1986); Gabor S. Boritt, *Why the Confederacy Lost* (1992); Richard N. Current, *Lincoln's Loyalists* (1992); William C. Davis, *Jefferson Davis* (1991); William C. Davis, *Diary of a Confederate Soldier* (1990); Robert F. Durden, *The Gray and the Black: The Confederate Debate on Emancipation* (1972); Paul D. Escott, *Many Excellent People* (1985); Paul D. Escott, *After Secession: Jefferson Davis and the Failure of Confederate Nationalism* (1978); Eli N. Evans, *Judah P. Benjamin* (1987); J. B. Jones, *A Rebel War Clerk's Diary*, 2 vols., ed. Howard Swiggett (1935); Ella Lonn, *Desertion During the Civil War* (1928); Mary Elizabeth Massey, *Refugee Life in the Confederacy* (1964); Larry E. Nelson, *Bullets, Ballots, and Rhetoric: Confederate Policy for the United States Presidential Contest of 1864* (1980); Alan T. Nolan, *Lee Considered* (1991); Harry P. Owens and James J. Cooke, eds., *The Old South in the Crucible of War* (1983); Frank L. Owsley, *State Rights in the Confederacy* (1925); Charles W. Ramsdell, *Behind the Lines in the Southern Confederacy*, ed. Wendell H. Stephenson (1944); James L. Roark, *Masters Without Slaves* (1977); Georgia Lee Tatum, *Disloyalty in the Confederacy* (1934); Emory M. Thomas, *The Confederate Nation* (1979); Emory M. Thomas, *The Confederacy as a Revolutionary Experience* (1971); William A. Tidwell, *Come Retribution: The Confederate Secret Service and the Assassination of Lincoln* (1989); Bell Irvin Wiley, *The Life of Johnny Reb* (1943); Bell Irvin Wiley, *The Plain People of the Confederacy* (1943); W. Buck Yearns, ed., *The Confederate Governors* (1985).

The War and the North

Ralph Andreano, ed., *The Economic Impact of the American Civil War* (1962); Robert Cruden, *The War That Never Ended* (1973); David Donald, ed., *Why the North Won the Civil War* (1960); James W. Geary, *We Need Men* (1991); Wood Gray, *The Hidden Civil War* (1942); Randall C. Jimerson, *The Private Civil War* (1988); Frank L. Klement, *The Copperheads in the Middle West* (1960); Susan Previant Lee and Peter Passell, *A New Economic View of American History* (1979); James M. McPherson, *Battle Cry of Freedom* (1988); James H. Moorhead, *American Apocalypse* (1978); Phillip S. Paludan, *"A People's Contest": The Union and the Civil War, 1861–1865* (1989); Robert Hunt Rhodes, ed., *All for the Union: The Civil War Diary and Letters of Elisha Hunt Rhodes* (1991); George Winston Smith and Charles Burnet Judah, *Life in the North During the Civil War* (1966); George Templeton Strong, *Diary*, 4 vols., ed. Allan Nevins and Milton Hasley Thomas (1952); Paul Studenski, *Financial History of the United States* (1952); Bell Irvin Wiley, *The Life of Billy Yank* (1952).

Women

John R. Brumgardt, ed., *Civil War Nurse: The Diary and Letters of Hannah Ropes* (1980); Beth Gilbert Crabtree and James W. Patton, eds., *"Journal of a Secesh Lady": The Diary of Catherine Ann Devereux Edmondston, 1860–1866* (1979); Jacqueline Jones, *Labor of Love, Labor of Sorrow* (1985); Mary Elizabeth Massey, *Bonnet Brigades* (1966); George C. Rable, *Civil Wars: Women and the Crisis of Southern Nationalism* (1989); Mary D. Robertson, ed., *Lucy Breckinridge of Grove Hill: The Journal of a Virginia Girl, 1862–1864* (1979); C. Vann Woodward and Elisabeth Muhlenfeld, eds., *Mary Chesnut's Civil War* (1981); Agatha Young, *Women and the Crisis* (1959).

African-Americans

Virginia M. Adams, ed., *On the Altar of Freedom: A Black Soldier's Civil War Letters from the Front* (1991); Ira Berlin, ed., *Freedom: A Documentary History of Emancipation, 1861–1867*, Series I, *The Destruction of Slavery* (1979), and Series II, *The Black Military Experience* (1982); David W. Blight, *Frederick Douglass' Civil War* (1989); Dudley Cornish, *The Sable Arm* (1956); Barbara Jeanne Fields, *Slavery and Freedom on the Middle Ground* (1985); Joseph T. Glatthaar, *Forged in Battle* (1990); Leon Litwack, *Been in the Storm So Long* (1979); James M. McPherson, *The Negro's Civil War* (1965); James M. McPherson, *The Struggle for Equality* (1964); Clarence L. Mohr, *On the Threshold of Freedom* (1986); Benjamin Quarles, *The Negro in the Civil War* (1953).

Military History

Nancy Scott Anderson and Dwight Anderson, *The Generals: Ulysses S. Grant and Robert E. Lee* (1987); Albert Castel, *Decision in the West* (1992); Bruce Catton, *Grant Takes Command* (1969); Bruce Catton, *Grant Moves South* (1960); Benjamin Franklin Cooling, *Forts Henry and Donelson* (1988); Peter Cozzens, *This Terrible Sound* (1992); William C. Davis, ed., *The Image of War*, multi-volume (1983–1985); Shelby Foote, *The Civil War, a Narrative*, 3 vols. (1958–1974); Douglas Southall Freeman, *Lee's Lieutenants*, 3 vols. (1942–1944); Douglas Southall Freeman, *R. E. Lee*, 4 vols. (1934–1935); Joseph T. Glatthaar, *The March to the Sea and Beyond* (1985); Herman Hattaway and Archer Jones, *How the North Won* (1983); Archer Jones, *Civil War Command and Strategy* (1992); Alvin M. Josephy, Jr., *The Civil War in the American West* (1991); Gerald F. Linderman, *Embattled*

Courage (1989); Thomas L. Livermore, *Numbers and Losses in the Civil War in America* (1957); John F. Marszalek, *Sherman* (1992); Grady McWhiney and Perry D. Jamieson, *Attack and Die* (1982); J. B. Mitchell, *Decisive Battles of the Civil War* (1955); Reid Mitchell, *Civil War Soldiers* (1988); Roy Morris, Jr., *Sheridan* (1992); Charles Royster, *The Destructive War* (1991); Stephen W. Sears, *To the Gates of Richmond* (1992); Stephen W. Sears, *George B. McClellan* (1988); Stephen Z. Starr, *The Union Cavalry in the Civil War*, 3 vols. (1985); Emory M. Thomas, *Bold Dragoon: The Life of J.E.B. Stuart* (1987); Noah Andre Trudeau, *The Last Citadel* (1991); Warren Wilkinson, *Mother, May You Never See the Sights I Have Seen* (1990); Steven E. Woodworth, *Jefferson Davis and His Generals* (1990).

Diplomatic History

Stuart L. Bernath, *Squall Across the Atlantic: American Civil War Prize Cases and Diplomacy* (1970); Kinley J. Brauer, "The Slavery Problem in the Diplomacy of the American Civil War," *Pacific Historical Review* XLVI, no. 3 (1977): 439–469; David P. Crook, *The North, the South, and the Powers, 1861–1865* (1974); Charles P. Cullop, *Confederate Propaganda in Europe* (1969); Norman A. Graebner, "Northern Diplomacy and European Neutrality," in David Donald, ed., *Why the North Won the Civil War* (1960); Frank J. Merli, *Great Britain and the Confederate Navy* (1970); Frank L. Owsley and Harriet Owsley, *King Cotton Diplomacy* (1959); Gordon H. Warren, *Fountain of Discontent: The Trent Affair and Freedom of the Seas* (1981); Gordon H. Warren, "The King Cotton Theory," in Alexander DeConde, ed., *Encyclopedia of American Foreign Policy*, 3 vols. (1978).

Abraham Lincoln and the Union Government

Allan G. Bogue, *The Earnest Men: Republicans of the Civil War Senate* (1981); Gabor S. Borit, ed., *The Historian's Lincoln* (1989); Fawn Brodie, *Thaddeus Stevens* (1959); Richard N. Current, *The Lincoln Nobody Knows* (1958); Leonard P. Curry, *Blueprint for Modern America: Non-Military Legislation of the First Civil War Congress* (1968); Christopher Dell, *Lincoln and the War Democrats* (1975); David Donald, *Charles Sumner and the Rights of Man* (1970); Ludwell H. Johnson, "Lincoln's Solution to the Problem of Peace Terms, 1864–1865," *Journal of Southern History* XXXIV (November 1968): 441–447; Peyton McCrary, *Abraham Lincoln and Reconstruction: The Louisiana Experiment* (1978); James M. McPherson, *Abraham Lincoln and the Second American Revolution* (1990); Mark Neely, *The Fate of Liberty* (1991); Joel Silbey, *A Respectable Minority: The Democratic Party in the Civil War Era* (1977); Benjamin P. Thomas, *Abraham Lincoln* (1952); Hans L. Trefousse, *The Radical Republicans* (1969); Glyndon G. Van Deusen, *William Henry Seward* (1967); T. Harry Williams, *Lincoln and His Generals* (1952); T. Harry Williams, *Lincoln and the Radicals* (1941).

16

Reconstruction: A Partial Revolution, 1865–1877

FOR BOTH MEN, WAR and Reconstruction brought stunning changes and swift reversals of fortune. In 1861 Robert Smalls was a slave in South Carolina, while Wade Hampton was a South Carolina legislator and one of the richest planters in the South. The events of the next fifteen years turned each man's world upside down more than once.

When Robert Smalls stole a Confederate ship from Charleston harbor and piloted it to the blockading federal fleet, he became a Union war hero. Thereafter Smalls guided Union gunboats and toured the North recruiting black troops. Though he enjoyed celebrity status, Smalls encountered harsh discrimination in the North and found in 1865 that neither his heroism nor his status as a free man entitled him to vote. But by 1868 that, too, had changed, and he began a career in politics. Robert Smalls helped write his state's constitution, served in the legislature, and won election to Congress. There he denounced white violence and worked for educational and economic opportunity for his people. But Smalls was helpless to prevent the end of Reconstruction or delay the return of white control in South Carolina.

Wade Hampton joined the Confederate army in 1861 and, in keeping with his wealth and social standing, rose to the rank of lieutenant-general. The South's defeat profoundly shocked him, and as Union forces closed in he spoke wildly of "forc[ing] my way across the Mississippi" with "a devoted band of Cavalry" and continuing the fight. The postwar years brought further painful and unexpected changes, including forced bankruptcy. In 1867 Hampton surprised other privileged whites by supporting suffrage for a few educated and propertied former slaves. By 1876 Hampton's fortunes were again on the rise: Democrats nominated him for governor, promising that he would "redeem" South Carolina from Republican misrule. While Hampton spoke misleadingly of respect for blacks' rights, each member of the paramilitary Red Shirts who supported him pledged to "control the vote of at least one Negro, by intimidation, purchase," or other means. Hampton won the governor's chair and then a seat in the U.S. Senate.

As the careers of Smalls and Hampton suggest, Reconstruction changed much and yet changed little. Robert Smalls rose from bondage to experience glory, emancipation, political

On January 6, 1874, Congressman Robert B. Elliott of South Carolina eloquently defended the proposed civil rights bill.

power, and, ultimately, disappointment. Wade Hampton fell from privilege to endure unaccustomed failure and powerlessness but eventually returned to a position of dominance. Similarly, American society experienced both extraordinary change and fundamental continuity. Unprecedented social, political, and constitutional changes took place, but the underlying realities of economic power, racial prejudice, and judicial conservatism limited Reconstruction's revolutionary potential.

Nowhere was the turmoil of Reconstruction more evident than in national politics. The president and Congress fought bitterly over the shaping of a plan for Reconstruction. When Andrew Johnson succeeded the martyred Abraham Lincoln, his first actions convinced both southern aristocrats and northern Republicans that he intended to be tough on traitors. Formerly a Democrat from Tennessee, Johnson had always been a combative foe of the South's wealthy planters. Before the end of 1865, however, Johnson's policies changed direction. Jefferson Davis stayed in prison for two years, but no Confederate leaders were executed, and southern aristocrats soon came to view Johnson as their friend and protector. He pardoned rebel leaders liberally and allowed them to occupy high offices. He also ordered tax officials to return plantations to their original owners, including abandoned coastal lands on which forty thousand freedmen had settled by order of General Sherman.

This turn of events alarmed northern voters. Republican congressmen began to discuss plans to keep rebels from regaining control of the South, and negotiations in Congress produced a new Reconstruction program, embodied in the Fourteenth Amendment. But southern intransigence blocked that program and forced the development of a more radical plan, the Reconstruction Act of 1867. When Congress put the act into effect, Johnson tried to subvert it, and by 1868 the president and Congress were bitterly antagonistic.

Before these struggles were over, Congress had impeached the president, enfranchised the freedmen, and given them a role in reconstructing the South. The nation also adopted the Fourteenth and Fifteenth Amendments. Yet nothing was done to open the doors of economic progress to black southerners. By 1877 hostile white Democrats in the South had regained control of every state government, undoing the political revolution. And

judicially, the Supreme Court was adopting interpretations of the Thirteenth, Fourteenth, and Fifteenth Amendments that crippled their power for decades.

Throughout this period of upheaval, few saw equal rights for African-Americans as the central aim of Reconstruction. During the war the federal government had been reluctant to grant fair treatment even to black troops. In Congress, northern Democrats continuously denounced the idea of equality. Republicans often differed among themselves, but a mixture of idealism, partisan motives, and southern intransigence drove them toward equal rights. The northern public, as a whole, had limited interest in black southerners, but war-born antipathy to rebellion swung most northern voters behind the policies of the Republican party.

Southern opposition to Reconstruction grew steadily, testing the North's determination. By 1869 the Ku Klux Klan had added large-scale violence to southern whites' repertoire of resistance. Despite new federal laws against the Klan, African-Americans were intimidated at the polls, robbed of their earnings, beaten, and murdered. Prosecution of Klansmen was spotty and often unsuccessful, and it did not stop the Democrats' march toward power in the southern states. By the early 1870s the failure of Reconstruction was imminent.

Voters had grown weary and suspicious of the use of federal power to prop up failing Republican governments in the South. Moreover, as the 1870s advanced, other issues drew attention away from Reconstruction. Industrial growth accelerated, creating new opportunities and raising new problems. Interest in territorial expansion revived. Political corruption became a nationwide scandal, and bribery a way of doing business. "Money has become the God of this country," wrote one disgusted observer, "and men, otherwise good men, are almost compelled to worship at her shrine." Eventually these other forces triumphed. As politics moved on to new concerns, the courts turned their attention away from civil rights, and even northern Republicans abandoned racial reforms in 1877.

Thus only limited change emerged from a period of tremendous upheaval. Congress asserted the principle of equality before the law for African-Americans and gave black men the right to vote. But more far-reaching measures to advance black freedom never had much support in Congress, and

• *Important Events* •

1865	President Johnson begins Reconstruction		**1870**	Congress passes first Enforcement Act

1865 President Johnson begins Reconstruction
Confederate leaders regain power
White southern governments pass restrictive black codes
Congress refuses to seat southern representatives
Thirteenth Amendment ratified

1866 Congress passes Civil Rights Act and renewal of Freedmen's Bureau over Johnson's veto
Congress approves Fourteenth Amendment
Most southern states reject Fourteenth Amendment
In *Ex parte Milligan* the Supreme Court reasserts its influence

1867 Congress passes Reconstruction Act and Tenure of Office Act
Secretary of State Seward arranges purchase of Alaska
Constitutional conventions called in southern states

1868 House impeaches Johnson; Senate acquits him
Most southern states gain readmission to Union
Fourteenth Amendment ratified
Ulysses S. Grant elected president

1869 Congress approves Fifteenth Amendment (ratified in 1870)

1870 Congress passes first Enforcement Act

1871 Congress passes a second Enforcement Act and the Ku Klux Klan Act
Treaty with England settles *Alabama* claims

1872 Amnesty Act frees almost all remaining Confederates from restrictions on holding office
Liberal Republicans organize
Debtors urge government to keep greenbacks in circulation
Grant re-elected

1873 *Slaughter-House* cases limit power of Fourteenth Amendment
Panic of 1873 damages economy

1874 Grant vetoes increase in paper money
Democrats win majority in House of Representatives

1875 Several Grant appointees indicted for corruption
Congress passes a weak Civil Rights Act
Congress requires that after 1878 greenbacks be convertible into gold

1876 *U.S.* v. *Cruikshank* and *U.S.* v. *Reese* further weaken Fourteenth Amendment
Presidential election disputed

1877 Congress elects Rutherford B. Hayes
Exodusters migrate to Kansas

when suffrage alone proved insufficient to remake the South, the nation soon lost interest. Reconstruction proclaimed anew the American principle of human equality but failed to secure it in reality.

EQUALITY: THE UNRESOLVED ISSUE

For America's former slaves, Reconstruction had one paramount meaning: a chance to explore freedom. A southern white woman admitted in her diary that the black people "showed a natural and exultant joy at being free." Former slaves remembered singing far into the night after federal troops reached their plantations. The slaves on a Texas plantation jumped up and down and clapped their hands as one man shouted, "We is free—no more whippings and beatings."

A few people gave in to the natural desire to do what had been impossible before. One grandmother who had long resented her treatment dropped her hoe and ran to confront the mistress. "I'm free!" she yelled. "Yes, I'm free! Ain't got to work for you no more! You can't put me in your pocket [sell me] now!" Another man recalled that he and others "started on the move," either to search for family members or just to exercise their new-found freedom of movement. As he traveled, one man sang about being free as a frog, " 'cause a frog had freedom to get on a log and jump off when he pleases."

Most freedmen reacted more cautiously and shrewdly, taking care to test the boundaries of their new condition. "After the war was over," explained one man, "we was afraid to move. Just like terrapins or turtles after emancipation. Just stick our heads out to see how the land lay." As slaves they had learned to expect hostility from white people, and they did not presume it would instantly disappear. Life in freedom might still be a matter of what was allowed, not what was right. "You got to say master?" asked a freedman in Georgia. "Naw," answered his fellows, but "they said it all the same. They said it for a long time."

One sign of this shrewd caution was the way freedmen evaluated potential employers. "Most all the Negroes that had good owners stayed with 'em, but the others left. Some of 'em come back and some didn't," explained one man. If a white person had been relatively considerate to blacks in bondage, they reasoned that he might prove a desirable employer in freedom. Others left their plantations all at once, for, as one put it, "that master am sure mean and if we doesn't have to stay we shouldn't, not with that master."

African-Americans' Desire for Land

In addition to a fair employer, the freedmen wanted opportunity through education and, especially, through land of their own. Land represented their chance to farm for themselves, to enjoy the independence valued by generations of American farmers. It represented compensation for generations of travail in bondage. A northern observer noted that freedmen in the Sea Islands of South Carolina and Georgia made "plain, straight-forward" inquiries as they settled the land set aside for them by Sherman. They wanted to be sure the land "would be theirs after they had improved it." Everywhere, blacks young and old thirsted for homes of their own. One white southerner noted with indignation in her diary that

> Uncle Lewis, the pious, the honored, the venerated, gets his poor old head turned with false notions of freedom and independence, runs off to the Yankees with a pack of lies against his mistress, and sets up a claim to part of her land!

Lewis simply wanted a new beginning. Like other freedmen, he hoped to leave slavery behind.

But how much of a chance would whites, who were in power, give to blacks? Northerners' racial attitudes were evolving but remained generally unfavorable. Abolitionists and many Republicans helped African-Americans fight for equal rights, and they won some victories. In 1864 the federal courts accepted black testimony, and the next year the Thirteenth Amendment won ratification. New York City and the District of Columbia desegregated their streetcars, and one state, Massachusetts, enacted a comprehensive public-accommodations law. Nevertheless, signs of resistance to racial equality abounded. The Democratic party fought hard against equality, charging that Republicans favored race-mixing and were undermining the status of the white worker. Voters in three states—Connecticut, Minnesota, and Wisconsin—rejected black suffrage in 1865.

Such evidence of northern prejudice was significant. The history of emancipation in the British Caribbean indicated that, if equality were to be won, the North would have to take a strong and determined stand. In 1833 Great Britain had abolished slavery in its possessions, providing slaveowners with £20 million in compensation and requiring all former agricultural slaves to work the land for six more years as apprentices. Despite such generosity to the slaveowners, the transition to free labor had not been easy. Everywhere in the British Caribbean planters had fought tenaciously to maintain control over their laborers, fashioning laws, taxes, and administrative decisions with an eye to keeping freedmen on the plantations. With equal determination, the former slaves had attempted to move onto small plots of land and raise food crops. They wanted independence and were not interested in raising sugar for export. The British, however—even abolitionists—judged the success of emancipation by the volume of sugar production for the world market. Their concern for the freedmen soon faded, and before long the authorities allowed planters to import indentured "coolie" labor from India.

In the United States, where white planters were far more numerous, some of the same tendencies had appeared even before the war ended. When federal forces occupied the Sea Islands, local planters had fled, leaving their slaves behind. These black people expressed a strong desire to move off the plantations and establish small, self-sufficient farms. Northern soldiers, officials, and missionaries of both races brought education and aid to the freedmen but also wanted them to grow cotton. They emphasized profit and the values of competitive capitalism. It would be "most unwise and injurious," wrote one worker in the Sea Islands, to give former slaves free land.

"The Yankees preach nothing but cotton, cotton!" complained one Sea Island black. "We wants land," wrote another, "this very land that is rich with the sweat of we face and the blood of we back." This man complained that tax officials "make the lots too big, and cut we out." Indeed, the government sold thousands of acres in the Sea Islands for nonpayment of taxes, but 90 percent of the land went to wealthy investors from the North. Even after blacks pooled their earnings, they were able to buy fewer than two thousand of the almost seventeen thousand acres sold in March 1863. Thus even from their northern supporters the former slaves had received only partial support. How much opportunity would freedom bring? That was a vital question, whose answer depended on the evolution of policy in Washington.

JOHNSON'S RECONSTRUCTION PLAN

When Reconstruction began under President Andrew Johnson, many expected his policies to be harsh. Throughout his career in Tennessee he had criticized the wealthy planters for holding down the small farmers, whose cause he championed. When an assassin's bullet thrust Johnson into the presidency, many former slaveowners shared the dismay of a North Carolina woman who wrote, "Think of Andy Johnson [as] the president! What will become of us—'the aristocrats of the South' as we are termed?" Northern Radicals also had reason to believe that Johnson would deal sternly with the South. When one of them suggested the exile or execution of ten or twelve leading rebels to set an example, Johnson replied, "How are you going to pick out so small a number? . . . *Treason* is a crime; and *crime* must be punished."

Through 1865 Johnson alone controlled Reconstruction policy, for Congress recessed shortly before he became president and did not reconvene until December. In the nearly eight months that intervened, Johnson devised and put into operation his own plan, forming new state governments in the South by using his power to grant pardons.

Wartime proposals for Reconstruction had produced much controversy but no consensus. In December 1863 Lincoln had proposed a "10 percent" plan for a government being organized in captured parts of Louisiana. Under this plan, a state government could be established as soon as 10 percent of those who had voted in 1860 took an oath of future loyalty to the Union. Only high-ranking Confederate officials would be denied a chance to take the oath, and Lincoln urged that at least a few well-qualified blacks be given the ballot. Radicals bristled, however, at such a mild plan, and Congress backed the much stiffer Wade-Davis bill, which required 50 percent of the voters to swear an "iron-clad" oath that they had never voluntarily supported the rebellion. Lincoln pocket-vetoed this measure.

Lincoln's Reconstruction Plan

Later, in 1865, Lincoln suggested but then abandoned even more lenient terms. At Hampton Roads, where he raised questions about the extent of emancipation (see page 445), Lincoln discussed compensation and restoration to the Union, with full rights, of the very state governments that had tried to leave it. In April he considered allowing the Virginia legislature to convene in order to withdraw its support from the Confederate war effort. Faced with strong opposition in his cabinet, Lincoln reversed himself, denying that he had intended to confer legitimacy on a rebel government. At the time of his death, he had given tentative approval to a plan, drafted by Secretary of War Stanton, to impose military authority and appoint provisional governors as steps toward the creation of new state governments. Beyond these general outlines, it is impossible to say what Lincoln would have done had he survived.

Johnson began with Stanton's plan. New governments would be created in the South, but which southerners would be allowed to vote? At a cabinet meeting in May 1865, Johnson's advisers split evenly on the question of voting rights for freedmen in the South. Johnson claimed that he favored black suffrage, but *only* if the southern states adopted it voluntarily. A champion of states' rights and no friend of African-Americans, he regarded this decision as too important to be taken out of the hands of the states.

This racial conservatism had an enduring effect on Johnson's policies. Where whites were

Combative and inflexible, President Andrew Johnson contributed greatly to the failure of his own reconstruction program. Library of Congress.

concerned, however, Johnson seemed to be pursuing radical changes in class relations. He proposed rules that would keep the wealthy planter class out of power. Every southern voter was required to swear an oath of loyalty as a condition of gaining amnesty or pardon, but Johnson barred several classes of southerners from taking the oath and gaining amnesty. Former federal officials who had violated their oaths to support the United States and had aided the Confederacy could not take the oath. Nor could graduates of West Point or Annapolis who had resigned their commissions to fight for the South. The same was true for high-ranking Confederate officers and political leaders. To this list Johnson added another important group: all southerners who aided the rebellion and whose taxable property was worth more than $20,000. Such individuals had to apply personally to the president for pardon and restoration of their political rights; otherwise, they risked legal penalties, which included confiscation of their land.

Oaths of Amnesty and New State Governments

Thus it appeared that the leadership class of the Old South would be removed from power, for virtually all the rich and powerful whites of prewar days needed Johnson's special pardon. Many observers in both South and North sensed that the president meant to take revenge on the haughty aristocrats whom he had always resented and to raise up a new leadership of deserving yeomen.

The provisional governors whom Johnson appointed began the Reconstruction process by calling constitutional conventions. The delegates chosen for these conventions had to draft new constitutions that eliminated slavery and invalidated secession. After ratification of these constitutions, new governments could be elected, and the states would be restored to the Union with full congressional representation. No southerner could participate in this process if he had not taken the oath of amnesty or if he had been ineligible to vote on the day the state seceded. Thus unpardoned whites and former slaves were not eligible.

If Johnson intended to strip the old elite of its power, his plan did not work as he hoped. The old white leadership proved resilient and influential; prominent Confederates (a few with pardons, but many without) won elections and turned up in various appointive offices. Then, surprisingly, Johnson helped to subvert his own plan: he started pardoning aristocrats and leading rebels who should not have been in office. By the fall of 1865 additional clerks had to be hired at the pardon office to churn out the necessary documents. These pardons, plus the return of planters' abandoned lands, restored the old elite to power.

Why did Johnson issue so many pardons? Perhaps vanity betrayed his judgment. Wealthy men of the type who had previously scorned him now waited on him for an appointment. Too long a lonely outsider, Johnson may have succumbed to the attention and flattery of the pardon seekers. He was also under great time pressure. It took months for the constitution drafting and elections to run their course; by the time the process was complete and Confederate leaders had emerged in powerful positions, the reconvening of Congress was imminent. To scrap his plan and remove the planters would be to admit failure. Since Johnson believed in white supremacy and wanted southern support in the next election, he decided to endorse the new governments and declare Reconstruction completed. Thus in December 1865 many Confederate congressmen traveled to Washington to claim seats in the U.S. Congress. Even Alexander Stephens, vice president of the Confederacy, returned to the capital as a senator-elect.

The election of such prominent rebels troubled many northerners, as did other results of Johnson's program. Some of the state conventions were slow to repudiate secession; others admitted only grudgingly that slavery was dead. Two refused to take any action to repudiate the large Confederate debt, which northerners felt should not be paid. Even Johnson admitted that these acts showed "something like defiance, which is all out of place at this time." Furthermore, to define the status of freedmen and control their labor, some legislatures merely revised large sections of the slave codes by substituting the word *freedmen* for *slave*. New laws written from scratch were also very restrictive. According to the new black codes, former slaves who were supposed to be free were compelled to carry passes, observe a curfew, live in housing provided by a landowner, and give up hope of entering many desirable occupations. Stiff vagrancy laws and restrictive labor contracts bound supposedly free laborers to plantations, and "anti-enticement" laws punished anyone who tried to lure these workers to other employment. Finally, state-supported institutions in the South, such as schools and orphanages, excluded blacks entirely. It seemed to northerners that the South was intent on returning African-Americans to a position of servility.

Black Codes

Thus it was not surprising that a majority of northern congressmen decided to take a closer look at the results of Johnson's plan. On reconvening, they voted not to admit the newly elected southern representatives, whose credentials were subject under the Constitution to congressional scrutiny. The House and Senate established a joint committee to examine Johnson's policies and advise on new ones. Reconstruction thus entered a second phase, one in which Congress would play the decisive role.

THE CONGRESSIONAL RECONSTRUCTION PLAN

Northern congressmen disagreed on what to do, but they did not doubt their right to play a role in Reconstruction. The Constitution mentioned nei-

ther secession nor reunion, but it gave Congress an important role in the federal government. Moreover, the Constitution declared that the United States shall guarantee to each state a republican government. This provision, the legislators thought, gave them the right to devise policies for Reconstruction, just as Johnson had used his power to pardon for the same purpose.

They soon found that other constitutional questions had a direct bearing on the policies they adopted. What, for example, had rebellion done to the relationship between southern states and the Union? Lincoln had always insisted that states could not secede and that the Union remained intact. Not even Andrew Johnson, however, accepted the southern position that the wartime governments of the South could simply re-enter the nation. Johnson argued that the Union had endured, though individuals had erred—thus the use of his power to grant or withhold pardons. Congressmen who favored vigorous Reconstruction measures tended to the view that war *had* broken the Union. They maintained that the southern states had committed legal suicide and reverted to the status of territories, or that the South was a conquered nation subject to the victor's will. Moderate congressmen held that the states had forfeited their rights through rebellion and had thus come under congressional supervision.

These diverse theories mirrored the diversity of Congress itself. Northern legislators fell into four major groups: Democrats, conservative Republicans, moderate Republicans, and those called Radical Republicans. No one of these groups had decisive power. Ideologically the majority of congressmen were conservative. In terms of partisan politics, the Republican party had a majority, but there were wide differences of opinion within its ranks. Conservative Republicans favored a limited federal role in Reconstruction and were fairly happy with Johnson's actions. The Radicals, led by Thaddeus Stevens, Charles Sumner, and George Julian, wanted to transform the South. Although they were a minority within their party, they had the advantage of a clearly defined goal. They believed it was essential to democratize the South, establish public education, and ensure the rights of freedmen. They favored black suffrage, often supported land confiscation and redistribution, and were willing to

The Radicals

exclude the South from the Union for several years if necessary to achieve their goals. Between the conservative Republicans and the Radicals lay the moderates, who held the balance of power.

One overwhelming political reality faced all four groups: the 1866 elections were approaching in the fall. Having questioned Johnson's program, Congress needed to develop an alternative plan and avoid going before the voters empty-handed. Thus, these politicians had to forge a majority coalition composed either of Democrats and Republicans or of various elements of the Republican party. The nature of the coalition would determine the kind of plan that Congress developed.

Johnson and the Democrats, ironically, sabotaged the possibility of a conservative coalition. They refused to cooperate with conservative or moderate Republicans and stubbornly insisted that Reconstruction was over, that the new state governments were legitimate, and that southern representatives should be admitted to Congress. These intransigent positions eliminated the Democrats' potential influence and blasted any possibility of bipartisan compromise. Bargaining over changes in Johnson's program therefore occurred within the Republican party. To devise a new program, conservative Republicans had to work with the Radicals. This development and subsequent events enhanced the Radicals' influence. In 1865, however, Republican congressmen were still reluctant to break with the president, who was, for better or for worse, the titular head of their party.

Trying to work with Johnson, Republicans thought a compromise had been reached in the spring of 1866. Under its terms Johnson would agree to two modifications of his program: an extension of the life of the Freedmen's Bureau, which Congress had established in 1865 to feed the hungry, negotiate labor contracts, and start schools, and passage of a civil-rights bill to counteract the black codes. This bill would force southern courts to practice equality before the law by giving federal judges the power to move from state courts into federal courts cases in which blacks were treated unfairly. Its provisions applied to discrimination by private individuals as well as government officials. As the first major bill to enforce the Thirteenth Amendment's abolition of slavery, it was a significant piece of

Congress Struggles for a Compromise

legislation, and it was to become very important in the twentieth century (see page 998).

Johnson destroyed the compromise, however, by vetoing both bills (they were later repassed). Denouncing any change in his program, the president condemned Congress's action. In inflammatory language he questioned the legitimacy of congressional involvement in policymaking and revealed his own racism. Because the civil rights bill defined U.S. citizens as native-born persons who were taxed, Johnson pronounced it discriminatory toward "large numbers of intelligent, worthy, and patriotic foreigners . . . in favor of the negro." The bill, he said, would "operate in favor of the colored and against the white race."

All hope of working with the president was now dead. But Republican congressmen sensed that their constituents remained dissatisfied with Reconstruction. Newspapers reported daily violations of blacks' rights in the South and carried troubling accounts of anti-black violence—notably in Memphis and New Orleans, where police aided brutal mobs in their attacks. Such violence convinced Republicans, and the northern public, that more needed to be done. The various factions of Republican lawmakers therefore continued bargaining among themselves until a plan emerged. It took the form of a proposed amendment to the Constitution and represented a compromise between radical and conservative elements of the party. The Fourteenth Amendment was Congress's alternative to Johnson's program of Reconstruction.

Of the four points in the amendment, there was near-universal agreement on one: the Confederate debt was declared null and void, and the war debt of the United States guaranteed. Northerners uniformly rejected the notion of paying taxes to reimburse those who had financed a rebellion, and business groups agreed on the necessity of upholding the credit of the U.S. government. There was also fairly general support for prohibiting prominent Confederates from holding political office. The amendment therefore barred Confederate leaders from state and federal office. Only Congress, by a two-thirds vote of each house, could remove the penalty.

Fourteenth Amendment

The first section of the Fourteenth Amendment, which would have the greatest legal significance in later years, conferred citizenship on freedmen and prohibited states from abridging their constitutional "privileges and immunities" (see the Appendix). It also barred any state from taking a person's life, liberty, or property "without due process of law" and from denying "equal protection of the laws." These clauses were phrased broadly enough to become powerful guarantees of African-Americans' civil rights—indeed, of the rights of all citizens—in the twentieth century. They also took on added meaning with court rulings that corporations were legally "persons" (see page 554).

The second section of the amendment, which dealt with representation, embodied the compromises and political motives that had produced the document. Northerners, in Congress and out, disagreed about whether black citizens should have the right to vote. As a citizen of Indiana wrote to a southern relative, there was strong feeling in favor of "humane and liberal laws for the government and protection of the colored population." But there was prejudice, too. "Although there is a great deal [of] profession among us for the relief of the darkey yet I think much of it is far from being cincere. I guess we want to compel you to do right by them while we are not willing ourselves to do so."

Republican congressmen shied away from confronting this ambivalence, but political reality required them to do something. The Constitution based congressional representation on population. Under slavery, each slave had counted as three-fifths of a person for this purpose. Emancipation made every former slave five-fifths of a person, a fact that would increase southern representation. Thus, the postwar South stood to *gain* power in Congress. And if white southerners did not allow blacks to vote, former secessionists would derive all the political benefit from emancipation.

What a strange result that would seem to most northerners! They had never planned to reward the South for rebellion, and Republicans in Congress were determined not to hand over power to their political enemies. So they offered the South a choice. According to the second section of the Fourteenth Amendment, states did not have to grant black men the right to vote. But if they did not do so, their representation would be reduced proportionally. (This clause has never been enforced, despite the clear intent of the amendment.)

If they did enfranchise black men, their representation would be increased proportionally—but, of course, Republicans could seek the support of the new black voters. This compromise protected northern interests and gave Republicans a chance to compete if freedmen gained the ballot.

The Fourteenth Amendment promoted the voting rights of black men but ignored female citizens, black and white. For this reason it provoked a strong reaction from the women's rights movement. Advocates of equal rights for women had worked with abolitionists for decades, often subordinating their cause to that of the slaves. During the drafting of the Fourteenth Amendment, however, female activists demanded to be heard. When legislators defined women as nonvoting citizens, prominent leaders such as Elizabeth Cady Stanton and Susan B. Anthony decided that it was time to end their alliance with abolitionists and fight more determinedly for themselves. Thus the amendment infused new determination into the independent women's rights movement.

In 1866, however, the major question in Reconstruction politics was how the public would respond to the amendment. Would the northern public support Congress's plan or the president's? Johnson did his best to block the Fourteenth Amendment and to convince northerners to reject it. Condemning Congress for its refusal to seat southern representatives, the president urged state legislatures in the South to vote against ratification. Every southern legislature except Tennessee's rejected the amendment by a wide margin. Its best showing was in Alabama, where it failed by a vote of 69 to 8 in the assembly and 27 to 2 in the senate. In three other states the amendment received no support at all.

Southern Rejection of the Fourteenth Amendment

To present his case to northerners, Johnson organized a National Union Convention and took to the stump himself. In an age when active personal campaigning was rare for a president, Johnson boarded a special train for a "swing around the circle" that carried his message deep into the Midwest and then back to Washington. In cities such as Cleveland and St. Louis, Johnson criticized the Republicans in a ranting, undignified style. Increasingly, audiences rejected his views and hooted and jeered at him.

The election of 1866 was a resounding victory for Republicans in Congress. Radical and moderate Republicans whom Johnson had denounced won re-election by large margins, and the Republican majority grew as new candidates defeated incumbent Democrats. The North had spoken clearly: Johnson's policies were giving the advantage to rebels and traitors. Although reformers who hoped to eliminate prejudice were only a minority, most northerners feared for "the future peace and safety of the Union." Thus Republican congressional leaders won a mandate to pursue their Reconstruction plan.

But, thanks to Johnson and southern intransigence, that plan had reached an impasse. All but one of the southern governments created by the president had rejected the Fourteenth Amendment and remained adamant. Nothing could be accomplished as long as those governments existed and the southern electorate was constituted as it was. The newly elected northern Republicans were not going to ignore their constituents' wishes and surrender to the South. To break the deadlock, Republicans had little choice but to form new governments in the South and enfranchise the freedmen. They therefore decided to do both. The unavoidable logic of the situation had forced the majority to accept part of the Radical plan.

The Radicals hoped Congress would do much more. Thaddeus Stevens, for example, argued that economic opportunity was essential to the freedmen. "If we do not furnish them with homesteads from forfeited and rebel property," Stevens declared, "and hedge them around with protective laws; if we leave them to the legislation of their late masters, we had better left them in bondage." Stevens therefore drew up a plan for extensive confiscation and redistribution of land. Only one-tenth of the land affected by his plan was earmarked for freedmen, in forty-acre plots. The rest was to be sold to generate money for veterans' pensions, compensation to loyal citizens for damaged property, and payment of the federal debt. By these means Stevens hoped to win support for a basically unpopular measure. But he failed, and in general the Radicals were not able to generate support from the public. Northerners were accustomed to a limited role for government, and the business community staunchly opposed any interference with private property rights. Thus black farmers were forced to seek work in a hostile environment in which landowners opposed their acquisition of land, even as renters.

The Reconstruction Act of 1867 incorporated only a small part of the Radical program. The act called for a return to military authority in the South until new governments could be set up. Five military districts were established, each headed by a Union general. Confederate leaders designated in the Fourteenth Amendment were barred from voting until new constitutions were ratified. The act guaranteed freedmen the right to vote in elections for state constitutional conventions and in subsequent elections under the new constitutions. In addition, each southern state was required to ratify the Fourteenth Amendment and to ratify its new constitution and submit it to Congress for approval. Thus African-Americans gained an opportunity to fight for a better life through the political process, but the only tool put into their hands was the ballot. The law required no redistribution of land and guaranteed no basic changes in southern social structure. It also permitted an early return to the Union.

Reconstruction Act of 1867

Congress's role as the architect of Reconstruction was not quite over, for its quarrels with Andrew Johnson were growing more bitter. To restrict Johnson's influence and safeguard its plan, Congress passed a number of controversial laws. First, it set the date for its own reconvening—an unprecedented act, for the president traditionally summoned legislators to Washington. Then it limited Johnson's power over the army by requiring the president to issue military orders through the General of the Army, Ulysses S. Grant, who could not be sent from Washington without the Senate's consent. Finally, Congress passed the Tenure of Office Act, which gave the Senate power to interfere with changes in the president's cabinet. Designed to protect Secretary of War Stanton, who sympathized with the Radicals, this law violated the tradition that a president controlled his own cabinet.

Johnson took several belligerent steps of his own. He issued orders to military commanders in the South limiting their powers and increasing the powers of the civil governments he had created in 1865. Then he removed officers who were conscientiously enforcing Congress's new law, preferring commanders who allowed disqualified Confeder-

Plans for Reconstruction Compared

	Johnson's Plan	Radicals' Plan	Fourteenth Amendment	Reconstruction Act of 1867
Voting	Whites only; Confederate leaders must seek pardons	Give vote to black males	Southern whites may decide but can lose representation	Black men gain vote; whites barred from office by Fourteenth Amendment cannot vote while new governments being formed
Office-holding	Many prominent Confederates regain power	Only loyal white and black males eligible	Confederate leaders barred until Congress votes amnesty	Fourteenth Amendment in effect
Time out of Union	Brief	Years; until South is thoroughly democratized	Brief	Brief
Other changes in southern society	Little; gain of power by yeomen not realized	Expand public education; confiscate land and provide farms for freedmen	Probably slight	Depends on action of new state government

ates to vote. Finally, he tried to remove Secretary of War Stanton. With that attempt the confrontation reached its climax.

Twice before, the House Judiciary Committee had considered impeachment, rejecting the idea once and then recommending it by only a 5-to-4 vote. That recommendation was decisively defeated by the House. After Johnson's last action, however, a third attempt to impeach the president carried easily. In 1868, the House was so determined to indict Johnson that it voted before drawing up specific charges. The indictment concentrated on his violation of the Tenure of Office Act, though modern scholars regard his efforts to impede enforcement of the Reconstruction Act of 1867 as a far more serious offense.

Impeachment of President Johnson

Johnson's trial in the Senate began promptly and lasted more than three months. The prosecution, led by such Radicals as Thaddeus Stevens and Benjamin Butler, attempted to prove that Johnson was guilty of "high crimes and misdemeanors." But they also argued that the trial was a means to judge Johnson's performance, not a judicial determination of guilt or innocence. The Senate ultimately rejected such reasoning, which could have made removal from office a political weapon against any chief executive who disagreed with Congress. Although a majority of senators voted to convict Johnson, the prosecution fell one vote short of the necessary two-thirds majority. Johnson remained in office, politically weakened and with only a few months left in his term. But his acquittal established the precedent that only serious misdeeds merited removal from office.

In 1869, in an effort to write democratic principles and colorblindness into the Constitution, the Radicals succeeded in presenting the Fifteenth Amendment for ratification. This measure forbade states to deny the right to vote "on account of race, color, or previous condition of servitude." Such wording did not guarantee the right to vote. It deliberately left states free to restrict suffrage on other grounds so that northern states could continue to deny suffrage to women and certain groups

Fifteenth Amendment

This lithograph celebrates the passage of the Fifteenth Amendment, which prohibited denial of the right to vote on grounds of "race, color, or previous condition of servitude." These words did not, however, guarantee the right to vote.   Library of Congress.

of men—Chinese immigrants, illiterates, and those too poor to pay taxes. Ironically, the votes of four uncooperative southern states—compelled by Congress to approve the amendment as an added condition to rejoining the Union—proved necessary to impose even this language on parts of the North. Although several states outside the South refused to ratify, the Fifteenth Amendment became law in 1870.

RECONSTRUCTION POLITICS IN THE SOUTH

From the start, Reconstruction encountered the resistance of white southerners. Their opposition to change appeared in the black codes and other poli-

White Resistance

cies of the Johnson governments as well as in private attitudes. Many whites stubbornly opposed emancipation, and—as was true in the British Caribbean—the former planter class proved espe-

cially unbending. In 1866 a Georgia newspaper frankly observed that "most of the white citizens believe that the institution of slavery was right, and . . . they will believe that the condition, which comes nearest to slavery, that can now be established will be the best." Unwillingness to accept black freedom would clearly have been a widespread problem in any circumstances; Andrew Johnson's encouragement of southern whites to resist Congress only intensified the problem.

Fearing loss of control over their slaves, some planters attempted to postpone freedom by denying or misrepresenting events. Former slaves reported that their owners "didn't tell them it was freedom" or "wouldn't let [them] go." Agents of the Freedmen's Bureau agreed. One agent in Georgia concluded, "I find the old system of slavery working with even more rigor than formerly at a few miles distant from any point where U.S. troops are stationed." To hold onto their workers, some landowners claimed control over black children and used guardianship and apprentice laws to bind black families to the plantation.

Whites also blocked blacks from acquiring land. A few planters divided up plots among their slaves, but most condemned the idea of making blacks landowners. One planter in South Carolina refused to sell as little as 1.5 acres to each family. Even a Georgia woman whose family was known for its support of religious education for slaves was outraged that two property owners planned to "rent their lands to the Negroes!" Such action was, she declared, "injurious to the best interest of the community." The son of a free black landowner in Virginia who sold nearly 200 acres to former slaves explained that "White folks wasn't lettin' Negroes have nothing." These realities severely limited the rewards of a supposedly free labor system.

Adamant resistance by propertied whites soon manifested itself in other ways, including violence. In one North Carolina town a local magistrate clubbed a black man on a public street, and bands of "Regulators" terrorized blacks in parts of that state and Kentucky. Such incidents were predictable in a society in which many planters believed, as a South Carolinian put it, that blacks "can't be governed except with the whip."

After President Johnson encouraged the South to resist congressional Reconstruction, white conservatives worked hard to capture the new state governments. Many whites also boycotted the polls in an attempt to defeat Congress's plans; since the new constitutions had to be approved by a majority of registered voters, registered whites could defeat them by sitting out the elections. This tactic was tried in North Carolina and succeeded in Alabama, forcing Congress to base ratification on a majority of those voting.

Very few black men stayed away from the polls. They seized the opportunity to participate in politics enthusiastically and hopefully, voting solidly Republican. Most agreed with one man who felt he should "stick to the end with the party that freed me." Illiteracy did not prohibit blacks (or uneducated whites) from making intelligent choices. Although Mississippi's William Henry could read only "a little," he testified that he and his friends had no difficulty selecting the Republican ballot. "We stood around and watched," he explained. "We saw D. Sledge vote; he owned half the county. We knowed he voted Democratic so we voted the other ticket so it would be Republican." Women, who could not vote, encouraged their husbands and sons, and preachers exhorted their congregations to use the franchise. Such community

Thomas Nast, in this 1868 cartoon, pictured the combination of forces that threatened the success of Reconstruction: southern opposition and the greed, partisanship, and racism of northern interests.   Library of Congress.

spirit helped to counter white pressure tactics, and zeal for voting spread through the entire black community.

Thanks to a large black turnout and the barring of prominent Confederates from politics, a new southern Republican party came to power in the constitutional conventions. Among the Republican delegates were a sizable contingent of blacks (265 out of the total of just over 1,000 delegates throughout the South), some northerners who had moved to the South, and native southern whites who favored change. Together these Republicans brought the South into line with progressive reforms that had been adopted in the rest of the nation. The new constitutions were more democratic. They eliminated property qualifications for voting and holding office, and they made elective state and local offices that had been appointive. They provided for public schools and institutions to care for

Thomas Waterman Wood, who had painted portraits of society figures in Nashville before the war, sensed the importance of Congress's decision in 1867 to enfranchise the freedmen. This oil painting, one of a series on suffrage, emphasizes the significance of the ballot for the black voter. Tennessee Botanical Gardens and Museum of Art, Nashville.

the mentally ill, the blind, the deaf, the destitute, and the orphaned. They also put an end to imprisonment for debt and to barbarous punishments such as branding.

The conventions broadened women's rights in property holding and divorce. Usually, the main goal was not to make women equal with men but to provide relief to thousands of suffering debtors. In families left poverty-stricken by the war and weighed down by debt, it was usually the husband who had contracted the debts. Thus, giving women legal control over their own property provided some protection to their families. There were some delegates, however, whose goal was to elevate

women. Blacks in particular called for laws to provide for women's suffrage, but they were ignored by their white colleagues.

Under these new constitutions the southern states elected new governments. Again the Republican party triumphed, putting new men in positions of power. For the first time in history, the ranks of state legislators in 1868 included some black southerners. Congress's second plan for Reconstruction was well under way. It remained to be seen what these new governments would do and how much social change they would bring about.

Triumph of Republican Governments

One way to achieve radical change would have been to disfranchise substantial numbers of Confederate leaders. If the Republican regimes had used their new power to exclude many whites from politics as punishment for rebellion, they would have enjoyed a solid electoral majority based on black voters and their white allies. Land reform and the assurance of racial equality would have been possible. But none of the Republican governments did this or even gave it serious consideration.

Why did the new legislators reject this course of action? First, they appreciated the realities of power and the depth of racial enmity. In most states, whites were in the majority and former slaveowners controlled the best land and other sources of economic power. James Lynch, a leading black politician from Mississippi, candidly explained why African-Americans shunned what he called the "folly" of disfranchisement. Unlike northerners who "can leave when it becomes too uncomfortable," landless former slaves "must be in friendly relations with the great body of the whites in the state. Otherwise . . . peace can be maintained only by a standing army." Despised and lacking economic or social power, southern Republicans saw mere acceptance and legitimacy as ambitious goals.

Second, blacks believed in the principle of universal suffrage and the Christian goal of reconciliation. Far from being vindictive toward the race that had enslaved them, they treated leading rebels with generosity and appealed to white southerners to adopt a spirit of fairness and cooperation. Henry McNeil Turner, like other black ministers, urged his fellow Georgians to "love whites . . . soon their prejudice would melt away, and with God for our

One notable success in Reconstruction efforts to stimulate industry was Birmingham, Alabama. Here workers cast iron into blocks called pigs.   Birmingham Public Library.

father, we will all be brothers." (Years later Turner criticized his own naiveté, saying that in the constitutional convention his motto had been "Anything to please the white folks.") Therefore southern Republicans quickly (in some cases immediately) restored the voting rights of former Confederates, as Congress steadily released more individuals from the penalties of the Fourteenth Amendment.

Thus the South's Republican party committed itself to a strategy of winning white support. To put the matter another way, the Republican party condemned itself to defeat if white voters would not cooperate. Within a few years Republicans were reduced to the embarrassment of making futile appeals to whites while ignoring the claims of their strongest supporters, blacks.

But for a time both Republicans and their opponents, who called themselves Conservatives or Democrats, moved to the center and appealed for support from a broad range of groups. Some propertied whites accepted congressional Reconstruction as a reality and declared themselves willing to compete under the new rules. While these Democrats angled for some black votes, Republicans sought to attract more white voters. And both

parties found an area of agreement in economic policies.

The Reconstruction governments devoted themselves energetically to stimulating industry. This policy reflected northern ideals, but it also sprang from a growing southern eagerness to build up the manufacturing capacity of their region. Confederates had seen how beneficial industry was to the North during the war. Accordingly, Reconstruction legislatures designed many tempting inducements to investment. Loans, subsidies, and exemptions from taxation for periods up to ten years helped to lure new industries into the region. The southern railroad system was rebuilt and expanded, and coal and iron mining made possible Birmingham's steel plants (see illustration). Between 1860 and 1880, the number of manufacturing establishments in the South nearly doubled. This emphasis on big business, however, produced higher state debts and taxes, drew money away from schools and other programs, and multiplied possibilities for corruption. It also locked Republicans into a conservative strategy. In appealing to elite whites who never

Industrialization

supported the Republican party, they lost the opportunity of making a strong class-based appeal to poorer whites.

Policies appealing to African-American voters never went beyond equality before the law. In fact, the whites who controlled the southern Republican party were reluctant to allow blacks a share of offices proportionate to their electoral strength. Aware of their weakness, black leaders did not push for revolutionary economic or social change. In every southern state, they led efforts to establish public schools but usually did not press for integrated facilities. Having a school to attend was the most important thing at the time, for the Johnson governments had excluded blacks from schools and other state-supported institutions. As a result, virtually every public school organized during Reconstruction was racially segregated, and these separate schools established a precedent. By the 1870s segregation was becoming a common but not universal practice in theaters, trains, and other public accommodations in the South.

Other Republican Policies

A few African-American politicians did fight for civil rights and integration. Most were mulattos from cities such as New Orleans or Mobile, where large populations of light-skinned free blacks had existed before the war. Their experience in such communities had made them sensitive to issues of status, and they spoke out for open and equal public accommodations. Laws requiring equal accommodations won passage throughout the Deep South, but they often went unenforced or required an injured party to bring legal action for enforcement.

Economic progress was uppermost in the minds of most freed people and black representatives from agricultural districts. Land, above all else, had the potential to benefit the former slave, but few black state legislators promoted confiscation. Some hoped that high taxes on large landowners would force portions of their estates onto the market. Small farmers' lands were protected by homestead exemptions. In fact, much land did fall into state hands for nonpayment of taxes and was offered for sale in small lots. But most freedmen had too little cash to bid against investors or speculators, and few acquired land in this way. South Carolina established a land commission, but its purpose was to assist in the purchase of land. Any widespread redistribution of land had to arise from Congress, which never supported such action.

Within a few years, as centrists in both parties met with failure, white hostility to congressional Reconstruction began to dominate. Some conservatives had always favored fierce opposition to Reconstruction through pressure and racist propaganda. They put economic and social pressure on blacks: one black Republican reported that "my neighbors will not employ me, nor sell me a farthing's worth of anything." Charging that the South had been turned over to ignorant blacks, conservatives deplored "black domination." The cry of "Negro rule" now became constant.

Such attacks were gross distortions. African-Americans participated in politics but did not dominate or control events. They were a majority in only two out of ten state conventions (transplanted northerners were a majority in one). Of the state legislatures, only in the lower house in South Carolina did blacks ever constitute a majority; among officials, their numbers were generally far inferior to their proportion in the population. Sixteen blacks won seats in Congress before Reconstruction was over, but none was ever elected governor. Only eighteen served in a high state office such as lieutenant governor, treasurer, superintendent of education, or secretary of state. Freedmen were participating in government, to be sure, but there was no justification for racist denunciations of "Ethiopian minstrelsy, Ham radicalism in all its glory."

Conservatives also stepped up their propaganda against the allies of black Republicans. "Carpetbagger," a derisive name for whites from the North, suggested an evil and greedy northern politician, recently arrived with a carpetbag into which he planned to stuff ill-gotten gains before fleeing. (The carpetbag, a popular travel bag whose frame was covered with carpet material, was presumably deep enough to hold loot stolen from southern treasuries and filched from hapless, trusting former slaves.) Immigrants from the North, who held the largest share of Republican offices, were all tarred with this brush.

Carpetbaggers and Scalawags

In fact, most northerners who settled in the South had arrived before Congress gave blacks the right to vote. They had come seeking business opportunities or a warmer climate, and most never entered politics. Those who did generally wanted to democratize the South and to introduce northern ways, such as industry, public education, and the spirit of enterprise. Hard times and ostracism by white southerners made many of these men dependent on officeholding for a living, a circumstance that increased Republican factionalism and damaged the party. Although carpetbaggers supported black suffrage and educational opportunities, most opposed social equality and integration.

Conservatives invented the term *scalawag* to discredit any native white southerner who cooperated with the Republicans. A substantial number of southerners did so, including some wealthy and prominent men. Most scalawags, however, were yeoman farmers, men from mountain areas and nonslaveholding districts that had been restive under the Confederacy. They saw that they could benefit from the education and opportunities promoted by Republicans. Banding together with freedmen, they pursued common class interests and hoped to make headway against the power of long-dominant planters. Cooperation even convinced a few scalawags that "there is but little if any difference in the talents of the two races," as one observed, and that all should have "an equal start."

Yet this black-white coalition was vulnerable to the issue of race, and most scalawags shied away from support for racial equality. Republican tax policies also cut into upcountry yeoman support, because reliance on the property tax hit many small landholders hard. In addition, poll taxes (whose proceeds were often earmarked for education) endangered the independence of subsistence farmers, pressuring them to participate in the market economy to obtain cash.

Taxation was a major problem for the Reconstruction governments. Financially the Republicans were doomed to be unpopular despite their achievements. Republicans wanted to maintain prewar services, repair the war's destruction, stimulate industry, and support important new ventures such as public schools. But the Civil War had destroyed much of the South's tax base. One category of valuable property—slaves—was entirely gone. And hundreds of thousands of citizens had lost much of the rest of their real and personal property—money, livestock, fences, and buildings—to the war. Thus an increase in taxes was necessary even to maintain traditional services, and new ventures required still higher taxes. Eventually and inevitably, Republican tax policies aroused strong opposition.

Corruption was another serious charge levied against the Republicans. Unfortunately, it was true. Many carpetbaggers and black politicians engaged in fraudulent schemes, sold their votes, or padded expenses, taking part in what scholars recognize as a nationwide surge of corruption (see page 484). Although white Democrats often shared in the guilt, and some Republicans tried to stop it, Democrats convinced many voters that scandal was the inevitable result of turning government over to unqualified blacks and greedy carpetbaggers.

All these problems hurt the Republicans, whose leaders also allowed factionalism along racial and class lines to undermine party unity. But in many southern states the deathblow came through violence. The Ku Klux Klan, a secret veterans' club that began in Tennessee, spread through the South and rapidly evolved into a terrorist organization. Its members engaged in intimidation (note the miniature coffin in the photograph on page 484) and reprisals against blacks who tried to improve their status. Violence against African-Americans had occurred throughout Reconstruction, but it became far more organized and purposeful after 1867. The Ku Klux Klan rode to frustrate Reconstruction and keep the freedmen in subjection. Nighttime harassment, whippings, beatings, and murder became common, and in some areas virtually open warfare developed despite the authorities' efforts to keep the peace.

Ku Klux Klan

Although the Klan persecuted blacks who stood up for their rights as laborers or individuals, its main purpose was political. Lawless nightriders made active Republicans the target of their attacks. Prominent white Republicans and black leaders were killed in several states. After freedmen who worked for a South Carolina scalawag started voting, terrorists visited the plantation and, in the words of one victim, "whipped every nigger man they could lay their hands on." Klansmen also attacked Union League Clubs—Republican organizations that mobilized the black vote—and schoolteachers who were aiding the freedmen.

Klan violence was not a spontaneous outburst of racism; very specific social forces shaped and

The Ku Klux Klan aimed to terrorize and intimidate its victims by violence and other methods. Mysterious regalia, such as the pointed hood (which was held up by a stick inside) contributed to a menacing atmosphere. The miniature coffin, typically left on a Republican's doorstep, conveyed a more direct threat. Collection of State Historical Museum, Mississippi Department of Archives and History. Photo by Gib Ford.

directed it. In North Carolina, for example, Alamance and Caswell counties were the sites of the worst Klan violence. They were in the Piedmont, where slim Republican majorities rested on cooperation between black voters and white yeomen, particularly those whose Unionism or discontent with the Confederacy had turned them against local Democratic officials. Together, these black and

white Republicans had ousted officials long entrenched in power. But the slim Republican majority would disappear if either whites or blacks faltered in their support.

In Alamance and Caswell counties the wealthy and powerful men who had lost their accustomed political control were the secret organization's county officers and local chieftains. They organized a deliberate campaign of terror, recruiting members and planning atrocities. By whipping up racism or frightening enough Republicans, the Ku Klux Klan could split the Republican coalition and restore a Democratic majority.

Klan violence injured Republicans across the South. No fewer than one-tenth of the black leaders who had been delegates to the 1867–1868 constitutional conventions were attacked, seven fatally. In one judicial district of North Carolina the Ku Klux Klan was responsible for twelve murders, over seven hundred beatings, and other acts of violence, including rape and arson. A single attack on Alabama Republicans in the town of Eutaw left four blacks dead and fifty-four wounded. In South Carolina five hundred masked Klansmen lynched eight black prisoners at the Union County jail, and in nearby York County the Klan committed at least eleven murders and hundreds of whippings. According to historian Eric Foner, the Klan "made it virtually impossible for Republicans to campaign or vote in large parts of Georgia."

Thus a combination of difficult fiscal problems, Republican mistakes, racial hostility, and terror brought down the Republican regimes. In most

Failure of Reconstruction

southern states so-called Radical Reconstruction lasted only a few years (see map on page 491). The most enduring failure of Reconstruction, however, was not political; it was social and economic. Reconstruction failed to alter the South's social structure or its distribution of wealth and power. Exploited as slaves, freedmen remained vulnerable to exploitation during Reconstruction. Without land of their own, they were dependent on white landowners who could and did use their economic power to compromise blacks' political freedom. Armed only with the ballot, African-Americans in the South had little chance to effect major changes.

To reform the southern social order, Congress would have had to redistribute land, but never did a majority of congressmen favor such a plan. Radical Republicans like Albion Tourgée condemned

Congress's timidity. Turning the freedman out on his own without protection, said Tourgée, constituted "cheap philanthropy." Indeed, freedmen who had to live with the consequences of Reconstruction considered it a failure. The North should have "fixed some way for us," said former slaves, but instead it "threw all the Negroes on the world without any way of getting along."

Freedom had arrived, but blacks knew they "still had to depend on the southern white man for work, food, and clothing," and it was clear that most whites were hostile. Unless Congress exercised careful supervision over the South, the situation of the freedmen was sure to deteriorate. Whenever the North lost interest, Reconstruction would collapse.

THE SOCIAL AND ECONOMIC MEANING OF FREEDOM

Black southerners entered into life after slavery hopefully and determinedly, but not naively. They had had too much experience with white people to assume that all would be easy. A Texas man recalled his father telling him, even before the war was over, "Our forever was going to be spent living among the Southerners, after they got licked." Expecting hostility, freedmen tried to gain as much as they could from their new circumstances. Often the changes they valued the most were personal—alterations in location, employer, or living arrangements that could make an enormous difference to individuals or families.

One of the first decisions was whether to leave the old plantation or remain. This meant making a judgment about where opportunities for liberty and progress were likely to be greatest. Former slaves drew on their experiences in bondage to assess the whites with whom they had to deal. Not surprisingly, cruel slaveholders usually saw their former property walk off en masse. "And let me tell you," added one man who abandoned a harsh planter, "we sure cussed ole master out before we left there." Freedmen continued to seek fair employment throughout Reconstruction, and as many as one-third changed employers at the end of a crop year.

After choosing an employer, ex-slaves reached out for valuable things in life that had been denied

them. One of these was education. Blacks of all ages hungered for the knowledge in books that had been permitted only to whites. With freedom, they started schools and filled classrooms both day and night. On log seats and dirt floors, freedmen studied their letters in old almanacs, discarded dictionaries, or whatever was available. (Note the simple construction of the Freedmen's School in the photograph.) Young children brought infants to school with them, and adults attended at night or after "the crops were laid by." Many a teacher had "to make herself heard over three other classes reciting in concert" in a small room, but the students kept coming. The desire to escape slavery's ignorance was so great that, despite their poverty, many blacks paid tuition, typically $1 or $1.50 a month. These small amounts constituted one-tenth of many people's agricultural wages and added up to more than $1 million by 1870.

Education for African-Americans

The federal government and northern reformers of both races assisted this pursuit of education. In its brief life the Freedmen's Bureau founded over four thousand schools, and idealistic men and women from the North established and staffed others. The Yankee schoolmarm—dedicated, selfless, and religious—became an agent of progress in many southern communities. Thus, with the aid of religious and charitable organizations throughout the North, freedmen began the nation's first assault on the problems created by slavery. The results included the beginnings of a public school system in each southern state and the enrollment of over 600,000 African-Americans in elementary school by 1877.

Blacks and their white allies also saw the need for colleges and universities to train teachers and equip ministers and professionals for leadership. The American Missionary Association founded seven colleges, including Fisk and Atlanta universities, between 1866 and 1869. The Freedmen's Bureau helped to establish Howard University in Washington, D.C., and northern religious groups such as the Methodists, Baptists, and Congregationalists supported dozens of seminaries, colleges, and teachers' colleges. By the late 1870s black churches had joined in the effort, founding numerous colleges despite limited resources.

Even during Reconstruction, African-American leaders often were highly educated individu-

Freed from slavery, blacks of all ages filled the schools to seek the educations that had been denied to them in bondage. Their education often cost one-tenth of each month's wages.   William Gladstone Collection.

als, many of whom came from the prewar elite of free people of color. This group had benefited from its association with wealthy whites, who were often blood relatives; some planters had given their mulatto children outstanding educations. Francis Cardozo, who served in South Carolina's constitutional convention and later as that state's secretary of the treasury and secretary of state, had attended universities in Scotland and England. P.B.S. Pinchback, who became lieutenant governor of Louisiana, was the son of a planter who had sent him to school in Cincinnati. The two black senators from Mississippi, Blanche K. Bruce and Hiram Revels, had both had privileged educations. Bruce was the son of a planter who had provided tutoring at home; Revels was the son of free North Carolina mulattos who had sent him to Knox College in Illinois. These men and many self-educated former slaves brought to political office their experience as artisans, businessmen, lawyers, teachers, and preachers.

Meanwhile, millions of former slaves concentrated on improving life on their farms and in their neighborhoods. Surrounded by an unfriendly white population, black men and women sought to insulate themselves from white interference and to strengthen the bonds of their own community. Throughout the South they devoted themselves to reuniting their families, moving away from the slave quarters, and founding black churches. Given the eventual failure of Reconstruction, the gains that African-Americans made in their daily lives often proved the most enduring.

The search for family members who had been sold away during slavery was awe-inspiring. With only shreds of information to guide them, thousands of freedmen embarked on odysseys in search of a husband, wife, child, or parent. By relying on the black community for help and information, many succeeded in their quest, sometimes almost miraculously. Others walked through several states and never found loved ones.

Reunification of African-American Families

Husbands and wives who had belonged to different masters established homes together for the first time, and parents asserted the right to raise their own children. One mother reclaimed a child whom the mistress had been raising in her own house, saying "You took her away from me and didn' pay no mind to my cryin', so now I'm takin' her back home." Another woman bristled when her old master claimed a right to whip her children, informing him that "he warn't goin' to brush none of her chilluns no more." One girl recalled that her mistress had struck her soon after freedom. As if to clarify the new ground rules, this girl "grabbed her leg and would have broke her neck." The freedmen were too much at risk to act recklessly, but, as one man put it, they were tired of punishment and "sure didn't take no more foolishment off of white folks."

Many black people wanted to minimize all contact with whites. "There is a prejudice against us . . . that will take years to get over," Reverend Garrison Frazier told General Sherman in January 1865. To avoid contact with overbearing whites who were used to supervising and controlling them, blacks abandoned the slave quarters and fanned out to distant corners of the land they worked. Some built new homes in the woods. "After the war my stepfather come," recalled Annie Young, "and got my mother and we moved out in the piney woods." Others described moving "across the creek to [themselves]" or building a "saplin house . . . back in the woods." Some rural dwellers established small all-black settlements that still exist today along the backroads of the South.

Even once-privileged slaves shared this desire for independence and social separation. One man turned down the master's offer of the overseer's house and moved instead to a shack in "Freetown." He also declined to let the former owner grind his grain for free, because it "make him feel like a free man to pay for things just like anyone else." One couple, a carriage driver and trusted house servant during slavery, passed up the fine cooking of the "big house" to move "in the colored settlement."

The other side of movement away from whites was closer communion within the black community. Freed from the restrictions and regulations of slavery, blacks could build their own institutions as they saw fit. The secret churches of slavery came out into the open; in countless communities throughout the South, ex-slaves "started a brush arbor." A brush arbor was merely "a sort of . . .

Founding of Black Churches

Born a free man and educated before the war in Illinois, Senator Hiram Revels of Mississippi took the seat formerly occupied by Jefferson Davis. A minister and fairly conservative in his views, Revels had some support among Mississippi whites.   National Portrait Gallery, Smithsonian Institution, Washington, D.C.

shelter with leaves for a roof," but the freedmen worshiped in it enthusiastically. "Preachin' and shouting sometimes lasted all day," they recalled, for the opportunity to worship together freely meant "glorious times." Within a few years independent branches of the Methodist and Baptist churches had attracted the great majority of black Christians in the South.

The desire to gain as much independence as possible also shaped the freedmen's economic arrangements. Since most former slaves lacked money to buy land, they preferred the next best thing: renting the land they worked. But few whites would consider renting land to blacks— there were strong social pressures against it—and most blacks had no means to get cash before the harvest. Thus other alternatives had to be tried.

Northerners and officials of the Freedmen's Bureau favored contracts between owners and laborers. To northerners who believed in "Free soil, Free labor, Free men," contracts and wages seemed

How do historians know

that African-Americans employed strategies to progress in postwar southern society? Professor Peter Rachleff has studied the records of the Freedmen's Saving and Trust Company to illuminate the efforts of blacks in Richmond, Virginia. These records reveal that extended kinship networks were a major resource for aid and security. Parents opened accounts for their children, to prepare for their future, or to help parents in their old age. Individuals directed that relatives could have access to their savings in time of need. "Mutual support," notes Rachleff, "flowed back and forth between parents and children, tying them together for their entire lives."   Photo: National Archives.

the key to progress. For a few years the Freedmen's Bureau helped draw up and enforce such contracts, but they proved unpopular with both races. Owners often filled the contracts with detailed requirements that reminded blacks of their circumscribed lives under slavery. Disputes frequently arose over efficiency, lost time, and other matters. Besides, cash was not readily available in the early years of Reconstruction; times were hard and the failure of Confederate banks had left the South with a shortage of credit facilities.

Black farmers and white landowners therefore turned to sharecropping, a system in which farmers kept part of their crop and gave the rest to the

Rise of the Sharecropping System

landowner while living on his property. The landlord or a merchant "furnished" food and supplies needed before the harvest, and he received payment from the crop. Republican laws gave laborers a first lien, or legal first claim, on the crop, enhancing their sense of ownership. Although landowners tried to set the laborers' share at a low level, black farmers had some bargaining power. By holding out and refusing to sign contracts at the end of the year, sharecroppers succeeded in keeping the owners' share at around one-half during Reconstruction.

The sharecropping system originated as a desirable compromise. It eased landowners' problems with cash and credit; blacks accepted it because it gave them more freedom from daily supervision. Instead of working under a white overseer, as in slavery, they farmed a plot of land on their own in family groups. But sharecropping later proved to be a disaster for all concerned. When the Democrats returned to power, they often changed the lien laws to favor landlords; when crop prices were low, landlords received their payment first, even if there was no money left over for the laborer. And in a discriminatory society whites had many opportunities to cheat sharecroppers. Owners and merchants frequently underpaid or overcharged them, and they manipulated records so that the sharecropper remained always in debt.

The fundamental problem, however, was that southern farmers were concentrating on cotton, a crop with a bright past and a dim future. During the Civil War, India, Brazil, **Overdependence** and Egypt had begun to supply **on Cotton** cotton to Britain, and not until 1878 did the South recover its prewar share of British cotton purchases. This temporary loss of markets reduced per capita income, as did a decline in the amount of labor invested by the average southern farmer. One aspect of the exploitation of slavery had been the sending of black women and children into the fields. In freedom, like their white counterparts, these women and children stayed at home when possible. Black families valued human dignity more highly than the levels of production that had been achieved under the lash.

But even as southerners grew more cotton, eventually surpassing prewar totals, their reward diminished. Cotton prices began a long decline whose causes merely coincided with the Civil War. From 1820 to 1860, world demand for cotton had grown at a rate of 5 percent per year, but from 1866 to 1895 the rate of growth slowed to only 1.3 percent per year. By 1860 the English textile industry, the world leader in production, had penetrated all the major new markets, and from that point on increases in demand were slight. As a result, when southern farmers planted more cotton they tended to depress the price.

In these circumstances overspecialization in cotton was a mistake, but for most southern farmers there was no alternative. Landowners required

sharecroppers to grow the prime cash crop, whose salability was certain. Because of the shortage of banks and credit in the South, white farmers often had to borrow from a local merchant, who insisted on cotton production to secure his loan. Thus southern agriculture slipped deeper and deeper into depression. Black sharecroppers struggled under a growing burden of debt that reduced their independence and bound them to landowners almost as oppressively as slavery had bound them to their masters. Many white farmers became debtors, too, and gradually lost their land. These were serious problems, but few people in the North were paying attention.

RECONSTRUCTION'S DECLINE AND FALL

Northerners had always been far more interested in suppressing rebellion than in aiding southern blacks, and by the early 1870s the North's partial commitment to bringing about change in the South was weakening. Criticism of the southern governments grew, new issues captured people's attention, and soon voters began to look favorably upon reconciliation with southern whites. In one state after another in the South, Democrats regained control, and they threatened to defeat Republicans in the North as well. Before long the situation had returned to "normal" in the eyes of southern whites.

The antagonism between Unionists and rebels was still very strong in 1868. That year Ulysses S. Grant, running as a Republican, defeated Horatio Seymour, a New York Democrat, for president. Grant was **Election of** not a Radical, but he realized **1868** that Congress's program represented the wishes of most northerners. He supported a platform that praised congressional Reconstruction and endorsed black suffrage in the South. (Significantly, the platform stopped short of endorsing it in the North.) The Democrats, meanwhile, vigorously denounced Reconstruction and thus renewed the sectional conflict. By associating themselves with rebellion and with Johnson's repudiated program, the Democrats went down to defeat in all but eight states, though the popular vote was fairly close.

In office Grant acted as an administrator of Reconstruction but not as its enthusiastic advocate. He vacillated in his dealings with the southern states, sometimes defending Republican regimes and sometimes currying favor with Democrats. On occasion Grant called out federal troops to stop violence or enforce acts of Congress, but only when he had to. Grant hoped to avoid confrontation with the South and to erase any image of dictatorship summoned up by his military background. In fact, neither he nor Johnson imposed anything approaching a military occupation on the South. Rapid demobilization had reduced a federal army of more than 1 million to 57,000 within a year of the surrender at Appomattox. Thereafter the number of troops in the South continued to fall, until in 1874 there were only 4,000 in the southern states outside Texas. Throughout Reconstruction, the strongest federal units were in Texas and the West, fighting Indians, not white southerners.

In 1870 and 1871 the violent campaigns of the Ku Klux Klan forced Congress to pass two Enforcement Acts and an anti-Klan law. These laws made acts by *individuals* against the civil and political rights of others a federal criminal offense for the first time. They also provided for election supervisors and permitted martial law and suspension of the writ of habeas corpus to combat murders, beatings, and threats by the Klan. But federal prosecutors used the laws rather selectively. In 1872 and 1873 Mississippi and the Carolinas saw many prosecutions, but in other states where violence flourished the laws were virtually ignored. (Meanwhile, the Republican party vigorously used the election-supervision provisions of the law to combat Democratic election fraud in northern cities.) Southern juries sometimes refused to convict Klansmen, and out of a total of 3,310 cases, only 1,143 ended in convictions. Though many Klansmen (roughly two thousand in South Carolina alone) fled their states to avoid prosecution, and the organization officially disbanded, the threat of violence did not end. Paramilitary organizations known as Rifle Clubs and Red Shirts often took the Klan's place.

Klan terrorism defied Congress in an especially clear-cut way, yet even on this issue there were ominous signs that the North's commitment to racial justice was fading. Some conservative but influential Republicans opposed the anti-Klan laws. Rejecting other Republicans' arguments that the Thirteenth, Fourteenth, and Fifteenth Amendments had made the federal government the protec-

tor of the rights of citizens, these dissenters echoed an old Democratic charge that Congress was infringing on states' rights. Lyman Trumbull of Illinois declared that the states remained "the depositories of the rights of the individual." If Congress could punish crimes like assault or murder, he asked, "what is the need of the State governments?" For years Democrats had complained of "centralization and consolidation"; now some Republicans seemed to agree with them. This opposition foreshadowed a more general revolt within Republican ranks in 1872.

Disenchanted with Reconstruction, a group calling itself the Liberal Republicans bolted the party in 1872 and nominated Horace Greeley, the well-known editor of the *New York Tribune*, for president. The Liberal Republicans were a varied group, including civil-service reformers, foes of corruption, and advocates of a lower tariff. Normally such disparate elements would not cooperate with each other, but they were united by two popular and widespread attitudes: distaste for federal intervention in the South and a desire to let market forces and the "best men" determine events there. The Democrats also gave their nomination to Greeley in 1872. The combination was not enough to defeat Grant, but it reinforced his desire to avoid confrontation with white southerners. Grant continued to use military force sparingly, and in 1875 he refused a desperate request for troops from the governor of Mississippi.

Liberal Republicans Revolt

The Liberal Republican challenge reflected growing dissatisfaction with Grant's administration. Strong-willed but politically naive, Grant made a series of poor appointments. His secretary of war, his private secretary, and officials in the Treasury and Navy departments were all involved in bribery or tax-cheating scandals. Instead of exposing the corruption, Grant defended some of the culprits. As the clamor against dishonesty in government grew, Grant's popularity and his party's prestige declined. In 1874 the Democrats recaptured the House of Representatives.

The Democratic gains further weakened congressional resolve on southern issues. Congress had already lifted the political disabilities of the Fourteenth Amendment from many former Confederates. In 1872 it had adopted a sweeping Amnesty Act, which pardoned

Amnesty Act

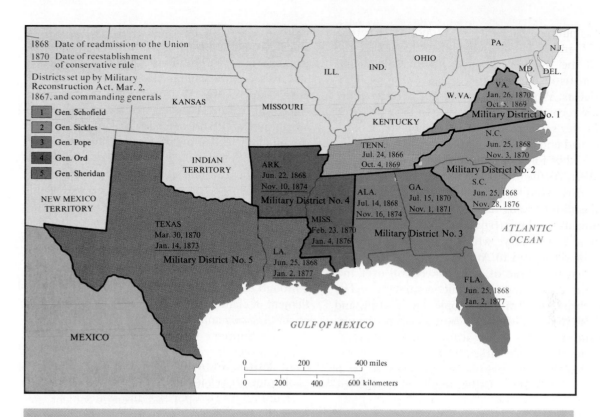

1868 Date of readmission to the Union
1870 Date of reestablishment of conservative rule
Districts set up by Military Reconstruction Act. Mar. 2. 1867, and commanding generals

1 Gen. Schofield
2 Gen. Sickles
3 Gen. Pope
4 Gen. Ord
5 Gen. Sheridan

The Reconstruction   *This map displays the five military districts established when Congress passed the Reconstruction Act of 1867. As the dates within each state indicate, conservative forces quickly regained control of government in four southern states. So-called Radical Reconstruction was curtailed in most of the others as factions within the weakened Republican party began to cooperate with Conservatives.*

most of the remaining rebels and left only five hundred barred from political officeholding. A Civil Rights Act passed in 1875 purported to guarantee black people equal accommodations in public places, such as inns and theaters, but the bill was watered down and contained no effective provisions for enforcement. (Later this law was struck down by the Supreme Court; see page 525.)

Democrats regained power in the South rather quickly, winning control of state government in four states before 1872 and a total of eight by January, 1876 (see map). Meanwhile, northern Republicans worried about their opponents' stress on the failure and scandals of Reconstruction governments. Northern magazines carried articles condemning the enfranchisement of blacks as "a wholesale creation of the most ignorant mass of voters to be found in the civilized world" (in the words of historian Brooks Adams, the grandson

and great-grandson of presidents). Many Republicans sensed that their constituents were tiring of southern issues.

In fact, new concerns were capturing the public's attention. Industrialization and immigration had both surged, hastening the pace of change in national life. Within only eight years, postwar industrial production had increased by an impressive 75 percent. For the first time, nonagricultural workers outnumbered farmers, and only Britain had a greater industrial output. Government financial policies had done much to bring about this rapid growth. Soon after the war Congress had shifted some of the government's tax revenues to pay off the interest-bearing war debt: the debt fell from $2.33 billion in 1866 to only $587 million in 1893, and every dollar repaid was a dollar injected into the economy for potential reinvestment. Thus approximately 1 percent of the gross national product was pumped back into the economy from 1866 to 1872, and only slightly less than that during the rest of the 1870s. Low taxes on investment and high tariffs on manufactured goods also aided industrialists. With such help, the northern economy quickly recovered its prewar rate of growth.

In the same period three million new immigrants had entered the country, most of them joining the labor force of industrial cities in the North and West. As the number of immigrants rose, there was a corresponding revival of ingrained suspicions and hostilities among native-born Americans. Also prominent was the question of how Utah's growing Mormon community, which practiced polygamy, could be reconciled to American law.

Then the Panic of 1873 ushered in over five years of continuing economic contraction. The panic threw three million people out of work, and the clash between labor and capital became the major issue of the day. Class attitudes diverged, especially in the larger cities. Debtors and the unemployed sought easy-money policies to spur economic expansion. Businessmen, disturbed by the strikes and industrial violence that accompanied the panic, became increasingly concerned about the defense of property.

The monetary issue aroused particularly strong controversy. Keeping Civil War paper money—called greenbacks—in circulation could expand the money supply and

Greenbacks versus Sound Money

raise prices. In 1872, Democratic farmers and debtors had urged such a policy, but they were overruled by "sound money" men—businessmen, bankers, and creditors. Now hard times swelled the ranks of the "greenbackers"—voters who favored greenbacks and easy money. Congress voted in 1874 to increase the number of greenbacks in circulation, but Grant vetoed the bill in deference to the opinions of financial leaders. The next year sound-money interests prevailed in Congress, winning passage of a law requiring that greenbacks be convertible into gold after 1878. This law limited the inflationary impact of the greenbacks and aided creditors rather than debtors (such as the hard-pressed and angry farmers).

In international affairs, meanwhile, there was renewed pressure for, and controversy about, expansion (see Chapter 22). In 1867 Secretary of State William H. Seward accomplished a major addition of territory to the national domain by arranging to purchase Alaska from the Russian government for $7.2 million. Opponents ridiculed Seward's venture, calling Alaska Frigidia, the Polar Bear Garden, and Walrussia. But Seward convinced important congressmen of Alaska's economic potential, and other lawmakers favored the dawning of friendship with Russia. The same year, the United States took control of the Midway Islands, a thousand miles from Hawaii. (They were scarcely mentioned again until the Second World War.) And in 1870, President Grant tried to annex the Dominican Republic, but Senator Charles Sumner blocked the attempt. Seward and his successor, Hamilton Fish, also resolved troubling Civil War grievances against Great Britain. Through diplomacy they arranged a financial settlement of claims on Britain for permitting the sale of the *Alabama* and other Confederate cruisers.

The Supreme Court also participated in the northern retreat from Reconstruction. During the Civil War the Court had been cautious and reluctant to assert itself. Reaction to the Dred Scott decision (see page 414) had been so violent, and the Union's wartime emergency so great, that the Court had refrained from blocking or interfering with government actions. The justices had breathed a collective sigh of relief, for example, when legal technicalities prevented them from reviewing the case of Clement Vallandigham, who had been convicted of aiding the enemy (see page 455).

But in 1866 a similar case, *Ex parte Milligan*, reached the Court through proper channels. Lambdin P. Milligan of Indiana had participated in a plot to free Confederate prisoners of war and overthrow state governments; for these acts a military court had sentenced Milligan, a civilian, to death. Milligan challenged the authority of the military tribunal, claiming that he had a right to a civil trial. The Supreme Court declared that military trials were illegal when civil courts were open and functioning, and the sweeping language of the decision indicated that the Court intended to reassert itself as a major force in national affairs. This case could have led to a direct clash with Congress, which established military districts and military courts in the 1867 Reconstruction Act. But Congress altered part of the Court's jurisdiction, removing such matters from its purview. Congress was constitutionally empowered to do so but had never taken such action before (and has not done so since). By altering the Court's jurisdiction, Congress protected its Reconstruction policy and avoided a confrontation.

By the 1870s, however, Congress was ready to acquiesce as the Supreme Court drastically narrowed the meaning and effectiveness of the Fourteenth Amendment. In 1873

Supreme Court Decisions on Reconstruction
———

the Court decided *Bradwell* v. *Illinois*, a case in which Myra Bradwell, a female attorney, had been denied the right to practice law in Illinois on account of her gender. Pointing to the Fourteenth Amendment, Bradwell's attorneys contended that the state had unconstitutionally abridged her "privileges and immunities" as a citizen. The Supreme Court rejected her claim, alluding to women's traditional role in the home.

The previous day, in the *Slaughter-House* cases, the Court had made its restrictive reading of the Fourteenth Amendment even more explicit. The *Slaughter-House* cases had arisen in 1869, when the Louisiana legislature granted one company a monopoly on the slaughtering of livestock in New Orleans. Rival butchers in the city promptly sued. Their attorney, former Supreme Court Justice John A. Campbell, pointed out that Louisiana had discriminated, violating the rights of some of its citizens in favor of others. More fundamentally, Campbell argued that the Fourteenth Amendment had revolutionized the constitutional system by bringing individual rights under federal protection. Campbell thus articulated an original goal of the Republican party: to nationalize civil rights and guard them from state interference. Over the years his argument would win acceptance, offering shelter from government regulation to corporate "persons" in the nineteenth century and providing protection for blacks and other minorities in the twentieth.

But in the *Slaughter-House* decision, the Supreme Court dealt a stunning blow to the scope and vitality of the Fourteenth Amendment and to the hopes of blacks. Refusing to accept Campbell's argument, it interpreted the "privileges and immunities" of citizens so narrowly that it reduced them almost to trivialities. State citizenship and national citizenship were separate, the Court declared. National citizenship involved only such matters as the right to travel freely from state to state and to use the navigable waters of the nation, and only these narrow rights were protected by the Fourteenth Amendment. With this interpretation, the words "No state shall make or enforce any law which shall abridge the privileges or immunities of citizens of the United States" disappeared, from that day until now, as a meaningful and effective part of the Constitution.

The Supreme Court also concluded that the butchers who sued had not been deprived of their rights or property in violation of the "due process" clause of the amendment. Shrinking from a role as "perpetual censor upon all legislation of the States, on the civil rights of their own citizens," the court's majority declared that the framers of the recent amendments had not intended to "destroy" the federal system, in which the states exercised "powers for domestic and local government, including the regulation of civil rights." Thus the justices dismissed Campbell's central contention and severely limited the amendment's potential for securing and protecting the rights of black citizens.

In 1876 the Court weakened the Reconstruction-era amendments even further by emasculating the enforcement clause of the Fourteenth Amendment and revealing deficiencies inherent in the Fifteenth Amendment. In *United States* v. *Cruikshank* the Court dealt with Louisiana whites convicted under the 1870 Enforcement Act of attacking a meeting of blacks and conspiring to deprive them of their rights. The justices ruled that the Fourteenth Amendment did not empower the federal government to act against whites who were oppressing blacks. The duty of protecting citizens' equal rights "was originally assumed by the States; and it still remains there." As for the protection of "unalienable rights," the Court said that "Sovereignty, for this purpose, rests alone with the States." In *United States* v. *Reese* the Court noted that the Fifteenth Amendment did not guarantee a citizen's right to vote but merely listed certain impermissible grounds for denying suffrage. Thus a path lay open for southern states to disfranchise blacks for supposedly nonracial reasons—lack of education, lack of property, or lack of descent from a grandfather qualified to vote before the Military Reconstruction Act. (So-called grandfather clauses became a means to give the vote to illiterate whites while excluding blacks, because the grandfathers of most black people had been slaves before Reconstruction and unable to vote.)

THE "STRONG" GOVERNMENT 1869–1877.   THE "WEAK" GOVERNMENT 1877–1881.

These cartoons reveal the North's readiness to give up on a strong Reconstruction policy. According to the images on the left, only federal bayonets could support the "rule or ruin" carpetbag regimes that oppressed the South. What do the background and foreground of the cartoon on the right suggest will be the results of Hayes' "Let 'Em Alone Policy"? Library of Congress.

As the 1876 elections approached, it was obvious to most political observers that the North was no longer willing to pursue the goals of Reconstruction. The results of a disputed presidential election confirmed this fact. Samuel J. Tilden, the Democratic governor of New York, ran strongly in the South and took a commanding lead in both the popular vote and the electoral college over Rutherford B. Hayes, the Republican nominee. Tilden won 184 electoral votes and needed only one more for a majority. Nineteen votes from Louisiana, South Carolina, and Florida were disputed; both Democrats and Republicans claimed to have won in those states despite fraud on the part of their opponents. One vote from Oregon was undecided due to a technicality (see map).

Election of 1876

To resolve this unprecedented situation, on which the Constitution gave no guidance, Congress established a fifteen-member electoral commission. In the interest of impartiality, membership on the commission was to be balanced between Democrats and Republicans. But one independent Republican, Supreme Court Justice David Davis, refused appointment in order to accept his election as a senator. A regular Republican took his place, and the Republican party prevailed 8 to 7 on every decision, along strict party lines. Hayes would become president if Congress accepted the commission's findings.

Congressional acceptance, however, was not certain. Democrats controlled the House and could filibuster to block action on the vote. Many citizens worried that the nation had entered a major constitutional crisis and would slip once again into civil war. The crisis was resolved when Democrats acquiesced in the election of Hayes. Scholars have found evidence of negotiations between Hayes supporters and southerners who wanted federal aid to railroads, internal improvements, federal patronage, and removal of troops from southern states. But studies of Congress conclude that these negotiations did not have a deciding effect on the outcome: neither party was well enough organized to implement and enforce a bargain between the sections. Northern and southern Democrats simply decided they could not win and did not contest the election. Thus Hayes became president, and southerners looked forward to the withdrawal of federal troops from the South. In 1877 Reconstruction was unmistakably over.

Southern Democrats rejoiced, but African-Americans grieved over the betrayal of their hopes for equality. Tens of thousands considered leaving the South, where freedom was

Exodusters Move West
———

no longer a real possibility. "[We asked] whether it was possible we could stay under a people who had held us in bondage," said Henry Adams, who led a migration to Kansas. "[We] appealed to the President . . . and to Congress . . . to protect us in our rights and privileges," but "in 1877 we lost all hopes." Thereafter many black southerners "wanted to go to a territory by ourselves." In South Carolina, Louisiana, Mississippi, and other southern states, thousands gathered up their possessions and migrated to Kansas. They were known as Exodusters, disappointed people still searching for their share in the American dream. Even in Kansas they met disillusionment, as the welcome extended by the state's governor soon gave way to hostile public reactions.

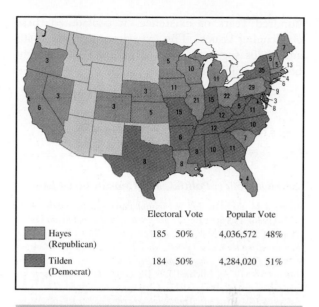

	Electoral Vote		Popular Vote	
Hayes (Republican)	185	50%	4,036,572	48%
Tilden (Democrat)	184	50%	4,284,020	51%

Presidential Election, 1876 *In 1876 a combination of solid southern support and Democratic gains in the North gave Samuel Tilden the majority of popular votes, but Rutherford B. Hayes won the disputed election in the electoral college.*

Thus the nation ended over fifteen years of bloody Civil War and controversial Reconstruction without establishing full freedom for African-Americans. This contradictory record typified the results of Reconstruction in many other ways. A tumultuous period had brought tremendous change, and yet many things remained the same. Because extraordinary situations had, for a time, required revolutionary changes, the North had acted. The Union victory brought about an increase in federal power, stronger nationalism, unprecedented federal intervention in the southern states, and landmark amendments to the Constitution. Yet, because there was no commitment to make these changes endure, the revolution remained partial.

The North had embraced emancipation, black suffrage, a powerful central government, and significant constitutional amendments. But it did so in order to defeat the rebellion, secure the peace, and prevent the rebellion from re-emerging. As the pressure of these crises declined, strong underlying continuities emerged and placed their mark on Reconstruction. The American people and the courts maintained a preference for state authority and a distrust of federal power. The ideology of free la-

bor dictated that property should be respected and that individuals should take care of themselves without much help from government. Racism endured and the black minority faced a difficult challenge in gaining the attention of the white majority. Concern for the human rights of African-Americans was strongest when their plight involved some danger to the interests of whites, and reform frequently had less appeal than money making in a diverse, individualistic, and enterprising society.

Thus the status of African-Americans would continue to be a major social and political issue. And a host of other issues would arise from industrialization. How would the country develop its immense resources in a growing and increasingly interconnected national economy? How would farmers, industrial workers, immigrants, and capitalists fit into the new social system? Industrialization promised not just a higher standard of living but also a different lifestyle in both urban and rural areas. Moreover, it increased the nation's power and laid the foundation for an enlarged American role in international affairs. Americans' thoughts again turned to expansion and the conquest of new frontiers. As the United States entered its second hundred years of existence, it confronted these challenging issues. The experiences of the 1860s and 1870s suggested that solutions, if any, might be neither clear nor complete.

SUGGESTIONS FOR FURTHER READING

National Policy, Politics, and Constitutional Law

Richard H. Abbott, *The Republican Party and the South, 1855–1877* (1986); Herman Belz, *Emancipation and Equal Rights* (1978); Herman Belz, *A New Birth of Freedom* (1976); Herman Belz, *Reconstructing the Union* (1969); Michael Les Benedict, *A Compromise of Principle: Congressional Republicans and Reconstruction, 1863–1869* (1974); Michael Les Benedict, *The Impeachment and Trial of Andrew Johnson* (1973); Charles S. Campbell, *The Transformation of American Foreign Relations, 1865–1900* (1976); Adrian Cook, *The Alabama Claims* (1975); Michael Kent Curtis, *No State Shall Abridge* (1987); David Donald, *Charles Sumner and the Rights of Man* (1970); Harold M. Hyman, *A More Perfect Union* (1973); Ronald J. Jensen, *The Alaska Purchase and Russian-American Relations* (1975); William S. McFeely, *Grant* (1981); William S. McFeely, *Yankee Stepfather: General O. O. Howard and the Freedmen* (1968); Eric L. McKitrick, *Andrew Johnson and Reconstruction* (1966); James M. McPherson, *The Abolitionist Legacy* (1975); Brooks D. Simpson, *Let Us Have Peace* (1991); Kenneth M. Stampp, *The Era of Reconstruction* (1965); Hans L. Trefousse, *Andrew Johnson* (1989).

The Freed Slaves

Roberta Sue Alexander, *North Carolina Faces the Freedmen* (1985); Ira Berlin, ed., *Freedom: A Documentary History of Emancipation, 1861–1867* (1984); Elizabeth R. Bethel, *Promiseland* (1981); Orville Vernon Burton, *In My Father's House Are Many Mansions* (1985); Edmund L. Drago, *Black Politicians and Reconstruction in Georgia* (1982); Paul D. Escott, *Slavery Remembered* (1979); Eric Foner, "Reconstruction and the Crisis of Free Labor," in *Politics and Ideology in the Age of the Civil War*, ed. Eric Foner (1980); Gerald Jaynes, *Branches Without Roots: The Genesis of the Black Working Class in the American South, 1862–1882* (1986); Peter Kolchin, *First Freedom* (1972); Leon Litwack, *Been in the Storm So Long* (1979); Edward Magdol, *A Right to the Land* (1977); Robert Morris, *Reading, 'Riting and Reconstruction* (1981); Howard Rabinowitz, ed., *Southern Black Leaders in Reconstruction* (1982); C. Peter Ripley, *Slaves and Freedmen in Civil War Louisiana* (1976); Willie Lee Rose, *Rehearsal for Reconstruction* (1964); Emma Lou Thornbrough, ed., *Black Reconstructionists* (1972); Okon Uya, *From Slavery to Public Service* (1971); Clarence Walker, *A Rock in a Weary Land* (1982).

Politics and Reconstruction in the South

Robert W. Coakley, *The Role of Federal Military Forces in Domestic Disorders, 1789–1878* (1988); Richard N. Current, *Those Terrible Carpetbaggers* (1988); Jonathan Daniels, *Prince of Carpetbaggers* (1958); W.E.B. Du Bois, *Black Reconstruction* (1935); Paul D.

Escott, *Many Excellent People: Power and Privilege in North Carolina, 1850–1900* (1985); W. McKee Evans, *Ballots and Fence Rails: Reconstruction on the Lower Cape Fear* (1966); Michael W. Fitzgerald, *The Union League Movement in the Deep South* (1989); Eric Foner, *Reconstruction: America's Unfinished Revolution, 1863–1877* (1988); Eric Foner, *Nothing but Freedom* (1983); William C. Harris, *William Woods Holden, Firebrand of North Carolina Politics* (1988); William C. Harris, *The Day of the Carpetbagger* (1979); Thomas Holt, *Black over White: Negro Political Leadership in South Carolina During Reconstruction* (1977); J. Morgan Kousser and James M. McPherson, eds., *Region, Race and Reconstruction* (1982); Robert Manson Myers, ed., *The Children of Pride* (1972); Elizabeth Studley Nathans, *Losing the Peace* (1968); Michael Perman, *The Road to Redemption* (1984); Michael Perman, *Reunion Without Compromise* (1973); Lawrence N. Powell, *New Masters* (1980); George C. Rable, *But There Was No Peace* (1984); James Roark, *Masters Without Slaves* (1977); James Sefton, *The United States Army and Reconstruction, 1865–1877* (1967); Mark W. Summers, *Railroads, Reconstruction, and the Gospel of Prosperity* (1984); Allen Trelease, *White Terror* (1967); Ted Tunnell, *Carpetbagger from Vermont* (1989); Ted Tunnell, *Crucible of Reconstruction* (1984); Michael Wayne, *The Reshaping of Plantation Society* (1983); Sarah Woolfolk Wiggins, *The Scalawag in Alabama Politics, 1865–1881* (1977).

Women, Family, and Social History

Virginia I. Burr, ed., *The Secret Eye* (1990); Ellen Carol Dubois, *Feminism and Suffrage* (1978); Herbert G. Gutman, *The Black Family in Slavery and Freedom, 1750–1925* (1976); Elizabeth Jacoway, *Yankee Missionaries in the South* (1979); Jacqueline Jones, *Labor of Love, Labor of Sorrow* (1985); Jacqueline Jones, *Soldiers of Light and Love* (1980); Robert C. Kenzer, *Kinship and Neighborhood in a Southern Community* (1987); Mary P. Ryan, *Women in Public* (1990); Rebecca Scott, "The Battle over the Child," *Prologue* 10 (Summer 1978): 101–113.

The End of Reconstruction

Michael Les Benedict, "Southern Democrats in the Crisis of 1876–1877," *Journal of Southern History* 66 (November 1980): 489–524; William Gillette, *Retreat from Reconstruction, 1869–1879* (1980); William Gillette, *The Right to Vote* (1969); Keith Ian Polakoff, *The Politics of Inertia* (1973); John G. Sproat, *"The Best Men": Liberal Reformers in the Gilded Age* (1968); C. Vann Woodward, *Reunion and Reaction* (1951).

Reconstruction's Legacy for the South

Robert G. Athearn, *In Search of Canaan* (1978); Edward L. Ayers, *The Promise of the New South* (1992); Norman L. Crockett, *The Black Towns* (1979); Stephen J. DeCanio, *Agriculture in the Postbellum South* (1974); Steven Hahn, *The Roots of Southern Populism* (1983); Jay R. Mandle, *The Roots of Black Poverty* (1978); Nell Irvin Painter, *Exodusters* (1976); Howard Rabinowitz, *Race Relations in the Urban South, 1865–1890* (1978); Roger L. Ransom and Richard Sutch, *One Kind of Freedom* (1977); Laurence Shore, *Southern Capitalists* (1986); Peter Wallenstein, *From Slave South to New South* (1987); Jonathan M. Wiener, *Social Origins of the New South* (1978); C. Vann Woodward, *Origins of the New South* (1951).

The Transformation of the West and South, 1877–1892

THEY CALLED THEMSELVES DINE', which meant "The People." The Spanish had named them *Apaches de Nabahu*, or "Strangers of the Cultivated Fields." White Americans called them *Navahos*. They lived in what would become northern Arizona and New Mexico and devoted themselves to achieving *k'e*—a universal harmony of love, peace, and cooperation. *K'e* was symbolized by motherhood and by everything that was life giving. Among the Navahos, said one of their tribespeople, "the earth is called mother, the sheep herd is called mother, corn is called mother, and the sacred mountain soil bundle is called mother." They tried to achieve *k'e* by living in unity with the land and all other facets of nature.

White people did not share the Navaho reverence for the earth. When they moved into territory inhabited by Navahos and other tribal peoples, whites took more than they needed simply to survive. They cut open the earth to remove tons of minerals, cut down forests for lumber to build homes, dammed the rivers, and plowed the soil to grow crops to sell at distant markets. The Indians did not understand why white people urged them to adopt these practices and im-

prove their lives by creating material wealth. When told he must grow crops for profit, a member of the Comanche tribe (who like the Navahos believed in the order of the natural environment) replied, "The earth is my mother. Do you give me an iron plow to wound my mother's breast? Shall I take a scythe and cut my mother's hair?" Whites, confronted with tribal resistance to their plans, responded with brutal violence.

Indian subsistence cultures withered in the face of coercive government policies and the triumph of market economies when white Americans transformed the western frontier in the late nineteenth century. The term *West* has had a shifting meaning in American history. In the eighteenth century, it meant the area beyond the Appalachian Mountains. By the late nineteenth century, it usually referred to the entire area between the Mississippi River and the Pacific Ocean, including the flat Plains region between the Mississippi and the Rockies, the Rocky Mountain regions themselves, and the mountains and valleys of the Far West. Between 1870 and 1890, settlement of the West proceeded at a furious pace. In those years, the population living between the Mississippi River and the Pacific Ocean swelled from 7 million to nearly 17 million. Growth charac-

A painting by the artist Thomas Moran (1874) shows a solitary American Indian dwarfed, but not threatened, by nature.

terized the new areas of the South as well. Shortly after Reconstruction ended, cotton production reached pre-Civil War levels and people were finding new ways to profit from the region's abundant natural resources.

By 1890 farms, ranches, mines, towns, and cities could be found in almost every corner of the present-day continental United States, some of which consisted of territories not yet eligible for statehood. That year, the superintendent of the census acknowledged that

> up to and including 1880, the country had a frontier of settlement, but at present the unsettled area has been so broken into by isolated bodies of settlement that there can hardly be said to be a frontier line. In the discussion of its extent and its westward movement, etc., it can not therefore, any longer have a place in the census reports.

What had happened to the frontier and what effect did its disappearance have on the nation?

In popular thought, the frontier represented the birthplace of American individualism. Historian Frederick Jackson Turner, influenced by the 1890 census announcement, asserted in "The Significance of the Frontier in American History" (1893) that the West, not the East or Europe, held the key to American character. According to Turner, as pioneers and settlers moved steadily across the continent, breaking through new frontiers at each stage, the environment of the West gave repeated rebirth to the American spirit. "What the Mediterranean Sea was to the Greeks," Turner exclaimed, "breaking the bonds of custom, offering new experiences, calling out new institutions and activities, that and more, the ever retreating frontier has been to the United States."

Conquering the wilderness and bringing forth food and raw materials, not to mention building cities within a single generation, filled white Americans with a sense of power and a faith that anyone eager and persistent enough could succeed. They spread their market economy across the North American continent—finding and extracting raw materials, harnessing water supplies for productive use, building railroads that carried raw materials to markets and manufactured products to farmers and miners, mechanizing agriculture to make the Plains the nation's breadbasket and meat supplier, and expanding both agriculture and industry in the South. In doing so, Americans exhibited their worst as well as their best character-

istics. Their self-confidence was easily transformed into an arrogant belief that white Americans were somehow special, and individualism often asserted itself at the expense of racial minorities and people without property—and at the expense of the environment. Americans rarely thought about conserving resources because there was always more territory to exploit and bring into the market economy.

The fading of the frontier, though of great symbolic importance, had little direct impact on people's behavior because vast stretches of land remained unsettled. Millions of people continued to stream into the West, and more land in the South fell under cultivation. Settlers who failed in one region rarely perished; they moved on and tried again somewhere else. Although life in the West was less comfortable than settlers might have wished, and the South failed to fulfill its potential, the western and southern frontiers gave Americans the feeling that they would always have a second chance. The belief in an infinity of second chances left a deep imprint on the American character.

THE TRANSFORMATION OF NATIVE AMERICAN CULTURES

Historians once defined the American frontier as "the edge of the unused," implying that the frontier faded when open land began to be used for farming or the building of cities. Now scholars emphasize that Native American tribes were using the land long before other Americans migrated there. Neither passive nor impotent in the face of nature, western Indians had been shaping their environment for centuries. Nevertheless, almost all tribal economic systems failed in the late nineteenth century. Why and how did these declines happen?

Western tribes' cultures varied—some were nomadic, others more settled—but all based their economies to differing degrees on four activities:

Subsistence Cultures

crop raising; livestock raising; hunting, fishing, and gathering; and raiding. Corn was the most common crop; sheep and horses, acquired from Spanish colonizers, were the livestock; and buffalo were the primary prey of hunts. Tribes raided each other for food, hides, and slaves. They also warred with and displaced each other over hunting grounds and

• Important Events •

1862	Homestead Act grants free land to citizens who live on and cultivate the land for five years Morrill Land Grant Act gives states public lands to finance agricultural and industrial colleges
1869	First transcontinental railroad, the Union Pacific, completed
1874	Barbed-wire fence patented, enabling easier control of cattle herds
1876	Custer's Last Stand (Battle of Little Big Horn): Sioux annihilate white troops led by Colonel George A. Custer
1878	Timber and Stone Act allows citizens to buy timber land cheaply but also enables large companies to acquire huge tracts of forest land
1880–81	George Manypenny's *Our Indian Wards* indicts the government's treatment of Indians Helen Hunt Jackson's *A Century of Dishonor* influences public conscience about poor government treatment of Indians
1882–83	Transcontinental routes of Santa Fe, Southern Pacific, and Northern Pacific railroads completed
1883	Supreme Court, in *Civil Rights Cases*, strikes down 1875 Civil Rights Act and reinforces claim that the federal government cannot regulate behavior of private individuals in matters of race relations National time zones standardized
1887	Dawes Severalty Act dissolves tribal lands and grants land allotments to individual families Hatch Act provides for agricultural experiment stations in every state
1889	Statehood granted to North Dakota, South Dakota, Washington, and Montana
1890	Wounded Knee massacre: final suppression of Plains tribes by U.S. Army Census Bureau announces closing of the frontier Statehood granted to Wyoming and Idaho Yosemite National Park established
1896	*Plessy* v. *Ferguson* upholds doctrine of "separate but equal" among blacks and whites in public facilities Rural Free Delivery made available Statehood granted to Vermont
1899	*Cummins* v. *County Board of Education* applies "separate but equal" doctrine to public schools

in defense of property. The goal of all these activities was *subsistence*, the maintenance of life at its most basic level. To achieve subsistence, Indians tried to balance their economic systems. Thus when a buffalo hunt failed, a tribe could still subsist on crops; when its crops failed, the tribe could still hunt buffalo and steal food in a raid on another tribe. Indians also traded with each other and with whites, mainly to obtain such necessities as horses and furs.

For Indians on the Plains, whether they were nomads such as the Lakotas (Sioux) or village-dwellers such as the Pawnees, everyday life focused on the buffalo. They cooked and preserved buffalo meat; fashioned hides into clothing, shoes, and blankets; used sinew for thread and bow-strings; and carved tools from bones and horns. The tribes also depended heavily on horses, which can be seen in the early photograph of a Sioux camp in South Dakota on page 502. Horses were used for transportation, and hunting, and symbols of wealth. To provide food for their herds, Pawnees and other tribes often set fire to tall-grass prairies. The fires burned away dead growth, facilitating new growth of grass in the spring so horses could feed all summer.

In the Southwest, Indians placed great value on sheep, goats, and horses. Old Man Hat, a Navaho, explained, "The herd is money. . . . You know that you have some good clothing; the sheep gave you that. And you've just eaten different kinds of food; the sheep gave that food to you.

This Sioux camp in South Dakota, photographed in 1891, typifies Sioux nomadic life; they carried out their subsistence economy in harmony with the natural environment. When they packed up and moved on, they left the landscape almost undisturbed. The photograph shows the temporary situation characteristic of their camps.   Library of Congress.

Everything comes from the sheep." He was not speaking of money in a business sense, though. To the Navahos, the herds were a means to achieve security. Like many Indians, they emphasized generosity and distrusted private property and wealth. Within the family, sharing was expected; outside the family, gifts and reciprocity governed personal relations.

This world of subsistence and ecological balance began to dissolve when whites entered the West to extract minerals and plow the soil. Perceiving the buffalo and the Indians as hindrances to their ambitions on the Plains, whites endeavored to eliminate both. As one U.S. army officer put it, "Kill every buffalo you can. Every buffalo dead is an Indian gone." Railroads sponsored hunts in which eastern sportsmen shot at the bulky targets from slow-moving trains. Some hunters collected $1 to $3 from tanneries for hides; others did not even stop to pick up their kill. By the 1880s only a few hundred remained of the estimated thirteen

Slaughter of Buffalo

million buffalo that had existed in 1850. As the buffalo herds dwindled, Pawnees and other Plains tribes had to hunt farther from their villages. In so doing, they clashed with rival tribes over scarce buffalo and left their own settlements vulnerable to raids by hostile tribes seeking food. The scarcity of buffalo disturbed the subsistence system by leaving Indians less food to supplement their diets if their crops failed or were stolen.

Government policy reinforced private efforts to remove Indians from the path of white ambitions. Since the treaty of Greenville in 1795, American government officials had considered Indian tribes to be separate nations with whom they could make treaties that ensured peace and defined the boundaries between tribal and white lands. But treaties seldom guaranteed the Indians' future land rights; whites assumed that eventually they could settle wherever they wished. As white settlers pressed into Indian territories in the West, treaties made one week were violated the next. Some tribes acquiesced; others resisted with attacks on settlements, herds, and troops. Whites responded with murders and massacres of entire villages. At Sand Creek, Colorado, in 1864 U.S. troops murdered about 150 Cheyennes, mostly women and children. In addition, whites openly stole Indian land claims and sold them smallpox-infested blankets and spoiled meat.

By the 1870s, federal officials and humanitarians, seeking more peaceful means of dealing with western tribes, began promoting policies that would treat Indians more like blacks and immigrants; instead of being considered foreign nations, the tribes would be "civilized" and "uplifted" through education. With government encouragement, white missionaries and teachers would attempt to inculcate in Indians the values of the white mobility ethic: ambition, thrift, and materialism. To achieve this transformation, however, Indians would have to abandon their traditional cultures.

From the 1860s to the 1880s, the federal government tried to force Indians onto reservations, where, it was thought, they could best be civilized.

Reservation Policy
———

Reservations usually consisted of those areas of a tribe's previous territory that were least desirable to whites (see map, page 513). In assigning Indians to specific territories, the government promised protection from white encroachment and agreed to provide food, clothing, and other necessities.

Buffalo kills and reservation policy were both means to extend the influence of the market economy, which more than any other feature of Anglo-American culture undermined tribal subsistence systems. In the early years of contact, trade had benefited both Indians and whites and had taken place on a nearly equal footing. Indians acquired clothing, guns, and tools in return for wool, hides, and, sometimes, military service. Gradually, however, the whites' needs and economic power grew disproportionate to the needs and power of Indians. The Indians became more dependent, and whites increasingly dictated what was to be traded and on what terms, and how the traded goods were to be used. To satisfy whites, for example, Navahos sold wool and hand-made blankets. White traders persuaded Navaho weavers to produce heavy rugs suitable for eastern customers and to adopt new designs and colors to boost sales. Meanwhile Navahos raised fewer crops and were forced to buy food because the market economy lured them away from subsistence agriculture. Soon

Intent on removing the huge buffalo herds that impeded their settlement, white Americans engaged in an orgy of killing. Some hunters removed the buffalo hides in order to sell them but left hundreds of thousands of carcasses to rot on the plains. Library of Congress.

tribespeople were selling their land and labor to whites as well, which made it easier to force them onto reservations.

Reservation policy had disturbing consequences. First, Indians had no say over their own affairs on reservations. Supreme Court decisions in 1884 and 1886 denied them the right to become U.S. citizens, leaving them unprotected by the Fourteenth and Fifteenth Amendments, which had extended to African-Americans the rights of citizenship. Second, it was impossible to protect reservations from the white farmers, miners, and herders who continually sought even remote Indian lands for their own purposes. Third, the government ignored tribal integrity, even combining on the same reservation tribes who had habitually waged war with each other. Rather than serving as civilizing communities, reservations came to resemble antebellum slave quarters.

Not all tribes succumbed to market forces and reservation restrictions. Pawnees, for example, resisted extensive trading as well as the liquor that white traders deliberately used to addict Indians and tempt them into disadvantageous deals. And some tribes tried to preserve their traditional cultures even as they became dependent on whites. Navahos traded for food in order to restore their subsistence way of life, and Pawnees agreed to leave their Nebraska homelands for a reservation in the hope that they could hunt buffalo and grow corn as they had once done.

Tribal Resistance

Indians also actively defended their homelands against white intrusion in a series of bloody conflicts and revolts. The most famous battle occurred in June 1876, when 2,500 Dakota led by Chiefs Rain-in-the-Face, Sitting Bull, and Crazy Horse annihilated white troops led by the rash Colonel George A. Custer near the Little Big Horn River in southern Montana. Other Indian victories followed, but shortages of supplies and relentless pursuit by white troops eventually overwhelmed armed Indian resistance.

These conditions kindled new efforts to reform Indian policy in the 1880s. Reform treatises—George Manypenny's *Our Indian Wards* (1880) and Helen Hunt Jackson's *A Century of Dishonor* (1881), for example—and unfavorable comparison with Canada's management of Indian affairs aroused the American conscience. Canada had granted tribal peoples the rights of British subjects, and the Royal Mounted Police defended them against whites. Canadian officials were more tolerant of tribal customs, and proceeded more slowly than Americans in efforts to acculturate Indians. A high rate of intermarriage between Indians and Canadian whites also promoted smoother relations in Canada.

In the United States, the two most important Indian reform organizations were the Women's National Indian Association (WNIA) and the In-

The Carlisle School in Pennsylvania was founded by the U.S. government in 1879 to teach Indians to behave and dress like whites. These photos show Tom Torleno, a Navaho, before he entered the Carlisle School and again after he had spent three years there. Smithsonian Institution, Washington, D.C.

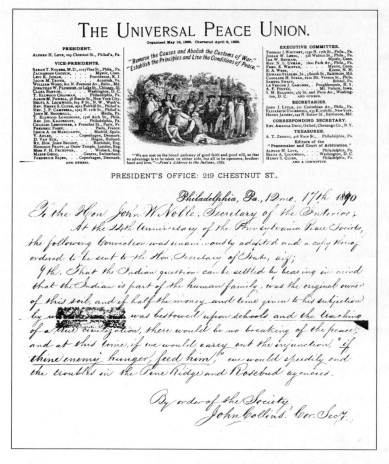

How do historians know

that the "Indian problem" of the late nineteenth century affected the public conscience? This letter was sent by the president of the Universal Peace Union, a humanitarian reform organization, to John W. Noble, secretary of the interior and the federal officer who ultimately oversaw U.S. policy toward the Native American tribes. The organization was forwarding its opinion that Indians were "part of the human family" and that the money and time being spent on subjecting them could be better spent on educating them. Though this organization was somewhat unique because its vice presidents included several women and foreigners, it was one of many whose meetings, resolutions, and publications catalyzed public opinion to favor a more humane and peaceful approach to disputes between the government and Native Americans. Letters such as this one reveal not only the method of petition the organization adopted but also the fervent language it used. National Archives

Reform of Indian Policy

dian Rights Association (IRA). The WNIA, a group composed mainly of white women who sought to put women's domestic skills and virtues at the service of people in need, urged gradual assimilation of Indians. The IRA, which numbered few Native Americans among its members, supported citizenship and landholding by individual Indians.

Most reform groups believed Indians were culturally but not racially inferior to whites, and they assumed Indians could succeed economically only if they adopted middle-class values of cleanliness, diligence, monogamy, and education.

Reformers particularly deplored Indians' sexual division of labor. Women seemed to do all the work—tending crops, raising children, cooking, curing hides, making tools and clothes—and to be servile to men, who hunted but were otherwise idle. Groups such as the WNIA and IRA wanted Indian men to bear more responsibilities and to become more like the heads of white middle-class households. While reformers urged that Indian women be treated more respectfully by their menfolk, the effect of their reforms would have been— and sometimes was—to curtail the economic independence of Indian women.

Prodded by reformers, Congress in 1887 reversed its reservation policy and passed the Dawes Severalty Act. The act dissolved community-owned tribal lands and granted **Dawes Severalty Act** land allotments to individual families according to family size, awarding citizenship (after a twenty-five-year waiting period) to all who accepted allotments. It also authorized the government to sell unallotted land and to set aside the proceeds for the education of Indians. These provisions applied to western tribes except the Pueblo peoples, who retained land rights granted to them by the Spanish.

U.S. Indian policy, as carried out by the Indian Bureau of the Interior Department, now took on three main features. First and foremost, land was distributed to individual families in the belief that they would acquire white people's wants and values by learning how to manage their own property. Second, bureau officials believed that Indians would abandon their "barbaric" habits more quickly if their children were educated in boarding schools away from the reservations. Third, officials tried to suppress what they believed were dangerous religious ceremonies by funding white church groups to establish religious schools among the Indians and teach them to become good Christians.

In 1890 the U.S. government made one last show of force—though such a demonstration was hardly necessary. Active resistance having become less feasible by then, some Sioux turned to the visionary religion of the Ghost Dance movement as a spiritual means of preserving native culture. Inspired by a prophet named Wovoka, the Ghost Dance promised a day when ancestors and buffalo would return and the land and water would swallow up all whites while the Indians danced as ghosts suspended above the calamity. All implements of white civilization, including guns and whiskey, would be buried, and all Indians— united as brothers—would return to reclaim the earth. The Ghost Dance expressed this vision in

a ritual involving five days of slow dancing and meditation.

Although the Ghost Dance foreswore violence, dancers appeared aggressive when they donned sacred shirts that they believed would repel the white man's bullets. Government agents became alarmed about the possibility of renewed Indian uprisings as Wovoka's vision became more popular. Charging that the cult was anti-Christian, they began arresting ghost dancers (meanwhile leaving alone Seventh-Day Adventists, who anticipated a messianic age, much as did the ghost dancers). Late in 1890, the government sent the Seventh Cavalry, Custer's old regiment, to apprehend some Sioux moving north from Pine Ridge, South Dakota, who were believed to be armed for revolt. During the encounter, at a creek called Wounded Knee, the troops massacred two hundred men, women, and children in the snow.

In one crucial respect, the Dawes Act effectively accomplished what whites wanted and Indians feared: it reduced tribal control over land. In spite of some protection against such practices, eager speculators induced Indians inexperienced in commercial dealings to sell their newly acquired property. Between 1887 and the 1930s, tribal landholdings dwindled from 138 million acres to 52 million. Land-grabbing whites were particularly cruel to the Ojibwas (Chippewas) of the northern Plains. In 1906, Senator Moses E. Clapp, a progressive Republican from Minnesota, attached a rider to an Indian appropriations bill declaring that mixed-blood adults on the White Earth reservation were "competent" enough to sell their land without having to observe the twenty-five-year waiting period stipulated in the Dawes Act. When the bill became law, white speculators duped many Chippewas, declared "mixed-bloods" by white experts on the basis of fraudulent evidence, into signing away their land in return for counterfeit money and worthless merchandise. More than half their original holdings passed from their control, and economic ruin overtook the tribe.

The Dawes Act had other drawbacks as well. The boarding-school program affected thousands of children, but most returned to their reservations rather than assimilate **Decline of Western Tribes** into white society. Efforts to suppress religious observances only drove them underground. Ultimately, however, the western tribes were overcome by political and ecological crises. Buffalo extinction, enemy raids, disease, and military force combined to hobble subsistence culture to the point that the Native American tribes were willing to yield their lands to market-oriented whites. Believing themselves superior, whites determined to turn Indians into "virtuous" farmers by making them appreciate the value of private property, educating them in American ideals, and forcefully eradicating their "backward" languages, lifestyles, and religions. By the end of the century, Indians had become what historian Richard White has called "a population without control over resources, sustained in its poverty by payments controlled by the larger society, and subject to increasing pressure to lose their group identity and disappear."

White military superiority was not the only factor contributing to defeat of the western tribes. Their economic systems had started to break down before the military defeats occurred. Although Indians tried to retain their culture by both adapting and yielding to the various pressures, the West was won at their expense, and they remain casualties of an aggressive age.

THE EXPLOITATION OF NATURAL RESOURCES

In sharp contrast to the Indians' use of the natural environment to meet subsistence needs, white migrants to the West and the Plains were driven by a get-rich-quick mentality. To their eyes, the continent's vast stretches of unsettled territory were untapped reservoirs of resources and profits. Extraction of these resources advanced settlement and created new markets; it also fueled the revolutions in transportation, agriculture, and industry that swept the United States in the late nineteenth century. At the same time, the exploitation of nature's wealth gave rise to a spirit of carelessness toward the environment, reinforced the sexual division of labor, and fed habits of racial oppression.

In the years just before the Civil War, eager prospectors began to comb remote forests and mountains for gold, silver, iron, coal, timber, oil, and copper. The mining frontier advanced rapidly, drawing thousands of people to California, Nevada, Idaho, Montana, and Colorado. Prospectors tended to be restless optimists, willing to tramp

Mining and Lumbering

mountains and deserts in search of a telltale glint of precious metal. They shot game for food and financed their explorations by convincing merchants to advance credit for equipment in return for a share of the as-yet-undiscovered lode. When their credit ran out, unlucky prospectors took jobs and saved up for another search for riches.

The prospectors' ultimate goal was to find and sell a large quantity of minerals. But because excavating and transporting minerals were extremely expensive, prospectors who did discover veins of metal seldom mined them. Instead, they sold their claims to mining syndicates, lived it up on their new wealth, and then set off on another quest. Financed by ample eastern capital the mining companies could bring in engineers, heavy machinery, railroad lines, and work crews. Although discoveries of gold and silver first drew attention to the West and its resources, mining companies usually moved into the Rocky Mountain states to exploit

By the 1880s, large-scale operation had replaced solitary prospectors in the extraction of minerals from western territories. Here, powerful hydraulic sluices are being used to recover silver from a promising deposit in Alma, Colorado. Colorado Historical Society.

less romantic but equally lucrative bonanzas of lead, zinc, tin, quartz, and copper.

Lumber production—another large-scale extractive industry—required vast amounts of forest land. As lumber companies moved into the Northwest, they grabbed millions of acres by exploiting the Timber and Stone Act (1878). This measure, passed by Congress to stimulate settlement in California, Nevada, Oregon, and Washington, allowed private citizens to buy (at the low price of $2.50 per acre) 160-acre plots "unfit for cultivation" and "valuable chiefly for timber." Taking advantage of the act, lumber companies hired seamen from waterfront boarding houses to register claims to timberland and turn them over to the companies. By 1900, claimants had bought over 3.5 million acres, but most of that land belonged to corporations.

While lumbermen were acquiring timberlands in the Northwest, oilmen were beginning to sink wells in the Southwest. In 1900 most of the nation's petroleum still came from the Appalachians and Midwest, but rich oil reserves had been discovered in southern California and eastern Texas. Although oil and kerosene were still used mostly for lubrication and lighting, discoveries in the Southwest later became a vital new source of fuel.

The natural-resource frontier was largely a man's world. In 1880, white men outnumbered white women by more than two to one in Colorado, Nevada, and Arizona.

Frontier Society

Many western communities did have substantial populations of women, who had come for the same reason as men: to find a fortune. But on the mining frontier as elsewhere, their independence was limited; they usually accompanied a husband or father and seldom prospected themselves. Even so, many women such as those in the photograph below realized opportunities to earn money in the towns, where they pro-

Though greatly outnumbered by men, women populated many western mining camps where they hauled water, cooked for gangs of miners, and stored gold dust in milk pails. In this photograph, which shows ramshackle living quarters—a tent and a flimsy shack—the women are carrying out a variety of domestic responsibilities. Historical Collection, University Archives, University of Colorado at Boulder.

vided cooking and laundering (and in some cases, sexual services) for the miners. Occasionally, a woman became the main breadwinner when her husband failed to strike it rich. Women also helped to bolster family and community life by campaigning against drinking, gambling, and prostitution.

Many mining and lumber communities had small numbers of Chinese, Mexican, Indian, and African-American residents. Most Chinese worked on the railroads, but some were employed in the camps to do cooking and cleaning. Blacks also held such jobs. Mexicans and Indians often had been the original settlers of land coveted by whites, and some resisted the white intruders. Each of these groups encountered prejudice, especially as whites tried to reserve for themselves the riches that the mines and forests might yield. Native-born whites in California generally welcomed European immigrants such as the Irish and Germans, who experienced rebuffs and violence elsewhere, but they held nonwhites in low esteem. The state imposed a tax on foreign miners, and denied blacks, Indians, and Chinese the right to testify or submit evidence in court. Just as land treaties with Indians were frequently broken, Mexicans' claims to land sought by white miners were often ignored or stolen. Blacks and Chinese who worked in mining camps often suffered abuse and violence, such as the attack on Chinese laborers by white miners at Rock Springs, Wyoming, in 1885. And in California, Mexican bandits also preyed on the Chinese even more than on the Anglos. Nonwhites defended themselves as well as they could against intimidation, but their most common tactic was to move on to jobs and homes in another town or mining camp.

Development of the nation's oil, mineral, and timber reserves raised serious questions about what resources belonged to the American people, as represented by the federal government, and what belonged to private interests whose motive was profit. Two factors operated at cross-purposes. First, much of the undeveloped territory west of the Mississippi was in the public domain, and some people believed that the federal government, as its owner, should receive some compensation for its exploitation. However, the government, lacking both the motivation and the means to dig mines, sink wells,

Use of Public Lands

and cut forests, sold the land to private interests that would take the initiative.

Developers of natural resources were seldom interested in landowning. They wanted trees, not forest land that would become useless once they had cut the trees. They wanted oil, not the scrubby plain that would be worthless if—as often happened—they dug wells but found no oil. To avoid purchase costs, oilmen and iron miners often leased property from private owners or the government and paid royalties on the minerals extracted. Some lumbermen simply cut trees on public lands without paying a cent (and used trickery to buy land cheaply under the Timber and Stone Act). Even when Congress and the U.S. Land Office tried to prevent fraud by passing new legislation and sending out investigators, many communities resisted in fear that such crackdowns would slow local economic growth.

Questions about natural resources caught Americans between the desire for progress and the fear of spoiling the land. By the late 1870s and early 1880s, people eager to protect the natural landscape began to coalesce into a conservation movement. Prominent among them was western naturalist John Muir, who helped establish Yosemite National Park in 1890. The next year, under pressure from Muir and others, Congress authorized President Benjamin Harrison to create forest reserves—public land protected from cutting by private interests. Such policies met with strong objections. Lumber companies, lumber dealers, and railroads were joined in their opposition by householders accustomed to cutting timber freely for fuel and building material. Public opinion on conservation also split along sectional lines. Most supporters of regulation came from the eastern states, where resources had already become less plentiful; opposition was loudest in the West, where people were still eager to take advantage of nature's bounty.

Development of the mining and forest frontiers, and of the farms and cities that followed, brought western territories to the threshold of statehood. In 1889, Republicans seeking to solidify their control of Congress pushed through an omnibus bill granting statehood to North Dakota, South Dakota, Washington, and Montana. Wyoming and Idaho were admitted the following year. Congress denied statehood to Utah until 1896,

Admission of New States

when the Mormons, who constituted a majority of the territory's population and controlled its government, agreed to abandon polygamy.

These states' mining towns and lumber camps spiced American folk culture and fostered a go-getter optimism that distinguished the American spirit. The lawlessness and hedonism of places like Deadwood, in Dakota Territory, and Tombstone, in Arizona Territory, gave the West notoriety and romance. Legends grew up almost immediately about inhabitants of these towns whose lives both typified and magnified western experience. One such character was Martha Jane Canary, known as Calamity Jane, who worked as a scout and wagon driver in Wyoming and South Dakota in the 1870s. Skilled with a rifle and dressed in men's clothes, Calamity Jane acquired a reputation for hard drinking and wild behavior that fiction writers later glorified. Yet according to an army captain who employed her, Jane was "eccentric and wayward rather than bad and had adopted male attire more to aid her in getting a living than for any improper purpose."

Arizona's mining towns, with their free-flowing cash and loose law enforcement, attracted gamblers, thieves, and opportunists whose names came to stand for the Wild West. Near Tombstone, the infamous Clanton family and their partner John Ringgold (known as Johnny Ringo) engaged in smuggling and cattle rustling. Inside the town, the Earp brothers—Wyatt, Jim, Morgan, Virgil, and Warren—and their friends William ("Bat") Masterson and John Henry ("Doc") Holliday operated on both sides of the law as gunmen, gamblers, and politicians. A feud between the Clanton and Earp clans climaxed on October 26, 1881, in a shootout at the OK Corral, where three Clantons were killed and Virgil and Morgan Earp were seriously wounded.

Mark Twain, Bret Harte, and other fiction writers captured for posterity the flavor of mining life, and characters like Wild Bill Hickok, Poker Alice, and Bedrock Tom became western folk heroes. But violence and eccentricity were far from common. Most miners and lumbermen worked seventy hours a week and had little time, energy, or money for gambling, carousing, or gunfights. Women worked as long or longer as teachers, cooks, laundresses, storekeepers, and housewives; only a few were sharpshooters or dance-hall queens. For most westerners, life was a matter of adapting and surviving.

WATER AND WESTERN AGRICULTURE

Glittering gold, tall trees, and gushing oil shaped the popular image of the West, but water gave it life. If the territories and states from the Rocky Mountains westward, plus Texas and Oklahoma, promised wealth from mining, cutting, and drilling, their agricultural potential promised more—if settlers could find a way to bring water to the arid land. Of most importance in the winning of the West is how engineering innovations, technology, and governmental and corporate effort developed the West's river basins and, in the process, made the land agriculturally productive.

For centuries, Native American tribes had irrigated the hot southwestern desert lands to sustain their subsistence farming. By the late sixteenth century, the Spanish had begun tapping the Rio Grande to irrigate their farms in southwest Texas and New Mexico; later they channeled water resources to support California mission communities like San Diego and Los Angeles. The first Americans of northern European ancestry to practice extensive irrigation were the Mormons. Arriving in Utah Territory in 1847, they quickly diverted streams and rivers into a network of canals, whose water enabled them to farm the hard-baked soil. By 1890, Utah could boast over 263,000 irrigated acres supporting more than 200,000 people.

Large-scale efforts at land reclamation through irrigation in Colorado and California raised controversies over rights to the precious streams that flowed through the West. **Who Owns the Water?** Americans had inherited the English common-law principle of *riparian rights*, which held that only people who owned land along the banks of a river could appropriate from the water's flow. The stream itself, according to riparianism, belonged to no one but God; those who lived on its banks could take water for normal needs, but they were not to diminish the river. This principle, intended to protect nature, discouraged economic development because it prohibited each property owner from "artificial" use, such as damming or diverting water at the expense of others who lived along the banks.

Americans, especially those who settled the West, snubbed this Old World view. They rejected riparianism in favor of the doctrine of *prior appropriation*, which awarded a river's water to the first person who claimed it. Westerners, taking their cues in part from earlier Americans who had appropriated waterways for use in eastern mills and factories, asserted that nature existed to advance human needs and profits. According to this capitalistic outlook, water resembled timber, minerals, and other natural resources: it could be held and used as private property. Western farmers wanted to be allowed, as nonriparian property owners, to dam rivers and transport water as far as they wished. Moreover, they believed—a belief eventually supported by the courts—that anyone intending a beneficial or "reasonable" (economically productive) use of river water should have the right to appropriation. This doctrine, then, fostered a new attitude toward nature in the West, a belief that natural resources existed for human appropriation.

Without appropriated water, agriculture could not have flourished in the West. Most lands were too dry for the rainfall farming that characterized the eastern Plains (see page 517). Allowing water-drawing rights only to farmers who lived along river banks would give them a monopoly and effectively prevent development of most of the land. The unspoken premise, however, was that *all* land existed for potential human development and that *all* natural resources should be used—even used up—to conquer the land and support maximum economic gain. Most white people assumed that the doctrine of appropriation made sense. But, as the Indians knew, there were other ways to view the land.

Riparianism did not permit use of water in a way that would diminish a river's flow. Under appropriation, by contrast, those who dammed and diverted water could and often did reduce the flow of water available to potential users downstream. People disadvantaged by such action could protect their interests either by suing those who deprived them of water or by establishing a public authority to regulate water usage. Thus in 1879 Colorado created a number of water divisions, each with a commissioner to determine and regulate water rights. An 1881 law established a state engineer's office to supervise water claims. In 1890 Wyoming enlarged the concept of state control with a constitutional provision declaring that the state's rivers were public property subject to state supervision of their use.

California, destined to become the most productive agricultural state, was the scene of the most dramatic water-related developments. In the 1860s a few individuals controlled huge tracts of land in the fertile Sacramento and San Joaquin river valleys, which they used for speculation, raising cattle, and growing wheat. But around the edges of the wheat fields lay unoccupied lands that could profitably support vegetable and fruit farming if irrigated properly.

Unlike other western states that had opted for appropriation rights over riparian rights, California maintained a mixed legal system that upheld riparianism while allowing for some appropriation. Such a system put irrigators at a disadvantage and prompted them to seek a change in state law. In 1887 the state legislature passed such a law, permitting farmers to organize into irrigation districts that would sponsor construction and operation of irrigation projects. An irrigation district could use its public authority to purchase water rights, seize private property by power of eminent domain to build irrigation canals, and finance its projects through taxation or by issuing bonds. As a result of this legislation, California became the nation's leader in irrigated acreage, with over one million irrigated acres by 1890. Each of these acres annually produced crops valued at $19, the most profitable agriculture in the country.

Though irrigation stimulated development, the federal government still owned most of the West in the 1890s, ranging from 64 percent of California to 96 percent of Nevada. The states, prodded by land-hungry developers, wanted the federal government to transfer to them all, or at least part, of its public-domain lands. States could then make these lands profitable through *reclamation*—providing them with irrigated water—which would expand the states' tax bases. For the most part, Congress refused such transfers. Even if federal lands were transferred to state control for the purpose of water development, who would regulate waterways that flowed through more than one state, or that could potentially provide water to a nearby state? If, for example, California received control of the Truckee River, which flowed westward out of Lake Tahoe, how would Nevadans be assured that California would give them any water? Only the federal government, it seemed, had the power to regulate water development.

In 1902, after many years of proposals and debates, Congress passed the National, or Newlands,

Reclamation Act. Named for Congressman Francis Newlands of Nevada, the act

Newlands Reclamation Act

allowed the federal government to sell western public lands to individuals in parcels not to exceed 160 acres, and to use the proceeds from such sales solely to finance irrigation projects. The Newlands act provided for control but not conservation of water, because some three-fourths of the water used in open-ditch irrigation, the most common form, was lost to evaporation. Thus the legislation fell squarely within the tradition of exploitation of nature for human profit. Often identified as an example of sensitivity to natural-resource conservation in the Progressive Era (see Chapter 21), the Newlands Reclamation Act represented a direct decision by the federal government to aid the agricultural and general economic development of the West, just as subsidies to railroads aided the settlement of the West.

THE AGE OF RAILROAD EXPANSION

The whole country knew what was happening at Promontory Summit in the mountains of Utah on May 10, 1869. On that day, the Central Pacific Railroad, built 689 miles eastward from Sacramento, California, joined with the Union Pacific Railroad, built 1,086 miles westward from Omaha, Nebraska, to form the nation's first transcontinental rail route. Work crews of six hundred Irish, Chinese, Mexicans, and African- and Anglo-Americans participated in the completion ceremony. A gold railroad spike was used to commemorate the event, but the last spike to be driven was made of steel: it was wired to a telegraph line, and when pounded it would signal to the world that the railroad had been completed. Governor Leland Stanford of California had the honor of driving the final spike. As the crowd hushed, he drew back his silver hammer, swung—and missed. The telegrapher sent the message anyway, and across the nation church bells rang and multitudes cheered.

The discovery and development of natural riches provided the base on which the nation's economy expanded. But raw wealth would have been of limited value without the means to carry it to factories and marketplaces. Railroads filled this need, spreading a web of tracks across the country and refashioning the economy in the process.

Railroad construction was extensive and complex. Between 1865 and 1890, total track in the United States grew from 35,000 to 200,000 miles (see map). By 1910 the nation

Effects of Railroad Construction

had one-third of all the railroad track in the world. A diverse mix of workers made up construction crews, such as the Union Pacific workers photographed in 1869 (see page 514). The Central Pacific imported seven thousand Chinese to build its tracks, and the Union Pacific used mainly Irish construction gangs. Workers lived in shacks and tents that could be dismantled, loaded on flatcars, and relocated at intervals of sixty or seventy miles. At one time, the Union Pacific needed forty railcars to supply its crews with rails, ties, bridge materials, and food. After 1880, when durable steel rails began to replace iron rails, railroads helped to boost the nation's steel industry to international leadership. Railroad expansion also spawned a number of related industries, including coal production, passenger- and freight-car manufacture, and depot construction.

Railroads also altered Americans' conceptions of time and space. First, by overcoming barriers of distance, railroads in effect transformed space into time. Instead of using miles to express the distance between places, people began to refer to the amount of time it took to travel from one place to another. Second, railroad scheduling required nationwide standardization of time. Before railroads, each locale had its own time. Local church bells and clocks struck noon when the sun was directly overhead, and people set their clocks and watches accordingly. But because the sun was not overhead at exactly the same moment everywhere, time varied from place to place. Clocks in Boston, for instance, differed from those in New York by almost twelve minutes. To impose some regularity, railroads created their own time zones. By 1880 there were still nearly fifty different standards, but in 1883 the railroads finally agreed—without consulting anyone in government—to establish four standard time zones for the whole country. Most communities adjusted their clocks accordingly (though Chicago held out briefly), and railroad time became national time.

Third, railroad construction brought about technological and organizational reforms. By the

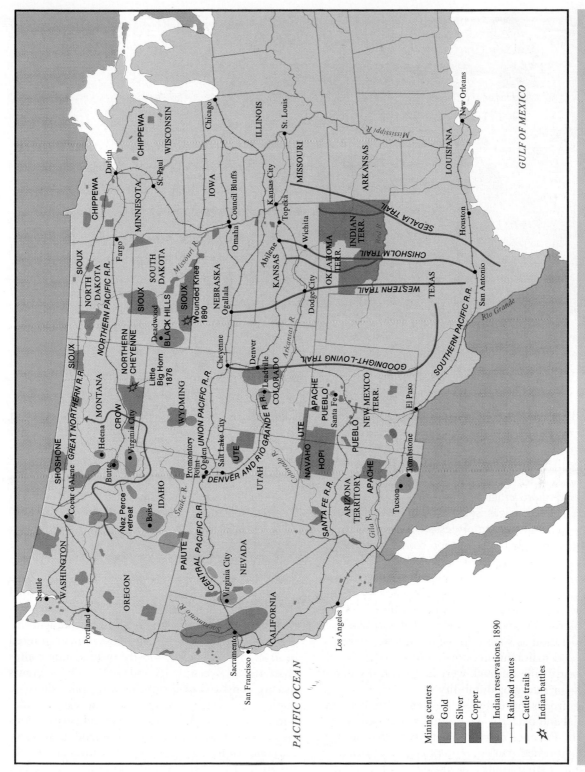

The American West, 1860–1890 *This map shows the dispersed nature of economic activity in the trans-Mississippi West and the importance of railroads in linking those activities.*

Construction crews on western railroads contained a variety of ethnic and racial workers. This work gang, posing on a handcar on the Union Pacific tracks in 1869, includes Chinese and African-American laborers as well as a white foreman.   Lightfoot Collection.

late 1880s, almost all lines had adopted standard-gauge rails so that their tracks could connect with one another. Westinghouse air brakes, automatic car couplers, standardized handholds on freight cars, and other devices made rail transportation safer and more efficient. The need for gradings, tunnels, and bridges spurred the growth of the American engineering profession. Organizational advances included systems for coordinating complex passenger and freight schedules, and the adoption of uniform freight-classification systems.

From other perspectives, the effects of railroads were less favorable. Because of the high costs of construction and equipment, new railroads began operation as soon as possible in order to repay debts and maintain investors' confidence. As a result, many miles of track were laid hastily, without regard for safety or durability.

Railroads nevertheless became extremely influential and performed a uniquely American function. In Europe, railroads were typically built to link established market centers and to improve or replace existing routes of traffic. In the United States, railroads often created many of the very communities they were meant to serve and carried traffic that had never before existed. Railroads such as the Southern Pacific and Louisville and Nash-

ville accelerated the growth of such western and southern regional centers as Omaha, Kansas City, Cheyenne, Los Angeles, Portland, Seattle, Atlanta, and Nashville.

Railroads accomplished these feats with the help of some of the largest government subsidies in American history. Executives argued that because railroads benefited the public,

Government Subsidy of Railroads
———

the government should aid them by giving them land from the public domain. Congress was sympathetic, as it had been when it aided canals earlier in the nineteenth century. To encourage railroad construction, the federal government granted over 180 million acres, mostly to interstate routes chartered between 1850 and 1871. These grants usually consisted of a right of way, plus alternate sections of land in a strip twenty to eighty miles wide along the right of way. Railroad corporations funded construction by using the land as security for bonds or by selling it for cash. States and localities heaped further subsidies on new routes. State land was frequently offered to railroads by legislators, many of whom were handsomely bribed by business executives and investors eager for the advantages railroads could bring. State grants totaled about 50 million acres. Counties, cities, and towns also assisted, usually by offering loans or by purchasing railroad bonds or stocks.

Government subsidies had mixed effects. Although capitalists argued against government interference, they nevertheless accepted government aid and pressured governments into meeting their needs. The Southern Pacific, for example, threatened to by-pass Los Angeles unless the city came up with a bonus and built a depot. Without public help, few railroads could have prospered sufficiently to attract private investment, yet public aid was not always salutary. During the 1880s, the policy of assistance haunted communities whose zeal for railroads had prompted them to commit too much to lines that were never built or to companies that defaulted on loans. Some laborers and farmers fought subsidies, arguing that companies like the Southern Pacific would become too powerful. Many communities boomed, however, because they had linked their fortunes to the iron horse. Moreover, railroads drew farmers deeper into the market economy.

FARMING THE PLAINS

"You are in a sea of wheat," rhapsodized the author of an 1880 magazine article about Oliver Dalrymple's farm in Dakota Territory's Red River valley. "The railroad train rolls through an ocean of grain. . . . We encounter a squadron of war chariots . . . doing the work of human hands. . . . There are 25 of them in this one brigade of the grand army of 115, under the marksmanship of this Dakota farmer." Dalrymple's farm exemplified two important achievements of the late nineteenth century: the taming of wide, windswept prairies so that the land would yield crops to benefit humankind; and the transformation of agriculture into big business by means of mechanization, long-distance transportation, and scientific cultivation.

These achievements did not come easily. The climate and landscape of the Plains presented formidable challenges, and overcoming them did not guarantee success or security. Agricultural development of the West and the Plains turned the United States into the world's breadbasket, but it also scarred the lives of hundreds of thousands of men and women who made that development possible.

Migration to the Plains

Settlement of the Plains and the West involved the greatest migration in American history. More acres were settled and put under cultivation between 1870 and 1890 than in the nation's previous 250 years. The number of farms tripled from 2 million to over 6 million between 1860 and 1910. During the 1870s and 1880s, hundreds of thousands of people streamed into states like Kansas, Nebraska, Texas, and California.

Most, though not all, migrants came from the eastern states or Europe. Several western states opened immigration bureaus in the East and in European ports to lure settlers westward. Labor-short railroads were especially aggressive, advertising cheap land, arranging credit terms, offering reduced fares, and promising instant success. Railroad agents—often former immigrants—traveled to places like Denmark, Sweden, and Germany to recruit prospective settlers, and they greeted newcomers at eastern ports. In California, fruit and vegetable growers imported laborers from Japan and Mexico to work in the fields and canneries.

Train schedules not only revised the American economy but also helped reorient how Americans timed their daily lives. People ordered their day according to the arrival and departure of trains and in 1883 the railroads established four uniform time zones across the country. Library of Congress.

Most migrants went west because opportunities there seemed to promise a better life. Railroad expansion made remote farming regions more accessible, and the construction of grain elevators eased problems of shipping and storage. As a result of population growth, the demand for farm products grew rapidly, and developments in transportation and storage made the prospects for commercial farming—growing crops for profit—more favorable than ever.

Life on the Plains, however, was much harder

In 1881 the Burlington & Missouri Railroad published this brochure in the Czech language to attract East European immigrants to Nebraska, "the best land in the West," where the railroad owned 600,000 acres and was selling farm plots at low prices and under "the most liberal credit terms ever offered by any company." Nebraska Historical Society.

than the advertisements and railroad agents suggested. Migrants often encountered scarcities of essentials they had once taken for granted. The open prairies contained little lumber for housing and fuel. Pioneer families were forced to build houses of sod and to burn manure for heat. Water was sometimes as scarce as timber. Few families were lucky or wealthy enough to buy land near a stream that did not dry up in summer and freeze in winter. Machinery for drilling wells was scarce until the 1880s, and even then it was very expensive: many wells were dug by hand.

Hardships of Life on the Plains

Even more formidable than the terrain was the climate of the Plains. The expanse between the Missouri River and the Rocky Mountains divides climatologically along a line running from Minnesota southwest through Oklahoma, then south, bisecting Texas. East of this line, annual rainfall averages about 28 inches, enough for most crops (see maps). To the west, life-giving rain was never certain; heartened by adequate water one year, farmers gagged on dust and broke their plows on hardened limestone soil the next.

Weather seldom followed predictable cycles. In summer, weeks of torrid heat and parching winds suddenly gave way to violent storms that washed away crops and property. Winter blizzards piled up mountainous snowdrifts that halted all outdoor movement. In March and April, melting snow swelled streams, and flood waters threatened millions of acres. In the fall, a week without rain could turn dry grasslands into tinder, and the slightest spark could ignite a raging prairie fire.

Even when the climate was favorable, nature could be cruel. Weather that was good for crops was also good for breeding insects. Worms and flying pests ravaged corn and wheat. In the 1870s and 1880s swarms of grasshoppers virtually ate up entire farms. Heralded only by the rising din of buzzing wings, a mile-long cloud of insects would smother the land and devour everything: plants, tree bark, and clothes. As one farmer lamented, the "hoppers left behind nothing but the mortgage."

Settlers of the Plains also had to contend with social isolation. In New England and in Europe farmers lived in villages and traveled each day to their nearby fields. This pattern was rare in the American West, where peculiarities of land division compelled Amer-

Social Isolation

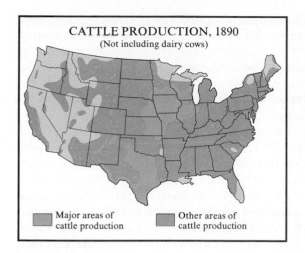

CATTLE PRODUCTION, 1890
(Not including dairy cows)

Major areas of cattle production — Other areas of cattle production

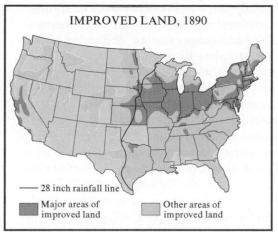

IMPROVED LAND, 1890

—— 28 inch rainfall line
Major areas of improved land — Other areas of improved land

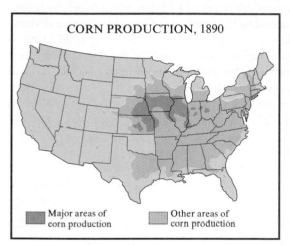

CORN PRODUCTION, 1890

Major areas of corn production — Other areas of corn production

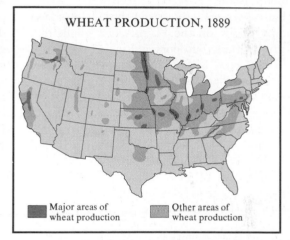

WHEAT PRODUCTION, 1889

Major areas of wheat production — Other areas of wheat production

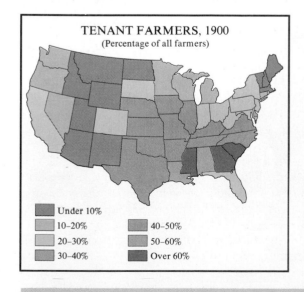

TENANT FARMERS, 1900
(Percentage of all farmers)

Under 10%
10–20%   40–50%
20–30%   50–60%
30–40%   Over 60%

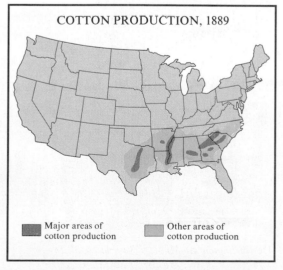

COTTON PRODUCTION, 1889

Major areas of cotton production — Other areas of cotton production

Agricultural Regions, 1889–1900 *Commercial agriculture concentrated certain kinds of production in specific regions: cattle and grain in the Midwest, cotton in the South.* Source: From Charles A. Paullin, *Atlas of the Historical Geography of the United States.* Used by permission of Carnegie Institution of Washington.

ican rural dwellers to live apart from each other. The Homestead Act of 1862 and other measures adopted to encourage western settlement offered cheap or free plots to people who would live on and improve their property. Because most plots acquired by small farmers were rectangular—usually encompassing 160 acres—at most four families could live near each other, but only if they congregated around the shared four-corner boundary intersection. In practice, farm families such as the grim-faced folk photographed in front of their sod house in Nebraska (below), usually lived back from their boundary lines, and at least a half-mile separated farmhouses. Land adjacent to farmhouses often was unoccupied, making neighbors even more distant.

Many observers wrote about the loneliness and monotony of life on the Plains. Men might find escape by working outdoors and taking occasional trips to sell crops or buy supplies. Women were more isolated, confined by domestic chores to the household, where, as one writer remarked, they were "not much better than slaves. It is a weary, monotonous round of cooking and washing and mending and as a result the insane asylum is 1/3d filled with wives of farmers."

The letters that Ed Donnell, a young Nebraska homesteader, wrote to his family in Missouri reveal how time and circumstances could dull optimism. In the fall of 1885, Donnell wrote to his mother: "I like Nebr first rate. . . . I have saw a pretty tuff time a part of the time since I have been out here, but I started out to get a home and I was determined to win or die in the attempt. . . . Have got a good crop of corn, a floor in my house and got it ceiled overhead." Already, though, Donnell was lonely. He went on: "There is lots of other bachelors here but I am the only one I know who doesn't have kinfolks living handy. . . . You wanted to know when I was going to get married. Just as quick as I can get money ahead to get a cow." A year and a half later, Donnell's dreams were dissolving and, still a bachelor, he was beginning to look for a second chance elsewhere. As he explained to his brother, "The rats eat my sod stable down. . . . I may sell out this summer, land is going up so fast. . . . If I sell I am going west and grow up with the country." By fall things had worsened, and Donnell wrote, "We have been having wet weather for 3 weeks. . . . My health has been so poor this summer and the wind and the sun hurts my head so. I think if I can sell I will . . . move to town for I can get $40 a month working in a grist mill and I would not be exposed to the weather." Donnell's doubts and hardships, shared by thousands of other people, fed the city-

Posing in front of their sod-house home, this proud Nebraska family affects an air of seriousness that derived from their hard lives on the Plains. Though tall bushes and other growth appear in the background, the absence of trees is notable. Nebraska State Historical Society.

ward migration of farm folk that characterized late-nineteenth-century urban growth (see pages 565–567).

Farm families survived by sheer resolve and by organizing churches and Grange clubs where they could socialize a few times a month. By the early 1900s, two developments had brought rural settlers into closer contact with modern consumer society (though people in sparsely settled regions west of the 28-inch rainfall line remained isolated for several more decades). First, mail-order houses—Montgomery Ward and Sears, Roebuck—made new consumer products available to almost everyone by the 1870s and 1880s. Emphasizing personal attention to customers, Ward's and Sears, Roebuck were outlets for sociability as well as material goods. Letters from customers to Mr. Ward often reported family news and sought advice on everything from gifts to childcare. A Washington State man wrote, "As you advertise everything for sale that a person wants, I thought I would write you, as I am in need of a wife, and see what you could do for me." Another wrote: "I suppose you wonder why we haven't ordered anything from you since the fall. The cow kicked my arm and broke it and besides my wife was sick, and there was the doctor bill. But now, thank God, that is paid, and we are all well again, and we have a fine new baby boy, and please send plush bonnet number 29d8077."

Mail-Order Companies and Rural Free Delivery

Second, scores of rural communities petitioned Congress for extension of the postal service during the 1890s, and in 1896 the government made Rural Free Delivery (RFD) widely available. Farmers would no longer lack news and information; they could receive letters, newspapers, and catalogues at home nearly every day. In 1913 the postal service inaugurated parcel post, which enabled people to receive packages, such as orders from Ward's and Sears, more cheaply. By 1920, rural families had regular access to the wider world through the mails.

The agricultural revolution that followed the Civil War would not have been possible without the expanded use of machinery. When the Civil War drew men away from farms in the upper Mississippi River valley, the women and men who remained behind began using reapers and other

Mechanization of Agriculture

mechanical implements to satisfy demand and take advantage of high grain prices. After the war, continued demand and high prices encouraged farmers to depend more on machines, and inventors worked hard to develop new implements for farm use. Seeders, combines, binders, mowers, and rotary plows were introduced on the Plains and in California in the 1870s and 1880s.

For centuries, the acreage of grain a farmer could plant had been limited by the amount that could be harvested by hand. Machines—driven first by animals, then by steam—increased productivity beyond farmers' wildest imaginations. Before mechanization, a farmer working alone could harvest about 7.5 acres of wheat a season. Using an automatic binder that cut and tied bundles of grain, the same farmer could harvest 135 acres. Machines dramatically reduced the time and cost of farming various other crops as well (see table, page 520).

Meanwhile, Congress and scientists worked to improve existing crops and develop new ones. The 1862 Morrill Land Grant Act (see page 440) granted each state federal lands to sell in order to finance agricultural and industrial colleges. The act discriminated against western states by linking land-grant acreage to the size of the congressional delegation (the formula of 30,000 acres for each senator and representative gave New York about 1 million acres, Kansas only 90,000), but it did promote the establishment of educational institutions that aided agricultural development. (A second Morrill Act in 1890 aided more schools, including a number of public black colleges.) The Hatch Act of 1887 provided for agricultural experiment stations in every state, further encouraging the advancement of farming technology.

Legislative and Scientific Aid to Farmers

Meanwhile, scientific advances enabled farmers to use the soil more efficiently. Agricultural researchers developed the technique of dry farming, a system of plowing and harrowing that prevented precious moisture from evaporating. Botanists perfected several varieties of "hard" wheat whose seeds could withstand northern winters, and millers invented an efficient process for grinding the tougher wheat kernels into flour. Agriculturists also adapted new varieties of alfalfa from Mongolia, corn from North Africa, and rice from Asia. Californian Luther Burbank developed a wide range of new plants by cross-breeding. Chemist George

By the late nineteenth century, the industrial revolution was making a significant impact on farming. This scene from a Colorado wheat farm shows a harvest aided by a steam tractor and belt-driven thresher, machines that enabled large-scale commercial crop production.   Colorado Historical Society.

Washington Carver of the Tuskegee Institute created hundreds of new products from peanuts, soybeans, sweet potatoes, and cotton wastes, and taught methods of soil improvement. Other scientists developed new means of combating plant and animal diseases. Turbulent times lay ahead for farmers, but in the meantime development of the agricultural hinterland by virtue of settlement, science, and technology made America what one journalist called "the garden of the world."

THE RANCHING FRONTIER

While commercial farming was spreading, one of the West's most romantic industries, cattle ranching, was evolving. Early in the nineteenth century huge herds of cattle, introduced by the Spanish and developed by Mexican ranchers, roamed southern Texas and bred with cattle brought by Anglo settlers. The resulting longhorn breed mul-

Time and Cost of Farming an Acre of Land by Hand and by Machine, 1890

	Hours Required		Labor Cost	
Crop	*Hand*	*Machine*	*Hand*	*Machine*
Wheat	61	3	$3.65	$ .66
Corn	39	15	$3.62	$1.51
Oats	66	7	$3.73	$1.07
Loose hay	21	4	$1.75	$ .42

Source: Ray Allan Billington, *Westward Expansion: A History of the American Frontier*, 2nd ed. (New York: Macmillan, 1960), p. 697.

tiplied and became valuable by the 1860s, when population growth increased demand for beef and railroads facilitated the transportation of food. By 1870, drovers were herding thousands of Texas cattle northward to Kansas, Missouri, and Wyoming (see map, page 513). On these long drives, mounted cowboys (as many as 25 percent of whom were African-American) supervised the herds, which fed on open grassland along the way. At the northern terminus—usually Abilene, Dodge City, or Cheyenne—the cattle were sold to northern ranches or loaded onto trains bound for Chicago and St. Louis for slaughter and distribution.

The long drive gave rise to romantic lore, but it was not very efficient. Trekking 1,500 miles made cattle sinewy and tough. Herds traveling through Indian lands and farmers' fields were sometimes shot at and later prohibited from such trespass by state laws. The ranchers' only alternative was to eliminate long drives by raising herds nearer to railroad routes. Thus when ranchers discovered that crossing sturdy Texas longhorns with heavier Hereford and Angus breeds produced cattle better able to survive northern winters, cattle raising spread across the Great Plains. Between 1860 and 1880 the cattle population of Kansas, Nebraska, Colorado, Wyoming, Montana, and the Dakotas increased from 130,000 to 4.5 million.

Cattle raisers needed vast stretches of land to graze their herds, and they wanted to incur as little expense as possible in using such land. Thus they

Open-Range Ranching

often bought a few acres bordering streams and turned their herds loose on adjacent public domain that no one wanted because it lacked water access. By this method, called *open-range ranching*, a cattle raiser could control thousands of acres by owning only a hundred or so.

Neighboring ranchers often formed associations and allowed their herds to graze together. Owners identified their own cattle by burning a brand into every animal's hide. Each ranch had its own brand—an improvised shorthand for labeling movable property. Cowboy crews rounded up the cattle twice each year to brand new calves in the spring and to drive mature animals to market in the fall.

Roundups delighted easterners with colorful images of western life: bellowing cattle, mounted rope-swinging cowboys, and smoky campfires. But roundups and open-range ranching proved short-lived because they lured too many ranchers into the business. Opportunities for profit at first enriched Civil War veterans in Texas and other states. As one publication explained:

The roundup, where cattle were branded, was one of the most vital activities of western ranching. In this photograph, taken in 1888 at the Cal Snyder ranch in Custer County, Nebraska, a woman and child observe while cowboys rope a steer and singe a brand into the animal's hide.   Nebraska State Historical Society.

A good sized steer when it is fit for the butcher market will bring from $45.00 to $60.00. The same animal at its birth was worth but $5.00. He has run on the plains and cropped the grass from the public domain for four or five years, and now, with scarcely any expense to its owner, is worth $40.00 more than when he started on his pilgrimage.

But as demand for beef kept rising and ranchers and capital flowed into the Plains, cattle began to overrun the range.

Meanwhile, sheepherders from California and New Mexico were moving onto the public-domain cattle ranges. Ranchers complained that sheep ruined grassland by eating down to the roots, and that cattle refused to graze where sheep had been because the "woolly critters" left a repulsive odor. Armed conflict occasionally erupted when cowboys and sheepherders resorted to violence rather than settle disputes in court, where a judge might discover that both were using public land illegally. More important than these disputes was the fact that the farming frontier was advancing and generating new demands for land.

Fearing loss of control, ranchers began to fence in pastures with barbed wire, a new invention— even though they had no legal title to the land. Fences eliminated the open range and often provoked disputes between competing ranchers, between cattle raisers and sheep raisers, and between ranchers and farmers who claimed use of the same land and who both wanted to appropriate waterways for irrigation. In 1885, President Grover Cleveland ordered the removal of illegal fences on public lands and Indian reservations. Enforcement was slow, but the order signaled that free use of public domain was ending.

Open-range ranching made beef a staple of the American diet and created a few fortunes, but its extralegal features could not survive the rush of history. Moreover, a devastating winter in 1886–1887 destroyed countless herds and drove small ranchers out of business. By 1890, big businesses were taking over the cattle industry and applying scientific methods of breeding and feeding. Most ranchers owned or leased the land they used, though some illegal fencing persisted. As the cowboy became just another corporate wage earner, the myth of his freedom and individualism became even more deeply rooted in the American psyche.

THE SOUTH AFTER RECONSTRUCTION

While the Plains and West were being transformed, the South was developing its own forms of resource exploitation and market economies. Ravaged by the Civil War, which had killed one-third of all draft animals and destroyed half of the region's farm equipment, southern agriculture recovered slowly. Rather than diversify, farmers concentrated on growing cotton even more single-mindedly than before the war. High prices for seed and implements, declining prices for crops, taxes, and, most of all, debt trapped many white families in poverty. Conditions were even worse for blacks, who had to endure brutal racial prejudice along with economic hardship.

To achieve sectional independence, some southern leaders tried to promote industrialization. Their efforts partially succeeded, but by the early 1900s many southern industries were mere subsidiaries of northern firms. Moreover, southern planters, shippers, and manufacturers depended heavily on northern banks to finance their operations. Equally important, low wages and stunted opportunities prevented inflows of people—laborers, farmers, businesspeople, and professionals—who would have brought inflows of capital. Thus although in some ways the South grew as rapidly as the North, it remained an isolated region, poorly integrated into the national economy.

During and after Reconstruction, a significant shift in the nature of agriculture swept through the South. Between 1860 and 1880, the total number of farms in southern states more than doubled, from 450,000 to 1.1 million. In 1880, four times as many farmers lived in the South as on the Plains. The number of landowners, however, did not increase, because a growing proportion of southern farmers rented, rather than owned, their farms. Meanwhile, the size of the average farm actually decreased—from 347 to 156 acres. Southern agriculture, once dominated by laborlords (slave owners), was now dominated by landlords, and the system was characterized by sharecropping and tenant farming (see page 523). Over one-third of the farmers counted in the 1880 census were sharecroppers and tenants, and the proportion increased to two-thirds by 1920.

Sharecropping and tenant farming entangled millions of southerners in a web of humiliation, at whose center was the crop lien. Most farmers, too poor ever to have cash on hand, borrowed in order to buy necessities. They could offer as collateral only what they could grow. A farmer in need of supplies would deal with a nearby "furnishing merchant," who would exchange supplies for a certain portion, or *lien*, of the farmer's forthcoming crop. After the crop was harvested and brought to market, the merchant collected his debt. All too often the farmer's debt exceeded his crop's value. Thus the farmer paid off the merchant, received no cash for the crop, and still needed food and supplies. His only choice was to commit his next crop to the merchant and sink deeper into debt.

Crop-Lien System

The merchants frequently took advantage of the customer's powerlessness by inflating prices, charging credit customers an average of 30 to 40 percent more than cash customers paid. Credit customers also had to pay interest ranging from 33 to 200 percent on the advances they received. Suppose, for example, that a farmer needed a 20-cent bag of seed or a 20-cent piece of cloth and had no cash. The furnishing merchant would extend credit for the purchase but would also boost the price to 28 cents. At year's end that 28-cent loan would have accumulated interest, raising the farmer's debt to, say, 42 cents—more than double the item's original cost. The farmer, having pledged more than his crop's worth against scores of such debts, fell behind in payments and never recovered. If he fell too far behind, he could be evicted. As one contemporary writer remarked, "When one of these mortgages has been recorded against the Southern farmer, he has usually passed into a state of helpless peonage."

The lien system caused hardship in former plantation areas where tenants and sharecroppers—black and white—grew cotton for the same markets that had existed before the Civil War. In the southern backcountry, which in the antebellum era had been characterized by small farms, relatively few slaves, and diversified agriculture, the crop-lien problem was compounded by other economic changes.

New spending habits of backcountry farmers illustrate the most important of these changes. In 1884, Jephta Dickson of Jackson County in the northern Georgia hills bought $53.37 worth of flour, meal, peas, meat, corn, and syrup from one merchant and $2.53 worth of potatoes, peas, and sugar from another. Such expenditures would have been rare in the upcountry before the Civil War, when most farmers grew almost all the food they needed. But after the war, yeoman farmers like Jephta Dickson shifted from semisubsistence agriculture to more commercialized farming; in the South that meant raising cotton. This change came about for two reasons: debts incurred during the war and Reconstruction forced farmers to grow a crop that would bring in cash, and railroad expansion enabled them to transport cotton to markets more easily than before. As backcountry yeomen devoted more acres to cotton, they raised less of what they needed on a day-to-day basis and found themselves more frequently at the mercy of merchants. In this respect, their economy resembled those of western Indians.

At the same time, backcountry farmers suffered from new laws that essentially closed the southern range (those lands owned by the federal government but used freely by southern herders). This change, too, resulted from the commercialization of agriculture. Before the 1870s southern farmers, like open-range ranchers in the West, had let their livestock roam freely on other people's land in search of food and water. By custom, farmers who wished to protect their crops from foraging animals were supposed to build fences around those crops. But as commercial agriculture reached the backcountry, large landowners and merchants induced county and state legislative bodies to require the fencing-in of animals rather than crops. These laws hurt poor farmers who had little land, requiring them to use more of their precious land for pasture. Though consistent with the concept of individual responsibility for private property, such laws undermined the cooperative customs that yeomen cherished. As one farmer put it, "God makes the grass . . . and corn in the valleys grow, so let's not try to deprive our poor neighbors from receiving his blessing." Increasingly, yeoman farmers came to resent merchants, large landowners, and other promoters of commercialized agriculture. Their disaffection

Closing the Southern Range

In the post-Reconstruction years, lynchings of African-American men occurred with increasing frequency, chiefly in sparsely populated areas where whites looked upon strangers, especially black strangers, with fear and suspicion. © R. P. Kingston Collection/The Picture Cube.

would eventually find political expression as populism (see Chapter 20).

Poor whites in the rural South, facing the economic threat of loss of the open range, also feared that newly enfranchised blacks could undermine whatever political and social superiority (real and imagined) they enjoyed. Wealthy white landowners and merchants fanned these fears, using racism to divide poor whites and blacks and to distract poor whites from protesting their economic subjugation.

The majority of the nation's African-Americans still lived in the South and worked in agriculture and, although the abolition of slavery had altered their legal status, it had not improved their opportunities relative to those of whites. In 1880, 90 percent of all southern blacks depended for a living on farming or personal

Condition of African-Americans

and domestic service—the same occupations they had held as slaves.

Moreover, the New South proved to be as violent a place for African-Americans as the Old South had been. Weapons, including a gun commonly known as a "nigger killer," were plentiful, and whites seldom hesitated to use them. One man wrote in his memoirs that all "young blades of the day . . . desired to have a pistol, a jack knife, and a pair of brass knucks." Such weaponry was often used in combination with a noose when a black man allegedly broke the racial code. Between 1889 and 1909 over 1,700 African-Americans were lynched in the South. Like the hanging photographed by an unknown observer or participant around 1880, most of these murders occurred in sparsely populated rural districts where whites felt threatened by an influx of blacks and where fast-changing communities left migrant blacks with no friends, black or white, to vouch for them. Most victims of lynchings were vagrants who had accidentally crossed the bounds of acceptable behavior, usually involving an alleged assault—rarely proved—on a white woman. But behind the accusations, a deeper fear drove whites to such an extreme form of retribution. As one Kentuckian wrote, "I think there can be no doubt that a considerable amount of crime on the part of colored men against white men and women is due to a spirit of getting even."

Threatened by violence, pushed into sharecropping, and burdened with crop liens, African-Americans also had to contend with new forms of social and political oppression. With slavery dead, white supremacists fashioned new ways to keep blacks in a position of inferiority. Southern leaders, embittered by northern interference in race relations during Reconstruction and eager to reassert their authority after the withdrawal of federal troops, instituted measures to discourage blacks from voting and to segregate them legally from whites. To humanitarians, discrimination and segregation seemed cruel and demeaning; to whites who supported these measures, the "new order" represented a modern, moderate way to maintain race relations between what they believed to be superior and inferior peoples.

The end of Reconstruction did not stop blacks from voting. Despite increasing threats and intimidation, blacks still formed the backbone of the Republican party and some still won elective offices.

In North Carolina, for example, eleven African-American men were elected to the state senate and forty-three to the house between 1877 and 1890. White politicians began to seek ways to discourage the "Negro vote" by imposing restrictions that appeared neutral but would actually bar blacks from the polls. Beginning with Georgia in 1877, southern states levied taxes of $1 to $2 on all citizens wishing to vote. These poll taxes proved prohibitive to most black voters, who were so deeply in debt to merchants and landlords that they never had cash for any purpose. Other schemes disfranchised black voters who could not read. Voters might be required, for instance, to deposit ballots for different candidates in different ballot boxes. To do so correctly, however, voters had to be able to read the instructions. Such measures also disqualified many poor whites, but their prime objective was to curtail voting by African-Americans.

Racial discrimination also stiffened in social affairs. Under slavery, a widespread informal system of separation had governed race relations. After the Civil War, this system was formalized in law. In a series of cases during the 1870s, the Supreme Court opened the door to discrimination by ruling that the Fourteenth Amendment protected citizens' rights only against infringement by state governments (see page 493). The federal government, according to the Court, had no authority over the actions of individuals or organizations. If blacks wanted protection under the law, the Court said, they must seek it from the states, which under the Tenth Amendment retained all powers not specifically assigned to Congress.

Spread of Jim Crow Laws

The climax to these rulings came in 1883, when in the *Civil Rights Cases* the Court struck down the 1875 Civil Rights Act, which had prohibited segregation in public facilities such as streetcars, hotels, theaters, and parks. Again the Court declared that the federal government could not regulate the behavior of private individuals in matters of race relations. Subsequent lower-court cases in the 1880s established the principle that blacks could be restricted to "separate-but-equal" facilities. The Supreme Court upheld the separate-but-equal doctrine in *Plessy* v. *Ferguson* (1896) and officially applied it to schools in *Cummins* v. *County Board of Education* (1899).

Thereafter, segregation laws—popularly known as "Jim Crow" laws—multiplied throughout the South, confronting African-Americans with daily reminders of their inferior status. State and local laws restricted them to the rear of streetcars, to separate drinking fountains and toilets, and to separate sections of hospitals, asylums, and cemeteries. A Birmingham, Alabama, ordinance required that the races be "distinctly separated . . . by well defined physical barriers" in "any room, hall, theatre, picture house, auditorium, yard, court, ballpark, or other indoor or outdoor place." Local laws defined certain neighborhoods as all-black or all-white. Mobile, Alabama, passed a curfew requiring blacks to be off the streets by 10 p.m, and Atlanta required separate Bibles for the swearing-in of black witnesses in court. Thus for thousands of black southerners race relations deteriorated after emancipation and would not improve markedly until the 1960s. African-Americans adapted to racial bias by creating and controlling their own social institutions: churches, schools, and family networks.

In industry, new initiatives brought breezes of change but there, too, a distinctively southern quality prevailed. Two of the South's leading industries in the late nineteenth century relied on traditional staple crops—cotton and tobacco. In the 1870s, textile mills began to appear in the Cotton Belt. Powered by the region's abundant rivers and streams, manned cheaply by poor whites eager to escape crop liens, and aided by low taxes, such mills multiplied. By 1900 the South had four hundred mills with a total of over four million spindles, and twenty years later the region was eclipsing New England in textile-manufacturing supremacy. Proximity to raw materials and cheap labor also aided the tobacco industry, and the invention in 1880 of a cigarette-making machine immensely enhanced the marketability of tobacco.

Industrialization of the South

Cigarettes were manufactured in cities by black and white workers (though in segregated sections of the factories); textile mills were concentrated in small towns and developed their own exploitative labor system. Financed mostly by local investors, mills employed women and children from poor white families and paid 50 cents a day for twelve or more hours of work. Such wages were barely half of the wage paid to northern workers.

Tobacco production was one industry that traditionally hired African-American laborers. This scene from a Richmond tobacco factory around 1880 shows women and children workers preparing the leaves for curing by tearing off the stems.   Valentine Museum.

Many companies built villages around their mills, where they controlled the housing, stores, schools, and churches. Criticism of the company was forbidden, and attempts at union organization were squelched. Mill families soon found that factory jobs changed their status very little: the company store replaced the furnishing merchant, and the mill owner replaced the landlord.

Other industries were launched in the South, under the sponsorship of northern or European capitalists. Between 1890 and 1900, northern lumber syndicates moved into the pine forests of the Gulf states, boosting production by 500 percent. During the 1880s, northern investors developed southern iron and steel manufacturing, much of it centered in the boom city of Birmingham. Coal mining and railroad construction also expanded rapidly, but New York and London financiers dominated the boards of directors of most southern companies. Moreover, the South lacked technological innovators, such as those in the machine-tool industry who had enabled northern industries to compete with other industrializing nations. Southern industries had to wait until techniques were developed elsewhere and then adapt them.

Industrialization, regardless of its outside origins, prompted southern boosters to herald the emergence of a New South ready to compete economically with other sections. Henry Grady, edi-

tor of the *Atlanta Constitution* and the most articulate voice of southern progress, proclaimed, "We have sowed towns and cities in the place of theories, and put business in place of politics. We have challenged your spinners in Massachusetts and your iron-makers in Pennsylvania. . . . We have fallen in love with work." Yet in 1900 the South remained as rural as it had been in 1860. Staple-crop agriculture supported its economy, and white supremacy permeated its social and political relations, barring blacks from industrial jobs and the polls. Furthermore, because of its low wages the South attracted few immigrants and thus enjoyed little of their energizing influence. In 1910 only about 2 percent of the southern population was foreign-born. A New South eventually would emerge, but not until after a world war and a massive black exodus had shaken up old attitudes.

The development of the West was accomplished with courage and creativity that amazed the rest of the world. The extraction of raw minerals, the use of irrigation and mechanization to bring forth agricultural abundance from the land, and the construction of railroads to tie the nation together transformed half the continent within half a century. The optimistic conquerors, however, employed power, violence, and greed that overwhelmed the culture of the land's original inhabitants, left many farmers feeling cheated and betrayed, and sacrificed environmental balance for market profits. In the South, recovery and growth kindled new optimism, but careless exploitation exhausted the soil and left poor farmers as downtrodden as ever. In an age of expansion, African-Americans saw their rights and opportunities narrowing. Industrialization failed to lessen the dominance of southern staple-crop agriculture, and by 1900 the South was more dependent economically on the North than it had been before the Civil War.

In both the West and the South, the appeal of commercial exchange drew tribal peoples, freedmen, and other Americans away from their subsistence ways of life and into the marketplace. The raw materials and agricultural products of both sections improved living standards and contributed to industrial progress, but not without human and environmental costs.

Cliffs of Green River *by Thomas Moran in 1874. A detail of this painting appears at the beginning of Chapter 17, on page 498.* Amon Carter Museum, Fort Worth, Texas.

SUGGESTIONS FOR FURTHER READING

The Western Frontier

Ray A. Billington and Martin Ridge, *Westward Expansion*, 5th ed. (1982); Sara Deutsch, *No Separate Refuge: Culture, Class, and Gender on an Anglo-Hispanic Frontier in the American Southwest* (1987); William S. Greever, *Bonanza West: Western Mining Rushes* (1963); Robert V. Hine, *The American West*, 2nd ed. (1984); Julie Roy Jeffrey, *Frontier Women* (1979); Patricia Limerick, *The Legacy of Conquest: The Unbroken Past of the American West* (1987); Ruth Moynihan, *Rebel for Rights: Abigail Scott Duniway* (1983); Rodman W. Paul, *The Far West and the Great Plains in Transition, 1859–1900* (1988); Rodman W. Paul and Richard W. Etulain, *The Frontier and the American West* (1977); Richard Slotkin, *The Fatal Environment: The Myth of the Frontier in the Age of Industrialization* (1985); Henry Nash Smith, *Virgin Land: The American West as Symbol and Myth* (1950, 1958); Kent Ladd Steckmesser, *The Western Hero in History and Legend* (1965).

Water and the Environment

Roderick Nash, *American Environmentalism* (1990); Joseph M. Petulla, *American Environmental History* (1977); Donald Worster, *Rivers of Empire: Water, Aridity, and the Growth of the American West* (1985).

Railroads

Alfred D. Chandler, ed., *Railroads: The Nation's First Big Business* (1965); Robert W. Fogel, *Railroads and Economic Growth* (1964); Edward C. Kirkland, *Men, Cities, and Transportation* (1948); George R. Taylor and Irene Neu, *The American Railroad Network* (1956); Alan Trachtenberg, *The Incorporation of America* (1982); O. O. Winther, *The Transportation Frontier* (1964).

Native American Tribes

Ralph K. Andrist, *The Long Death: The Last Days of the Plains Indians* (1964); Leonard A. Carlson, *Indians, Bureaucrats, and Land: The Dawes Act and the Decline of Indian Farming* (1981); Frederick E. Hoxie, *A Final Promise: The Campaign to Assimilate the Indians, 1880–1920* (1984); Francis Paul Prucha, *The Great Father: The United States Government and the American Indians* (1984); Edward H. Spicer, *Cycles of Conquest: The Impact of Spain, Mexico, and the United States on the Indians of the Southwest* (1962); Robert M. Utley, *The Indian Frontier of the American West, 1846–1890* (1984); Philip Weeks, *Farewell, My Nation: The American Indian and the United States* (1990); Richard White, *The Roots of Dependency* (1983).

Ranching and Settlement of the Plains

Lewis Atherton, *The Cattle Kings* (1961); Allan G. Bogue, *From Prairie to Corn Belt* (1963); David Dary, *Cowboy Culture: A Saga of Five Centuries* (1981); Everett Dick, *The Sod-House Frontier* (1937); Gilbert C. Fite, *The Farmer's Frontier* (1963); J. Stanford Rikoon, *Threshing in the Midwest* (1988); Walter Prescott Webb, *The Great Plains* (1931).

The New South

Edward L. Ayers, *The Promise of the New South* (1992); Orville Vernon Burton and Robert C. McMath, Jr., eds., *Toward a New South?: Post-Civil War Southern Communities* (1982); Paul Gaston, *The New South Creed* (1970); Dewey Grantham, Jr., *The Democratic South* (1963); Steven Hahn, *The Roots of Southern Populism: Yeoman Farmers and the Transformation of the Georgia Upcountry, 1850–1890* (1983); Stanley P. Hirshson, *Farewell to the Bloody Shirt: Northern Republicans and the Southern Negro* (1962); J. Morgan Kousser, *The Shaping of Southern Politics* (1974); Melton A. McLaurin, *Paternalism and Protest: Southern Cotton Mill Workers and Organized Labor* (1971); Howard N. Rabinowitz, *Race Relations in the Urban South, 1865–1890* (1978); Theodore Saloutos, *Farmer Movements in the South, 1865–1933* (1960); C. Vann Woodward, *The Strange Career of Jim Crow* (1966); C. Vann Woodward, *Origins of the New South*, rev. ed. (1951); Gavin Wright, *Old South, New South* (1986).

The Machine Age, 1877–1920

CONRAD CARL TRIED TO appear calm, but he was understandably nervous. It was 1882, and Carl, a tailor who for nearly thirty years had done piecework in his New York City tenement apartment, was appearing before a Senate committee in Washington, D.C. The Committee on Education and Labor was investigating the causes of recent labor unrest, and Senator James L. Pugh of Alabama was asking Carl to explain changing work conditions in the tailoring business.

Admitting that his testimony would probably cost him his job, Carl nevertheless answered candidly. When he first began tailoring, Carl explained, he and his wife and children had pieced together garments by hand. The pace of their work was relaxed, yet he was able to save a few dollars each year. Then, said Carl, "in 1854 or 1855, . . . the sewing machine was invented and introduced, and it stitched very nicely, nicer than the tailor could do; and the bosses said: 'We want you to use the sewing machine; you have to buy one.'"

Carl and his fellow tailors used their meager savings to buy machines, hoping they could earn more by producing more. But then employers cut wages. The tailors "found that we could earn no more than we could without the machine; but the money for the machine was gone now, and we found that the machine was only for the profit of the bosses; that they got their work quicker, and it was done nicer." Moreover, Carl, now old and discouraged, had seen that mechanization had other troubling effects on workers and those around them. "The machine makes too much noise and the neighbors want to sleep," he explained, "and we have to stop sewing earlier, so we have to work faster. We work now in excitement—in a hurry; . . . It is not work at all; it is a hunt."

Conrad Carl's testimony to the Senate committee was one worker's account of the industrialization that was relentlessly overtaking American society. The new order was both inspiring and ominous. The factory and the machine broke down manufacturing into minute routinized tasks, and organized work according to the dictates of the clock. Workers, who had long thought of themselves as valued producers, found themselves struggling to avoid becoming slaves to machines. Meanwhile, in the quest for productivity and profits, corporations merged and amassed awesome power. Defenders of the new system devised new theories to justify it, while critics tried to combat what they thought were abuses of power.

Industrialization was and is a complex process whose chief feature is the production of goods by machine rather than by hand. By using machines,

A huge machine dwarfs a worker at the General Electric Main Street Station in Minneapolis.

manufacturers could lower production costs and significantly raise each worker's output. Mechanization relied on the use of standardized parts and brought about specialization in production. In America, industrialization was characterized by the following phenomena:

- Concentration of production in large, intricately organized factories
- Growth of large enterprises and specialization in all forms of economic activity
- Involvement of an increasing proportion of the work force in manufacturing
- Increased accumulation of capital for investment in the expansion of production
- Accelerated technological innovation, emphasizing new inventions and applied science
- Expanded markets, no longer merely local and regional in scope
- Growth of a nationwide transportation network based on the railroad, and an accompanying communications network based on the telegraph and telephone
- Rapid increase in population
- Steady increase in the size and predominance of cities

In 1860 only about one-fourth of the American labor force worked in manufacturing and transportation; by 1900 over half did so. By the dawn of the twentieth century, the United States was not only the world's largest producer of raw materials and food but also the most productive industrial nation. Between 1879 and 1920 the value of exports increased twelvefold. Accelerated migration from farms and mass immigration from abroad swelled the industrial work force (see Chapter 19); but machines, more than people, boosted American productivity. Moreover, business innovations, in organization and marketing as well as in technology, drove the quest for profits.

These developments had momentous effects on standards of living and on the nature of everyday life. During the half-century between the end of Reconstruction and the end of the First World War, a new consumer society took shape. The nation's farms and factories were producing so much that Americans could afford to satisfy their material wants. What had once been accessible only to a few was becoming available to many; what had formerly been dreams were becoming necessities.

Yet the accomplishments of industrial expansion, like expansion into the natural resources and agricultural frontiers (see Chapter 17), involved waste and greed. The vigor and creativity that marked the half-century after the end of the Civil War gave rise to both constructive and destructive forces.

TECHNOLOGY AND THE TRIUMPH OF INDUSTRIALISM

In 1876, Thomas A. Edison and his associates moved into a long wooden shed in Menlo Park, New Jersey, where Edison intended to turn out "a minor invention every ten days and a big thing every six months or so." Edison envisioned his Menlo Park laboratory as an invention factory, where creative people would pool their ideas and skills to fashion marketable products. Here was the brash American spirit adapting itself to a more systematic work ethic. If Americans wanted new products, they had to organize and work purposefully to bring about progress. Such efforts reflected a forward-looking energetic spirit that enlivened American industrialization at the end of the nineteenth century.

In the years between 1865 and 1920, the machine fired American optimism. The machine, like the West, embodied opportunity. Technological adaptation of existing devices, such as the steam engine and sewing machine, plus new inventions in fields like electricity and industrial chemistry enabled the United States to surpass all rivals in industrial and agricultural production. The patent system, created by the Constitution to "promote the Progress of science and useful Arts," testifies to an outburst of American inventiveness. Between 1790 and 1860 the U.S. Patent Office had granted a total of 36,000 patents. In 1897 alone it granted 22,000 patents, and in the seventy years after 1860 it registered 1.5 million. As innovative as the inventions themselves was the marriage between technology and business organization. The harnessing of electricity, internal combustion, and industrial chemistry illustrate how this marriage worked.

Many of Thomas Edison's more than one thousand inventions used electricity to transmit light, sound, and images. Perhaps the biggest of his "big

• Important Events •

1859	Great Atlantic Tea Company (the A&P), nation's first chain store, is founded
1873–78	Overly rapid expansion causes economic decline
1877	Widespread railroad strikes protest wage cuts
1879	Henry George's *Progress and Poverty* argues against economic inequality Edison perfects incandescent light bulb
1880s	Chain-pull toilets spread across U.S. Doctors accept germ theory of disease Mass production of tin cans begins
1881	First federal trademark law begins spread of brand names
1882	Standard Oil Trust formed
1884–85	Economic decline results from numerous causes
1886	Haymarket riot in Chicago protests police brutality against labor demonstrators; seven people killed, eight anarchists tried and convicted American Federation of Labor (AFL) founded
1888	Edward Bellamy's *Looking Backward* depicts utopian world free of monopoly, politicians, and class divisions
1890	Sherman Anti-Trust Act outlaws "combinations in restraint of trade"
1892	Homestead (Pennsylvania) steel workers strike against Carnegie Steel Company
1893–97	Severe economic depression causes high unemployment and numerous business failures

1894	Workers at Pullman Palace Car Company in company town of Pullman, Illinois, strike against exploitative policies Henry Demarest Lloyd's *Wealth Against Commonwealth* proposes cooperative commonwealth with government ownership of factories
1895	*U.S.* v. *E.C. Knight Co.* limits Congress's power to regulate manufacturing
1896	*Holden* v. *Hardy* upholds law regulating miners' working hours because of mining dangers
1898	Frederick W. Taylor promotes scientific management (rigid schedules and repetitive routines) as efficiency measure in industry
1901–03	U.S. Steel Corporation founded E. I. du Pont de Nemours and Company reorganized Ford Motor Company founded
1905	*Lochner* v. *New York* overturns law limiting bakery workers' work hours and limits scope of labor protection laws Industrial Workers of the World founded
1908	*Muller* v. *Oregon* upholds law limiting women to ten-hour workday First Ford Model T built
1911	Triangle Shirtwaist Company fire in New York City leaves 146 workers dead
1913	First moving assembly line begins operation at Ford Motor Company

Birth of the Electrical Industry

thing" projects began in 1878 when he formed the Edison Electric Light Company and embarked on a search for a cheap, efficient means of indoor lighting. Gas, candles, and oil lamps had all proved impractical for lighting large buildings, as had electric current flowing between two carbon rods. After a tedious trial-and-error search for a better filament, Edison perfected an incandescent bulb that used a filament in a vacuum. At the same time he worked out a *system* of power production and distribution—an improved dynamo and a parallel circuit of wires—to provide cheap, convenient power to a large number of customers.

To make his ideas marketable, Edison acted as his own publicist. During the 1880 Christmas season he illuminated Menlo Park with forty incandescent bulbs, and in 1882 he built a power plant that would light eighty-five buildings in New York's financial district around Wall Street. When the

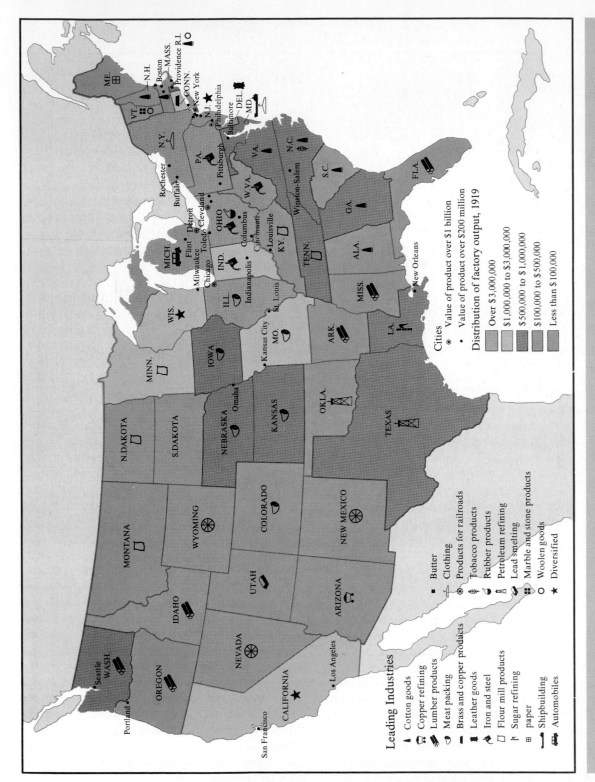

Industrial Production, 1919 *By the early twentieth century, each state was dominated by one or a few kinds of industrial production. Although the value of goods produced was still highest in the Northeast, states like Minnesota and California had impressive dollar values of outputs.* Source: © American Heritage Publishing Co., Inc., *American Heritage Pictorial Atlas of United States History*; data from U.S. Bureau of the Census, *Fourteenth Census of the United States, 1920.* Vol. IX: *Manufacturing* (Washington: U.S. Government Printing Office, 1921).

Pearl Street Station began service, a *New York Times* reporter marveled that working in his office at night "seemed almost like writing in daylight."

Because Edison's system used direct current at low voltage, it could send electric power only a mile or two. George Westinghouse, a young inventor from Schenectady, New York, who had become famous for devising an air brake for railroad cars, solved the problem. Westinghouse purchased patent rights to generators that used alternating current and transformers that reduced high-voltage power to lower voltage levels, thus making transmission over long distances cheaper.

Once Edison and Westinghouse had made their technological breakthroughs, others introduced new business practices to market and refine their inventions. Samuel Insull, Edison's private secretary, who later amassed a huge electric-utility empire, deftly attracted investments and organized Edison power plants across the country, turning energy into big business. In the late 1880s and early 1890s financiers Henry Villard and J. P. Morgan enlarged the manufacturing scope of the industry when they consolidated patents in electric lighting and merged small equipment-manufacturing companies into the General Electric Company. Equally important, General Electric and Westinghouse Electric encouraged the practical application of electricity, formerly an experimental field for scientists, when they established research laboratories that paid scientists to find new everyday uses for electricity.

Even while corporations in the electricity industry were organizing the process of invention in a systematic way, a number of inventors continued to work independently and tried, sometimes successfully and sometimes not, to sell their handiwork to manufacturing companies. One such inventor was Granville T. Woods, an African-American engineer from Columbus, Ohio. Working in machine shops, first in Cincinnati and then in New York City, Woods patented thirty-five devices vital to electronics and communications. Among his inventions, most of which he sold to companies such as General Electric, were an automatic circuit breaker, electric incubator, electromagnetic brake, and various instruments to aid communications between railroad trains.

Development of the internal-combustion engine produced the era's most visionary manufacturer, Henry Ford. In the 1890s Ford, then an

Thomas A. Edison was not only an inventor extraordinaire but also a skilled entrepreneur and promoter. In this photograph, taken after his rise to fame, he poses in his laboratory with gadgets and inventing tools all around him, conveying the image of a confident technician.   Library of Congress.

electrical engineer in Detroit's Edison Company, experimented in his spare time with a gasoline-burning internal-combustion engine to power a vehicle. George Selden, a lawyer from Rochester, New York, had been tinkering with internal-combustion engines since the 1870s. But Ford applied his organizational genius to this invention and spawned a massive industry.

Like Edison, Ford had a scheme as well as a product. In 1909 he declared, "I am going to democratize the automobile. When I'm through

The idea of the assembly line, as perfected at the Ford plant in Highland Park, Michigan, outside of Detroit, was to break down the production process so that individual workers efficiently repeated the same task. In this photograph, taken around 1914, assembly-line workers are installing pistons in engines of the Ford Model T. Henry Ford Museum and Greenfield Village.

Mass Production of the Automobile
———

everybody will be able to afford one, and about everyone will have one." Ford proposed to reach this goal by means of *mass production:* producing millions of identical cars in exactly the same way. The key to mass production was *flow*. Adapting the methods of the meat-packing and metalworking industries, Ford engineers set up assembly lines that drastically reduced the time and cost of producing cars. Instead of performing numerous tasks, each worker—like those photographed installing pistons—was given responsibility for only one task, performed repeatedly, using the same specialized machine. By means of a continuous flow of these tasks, each component part was fashioned and the car was progressively assembled. The Ford Motor Company began operation in 1903, and in 1908, the first year the famous Model T was built, Ford sold 10,000 cars. By 1914, the year after the first moving assembly line was inaugurated, 248,000 Fords had been sold. The value of automobiles manufactured, only $6 million in 1900, reached $420 million by 1914.

Moreover, rising automobile production created more jobs, higher earnings, and higher profits in such related industries as oil, paint, rubber, and glass. The Model T was indeed replacing the horse.

By 1914, many Ford cars cost $490, only about one-fourth of their cost a decade earlier. Yet even $490 was too much for many workers, who earned at best $2 a day. In 1914, however, Ford tried to spur productivity, prevent high labor turnover, head off unionization, and better enable his workers to buy the cars they produced by offering them the Five-Dollar-Day plan—combined wages and profit sharing equal to $5 a day.

During the same period, the du Ponts were doing for the chemical industry what Edison and Ford did for the electrical and automobile industries. The du Pont family had been manufacturing gunpowder and other explosives in America since the early 1800s. In 1902 three du Pont cousins, Alfred, Coleman, and Pierre, took over the company and broadened production. In 1911, du Pont laboratories began to adapt cellu-

Du Ponts and the Chemical Industry
———

lose to the eventual production of such materials as photographic film, rubber, lacquer, and textile fibers. The company also pioneered in efficient methods of management, accounting, and reinvestment of earnings, all of which contributed to controlled production, better recordkeeping, and, of course, higher profits.

The timing of technological innovation varied from one industry to another, but machines altered the nation's economy and everyday life in a pervasive way between 1865 and 1900 by creating new industries. The telephone and typewriter revolutionized communications, making face-to-face conversations less important and facilitating correspondence and recordkeeping. Sewing machines made mass-produced clothing available to almost everyone. Refrigeration changed American dietary habits by making it easier to preserve meat, fruit, vegetables, and dairy products. Streetcars, elevated railroads, and subways enabled people to live farther from their workplaces. Cash registers and adding machines revamped accounting and created new clerical jobs.

Profits from these products resulted from higher production at lower costs. As technological innovations made large-scale production more economical, some owners used part of their profits to replace small factories with larger ones. Between 1850 and 1900 the average capital investment in a manufacturing firm increased from $700,000 to $1.9 million. Only large factories could afford to buy new machines and operate them at full capacity. And large factories could best take advantage of discounts for shipping products in bulk and for buying raw materials in quantity. Economists call such advantages *economies of scale*.

But profitability was a matter of organization as well as mechanics. Running a successful factory depended as much on how production was ar-

New Emphasis on Efficiency

ranged as on the machines in use. Where once shop-floor workers had made basic decisions about how a product was to be made, by the 1890s engineers and managers with specialized scientific knowledge had assumed this responsibility and planned every work task to increase output. Their efforts standardized tasks and quality in mass production, which then required less skill and independent judgment from workers.

The most influential advocate of efficient production was Frederick W. Taylor. As foreman and engineer for the Midvale Steel Company in the 1880s, Taylor concluded that the only way a company could lessen fixed costs and increase profits was to apply scientific studies of "how quickly the various kinds of work . . . ought to be done." The "ought" in Taylor's formulation was momentous because it signified the goal of producing more for a lower cost per unit—by eliminating unnecessary workers. Similarly, "how quickly" signified that time and money were equivalent.

In 1898 Taylor took his stopwatch to the Bethlehem Steel Company to illustrate how his principles of scientific management worked. His experiments, he explained, involved identifying the "elementary operations of motions" used by specific workers, selecting better tools, and devising "a series of motions which can be made quickest and best." Applying this technique to the shoveling of ore, Taylor designed fifteen kinds of shovels and prescribed the proper motions for using each one. He succeeded in reducing a crew of 600 men to 140, who received higher wages, though their new jobs were more stressful.

Time, as much as quality, became the measure of acceptable work as a result of Taylor's writings and experiments, and science rather than tradition determined the right ways of doing things. As integral features of the assembly line, where work was divided into specific time-determined tasks, employees had become another kind of interchangeable part.

MECHANIZATION AND THE CHANGING STATUS OF LABOR

Technological innovation and assembly-line production created new jobs, but because most machines were labor-saving devices, fewer workers could produce more in less time—as Conrad Carl knew all too well. Mechanization destroyed time-honored crafts such as glassmaking and iron molding; it also subordinated men and women workers to rigid schedules and repetitive routines that transformed the nature of work.

By 1880, the status of labor had undergone a dramatic shift in the course of a single generation. Almost 5 million Americans now worked in manufacturing, construction, and transportation, an increase of over 300 percent in those industries. Most workers could no longer accurately be termed *producers*, as craftsmen and farmers had traditionally thought of themselves. The enlarged working class consisted mainly of *employees*—people who worked only when someone else hired them. Producers were paid by consumers according to the quality of what they produced; employees were paid wages based on time spent on the job.

As mass production subdivided manufacturing into small tasks, workers spent their time repeating one specialized operation. One investigator who looked into the effects of specialization on a typical laborer found that he became

> a mere machine. . . . Take the proposition of a man operating a machine to nail on 40 to 60 cases of heels in a day. That is 2,400 pairs, 4,800 shoes in a day. One not accustomed to it would wonder how a man could pick up and lay down 4,800 shoes in a day, to say nothing of putting them . . . into a machine. . . . That is the driving method of the manufacture of shoes under these minute subdivisions.

Even as work became more routinized, workers fought to retain their workplace customs. In this photograph a cigar maker reads the newspaper to his fellow workers, according to tradition. George Eastman House, International Museum of Photography.

By reducing the manufacturing process to numerous simplified tasks constantly repeated, and by coordinating production to the running of machinery, assembly-line production also deprived employees of their independence. Workers could no longer decide when to begin and end the workday, when to rest, and what tools and techniques to use. As a Massachusetts factory worker complained in 1879, "During working hours the men are not allowed to speak to each other, though working close together, on pain of instant discharge. Men are hired to watch and patrol the shop." And workers were now surrounded by others who labored at the same rate for the same pay, regardless of the quality of their work.

Men and women affected by these changes did not accept them passively. Workers reacted by struggling to retain independence and self-respect in the face of employers' ever-increasing power. As new groups encountered the industrial system, they resisted in various ways. Artisans such as cigar makers, glass workers, and coopers (barrel makers), caught in the transition from hand labor to machine production, fought to preserve the pace and quality of their jobs and to retain such customs as appointing a fellow worker to read aloud while they worked. When immigrants went to work in factories, they often convinced foremen to hire their relatives and friends, thus preserving the on-the-job family and village ties they had always known. Off the job, workers continued to gather for leisure-time activities like social drinking and holiday celebrations, shunning employers' attempts to control their social lives.

Employers took steps to establish standards of behavior and work incentives that they thought would enhance efficiency and productivity. To make workers docile (like the machines they operated), employers supported temperance and moral-reform societies, dedicated to combating supposed drinking and debauchery on and off the job. Managers at Ford Motors required workers to meet the company's behavior code before they could earn the profit-sharing segment of the Five-Dollar-Day plan. Other employers established piecework rates, paying workers an amount per item produced, rather than an hourly wage, to encourage maximum use of machines. And they lowered wages, forcing people to work harder and longer just to maintain the same income.

As machines and assembly-line production reduced the need for skilled workers, employers cut

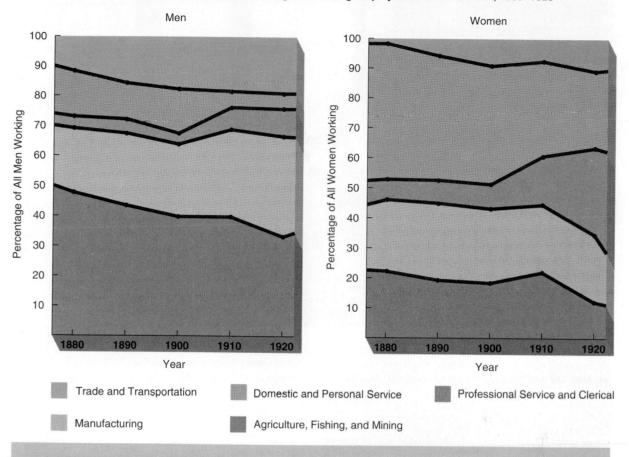

Distribution of Occupational Categories among Employed Men and Women, 1880–1920

Distribution of Occupational Categories, Males and Females, 1880–1920   The changing thickness of each part of this graph represents trends in male and female employment. The agriculture, fishing, and mining and the domestic service sectors declined the most, while notable increases occurred in professional service and clerical, and trade and transportation.   Source: U.S. Bureau of the Census, *Census of the United States, 1880, 1890, 1900, 1910, 1920* (Washington: U.S. Government Printing Office).

Employment of Women

wage costs by hiring more women and children. Between 1880 and 1900, the numbers of employed women grew from 2.6 million to 8.6 million, and at the same time their occupational patterns underwent striking changes. The proportion of women in domestic-service jobs (maids, cooks, laundresses)—traditionally the most common and lowest-paid form of female employment—dropped dramatically as jobs opened in other sectors. In manufacturing, these jobs were usually menial positions in textile mills and food-processing plants that paid women as little as $1.56 a week for seventy hours of labor. Though the number of female factory hands tripled between 1880 and 1900, the

proportion of women workers in these jobs remained about the same.

More importantly, a major shift was occurring that set the pattern for female workers in the twentieth century. The enormous expansion in the industrial and retail sectors caused the numbers and percentages of women in clerical jobs—typists, bookkeepers, sales clerks—to skyrocket. By 1920 nearly half of all clerical workers were women; in 1880 only 4 percent had been women. Previously, when sales and office positions had demanded accounting, drafting, and letter-writing skills, men had dominated such jobs. Then new inventions such as the typewriter, cash register, and adding machine simplified such tasks. Companies eagerly hired women who streamed into the labor market,

The rise of clerical occupations was one of the most important developments in employment for women at the beginning of the twentieth century. Employers readily hired women to operate typewriters and adding machines and paid them less than male employees. Note the male supervisors in this photograph.   Minnesota Historical Society.

having taken courses in typing and shorthand in preparation for the better pay and conditions that these jobs offered relative to factory and domestic work. An official of a sugar company observed in 1919 that "all the bookkeeping of this company . . . is done by three girls and three bookkeeping machines . . . one operator takes the place of three men." Because office machines made tasks simpler and schools prepared women in office skills, employers did not have to invest much in training; men who previously would have held clerical positions could now be shifted into higher managerial positions.

In sales, as in the office, women needed little training and could be paid low wages. Women were attracted to the respectability, pleasant surroundings, and contact with affluent customers sales jobs offered. They were given no responsibility for billing or counting money; in department stores male cashiers took in cash and made change. Sex discrimination thus pervaded the clerical sector. The new jobs offered women some opportunities for advancement to supervisory positions, but women posed no threat to men's managerial jobs.

Although most working children toiled on their parents' farms, the number in nonagricultural occupations tripled between 1870 and 1900.

Employment of Children

In 1890, over 18 percent of all children between ages ten and fifteen were gainfully employed. In textile factories in particular, many workers were below age sixteen. Mechanization created a number of light tasks, such as running errands and helping machine operators, that children such as those in the opposite photograph could handle at a fraction of adult wages. Conditions were especially bad for child laborers in the South, where burgeoning textile mills needed unskilled hands. Mill owners induced poor white farm families, who otherwise might not have had any jobs or income, to bind their children over to the factories at miserably low wages.

Several states, especially in the Northeast, had laws specifying the minimum age and maximum workday hours for child labor. But because state statutes did not apply to firms engaged in interstate commerce, most large companies could avoid state regulations. Furthermore, it was difficult to enforce age requirements, and to supplement the family income many parents lied about children's ages. One woman who had worked in the Amoskeag Mills of Manchester, New Hampshire, recalled how easy it was to get a job without proof of age. "I was twelve years old when I arrived here and started work," she recalled. "All we had to do was show them that we were fourteen years old. Tall or short, it didn't matter; they'd just ask, 'Are you fourteen years old?' OK. That's all. So that's how I went in to work."

In the South, mill operators staunchly opposed state interference and insisted that only parents should decide what was best for their children. By 1900, state laws and further automation had reduced the number of children working in manufacturing, but many more worked at street trades—shining shoes and peddling newspapers and other merchandise—and as helpers in stores. Not until the Progressive era did reformers turn to federal legislation as the remedy for child labor (see Chapter 21).

Although working conditions were often dangerous and unhealthy, low wages were usually the immediate catalyst of worker unrest. Many employers believed in "the iron law of wages," which dictated that employees be paid according to conditions of supply and demand. Theoretically, because laborers were free to make their own choices and employers competed for their labor, workers would receive the highest wages the employer could pay without being driven out of business. In reality, the "iron law" meant that employers did not have to raise wages—and could even cut them—as long as there were workers who would accept low pay. Employers justified the system by invoking individual freedom: a worker who did not like the wages being offered was free to quit and find a job elsewhere.

Courts reinforced the principle, denying workers the right to organize and bargain collectively on the grounds that an employee's wages should be the result of an individual negotiation between employee and employer. Wage earners saw things differently; they believed the system trapped them. As one Massachusetts factory worker testified in 1879, "The market is glutted, and we have seasons of dullness; advantage is taken of men's wants, and the pay is cut down; our tasks are increased, and

Factories employed children from the early nineteenth century well into the twentieth. In textile mills like the one pictured here, girls operated machines and boys ran messages and carried materials back and forth. Mill girls had to wear their hair tied up so that it would not get caught in the machines; the girl above with the shawl over her head would never have worn that garment while she was working. National Archives.

Children in the Labor Force, 1880–1930

━━━ Total Number of Children Aged 10–15
━━━ Total Number of Children Employed

Children in the Labor Force, 1880–1920 *The total number and percentage of children in the labor force peaked around the turn of the century. Thereafter, the passage of state laws requiring children to attend school until age fourteen and limiting the ages at which children could be employed caused child labor to decline.* Source: *The Statistical History of the United States from Colonial Times to the Present* (Stamford, Conn.: Fairfield Publishers, 1965).

if we remonstrate, we are told our places can be filled. I work harder now than when my pay was twice as high."

Even steady employment was insecure. Repetitive tasks using high-speed machinery dulled concentration, and the slightest mistake could cause serious injury. Industrial acci-

Industrial Accidents

dents rose steadily before 1920, killing or maiming hundreds of thousands of people each year. As late as 1913, after factory owners had installed safety devices, some 25,000 people died each year in industrial mishaps, and close to 1 million were injured. Each year sensational disasters, such as explosions, mine cave-ins, and fires, aroused public clamor for better safety regulations. The most notorious tragedy was the fire at New York City's Triangle Shirtwaist Company in 1911, which killed 146 workers, most of them Jewish immigrant women. Equally tragic, however, were the countless accidents that resulted in mangled limbs, infected cuts, chronic illness, and death. A railroad brakeman described his accident in 1888:

> It was four or five months before I "got it." I was making a coupling one afternoon. . . . Just before the two cars were come together, the one behind me left the track. . . . Hearing the racket, I sprang to one side, but my toe caught the top of the rail. I was pinned between the corners of the cars as they came together. I heard my ribs cave in like an old box smashed with an ax.

Because disability insurance and pensions were almost nonexistent, families stricken by such accidents suffered acutely. Prevailing free market views stifled protective legislation for workers, and employers denied responsibility for employees' well-being. As one railroad manager declared, "The regular compensation of employees covers all risk or liability to accident. If an employee is disabled by sickness or any other cause, the right to claim compensation is not recognized." The only recourse for a stricken family was to sue and prove in court that the killed or injured worker had not realized the risks involved and had not caused the accident, an expensive route that very few ever took.

Reformers and union leaders in several states lobbied Congress successfully for laws to improve working conditions, but the Supreme Court lim-

Courts Restrict Labor Reform

ited the scope of such legislation by narrowly defining what jobs were dangerous and which workers needed protection. Initially, in *Holden* v. *Hardy* (1896), the Court upheld a law regulating the working hours of miners because their work was so dangerous that overly long hours would increase the threat of injury. In *Lochner* v. *New York* (1905), however, the Court struck down a law limiting bakery workers to a sixty-hour week and a ten-hour day. In response to the argument that states had the authority to protect workers' health and safety, the Court ruled that baking was not a dangerous enough occupation to justify restricting the right of workers to sell their labor freely. According to the Court, interference with the right of individuals to make contracts for their labor would violate the Fourteenth Amendment's guarantee that no state could "deprive any person of life, liberty, or property without due process of law."

In *Muller* v. *Oregon* (1908), the Court used a different rationale to uphold a law limiting women to ten hours of work a day. In this case, setting aside its *Lochner* argument, the Court asserted that women's health and reproductive functions required protection. According to the Court, a woman's health "becomes an object of public interest and care in order to preserve the strength and vigor of the race." As a result, women were barred from such occupations as printing and transportation, which required long hours or night work, and thus were confined to the menial jobs they had always held.

Throughout the nineteenth century, tensions rose and fell as workers confronted mechanization. Different adjustments were made as different groups—rural migrants, foreign immigrants, women, and children—entered the industrial labor force. Some people bent to the demands of the factory, machine, and time clock. Some tried to blend old ways of working into the new system. Some never adjusted and wandered from place to place, job to job. Others, however, turned to organized resistance.

The year 1877 was in many ways a watershed. In July a series of strikes broke out among unionized railroad workers who were protesting wage

Strikes of 1877

cuts. Violence spread from Pennsylvania to the Midwest, Texas, and California. Venting pent-up anger, rioters attacked railroad property, derailing trains and burning railroad yards. State militia companies, organized and commanded by employers, broke up picket lines and fired into threatening crowds. In several communities, factory workers, wives, and even local merchants aided the strikers, while railroads enlisted strikebreakers to replace union men.

The worst violence occurred in Pittsburgh, where on July 21 militiamen from Philadelphia bayoneted and fired on a crowd of rock-throwing demonstrators, killing ten and wounding many more. Infuriated, the mob drove the soldiers into a railroad roundhouse and set a series of fires that destroyed 39 buildings, 104 engines, and 1,245 freight and passenger cars. The next day, the troops shot their way out of the roundhouse and killed twenty more citizens before fleeing the city. After more than a month of unprecedented carnage, President Rutherford B. Hayes sent federal troops to end the strikes—the first significant use of troops to quell labor unrest.

The immediate cause of these strikes was the squeeze of hard times. In the economic slump that followed the Panic of 1873, railroad managers cut wages, increased workloads, and laid off workers, especially those who had joined unions. Such actions drove workers to strike and riot. Laborers in other industries sympathized with the strikers, as did other residents of their communities. A Pittsburgh militiaman, ordered out to break the 1877 strike by his fellow townsmen, recalled, "I talked to all the strikers I could get my hands on, and I could find but one spirit and one purpose among them—that they were justified in resorting to any means to break down the power of the corporations."

THE UNION MOVEMENT

After 1877, anxiety over the loss of independence and a desire for better wages, hours, and working conditions attracted more workers into unions to protect their interests. The union movement had precedents but few successes. Craft unions composed of skilled workers in a particular trade dated from the early nineteenth century, but the narrowness of their membership left them without broad power. The National Labor Union, founded in 1866, claimed 640,000 members in 1868 but died when its members' loyalty seeped away during the hard times of the 1870s. The only broad-based labor organization to survive that depression was the Knights of Labor. Founded in 1860 by Philadelphia garment cutters, the Knights opened their doors to other workers in the 1870s. In 1879, when the union still had fewer than 10,000 members and the factory system was not yet firmly established, Terence V. Powderly, a machinist and former mayor of Scranton, Pennsylvania, was elected grand master. Under his forceful guidance, Knights membership mushroomed, peaking at 730,000 in 1886. At a time when most labor organizations were trade unions—which excluded everyone except skilled workers in particular crafts—the

Knights recruited women, African-Americans, immigrants, and unskilled and semiskilled workers.

Under Powderly, the Knights of Labor tried to avert the bleak future that they believed industrialism portended by building an alliance among all producers—workers and employers—that would offer an alternative to industrial capitalism and the profit system. They believed they could eliminate conflict between workers and employers by establishing a cooperative society in which laborers worked for themselves, not for those who possessed capital. The goal, argued Powderly, was to "eventually make every man his own master—every man his own employer. . . . There is no good reason why labor cannot, through cooperation, own and operate mines, factories, and railroads."

Knights of Labor

Technological and economic changes were making it impossible for each worker to be his or her own employer. But like many farmers, the Knights saw producer and consumer cooperatives as preferable to the forces of greed that surrounded them. They concluded that a society in which all groups lived cooperatively was achievable. This view was the source of both the organization's strength and of its weakness. The cooperative idea, attractive in the abstract, gave laborers little bargaining power. It was too vague a concept, and employers held most of the economic leverage. Strikes were a means of seeking immediate goals, but Powderly and other Knights leaders opposed strikes for two reasons: they tended to divert attention from the long-term goal of a cooperative society, and workers tended to lose more strikes than they won.

But some Knights leaders and the rank and file did engage in militant actions, including a demand for higher wages and union recognition from railroads in the Southwest in 1886. Railroad magnate Jay Gould refused to negotiate, and a strike that began on March 1 in several Texas communities spread to Kansas, Missouri, and Arkansas. As violence increased, Powderly met with Gould and called off the strike, hoping to settle the conflict. But Gould again refused concessions, and the Knights had no choice but to give in. By mid-1886, when Powderly began to denounce radicalism and violence, the more militant craft unions broke away, upset by Powderly's compromising position and confident that they could attain more on their own. Membership in the Knights dwindled, although the union survived in a few small towns, where it made a brief attempt to unite with Populists in the 1890s. The special interests of craft unions overcame the Knights' broad-based and often vague appeal, and dreams of labor unity faded.

As the hard times of the 1870s gave way to better conditions in the early 1880s, a number of labor groups, including the Knights, began to campaign for an eight-hour workday, partly as a means of creating more jobs so as to reduce unemployment. This effort on the part of laborers to regain control of their work gathered momentum in Chicago, where radical anarchists—who believed that voluntary cooperation should replace all government—as well as various craft unions agitated for the cause. Finally, on May 1, 1886, mass strikes and the largest spontaneous labor demonstration in the country's history took place. Some one-hundred thousand workers turned out, and Chicago police mobilized to prevent disorder, especially among striking workers at the huge McCormick reaper factory. The day passed calmly, but two days later police stormed an area near the McCormick plant and broke up a battle between striking unionists and nonunion strikebreakers. Police shot and killed two unionists and wounded several others. The next evening, labor groups rallied at Haymarket Square, near downtown Chicago, to protest police brutality. As a company of police officers approached, a bomb exploded near their front ranks, killing seven and injuring sixty-seven. Mass arrests of anarchists and unionists followed. Eventually eight men, all anarchists, were tried and convicted of the bombing, though the evidence of their guilt was questionable. Four were executed and one committed suicide in prison. The remaining three were pardoned in 1893 by Illinois governor John P. Altgeld, who believed they had been victims of the "malicious ferocity" of the courts. Altgeld's act of conscience ruined his political career when law-and-order advocates across the country denounced him as a friend of anarchy.

Haymarket Riot

The Haymarket bombing, like the 1877 railroad strikes, drew public attention to the growing discontent of labor and also revived middle-class fear of radicalism. The participation of anarchists and socialists, many of them foreign-born, created a sense of crisis, a feeling that the forces of law and

The Haymarket Riot of 1886 was one of the most violent incidents connected with labor unrest in the late nineteenth century. This drawing, taken from Frank Leslie's Illustrated Newspaper, *shows workers fleeing while police beat demonstrators with night-sticks. As all of this occurred, a bomb, allegedly set off by anarchists, exploded, killing both police and workers.* Library of Congress.

order had to act swiftly to prevent social turmoil. To protect their city, private Chicago donors helped to establish the military base at Fort Sheridan and the Great Lakes Naval Training Station. Elsewhere, police forces and armories were strengthened. Employer associations—coalitions of manufacturers in the same industry—worked to counter labor militancy by agreeing to resist strikes and by purchasing strike insurance.

The American Federation of Labor (AFL) emerged from the 1886 upheavals as the major workers' organization. A federation of national

American Federation of Labor

craft unions, the AFL initially had about 140,000 members, most of them skilled native-born workers. Led by Samuel Gompers, the pragmatic and opportunistic immigrant who headed the Cigar Makers' Union, the AFL avoided the idealistic rhetoric of worker solidarity to press for concrete goals—specifically higher wages, shorter hours, and the right to bargain collectively. As Gompers's associate Adolph Strasser explained, "We have no ultimate ends. We are going from day to day. We are fighting only for immediate objects—objects that can be realized in a few years." In contrast to the Knights of Labor, the AFL accepted industrialism and worked to achieve better conditions within the wage-and-hours system. Member unions retained autonomy in their own areas of interest but tried to develop a general policy that would suit all members. Since these unions were organized by craft (skill) rather than

by workplace, they had little interest in including unskilled workers.

Under Gompers the AFL grew to over 1 million members by 1901 and 2.5 million by 1917, when it represented 111 national unions and 27,000 local unions. The national organization required all constituent unions to hire organizers to expand membership, and it collected dues for a fund to aid members on strike. The AFL avoided party politics, adhering instead to Gompers's dictum to support labor's friends and oppose its enemies, regardless of party.

The AFL and the labor movement in general suffered a series of setbacks in the early 1890s, when once again labor violence stirred public fears. In July 1892, when the AFL-affiliated Amalgamated Association of Iron and Steelworkers refused to accept pay cuts and went on strike in Homestead, Pennsylvania, Henry C. Frick, the president of Carnegie Steel Company, closed the plant. Shortly thereafter, Frick tried to protect the plant by hiring three hundred Pinkerton guards and floating them in by barge under cover of darkness. Angry workers, lying in wait on the shore of the Monongahela River, attacked and routed the guards. State militia were summoned, and after five months the strikers gave in. By then public opinion had turned against the strike because of an attempt on Frick's life by a young anarchist who was not a striker.

In 1894, workers at the Pullman Palace Car Company walked out in protest over exploitative policies at the company town near Chicago. The

Pullman Strike

paternalistic George Pullman provided everything for the twelve thousand residents of his so-called model town. His company owned and controlled all land and buildings, the school, the bank, and the water and gas systems. It paid wages, fixed rents, and employed spies to report on disgruntled employees. As one laborer grumbled, "We are born in a Pullman house, fed from the Pullman shop, taught in the Pullman school, catechized in the Pullman church, and when we die we shall be buried in the Pullman cemetery and go to the Pullman hell."

One thing Pullman would not do was negotiate with workers. When the hard times that began in 1893 threatened his business, Pullman maintained profits and stock dividends by cutting wages 25 to 40 percent while holding firm on rents and prices in the model town. Workers, pressed into debt and deprivation, sent a committee to Pullman to protest his policies. He reacted by firing three members of the committee. Enraged workers, most of whom had joined the American Railway Union, called a strike; Pullman retaliated by closing the plant. When the American Railway Union, led by the charismatic young organizer Eugene V. Debs, voted to aid the strikers by refusing to handle all Pullman cars, Pullman stood firm and rejected arbitration. The railroad owners' association then enlisted the aid of U.S. Attorney General Richard Olney, who obtained a court injunction to prevent the union from "obstructing the railways and holding up the mails." President Grover Cleveland sent troops to Chicago, ostensibly to protect the mails but in reality to crush the strike. Within a month the strike was over and Debs was jailed for contempt in defying the injunction. The Supreme Court upheld Debs's six-month sentence on the grounds that the federal government had the power to remove obstacles to interstate commerce.

In the West, more radical labor activity arose among metal miners in Colorado, who participated in a series of bitter struggles and violent strikes. Their union, the Western Federation of Miners, helped form a new labor organization, the Industrial Workers of the World (IWW). Unlike the AFL, the IWW strove like the Knights of Labor to unify all American laborers, including the unskilled who were not in craft unions; its motto was "an injury to one is an injury to all." But the "Wobblies," as the IWW was known, went beyond the goals of the Knights and espoused the goal of so-

cialism and the tactics of violence and sabotage. Using the rhetoric of class conflict—"The final aim is revolution," according to an IWW organizer—the Wobblies believed workers should seize and run the nation's industries. "Mother" Jones, an Illinois coalfield union organizer, Elizabeth Gurley Flynn, a fiery orator known as the "Joan of Arc" of the labor movement, and William D. (Big Bill) Haywood, the brawny, one-eyed founder of the Western Federation of Miners, led a series of IWW-organized strife-torn strikes. Demonstrations erupted in western lumber and mining camps, in the steel town of McKees Rocks, Pennsylvania (1907), and in the textile mills of Lawrence, Massachusetts (1912). Though their anticapitalist goals and aggressive tactics attracted considerable publicity, IWW members probably never exceeded 150,000. The organization faded during the First World War when federal prosecution—and persecution—sent many of its leaders to jail.

Many unions, notably those of the AFL, were openly hostile to women. Of the 6.3 million employed women in 1910, fewer than 2 percent belonged to unions. Male unionists often rationalized the exclusion of women by insisting that women should not be employed. According to one labor leader, "Woman is not qualified for the conditions of wage labor. . . . The mental and physical makeup of woman is in revolt against wage service. She is competing with the man who is her father or husband or is to become her husband." Fear of competition was the crucial issue. Because women were paid less than men, males worried that their own wages would be lowered or that they would lose their jobs altogether if women invaded the workplace. Moreover, male workers accustomed to sex segregation in employment could not imagine women and men working side by side.

Women and the Labor Movement

Yet female employees could organize and fight employers as strenuously as men could. Since the early years of industrialization, female workers had formed their own unions. Some, such as the Collar Laundry Union of Troy, New York, organized in the 1860s, had successfully struck for higher wages. The "Uprising of the 20,000" in New York City, a 1909 strike by young immigrant members of the International Ladies Garment Workers Union (ILGWU), was one of the largest strikes in the country to that time. Women were also prominent in the Lawrence (Massachusetts) textile workers' strike of 1912. Female trade-union membership swelled during the 1910s, but the national trade unions were still led by men, even in industries with large female work forces, such as the garment industry, textiles, and boots and shoes.

Women did dominate, however, in both membership and leadership in one union—the Telephone Operators' Department of the International Brotherhood of Electrical Workers. First organized in Montana and San Francisco early in the twentieth century, the union spread throughout the Bell system, the nation's major telephone company and single largest employer of women. To promote solidarity among their mostly young members, union leaders sponsored dances, excursions, and bazaars. Influenced by the women's rights movement, they also undertook educational programs to enhance members' assertiveness and leadership skills. The main focus was workplace issues. Intent on developing pride in the craft of telephone operators, the union opposed scientific management techniques and tightening of supervision. In 1919 several particularly militant unions, such as the one pictured

in the accompanying photo, paralyzed phone service in five New England states; the strike was the country's largest since 1909. The union collapsed after a failed strike, again in New England, in 1923, but not until women had proved that they could advance their own cause.

The first women's labor federation to parallel the AFL was the Women's Trade Union League (WTUL), founded in 1903 and patterned after a similar union in England. The WTUL worked for protective legislation for female workers, sponsored educational activities, and campaigned for women's suffrage. It helped the telephone operators organize their union, and in 1909 it supported the ILGWU's massive strike against New York City sweatshops. Initially the union's highest offices were held by middle-class women who sympathized with female wage laborers, but control shifted in the 1910s to forceful working-class leaders—notably Agnes Nestor, a glove maker, Rose Schneiderman, a cap maker, and Mary Anderson, a shoe worker. The WTUL advocated such changes as opening apprenticeship programs to women so they could enter skilled trades and providing leadership training for female workers. It

In 1919, telephone operators, mostly female, went out on strike and shut down phone service throughout New England. The workers above, who interrupted their picketing to pose for the photograph, showed that women could take forceful action in support of their labor interests.   UPI/Bettmann Archive.

served as a vital link between the labor and women's movements into the 1920s (see Chapter 24).

Organized labor also excluded most immigrant and African-American workers. Some trade unions welcomed skilled immigrants—in fact, foreign-born craftsmen were prominent leaders of several unions—but only the Knights of Labor and the IWW had firm policies of accepting immigrants and blacks. Blacks were among the organizers of the coal miners' union, and they were partially unionized in trades such as construction, barbering, and dock work, which had large numbers of black workers. But they could belong only to segregated local unions in the South, and the majority of northern AFL unions also had exclusion policies. Long-held prejudices were reinforced when blacks and immigrants worked as strikebreakers, hired to take the jobs of striking workers. Probably few strikebreakers understood the full effects of their actions, but even those who did found the lure of employment too great to resist.

Immigrants, African-Americans, and the Labor Movement

The drama that characterized the struggles of the labor movement in the half-century following the Civil War makes it easy to forget that only a small fraction of American workers belonged to unions. In 1900, only about 1 million out of a total of 27.6 million workers were unionized. By 1920, total union membership had grown to 5 million—still only 13 percent of the work force. Unionization was strong in building trades, transportation, communications, and, to a lesser extent, manufacturing. For many workers, issues of wages and hours were meaningless; getting and holding a job was the first priority. Job instability and the seasonal nature of work seriously hindered union organizing efforts. Few companies employed a full work force all year round; most employers hired workers during peak seasons and laid them off during slack periods. Thus employment rates often fluctuated wildly. The 1880 census showed that in some communities 30 percent or more of adult males had been unemployed at some time during the previous year. And organizers took no interest in large segments of the industrial labor force and intentionally excluded others.

The millions of men, women, and children who were not unionized tried in their own ways to cope with the pressures of the new machine age. Increasing numbers of workers, both native-born and immigrant, turned to fraternal societies such as the Polish Roman Catholic Union and the Jewish B'nai B'rith. These organizations, which for small monthly or yearly contributions provided their members life insurance, sickness benefits, and funeral expenses, became widespread by the early twentieth century.

For most American workers, then, the machine age had mixed results. Industrial wages rose between 1877 and 1914, boosting purchasing power and creating a mass market for standardized goods. Yet in 1900 most employees worked sixty hours a week at wages that averaged twenty cents an hour for skilled work and ten cents an hour for unskilled. Moreover, as wages rose, living costs increased even faster.

STANDARDS OF LIVING

Though some Americans were deeply suspicious of the advent of machines and the pursuit of profits, few could resist the changes that mechanization brought to everyday life. The rapid spread of railroad, postal, telephone, and electrical service drew even isolated communities into the orbit of a consumer-oriented society. American ingenuity combined with mass production and mass marketing to make available myriad goods that had not previously existed or had been the exclusive property of the wealthy. This new material well-being, brought about by the advent of such products as ready-made clothes, canned foods, and home appliances, had a dual effect: it drew Americans of differing status into communities of consumers—communities defined not by place or class but by possessions—and it accentuated differences between those who could afford such goods and services and those who could not.

If a society's affluence can be measured by how quickly it converts luxuries into commonplace articles, the United States was indeed becoming affluent in the years between 1880 and 1920. In 1880, for example, smokers rolled their own cigarettes; only wealthy women could afford silk stockings; only residents of Florida, Texas, and California could enjoy fresh oranges; and people made such goods as candy and soap at home. By 1899, manufactured goods and perishable foodstuffs were becoming increasingly widespread. That year Ameri-

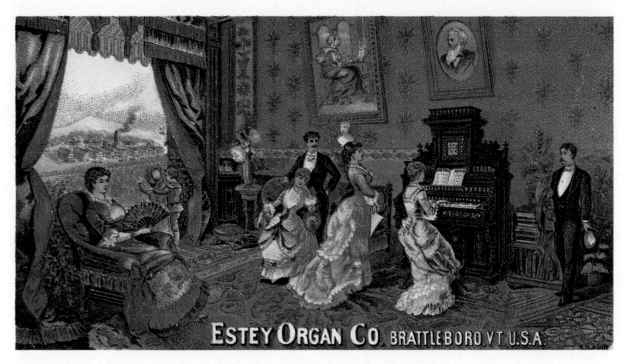

Industrialization enhanced the incomes and luxuries of the factory-owning classes, enabling them to purchase spacious homes and lavish furnishings. In this advertisement for a fancy organ, children gaze out the window at the nearby factory while adults admire the music being played. Collection of Sally Fox.

cans bought 2 billion machine-produced cigarettes (an average of 27 per person) and 151,000 pairs of silk stockings, consumed oranges at the rate of 100 crates for every 1,000 people, and spent an average of $1.08 per person on store-bought candy and pastries and 63 cents on soap. By 1921 the transformation was even more advanced. Americans smoked 43 billion cigarettes that year (403 per person), ate 248 crates of oranges per 1,000 people, bought 217 million pairs of silk stockings, and spent $1.66 per person on confectionery goods and $1.40 on soap. How did people afford to make these changes in their standard of living?

What people can afford obviously depends on their resources and incomes. Data for the period are incomplete, but there is no doubt that incomes rose. The rapidly expanding **Rising Personal** economy spawned massive for-**Income** tunes and created a new industrial elite. "The Coming Billionaire," published in *Forum* magazine in 1891, estimated that 120 Americans already were worth at least $10 million. By 1920, when income-tax figures made possible the accurate tabulation of income distribution, the richest 5 percent of the population was receiving almost one-fourth of all earned income. Returns on investments were even more skewed; the same 5 percent received almost half of all interest payments and 85 percent of all stock and bond dividends.

Incomes also rose among the middle classes. For example, average pay for clerical workers rose 36 percent between 1890 and 1910 (see table, page 549). After the turn of the century, employees of the federal executive branch were averaging $1,072 a year, and college professors $1,100—not handsome sums, but much more than manual workers received. With such incomes, the middle class, whose numbers were increasing as a result of new job opportunities, could afford relatively comfortable housing. A six- or seven-room house cost around $3,000 to buy or build and $15 to $20 per month to rent.

Though wages for industrial workers increased as well, income figures were deceptive because jobs were not always stable and workers had to expend a disproportionate amount of their income on necessities. On average, annual wages of factory workers rose from $486 in 1890 to $630 in 1910, about 30 percent. In industries with large female work forces, such as shoe and paper manufacturing, hourly rates remained lower than in male-dominated industries such as coal mining and iron production. Regional variations were also wide. Nevertheless, most wages moved upward (see table). Income for farm laborers followed the same trend, though wages remained relatively low because farm workers generally received free room and board.

Wage increases mean little, however, if living costs rise as fast as or faster than wages, and that is what happened. According to one economic index, the weekly cost of living

Cost of Living

for a typical wage earner's family of four rose over 47 percent between 1889 and 1913. In other words, a combination of food and other goods that cost $6.78 in 1889 increased, after a slight dip in the mid-1890s, to $10 by 1913 (see table for specific food prices). In very few working-class occupations did income rise at the same rate as the cost of living.

How then could working-class Americans afford the new goods and services that the machine age offered? Many could not. The daughter of a textile worker, recalling her school days, described how "some of the kids would bring bars of chocolate, others an orange. . . . I suppose they were richer than a family like ours. My father used to buy a bag of candy and a bag of peanuts every payday. . . . And that's all we'd have until the next payday. If we asked for something my mother would say, 'Well, we're too poor. We can't afford to buy that.' " Another woman explained how her family coped with high prices and low wages: "My mother made our clothes. People then wore old clothes. My mother would rip them out and make them over."

Still, a working-class family could raise its income and partake modestly in the consumer society by sending children and women into the labor market (see pages 537–539). In a

Supplements to Family Income

household where the father made $600 a year, the wages of other family members might lift total income to $800 or $900. Many families also rented rooms to boarders and lodgers, a practice that could yield up to $200 a year. These means of increasing family income enabled people to spend more and save more. Between 1889 and 1901, working-class families markedly increased expenditures for such items as life

insurance, amusements, alcoholic beverages, and union dues. Thus workers were able to improve their living standards, but not without sacrifices.

The work people did was part of a highly developed wage and money economy. Between 1890 and 1920, the American labor force increased by 50 percent, from 28 million workers to 42 million. These figures, however, are somewhat misleading: in general, they represent a change in the nature of work, rather than an increase in the number of available jobs. In the rural society that predominated in the United States in the nineteenth century, women and children performed work that was crucial to the family's daily existence—cooking, cleaning, planting, and harvesting—but often hard to define; they seldom appeared in employment figures because they earned no wages. But as the nation industrialized, and the agricultural sector's share of national income and population declined, paid employment became more common. Jobs in industry and commerce were easier to define and easier to count. It is probable that the proportion of Americans who worked was not increasing markedly—most Americans, male and female, had always worked. What was new was the increase in paid employment, making purchases of consumer goods and services more affordable.

Scientific and technological developments eased some of life's struggles, and their impact on living standards increased after 1900. Advances

Higher Life Expectancy

in medical care, better diets, and improved living conditions sharply reduced death rates and extended the life span. Between 1900 and 1920, life expectancy rose by fully six years and the death rate dropped by 24 percent (see table). During the same period there were notable declines in death from typhoid, diphtheria, influenza (except for a harsh pandemic in 1918 and 1919), tuberculosis, and intestinal ailments—diseases that had been scourges of earlier generations. There were, however, significantly more deaths from cancer, diabetes, and heart disease, afflictions of an aging population and perhaps also of new environmental factors. Americans also found more ways to kill one another: although the suicide rate remained about the same, homicides and automobile deaths, effects of a fast-paced urban society, increased dramatically between 1900 and 1920.

Not only were amenities and luxuries more readily available in the early 1900s than they had

American Living Standards, 1880–1920

	1880	1890	1900	1910	1920
Income and earnings:					
Annual income:					
Clerical worker		$848		$1,156	
Public school teacher		$256		$492	
Industrial worker		$486		$630	
Farm laborer		$233		$336	
Hourly wage:					
Soft-coal miner		$0.18[a]		$0.21	
Iron worker		$0.17[a]		$0.23	
Shoe worker		$0.14[a]		$0.19	
Paper worker		$0.12[a]		$0.17	
Labor statistics					
Number of people in labor force	17.4 million	28.5 million			41.7 million
Average workweek, manufacturing		60 hours		51 hours	47.4 hours
Food costs					
10 pounds potatoes		$0.16		$0.17	
1 dozen eggs		$0.21		$0.34	
1 pound bacon		$0.12½		$0.25	
Demographic data					
Life expectancy at birth:					
Women			48.3 years		54.6 years
Men			46.3 years		53.6 years
Death rate per 1,000 people			172		130
Birthrate per 1,000 people	39.8		32.3		27.7
Other					
Number of students in public high schools		203,000			2.3 million
Advertising expenditures	$20 million		$95 million		$500 million
Telephones per 100 people		0.3[b]	2.1[c]		12.6[d]

[a] 1892 [b] 1891 [c] 1901 [d] 1921

been a half-century earlier, but the means to upward mobility seemed more accessible as well. Education was increasingly becoming the key to success. The spread of public education—fueled by construction of new schools, particularly high schools, and passage of compulsory-attendance laws that required children to stay in school to age fourteen—helped equip young people to achieve a standard of living higher than their parents'. Between 1890 and 1922 the number of students enrolled in public high schools grew dramatically (see table). The creation of new white-collar jobs in growing service industries helped to stem the downward mobility that resulted when mechanization pushed skilled workers out of their crafts. Yet

the inequities that had pervaded earlier eras remained in place. Race, gender, religion, and ethnicity still determined access to opportunity.

THE QUEST FOR CONVENIENCE

One of the most representative agents of the revolution in American lifestyles at the end of the nineteenth century was the toilet. The chain-pull washdown water closet, invented in England around 1870, was adopted in the United States in the 1880s. Shortly after 1900 the flush toilet appeared;

thanks to the mass production of enamel-coated fixtures, it soon became standard in American homes and buildings.

The indoor toilet, suddenly cheap and easy to install, brought about a shift in habits and attitudes. Before 1880, only luxury hotels and estates had private bathrooms. By the 1890s, however, acceptance of the germ theory of disease had raised fears about carelessly disposed human waste as a source of infection and water contamination. Much more rapidly than Europeans did, Americans combined a desire for cleanliness with an urge for convenience, and water closets became common, especially in middle-class urban houses. Now bodily functions took on an unpleasant image, and the home bathroom became a place of utmost privacy. Edward and Clarence Scott, who produced white tissue in small perforated rolls, provided Americans a more convenient form of toilet paper than the rough paper they had previously used. At the same time, the toilet and the private bathtub gave Americans new ways to use—and waste—water. These advances in plumbing were part of a broader democratization of convenience that accompanied mass production and consumerism.

Processed and Preserved Foods

The tin can also altered lifestyles. Before the mid-nineteenth century, Americans typically ate only foods that were in season. Drying, smoking, and salting could preserve meat for a short time, but the availability of fresh meat, like that of fresh milk, was limited; there was no way to prevent spoilage. A French inventor developed the cooking-and-sealing process of canning around 1810, and in the 1850s an American man named Gail Borden developed a means of condensing and preserving milk. Canned goods and condensed milk became more common during the 1860s, but supplies remained low because cans had to be made by hand. By 1880, however, inventors had fashioned stamping and soldering machines to mass-produce cans from tin plate. Now, even people remote from markets, like sailors and cowboys, could readily consume tomatoes, milk, oysters, and other alternatives to previously monotonous diets. Housewives also did their own preserving of fruits and vegetables, "putting up" foods in glass jars.

Other trends and inventions helped broaden Americans' diets. Growing urban populations created the demand that encouraged fruit and vegetable farmers to raise more produce. Railroad refrig-erator cars enabled growers and meatpackers to ship perishables greater distances and to preserve them for longer periods. By the 1890s, northern city dwellers could enjoy southern and western strawberries, grapes, and tomatoes for up to six months of the year. Home iceboxes enabled middle-class families to store perishables. An easy means of producing ice commercially was invented in the 1870s, and by 1900 the nation had over two thousand commercial ice plants, most of which made home deliveries.

The availability of new foods also inspired health reformers to correct the American diet. In the 1870s, John H. Kellogg, a nutritionist and manager of the Western Health Reform Institute in Battle Creek, Michigan, began serving patients new health-providing foods, including peanut butter and wheat flakes. Several years later his brother, William K. Kellogg, invented Corn Flakes, and Charles W. Post introduced Grape-Nuts, revolutionizing breakfast by replacing eggs, potatoes, meats, and breads with ready-to-eat cold cereal, which supposedly was healthier. Just before the First World War, scientists discovered the dietetic value of vitamins A and B (C and D were discovered after the war). Growing numbers of published cookbooks and the opening of new cooking schools reflected heightened interest in food and its possibilities for health and enjoyment.

Even the working class enjoyed a more diversified diet. As in the past, the poorest people still ate cheap foods, heavy in starches and carbohydrates. Southern textile workers, for example, ate corn mush and fatback (the strip of meat from a hog's back) almost every day. Poor urban families seldom could afford meat. Now, however, many could buy previously unavailable fruits, vegetables, and dairy products. Workers had to spend a high percentage of their income on food—almost half the breadwinner's wages—but they never suffered the severe malnutrition that plagued other developing nations.

Ready-made Clothing

Just as tin cans and iceboxes made many foods widely available, the sewing machine was bringing about a revolution in clothing. In the eighteenth century, nearly all the clothes Americans wore were made at home or by seamstresses and tailors, and a person's social status was apparent in what he or she wore. Then in the 1850s the sewing machine, invented in Europe but refined by Americans Elias Howe, Jr., and Isaac M. Singer, came into use in clothing and shoe manufacture. Demand for uniforms during the Civil War boosted the ready-made clothing industry, and by 1890 annual retail sales of mass-produced garments reached $1.5 billion. Mass production enabled manufacturers to turn out good-quality apparel at relatively low cost and to standardize sizes to fit different body shapes. By 1900, only the poorest families could not afford "ready-to-wear" clothes. Tailors and seamstresses, once the originators of fashion, had been relegated to repair work. The advent of dress patterns intended for use with a sewing machine simplified the remaining home production of clothing and gave even those who could not afford ready-made clothes access to stylish fashions.

With mass-produced clothing and dress patterns came a concern for style. Restrictive Victorian fashions still dominated women's clothing, but some of the most burdensome features were beginning to be abandoned. As women's participation in work and leisure activities became more active, dress styles began to place greater emphasis on comfort. By the end of the nineteenth century, long sleeves and skirt hemlines receded, and high-boned collars disappeared. Designers used less fabric; by the 1920s a dress required three yards of material instead of ten. Petite was still the ideal, however: the most desirable waist measurement was 18 to 20 inches, and corsets were big sellers at 79 cents. Meanwhile, health reformers complained that women often tried to squeeze into dresses, gloves, and shoes that were a size too small. In the early 1900s, long hair tied at the back of the neck was the most popular style. By the First World War, when many women worked in hospitals and factories, shorter and more manageable styles had become fashionable.

Men's clothes, too, became more lightweight and stylish. Before 1900, among the middle and affluent working classes, a man would have owned no more than two suits, one for Sundays and special occasions and one for everyday wear. After 1900, however, manufacturers began to produce garments from fabrics of different weights and for different seasons. Men replaced stiff derbies with soft felt hats, and stiff collars and cuffs with soft ones; dark-blue serge gave way to softer shades and more intricate weaves. Workingmen's clothes did not change markedly: laborers still needed the most durable, least expensive overalls, shirts, and shoes.

By the end of the nineteenth century, a great variety of canned foods became common ingredients in the diet of millions of Americans. Often advertising in women's magazines, some food processors made recipe books available to consumers who bought their products. Collection of Sally Fox.

But even for those of modest means, clothing was becoming something to be bought instead of made and remade at home.

Department stores and chain stores helped to create and serve this new consumerism. The great boom occurred between 1865 and 1900, when

Department and Chain Stores
———

companies like Macy's, Wanamaker's, Jordan Marsh, and Marshall Field became fixtures of metropolitan America. Previously, working-class people had bought their goods in shabby stores and wealthier types had patronized fancy shops; each was discouraged by price, quality of goods, and social custom from shopping at the other's establishments. Now department stores, with their open displays of clothing, housewares, and furniture—all available in large quantities to anyone with the purchase price—caused a merchandising revolution. They offered not only a wide variety but also home deliveries, liberal exchange policies, and charge accounts.

In their quest for convenience, Americans shopped for mass-produced, standard-size clothing in department stores. Still, however, many women continued to make their own clothing, often from standardized dress patterns. This drawing shows a large millinery shop in New York, where women purchased the cloth they used to fashion dresses from patterns.   New York Historical Society.

Meanwhile, the Great Atlantic Tea Company, founded in 1859, became the first grocery-store chain. Renamed the Great Atlantic and Pacific Tea Company in 1869 (more familiarly known as the A&P), the firm's stores could buy in volume and thus sell to the public at low prices. By 1915 there were almost eighteen hundred A&P stores, and twelve thousand more were built in the next ten years. Other chains, such as Woolworth's, grew rapidly during the same period.

THE TRANSFORMATION
OF MASS
COMMUNICATIONS

With so many new things to do and buy, how did Americans decide what they wanted? Consumer tastes and public opinion were being influenced by two new types of communication: modern advertising and popular journalism.

A society of scarcity does not need advertising. When demand exceeds supply, producers have no trouble selling what they market. But in a society

Advertising

of abundance such as industrial America, supply frequently outstrips demand, making necessary a means of increasing or even creating demand. Thus advertising took on a new scale and function in the late nineteenth century. In 1865 about $9.5 million was spent on advertising; that sum had reached $95 million by 1900, and nearly $500 million by 1919.

The American salesperson's function has traditionally been to convince a customer that a certain product—whether an insurance policy, article of clothing, or home appliance—is uniquely suited to fill a need that the customer has identified. Advertisers, on the other hand, aim to *invent* a need by convincing entire groups that everyone in that group should buy a specific product—a brand of cigarettes, a particular cosmetic, a certain company's canned foods. Indeed, the growth in the late nineteenth century of large companies that mass-produced consumer goods gave advertisers the task of creating "consumption communities"—bodies of consumers loyal to a particular brand name.

In 1881, Congress passed a federal trademark law enabling producers to register and protect brand names. Thousands of companies eventually registered such well-known products as Hires Root Beer, Uneeda Biscuits, and Carter's Little Liver Pills. Advertising agencies—a new service industry pioneered by N. W. Ayer & Son of Philadelphia—in turn offered expert advice to companies that wished to cultivate brand loyalty. By the turn of the century, advertising techniques had been perfected to such an extent that French composer Jacques Offenbach observed, "Decidedly the American advertising men play upon the human mind as a musician plays on his piano."

The prime vehicle for advertising was the newspaper. In the mid-nineteenth century, publishers began to pursue higher revenues from advertising by selling more ad space, especially to big urban department stores. Wanamaker's placed the first full-page ad in 1879, and at about the same time newspapers began to allow advertisers to print pictures of products. Such attention-getting techniques transformed advertising into news. More than ever before, people read newspapers to find out what was for sale as well as what was happening (see pages 583–584).

At the same time, large manufacturers were adding new marketing techniques to their technological and organizational innovations. Meat processor Gustavus Swift used branch slaughterhouses and refrigeration to enlarge the market for fresh meat. James B. Duke, whose American Tobacco Company made cigarettes a big business, saturated communities with billboards and free samples and offered premium gifts to retailers for selling more cigarettes. Companies like International Harvester and Singer Sewing Machine set up systems for servicing their products and introduced financing schemes to permit customers to buy the machines more easily. In many instances marketing innovations enabled producers to sell directly to retailers, squeezing out wholesalers and eliminating the excess costs that wholesaling entailed.

THE CORPORATE CONSOLIDATION MOVEMENT

Neither the wonders of industrial production nor the new techniques of market promotion masked unsettling factors in the American economy. The race for higher productivity and new markets had costs as well as benefits. New technology demanded that factories operate at near capacity in order to produce goods most economically. But the more manufacturers produced, the more they had to sell. And to sell more, they had to reduce prices. To increase profits and compensate for reduced prices, they further expanded production and often

reduced wages. To expand, they had to borrow money. And, to repay the loans, they had to produce and sell even more. This circular process strangled small firms that could not keep pace, and thrust workers into conditions of constant uncertainty. The same cycle affected commerce, banking, and transportation as well as manufacturing.

This environment encouraged rapid growth, but optimism could dissolve at the hint that debtors could not meet their obligations. In the final third of the nineteenth century, financial panics afflicted the economy at least once a decade, ruining businesses and putting workers out of jobs. The economic declines that began in 1873, 1884, and 1893 each lingered for several years. Business leaders disagreed on what caused them. Some blamed overproduction; others pointed to underconsumption; still others blamed lax credit and investment practices. Whatever the explanation, businesspeople began seeking ways to combat the uncertainty of the boom-and-bust business cycle. Many turned to centralized and cooperative forms of business organization, notably corporations, pools, trusts, and holding companies.

Unlike laborers, industrialists never questioned the capitalist system or lost faith in their leadership abilities. They looked for new ways to build on the corporate base **Role of Corporations** that had supported economic growth since the early 1800s, when states had adopted incorporation laws to encourage commerce and industry. Under such laws, almost anyone could start a company and raise money by selling stock to investors. Stockholders could share in profits without high risk because the laws limited their liability for company debts to the amount of their own investment; the rest of their wealth was protected should the company fail. Nor did they need to concern themselves with the day-to-day operation of the firms; full responsibility for company administration was left in the hands of managers. The corporation proved to be the best instrument to raise capital for industrial expansion, and by 1900 corporations were responsible for two-thirds of all goods manufactured in the United States. Moreover, corporations won broad judicial protection in the 1880s and 1890s when the Supreme Court ruled that they, like individuals, are protected by the Fourteenth Amendment. In other words, states could not deny corporations equal protection under the law and could not deprive them of rights or property without due process of law. Such rulings insulated corporations against vigorous government interference in their operations.

But as both economic disorder and the urge for profits mounted, corporation managers began to seek greater stability in new and larger forms of economic concentration. Between the late 1880s and early 1900s, an epidemic of business consolidation swept the United States, eventually resulting in the massive conglomerates that have dominated the American economy in the twentieth century. At first such efforts were tentative and informal, consisting mainly of cooperative agreements among firms that manufactured the same product or offered the same service. Through these arrangements, called *pools*, competing companies tried to control the market by agreeing how much each should produce and what prices should be charged. Employed mainly by railroads (to divide up traffic), steel producers, and whiskey distillers, pools depended on their members' honesty. Such "gentlemen's agreements" worked during good times when there was enough business for all; but during slow periods, the desire for profits often tempted pool members to evade their commitments by secretly reducing prices or by selling more than the agreed quota. The Interstate Commerce Act of 1887 outlawed pools (see page 602), but by then their usefulness was already fading.

John D. Rockefeller disliked pools, calling them "ropes of sand"—that is, weak and undependable instruments. In 1879 one of his lawyers, Samuel Dodd, devised a more stable means of dominating the market. Since state laws prohibited one corporation from holding stock in another corporation, Dodd adapted an old device called a *trust*, which in law existed as an arrangement whereby responsible individuals would manage the financial affairs of a person unwilling or unable to handle them alone. Dodd reasoned that one company could achieve control of an industry by luring or forcing the stockholders of smaller companies in the industry to yield control of their stock "in trust" to the larger company's board of trustees. This device allowed Rockefeller to achieve *horizontal integration* of the highly profitable petroleum industry in 1882 by combining his Standard Oil Company of Ohio with other refineries he bought up, thus strengthening his grip.

In 1888 New Jersey adopted new laws allowing corporations chartered there to own property in other states and to own stock in other corporations. (Trusts provided for trusteeship, but not ownership.) This liberalization facilitated the creation of the *holding company*, which owned a partial or complete interest in other companies. Holding companies could in turn merge their constituent companies' assets (buildings, equipment, inventory, and cash) as well as their management. Under this arrangement, Rockefeller's holding company, Standard Oil of New Jersey, merged forty constituent companies. By 1898, Standard Oil refined 84 percent of all oil produced in the nation, controlled most pipelines, and had moved into natural-gas production and ownership of oil-producing properties.

Standard Oil's expansion into operations besides oil refining exemplified a new form of economic integration. In an effort to dominate their markets, many holding companies sought control over all aspects of their operations, including raw materials, production, and distribution. The prime example of such *vertical integration*, which fused a broad range of business activities into one entity under unified management, was Gustavus Swift's meat-processing operation. During the 1880s, Swift boldly invested in livestock, slaughterhouses, refrigerator cars, and marketing to ensure the sale of his beef without unexpected inconvenience.

Mergers became the answer to industry's search for order. Between 1889 and 1903, some three hundred combinations were formed, most of them trusts and holding companies. The most spectacular was the U.S. Steel Corporation, formed in 1901 and financed by J. P. Morgan. This new enterprise, made up of iron-ore properties, freight carriers, wire mills, plate and tubing companies, and other firms, was capitalized at over $1.4 billion. Other mammoth combinations included the Amalgamated Copper Company, American Sugar Refining Company, American Tobacco Company, and U.S. Rubber Company, each worth over $50 million.

The merger movement created a new species of businessman, whose vocation was financial organizing rather than producing a particular good or service. Shrewd operators sought opportunities for combination, formed corporations, and then persuaded producers to sell their firms to the new

Pools, Trusts, and Holding Companies

Role of Financiers

company. These financiers usually raised money by selling stock and borrowing from banks. Uncommitted to any particular industry, their attention ranged widely. Thus W. H. Moore organized the American Tin Plate Company, Diamond Match Company, and National Biscuit Company, and he acquired control of the mighty Rock Island Railroad. Elbert H. Gary similarly participated in consolidation of the barbed-wire industry and then of U.S. Steel. Investment bankers like J. P. Morgan and Jacob Schiff piloted the merger movement, inspiring awe with their financial power and organizational skills.

The growth of corporations in the late nineteenth century turned financial exchanges into hubs of activity where investors bought and sold stocks and bonds feverishly. By the end of 1886, trading on the New York Stock Exchange had reached 1 million shares a day. By 1914 the number of industrial stocks traded had reached 511, compared with 145 in 1869. Investment could not have occurred without attracting the capital necessary for such purposes. Between 1870 and 1900 foreign investment in American companies rose from $1.5 billion to $3.5 billion. Personal savings and institutional investment also mushroomed: assets of savings banks, concentrated in the Northeast and on the West Coast, rose by 700 percent between 1875 and 1897 to a total of $2.2 billion. States gradually loosened their regulations to enable banks to invest in railroads and industrial enterprises. Commercial banks, insurance companies, and corporations also invested heavily. As one journal proclaimed, "Nearly the whole country (including the typical widow and orphan) is interested in the stock market." Though a gross exaggeration, this assertion reflected what optimistic capitalists wanted to believe.

THE GOSPEL OF WEALTH AND ITS CRITICS

To corporate investors and executives, profits depended on growth, and profits meant everything. Pursuit of wealth, which drove corporate competition, had become the purpose of existence. As Milton H. Smith of the Louisville and Nashville Railroad put it, "Society, as created, was for the purpose of one man's getting what the other fellow has, if he can, and keep out of the penitentiary."

The merger movement that resulted in trusts and holding companies contradicted the philosophy of open competition. Business leaders turned to consolidation under new corporate forms not to promote competition but to mimimize it. To justify the size and power of the resulting monopolistic companies to a public raised on the ideology of open competition, defenders of business eagerly embraced the doctrine of Social Darwinism. Developed by English philosopher Herbert Spencer and preached in the United States by Yale professor William Graham Sumner, Social Darwinism loosely grafted Charles Darwin's theory of the evolutionary survival of the fittest onto laissez faire, the doctrine that government should not interfere in economic private affairs. Social Darwinists reasoned that, in an unconstrained economy, power would flow naturally to the most capable. The acquisition and possession of property were therefore sacred rights, and wealth was a mark of well-deserved power and responsibility. Civilization depended on this system, explained Sumner. "If we do not like the survival of the fittest," he wrote, "we have only one possible alternative, and that is survival of the unfittest." Monopolies, therefore, resulted from the natural accumulation of economic power by those most capable of wielding it. Many clergymen and journalists supported this argument.

Social Darwinism

Social Darwinists reasoned, too, that wealth carried moral responsibilities: captains of industry should provide for the needs of those less fortunate or less capable. Steel baron Andrew Carnegie asserted what he called "the Gospel of Wealth"—that he and other powerful industrialists were trustees for society's wealth and that they had a duty to fulfill that trust in humane ways. Over his lifetime, Carnegie donated more than $350 million to libraries, educational institutions, peace initiatives, and the arts. Such philanthropy, however, also implied a right for men like Rockefeller and Carnegie to define what they believed was good and necessary for society. It meant that the wealthy could and should raise "moral culture" by endowing churches, hospitals, and schools; it also meant that government should not tax or regulate the rich or their activities.

Paradoxically, business executives who extolled individual initiative and independence also pressed for government assistance. While denounc-

Government Assistance to Business
———

ing measures to aid unions or regulate factory conditions as interference with natural economic laws, they lobbied forcefully and successfully for subsidies, loans, and tax relief to encourage business growth. By far the most extensive form of government assistance to American industry was tariffs, which raised the price of foreign products by placing an import tax on them. When Congress imposed high import duties on foreign goods like kerosene, steel rails, worsted wools, and tin plate, American producers could continue to sell their goods at relatively high prices. Industrialists argued that tariff protection encouraged the development of new products and the founding of new enterprises. But tariffs also forced consumers to pay artificially high prices for many goods.

Critics who opposed trusts and other new forms of business organization based their arguments on traditional American beliefs in independence and opportunity. In do-

Dissenting Voices
———

ing so, they argued within the same framework of values as did the corporate leaders they opposed. While defenders of trusts insisted that they were a natural and efficient outcome of economic development, critics charged that trusts were unnatural because they were created by greed and inefficient because they stifled opportunity. Such charges gave voice to an ardent fear of *monopoly*, the domination of an economic activity by one powerful company, such as Standard Oil. Those who feared monopoly believed that large corporations could manipulate consumers by fixing prices, exploit workers by cutting wages, destroy opportunity by crushing small businesses, and threaten democracy by corrupting politicians—all of which was not only unnatural but immoral. To critics, ethics eclipsed economics.

Many believed there was a better way to achieve progress. By the mid-1880s, a number of young professors began to challenge Social Darwinism and laissez faire economics. Brown University sociologist Lester Ward attacked the application of evolutionary theory to social and economic relations. In *Dynamic Sociology* (1883), Ward argued that human control of nature, not natural law, accounted for the advance of civilization. To Ward, a system that guaranteed survival only to the fittest was wasteful and brutal; instead, he reasoned, co-

operative activity fostered by planning and government intervention was the best route to progress. Economists Richard Ely, John R. Commons, and Edward Bemis agreed that natural forces should be harnessed for the public good. They denounced the laissez-faire system for its "unsound morals" and praised the positive assistance that government could offer. These views formed the philosophical underpinning for government action during the Progressive era in the early twentieth century (see Chapter 21).

While academics endorsed intervention in the natural economic order, others proposed more utopian schemes for combating monopolies. Though

Utopian Economic Schemes
———

they opposed the industrial system, they did not shun the technology that had made it possible. Rather, they believed humans could harness their skills and machines in a better way. Reformer Henry George, whose background as a printer and writer had sensitized him to the exploitative power of large enterprises, declared that economic inequality stemmed from the ability of a few to profit from rising land values. George argued that rising land values made owners rich simply because of increased demand for living and working space, especially in cities. To prevent profiteering, George proposed to replace all taxes with a "single tax" on the "unearned increment"—the rise in property values caused by increased market demand rather than by owners' improvements. George's scheme, argued forcefully in *Progress and Poverty* (1879), had great popular appeal and almost won him the mayoralty of New York City in 1886.

Unlike George, who accepted private ownership, novelist Edward Bellamy envisioned a state in which government would own and oversee the means of production and would unite all citizens under moral laws. Bellamy outlined his dream in *Looking Backward, 2000–1887* (1888). The novel, which sold over a million copies, depicted Boston in the year 2000 as a peaceful community where everyone belonged to an industrial army and people were paid not in money but in credits enabling them to obtain consumer goods and entertainment. By depicting a utopian world free of politicians and class divisions, Bellamy tried to convince readers that a "principle of fraternal cooperation" could replace vicious competition and wasteful monopoly.

How do historians know

what turn-of-the-century Americans thought about big business? Political cartoons and the symbols used by cartoonists often represent prevailing attitudes and can serve as a kind of shorthand for understanding how the same historical circumstance can arouse differing opinions. These two cartoons illustrate two quite different points of view. The one on the top depicts the Standard Oil Trust as a greedy octopus with sprawling tentacles that are snaring Congress, state legislatures, and the taxpayer in their grasp and are reaching for the White House. The cartoonist obviously saw dangerous and wide-reaching power being exercised by such an economic giant. The second cartoon portrays a much more benevolent view. In this version, the cartoonist depicts John D. Rockefeller of Standard Oil and Andrew Carnegie of U.S. Steel at work, using their profits to nurture a garden of colleges and libraries, thereby showing the social good that could result from trusts.   Octopus: Library of Congress; garden: Baker Library, Harvard Business School.

This vision, which he called Nationalism, sparked the formation of Nationalist clubs around the country and kindled popular appeals for civil service reform, social welfare measures, and government ownership of railroads and utilities.

Journalist and reformer Henry Demarest Lloyd arrived at a similar conclusion by a different route. His *Wealth Against Commonwealth* (1894) indicted John D. Rockefeller and Standard Oil for exploiting the poor and crushing competition. As an alternative to ruthless monopolies and enslavement of labor, Lloyd proposed a cooperative commonwealth, similar to Bellamy's, in which government would own and operate factories for the common good.

Before 1900 few people supported the kind of government ownership envisioned by Bellamy and Lloyd, but several state governments did take steps to prohibit monopolies and regulate big business. By the end of the century, fifteen states had constitutional provisions outlawing trusts, and twenty-seven had laws forbidding pools. Most were agricultural states in the South and West that were responding to antimonopolistic pressure from various farm organizations (see page 602). But state attorneys general lacked the staff and judicial support for an effective attack on big business, and corporations always found ways to evade restrictions. Consequently a need for national legislation became more pressing.

Antitrust Legislation

Congress moved hesitantly toward such legislation in the 1880s and in 1890 finally passed the Sherman Anti-Trust Act. Introduced by Senator John Sherman of Ohio and rewritten by probusiness eastern senators, the law made illegal "every contract, combination in the form of trust or otherwise, or conspiracy in the restraint of trade." People found guilty of violating the law faced fines and jail terms, and those wronged by illegal combinations could sue for triple damages. However, the law was left purposely vague so all factions could support at least part of it. It did not define clearly what a restraint of trade was. Moreover, it consigned interpretation of its provision to the courts, which at the time were strong allies of business.

Judges thus used the law's vagueness to blur distinctions between reasonable and unreasonable restraints of trade. When in 1895 the federal government prosecuted the so-called Sugar Trust for owning 98 percent of the nation's sugar-refining capacity, eight of the nine Supreme Court justices ruled that control of manufacturing did not necessarily mean control of trade (*U.S.* v. *E.C. Knight Co.*). According to the Court, the Constitution empowered Congress to regulate interstate *commerce*, but *manufacturing* (which in the *Knight* case took place entirely within the state of Pennsylvania) did not fall under congressional control.

Between 1890 and 1900 the federal government prosecuted only eighteen cases under the Sherman Anti-Trust Act. The most successful cases were those aimed at railroads directly involved in interstate commerce. Ironically, the act did equip government officials with a tool for breaking up labor unions; courts that did not consider monopolistic production a restraint on trade willingly applied antitrust provisions to strikes.

Mechanization and a burst of new inventions thrust the United States into the vanguard of industrial nations and immeasurably altered daily life between 1877 and 1920. Other effects were less positive. In industry, as in farming and mining, bigness and consolidation engulfed the individual, changing the nature of work from individual activity undertaken by producers to mass production undertaken by employees. Workers fought to regain control of their efforts, but they failed to develop well-organized unions that could meet their needs on a large scale. The outpouring of new products created a new mass society based on consumerism, but even the "democratization of consumption" did not benefit all social groups.

The problems of enforcing the Sherman Anti-Trust Act reflected the uneven distribution of power among American interest groups. Corporate enterprises had effectively consolidated, and they controlled great resources of economic and political power. Other groups—farmers, laborers, and reformers—had numbers and ideas but lacked power. Almost all members of these groups desired the material gains that technology and large-scale production were providing, but they increasingly feared that business was acquiring too much influence. In factories and on farms, some people were celebrating the industrial transformation while others were struggling with the dilemma of American industrialism: whether a system based on ever-greater profits was the best way for Americans to achieve the nation's democratic destiny.

SUGGESTIONS FOR FURTHER READING

General

Daniel J. Boorstin, *The Americans. The Democratic Experience* (1973); Carl N. Degler, *The Age of the Economic Revolution* (1977); Ray Ginger, *The Age of Excess* (1965); Samuel P. Hays, *The Response to Industrialism* (1975); Thomas J. Schlereth, *Victorian America: Transformations in Everyday Life* (1991).

Technology and Invention

Robert W. Bruce, *Bell: Alexander Graham Bell and the Conquest of Solitude* (1973); Roger Burlingame, *Henry Ford* (1957); Robert Friedel and Paul Isaacs, *Edison's Electric Light: Biography of an Invention* (1986); David Hounshell, *From the American System to Mass Production* (1984); Thomas Parke Hughes, *American Genesis: A Century of Technological Enthusiasm* (1989); Thomas Parke Hughes, *Networks of Power: Electrification in Western Society* (1983); John P. Kasson, *Civilizing the Machine: Technology and Republican Values in America* (1976); Leo Marx, *The Machine in the Garden: Technology and the Pastoral Ideal* (1964); Andre Millard, *Edison and the Business of Innovation* (1990); David E. Nye, *Electrifying America* (1990); Howard Segal, *Technological Utopianism in American Culture* (1985); Peter Temin, *Steel in Nineteenth-Century America* (1964).

Industrialism, Industrialists, and Corporate Growth

W. Eliot Brownlee, *Dynamics of Ascent: A History of the American Economy*, 2nd ed. (1979); Stuart Bruchey, *Growth of the Modern Economy* (1973); Vincent P. Carosso, *The Morgans* (1987); Alfred D. Chandler, *The Visible Hand: The Managerial Revolution in American Business* (1977); Alfred D. Chandler, *Strategy and Structure: Chapters in the History of American Industrial Enterprise* (1966); Thomas C. Cochran, *Business in American Life* (1972); Francis L. Eames, *The New York Stock Exchange* (1968); David F. Hawkes, *John D.: The Founding Father of the Rockefellers* (1980); Robert Higgs, *The Transformation of the American Economy, 1865–1914* (1971); Matthew Josephson, *The Robber Barons* (1934); Harold C. Livesay, *Andrew Carnegie and the Rise of Big Business* (1975); Daniel Nelson, *Managers and Workers: Origins of the New Factory System in the United States, 1800–1920* (1975); Allan Nevins, *Study in Power: John D. Rockefeller*, 2 vols. (1953); Glen Porter, *The Rise of Big Business* (1973); Martin J. Sklar, *The Corporate Reconstruction of American Capitalism* (1988); Joseph Wall, *Alfred I. du Pont: The Man and His Family* (1990); Joseph Wall, *Andrew Carnegie* (1970).

Work and Labor Organization

Alan Dawley, *Class and Community* (1977); Alan Derickson, *Workers' Health, Workers' Democracy: The Western Miners' Struggle, 1891–1925* (1988); Melvin Dubofsky, *We Shall Be All: A History of the Industrial Workers of the World* (1969); Sarah Eisenstein, *Give Us Bread, Give Us Roses: Working Women's Consciousness in the United States, 1890 to the First World War* (1983); Leon Fink, *Workingmen's Democracy: The Knights of Labor and American Politics* (1982); Philip S. Foner, *The Great Labor Uprising of 1877* (1977); Herbert G. Gutman, *Work, Culture and Society in Industrializing America* (1976); Tamara K. Hareven, *Family Time and Industrial Time: The Relationship Between the Family and Work in a New England Industrial Community* (1982); Alice Kessler-Harris, *Out to Work: A History of Wage Earning Women in the United States* (1982); Susan Lehrer, *Origins of Protective Labor Legislation for Women* (1987); Harold Livesay, *Samuel Gompers and Organized Labor in America* (1978); Milton Meltzer, *Bread and Roses: The Struggle of American Labor, 1865–1915* (1967); Stephen Meyer III, *The Five Dollar Day: Labor Management and Social Control in the Ford Motor Company, 1908–1921* (1981); Ruth Milkman, ed., *Women, Work, and Protest* (1985); David Montgomery, *The Fall of the House of Labor: The Workplace, the State, and American Labor Activism, 1865–1925* (1987); David Montgomery, *Workers' Control in America: Studies in the History of Work, Technology, and Labor Struggles* (1979); Stephen H. Norwood, *Labor's Flaming Youth: Telephone Operators and Worker Militancy* (1990); Elizabeth Ann Payne, *Reform, Labor, and Feminism: Margaret Dreier Robins and the Women's Trade Union League* (1988); Daniel J. Walkowitz, *Worker City, Company Town* (1978); Leon J. Wolff, *Lockout: The Story of the Homestead Strike of 1892* (1965).

Living Standards and New Conveniences

Susan Porter Benson, *Counter Cultures: Saleswomen, Managers, and Customers in American Department Stores, 1890–1940* (1986); Daniel J. Boorstin, *The Americans: The Democratic Experience* (1973); Stephen Fox, *The Mirror Makers: A History of American Advertising and Its Creators* (1984); T. J. Jackson Lears and Richard W. Fox, eds., *The Culture of Consumption* (1983); Godfrey M. Lebhar, *Chain Stores in America* (1962); Harvey A. Levenstein, *Revolution at the Table: The Transformation of the American Diet* (1988); Daniel Pope, *The Making of Modern Advertising* (1983); Peter R. Shergold, *Working Class Life: The "American Standard" in Comparative Perspective, 1899–1913* (1982); Susan Strasser, *Satisfaction Guaranteed: The Making of the American Mass Market* (1989); Gwendolyn Wright, *Building the Dream: A Social History of Housing in America* (1983); Lawrence Wright, *Clean and Decent* (1960).

Attitudes Toward Industrialism

Sidney Fine, *Laissez Faire and the General Welfare State* (1956); Louis Galambos and Barbara Barron Spence, *The Public Image of Big Business in America* (1975); Richard Hofstadter, *Social Darwinism in American Thought*, rev. ed. (1955); T. J. Jackson Lears, *No Place of Grace: Antimodernism and the Transformation of American Culture* (1981); Henry Demarest Lloyd, *Wealth Against the Commonwealth* (1894); Robert McCloskey, *American Conservatism in the Age of Enterprise* (1951); John L. Thomas, *Alternative America: Henry George, Edward Bellamy, Henry Demarest Lloyd, and the Adversary Tradition* (1983).

The Vitality and Turmoil of Urban Life, 1877–1920

F OR NEARLY THIRTY YEARS, Frank Ventrone had successfully pursued his dream. Then, one night in August 1914, his world literally shattered. Ventrone had emigrated in the 1880s from Isernia, in southern Italy, to Providence, Rhode Island, a bustling, industrializing city. By saving money and buying property, Ventrone became a prominent businessman in the city's fast-growing Italian immigrant community, many of whose residents had also come from Isernia. Ventrone's biggest success was a pasta business that furnished the community's staple food. This business was also the source of his trouble.

Food prices were rising in the summer of 1914, and Ventrone followed the trend by raising the price of his pasta. Angered by the added pressure to their already overburdened incomes, the people of Providence's Italian section vented their frustration on Ventrone. One August weekend they marched through the neighborhood, broke windows in a block owned by Ventrone, broke into his shop and dumped his stock of macaroni in the street. When police arrived, the rioters insisted that the matter was an internal one to be resolved by their community. Ventrone had violated the code

of ethnic loyalty. The next Monday, Ventrone's agent met with community members and agreed to lower his prices. "Signor Ventrone . . . owes everything to our colony," declared the neighborhood newspaper. "Our brave colony, when we all stand together, will be given justice."

The Providence "macaroni riot," with its various dimensions—the transfer of immigrant cultures from Old World to New, the mobility of some people from rags to respectability, the continued poverty of others amid economic uncertainty, the eruption of violence—was just one of millions of events that characterized life in an American city. A similar protest could have occurred in Italy, but the American context amplified its drama. By 1900, Providence was a rapidly growing city, and the United States was the most rapidly urbanizing nation in the Western world. The hopes, frustrations, and conflicts that urban growth generated seemed both dazzling and bewildering. Clanging trolleys, smoky air, crowded streets, a jumble of languages—these sensations and more contrasted with the slow, quiet pace of village and farm life. As cities grew, they became places of both opportunity and misery.

"Jefferson Market," a depiction of modern Philadelphia, was painted in 1922 by painter and illustrator, John Sloan.

In the 1830s and 1840s, the nation's urban population started to grow much faster than its rural population. But not until the 1880s did the United States begin to become a truly urban nation. By 1920 a symbolic milestone of urbanization had been passed: that year's census showed that, for the first time, a majority of Americans (51 percent) lived in cities (any settlement with more than 2,500 people). This new fact of national life was as symbolically significant as the disappearance of the frontier in 1890. The era of the yeoman farmer was over, and urban growth joined with the development of natural resources (Chapter 17) and industrialization (Chapter 18) as an identifiable feature of American expansion in the late nineteenth and early twentieth centuries.

Cities served as marketplaces and forums, bringing together the people, resources, and ideas responsible for many of the changes American society was experiencing. By 1900 a network of small, medium, and large cities spanned every section of the country and attracted exuberant admirers and sneering detractors. Some people relished the opportunities and excitement cities offered. As one newspaper editor wrote, it was "better [to] be the 1/1,000,000,000 of New York than the 1/1 of Aroostook County." Others found the crudeness of American cities disquieting. "Having seen it," British poet Rudyard Kipling wrote of Chicago, "I urgently desire never to see it again." But whatever people's personal impressions, the city had become central to American life. Modern American society has been shaped by the ways people built their cities and adjusted to the new urban environment.

TRANSPORTATION AND INDUSTRIAL GROWTH IN THE MODERN CITY

By 1900, the compact American city of the early nineteenth century, where residences were mixed in among shops, factories, and warehouses, had burst open. From Boston to Los Angeles, development had sprawled several miles beyond the original central core. No longer did walking distance determine a city's size, and no longer did different social groups live close together: poor near rich, immigrant near native-born, black near white. Instead, cities subdivided into distinct districts: working-class neighborhoods, African-American

Electric trolley cars and other forms of mass transit enabled middle-class people like the women and men in this photograph to reside on the urban outskirts and ride public transportation into the city center for work, shopping, and entertainment. Museum of the City of New York.

• *Important Events* •

1867	First law regulating tenements passes, in New York State	**1895**	William Randolph Hearst buys the *New York Journal*, another major popular "yellow press" newspaper
1876	National League of Professional Baseball Clubs founded	**1898**	Race riot erupts in Wilmington, North Carolina
1880s	"New" immigrants from eastern and southern Europe begin to arrive in large numbers	**1900–10**	Immigration reaches peak Vaudeville rises in popularity
1883	Brooklyn Bridge completed Joseph Pulitzer buys *New York World* and creates a major vehicle for "yellow journalism"	**1903**	Boston plays Pittsburgh in first baseball World Series
1885	Safety bicycle invented	**1905**	Intercollegiate Athletic Association, forerunner of National College Athletic Association (NCAA) is formed and restructures rules of football
1886	First settlement house opens in New York City	**1906**	Race riot erupts in Atlanta, Georgia
1889	Thomas A. Edison invents the motion picture and viewing device	**1915**	D. W. Griffith directs *Birth of a Nation*, one of first major technically sophisticated movies
1890s	Electric trolleys replace horse-drawn mass transit	**1920**	Majority (51.4 percent) of Americans now live in cities
1893	World's Columbian Exposition opens in Chicago		

ghettos, business districts, a ring of suburbs. Two forces were responsible for this new arrangement. One, mass transportation, was centrifugal, propelling people and enterprises outward. The other, economic change, was centripetal, drawing human and economic resources inward.

Mass transportation moved people faster and farther. Before the 1870s, horse- and mule-drawn vehicles had been the main means of transport in cities. But they were inefficient. They could carry relatively few riders, and purchasing and feeding the animals was costly. Once the technology was developed, entrepreneurs adopted better ways to transport people. During the 1850s and 1860s, steam-powered commuter railroads had appeared in a few cities, such as New York and Boston, but not until the late 1870s did mechanized mass transit begin to appear. The first power-driven devices were cable cars, carriages that clamped onto a moving underground wire. Cheaper than horse cars, cable cars were also more efficient at hauling passengers up and down

Mechanization of Mass Transportation

steep hills. By the 1880s, cable-car lines operated in Chicago, San Francisco, and many other cities.

In the 1890s, electric-powered streetcars began replacing early forms of mass transit. Designed in Montgomery, Alabama, and Richmond, Virginia, electric trolleys spread quickly to nearly every large American city. Between 1890 and 1902, total mileage of electrified track grew from 1,300 to 22,000 miles. Meanwhile horse-railway track shrank. In a few cities, trolley companies raised part of the track onto stilts, enabling vehicles to travel without interference above jammed downtown districts. In Boston, New York, and Philadelphia, transit firms dug underground passages for their cars, also to avoid delays. Because elevated railroads and subways were extremely expensive to construct, they appeared only in the few cities where transit companies could amass enough capital to lay track and buy equipment and where there were enough riders to ensure profits.

Another form of mass transit, the electric interurban railway, not only provided greater convenience for riders but also helped link nearby cities. Usually built over shorter distances than steam

Along with mass-produced consumer goods such as clothing and appliances, Sears, Roebuck and Company marketed architectural plans for middle-class suburban housing. The drawing above, taken from the Sears catalogue for 1911, illustrates the look of the kind of housing developed on the urban outskirts in the early twentieth century.   Sears, Roebuck and Company.

railroads, the interurbans operated between cities in areas with growing populations and furthered urban development by making such regions more attractive for settlers and businesses. The extensive network of the Pacific Electric Railway in southern California, for example, facilitated both travel and economic development in that region.

Mass-transit lines launched millions of urban dwellers into outlying neighborhoods and created a commuting public. Those who could afford the fare—usually five cents a ride—could live outside the crowded central city but return there for work, shopping, and entertainment. Working-class families, whose incomes rarely topped a dollar a day, found the fare too high and could not benefit from streetcars. But for the growing middle class, bungalows, like the one that could be built from the Sears, Roebuck design, offered homes in quiet tree-lined neighborhoods on the urban outskirts. Real-estate development boomed around the peripheries of scores of cities. Between 1890 and 1920, for example, developers in the Chicago area

Beginnings of Urban Sprawl

opened 800,000 new lots—enough to house at least three times the city's 1890 population. A home several miles from downtown was inconvenient, but the benefits seemed to outweigh the costs. As one suburbanite wrote in 1902, "It may be a little more difficult for us to attend the opera, but the robin in my elm tree struck a higher note and a sweeter one yesterday than any prima donna ever reached."

Urban sprawl was essentially unplanned, but certain patterns did emerge. Eager to capitalize on commuting possibilities, thousands of small investors who bought land in anticipation of settlement paid little attention to the need for parks, traffic control, and public services. Construction of mass transit was guided by the profit motive and thus benefited the urban public unevenly. Streetcar lines serviced mainly those districts that promised the most riders—whose fares, in other words, would increase dividends for stockholders.

Streetcars, elevateds, and subways altered commercial as well as residential patterns. When consumers moved outward, businesses followed. Secondary commercial centers sprouted at trolley-line intersections and elevated-railway stations.

Branches of department stores and banks joined groceries, theaters, drugstores, taverns, and specialty shops to create neighborhood shopping centers, the forerunners of today's suburban malls. Meanwhile, the urban core became the work zone, where offices and stores loomed over streets clogged with traffic. Districts like Chicago's Loop and New Orleans's Canal Street contained practically every kind of business and cultural institution.

Cities also became the main arenas for industrial growth. As centers of resources, labor, transportation, and communications, cities provided everything factories needed. **Urban-Industrial Development** Once mass production became possible, capital accumulated by the cities' commercial enterprises—gathering and distributing raw materials and finished goods—fed industrial investment. Urban populations also furnished consumers for myriad new products. Thus urban growth and industrialization wound together in a mutually beneficial spiral. The further industrialization advanced, the more opportunities it created for work and investment in cities. Increased opportunity in turn drew more people to cities; as workers and as consumers, they fueled further industrialization.

Most cities housed a variety of industrial enterprises, but product specialization gradually became common. Mass production of clothing was concentrated in New York; the shoe industry in Philadelphia; and textiles in several New England cities. Other cities processed products from surrounding agricultural regions: flour in Minneapolis, cottonseed oil in Memphis, beer in Milwaukee. Still others processed natural resources: gold and copper in Denver, fish and lumber in Seattle, coal and iron in Pittsburgh and Birmingham, oil in Houston and Los Angeles. Such activities increased the magnetic attraction of cities for people in search of steady employment.

Urban and industrial growth transformed the national economy and freed the United States from dependence on European capital and manufactured goods. Imports and foreign investments still flowed into the United States. But by the early 1900s, cities and their factories, stores, and banks were converting America from a debtor agricultural nation into a major industrial, financial, and exporting power.

PEOPLING THE CITIES: MIGRANTS AND IMMIGRANTS

Economist Edmund J. James had good reason to assert in 1899 that the era he was living in was "not only the age of cities but the age of great cities." Between 1870 and 1920, the number of Americans living in cities exploded almost 550 percent, from 10 million to 54 million. During the same period, the number of cities with more than 100,000 people grew from fifteen to sixty-eight, and the number with more than 500,000 swelled from two to twelve (see maps). These figures, dramatic in themselves, represent millions of stories of hope and frustration, adjustment and confusion, success and failure.

The population of a place can grow in three ways: by extension of its borders to annex land and people; by natural increase (an excess of births over deaths); and by net migration **How Cities Grew** (an excess of in-migrants over out-migrants). Between the 1860s and early 1900s, many cities annexed nearby suburbs, thereby instantly increasing their populations. The most notable consolidation occurred in 1898 when New York City, which had previously consisted only of Manhattan and the Bronx, merged with Brooklyn, Staten Island, and part of Queens and grew overnight from 1.5 million to over 3 million people. The thirst for expansion was insatiable. As one observer remarked, "Those who locate near the city limits are bound to know that the time may come when [the city] will extend the limits and take them in." Moreover, suburbs often desired annexation because they needed the schools, water, fire protection, and sewer systems that cities had developed. Annexation also added vacant land where new city dwellers could live. Cities like Chicago, Minneapolis, and Cincinnati incorporated hundreds of undeveloped square miles into their borders in the 1880s, only to see them fill up with new residents in succeeding decades. Annexation did increase urban populations, but its major effect was to enlarge the physical size of cities.

Natural increase did not account for much of any city's population growth. In the late nineteenth century, death rates declined in most regions of the

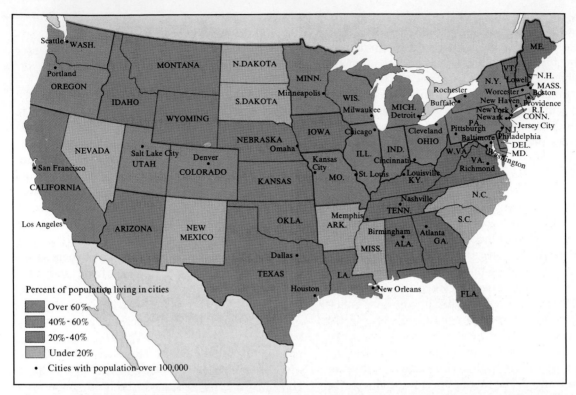

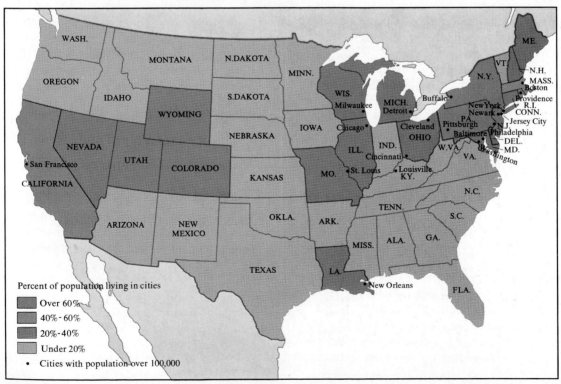

Urbanization, 1880; Urbanization, 1920   *Whereas in 1880 the vast majority of states still were heavily rural, by 1920 only a few had less than twenty percent of their population living in cities.*

country, but birthrates fell rapidly as well (see the Appendix). In urban areas, birthrates decreased more rapidly than in rural areas. In cities, the number of people who were born in a given year was roughly equal to the number who died that year.

Migration and immigration made by far the greatest contribution to urban population growth. In fact, migration to cities nearly matched the massive migration to the West that was occurring at the same time. Urban newcomers arrived from two major sources: the American countryside and Europe. Asia, Canada, and Latin America also supplied immigrants, though in smaller numbers.

In general, rural populations were declining as urban populations burgeoned. A variety of factors such as low crop prices and high debts dashed farmers' hopes and drove them **Major Waves of Migration and Immigration** off the land toward the opportunities that cities seemed to offer. Their migrations affected not only cities like Detroit, Chicago, and San Francisco but also scores of secondary cities like

Toledo, Indianapolis, Salt Lake City, Birmingham, and San Diego. The thrill of city life beckoned especially to young people. A character in the play *The City* spoke for many youths when she exclaimed, "Who wants to smell new-mown hay, if he can breathe in gasoline on Fifth Avenue instead! Think of the theaters! The crowds! *Think* of being able to go out on the street and *see some one you didn't know by sight!*"

Many more of the newcomers were immigrants who had fled foreign farms, villages, and cities for American shores. The dream of a large number was not to stay but to make enough money to return home and live in greater comfort and security. For every hundred foreigners who entered the country, around thirty left. Still, most of the 26 million immigrants who arrived between 1870 and 1920 remained, and the great majority settled in cities, where they helped reshape American culture.

These immigrants to the United States were participants in a worldwide movement that had two components. One pushed people away from traditional means of support; the other pulled them

Arriving at Ellis Island in New York Harbor, probably to rejoin their husband and father who already had settled in the United States, this mother and her children put on their best clothes to match their determined look. Relatives and fellow villagers often advised immigrants to do everything possible to impress inspectors who examined them upon arrival.   Brown Brothers.

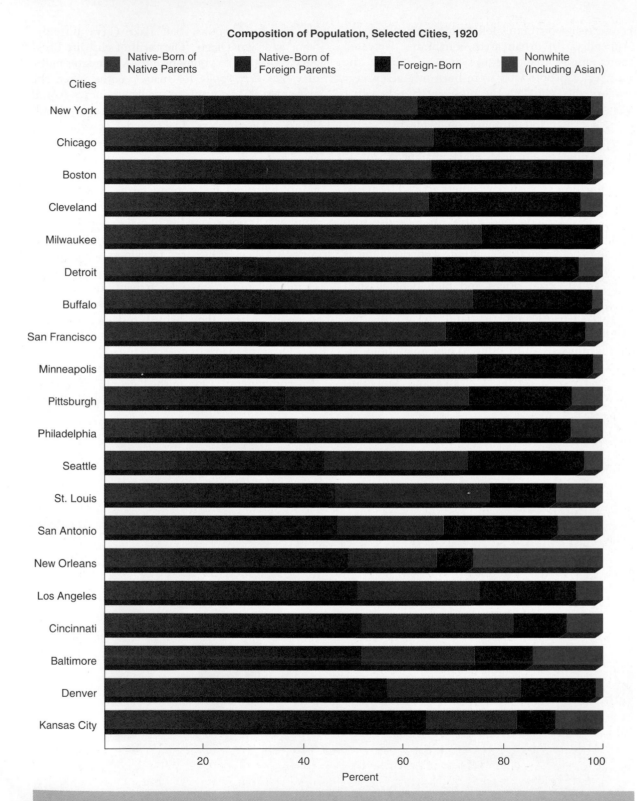

Composition of Population, Selected Cities, 1920   *As a result of immigration and migration, in almost every major city by the early twentieth century native-born whites of native-born parents were distinct minorities. Moreover, foreign-born residents and native-born whites of foreign parents (combining the green and purple segments of a line) constituted absolute majorities in numerous places.*

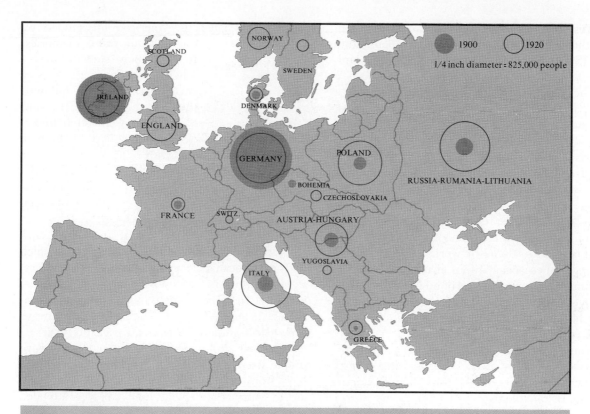

Sources of European-Born Population, 1900 and 1920   *In just a few decades, the proportion of European immigrants to the United States who came from northern and western Europe decreased, while the proportion from eastern and southern Europe increased.*

toward the opportunity for a better life. As industrialization undercut local crafts like weaving and shoemaking, artisans found it more difficult to supplement their agricultural income with household production. In addition, the growth of cities worldwide increased demand for agricultural goods, thereby encouraging large-scale production, which in turn made small farms less profitable. Population pressures and economic changes resulting from land redistribution and industrialization induced millions of small farmers and craftsmen to leave Europe and Asia. They traveled to Canada, Australia, Brazil, Argentina, and other relatively unsettled places, as well as the United States, in search of a better life. Also, religious persecution, particularly the violent pogroms and merciless military conscription that Russian Jews suffered, caused people to flee across the Atlantic. Countless others, particularly the poorest peasants, migrated shorter distances in search of better conditions, usually from a rural village or town to an industrial city. Migration has always been present in human

history, but now technology in the form of the telegraph, railroad, and steamship made communications and travel cheaper, quicker, and safer.

The United States had been the destination of immigrants from northern and western Europe since the 1840s, but after 1880 economic and demographic changes propelled a second massive wave of immigrants from other regions. Northern and western Europeans continued to arrive, but the new wave brought more people from eastern and southern Europe, plus smaller contingents from Canada, Mexico, and Japan (see map and figure). Two-thirds of the newcomers who arrived in the 1880s were from Germany, England, Ireland, and Scandinavia; between 1900 and 1909, two-thirds were from Italy, Austria-Hungary, and Russia. By 1910, arrivals from Mexico were beginning to outnumber arrivals from Ireland, and large numbers of Japanese had moved to the West Coast and Hawaii. Foreign-born blacks, chiefly from

The New Immigration

the West Indies, also increased in number, from forty thousand in 1910 to seventy-four thousand in 1920. (See the Appendix for nationalities of immigrants.)

The immigrants varied widely in age, marital status, and other social characteristics, but certain traits stand out. Approximately two-thirds of the newcomers were males, especially after 1900, and about two-thirds were between the ages of fifteen and thirty-nine. Not all groups were equally educated, but almost three-fourths of the immigrants could read and write, at least in their native languages. Among those reporting occupations at the time of entry, half identified themselves as unskilled laborers or domestic workers (maids, cooks, cleaners). These occupations may have reflected the immigrants' expectations of how they would be employed in America, but they also suggest that many had lived in cities for at least a short time before emigrating.

Many Americans feared the strange customs, Catholic and Jewish faiths, illiteracy, and poverty of "new" immigrants, considering them less desirable and assimilable than "old" immigrants, whose languages and beliefs seemed less alien. This view received sober support from authorities like future president Woodrow Wilson, who wrote in his *History of the American People* (1902), "The immigrant newcomers of recent years are men of the lowest class from the South of Italy, and men of the meaner sort out of Hungary and Poland, men out of the ranks where there was neither skill nor energy, nor any initiative or quick intelligence."

In reality, however, old and new immigrants resembled each other more closely than many Americans believed. The majority of both groups came from a world in which family was the focus of all decisions and undertakings. Whether and when to emigrate was decided in light of the family's needs, and family bonds and interests continued to prevail after immigrants reached the New World. New arrivals almost always knew where they wanted to go and how to get there because they received aid from relatives who had already immigrated. In many instances, workers helped kin obtain jobs, and family members pooled their resources to maintain, if not improve, their standard of living. The bywords for all immigrants were "cooperate and survive."

Perhaps of most importance, all immigrants brought with them memories of their homelands, and they adjusted to American life guided by the light of those memories.

Immigrant Cultures

In their new surroundings—where the language was a struggle, the workday followed the clock rather than the sun, and housing and employment were often uncertain—immigrants anchored their lives to the rock they knew best: their culture. Old World customs persisted in immigrant enclaves of Italians from the same province, Japanese from the same island district, or Russian Jews from the same *shtetl* (village). Mutual benefit and fraternal societies were recreated along village and provincial lines. For example, Japanese transferred their *ken* societies, which organized social celebrations and relief services, and Chinese from Canton brought *hui* institutions, which raised money to help members acquire businesses. People practiced religion as they always had, held traditional feasts and pageants, married within their group, and pursued old feuds with people from rival villages and provinces. Among Jews from eastern Europe, men grew long sidelocks, women wore wigs, and children attended afternoon religious training. Southern Italians transplanted the system whereby a boss, or *padrone*, found jobs for unskilled workers by negotiating with an employer. They also recreated their Old World mutual benefit associations to provide families emergency aid as well as sickness and death benefits. Pasquale Cruci, an immigrant from Salerno, explained that he helped to found such an association in Bridgeport, Connecticut, because

> I felt that the Italian people of this city should have some security from death and accidents. The Italian people of this time didn't trust the big insurance companies because they thought they would get cheated. They felt that if some organization was Italian that it was all right.

Yet the very diversity of American cities forced immigrants to modify their attitudes and habits. Few newcomers could avoid contact with people different from themselves, and few could prevent such contacts from altering their traditional ways of life. Although many foreigners identified themselves by their village or region of birth, native-born Americans categorized them by nationality. People from County Cork and County Limerick were lumped together as Irish; those from Schleswig and Wurttemberg were Germans; those from Calabria and Campobasso were Italians. Immigrant institutions, such as newspapers and churches, found they had to appeal to the entire nationality in order to survive.

Everywhere, Old World culture persisted alongside New World realities. Although immigrants struggled to maintain their native languages and to pass them down to younger generations, English was taught in the schools and needed on the job; it soon penetrated nearly every community. Foreigners cooked ethnic meals using American foods and fashioned American fabrics in European styles. Italians went to American doctors but still carried traditional amulets in their pockets to ward off evil spirits. Chinese expanded their traditional gambling games to include poker. Music especially revealed adaptations. Polka bands still entertained at Polish social gatherings, but their repertoires expanded to blend American and Polish folk music; the bands, once dominated by violins, added accordions, clarinets, and trumpets to enable them to play more loudly. Mexican ballads acquired new themes that described the adventures of border crossing and the hardship of labor in the United States. Eventually most immigrants grew accustomed to trusting American institutions. An Italian woman in Bridgeport, Connecticut, admitted

> that time [previously] they had all the societies that give you the money if you die, and that's . . . why all the women they were belonging to these societies. . . . Now they don't do this so much, they get the insurance from the Metropolitan and the other companies. . . . Now us Italian people we are more "Americanizzata."

The influx of so many immigrants between 1870 and 1920 transformed the United States from a basically Protestant nation into one composed of Protestants, Catholics, and Jews. Newcomers from Italy, Hungary, Poland, and the present-day Czech Republic and Slovakia joined Irish and Germans to boost the proportion of Catholics in a number of cities. In places like Buffalo, Cleveland, Chicago, and Milwaukee, Catholic immigrants and their offspring approached a majority of the population. Catholic Mexicans constituted over half the population of El Paso. German and Russian immigrants gave New York one of the largest Jewish populations in the world.

Influence on Religion

Believing that assimilation under one language was the end product of immigration, those who wished to "Americanize" the immigrants felt the schools could provide the best setting for the process. This 1917 poster from the Cleveland Board of Education and the Cleveland Americanization Committee used languages most common to the new immigrants—Slovene, Italian, Polish, Hungarian, and Yiddish—besides English to invite newcomers to free classes in the schools, where they could learn "the language of America" and "citizenship."   National Park Service Collection, Ellis Island Immigration Museum. Photo by Chermayeff & Geismar/MetaForm.

Partly in response to Protestant charges that they could not retain Old World religious beliefs and still assimilate into American society, many Catholics and Jews tried to accommodate their faiths to the new environment. Some Catholic and Jewish leaders from older, more established immigrant groups supported liberalizing trends—the use of English in sermons, the phasing-out of Old World rituals such as saints' feasts, and a preference for public over religious schools. As long as new immigrants continued to arrive, however, these tendencies met stiff opposition. Newcomers usually sought to retain familiar practices, whether the folk Catholicism of southern Italy or the orthodox Judaism of eastern Europe. Catholic immigrants pressed for ethnically separate parishes in spite of Church attempts to make American Catholicism more uniform. Bishops acceded to pressures from predominantly Polish congregations for Polish- rather than German-born priests. Eastern European Jews, convinced that Reform Judaism sacrificed too much to American ways, established the Conservative branch, which retained traditional ritual, though it abolished the segregation of women in synagogues and allowed English prayers.

In the 1880s, another group of migrants began to move into American cities. Thousands of rural African-Americans moved northward and westward, seeking better employment and fleeing crop liens, the ravages of the boll weevil on cotton crops, racial violence, and political oppression. Although black urban dwellers would grow more numerous after 1915, thirty-two cities had ten thousand or more black residents by 1900, and 79 percent of all blacks outside the South lived in cities. These migrants resembled foreign immigrants in their rural backgrounds and economic motivations, but they differed in several important ways. Because few factories would employ African-Americans, most found jobs in the service sector—cleaning, cooking, and driving—rather than in the industrial trades. Also, because most domestic and personal service openings were traditionally female jobs, black women outnumbered black men in cities like New York, Baltimore, and New Orleans.

African-American Migration to the Cities

Each of the three major migrant groups that peopled American cities—native-born whites, foreigners of various races, and native-born blacks—helped build modern American culture. The cities nurtured rich cultural variety: American folk music and literature, Italian and Mexican cuisine, Irish comedy, Yiddish theater, African-American jazz and dance, and much more. Like their predecessors, newcomers in the late nineteenth century changed their environment as much as they were changed by it.

LIVING CONDITIONS IN THE INNER CITY

Urban population growth created intense pressures on the public and private sectors. The masses of people who jammed inner-city districts were known more for the problems they bred than for their cultural contributions. American cities seemed to harbor all the afflictions that plague modern society: poverty, disease, crime, and other unpleasant conditions that develop when large numbers of people live close together. City dwellers adjusted as best they could. Although technology, science, private enterprise, and public authority failed to relieve all of these problems, some remarkable successes were achieved. In the late nineteenth and early twentieth centuries, construction of buildings, homes, streets, sewers, and schools proceeded at a furious pace. American cities set world standards for fire protection and water purification. But many other hardships and ills still await solution.

One of the most persistent shortcomings of American cities—their failure to provide adequate housing for all who need it—has its roots in nineteenth-century urban development. In spite of massive construction in the 1880s and early 1900s, population growth outpaced housing supplies. This situation weighed most heavily on working-class families who, because of low wages, had to rent their living quarters. As cities grew, landlords took advantage of shortages in low-cost rental housing by splitting up existing buildings to house more people, constructing multiple-unit tenements, and hiking rents. Low-income families adapted to high costs and short supply by sharing space and expenses. Thus it became common in many big cities for a "one-family" apartment to be occupied by two or three families or a single family plus a number of boarders.

Housing Problems

Such conditions created unprecedented crowding. In 1890, New York City's immigrant-packed Lower East Side, pictured opposite, averaged 702 people per acre, one of the highest population densities in the world. Low-rent districts had distinctive physical appearances in different cities:

six- to eight-story barracks-like buildings in New York; dilapidated row houses in Baltimore and Philadelphia; converted slave quarters in Charleston and New Orleans; and crumbling two- and three-story frame houses in Boston and San Francisco.

Inside many buildings, living conditions were harsh. The largest rooms were barely ten feet wide, and interior rooms either lacked windows or opened onto narrow shafts that bred vermin and rotten odors. Describing such a shaft, one immigrant housekeeper said, "It's damp down there, and the families, they throw out garbage and dirty papers and the insides of chickens, and other unmentionable filth. . . . I just vomited when I first cleaned up the air shaft." Few buildings had indoor plumbing, and the only source of heat was dangerous, polluting coal-burning stoves.

Housing problems aroused concerned citizens to mount reform campaigns in several places. New York State took the lead by legislating light, venti-

Housing Reform

lation, and safety codes for new tenement buildings in 1867, 1879, and 1901. These and similar laws in other states could not remedy the ills of existing buildings, but they did impose minimal obligations on landlords. A few reformers, such as journalist Jacob Riis and humanitarian Lawrence Veiller, advocated housing low-income families in "model tenements," with more spacious rooms and better facilities. Model tenements, however, required landlords to accept lower profits—a sacrifice few were willing to make. Neither reformers nor public officials would consider government financing of better housing, fearing that such a step would undermine private enterprise. Still, the housing codes and regulatory commissions that resulted from reform campaigns did strengthen the power of local government to oversee construction. And reformers' earnest concern for the lives of inner-city residents gradually made a difference.

Just as they used indoor space as efficiently as possible, inner-city dwellers adapted what little outdoor space they had to their needs. In this cramped block of six-story tenements in New York, scores of families hung their wash in the spaces behind the buildings. Note that there is virtually no space between buildings, meaning that only the rooms in front and back, not those on the sides, were exposed to light and air. Library of Congress.

As Veiller urged, "We must stop people living in cellars before we concern ourselves with changes in methods of taxation. We must make it impossible for builders to build dark rooms in new houses before we urge the government to subsidize the building of houses. We must abolish privy vaults [latrines] before we build model tenements."

Efforts at housing reform had only limited success, but scientific and technological advances eventually enabled city dwellers and the nation in general to live and work in greater comfort and safety. By the 1880s, most doctors had accepted the germ theory of disease. In response, cities established more efficient systems of water purification and sewage disposal. Although disease and death rates remained higher in cities than in the countryside, and tuberculosis and other respiratory ills continued to plague inner-city districts, public health regulations helped to control such dread diseases as cholera, typhoid fever, and diphtheria.

Meanwhile, street paving, modernized firefighting equipment, and electric street lighting spread rapidly across urban America. Previously, the number of rooms in a house had been limited by the number of fireplaces the house contained; now central heating and electricity made it possible to heat and light separate rooms, enabling some urban dwellers to enjoy unprecedented privacy in their own bedrooms. Indoor plumbing, which allowed for construction of a separate room with toilet and bathtub, also affected attitudes about privacy and personal hygiene.

Steel-frame construction, which supported a building by a metal skeleton rather than by masonry walls, made possible the construction of skyscrapers—and thus more efficient use of scarce and costly urban land. Electric elevators and steam-heating systems serviced these buildings. Steel-cable suspension bridges, developed by John A. Roebling and epitomized by the great Brooklyn Bridge (completed in 1883), linked metropolitan sections more closely.

None of these improvements, however, lightened the burden of poverty. The urban economy, though generally expanding, advanced erratically.

Urban Poverty

Employment, especially for unskilled workers in manufacturing and construction, rose and fell with business cycles and changing seasons. An ever-increasing number of families lived on the margins of survival.

Ever since colonial days, Americans have disagreed on how much responsibility the public should assume for poor relief. According to traditional beliefs, still widespread in the late nineteenth and early twentieth centuries, anyone could escape poverty through hard work and clean living; poverty was inevitable only because some people were weaker than others. Such reasoning bred fear that aid to poor people would encourage paupers to rely on public relief rather than their own efforts. This attitude hardened as poverty increased, and city governments discontinued direct grants of food, fuel, and clothing to needy families. Instead, cities provided relief in return for work on public projects and sent special cases to such state-run institutions as almshouses, orphanages, and homes for the blind, deaf, and mentally ill.

Private philanthropic agencies concerned themselves only with helping "the worthy poor," but their efforts to professionalize relief did foster some change in attitude. Between 1877 and 1892, philanthropists in ninety-two cities formed Charity Organization Societies, an attempt to put social welfare on a more systematic basis by merging disparate charity groups into a coordinated unit. Believing poverty to be caused by personal defects like alcoholism and laziness, members of these organizations spent most of their time visiting poor families and encouraging them to be thriftier and more virtuous.

Close observation of the poor, however, caused some welfare workers to conclude that people's environments, not their personal shortcomings, caused poverty. In turn, they came to believe that the ills of poverty could be cured by improving housing, education, and sanitation, and by expanding job opportunities rather than admonishing the poor to be more moral. This new attitude, which had been gaining ground since the mid-nineteenth century, fueled drives for building codes, factory regulations, and public health measures. But most middle- and upper-class Americans continued to endorse the creed that in a society of abundance only the unfit were poor and that poverty relief should be tolerated but never encouraged. As one charity worker put it, relief "should be surrounded by circumstances that shall . . . repel every one . . . from accepting it."

Even more than crowding and pauperism, crime and disorder nurtured fears that urban growth, especially the immigrant slums, threat-

Crime and Violence

ened the nation. The more cities grew, it seemed, the more they shook with violence. While homicide rates declined in industrialized nations like England and Germany, those in America rose alarmingly: 25 murders per million people in 1881; 107 per million in 1898. Pickpockets, swindlers, and burglars roamed every city. Some acquired as much notoriety as western desperadoes (see Chapter 17). One infamous urban outlaw was Rufus Minor, alias Rufus Pine. Short, stocky, and bald, Minor resembled an obscure clerk, but one police chief labeled him "one of the smartest bank sneaks in America." A sometime associate of Billy "The Kid" Burke, he often grew a heavy beard before holding up a bank, then shaved afterward to avoid identification by eyewitnesses to the robbery. Minor was implicated in bank heists in New York City, Cleveland, Detroit, Providence, Philadelphia, Albany, Boston, and Baltimore—all between 1878 and 1882.

Despite the fear of increases in robberies and violence, urban crime may simply have become more conspicuous and sensational, rather than more prevalent. To be sure, concentrations of wealth and the mingling of different peoples provided new opportunities for organized thievery, petty larceny, vice, and violent grudge settling. But did urban lawlessness and brutality exceed that of backwoods mining camps and southern plantations? Native-born whites were quick to blame Irish bank-robbery gangs, German pickpockets, and Italian Black Hand murderers for urban disorder, but there is little evidence that more immigrant than native-born Americans populated the rogues' gallery. One investigation of jails in 1900 concluded that "we have ourselves evolved as cruel and cunning criminals as any that Europe may have foisted upon us."

Whatever the extent of criminality, city life in this period supported the thesis that the United States has a tradition of violence. Cities served as arenas for many of the era's worst riots. As laborers and employers tried to adjust to the uncertainties of industrialization, violence became, in the words of one observer, "a sort of natural and inevitable concomitant." Ethnic and racial minorities were often victims of violent bigotry that lurked beneath the American myth of equality. The cityward movement of African-Americans roused white fears, and as the twentieth century dawned, a series of race riots spread across the nation: Wilmington, North Carolina, 1898; Atlanta, Georgia, 1906; Springfield, Illinois, 1908. In cities of the Southwest and Pacific Coast, Chinese and Mexican immigrants often felt the sting of intolerance. And innumerable disruptions ranging from domestic violence to muggings to gang fights made cities scenes of constant turbulence.

Role of the Police

Since the mid-nineteenth century, city dwellers had gradually overcome their resistance to professional law enforcement and increasingly depended on the police to protect life and property. By the early 1900s, however, law enforcement had become complicated and controversial because various groups differed in their views of the law and how it should be enforced. Disadvantaged groups—notably ethnic and racial minorities—could not escape arrest as easily as those with economic or political influence. And police officers applied the law less harshly to members of their own ethnic groups and to people who bought exemptions with bribes.

As the chief urban law-enforcement agency, the police were often caught between conflicting pressures for swift and severe action on the one hand and leniency on the other. Some people clamored for crackdowns on drinking, gambling, and prostitution at the same time that others privately supported loose law enforcement so they could indulge in these so-called "customer crimes." Urban American society became more diversified, and different groups tried to protect their particular interests—such as keeping saloons open late at night, indulging in social gambling, or even applying their own notions of law and order, as happened in the case of Frank Ventrone. Achieving a balance between the idealistic intentions of criminal law and people's desire for individual freedom grew increasingly difficult, and it has remained so to this day.

The mounting problems of city life seemed to demand greater government action. Thus city governments passed more ordinances that regulated housing, provided poverty relief, and expanded police power to protect health and safety. Yet public responsibility always ended at the boundaries of private property. Eventually some advances in housing construction, sanitation, and medical care did reach slum dwellers. But for most people, the only hope was that their children would do better or that opportunities would be better somewhere else.

FAMILY LIFE

Although the overwhelming majority of Americans continued to live within families, this most basic of social institutions suffered considerable strain during the era of urbanization and industrialization. New institutions—schools, social clubs, political organizations, and others—increasingly competed with the family to provide nurturance, education, and security. Many observers warned that rising divorce rates, the growing separation between home and work, the entrance of large numbers of women into the work force, and loss of parental control over children spelled peril for home and family. Yet the family retained its fundamental role as a cushion in a hard, uncertain world.

Family and Household Structures

Throughout modern Western history, most people have lived in two overlapping social units: household and family. A *household* is a group of people, related or unrelated, who share the same residence. A *family* is a group of people related by kinship, some of whom typically live together. The distinction helps describe how Americans lived in the late nineteenth and early twentieth centuries, because different patterns characterized the two institutions.

At the most elementary level, Americans continued to group themselves in traditional ways. As in the past, the vast majority of households (75 to 80 percent) consisted of *nuclear families*—usually a married couple, with or without children. About 15 to 20 percent of households consisted of *extended families*—usually a married couple, with or without children, plus one or more relatives such as parents, adult siblings, grandchildren, aunts, uncles, or in-laws. About 5 percent of households consisted of people who lived alone. Despite slight

Family life provided stability in an age of change, though often its activities were romanticized. This photograph, taken in a middle-class home in Natchez, Mississippi, shows parents and five children posing happily together and surrounded by the comforts of home, including gaslight, an oil lamp, and coal-stove heat.   Collection of Joan W. Gandy & Thomas H. Gandy.

variations among ethnic, racial, and socioeconomic groups, this pattern held relatively constant.

Several factors explain this pattern. Because immigrants tended to be young, the U.S. population as a whole was young. In 1880 the median age was under twenty-one, and by 1920 it was still only twenty-five. (Median age at present is over thirty-one.) Moreover, in 1900 the death rate among people aged forty-five to sixty-four was over twice what it is today. As a result, there were relatively few old people: only 4 percent of the population was sixty-five or older, compared with about 15 percent today. Thus few families could form extended three-generation households. Fewer children than today knew their grandparents, and the experience of being a grandparent was rarer. Migration separated many families, and the ideal of a home of one's own encouraged nuclear household organization. (In spite of the urban tenements, most Americans, rich and poor, lived in single-family homes; between 1890 and 1930, from 56 to 80 percent of all housing starts were single-family residences.)

The average size of nuclear families did change over time, though. Most of Europe and North America experienced a fall in birthrates in the nineteenth century. The decline began early in the 1800s in the United States, and accelerated toward the end of the century. In 1880 the birthrate was 40 live births per 1,000 people; by 1900 it had dropped to 32; by 1920 to 28. Several factors explain this decline. First, the United States was becoming an urban nation, and birthrates in cities are generally lower than in rural areas. On farms, where children could work at home or in the fields at an early age, each child born represented a new set of hands for the family work force. In the wage-based urban economy, children could not contribute significantly to the family income for many years, and a new child simply represented another mouth to feed. Second, infant mortality fell as diet and medical care improved, and families did not have to bear many children just to ensure that some would survive. Third, growing awareness that smaller families meant an improved quality of life seems to have stimulated decisions to limit family size—either by abstaining from sex during the wife's fertile period or by using contraception and abortion. Although fertility was consistently higher among blacks, immigrants, and rural people

Declining Birthrates

than among white native-born city dwellers, birthrates of all groups fell. As a result, families with six or eight children became less common; three or four became more usual. Thus the nuclear family tended to reach its maximum size and then shrink faster than in earlier eras.

Though the nuclear family predominated, the household tended to expand and contract over the lifetime of a given family. Family size grew as children were born. Later, especially in working-class families, it shrank, as children of both sexes left home before they were twenty years old, usually to work. The process of leaving home also changed households; huge numbers of young people—and some older people—lived as boarders and lodgers, especially in cities. Middle- and working-class families commonly took in boarders to occupy rooms vacated by grown children and to help pay the rent. Immigrants often lodged newly arrived relatives and fellow villagers until they could establish themselves. Historians have estimated that at the end of the nineteenth century 50 percent of city residents had lived either as or with boarders at some point during their lifetime. Housing reformers charged that boarding caused overcrowding and loss of privacy. Yet for those who boarded, the practice was highly useful. As one immigrant woman recalled:

Boarding

> We had four boarders and I had to cook for them. When I first came here I didn't want to do this because everybody want to have their own house. Well, I change my mind because everybody was doing this thing. That time some of the people that came from the other side didn't have no place to stay and we took some of the people in the house that we knew. . . . This is the way that everybody used to do it that time.

For immigrants and young people, boarding was a transitional stage, providing them with a quasi-family environment until they set up their own households. Also, growing numbers of young people lived independently, away from any family. The "efficiency apartment"—one room with a disappearing or folding bed and collapsible furniture—originated in San Francisco around 1900 to house such people and quickly spread eastward.

Some households took in extended-family members who lived as quasi-boarders. Especially in communities where economic hardship or rapid growth made housing expensive or scarce, newlyweds sometimes lived temporarily with one spouse's parents. Families also took in widowed parents or unmarried siblings who would otherwise have lived alone.

For immigrants and migrants, the family served as a refuge in a strange new place. Having moved from the Old World to the New, or from one region to another, they sought out relatives who had preceded them. A Russian woman prepared for emigration by writing to relatives in New York. "When I came off the ship, an uncle of mine was supposed to pick me up. . . . But I didn't live with this uncle because I had my mother's sister so I stayed with her."

At a time when welfare and service agencies were rare, the family continued to be the institution to which people in need could turn. Even

Importance of Kinship

when relatives did not live together, they often lived nearby and aided each other with childcare, meals, shopping, advice, and consolation. They also obtained jobs for each other. Factory foremen who had responsibility for hiring often recruited new workers recommended by their employees. According to one new arrival, "After two days my brother took me to the shop he was working in and his boss saw me and he gave me the job." A woman who worked in an optical factory recalled, "My uncle was foreman there. . . . That was my first job. I worked there with my mother. . . . My sister worked there a while too."

But obligations of kinship were not always welcome or even helpful. Immigrant families often put pressure on last-born children to stay at home to care for aging parents, a practice that stifled opportunities for education, marriage, and economic independence. As an aging Italian-American father confessed, "One of our daughters is an old maid [and] causes plenty of troubles. . . . It may be my fault because I always wished her to remain at home and not to marry for she was of great financial help." Tensions also developed when one relative felt another was not helping out enough. One woman, for example, complained that her brother-in-law "resented the fact that I saved my money in a bank instead of handing it over to him." Nevertheless, for better or worse, kinship provided people a means of coping with the many stresses caused by an urban industrial society. Social and economic change did not burst family ties.

While the family remained resilient and adaptable, subtle but momentous changes began to occur in individual life patterns. Before the twentieth

Stages of Life

century, stages of life were less distinct than they are today, and generations blended into each other with relatively little differentiation. Childhood, for instance, was regarded as a period during which young people prepared for adulthood by gradually assuming more adult roles and responsibilities. The various subdivisions of youth—toddlers, schoolchildren, adolescents, and the like—were not nearly as sharp as they are today. Married couples had more children over a longer time span than is common in the twentieth century, so active parenthood occupied most of their adult lives. Older children, who often cared for their younger sisters and brothers, might begin parenting even before reaching adulthood. And because relatively few people lived beyond age 65 or 70 or left work voluntarily, and because homes for the elderly were rare, older people were not isolated as frequently as they are today.

By the turn of the century, demographic and social changes had altered these patterns. Decreasing birthrates shortened the period of parental responsibility, so more middle-aged couples experienced a stage when all their children had grown up and left home. Longer life expectancy and a tendency among employers to force aged workers to retire, especially in manufacturing, separated the old from the young. At the same time, work became more specialized and education in graded schools more formalized—especially after states passed compulsory school-attendance laws in the 1870s and 1880s. Childhood and adolescence therefore became more distinct from adulthood. As a result of these and other trends (including the lower birthrate, which gave people fewer sisters and brothers to relate to), Americans became more conscious of age and peers. People's roles in school, in the family, on the job, and in the community came to be defined by age more than by any other characteristic.

Thus by the early 1900s, family life and its functions were both changing and holding firm. New institutions were assuming tasks formerly performed by the family. Schools were making education more of a community responsibility. Employment agencies, personnel offices, labor unions, and legislatures were taking responsibility for employee recruitment and job security. Age-based peer groups were exerting greater influence over people's values and activities. In addition, migration and a soaring divorce rate seemed to be splitting families apart: 19,633 divorces were granted nationwide in 1880; by 1920, that number had grown to 167,105. Popular and scholarly writers predicted the decline of the family, just as they do today. Yet in the face of these pressures, the family adjusted by expanding and contracting to meet temporary needs, and kinship remained a dependable though not always appreciated institution. For the majority of people, family life was vital. "As I grew up, living conditions were a bit crowded," one woman reminisced, "but no one minded because we were a family . . . thankful we all lived together."

THE NEW LEISURE AND MASS CULTURE

On December 2, 1889, as hundreds of workers paraded through Worcester, Massachusetts, in support of shorter working hours, a group of carpenters hoisted a banner proclaiming, "Eight Hours for Work, Eight Hours for Rest, Eight Hours for What We Will." The phrase, "for What We Will," was significant, for it laid claim to a special segment of daily life that belonged to the individual. Increasingly, among all social classes, leisure activities filled this time segment.

American inventors had long tried to create labor-saving devices, but not until the late 1800s did technological development become truly time-saving. Mechanization and as-

Increase in Leisure Time

sembly-line production helped to cut the average workweek in manufacturing from sixty-six hours in 1860 to sixty in 1890 and forty-seven in 1920. These reductions meant both shorter workdays and freer weekends. White-collar workers spent eight to ten hours a day on the job and often worked only half a day or not at all on weekends. To be sure, thousands still spent twelve- or fourteen-hour shifts in steel mills and sweatshops and had no time or energy for leisure. But more Americans began to partake of a variety of diversions, and for the first time a substantial segment of the economy began providing for—and profiting from—leisure. By the early 1900s, many Americans were enmeshed in the business of play.

After the Civil War, amusement became an organized activity comparable to production and consumption. The vanguard of this trend was sports. Formerly a fashionable indulgence of the genteel class, organized sports quickly became the most popular pastime of all classes, attracting huge numbers of participants and spectators. Even those who could not play or watch became involved by reading about sports in the newspapers.

The most popular organized sport was baseball. An outgrowth of older games using bats, balls, and base circling, baseball was formalized in

Baseball

1845 when a group of wealthy New Yorkers organized the Knickerbocker Club and codified the rules of play. By 1860 there were at least fifty baseball clubs, and pick-up games were being played on city lots and rural fields across the nation. In 1869 a professional club, the Cincinnati Red Stockings, went on a national tour, and other clubs quickly followed suit. The National League of Professional Baseball Clubs, founded in 1876, gave the sport a stable, business-like structure. By the 1880s, professional baseball was a big business. In 1887, over 51,000 people paid to watch a championship series between St. Louis and Detroit. In 1903, the National League and competing American League (formed in 1901) began a World Series between their championship teams, entrenching baseball as the national pastime. The Boston Red Socks beat the Pittsburgh Pirates in that first series.

Baseball appealed mostly to men. But croquet, which also swept the nation after the Civil War, attracted both sexes. Middle- and upper-class peo-

Croquet and Cycling

ple held croquet parties and even outfitted wickets with candles for night games. In an era when the departure of paid work from the home had separated men's from women's spheres, croquet increased opportunities for social contact between the sexes.

Meanwhile, bicycling achieved a popularity rivaling that of baseball—especially after 1888, when the cumbersome velocipede, with its huge front wheel and tall seat, gave way to the safety bicycle with pneumatic tires and wheels of identical size. By 1900 Americans owned over 10 million bicycles, and clubs like the League of American Wheelmen were pressing state and local governments to build more paved roads. One journal boasted that cycling cured dyspepsia, headaches, insomnia, and sciatica and gave "a vigorous tone to the whole system." Professional competition in bicycle races brought success to racers such as Major Taylor, an African-American who won fame in Europe and the United States. Like croquet, bicycling brought men and women together, combining opportunities for courtship and exercise. Moreover, the bicycle played an influential role in freeing women from the constraints of Victorian fashions. In order to ride bikes, even the dropped-frame female models, women had to wear divided skirts and simple undergarments. Gradually, freer styles of cycling costumes began to have an influence on everyday fashions. As the 1900 census declared, "Few articles . . . have created so great a revolution in social conditions as the bicycle."

Other sports had their own supporters. Tennis and golf attracted both sexes from the 1880s onward but remained pastimes of the wealthy. Played mostly at private clubs, these sports lacked baseball's team competition and cycling's informality. American football also began as a sport for people of high social rank. As an intercollegiate sport, football attracted players and spectators wealthy enough to have access to higher education. By the end of the century, however, the game was appealing to a broader audience. The 1893 Princeton-Yale game drew fifty thousand spectators, and informal games were being played in yards and playgrounds throughout the country.

Football

At the same time, college football was becoming a national scandal because of its violence and use of "tramp athletes," nonstudents whom colleges hired to help their teams win. Critics charged that football mirrored the worst features of American society. An editor of *The Nation* charged in 1890 that "the spirit of the American Youth, as of the American man, is to win, to 'get there,' by fair means or foul; and the lack of moral scruple which pervades the struggles of the business world meets with temptations equally irresistible in the miniature contests of the football field." The scandals climaxed in 1905, when 18 players died from game-related injuries and over 150 were seriously injured. President Theodore Roosevelt, a strong advocate of athletics, convened a White House conference to discuss ways of eliminating brutality and foul play. The conference founded the Intercollegiate Athletic Association (renamed the National College Athletic Association in 1910) to police college sports. In 1906 the association altered the rules of football to make it less violent and more open. New rules outlawed "flying wedge" rushes, extended from 5 to 10 yards the distance needed to earn a first down, legalized the forward pass, and tightened player eligibility requirements.

As more women enrolled in college, they began to pursue forms of physical activity besides croquet, horseback riding, and bicycling. Believing that to succeed intellectually they needed to be active and healthy, college women participated in such sports as rowing, track, and swimming. Eventually basketball, pictured opposite, became the most popular sport among college women. Invented in 1891 as a winter sport for men, basketball was given women's rules (that limited dribbling and running and encouraged passing) by Senda Berenson of Smith College in the 1890s, and intercollegiate games became common.

Paralleling the rise of sports, American show business also became a mode of leisure created by and for common people. Circuses—traveling shows of acrobats and animals—had existed since the 1820s. But after the Civil War, railroads enabled circuses to reach more of the country, and the popularity of "the big show" increased enormously. Circuses offered two main attractions: so-called freaks of nature, both human and animal, and the temptation and conquest of death. At the heart of their appeal was the sheer astonishment aroused by the trapeze artists, lion tamers, acrobats, and clowns. Writer Hamlin Garland captured the circus's effect on a thousand communities:

Circuses

> From the time the "advance man" flung his highly colored posters over the fence till the coming of the glorious day, we thought of little else. . . . It was our brief season of imaginative life. In one day—in a part of one day—we gained a thousand new conceptions of the world and of human nature. It was the embodiment of all that was skillful and beautiful in human action. . . . It gave us something to talk about.

Three branches of American show business matured with the growth of cities. Popular drama, musical comedy, and vaudeville offered audiences a chance to escape the harsh realities of urban-industrial life into melodrama, adventure, and comedy. The plots were simple, the heroes and villains recognizable. For urbanized

Popular Drama and Musical Comedy

people increasingly distant from the frontier, popular plays brought to life the mythical Wild West and Old South through stories of Davy Crockett, Buffalo Bill, and Civil War romances. Virtue, honor, and justice always triumphed in melodramas like *Uncle Tom's Cabin* and *The Old Homestead*, reinforcing the popular faith that even in an uncertain and disillusioning world, goodness would nevertheless prevail.

Musical comedies raised audiences' spirits with song, humor, and dance. American musical comedy grew out of the lavishly costumed operettas popular in Europe. By introducing American themes (often involving ethnic groups), folksy humor, and catchy tunes and dances, these shows launched the nation's most popular songs and entertainers. George M. Cohan, a spirited singer, dancer, and songwriter born into an Irish family of vaudeville entertainers, became the master of American musical comedy after the turn of the century. Drawing on urbanism, patriotism, and traditional values in songs like "Yankee Doodle Boy" and "You're a Grand Old Flag," Cohan helped bolster national morale during the First World War. Comic opera, too, became a fad, and the talented, beautiful, dignified Lillian Russell was its most admired performer. The first American comic operas imitated European musicals, but by the early 1900s composers like Victor Herbert were writing for American audiences. Shortly thereafter Jerome Kern began to write more sophisticated musicals, and American musical comedy came into its own.

Vaudeville, which originated in France as light drama with musical interludes, became a uniquely American entertainment form. Originally staged by saloonkeepers to attract customers, vaudeville variety shows were developed by skilled promoters who gave it respectability and mass appeal. Because of its variety, vaudeville was probably the most popular entertainment in early-twentieth-century America. Shows included magic and animal acts, juggling, comedy (especially ethnic humor), and song and dance. Around 1900, the number of vaudeville theaters and troupes skyrocketed. Fostered by sharp entrepreneurs who did for entertainment what Edison and Ford did for technology, vaudeville quickly became big business. Its most famous promoter, Florenz Ziegfeld, brilliantly packaged popular entertainment in a stylish format—the Ziegfeld Follies—and gave the nation a new model of

Vaudeville

While baseball, football, boxing, and racing became popular sports for men, basketball became the most appealing sport for women, especially those in college. Special rules were established in 1897 to lessen supposed dangers of rough, vigorous play by limiting the number of dribbles, confining players to particular zones on the court, and encouraging passing. Collection of Sally Fox.

femininity, the Ziegfeld Girl, whose graceful dancing and alluring costumes were meant to suggest a haunting sensuality.

Show business provided new economic opportunities for women, African-Americans, and immigrants, but it also encouraged stereotyping and exploitation. Lillian Russell, vaudeville singer and comedienne Fanny Brice, and burlesque queen Eva Tanguay attracted intensely loyal fans, commanded handsome fees, and won respect for their genuine talents. In contrast to the demure Victorian female, they conveyed pluck and creativity. There was something both shocking and refreshingly confident about Eva Tanguay when she sang earthy songs like "I Want Someone to Go Wild with Me," "It's All Been Done Before But Not the

Lavish musical reviews and vaudeville shows became a very popular form of American entertainment. Filled with song, dance, and comedy, these performances reflected the new scale and organization of the American economy and culture. Culver Pictures.

Way I Do It," and her theme song "I Don't Care." But lesser female performers were often exploited by male promoters and theater owners, many of whom wanted only to titillate the public with the sight of scantily clad women.

Before the 1890s, the chief form of commercial entertainment open to African-American performers was the minstrel show. By century's end, however, minstrel shows had given

African-Americans and Immigrants in Vaudeville

way to more sophisticated musicals, and blacks had begun to break into vaudeville. As stage settings shifted from the plantation to the city, music shifted from folk tunes to ragtime. Pandering to the prejudices of white audiences, composers and performers of both races ridiculed blacks. As the popularity of songs like "He's Just a Little Nigger, But He's Mine All Mine," and "You May Be a Hawaiian on Old Broadway, But You're Just Another Nigger to Me" confirm, blacks on the stage suffered much as they did in society at large. Even Burt Williams, a talented and highly paid black comedian and dancer who achieved success mainly by playing the stereotypical roles of

darky and dandy, was tormented by the humiliation he had to suffer.

Much of the uniqueness of American mass entertainment arose from its ethnic flavor. Indeed, immigrants occupied the core of American show business. Vaudeville in particular drew on and embellished ethnic humor, exaggerating dialects and other national traits. Skits and songs reinforced ethnic stereotypes and made fun of ethnic groups, but such distortions were more self-conscious and sympathetic than those directed at blacks. Ethnic humor often focused on difficulties faced by immigrants. A typical scene involving Italians, for example, revolved around a character's uncertain grasp of English, which caused him to confuse *mayor* with *mare*, *diploma* with *the plumber*, and *pallbearer* with *polar bear*. Other routines depicted common experiences like the interplay between a doctor and a patient:

Doctor: Do you have insurance?
Patient: I ain't got one nickel insurance.
Doctor: If you die, what will your wife bury you with?
Patient: With pleasure.

or

> Doctor: You owe me $10 for my advice.
> Patient: Here's $2. Take it, that's my advice.

Such scenes allowed audiences to laugh at the human condition and reminded them that, deep down, all people—at least all white people—were the same. Blacks, however, were never assumed to share the same hopes and frustrations as whites.

Shortly after 1900, live entertainment began to yield to an even more accessible form of amusement: moving pictures. Perfected by Thomas Edison in the late 1880s, movies began as slot-machine peepshows in penny arcades and billiard parlors. Eventually images were projected onto a screen so that large audiences could view them, and a new medium was born. At first, the subjects of films hardly mattered; it was enough merely to awe viewers with scenes of speeding trains, galloping horses, and writhing belly dancers.

Movies
———

Producers soon discovered that a film could tell a story—and tell it with flair. By 1910 motion pictures had become a distinct art form, thanks to creative directors like D. W. Griffith. Griffith's most famous work, *The Birth of a Nation* (1915), an epic film about the Civil War and Reconstruction, fanned racial prejudice by depicting African-Americans as a threat to white moral values. An organized black protest against it was led by the infant National Association for the Advancement of Colored People (NAACP) (see page 640). But the film's innovative techniques—close-ups, fade-outs, and battle scenes—gave viewers heightened drama and excitement. From the beginning, movies were popular among all classes (admission usually cost a nickel), and audiences idolized film stars like Mary Pickford, Lillian Gish, and Charlie Chaplin with a fervor no stage performer had ever evoked.

The still camera, modernized by inventor George Eastman, enabled ordinary people to make their own photographic images, especially useful for preserving family memories; and the phonograph, another Edison invention, brought musical performances into the home. The spread of movies, photography, and phonograph records meant that access to live performances no longer limited people's exposure to art and entertainment. By making it possible to mass-produce sound and images, technology dissolved the uniqueness of experience. Entertainment became a consumer good more widely available than ever before.

News also became a consumer good. Canny publishers made people crave news just as they craved amusements and new products. City life and increased leisure time seemed to nurture a fascination with the sensational, and from the 1880s onward popular newspapers increasingly whetted that appetite and catered to it.

Joseph Pulitzer, a Hungarian immigrant who bought the *New York World* in 1883, pioneered journalism as a branch of mass culture. Believing that newspapers should be "dedicated to the cause of the people rather than to that of the purse potentates," Pulitzer filled the *World* with stories of disasters, crimes, and scandals. Sensational headlines, set in large bold type like that used for advertisements, screamed from every page. Pulitzer's journalists not only reported news but sought it out—and sometimes even created it. *World* reporter Nellie Bly (whose real name was Elizabeth Cochrane) faked her way into an insane asylum and wrote a sensational exposé of the sordid conditions she found. Other reporters staged stunts and sought out heart-rending human-interest stories. Pulitzer also popularized the comics, and the yellow ink they were printed in gave rise to the term *yellow journalism* as a synonym for sensationalism.

Yellow Journalism
———

Pulitzer's strategy was immensely successful. In just one year he increased the *World*'s daily circulation from 20,000 to 100,000, and by the late 1890s it had reached 1 million. Soon other publishers, such as William Randolph Hearst, who bought the *New York Journal* in 1895 and started an empire of mass-circulation newspapers, adopted Pulitzer's techniques. Yellow journalism became a nationwide phenomenon, feeding interest in bizarre aspects of the human condition and kindling sentiments for reform.

Pulitzer and his rivals boosted circulation even further by emphasizing sports and women's news. Newspapers had always reported on sporting events, but yellow-journalism papers gave such stories far greater prominence by printing separate, expanded sports sections. Such sections did more than anything else to promote sports as a leisure-time attraction. Sports news became a new addiction, re-creating a particular game's drama through narrative and statistics. While they were expanding sports news, mostly for male readers, newspapers were adding special sections devoted to household tips, fashion, decorum, and club news to capture the interest of female readers. Like crime and disaster stories, sports and women's sections helped to make news a mass commodity.

By the early twentieth century, mass-circulation magazines made possible by the steam-driven high-speed rotary printing press—an important technological innovation—were **Magazines for** overshadowing the expensive **the Mass** elitist journals of earlier eras. **Market** Publications like *McClure's, Saturday Evening Post*, and *Ladies' Home Journal* offered human-interest stories, muckraking exposés (see page 629), titillating fiction, numerous photographs, colorful covers, and eye-catching ads to a growing mass market. These magazines had much

Frank Merriwell, the fictional hero of hundreds of sports and adventure stories written by Burt Standish (the pen name used by Gilbert Patten), was a popular character model for young men in the early 1900s. In a series of adventures, mostly involving sports, Frank used his physical skills, valor, and moral virtue to lead by example, accomplish the impossible, and influence others to behave in an upstanding way. Collection of Picture Research Consultants.

higher sales than their predecessors. Meanwhile, the total number of books published more than quadrupled between 1880 and 1917. This rising popular consumption of news and books reflected growing literacy. Between 1870 and 1920, the proportion of Americans aged ten or over who could not read or write fell from 20 percent to 6 percent.

Other forms of communication were also expanding. In 1891 there was less than one telephone for every 100 people in the United States; by 1901 the number had grown to 2.1, and by 1921 it had swelled to 12.6. In 1900 Americans used 4 billion postage stamps; in 1922 they used 14.3 billion. Little wonder, then, that the term *community* took on new dimensions, as people used the media, mail, and telephone to extend their horizons far beyond their place of residence. More than ever before, people in different parts of the country knew about and discussed the same news event, whether it was a sensational murder, a sex scandal, or the fortunes of a particular entertainer or athlete. America was becoming a mass society.

To some extent, new amusements and pastimes had a homogenizing influence, bringing together disparate ethnic and social groups to share a common experience. Parks, ball fields, vaudeville shows, movies, and feature sections of newspapers and magazines were nonsectarian and apolitical, designed to appeal to everyone. Yet, even though promoters and entrepreneurs were responsible for the spread of amusements, different groups of consumers often used them to reinforce their own cultural habits. In some communities, for example, working-class immigrants used parks and amusement areas as sites for family and ethnic gatherings. Much to the dismay of reformers who hoped that recreation would help assimilate newcomers and teach them habits of restraint, immigrants used picnics and Fourth of July celebrations as occasions for boisterous drinking and sometimes violent behavior. Similarly, young working-class men and women resisted parents' and reformers' warnings and frequented urban dance halls, where they explored less formal forms of courtship and sexual behavior.

The most provocative issue was the use of leisure time on Sunday, the Lord's day. In the Puritan tradition, native-born Americans supported blue laws designed to prevent desecration of the Sabbath by prohibiting various commercial and recreational activities. Immigrants, accustomed to feasting and playing after church, fought the closing of saloons and other restrictions on the only day they had free for fun and relaxation. Thus in 1913, when the New York legislature proposed a law granting cities authority to end restrictions on Sunday baseball games and liquor sales, both sides argued vehemently. One rural Republican charged that such a measure amounted to "amending Moses' law," while a New York City Democrat of Irish lineage retorted that "Moses was an organization Democrat" who wrote the commandment "Don't covet your neighbor's rights." At about the same time, the Illinois and Ohio legislatures split over whether to legalize boxing, which small-town Protestants opposed and urban Catholics and Jews favored. Similar splits developed over public versus parochial schools and prohibition versus free availability of liquor. Thus as Americans learned to play, their leisure—like their work and politics—was shaped by and expressed pluralistic forces.

PROMISES OF MOBILITY

Baptist minister Russell Conwell delivered the same sermon more than six thousand times to countless listeners across the United States between the Civil War and the First World War. Titled "Acres of Diamonds," this popular lecture affirmed the faith that any American could achieve success. People did not have to look far for riches, Conwell preached; acres of diamonds lay at everyone's feet. Night after night he would insist to his audience, "the opportunity to get rich, to attain unto great wealth, is here . . . within the reach of almost every man and woman who hears me speak tonight. . . . I say you ought to get rich, and it is your duty to get rich. . . . If you can honestly attain unto riches it is your Christian and Godly duty to do so." Success was not only possible; it was a religious obligation.

Was it really possible for people to improve their lot and fulfill that duty? The answer is a mixed story of small triumphs but also dashed hopes, discrimination, and failure. Basically, there were three ways a person could get ahead: occupational advancement (and the higher income that accompanied it); acquisition of property (and the wealth it represented); and migration to an area that offered better conditions and greater opportunity. All these options were open chiefly to white men. Although many women held paying jobs, owned property, and migrated, their economic standing was usually defined by the men in their lives—husbands, fathers, or other kin. Women could improve their economic status by marrying men with wealth or potential, but other avenues were mostly closed. Laws restricted women's economic rights by limiting what they could inherit; educational institutions blocked their training in professions such as medicine and law; and prevailing assumptions attributed higher aptitude for manual skills and business to men than to women. Men and women who were African-American, American Indian, Mexican-American, or Asian-American had even fewer opportunities. Pinned to the bottom of society by prejudice, these groups were forced to accept their imposed station.

Occupational mobility was a reality, however, for large numbers of people, thanks to urban and industrial expansion. Thousands of small businesses were needed to supply

Occupational Mobility

goods and services to burgeoning urban populations. As corporations grew and centralized their operations, they required new managerial personnel. Capital for a large business was hard to amass, but a saloon or small shop such as the one festively decorated by its new Polish owners could be opened for only $200 or $300. Knowledge of accounting could qualify one for new white-collar jobs that sometimes paid better than manual labor. Thus nonmanual work and the higher social status and income that tended to accompany it were attainable.

Such advancement occurred often. To be sure, only a very few traveled the rags-to-riches track that Andrew Carnegie and Henry Ford discovered. Studies of the era's wealthiest businessmen show that the vast majority began their careers with distinct advantages: American birth, Protestant religion, better-than-average education, and relatively affluent parents. Yet considerable movement occurred along the path from rags to moderate success as men climbed from manual to nonmanual jobs or saw their children do so. Thus personal successes like that of Meyer Grossman, a Russian immigrant to Omaha, Nebraska, who worked as a teamster before saving enough to open a successful furniture store, were common.

Rates of occupational mobility in American communities were slow but steady between 1870 and 1920. In new, fast-growing cities like Atlanta,

Becoming the proprietor of one's own business was one of the most visible forms of social mobility for immigrants as well as native-born Americans. In this photograph, Polish immigrants have decorated a new business establishment opened by one of their neighbors in an ethnic neighborhood of Chicago.   Chicago Historical Society.

Los Angeles, and Omaha, approximately one in five white manual workers rose to white-collar or owner's positions within ten years—provided they stayed in the city that long. In older northeastern cities like Boston and Newburyport, upward mobility averaged closer to one in six in ten years. Some people slipped from a higher to a lower rung on the occupational ladder, but rates of upward movement were almost always twice that of downward rates. Though patterns were not consistent, immigrants generally experienced less upward and more downward mobility than the native-born did. Still, regardless of birthplace, the chances for a white male to rise occupationally over the course of his career or to have a higher-status job than his father had were relatively good.

It must be remembered, however, that what constitutes a better job depends on one's definition of improvement. Many an immigrant artisan, such as a German carpenter or an Italian shoemaker, would have considered an accountant's job demeaning and unproductive. People with traditions of pride in manual skills neither wanted nonmanual jobs nor encouraged their children to seek them. As one Italian tailor explained, "I learned the tailoring business in the old country. Over here, in America, I never have trouble finding a job because I know my business from the other side [Italy]. . . . I want that my oldest boy learn my trade because I tell him that you could always make at least enough for the family."

Business ownership, moreover, entailed risks. Rates of failure were high among shopkeepers, saloon owners, and other small proprietors in working-class neighborhoods because the low incomes of their customers made business uncertain. Many manual workers sought security rather than mobility, preferring a steady wage to the risks of ownership. A Sicilian who lived in Bridgeport, Connecticut, observed that "the people that come here they afraid to get in business because they don't know how that business goes. In Italy these people don't know much about these things because most of them work on farms or in [their] trade."

In addition to or instead of advancing occupationally, a person could achieve social mobility by the acquisition of property. But property was not

Acquisition of Property

easy to acquire. Banks and savings and loan institutions were far stricter in their lending practices than they would become after the 1930s, when the federal government began to insure real-estate financing. Before then, however, mortgage loans carried relatively high interest rates and short repayment periods. Thus renting, even of single-family houses, was common, especially in big cities. A general rise in wage rates nevertheless enabled many families to amass savings, which could be used as down payments on property. Among working-class families who stayed in Newburyport at least ten years, for example, a third to a half managed to accumulate some property; two-thirds did so within twenty years. Ownership rates varied regionally—higher in western cities, lower in eastern cities—but 36 percent of urban American families owned their homes in 1900, the highest homeownership rate of any Western nation with the exceptions of Denmark, Norway, and Sweden.

Following the maxim that movement means improvement, millions of families each year packed up and moved elsewhere. As early as 1847, a foreign visitor, amazed by American transiency, wrote, "If God were suddenly to call the world to judgment He would surprise two-thirds of the American population on the road like ants." This urge to move affected every region, every city. From Boston to San Francisco, from Minneapolis to San Antonio, no more than half the families residing in a city at any one time could be found there ten years later.

Residential Mobility

Many people who migrated, particularly unskilled workers, did not improve their status; they simply floated from one low-paying job to another. Others did find greener pastures. Studies of Boston, Omaha, Atlanta, and other cities show that most men who rose occupationally or acquired property had migrated from somewhere else. Thus, while cities frustrated the hopes of some, they offered opportunities to others.

In addition to movement between cities, extraordinary numbers of people moved within the same city. In American communities today, one in every five families changes residence in a given year. A hundred years ago, the proportion was closer to one in four, or even one in three. In Omaha between 1880 and 1920, for example, nearly 60 percent of families who remained in the city for as long as fourteen years had lived at three or more addresses during that span of time. Population turnover affected almost every neighborhood, every ethnic and occupational group.

Rapid residential flux undermined the stability of even the most homogeneous neighborhoods. Rarely did a single nationality make up a clear majority in any large area, even when that area was known as Little Italy, Jewtown, Polonia, or Greektown. Even in heavily ethnic Chicago, a survey of one district found a kaleidoscope of immigrants packed tightly together:

Ethnic Neighborhoods and Ghettos

> Between Halsted Street and the river live about ten thousand Italians, Neapolitans, Sicilians, and Calabrians. . . . To the South on Twelfth Street are many Germans, and the side streets are given over almost entirely to Polish and Prussian Jews.

> Further south, three Jewish colonies merge into a huge Bohemian colony. . . . To the north-west are many Canadians . . . and to the north are many Irish.

Moreover, immigrants rapidly dispersed from their original areas of settlement. The families who inhabited a certain neighborhood at one point were not likely to be living there five or ten years later. Ethnically homogeneous districts did exist in New York, Boston, and other eastern ports, and people tended to change residences within those districts rather than move away from them. Elsewhere, however, most white immigrant families lived in ethnically mixed neighborhoods rather than in ghettos.

In most cities an area's institutions and enterprises, more than the people who actually lived there, identified a district as an ethnic neighborhood. A certain part of town, familiar and accessible to a particular group, became the location of its churches, clubs, bakeries, markets, and other establishments. Some members of a particular group lived near a certain part of town, others lived farther away but could travel there on streetcars or on foot. Thus some of the secondary business centers that formed at the intersections of mass-transit routes became locations of ethnic business and social activity. A Bohemian Town, for example, received its nickname because it was the location of Swoboda's Bakery, Cermak's Drug Store, Cecha's Jewelry, Knezacek's Meats, St. Wenceslaus Church, and the Bohemian Benevolent Association. Such institutions gave the district an ethnic identity even though the surrounding neighborhood was mixed and unstable.

Residential dispersion did not necessarily mean acceptance; immigrants and their children often encountered hostility in all walks of life. In many communities during the depression of the 1890s, the American Protective Association attracted attention by attacking "the diabolical works of the Catholic Church" and demanding an end to immigration. Such sentiment influenced national legislation. In 1882, Congress bowed to pressure from West Coast nativists and prohibited Chinese immigration for ten years. In 1902 a new law excluded the Chinese indefinitely; not until 1943 was the ban lifted. Also, periodic attempts were made to prevent foreign-born citizens from voting by imposing literacy tests on them.

If a *ghetto* is defined as a place of enforced residence from which escape is difficult at best, only nonwhites experienced true ghetto life in this era. Wherever Asians and Mexicans settled, they encountered discrimination in housing, employment, and other facets of public life. Although these groups often preferred to remain separate in Chinatowns and *barrios*, white Americans also made every effort to keep them confined. In the 1880s the city of San Francisco, for example, tried to prohibit Chinese laundries from locating in most neighborhoods, and its school board tried to isolate Japanese and Chinese children in Chinatown schools. In the *barrios* of Los Angeles and San Antonio, Anglo teachers and administrators who dominated the schools were insensitive to the needs of Hispanic students and insisted on teaching in English even when the children had no knowledge of the language.

The same prejudice and discrimination that trapped African-Americans at the bottom of the occupational ladder also limited housing opportunities. Whites organized protective associations that pledged not to sell homes to blacks and occasionally used violence to scare them away from white neighborhoods. Such efforts seldom worked. Whites who lived on the edge of black neighborhoods often fled, leaving homes and apartments to be sold and rented to black occupants. In almost every city, totally black residential districts expanded while white native and ethnic neighborhoods dispersed. By 1920 in Chicago, Detroit, Cleveland, and other cities outside the South, two-thirds or more of the total African-American population lived in only 10 percent of the residential area. Within these districts, they nurtured cultural institutions that helped them adjust to urban life: storefront churches, business and educational organizations, social clubs, and saloons. But the ghettos also bred frustration, the result of stunted opportunity and racial bigotry. Color, more than any other factor, made the urban experiences of blacks different from those of whites.

All groups, however, including blacks, could and did move—if not from one part of the city to another, then from one city to another. Americans were always seeking greener pastures, and hope that things might be better elsewhere acted as a safety valve, relieving some of the tensions and frustrations that simmered inside the city. At times these emotions erupted into violence; more often, people simply left. A railroad ticket from one city to another cost a few dollars; there was little to lose by moving.

The possibilities of upward mobility, moreover, seemed to temper people's dissatisfaction. Although the gap between the very rich and very poor widened, the expanding economies of American cities created room in the middle of the socioeconomic scale. Few could hope to become another Rockefeller, and failed or blocked mobility frustrated others. But many did become respectable shopkeepers, foremen, clerks, and agents; if advancement was not possible in one generation, it might be in the next. Finally, if migration, occupational mobility, and property acquisition offered little hope of improvement or relief, there was still one sphere to which city dwellers could turn: politics.

THE POLITICS OF BOSSISM AND CIVIC REFORM

The sudden growth and mounting rivalry among social and economic interest groups that occurred in the late nineteenth century mired cities in a governmental swamp. Burgeoning populations, business expansion, and technological change created urgent needs for sewers, police and fire protection, schools, parks, and other services. Such needs strained municipal governments beyond their capacities. Furthermore, city governments approached these needs in a disorganized fashion. Legislative and administrative functions were typically scattered among a mayor, city council, and independent boards that administered health regulations, public works, poverty relief, and other services. Philadelphia at one time had thirty different boards, plus a mayor and council. Furthermore, state governments often imposed their will on city administrations, appointing board members and limiting local rights to levy taxes and borrow money.

Power thrives on confusion, and out of this governmental chaos arose political machines, organizations whose main goals were the rewards—whether money, influence, or prestige—of getting and keeping political power. Machine politicians routinely used bribery and graft to further their ends. But machines needed popular support, and they could not have succeeded if they had not provided relief, security, and services to large numbers of people. By doing so, machine politicians accom-

Political Machines

plished things that other agencies had been unable or unwilling to attempt.

Machines were also beneficiaries of new urban conditions. As cities grew larger and economically more complex, some business leaders vied to use local government to advance their interests; others withdrew from local affairs to pursue their interests through interurban or interregional economic organizations. At the same time, hordes of newcomers, often unskilled and foreign-born, crowded into cities. As they acquired citizenship and voting rights, the men in these groups became a substantial political force.

These circumstances bred a new kind of leader: the political boss. Special-interest groups needed brokers who could facilitate their goals, and urban newcomers had needs that required public attention. Bosses and machines established power bases among new immigrant voters and used politics to solve important urban problems. Most bosses had immigrant backgrounds themselves and had grown up in the inner city, so they knew their constituents' needs firsthand. Machines made politics a full-time profession. According to George

Washington Plunkett, a small-time boss in New York City who published his memoirs in 1905, "As a rule [the boss] has no business or occupation other than politics. He plays politics every day and night in the year and his headquarters bears the inscription, 'Never closed.'"

Bosses and machines were rarely as dictatorial or corrupt as critics charged. To be sure, fraud, bribery, and thievery tainted the system. Bosses such as Philadelphia's "Duke" Vare, Kansas City's Tom Pendergast, and New York's Richard Croker lived like kings, though their official incomes were slim. A few bosses had no permanent organization; they were freelance opportunists who bargained for power, sometimes winning and sometimes losing. But from the 1880s onward, most machines evolved into highly organized political structures that wedded solid accomplishments with personal gain.

The system rested on a popular base and was held together by loyalty and service. City machines were coalitions of smaller machines that derived power directly from inner-city neighborhoods inhabited by native and immigrant working classes.

Urban political bosses constructed their political support in inner-city neighborhoods by providing employment and personal assistance to people in need. In this photograph, a line of unemployed men extends along a street leading to Chicago's city hall, where the men hope the political machine will have jobs to distribute to them.   Chicago Historical Society.

In return for votes, bosses provided jobs, built parks and bathhouses, distributed food and clothing to the needy, and helped when someone ran afoul of the law. Such personalized service cultivated mass attachment to the boss; never before had public leaders assumed such responsibility for people in need.

Bosses, moreover, were genuinely public people. They attended weddings and wakes, joined clubs, and held open houses in saloons where neighborhood folk could talk to them personally. Each boss had his own style. Pittsburgh's Christopher Magee gave his city a zoo and a hospital. Brooklyn's Hugh McLaughlin provided free burial services. Boston's James Michael Curley would approach a haggard old woman and tell her that "a woman should have three attributes. . . . beauty, intelligence, and money." Then he would press a silver dollar into her hand and say, "Now you have all three."

Techniques of Bossism

To finance their largess and support the system they had created, bosses exchanged favors for votes or money. Power over local government enabled machines to control the letting of public contracts, the granting of utility or streetcar franchises, and the distribution of city jobs. Recipients of city business and jobs were expected to repay the machine with a portion of their profits or salaries and to cast supporting votes on election day. Critics called this process graft; bosses called it gratitude. Machines constructed public buildings, sewer systems, and mass-transit lines that otherwise might not have been built; but bribes and kickbacks made such projects costly to taxpayers. In the late nineteenth century, cities financed their expansion with loans from the public in the form of municipal bonds. Critics of bosses charged that these loans were inflated or unnecessary. Whether necessary or not, these bonds caused public debts to soar, and taxes had to be raised to repay their interest and principal. In addition, machines dispersed favors to both legal and illegal businesses. Payoffs from gambling, prostitution, and illegal liquor traffic became important sources of machine revenue.

Bosses held their power because they knew people's needs and they tended to problems of everyday life. Martin Lomasney, boss of Boston's South End, explained, "There's got to be in every ward somebody that any bloke can come to—no matter what he's done—and get help. Help, you understand, none of your law and justice, but help." The boss system, however, was neither innocent nor fair. Jobs, Christmas turkeys, and funeral money were accompanied by thievery and extortion. Bosses seldom distributed favors equitably. Racial minorities and new immigrant groups like Italians and Poles received only token recognition, if any. Also, because machines emphasized personal and neighborhood issues, they deflected working-class attention from workplace issues and may have prevented unions from growing more rapidly. But in an age of economic individualism, bosses were no more guilty of self-interest and discrimination than were business leaders who exploited workers, spoiled the landscape, and manipulated government in pursuit of profits. Sometimes humane and sometimes criminal, bosses were brokers between various sectors of urban society and an uncertain world.

While bosses were consolidating their power, others were attempting to destroy political machines. Many middle- and upper-class Americans feared that immigrant-based political machines menaced the republic and that unsavory alliances between bosses and businesses undermined municipal finances. Anxious over the poverty, crowding, and disorder that seemed to accompany population expansion, and convinced that urban services were making taxes too high, civic reformers organized to install more responsible leaders at the helm of urban administrations.

Urban reform arose in part from the industrial system's emphasis on eliminating waste and inefficiency. Government could be made more efficient, business-minded reformers were convinced, if it were run like a business. The only way to prevent civic decay, they believed, was to elect officials who would hold down expenses and prevent corruption. Thus their main goals were to reduce city budgets, make public employees work more efficiently, and cut taxes.

To impose sound business principles on government, civic reformers supported structural changes such as the city-manager and commission forms of government and non-partisan citywide election of officials. These reforms were meant to abolish party politics and to put decision making in the hands of experienced experts. Armed with such strategies, reformers believed they could centralize and systematize admin-

Structural Reforms in Government

istration and thereby undermine bosses' power bases in the wards and neighborhoods. They rarely realized, however, that bosses succeeded because they used government to meet people's needs. Reformers only noticed the waste and corruption that machines bred.

A few reform mayors did look beyond structural changes to a genuine concern for social problems. Hazen S. Pingree of Detroit, Samuel "Golden Rule" Jones of Toledo, and Tom Johnson of Cleveland worked to provide jobs for poor people, reduce charges by transit and utility companies, and promote greater governmental responsibility for the welfare of all citizens. They also supported public ownership of gas, electric, and telephone companies, a quasi-socialist reform that alienated their business allies. But Pingree, Jones, and Johnson were exceptions. Most civic reformers were narrow of vision. They achieved temporary success but could not match the bosses' political savvy; they soon found themselves out of power.

URBAN PROFESSIONALS: ENGINEERS AND SOCIAL WORKERS

Meanwhile, a different type of reform was beginning to take hold outside of politics. Driven by an urge to identify and address urban problems, and convinced that lais-

Social Reform sez-faire ideology was not applicable in a complex urban-industrial world, social reformers—mostly young and middle-class—embarked on campaigns for social betterment. Housing reformers pressed local governments for building codes to ensure safety in tenements. Protestant reformers influenced by the Social Gospel movement, which emphasized social responsibility as a means to salvation, built churches in slum neighborhoods and urged businesses to be socially responsible. Believing that service to fellow humans was a Christian duty, Social Gospel clergymen such as Washington Gladden of Columbus, Ohio, and Walter Rauchenbusch of Rochester, New York, worked to alleviate poverty and to make peace between employers and labor unions. Educational reformers such as William T. Harris of St. Louis saw public schools as a means of preparing immigrant children for citizenship by teaching

them American values as well as the English language.

Perhaps the most ambitious and inspiring feature of the urban reform movement was the settlement house. Run mostly by women, settlements were efforts by educated, middle-class young adults to bridge the gulf between social classes by going to live in slum neighborhoods. The first American settlement house, patterned after London's Toynbee Hall, opened in New York City in 1886, and others quickly appeared in Chicago, Boston, and elsewhere. Early settlement leaders such as Jane Addams, the founder of Hull House in Chicago and one of country's most revered women, and Florence Kelley, a brilliant socialist who always dressed in black, wanted to improve the lives of slum dwellers by helping them to obtain education, appreciation of the arts, better jobs, and better housing. Although working-class and immigrant neighborhood residents sometimes mistrusted them as outsiders, settlement workers offered activities ranging from vocational classes to childcare for working mothers and ethnic art exhibits and pageants.

As they broadened their scope to fight for school nurses, building safety codes, public playgrounds, and support for labor unions, settlement workers became reform leaders in cities and in the nation. Their efforts to involve national and local governments in the solution of social problems later made them the vanguard of the Progressive era when a reform spirit swept the nation (see Chapter 21). Moreover, the activities of settlement houses helped create new professional opportunities for women in social work, public health, and child welfare. These professions enabled female reformers to build a dominion of influence over aspects of social policy independent of male-dominated professions and to make valuable contributions to national as well as inner-city life.

A contrast developed between white female reformers, who worked mainly in northern cities, and black female reformers who operated both in the South and, increasingly, in northern cities. Middle-class white women lobbied for government programs to aid needy people and focused on "helping others"—that is, the immigrant and native-born working classes. Black women, barred by their race from white political institutions, raised funds from private institutions and focused on helping members of their own race. These African-American women were especially active in raising

SCHEDULE OF OCCASIONS

LIST OF MEETINGS, CLASSES, CLUBS AND OTHER APPOINTMENTS OF
THE WEEK AT CHICAGO COMMONS AND THE TABERNACLE
DURING THE PAST WINTER.

AT THE COMMONS,
140 NORTH UNION STREET.

DAILY
All Day—House open for neighbors and friends.
9:00–12:00 a. m.—Free Kindergarten (except Saturday and Sunday). Mrs. Bertha Hofer Hegner, head kindergartner; Miss Alice B. Coggswell, assistant.
2:00–5:00 p. m.—Kindergarten Training Classes.
7:00 p. m.—Family Vespers (except Saturday).

SUNDAY
3:30 p. m.—Pleasant Sunday Afternoon.

MONDAY
4:00 p. m.—Manual Training (Girls.) Mr. N. H. Weeks.
7:30 p. m.—Penny Provident Bank.
8:00 p. m.—Girls' Clubs. Misses Coggswell, Taylor and Purnell.
Cooking Class (Girls). Miss Manning.
Girls' Progressive Club (Young Women). Classes in Art, Miss Cushman; Embroidery, Mrs. Gavit; Greek Mythology, Mrs. Follett; English History and Constitution, Miss Allen.
Shakespere Class. Mr. Gavit.

TUESDAY
2:00 p. m.—Woman's Club.
4:00 p. m.—Cooking Class (Girls). Miss Cookinham.
Manual Training. Mr. Weeks.
7:30 p. m.—Boys' Club. Mr. Weeks, Misses Alexander and Holdridge.
French. Miss Sayer.
Rhetoric. Mr. Wyatt.
Stenography. Mr. Fisher.
Cooking Class (Girls) Miss Thayer.
8:00 p. m.—Choral Club. Miss Hofer and Mr. C. E. Weeks.
8:15 p. m.—"The Tuesday Meeting," for Economic Discussion.

WEDNESDAY
4:00 p. m.—Kindergarten Clubs (children). Miss Purnell and Abbott.
Dressmaking Class (Girls). Miss Temple.
Piano. Miss Gavit.
7:00 p. m.—Piano. Miss Bemiss.
7:30 p. m.—Penny Provident Bank.
Girls' Clubs. Misses Coggswell, Gavit, Bosworth, Bemiss, Etheridge.
Boys' Club. Mr. Grant.
Cooking Class (Young Women). Miss Temple.

THURSDAY
4:00 p. m.—Cooking Class (for Women). Miss Temple.
Elocution. Miss Ellis.
Manual Training (Girls). Mr. Weeks.
7:30 p. m.—Girls' Club. Miss Chandler.
Good Will ("Blue Ticket") Club. Mr. Weeks.
Elocution. Miss Ellis.
Grammar. Mr. Carr.
Cooking (for Girls). Miss Manning.
Mothers' Club (Fortnightly).
Seventeenth Ward Municipal Club (Monthly).

FRIDAY
4:00 p. m.—Manual Training (Boys'). Mr. Weeks.
7:30 p. m.—Penny Provident Bank.
Cooking Class (Girls). Miss Manning.
Boys' Clubs. Messrs. Burt, Carr, Crocker, Young, C. E. Weeks, N. H. Weeks.
Dressmaking. Mrs. Strawbridge.

SATURDAY
10:00 a. m.—Manual Training (Boys). Mr. Weeks.
2:00 p. m.—Manual Training (Boys). Mr. Weeks.
3:00 p. m.—Piano Lessons. Miss Bemiss.
6:30 p. m.—Residents' Meeting (for residents only).

Other Appointments, for Clubs, Study Classes, Social Gatherings, etc., are made from time to time and for special occasions.

How *do* historians know

the intent of settlement-house activities? This document presents an actual listing of one week's activities at the Chicago Commons settlement house in 1896. There are at least three ways to interpret these activities. First is the nature of the activities themselves: a blend of practical (savings bank, cooking, manual training) with intellectual (Shakespeare, French, elocution). Second is the age factor: note that the majority of entries are for children. Third is the gender factor: *though there are a few activities for males, they are almost exclusively for boys, not adult men. Moreover, the female activities reinforce prevailing stereotypes of women's role as housekeeper—though the daily kindergarten might be used as a form of childcare for working mothers of young children. A reader might also consider the significance of the time for which each activity is scheduled.* Photo: Library of Congress.

money for schools, old-age homes, and hospitals, but they also worked for advancement of the race and protection of black women from sexual exploitation. Their ranks included women such as Jane Hunter, who founded a home for unmarried black working women in Cleveland in 1911 and influenced the founding of similar homes in other cities, and Modjeska Simkins, who founded a program to address health problems among blacks in South Carolina.

While female reformers tried to revive the neighborhoods, a group of male reformers worked to beautify whole cities in the City Beautiful movement. Inspired by the World's Columbian Exposition of 1893, a dazzling world's fair held in a specially built White City on Chicago's South Side, architects and city planners worked to redesign the urban landscape. Led by architect Daniel Burnham,

Beautification Campaigns

City Beautiful advocates built civic centers, parks, boulevards, and transportation systems that would make cities more attractive as well as economically efficient. "Make no little plans," Burnham urged city officials. "Make big plans; aim high in hope and work." This attitude spawned beautifying projects in Chicago, San Francisco, and Washington, D.C., in the early 1900s. Yet most of these big plans turned out to be only big dreams. Neither government nor the private sector could finance large-scale projects, and the planners disagreed among themselves and with social reformers over whether beautification would really solve urban problems.

Whether they concentrated on government, social services, or city design, urban reformers wanted to save cities, not abandon them. They believed they could improve urban life by restoring cooperation among all citizens. They often failed to realize, however, that cities were places of great diversity and that different people held very different views about what reform actually meant. To civic reformers, distributing city jobs on the basis of civil service exams rather than party loyalty meant progress; to working-class men it signified reduced employment opportunities. Moral reformers tried to prohibit the sale of alcoholic beverages to prevent working-class breadwinners from wasting their wages and ruining their health, but immigrants saw such crusades as interference in their wine- and beer-drinking customs. Planners saw civic buildings and transportation systems as modern necessities, but such structures often displaced the poor. Well-meaning humanitarians criticized immigrant mothers for the way they shopped, dressed, did housework, and raised children, without regard for the inability of these mothers to afford the products that the consumer economy created. Thus early urban reform merged idealism with naiveté and insensitivity.

At the same time, efforts that took place outside the context of bossism and reform were making cities more livable. Technical and professional creativity, not political or humanitarian action, were required to address sanitation, street lighting, bridge and street building, and other such needs. In addressing these issues, American urban dwellers, and the engineering profession in particular, developed new systems and standards of worldwide significance.

Engineering Reforms

Take, for example, the problem of refuse. Experts in 1900 estimated that every New Yorker generated annually some 160 pounds of garbage (food and bones), 1,200 pounds of ashes (from stoves and furnaces), and 100 pounds of rubbish (old shoes, furniture, and other items). Europeans of that era produced only about half as much trash. At the same time, there were as many as 3.5 million horses in American cities, each of which produced about 20 pounds of manure and a gallon of urine daily. City horses worked so hard that they lived only a few years, and each city also had to dispose of thousands of carcasses every year. In past eras, trash and excrement could be dismissed as nuisances; by the twentieth century they were threats to public health and safety, and citizens' groups were raising loud protests against inadequate refuse collection and disposal.

Most people agreed that government had the ultimate responsibility, but the problem raised difficult questions. Who should be responsible for waste removal, city workers or a private contractor hired by the city? Previously, cities had dumped refuse on vacant land and in nearby rivers and lakes. What alternatives were there to these unsafe practices? Should trash be sorted so that some could be salvaged and sold or recycled? How frequently should streets be cleaned, and by whom?

To solve their problems, cities increasingly depended on engineers, who had become, except for teachers, the largest profession in the country by 1900. Engineers applied their technical expertise to devise systems for incinerating refuse, dumping trash while ensuring safe water supplies, constructing efficient sewers, and providing for regular street cleaning and snow removal. Engineers also advised officials on budgetary matters and contracts. They had similar influence in matters of street lighting, parks, fire protection, and more. City officials, whether bosses or reformers, came to depend on the expertise of engineers, who seemed best qualified to supervise a city's expansion. Insulated within professional bureaucratic agencies from tumultuous party strife, engineers generally carried out their responsibilities efficiently and without great publicity.

Much of what American society is today originated in the urbanization of the late nineteenth century. American cities may have been less orderly and beautiful than European cities, but they hummed with energy and excitement. Virtually ungovernable in the 1860s and 1870s, American cities experienced an "unheralded triumph" by the early twentieth century. Amid corruption and political conflict, urban engineers modernized the local infrastructure with construction of new sewer, water, and lighting services, and urban governments made the environment safer by expanding professional police and fire departments. When old-fashioned native inventiveness met the traditions of European, African, and Asian cultures, a new kind of society emerged. This society seldom functioned smoothly; in fact, there really was no coherent urban community, only a collection of subcommunities. Yet its jumble of social classes, ethnic and racial groups, political organizations, and other components left important legacies.

By the early 1900s, American cities exhibited bewildering diversity. Fearful and puzzled, native-born whites tried to Americanize and uplift immigrants, but the newcomers stubbornly strained to protect their cultures. Optimists had envisioned the American nation as a melting pot, where various nationalities would blend to become a new unified people. Instead, many ethnic groups proved unmeltable, and racial minorities got burned on the bottom of the pot. As a result of immigration and urbanization, the United States became a culturally pluralistic society—not so much a melting pot as a salad bowl. As one immigrant priest told a social worker, "There is no such thing as an American." He meant the same thing that literary critic Randolph Bourne meant when he dubbed the United States "a cosmopolitan federation of national colonies." This kind of reasoning produced hyphenated identifications: people considered themselves Irish-American, Italo-American, Polish-American, and the like.

Pluralism and its attendant interest-group loyalties enhanced the importance of politics. If America was not a melting pot, then different groups were competing for power, wealth, and status. Adherents of diverse cultural traditions battled over how much control government should exercise over people's lives. Such conflicts, fueled by hard times as well as the ever-growing diversity of the American population, illustrate why local politics and state politics were so heated. Some people carried polarization to extremes and tried to suppress everything allegedly un-American.

Efforts to enforce homogeneity generally failed, however, because the country's cultural diversity prevented domination by a single ethnic majority. By 1920, immigrants and their offspring outnumbered the native-born in many cities, and the national economy depended on new workers and consumers. These new Americans had transformed the United States into an urban nation. They had given American culture its rich and varied texture, and had laid the foundations for the liberalism that would characterize American politics in the twentieth century.

SUGGESTIONS FOR FURTHER READING

Urban Growth

Howard P. Chudacoff and Judith E. Smith, *The Evolution of American Urban Society*, 4th ed. (1993); Howard Gillette, Jr., and Zane L. Miller, eds., *American Urbanism: A Historiographical Review* (1987); David Goldfield and Blaine Brownell, *Urban America*, 2nd ed. (1990); Kenneth T. Jackson, *The Crabgrass Frontier: The Suburbanization of the United States* (1985); Raymond A. Mohl, *The New City: Urban America in the Industrial Age* (1985); Jon Teaford, *City and Suburb: The Political Fragmentation of Metropolitan America, 1850–1970* (1979); Sam Bass Warner, Jr., *The Urban Wilderness* (1982).

Immigration, Ethnicity, and Religion

Aaron I. Abell, *American Catholicism and Social Action* (1960); Josef J. Barton, *Peasants and Strangers: Italians, Rumanians, and Slovaks in an American City* (1975); John Bodnar, *The Transplanted* (1985); John Bodnar, Roger Simon, and Michael P. Weber, *Lives of Their Own: Blacks, Italians, and Poles in Pittsburgh, 1900–1960* (1982); John W. Briggs, *An Italian Passage* (1978); Sucheng Chan, ed., *Entry Denied: Exclusion and the Chinese Community in America, 1882–1943* (1990); Jack Chen, *The Chinese of America* (1980); Hasia Diner, *Erin's Daughters in America* (1983); John B. Duff, *The Irish in the United States* (1971); Elizabeth Ewen, *Immigrant Women in the Land of Dollars* (1985); Mario T. Garcia, *Desert Immigrants: The Mexicans of El Paso, 1880–1920* (1981); Caroline Golab, *Immigrant Destinations* (1977); Milton Gordon, *Assimilation in American Life* (1964); Victor Greene, *For God and Country: The Rise of Polish and Lithuanian Ethnic Consciousness in America* (1975); Oscar Handlin, *The Uprooted*, 2nd ed. (1973); John Higham, *Strangers in the Land: Patterns of American Nativism* (1955); Yusi Ichioka, *The Issei: The World of the First Japanese Immigrants, 1885–1924* (1988); Harry Kitano, *Japanese Americans: The Evolution of a Subculture* (1969); Alan M. Kraut, *The Huddled Masses: The Immigrant in American Society, 1880–1921* (1982); Matt S. Maier and Felciano Rivera, *The Chicanos* (1972); Henry F. May, *Protestant Churches and Industrial America* (1949); Ewa Morawska, *For Bread with Butter: Life-Worlds of East Europeans in Johnstown, Pennsylvania, 1890–1940* (1986); Humbert S. Nelli, *The Italians of Chicago* (1970); Moses Rischin, *The Promised City: New York's Jews* (1962); Judith E. Smith, *Family Connections* (1985); Werner Sollors, *Beyond Ethnicity* (1986); Stephan Thernstrom, ed., *Harvard Encyclopedia of American Ethnic Groups* (1980).

Urban Needs and Services

James H. Cassedy, *Charles V. Chapin and the Public Health Movement* (1962); Charles W. Cheape, *Moving the Masses* (1980); Lawrence A. Cremin, *American Education: The Metropolitan Experience* (1988); Marvin Lazerson, *Origins of the Urban School* (1971); Martin V. Melosi, *Garbage in the Cities* (1981); Eric Monkkonen, *America Becomes Urban* (1988); Thomas L. Philpott, *The Slum and the Ghetto* (1978); James F. Richardson, *The New York Police* (1970); Barbara Gutmann Rosencrantz, *Public Health and the State* (1972); Stanley K. Schultz, *Constructing Urban Culture: American Cities and City Planning* (1989); Mel Scott, *American City Planning Since 1890* (1969); David B. Tyack, *The One Best System: A History of American Urban Education* (1974).

Family and Individual Life Cycles

W. Andrew Achenbaum, *Old Age in the New Land* (1979); Howard P. Chudacoff, *How Old Are You? Age in American Culture* (1989); Carl N. Degler, *At Odds: Women and the Family in America* (1980); John D'Emilio and Estelle B. Freedman, *Intimate Matters: A History of Sexuality in America* (1988); David H. Fischer, *Growing Old in America* (1977); Michael Gordon, ed., *The American Family in Social-Historical Perspective*, 3rd ed. (1983); Carole Haber, *Beyond Sixty-five: Dilemmas of Old Age in America's Past* (1983); Tamara K. Hareven, *Family Time and Industrial Time: The Relationship Between the Family and Work in a New England Industrial Community* (1981); Joseph Kett, *Rites of Passage: Adolescence in America* (1979); Ellen K. Rothman, *Hands and Hearts: A History of Courtship in America* (1986).

Mass Entertainment and Leisure

Robert Clyde Allen, *Vaudeville and Film, 1895–1915: A Study in Media Interaction* (1977); Gunther Barth, *City People* (1980); Foster R. Dulles, *America Learns to Play* (1966); Allen Guttmann, *A Whole New Ball Game: An Interpretation of American Sports* (1988); John F. Kasson, *Amusing the Million: Coney Island at the Turn of the Century* (1978); Donald J. Mrozek, *Sport and American Mentality, 1880–1910* (1983); Joseph A. Musselman, *Music in the Cultured Generation: A Social History of Music in America, 1870–1900* (1971); Kathy Peiss, *Cheap Amusements: Working Women and Leisure in Turn-of-the-Century New York* (1986); Benjamin G. Rader, *American Sports* (1983); Steven A. Riess, *City Games* (1989); Roy Rosenzweig, *Eight Hours for What We Will! Workers and Leisure in an Industrial City, 1870–1920* (1983); Harold Seymour, *Baseball*, 2 vols. (1960–1971); Robert Sklar, *Movie-Made America* (1976); Ronald A. Smith, *Sports and Freedom: The Rise of Big-Time College Athletics* (1988); Robert V. Snyder, *The Voice of the City: Vaudeville and Popular Culture in New York City, 1880–1920* (1990); Robert C. Toll, *On with the Show: The First Century of Show Business in America* (1976).

Journalism

George Juergens, *Joseph Pulitzer and the New York World* (1966); Frank L. Mott, *American Journalism*, 3rd ed. (1962); Frank L. Mott, *A History of American Magazines*, 5 vols. (1930–1968); W. A. Swanberg, *Citizen Hearst* (1961); Bernard A. Weisberger, *The American Newspaperman* (1961).

Mobility and Race Relations

James Borchert, *Alley Life in Washington* (1980); Howard P. Chudacoff, *Mobile Americans* (1972); Clyde Griffen and Sally Griffen, *Natives and Newcomers* (1977); Jacqueline Jones, *Labor of Love, Labor of Sorrow: Black Women, Work and the Family from Slavery to the Present* (1985); David M. Katzman, *Before the Ghetto* (1973); Thomas Kessner, *The Golden Door* (1977); Kenneth L. Kusmer, *A Ghetto Takes Shape* (1976); Gilbert Osofsky, *Harlem: The Making of a Ghetto* (1966); Elizabeth H. Pleck, *Black Migration and Poverty: Boston, 1865–1900* (1979); Howard N. Rabinowitz, *Race Relations in the Urban South* (1978); Allan H. Spear, *Black Chicago* (1967); Stephan Thernstrom, *The Other Bostonians: Poverty and Progress in the American Metropolis* (1973); Olivier Zunz, *The Changing Face of Inequality: Urbanization, Industrial Development and Immigrants in Detroit, 1880–1920* (1982).

Boss Politics

John M. Allswang, *Bosses, Machines and Urban Voters* (1977); Blaine Brownell and Warren E. Stickle, eds., *Bosses and Reformers* (1973); Alexander B. Callow, Jr., ed., *The City Boss in America* (1976); Lyle Dorsett, *The Pendergast Machine* (1968); Leo Hershkowitz, *Tweed's New York: Another Look* (1977); Terrence J. McDonald, *The Parameters of Urban Fiscal Policy: Socioeconomic Change and Political Culture in San Francisco, 1860–1906* (1986); Zane L. Miller, *Boss Cox's Cincinnati* (1968); Bruce M. Stave and Sondra Stave, eds., *Urban Bosses, Machines, and Progressive Reformers* (1984).

Urban Reform

Ruth Bordin, *Women and Temperance* (1981); John D. Buenker, *Urban Liberalism and Progressive Reform* (1973); James B. Crooks, *Politics and Progress* (1968); Doris Groshen Daniels, *Always a Sister: The Feminism of Lillian D. Wald* (1989); Allen F. Davis, *American Heroine: The Life and Legend of Jane Addams* (1973); Allen F. Davis, *Spearheads for Reform* (1967); Michael Ebner and Eugene Tobin, eds., *The Age of Urban Reform* (1977); Lori Ginzberg, *Women and the Work of Benevolence* (1991); Melvin Holli, *Reform in Detroit* (1969); Roy M. Lubove, *The Progressives and the Slums* (1962); Clay McShane, *Technology and Reform* (1974); Robyn Muncy, *Creating a Female Dominion in American Reform* (1991); Martin J. Schiesl, *The Politics of Efficiency: Municipal Administration and Reform in America* (1977).

Chapter

20

Gilded Age Politics,
1877–1900

RUTHERFORD B. HAYES, nineteenth president of the United States (1877–1881), knew he lived in a time of transition. "We are in a period when old questions are settled," he wrote in his diary in 1878, "and the new are not yet brought forward." A dignified man of restrained passions, Hayes tried hard to move the nation beyond the tumult of the Civil War and Reconstruction as well as the scandals of the Grant presidency. In his speeches and writings, he emphasized social harmony, individual effort, and "character," meaning qualities of virtue and morality, as the goals of human development. He also protested exploitative treatment of Indians, discrimination toward blacks, and the corrupt spoils system.

But soon after he left office, Hayes found that two obstacles thwarted his faith in individual character and his worship of the "self-made man." One was "a system that fosters the giant evils of great riches and hopeless poverty." The other was "a government the exact opposite of the popular government for which Lincoln had lived and died—'a government of the people, by the people, and for the people'—and instead of it . . . a 'government of the rich, by the rich, and for the rich.'" Hayes's faith in property ownership as a route to virtue eroded when he discovered that property was becoming concentrated in the hands of a few and that economic opportunity was fading. These new conditions, moreover, undermined Hayes's conception of responsible government. In 1888, seven years after leaving the White House, he wrote that "vast accumulations of wealth in a few hands" tended "to corrupt politics, to bribe conventions, legislative bodies, courts and juries."

But however much he fretted, Hayes would not abandon his faith in individualism. He rejected a view that government regulation in the name of the public interest could alleviate problems of poverty and the unequal distribution of wealth. Ironically, Hayes died in 1893, just as a mass democratic movement called Populism was preparing the nation for a new century in which government was to take much greater responsibility for solving the problems that so troubled him.

Between 1877 and 1900, transformation of the nation by the commercialization of agriculture, industrialization, and urbanization (see Chapters 17, 18, and 19) generated forces that upset time-honored customs and values. Corruption and greed tugged at the fabric of democracy, and the era's venality prompted novelists Mark Twain and Charles Dudley Warner to

During the late nineteenth century, electoral politics was a major community activity in cities and towns across the country.

dub the 1870s and 1880s the Gilded Age. Office-holders used their positions to amass personal fortunes and dispense patronage appointments to their supporters. Congress, though split by powerful partisan and regional rivalries, did grapple with important issues, such as railroad regulation, tariffs, and currency, and legislated some reforms; but many of its accomplishments proved to be either weak compromises or favors to special interests. Meanwhile, the judiciary became active in shaping public policy. By consistently defending vested property rights against state and federal regulation, the courts supported big business. The presidency was occupied by a series of honest, respectable men who seldom took initiative; when they did, they often found themselves blocked by Congress and the courts.

Several major themes characterized politics. The influence of powerful special interests and the conflict between these private interests and the public interests, especially of those who lacked power, emerged as the most prominent theme.

President Rutherford B. Hayes (1822–1893) entered office after an electoral dispute and amid numerous claims on him by special interests. This cartoon shows Hayes making the precarious (to say the least!) journey from the Ohio State House, where he had served as governor, across a field of bayonets to his presidential chair, which is outfitted with a seat of spikes and propped up by the Republican party. Library of Congress.

Manufacturers, railroad managers, creditors, and wealthy men in general directed political affairs, so much so that humorist Ambrose Bierce caustically defined politics as "the conduct of public affairs for private advantage." Corruption flourished as the special interests vied for favors. Vote fraud, bribery, and unfair influence sparked calls for reform and defined several major legislative issues. Exclusion was another theme of politics, because the majority of Americans—including women, southern blacks, Indians, uneducated whites, and unnaturalized immigrants—could not vote and therefore could not use the tools of democracy to redress their grievances. These phenomena—powerful special interests, corruption, and exclusion—contributed to a delicate equilibrium characterized by a stable party system and a regional balance of power.

Then in the 1890s two developments shattered the equilibrium: the rural discontent that accompanied the transformation of the West and South erupted, and a deep economic depression bared flaws in the industrial system. Amid these crises, a presidential campaign stirred Americans as they had not been stirred for a generation. A new party arose, old parties split, sectional unities dissolved, and fundamental questions about the nation's future came to a head. The nation emerged from the turbulent 1890s with new political alignments, just as it had developed new economic configurations.

THE NATURE OF PARTY POLITICS

The historian Henry Adams, a grandson and a great-grandson of presidents, observed that in American political history, the period between 1870 and 1895 "was poor in purpose and barren in results." Adams was only partially right, for he overlooked the spirited competition between the major parties and the emotional commitments that Americans, even those who could not vote, made to the electoral process.

At no other time in the nation's history was public interest in elections more avid. Consistently, 80 to 90 percent of eligible voters (white and black males in the North, mostly white males in the South) cast ballots in local and national elections. (Fewer than 50 percent typically do so to-

Party Allegiances

• *Important Events* •

1873	Congress ends coinage of silver dollars
1873–78	Economic hard times hit
1876	Rutherford B. Hayes elected president
	U.S. v. *Reese* affirms that Congress has no control over states wishing to disfranchise black voters
1877	*Munn* v. *Illinois* upholds state regulation of railroad rates
1878	Bland-Allison Act requires U.S. Treasury to buy between $2 million and $4 million worth of silver each month
	Susan B. Anthony-backed bill for women's suffrage amendment is defeated in Congress
1880	James Garfield elected president
1881	Garfield assassinated; Chester Arthur assumes the presidency
1883	Pendleton Civil Service Act creates Civil Service Commission to oversee competitive examinations for government positions
1884	Grover Cleveland elected president
1886	*Wabash* case declares that only Congress can limit interstate commerce rates
1887	Farm prices collapse
	Interstate Commerce Act creates commission to regulate rates and practices of interstate shippers
1888	Benjamin Harrison elected president
1890	McKinley Tariff raises tariff rates and introduces reciprocity
	Sherman Silver Purchase Act commits U.S. Treasury to buying 4.5 million ounces of silver each month
	"Billion-Dollar Congress" passes first federal budget surpassing $1 billion
	"Mississippi Plan" disfranchises African-Americans by imposing poll tax, property, and literacy requirements
1892	Populist convention in Omaha draws up reform platform
	Cleveland elected president
1893–97	Worst depression in country's history hits United States
1893	Sherman Silver Purchase Act repealed
1894	Wilson-Gorman Tariff attempts to reduce tariff rates; Senate Republicans restore cuts made by House
	Pullman strike; Eugene V. Debs arrested and turns to socialism
	Coxey's army marches on Washington, D.C.
1895	President Cleveland deals with bankers to save the gold reserve
1896	William McKinley elected president
1897	Dingley Tariff raises duties but expands reciprocity provisions
	Maximum Freight Rate decision rules that the Interstate Commerce Commission has no power to set rates
1898	Louisiana enacts first "grandfather clause," using literacy and property qualifications to prevent blacks from voting
1900	Gold Standard Act requires all paper money to be backed by gold
	McKinley re-elected president

day.) Even among those who could not vote, politics was a form of recreation, more popular than baseball, vaudeville, or circuses. Actual voting was only the final stage in a process that included rallies, parades, picnics, and speeches, all of which were as much public amusement as civic responsibility. As one observer remarked, "What the theatre is to the French, or the bull fight . . . to the Spanish . . . [election campaigns] and the ballot box are to *our* people."

Politics was a personal as well as a community activity. In an era before advertising, polls, and media influenced voters' choices, people formed strong loyalties to individual politicians, loyalties that often overlooked crassness and corruption. James G. Blaine—a flamboyant and powerful congressman, senator, and frequent presidential aspirant from Maine who served twice as secretary of state—typified this appeal. Blaine's followers named him "the Plumed Knight," composed songs and organized parades in his honor, and sat mesmerized by his long speeches, while disregarding his corrupt alliances with businesses and railroads, his animosity toward laborers and farmers, and his ignorance of economic issues.

Allegiances to parties and candidates were distributed so evenly on the national level that no major faction or party gained control for any sustained period of time. Between 1877 and 1897, Republicans held the presidency for three terms, Democrats for two. Only briefly and rarely did the same party control the presidency and both houses of Congress simultaneously: the Republicans twice, the Democrats once, for two years at a stretch. In the 1880s and early 1890s, elections were extremely close, especially on the national level. The outcome of presidential elections often hinged on a few states—Connecticut, New York, New Jersey, Ohio, Indiana, and Illinois. Both parties tried to gain advantages by nominating presidential and vice-presidential candidates from these states (and also by committing vote frauds there on their candidates' behalf).

Republicans and Democrats competed avidly for office, but quarrels split both parties from within. Among Republicans, factional feuds and personal rivalries often took
Party Factions precedence over national concerns. On one side stood "the Stalwarts," led by New York's pompous Senator Roscoe Conkling. A physical-fitness devotee and former boxer once labeled "the finest torso in public life," Conkling worked the spoils system to win government jobs for his supporters. On the other side stood "the Half Breeds," led by James G. Blaine. Blaine pursued influence with the Republican party as blatantly as Conkling did, but he disguised his self-serving aims by courting support from independents. On the sidelines were the more idealistic Republicans, or "Mugwumps" (an Indian term meaning "mug on one side of the fence, wump on the other"). Mugwumps such as Senator Carl Schurz of Missouri disliked the political roguishness that tainted their party and believed that only righteous, educated men like themselves should govern. Meanwhile, the Democrats tended to subdivide into white-supremacy southerners, immigrant-stock urban machine members, and business-oriented advocates of low tariffs. Like Republicans, Democrats eagerly pursued the spoils of office.

At the state level, one party usually dominated, and within that party one or two men typically dictated political affairs. Often the state "boss" was a senator: senators were elected by the legislature, not the voters, until the Seventeenth Amendment to the Constitution was ratified in 1913, and a powerful senator could wield enormous influence over the legislature and over federal patronage jobs. Many senators parlayed their state power into national influence. Besides Conkling and Blaine, their ranks included Thomas C. Platt of New York, Nelson W. Aldrich of Rhode Island, Mark A. Hanna of Ohio, Matthew S. Quay of Pennsylvania, and William Mahone of Virginia. Some were Republicans, some Democrats. But party affiliation was often merely a route to power, and private interests forged alliances among these leaders regardless of party.

NATIONAL ISSUES

In Congress, parties split over long-standing political and economic issues. Sectional controversies, patronage abuses, railroad regulation, tariffs, and
Sectional Conflict currency provoked heated debates. Long after Reconstruction ended, the bitter hostilities that the Civil War had engendered continued to haunt Americans. Republicans capitalized on war memories by "waving the bloody shirt" in response to Democratic challenges. As one Republican orator harangued in 1876, "Every man that tried to destroy this nation was a Democrat. . . . Soldiers, every scar you have on your heroic bodies was given you by a Democrat." In the South, voters also waved the bloody shirt, calling Republicans traitors to white supremacy. Such emotional appeals persisted well into the 1880s.

Politicians were not the only Americans who attempted to profit by invoking the war. The Grand Army of the Republic, an organization of Union army veterans numbering over 400,000, allied with the Republican party in the 1880s and 1890s and lobbied Congress into legislating generous pensions for former Union soldiers and their widows. Many pensions were deserved: Union soldiers had been poorly paid, and thousands of wives had been widowed. But for many veterans, the war's emotional wake provided an opportunity to

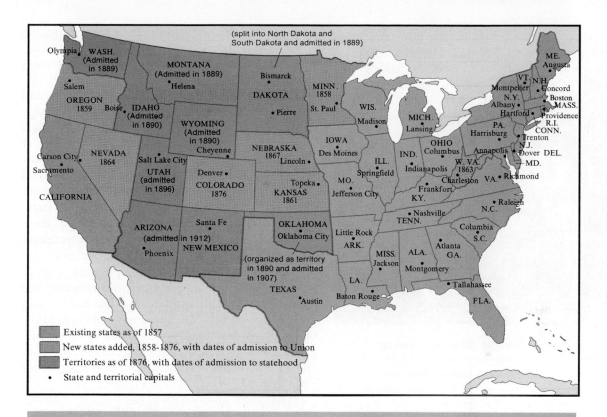

Existing states as of 1857

New states added, 1858-1876, with dates of admission to Union

Territories as of 1876, with dates of admission to statehood

• State and territorial capitals

The United States, 1876–1912 *A wave of admissions between 1889 and 1912 brought remaining territories to statehood and marked the final creation of new states until Alaska and Hawaii were admitted in the 1950s.*

profit at the public's expense. By the 1890s the federal government was spending $157 million annually for soldiers' pensions, one of the largest welfare commitments it has ever made. Confederate veterans received none of this money, though some southern states did fund small pensions and build old-age homes for ex-soldiers.

Few politicians could afford to oppose Civil War pensions, but a number of reformers attempted to dismantle the spoils system. The prac-

Civil Service Reform
_____

tice of awarding government jobs to party workers, regardless of their qualifications, had taken root before the Civil War and flourished after it. As the postal service, the diplomatic and consular corps, and other government activities expanded, so did the public payroll. Between 1865 and 1891 the number of federal government jobs tripled, from 53,000 to 166,000. Elected officials, often lampooned in cartoons in the media, scrambled to control new appointments as a means of cementing

support for themselves and their parties. In return for the comparatively short hours and high pay of government jobs, appointees pledged their votes and a portion of their earnings.

Shocked by such blatant corruption, a growing number of independents began advocating appointments and promotions based on merit rather than political connections. The movement for civil service reform grew during the 1870s, when scandals in the Grant administration exposed the defects of the spoils system. It became a fervent reform crusade in 1881 with the formation of the National Civil Service Reform League, led by George W. Curtis, editor of *Harper's Weekly*, and E. L. Godkin, editor of the *Nation*. The same year, a frustrated and demented job seeker assassinated President James Garfield. The murder hastened the drive for civil service reform.

The Pendleton Civil Service Act, passed by Congress in 1882 and signed by President Chester Arthur in 1883, outlawed political contributions by officeholders and created the Civil Service Com-

Before passage of the Pendleton Act of 1883, many government positions were filled by patronage; hat in hand, job seekers beseeched political leaders to find a place for them. Here a member of Congress presents office-seeking friends and constituents to President Hayes.   Library of Congress.

mission to oversee competitive examinations for government positions. The act gave the commission jurisdiction, however, over only about 10 percent of federal jobs, though the president could expand the list, and it also applied only to the federal government. The Constitution barred Congress from interfering in state affairs, and thus civil service at the state and local levels developed in an even more haphazard manner.

Meanwhile, economic development was causing political problems at both the state and national levels. Railroad expansion was a particularly controversial area. As the nation's rail network spread, so did competition. In their quest for customers, railroad lines reduced rates to outmaneuver rivals, but rate wars soon cut into profits and wild vacillations of rates angered shippers and farmers.

Ironically, as rates generally fell, complaints about excessively high rates rose. On noncompetitive routes, railroads often boosted rates as high as possible to compensate for unprofitably low rates on competitive routes, making pricing disproportionate to distance. Charges on short-distance shipments served by only one line could be far higher than those on long-distance shipments served by

competing lines. Railroads also played favorites: they gave reduced rates to large shippers and offered free passenger passes to preferred customers and politicians.

Such favoritism stirred farmers, shippers, and reform politicians to demand that government regulate railroad practices, especially rates. Attempts at regulation occurred first at the state level. By 1880, fourteen states had established commissions to limit freight and storage charges of state-chartered lines. Railroads bitterly fought these measures, arguing that rights of private property superseded public authority. This belief in the sacred freedom to acquire and use property without government restraint prevented the ultimate step —public ownership of railroads—but did not halt regulation. In 1877 the Supreme Court upheld the principle of rate regulation in *Munn* v. *Illinois*, declaring that railroads were acting in the public interest and therefore must submit to regulation for "the common good."

Railroad Regulation

But state agencies could not regulate large interstate lines, a limitation affirmed by the Supreme Court in the *Wabash* case of 1886, in which the Court declared that only Congress could limit rates involving interstate commerce. Reformers thereupon demanded federal regulation. Congress responded in 1887 by passing the Interstate Commerce Act. The act prohibited pools (see Chapter 18), rebates, and long haul–short haul rate discrimination, and it directed that "charges . . . shall be reasonable and fair." It also created the Interstate Commerce Commission (ICC) and empowered it to investigate railroad rate-making practices, issue "cease-and-desist" orders against illegal practices, and seek court aid to enforce compliance. The legislation proved, however, to be a flimsy roadblock to business interests: lack of provisions for enforcement left the railroads ample room for evasion, and federal judges chipped away at ICC powers. In the *Maximum Freight Rate* case of 1897, the Supreme Court ruled that the ICC did not have the power to set rates, and in the *Alabama Midlands* case the same year the Court overturned prohibitions against long haul–short haul discrimination. Even so, the principle of government regulation, though weakened, remained in force.

Tariffs were another economic issue with political implications. Congress had initially created tariffs to protect American manufactured goods

Tariff Policy

———

and some agricultural products from European competition. But tariffs quickly became a tool with which special interests could protect and enhance their profits. By the 1880s separate tariffs applied to over four thousand items, and the resulting revenues were producing an embarrassing surplus in the federal Treasury. A few economists and farmers argued for free trade, but most politicians still insisted that tariffs were necessary to support industry and preserve jobs.

The Republican party, claiming responsibility for economic growth, put protective tariffs at the core of its political agenda. The Democrats complained that tariffs made prices artificially high by keeping out less expensive foreign goods, thereby benefiting manufacturers while hurting farmers whose crops were not protected and consumers who had to buy manufactured goods. For example, a yard of flannel that might have cost 10 cents (including profits) to produce abroad and ship to the United States cost consumers 18 cents after the imposition of an 8-cent tariff. A U.S. manufacturer of a similar yard of flannel could charge 17 cents, underselling the foreign competition while still pocketing a large profit at the consumers' expense, especially since only about 3 cents was used to pay laborers. Although Democrats acknowledged a need for some protection of manufactured goods and raw materials, they favored lower tariff rates to encourage foreign trade and to reduce the Treasury surplus.

Manufacturing interests and their congressional allies successfully fought off objections and maintained control over tariff policy. The McKinley Tariff of 1890 boosted already-high rates by another 4 percent. When House Democrats supported by President Grover Cleveland passed a bill to reduce tariff rates in 1894, Senate Republicans, aided by southern Democrats eager to protect their region's infant industries, added some six hundred amendments restoring most cuts (Wilson-Gorman Tariff). In 1897 a new tariff bill, the Dingley Act, raised rates further, though it expanded reciprocity provisions. Reciprocity, introduced in the McKinley Tariff of 1890 and designed to encourage foreign trade and discourage foreign retaliation against high American duties, authorized the president to remove items from the free list if their countries of origin placed unreasonable tariffs on American goods. Attacks on the tariff, though unsuccessful, did make tariffs the symbol of privileged business in the public mind, and a target of progressive reformers after 1900 (see Chapter 21).

The currency controversy was even more tangled than the tariff issue. When prices fell after the Civil War, as a result of increased industrial and agricultural production, debtors and creditors had opposing reactions. Farmers, most of whom were debtors, suffered because they had to pay fixed mortgage and interest payments while prices for their crops were dropping. Correctly perceiving that an insufficient money supply made debts more expensive relative to other costs, farmers favored schemes like the coinage of silver to increase the amount of currency in circulation. With an expanded money supply, debts would be less burdensome because interest rates would be lower. Thus farmers' costs would be lower relative to the prices they could receive for their crops. Creditors, on the other hand, believed that overproduction had caused prices to decline. They favored a more stable, limited money supply backed only by gold. They opposed an expanded money supply because, without gold to back it, money's value would become more uncertain and susceptible to fluctuation, thereby undermining investors' confidence in the American economy.

Monetary Policy

———

But the issue of the quantity and quality of money involved more than a question of economics. It grew from a series of conflicts—social, regional, and emotional. First, creditor-debtor conflict translated into haves versus have-nots. The debate also represented a sectional cleavage: western silver-mining areas and agricultural regions of the South and West against the more conservative industrial Northeast. Finally, the issue carried moral, almost religious, overtones, as can be seen in some of the "Gold Bug" (and "Silver Bug") jewelry worn at the time (see page 604). For some Americans, the beauty, rarity, and durability of gold gave it a magical potency and made it seem a God-given symbol of value. For others, the gold standard for currency was too limiting for the machine age; sustained prosperity, they believed, demanded new attitudes.

By the early 1870s, the currency controversy boiled down to gold versus silver. Until that time the government had coined both gold and silver dollars. A silver dollar weighed sixteen times more than a gold dollar, meaning that gold was officially worth sixteen times as much as silver. Gold discoveries after 1848, however, had increased the supply and lowered gold's market price relative to that of silver. Because silver came to be worth more than one-sixteenth the value of gold, silver producers preferred to sell their metal on the open market rather than to the government. Silver dollars disappeared from circulation—because of their inflated value owners hoarded them rather than spending them—and in 1873 Congress officially stopped coining silver dollars, an act that partisans of silver called "the Crime of '73." At about the same time, European nations also stopped buying silver. Thus the United States and many of its trading partners unofficially adopted the gold standard, meaning that their currency was backed chiefly by gold.

During the 1880s and 1890s the kind and content of money dominated political debates. These pins of "Gold Bugs" and "Silver Bugs"—the names given to supporters of the gold standard and the silver standard for American currency—were common to the age and reflected the dedication that supporters of each side had to their cause. Museum of American Political Life, University of Hartford.

Within a few years, new mines in the American West began to flood the market with silver, and its price dropped accordingly. Once again gold was worth more than sixteen times the value of silver. It became profitable to spend silver dollars, and it would have been worthwhile to sell silver to the government in return for gold—but the government was no longer buying silver. Debtors, hurt by falling prices and the economic hard times of the mid-1870s, saw silver as a means of expanding the currency supply. They joined with silver producers to denounce "the Crime of '73" and press for the resumption of coinage at the old sixteen-to-one ratio.

Split into silver and gold factions, Congress tried to achieve a compromise. The Bland-Allison Act of 1878 required the Treasury to buy between $2 million and $4 million worth of silver each month, and the Sherman Silver Purchase Act of 1890 fixed the government's monthly purchase of silver in weight (4.5 million ounces) rather than dollars. But neither act satisfied the different interest groups. The minting of silver dollars, which these laws allowed, failed to expand the money supply as substantially as debtors had hoped, and it also failed to erase the impression that the government favored the creditors' interests. Not until after a depression in the 1890s and an emotional presidential election did the money issue subside.

Amid debates over tariffs and money, supporters of women's suffrage pressed Congress and state legislatures more fervently than ever before. Win-

Women's Suffrage

ning the vote had preoccupied women reformers since the 1840s. In 1869, adoption of the Fifteenth Amendment forbidding states to deny the vote "on account of race, color or previous condition" had omitted reference to women, disappointing those who advocated female suffrage and provoking a split in the women's movement. For the next twenty years, two organizations—the National Woman Suffrage Association (NWSA) and the American Woman Suffrage Association (AWSA)—competed for support. The NWSA, led by militants Elizabeth Cady Stanton and Susan B. Anthony, mounted a drive for comprehensive women's rights in courts and workplaces as well as at the ballot box. Meanwhile, the AWSA, led by former abolitionists such as Lucy Stone and Thomas Wentworth Higginson, focused more narrowly on suffrage.

American Woman and Her Political Peers.
COPYRIGHT, 1893, BY HENRIETTA BRIGGS-WALL.

How *do historians know*

the extent of opposition to women's suffrage in the late nineteenth century? In addition to numerous newspaper articles, editorials, and other publications, political posters and broadsides often got across messages with brutal force. Opponents of women's suffrage sometimes used vicious and racist propaganda in support of their cause. This 1893 illustration equated a stern-faced, tightly garbed suffragette to a variety of other individuals deemed inferior and prohibited from voting. She is surrounded (clockwise, from upper left) by an immigrant, a convict, a hobo, and a Native Indian. Note how the artist depicted the personality of each figure in the drawing by presenting faces and clothing that represent extreme stereotypes. Photo: Sophia Smith Collection, Smith College.

In 1878 Susan B. Anthony, who had been rebuffed by the courts when she tried to vote in 1872, persuaded Senator A. A. Sargent of California, a proponent of women's suffrage, to introduce a constitutional amendment stating that "the right of citizens of the United States to vote shall be denied or abridged by the United States or by any state on account of sex." A Senate committee killed the bill, but the NWSA had it reintroduced repeatedly over the next eighteen years. On the few occasions when the bill reached the Senate floor, it was voted down by senators who expressed fears that suffrage would interfere with women's family obligations and ruin female virtue.

While the NWSA fought for the vote on the national level, the AWSA worked for constitutional amendments at the state level. (The two groups merged in 1890 to form the National American Woman Suffrage Association.) Between 1870 and 1910, eleven states held referenda (all but three of them west of the Mississippi River) to legalize women's suffrage. Though few of these attempts succeeded, they helped to train a corps of female leaders in political organizing and public speaking. Women did win partial victories: by 1890 nineteen states allowed women to vote on school issues, and three granted suffrage on tax and bond issues. But broader rights would have to await a later generation.

Throughout the Gilded Age, legislators focused chiefly on protection of private property and the stability of the investment climate—deemed essential for economic progress. Debtors, farmers, laborers, women, racial minorities, and others who believed themselves disadvantaged expressed their political interests in increasingly organized and articulate ways, but Congress and the state legislatures catered to those who already had social and economic privileges.

THE PRESIDENCY
IN ECLIPSE

American presidents in the years between 1877 and 1900 bore little resemblance to forceful predecessors like Andrew Jackson and Abraham Lincoln. Operating under the cloud of Andrew Johnson's impeachment, Grant's scandals, and doubts about the legitimacy of the election of 1876 (see Chapter 16), these presidents proceeded gingerly to restore the authority of their office in the eyes of Congress and the public. Proper, honorable, and honest, Presidents Rutherford Hayes (1877–1881), James Garfield (1881), Chester Arthur (1881–1885), Grover Cleveland (1885–1889 and 1893–1897), Benjamin Harrison (1889–1893), and William McKinley (1897–1901) won respect but seldom elicited strong emotions. Like other politicians, they used symbols. Hayes served lemonade at the White House to emphasize that he, unlike his predecessor Ulysses Grant, was no hard drinker. McKinley put aside his cigar in public so photographers would not catch him setting a bad example for youth. But none of the era's presidents was an inspiring personality, nor could any dominate the factional chieftains of his party. Each president initiated legislation and used the veto to combat Congress, but the major presidential actions were in foreign policy (see Chapter 22).

Rutherford B. Hayes had been a Union general and an Ohio congressman and governor before his disputed election to the presidency, an event that prompted opponents to label him "Rutherfraud B. Hayes." Though most contemporaries regarded him as a staunch ally of business, Hayes played a quiet role as a reformer and conciliator. He emphasized national unity over sectional rivalry and opposed violence of all kinds. When Hayes ordered out troops to disperse railroad strikers in 1877, it was not to suppress their cause but because he believed the rioting and looting that accompanied the strikes threatened social harmony. He tried also to honor his pledge to overhaul the spoils system by appointing civil service reformer Carl Schurz to his cabinet and by battling New York's patronage king, Senator Roscoe Conkling. (He fired Conkling's protégé, Chester Arthur, from the post of New York customs house collector.) Hayes believed society was obligated to help those whom it had formerly oppressed, including American Chinese and Indians, and after retiring from the presidency he worked diligently to help former slaves. But his Victorian sense of propriety caused him to avoid publicity so assiduously that, according to poet-journalist Eugene Field, the only person who would recognize Hayes at a public meeting would be a policeman who would ask him to get off the grass.

Hayes, Garfield, and Arthur

When Hayes declined to run for re-election in 1880, the Republicans nominated another Ohio congressman and Civil War hero, James A. Garfield. A solemn and cautious man, Garfield defeated Democrat Winfield Scott Hancock, also a Civil War hero, by just 40,000 votes out of more than 9 million cast. By carrying the pivotal states of New York and Indiana, however, Garfield won in the electoral college by a comfortable margin of 214 to 155. Garfield spent most of his brief presidency trying to secure an independent position among party potentates. He hoped to reduce the tariff and develop American economic interests in Latin America (see Chapter 22), but he had to spend most of his time dealing with hordes of office seekers. "Once or twice I felt like crying out in the agony of my soul," Garfield admitted, "against the greed for office and its consumption of my time." Garfield pleased civil service reformers by rebuffing Conkling's patronage demands, but his chance to make lasting contributions ended in July

1881 when Charles Guiteau, a disappointed patronage seeker, shot him in a Washington railroad station. Garfield lingered for seventy-nine days while doctors tried vainly to remove a bullet lodged in his back. His condition steadily deteriorated, and he succumbed to infection on September 19.

Garfield's vice president and successor was New York politician Chester A. Arthur, the spoilsman Hayes had fired in 1878. Arthur had been nominated as vice president only to help the Republican party carry New York State. Though his elevation to the presidency made reformers shudder, he became a dignified and temperate executive. Arthur signed the Pendleton Civil Service Act, urged Congress to modify outdated tariff rates, and supported federal regulation of railroads. He wielded the veto aggressively, killing a number of bills that excessively benefited privileged interests. But congressional partisans frustrated his hopes for reducing the tariff and building up the navy. Arthur wanted to run for re-election in 1884 but lost the nomination to James G. Blaine on the fourth ballot at the Republican national convention.

The 1884 presidential campaign magnified the era's political banalities. To run against Blaine, the Democratic party named New York's Governor Grover Cleveland, a bachelor whose respectable reputation was tainted by his having fathered an illegitimate son—a fact he admitted openly during the campaign. Both parties focused on the sordid. (Alluding to Cleveland's illegitimate son, Republicans chided him with catcalls of "Ma! Ma! Where's my pa?" To which Democrats replied, "Gone to the White House, Ha! Ha! Ha!" Distaste for Blaine was so strong that a number of Mugwump Republicans deserted their party for Cleveland. On election day Cleveland beat Blaine by only 23,000 popular votes; his tiny margin of 1,149 votes in New York gave him that state's 36 electoral votes, enough for a 219-to-182 vote victory in the electoral college. Cleveland may have won New York thanks to the last-minute efforts of a local Protestant minister, who publicly equated Democrats with "rum, Romanism, and rebellion" (drinking, Catholicism, and the Civil War). The Democrats eagerly publicized the slur among New York's large Irish-Catholic population, urging voters to protest by turning out for Cleveland.

Cleveland, the first Democratic president since James Buchanan (1857–1861), echoed his Republican counterparts' complaints about the "cursed

James A. Garfield (1831–1881), pictured on this trade card, was a Civil War hero from Ohio who won a narrow electoral victory in 1880 to become the nation's twentieth president. His death at the hand of an assassin in 1881 spurred efforts to establish civil service as a means of appointing federal employees. Museum of American Political Life, University of Hartford.

Cleveland and Harrison

constant grind" of his office and the "want of rest." He did, however, exert more vigorous leadership. He used the veto against excessive pension bills —in fact, he vetoed two-thirds of all the bills Congress passed—and he expanded the merit-based civil service. His most forceful action was in the interest of tariff reform. Worried about the growing Treasury surplus, Cleveland urged Congress to cut duties on raw materials and manufactured goods. When advisers warned him that his stand might weaken his chances for re-election, the president retorted, "What is the use of being elected or re-elected, unless you stand for something?" But the Mills tariff bill of 1888, passed by the House in response to Cleveland's wishes, died in the Senate. When Democrats renominated Cleveland for the

This handkerchief from the presidential campaign of 1892 depicts Democratic candidate Grover Cleveland as a just and patriotic statesman. He remains the only president to have served two nonconsecutive terms, 1885–1889 and 1893–1897. Museum of American Political Life, University of Hartford.

presidency in 1888, protectionists in the party convinced him to temper his attacks on high tariffs.

The Republicans in 1888 nominated Benjamin Harrison, an intelligent but dull former senator from Indiana and grandson of President William Henry Harrison (1841). The campaign was less savage than that of 1884 but far from clean. Some shrewd Republicans manipulated the British minister in Washington into stating that Cleveland's re-election would be good for England. Irish Democrats took offense, as intended, and Cleveland's campaign was weakened. Perhaps more helpful to Harrison was the bribery and multiple voting that helped him to win Indiana by 2,300 votes and New York by 14,000. (Democrats also indulged in bribery and vote fraud, but this time Republicans proved more successful at it.) Those crucial states assured Harrison's victory; though Cleveland out-

polled Harrison by 90,000 popular votes, Harrison carried the electoral vote by 233 to 168. After the election, Harrison exclaimed to Matthew Quay, the Republican national chairman, "Providence has given us the victory." Quay later quipped to a friend, "Think of the man. He ought to know that Providence hadn't a damned thing to do with it. . . . [He] would never learn how close a number of men were compelled to approach the gates of the penitentiary to make him president."

Though Harrison was the first president since 1875 whose party had majorities in both houses of Congress, he had little control over legislators, and he alienated supporters. "Harrison can make a speech to ten thousand men," mused an associate, "and every man of them will go away his friend. Let him meet the same ten thousand in private, and every one will go away his enemy." Harrison professed support for civil service and appointed the reformer Theodore Roosevelt a civil service commissioner, but the president's lackluster character prompted the reform-minded and impatient Roosevelt to call him a "cold-blooded, narrow-minded, prejudiced, obstinate, timid, old psalm-singing Indianapolis politician." Harrison also signed the Dependents' Pension Act, which provided disability pensions for all Union veterans of the Civil War and granted aid for their widows and minor children. The bill doubled the number of pensioners from 490,000 to 966,000. By 1911, the nation had spent over $4 billion on Civil War pensions, a sum that vastly exceeded the war's entire cost. Politics had met the demands of another special interest.

As a consequence of the Pension Act and other grants and appropriations, the federal budget surpassed $1 billion in 1890 for the first time in the nation's history. Democrats blamed the "Billion-Dollar Congress" on spendthrift Republicans. Voters reacted by unseating seventy-eight Republicans in the congressional elections of 1890. Seeking to capitalize on voter unrest, Democrats nominated Cleveland to run against Harrison again in 1892. This time Cleveland attracted large contributions from business and beat Harrison by 380,000 popular votes (3 percent of the total) and by a 277-to-145 electoral vote.

In office once more, Cleveland took bolder steps to address the problems of currency, tariffs, and labor unrest. But his actions reflected a narrow orientation toward the interests of business, and it bespoke political weakness. To protect the nation's dwindling gold reserve, which was shrinking during the Panic of 1893, Cleveland enlisted aid from bankers, who in 1895 bailed out the nation on terms highly favorable to themselves. During his campaign Cleveland had promised sweeping tariff reform, but he made little effort to line up support for such reform in the Senate, where protectionists undercut all efforts to reduce rates. And when 120,000 boycotting railroad workers paralyzed western commerce in the Pullman strike of 1894 (see Chapter 18), Cleveland bowed to requests from railroad managers and Attorney General Richard Olney to send in troops. Throughout Cleveland's second term, events—particularly economic downturn and Populist ferment—seemed too much for the president, and in 1896 his party abandoned him.

STIRRINGS OF AGRARIAN UNREST AND POPULISM

While the federal government labored to sustain harmony and prosperity, debates about the nature of democracy were occurring outside the political system. Inequities in the new agricultural and industrial order were stirring up a mass movement that was to shake American society. The agrarian revolt—a complex mixture of strident rhetoric, nostalgic dreams, desires for economic security, and hard-headed egalitarianism—began in Grange organizations in the early 1870s. The revolt accelerated when farmers' alliances formed in Texas in the late 1870s and then spread across the Cotton Belt and Plains in the 1880s. The movement caught on chiefly in areas where farm tenancy, crop liens, merchants, railroads, banks, weather, and insects threatened the ambitions and economic well-being of hopeful farmers. Once under way, the agrarian rebellion inspired visions of a truly cooperative and democratic society.

Agricultural expansion in the West and South exposed millions of people to the hardships of rural life (see Chapter 17). The uncertainties might have been more bearable if rewards had been more promising, but such was not the case for farmers of small and middle-size landholdings. As growers put more land under cultivation, as mechanization boosted productivity, and as foreign competition increased, supplies exceeded national and world-wide demand for agricultural products. Consequently, prices for staple crops dropped steadily. A bushel of wheat that sold for $1.45 in 1866 brought only 80 cents in the mid-1880s and 49 cents by the mid-1890s. Meanwhile, transportation, storage, and sales fees remained high relative to other prices. Combined with social isolation, high expenses—for seed, fertilizer, manufactured goods, taxes, and mortgage interest—trapped many farm families in disadvantageous and sometimes desperate circumstances. In order to buy necessities and pay bills, farmers had to produce more. But the spiral wound ever more tightly: the more farmers produced, the lower prices dropped.

Even before the full impact of these developments was felt, small farmers had begun to organize. With aid from Oliver H. Kelley of the Department of Agriculture, farmers founded a network of local organizations called Granges in almost

Grange Movement

every state during the 1860s and 1870s. By 1875 the Grange had nearly twenty thousand local branches and more than one million members. Strongest in the Midwest and South, Granges served a chiefly social function, sponsoring meetings and educational events to help relieve the loneliness of farm life. Family-oriented and open to all, local Granges made specific provisions for women's participation.

As membership flourished, Granges moved into economic and political action. Encouraged by the national Grange, local branches formed cooperatives to buy equipment and supplies directly from manufacturers. Granges also organized sales cooperatives, whereby farmers would divide the profits

from the sale of their pooled grain and dairy products. In a few instances, Grangers even operated farm-implements factories and insurance companies. Most of these enterprises failed, however, because farmers lacked cash for cooperative buying and because ruthless competition from large manufacturers and dealers undercut them. In politics, Grangers used their numbers to some advantage, electing sympathetic legislators and pressing for so-called Granger laws to regulate transportation and storage rates.

Despite their efforts, Granges declined in the late 1870s. A requirement that cooperatives run on a cash-only basis excluded large numbers of farmers who rarely had cash. Legislative efforts to regulate business and transportation withered when

Shifting Gap between Farm Income and Consumer Costs, 1865–1913

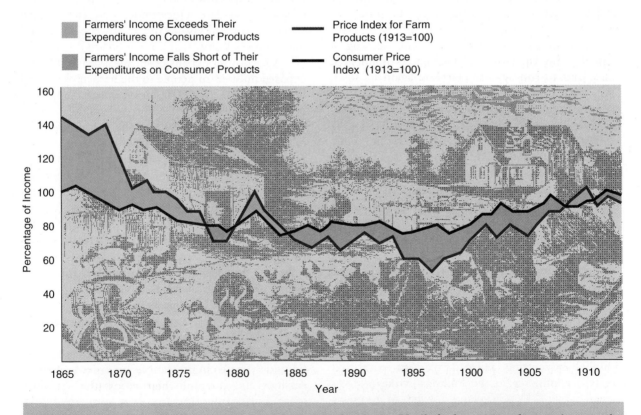

Legend:
- Farmers' Income Exceeds Their Expenditures on Consumer Products
- Farmers' Income Falls Short of Their Expenditures on Consumer Products
- Price Index for Farm Products (1913=100)
- Consumer Price Index (1913=100)

Consumer Prices and Farm Product Prices, 1865–1913 Until the late 1870s, farmers in general were able to receive more income for their crops than they spent on consumer goods in spite of falling farm prices. But beginning in the mid-1880s, consumer prices began leveling off and then rose, while prices for farm products continued to drop. As a result, farmers found it increasingly difficult to afford consumer goods, a problem that plagued them until well into the twentieth century.

corporations won court support against such "Granger laws." Politically, Granges disavowed third parties but could not withstand the power of business interests within the two major parties. Finally, the Grange's promotion of thrift and hard work hardly helped families already overburdened with both virtues. Thus, after a brief assertion of influence, the Grange reverted to an organization of farmers' social clubs.

Rural political activism then shifted to the Farmers' Alliances, two networks of organizations—one in the Plains and one in the South—

Farmers' Alliances
———

that by 1890 constituted a genuine mass movement. The first Alliances sprang up in Texas, where hard-pressed small farmers rallied against crop liens, merchants, and railroads in particular, and against "money power" in general. Using traveling lecturers to recruit members, Alliance leaders extended the movement to other southern states. By 1889 the Southern Alliance boasted over three million members, including the powerful Colored Farmers' National Alliance, which claimed over one million black members. A similar movement flourished in the Plains, where by the late 1880s two million members were organized in Kansas, Nebraska, and the Dakotas.

Alliances sponsored rallies, educational meetings, and cooperative buying and selling agreements and pushed the Grange concept of cooperation to new limits. Seeing themselves as laborers battling capitalists in a new age, some Alliance members advocated unity with the Knights of Labor and other workers' groups in the campaign against unfair privilege. Beyond urging democratic cooperation, the Alliance movement proposed a scheme to relieve the most serious rural problems: lack of cash and lack of credit. The subtreasury plan, adapted from French and Russian precedents, called for the federal government to construct warehouses in every major agricultural county. At harvest time, farmers could store crops in these "subtreasuries" while awaiting higher prices, and the government would loan farmers Treasury notes amounting to 80 percent of the market price the stored crops would bring. Farmers could use these Treasury notes as legal tender to pay debts and make purchases. Once the stored crops were sold, farmers would pay back the loans plus small interest and storage fees.

THE NEW UNCLE SAM.
How the Farmers' Alliance propose to have the Government run when they get the power.

The Farmers' Alliance movement organized agrarian unrest into a cogent list of reforms. This cartoon shows how alliance members hoped to protect their mortgages and crops with a series of economic proposals that would make the currency system more flexible. Library of Congress.

The subtreasury plan was meant to replace the crop-lien system by giving farmers greater control over their financial affairs and freeing them from dependence on exploitative storage operators and purchasers.

Subtreasury Plan
———

No longer would merchants be able to take advantage of farmers at harvest time, when market gluts depressed prices. No longer would farmers have to mortgage their crops (through crop liens) at high interest. No longer would they lack cash to buy supplies. And by issuing Treasury notes, the government would be injecting money into the economy and encouraging the kind of inflation that would supposedly raise crop prices without raising the prices of supplies and rents. If the government subsidized business, reasoned

Shifting Population Urban vs. Rural, 1870–1920

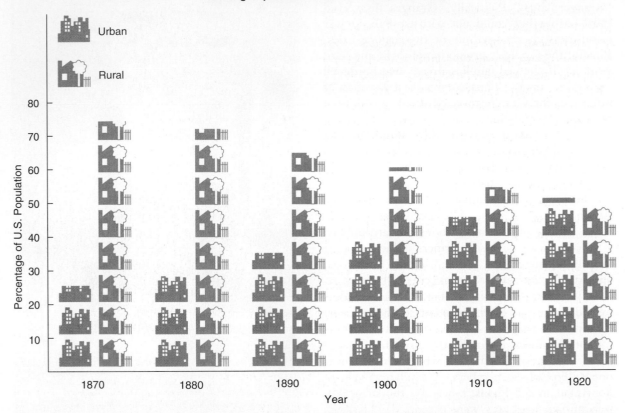

Shifting Population, Urban vs. Rural, 1870–1920 *Throughout the years between 1870 and 1920, the percentage of the population living in rural areas (places with less than 2,500 people) declined steadily, reflecting further the declining attractiveness of farming as a means of earning a living. Meanwhile the proportion in urban areas rose, becoming a majority in 1920 and signaling the emergence of the United States as an urban-industrial nation.*

Alliance members, why should it not help farmers earn a decent living, too?

If the various Alliances in the North and South had been able to unite, they would have made a formidable political force; but sectional differences and personality clashes thwarted early attempts at merger. At an 1889 meeting in St. Louis, white southerners, fearing reprisals from landowners and objecting to participation by blacks, rejected proposals that would have ended secret Alliance activities and whites-only membership rules. Northerners, too, shied away from amalgamation, fearing domination by the more experienced southern leaders. Differences on issues also prevented unity. Northern farmers, who were mostly Republicans, wanted protective tariffs to keep out foreign grain;

white southerners, mostly Democrats, wanted low tariffs to hold down the costs of foreign manufactured goods. Both Alliances did favor governmental regulation of transportation and communications, liberal credit policies, equitable taxation, prohibition of landownership by foreign investors, and currency reform.

Growing membership and rising confidence nonetheless drew the Alliances more deeply into politics. By 1890, farmers had elected a number of officeholders sympathetic to their programs—especially in the South, where Alliance members controlled four governorships, eight state legislatures, forty-four seats in the U.S. House of Representa-

Rise of Populism

tives, and three seats in the U.S. Senate. In the Midwest, Alliance candidates often ran on independent third-party tickets and achieved some success in Kansas, Nebraska, and the Dakotas. Alliance rallies and parades resounded with songs and orations; their banners proclaimed "We Are All Mortgaged But Our Votes." During the summer of 1890, the Kansas Alliance held a "convention of the people" and nominated candidates who swept the state's fall elections. Formation of this People's party, whose members were called Populists (from *populus*, the Latin word for "people"), gave a name to Alliance political activism.

Election results in 1890 energized efforts to unite Alliance groups into a single Populist party. A meeting in May 1891 of northern and southern Alliances in Cincinnati failed when southerners chose to remain Democrats rather than risk joining a third party. But by early 1892 southern Alliance members were ready for independent action. Meeting with northern counterparts in St. Louis, they summoned a People's party convention in Omaha on July 4 to draft a platform and nominate a presidential candidate.

The new party's platform was one of the most comprehensive reform documents in American history. Its preamble charged that the nation had been "brought to the verge of moral, political, and material ruin. Corruption dominates the ballot box, the legislatures, the Congress, and touches . . . even the [judiciary] bench." More importantly, corruption fostered inequality that threatened to split American society. "The fruits of the toil of millions," the platform declared, "are boldly stolen to build up colossal fortunes for a few."

Claiming that "wealth belongs to him that creates it," the Omaha platform presented a host of proposals addressing the three central sources of rural unrest: transportation, land, and money. Frustrated with weak state and federal regulation, Populists demanded government ownership of railroad and telegraph lines. They urged the federal government to reclaim all land owned for speculative purposes by railroads and foreigners. The monetary plank called for a flexible currency system based on free and unlimited coinage of silver, which would increase the money supply and enable farmers to pay their debts more easily. Other planks advocated a graduated income tax, postal savings banks, direct election of U.S. senators, and shorter hours for workers. As its presidential can-

Mary E. Lease (1850–1933) was a fiery and controversial speaker for the Farmers' Alliance and Populist party in Kansas. Tall and intense, she had a deep, almost hypnotic voice that made her an effective publicist for the farmers' cause. She was one of the founders of the Populist party and gave a seconding speech to the presidential nomination of James B. Weaver at the party convention in 1892. Library of Congress.

didate, the party nominated James B. Weaver of Iowa, a former Union general and supporter of a liberally increased money supply.

The Populist campaign featured colorful personalities and vivid rhetoric. The Kansas plains rumbled with the speeches of "Sockless Jerry" Simpson, an unschooled but canny rural reformer, and of Mary Ellen Lease, a fiery orator who allegedly urged farmers to "raise less corn and more hell." The South produced equally forceful leaders, such as Charles W. Macune of Texas, Thomas Watson of Georgia, and Leonidas Polk of North Carolina. Minnesota's Ignatius Donnelly, pseudo-scientist and writer of apocalyptic novels, became the chief ideologue of the northern Plains and was responsible for the thunderous language in the Omaha platform. Finally, the campaign had opportunists like James Hogg, the three-hundred-pound governor of Texas, and one-eyed Senator "Pitchfork Ben" Tillman of South Carolina, who were not genuine Populists but used the rising agrarian fervor for their own political ends.

Though Weaver lost badly in 1892, he garnered over one million popular votes (8 percent of the total), majorities in four states and twenty-two electoral votes. Not since 1856 had a third party won so many votes in its first national effort. The party's central dilemma—whether to stand by its principles at all costs or compromise in order to gain power—still loomed ahead. But in the early 1890s, rural dwellers in the South and Plains had an emotional faith in the future. Although Populists were flawed democrats—their mistrust of blacks and foreigners gave them a reactionary streak—they sought change in order to fulfill their version of American ideals. Amid hardship and desperation, millions of people had begun to believe that a cooperative democracy in which government would ensure equal opportunity could overcome corporate power. A banner draped above the stage at the Omaha convention captured the movement's spirit: "We do not ask for sympathy or pity. We ask for justice."

THE DEPRESSION OF THE 1890s

Shortly before Grover Cleveland became president for the second time in 1893, an apparently minor but ominous event occurred: the Philadelphia and Reading Railroad, once a thriving and profitable line, went bankrupt. Like other railroads, the Philadelphia and Reading had borrowed heavily to lay track and build stations and bridges. But overexpansion cut into profits, and ultimately the company was unable to pay its debts.

The same problem beset manufacturers. Output at McCormick farm machinery factories was nine times greater in 1893 than it had been in 1879, for example, but revenues only tripled. To compensate, the company bought more machines and squeezed more work out of fewer laborers. This strategy, however, only enlarged the debt and increased unemployment. The unemployed workers found themselves in the same plight as their employers: they could not pay their creditors. Banks suffered, too, when their customers defaulted. The failure of the National Cordage Company in May 1893 accelerated a chain reaction of business and bank closings. During the first four months of

1893, 28 banks failed. By June the number reached 128. The next year an adviser warned President Cleveland, "We are on the eve of a very dark night." He was right; between 1893 and 1897, the nation suffered the worst economic depression it had ever experienced.

Personal hardship followed the business failures. Although records are sketchy, it appears that nearly 20 percent of the labor force was jobless for a significant time during the depression. Falling demand caused the cost of living to drop between 1892 and 1895, but layoffs and wage cuts more than offset declining living costs. Many people could not afford basic necessities. The New York police estimated that twenty thousand homeless and jobless people roamed the city's streets. Surveying the depression's impact on Boston, Henry Adams wrote, "Men died like flies under the strain, and Boston grew suddenly old, haggard, and thin."

As the depression deepened, the currency problem reached a critical stage. The Sherman Silver Purchase Act of 1890 had committed the government to buy 4.5 million **Currency** ounces of silver each month **Problems** (see page 604). Payment was to be in gold, at the ratio of one ounce of gold for every sixteen ounces of silver. But a western mining boom made silver more plentiful, causing its value relative to gold to fall. Thus every month the government exchanged gold, whose worth remained fairly constant, for less valuable silver. Fearing a decrease in the value of the dollar, which was based on Treasury holdings in silver and gold, merchants at home and abroad began to cash in paper money and securities for gold. The nation's gold reserve soon dwindled, falling below $100 million in early 1893.

The $100 million level was psychologically significant. If investors believed that the country's gold reserve was disappearing, they would lose confidence in its economic stability and refrain from investing. For example, British capitalists owned some $4 billion in American stocks and bonds. If the dollar were to depreciate too much, they would sell their holdings and stop investing in American economic growth. In fact, the lower the gold reserve dropped, the more people rushed to redeem their money and securities—to get gold before it disappeared. Panic spread, causing further bankruptcies and unemployment.

President Cleveland, vowing to protect the

gold reserve, called a special session of Congress to repeal the Sherman Silver Purchase Act. Repeal passed in late 1893, but the run on the Treasury continued through 1894. By early 1895 gold reserves had fallen to $41 million. In desperation, Cleveland accepted an offer of 3.5 million ounces of gold in return for $62 million worth of federal bonds from a banking syndicate led by financier J. P. Morgan. When the bankers resold the bonds to the public, they profited handsomely at the nation's expense. Cleveland claimed that he had saved the gold reserves, but discontented farmers, workers, silver miners, and even some members of Cleveland's own party saw only humiliation in the president's deal with big businessmen. "When Judas betrayed Christ," charged South Carolina's Senator "Pitchfork Ben" Tillman, "his heart was not blacker than this scoundrel, Cleveland, in betraying the [Democratic party]."

No one knew what the president was really enduring. At about the time Cleveland called the special session of Congress, doctors had discovered a malignant tumor on his palate that required immediate removal. Fearful that public knowledge of his illness would hasten the run on gold, and intent on preventing Vice President Adlai E. Stevenson, a silver supporter, from gaining influence, Cleveland kept his condition a secret. He announced that he was going sailing, and doctors removed his cancerous upper left jaw while the yacht floated up the East River from New York City. Outfitted with a rubber jaw, Cleveland resumed a full schedule five days later, hiding terrible pain to dispel rumors that he was seriously ill. He eventually recovered, but those who knew of his surgery believed it had sapped his vitality.

The deal between Cleveland and Morgan did not end the depression. After improving slightly in 1895, the economy plunged again. Farm income, on the decline since 1887, continued to slide; factories closed; banks that remained open restricted withdrawals. The tight money supply depressed housing construction, drying up an important source of jobs and reducing immigration. Cities such as Detroit allowed citizens to cultivate "potato patches" on vacant land to help alleviate food shortages. Each night police stations in almost every city filled up with vagrants who had no place to stay.

As in previous hard times, the depression finally ran its course. In the final years of the century, new gold discoveries in Alaska, good har-

Effect of New Economic Structures

vests, and industrial growth brought relief. But the downturn of the 1890s had hastened the crumbling of the old economic system and the emergence of a new one. Since the 1850s, railroads had been the prime mover of American economic development, opening up new markets, boosting steel production, and invigorating banking. But the central features of the new business system—consolidation and a trend toward bigness—were beginning to solidify just when the depression hit.

The nation's economy had become interdependent rather than sectional; the fortunes of a large business in one part of the country now had repercussions elsewhere. By the 1890s many companies had expanded too rapidly. When contraction occurred, their reckless assumption of debt dragged them down, and they pulled other industries down with them. In early 1893, for example, thirty-two steel companies failed; five hundred banks and sixteen thousand businesses filed for bankruptcy that year. European economies also slumped, and more than ever before the fortunes of one country affected those of other countries.

To complicate matters, American farmers had to contend not only with fluctuating transportation rates and falling crop prices at home, but also with Canadian and Russian wheat growers, Argentine cattle ranchers, Indian and Egyptian cotton producers, and Australian wool producers. When farmers fell deeper into debt and lost purchasing power, their depressed condition in turn affected the economic health of railroads, farm-implements manufacturers, banks, and other businesses. The downward spiral ended late in 1897, but the depression exposed problems that demanded reform and set an agenda for the years to come (see Chapter 21).

DEPRESSION-ERA PROTESTS

The depression exposed fundamental tensions in the industrial system. The gap between employees and employers had been widening steadily for half a century in response to technological and organizational changes. By the 1890s workers' protests against exploitation were threatening to become a full-fledged economic and political upheaval. In 1894, the year the American economy plunged into depression, there were over thirteen hundred strikes and countless riots. Labor violence reached an alarming pitch, and radical rhetoric escalated. Contrary to the fears of business leaders, only a few of the protesters were anarchists or communists from Europe come to sabotage American democracy. The disaffected included hundreds of thousands of men and women who believed that in a democracy their voices should be heard.

The era of protest began with the railroad strikes of 1877. The vehemence of those strikes, and the support they drew from working-class people, raised fears that the United States would experience a popular uprising like the one in France six years earlier, which had briefly overturned the government and introduced communist principles. Anxieties were heightened by the Haymarket riot of 1886, a general strike in New Orleans in 1891, and a prolonged strike at the Homestead Steel plant in 1892. In the West, too, workers became embittered. In 1892 violence broke out at a silver mine in Coeur d'Alene, Idaho; angered by wage cuts and a lockout, striking miners seized the mines and battled federal troops sent to subdue them. Such defiance convinced some business owners that only force could counter the radicalism allegedly promoted by socialists and anarchists.

Small numbers of socialists did participate in these and other confrontations. Furthermore, many workers who never became socialists had been convinced by their own experience to agree with Karl Marx (1818–1883), the German philosopher and father of communism, that whoever controls the means of production holds the power to determine how well people live. Marx had written that industrial capitalism generates profits by paying workers less than the value of their labor. Furthermore, mechanization and the division of labor alienate workers from the means of production. Thus, Marx contended, capitalists and laborers are engaged in an inescapable conflict over whether workers will receive the true value of their labor. According to Marx, only by abolishing return on capital—profits—could labor receive its true value. This would be possible, of course, only if workers owned the means of production. Marx predicted that workers throughout the world would become so discontented that they would revolt and seize factories, farms, banks, and

Socialism
———

transportation lines. The societies resulting from this revolution would establish a new socialist order of justice and equality. Marx's vision appealed to some workers because it promised them independence and abundance; it appealed to some intellectuals because it promised an end to class conflict and crude materialism.

American socialism suffered from internal schisms and a lack of strong leadership. It splintered into a number of small groups, such as the Socialist Labor party, led by Daniel DeLeon, a fiery West Indian-born lawyer. DeLeon and other socialist leaders failed to attract the mass of unskilled workers, even though many immigrant workers had been exposed to socialism in Europe. American socialists often focused on fine points of doctrine while ignoring the everyday needs of workers, and they could not rebut the clergy and business leaders who celebrated opportunity, self-improvement, and consumerism. Social mobility and the philosophy of individualism also undermined socialist aims. Workers hoped that they or their children would improve their lives through education or acquisition of property or by becoming their own boss; thus most workers sought individual advancement rather than the betterment of all workers.

Events in 1894 triggered changes within the socialist movement. That year the government's quashing of the Pullman strike and of the newly formed American Railway Union elevated an inspiring new socialist leader. Eugene V. Debs, the intense and animated president of the railway union, had become a socialist while serving a six-month prison term for defying an injunction against the strike. Once released, Debs became the leading spokesman for American socialism, combining visionary Marxism with Jeffersonian and Populist antimonopolism. Though never good at organizing, Debs (see photo, opposite) captivated huge audiences with his passionate eloquence and indignant attacks on the free enterprise system. "Many of you think you are competing," he would lecture. "Against whom? Against Rockefeller? About as I would if I had a wheelbarrow and competed with the Santa Fe [railroad] from here to Kansas City." By 1900 the group soon to be called the Socialist Party of America was beginning to unite around Debs. It soon would make its presence felt more forcefully in the new century.

In 1894, however, Debs had to share public attention with a quiet businessman from Mas-

Eugene V. Debs (1855–1926) was the country's leading socialist at the turn of the century. His forceful oratorical style and keen intellect not only attracted large audiences but also prompted the Socialist party to nominate him for president five times. Brown Brothers.

Coxey's Army

sillon, Ohio. Like Debs, Jacob S. Coxey had a vision. Coxey was convinced that, to aid debtors, the government should issue paper money unbacked by gold—in other words, the government should deliberately stimulate inflation. As the depression deepened, Coxey also advocated a federal public works program—financed with $500 million of this "legal tender" paper money—to relieve unemployment and revive consumer spending. He planned to publicize his scheme by leading a march from Massillon to Washington, D.C., gathering a "petition in boots" of unemployed workers along the way. Coxey even christened his newborn son Legal Tender and proposed that his teenage daughter lead the procession on a white horse.

Coxey's army, about two hundred strong, left Massillon in late March 1894. Moving across Ohio and into Pennsylvania, they were given food and housing, and they won new recruits from de-

pressed industrial towns and rural villages. Many participants succumbed to boredom or the weather and dropped out of the march, but elsewhere in the country similar armies organized and began the trek toward the Capitol.

Coxey's troops, including women and children, entered Washington on April 30. The next day (May Day, a date traditionally associated with socialist demonstrations), the citizen army of five hundred marched to the Capitol, armed with "war clubs of peace." When Coxey and a few others vaulted the wall surrounding the Capitol grounds, mounted police moved in and routed the crowd. Coxey tried to speak from the Capitol steps, but police dragged him away. As arrests and clubbings continued, Coxey's dream of a demonstration of 400,000 jobless workers dissolved. Like the strikes, the first people's march on Washington had yielded to police muscle.

Coxey's march expressed the frustration of people seeking relief from uncertainty. Unlike socialists, who wished to alter the economic system fundamentally, Coxey's troops merely wanted more jobs and better living standards. Today, in an age of union contracts, regulation of business, and government-sponsored unemployment relief, their goals do not appear radical. Yet the brutal reactions of officials reveal how threatening the dissenters, from Coxey to Debs, must have appeared to the defenders of the existing social order.

POPULISTS AND THE SILVER CRUSADE

The Populists did not elicit the kinds of suppression experienced by unions and Coxey's army, but they encountered problems just when their political goals seemed attainable. As late as 1894, Populist candidates made good showings in local and state elections in the West and South. Like earlier third parties, though, Populists were underfinanced and underorganized. They had strong and colorful candidates but not enough of them to wrest control from the major parties. Many voters were reluctant to abandon old loyalties to the Republicans or Democrats.

Moreover, the two major parties took steps to destroy Populist voting strength, especially in the South. The threat of biracial political dissent posed by the Farmers' Alliances in the 1890s prompted southern white Democrats to take urgent action. Southern legislatures had already enacted several measures to curtail black voting, including poll taxes and literacy tests (see Chapter 17). Not confident that these measures would thwart a Populist coalition of black and white voters, and fearful that northern Republicans might revive federal supervision of elections, southern white legislators took steps to prevent all blacks from voting.

Curtailment of African-American Voting

Disfranchisement was accomplished in clever and devious ways. The Supreme Court affirmed in 1876 that the Fifteenth Amendment prohibited states from denying the vote "on account of race, color, or previous condition of servitude." But, said the Court in *U.S.* v. *Reese*, Congress had no control over state elections other than the provisions of the Fifteenth Amendment. State legislatures thus found ways to exclude black voters without mentioning race, color, or servitude. For instance, an 1890 state constitutional convention established the "Mississippi Plan," which required all voters to pay a poll tax eight months before each election, to present the receipt at election time, and to prove that they could read and interpret the state constitution. Registration officials applied much stiffer standards to blacks than to whites, even declaring college graduates ineligible on grounds of illiteracy. In 1898 Louisiana enacted the first "grandfather clause," which established literacy and property qualifications for voting but exempted sons and grandsons of those eligible to vote before 1867. The law effectively excluded African-Americans from voting, because few could meet the qualifications and none had been able to vote after 1835. Other southern states initiated similar measures.

Such restrictions proved highly effective. In South Carolina, for example, 70 percent of eligible blacks had voted in the presidential election of 1880; by 1896 the voting rate had dropped to 11 percent. By the early 1900s, African-Americans had effectively lost their political rights in every southern state except Tennessee. Disfranchisement also affected poor whites, few of whom could meet poll tax, property, and literacy requirements. Thus by 1892 the total number of eligible voters in Mississippi had shrunk from 257,000 to 77,000.

White fears of a biracial Populist coalition were largely unjustified, for fundamental racism impeded the acceptance of blacks by white Populists. To be sure, some Populists sought a coalition of distressed black and white farmers. Tom Watson, Georgia's most prominent Populist, noted that "the crushing burdens which now oppress both races in the South will cause each to . . . see a similarity of cause and a similarity of remedy." But even poor white farmers could not put aside their racism. Many came from families that had supported the Ku Klux Klan during Reconstruction. Some had once owned slaves, and they considered African-Americans a permanently inferior people who would never be able to act for themselves. They seemed to take comfort in the belief that there would always be people worse off than they were. Thus few Populists addressed the needs of black farmers, and many used white-supremacist rhetoric to avoid charges that they encouraged racial mingling.

In the national arena, the Populist crusade against "money power" settled on the issue of silver. Many people saw silver as a simple solution to the nation's complex ills. To

Free Silver
———

them, free coinage of silver (not held to the gold standard) meant the end of special privileges for the rich and the return of government to the people. William H. Harvey, author of the immensely popular *Coin's Financial School* (1894), preached that by coining silver "you increase the value of all property by adding to the number of money units in the land. You make it possible for the debtor to pay his debts [and for] business to start anew, and revivify all the industries of the country."

Adopting this reasoning, Populists made free coinage of silver their political battle cry. But as the election of 1896 approached, they had to settle on a strategy to translate their few previous electoral victories into larger success. Should they join forces with sympathetic factions of the major parties, thus risking a loss of identity, or should they remain an independent third party and settle for minor successes at best? Except in the Rocky Mountain states, where free coinage of silver had strong support, Republicans were unlikely allies. Although Republican politicians could be as moralistic as Populists, their anti-inflationist conservatism, support for the gold standard, and big-business orientation represented everything Populists opposed. In the North and West, alliance with Democrats was more plausible. In many areas the Democratic party retained vestiges of antimonopoly ideology and some sympathy for a looser currency system, although "gold Democrats" like

Critics of the free silver policy advocated by Populists and Democrats in the 1896 presidential election tried to convince voters that such a policy would result in poverty and low wages. The message of this broadside is that free silver would make Americans as downtrodden as peasants in the most underdeveloped countries. Smithsonian Institution, Division of Political History, Washington, D.C.

President Cleveland and Senator David Hill of New York did exert powerful opposition. Populists assumed they also shared common interests with traditionally Democratic urban workers, whom they believed suffered from the same oppression that stifled farmers. In the South, fusion with Democrats seemed less likely, since there the party constituted the very power structure against which Populists had revolted in the late 1880s. Whichever option they chose, coalition building or independence, Populists made certain that the political campaign of 1896 would be like none before it.

THE ELECTION OF 1896

The presidential election of 1896, the most issue-oriented election since 1860, brought the political turbulence to a climax. Each party was divided.

McKinley and Bryan

Republicans, directed by political boss Marcus Alonzo Hanna, a prosperous Ohio industrialist, had only minor problems. For over a year, Hanna had been maneuvering to win the nomination for Ohio's governor, William McKinley. By the time the party convened in St. Louis, Hanna had corralled enough delegates to succeed. "He had advertised McKinley," quipped Theodore Roosevelt, "as if he were a patent medicine." The Republicans' only distress occurred when the party adopted a moderate platform supporting gold, rejecting a prosilver stance proposed by Senator Henry M. Teller of Colorado. Teller, who had been among the party's founders forty years earlier, walked out of the convention in tears, taking a small group of silver Republicans with him.

At the Democratic convention, prosilver delegates paraded through the Chicago Amphitheatre wearing silver badges and waving silver banners. Observing their tumultuous demonstrations, one eastern delegate wrote, "For the first time I can understand the scenes of the French Revolution!" A *New York World* reporter remarked that "All the silverites need is a Moses." They soon found one in William Jennings Bryan.

Bryan arrived at the Democratic convention as a member of a contested Nebraska delegation. A former congressman whose support for free coinage of silver had annoyed President Cleveland, he was only thirty-six years old, deeply religious, and highly distressed by what the depression had done to midwestern farmers. The convention seated Bryan and his colleagues instead of a competing faction that supported the gold standard. Shortly afterward, as a member of the party's resolutions committee, Bryan helped write a platform calling for free coinage of silver.

When the committee presented the platform to the full convention, Bryan rose to speak on its behalf. In the heat and humidity of the Chicago summer, Bryan's now-famous closing words ignited the delegates:

> Having behind us the producing masses of this nation and the world, supported by the commercial interests, the laboring interests, and the toilers everywhere, we will answer their [the wealthy classes'] demand for a gold standard by saying to them: You shall not press down upon the brow of labor this crown of thorns, you shall not crucify mankind upon a cross of gold.

The speech could not have been timed better; indeed, Bryan planned it to be that way. Friends who had been pushing Bryan for the presidential nomination now had no trouble enlisting support, in spite of Bryan's youthful appearance, which can be seen in the photo, opposite, taken in 1896. It took five ballots to win the nomination, but the magnetism of the "Boy Orator" proved irresistible. In bowing to the silverite will of southerners and westerners and repudiating Cleveland's policies in its platform, the party became more attractive to discontented farmers. But like the Republicans, it, too, drove away a dissenting minority wing. A faction of gold Democrats withdrew and nominated their own candidate.

Bryan's nomination presented the Populist party with a serious dilemma. Should Populists join Democrats in support of Bryan, or should they nominate their own candidate? Tom Watson of Georgia, expressing southern sentiment against fusion with Democrats, warned that "the Democratic idea of fusion [is] that we play Jonah while they play whale." Others reasoned that supporting a different candidate would split the anti-McKinley vote and guarantee a Republican victory. In the end the convention compromised, first naming Watson as its vice-presidential nominee to preserve party identity (Democrats had nominated Maine shipping magnate Arthur Sewall for vice president) and then nominating Bryan for president.

The campaign, in the words of journalist William Allen White, "took the form of religious frenzy. . . . Far into the night, the voices rose—

women's voices, children's voices, the voices of old men, of youths and of maidens, rose on the ebbing prairie breezes, as the crusaders of the revolution rode home, praising the people's will as though it were God's will and cursing wealth for its iniquity." The issues were free silver and moneyed privilege, but campaign rhetoric rang with emotionalism. Bryan repeatedly preached that "every great economic question is in reality a great moral question." Republicans countered Bryan's moral evangelism and attacks on privilege by predicting chaos if he should win. While Bryan raced around the country giving twenty speeches a day, Hanna invited thousands of people to McKinley's home in Canton, Ohio, where the candidate plied them with speeches on moderation and prosperity, promising something for everyone. In an appeal to working-class voters, Republicans particularly stressed the new jobs that a protective tariff would create.

Election Results
——

The election results revealed that the political stand-off had finally ended. McKinley, symbol of Republican pragmatism and a new economic order of corporate ascendancy, beat Bryan by over 600,000 popular votes and won in the electoral college by 271 to 176 (see map, page 622). It was the most lopsided presidential election since 1872.

Bryan had worked hard to rally the nation and to offset the huge Republican campaign chest, estimated at between $3.5 million and $7 million, by traveling eighteen thousand miles and delivering more than six hundred speeches. But lean campaign finances and obsession with silver undermined his effort. The silver issue in particular prevented Populists from building the urban-rural coalition that would have given them political breadth. Reformer Henry Demarest Lloyd summarized the matter succinctly: "Free silver," he wrote, "is the cowbird of the reform movement. It waited till the nest had been built by the sacrifices and labor of others, and then it laid its eggs in it, pushing out the others which it smashed to the ground." Farmers' demands for an expanded currency found little support. Urban workers shied away from the silver issue out of fear that free coinage would inflate prices. Labor leaders like Samuel Gompers of the AFL, though partly sympathetic, would not join forces with Populists because they viewed farmers as businessmen, not workers. And socialists such as Daniel DeLeon denounced Popu-

William Jennings Bryan (1860–1925) poses for a photograph taken in 1896 when he first ran for president at the age of thirty-six. Bryan was an emotional speaker who turned agrarian unrest and the issue of free silver into a moral crusade. Library of Congress.

lists as "retrograde" because they, unlike socialists, still believed in free enterprise. Thus the Populist crusade collapsed in 1896. Although Populists and fusion candidates won a few state and congressional elections, the Bryan-Watson ticket of the Populist party polled only 222,600 votes nationwide.

The McKinley Presidency
——

As president, McKinley signed the Gold Standard Act (1900), which required that all paper money be backed by gold. A seasoned and personable politician, McKinley was best known for his expertise in crafting high protective tariffs; as a congressman from Ohio, he had guided passage of record-high tariff rates in 1890. He accordingly supported the Dingley Tariff of 1897, which raised

William McKinley (1843–1902) ran for president in 1896 on a platform that linked business prosperity with national prestige and economic well-being. Library of Congress.

duties even higher—though it did expand reciprocity provisions. Domestic tensions subsided during McKinley's presidency; an upward swing of the business cycle and a money supply enlarged by new gold discoveries in Alaska, Australia, and South Africa helped restore prosperity. A strong believer in the need to open new markets abroad in order to sustain prosperity at home, McKinley encouraged imperialistic ventures in Latin America and the Pacific (see Chapter 22). Good times and victory in the Spanish-American War enabled him to beat Bryan again in 1900, using the slogan "The Full Dinner Pail."

The 1896 election destroyed the old equilibrium and realigned national politics. The Republican party, founded in the 1850s as a party of moral evangelism against slavery, had become the major-

ity party by emphasizing freedom for big business, broadening its social base to include urban workers, and playing down its moralism. The Democratic party had miscalculated on the silver issue and held onto its traditional support only in the South; it would take three decades to refashion a broader appeal. After 1896, however, party loyalties were not as potent as they once had been. Suspicion of party politics increased, and voter participation rates declined. A new kind of politics was brewing, one in which technical experts and scientific organization would attempt to supplant the back-room deals and favoritism that had characterized the previous age.

The Populists had made a concerted effort to combat special privilege and corruption, but they foundered because too many people were benefiting from a generally expanding economy. Rural depopulation and migration to the cities, moreover, was removing some of the Populist base. Ironically, by 1920 many Populist reform goals would be achieved, including regulation of railroads, banks, and utilities; shorter working hours; a variant of the subtreasury system; a graduated income tax; direct election of senators; and the secret bal-

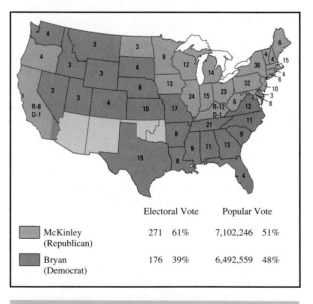

	Electoral Vote		Popular Vote	
McKinley (Republican)	271	61%	7,102,246	51%
Bryan (Democrat)	176	39%	6,492,559	48%

Presidential Election, 1896 *Though William Jennings Bryan had strong voter support in the South and West, the numerically-superior industrial states, including California, created large majorities for William McKinley.*

lot. These reforms succeeded because a variety of groups united behind them. Immigration, urbanization, and industrialization had transformed the United States into a pluralistic society in which compromise among interest groups had become a political fact of life. As the Gilded Age ended, business was still in the ascendancy and large segments of the population were still excluded from the political system and from economic opportunity. But the winds of dissent and reform had begun to blow more strongly.

SUGGESTIONS FOR FURTHER READING

General

Sean Denis Cashman, *America in the Gilded Age* (1984); Harold U. Faulkner, *Politics, Reform, and Expansion, 1890–1900* (1959); Ray Ginger, *The Age of Excess*, 2nd ed. (1975); H. Wayne Morgan, ed., *The Gilded Age* (1970); H. Wayne Morgan, *From Hayes to McKinley* (1969); Nell Irvin Painter, *Standing at Armageddon: The United States, 1877–1919* (1987); Alan Trachtenberg, *The Incorporation of America: Culture and Society in the Gilded Age* (1982); R. Hal Williams, *Years of Decision: American Politics in the 1890s* (1978).

Parties and Political Issues

Paula Baker, *The Moral Framework of Public Life* (1991); Beverly Beeton, *Women Vote in the West: The Suffrage Movement, 1869–1896* (1986); Christine Bolt, *American Indian Policy and American Reform* (1987); Eleanor Flexner, *Century of Struggle: The Women's Rights Movement in the United States* (1959); Elisabeth Griffith, *In Her Own Right: The Life of Elizabeth Cady Stanton* (1984); J. Rogers Hollingsworth, *The Whirligig of Politics: The Democracy of Cleveland and Bryan* (1963); Ari A. Hoogenboom, *Outlawing the Spoils: The Civil Service Movement* (1961); Richard J. Jensen, *The Winning of the Midwest* (1971); David M. Jordan, *Roscoe Conkling of New York* (1971); Matthew Josephson, *The Politicos* (1938); Morton Keller, *Affairs of State* (1977); Paul Kleppner, *The Third Electoral System, 1853–1892* (1979); Paul Kleppner, *The Cross of Cul-*

ture (1970); Robert D. Marcus, *Grand Old Party* (1971); Michael E. McGerr, *The Decline of Popular Politics* (1986); Walter T. K. Nugent, *Money and American Society* (1968); A. M. Paul, *Conservative Crisis and the Rule of Law: Attitudes of Bar and Bench, 1887–1895* (1969); David J. Rothman, *Politics and Power: The United States Senate, 1869–1901* (1966); John G. Sproat, *The Best Men: Liberal Reformers in the Gilded Age* (1968).

The Presidency

Kenneth E. Davison, *The Presidency of Rutherford B. Hayes* (1972); Lewis L. Gould, *The Presidency of William McKinley* (1981); Margaret Leech and Harry J. Brown, *The Garfield Orbit* (1978); Horace Samuel Merrill, *Bourbon Leader: Grover Cleveland and the Democratic Party* (1957); H. Wayne Morgan, *William McKinley and His America* (1963); Allan Peskin, *Garfield* (1978); Thomas C. Reeves, *Gentleman Boss: The Life of Chester Alan Arthur* (1975); H. J. Sievers, *Benjamin Harrison*, 3 vols. (1952–1968).

Currents of Protest

William M. Dick, *Labor and Socialism in America* (1972); John P. Diggins, *The American Left in the Twentieth Century* (1973); Ray Ginger, *Bending Cross: A Biography of Eugene Victor Debs* (1969); John Laslett, *Labor and the Left* (1970); Nick Salvatore, *Eugene V. Debs: Citizen and Socialist* (1982); Carlos A. Schwantes, *Coxey's Army* (1985); David Shannon, *The Socialist Party of America* (1955).

Populism and the Election of 1896

Peter H. Argersinger, *Populism and Politics: William Alfred Peffer and the People's Party* (1974); Paolo Coletta, *William Jennings Bryan: Political Evangelist* (1964); Paul W. Glad, *McKinley, Bryan, and the People* (1964); Paul W. Glad, *The Trumpet Soundeth: William Jennings Bryan and His Democracy* (1964); Lawrence Goodwyn, *Democratic Promise: The Populist Moment in America* (1976); Sheldon Hackney, *Populism to Progressivism in Alabama* (1969); Steven Hahn, *The Roots of Southern Populism* (1983); John D. Hicks, *The Populist Revolt* (1931); Richard Hofstadter, *The Age of Reform: From Bryan to FDR* (1955); J. Morgan Kousser, *The Shaping of Southern Politics* (1974); Scott G. McNall, *The Road to Rebellion: Class Formation and Kansas Populism* (1988); Walter T. K. Nugent, *The Tolerant Populists* (1963); Norman Pollack, *The Populist Response to Industrial America* (1962); Allan Weinstein, *Prelude to Populism: Origins of the Silver Issue* (1970); C. Vann Woodward, *Tom Watson* (1938).

21

The Progressive Era,
1895–1920

A<small>N ASSOCIATE DESCRIBED</small> Florence Kelley as a "guerrilla warrior" in the "wilderness of industrial wrongs." A woman of sharp wit and commanding presence who always dressed in black, Kelley accomplished as much as anyone in guiding the United States out of the tangled swamp of unregulated industrial capitalism into the uncharted seas of the twentieth-century welfare state.

Kelley's career traced a remarkable odyssey. Raised in middle-class comfort in Philadelphia as the daughter of a Republican congressman, Kelley embarked on a tour of Europe in 1883 after graduating from Cornell. She had hoped to prepare for the study of law, but the University of Pennsylvania had denied her admission to its graduate school because of her gender. In Zurich, Kelley fell in with a group of socialists who opened her eyes to the plight of the underprivileged, especially working women and children. She married a Russian medical student and returned to the United States with her husband and infant son in 1886. When debts and other problems ended the marriage five years later, Kelley took her three children from New York to Chicago to obtain a divorce under Illinois's more permissive laws. Later that year she moved into Hull

House, a residence in the slums where middle-class reformers went to live in order to help and learn from working-class immigrants. There her transforming work truly began.

Until the 1890s, Kelley's life had been male-oriented, influenced first by her father and then by her husband, who was a socialist as well as a medical student. Kelley had tried to enter public life as men did, by attending law school and participating in political organizations. But men had blocked her path at every turn. At Hull House, however, she became immersed in a female-oriented world, where women sought to transfer their traditional helping skills to the betterment of society. This environment encouraged Kelley to assert her powerful abilities.

Over the next decade, Kelley became one of the nation's most ardent advocates of better conditions for working-class women and children. She investigated and publicized abuses of the sweatshop system in Chicago's garment industry, lobbied for laws to prohibit child labor and regulate women's working hours, and served as Illinois's first chief factory inspector. Her work helped create new professions for women in social reform, and her strategy of investigating, publicizing, and crusading for action became a

Vigorous and persuasive, Theodore Roosevelt epitomized the spirit of Progressive reform.

model for progressive reform initiatives. Perhaps most significant, she helped involve government in the solution of pressing social problems.

During the 1890s a severe depression, bitter labor violence, political upheaval, and foreign entanglements shook the nation. Many of the promises of technology had been fulfilled, but great numbers of Americans continued to suffer from poverty and disease. Many people regarded industrialists as monsters who controlled markets, wages, and prices for the sole purpose of maximizing profits. Government seemed corroded by bosses and their henchmen who used politics to enrich themselves rather than address the nation's problems. Tensions created by urbanization and industrialization seemed to be fragmenting society into conflicting interest groups.

By 1900, however, there was cause for optimism. The tumult of Populism had died down, and the depression seemed to be over. The nation had just emerged victorious from a war (see Chapter 22), and a new political era of dynamic leaders such as Theodore Roosevelt and Woodrow Wilson was dawning. The resulting sense of renewal served both to heighten anxiety over continuing social and political problems and to raise hopes that such problems could somehow be fixed.

From these circumstances there emerged a broad and complex reform campaign, so many-sided that it is hard even to identify its unifying characteristics. By the 1910s many reformers were calling themselves "progressives," and a new political party by that name had formed to embody their principles. Since that time historians have used the term *progressivism* to refer to the era's reformist spirit while disagreeing over the movement's meaning and membership. The era between 1895 and 1920 can nonetheless be characterized by a series of movements, each aimed in one way or another at renovating or restoring American society, its values, and its institutions.

The urge for reform had many sources. Industrialization had brought awesome technology, unprecedented productivity, and a cornucopia of consumer goods. But it also brought labor strife, spoiling of natural resources, and abuse of corporate power. Rapidly growing cities facilitated the amassing and distribution of goods, services, and cultural amenities; they also bred poverty, disease, crime, and political corruption. The old social order was shaken by massive influxes of immigrants

and the rise of a new class of managers and professionals. And the crippling depression of the 1890s forced many leading citizens to realize what working people had known for some time: the central promise of American life was not being kept. Equality of opportunity was a myth.

Progressives tried to address these problems by organizing their thinking and actions around three basic goals. First, they sought to end abuses of power. Attacks on unfair privilege, monopoly, and corruption were not new in 1900; the Jacksonian reformers of the 1830s and 1840s and the Populists of the 1890s belonged to the same tradition. In the Progressive era, however, the attacks intensified. Trustbusting, consumers' rights, and good government became compelling political issues.

Second, progressives aimed to supplant corrupt power with reformed versions of such traditional institutions as schools, charities, medical clinics, and the family. Although eager to protect individual rights, they abandoned the old individualistic notions that hard work and good character automatically ensured success and that the poor had only themselves to blame for their plight. Instead, progressives acknowledged that society and its institutions had power to help or harm the individual, and they believed society must provide opportunity for everyone. Their revolt against fixed categories of thought challenged entrenched views on women's role, race relations, public education, legal and scientific thought, and morality.

Third, progressives wanted to apply scientific principles and efficient management to economic, social, and political institutions. Their aim was cooperation, especially between business and government, that would end wasteful competition and labor conflict and minimize social and economic disorder.

Befitting their name, progressives had a deep faith in the ability of humankind to create a better world. They used such phrases as "humanity's universal growth" and "the upward spiral of human development." Judge Ben Lindsey of Denver, who spearheaded reform in the treatment of juvenile delinquents, expressed the progressive creed when he wrote, "In the end the people are bound to do the right thing, no matter how much they fail at times." More than ever before, Americans looked to government as an agent of the people. As such, government could and should intervene in society and the economy to protect the common good and elevate the public interest above self-interest.

• Important Events •

1893	Anti-Saloon League founded
1895	Booker T. Washington gives Atlanta Compromise speech
1898	*Holden* v. *Hardy* upholds Utah's mining regulations
1900	William McKinley re-elected
1901	McKinley assassinated; Theodore Roosevelt assumes the presidency
1903	Elkins Act
1904	*Northern Securities* case dissolves railroad trust Theodore Roosevelt elected president
1905–06	Niagara Falls Convention promotes more militant pursuit of African-American rights *Lochner* v. *New York* revoked, removes limits on bakers' work hours Hepburn Act tightens control over railroads Pure Food and Drug Act requires ingredient labels on patent-medicines
1907	Reckless speculation causes economic panic
1908	William H. Taft elected president *Muller* v. *Oregon* upholds limits on women's work hours
1909	NAACP founded Payne-Aldrich Tariff passed
1910	Mann-Elkins Act reinforces ICC powers
	White Slave Traffic Act prohibits transportation of women for "immoral purposes" Ballinger-Pinchot controversy angers conservationists
1912	Theodore Roosevelt runs for president on the Progressive (Bull Moose) ticket Woodrow Wilson elected president
1913	Sixteenth Amendment ratified; legalizes federal income tax Seventeenth Amendment ratified; provides for direct election of U.S. senators Underwood Tariff institutes income tax Federal Reserve Act establishes central banking system
1914	Federal Trade Commission created to investigate unfair trade practices Clayton Anti-Trust Act outlaws monopolistic business practices Margaret Sanger indicted for sending articles on contraception through the mail
1916	Wilson re-elected Federal Farm Loan Act provides credit to farmers
1919	Eighteenth Amendment ratified; prohibits manufacture, sale, and transportation of alcoholic beverages
1920	Nineteenth Amendment ratified; gives women the vote in federal elections

THE CONTRADICTIONS OF PROGRESSIVISM

The Progressive era emerged in the aftermath of the tumultuous election of 1896 to address the issues raised by urban reformers in the previous half-century (see Chapters 19 and 20). As the twentieth century dawned, party loyalty eroded and voter turnout declined. Voter participation in presidential elections dropped from Gilded Age levels of over 80 percent of the eligible electorate to less than 60 percent in northern states and under 30 percent in southern states, where African-Americans had been excluded from the polls. Parties and elections, it seemed, were losing their function of providing Americans a means of influencing government policies.

The political system was opening up to multiple and shifting interest groups, each of which championed its own brand of reform. Although local voluntary associations had been widespread since the 1790s, many such organizations became nationwide in scope after the 1890s and began trying to shape government policy to meet

Issues of Reform

Judge Ben Lindsey (1869–1943) of Denver was a progressive reformer who worked for better legal protection for children. Typical of many reformers of his era, Lindsey had an earnest faith in the ability of humankind to build a better world. Library of Congress.

their own needs and goals. These organizations included professional associations such as the American Bar Association; women's organizations such as the National American Woman Suffrage Association; issue-oriented lobbies such as the National Consumers League; civic clubs such as the National Municipal League; and associations oriented toward minority groups, such as the National Negro Business League and the Society of American Indians. Because they were not usually tied to either of the established political parties, these organizations made politics much more fragmented and issue-focused than in earlier eras.

Although some of the cherished values of the rural-based Populist movement lingered—notably moral regeneration, political democracy, and antimonopolism—the prevailing values of the Progressive era were urban. The progressive quest for social justice, educational and legal reform, and streamlining of government drew on the urban-reform goals of the previous half-century. Between 1890 and 1920 the proportion of the nation's population living in cities rose from 35 percent to over 51 percent. During the same period, the number of cities with populations of fifty thousand or more rose from 58 to 144. Recognition of the consequences of such changes, plus easier communications by mail, telephone, and telegraph, stimulated urban reformers to share information and consolidate their efforts. Formation of the National Municipal League in 1895 and the National Civic Federation in 1900 signaled the beginning of the new reform era. The National Municipal League served as a forum for debate on civic reform issues such as civil service, nonpartisan elections, and municipal ownership of public utilities. The National Civic Federation fostered discussion of social reforms, such as workers' compensation and arbitration of labor disputes.

Organizations and individuals who accepted the three progressive themes—opposition to abuse of power, reform of social institutions, quest for cooperation and scientific efficiency—existed in almost all levels of society. But the new middle class—men and women in the professions of law, medicine, engineering, social work, religion, teaching, and business—formed the vanguard of reform. Offended by inefficiency and immorality in business, government, and human relations, these people set out to apply the scientific techniques they had learned in their professions to the problems of the larger society.

Motivated by personal indignation at corruption and injustice, many middle-class progressive reformers sought an end to abuses of power. Their views were voiced by journalists whom Theodore Roosevelt dubbed *muckrakers* (after a character in the medieval allegory *Pilgrim's Progress* who rejected a crown for a muckrake). Muckrakers fed the public's taste for scandal and sensation by investigating and attacking social, economic, and political wrongs. Their fact-filled articles in *McClure's*, *Cosmopolitan*, and other popular magazines exposed such offenses as adulterated foods, fraudulent insurance, and prostitution. Lincoln Steffens's articles in *McClure's*, later published as *The Shame of the Cities* (1904), ranked among the highlights. Steffens hoped his exposés of bosses' misrule would inspire mass outrage and, ultimately, reform. Other well-known muckraking efforts included Upton Sinclair's *The Jungle* (1906), a novel that attacked the meat-packing industry; Ida M. Tarbell's scathing history of Standard Oil (1904); Burton J. Hendrick's *Story of Life Insurance* (1907); and David Graham Phillips's *Treason of the Senate* (1906).

Middle-class indignation also expressed itself as opposition to party politics, a reflection of the interest-group political system that arose in the 1890s. Male political reformers deplored the bargaining and self-serving that they believed infected boss-ridden parties. (Women could not vote and therefore were seldom involved in these discussions.) As journalist William Allen White put it, machines and bosses should be "reduced to mere political scrap iron by the rise of the people." By "the people," however, reformers all too often meant middle-class people like themselves, excluding blacks, immigrants, and the white native-born working class. To improve the political process, the progressives advocated nominating candidates through direct primaries instead of party caucuses and holding nonpartisan elections to prevent the fraud and bribery bred by party loyalties.

Political Reformers

To make legislators more responsible, they advocated three reforms: the initiative, which would permit voters to propose new laws on their own; the referendum, which would enable voters to accept or reject a law; and the recall, which would allow voters to remove offending officials and judges from office before their terms were up. Their goal, like that of the business-consolidation movement, was efficiency: they would reclaim government by replacing the boss system with rational, accountable management chosen by a responsible electorate.

Middle-class progressive reformers recoiled from party politics but not from government. In fact, they turned to government for aid in achieving most of their goals, for they were convinced that only government offered the leverage they needed. Members of professions founded on systematic investigation and efficient management also agreed with muckrakers that knowledge was the key to progress. Science and scientific method—planning, control, and predictability—were central to their values. Just as corporations applied scientific management to achieve economic efficiency (see Chapter 18), progressives favored using expertise and planning to achieve social and political efficiency.

The progressive spirit also stirred some elite business leaders. Certain successful executives, like Alexander Cassatt of the Pennsylvania Railroad, supported some government regulation and political reforms to protect their interests from more radical political elements. Others, like E. A. Filene, founder of a Boston department store, and Tom Johnson, a Cleveland streetcar magnate, were humanitarians who worked unselfishly for social justice. Business-dominated organizations like the Municipal Voters League and U.S. Chamber of Commerce supported limited political and economic reform. They aimed to stabilize society by running schools, hospitals, and local government like efficient businesses. Elite women often led reform organizations like the Young Women's Christian Association, which aided growing numbers of unmarried working women who had moved away from their families, and the Women's Christian Temperance Union, the largest women's organization of its time, which participated in numerous causes besides abstinence from drinking.

Upper-Class Reformers

But not all progressive reformers were middle- or upper-class. Vital elements of what would be-

Working-Class Reformers

come modern American liberalism grew out of the working-class urban experience in this era. By 1900, many urban workers were pressing for government intervention to ensure safety and promote welfare. They wanted safe factories, shorter working hours, workers' compensation, better housing, health safeguards, and other "bread-and-butter" reforms. Often these were the same people who supported political bosses, supposedly the enemies of reform. Workers understood that bosses needed to cultivate allegiance among their constituents and thus would cater to everyday needs. In fact, bossism was not necessarily at odds with humanitarianism. When "Big Tim" Sullivan, an influential boss in New York City's Tammany Hall political machine, was asked why he supported shorter working hours for women, he explained, "I had seen me sister go out to work when she was only fourteen and I know we ought to help these gals by giving 'em a law which will prevent 'em from being broken down while they're still young."

After 1900, voters from inner-city districts populated by working-class families elected a number of progressive legislators who had trained in the trenches of machine politics. New York's Alfred E. Smith and Robert F. Wagner, Massachusetts's David I. Walsh, and Illinois's Edward F. Dunne—all from immigrant backgrounds—became spokesmen for reform at the state and national levels. Their chief goal was to have government take responsibility for alleviating hardships that resulted from urban-industrial growth. They opposed such reforms as prohibition, Sunday closing laws, civil service, and nonpartisan elections, all of which conflicted with their constituents' interests. They were most successful when they joined forces with other reformers to pass laws aiding labor and promoting social welfare.

Some deeply frustrated workers wanted more than progressive reform; they wanted a different society. These people turned to the socialist movement, a blend of immigrant intellectuals, industrial workers, disaffected Populists, miners, lumbermen, and some women's rights activists. The majority of socialists united behind Eugene V. Debs (see Chapter 18), the tall, dynamic American Railway Union organizer who drew nearly 100,000 votes in the 1900 presidential election. Although Debs failed to de-

Socialists

velop a consistent program beyond opposition to war and bourgeois materialism, he was a spellbinding speaker for the radical cause. His speaking tours activated increasing numbers of disenchanted workers and intellectuals. As the Socialist party's presidential candidate Debs won 400,000 votes in 1904, and in 1912, at the pinnacle of his and his party's career, he polled over 900,000.

With stinging rebukes of exploitation and unfair privilege, Debs and other socialists like Milwaukee's Victor Berger and New York's Morris Hilquit made compelling overtures to reform-minded people. Some, such as Florence Kelley, joined the socialist cause. But most progressives avoided radical attacks on free enterprise. Municipal ownership of public utilities was as far as they would go toward fundamental change in the system. Indeed, progressives had too much at stake in the capitalist system to overthrow it. Even in Wisconsin, where progressivism was most highly developed, progressives refused to join forces with Berger's more radical group. California progressives even formed a temporary alliance with reactionaries to prevent socialists from gaining power in Los Angeles. And few humanitarian reformers objected when Debs was jailed for giving an antiwar speech in 1918.

It would be a mistake to assume that a progressive spirit captured all of American society between 1895 and 1920. Large numbers of people who were heavily represented in Congress disliked government interference in economic affairs—except to strengthen the tariff—and they found no fault with existing power structures. "Old-guard" Republicans like Senator Nelson W. Aldrich of Rhode Island and House Speaker Joseph Cannon of Illinois championed this ideology. Outside of Washington, D.C., this outlook was represented by tycoons like J. P. Morgan, John D. Rockefeller, and E. H. Harriman, and by countless other capitalists who insisted that the most genuine progress would result from maintaining the profit incentive.

Progressive reformers operated from the center of the ideological spectrum. Moderate, socially aware, sometimes contradictory, they believed on the one hand that the laissez-faire system was obsolete and on the other that a radical shift away from capitalism was dangerous. Like Jeffersonians, they believed in the conscience and will of the people; like Hamiltonians, they opted for a strong central government to act in the interests of conscience. The goals of progressive reformers were both ideal-

Though their objectives sometimes differed from those of middle-class progressive reformers, socialists also became a more active force in the early twentieth century. Socialist parades on May Day, such as this one in 1910, were meant to express the solidarity of all working people. Library of Congress.

istic and realistic. As minister-reformer Walter Rauschenbusch wrote, "We shall demand perfection and never expect to get it."

GOVERNMENTAL AND LEGISLATIVE REFORM

What should be the responsibilities of government? Early-twentieth-century answers to this question diverged from those of the previous century. Traditionally, theorists and ordinary citizens had held that because the United States had been born from mistrust of government authority, democratic government should be small and unobtrusive. It should interfere in private affairs only in unique circumstances and should withdraw when balance had been restored. But in the late 1800s this point of view lost adherents. Corporations pursued government aid and protection for their enterprises. Discontented farmers organized to seek government regulation of railroads and other monopolistic businesses. City dwellers, accustomed to the favors performed by political machines, came to expect government to act on their behalf.

By the turn of the century, professionals and intellectuals were concluding that government should exert more power to ensure justice and well-being. Increasingly aware of the ineffectiveness of a simple, inflexible government in a complex industrial age, they reasoned that public authority was needed to counteract inefficiency, corruption, and exploitation. But before reformers could effectively use such power, they would have to capture government from politicians whose greed had soiled the democratic system. Thus, eliminating corruption from government was a central thrust of progressive activity.

Reformers first attacked corruption in cities (see Chapter 19). Between 1870 and 1900, opponents of the boss system tried to restructure government through reforms such as civil service hiring, nonpartisan elections, and tighter scrutiny of public expenditures. A few reformers actively supported poverty relief, housing improvement, and prolabor laws, but most worked chiefly for efficient—meaning economical—government. After 1900 growing momentum for reform brought into being the city-manager and city-commission forms of government (in which urban officials were chosen for professional expertise, rather than political

Robert M. La Follette (1855–1925) was one of the most dynamic of progressive politicians. As governor of Wisconsin, he sponsored a program of political reform and business regulation known as the Wisconsin Plan. In 1906 he entered the U.S. Senate and continued to champion progressive reform. The National Progressive Republican League, which La Follette founded in 1911, became the core of the Progressive party.   Library of Congress.

connections) and public ownership of utilities (to prevent gas, electric, and streetcar companies from profiting at the public's expense and to circumscribe their monopoly power).

Reformers found, however, that the city was too small an arena for the changes they sought. Frustrated by only limited victories, they came to believe that state and federal governments offered more opportunities for enacting sweeping reform through legislation. Because of their faith in a strong, fair-minded executive, progressives looked to governors and other elected officials to extend and protect reforms achieved at the local level. Their goals tended to vary regionally. In the Plains and Far West, they rallied behind railroad regulation and such governmental reforms as the initiative and referendum. In the South reformers continued the Populist crusade against big business and autocratic politicians. In the urban-industrial Northeast and Midwest, they attacked corrupt political machines and unsafe labor conditions.

The reform movement produced a number of skillful, influential, and charismatic governors who used executive power to achieve change. Their ranks included Braxton Bragg **Progressive** Comer of Alabama and Hoke **Governors** Smith of Georgia, who introduced business regulation and other reforms in the South; Albert Cummins of Iowa and Hiram Johnson of California, who battled the railroads that dominated their states; and Woodrow Wilson of New Jersey, whose administrative reforms were imitated by other governors. Such men were not saints, however. Smith, bowing to prevailing racist sentiments, supported disfranchisement of African-Americans, and Johnson promoted discrimination against Japanese-Americans.

The most forceful of the progressive governors was Wisconsin's Robert M. La Follette. A self-made small-town lawyer whose compact build and thick, bristling hair suited his combative personality, La Follette rose through the ranks of the state Republican party and won the governorship in 1900. As governor he initiated a multipronged reform program distinguished by direct primaries, more equitable taxes, and regulation of railroad rates. He also appointed numerous commissions staffed by experts, whose investigations supplied La Follette with the facts and figures he used in fiery speeches to arouse public support for his policies. After three terms as governor, La Follette was elected to the U.S. Senate and carried his progressive ideals into national politics. "Battling Bob" displayed a rare ability to approach reform in a tempered, scientific way while still stirring up the people with moving rhetoric. His goal, he once asserted, "was not to 'smash' corporations, but to drive them out of politics, and then to treat them exactly the same as other people are treated."

Few state leaders were as successful as La Follette. To be sure, the crusade against corrupt politics did bring about some permanent changes. By 1916 all but three states had direct primaries, and many had adopted the initiative, referendum, and recall. Political reformers achieved one of their major goals in 1912 when the states ratified the Seventeenth Amendment, which provided for direct election of U.S. senators. (They were formerly elected by state legislatures, which were often corrupted by private interests.) But political reforms did not always help. Party bosses, better organized and more experienced than reformers, were still able to control elections. Efforts to use the initiative, referendum, and recall often failed because special-interest groups expended large sums to lobby the public and influence the voting. Political reformers also found that the courts aided entrenched power in stifling change.

New state laws aimed at promoting social welfare had greater impact, especially in factories, than did political reforms. Broadly interpreting their constitutional powers to protect the health and safety of their citizens, many states enacted factory inspection laws, and by 1916 nearly two-thirds of the states required compensation for victims of industrial accidents. A coalition of labor and humanitarian groups supported these laws and even induced some legislatures to grant aid to mothers with dependent children. Under pressure from the National Child Labor Committee, nearly every state set a minimum age for employment (varying from twelve to sixteen) and prohibited employers from working children more than eight or ten hours a day. Such laws were hard to enforce, though, because they seldom provided for the close inspection of factories that full enforcement required. And families that needed extra income evaded the laws by encouraging their children to work and to lie about their ages.

Progressive Legislaton

Several groups also joined forces to limit working hours for women. After the Supreme Court upheld Oregon's ten-hour limit in 1908 (see Chapter 18), many more states passed laws protecting female workers. Meanwhile, in 1914 efforts of the American Association for Old Age Security showed signs of success when Arizona established old-age pensions. The courts struck down the law, but demand for pensions did not diminish, and in the 1920s many states enacted laws to provide for needy elderly people.

Defenders of free enterprise opposed most of the new regulatory measures out of self-interest and fear that such government programs would undermine the individual initiative and competition that they believed to be the basis of the free market system. Government interference, they contended, also contradicted the natural law of survival of the fittest. The National Association of Manufacturers coordinated the campaign against regulation of business and working conditions. And legislators friendly to special interests connived to weaken new laws by withholding the funds for their enforcement.

Reformers themselves were not always certain about what was progressive, especially in human behavior. The main question was whether it was possible to create a desirable moral climate through legislation. Some reformers, notably adherents of the Social Gospel movement (see Chapter 19), believed that only church-based inspiration and humanitarian work, rather than legislation, could transform society. Others believed that state intervention was necessary to enforce purity, especially in drinking habits and sexual behavior.

Moral Reform

The Anti-Saloon League, formed in 1893, intensified the long-standing campaign against drunkenness and its costs to society. This organization joined forces with the Woman's Christian Temperance Union (founded in 1873) to publicize the role of alcoholism in liver disease and other health problems. But the League was especially successful in shifting attention from the individual's responsibility for temperance to the alleged link between the drinking that saloons encouraged and the accidents, poverty, and threat to industrial productivity that were consequences of drinking.

The war on saloons prompted many states, counties, towns, and city wards to restrict the sale and consumption of liquor. By 1900 almost one-fourth of the nation's population lived in "dry" communities (which prohibited the sale of liquor). But consumption of alcohol, especially beer, increased after 1900, convincing prohibitionists that a nationwide ban on alcohol was the only solution. By 1917 they had converted to their cause such notables as Supreme Court Justice Louis D. Brandeis and former president William Howard Taft. In 1918 prohibitionists induced Congress to pass the Eighteenth Amendment (ratified in 1919 and implemented in 1920) outlawing the manufacture, sale, and transportation of intoxicating liquors. Not all prohibitionists were progressive reformers, and not all progressives were prohibitionists. Certainly not all Americans supported prohibition, and social satirists of the time voiced protests in the media and in music. Nevertheless, the Eighteenth Amendment can be seen as an expression of the progressive urge to cleanse society and elevate morality through reform legislation.

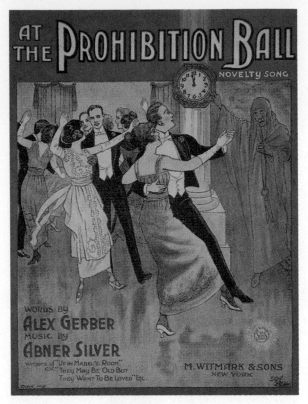

Though not supported by all progressive reformers, the Eighteenth Amendment to the Constitution passed during this era. The measure, which prohibited the manufacture, sale, and transportation of alcoholic beverages, was intended to uplift morality and protect health. Social satirists exaggerated the belief that no fun could be had after prohibition went into effect. This sheet music cover from 1919 shows party-goers trying to squeeze in one last minute before the new law would take effect at midnight. Sheet Music Collection, The John Hay Library, Brown University. Photo by Brooke Hammerle.

women, especially immigrants and blacks, into prostitution. Above all, however, it asserted that

> it is a man and not a woman problem which we face today—commercialized by men—supported by men—the supply of fresh victims furnished by men. . . . So long as there is lust in the hearts of men [the Social Evil] will seek out some method of expression. Until the hearts of men are changed we can hope for no absolute annihilation of the Social Evil.

Such investigations found apparently rising numbers of prostitutes but failed to prove that organized rings of men deliberately entrapped young women into prostitution. It appeared instead that women were making their own choices to enter "the life"—choices that clearly reflected economic needs but that also alarmed moralists about the alleged dangers of young women's sexuality. Reformers nonetheless believed they could attack prostitution by punishing those who promoted it. In 1910 Congress passed the White Slave Traffic Act, known as the Mann Act, prohibiting interstate and international transportation of women for immoral purposes. By 1915 nearly every state had outlawed brothels and solicitation of sex.

Like prohibition, the Mann Act reflected growing sentiment that government could improve human behavior by restricting it. Reformers believed that the source of evil was not original sin or human nature but the social environment. And if evil was created by human beings, it followed that it could be eradicated by human effort. Intervention in the form of laws could help build a heaven on earth.

Public outrage erupted in another area when muckraking journalists charged that interstate and international rings kidnaped young women and forced them into prostitution, a practice called white slavery. Middle-class moralists, already alarmed by a perceived link between immigration and prostitution and fearful that prostitutes were producing genetically inferior children, prodded governments to investigate the problem and recommend corrective legislation. The Chicago Vice Commission, for example, undertook a "scientific" survey and published its findings, called *The Social Evil in Chicago*, in 1911. The report underscored the poverty, ignorance, and desperation that drove

NEW IDEAS IN EDUCATION, LAW, AND THE SOCIAL SCIENCES

While legislation anchored the reform impulse, equally important changes occurred in schools, courts, and settlement houses. The prevailing preoccupation with efficiency and scientific management challenged educators, judges, and social scientists to come to grips with the problems of modern mass society. New ways of thinking and new forms of social organization were necessary. Darwin's theory of evolution had undermined traditional beliefs in a God-created world; immigration had replaced social uniformity with diversity; and technology had made old habits of production and consumption obsolete. Thoughtful people in a number of professions grappled with how to respond to the new era yet preserve what was best from the past.

In education, changing patterns of school attendance called for new ways of thinking. As late as the 1870s, when rural families needed their children at home to do farm work, Americans attended school for an average of only four years. By 1900, however, swelling cities contained multitudes of children who had more time for school. Also, urban taxpayers were providing sufficient revenues to make mass education possible. Boosted by compulsory-attendance laws, enrollments in public schools rose from seven million in 1870 to eighteen million in 1910. Meanwhile, the number of public high schools grew from five hundred to over ten thousand.

Reformers had long envisioned education as a means of bettering society. In 1883, psychologist G. Stanley Hall noted that the experiences of modern urban schoolchildren differed greatly from those of their farm-bred parents and grandparents. In the early nineteenth century, school curricula had consisted chiefly of moralistic pieties. *McGuffey's Reader*, used throughout the nation, contained homilies such as "By virtue we secure happiness," and "One deed of shame is succeeded by years of penitence." Hall and the influential educational philosopher John Dewey asserted that modern education ought to prepare children for productive citizenship and fulfilling lives. The development of the child, not the subject matter, should be the focus of the curriculum. Moreover, schools should serve as community centers and instruments of social progress. Above all, said Dewey, education must relate directly to experience; children should be encouraged to discover knowledge for themselves. Learning relevant to students' lives should replace rote memorization and outdated subjects.

Progressive education, based on Dewey's *The School and Society* (1899) and *Democracy and Education* (1916), was a uniquely American phenomenon. Dewey believed that learning should focus on real-life problems and that children should be taught to

Progressive Education

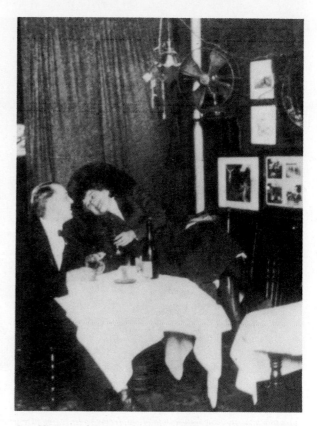

In addition to their crusade against drunkenness, moral reformers stirred up emotions over accusations that evil men were seducing innocent young women into prostitution—or white slavery, as it was called. In this posed photograph printed in a 1910 antivice publication, The White Slave Hell: or, With Christ at Midnight in the Slums of Chicago, *the man supposedly has gotten the woman drunk and is about to lure her into a life of sin.* Collection of Perry R. Duis, from The Saloon.

use their intelligence and ingenuity as instruments for controlling their environment. Such theories rested solidly in the progressive tradition. From kindergarten through high school, Dewey asserted, children should learn through direct experience. Dewey and his wife Alice put these ideas into practice in the Laboratory School that they directed at the University of Chicago. In classrooms such as the one in the photograph on page 636, children examined, built, and discussed tools, toys, and other objects just as they would outside school.

Personal growth became the driving principle behind college education as well. The purpose of American colleges and universities had tradition-

The objective of progressive education was to free children from the rigid classrooms of the past, where pupils had to sit quietly at attention, and enable them to learn by doing and making things. Rather than make the subject matter the major focus of the learning process, progressives made children the center of attention.   Library of Congress.

Growth of Colleges and Universities

ally been that of their European counterparts: to train a select few for the professions of law, medicine, teaching, and religion. But in the late 1800s, institutions of higher education multiplied, spurred by land grants and more people who could afford tuition. Between 1870 and 1910 the number of colleges and universities in the United States grew from 563 to nearly 1,000. Curricula expanded as educators sought to make learning attractive and to keep up with technological and social changes. Harvard University, under President Charles W. Eliot, pioneered in substituting electives for required courses and experimenting with new teaching methods. The University of Wisconsin and other public universities achieved distinction in new areas of study such as political science and sociology.

Much of the expansion in college enrollments, especially in the Midwest and West, was prompted by the Morrill Land Grant Act of 1862. Land-grant colleges offered a wide variety of courses, ranging from classics and natural science to carpentry and

farming. Many of these schools considered athletics vital to a student's growth, and intercollegiate sports became a permanent feature of student life as well as a source of school pride and alumni contributions. Southern states, in keeping with separate-but-equal policies, set up segregated land-grant colleges for blacks. *Separate* was a more accurate description of these institutions than *equal*. African-Americans continued to suffer the consequences of inferior educational opportunities in both state institutions and private all-black colleges.

As colleges and universities expanded, so did their female enrollments. Between 1890 and 1910 the number of women in institutions of higher learning swelled from 56,000 to 140,000. Of these women, 106,000 attended coeducational institutions (mostly state universities aided by the Morrill Act); the rest attended women's colleges. By 1920, 283,000 women were attending college, accounting for 47 percent of total enrollment. These numbers disproved earlier objections that women were unfit for higher learning because they were mentally and physically inferior to men, but discrimination lingered in admissions and curriculum policies. Women were encouraged (indeed, they usually sought) to take home economics and education courses rather than science and mathematics, and most medical schools, including Harvard and Yale, refused to admit women.

American educators tended to adopt the prevailing attitude of business: more is better. They justifiably congratulated themselves for increasing enrollments and making instruction more meaningful. By 1920, 78 percent of all children between ages five and seventeen were enrolled in public elementary and high schools; another 8 percent attended private and parochial schools. These figures represented a huge increase over the 1870 attendance rate. And there were 600,000 college and graduate students in 1920, compared with only 52,000 in 1870. Yet few people looked beyond the numbers to assess how well schools were doing their job. Very little critical analysis was brought to bear on the faith that schools could promote equality and justice as well as personal growth and responsible citizenship.

The legal profession also embraced a new emphasis on experience and scientific principles. Harvard law professor Roscoe Pound, an influential proponent of the new point of view, urged that social reality should influence legal thinking. Oliver Wendell Holmes, Jr., an associate justice of the Supreme Court between 1902 and 1932, led the attack on the traditional view of law as universal and unchanging, like the Ten Commandments. "The life of the law," said Holmes, sounding like Dewey, "has not been logic; it has been experience." The view that law should reflect society's needs challenged the practice of invoking legal precedents in an inflexible way that often obstructed social legislation. Louis D. Brandeis, a brilliant lawyer who later joined Holmes on the Supreme Court, carried legal reform one step further by insisting that judges' opinions be based on factual, scientifically gathered information about social realities. In the landmark case *Muller* v. *Oregon* (1908), Brandeis collected extensive scientific data on the harmful effects of long hours to convince the Supreme Court to uphold Oregon's law limiting women's working hours.

The new legal thinking met with some resistance. Judges raised on laissez-faire economic theory and strict construction of the Constitution con-

Progressive Legal Thought

tinued to overturn the laws progressives thought necessary for effective reform. Thus despite Holmes's forceful dissent, the Supreme Court in 1905 revoked a New York law limiting bakers' working hours (*Lochner* v. *New York*). As in similar cases, the Court's majority argued that the Fourteenth Amendment protected an individual's right to make contracts without government interference, and that this protection superseded reform sentiments. Judges also weakened federal regulations by invoking the Tenth Amendment, which prohibited the federal government from interfering in matters reserved to the states.

The judiciary was not entirely reactionary during the Progressive era. Courts upheld some regulatory measures, particularly those protecting general public safety. A string of decisions beginning with *Holden* v. *Hardy* (1898), in which the Supreme Court upheld Utah's mining regulations, supported the use of state police powers to protect health, safety, and morals. Judges also affirmed federal police powers and Congress's authority over interstate commerce in sustaining such federal legislation as the Pure Food and Drug Act, the Meat Inspection Law (see page 647), and the Mann Act (see page 634). In these instances citizens' welfare took precedence over the Tenth Amendment.

But the concept of general welfare posed thorny legal problems. Even if one agreed that laws should address society's needs, whose needs should prevail? The United States was a mixed nation, and religion and ethnicity deeply influenced law. In many localities a native-born white Protestant majority imposed Bible reading in public schools (offending Catholics and Jews), required business establishments to close on Sundays, restricted the religious practices of Mormons and other groups, prohibited interracial marriage, and enforced racial segregation. Holmes asserted that laws should be made for "people of fundamentally differing views," but were such laws possible in a nation of so many ethnic, racial, and religious interest groups?

At about the same time, social science—the study of society and its institutions—experienced changes as deep as those overtaking law and education. In economics a group of young scholars used statistics to argue that the laws governing economic relationships were not carved in stone. Instead, they claimed,

Social Science

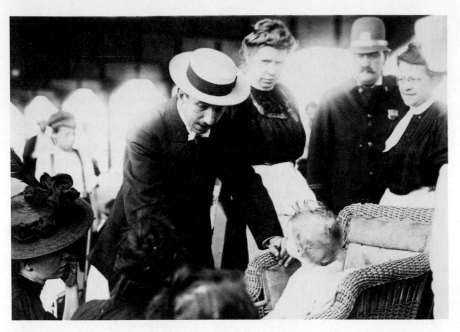

Health reform, especially the medical care of children, constituted a primary focus of social reform during the Progressive era. Boards of health employed nurses and physicians, like those above, to open clinics in inner-city tenement neighborhoods and to visit the homes of poor people to examine children and make sure they were receiving health care.   Library of Congress.

economic theory should reflect prevailing social conditions. Richard T. Ely of Johns Hopkins University and the University of Wisconsin, an early spokesman for this point of view, argued that the poverty and impersonality promoted by industrialization required interference in social and economic affairs by "the united efforts of Church, state, and science." A new breed of sociologists led by Lester Ward, Albion Small, and Edward A. Ross agreed, adding that citizens should engage in planning to cure social ills rather than passively waiting for problems to solve themselves. In the field of psychology, female researchers challenged age-old beliefs that women's minds were different from, and inferior to, men's.

Meanwhile, the progressive historians Frederick Jackson Turner, Charles A. Beard, and Vernon L. Parrington were examining the past as a means of explaining current issues in American society and of promoting social change. Beard and other progressives believed, for example, that the American Constitution was a flexible document amenable to growth and change, not an inviolable code imposed by wise forefathers. His influential *Economic Interpretation of the Constitution* (1913) argued that a group of merchants and business-oriented lawyers had created the Constitution to defend private property. Thus, if it had served special interests in one age, it could be changed to serve broader interests in another age. Meanwhile, political scientists like Woodrow Wilson emphasized the practical over the theoretical, advocating expansion of governmental power to ensure justice and progress.

In public health, organizations like the National Consumers League (NCL) joined with physicians and social scientists to bring about some of the most far-reaching progressive reforms. Founded by Josephine Shaw, a socially prominent Massachusetts widow, the NCL initially focused on improving the wages and working conditions of young women employed in department stores. After Florence Kelley became the NCL's general secretary, the organization expanded its activities to encompass women's suffrage, protection of child laborers, and elimination of potential health hazards. Local branches supported such consumer-protection measures as the licensing of food ven-

National Consumers League and Public Health Reform

dors and inspection of dairies. They also urged city governments to fund neighborhood clinics that provided health education and medical care to the poor. The NCL's efforts spurred a broad-based consumer and health-awareness movement that has persisted to the present day. Another important consumer-related reform involved regulation of life insurance companies, epitomized by Wisconsin's establishment of a program of state life insurance protection in 1911.

Thus a new breed of men and women pressed for institutional change as well as political reform between the end of the nineteenth century and the First World War. Largely middle class in background, trained by new professional standards, confident that new ways of thinking could bring about progress, these people helped to broaden government's role in meeting the needs of a mature industrial society. Their questioning of prevailing assumptions extended beyond their immediate goals and unsettled conventional attitudes toward race and gender.

CHALLENGES TO RACIAL AND SEXUAL DISCRIMINATION

W. E. B. Du Bois, the forceful black scholar and writer, ended an essay in *The Souls of Black Folk* (1903) with a call that heralded the twentieth-century civil rights movement: "By every civilized and peaceful method," Du Bois wrote, "we must strive for the right which the world accords to men."

By "men" Du Bois meant all free human beings, not just one gender. But his assertion expresses well the circumstances of the two largest groups of underprivileged Americans in the early 1900s: women and people of color. Both lived in a society dominated by native-born white males. Both experienced disfranchisement, discrimination, and humiliation. And for centuries both had been striving for "the right which the world accords to men"—freedom and equality. The progressive challenge to entrenched ideas and customs gave impetus to African-Americans' and women's struggles for their rights, but it posed a dilemma as well. Should women and people of color strive to become just like white men, with white men's

values and power as well as their rights? Or was there something unique about their racial and sexual identities that should be preserved at the risk of sacrificing some gains? Both groups fluctuated between attraction to and rejection of the culture from which they had been excluded.

The problems of African-Americans in white American society remained largely regional. In 1900 nine out of ten blacks lived in the South, where fear of the African-American presence prevailed and where repressive Jim Crow laws had multiplied in the 1880s and 1890s. Southern blacks were denied legal and voting rights and were officially segregated in almost all walks of life. They faced constant exclusion; in 1910 only 8,000 out of 970,000 high-school-age blacks in the entire South were enrolled in high schools. And they met with constant violence. Between 1900 and 1914 white mobs lynched over a thousand blacks. Vigilantes in countless southern communities, usually incensed over rumored sexual assaults by black men on white women, seized alleged offenders and viciously murdered them by hanging, burning, or shooting while authorities looked the other way.

Blacks began to migrate northward in the 1880s, accelerating their rate of departure after 1900. The conditions they found represented a relative improvement over their rural sharecropping existence, but job discrimination, inferior schools, and segregated neighborhoods characterized northern as well as southern cities. White humanitarians perpetuated segregation by maintaining separate and inferior institutions, such as hospitals and schools, for blacks, rather than integrating them with whites. A half-century after the abolition of slavery, most whites still agreed with historian James Ford Rhodes, who wrote that blacks were "innately inferior and incapable of citizenship."

African-American leaders differed sharply over how—and whether—to pursue assimilation. In the wake of emancipation, ex-slave Frederick Douglass had urged "ultimate assimilation through self-assertion, and on no other terms." Those who favored isolation from cruel white society supported migration to Africa or the establishment of all-black communities in Oklahoma Territory and Kansas. Others advocated militancy, believing, as one writer stated, "Our people must die to be saved and in dying must take as many along with them as it is possible to do with the aid of firearms and all other weapons."

Most blacks, however, could neither escape nor conquer white society. They had to find other routes to economic and social improvement. Self-help, a strategy articulated by educator Booker T. Washington, was one of the most popular alternatives. Born to slave parents in 1856, Washington worked his way through school and in 1881 founded Tuskegee Institute in Alabama, a vocational school for blacks. There he developed the philosophy that blacks' best hopes for assimilation lay in at least temporarily accommodating to whites. Rather than fighting for political rights, he said, blacks should work hard, acquire property, and prove they were worthy of their rights. Washington voiced his views in a widely acclaimed speech at the Atlanta Exposition in 1895. "Dignify and glorify common labor," he urged in what became known as the Atlanta Compromise. "Agitation of questions of racial equality is the extremest folly." Envisioning a society where blacks and whites would remain apart but share the same goals, Washington observed that "in all things that are purely social we can be as separate as the fingers, yet one as the hand in all matters essential to mutual progress."

Booker T. Washington

Whites, including progressives, welcomed Washington's policy of accommodation because it urged patience and reminded black people to stay in their place. Because he said what they wanted to hear, white businesspeople, reformers, and politicians chose to regard Washington as representative of all African-Americans. Yet though Washington endorsed a separate-but-equal policy, he projected a subtle racial pride that would find more direct expression in black nationalism later in the twentieth century, when some African-Americans would advocate control of their own businesses and schools. Washington never argued that blacks were inferior to whites; he instead asserted that they could enhance their dignity through self-improvement.

But Booker T. Washington seemed to some blacks to favor second-class citizenship, which they considered degrading. His southern-based philosophy did not attract well-educated northern African-Americans, such as William Monroe Trotter, the fiery editor of the *Boston Guardian*, or social scientist T. Thomas Fortune. In 1905 a

W. E. B. Du Bois

group of "anti-Bookerites" convened near Niagara Falls and pledged a more militant pursuit of such rights as unrestricted voting, equal economic opportunity, integration, and equality before the law. The spokesperson for the Niagara movement was W. E. B. Du Bois, an outspoken critic of the Atlanta Compromise. A New Englander with a Ph.D. from Harvard, Du Bois was both a progressive and a member of the black elite. He held an undergraduate degree from all-black Fisk University and had studied in Germany, where he learned about scientific investigation. When he joined the faculty at all-black Atlanta University, Du Bois compiled rigorous fact-filled sociological studies of black ghetto dwellers and wrote poetically in support of civil rights. Du Bois initially supported the Atlanta Compromise and treated Washington politely, but he could not accept white domination. "The way for a people to gain their reasonable rights," Du Bois asserted, "is not by voluntarily throwing them away." Instead blacks must agitate for what was rightfully theirs.

Du Bois demonstrated that accommodation was an unrealistic strategy, but his own solution may have been just as fanciful. A blunt elitist, Du Bois believed that an intellectual vanguard of cultivated, highly trained blacks, the "Talented Tenth," would save the race by setting an example to whites and uplifting other blacks. Such sentiment had more appeal for middle-class white liberals than for African-American sharecroppers. Thus in 1909 when Du Bois and his allies formed the National Association for the Advancement of Colored People (NAACP), which aimed to end racial discrimination by pursuing legal redress in the courts, the leadership consisted chiefly of white progressives. By 1914 the NAACP had fifty branch offices and over six thousand members, but only its fight against lynching affected sharecropping and laboring families in the South.

Whatever their views, African-Americans faced continued oppression. In fact, those who managed to acquire property and education encountered increased resentment, especially when they fought openly for civil rights. Black editor and reformer Ida B. Wells, whose *On Lynching* was written in support of antilynching legislation, suffered destruction of her property and threats against her life. The federal government only aggravated biases. Under the administration of Woodrow Wilson, discrimination within the federal government expanded—southern cabinet

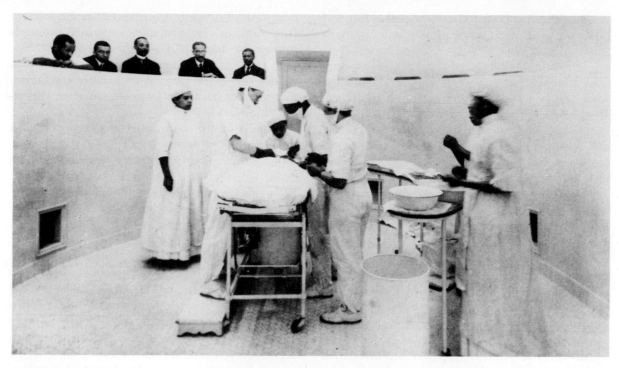

During the Progressive era, African-Americans struggled to partake of the various advances in the reform of society. Part of this struggle involved their own assertion of ability in science and economics. This photograph, taken at the surgical amphitheater of the Moorland-Spingarn Research Center at all-black Howard University, shows African-American medical personnel learning and performing medical skills.   Moorland-Spingarn Research Center, Howard University, Howard University Archives.

members supported racial separation in rest rooms, restaurants, and government office buildings, and they balked at hiring black workers. Commenting on Wilson's racism in 1913, Booker T. Washington wrote, "I have never seen the colored people so discouraged and so bitter as they are at the present time." Disfranchisement, instituted by southern states in the late nineteenth century (see Chapter 20), still prevented blacks from becoming full-fledged American citizens. Washington seemed to accept disfranchisement, hoping blacks would eventually regain the vote through education and hard work. Du Bois believed suffrage was essential to protect social and economic rights.

African-Americans still sought to fulfill the American dream of success, but many wondered whether their goals should include membership in a corrupt white society. Du Bois voiced these doubts poignantly, writing that "one ever feels his twoness—an American, a Negro, two souls, two thoughts, two unreconciled strivings, two warring ideals in one dark body." Somehow blacks would

have to reconcile that "twoness" by combining racial pride with national identity. As Du Bois wrote in 1903, a black

> would not Africanize America, for America has too much to teach the world and Africa. He would not bleach his Negro soul in a flood of white Americanism, for he knows that Negro blood has a message for the world. He simply wishes to make it possible for a man to be both a Negro and an American.

That simple unfulfilled wish would haunt the nation for decades to come.

The dilemma of identity haunted Native Americans as well, but it had an added dimension of tribal loyalty. Since the 1880s, Native American reformers had belonged to white-led Indian organizations. In 1911 educated, middle-class Indian men and women formed their own association, the Society of American Indians (SAI); men held most leadership positions. SAI worked for better education, civil rights, and health care. It also sponsored

American Indian Days to cultivate native pride and offset the Anglo images of tribal peoples promulgated in Wild West shows.

The SAI's emphasis on racial pride, however, was squeezed between pressures for assimilation from one side and tribal allegiance on the other. Its small membership did not genuinely represent the diverse and unconnected nations and tribes, and its attempt to establish a governing body representing all of them faltered. Some tribal governments no longer existed to select representatives, and most SAI members simply promoted their own points of view. At the same time, the goal of achieving acceptance in white society proved elusive. Individual hard work was not enough to overcome white prejudice and condescension, and attempts to redress grievances through legal action bogged down for lack of funds. Ultimately, the SAI had to rely on rhetoric and moral exhortation, which had little effect on poor and powerless Indians who seldom knew the SAI even existed. Torn by doubts and internal disputes, the association folded in the early 1920s.

During the same period, the progressive challenge to established social assumptions also stirred women to seek liberation from the confines of hearth and home. Their struggle raised questions of identity like those faced by blacks: what tactics should women use to achieve equality, and what should be their role in society? Novelist Henry James expressed the dilemma from a male point of view when he complained that women who wanted to become just like men were disregarding their own uniqueness. Or, as some women put it, could women achieve equality with men and at the same time change male-dominated society?

The answers women found involved a subtle but important shift in women's politics. Before about 1910, those engaged in the quest for women's rights referred to themselves as **"The Woman Movement"** "the woman movement." This label was used to characterize middle-class women striving to move beyond the home into social-welfare activities, higher education, and paid labor. Like some African-American and Indian leaders, they argued that legal and voting rights were indispensable accompaniments to such moves. These women's-rights advocates based their claims on the theory that women's special, even superior, traits as guardians of family and morality would humanize all of society. Settlement-house founder Jane Addams, for example, supported women's suffrage by asking, "If women have in any sense been responsible for the gentler side of life which softens and blurs some of its harsher conditions, may not they have a duty to perform in our American cities?"

The women's club movement represented a uniquely female dimension of Progressive era reform. Originating as literary and educational organizations, women's clubs consisted of middle-class women who began taking stands on public affairs in the late nineteenth century. Because they were excluded from holding office, these reformers were drawn less to efforts to revise government than to drives for social betterment, an enterprise called "social housekeeping." Rather than pressing for reforms such as trustbusting and direct primaries, women tended to work for goals such as factory inspection, regulation of children's and women's labor, housing reform, upgrading of education, and pure food and drug laws. Such efforts were not confined to white women. The National Association of Colored Women, founded in 1895, fourteen years before the NAACP, was the nation's first African-American social-service organization; it concentrated on establishing nurseries, kindergartens, and retirement homes.

Around 1910 some of those concerned with women's place in society began using a new term, *feminism*, to refer to their efforts. Whereas members of the woman movement spoke of duties and moral purity, feminists, more explicitly conscious of their identity as women, spoke of rights and self-development. Feminism, however, contained an inherent contradiction, arguing on the one hand that all women should unite in the struggle for rights because of their shared disadvantages as women, and on the other, that sex-typing—differential treatment of women and men—must wither because it resulted in discrimination. Thus feminists were advancing the self-contradictory position that women should unite as a gender group for the purpose of abolishing all gender-based distinctions.

Feminism focused in particular on economic and sexual independence. Charlotte Perkins Gilman articulated feminist goals in *Women and Eco-*

BIRTH CONTROL REVIEW

Edited by Margaret Sanger

TWENTY CENTS A COPY   NOVEMBER, 1923   TWO DOLLARS A YEAR

Official Organ of
THE AMERICAN BIRTH CONTROL LEAGUE, INC., 104 FIFTH AVENUE, NEW YORK CITY

How do historians know

about Margaret Sanger and the birth-control movement of the Progressive era? The issue of unwanted pregnancy has long vexed American women, families, and all of society. In the early 1900s the issue was fraught with moral and social controversy. Would common practice of birth control violate God's law and promote promiscuity? If women intentionally reduced the numbers of children born, would the American population eventually fail to replace itself or, as Theodore Roosevelt termed it, experience "race death"? Margaret Sanger, a young socialist and feminist mother of three living in New York City's Greenwich Village, did not believe so. She saw women dying from self-induced abortions, and she herself had been warned of possible death if she were to become pregnant again. Her re-sponse was to promote birth control (a term she first used in 1914) as a means of helping women, especially poor working-class women, to make choices about bearing children. After being forced to flee government prosecution for her ideas, Sanger returned to the United States and in 1916 organized the New York Birth Control League to lobby for the prerogative of physicians to advise women about contraception. In 1921 the movement nationalized when Sanger formed the American Birth Control League and began selling the "Birth Control Review," which contained articles on the medical, as well as the social, issues involved in contraception. Photo: The Schlesinger Library, Radcliffe College.

nomics (1898), declaring that domesticity and female innocence were obsolete and attacking the male monopoly on economic opportunity. Gilman argued that women must enter the modern age by taking paid jobs in industry and the professions, and that domestic chores such as cooking, cleaning, and child care should be handled by paid employees.

Feminists also supported what they called "sex rights," or a single standard of social behavior for men and women in conjunction with recognition of women's sexual drives. A number of feminists joined the birth-control movement led by Margaret Sanger. As a visiting nurse in New York's East Side immigrant neighborhoods, Sanger distributed information about contraception, in hopes of preventing unwanted pregnancies and their tragic consequences among poor women. Sanger's crusade won the support of middle-class women who wanted both to limit their own families and to control the growth of immigrant masses. It also aroused the opposition of those who saw birth control as a threat to the family and to morality. In 1914, Sanger's opponents caused her to be indicted for defying an 1873 law that prohibited the sending of obscene literature (articles on contraception) through the mails, and she was forced to flee the country for a year. Sanger persevered and in 1921 formed the American Birth Control League, which enlisted physicians and social workers to convince judges to allow distribution of birth-control information. Most states still prohibited the sale of contraceptives, but Sanger had succeeded in introducing the issue into the realm of public discussion.

Women's Suffrage

Feminist debates over work and class pervaded the suffrage movement, which achieved victory in 1920 when enough states ratified the Nineteenth Amendment to give women the vote in federal elections. Until the 1890s, the suffrage crusade was led by elite women who believed that the political system needed more participation by refined and educated people like themselves, and that working-class women would defer to better-educated women on political matters. Elizabeth Cady Stanton, a stalwart of the woman movement who had long fought for equality, voiced this viewpoint when she said that enfranchisement of "educated women" would best promote "woman's influence in public life."

The younger generation of feminists, represented by Stanton's daughter Harriot Stanton Blatch, ardently opposed this logic. Blatch focused on work, declaring that all women worked, whether they performed paid labor or unpaid housework (like Gilman, she urged that women be paid for whatever work they did), and that all women's efforts contributed to society's betterment. To Blatch, achievement rather than wealth and refinement was the best criterion for public influence. Thus women should exercise the vote not to increase the role of elites in public life but to promote and protect women's economic roles. This rationale, too, contained ambiguities. It implicitly (and sometimes explicitly) advocated that all women work for pay, especially outside the home. But in doing so, it overlooked the exploitation of working-class women already in the labor force. The tension between the needs of middle- and upper-class women and those of poor laboring women haunted the suffrage movement.

Despite internal differences, suffragists achieved some successes. Nine states, all in the West, allowed women to vote in state and local elections by 1912, and women continued to press for national suffrage. Their tactics ranged from the moderate but persistent propaganda campaigns of the National American Woman Suffrage Association, led by Carrie Chapman Catt, to the open-air meetings and marches of the National Woman's party, led by feminist Alice Paul. All these activities heightened public awareness. More decisive, however, were women's efforts during the First World War as factory laborers, medical volunteers, and municipal workers (see pages 703–704). By convincing legislators that women could shoulder public responsibilities, women's wartime contributions gave final impetus to passage of the suffrage amendment.

The activities of women's clubs, suffragists, and feminists failed to create an interest group united or powerful enough to dent the political, economic, and social ascendancy of men. Like blacks, women knew that voting rights meant little until people's attitudes changed. The Progressive era helped women to clarify the issues that concerned them, but major reforms would have to await a later era. As the feminist Crystal Eastman observed, echoing W. E. B. Du Bois, in the aftermath of the suffrage crusade:

> Men are saying perhaps, "Thank God, this everlasting women's fight is over!" But women, if I know them, are saying, "Now at last we can begin." . . . Now they can say what they are really after, in common with all the rest of the struggling world, is *freedom*.

THEODORE ROOSEVELT AND THE REVIVAL OF THE PRESIDENCY

The Progressive era's theme of reform—in politics, institutions, and social relations—drew attention to government, especially the federal government, as the foremost agent of change. At first, however, the federal government seemed incapable of assuming such responsibility. Dominated by two political parties that resembled private clubs more than bodies of statesmen, the federal government acted mainly on behalf of special interests when it acted at all. Then, in September 1901, the political climate suddenly changed. The assassination of President William McKinley by anarchist Leon Czolgosz vaulted Theodore Roosevelt, the vigorous young vice president, into the White House.

Political manager Mark Hanna had warned fellow Republicans against nominating Roosevelt for the vice presidency in 1900. "Don't any of you realize," Hanna asked after the nominating convention, "that there's only one life between that madman and the presidency?" As governor of New York, Roosevelt had angered state Republican bosses by showing sympathy for regulatory legislation, so they had rid themselves of their pariah by pushing him into national politics. Little did they realize that they were presenting the nation with its most forceful president since Lincoln, a man who would infuse the office with much of its twentieth-century character.

In marked contrast to his predecessors, Theodore Roosevelt lacked the dignified appearance of a president. Nearsighted, he was helpless without his metal-rimmed glasses. He

Theodore Roosevelt

had prominent teeth, talked in a high-pitched voice, and stood five-foot-nine but looked shorter. As a youth he had suffered from asthma; as his photo suggests, he was driven throughout his later life by an obsession to overcome his physical limitations and exert what he and his contemporaries called "manliness." In his teens he practiced diligently to become an expert marksman and horseman and later competed on Harvard's boxing and wrestling teams. In the 1880s he went to live on a Dakota ranch, where he roped cattle and brawled with other cowboys.

As a descendant of a Dutch aristocratic family, Roosevelt had the wealth to indulge in such pursuits. But he also inherited a sense of civic responsibility that he translated into a career in public service. He served three terms in the New York State Assembly, ran for mayor of New York City in 1886 (finishing third), served on the federal Civil Service Commission (as New York City's police commissioner) and was assistant secretary of the navy. In this series of offices Roosevelt earned a reputation as a combative, politically crafty leader. He also distinguished himself as a historian with

Theodore Roosevelt (1858–1919) liked to think of himself as a great outdoorsman, one who loved the most rugged countryside and one who believed that he and his country should serve as examples of "manliness." California Museum of Photography, University of California.

The Naval War of 1812 (1882) and *The Winning of the West* (1889).

In 1898, Roosevelt thrust himself into the Spanish-American-Cuban-Filipino War by organizing a volunteer cavalry brigade, called the Rough Riders, to fight in Cuba (see page 670). Though it had little impact on the war's outcome, his dramatic act excited the public's imagination. A publicity hound who craved being the center of attention, Roosevelt returned a folk hero (people called him Teddy, a name he disliked) and was elected governor of New York, then vice president.

As president, Roosevelt came to conclusions about the role of government similar to those reached by progressives. His sense of history convinced him that the small government Jefferson had envisioned would not suffice in the industrial era. Instead, economic development necessitated a Hamiltonian system of government powerful enough to guide national affairs. Like his progressive supporters, Roosevelt believed in the wisdom and talents of a select few, whose superior backgrounds and education qualified them to coordinate public and private enterprise. "A simple and poor society," he observed, "can exist as a democracy on the basis of sheer individualism. But a rich and complex society cannot so exist."

Roosevelt became a hero, attracting the loyal support of those who believed his progressivism was heartfelt. In action, though, he deviated from the progressive path. His brash patriotism, admiration for big business, and dislike of anything he considered effeminate recalled the previous era of unbridled expansion when raw power prevailed in social and economic affairs.

The federal regulation of economic affairs that has characterized twentieth-century American history began with Roosevelt's presidency. Roosevelt

Regulation of Trusts

——

turned his attention first to big business, where the combination movement had produced giant trusts that controlled almost every sector of the economy. Although Roosevelt won a reputation as a trustbuster, he actually considered consolidation the most efficient means to achieve material progress. Rather than tolerate uncontrolled competition, he believed in distinguishing between good and bad trusts and preventing bad ones from manipulating markets. Thus he instructed the Justice Department to use antitrust laws to prosecute the railroad, meat-packing, and oil trusts, which he believed had unscrupulously exploited the public. Roosevelt's policy triumphed in 1904 when the Supreme Court, convinced by the government's arguments, ordered the breakup of the Northern Securities Company, the huge railroad combination created by J. P. Morgan and his powerful business allies. (Roosevelt chose, however, not to attack other gigantic trusts, such as U.S. Steel, another of Morgan's creations.)

When prosecution of Northern Securities began, Morgan reportedly collared Roosevelt and offered, "If we have done anything wrong, send your man to my man and they can fix it up." The president refused, but he was more sympathetic to cooperation between business and government than his rebuff might suggest. Rather than prosecute, he urged the Bureau of Corporations (part of the newly created Department of Labor and Commerce) to work with companies on mergers and other forms of expansion. Through investigation and cooperation the administration exerted pressure on business to regulate itself.

Roosevelt also pushed for regulatory legislation—especially after his resounding electoral victory in 1904, in which he won the votes of progressives and businesspeople alike. After a year of wrangling with business lobbyists in Congress, Roosevelt persuaded Congress to pass the Hepburn Act (1906), which imposed stricter control over railroads. The act gave the Interstate Commerce Commission (ICC) more authority to set railroad rates (though it did allow the courts to overturn rate decisions). Progressives like Robert La Follette complained that Roosevelt had compromised with business allies like Senator Nelson W. Aldrich of Rhode Island to assure the bill's passage. But Roosevelt's aim was to reaffirm the principle of government regulation rather than risk defeat over more idealistic objectives.

Roosevelt showed similar willingness to compromise on legislation to ensure the purity of food and drugs. Reformers had been urging government

Pure Food and Drug Laws

——

regulation of patent medicines and processed meat for decades. Public outrage at fraud and adulteration heightened in 1906 when Upton Sinclair published *The Jungle*, a fictionalized exposé of Chicago meat-packing plants. Sinclair, a young socialist whose prime objective was to improve working conditions in the plants, shocked public sensibilities with his vivid and scandalous descriptions:

> There was never the least attention paid to what was cut up for sausage; there would come all the way back from Europe old sausage that had been rejected, and that was mouldy and white—it would be dosed with borax and glycerine, and dumped into the hoppers, and made over again for home consumption. . . . There would be meat stored in great piles in rooms; and the water from the leaky roofs would drip over it, and thousands of rats would race about on it. It was too dark in these storage places to see well, but a man could run his hand over these piles of meat and sweep off handfulls of dried dung of rats. These rats were a nuisance, and the packers would put poisoned bread out for them; they would die, and then rats, bread, and meat would go into the hoppers together.

On reading the novel, Roosevelt ordered an investigation. Finding Sinclair's descriptions accurate, the president supported the Meat Inspection Act, which passed in 1906. Like the Hepburn Act, this law reinforced the principle of government regulation. But as part of the compromise to obtain its passage, the government had to pay for inspections, and meatpackers could appeal adverse decisions in court. Nor were companies required to provide date-of-processing information on their canned goods. Most large companies welcomed the legislation anyway, because it helped them regularize their business, force out smaller competitors, and restore falling confidence in American meat products in foreign markets.

The Pure Food and Drug Act (1906) addressed consumer abuses of the patent medicine industry. Makers of various tonics and pills were not only making wild claims about the effects of their products but also liberally using alcohol and narcotics as ingredients. Ads in popular publications, including the Sears, Roebuck catalogue claimed that such medicines had "cure-all" qualities. A typical ad touted a "Brain Stimulator and Nerve Tonic." Although the Pure Food and Drug Act did not ban such products, it did require the use of labels listing the ingredients—a goal consistent with the progressive confidence that if the people knew the truth, they would act on it and stop buying these medicines.

Roosevelt's approach to labor issues resembled his stance toward business. When the United Mine Workers in Pennsylvania called a strike against coal-mine owners in 1902 in pursuit of an eight-hour day and higher pay, the president employed the progressive tactics of investigation and arbitration. Owners stubbornly refused to recognize the union or arbitrate grievances. As winter approached and fuel shortages threatened, Roosevelt mustered public opinion. He would use federal troops to reopen the mines, he warned, thus forcing management to accept arbitration of the dispute by a special commission. The commission decided in favor of higher wages and reduced hours and required management to deal with grievance committees elected by the miners, but it did not require recognition of the union. The decision, according to Roosevelt, provided a "square deal" for all. The settlement also embodied Roosevelt's belief that the president or his representatives should have a say in which labor demands were legitimate and which were not—comparable to his role in business regulation. In Roosevelt's mind there were good and bad labor organizations (socialists, for example, were bad), just as there were good and bad business combinations.

In matters of conservation and the environment, Roosevelt employed the same mix of flamboyant executive action and quiet compromise. He built a reputation as a determined conservationist, warning Congress in 1907, "We are prone to think of the resources of this country as inexhaustible; this is not so." A lover of the outdoors, Roosevelt used presidential authority to add almost 150 million acres to the national forests and to preserve vast areas of water and coal from private plunder. In 1902 he influenced passage of the National (Newlands) Reclamation Act, which set aside proceeds from western public-land sales for the purpose of financing irrigation projects. Roosevelt thought highly of conservationist Gifford Pinchot, the government's chief forester, and in 1908 called forty-four governors and five hundred natural-resource experts to a national Conservation Congress. True to the progressive spirit of efficiency, Roosevelt wanted a "well-conceived plan" for resource management—that is, for ordered growth, rather than preservation of nature as it was. But compromises and factors beyond his control weakened his scheme. Timber and mining companies evaded supervision of their wasteful practices, and Congress never authorized enough funds to enforce regulations.

Conservation and the Environment

Roosevelt also had to compromise his principles in the face of economic crisis. In 1907 a financial panic caused by reckless speculation forced some New York banks to close to prevent frightened depositors from withdrawing money. J. P. Morgan helped to stem the panic by persuading other financiers to stop dumping their securities. In return for Morgan's aid, Roosevelt approved a deal allowing U.S. Steel to absorb a competitor, the Tennessee Iron and Coal Company—a deal that contradicted Roosevelt's professed trustbusting aims.

During his last year in office, Roosevelt drew away from the Republican party's traditional friendliness to big business. He lashed out at the irresponsibility of "malefactors of great wealth" and supported stronger regulation of business and heavier taxation of the rich. Having promised that he would not seek re-election, Roosevelt backed his friend Secretary of War William Howard Taft for the nomination in 1908, hoping that Taft would continue to pursue Roosevelt's initiatives. Democrats nominated William Jennings Bryan for the third time, but "the Great Commoner" lost again. Aided by Roosevelt, who still enjoyed great popularity, Taft won by 1.25 million popular votes and a 2-to-1 margin in the electoral college.

Early in 1909 Roosevelt went to Africa to shoot game (he saw no contradiction between hunting and conservation), leaving Taft to face political problems that his predecessor had managed to postpone. Foremost among them was the tariff; rates had risen to excessive levels. Honoring Taft's pledge to cut rates, the House passed a bill sponsored by Representative Sereno E. Payne that provided for numerous downward revisions. Protectionists in the Senate prepared, as in the past, to amend the House bill and revise rates upward. But Senate progressives, led by La Follette, organized a stinging attack on the tariff for benefiting vested interests. Taft was caught between reformers who claimed to be preserving Roosevelt's antitrust campaign and protectionists who still controlled the Republican party. In the end, Senator Aldrich and other protectionists restored many of the tariff cuts the Payne bill had made, and Taft—more reluctant than Roosevelt to interfere in the legislative process—signed what became known as the Payne-Aldrich Tariff. In the eyes of many progressives, Taft had failed the test of filling Roosevelt's shoes.

Taft Administration

The progressive and conservative wings of the Republican party were rapidly drifting apart. Soon after the tariff controversy, a group of insurgents in the House led by George Norris of Nebraska mounted a challenge to Speaker "Uncle Joe" Cannon of Illinois, whose power over committee assignments and the scheduling of debates could make or break a piece of legislation. Taft first supported and then abandoned the insurgents, who nevertheless managed to liberalize procedures by enlarging the influential Rules Committee and removing selection of its members from Cannon's control. Taft also angered conservationists by allowing Secretary of the Interior Richard A. Ballinger to remove one million acres of forest and mineral land from the reserved list and to fire Gifford Pinchot when he protested a questionable sale of coal lands in Alaska.

In reality Taft was as sympathetic to reform as Roosevelt was. He prosecuted more trusts than Roosevelt, expanded the national forest reserves, signed the Mann-Elkins Act of 1910 bolstering the regulatory powers of the ICC, and supported such labor reforms as the eight-hour day and mine safety legislation. The Sixteenth Amendment, which legalized federal income tax, and the Seventeenth Amendment, which provided for the direct election of U.S. senators, were initiated during Taft's presidency (and ratified in 1913). Like Roosevelt, Taft was forced to compromise with big business, but unlike Roosevelt he lacked the ability to maneuver and publicize his positions. Roosevelt had worked to expand presidential power and had infused the office with vitality. "I believe in a strong executive," he once asserted. "I believe in power." Taft, by contrast, believed in the strict restraint of law. He had been a successful lawyer and judge (and subsequently returned to the bench as chief justice of the United States between 1921 and 1930). His caution and unwillingness to offend disappointed those accustomed to Roosevelt's impetuosity.

In 1910, when Roosevelt returned from Africa boasting over three thousand animal trophies, he found his party worn and tormented. Reformers angered by Taft's apparent insensitivity to their cause formed the National Progressive Republican League and rallied behind Robert La Follette for president in 1912, though many hoped Roosevelt would run. Another wing of the party remained loyal to Taft. Disappointed by Taft's performance (particularly his refusal to back Pinchot), Roosevelt soon began to speak out and to rekindle public attention. He filled his speeches with references to "the welfare of the people" and stronger regulation of business. When La Follette became ill early in 1912, Roosevelt, proclaiming himself fit as a "bull moose," threw his hat in the ring for the Republican presidential nomination.

Taft's supporters controlled the convention and nominated him for a second term, but Roosevelt forces formed a third party—the Progressive or Bull Moose party—and nominated the fifty-three-year-old former president. Meanwhile, it took Democrats forty-six ballots to select as their candidate New Jersey's progressive governor Woodrow Wilson. The Socialists, by now an organized and growing party, again nominated Eugene V. Debs. The ensuing campaign exposed voters to the most thorough evaluation of the American system in nearly a generation.

WOODROW WILSON AND THE EXTENSION OF REFORM

In his acceptance speech before the Progressive party, Theodore Roosevelt had proclaimed, "We stand at Armageddon and we battle for the Lord." But on inauguration day 1913, it was Woodrow Wilson who assumed command of the forces of good. "The Nation," he exhorted,

> has been deeply stirred by a solemn passion. Stirred by the knowledge of wrong, of ideals lost, of government too often debauched and made an instrument of evil. The feelings with which we face this new age of right and opportunity sweep across our heartstrings like some air out of God's own presence, where justice and mercy are reconciled and the judge and the brother are one.

The election's outcome illustrated the extent to which the electorate had been swept up by the moral fervor of such pronouncements. Wilson won with 42 percent of the popular vote—he was a minority president, though he did capture 435 out of 531 electoral votes (see map). Roosevelt received about 27 percent of the popular vote. Taft finished a poor third, polling 23 percent of the popular vote and only 8 electoral votes. Debs won 902,000 votes, or 6 percent of the total, but no electoral votes. Fully three-quarters of the electorate thus supported some alternative to the restrained approach to government that Taft represented.

Sharp debate over the fundamentals of progressive government had characterized the campaign. Roosevelt had offered voters a system called New Nationalism, a term coined by reform editor Herbert Croly. Roosevelt foresaw a new era of national unity in which governmental authority would coordinate and regulate economic activity. He would not destroy big business, which he saw as an efficient way to organize production. Instead, he would establish regulatory commissions, groups of experts who would protect citizens' interests and ensure wise use of concentrated economic power. "The effort at prohibiting all combinations has sub-

The New Nationalism and the New Freedom

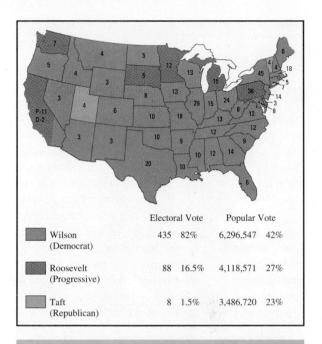

	Electoral Vote		Popular Vote	
Wilson (Democrat)	435	82%	6,296,547	42%
Roosevelt (Progressive)	88	16.5%	4,118,571	27%
Taft (Republican)	8	1.5%	3,486,720	23%

Presidential Election, 1912 *Though he won only a minority of the popular votes, Woodrow Wilson captured so many states that he achieved an easy victory in the electoral college.*

stantially failed," he claimed. "The way out lies . . . in completely controlling them."

Wilson offered a more idealistic scheme in the New Freedom, based on the ideas of progressive lawyer Louis D. Brandeis. Wilson believed that concentrated economic power threatened individual liberty and that monopolies had to be broken up so that the marketplace could again become genuinely open. But he did not want to restore laissez faire. Like Roosevelt, Wilson proposed to enhance governmental authority to protect and regulate. "Freedom today," he declared, "is something more than being let alone. Without the watchful . . . resolute interference of the government, there can be no fair play between individuals and such powerful institutions as the trust." But Wilson stopped short of advocating the cooperation between business and government inherent in Roosevelt's New Nationalism. In the campaign at least, he spoke in evangelical tones of economic emancipation, the need to "come out of a stifling cellar into the

Looking sober and stubborn, Woodrow Wilson (1856–1924) used a preacher's moralism and an academic's reasoning to raise citizens' expectations for the fulfillment of his idealistic promises. National Portrait Gallery, Smithsonian Institution. Transfer from the National Museum of American Art, Gift of the City of New York through the National Art Committee, 1923.

open . . . breathe again and see the free spaces of the heavens.''

Roosevelt and Wilson stood closer together than their rhetoric implied. In spite of his faith in experts as regulators, Roosevelt harbored a belief in individual freedom at least as strong as Wilson's. And Wilson was not really hostile to concentrated power. Both men strongly supported equality of opportunity (though chiefly for white males), conservation of natural resources, fair wages, and social betterment for all classes. And neither would hesitate to expand the scope of governmental activity through strong personal leadership and bureaucratic reform. Thus, even though he received a minority of the total vote in 1912, Wilson could interpret the election results as a popular mandate to subdue trusts and broaden the federal government's role in social reform.

The public had often fondly referred to Roosevelt as Teddy or TR, but no one ever called Thomas Woodrow Wilson Tommy or WW. The son of a Presbyterian minister, Wilson was born in 1856 and raised in the South. Both his mother and his first wife were daughters of Presbyterian ministers. Wilson chose instead to become an academic. He earned a B.A. at Princeton, studied law at Virginia, received a Ph.D. from Johns Hopkins, and became a professor of history, jurisprudence; and political economy. Between 1885 and 1908 he published several books on American history and government that established him as a respected scholar.

Woodrow Wilson

Wilson's manner and bearing reflected his background. Tall, lean, and stiff, he seemed to stare coldly through his pince-nez glasses, an image that lingers in the painting now kept in the Smithsonian. He exuded none of Roosevelt's flamboyance; in contrast to Roosevelt's lecturing, Wilson sermonized. Yet Wilson was an effective and charismatic leader. A superb orator, he could inspire intense loyalty with religious imagery and an eloquent expression of American ideals. Wilson's convictions had led him early into reform. In 1902 he became president of Princeton, where he upset tradition with curricular reforms and battles against aristocratic elements in the university. In 1910 New Jersey's Democrats, eager for respectability, nominated Wilson for governor. After winning the election, Wilson repudiated the party bosses and directed passage of progressive legislation. A poor administrator, he often lost his temper and stubbornly refused to compromise. His accomplishments nevertheless attracted national attention and won him the Democratic nomination for president in 1912.

As president, Wilson found it necessary to blend New Freedom commitment to competition with New Nationalism regulation, and in so doing he set the direction of federal economic policy for much of the twentieth century. The corporate merger movement had proceeded so far that restoration of free competition proved impossible. Thus Wilson could only acknowledge economic concentration and try to prevent abuses by expanding government's regulatory

Wilson's Policy on Business Regulation

powers. His administration moved toward that end with passage in 1914 of the Clayton Anti-Trust Act and a bill creating the Federal Trade Commission (FTC). The Clayton Act extended the Sherman Anti-Trust Act of 1890 by outlawing quasi-monopolistic practices such as price discrimination (efforts to destroy competition by lowering prices in some regions but not others) and interlocking directorates (management of two or more competing companies by the same executives). The FTC, which replaced the Bureau of Corporations, was to investigate corporations and issue cease-and-desist orders against unfair trade practices. As in ICC rulings, accused companies could appeal FTC orders in the courts. Nevertheless, the FTC represented a further step in consumer protection.

Wilson broadened federal regulation of finance with the Federal Reserve Act of 1913, which established the nation's first central banking system since Andrew Jackson had destroyed the Second Bank of the United States in 1832. Twelve new district banks were created to hold the reserves of member banks throughout the nation. (The act created many banks rather than one to allay the agrarian fear of a monolithic eastern banking power, which had doomed the central bank in Jackson's time.) The district banks would loan money to member banks at a low interest rate called the *discount rate*. By adjusting this rate (and thus the amount of money a bank could afford to borrow), district banks could increase or decrease the amount of money in circulation. In other words, depending on the nation's needs, the reserve bank could loosen or tighten credit. Monetary affairs would no longer depend on the supply of gold, and interest rates would be fairer, especially for small borrowers.

Perhaps the only act of Wilson's first administration that promoted free competition was the Underwood Tariff, passed in 1913. Rising prices had

Tariff and Tax Reform
———

for years thwarted consumers' desires for the material benefits of the industrial age. Some prices were unnaturally high because tariffs had discouraged the importation of cheaper foreign materials and manufactured products. By drastically reducing or eliminating tariff rates, the Underwood Tariff encouraged imports. To replace revenues that were lost due to reductions, the act levied a graduated income tax on U.S. residents—an option made possible when the Sixteenth Amendment was ratified earlier that year. The income tax was tame by today's standards. Incomes under $4,000 were exempt; thus almost all factory workers and farmers escaped taxation. Individuals and corporations earning between $4,000 and $20,000 had to pay a 1 percent tax, and rates for higher incomes rose gradually to a maximum of 6 percent on earnings over $500,000. Such rates tore no holes in pockets of the rich, but the income tax did become an institutional feature of American life.

The outbreak of the First World War in 1914 (see Chapter 23) and the approaching presidential campaign prompted Wilson to support stronger reforms in 1916. Concerned that farmers needed a better system of long-term mortgage credit to sustain production, the president backed the Federal Farm Loan Act. This measure created twelve federally supported banks (not to be confused with the Federal Reserve banks) that would lend money at moderate interest to farmers who belonged to credit institutions—a watered-down version of the subtreasury scheme that Populists had agitated for a generation earlier. To stave off railroad strikes that might disrupt transportation at a time of national emergency, Wilson pushed passage of the Adamson Act, which mandated an eight-hour day and time-and-a-half overtime pay for railroad laborers. He also pleased progressives by appointing Louis D. Brandeis, "the people's advocate," to the Supreme Court, though an anti-Semitic backlash almost blocked Senate approval of the first Jewish justice on the Court. Finally, Wilson courted the support of social reformers by backing laws that outlawed child labor and provided workers' compensation for federal employees who suffered work-related injuries or illness.

In selecting a candidate to oppose Wilson in 1916, Republicans snubbed Theodore Roosevelt, who wanted the nomination, in favor of Charles

Election of 1916
———

Evans Hughes, a Supreme Court justice and former reform governor of New York. Acutely aware of the influence of the First World War on national affairs, Wilson ran on a platform of peace, progressivism, and preparedness, and his supporters used the campaign slogan "He Kept Us Out of War." Hughes and his fractured party could not muzzle Roosevelt, whose bellicose speeches suggested that Republicans would drag Americans into the world war. Wilson received 9.1 million votes to Hughes's 8.5 million, and the president barely won the electoral college—by 277 to 254. The Socialist party, which had earned 902,000 votes four years earlier, dropped to 600,000, largely because Wilson's reforms had won over some socialists and the ailing Eugene Debs was no longer the party's standard-bearer.

U.S. involvement in the First World War during Wilson's second term brought about a shift away from competition toward interest-group politics and government regulation. During his first term Wilson had become convinced that regulatory commissions, which could easily fall under the influence of the very interests they were meant to regulate, should not govern social and economic behavior. The war effort, he came to believe, required government coordination of production, and cooperation between the public and private sectors. The War Industries Board (see Chapter 23) exemplified this cooperation: the private businesses regulated by the board submitted to its control on condition that their own profit motives would continue to be satisfied.

After the war the Wilson administration dropped most cooperative and regulatory measures, including farm price supports, guarantees of collective bargaining, and high taxes. This move away from regulation would stimulate a new era of business ascendancy in the 1920s (see Chapter 24).

By 1920, a quarter-century of reform had wrought momentous changes. Government, economy, and society as they had existed in the nineteenth century were gone forever. The progressives had established the principle of government intervention to ensure fairness, health, and safety for all citizens. Public concern over poverty and injustice had risen to new heights. But for every American who suffered some form of deprivation, three or four enjoyed unprecedented material comforts; and amid growing affluence, reformers could not sustain their efforts indefinitely. Although progressive values lingered and even spread after the First World War, a mass consumer society had begun to refocus people's attention from reform to materialism.

The Progressive era was characterized by multiple and sometimes contradictory goals. By no means was there a single progressive movement.

Reform programs on the national level ranged from Roosevelt's New Nationalism, with its faith in big government as a coordinator of big business, to Wilson's New Freedom, with its promise to dissolve economic concentrations and legislate open competition. At the state and local levels, reformers pursued causes as varied as neighborhood improvement, government reorganization, public ownership of utilities, betterment of working conditions, and moral revival. Local organizations and national associations coordinated their efforts on specific issues, but reformers with different goals often worked at cross-purposes.

The failure of many progressive initiatives testifies to the strength of opposition to reform, as well as to weaknesses within the reform movements themselves. Courts asserted constitutional and liberty-of-contract maxims in striking down some key progressive legislation, notably the federal law prohibiting child labor. In states and cities, adoption of the initiative, referendum, and recall did not encourage greater participation in government as had been hoped; those mechanisms were either seldom used or became tools of special interests. On the federal level, regulatory agencies rarely had enough resources for thorough investigations; they had to obtain information from the companies they were meant to police. Progressives thus failed in many respects to redistribute power. In 1920 as in 1900, government remained under the influence of business and industry, a state of affairs that many people considered quite satisfactory.

Yet the numerous reform movements that characterized the Progressive era did refashion the nation's future. Trustbusting, however faulty, forced industrialists to become more sensitive to public opinion, and insurgents in Congress partially diluted the power of dictatorial politicians. Progressive legislation equipped government with tools to protect consumers against price fixing and dangerous products. The income tax became a means for building government revenues and redistributing wealth. Social reformers eased some of the ills of urban life. And perhaps most important, progressives challenged old ways of thinking: though the questions they raised about the quality of American life remained largely unresolved, they made the nation more acutely aware of its principles and its promise.

SUGGESTIONS FOR FURTHER READING

General

Richard Abrams, *The Burden of Progress* (1978); John W. Chambers, *The Tyranny of Change: America in the Progressive Era* (1980); Arthur Ekirch, *Progressivism in America* (1974); Louis Filler, *The Muckrakers*, rev. ed. (1980); Samuel P. Hays, *The Response to Industrialism* (1957); Richard Hofstadter, *The Age of Reform: From Bryan to FDR* (1955); William R. Hutchinson, *The Modernist Impulse in American Protestantism* (1976); Morton Keller, *Regulating a New Economy* (1990); Gabriel Kolko, *The Triumph of Conservatism* (1963); David W. Noble, *The Progressive Mind*, rev. ed. (1981); James Weinstein, *The Corporate Ideal in the Liberal State, 1900–1918* (1968); Robert Wiebe, *The Search for Order* (1968).

Regional Studies

Dewey Grantham, *Southern Progressivism: The Reconciliation of Progress and Tradition* (1983); Sheldon Hackney, *Populism to Progressivism in Alabama* (1969); Richard L. McCormick, *From Realignment to Reform: Political Change in New York State, 1893–1910* (1981); George E. Mowry, *The California Progressives* (1951); David P. Thelen, *Robert La Follette and the Insurgent Spirit* (1976); David P. Thelen, *The New Citizenship: Origins of Progressivism in Wisconsin* (1972); C. Vann Woodward, *Origins of the New South* (1951).

Legislative Issues and Reform Groups

Allen F. Davis, *Spearheads for Reform: The Social Settlements and the Progressive Movement, 1890–1914* (1967); Ruth Rosen, *The Lost Sisterhood: Prostitution in America, 1900–1918* (1982); James H. Timberlake, *Prohibition and the Progressive Crusade* (1963); Walter I. Trattner, *Crusade for the Children* (1970); Irwin Yellowitz, *Labor and the Progressive Movement in New York State* (1965); James Harvey Young, *Pure Food: Securing the Federal Food and Drug Act of 1906* (1989). (For works on socialism, see the listings under "Currents of Protest" at the end of Chapter 20.)

Education, Law, and the Social Sciences

Jerold S. Auerback, *Unequal Justice: Lawyers and Social Change in Modern America* (1976); Lawrence Cremin, *The Transformation of the School: Progressivism in American Education* (1961); Martin S. Dworkin, ed., *Dewey on Education* (1959); Paula S. Fass, *Outside In: Minorities and the Transformation of American Education* (1989); Ellen Fitzpatrick, *Endless Crusade: Women Social Scientists and Progressive Reform* (1990); Lynn D. Gordon, *Gender and Higher Education in the Progressive Era* (1990); Thomas L. Haskell, *The Emergence of Professional Social Science* (1977); David W. Marcell, *Progress and Pragmatism: James, Dewey, Beard, and the American Idea of Progress* (1974); Sheldon Novick, *Honorable Justice: The Life of Oliver Wendell Holmes* (1989); Philippa Strum, *Louis D. Brandeis, Justice for the People* (1984); Lawrence Veysey, *The Emergence of the American University* (1970).

Women

Lois Banner, *Women in Modern America: A Brief History*, 2nd ed. (1984); Ruth Borden, *Women and Temperance* (1980); Nancy F. Cott, *The Grounding of American Feminism* (1987); Carl N. Degler, *At Odds: Women and the Family in America* (1980); Eleanor Flexner, *Century of Struggle: The Women's Rights Movement in the United States* (1959); Linda Gordon, *Woman's Body, Woman's Right: A Social History of Birth Control in America* (1976); David Kennedy, *Birth Control in America: The Career of Margaret Sanger* (1970); Alice Kessler-Harris, *Out to Work: A History of Wage-Earning Women in the United States* (1982); Aileen Kraditor, *The Ideas of the Women's Suffrage Movement* (1965); Robyn Muncy, *Creating a Female Dominion in American Reform* (1991); William L. O'Neill, *Everyone Was Brave: The Rise and Fall of Feminism in America* (1969); William L. O'Neill, *Divorce in the Progressive Era* (1967); Rosalind Rosenberg, *Beyond Separate Spheres: Intellectual Roots of Modern Feminism* (1982); Sheila M. Rothman, *Woman's Proper Place* (1978).

African-Americans

John Dittmer, *Black Georgia in the Progressive Era, 1900–1920* (1977); George Frederickson, *The Black Image in the White Mind* (1971); Louis R. Harlan, *Booker T. Washington: The Wizard of Tuskegee, 1901–1915* (1983); Louis R. Harlan, *Booker T. Washington: The Making of a Black Leader, 1856–1901* (1972); Jacqueline Jones, *Labor of Love, Labor of Sorrow: Black Women, Work and the Family from Slavery to the Present* (1985); Charles F. Kellogg, *NAACP* (1970); August Meier, *Negro Thought in America, 1880–1915* (1963); Elliot M. Rudwick, *W.E.B. Du Bois* (1969); Donald Spivey, *Schooling for the New Slavery: Black Industrial Education* (1978).

Roosevelt, Taft, and Wilson

John M. Blum, *Woodrow Wilson and the Politics of Morality* (1956); John M. Blum, *The Republican Roosevelt*, 2nd ed. (1954); Francis L. Broderick, *Progressivism at Risk: Electing a President in 1912* (1989); Paolo E. Coletta, *The Presidency of William Howard Taft* (1973); John Milton Cooper, Jr., *The Warrior and the Priest: Woodrow Wilson and Theodore Roosevelt* (1983); Lewis Gould, *The Presidency of Theodore Roosevelt* (1991); August Hecksher, *Woodrow Wilson* (1991); Edmund Morris, *The Rise of Theodore Roosevelt* (1979); James Pednick, Jr., *Progressive Politics and Conservation: The Ballinger-Pinchot Affair* (1968).

22

The Quest for Empire, 1865–1914

U.S. fleet,
the Straits of
Magellan, 1908,
by Henry
Reuterdahl.

THE WHITE AMERICAN LAWYERS, businessmen, and sugar planters, many of them the sons of Protestant missionaries, were certainly not the sort of people one would think of as revolutionaries. But these *haole* (foreigners) who plotted against Queen Liliuokalani sought the overthrow of the native Hawaiian government and the creation of a new order that favored their interests. In January 1893, members of Hawaii's white American elite made their treasonous move.

Americans had long coveted opportunities in the Hawaiian Islands, the Pacific Ocean archipelago of eight major islands located two thousand miles from the west coast of the United States. In the late eighteenth and early nineteenth centuries, American traders cut sandalwood for export to Asia, where it was used for ointments and perfumes. Then came fleets of whaling ships. In the 1830s, Presbyterian and Congregational missionaries from New England founded schools to Christianize—and Americanize—the Hawaiians. The cultivation of sugar cane and fruit eventually drew other adventurous Americans.

The descendants of the missionaries prospered both economically and politically. As one wag put it, "They came to do good and they did well."

By 1890 Americans owned about three-quarters of the islands' wealth, though they represented less than 10 percent of the population. Because diseases brought by foreigners had diminished the native population, causing a labor shortage, the American oligarchy imported Chinese and Japanese workers for the expanding sugar industry. By 1890 native Hawaiians accounted for only 40 percent of the islands' population. Hawaii became a multiracial society dominated by white Americans who subordinated its economy to that of the United States through sugar exports that entered the American marketplace duty-free.

Many native Hawaiians joined King Kalakaua in the 1870s and 1880s in resisting the "grasping" foreigners, who were organizing secret clubs and military units to contest the royal government. In 1887 the American conspirators forced the king to accept a new constitution—the so-called Bayonet Constitution—which granted foreigners the right to vote and shifted decision-making authority from the monarchy to the legislature. The same year, Hawaii empowered the United States to develop Pearl Harbor. Hawaiians were losing control of their land, their economy, their politics, and their sovereignty.

The McKinley Tariff of 1890 created an economic crisis for Hawaii that further undermined the native government. The tariff eliminated Hawaiian sugar's favored status by admitting all foreign sugar into the United States duty-free. The measure also provided a bounty of 2 cents a pound to domestic U.S. growers, making it possible for them to sell their sugar at a price lower than that charged for foreign sugar. With this new competition from other foreign producers and this advantage for U.S. producers, planters and their allies in Hawaii suffered declining profits. To relieve their economic woes, prominent Americans in Hawaii soon pressed for annexation of the Hawaiian Islands to the United States so that their sugar would be classified as domestic rather than foreign.

When Kalakaua's sister Princess Liliuokalani assumed the throne upon his death in 1891, "they were lying in wait," she remembered. The new queen wanted to roll back the political power of the *haole*. She also supported the legalization of opium and a lottery to raise revenues. The next year, the white oligarchy—questioning her moral rectitude, fearing Hawaiian nationalism, and reeling from the McKinley Tariff—formed a subversive Annexation Club.

In collusion with the chief U.S. diplomat in Hawaii, John L. Stevens, the conspirators struck in January 1893—but only after U.S. troops from the U.S.S. *Boston* occupied key sites in Honolulu. The queen reluctantly surrendered to what she acknowledged as the "superior force" of the United States, but she refused to deal with the new regime headed by Sanford B. Dole, son of missionaries and a prominent attorney. On February 1, with Stevens's blessing, the American flag was raised over the Government Building in Honolulu. "The Hawaiian pear is now fully ripe and this is the golden hour to pluck it," a triumphant Stevens informed the U.S. Department of State.

Seizing foreign opportunities was common practice for those who governed in Washington, D.C., during the late nineteenth and early twentieth centuries. They were unabashed expansionists and imperialists whose "destiny is always to expand," as the Russian diplomat who negotiated the sale of Alaska to the United States remarked. In the early nineteenth century, Americans had pur-

chased Louisiana; annexed Florida, Oregon, and Texas; pushed Indians out of the path of white migration westward; seized California and other western areas from Mexico; and acquired the Gadsden Purchase. Since the founding of the republic, moreover, they had developed a lucrative foreign trade with most of the world. Very little, the Russian observed, "escaped the lust of Americans."

From the Civil War to the First World War the United States became one of the world's premier expansionist nations, ultimately building, managing, and protecting an overseas empire. The international system at the time was becoming multipolar, with several countries sharing power in an age of active imperialism throughout the world. Germany rose to challenge a declining Great Britain, the economic and military giant of the world, and Japan in Asia and the United States in Latin America emerged as regional powers. The U.S. empire ultimately stretched from Latin America to Asia, but not without opposition. Proud nationalists, commercial competitors, and other imperial nations tried to block the spread of U.S. influence, while anti-imperialists at home stimulated a momentous debate over the fundamental course of American foreign policy.

Most Americans applauded *expansionism*—the outward movement of goods, ships, dollars, people, and ideas—as a traditional feature of their nation's history. But many became uneasy whenever expansionism gave way to *imperialism*—the imposition of control over other peoples, undermining their sovereignty so that they lose the freedom to make their own decisions. Imperial control could be imposed either formally (by annexation, colonialism, or military occupation) or informally (by economic domination, political manipulation, or the threat of intervention). As the informal methods indicate, imperialism did not necessarily mean the taking of territory.

Critics in the late nineteenth century disparaged territorial imperialism as unbefitting the United States, and they opposed joining other great powers in the scramble for colonies in Asia and Africa. Would not an overseas territorial empire, with lands and peoples noncontiguous to the United States, undermine institutions at home, invite perpetual war, and violate honored principles? Although the United States preferred the "annexation of trade" to the annexation of territory, as Secretary of State James G. Blaine once declared,

• Important Events •

1861–69	Secretary of State Seward sets expansionist course		First Open Door note, calling for equal trade opportunity in China
1866	Transatlantic cable completed France withdraws from Mexico		Outbreak of Philippine Insurrection against the United States
1867	Alaska and Midway acquired	**1900**	Second Open Door note requests respect for China's sovereignty
1868	Burlingame Treaty with China regulates immigration		Foraker Act organizes Puerto Rico's government
1870	Senate rejects annexation of Dominican Republic		U.S. exports total $1.5 billion McKinley re-elected
1871	*Alabama* claims settled with Great Britain	**1901**	Theodore Roosevelt becomes president Aguinaldo captured in Philippines Hay-Pauncefote Treaty allows sole U.S. development of isthmian canal
1878	U.S. products monopolize awards at Paris World's Fair		
1883	Advent of the New Navy	**1903**	Panama breaks from Colombia and grants canal rights to United States
1887	United States gains naval rights to Pearl Harbor		Platt Amendment subjugates Cuba
1889	First Pan-American Conference	**1904**	Roosevelt Corollary declares United States a "police power"
1890	Mahan's *The Influence of Sea Power upon History* is published McKinley Tariff hurts Hawaiian sugar exports	**1905**	Taft-Katsura Agreement gains Japanese pledge not to molest the Philippines Portsmouth Conference under Roosevelt's guidance ends Russo-Japanese War United States imposes financial supervision on the Dominican Republic
1893	Severe depression begins Turner's frontier thesis expounded Hawaiian revolution overthrows Queen Liliuokalani	**1906**	San Francisco segregates Asian schoolchildren United States invades Cuba to put down rebellion
1894	Wilson-Gorham Tariff imposes tariff on Cuban sugar	**1907**	"Great White Fleet" makes world tour "Gentleman's agreement" with Japan restricts immigration
1895	Venezuelan crisis with Britain Cuban revolution against Spain begins Japan defeats China to become major Asian power	**1908**	Root-Takahira Agreement made with Japan for security of the Philippines
1896	William McKinley elected president on imperialist platform	**1910**	Mexican Revolution begins against Díaz and U.S. interests
1898	Sinking of the *Maine* heightens chances of war Spanish-American-Cuban-Filipino War Hawaii annexed (Newlands Resolution)	**1912**	U.S. troops invade Cuba again U.S. troops occupy Nicaragua
1899	Treaty of Paris approved United Fruit Company forms and becomes influence in Central America	**1914**	U.S. troops invade Mexico First World War begins Panama Canal opens

it became clear that economic expansionism sometimes led to both formal and informal imperialism and even to the grabbing of colonies. Most Americans endorsed economic expansion as essential to the nation's prosperity and security, but anti-imperialists drew the line between expansionism and imperialism: profitable and fair trade relationships, yes; exploitation, no. And, some advised, American business activity abroad should not draw the United States into unwanted diplomatic crises and wars. But it did.

In the late nineteenth century the federal government sometimes failed to fund adequately the vehicles of expansion. Washington neglected the navy until the 1880s and continued to tolerate a foreign service weakened by the political spoils system. Most businessmen ignored foreign commerce in favor of the dynamic domestic marketplace. Still, the direction of American foreign policy after the Civil War became unmistakable: Americans intended to exert their influence beyond the continental United States, to reach for more space, more land, more markets, and more international power. A pattern of accelerating activity abroad culminated in the tumultuous decade of the 1890s, when doubters' voices were drowned out by calls for war and foreign territory, and when American power was sufficient to deliver both. U.S. entry into the Spanish-American-Cuban-Filipino War in 1898 and the subsequent subjugation of other peoples set off one of the major controversies in American history. The experience also helped carry the United States to great-power status.

THE DOMESTIC ROOTS OF EXPANSIONISM AND EMPIRE

Foreign policy has always sprung from the domestic setting of a nation—its needs, wants, moods, prejudices, and ideals. The leaders who guided America's expansionist foreign relations were the same people who kindled the spirit of national growth at home, celebrated the machine age, forged the transcontinental railroad, shoved Native Americans aside, and built America's bustling cities and giant corporations.

Unlike domestic policy, foreign policy is seldom shaped by "the people." Most Americans simply do not follow international relations or express themselves on foreign issues. Most Americans in the late nineteenth century were too caught up in the daily bustle of machine-age life to give much attention to foreign matters. Indeed, at the time no more than 10 to 20 percent of the voting public was alert to world affairs. Thus the making of foreign policy was dominated by what scholars have labeled the foreign policy elite—opinion leaders in politics, business, labor, agriculture, religion, journalism, education, and the military. This small group, whom Secretary of State Walter Q. Gresham called "the thoughtful men of the country," expressed the opinion that counted. Better read and better traveled than most Americans, more cosmopolitan in outlook, and politically active, they believed that U.S. prosperity and security depended on the exertion of American influence abroad. Increasingly in the late nineteenth century, and especially in the 1890s, the foreign policy elite urged not only expansionism, but both formal and informal imperialism. Those members of the political elite, like President Grover Cleveland, who favored economic expansion but not the annexation of territory gradually lost ground.

Foreign Policy Elite

Ambitious and clannish, the imperialists often met in Washington, D.C., at the homes of Henry Adams or John Hay (who became secretary of state in 1898) or at the Metropolitan Club. They talked about building a bigger navy and an isthmian canal, establishing colonies, and selling surpluses abroad. Theodore Roosevelt, appointed assistant secretary of the navy in 1897, was among them; so were Senator Henry Cabot Lodge, who became a member of the Foreign Relations Committee in 1895, and the corporate lawyer Elihu Root, who would later serve as both secretary of war and secretary of state. These luminaries kept up the drumbeat for empire.

American leaders understood the close relationship between domestic developments and foreign relations. They knew that railroads made it possible for midwestern farmers to transport their crops to seaboard cities and then on to foreign markets—"feeding the world." One result was that the farmers' livelihood became tied to world market conditions and the outcomes of foreign wars. Periodic depressions—especially the monster of the 1890s—fostered the belief among industrialists and others that the country's surplus production must be sold in foreign markets to restore and sustain economic well-being at home. By promoting economic health, these markets would also contribute to domestic social and political stability. Blaine made the point: "With these markets secured, new life would be given to our manufactories, the product of the Western farmer would be in demand, the reasons for and inducements to strikers with all their attendant evils would cease." The tariff question also linked domestic and world affairs. Tariff increases designed to protect American industry and agriculture from foreign competition adversely affected those who sold to America, prompting them to enact retaliatory tariffs on American products. American tariff revisions actually induced economic crises—in Hawaii and Cuba, for example—which fed revolutions that ultimately served U.S. interests.

The Civil War had temporarily interrupted expansionism, but after that searing conflict leaders once again put the United States on an expansionist

Nationalism and Exceptionalism
——

course. Their kindling of a spirit of nationalism helped heal sectional wounds at the same time that it resuscitated an expansionist mood. The 1876 centennial celebration emphasized national unity. Confederate and Union soldiers met to exchange captured flags. Pride welled up when at the 1878 Paris World's Fair American exhibitors won more awards than any other nation's representatives. Patriotic societies like the Daughters of the American Revolution (founded in 1890) championed nationalism.

The inflated rhetoric of American exceptionalism and manifest destiny revived, giving intensified voice to racist explanations for expansion. The Reverend Josiah Strong's influential *Our Country* (1885) characterized Americans as a special God-favored Anglo-Saxon race destined to lead others. "As America goes, so goes the world," he declared. Social Darwinists saw Americans as a superior people who would surely overcome all competition and thrive. "The rule of the survival of the fittest applies to nations as well as to the animal kingdom," claimed the American diplomat John Barrett. The humorist Finley Peter Dunne conveyed the American mood by putting words in the mouths of his fictional Irish-American characters: "'We're a gr-reat people,' said Mr. Hennessy, ear-

nestly. 'We ar-re,' said Mr. Dooley. 'We ar-re that. An' th best iv it is, we know we are.'"

Missionaries
——

Missionaries, a majority of whom were women, contributed to expansionist ideology by spurring the transfer of American culture and power abroad. Like Grace Roberts in China, they taught the Bible, hoping to convert "natives" and "savages" to Christianity. "Don't stay in this country theorizing," implored an officer of the Student Volunteer Movement, founded by college students in the 1880s. "A hundred thousand heathen a day are dying without hope because we are not there teaching the Gospel to them." The *Mother Goose Missionary Rhymes* captured the familiar blend of American evangelism, nationalism, and cultural arrogance:

> Ten little heathen standing in a line;
> One went to mission school, then there were but
> nine. . . .
> Three little heathen didn't know what to do;
> One learned our language, then there were
> two. . . .
> One little heathen standing all alone;
> He learned to love our flag, then there were none.

The arguments for expansion seemed all the more urgent when Americans anticipated the closing of the frontier at home. In 1893 the historian

Turner's Frontier Thesis
——

Frederick Jackson Turner of the University of Wisconsin postulated the thesis that an ever-expanding continental frontier had shaped the American character. That "frontier has gone," Turner wrote, "and with its going has closed the first period of American history." He did not explicitly say that a new frontier had to be found overseas, but he did write that "American energy will continually demand a wider field for its exercise."

With a mixture of self-interest and idealism typical of American thinking on foreign policy, advocates of expansion and empire believed that

Remaking Societies
——

imperialism benefited both Americans and those who came under their control. When the United States intervened in other lands or lectured weaker states, Americans defended such behavior on the grounds that they were extending the blessings of liberty and prosperity to less fortunate

The missionary Grace Roberts taught the Bible to Chinese in Manchuria in 1903. The prominent American flag reveals that Americanism went hand in hand with overseas religious work. The mission force was feminized—in fact, a majority of missionaries were women. ABCFM pictures. Courtesy of Houghton Library, Harvard University.

people. For those imperialists who were also progressive reformers, interventions seemed to offer opportunities for Americans to remake foreign societies in the U.S. model.

To the critics at home and abroad, however, American paternalism appeared hypocritical—a violation of cherished principles. To impose on Filipinos an American-style political system, for example, U.S. officials censored the press, jailed critics, and picked candidates for public office. From this coercive experience, Filipinos probably learned more about how to fix elections than about how to make democracy work. The persistent American belief that other peoples cannot solve their own problems and that only the American model of development is appropriate produced what the historian William Appleman Williams has called "the tragedy of American diplomacy."

FACTORY, FARM, AND FOREIGN AFFAIRS

American political leaders shared the views of the many businesspeople and farmers who believed that selling, buying, and investing in foreign marketplaces were important to the United States. Why? First, because of profits from foreign sales. "It is my dream," cried the governor of Georgia in 1878, to see "in every valley . . . a cotton factory to convert the raw material of the neighborhood into fabrics which shall warm the limbs of Japanese and Chinese." Fear helped make the case for foreign trade as well, because the nation's farms and factories produced more than Americans could consume. Foreign commerce, it was thought, could serve as a safety valve to relieve the domestic pressures of overproduction, unemployment, economic depression, and the social tensions that arise from them. Surpluses had to be exported, the economist David A. Wells warned, or "we are certain to be smothered in our own grease." Economic ties also permitted political influence to be exerted abroad and helped spread the American way of life, creating a world more hospitable to Americans. In an era when the most powerful nations in the world were also the greatest traders, vigorous foreign economic expansion symbolized national stature.

One of the major components of the tremendous economic growth of the United States after

Growth of Foreign Trade

the Civil War was foreign trade. Foreign trade expansion produced important consequences: the building of a larger navy to protect this lucrative commerce; reform of the foreign service to make it more efficient; calls for more colonies; and a more interventionist foreign policy. In 1865 United States exports totaled $234 million; by 1900, they had climbed to $1.5 billion (see figure). By 1914, at the outbreak of the First World War, American exports had reached $2.5 billion, prompting some Europeans to protest an "American export invasion." In the 1870s the United States reversed its

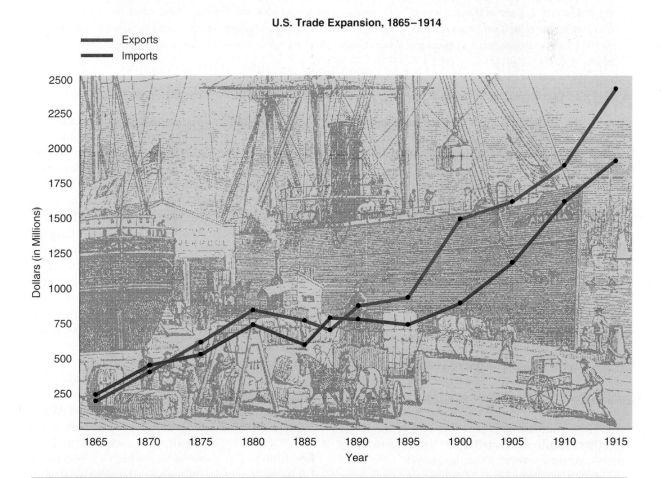

U.S. Trade Expansion, 1865–1914

— Exports
— Imports

Dollars (in Millions) — Year (1865–1915)

United States Trade Expansion, 1865–1914   *This figure illustrates two key characteristics of U.S. foreign trade: first, that the United States began in the 1870s to enjoy a favorable balance of trade (exporting more than it imported); second, that U.S. exports expanded tremendously, making the United States one of the world's economic giants.*   Source: From Thomas G. Paterson, J. Garry Clifford, and Kenneth J. Hagan, *American Foreign Policy: A History.* 3rd edition. Copyright 1988. Used by permission of D.C. Heath and Company.

The Rise of U.S. Economic Power in the World

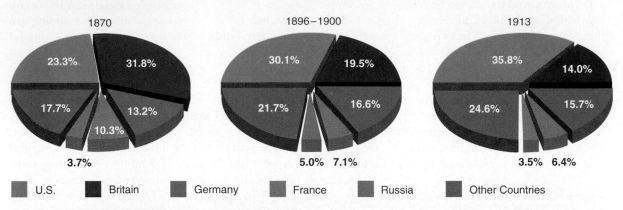

The Rise of U.S. Economic Power in the World *These data—percentage shares of world manufacturing production for the major nations of the world—demonstrate that the United States came to surpass Great Britain in this significant measurement of power.* Source: League of Nations data presented in Aaron L. Friedberg, *The Weary Titan: Britain and the Experience of Relative Decline, 1895–1905* (Princeton, NJ: Princeton University Press, 1988), p. 26.

historically unfavorable balance of trade (importing more than it exported) and began to enjoy a long-term favorable balance (exporting more than it imported). Most of America's products went to Britain, other parts of Europe, and Canada, but increasing amounts flowed to new markets in Latin America and Asia. Meanwhile, direct American investments abroad reached $3.5 billion by 1914, placing the United States among the top four investor countries.

Agricultural goods accounted for about three-fourths of total exports in 1870 and about two-thirds in 1900, with grains, cotton, meat, and dairy products topping the export list that year. More than half the annual cotton crop was exported each year. Wisconsin cheesemakers shipped to Britain; the Swift and Armour meat companies exported refrigerated beef to Europe; and American farmers became Europe's largest supplier of wheat. To sell American grain abroad, James J. Hill of the Great Northern Railroad distributed wheat cookbooks translated into several Asian languages.

America's ambitious entrepreneurs and large businesses increasingly looked to foreign markets, especially during the depression-ridden 1890s, when it became clear that industrial production was outdistancing consumption. The photography baron George Eastman, whose business operated around the globe, once remarked that greater foreign sales allowed Americans to "distribute our eggs and pad the basket at the same time." Manufactured goods led foreign sales for the first time in 1913, when the United States ranked third behind only Britain and Germany in such exports. In the 1870s and 1880s about two-thirds of all American petroleum was exported, and in succeeding decades the figure was about one-half. Fifteen percent of America's iron and steel and 50 percent of its copper were sold abroad by the turn of the century, making many workers in those industries dependent on exports. George Westinghouse marketed his air brakes in Europe; almost as many Singer sewing machines were exported as were sold at home; and Cyrus McCormick's "reaper kings" harvested the wheat of Russian fields.

Especially in Latin America, U.S. economic expansion grew impressively and aroused Washington's diplomatic interest in its neighbors to the

Economic Links with Latin America

South. U.S. exports to Latin America, which exceeded $50 million in the 1870s, rose to more than $120 million in 1900 and reached $300 million in 1914. Investments by U.S. citizens in Latin America amounted to a towering $1.26 billion in 1914. In 1899 two large banana

The Singer Manufacturing Company handed out this promotional postcard as a souvenir from the firm's display at the 1893 Columbian Exposition, a mammoth world's fair in Chicago where Americans showed off their technological and industrial genius. Singer sewing machines joined many other U.S. products in penetrating world markets, where three-quarters of all sewing machines sold were Singers. This machine was marketed in South Africa, where, the company advised, the "Zulus are a fine warlike people" who were moving toward "civilization" with Singer's help. State Historical Society of Wisconsin.

importers merged to form the United Fruit Company. In Central America, United Fruit owned much of the land (more than one million acres in 1913) and the railroad and steamship lines, and the firm became an influential economic and political force in the region. The company developed transportation, cultivated land, and worked to eradicate yellow fever and malaria while it manipulated Central American politics to gain governmental favors. As for Mexico, American capitalists came to own its railroads and mines. By 1910, Americans controlled 43 percent of Mexican property and produced more than half of Mexico's oil.

Economic expansion abroad became both a reason and a mechanism for exerting political influence. Dunne's Mr. Dooley put it simply: "I tell ye, th' hand that rocks th' scales in th' grocery store is th' hand that rules th' wurruld." Indeed, by the early twentieth century American economic interests were influencing policies on taxes and natural resources in Cuba and Mexico, drawing Hawaii into the U.S. imperial net, and spreading American cultural values abroad. Religious missionaries and Singer executives, for example, joined hands

in promoting the "civilizing medium" of the sewing machine. "The world is to be Christianized and civilized," declared Josiah Strong. "And what is the process of civilizing but the creating of more and higher wants."

A WIDER FIELD ABROAD, 1860s–1880s

The American empire grew gradually, sometimes haltingly. William H. Seward, one of its chief architects, argued articulately for extension of the American frontier as senator from New York (1849–1861) and secretary of state (1861–1869). "There is not in the history of the Roman Empire an ambition for aggrandizement so marked as that which characterizes the American people," he once said. Seward envisioned a large, coordinated U.S. empire encompassing Canada, the Caribbean, Cuba, Cen-

Grand Expansionist: William H. Seward

tral America, Mexico, Hawaii, Iceland, Greenland, and Pacific islands. This empire would be built not by war but by a natural process of gravitation toward the United States. Commerce would hurry the process, he thought, noting that in earlier centuries the merchants of Venice and Britain had become "masters of the world." To ensure the unity of this new empire, Seward appealed for a canal across Central America, a transcontinental American railroad to link up with Asian markets, and a telegraph system to speed communications.

Most of Seward's grandiose plans did not reach fruition in his own day. In 1867, for example, he signed a treaty with Denmark to buy the Danish West Indies (the Virgin Islands). Shortly afterward a hurricane and tidal wave wrecked St. Thomas, diminishing its value in the eyes of many senators. (They were also reluctant to hand Republican Seward a diplomatic triumph while he was supporting Democrat Andrew Johnson during the president's impeachment proceedings.) The treaty was shelved, and the Virgin Islanders, who had voted for annexation, had to wait until 1917.

Most of Seward's plans for acquiring territory were blocked by a combination of anti-imperialists and political foes. Anti-imperialists like Senator Carl Schurz and E. L. Godkin, editor of the magazine *The Nation*, argued that the country already had enough unsettled land and that the creation of a showcase of democracy and prosperity at home would best persuade other peoples to adopt American institutions and principles. Some anti-imperialists, sharing the racism of the times, opposed the annexation of territory populated by "inferior" dark-skinned people.

But Seward did enjoy some successes. In 1867 he paid Russia $7.2 million for the 591,000 square miles of Alaska—a real bargain for land twice the size of Texas. Some critics lampooned "Seward's Icebox," but the secretary of state extolled the Russian territory's rich natural resources, and the Senate voted overwhelmingly for the treaty. That same year, when an American naval officer seized the Midway Islands, Seward laid claim to them for the United States.

The secretary's forceful handling of French interference in Mexico also furthered his reputation. Napoleon III had made Archduke Ferdinand Maximilian of Austria Mexico's monarch in 1861. Preoccupied with the Civil War, Seward could do little. But in 1866, as U.S. troops headed for the

Mexican border, Seward cited the Monroe Doctrine and told the French to get out. Napoleon, troubled at home and now opposed by both Mexicans and Americans, abandoned his venture. Seward also shepherded the Burlingame Treaty (1868) through the Senate. This treaty with China provided for free immigration between the two countries and pledged Sino-American friendship. (A new treaty in 1880 permitted Congress to suspend Chinese immigration to the United States; it did so two years later to satisfy anti-Asian bias in the American West, which was sometimes expressed violently, as at Rock Springs, Wyoming, in 1885, when white coal miners and railway workers rioted and killed at least twenty-five Chinese.)

International Communications — Seward realized his dream of a world knit together into a giant communications system. In 1866, through the persevering efforts of financier Cyrus Field, an underwater transatlantic cable linked European and American telegraph networks. Diplomats soon put it to good use. In 1873, for example, during a Cuban rebellion against Spain, the Spanish seized the gun-running Cuban ship *Virginius* and executed some Americans on board. Washington quickly used the telegraph to manage the crisis before war fever carried the United States into a serious conflict. Spain later paid an indemnity of $80,000, and the crisis passed.

Backed by J. P. Morgan's capital, the communications pioneer James A. Scrymser strung telegraph lines to Latin America, reaching Chile in 1890. In 1903 a submarine cable reached across the Pacific to the Philippines, and three years later, to Japan and China. Information about markets, crises, and war flowed steadily and quickly. Drawn closer to one another by improvements in communications and transportation, nations found that faraway events became more important to their prosperity and security. Wire telegraphy—like radio (wireless telegraphy) later—shrank the globe.

Anglo-American Issues — Seward's successor, Hamilton Fish (1869–1877), inherited the knotty and emotional problem of the *Alabama* claims. The *Alabama* and other vessels built in Great Britain for the Confederacy during the Civil War had preyed on Union shipping. Senator Charles Sumner demanded that Britain pay $2 billion in damages or cede Canada to the United

States, but Fish favored negotiations. In 1871 Britain and America signed the Washington Treaty, whereby the British apologized and agreed to the creation of a tribunal, which later awarded the United States $15.5 million. Disputes over fishing rights along the North Atlantic coast and the hunting of seals in the Bering Sea near Alaska also dogged Anglo-American relations and would continue to do so for decades. Yet the two powers were coming to the conclusion that rapprochement rather than confrontation best served their interests. American politicians still tried to "twist the lion's tail" to score political points at home, but the trend toward Anglo-American accommodation was not reversed.

Secretary Fish also had to deal with President Grant's ambitious designs on the Dominican Republic. The president was impressed by the island's raw materials and its potential as a market for American textiles, and the navy liked the harbor at Samaná Bay. Grant's personal secretary, Orville Babcock, negotiated a treaty of annexation. But Senator Sumner smelled a rat in Babcock, who through private intrigue stood to gain financially from the venture. Civil war, moreover, engulfed the Dominican Republic. Political rivalry in the United States also complicated the question. "No wild bull ever dashed more violently at a red rag than he does at anything that he thinks the President is interested in," Fish said of Sumner's political motives. In 1870 the Senate rejected the treaty.

Another venture succeeded, this time in the Pacific. In 1878 the United States gained rights to a naval station at the strategic port of Pago Pago in Samoa, a group of islands four thousand miles from San Francisco on the trade route to Australia. The Germans and British also coveted the islands. Year by year tensions grew. To avoid war, Germany, Britain, and the United States met in Berlin in 1889 and, without consulting the Samoans, carved Samoa into three parts. A decade later the United States annexed part of the islands, including Pago Pago.

In Latin America, meanwhile, the convening in 1889 of the first Pan-American Conference in Washington, D.C., bore witness to the growing ties of the United States with its hemispheric neighbors. Conferees from Latin America toured U.S. factories and then negotiated several commercial

Pan-American Conference

agreements. To encourage inter-American cooperation, they founded the Pan American Union, which in 1907 moved into elegant new Washington quarters financed by Andrew Carnegie. But Pan-Americanism did not prevent growing Latin American resentment toward U.S. influence in the hemisphere.

As the United States acquired new territories and markets, expansionists bemoaned the condition of the U.S. Navy. Captain Alfred T. Mahan became a major popularizer for a "New Navy." Because foreign trade was vital to U.S. well-being, he argued, the nation required an efficient navy to protect its shipping; in turn, a navy required colonies for bases. "Whether they will or no," Mahan wrote, "Americans must now begin to look outward. The growing production of the country demands it." Mahan became president of the Naval War College in Newport, Rhode Island, founded in 1884, and there gave lectures that were published as *The Influence of Sea Power upon History* (1890). This widely read book sat on every serious expansionist's shelf. German, Japanese, and British leaders turned its pages. Theodore Roosevelt and Henry Cabot Lodge eagerly consulted Mahan, sharing his belief in the links between trade, navy, and colonies.

Mahan and the New Navy

Until its modernization, the navy was in a sorry state. Many of its wooden ships were rotting, and its shipyards had become infamous for political patronage and waste. But in 1883 Congress authorized construction of the first steel-hulled warships. American factories went to work to produce steam engines, high-velocity shells, powerful guns, and precision instruments. Andrew Carnegie, displaying none of his later pacifism and seeing "millions for us in armor," signed a highly profitable naval contract. Businesspeople seeking men-of-war escorts for their commercial vessels and scouts for new trade opportunities cheered the birth of the New Navy. Gradually, but especially in the 1880s, the Navy shifted from sail to steam and from wood to steel. Often named for states and cities to kindle patriotism and local support for naval expansion, New Navy ships like the *Maine*, the *Oregon*, and the *Boston* thrust the United States into naval prominence. When the United States faced crises in the 1890s, the New Navy warships were put to the test.

CRISES IN THE 1890s: HAWAII, VENEZUELA, AND CUBA

In the depression-plagued 1890s, crises in Hawaii, Venezuela, and Cuba gave expansionist Americans opportunities to act on their zealous arguments for what Senator Lodge called a "large policy." The Hawaiian Islands had long commanded American attention—commercial, missionary, naval, and diplomatic. Secretary Blaine warned other nations away from the archipelago, declaring them "essentially a part of the American system." That is what many Americans living in Hawaii believed, only to find obstacles placed in their way by Congress (the McKinley Tariff) and by native Hawaiians (Queen Liliuokalani). As discussed earlier in this chapter, in 1893 wealthy Americans overthrew the queen and immediately sought annexation to the United States.

Annexation of Hawaii

Against the fervent protests of Queen Liliuokalani and of Japan, whose nationals far outnumbered Americans in Hawaii's population, President Benjamin Harrison hurriedly sent a treaty of annexation to the Senate. But incoming President Grover Cleveland, who disapproved of forced annexation, withdrew it. He dispatched an investigator whose report confirmed a conspiracy by a self-interested white economic elite in league with the U.S. diplomat John Stevens and noted that a majority of Hawaiians opposed annexation. Down came the American flag.

When the Cleveland administration tried diplomacy to reverse this "abuse of power," the Dole government rejected U.S. attempts to restore the monarchy. Dole and his co-conspirators in Honolulu arrested the queen and confined her to her quarters for months. After gaining her freedom, she continued to speak out, making the Hawaiian nationalist case against annexation. But, in 1898, during the Spanish-American-Cuban-Filipino War, Hawaii gained renewed attention as a strategic and commercial waystation to Asia and the Philippines. Wide-eyed expansionists envisioned ships sailing from the eastern seaboard through a Central American canal to Hawaii and then on to China. On

July 7 President William McKinley successfully maneuvered annexation through Congress by means of a majority vote (the Newlands Resolution) rather than by a treaty, which would have required a two-thirds count. In part because of Hawaii's mixed racial composition, statehood did not come until 1959.

Venezuelan Crisis

The Venezuelan crisis of 1895 also saw the United States in an expansive mood. For decades Venezuela and Great Britain had squabbled over the border between Venezuela and British Guiana. The disputed territory contained rich gold deposits, and the mouth of the Orinoco River was the commercial gateway to northern South America. Venezuela asked for American help. President Cleveland decided that the "mean and hoggish" British had to be warned away. In July 1895, Secretary of State Richard Olney sent the British a brash message that Cleveland compared to a twenty-inch gun—in the naval parlance of the time, a huge weapon. Olney lectured the British that the Monroe Doctrine prohibited European intervention in the Western Hemisphere, whose states "are friends and allies, commercially and politically, of the United States." The spread-eagle words that followed were clearly directed at an international audience: "To-day the United States is practically sovereign on this continent, and its fiat is law upon the subjects to which it confines its interposition."

This bold statement of U.S. hegemony did not impress the British, who rejected American interference in their affairs. American jingoistic nationalists clamored for action. "Let the fight come if it must; I don't care whether our seacoast cities are bombarded or not; we would take Canada," snorted Theodore Roosevelt. But neither London nor Washington wanted war. The British, seeking international friends to help counter intensifying competition from Germany, quietly retreated from the crisis. In 1896 an Anglo-American arbitration board divided the disputed territory between Britain and Venezuela. The Venezuelans were barely consulted. Thus the United States displayed a trait common to imperialists: a disregard for the rights and sensibilities of small nations.

In 1895 another crisis rocked Latin America: the Cuban revolution against Spain. From 1868 to 1878 the Cubans had battled their mother country.

How do historians know

that wealthy white Americans in Hawaii plotted in 1893 to overthrow the native government of Queen Liliuokalani? Both the queen (on the right) and the new president after her ouster, Sanford B. Dole (shown with Anna, his wife), have written memoirs. Autobiographies must be read with skepticism, for their authors often embellish their performances and hide their blemishes. Memoirs are too frequently self-serving, presenting selective and faulty memories. Still, autobiographies can be valuable sources. Their accuracy can be tested and corroborated through comparison with other accounts and records, including private papers in archives. Memoirs also reveal the flavor of the times and the factors that influenced decisions. Sanford B. Dole (1844–1926) actually left several memoirs. After writing the unpublished "Reminiscences" for his family, he remembered events for the librarian of the Hawaiian Archives. Then, about 1914, he prepared articles for a Honolulu newspaper that never published them. In 1936, ten years after Dole's death, these articles were published as Memoirs of the Hawaiian Revolution. Dole detailed the revolution against the queen, whom he called corrupt and politically inept, and claimed that he was a reluctant participant in the scheme. He also downplayed contacts with U.S. officials who welcomed the plot. Queen Liliuokalani (1838–1917) also left her recollections—in letters, diaries, interviews, and a memoir, Hawaii's Story by Hawaii's Queen (1898). She chastised Dole as a conspirator, defended Hawaiian nationalism, and emphasized the interventionist role of the U.S. diplomat John L. Stevens. The Dole and Liliuokalani autobiographies differ markedly, but together with contemporary official documents, they have helped historians explain the great divide between foreigners and Hawaiians in the 1890s.
Photo: Hawaiian Historical Society.

When the Spanish General Valeriano Weyler arrived in Cuba in 1896 with fresh troops to quell the rebellion for independence, he soon determined that Spain could win only if it severed the nurturing ties between the people and the insurgents. So, under a harsh policy called reconcentration, he ordered rural folk to leave their lands and relocate in fortified camps controlled by Spanish authorities. Tens of thousands died. W. A. Rogers captured some of the tragedy in this painting he titled Starvation by Proclamation. *Chicago Historical Society.*

Economic and Cultural Ties with Cuba

Slavery was abolished but independence denied. While the Cuban economy suffered depression, Spanish rule continued to be repressive. Insurgents committed to "Cuba Libre" waited for another chance. José Martí, one of the heroes of Cuban history, collected money, arms, and men in the United States. This was but one of the many ways the lives of Americans and Cubans were linked. Their economies, for example, became integrated. U.S. investments of $50 million, mostly in sugar plantations, dominated the Caribbean island. More than 90 percent of Cuba's sugar was exported to the United States, and most island imports came from the United States. The Florida and Cuban economies also fused. Havana's famed cigar factories relocated to Key West and Tampa to get under protectionist U.S. tariff laws. Martí

worried about the close economic relationship, because "economic union means political union. The nation that buys, commands. The nation that sells, serves."

Because most of the 100,000 Cubans (10 percent of the population) who emigrated from the troubled island for economic and political reasons in the last half of the nineteenth century went to the United States, Cuban-American cultural ties also developed. Cubans of all classes settled in Baltimore, New York, Boston, and Philadelphia. Prominent Cubans on the island sent their children to U.S. schools. When Cuban expatriates returned home, many came in American clothes, spoke English, decorated their houses with American furniture, and played baseball, which became a popular sport on the island.

As in the case of Hawaii, a change in American tariff policy hastened the Cuban revolution and the island's further incorporation into "the American system." The Wilson-Gorman Tariff (1894) imposed a duty on Cuban sugar, which had been entering the United States duty-free under the McKinley Tariff (1890). The Cuban economy, highly dependent on exports, plunged into deep crisis.

Martí and the Cuban Revolution

From American soil, Martí launched a revolution in 1895 that became gruesome in its human and material costs. Rebels burned sugar-cane fields and razed mills, conducting an economic war and using guerrilla tactics to avoid head-on clashes with Spanish soldiers. "It is necessary to burn the hive to disperse the swarm," explained the insurgent leader Máximo Gomez. The Spanish retaliated under the command of the ruthless General Valeriano Weyler, who instituted a policy of "reconcentration": to separate the insurgents from their supporters among the Cuban people, an estimated 300,000 Cubans of all ages were herded into fortified towns and camps. Hunger, starvation, and disease led to mass deaths in the camps, where tens of thousands perished. Weyler's forces also ransacked the countryside. U.S. investments were jeopardized and Cuban-American trade dwindled. As reports of atrocity and destruction became headline news in the U.S. yellow press (see Chapter 20), Americans sympathized increasingly with the insurrectionists, whose ranks were swelling with each Weyler barbarity. In late 1897, a new government in Madrid modified reconcentration and promised some autonomy for Cuba.

Americans joined President William McKinley in wondering if the new reforms would subdue the rebellious island and restore peace. McKinley had come to office an imperialist. He wanted foreign bases for a larger navy; he recognized that surplus production had to be exported; and he echoed the belief that U.S. supremacy was essential in the Western Hemisphere. The 1896 Republican platform on which McKinley ran demanded an enlarged American empire—Hawaii, the Virgin Islands, and a Nicaraguan canal. As for Cuba, McKinley wanted independence achieved without a U.S. war if at all possible.

Events in early 1898 sabotaged the Spanish reforms and exhausted American patience. In January, when antireform pro-Spanish loyalists and army personnel rioted in Havana, many Americans lost faith in Madrid's ability to make its reforms work. After the riots, Washington officials ordered the battleship *Maine* to Havana harbor to demonstrate U.S. concern and protect American citizens. On February 15 an explosion under the enlisted men's quarters ripped the *Maine*, killing 266 of 354 American officers and crew.

Sinking of the Maine

A week earlier, Spain's image in the United States had been further tarnished when William Randolph Hearst's inflammatory *New York Journal* published a stolen private letter from the Spanish minister in Washington, Enrique Dupuy de Lôme. The de Lôme letter scorned McKinley as "weak and a bidder for the admiration of the crowd" and revealed Spain's determination to fight on in Cuba. An irritated McKinley soon asked for $50 million in defense funds, and Congress complied unanimously. The naval board created to investigate the sinking of the *Maine* then reported that a mine had caused the explosion. (A study by Admiral Hyman G. Rickover in 1976 challenged that conclusion, blaming the explosion on an internal accident.)

The impact of these events narrowed McKinley's diplomatic options. He decided to send Spain an ultimatum. In late March the United States insisted that Spain accept an armistice, end reconcentration altogether, and designate McKinley as arbiter. Implicit was the demand that Spain grant Cuba its independence. No Spanish government could have given up Cuba and remained in office, but Madrid nonetheless made concessions. It abolished reconcentration and accepted an armistice on the condition that the insurgents agree first.

Wanting more, McKinley began to draft a war message to Congress. After completing it, he received news that Spain had gone a step further and declared a unilateral armistice. The weary McKinley—who was taking medication in order to sleep—hesitated, but he would no longer tolerate chronic disorder just ninety miles off the American coast. As Senator Lodge explained, "We cannot go on indefinitely with this strain, this suspense, and this uncertainty, this tottering upon the verge of war."

On April 11, the president asked Congress for authorization to use force against Spain. McKinley listed the reasons why the United States had to end the turmoil: first, the "cause of humanity"; second, the protection of American life and property; third, the "very serious injury to the commerce, trade, and business of our people"; fourth, referring to the destruction of the *Maine*, the "constant menace to our peace." At the very end of his message the president mentioned Spain's recent concession but made little of it.

McKinley's War Message

After a week of debate, Congress on April 19 declared Cuba free and independent and directed the president to use force to remove Spanish authority from the island. The legislators also passed the Teller Amendment, which disclaimed any American intention to annex Cuba. McKinley beat back a congressional amendment to recognize the rebel government. Believing that the Cubans were not ready for self-government, he argued that they needed a period of American tutoring.

THE SPANISH-AMERICAN-CUBAN-FILIPINO WAR

Diplomacy had failed. By the time the Spanish concessions came forth, events had already pushed the antagonists to the brink. Washington might have been more patient, and Madrid might have faced the fact that its once-grand empire had disintegrated. Still, prospects for compromise appeared dim, because the advancing Cuban insurgents would settle for nothing less than full independence. That Spain could not easily accept. Nor did the United States welcome a wholly independent Cuban government that might attempt to reduce U.S. interests. In the Cuban crisis, as in the Venezuelan crisis, the United States claimed the right to set the rules for nations in the Western Hemisphere. The British had backed down in 1895, but the Spanish and Cubans stood firm in 1898.

The motives of Americans who favored war were mixed and complex. McKinley's April message expressed a humanitarian impulse to stop the bloodletting, a concern for commerce and property, and the psychological need to end the nightmarish anxiety once and for all. Republican politicians advised McKinley that their party would lose the upcoming congressional elections unless the Cuban question was solved. Many businesspeople, who had been hesitant before the crisis of early 1898, joined many farmers in the belief that ejecting Spain from Cuba would open new markets for surplus production—to which the depression of the 1890s had given urgency.

Motives for War

Inveterate imperialists saw war as an opportunity to fulfill expansionist dreams. Naval enthusiasts could prove the worth of the New Navy. Some religious leaders also saw merit in war. Social Gospel advocate Washington Gladden remarked that "in saving others we may save ourselves." Conservatives, alarmed by Populism and violent labor strikes, welcomed war as a national unifier. One senator commented that "internal discord" was disappearing in the "fervent heat of patriotism. . . . You will not see another [Eugene] Debs riot for many years." Sensationalism also figured in the march to war, with the yellow press in particular exaggerating stories of Spanish misdeeds. Assistant Secretary of the Navy Theodore Roosevelt and others too young to remember the bloody Civil War looked on war as adventure and used inflated rhetoric to trumpet the call to arms. Anglo-Saxon supremacists like politician Albert Beveridge shouted, "God's hour has struck." Overarching all explanations for this war were expansionism and imperialism, whose momentum had been moving the nation ever outward in the last half of the nineteenth century.

More than 263,000 regulars and volunteers served in the army and another 25,000 in the navy during the war. The typical volunteer was young (early twenties), white, unmarried, native-born, and working-class. Most never left the United States, and few found glory in what John Hay

U.S. Military Forces

called "a splendid little war." More than 5,400 Americans died, but only 379 of them in combat. The rest fell to malaria and yellow fever spread by mosquitoes. Food was bad and medical care was unsophisticated. Soldiers were issued heavy woolen uniforms in a tropical climate, and the stench of body odor was sickening. Still, Roosevelt could hardly contain himself. The Rough Riders, his motley unit of Ivy Leaguers and cowboys, in his words were "children of the dragon's blood, and if they had no outland foe to fight and no outlet for their vigorous and daring energy, there was always the chance of their fighting one another." The Rough Riders were undisciplined and not always effective warriors, but largely because of Roosevelt's self-serving publicity efforts they got a good press.

About 10,000 African-American troops, assigned to segregated regiments, found no relief from racism and Jim Crow. Whites in the South, where most troops were stationed, resented the appearance of status that the military uniform gave to blacks and used threats and violence to intimidate those who suggested that a war to free the Cubans might help to break down the color line at home. Race riots broke out; one in Tampa in June sent twenty-seven blacks and several whites to the hospital. In Macon, Georgia, African-American soldiers tore down a park sign reading "No Dogs and Niggers Allowed" and chopped down a persimmon tree famous as a lynching site. One black Iowan announced: "I will not go to war. I have no country to fight for. I have not been given my rights." But most volunteers, black and white, shared the attitude of a soldier who wrote to his parents back in Pennsylvania: "The boys are all in good health and spirits, and think they can whip the world."

To the surprise of most Americans, the first war news actually came from faraway Asia, from the Spanish colony of the Philippines. On May 1, 1898, Commodore George Dewey's New Navy ship the *Olympia*, leading an American squadron, steamed into Manila Bay and wrecked the outweighed and outgunned Spanish fleet. Dewey's sailors had to be handed volumes of the *Encyclopaedia Britannica* to acquaint them with this strange land, but officials in Washington knew better. Manila ranked with Pearl Harbor and Pago Pago as a

Dewey in the Philippines

On July 1, 1898, U.S. troops stormed Spanish positions on San Juan Hill near Santiago, Cuba. Both sides suffered heavy casualities. A Harper's *magazine correspondent reported a "ghastly" scene of hundreds killed and thousands wounded. The American painter William Glackens (1870–1938) put to canvas what he saw. Because Santiago surrendered on July 17, propelling the United States to victory in the war, and because the Rough Rider Theodore Roosevelt fought at San Juan Hill and later gave a self-congratulatory account, the human toll of the battle has often gone unnoticed.* Wadsworth Atheneum, Hartford, Gift of Henry Schnakenberg.

choice harbor and the Philippines sat conveniently on the way to China and its potentially huge markets. Histories used to credit (or blame) Assistant Secretary of the Navy Theodore Roosevelt for having ordered Dewey to Manila. The story goes that Roosevelt usurped authority in the navy secretary's absence and cabled Dewey to head for Manila the moment war with Spain broke out. Actually Roosevelt was following established policy; McKinley himself approved Roosevelt's instructions to Dewey.

The writer Sherwood Anderson observed that fighting Spain was "like robbing an old gypsy woman in a vacant lot at night after a fair." Facing rebels and Americans in both Cuba and the Philippines, Spanish resistance collapsed rapidly. American ships had early blockaded Cuban ports to prevent Spain from reinforcing and resupplying its army on the island. American troops saw their first ground-war action on June 22, the day several thousand of them landed near Santiago de Cuba and laid siege to the city. On July 3, the Spanish Caribbean squadron, trapped in Santiago harbor, made a desperate attempt to escape but was destroyed by American warships. Two weeks later the Spanish garrison at Santiago capitulated. Several days after that dramatic U.S. victory, American forces assaulted the Spanish Caribbean colony of Puerto Rico. Losing on all fronts, Madrid sued for peace. On August 12, Spain and the United States signed an armistice to end the Spanish-American-Cuban-Filipino War. "Let's see what we get by this," said Secretary of State William R. Day as he twirled the large globe in his office.

In Paris in December 1898, American and Spanish negotiators agreed on the peace terms: independence for Cuba; cession of the Philippines, Puerto Rico, and Guam (an island in the Pacific) to the United States; and American payment of $20 million to Spain for the territories. Filipino nationalists failed to persuade U.S. officials to grant their nation its freedom. The American empire now stretched deep into Asia; and the annexation of Wake Island (1898), Hawaii (1898), and Samoa (1899) gave American traders, missionaries, and naval promoters other steppingstones to China.

Treaty of Paris

THE TASTE OF EMPIRE: IMPERIALISTS VERSUS ANTI-IMPERIALISTS

During the war, the *Washington Post* detected "a new appetite, a yearning to show our strength. . . . The taste of empire is in the mouth of the people." But as the nation debated the Treaty of Paris, it became evident that many Americans found the taste bitter. Anti-imperialists like Mark Twain, William Jennings Bryan, William Graham Sumner, Jane Addams, Andrew Carnegie, and Senator George Hoar of Massachusetts argued vigorously against annexation of the Philippines. They were disturbed that a war to free Cuba had led to empire.

Some critics of U.S. policy appealed to principle, citing the Declaration of Independence and the Constitution: the conquest of people against their will violated the concept of self-determination. Other anti-imperialists argued that the United States could acquire markets without having to subjugate foreign peoples. The philosopher William James charged that the United States was throwing away its special place among nations; it was, he

Anti-Imperialist Arguments

warned, about to "puke up its heritage." To those who argued that the Filipinos were not yet fit for self-government, former Senator Carl Schurz retorted that Manila's city council was probably less corrupt than Chicago's. Others claimed that to maintain empire, the president would repeatedly have to dispatch troops overseas. Because he could do so as commander-in-chief, he would not have to seek congressional approval, thus subverting the constitutional checks-and-balances system.

Reform-minded critics of the treaty insisted that domestic issues—including race relations—deserved first priority on the national agenda. "Until our nation has settled the Negro and Indian problems," said Booker T. Washington, "I do not believe that we have a right to assume more social problems." An African-American politician from Massachusetts who had just protested a lynching in Georgia cried that the United States was exhibiting quite a spectacle to the world, "offering liberty to the Cubans with one hand, cramming liberty down the throats of the Filipinos with the other, but with both feet planted upon the neck of the negro." Meanwhile, some anti-imperialists, believing in a racial hierarchy with white Americans positioned at the top, warned that the absorption of people of color would undermine Anglo-Saxon purity and supremacy.

Samuel Gompers and other labor leaders worried about the possible undercutting of American labor by what Gompers called the "half-breeds and semi-barbaric people" of the new colonies. Might not the new colonials be imported as cheap contract labor to drive down the wages of American workers? Would not exploitation of the weak abroad become contagious and lead to further exploitation of the weak at home? Would not an overseas empire drain interest and resources from pressing domestic problems, delaying reform? Gompers charged, in fact, that imperialism was an attempt "to divert the attention of our people from the ills from which we suffer at home."

The anti-imperialists entered the debate with many handicaps and never launched an effective campaign. Although they organized the Anti-Imperialist League, they differed so profoundly on domestic issues that they found it difficult to speak with one voice on a foreign question. They also appeared inconsistent: Gompers favored the war but not the postwar annexations; Carnegie would accept colonies if they were not acquired by force;

Hoar voted for annexation of Hawaii but not of the Philippines. Finally, possession of the Philippines was an established fact, very hard to undo.

The imperialists answered their critics with appeals to patriotism, destiny, and commerce. They sketched a scenario of American greatness:

The Case for Empire

merchant ships plying the waters to boundless Asian markets; naval vessels cruising the Pacific to protect American interests; missionaries uplifting inferior peoples. It was America's duty, they insisted, quoting a then-popular Rudyard Kipling poem, to "take up the white man's burden." Furthermore, insurgents were beginning to resist U.S. rule, and it was cowardly to pull out under fire. Germany and Japan, two powerful international competitors, were snooping around the Philippine Islands, apparently ready to seize them if the United States did not. National honor dictated that Americans keep what they had shed blood to take. Senator Beveridge asked: "Shall [history] say that, called by events to captain and command the proudest, ablest, purest race of history in history's noblest work, we declined that great commission?"

In February 1899, the Senate passed the Treaty of Paris by a 57-to-27 vote. Except for Hoar and Senator Eugene Hale of Maine, Republicans voted with their president; 22 Democrats voted no, but 10 voted for the treaty. The latter group was probably influenced by Bryan, who had served as a colonel during the war; he urged a favorable vote in order to end the war and then push for Philippine independence. An amendment promising independence as soon as the Filipinos formed a stable government was defeated only by the tie-breaking ballot of the vice president.

The anti-imperialists lost, but Bryan carried the debate into the election of 1900 as the Democratic standard-bearer against McKinley. In that unsuccessful campaign Bryan charged that imperialism benefited only American economic interests. To repudiate the principle of self-government in the Philippines, he said, would weaken it at home. "It is not necessary to own people to trade with them," Bryan asserted. But McKinley would not apologize for American imperialism. "It is no longer a question of expansion with us," he told a midwestern audience. "If there is any question at all it is a question of contraction; and who is going to contract?"

26. Spain's "Sense of Justice"
C. G. Bush, *New York World*, 1898.

This magazine reflected the jingoistic warrior mentality of many Americans in 1898. The war with Spain, fought in Cuba and the Philippines, gave the New Navy ships shown here a chance to display the nation's military might and gave Americans a chance to cheer the result. New York World, 1898.

ASIAN ENCOUNTERS: OPEN DOOR IN CHINA, PHILIPPINE INSURRECTION, AND JAPAN

In 1895, the same year as the Venezuelan crisis and the advent of the Cuban revolution, Japan claimed victory over China in a war of only eight months. Outsiders had been pecking away at China—known as "the Sick Man of Asia"—since the 1840s, but the Japanese onslaught intensified the international scramble. The Germans carved out a sphere of interest in Shandong; the Russians moved into Manchuria and the Liaodong peninsula; the French and the British drove in stakes, too. Japan controlled Formosa and Korea as well as parts of China proper (see map). Within their spheres, the imperial powers built fortified bases and claimed exclusive economic privileges. American religious leaders, whose missions in China had doubled to one thousand in the 1890s, and business interests, which saw trade opportunities threatened, petitioned Washington to halt the dismemberment before they were closed out. What good were the Philippines as steppingstones to China if there was nothing left to step into?

Secretary Hay knew that the United States could not force the imperial powers out of China, but he was determined to protect American commerce. In September 1899 Hay sent the imperial nations a note asking them to respect the principle of equal trade opportunity—an Open Door—for all nations in their spheres. The recipients sent evasive replies, privately complaining that the United States was seeking for free the trade rights they had gained at considerable military and administrative cost. The next year, a Chinese secret society called the Boxers laid siege to the foreign legations in Beijing (Peking). The United States joined the imperial powers in sending troops to lift the siege and sent a second Open Door note in July that instructed other nations to preserve China's territorial integrity and to honor "equal and impartial trade." Hay's protests notwithstanding, China continued for years to be fertile soil for foreign exploitation, especially for the Japanese.

Open Door Policy

Though Hay's foray into Asian politics settled little, the Open Door policy became established as a cornerstone of U.S. diplomacy. Actually, the "open door" had long been an American principle, for as a trading nation the United States opposed barriers to international commerce and demanded equal access to markets. After 1900, however, when the United States began to emerge as the premier world trader, the Open Door policy became an instrument first to pry open markets and then to dominate them, not just in China but throughout the world. But the Open Door was not just a policy. It was also an ideology with several tenets: first, that America's domestic well-being required exports; second, that foreign trade would suffer interruption unless the United States intervened abroad to implant American principles and keep foreign markets open; and, third, that the closing of any area to American products, citizens,

or ideas threatened the survival of the United States itself.

In the Philippines, meanwhile, the United States soon antagonized its new "wards," as McKinley labeled them. Emilio Aguinaldo, the Philippine nationalist leader who had been battling the Spanish for years, believed that U.S. officials had promised independence for his country. But after the victory, Aguinaldo was ordered out of Manila and isolated from decisions affecting his nation. American racial slurs and paternalistic attitudes infuriated nationalistic Filipinos, and they felt betrayed by the Treaty of Paris. Once again Mr. Dooley caught the imperious U.S. mood: "In ivry city in this unfair land we will erect schoolhouses an' packin' houses an' houses of correction; and we'll larn ye our language, because 'tis aisier to larn ye ours than to larn oursilves yours. An' we'll give ye clothes, if ye pay f'r them; an' if ye don't, ye can go without."

Philippine Insurrection

In January 1899, an uncowed Aguinaldo proclaimed an independent Philippine Republic and took up arms. Before the Philippine Insurrection was suppressed in 1902, more than two hundred thousand Filipinos and five thousand Americans lay dead. U.S. troops burned villages, tortured captives, and introduced a variant of the reconcentration policy. In the province of Batangas south of Manila, for example, U.S. troops forced residents to live in designated zones in an effort to separate the insurgents from local supporters. Disaster followed. Poor sanitation, starvation, and malaria and cholera killed several thousand people. Outside the secure areas, Americans destroyed food supplies to starve out the rebels. At least one-quarter of the population of Batangas died or fled.

Anti-imperialists cried foul, but President Roosevelt remarked that there had not been "a single incident in the Philippines as bad as the massacre at Wounded Knee." His reference to the massacre of Native Americans in South Dakota (see Chapter 17) revealed an apt comparison. Americans stationed at the Philippine front often spoke of the "savage" Filipino insurgents who might "injun up" on them. One U.S. soldier declared that the Philippines "won't be pacified until the niggers [Filipinos] are killed off like the Indians." Twenty-six of the thirty U.S. Army generals ordered to the Philippines from 1898 through 1902 had had prior experience battling Native Americans.

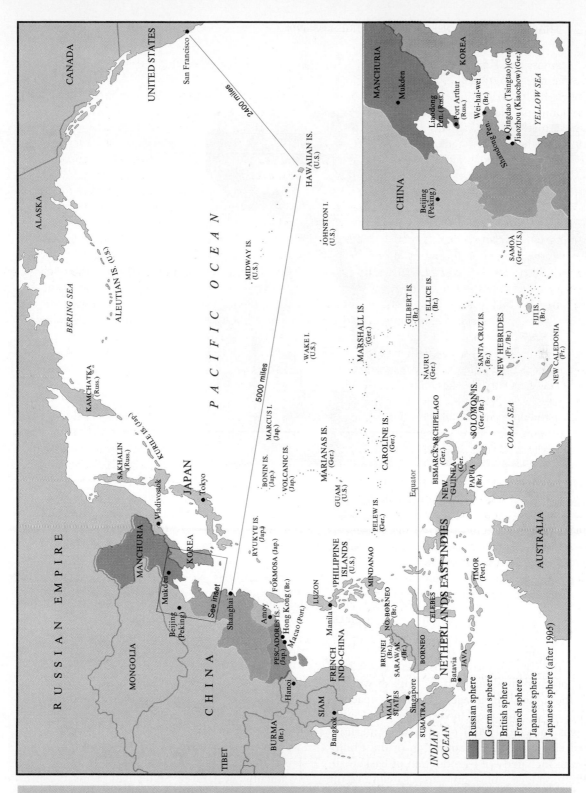

Imperialism in Asia: Turn of the Century *China and the Pacific region had become imperialist hunting grounds by the turn of the century. The European powers and Japan controlled more areas than the United States did, but it participated in the race for influence by annexing the Philippines, Wake, Guam, and Hawaii, announcing the Open Door policy, and expanding trade in the area. As the "spheres" in China demonstrate, that besieged nation succumbed to imperial outsiders despite the Open Door policy.*

Map labels:

CANADA
UNITED STATES
San Francisco
2400 miles
ALASKA
BERING SEA
KAMCHATKA (Russ.)
ALEUTIAN IS. (U.S.)
PACIFIC OCEAN
HAWAIIAN IS. (U.S.)
JOHNSTON I. (U.S.)
MIDWAY IS. (U.S.)
5000 miles
SAKHALIN (Russ.)
KURILE IS. (Jap.)
Vladivostok
JAPAN
Tokyo
RUSSIAN EMPIRE
MONGOLIA
MANCHURIA
Mukden
Beijing (Peking)
KOREA
See inset
Shanghai
CHINA
Amoy
FORMOSA (Jap.)
Hong Kong (Br.)
Macao (Port.)
PESCADORES IS. (Jap.)
RYUKYU IS. (Jap.)
BONIN IS. (Jap.)
VOLCANIC IS. (Jap.)
MARCUS I. (Jap.)
WAKE I. (U.S.)
MARSHALL IS. (Ger.)
GILBERT IS. (Br.)
ELLICE IS. (Br.)
MARIANAS IS. (Ger.)
GUAM (U.S.)
CAROLINE IS. (Ger.)
PELEW IS. (Ger.)
NAURU (Ger.)
SANTA CRUZ IS. (Br.)
NEW HEBRIDES (Fr./Br.)
FIJI IS. (Br.)
NEW CALEDONIA (Fr.)
SAMOA (Ger./U.S.)
Equator
BISMARCK ARCHIPELAGO (Ger.)
SOLOMON IS. (Ger./Br.)
NEW GUINEA (Ger.)
PAPUA (Br.)
CORAL SEA
AUSTRALIA
PHILIPPINE ISLANDS (U.S.)
LUZON
Manila
MINDANAO
CELEBES
NO. BORNEO (Br.)
BRUNEI (Br.)
SARAWAK (Br.)
BORNEO
NETHERLANDS EAST INDIES
TIMOR (Port.)
JAVA
Batavia
SUMATRA
FRENCH INDO-CHINA
Hanoi
SIAM
Bangkok
BURMA (Br.)
TIBET
MALAY STATES
Singapore
INDIAN OCEAN

Legend:
Russian sphere
German sphere
British sphere
French sphere
Japanese sphere
Japanese sphere (after 1905)

Inset:
MANCHURIA
Mukden
Liaodong Pen. (Russ.)
Port Arthur (Russ.)
KOREA
Wei-hai-wei (Br.)
Qingdao (Tsingtao) (Ger.)
Jiaozhou (Kiaochow) (Ger.)
Shandong Pen.
YELLOW SEA
CHINA
Beijing (Peking)

This 1900 photograph was titled "Our young Filipinos in holiday attire at the Fourth of July celebration, Manila, P.I." The quizzical looks on the faces of these children suggest that they may not have fully understood life as colonials in the U.S. empire. But their parents certainly did. After taking the Philippines from Spain, the United States blocked Philippine independence, went to war against Filipino nationalists, and imposed American rule on the islands. Library of Congress.

After capturing Aquinaldo in 1901, the United States soon imposed its regime on the Philippines. A policy of "bread and guns" introduced public works programs. The architect Daniel Burnham, leader of the City Beautiful movement (see Chapter 19), planned modern Manila. English was declared the official language, American teachers were imported, and the University of the Philippines was founded (1908) to train an American-oriented elite. The Americanization of the Philippines even included the introduction of basketball. The Philippine economy grew as a satellite of the U.S. economy, and a sedition act silenced critics of U.S. authority by sending them to prison. But fiercely independent Muslim Filipinos, the vast majority of the inhabitants of Moro Province, refused to knuckle under. Comparing the "uncivilized" Moros to American Indians, the U.S. military ordered them to submit or be exterminated. The Moros were finally defeated in 1906; six hundred of them, including many women and children, were slaughtered at the Battle of Bud Dajo. "Work of this kind," General Leonard Wood wrote Roosevelt, "has its disagreeable side." In 1916 the Jones Act promised independence to the Philippines, but it did not become a reality until thirty years later.

As the United States disciplined the Filipinos, Japan was becoming the dominant power in Asia. Gradually the United States had to make concessions to Japan in efforts to protect the vulnerable Philippines (Roosevelt soon regarded the islands as America's Achilles heel) and to salvage the Open Door policy. Japan had carved

Japanese-American Rivalry

out interests in China long before it smashed the Russians in the Russo-Japanese War (1904–1905). Roosevelt mediated the crisis at the Portsmouth Conference in New Hampshire in the hope that the peace settlement would preserve a balance of power in Asia. Although the president won the Nobel Peace Prize for his efforts, peace did not come to Asia, and U.S. interests remained jeopardized. In 1905, in the Taft-Katsura Agreement, the United States conceded Japanese hegemony over Korea in return for Japan's pledge not to undermine the American position in the Philippines. Two years later, in the Root-Takahira Agreement, the United States recognized Japan's interests in Manchuria, whereas Japan again pledged the security of American possessions in the Pacific and promised to honor the Open Door in China. Roo-

sevelt also built up U.S. naval power to deter the Japanese; in 1907 he sent the "Great White Fleet" on a world tour. Duly impressed, the Japanese began to build a bigger navy of their own.

President William Howard Taft thought he might counter Japanese advances in Asia through *dollar diplomacy*—the use of private funds to serve American diplomatic goals and at the same time to garner profits for American financiers. In this case, Taft induced American bankers to join an international consortium to build a Chinese railway. Taft's venture seemed only to embolden Japan to solidify and extend its holdings in China, whose nationalistic revolution of 1911 proved incapable of stopping relentless Japanese aggression.

Japanese-American relations also became tense over the treatment of Japanese citizens in the

This cloth bandanna celebrated President Theodore Roosevelt's receipt of the Nobel Peace Prize in 1906 for helping to negotiate an end to the Russo-Japanese War. A bequest of the Swedish inventor-industrialist Alfred Bernhard Nobel created the prize, which was first awarded in 1901. The irony of giving a peace prize to a man who often seemed eager for war was well illustrated at the top of this work, when Roosevelt the Rough Rider charges on horseback into battle in the Spanish-American-Cuban-Filipino War. Museum of American Political Life, University of Hartford.

Latin America, then set out to reclaim their nation's sovereignty by ending their economic dependency on the United States (see Chapter 26).

In its relations with Europe, the United States reaffirmed the Monroe Doctrine and demonstrated the power to enforce it. Another guiding principle

Relations with Europe

of U.S.-European relations was that the United States should stand outside continental embroilments. The balance of power in Europe was precarious, and seldom did an American president involve the United States directly. At Germany's request, Roosevelt helped to settle a Franco-German clash over Morocco by mediating a settlement at Algeciras, Spain (1906). But the president drew American criticism for entangling the United States in a European problem. Americans endorsed the ultimately futile Hague peace conferences (1899 and 1907) and negotiated various arbitration treaties, but on the whole they stayed outside Europe's embittered arena.

A third principle of American-European relations was that America's best interests lay in cooperation with Great Britain. One outcome of the

Anglo-American Rapprochement

German-British rivalry was London's quest for American friendship. The makings of rapprochement had been developing since the late nineteenth century as Britain grew more wary of Germany and recognized the increasing power of the United States. Americans warmed to Britain when the British supported the United States in the war of 1898, stepped aside in the Hay-Pauncefote Treaty (1901) to permit construction of a U.S. canal, virtually endorsed the Roosevelt Corollary, and withdrew their warships from the Caribbean. The British overtures were to pay off in 1917 when the United States threw its weapons and soldiers into the First World War on the British side.

In the years from the Civil War to the First World War, expansionism and imperialism had elevated the United States to the status of a major world power. The victory over Spain at the end of the century was but the most dramatic moment in the long process. By 1914 Americans held extensive economic, strategic, and political interests in a world made smaller by modern technology. The belief that the nation needed foreign markets to absorb surplus production so that the domestic economy could thrive joined a missionary zeal to reform other societies. Notions of racial supremacy and emotional appeals to national greatness also fed the appetite for foreign adventure and commitments. American entrepreneurs and inventors produced the instruments of expansion and empire: underwater cables, steel warships, and the Panama Canal. The American products and dollars that penetrated markets across the globe and the rifles toted by American soldiers into Philippine jungles and into the streets of Latin American capitals—all facilitated the imperial odyssey.

The outward reach of U.S. foreign policy from Secretary of State Seward to President Wilson sparked opposition from domestic critics, other imperial nations, and foreign nationalists, but the trend was never seriously diverted. In the future, Americans who sincerely believed that they had been helping foreign peoples to enjoy a better life would come to feel betrayed when their foreign clients questioned American tutelage or openly rebelled. Meanwhile, August 1914 presented a much different problem: the outbreak of war in Europe.

SUGGESTIONS FOR FURTHER READING

General

Robert L. Beisner, *From the Old Diplomacy to the New, 1865–1900*, 2nd ed. (1986); Charles S. Campbell, *The Transformation of American Foreign Relations, 1865–1900* (1976); Richard D. Challener, *Admirals, Generals, and American Foreign Policy, 1889–1914* (1973); Willard B. Gatewood, Jr., *Black Americans and the White Man's Burden* (1975); Daniel R. Headrick, *The Invisible Weapon: International Communications and International Politics, 1851–1945* (1991); David Healy, *United States Expansionism* (1970); Patricia Hill, *The World Their Household* (1985) (on women missionaries); Ronald J. Jensen, *The Alaska Purchase and Russian-American Relations* (1975); George F. Kennan, *American Diplomacy, 1900–1950* (1951); Paul Kennedy, *The Rise and Fall of the Great Powers* (1987); Walter LaFeber, *The New Empire* (1963); Ernest R. May, *American Imperialism* (1968); Thomas G. Paterson and Stephen G. Rabe, eds., *Imperial Surge* (1992); Milton Plesur, *America's Outward Thrust* (1971); David M. Pletcher, *The Awkward Years* (1962); Emily Rosenberg, *Spreading the American Dream* (1982); Richard E. Welch, *The Presidencies of Grover Cleveland* (1988); Rubin F. Weston, *Racism in United States Imperialism* (1972); William Appleman Williams, *The Tragedy of American Diplomacy*, new ed. (1988).

Theodore Roosevelt and Other Expansionists

Howard K. Beale, *Theodore Roosevelt and the Rise of America to World Power* (1956); John M. Blum, *The Republican Roosevelt* (1954); John M. Cooper, Jr., *The Warrior and the Priest: Woodrow*

Wilson and Theodore Roosevelt (1983); Louis L. Gould, *The Presidency of Theodore Roosevelt* (1991); Lewis L. Gould, *The Presidency of William McKinley* (1981); William H. Harbaugh, *The Life and Times of Theodore Roosevelt* (1975); Frederick Marks III, *Velvet on Iron* (1979) (on Roosevelt); Frank Merli and Theodore A. Wilson, eds., *Makers of American Diplomacy* (1974); Edmund Morris, *The Rise of Theodore Roosevelt* (1979); Ernest N. Paolino, *The Foundations of the American Empire* (1973) (on Seward); William C. Widenor, *Henry Cabot Lodge and the Search for an American Foreign Policy* (1980).

Economic Expansion

See the works by Beisner, Campbell, and LaFeber cited above; William H. Becker, *The Dynamics of Business-Government Relations* (1982); Robert B. Davies, *Peacefully Working to Conquer the World: Singer Sewing Machines in Foreign Markets, 1854–1920* (1976); Tom Terrill, *The Tariff, Politics, and American Foreign Policy, 1874–1901* (1973); Mira Wilkins, *The Emergence of the Multinational Enterprise* (1970); William Appleman Williams, *The Roots of the Modern American Empire* (1969).

The U.S. Navy

Benjamin F. Cooling, *Gray Steel and Blue Water Navy* (1979); Frederick C. Drake, *The Empire of the Seas* (1984) (on Shufeldt); Kenneth J. Hagan, ed., *In Peace and War*, 2nd ed. (1984); Kenneth J. Hagan, *American Gunboat Diplomacy and the Old Navy, 1877–1889* (1973); Walter R. Herrick, *The American Naval Revolution* (1966); Peter Karsten, *The Naval Aristocracy* (1972); Robert Seager II, *Alfred Thayer Mahan* (1977); Ronald Spector, *Admiral of the New Empire* (1974) (on Dewey).

The Spanish-American-Cuban-Filipino War

Graham A. Cosmas, *An Army for Empire* (1971); Richard Hofstadter, "Cuba, the Philippines, and Manifest Destiny," in *The Paranoid Style in American Politics*, ed. Richard Hofstadter (1967); Gerald F. Linderman, *The Mirror of War: American Society and the Spanish-American War* (1974); Ernest R. May, *Imperial Democracy* (1961); Joyce Milton, *The Yellow Kids* (1989); John Offner, *An Unwanted War: The Diplomacy of the United States and Spain over Cuba, 1895–1898* (1992); Julius Pratt, *Expansionists of 1898* (1936); David F. Trask, *The War with Spain in 1898* (1981).

Anti-Imperialism and the Peace Movement

Robert L. Beisner, *Twelve Against Empire* (1968); Kendrick A. Clements, *William Jennings Bryan* (1983); Merle E. Curti, *Peace or War* (1936); Charles DeBenedetti, *Peace Reform in American History* (1980); C. Roland Marchand, *The American Peace Movement and Social Reform, 1898–1918* (1973); Thomas J. Osborne, *"Empire Can Wait": American Opposition to Hawaiian Annexation, 1893–1898* (1981); David S. Patterson, *Toward a Warless World* (1976); E. Berkeley Tompkins, *Anti-Imperialism in the United States* (1970).

Cuba, Mexico, Panama, and Latin America

Samuel F. Bemis, *The Latin American Policy of the United States* (1943); Arturo M. Carrión, *Puerto Rico* (1983); Richard H. Collin, *Theodore Roosevelt's Caribbean* (1990); David Healy, *Drive to Hegemony: The United States in the Caribbean, 1898–1917* (1989); Walter LaFeber, *The Panama Canal*, rev. ed. (1990); Walter LaFeber, *Inevitable Revolutions*, 2nd ed. rev. (1993) (on Central America); Lester D. Langley, *Struggle for the American Mediterranean* (1980); Lester D. Langley, *The United States and the Caribbean, 1900–1970* (1980); David McCullough, *The Path Between the Seas* (1977) (on the Panama Canal); Allan R. Millett, *The Politics of Intervention* (1968) (on Cuba); Louis A. Pérez, Jr., *Cuba and the United States* (1990); Louis A. Pérez, Jr., *Cuba* (1988); Louis A. Pérez, Jr., *Cuba Under the Platt Amendment, 1902–1934* (1986); Dexter Perkins, *The Monroe Doctrine, 1867–1907* (1937); Brenda G. Plummer, *Haiti and the Great Powers, 1902–1915* (1988); Ramón E. Ruíz, *The People of Sonora and Yankee Capitalists* (1988); Karl M. Schmitt, *Mexico and the United States, 1821–1973* (1974); Josefina Vázquez and Lorenzo Meyer, *The United States and Mexico* (1985).

Hawaii, China, Japan, and the Pacific

Helena G. Allen, *Sanford Ballard Dole* (1988); Helena G. Allen, *The Betrayal of Liliuokalani* (1982); Charles S. Campbell, *Special Business Interests and the Open Door Policy* (1951); Warren I. Cohen, *America's Response to China*, 3rd ed. (1989); John K. Fairbank, *The United States and China*, 4th ed. (1983); Michael Hunt, *The Making of a Special Relationship* (1983) (on China); Jane Hunter, *The Gospel of Gentility: American Women Missionaries in Turn-of-the-Century China* (1984); Akira Iriye, *Across the Pacific* (1967); Jerry Israel, *Progressivism and the Open Door* (1971); Paul M. Kennedy, *The Samoan Tangle* (1974); Ralph S. Kuykendall, *The Hawaiian Kingdom* (1967); Robert McClellan, *The Heathen Chinee* (1971); Thomas J. McCormick, *China Market* (1967); Charles E. Neu, *The Troubled Encounter* (1975) (on Japan); Craig Storti, *Incident at Bitter Creek: The Story of the Rock Springs Chinese Massacre* (1991); Merze Tate, *Hawaii: Reciprocity or Annexation* (1968); Merze Tate, *The United States and the Hawaiian Kingdom* (1965); Marilyn Blatt Young, *The Rhetoric of Empire* (1968).

The Philippines: Insurrection and Colony

John M. Gates, *Schoolbooks and Krags: The United States Army in the Philippines, 1898–1902* (1973); Stanley Karnow, *In Our Image: America's Empire in the Philippines* (1989); Brian M. Linn, *The U.S. Army and Counterinsurgency in the Philippine War, 1898–1902* (1989); Glenn A. May, *Battle for Batangas* (1991); Glenn A. May, *Social Engineering in the Philippines* (1980); Stuart C. Miller, *"Benevolent Assimilation"* (1982); Daniel B. Schirmer, *Republic or Empire?* (1972); Peter Stanley, *A Nation in the Making* (1974); Richard E. Welch, *Response to Imperialism: American Resistance to the Philippine War* (1972); Walter L. Williams, "United States Indian Policy and the Debate over Philippine Annexation," *Journal of American History* 66 (1980): 810–831.

Great Britain and Canada

Kenneth Bourne, *Britain and the Balance of Power in North America, 1815–1908* (1967); Robert C. Brown, *Canada's National Policy, 1883–1900* (1964); Alexander E. Campbell, *Great Britain and the United States, 1895–1903* (1960); Charles S. Campbell, *From Revolution to Rapprochement: The United States and Great Britain, 1783–1900* (1974); Adrian Cook, *The Alabama Claims* (1975); Bradford Perkins, *The Great Rapprochement* (1968).

23

Americans at War, 1914–1920

T HE MEDICAL CASE FILES listed him as "A.P." An eighteen-year-old Marine Corps private who had volunteered to fight in the First World War, he thrived on the military life. Like other young American soldiers, A.P. was ordered to the Western front in France. During early 1918 the Germans relentlessly bombarded his position at Château-Thierry, where screeching shells and deafening explosions punished the fresh American troops.

In June, A.P.'s company trudged closer to the forward battle lines, past the bodies of French soldiers dismembered by the pounding of the big guns. His commanding officer detailed him to bury the mangled corpses. For several nights thereafter A.P. could not sleep. Artillery fire now frightened him. During a bombardment on June 14, he began to tremble uncontrollably. A.P. was evacuated to a hospital, where noise easily startled him and horrifying dreams haunted him.

Doctors who treated military casualties were seeing tens of thousands of such patients, whom they diagnosed as suffering from a mental illness they called war neurosis or war psychosis. Almost everyone else called it shell shock. The symptoms became all too familiar: a fixed empty stare, violent tremors, paralyzed limbs, listlessness,

jabbering, screaming, and terrifying dreams. The illness could strike anyone; even those soldiers who appeared most virile and courageous cracked after days of noisy shelling. "There was a limit to human endurance," one lieutenant explained.

Their nervous systems shattered by explosives, some one hundred thousand victims went to special military hospitals staffed by psychiatrists. A regimen of rest, military discipline, constant reminders about patriotic duty, recreation, exercise, and counseling restored many shell-shock victims to health. Although some returned to the front lines, others suffered persistent anxiety and were assigned to noncombat duties. The very ill were sent home to the United States. According to follow-up studies, even cured shell-shock victims suffered lingering mental problems—flashbacks, nightmares, and a persistent disorientation that made it difficult for them to make decisions or organize their lives. Thousands of the most severely afflicted remained in veterans' hospitals.

For the generation that lived through the First World War, the glory of saving civilization from the Germans dissolved into the tragedy of human hurt. For many Americans

Harvey Dunn's painting of casualties in the First World War.

who had heeded President Woodrow Wilson's call to "make the world safe for democracy," the war's results seemed more a national disaster than an ennobling experiment. Like the British poet Robert Graves, many came to see the war as "the Sausage Machine, because it was fed with live men, churned out corpses, and remained firmly screwed in place."

Still, many Progressive era professionals and reformers found rewards in the wrenching national emergency. For some the war presented an opportunity. The psychiatrists who treated the shell-shock victims, for example, wanted to apply their mental health expertise to help win the war. They also hoped to use their wartime medical experience later, at home, to improve care for the mentally ill. For them, the cataclysm of foreign crisis and the opportunity for domestic social betterment went hand in hand.

The outbreak of the Great War in Europe in 1914 at first stunned Americans. For years they had witnessed and participated in the international competition for colonies, markets, and weapons supremacy. But full-scale war seemed unthinkable in the modern age of progress. "Civilization is all gone, and barbarism come," moaned one social reformer. The French and Germans were using "huge death engines to mow down men and cities," observed *Harper's Weekly.* "We go about in a daze, hoping to awake from the most horrid of nightmares." Articulated by well-organized groups, peace sentiment in the United States strengthened with each grisly report from the European battlefield.

For almost three years President Wilson kept America out of the war. During this time, he sought to protect U.S. interests as a neutral trader and to improve the nation's military posture should the United States ever decide to join the fight. He lectured the belligerents to rediscover their humanity and to respect international law. But American neutrality, lives, and property fell victim to British and German naval warfare. In early 1917, when the president finally asked Congress for a declaration of war, he did so with his characteristic crusading zeal. America entered the battle not just to win the war but to reform the postwar world.

Even after more than a decade of progressive reform, Americans remained a heterogeneous and fractious people at the start of the Great War. Headlines still trumpeted labor-capital confrontations like the Ludlow Massacre in Colorado, in which two women and eleven children were killed when state militia attempted to break a miners' strike. Racial antagonisms were evident in Wilson's decision to segregate federal buildings in Washington and in continued lynchings of African-Americans (fifty-one in 1914). Nativists protested the pace of immigration; 1.2 million immigrants entered the United States in 1914 alone. Ethnic groups eyed one another suspiciously. Many women argued for equality among the sexes and for female suffrage, while many men wanted to sustain the tradition of the subordination of women.

The war experience accentuated and intensified the nation's social divisiveness. Many whites did not like the northward migration of southern blacks to work in defense plants, and race riots revealed once again the depth of racial prejudice. German-Americans were denounced as traitors, and war hawks harassed pacifists. The federal government itself, eager to stimulate patriotism, trampled on civil liberties to silence critics. And, as communism implanted itself in Russia, a postwar Red Scare in the United States further undermined America's reputation as a free and democratic society. In the aftermath of war, groups that sought to consolidate gains made during the war vied with those who sought to restore the prewar status quo.

America's participation in the war wrought massive changes and accelerated trends already in motion. Wars are emergencies, and during such times normal ways of doing things surrender to the extraordinary and exaggerated. The U.S. government, more than ever before, became a manager—of people, prices, production, and minds. A compulsory draft pulled men into the armed services. The presidency assumed greater powers. Unprecedented centralization and integration of the economy, increased standardization of products, and unusual cooperation between government and business also characterized the times. Although reformers did continue to devote themselves to such issues as prohibition and women's suffrage, the war experience also helped splinter and thus undermine the progressive movement. As Jane Addams sadly remarked, "the spirit of fighting burns away all those impulses . . . which foster the will to justice."

The United States emerged from the war a major power in a disrupted and economically hobbled world. Yet Americans who had marched to battle as if on a crusade grew disillusioned. They recoiled from the spectacle of the victors squab-

• *Important Events* •

1914 During Mexican Revolution U.S. troops invade Mexico

First World War begins in Europe

1915 Germany declares war zone around British Isles

Wilson denounces German U-boat sinking of *Lusitania*

Secretary of State Bryan resigns in protest against Wilson's policies

1916 Gore-McLemore resolution barring Americans from travel on belligerent ships is defeated

U.S. troops invade Mexico again

After *Sussex* is torpedoed, Germany pledges not to attack merchant ships without warning

National Defense Act provides for larger military

Wilson re-elected on platform of peace, progressivism, and preparedness

1917 Germany declares unrestricted submarine warfare

Zimmermann telegram tries to stir up Mexican-U.S. troubles

Russian Revolution ousts the czar

U.S. enters First World War

Selective Service Act sets up compulsory military service (the draft)

Espionage Act limits First Amendment rights

Whites attack African-Americans in race riot in East St. Louis, Illinois

War Industries Board created to manage the economy

War Revenue Act raises taxes to avoid war profiteering

Fuel crisis in severe winter

1918 Wilson announces Fourteen Points to guide future international relations

Sedition Act further limits free speech

Eugene Debs imprisoned for speaking against the war

U.S. troops at Château-Thierry help turn back German offensive

U.S. troops intervene in Russian civil war

Deadly flu epidemic sweeps world and the United States

Republicans hand Wilson setback by winning congressional elections

Armistice ends the First World War

1919 Paris Peace Conference punishes Germany and plans new world order

May Day bombings contribute to fears and stimulate Red Scare

American Legion organizes for veterans' benefits and antiradicalism

Chicago race riot one of many in the "Red Summer"

Workers strike against the steel industry

Communist Party of the United States of America founded

Wilson suffers stroke after speaking tour

Senate rejects Treaty of Paris and U.S. membership in League of Nations

Schenck v. *U.S.* upholds Espionage Act

1920 Palmer Raids of the Red Scare round up suspected radicals

Nineteenth Amendment ratified, giving women the vote

---

bling over the spoils, and they chided Wilson for failing to deliver the "peace without victory" he promised. As in the 1790s, the 1840s, and the 1890s, Americans engaged in a searching national debate about the fundamental direction of their foreign policy. The president appealed for American membership in the League of Nations, which he touted as a vehicle for reforming world politics. But the Senate killed his diplomatic offspring, fearful that the League might entangle Americans once again in Europe's problems, impede the growth of the U.S. empire, and compromise the country's traditional unilateralism. On many fronts, then, Americans during the era of the First World War were at war with themselves.

STRUGGLING WITH NEUTRALITY

The war that erupted in August 1914 grew from years of European competition over trade, colonies, allies, and armaments. Two powerful alliance systems had formed: the Triple Alliance of Germany, Austria-Hungary, and Italy, and the Triple

nal and bank. Americans, however, faced a dilemma: cutting their economic ties with Britain would constitute an unneutral act in favor of Germany. Under international law, Britain—which controlled the seas—could buy both contraband (war-related goods) and noncontraband from neutrals. It was Germany's responsibility, not America's, to stop such trade in ways that international law prescribed—that is, by an effective blockade of the enemy's territory, by the seizure of contraband from neutral (American) ships, or by the confiscation of any goods from belligerent (British) ships. Germans, of course, judged the huge U.S. trade with the Allies an act of unneutrality that had to be stopped.

The pro-Allied sympathies of Woodrow Wilson and his advisers were the third reason why neutrality did not work. On August 4, 1914, as

Pro-Allied Sympathies
Wilson kept vigil at his dying wife's bedside, he drafted a message offering U.S. mediation to end the war the European nations had just begun.

Two days later Ellen Axson Wilson died from kidney disease. Seldom have such painful personal and official burdens fallen on a president at the same time. He soon received a note from another man who had lost his wife, British Foreign Secretary Edward Grey. Moved by the thoughtful message, Wilson replied "that we are bound together by common principle and purpose." The president was talking not only about their personal tragedies but also about their shared conviction that a German victory would destroy free enterprise and government by law. If Germany won the war, Wilson prophesied, "it would change the course of our civilization and make the United States a military nation." Wilson's chief advisers and diplomats—his assistant Edward House, Secretary of State Robert Lansing, and Ambassador to London Walter Hines Page—held similar anti-German views that often translated into pro-Allied policies.

The president and his aides also believed that Wilsonian principles stood a better chance of international acceptance if Britain, rather than the

Wilsonianism
Central Powers, sat astride the postwar world. "Wilsonianism"—the cluster of ideas Wilson espoused—consisted of traditional American principles and an evolving ideology of internationalism whose central tenet was that the United States had become such a spe-

cial nation that it could best lead world affairs into a new, peaceful era. Wilson's ideal world was to be open in every sense: no barriers to commerce, no impediments to democratic politics, no secret diplomatic deals. Empires were to be dismantled in keeping with the principle of self-determination. Armaments were to be reduced. Wilson also envisioned free-market nonexploitative capitalism and political constitutionalism for all nations, to ensure the good society and world peace. His critics charged that Wilson often violated his own tenets in his eagerness to force them on others. All agreed, though, that such ideals served the American national interest; in this way idealism and realism were married.

Wilson also articulated the traditional belief in American exceptionalism. America had a mission, he believed, to restructure international relations and to reform other societies. American progressivism was to be projected onto the world. "We created this Nation," he intoned, "not to serve ourselves, but to serve mankind." Wilson's missionary zeal, however, blended with a pragmatic understanding of the balance of world power and of America's prominent position in the world economy. His inheritance was the expansionism and imperialism that characterized American foreign policy before the First World War. Like his predecessors, he believed that even unsavory methods—such as military intervention—sometimes became necessary in the short term to protect U.S. interests.

To say that American neutrality was never a real possibility given ethnic loyalties, economic ties, and Wilsonian preferences is not to say that Wilson sought to enter the war. He emphatically wanted to keep the United States out. Time and again, Wilson tried to mediate the crisis to prevent one power from crushing another. In early 1917, the president remarked that "we are the only one of the great white nations that is free from war today, and it would be a crime against civilization for us to go in." But go in the United States finally did. Why?

Americans got caught in the Allied-Central Power crossfire. British naval policy was designed to sever neutral trade with Germany in order to cripple the German economy.

British Naval Policy
The British, "ruling the waves and waiving the rules," declared a blockade of water entrances to Germany and mined

the North Sea. They also harassed neutral shipping by seizing cargoes and defined a broad list of contraband (including foodstuffs) that they prohibited neutrals from shipping to Germany; American vessels bearing goods for Germany seldom reached their destination. Furthermore, to counter German submarines (U-boats), the British flouted international law by arming their merchant ships and flying neutral (sometimes American) flags. Wilson frequently protested British violations of neutral rights, pointing out that neutrals had the right to sell and ship noncontraband goods to belligerents without interference. But London often deftly defused American criticism by paying for confiscated cargoes, and German provocations made British behavior appear less offensive by comparison.

Germany, unable to win the war on land and determined to lift the blockade and halt American-Allied commerce, looked for victory at sea by using submarines. In February 1915 Berlin announced that it was creating a war zone around the British Isles; all enemy ships in the area would be sunk. Neutral vessels were warned to stay out so as not to be attacked by mistake, and passengers from neutral nations were advised to stay off Allied ships. President Wilson stiffly informed Germany that the United States was holding it to "strict accountability" for any losses of American life and property.

Wilson was interpreting international law in the strictest possible sense. The law that an attacker had to warn a passenger or merchant ship before attacking, so that passengers and crew could disembark safely into lifeboats, predated the emergence of the submarine as a major weapon. When Wilson refused to make adjustments, the Germans thought him unfair. As they saw the issue, the slender, frail, and sluggish *unterseebooten* should not be expected to surface to warn ships of their imminent destruction. Surfacing would deny the U-boats the advantage of surprise and a surfaced submarine would become a sitting target for a British deck gun or even a hand grenade. British vessels also had standing orders to ram U-boats and sink them. Finally, the time required to evacuate passengers usually gave the distressed ship adequate opportunity to radio for help to a British destroyer in nearby waters. Berlin frequently complained to Wilson that he was denying the Germans the one

The Submarine and International Law

weapon they could use to break the British economic stranglehold, disrupt the Allies' substantial connection with U.S. producers and bankers, and win the war. To all concerned—British, Germans, and Americans—this naval warfare became a matter of life and death.

WILSON, THE SUBMARINE, AND THE DECISION FOR WAR

Over the next few months the U-boats sank ship after ship. In May 1915 the swift, luxurious British passenger liner *Lusitania* left New York City carrying more than twelve hundred passengers and a cargo of food and contraband, including 4.2 million rounds of ammunition for Remington rifles. Before "Lucy's" departure, the newspapers printed an unusual announcement from the German embassy: travelers on British vessels were warned that Allied ships in war-zone waters "are liable to destruction." Few passengers paid attention to the notice; few shifted to an American vessel for the transatlantic trip. On May 7, off the Irish coast, submarine U-20 unleashed torpedoes at the four-stacked vessel. The *Lusitania* sank quickly, taking to their deaths 1,198 people, 128 of them Americans.

Sinking of the *Lusitania*

Even if the ship was carrying armaments, argued Wilson, the sinking was a brutal assault on innocent people. But he ruled out a military response. Secretary of State William Jennings Bryan advised that Americans be prohibited from travel on belligerent ships and that passenger vessels be prohibited from carrying war goods. "Germany has a right to prevent contraband going to the Allies," wrote Bryan, "and a ship carrying contraband should not rely on passengers to protect her from attack—it would be like putting women and children in front of an army."

The president rejected Bryan's counsel, insisting on the right of Americans to sail on belligerent ships and demanding that Germany cease its inhumane submarine warfare. "Weasel words" from "the word-lover in the White House," shouted Theodore Roosevelt, one of many jingoists who clamored for war. When the Germans urged Wilson to rethink the relationship between interna-

*"Here's money for your Americans. I may drown some more,"
says the German kaiser to President Woodrow Wilson. This
anti-German cartoon appeared in early 1916 after Germany
finally expressed regret for having taken American lives almost
a year earlier when a U-boat sank the* Lusitania. *The Germans
offered an indemnity, but not until 1925 did a claims commission determine that Germany should pay $2.5 million to Ameri-
can claimants who had suffered losses because of the* Lusitania
tragedy. Life *magazine, April 13, 1916. The Boston Athenaeum.*

tional law and the submarine, the president fumed.
After a stormy White House meeting marked by
Bryan's charge that the cabinet was pro-Allied,
Wilson reiterated his demand that submarines be
kept in port. When the president refused to ban
American travelers from belligerent ships, Bryan
resigned in protest—an uncommon act for unhappy secretaries of state, who usually leave quietly. (The pro-Allied Robert Lansing, a lawyer
with experience in the international field, took
Bryan's place.) When criticized for pursuing a
double standard in favor of the Allies, Wilson
responded that the British were taking cargoes
and violating property rights but the Germans
were taking lives and violating human rights.
Wilson's attitude toward Germany had noticeably
hardened.

Germany, seeking to avoid war with America,
ordered its U-boat commanders to halt attacks on
passenger liners. But in mid-August another British vessel, the *Arabic*, was sunk and two American
lives were lost. The Germans hastened to pledge
that an unarmed passenger ship would never again
be attacked without warning. But the sinking of
the *Arabic* fueled debate over American passengers
on belligerent vessels. Why not require Americans
to sail on American craft? asked critics. From August 1914 to March 1917 only three Americans
died on an American ship (the tanker *Gulflight* in
May 1915), whereas about 190 were killed on belligerent ships.

In early 1916 Congress began to debate the
Gore-McLemore resolution to prohibit Americans
from traveling on armed merchant vessels or ships
carrying contraband. The reso-
lution, it was hoped, would
prevent incidents like the sinking of the *Lusitania* from hur-
tling the United States into
war. But Wilson would tolerate no interference in
the presidential making of foreign policy (he had
just sent Edward House to Europe to mediate an
end to the war) and no restrictions on American
travel. The resolution, he argued, would destroy
the "whole fine fabric of international law." After
heavy politicking, Congress soundly defeated the
resolution. Wilson's critics have pointed out that
passage of the Gore-McLemore resolution would
have avoided or at least delayed a German-
American confrontation over the submarine without undercutting U.S. interests or besmirching national honor.

In March 1916 a U-boat attack on the *Sussex*,
a French vessel crossing the English Channel, took
the United States a step closer to war. Four Americans were injured on that ship, which the U-boat
commander mistook for a minelayer. Stop the marauding submarines, Wilson lectured Berlin, or he
would sever diplomatic relations. Again the Germans backed off, pledging not to attack merchant
vessels without warning. At about the same time,
relations with Britain soured. The British crushing
of the Easter Rebellion in Ireland and further restriction of U.S. trade with the Central Powers
aroused American anger.

As the United States became more entangled
in the Great War, many Americans urged Wilson
to keep the nation out of the conflict. In late 1915,

**Gore-McLemore
Resolution**

Peace Movement
———

some pacifist progressives—like Oswald Garrison Villard, Paul Kellogg, and Lillian Wald—had organized an antiwar coalition, the American Union Against Militarism. Jane Addams, Carrie Chapman Catt, and other suffragists had helped found the Woman's Peace party. The businessman Andrew Carnegie, who in 1910 had established the Carnegie Endowment for International Peace with $10 million in U.S. Steel bonds, helped finance peace groups. So did Henry Ford, who spent half a million dollars in late 1915 to send a "peace ship" to Europe to propagandize for a negotiated settlement. "If I had my way," said Ford, "I'd throw every ounce of gunpowder into the sea and strip soldiers of their insignias." Socialists like Eugene Debs added their voices to the peace movement.

The various messages of these antiwar advocates were that war drained a nation of its youth, resources, and impulse for reform; that it fostered a repressive spirit at home; that it violated Christian morality; and that wartime business barons reaped huge profits at the expense of the people. Militarism and conscription, Addams pointed out, were what millions of immigrants had left behind in Europe. Were they now—in the United States—to be forced into the decadent system they had escaped? Although the peace movement was splintered—some of its followers endorsing peace but not pacifism—it carried political and intellectual weight that Wilson could not ignore and articulated several ideas that he shared. In fact, he campaigned on a peace platform in the 1916 presidential election. After his triumph, Wilson futilely labored once again to bring the belligerents to the conference table. In early 1917 he advised them to temper their acquisitive war aims, appealing for a "peace without victory."

In early February 1917, Germany launched unrestricted submarine warfare. All vessels—belligerent or neutral, warship or merchant—

Unrestricted Submarine Warfare
———

would be attacked if sighted in the declared war zone. This bold decision represented a calculated risk that submarines could impede U.S. munitions shipments to England and thus defeat the Allies before American troops could be ferried across the Atlantic. Wilson quickly broke diplomatic relations with Berlin. Everybody waited for the inevitable collision.

This German challenge to American neutral rights and economic interests was soon followed by a German threat to U.S. security. In late February, British intelligence intercepted, decoded, and passed to officials in Washington a telegram addressed to the German minister in Mexico from German Foreign Secretary Arthur Zimmermann. If the Mexican government joined a military alliance against the United States, the minister was instructed to tell Mexican leaders, Germany would help Mexico recover the territories it had lost to its northern neighbor in 1848, including several western states. Zimmermann hoped, he told other German officials, to "*set new enemies on America's neck—enemies which give them plenty to take care of over there.*"

American officials took the message seriously, because Mexican-American relations had recently deteriorated. The Mexican Revolution, a bloody

Mexican Revolution and Zimmermann Telegram
———

civil war with strong anti-Yankee overtones, threatened U.S. interests when the Mexican government began to take steps toward the nationalization of extensive American-owned properties (see Chapters 22 and 26). Wilson had twice ordered U.S. troops onto Mexican soil: in 1914, at Veracruz, to avenge a slight to the American uniform and flag and to destabilize a government he did not like; and again in 1916, in northern Mexico, where General John J. "Black Jack" Pershing spent months pursuing the elusive Pancho Villa after the Mexican rebel had raided an American border town. The nationalistic president of Mexico, Venustiano Carranza, demanded that the U.S. invaders depart, which they did in January 1917 as Washington's attention was drawn to the prospect of U.S. participation in the European war. Lansing and Wilson agreed that Zimmermann's telegram constituted "a conspiracy against this country."

Soon after learning of Zimmermann's ploy, Wilson asked Congress for "armed neutrality" to defend American lives and commerce. He requested authority to arm American merchant ships and to "employ any other instrumentalities or methods that may be necessary." In the midst of the debate, Wilson released Zimmermann's telegram to the press; Americans expressed outrage.

The United States disapproved of the government of Venustiano Carranza (1859–1920), who came to power in 1914 during the stormy Mexican Revolution. Twice, in 1914 and 1916, U.S. troops invaded Mexico, only adding to the turmoil. Here Carranza once again tells Uncle Sam to withdraw U.S. Army forces, which departed Mexico in January 1917.   Library of Congress.

Still, the antiwar Senators Robert M. La Follette and George Norris, among others, saw the armed-ship bill as a blank check for the president to move the country to war, and they filibustered it to death. Wilson, denouncing them as a "little group of willful men," proceeded to arm America's commercial vessels anyway. The action came too late to prevent the sinking of several American ships. War cries echoed across the nation. In late March, after agonizing in private for some time, Wilson called Congress into special session.

On April 2, 1917, the president stepped before a hushed Congress. Solemnly he accused the Germans of "warfare against mankind." Passionately and eloquently, Wilson ex-

Wilson's War Message

plained American grievances: Germany's violation of freedom of the seas, disruption of commerce, attempt to stir up trouble in Mexico, and breach of human rights by killing innocent Americans. The "Prussian autoc-

racy" had to be punished by "the democracies." Russia was now among the latter, he was pleased to report, because the Russian Revolution had ousted the czar just weeks before. Wilson's most famous words rang out: "The world must be made safe for democracy." Congress quickly declared war against Germany by a vote of 373 to 50 in the House and 82 to 6 in the Senate. The first woman ever to sit in Congress, Montana's Jeannette Rankin, cast a ringing "no" vote that won her high ranking in the pantheon of American pacifism. "Peace is a woman's job," she declared, "because men have a natural fear of being classed as cowards if they oppose war" and because mothers should protect their children from death-dealing weapons.

For principle, for morality, for honor, for commerce, for security, for reform—for all of these reasons, Wilson took the United States into World War I. The submarine was certainly the culprit that drew a reluctant president and nation into the maelstrom. Yet critics like Bryan, Gore,

McLemore, La Follette, and Rankin did not attribute the American descent into war to the U-boat alone. They emphasized Wilson's rigid definition of international law, which did not take account of the submarine's tactics. They faulted his contention that Americans should be entitled to travel anywhere, even on a belligerent ship loaded with contraband, in time of war. They criticized his policies as unneutral. But they lost the debate. Although Americans might agree that Wilson's decisions were anti-German, they seemed to accept his view that the Germans had to be checked to ensure an open and orderly world in which American principles and interests would be safe.

In the broadest sense, America went to war to reform world politics, not to destroy Germany. By early 1917 Wilson seemed to believe that America would not be able to claim a seat at the postwar peace conference unless it had become a combatant. At the peace conference, Wilson intended to promote the principles he thought essential to a stable world order, to advance democracy and the Open Door, and to outlaw revolution and aggression. If he remained the representative of a neutral nation, he could only "call through a crack in the door" at the postwar conference. In the end, Woodrow Wilson decided for war to gain an American-fashioned peace.

Jeanette Rankin (1880–1973) of Montana was the first woman to sit in the House of Representatives (elected in 1916) and the only member of Congress to vote against U.S. entry into both world wars (1917 and 1941). A life-long pacifist, she led a march in Washington, D.C.—at age eighty-seven—against U.S. participation in the Vietnam War.   Brown Brothers.

TAKING UP ARMS AND WINNING THE WAR

Even before the U.S. declaration of war, the Wilson administration—encouraged by such groups as the National Security League and the Navy League and by mounting public outrage against Germany's submarine warfare—had been beefing up the military. "Preparedness" seemed prudent to many, but Senator La Follette and House Majority Leader Claude Kitchin, among others, vowed to prevent passage of the National Defense Act of 1916. They failed. This legislation provided for increases in the army and National Guard and for summer training camps modeled on the one in Plattsburg, New York, where a slice of America's social and economic elite had trained in 1915 as "citizen soldiers." The Navy Act, providing for a three-year naval expansion program, soon followed. To pay part of the huge cost of these undertakings, Congress passed the Revenue Act in 1916.

Backers of the bill believed that businesspeople should pour back into the national treasury a portion of the profits they were sure to derive from the new defense contracts. The act raised the surtax on high incomes and corporate profits, imposed a federal tax on large estates, and significantly increased the tax on the gross receipts of munitions manufacturers.

To raise an army after the declaration of war, Congress in May 1917 passed the Selective Service Act, requiring the registration of all males between the ages of twenty and thirty

The Draft

(later changed to eighteen and forty-five). National service, proponents believed, would not only prepare the nation for battle but instill respect for order, democracy, personal sacrifice, and nationalism. One general claimed that compulsory national service would "heat up the melting pot." Where else but in an army tent could a Boston Brahmin, an immigrant laborer, a college student, a dairy farmer, and the son of a domestic

American Soldiers in the First World War

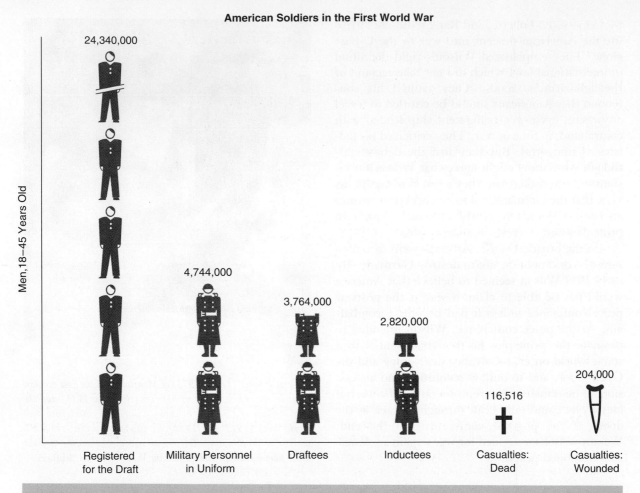

Men, 18–45 Years Old

24,340,000

4,744,000

3,764,000

2,820,000

116,516

204,000

Registered for the Draft | Military Personnel in Uniform | Draftees | Inductees | Casualties: Dead | Casualties: Wounded

American Soldiers in the First World War *As this figure shows, although many men were required to register for the draft under the Selective Service Act, only a small number (about 15 percent) were actually drafted and even fewer (about 12 percent) were inducted into the military. About half of the death casualties were caused by disease (especially by the flu).*

servant be brought together? Critics, on the other hand, feared that "Prussianism," not democratization, would be the likely outcome.

On June 5, 1917, more than 9.5 million men signed up for the "great national lottery." By war's end, 24 million men had been registered by local draft boards and more than 4.8 million had served in the armed forces, 2 million of them in France (see figure). Millions of laborers received deferments from military duty because they worked in war industries or had personal dependents.

Approximately 3 million men evaded draft registration. Some were arrested and others fled to

Mexico or Canada, but most stayed at home and were never discovered. Another 338,000 men who had registered and been summoned by their draft boards failed to show up for induction. Most of these "deserters" and the more numerous "evaders" were, according to arrest records, lower-income agricultural and industrial laborers. Some simply felt overwhelmed by the government bureaucracy and stayed away; others were members of minority or ethnic groups who felt alienated. Although nearly 65,000 draftees initially applied for conscientious-objector status (refusing to bear arms on religious or pacifistic grounds), some changed their minds or, like so many others, failed pre-induction examinations. Quakers and Mennonites were numerous among the 4,000 inductees actually classified as conscientious objectors (COs). General Leonard Wood called COs "enemies of the Republic," and the military harassed them. COs who refused noncombat service, such as in the Medical Corps, faced imprisonment.

Before December 1917, when the government prohibited enlistment, hundreds of thousands of citizens volunteered to the sound of the popular song "Johnny Get Your Gun." Asked why he had joined the army, one soldier replied that he was eager "to see a little of the biggest scrap the world has ever known." Other volunteers gave different answers: "Girls like soldiers"; they wanted to become "men"; they were homeless.

The typical American soldier in the First World War was a draftee between twenty-one and twenty-three years old, white, single, and poorly educated (most had not attended high school). Perhaps as many as 18 percent were foreign-born, and 400,000 were African-American. Though women were excluded from military service, some women became navy clerks; others served as telephone operators in the Army Signal Corps or as nurses and physical therapists. On college campuses, 150,000 students joined the Student Army Training Corps or similar navy and marine units.

Camp life for the new soldiers was demanding. They put in seventeen-hour days doing calisthenics, kitchen duty, target practice, grounds maintenance ("policing the area"), and bayonet drills. They ate well but slept on straw mattresses and marched around in olive-drab uniforms and leggings. There were never enough weapons to go around, so some trained without. At officer training camps, the army turned out "ninety-day wonders." Some soldiers imbibed Wilson's idealism, but others were so ignorant of the reasons they were going to war that U.S. officials put a copy of the president's war message in every knapsack.

American leaders worried that the young soldiers, once away from home, would be tempted by vice—especially by the saloons and houses of prostitution that quickly surrounded training centers. To protect the supposed novices with "invisible armor," the government created the Commission on Training Camp Ac-

Commission on Training Camp Activities

During the First World War, the War Department promoted a film to combat sexually transmitted disease. After the war, the New York State Board of Censors declared the film obscene. Social Welfare History Archives Center, University of Minnesota.

tivities to coordinate the work of the YMCA and other groups that dispensed food, showed movies, held athletic contests, and distributed books. Men in uniform were not permitted to drink. Alarmed by the spread of venereal disease, commission officials declared "sin-free" zones around military bases and exhorted soldiers to abstain from sex: besides the dangers of a disabling disease, the recruits were told, "a man who is thinking below the belt is not efficient." American Federation of Labor President Samuel Gompers thought the moralizing ridiculous and the prohibitions unenforceable because "real men will be men." Navy Secretary Josephus Daniels replied that "men must live straight if they would shoot straight."

Jim Crow was in the army too. Fearing "arrogant, strutting representatives of black soldiery in every community," as Senator James K. Vardaman of Mississippi growled, many politicians opposed the drafting of African-Americans. But the army needed men, white and black. The NAACP and W. E. B. Du Bois urged blacks to join the fight for "world liberty," in the hope that a war to make the world safe for democracy might also blur the color line at home. Instead, blacks encountered conscious discrimination. Draft boards frequently denied African-Americans' legitimate requests for occupational or dependency deferments. Military leaders segregated camp facilities, discouraged blacks from becoming officers, and assigned black soldiers to menial labor. Racist slang became common in the camps. In August 1917 in Houston, Texas, angry African-American soldiers retaliated against whites who had been harassing them, killing sixteen. Nineteen black soldiers were ultimately executed; others were court-martialed and given long prison terms.

In Europe, General John J. Pershing, the head of the American Expeditionary Forces (AEF), insisted that his troops remain an independent army. He was not about to put his "doughboys"—so called by the French because they looked so clean—under the leadership of Allied commanders, who had become wedded to unimaginative and deadly trench warfare, producing a military stalemate and ghastly casualties on the Western front. Zigzag trenches fronted by barbed wire and mines stretched across France. Beyond the muddy and stinking trenches lay "no man's land," denuded by artillery fire. When ordered out, soldiers would charge the German lines, also a maze of trenches. Machine guns mowed them down; chlorine gas, first used by Germany in 1915, poisoned them. Little was gained. At the Battle of the Somme in 1916 the British and French suffered 600,000 dead or wounded to earn only 125 square miles; the Germans lost 500,000 men.

The influx of American men and materiel decided the outcome of the First World War. With both sides virtually exhausted, the Americans tipped the balance toward the Allies. American forces, successfully convoyed across the Atlantic by the U.S. Navy, did not actually engage in much combat until after the lull in the fighting during the severe winter of 1917–1918. The Germans launched a major offensive in March 1918, after they had knocked Russia out of the war and shifted troops from the eastern front to France. By May, Kaiser Wilhelm's forces had stormed to within fifty miles of Paris. Late that month, troops of the U.S. First Division helped blunt the German advance at Cantigny (see map). In June the U.S. Third Division helped the French hold positions along the Marne River at Château-Thierry, and the U.S. Second Division soon attacked the Germans west of Château-Thierry in the Belleau Wood. American soldiers won the battle after three weeks, but 5,183 of 8,000 Marines died or were wounded after they made almost sacrificial frontal assaults against German machine guns. From this

AEF Battles in France

costly victory, the AEF learned to adopt more flexible attack methods.

Firsthand war, American soldiers in France quickly learned, differed starkly from popular slogans that glorified American participation. They came to know the muck and putrid smell of trench warfare and the devastation wrought by technological innovations: poison gas, machine guns, artillery. Many suffered shell shock, and by today's standards army medicine and psychiatry were primitive. Away from the front lines, Red Cross canteens staffed by women volunteers served the soldiers as way stations in a strange land, offering haircuts, food, and recreation. Some 10,000 Red Cross nurses also cared for the doughboys. American troops might even have met some American literary figures. Early in the war Ernest Hemingway, e e cummings, John Dos Passos, and other writers had volunteered for ambulance service in Allied countries because they thought it a humane thing to do. But another motive drove them, too, as Dos Passos explained candidly: "What was war like? We wanted to see with our own eyes. . . . I wanted to see the show."

For some young warriors, "the show" played in cafés and brothels—just as officials had feared. In Paris, where no fewer than forty large houses of prostitution thrived, it became commonplace to hear that the British were drunkards, the French were whoremongers, and the Americans were both. Venereal disease became a serious problem. French Prime Minister Georges Clemenceau offered licensed, inspected prostitutes in "special houses" to the American army. When the generous Gallic offer was received in Washington, Secretary of War Newton Baker gasped, "For god's sake . . . don't show this to the President or he'll stop the war." By war's end, about 15 percent of America's soldiers had contracted venereal disease, costing the army $50 million and 7 million days of active duty. Periodic inspections, chemical prophylactic treatments, and the threat of court-martial for infected soldiers kept the problem from being even more disastrous.

Problem of Venereal Disease

Allied victory in the Second Battle of the Marne in July 1918 seemed to turn the tide against the Germans. In September French and American forces took St. Mihiel and the Allies began their massive Meuse-Argonne offensive. More than 1 million Americans joined British and French

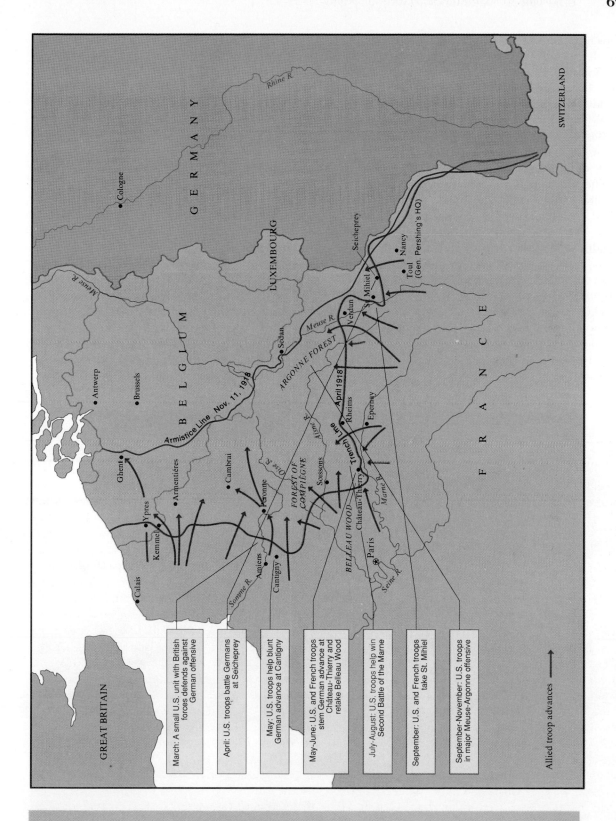

American Troops at the Western Front, 1918 *America's two million troops in France met German forces head-on, ensuring the defeat of the Central Powers in 1918.*

troops in weeks of fierce combat made all the more difficult by cold, rainy weather. More than 26,000 Americans died before the Allies claimed the Argonne Forest on October 10. For Germany, its ground war a shambles, its submarine warfare a dismal failure, its troops and cities mutinous, and its allies Turkey and Austria dropping out, peace became imperative. The Germans accepted an armistice on November 11, 1918.

The belligerents counted awesome casualties: 8 million soldiers and 6.6 million civilians dead and 21.3 million people wounded. Fifty thou-

Casualties
————

sand American soldiers died in battle, and another 62,000 died from disease—many from the influenza pandemic (see page 705). More than 200,000 Americans were wounded.

For the surviving doughboys, the army years were memorable, a turning point in their lives. They shed some of their parochialism, as the title of a popular song noted: "How 'Ya Gonna Keep 'Em Down on the Farm, After They've Seen Paree?" And they made lasting friendships that would later be cemented by membership in the American Legion. A young soldier from Missouri, Harry S Truman of Battery D, would never lose touch with his wartime buddies, and when he became president in 1945 he would bring some of them into the White House as advisers.

President Wilson welcomed the armistice, not only because it ended the bloodletting but also because it was signed on his terms. The combatants agreed that the president's

The Fourteen Points
————

Fourteen Points, which he had enunciated in January, would guide the peace negotiations. The Allies initially balked, but Wilson scared them into acceptance by threatening a separate peace with Germany. The Fourteen Points summarized Wilsonian internationalism. The first five called for diplomacy "in the public

A U.S. soldier of Company K, 110th Infantry Regiment, receives aid during fighting at Verennes, France.   National Archives.

view," freedom of the seas, lower tariffs, reductions in armaments, and the decolonization of empires. The next eight points specified the evacuation of foreign troops from Russia, Belgium, and France and appealed for self-determination for nationalities in Europe, such as the Poles. For Wilson, the fourteenth point was the most important—the mechanism for achieving all the others: "a general association of nations" or League of Nations. Having won the war, the resolute Wilson set out to win the peace and build a stable world order in accordance with American principles.

MANAGING THE HOME FRONT

"It is not an army that we must shape and train for war," declared President Wilson, "it is a nation." The United States was a belligerent for only nineteen months, but the war had a tremendous impact at home. The federal government quickly geared the economy to war needs and marshaled public opinion for sacrifices and adjustments. The state intervened in American life as never before. An unprecedented concentration of bureaucratic power developed in Washington as the federal government sought to manage the economy, the labor force, the military, public opinion, and more. In the period from 1916 to 1919, annual federal expenditures increased 2,500 percent, and war expenses ballooned to $33.5 billion. The total cost of the war was probably triple that figure, since future generations would have to pay veterans' benefits and interest on loans. To progressives of the New Nationalist persuasion, the expansion and centralization of government power were welcome (see Chapter 21). To others, these developments seemed excessive and dangerous. "War is the health of the state," protested the radical intellectual Randolph Bourne.

The federal government and private business became partners during the war. Dollar-a-year executives flocked to the nation's capital from major companies; they retained their corporate salaries while serving in official administrative and consulting capacities. Early in the war, the government relied on several industrial commit-

Business-Government Cooperation

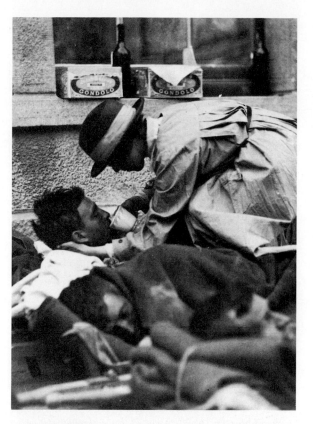

This American Red Cross worker, identified by the photographer as "Mrs. Hammond," served water to a badly wounded British soldier on a French railroad platform, May 31, 1918. National Archives.

tees for advice on purchases and prices. But evidence of self-interested businesspeople cashing in on the national interest aroused public protest. The head of the aluminum advisory committee, for example, was also president of the largest aluminum company. The committees were disbanded in July 1917 in favor of the War Industries Board (see page 702). But the government continued to work closely with business through trade associations, which grew significantly, numbering two thousand by 1920. Business-government cooperation was also stimulated by the suspension of antitrust laws and by cost-plus contracts, which guaranteed companies a healthy profit and a means to pay higher wages to head off labor strikes. Competitive bidding was virtually abandoned and a floor was placed under prices to ensure profits. Under these wartime practices, big business got bigger.

Hundreds of new government agencies, staffed largely by businesspeople, placed controls on the

The U.S. Fuel Administration during the First World War promoted economic mobilization at home through this poster in several languages.   National Park Service Collection, Ellis Island Immigration Museum. Photo Chermayeff & Geismar MetaForm.

economy in order to shift the nation's resources to the Allies, AEF, and war-related production. The Food Administration, led by Herbert Hoover, launched voluntary programs to increase production and conserve food—Americans were urged to grow "victory gardens" and to eat meatless and wheatless meals—but it also set prices and regulated distribution. The Railroad Administration took over the snarled railway industry. The Fuel Administration controlled coal supplies and rationed gasoline. When strikes threatened the telephone and telegraph companies, the federal government seized and ran them.

The largest of the superagencies was the War Industries Board (WIB), headed by the financier Bernard Baruch. Although the WIB seemed all-

War Industries Board
——

powerful, in reality it had to conciliate competing interest groups and compromise with the businesspeople whose advice it so valued. Designed as a clearing-house to coordinate the national economy,

the WIB made purchases, allocated supplies, and fixed prices at levels that business requested. The WIB ordered the standardization of goods to save materials and streamline production. The number of colors of typewriter ribbon, for example, was reduced from 150 to 5.

The performance of the mobilized economy was mixed, but it delivered enough men and materiel to France to ensure the defeat of the Central Powers. About a quarter of all American production was diverted to war needs. Farmers enjoyed boom years as they put more acreage into production and received higher prices. Encouraged to produce more at a faster pace, farmers mechanized as never before. From 1915 to 1920 the number of tractors in American fields jumped tenfold. Gross farm income for the period from 1914 to 1919 increased more than 230 percent. Although manufacturing output leveled off in 1918, some industries realized substantial growth because of wartime demand. Steel reached a peak production of 45 million tons in 1917, twice the prewar figure. The cigarette industry profited from a marked wartime increase in smoking: sales rose from 26 billion cigarettes in 1916 to 48 billion in 1918. Overall, the gross national product in 1920 was 237 percent higher than in 1914.

Massive assignments had to be completed in a hurry, and mistakes were made. Weapons deliveries fell short of demand; the bloated bureaucracy of the War Shipping Board failed to build enough ships. In the severe winter cold of 1917–1918, millions of Americans could not get coal because the coal companies had held back on production to raise prices and railroads did not have enough coal cars. Harbors froze, closing out coal barges. In January, blizzards shut down midwestern railroads and factories, impeding the war effort. People died from pneumonia and freezing. A Brooklyn man went out in the morning to forage for coal and returned to find his two-month-old daughter frozen to death in her crib. "COME TO FLORIDA—The Permanent Solution to the Coal Problem" read an advertisement for real estate in Lakeland, Florida.

If the fuel crisis could be blamed on the weather, inflation was directly attributable to government policy. The wholesale price index was 98

Inflation
——

percent higher in 1918 than it had been in 1913. Although partly stimulated by demand exceeding supply because of increases in Allied buying, inflation was also caused by the government's liberal credit policies and setting prices at high levels. By fixing prices on raw materials rather than on finished products, moreover, the government lost control of inflation. By bowing to the political pressure of southerners who wanted cotton left unregulated, the government permitted runaway cotton prices. Clothing tripled in cost and food prices more than doubled. A quart of milk that cost 9 cents in 1914 climbed to 17 cents in 1920. Fuel prices also skyrocketed: The price for a 100-pound sack of coal rose 100 percent. Inflation pinched household budgets.

Tax policies during the war were designed to pull some of the profits reaped from high prices into the treasury. The Wilson administration believed that wealth as well as labor should be conscripted. Still, the government financed only one-third of the war through taxes. The other two-thirds came from loans, including Liberty Bonds sold to the American people through aggressive campaigns. The War Revenue Act of 1917 provided for a more steeply graduated personal income tax, a corporate income tax, an excess-profits tax, and increased excise taxes on alcoholic beverages, tobacco, and luxury items. Although these taxes did curb excessive corporate profiteering, they had several loopholes. Sometimes companies inflated costs to conceal profits or paid high salaries and bonuses to their executives. Four officers of Bethlehem Steel, for example, divided bonuses of $2.3 million in 1917 and $2.1 million the next year. Corporate net earnings for 1913 totaled $4 billion; in 1917 they had risen to $7 billion; and in 1918, after the tax bite and the war's end, they still stood at $4.5 billion. Profits and patriotism went hand in hand in America's war experience.

Organized labor sought a partnership with government too, but its gains were far less spectacular. Laborers benefited from the full-employment

Labor and the War

wartime economy, which increased their total earnings and gave many of them time-and-a-half pay for overtime work. Given the high cost of living, however, workers saw little improvement in their economic standing. For unions, the war seemed to offer opportunities for recognition and better pay. Samuel Gompers threw the AFL's loyalty to the Wilson administration, promising to deter strikes. He and other moderate labor leaders were rewarded with appointments to high-level wartime government agencies. The National War Labor Board, created to mediate labor disputes, forbade strikes and lockouts and required management to negotiate with existing unions. Union membership climbed from roughly 2.5 million in 1916 to more than 4 million in 1919. The AFL could not curb strikes by the radical Industrial Workers of the World (IWW) or rebellious AFL locals, especially those with a high proportion of antiwar socialists as members. In the nineteen war months, more than six thousand strikes expressed workers' discontent with their wages, working conditions, and inflation.

When 16 percent of the male work force trooped off to battle, and when immigration dropped off and some aliens returned to Europe to

Women in the Work Force

fight for their homelands, business recruited women to fill the vacancies. Munitions makers in Bridgeport, Connecticut, for example, dropped leaflets from airplanes urging women to work in their factories. Although the total number of women in the work force increased slightly, the real story was that many changed jobs, sometimes moving into formerly male domains. Some white women left domestic service for factories, shifted from clerking in department stores to stenography and typing, or departed textile mills for employment in firearms plants. At least 20 percent of all workers in the wartime electrical-machinery, airplane, and food industries were women. As white women took advantage of these new opportunities, black women took some of their places in domestic service and in textile factories. For the first time, department stores employed black women as elevator operators and cafeteria waitresses (though they favored those with light skin color for these highly visible positions). Overall, most working women remained concentrated in sex-segregated occupations ("women's jobs") as typists, nurses, teachers, and domestic servants.

Some male workers, unaccustomed to working beside women, complained that women were destabilizing the work environment with their higher productivity; women answered that they were used to seasonal employment and piecework and hence worked at a faster pace. Some men protested that women were undermining the wage system by working for lower pay; women pointed out that male-dominated companies discriminated against them and unions denied them membership. Finally, male employees resented the spirit of inde-

One of many examples of posters issued during the war to mobilize the American people. This one from the Young Women's Christian Association reflects well the wartime movement of women into the work force and into military uniform. Museum of American Political Life, University of Hartford.

pendence evident among women, whose labor was now greatly valued. The women in a Vermont machine-tool company addressed a crude poem to their harping male co-workers:

> We're independent now you see,
> Your bald head don't appeal to me,
> I love my overalls;
> And I would rather polish steel
> Than get you up a tasty meal.
> Or go with you to balls.
> Now, only premiums good and big,
> Will tempt us maids to change our rig.
> And put our aprons on;
> And cook up all the dainty things,
> That so delighted men and kings
> In days now past and gone.[1]

[1] Originally appeared in the *Springfield Reporter*, December 5, 1917. Reprinted by permission of *The Eagle Times*.

When the war was over, women lost many of the gains they had made. The attitude that women's proper sphere was the home had changed very little. Married working women found their family relationships growing tense; their husbands and children resented the disruption of home life. Reformers complained, moreover, that working mothers were neglecting their children, failing to prepare good meals, and coming home so tired that they neglected their housework. Day nurseries were scarce and beyond the means of most working-class families, and few employers provided childcare facilities. Whether married or single— and the great majority of working women were unmarried—women lost their jobs to the returning veterans. "During the war they called us heroines," observed Mary McDowell of the University of Chicago Settlement, "but they throw us on the scrapheap now."

Women participated in the war effort in other ways. As volunteers, they made clothing for refugees and soldiers, rolled bandages, served at Red Cross facilities, and taught French to nurses assigned to the war zone. Many joined the activities of the Women's Committee of the Council of National Defense, whose leaders included Ida Tarbell and Carrie Chapman Catt. A vast network of state, county, and town volunteer organizations, the council publicized government mobilization programs, encouraged home gardens, sponsored drives to sell Liberty Bonds, and continued the push for social-welfare reforms. This patriotic work won praise from men and improved the prospects for passage of the Nineteenth Amendment (see Chapter 21).

Because southern blacks undertook a great migration to northern cities to work in railroad yards, packing houses, steel mills, shipyards, and coal mines, war mobilization wrought significant change for the African-American community. Between 1910 and 1920, Cleveland's black population swelled by more than 300 percent, Detroit's by more than 600 percent, and Chicago's by 150 percent; much of the increase occuring between 1916 and 1919. All told, about a half-million African-Americans uprooted themselves to move to the North. Labor agents from the South helped some find jobs. Families sometimes pooled savings to send one mem-

African-American Migration to the North

ber; others sold their household goods to pay for the journey north. Most of the migrants were males—young (in their early twenties), unmarried, and skilled or semiskilled. Many had first moved from rural areas to southern cities before venturing north. Wartime jobs in the North provided an escape from low wages, sharecropping, tenancy, crop liens, debt peonage, floods, boll-weevil-stricken cotton crops, lynchings, and political disenfranchisement. To a friend back in Mississippi, one African-American wrote: "I just begin to feel like a man. . . . I don't have to humble to no one. I have registered. Will vote the next election."

New opportunities could not erase the fact that African-Americans continued to experience blatant discrimination in both the North and the South. When the United States entered the First World War, there was not one black judge in the entire country. Segregation was social custom. The Ku Klux Klan was reviving, and racist films like D. W. Griffith's *The Birth of a Nation* (1915) fed prejudice. Lynching statistics exposed the wide gap between wartime declarations of humanity and the American practice of inhumanity at home: between 1914 and 1920, 382 blacks were lynched, some of them in military uniform.

Northern whites who resented "the Negro invasion" vented their anger in riots. In East St. Louis, Illinois, whites opposed to black employment in a defense plant rampaged through the streets in July 1917; forty blacks and nine whites lost their lives. During the bloody "Red Summer" of 1919, race riots rocked two dozen cities and towns. The worst violence occurred in Chicago, a favorite destination for migrating blacks. In the very hot days of July 1919, a black youth swimming at a segregated white beach was hit by a thrown rock and drowned. Rumors spread, tempers flared, and soon blacks and whites were battling one another. Stabbings, burnings, and shootings went on for days until state police restored some calm. Thirty-eight people died, twenty-three African-Americans and fifteen whites.

Some Americans concluded that the nation should direct its missionary zeal at the reform not of foreign societies but of its own. Insisting on equality and an end to segregation, W. E. B. Du Bois vowed a struggle: "We return. We return from fighting. We return fighting." In 1919 the black poet Claude McKay of New York expressed a self-assertiveness that prefigured later black protest:

Another poster of the First World War era, this one appeals to black women to move north to find new employment. Messages like this helped spur the great migration of African-Americans from the South to the North. National Archives.

If we must die—let it not be like hogs
Hunted and penned in an inglorious spot,
While round us bark the mad and hungry gods,
Making their mock at our accursed lot.

. . .

Like men we'll face the murderous, cowardly pack,
Pressed to the wall, dying but fighting back![2]

Added to the nation's unsettling war experience was a home-front crisis that cut across race, gender, and class lines: the influenza pandemic that engulfed the world in 1918–1919. Before it abated, as many as 40 million people—nobody knows for sure—died worldwide. The extremely contagious flu virus first unleashed an epidemic in the United States in spring 1918 and then spread to

Influenza Pandemic

[2] From "If We Must Die," by Claude McKay. Reprinted by permission of Twayne Publishers.

Europe. High fevers, aching muscles, and headaches made people feel as if they had been "beaten all over with a club." To fend off the virus, people received flu vaccines of questionable value or wore gauze masks. But mostly they had to wait until the virus tailed off. In many cases, severe pneumonia set in; victims' lungs filled with fluid and they died a "purple death." Seven hundred thousand people died from the killer disease in the United States. Compared to this huge human tragedy, other home-front problems seemed quite manageable.

TRAMPLING ON CIVIL LIBERTIES

"Woe be to the man that seeks to stand in our way in this day of high resolution," warned President Wilson. An official and unofficial campaign soon began to silence dissenters who questioned Wilson's decision for war or protested the draft. An "Americanization" crusade cut a gaping wound in American democracy, while jingoists warped truth and incited violence. Civil liberties were trampled. The targets of abuse were the hundreds of thousands of Americans and aliens who refused to support the war: pacifists from all walks of life, conscientious objectors, socialists, the Industrial Workers of the World, the debt-ridden tenant farmers of Oklahoma who staged the Green Corn Rebellion against the draft, the Non-Partisan League, reformers like Robert La Follette and Jane Addams, and countless others.

Shortly after the declaration of war in 1917, the president appointed George Creel, a progressive journalist, to head the Committee on Public Information (CPI). Employing some of the nation's most talented writers and scholars, the CPI set out to shape and mobilize public opinion. Its propaganda included anti-German tracts and films like *America's Answer* (1918). CPI "four-minute men" spoke at schools and churches. The committee also urged the press to practice "self-censorship" and encouraged people to spy on their neighbors and report any suspicious behavior. "Not a pin dropped in the home of any one with a foreign name," Creel claimed with satisfaction, "but that it rang like thunder on the inner ear

Committee on Public Information

of some listening sleuth." Exaggeration, fear-mongering, distortion, half-truths—such were the stuff of the CPI's "mind mobilization."

The Wilson administration also guided through an obliging Congress the Espionage Act (1917) and the Sedition Act (1918). The first statute forbade "false statements" designed to impede the draft or promote military insubordination and banned from the mails materials considered treasonous. The Sedition Act made it unlawful to obstruct the sale of war bonds and to use "disloyal, profane, scurrilous, or abusive" language to describe the government, the Constitution, the flag, and the military uniform. These loosely worded laws gave the government wide latitude to crack down on those with whom it differed. Fair-minded people could disagree over what constituted false or abusive language, but in the feverish home-front atmosphere of the First World War and under the threat of federal prosecution, the Justice Department's definition prevailed. More than two thousand people were prosecuted under the acts and many others were intimidated into silence.

Espionage and Sedition Acts

Stories of an intellectual reign of terror built up. Three Columbia University students were picked up in mid-1917 for circulating an antiwar petition. The liberal-left journal *The Masses* and Tom Watson's *The Jeffersonian* were denied use of the mails and forced to shut down. Jane Addams was put under Justice Department surveillance, causing her, by her own admission, to moderate her appeals for peace. The producer of *The Spirit of '76*, a film about the American Revolution complete with redcoats shooting minutemen, was given a ten-year prison sentence for, said the judge, questioning the "good faith of our ally, Great Britain."

In the summer of 1918, with a government stenographer present, Socialist party leader Eugene Debs delivered a spirited oration extolling socialism and freedom of speech—including the freedom to criticize the Wilson administration for taking America into the war. Federal agents arrested him. Debs told the court what many dissenters—and, later, many jurists and scholars—thought of the Espionage Act: it was "a despotic enactment in flagrant conflict with democratic principles and with the spirit of free institutions."

Imprisonment of Eugene Debs

Handed a ten-year sentence, Debs remained in prison until late 1921, when he received a pardon.

State and local governments joined the campaign. Because towns had Liberty Bond quotas to fill, they sometimes bullied "slackers" into making purchases. School boards dismissed teachers who questioned the war. German-Americans suffered floggings and other public humiliations; some were tarred and feathered. Everywhere, sauerkraut became known as "liberty cabbage." The governor of Iowa prohibited the use of any language but English in schools, and Pittsburgh banned Beethoven's music. In Hilger, Montana, citizens burned history texts that mentioned Germany. A German-American miner in Illinois was wrapped in a flag and lynched.

Advocates of "Americanization" or "100% Americanism" exploited the emotional atmosphere to exhort immigrants to throw off their Old World cultures. To fuse a superpatriotic national unity, the CPI set up Loyalty Leagues in ethnic communities. Companies offered English-language and naturalization classes in their factories and refused jobs and promotions to those who did not make adequate strides toward learning English. What began as education gave way to repression.

Encouraged by official behavior, groups like the American Protective League, the Sedition Slammers, and the American Defense Society took it upon themselves to cleanse the nation through vigilantism. In Tulsa, a mob whipped IWW members and poured tar into their bleeding sores. Nor did universities provide shelter for unorthodox ideas. In a celebrated case, Professor J. M. Cattell, a distinguished psychologist at Columbia University, was fired for his antiwar views. His colleague Charles Beard, a historian with a prowar perspective, resigned in protest: "If we have to suppress everything we don't like to hear, this country is resting on a pretty wobbly basis."

The point was just that: President Wilson and U.S. officials tried to crush what they did not like to hear. They concentrated their efforts on the IWW and the Socialist party. The war emergency and the frank opposition of those two radical organizations gave progressives and conservatives alike an opportunity to throttle their political rivals. The IWW, which stood for revolution against capitalism and was often violent in its tactics, aroused bitter opposition. Government agents raided union meetings and arrested IWW leaders. The army was

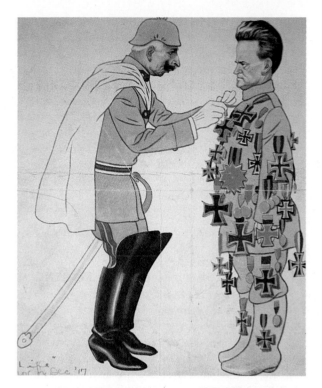

Some critics thought Senator Robert La Follette (1885–1925) a traitor because he opposed U.S. entry into the First World War. This harsh cartoon from Life magazine shows the German kaiser pinning medals on the Wisconsin reformer. La Follette believed that a majority of Americans, if asked in a referendum, would vote his way. "The poor . . . who are the ones called upon to rot in the trenches, have no organized power." The State Historical Society of Wisconsin.

dispatched to western mining and lumber regions to put down IWW strikes. Alien members of the IWW were deported. By the end of the war most of the union's leaders were in jail. The Socialist party fared little better; some socialists supported Wilson, but others besides Debs went to prison for their dissent. The new Civil Liberties Bureau (the forerunner of the American Civil Liberties Union) defended many antiwar people, but even its head, Roger Baldwin, ended up in jail as a conscientious objector.

The Supreme Court, itself attuned to the pulse of the times, upheld the Espionage Act. Justice Oliver Wendell Holmes, in *Schenck* v. *U.S.* (1919), expressed the Court's unanimous opinion that in time of war the First Amendment could be restricted: "Free speech would not protect a man falsely shouting fire in a theater and causing panic."

If, according to Holmes, words "are of such a nature as to create a clear and present danger that they will bring about the substantial evils that Congress has a right to prevent," free speech could be limited. In another case, *Abrams* v. *U.S.* (1919), the Court voted 7 to 2 (with Holmes and Louis Brandeis in the minority) that the Sedition Act was constitutional. This time Holmes expressed concern that the "free trade in ideas" was being jeopardized. Many agreed in the end that the Wilson administration compiled one of the worst civil liberties records in American history.

THE RED SCARE

The line between wartime suppression of dissent and the postwar Red Scare is not easily drawn. Both put on the mask of patriotism to harass suspected internal enemies and deprive them of their constitutional rights; both had government sanction. Together they stabbed at the Bill of Rights and crippled radicalism in America. In the last few months of the war, guardians of Americanism began to label dissenters not only pro-German but pro-Bolshevik. After the Bolshevik Revolution in the fall of 1917, American hatred for the Kaiser's Germany was readily transferred to Communist Russia. When the new Russian government under V. I. Lenin made peace with Germany in early 1918, Americans grew angry that the closing of the eastern front would permit the Germans to move troops west. Many lashed out at American radicals, casually applying the term "Red" to people of varying beliefs, including anarchists, Wobblies, Socialists, pacifists, Communists, union leaders, and reformers.

The ordeal of Victor Berger illustrates the blending of the wartime and postwar suppression of civil liberties. A Socialist of German descent and a former congressman from **Case of Victor Berger** Wisconsin, Berger was indicted under the Espionage Act for denouncing U.S. entry into the European war. The voters of Milwaukee nonetheless elected him once again to Congress in 1918. Early the next year Berger was convicted and sentenced to twenty years in federal prison. The House of Representatives thereupon refused to admit him, its members absurdly charging that he was both pro-German and pro-Bolshevik. While out on bail pending an appeal, Berger won the special election held to replace him. The House again blocked his admission. Berger's nightmare did not end until 1921, when the Supreme Court reversed his conviction. He was elected to Congress again in 1924. This time he took his seat.

The Wilson administration's ardent anti-Bolshevism became clear in mid-1918 when the president ordered five thousand American troops to northern Russia and ten **Intervention in Russian Civil War** thousand more soldiers to Siberia, where they joined other Allied contingents, including a large one from Japan. Wilson did not consult Congress. He announced that the military expeditions were intended to guard Allied supplies and Russian railroads from German seizure and to rescue a group of Czechs who wished to return home to fight the Germans. Worried that the Japanese were building influence in Siberia and closing the Open Door, Wilson also hoped to deter Japan from further advances in Asia. Mostly he wanted to smash the infant Bolshevik government. The Allied governments were blunter than Wilson about this goal, for they feared the spread of Bolshevism across Europe. (Short-lived uprisings did occur in Germany and Hungary in early 1919.)

Wilson went beyond attempting to subvert Lenin's regime by military means. The United States participated in an economic blockade of Russia, sent arms to anti-Bolshevik forces, and refused to recognize the Bolshevik government. Later, at the Paris Peace Conference, Russia was denied a seat. U.S. troops did not leave Siberia until spring 1920. These interventions in civil war–torn Russia immediately embittered Washington-Moscow relations—a legacy that would persist deep into the twentieth century.

At home, too, the Wilson administration moved against radicals and others imprecisely defined as Bolsheviks or Communists. By the war's close, Americans had become edgy. The war had exacerbated racial tensions. It had disrupted the workplace and the family. Americans had suffered an increase in the cost of living, and postwar unemployment loomed. To add to Americans' worries, the Russian Communists in 1919 established the Comintern to promote world revolution. Already hardened by wartime violations of civil liberties, Americans found it easy to blame their postwar troubles on new scapegoats.

During the Boston police strike in September 1919, looters and demonstrators took to the streets for two days. The Boston government organized a volunteer citizen force and Governor Calvin Coolidge of Massachusetts mobilized the State Guard to restore order, as in this scene from the Boston Common. At a time when fears of radicalism thrived in the United States, many Americans denounced the striking policemen as Bolsheviks and cheered Coolidge when he declared that "there is no right to strike against the public safety by anybody, anywhere, any time." UPI/ Bettmann Archives.

A rash of labor strikes in 1919 sparked the Red Scare. All told, more than 3,300 strikes involving 4 million laborers jolted the nation that year, including the Seattle general strike in January. America, Wilson's press secretary declared, was poised between "organization and anarchy." On May 1, traditionally a day of celebration for workers around the world, bombs were sent through the mails to prominent Americans. Although most of the devices were intercepted and dismantled, police never captured the conspirators. Most people assumed, not unreasonably, that anarchists and others bent on the destruction of the American way of life were responsible. Next came the Boston police strike in September. Some sniffed a Bolshevik conspiracy, but others thought it ridiculous to label Boston's Irish-American Catholic cops "radicals." The conservative governor of Massachusetts, Calvin Coolidge, gained fame by proclaiming that nobody had the right to strike

Labor Strikes, 1919

against the public safety. State guardsmen were brought in to replace the striking policemen.

Unrest in the steel industry in September seemed more ominous. Many steelworkers still put in twelve-hour days, seven days a week, and lived in squalid housing. They looked to local steel unions, organized by the National Committee for Organizing Iron and Steel Workers, to help them improve their lives. When postwar unemployment in the industry climbed and the U.S. Steel Corporation refused to meet with committee representatives, some 350,000 workers walked off the job demanding the right to collective bargaining, shorter hours, and a living wage. Besides hiring strikebreakers and sending agents to club strikers, the steel barons depicted strike leaders as Bolsheviks bent on revolution. The steel companies won; the strike collapsed in early 1920.

One of the leaders of the steel strike was William Z. Foster, an IWW member and militant labor organizer who later joined the Communist party. His presence in a labor movement seeking bread-and-butter goals permitted political and business leaders to dismiss the steel strike as a foreign threat orchestrated by American radicals. There was in fact no conspiracy, and the American left was badly splintered. Two defectors from the Socialist party, John Reed and Benjamin Gitlow, founded the Communist Labor party in 1919. The rival Communist Party of the United States of America, composed largely of aliens, was launched the same year. Neither party commanded much of a following—their combined membership probably did not exceed 70,000—and in 1919 the harassed Socialist party could muster no more than 30,000 members.

Although divisiveness among radicals actually signified weakness, progressives and conservatives both interpreted the advent of the new parties as a strengthening of the radical

American Legion

menace. That is certainly how the American Legion saw the question. Organized in May 1919 to lobby for veterans' benefits, the legion soon preached an antiradicalism that fueled the Red Scare. By 1920, the legion's 843,000 members, mostly middle and upper class, had become stalwarts of an impassioned Americanism that demanded conformity.

Wilson's attorney general, A. Mitchell Palmer, also insisted that Americans think alike. A progressive reformer, a Quaker, and an aspirant to the 1920 Democratic presidential nomination, Palmer claimed that "the blaze of revolution" was "eating its way into the homes of the American workmen, its sharp tongues of revolutionary heat . . . licking the altars of the churches, leaping into the belfry of the school bell, crawling into the sacred corners of American homes, burning up the foundations of society." To stamp out the radical fire, Palmer created a new Bureau of Investigation and appointed J. Edgar Hoover to run it. Hoover had joined the Justice Department just two years earlier after studying law at George Washington University. The young ambitious official compiled index cards bearing the names of allegedly radical individuals and organizations. During 1919, agents jailed IWW members; Palmer also saw to it that 249 alien radicals, including the anarchist Emma Goldman, were deported to Soviet Russia.

Again, state and local governments took their cue from Washington. States passed peacetime sedition acts under which hundreds of people were

arrested. Vigilante groups and mobs flourished once again, their numbers swelled by returning veterans. In November 1919, in Centralia, Washington, American Legionnaires broke from a parade to storm the IWW hall. Several were wounded. A number of Wobblies were soon arrested. One, an ex-soldier, was taken from jail by a mob, then beaten, castrated, and shot. The New York State legislature expelled five duly elected Socialist members in early 1920.

The Red Scare reached a climax in January 1920 when the attorney general staged his Palmer Raids. Using Hoover's file, government agents in

Palmer Raids

thirty-three cities broke into meeting halls and homes without search warrants. More than four thousand people were jailed and denied counsel. In Boston, some four hundred people were kept in detainment on bitterly cold Deer Island; two died of pneumonia, one leaped to his death, and another went insane. Because of court rulings and the courageous efforts of Assistant Secretary of Labor Louis Post, who deliberately held up paperwork, most of the Palmer Raid arrestees were released, although in 1920–1921 nearly six hundred were deported.

Palmer's disregard for elementary civil liberties drew criticism. Civil libertarians and lawyers charged that his tactics violated the Constitution. Many of the arrested "Communists" had committed no crimes. When Palmer called for a peacetime sedition act, he alarmed leaders of many political persuasions. His dire prediction that serious violence would mar May Day 1920 proved mistaken. Palmer's exaggerated scenarios of Bolshevik conspiracy simply exceeded the truth so far that he lost credibility. With the steel strike over, the threat of Bolshevism in Europe receding, and the nation returning to postwar "normalcy," Palmer could no longer count on stampeding the public. Finally, even officials in the Wilson administration refused to tolerate his gross violations of human rights.

The campaigns against free speech in the period from 1917 through 1920 left casualties. Antiwar critics, radicals, and others out of step with government policies became afraid to speak their minds and faced harassment and jail if they did. Debate, so essential to democracy, was wounded. Reform suffered as reformers either joined in the antiradicalism or became victims of it. Radical groups were badly weakened: the IWW became virtually extinct and the Socialist party was paralyzed. Throughout, the president made it appear that his critics were attacking the nation itself, when they were actually questioning the policies of his administration. Wilson's intolerance of those who disagreed with him seemed to bespeak a fundamental distrust of democracy. At the very least, it illustrated that some progressives were willing to use coercion to achieve their goal of a reformed society. Senator La Follette thought the sorry experience demonstrated the dangerous "encroachment of the powerful few upon the rights of the many."

THE PEACE CONFERENCE, LEAGUE FIGHT, AND POSTWAR WORLD

As the Red Scare threatened American democracy, Woodrow Wilson was struggling to make his Fourteen Points a reality. When the president departed for the Paris Peace Conference in December 1918, he faced obstacles erected by his political enemies, by the Allies, and by himself. Some observers suggested that the ambitious and self-confident Wilson underestimated his task. During the 1918 congressional elections, Wilson had urged a vote for the Democrats as a sign of support for his peace goals. But the American people did just the opposite, although probably less in response to foreign-policy issues than to domestic questions like inflation. The Republicans gained control of both houses, signaling trouble for Wilson in two ways. First, a peace treaty would have to be submitted for approval to a potentially hostile Senate. Second, Wilson's stature had been diminished in the eyes of foreign leaders.

Wilson aggravated his political problems by not naming a senator to his advisory American Peace Commission. He also refused to take any prominent Republican with him to Paris or to consult with the Senate Foreign Relations Committee before the conference. Analysts thought he had lost his political senses.

Another obstacle in Wilson's way was the Allies' determination to impose a harsh, vengeful peace on the Germans. Georges Clemenceau of France, David Lloyd George of Britain, and Vittorio Orlando of Italy—with Wilson, the Big Four—became formidable adversaries. They had signed secret treaties during the war to grab German-controlled territories, and they scoffed at the pious, headstrong, self-impressed president who wanted to deny them the spoils of war while he sought to expand U.S. power. "How can I talk to a fellow who thinks himself the first man for two thousand years who has known anything about peace on earth," snarled Clemenceau. "Wilson imagines that he is a second Messiah."

The Paris Peace Conference, held at the ornate palace of Versailles, was a meeting of the titans— "the clearing house of the Fates," as a contemporary put it. When the Big Four met behind closed doors, critics quickly pointed out that Wilson had abandoned the first of his Fourteen Points, which urged diplomacy "in the public view." The victors demanded that Germany pay a huge reparations bill. Wilson instead called for a small indemnity, fearing that a resentful and economically hobbled Germany might turn to Bolshevism or disrupt the postwar community in some other way. Unable to moderate the Allied position, the president reluctantly gave way, agreeing to a clause blaming the war on the Germans and to the creation of a commission to determine the amount of reparations (later set at $33 billion).

Paris Peace Conference

As for the breaking up of empires and the principle of self-determination, Wilson could deliver on only some of his goals. Creating a League-administered "mandate" system, the conferees placed former German and Turkish colonies under the control of other imperial nations. France and Britain, for example, obtained parts of the Middle East, and Japan gained authority over Germany's colonies in the Pacific. In other arrangements, Japan replaced Germany as the imperial overlord of China's Shandong peninsula, and France was permitted occupation rights in Germany's Rhineland. Elsewhere in Europe, Wilson's prescriptions fared better. Out of Austria-Hungary and Russia came the newly independent states of Austria, Hungary, Yugoslavia, Czechoslovakia, and Poland. Wilson and his colleagues also built a *cordon sanitaire* (buffer zone) of new westward-looking nations (Finland, Estonia, Latvia, and Lithuania) around Russia to quarantine the Bolshevik contagion (see map on page 713).

Wilson worked hardest on the charter for the League of Nations. In the long run, he believed, such an organization would moderate the harshness of the Allied peace terms and temper imperial ambitions. The League reflected the power of large nations like the United States: it consisted of an influential council of five permanent members and elected delegates from smaller states, an assembly of all members, and a World Court. The "backbone" of the League covenant, said Wilson, was Article 10:

League of Nations

> The Members of the League undertake to respect and preserve as against external aggression the territorial integrity and existing political independence of all Members of the League. In case of any such aggression or in case of any threat or danger of such aggression the Council shall advise upon the means by which this obligation shall be fulfilled.

This collective-security provision, along with the entire League charter, became part of the peace treaty.

German representatives at first refused to accept the punitive Treaty of Paris but ultimately signed it in June 1919. In so doing they gave up 13 percent of Germany's territory, 10 percent of its population, all of its colonies, and a huge portion of its national wealth. Secretary Lansing and others wondered how the League could function in the poisoned postwar atmosphere of revenge and humiliation. But Wilson waxed euphoric: "The stage is set, the destiny disclosed. It has come about by no plan of our conceiving, but by the hand of God."

Americans vigorously debated the treaty. In March 1919, while the conferees in Paris were still hammering out the accord, thirty-nine senators (enough to deny the treaty the necessary two-thirds vote) had signed a petition stating that the League's structure did not adequately protect U.S. interests. Wilson denounced his critics as "pygmy" minds, but he persuaded the peace conference to exempt the Monroe Doctrine and domestic matters from League jurisdiction. Having made these concessions to senatorial advice, Wilson would budge no more.

The journalist Walter Lippmann asked: "How in our consciences are we to square the results with the promises?" Criticism of the peace process and

Critique of the Treaty

the treaty mounted: Wilson had bastardized his own principles. He had conceded Shandong to Japan. He had personally killed a provision affirming the racial equality of all peoples. The treaty did not mention freedom of the seas, and tariffs were not reduced. Negotiations had been conducted in private, and reparations promised to be punishing. Senator La Follette complained that the League was an imperialists' club that would perpetuate empire. Conservative critics like Senator Henry Cabot Lodge of Massachusetts feared that the League would limit American freedom of action in world affairs, stymie U.S. expansion, and intrude on domestic questions. And Article 10 raised serious questions: Would the United States be obligated to use armed force to ensure collective security? And what about colonial rebellions, such as in Ireland or India? Would the League feel compelled to crush them?

Wilson pleaded for understanding and lectured his opponents. How could they fail to realize that compromises were necessary given the stubborn resistance of the Allies, who had threatened to jettison the conference unless Wilson made concessions? Did they not recognize that the League would rectify wrongs? Could they not see that membership in the League would give the United States "leadership in the world"? Senator Lodge remained unimpressed. A Harvard-educated Ph.D. and partisan Republican, he ridiculed the charter as poor scholarship on the part of Wilson, a former Princeton professor. Lodge packed the Foreign Relations Committee with critics and prolonged public hearings. He introduced reservations to the treaty: one stated that the nation's immigration acts could not be subject to League decision; another held that Congress had to approve any obligation under Article 10.

In September 1919, Wilson embarked on a speaking tour of the United States. Growing more exhausted every day, he dismissed his antagonists as "absolute, contemptible quitters." Provoked by Irish-American and German-American hecklers, he lashed out in Red Scare terms: "I cannot say too often—any man who carries a hyphen about him carries a dagger which he is ready to plunge into the vitals of the Republic." In Colorado, while delivering another passionate speech, the president collapsed. A few days later, back in Washington,

Europe Transformed by War and Peace *After President Wilson and the other conferees at Versailles negotiated the Treaty of Paris, empires were broken up. In Eastern Europe, in particular, new nations were established.*

he suffered a stroke that paralyzed his left side. He became peevish and stubborn, increasingly unable to conduct the heavy business of the presidency. Advised to placate senatorial critics so the treaty would have a chance of passing, Wilson rejected "dishonorable compromise." From Senate Democrats he demanded utter loyalty—a vote against all reservations.

Twice in November the Senate rejected the Treaty of Paris. In the first vote, Democrats joined a group of sixteen "Irreconcilables," mostly Repub-

Senate Rejection of the Treaty
———

licans who opposed any treaty whatsoever, to defeat the treaty *with* reservations (39 for and 55 against). In the second vote, Republicans and Irreconcilables turned down the treaty *without* reservations (38 for and 53 against). Had Wilson permitted Democrats to compromise—to accept reservations—he could have achieved his fervent goal of U.S. membership in the League of Nations.

Who or what was responsible for the defeat of the treaty? Wilson's stroke incapacitated the president, sapping his energy and his ability to lead effectively. Yet even a healthy Wilson would probably have set his jaw against compromise. The bitter personal feud between Wilson and Lodge accounts for some conflict, but it does not explain the determination of the Irreconcilables. Certainly Wilson's concessions to a harsh peace at Paris undercut his case in the United States, but, even so, two-thirds of the senators seemed willing to forgive his errors in Versailles if he would only accept some reservations. The uncompromising Wilson had become "a slave to vanity," regretted Secretary Lansing. But Wilsonian "vanity" also lacks adequate explanatory power. Of what was he so proud?

At the core of the debate lay a basic issue in American foreign policy: whether the United States would endorse collective security or con-

Collective Security vs. Unilateralism
———

tinue to travel the path of unilateralism articulated in George Washington's Farewell Address and in the Monroe Doctrine. In a world dominated by imperialist states unwilling to subordinate their selfish acquisitive ambitions to an international organization, Americans preferred their traditional nonalignment and freedom of choice over binding commitments to collective action. That is why so many of Wilson's critics targeted Article 10 and why the president was so adamant against its revision.

In the end, Woodrow Wilson failed to create a new world order through reform. He promised more than he could deliver. Still, the United States emerged from the First World War an even greater world power. By 1920 the United States had be-

come the world's leading economic power, producing 40 percent of its coal, 70 percent of its petroleum, and half of its pig iron. It also rose to first rank in world trade. During the war years, American companies expanded overseas. Goodyear went into the Dutch East Indies for rubber; copper interests dug new mines in Chile; and Swift and Armour reached into South America. American economic expansionists took advantage of the war to nudge the Germans and British out of foreign markets, especially in Latin America. Meanwhile, the United States shifted from being a debtor to a creditor nation, becoming the world's leading banker.

The disillusionment widespread among Americans after the disappointment of Versailles did not cause the United States to adopt a policy of isolationist withdrawal (see Chapter 26). Although the League of Nations began to operate without U.S. membership, American diplomats became curious onlookers who occasionally even participated in League activities. But in general Americans stood against intervening in European affairs until the Europeans first set their own house in order.

The carnage of the war stimulated new appeals for arms control and revitalized the peace movement. At the same time, the military became more professional. The Reserve Officers' Training Corps (ROTC) became permanent; military "colleges" provided upper-echelon training; and the Army Industrial College, founded in 1924, pursued business-military cooperation in the area of logistics and planning. The National Research Council, created in 1916 with government money and Carnegie and Rockefeller funds, continued after the war as an alliance of scientists and businesspeople engaged in research relating to national defense. As before the war, the tendencies toward disarmament on the one hand and preparedness on the other continued to compete.

The international system born in these years was unstable and fragmented. Espousing decolonization and taking to heart the Wilsonian principle of self-determination, national-

Unstable International System
———

ist leaders like Ho Chi Minh of Indochina and Mohandas K. Gandhi of India vowed to achieve independence for their peoples. Communism became a disruptive force in world politics, and the Russians bore a grudge against those invaders who had tried to thwart their revolution. The new states in

How do historians know

that President Woodrow Wilson's ill health contributed to the Senate's defeat of U.S. membership in the League of Nations? Although scholars differ on whether Woodrow Wilson's ill health and behavior stemmed primarily from physiological or psychological conditions, they agree that Wilson had been an ill man long before a massive stroke on October 2, 1919, incapacitated him during national debate on the League of Nations. His medical history included arteriosclerosis (hardening of the arteries) and several strokes (the first in 1896). He and his doctors conspired to keep this information from the American people, who might have hesitated to vote him into the presidency had they known how frail he was. During the League fight, Wilson's health further deteriorated. Nervous and trembling, he suffered headaches and insomnia. After a speech in Colorado, he collapsed. In tears, the president muttered, "I seem to have gone to pieces." After Wilson returned to Washington, D.C., a massive stroke soon left him paralyzed and haggard. He could not lead because he could seldom concentrate on any subject for very long and he secluded himself from cabinet members. But this irascible, stubborn, very sick man would not resign. Nor would he compromise with senators who said they would vote for U.S. membership in the League of Nations if only the president would accept changes in the Treaty of Paris. Given the serious issues raised by the collective security provision of the treaty, some historians continue to wonder whether even a healthy Wilson could have changed the outcome of the Senate vote.   Photo: Brown Brothers.

central and eastern Europe proved weak, dependent on outsiders for security. Germans bitterly resented the harsh peace settlement, and the war debts and reparations problems would dog international order for years. As it entered the 1920s, the international system that Woodrow Wilson vowed to reform seemed extremely unstable on many fronts.

At the close of the First World War, the historian Albert Bushnell Hart observed that "it is easy to see that the United States is a new country."

The British painter Paul Nash captured the mood of many after the First World War with this somber, devastated landscape titled We Are Making a New World. Imperial War Museum, London.

What had changed? America emerged from the war years an unsettled mix of the old and the new. The war exposed deep divisions among Americans: white versus black, nativist versus immigrant, capital versus labor, "dry" versus "wet," men versus women, radical versus progressive and conservative, pacifist versus interventionist, nationalist versus internationalist. It is little wonder that Americans—having experienced race riots, labor strikes, disputes over civil liberties, and the League fight—wanted to escape from what the education reformer John Dewey called the "cult of irrationality" to what President Warren G. Harding called "normalcy."

During the war the federal government intervened in the economy and influenced people's everyday lives as never before. Centralization of control in Washington, D.C., and mobilization of the home front served as a model for the future. The partnership of government and business in managing the wartime economy contributed to the further development of a mass society through the standardization of products and the promotion of efficiency. Wilsonian wartime policies also nourished the continued growth of oligopoly through the suspension of antitrust laws. After a short postwar recession, business power revived to dominate the next decade. American labor, by contrast, entered what one historian has called its lean years.

The war experience also changed Americans' mood. The war was grimy and ugly, far less glorious than Wilson's lofty rhetoric suggested it would be. People recoiled from photographs of shell-shocked faces and of bodies dangling from barbed wire. American soldiers, tired of idealism and cynical about their ability to right wrongs, craved the latest baseball scores, their regular jobs, and renewed participation in America's famed consumer culture. Those progressives who had believed that entry into the war would deliver the millennium, later marveled at their naiveté. Many lost their enthusiasm for crusades, and many others turned away in disgust from the bickering of the victors. Randolph Bourne commented that progressives felt "like brave passengers who have set out for the Isles of the Blest only to find that the first mate has gone insane and jumped overboard." Some felt betrayed. The journalist William Allen White angrily wrote to a friend that the Allies "have—those damned vultures—taken the heart out of the peace, taken the joy out of the great enterprise of the war, and have made it a sordid malicious miserable thing like all the other wars in the world."

Woodrow Wilson himself had remarked, soon after taking office in 1913 before the Great War, that "there's no chance of progress and reform in an administration in which war plays the principal part." From the perspective of 1920, looking back on distempers at home and abroad, Wilson would have to agree with other Americans that progress and reform had been dealt blows.

SUGGESTIONS FOR FURTHER READING

General

John W. Chambers, *The Tyranny of Change*, 2nd ed. (1992); Otis L. Graham, Jr., *The Great Campaigns* (1971); Ellis W. Hawley, *The Great War and the Search for a Modern Order*, 2nd ed. (1992); Henry F. May, *The End of American Innocence* (1964); Emily S. Rosenberg, *Spreading the American Dream* (1982); Bernadotte Schmitt and Harold E. Vedeler, *The World in the Crucible: 1914–1919* (1984); Ronald Steel, *Walter Lippmann and the American Century* (1980); David P. Thelan, *Robert M. La Follette and the Insurgent Spirit* (1976); John A. Thompson, *Reformers and War* (1987).

Woodrow Wilson, His Diplomacy, and the First World War

Lloyd E. Ambrosius, *Wilsonian Statecraft* (1991); Thomas A. Bailey and Paul B. Ryan, *The Lusitania Disaster* (1975); Frederick S. Calhoun, *Power and Principle* (1986); Kendrick A. Clements,

The Presidency of Woodrow Wilson (1992); John W. Coogan, *The End of Neutrality* (1981); John M. Cooper, Jr., *The Warrior and the Priest* (1983); Patrick Devlin, *Too Proud to Fight* (1975); Robert H. Ferrell, *Woodrow Wilson and World War I* (1985); Lloyd C. Gardner, *Safe for Democracy* (1984); Ross Gregory, *The Origins of American Intervention in the First World War* (1971); Manfred Jonas, *The United States and Germany* (1984); Thomas J. Knock, *To End All Wars* (1992); N. Gordon Levin, Jr., *Woodrow Wilson and World Politics* (1968); Arthur S. Link, ed., *Woodrow Wilson and a Revolutionary World, 1913–1921* (1982); Arthur S. Link, *Woodrow Wilson: Revolution, War and Peace* (1979); Arthur S. Link, *Wilson*, 5 vols. (1947–1965); Ernest R. May, *The World War and American Isolation, 1914–1917* (1959); J. W. Schulte Nordholt, *Woodrow Wilson: A Life in World Peace* (1991); David Stevenson, *The First World War and International Politics* (1988); Edwin A. Weinstein, *Woodrow Wilson: A Medical and Psychological Biography* (1981).

The U.S. Military

John W. Chambers, *To Raise an Army* (1987); J. Garry Clifford, *The Citizen Soldiers* (1972); Edward M. Coffman, *The War to End All Wars* (1968); Harvey A. DeWeerd, *President Wilson Fights His War* (1968); Thomas C. Leonard, *Above the Battle* (1978); Donald Smythe, *Pershing* (1986); Russell F. Weigley, *The American Way of War* (1973).

The Home Front

Allan M. Brandt, *No Magic Bullet* (1985) (on venereal disease); William J. Breen, *Uncle Sam at Home* (1984); Valerie Jean Conner, *The National War Labor Board* (1983); Alfred W. Crosby, *America's Forgotten Pandemic: The Influenza of 1918* (1989); Robert D. Cuff, *The War Industries Board* (1973); Charles Gilbert, *American Financing of World War I* (1970); Frank L. Grubbs, Jr., *The Struggle for Labor Loyalty* (1968); David M. Kennedy, *Over Here* (1980); Seward W. Livermore, *Politics Is Adjourned* (1966); Frederick C. Luebke, *Bonds of Loyalty: German-Americans and World War I* (1974); John F. McClymer, *War and Welfare: Social Engineering in America, 1890–1925* (1980); Ronald Schaffer, *America in the Great War: The Rise of the War Welfare State* (1991); Stephen L. Vaughn, *Holding Fast the Inner Lines* (1979) (on CPI); Neil A. Wynn, *From Progressivism to Prosperity: World War I and American Society* (1986).

Women, the War, and the Peace

Allen F. Davis, *American Heroine* (1974) (on Addams); Maurine W. Greenwald, *Women, War, and Work* (1980); Dorothy Schneider and Carl J. Schneider, *Into the Breach: American Women Overseas in World War I* (1991); Barbara J. Steinson, *American Women's Activism in World War I* (1982).

African-Americans at Home and Abroad

Arthur E. Barbeau and Florette Henri, *The Unknown Soldiers: Black American Troops in World War I* (1974); Marvin E. Fletcher, *The Black Soldier and Officer in the United States Army, 1891–1917* (1974); James B. Grossman, *Land of Hope: Chicago, Black Southerners, and the Great Migration* (1989); Robert V. Haynes, *A Night of Violence: The Houston Riot of 1917* (1976); Carole Marks, *Farewell—We're Good and Gone: The Great Black Migration* (1989); Elliot M. Rudwick, *Race Riot at East St. Louis, July 2, 1917* (1964); William M. Tuttle, Jr., *Race Riot: Chicago in the Red Summer of 1919* (1970).

Antiwar Critics, Antiradicalism, Civil Liberties, and the Red Scare

David Brody, *Labor in Crisis: The Steel Strike of 1919* (1965); Charles Chatfield, *The American Peace Movement* (1992); Stanley Coben, *A. Mitchell Palmer* (1963); Charles DeBenedetti, *Origins of the Modern Peace Movement* (1978); Robert L. Friedheim, *The Seattle General Strike* (1965); Sondra Herman, *Eleven Against War* (1969); Donald Johnson, *The Challenge to American Freedoms* (1963); C. Roland Marchand, *The American Peace Movement and Social Reform, 1898–1918* (1973); Paul L. Murphy, *World War I and the Origin of Civil Liberties* (1979); Robert K. Murray, *Red Scare* (1955); William Pencak, *For God and Country: The American Legion, 1919–1941* (1989); H. C. Peterson and Gilbert C. Fite, *Opponents of War, 1917–1918* (1968); Richard Polenberg, *Fighting Faiths* (1987) (the *Abrams* case); William Preston, *Aliens and Dissenters* (1966); Francis Russell, *A City in Terror: 1919—The Boston Police Strike* (1975); James Weinstein, *The Decline of Socialism in America, 1912–1923* (1967).

The United States and the Bolshevik Revolution

Peter G. Filene, *Americans and the Soviet Experiment, 1917–1933* (1967); John L. Gaddis, *Russia, the Soviet Union, and the United States*, 2nd ed. (1990); George F. Kennan, *The Decision to Intervene* (1958); George F. Kennan, *Russia Leaves the War* (1956); Christopher Lasch, *The American Liberals and the Russian Revolution* (1962); David McFadden, *Alternative Paths: Soviets and Americans, 1917–1920* (1993); John Thompson, *Russia, Bolshevism, and the Versailles Peace* (1966); Betty M. Unterberger, *The United States, Revolutionary Russia, and the Rise of Czechoslovakia* (1989); Betty M. Unterberger, *America's Siberian Expedition, 1918–1920* (1956).

Paris Peace Conference and League Fight

Lloyd Ambrosius, *Woodrow Wilson and the American Diplomatic Tradition* (1987); Thomas A. Bailey, *Woodrow Wilson and the Great Betrayal* (1945); Thomas A. Bailey, *Woodrow Wilson and the Lost Peace* (1944); Inga Floto, *Colonel House in Paris* (1973); Herbert Hoover, *The Ordeal of Woodrow Wilson* (1958); Warren F. Kuehl, *Seeking World Order* (1969); Arno Mayer, *Politics and Diplomacy of Peacemaking* (1967); Keith Nelson, *Victors Divided* (1973); Ralph A. Stone, *The Irreconcilables* (1970); Arthur Walworth, *Wilson and the Peacemakers* (1986); William C. Widenor, *Henry Cabot Lodge and the Search for an American Foreign Policy* (1980).

The Aftermath of War

Stanley Cooperman, *World War I and the American Mind* (1970); Malcolm Cowley, *Exile's Return* (1951); Paul Fussell, *The Great War and Modern Memory* (1975); Stuart I. Rochester, *American Liberal Disillusionment in the Wake of World War I* (1977); Stephen R. Ward, ed., *The War Generation: Veterans of the First World War* (1975).

24

The New Era of the 1920s

IT TOOK THE JURY of Chicagoans less than three hours to decide on acquittal. When they announced their verdict, on August 2, 1921, the packed courtroom erupted. "Hats sailed high in the air, papers were thrown around," a reporter wrote, "and the courtroom was the scene of the wildest confusion in any recent Cook County criminal case." Jurors lifted some of the defendants onto their shoulders, and even the judge joined the crowd in whistling and cheering.

The defendants were seven members of the Chicago White Sox and two alleged gamblers accused of conspiring to defraud the public by intentionally losing the 1919 World Series to the Cincinnati Reds. The "Black Sox scandal" had wracked baseball, the "national pastime" and most popular sport in the country, for almost two years. The accused included such heroes as pitcher Ed Cicotte, infielder Buck Weaver, and outfielder Joe Jackson, who rivaled Ty Cobb and Babe Ruth as the game's greatest hitter. No wonder the public celebrated when their idols were exonerated. Still recovering from a world war, eager to partake in new opportunities for amusement and consumer comfort, Americans wanted to put the darker realities behind them.

But was exoneration the answer? Judge Kennesaw Mountain Landis, a thin, craggy-faced former federal judge who was baseball's newly appointed commissioner, did not think so. An accumulation of evidence had prompted a grand jury to indict eight players, three of whom had confessed to taking a bribe, though their confessions mysteriously disappeared prior to the trial. (Charges were dropped against one of the eight.) The day after the trial, Landis declared that "Regardless of the verdict of juries, no player that throws a ball game; no player that undertakes or promises to throw a ball game; no player that sits in a conference with a bunch of crooked players and gamblers where the ways and means of throwing games are planned and discussed and does not promptly tell his club about it, will ever play professional baseball." With the same fearless rectitude and controlled temper he had used as judge in the trustbusting case against Standard Oil, Landis made a severe decision. As a lesson to present and future players and to the fans who revered the game, he banned all eight from ever playing professional baseball again. Landis's act illustrates the clash of values that characterized the decade of the 1920s: the tension between the urge for release, fun, and consumerism and the tug of old-fashioned values, moral purity, and order.

During the 1920s the flower of consumerism reached full bloom. Although poverty dogged small farmers, workers in declining industries, and nonwhites in inner cities, most of the population enjoyed a high standard of living. Spurred by advertising and new forms of credit, Americans eagerly bought radios, automobiles, real estate, and stocks. As in the Gilded Age, government policies supported the interests of business; Congress, three Republican presidents, and even the Supreme Court acted to maintain a favorable climate for profits. Yet important reforms were undertaken at state and local levels of government, solidifying and extending reforms of the Progressive era.

Complexity characterized the 1920s. Its frivolous stunts and fads were accompanied by an outburst of creativity in the arts and by significant advances in science and technology. Changes in work habits, family responsibilities, and health care fostered new uses of time and new attitudes about proper behavior. While material bounty and increased leisure time enticed Americans into a variety of new amusements, winds of change also stirred up waves of reaction. New liberal values repelled various groups such as the Ku Klux Klan, immigration restrictionists, and religious fundamentalists. They reacted by trying to restore a society in which everyone had the same beliefs, people knew their places, and deviants were not tolerated.

Other troubling clouds were gathering as well. The consumer culture that dominated everyday life caused Americans to ignore rising debts and other negative economic signs. Just before the decade closed, the whole system came crashing down, bringing the new era to a brutal close.

BIG BUSINESS TRIUMPHANT

The decade of business ascendancy began with a frightening economic decline. For two years after the First World War, heavy consumer spending drove prices up. Then in 1920 people abruptly stopped buying. Export trade and industrial output both dropped as wartime orders dried up. Farm income plunged due to falling exports, and farmers' share of the national wealth dropped. Unemployment, around 2 percent in 1919, passed 12 percent

in 1921. Profits declined in the railroad and mining industries, and layoffs spread through New England as textile companies abandoned outdated factories for the convenient raw materials and cheap labor of the South.

Electric motors helped drive the recovery that began in 1922 and continued unevenly until 1929. Electricity powered 70 percent of American industry by 1929, and thousands of steam engines had been relegated to the scrap heap. Assembly-line production also contributed to economic health, adding countless new consumer products such as vacuum cleaners and refrigerators to the market. New metal alloys, chemicals, synthetic materials such as rayon, and preserved foods became commonplace. As Americans acquired more spending money and leisure time, service industries boomed. More people could afford the goods and services of department stores, restaurants, beauty and barber shops, and movie theaters. This new consumerism was fueled by refined methods of credit, especially the installment or time-payment plan ("a dollar down and a dollar forever," as one critic quipped). Of 3.5 million automobiles sold in 1923, some 80 percent were bought on credit.

Beneath the prosperity, an economic revolution was rumbling. The consolidation movement that had bred trusts and holding companies in the late nineteenth century had reached a new stage. Although Progressive-era trustbusting had to some extent harnessed big business, it had not eliminated oligopoly—control of an entire industry by a few large firms. By the 1920s oligopolies dominated not only production but also marketing, distribution, and even finance. In such basic industries as automobile manufacturing, steel production, and electrical equipment, a few sprawling companies such as General Motors, U.S. Steel, and General Electric predominated.

The organizational movement and professionalization of management that had begun around 1900 also matured in the 1920s. Myriad business and professional associations sprang up to protect members' interests. Retailers and manufacturers formed trade associations to pool information and coordinate planning. Farm bureaus promoted scientific agriculture, lobbied for government protection, and tried to stabilize markets. Lawyers, engineers, and social scientists cooperated with business to promote economic growth by serving on boards of directors and providing research infor-

• *Important Events* •

1919	Eighteenth Amendment ratified, establishing Prohibition			Ku Klux Klan activity peaks

1919 — Eighteenth Amendment ratified, establishing Prohibition

1920 — Nineteenth Amendment ratified, legalizing the vote for women in federal elections
Warren G. Harding elected president
KDKA transmits first commercial radio broadcast

1920–21 — Postwar deflation and depression occurs

1921 — Federal Highway Act funds national highway system
Johnson Act establishes immigration quotas
Sacco and Vanzetti convicted
Sheppard-Towner Act allots funds to states to set up maternity and pediatric clinics

1922 — Economic recovery raises standard of living

1923 — Harding dies; Calvin Coolidge assumes the presidency
Ku Klux Klan activity peaks
Equal rights amendment introduced in Congress but not passed

1923–24 — Government scandals exposed

1924 — Johnson-Reid Act revises immigration quotas
Coolidge elected president

1925 — Scopes trial highlights battle between religious fundamentalists and religious liberals

1927 — Sacco and Vanzetti executed
Lindbergh pilots solo transatlantic flight
Babe Ruth hits sixty home runs
The Jazz Singer, the first movie with sound, is released

1928 — Stock market soars
Herbert Hoover elected president

1929 — Stock market crashes; Great Depression begins

mation. Big business had dominated American economic life since the late nineteenth century; these consolidated, corporate forms of initiative that now pervaded so many segments of the economy were what distinguished the twentieth century from the nineteenth.

In the course of this expansion, many Americans shed their fears of big business, swayed in part by the testimonials of probusiness propagandists. "Among the nations of the earth today," one writer proclaimed in 1921, "America stands for one idea: *Business*. . . . Thru business, properly conceived, managed and conducted, the human race is finally to be redeemed."

Government reflected this outlook. As corporations became more national in scope, they looked increasingly to the federal government to promote economic growth. Congress reduced taxes on corporations and wealthy individuals in 1921, and the next year it raised tariff rates in the Fordney-McCumber Tariff Act. Presidents Warren G. Harding, Calvin Coolidge, and Herbert Hoover appointed influential cabinet officers who pursued policies favorable to business. Regulatory agencies such as the Federal Trade Commission and Interstate Commerce Commission cooperated with corporations more than they regulated them.

The Supreme Court, led by Chief Justice William Howard Taft, the former president, exerted its authority as aggressively as it did in the Gilded Age to protect business and private property. Its key decisions sheltered business from government regulation and undermined attempts by organized labor to achieve its ends through strikes and legislation. In *Coronado Coal Company* v. *United Mine Workers* (1922), Taft ruled that a striking union, like a trust, could be prosecuted for illegal restraint of trade. Yet in *Maple Floor Association* v. *U.S.* (1929), the Court exempted from antitrust laws trade associations that collected and disseminated antiunion information. The Court also voided restrictions on child labor (*Bailey* v. *Drexel Furniture Company*, 1922) and overturned a minimum-wage law for women because it infringed on liberty of contract (*Adkins* v. *Children's Hospital*, 1923).

Organized labor, which had gained ground during the Progressive era, suffered other setbacks during the 1920s. Public opinion, influenced by a fear of Bolshevism—allegedly brought into the country after World War I by radical immigrants from eastern Europe—turned against workers who disrupted everyday life with strikes. Perpetuating tactics used during the Red Scare (see Chapter 23), the federal government frequently stifled union attempts to exercise power. In 1922, for instance, the Harding administration obtained a severe and sweeping court injunction to quash a strike by 400,000 railroad shop workers. The same year, the Justice Department helped put down a nationwide strike by 650,000 miners.

Meanwhile, large corporations counteracted the appeal of unions by offering pensions, profit sharing (which actually amounted to withholding wages for later distribution), and company-sponsored social and sporting events—a policy known as welfare capitalism. State legislators lent their support to employers by prohibiting closed shops (workplaces where union membership was mandatory). Concerned about secure employment, workers in turn shied away from unions and the uncertain class solidarity they promoted. In such a climate, union membership fell from 5.1 million in 1920 to 3.6 million in 1929.

A BUSINESS-MINDED PRESIDENCY

A series of Republican presidents in the 1920s extended Theodore Roosevelt's notion of government-business cooperation—but they typically made government a compliant coordinator rather than the active director Roosevelt had advocated. A symbol of the decade's good will toward business was President Warren G. Harding, a Republican elected in 1920 when the populace had no appetite for national or international crusades. Democrats had nominated Governor James M. Cox of Ohio, who supported Woodrow Wilson's fading hopes for U.S. membership in the League of Nations (see Chapter 23). But Cox and his running mate, Franklin D. Roosevelt of New York, failed to attract voters. Harding, who kept his position on the League vague, captured 16 million popular votes to only 9 million for Cox. (The total vote in the 1920 presidential election was 36 percent higher than in 1916, reflecting the participation of women voters for the first time.)

A small-town newspaper publisher and senator from Ohio, Harding selected some capable assistants, notably Secretary of State Charles Evans Hughes, Secretary of Commerce Herbert Hoover, Secretary of the Treasury Andrew Mellon, and Secretary of Agriculture Henry C. Wallace. Harding also backed some reforms that represented an extension of progressivism into the 1920s. He helped streamline the federal budget with the Budget and Accounting Act of 1921, supported antilynching legislation, approved bills assisting farm cooperatives and liberalizing farm credit, and, unlike his predecessor Wilson, was generally tolerant on civil liberties issues.

Harding Administration

Harding's problem was that he had too many predatory friends. "Warren, it's a good thing you wasn't born a gal," his father once reputedly remarked. "You'd be in the family way all the time—you can't say no." Indeed, Harding said yes far too often, appointing friends who saw officeholding as an invitation to corruption. Charles Forbes of the Veterans Bureau served time in federal prison after being convicted of fraud and bribery in connection with government contracts. Thomas W. Miller, custodian of alien property, was jailed for accepting bribes. Attorney General Harry Daugherty was implicated in a bribery scheme and in other fraudulent acts; he escaped prosecution only by refusing to testify against himself. In the most notorious case, a congressional inquiry in 1923 and 1924 revealed that Secretary of the Interior Albert Fall had accepted bribes to lease government property to private oil companies. For his role in the affair—called the Teapot Dome scandal after a Wyoming oil reserve that had been turned over to Mammoth Oil Company—Fall was fined $100,000 and spent a year in jail, the first cabinet officer ever to be so disgraced.

In mid-1923, few Americans knew how corrupt Harding's administration had become. The president, however, was disillusioned. Amid rumors of mismanagement and crime, he told journalist William Allen White, "My God, this is a hell of a job. I have no trouble with my enemies. . . . But my friends, my God-damned friends . . . they're the ones that keep me walking the floor nights." On a speaking tour that summer, Harding became ill, and he died in San Francisco on August 2. Though his death preceded revelation of the

Teapot Dome scandal, some people later speculated that Harding had committed suicide rather than face the brewing storm. Most evidence, however, points to death from natural causes, probably a heart attack. At any rate, Harding was truly mourned. A warm, dignified-looking man who relished a good joke and an evening of poker, he seemed suited to a nation that had just experienced wracking upheaval at home and abroad.

Vice President Calvin Coolidge, Harding's successor and a dour New Englander, was far more solemn. (Alice Roosevelt Longworth, Teddy's daughter, quipped that Coolidge looked as if he had been weaned on a pickle.) Coolidge had an undistinguished record as Republican governor of Massachusetts. He first attracted national attention in 1919 with his firm stand against striking Boston policemen, a policy that won him the vice-presidential nomination in 1920. Ordinarily, however, he was content to let events take their course, prompting columnist Walter Lippmann to remark on the "grim, determined, alert inactivity, which keeps Mr. Coolidge occupied constantly."

Coolidge had great respect for private enterprise. "The man who builds a factory builds a temple," he once declared. "The man who works there, worships there." Fortunately his presidency coincided with unusual business prosperity. Aided by Andrew Mellon, whom he retained as secretary of the treasury, Coolidge's administration balanced the budget, reduced government debt, lowered income-tax rates (especially for the rich), and began construction of a national highway system. His generally tightfisted fiscal policies won business support. Congress took little initiative during these years, assenting to most measures recommended by the cabinet and by business associations such as the U.S. Chamber of Commerce. The only disruptions arose over farm policy. Responding to farmers' complaints of falling prices, Congress twice passed bills to establish government-backed price supports for staple crops (the McNary-Haugen bills of 1927 and 1928). Coolidge, however, vetoed the measure both times.

"Coolidge prosperity" was the decisive issue in the presidential election of 1924. Both major parties ran candidates who accepted business supremacy. Republicans nominated Coolidge with little dissent. At their national convention Democrats

Coolidge Prosperity

Basically a shy and introverted person, Calvin Coolidge was content to let business have free rein in the pursuit of profits. This cartoon shows Coolidge accompanying the lively performance of big business with an instrument and a song of praise. Harvard University Art Museums.

first debated heatedly whether to condemn the Ku Klux Klan, voting 542 to 541 against condemnation. They then endured 103 ballots before breaking a deadlock between southern prohibitionists who supported former Secretary of the Treasury William G. McAdoo and antiprohibition easterners who backed New York's Governor Alfred E. Smith. They finally settled on John W. Davis, a corporation lawyer from New York. Remnants of the progressive movement, along with various farm, labor, and socialist groups, formed a new Progressive party and nominated Robert M. La Follette, the aging reformer from Wisconsin. The party revived issues unresolved by previous generations: public ownership of utilities, aid to farmers, more rights for organized labor, and increased regulation of business.

The election results resembled those of 1912 in reverse: the two probusiness candidates captured most of the votes. Coolidge beat Davis by 15.7

million to 8.4 million popular votes, 382 to 136 electoral votes. Like Taft in 1912, La Follette finished a poor third, receiving a respectable but ineffective 4.8 million popular votes and only 13 electoral votes. The electorate had endorsed the status quo and voiced its expectation of a period of extended prosperity.

EXTENSIONS OF REFORM

Some political analysts, struck by the triumph of business influence, claimed that progressivism had died. They were partly right; the urgent thrust for

Extension of Progressive Reforms

political and economic reform that had moved the previous generation faded in the 1920s. Yet many of the Progressive era's achievements were sustained and extended in these years. Federal trustbusting declined, but regulatory commissions and other government agencies still monitored business activities and worked to reduce wasteful business practices. A corps of congressional reformers led by George Norris of Nebraska and Robert La Follette of Wisconsin kept progressive causes alive by supporting labor legislation, aid to farmers, and a government-owned hydroelectric dam at Muscle Shoals, Alabama. (Business-oriented politicians wanted to sell or lease the dam and its nitrate plant to private interests.)

Most reform, however, occurred at state and local levels. Following initiatives begun before the First World War, thirty-four states instituted or expanded workers' compensation laws in the 1920s. Many states established employee-funded old-age pensions and welfare programs for the indigent. In the cities, social scientists gathered data in a systematic effort to identify and solve urban problems such as poverty and substandard housing. By 1926 every major city and many smaller ones had planning and zoning commissions that aimed to harness physical growth to the common good. Social workers continued to strive for better housing and poverty relief. During the 1920s the nation's state houses, city halls, and universities trained a new generation of reformers who would later influence national affairs during the New Deal.

Indian affairs also stirred reformers, who were forced by the generally apathetic stance of the federal government to take adversarial positions toward federal officials. No

Indian Affairs

longer a threat to whites' ambitions, Native Americans were now treated like other minorities: as objects of discrimination and of pressures to assimilate. Severalty, the policy of allotting land to individuals rather than to tribes, had failed to make Indians self-supporting. Indian farmers had to contend with poor soil, lack of irrigation, poor medical care, overcut forests, and cattle thieves. Deeply attached to their land, they showed little inclination to move to cities. Whites still hoped to convert tribal peoples into "productive" citizens but in a way that remained insensitive to indigenous cultures. Reformers were especially critical of Indian women, who refused to adopt middle-class homemaking methods and balked at sending their children to boarding schools.

Reform organizations such as the Indian Rights Association, the Indian Defense Association, and the General Federation of Women's Clubs worked to obtain racial justice and social services, including better education and return of tribal lands. Meanwhile, the federal government struggled to clarify Indians' citizenship status. The Dawes Act had conferred citizenship on all Indians who accepted land in severalty but not on those who remained on reservations. The government retained control over Indian citizens that it did not exercise over other citizens. (For example, in the early 1900s, before prohibition, federal law prevented the sale of liquor to Indians.) Congress finally clarified the issue in 1924 with a law granting full citizenship to all Indians who had not previously received it. Also, the Bureau of Indian Affairs was reorganized under President Herbert Hoover, and expenditures were increased for health, education, and welfare. Much of the money, however, went to enlarge the bureaucracy rather than into Indian hands, and paternalism continued to characterize federal policy.

Even after the achievement of suffrage in 1920 (see Chapter 21), politically active women tended to shun party politics in favor of voluntary organizations whose memberships

Women and Politics

helped develop the techniques of modern pressure-group politics. Whether the issue was birth control, peace, education, Indian affairs, or opposition to lynching,

Though armed with the vote for the first time in the 1920s, women generally failed to participate in elections in proportions higher than those of men. Nevertheless, some women took their new responsibilities seriously. These members of a women's political organization are prepared to attend a convention. UPI/ Bettmann Archives.

women active in these associations publicized their cause and lobbied legislators rather than trying to elect their own candidates. At times they allied with men's organizations working for similar ends and achieved legislative victories especially valuable to women. Lobbying by several women's groups persuaded Congress to pass the Sheppard-Towner (Maternity and Infancy) Act (1921), which allotted funds to states to help set up maternity and pediatric clinics. (The measure was rescinded in 1929 when Congress, under pressure from private physicians, cut off funding.) The Cable Act of 1922 reversed an old law under which an American woman who married a foreigner assumed her husband's citizenship; under the new law such a woman could retain U.S. citizenship.

As new voters, however, women faced a dilemma in electoral politics. Since male party leaders were not likely to yield their power and would welcome only those women who accepted the party's platform and candidates, should women form their own party? The National Woman's party, which before suffrage had been the champion of feminism, still stressed female solidarity in the quest for equal rights. In doing so, it perpetuated the old paradox of mobilizing women as a class to erase discrimination against the class of women (see Chapter 21). Other groups such as the League of Women Voters, which evolved out of the National American Woman Suffrage Association, did not attempt to create a female voting bloc. Instead, they preferred to lobby for issues of interest to women while at the same time integrating women into politics with men, rather than constantly struggling against them. To the dismay of women's political groups, however, newly enfranchised female voters participated in elections in the same small proportions as did men. Like men, they seemed preoccupied by the diversions of the new era's materialism.

The above illustration represents two major themes of the 1920s: the use of electricity for an ever-increasing variety of consumer products and the advertising that promoted expanding consumerism. Note the way in which the ad directs its appeal to women. Courtesy of The Strong Museum, Rochester, New York © 1993.

MATERIALISM UNBOUND

Poor Richard's Almanac would have sold poorly in the 1920s. Though traditional values persisted, many Americans found it difficult to reconcile the virtues of thrift and sobriety that Benjamin Franklin had preached with the new emphasis on acquisition, amusement, and salesmanship. Raised on traditional homilies like "Waste not, want not," they nevertheless succumbed to the advice of an advertising executive: "Make the public want what you have to sell. Make 'em pant for it." And, though confused about values, Americans attained the highest standard of living they had yet experienced. Poverty and social injustice still blighted the country, but the belief prevailed that, as journalist Joseph Wood Krutch put it, "the future was bright and the present was good fun at least."

Between 1919 and 1929 the gross national product—the total value of all goods and services produced in the United States—swelled by 40 percent. Wages and salaries also grew (though not as drastically), while the cost of living remained relatively stable. People had more purchasing power, and they spent as Americans had never spent. In an article in *Survey* magazine, Eunice Fuller Barnard contrasted one family's expenditures in 1900 with those of 1928:

Expansion of the Consumer Society

1900

2 bicycles	$ 70[1]
wringer and washboard	$ 5
brushes and brooms	$ 5
sewing machine (mechanical)	$ 25
Total	$ 105

1928

automobile	$ 700
radio	$ 75
phonograph	$ 50
washing machine	$ 150
vacuum cleaner	$ 50
sewing machine (electric)	$ 60
other electrical equipment	$ 25
telephone (year)	$ 35
Total	$1,145

Barnard added that education and medical care had become costlier. Nevertheless, she regarded the change as worthwhile, explaining that she would gladly pay more for a quart of milk she knew was safer and purer than the product of a generation earlier. "When some of us bewail the higher cost of living, we may be talking about the higher cost of *better* living," Barnard concluded.

The benefits of modern technology were reaching more people than ever before. By 1929 two-thirds of all Americans lived in dwellings that had electricity, compared with one-sixth in 1912. In 1929 one-fourth of all families owned electric vacuum cleaners and one-fifth had toasters. Many could afford these and other goods such as radios, washing machines, and movie tickets only because more than one family member worked or because the breadwinner took a second job. Nevertheless,

[1]From Paul Carter, *Another Part of the Twenties,* © 1977, Columbia University Press. By permission.

During the 1920s, the desire to own an automobile spread to all classes, races, and ethnic groups. Low prices and available credit enabled families such as this one from Beaumont, Texas, to own a "touring car."   Tyrrell Historical Library.

new products and services were available to more than just the rich.

Of all the era's material wonders, the automobile was the vanguard. During the 1920s automobile registrations soared from 8 million to 23 million. Mass production and competition brought down prices, making cars affordable even to some working-class families. A Ford Model T cost less than $300 and a Chevrolet sold for $700 by 1926—when workers in manufacturing earned about $1,300 a year and clerical workers about $2,300. At these prices, people could consider the car a necessity rather than a luxury. "There is no such thing as a 'pleasure automobile,'" proclaimed an ad in a Nashville newspaper in 1925. "You might as well talk of 'pleasure fresh air,' or of 'pleasure beef steak.' . . . The automobile increases length of life, increases happiness, represents above all other achievements the progress and the civilization of our age."

Effects of the Automobile

The car altered American life as much as the railroad had seventy-five years earlier. Women achieved newfound independence as high numbers learned to drive. Changes in design provided new opportunities for youths to escape from watchful parents: by 1927, most autos were enclosed (most had had open tops in 1919), making for a privacy that bred fears of "houses of prostitution on wheels." The vast choice of models (there were 108 automobile manufacturers in 1923) and colors allowed owners to express their personal tastes. And most important, the car was the ultimate symbol of social equality, as illustrated above in the photograph of the Texas family. As one writer observed in 1924, "It is hard to convince Steve Popovich, or Antonio Branca, or plain John Smith that he is being ground into the dust by Capital when at will he may drive the same highways, view the same scenery, and get as much enjoyment from his trip as the modern Midas."

Americans' new passion for driving necessitated extensive construction of roads and abundant supplies of fuel. Since the late 1800s farmers and bicyclists had been pressing for improved roads; after the First World War motorists joined the campaign to improve local arteries. Important advances came in 1921 when Congress passed the Federal Highway Act, which provided federal aid for state roads; and in 1923 when the Bureau of Public Roads planned a national highway system. The advent of the automobile also forced public officials to pay more serious attention to safety regulations and traffic control. (General Electric Company produced the first timed stop-and-go traffic light in 1924.)

The oil industry, already vast and powerful, shifted its emphasis from illumination and lubrication to propulsion. In 1920 the United States produced about 65 percent of the world's oil, much of it controlled by the Standard Oil trust. But corporate and government officials were already warning of fuel shortages and shrinking reserves. A 1920 U.S. Geological Survey report predicted that "unless our consumption is checked, we shall by 1925 be dependent on foreign oilfields." In some parts of the country oil companies doubled the price of gasoline and imposed limits on the amount people could buy. But the crisis appeared to be fabricated to help an American company. Just after price hikes, the State Department persuaded the British to grant Standard Oil a share in British-controlled Iraqi oilfields. Immediately thereafter, the crisis ended.

More than ever, demand for automobiles and other goods and services was whetted by advertising. By 1929 total advertising expenditures reached

Advertising $3.4 billion, more than was spent on all types of formal education. Advertising became a new gospel for many business-minded Americans. In his best-selling *The Man Nobody Knows* (1925), advertising executive Bruce Barton called Jesus "the founder of modern business" because he "picked up twelve men from the bottom ranks of business and forged them into an organization that conquered the world." About the same time, a pamphlet entitled *Moses, Persuader of Men* declared, "Moses was one of the greatest salesmen and real-estate promoters that ever lived," demonstrating that advertising could be ecumenical. Blending psychological principles with practical cynicism, advertising theorists asserted confidently that any person's tastes could be manipulated.

As daily newspaper circulation declined in the 1920s, other media assumed vital advertising functions. By 1929 over 10 million families owned radios, which bombarded them with advertisements. Radio was one of the most influential cultural and technological developments in the 1920s. Station KDKA in Pittsburgh pioneered commercial radio broadcasting beginning in 1920; within two years there were 508 such stations. By 1929 Americans were spending $850 million a year on radio equipment, and the National Broadcasting Company, which had begun to assemble a network of radio stations three years earlier, was charging advertisers $10,000 to sponsor an hour-long show. Highway billboards and commercials projected during intermissions at movie houses also reminded viewers to buy. Packaging and product display became sciences, with the objective of creating demand.

Although poor people could not afford all these new products and services, some new trends touched the working classes, especially those living in cities. Indoor plumbing and electricity became more common in private residences, and canned foods, ready-made clothes, and mass-produced shoes became more affordable. A little cash and a lot of credit enabled many wage earners to purchase an automobile. And even if a family could not afford a radio, vacuum cleaner, or vacation right away, there was always hope. Spending became a national pastime. No wonder many Americans wanted Henry Ford to run for president in 1924.

CITIES, MIGRANTS, AND SUBURBS

Consumerism signified not merely an economically mature nation but an urbanized one. The 1920 federal census revealed that for the first time a majority of Americans, 51.4 percent,

Continuing Urbanization lived in urban areas (defined as places with 2,500 or more people), a sign that the city had become the locus of national experience. Indeed, the growth of both services and industry was closely tied to urbanization. Industries such as steel, oil, and auto production invigorated cities like Detroit, Birmingham, and Houston; services and retail trades aided expansion

In 1922, only 60,000 families owned radios; by 1930, the number had swelled to 13.75 million. In cities and towns across the country eager buyers flocked to radio shops to listen to the new device through speakers and earphones.   Brown Brothers.

in Seattle, Atlanta, and Minneapolis. The most explosive growth occurred in cities with warm climates—notably Miami and San Diego—where the promise of comfort and profit attracted thousands of speculators.

The trend toward urbanization continued during the 1920s, when an estimated 6 million Americans left their farms for nearby or distant cities. Midwestern migrants, particularly young single people, moved to regional centers like Kansas City and Indianapolis or to the West. Between 1920 and 1930 California's population increased 67 percent; in the process it became one of the nation's most urbanized states while retaining its status as a leading agricultural state. Meanwhile a steady stream of rural southerners moved to the burgeoning industrial cities of the South or followed railroad lines northward to Chicago and Cleveland.

African-Americans accounted for a sizable portion of the migrants. Pushed out of cotton farming by a plague of boll weevils and lured by industrial jobs, 1.5 million blacks moved cityward during the 1920s, accelerating a trend that had begun a decade earlier (see Chapter 23). The African-American populations of New York, Chicago, Detroit, and Houston doubled during these years. Forced by low wages and discrimination to seek the cheapest housing, newcomers squeezed into ghettos—low-rent districts from which escape was difficult at best. Unlike white migrants, who were free to move away from inner-city districts when they could afford to, blacks found better housing closed to them. The only way they could expand their housing opportunities was to spill into nearby neighborhoods, a process that sparked resistance and violence. Fears of such expansion prompted white neighborhood associations to adopt restrictive covenants, whereby homeowners pledged not to sell their property to blacks.

In response to discrimination, race riots, and threats, thousands of blacks in northern cities joined movements that glorified black independence. The most influ-

Marcus Garvey ential of these black nationalist groups was the Universal Negro Improvement Association (UNIA), headed by Marcus Garvey, a visionary Jamaican immigrant who believed blacks should separate themselves from corrupt white society. Proclaiming "I am the equal of any white man," Garvey cultivated racial pride with mass meetings and parades. He also promoted black cap-

Cinco de Mayo Mogollon, N.M.

Mexican immigrants, like other immigrants, brought their homeland customs with them to the United States. One holiday, called Cinco de Mayo, commemorated the Mexican victory over French troops in the Battle of Puebla on May 5, 1862, with a parade such as this one in Mogollon, New Mexico. Library of Congress.

italism to foster blacks' management skills. His newspaper, the *Negro World*, refused to publish ads for hair straighteners and skin-lightening cosmetics, and his Black Star shipping line was intended to help blacks emigrate to Africa.

The UNIA declined in the mid-1920s when the Black Star line went bankrupt (unscrupulous dealers had sold the line dilapidated ships) and when antiradical fears prompted government prosecution (ten of the organization's leaders were arrested on charges of anarchism and Garvey was deported for mail fraud). Black middle-class leaders like W. E. B. Du Bois opposed the UNIA, as did black socialists like A. Philip Randolph and Chandler Owen. Nevertheless, in New York, Chicago, Detroit, and other cities, the organization attracted a huge following. (Contemporaries estimated it at 500,000; Garvey claimed 6 million.) Garvey's speeches had served notice that blacks had their own aspirations, which they could and would translate into action.

The newest immigrants to American cities came from Mexico and Puerto Rico. As in the nineteenth century, Mexicans continued to move north

Mexican and Puerto Rican Immigrants

to work as agricultural laborers in the Southwest, but in the 1920s many were also drawn to growing cities like Denver, San Antonio, Los Angeles, and Tucson. Like other immigrant groups, Mexicans generally lacked resources and skills, and men greatly outnumbered women. Victims of Anglo prejudice, Mexicans crowded into low-rent inner-city districts plagued by poor city services, such as sanitation, police protection, and schools. Yet in their communities, called *barrios*, immigrants could maintain the customs and values of the homeland and develop businesses and social organizations to help them adapt to American society.

The 1920s also witnessed an influx of Puerto Ricans to the mainland. (Puerto Rico had been a U.S. possession since 1898, and its natives were made U.S. citizens in 1917; see Chapter 22.) A shift in the island's economy from sugar to coffee production had created a surplus of workers. Attracted by contracts from employers seeking cheap labor, most Puerto Rican migrants moved to New

York City where they created barrios in parts of Brooklyn and Manhattan. Besides manufacturing, Puerto Ricans found jobs in hotels, restaurants, and domestic service. In both Puerto Rican and Mexican barrios, the educated elite—doctors, lawyers, business owners—tended to serve as community leaders. The Puerto Rican barrios also developed their own businesses, such as *bodegas* (grocery stores), restaurants, and boarding houses.

As urban growth peaked, suburban growth accelerated. Although towns had clustered around the edges of urban centers since the nation's

Growth of the Suburbs

earliest years, prosperity and easier transportation—mainly the automobile—made the urban fringe more accessible to those wishing to flee crowded cities in the 1920s. Between 1920 and 1930, the suburbs of Chicago (such as Oak Park and Evanston), Cleveland (such as Shaker Heights), and Los Angeles (such as Burbank and Inglewood) grew five to ten times as fast as did the central cities. Most suburbs were middle- and upper-class bedroom communities; some, like Highland Park (near Detroit) and East Chicago, were industrial suburbs.

Increasingly, suburbs resisted annexation to core cities. Suburbanites wanted to escape big-city crime, dirt, and taxes, and they fought to preserve local control over their own police, fire protection, and water and gas services. Particularly in the Northeast and Midwest, the suburbs' fierce independence choked off expansion by the central city and divided metropolitan areas in ways that would cause problems for future generations. Nevertheless, with the suburbs' dependence on automobiles and the dispersal of population away from urban cores, the environmental problems of city life—trash, air pollution, water pollution, and noise—spread across the entire metropolitan area.

Both bulging cities and suburbs fostered the mass culture that gave the decade its character. Most of the consumers who jammed shops, movie houses, and sporting arenas and embraced fads like crossword puzzles, miniature golf, and marathon dancing were city and suburban dwellers. Cities and suburbs were the places where people defied law and morality by patronizing speakeasies (illegal saloons), wearing outlandish clothes, and listening to jazz. They were also the places where women, ethnic and racial minorities, and devout moralists strained hardest to adjust to the new era. Yet the

Wide highways, cheap land, and affordable housing allowed automobile commuters to move to the urban periphery, such as Culver City, outside Los Angeles. In this photo, young women in 1920s flapper attire celebrate their suburbs' phenomenal growth. Note the strong presence of the motor car.   Security Pacific National Bank Collection, Los Angeles Public Library.

sentimental ideal of small-town society survived and contributed to the clash of values that characterized the era. While millions thronged cityward, Americans reminisced about the innocence and simplicity of a world gone by. This was the dilemma the modern nation faced: how does one anchor oneself in a world of rampant materialism and social change?

NEW RHYTHMS OF EVERYDAY LIFE

Amid all the change, Americans developed new ways of using time. People increasingly split their daily lives into distinct compartments: work, family, and leisure. Each type of time was altered in the 1920s. For many people, time on the job shrank. Among industrial workers the five-and-a-half-day workweek (half a day on Saturday) was becoming common. Many white-collar employees worked a forty-hour week and enjoyed two days off. Annual vacations were becoming a standard job benefit for white-collar workers, whose numbers grew by 40 percent.

Family time is harder to measure, but certain trends are clear. Birthrates dropped noticeably between 1920 and 1930 as birth control became more widely practiced and, as a result, family size decreased. Among American women who had married in the 1870s and 1880s, well over half who survived to age fifty had five or more children; of their counterparts who married in the 1920s, however, just 20 percent had five or more children. Meanwhile the divorce rate rose. In 1920 there was 1 divorce in every 7.5 marriages; by 1929 the national ratio was 1 in 6, and in many cities it was 2 in 7. In conjunction with longer life expectancy, lower birthrates and more divorce meant that adults were devoting a smaller portion of their lives to parental and other family tasks.

The availability of ready-to-wear clothes, canned foods, and mass-produced furniture meant that family members spent less time producing household necessities. Wives still spent long hours cleaning, cooking, and raising children, but machines now lightened some of their tasks. Especially in middle-class households, electric irons and washing machines simplified some chores. Gas-

Household Management

and oil-powered central heating and hot-water heaters eliminated the hauling of wood, coal, and water, the upkeep of a kitchen fire, and the removal of ashes.

Housewives thus used their time differently than their forebears had—though they spent as many, if not more, hours on domestic responsibilities. Although new technology was supposed to make life easier for women, it also created new demands on their time. By eliminating servants, who had helped with cleaning, cooking, and childcare, machines shifted the entire task of household management to the wife. No longer a producer of food and clothing as her predecessors had been, the wife now became the chief consumer, responsible for making sure the family spent its money wisely.

Prudent expenditure of family money was related to a major revolution in American eating habits. Before 1920, nutritionists had attributed poor health to harmful foods; their remedy was to cut down on or abstain from tangy foods like spices, garlic, and onions. With the discovery of vitamins between 1915 and 1930, nutritionists began advocating the consumption of certain foods to prevent illness. Giant food companies scrambled to advertise their products as filled with vitamins and minerals beneficial to growth and health. Not only did the producers of milk and canned fruits and vegetables exploit the vitamin craze, but other companies made lofty claims that were hard to dispute because little was known about these invisible, tasteless ingredients. Fleischmann's, for example, advertised its yeast cakes as the ultimate health food, "the richest known source of water soluble vitamins." C. W. Post claimed that his Grape-Nuts contained "*iron, calcium, phosphorus,* and *other mineral elements* that are taken right up as vital food by the millions of cells in the body." This new emphasis on nutrition added a scientific dimension to housewives' roles.

In addition, the availability of washing machines, hot water, and commercial soap put pressure on wives to keep everything clean. Advertisers tried to coax women to buy products by making them feel guilty and inadequate. "Are you unpopular with your own children?" asked the makers of Listerine mouthwash. If so, the ad advised, "more often than you would imagine . . . halitosis is at fault. Children are quick to resent it. . . . Realizing this, [caring mothers] eliminate any risk of offending by the systematic use of Listerine in the mouth. Every morning. Every night." Thus, even while the industrial and service sectors became more specialized as a result of technological advances, housewives like the commuter's wife in the *Life* illustration retained a wide variety of tasks and added new ones as well.

Better diets and shorter workdays made Americans generally healthier. Life expectancy at birth increased from fifty-four to sixty years between 1920 and 1930, and infant mortality decreased by two-thirds. Sanitation and research in bacteriology and immunology combined with better nutrition to reduce the risks of life-threatening diseases such as tuberculosis and diphtheria. But medical progress did not benefit all groups equally. Rates of stillbirth and infant mortality were 50 to 100 percent higher among blacks than among whites, and the incidence of tuberculosis in inner cities remained alarmingly high. Moreover, deaths from car accidents rose 150 percent, and deaths from heart disease and cancer—diseases of old age—increased about 15 percent. Nevertheless, Americans in general were living longer: the total population over age sixty-five grew 35 percent between 1920 and 1930, while the rest of the population increased only 15 percent.

These rising numbers and the worsening economic status of the elderly stirred interest in old-age pensions and other forms of assistance. The

Older Americans and Retirement

industrial system put a premium on youth and agility, pushing older people into poverty from forced retirement and reduced income. Recognizing the needs of aging citizens, most European countries had established state-supported pension systems in the early 1900s. Many Americans believed, however, that individuals should prepare for old age by saving in their youth; pensions, they felt, smacked of socialism. As late as 1923 the Pennsylvania Chamber of Commerce labeled old-age assistance "un-American and socialistic . . . an entering wedge of communistic propaganda."

Yet something had to be done. Most of the inmates in state poorhouses were older people, and almost one-third of Americans age sixty-five and older depended financially on someone else. Only a few employers offered pension plans; most, including the federal government, did not provide for retired employees. Noting that the government fed retired horses until they died, one postal

Suburbanization and the demands of white-collar work created new schedules and roles in the middle-class family. Here the housewife, now the chief consumer and household manager, sews a button on the sleeve of the breadwinner husband while he gulps coffee and reads his paper before rushing to catch his commuter train.   Library of Congress.

worker complained, "For the purpose of drawing a pension, it would have been better had I been a horse than a human being." Resistance to pension plans finally broke at the state level in the 1920s. Led by Isaac Max Rubinow and Abraham Epstein, reformers persuaded voluntary associations, labor unions, and legislators to endorse the principle of old-age assistance through pensions, insurance, and retirement homes. By 1933 almost every state provided at least minimal assistance to needy elderly people, and a path had been opened for a national program of old-age insurance.

As people spent more time away from both work and family and were thus exposed to new influences, new habits and values were inevitable.

Social Values

Especially among the middle class but among the working class, too, clothes became a means of self-expression and a banner of personal freedom. Both men and women wore more casual and gaily colored styles than their parents would have considered. The line between acceptable and inappropriate behavior

DEPARTMENT OF COMMERCE-BUREAU OF THE CENSUS
FOURTEENTH CENSUS OF THE UNITED STATES: 1920-POPULATION

STATE _Massachusetts_   ENUMERATOR _Harry Hoffman_
COUNTY _Suffolk_   ENUMERATED BY ME AN THE _7_ DAY OF _Jan_ 1920

TOWNSHIP OR OTHER DIVISION OF COUNTY _Tract 33 1413_   NAME OF INCORPORATED PLACE _Boston_

STREET	HOUSE NUMBER	NAME	RELATION	SEX	COLOR OR RACE	AGE	SINGLE, MARRIED, WIDOWED OR DIVORCED	CITIZENSHIP	YEAR OF IMMIGRATION	PERSON PLACE OF BIRTH	FATHER PLACE OF BIRTH	MOTHER PLACE OF BIRTH	ENGLISH SPEAKING	OCCUPATION
Stamford Street	22	Garrigan, James	step-son	M	W	20	S			Mass.	New York	Ireland	yes	Chauffeur
		— Ellen	step-daughter	F	W	16	S			Mass.	New York	Ireland	yes	Laundry
	16	Bradley, George	Head	M	W	53	M			Mass.	Mass.	Mass.	yes	Railroad
		— Bella A.	wife	F	W	52	M		1880	New Brunswick	New Brunswick	New Brunswick	yes	none
		Hart, Dennis	Lodger	M	W	49	wid.			Mass.	Ireland	Ireland	yes	Painter
	12	Sidlinger, Albert	Head	M	W	65	M			Maine	Maine	Maine	yes	none
		— Catherine	wife	F	W	49	M		1886	Scotia	Ireland	Scotia	yes	none
		— Albert K.	son	M	W	29	S			Mass.	Maine	Nova Scotia	yes	Insurance broker
	10	Milkowski, John	Head	M	W	34	M		1906	Russia	Russia	Russia	yes	cook
		— Mary	wife	F	W	27	M		1908	Russia	Russia	Russia	yes	none
		— Helen	daughter	F	W	6½	S			Mass.	Russia	Russia		none
		— Jennie	daughter	F	W	5½	S			Mass.	Russia	Russia		none
		— Peter	son	M	W	1½	S			Mass.	Russia	Russia		none
		McQuaid, Francis	Lodger	M	W	33	M			Mass.	Ireland	Ireland	yes	Reporter
		— Frieda	wife	F	W	22	M		1899	Switzerland	Italy	Germany	yes	none
		White, Irwin	Lodger	M	W	37	M		1897	England	England	England	yes	Hospital handyman
		Blake, John	Lodger	M	W	38	M		1894	Ireland	Ireland	Ireland	yes	Laborer
		Miller, Harry	Lodger	M	W	44	S		1910	Norway	Norway	Norway	yes	waiter ship
	8	Ling, Chintung	Head	M	Ch	60	M		1890	China	China	China	no	Laundry
	6	Ross, Frank	Head	M	W	45	M		1889	Italy	Italy	Italy	yes	Machine fitcher
		— Effie	wife	F	W	43	M			New Hampshire	New Hampshire	Maine	yes	none

How do historians know

about individual and family life in the 1920s? The manuscript census schedules (the pages on which census takers actually recorded information) from the 1920 federal census contain extraordinarily rich information. By sampling, tabulating, and analyzing large numbers of census entries—after trying to decipher often illegible handwriting—historians raise and attempt to answer questions about everyday life and the environments in which ordinary people lived. The excerpt on this page reproduces the records from a few families living on Stamford Street in Boston and yields numerous insights into how these households were organized. For example, the Bradley household at 16 Stamford contained only a middle-aged husband, who was born in Massachusetts and worked as a railroad baggage master, his wife, born in New Brunswick (Nova Scotia) and of British descent, and a middle-aged boarder, who worked as a painter. Why was the boarder living there? Did the Bradleys have extra space because their children had grown up and moved away? The Milkowski household at 10 Stamford was larger and more complex. It contained ten people, including three young children and five lodgers. Mr. and Mrs. Milkowski were from Russia, but their lodgers came from a variety of places. What kinds of social and economic relationships might have existed in this household? A lone Chinese man lived at 8 Stamford. He worked in a laundry, and the census notes that he was married. But where was his wife? Census data often must be combined with other sources in order to answer these questions, but manuscript censuses have helped to provide an important place for people previously excluded from the historical record because they did not leave diaries or letters and were not famous enough to be the subject of newspaper stories.   Photo: National Archives Records and Census Bureau.

blurred as smoking, swearing, and frankness about sex became fashionable. Thousands who had never read psychoanalyst Sigmund Freud's theories were certain that he prescribed an uninhibited sex life as the key to mental health. Birth-control advocate Margaret Sanger, who a decade earlier had been accused of promoting race suicide, gained a large following in respectable circles. Newspapers, magazines, motion pictures, and popular songs (such as "Hot Lips" and "Burning Kisses") made certain that Americans did not suffer from "sex starvation." A typical movie ad promised "brilliant men, beautiful jazz babies, champagne baths, midnight revels, petting parties in the purple dawn, all ending in one terrific smashing climax that makes you gasp."

Other trends contributed to the breakdown of old values. Because child-labor laws and compulsory-school-attendance laws kept children in school longer than ever before, peer groups played a more influential role in socializing children. In earlier eras, different age groups had shared the same activities: children had worked with older people in the fields, and young apprentices had worked with older journeymen and craftsmen. Now, graded school classes, sports, and other organized activities constantly brought together children of the same age, separating them from the company and influence of adults. Meanwhile parents tended to rely less on family tradition and more on childcare manuals in raising children. Old-age homes, public health clinics, and workers' compensation reduced family responsibilities even further.

After the First World War, women continued to stream into the labor force. By 1930, 10.8 million women held paying jobs, an increase of over

Jobs for Women

2 million since the war's end. The sex segregation that had long characterized the workplace persisted; most female workers held jobs in which men were rare. Over 1 million women were teachers and nurses. Some 2.2 million were typists, bookkeepers, and office clerks, a tenfold increase since 1920; another 736,000 were store clerks, and growing numbers took jobs as waitresses and hairdressers. Though almost 2 million women worked at mostly sex-segregated jobs in factories, their numbers grew very little over the decade. Wherever they were employed, women's wages seldom exceeded half of the wages paid to men.

For many women, employment outside the home represented an extension of their family roles. Although women worked for a variety of reasons, the economic needs of their families were paramount. The consumerism of the 1920s tempted working-class and middle-class families to satisfy their wants by living beyond their means or by sending women and children into the labor force. In previous eras, most of these extra wage earners had been young and single. In the 1920s,

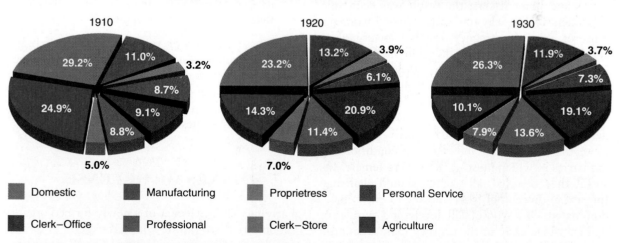

Changing Dimensions of Paid Women's Labor, 1910, 1920, 1930

Changing Dimensions of Paid Female Labor, 1910–1930 These charts reveal the extraordinary growth in clerical and professional occupations among employed women and the accompanying decline in agricultural labor in the early twentieth century. Note also that manufacturing employment peaked in 1920 and that domestic service fluctuated as white immigrant women began to move out of these jobs, only to be replaced by women of color.

married women as a proportion of the work force rose by 30 percent, and the number of employed married women swelled from 1.9 million to 3.1 million. These figures omit countless widowed, divorced, and abandoned women who held jobs and who, like married women, often had children to support. The vast majority of married women remained outside the work force (only 12 percent were employed in 1930), largely because of social pressure—it was a confession of failure if a wife had to take a paid job—and because the demands of housework and childcare prevented them from joining. African-American women were the exception; the proportion of black women who worked for pay was double that of white women. Kin such as grandmothers and aunts helped with childcare while mothers took outside employment, but such arrangements did not lessen the economic burdens of African-American households beset by poverty and discrimination.

Economic Feminism

A group of women known as economic feminists in the 1920s addressed the issue of women in the labor force, but they took a somewhat narrow view of the motivations of many female workers. According to these feminists, women who had formerly functioned as producers of food and clothes had lapsed into passive roles as child nurturers and homemakers; the result was economic dependency. The way to restore married women's sense of worth in a money-oriented society, they argued, was through gainful employment. A job, wrote *Harper's* editor Dorothy Bromley, would make a married woman "a full-fledged individual who is capable of molding her own life."

Because economic feminists stressed independence, they tended to oppose protective legislation to regulate the hours and working conditions in industries in which most workers were female. Instead, they believed, all women should challenge the sexual division of labor and try to enter male-dominated jobs whose skill levels and pay were higher. Since early in the century many feminists had called for equal pay and equal opportunity; in the 1920s their goals were voiced by Alice Paul, leader of the National Woman's party, who in 1923 supported an equal-rights amendment to the Constitution. But other women, including some feminists and some working-class women, had doubts. They did not trust the competitive, individualistic environment of the job market, and they had been raised in cultures that assigned women the responsibility of fostering cooperation within their families and neighborhoods. Once again the question of whether women should seek to resemble men posed thorny questions.

Alternative Images of Femininity

Employed or not, women confronted choices among alternative images of femininity. In contrast to the heavy floor-length dresses and long hair of previous generations, the short skirts and bobbed hair of the 1920s flapper signified independent-mindedness and sexual freedom. The flapper look became fashionable among office workers and store clerks as well as college coeds. As models of female behavior, chaste, modest heroines were eclipsed by movie vamps like Clara Bow, known as the "It Girl," and Gloria Swanson, known for her torrid love affairs on and off the screen. Many women—not just flappers—were asserting a new social equality with men. As one observer described "the new woman":

> She takes a man's point of view as her mother never could. . . . She will never make you a hatband or knit you a necktie, but she'll drive you from the station . . . in her own little sports car. She'll don knickers and go skiing with you, . . . she'll dive as well as you, perhaps better, she'll dance as long as you care to, and she'll take everything you say the way you mean it.

These new trends represented a sharp break with the more restrained culture of the nineteenth century. But social change rarely proceeds smoothly. As the decade wore on, various groups prepared to defend against threats to older and more familiar values.

LINES OF DEFENSE

Early in 1920 the leader of a newly formed organization hired two public relations experts to recruit members. The experts, Edward Clarke and Elizabeth Tyler, used modern advertising techniques to canvass communities in the South, Southwest, and Midwest, where they found thousands of men eager to pay a $10 membership fee and another $6 for a white uniform. For their efforts, Clarke and Tyler pocketed $2.50 from each membership they sold. No one could argue with their success. By 1923 the organization claimed 5 million members.

This was no ordinary civic club like the Lions or Kiwanis. It was the Ku Klux Klan, a revived version of the hooded order that had terrorized southern communities after the Civil War, and its appeal was based on fear. As one pamphlet distributed by Clarke and Tyler put it, "Every criminal, every gambler, every thug, every libertine, every girl ruiner, every home wrecker, every wife beater, every dope peddler, every moonshiner, every white slaver, every Rome-controlled newspaper, every black spider—is fighting the Klan. Think it over, which side are you on?"

The most sinister reactionary movement of the 1920s, the Klan was reconstituted in 1915 by William J. Simmons, an Atlanta evangelist and insurance salesman. The new Invisi-

Ku Klux Klan
━━━

ble Empire revived the hoods, intimidating tactics, and mystical terminology of its forerunner. (Its leader was the Imperial Wizard, its book of rituals the kloran.) But the new Klan had broader membership and objectives than the old. Its chapters fanned outward from the deep South and for a time wielded frightening power in every region of the country. Unlike the original Klan, which directed its terrorist tactics at emancipated blacks, the new Klan targeted a variety of racial and religious groups.

One brief phrase summed up the Klan's goals: "Native, white, Protestant supremacy." *Native* meant no immigration, no "mongrelization" of American culture. According to Imperial Wizard Hiram Wesley Evans, *white* supremacy was a matter of survival. "The world," he warned, "has been so made so that each race must fight for its life, must conquer, accept slavery, or die. The Klansman believes the whites will not become slaves, and he does not intend to die before his time." Evans praised *Protestantism* for fostering "unhampered individual development," and he accused the Catholic church of discouraging assimilation and enslaving people to priests and a foreign pope.

Using threatening assemblies, violence, and political pressure, Klan members menaced many communities in the early 1920s. Assuming the role of moral protector, the Klan meted out vigilante justice to suspected bootleggers, wife beaters, and adulterers; forced schools to adopt Bible reading and to stop teaching the theory of evolution; and

campaigned against Catholic and Jewish political candidates. By the mid-1920s, however, the Invisible Empire was on the wane, outnumbered by immigrants and their offspring and rocked by scandal. (In 1925 Indiana Grand Dragon David Stephenson kidnaped and raped a woman who later died either from taking poison or from infection caused by bites on her body; Stephenson was convicted of second-degree murder on the grounds that he was responsible for her suicide.) The Klan's negative, exclusive brand of patriotism and purity could not compete in a pluralistic society.

The Ku Klux Klan had no monopoly on bigotry in the 1920s; intolerance pervaded American society. A number of groups had been urging an end to free immigration since the 1880s. Nativists charged that Catholic and Jewish immigrants clogged city slums, flouted community norms, and stubbornly held to alien religious and political beliefs. As self-styled expert Madison Grant wrote in *The Passing of the Great Race* (1916): "These immigrants adopt the language of the native American, they wear his clothes, they steal his name and they are beginning to take his women, but they seldom adopt his religion or understand his ideals."

Fear of radicalism, left over from the Red Scare of 1919, fueled antiforeign sentiment. The most notorious outburst of hysteria occurred in

Sacco and Vanzetti
━━━

1921, when a court convicted Nicola Sacco and Bartolomeo Vanzetti, two immigrant anarchists, of murdering a guard and paymaster during a robbery in South Braintree, Massachusetts. Sacco and Vanzetti's main offenses seem to have been their political beliefs and Italian origins. Though the evidence failed to prove their involvement in the robbery, Judge Webster Thayer openly sided with the prosecution and privately called the defendants "anarchist bastards." Appeals and protests failed to win a new trial, and the two defendants, who remained calm and dignified throughout their ordeal, were executed in 1927. Their deaths touched off mass rallies and riots in Europe, Asia, and South America, chilling those who had looked to the United States as the land that nurtured freedom of belief.

Meanwhile, the movement to restrict immigration gathered support. Labor leaders warned that a flood of aliens would depress wages and raise unemployment. Business executives who had for-

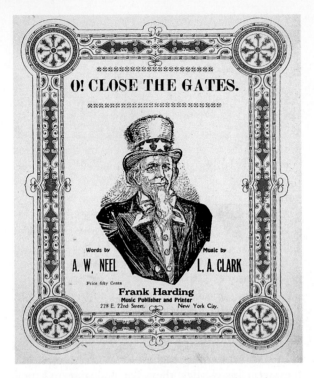

Anti-immigrationists used songs, as well as speeches and posters, to promote their cause. This 1923 tune urges the government to "Close the Gates" lest foreigners betray the hard-won rights of Americans and "drag our Colors down." National Park Service Collection, Ellis Island Immigration Museum. Photo Chermayeff & Geismar MetaForm.

merly opposed restrictions because immigrant laborers were easy to exploit now changed their minds, having realized that they could keep labor costs low by mechanizing and by hiring black workers.

Drawing support from such groups, Congress drastically reversed previous immigration policy and set yearly immigration quotas for each nationality. The quotas favored northern and western Europeans, in keeping with nativist prejudices against immigrants from southern and eastern Europe. By stipulating that annual immigration of a given nationality could not exceed 3 percent of the number of immigrants from that nation residing in the United States in 1910, the Quota (Johnson) Act of 1921 made it more difficult for immigrants from southern and eastern Europe, whose numbers were small in 1910 relative to those from northern Europe, to enter the country. The law also intro-

Immigration Quotas
———

duced a "non-quota" category that exempted from the quotas individuals with desirable professions, such as artists, nurses, ministers, and professors.

The Johnson Act, meant to be temporary, did not satisfy restrictionists, so Congress replaced it with the Immigration Act (Johnson-Reid Act) in 1924. This law limited annual immigration to 165,000 (less than one-fifth of prewar annual totals) and set quotas at 2 percent of each nationality residing in the United States in 1890. It thus further restricted southern and eastern Europeans, since fewer of those groups lived in the United States in 1890 than in 1910, though it did allow wives and dependent children of U.S. citizens to enter as nonquota immigrants. The act also established a "national-origins" system, to become effective in 1927. Instead of basing quotas on the 1890 census, national-origins policy fixed an annual limit of 150,000 immigrants, with each country receiving a fraction of that number equal to the percentage of people in the U.S. population in 1920 who derived from that country by *birth or descent*. This system fixed quotas of roughly 66,000 from Great Britain and 26,000 from Germany, but it allowed only 6,000 from Italy and 2,700 from Russia. It also excluded almost all Asians but set no quotas for peoples from the Western Hemisphere. Soon Canadians, Mexicans, and Puerto Ricans became the largest groups of newcomers (see figure).

While various groups lobbied for racial purity, the pursuit of moral purity stirred religious fundamentalists. As they had for many years, millions of Americans sought certainty in a rapidly changing world by following evangelical branches of Protestantism that accepted a literal interpretation of the Bible. For them, religion provided not only salvation but also a bulwark against the skepticism and irreverence of a materialistic, hedonistic society.

In 1925 Christian fundamentalism clashed with new scientific theory in a celebrated case in Dayton, Tennessee. Early that year the state legislature passed a law forbidding public school instructors to teach the theory that humans had evolved from lower forms of life, rather than from Adam and Eve. Shortly thereafter, high school teacher John Thomas Scopes was arrested for violating the law. (He had volunteered to serve in a test case.) Scopes's trial that summer became a headline event, with William Jennings Bryan, the former secretary of state and three-time presidential candidate, arguing for

Scopes Trial
———

Sources of Immigration, 1907 and 1927

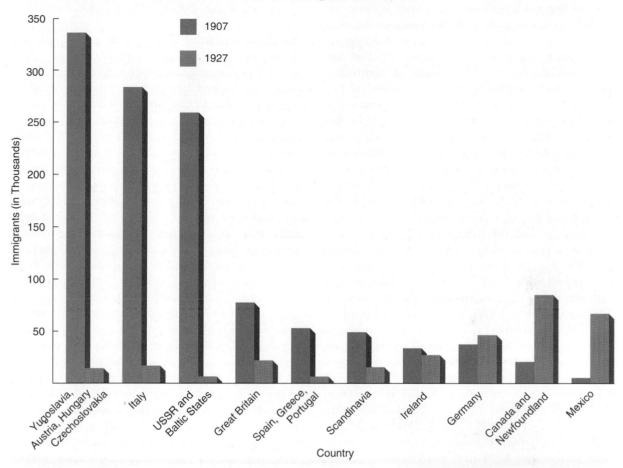

Sources of Immigration, 1907 and 1927   *Immigration peaked in the years 1907–1908, when newcomers from southern and eastern Europe poured into the United States. Then, after the immigration restriction laws were passed in the 1920s, the greatest number of immigrants came from the western hemisphere (Canada and Mexico) which was exempted from the quotas, while the number coming from eastern and southern Europe shrank.*

the prosecution, and a team of civil liberties lawyers headed by Clarence Darrow arguing for the defense. Hordes of news correspondents crowded into town, and radio stations broadcast the trial.

Although Scopes was convicted—clearly he had broken the law—modernists claimed victory. The testimony, they believed, had shown fundamentalism to be illogical. The trial's climax occurred when Bryan took the witness stand as an expert on religion and science. Responding to Darrow's probing, Bryan asserted that Eve had truly been created from Adam's rib, that the Tower of Babel was responsible for the diversity of lan-

guages, and that a big fish had swallowed Jonah. The liberal press mocked Bryan's uncritical faith; humorist Will Rogers quipped, "I see you can't say that man descended from the ape. At least that's the law in Tennessee. But do they have a law to keep a man from making a jackass of himself?" Nevertheless, fundamentalists nursed their wounds and steadfastly maintained their faith in ultimate salvation.

Klan rallies, immigration restriction, and fundamentalist literalism might have been interpreted as the last gasps of a rural society yielding to modern urban-industrial values. Yet city dwellers swelled the ranks of all these defensive movements. Nearly half the Klan's members lived in cities, especially in working-class neighborhoods where fear of invasion by African-Americans and foreigners was strong. Even urban reformers backed immigration restriction as a means of controlling poverty and quickening the assimilation of foreigners. Cities also housed hundreds of pentecostal churches, which attracted whites struggling between the lower and middle classes. Such people were swayed by the pageantry and closeness to God offered by such churches. Using modern advertising techniques and elaborately staged services broadcast live on radio, cult leaders such as the comely and magnetic Aimee Semple McPherson of Los Angeles and the former baseball player Billy Sunday stirred revivalist fervor. And many urban dwellers supported prohibition. Middle-class Protestants and some Catholics and Jews believed that eliminating the temptation of drink would help win the battle against poverty, vice, and corruption.

These defensive and emotional responses to events in the 1920s represented an attempt to sustain time-tested ways in a fast-moving and materialistic world. Some Americans lashed out at minority cultures and hedonistic trends in behavior. Millions of otherwise decent Americans firmly believed that nonwhites and immigrants were inferior people who imperiled existing values. And clergy and teachers of all faiths condemned drinking, dancing, new styles of dress, and new sexual habits.

Even while worrying about the decline of old values, most Americans tried to adjust to the new order in one way or another. Few refrained from listening to the radio and attending movies, activities that proved less corrupting than critics feared. Radio featured harmless music, news, and homey dramas, many of which endorsed traditional values. Movie producers, bowing to pressure from legislators, instituted self-censorship in 1927, forbidding nudity, rough language, and plots that did not end with justice and morality triumphant. More than ever, Americans sought fellowship rather than release of aggressive impulses in civic organizations. Membership swelled in Rotary, Kiwanis, Elks, and women's clubs, and the number of Community Chests—associations that coordinated civic and welfare projects—grew from 12 in 1919 to 361 in 1930. Perhaps most important, more people were finding release in a world of leisure.

THE AGE OF PLAY

An almost insatiable thirst for recreation gripped Americans in the 1920s. In 1919 they spent $2.5 billion on leisure activities; by 1929 such expenditures topped $4.3 billion, a figure not again equaled until after the Second World War. Spectator amusements—movies, music, and sports—accounted for about 21 percent of the 1929 total; the rest was individual recreation, from participatory sports to reading, hobbies, music, and travel.

Entrepreneurs responded quickly to Americans' apparently insatiable appetite for fads, frivolities, and what was called ballyhoo, a blitz of publicity that lent exaggerated importance to some person or event. New games and fancies particularly attracted middle-class families with large spendable incomes. Mahjong, a Chinese tile game, was all the rage in the early 1920s. Merchants could not import enough sets of the game, so dozens of American manufacturers began to produce them. By the mid-1920s people were turning to crossword puzzles, which mass-circulation newspapers and magazines had begun printing a decade earlier. When Simon and Schuster published a book of crossword puzzles with a pencil attached—people who did a crossword puzzle with a pen were labeled foolish optimists—the volume became an instant best seller. A few years later fun seekers adopted miniature golf as their new craze. By 1930 the nation had acquired some thirty thousand miniature golf courses featuring tiny castles, windmills, and waterfalls. Dance crazes like the Charleston riveted public attention throughout the country, aided by live and recorded band music on radio and the growing popularity of jazz.

In addition to participating actively in leisure activities, Americans were avid spectators, particularly of movies and sports. In total capital investment, motion pictures quickly became one of the nation's leading industries. Nearly every community had at least one theater, whether it was a hundred-seat Bijou on Main Street or a big-city "picture palace" with ornate walls, fountains in the lobby, and thousands of cushioned seats. In 1922 movies attracted 40 million viewers a week; by 1930 that number had reached 100 million—at a time when the total population was just over 120 million and total weekly

Movies

church attendance was under 60 million. The introduction of sound in *The Jazz Singer* in 1927, and of color a few years later, made movies even more attractive and realistic. The technology for making "talkie" movies had existed long before the 1920s, but producers had continued to make silent movies to appeal to the broadest possible broad audience, including immigrants who did not speak English. By the late 1920s, after immigration had been restricted and English-speaking offspring had increased, "talkies" could be better understood and had wider appeal.

Responding to the tastes of mass audiences, the movie industry produced more escapist entertainment than art. The most popular films were mass spectacles such as Cecil B. DeMille's *The Ten Commandments* (1923) and *The King of Kings* (1927); lurid dramas such as *Souls for Sale* (1923) and *A Woman Who Sinned* (1924); and slapstick comedies starring Fatty Arbuckle, Harold Lloyd, Buster Keaton, and Charlie Chaplin. Ironically, the comedies, with their poignant satire of the human condition, carried the most thought-provoking messages.

Spectator sports also boomed. Each year millions packed stadiums and parks to watch athletic events. Gate receipts from college football alone had surpassed $21 million by the late 1920s. In an age when technology and mass production had robbed experiences and objects of their uniqueness, sports provided the unpredictability and drama that people craved. Newspapers and radio captured and magnified this drama, feeding news to an eager public and glorifying events with unrestrained narrative. Thus the otherwise staid *New York Times* resorted to wild hyperbole to summarize a 1920 tennis match between Bill Tilden, the national champion, and challenger William Johnston:

> The Tilden-Johnston struggle will go down on the records as the most astounding exhibition of tennis, the most nerve-wracking battle that the courts have ever seen. . . . Tilden and Johnston played five acts of incredible melodrama, with a thrill in every scene, with horrible errors leading suddenly to glorious achievements, with skill and courage and good and evil fortune. . . . Tilden's victory was a triumph for supertennis.

With reporting like this, sports promoters did not need to buy advertising.

Baseball's drawn-out suspense, infinite variety of plays, and potential for keeping statistics attracted a huge following. After the "Black Sox

The consumerism and ballyhoo of the 1920s inspired a diverse array of fads and stunts, and the popular media were all too eager to publicize every impulsive event, such as this 1927 ride by a newlywed on an "aquaplane" in New York Harbor. Underwood & Underwood.

scandal" of 1919, baseball not only regained its respectability but also altered the nature of the game. Discovering that home runs excited fans, the leagues redesigned the ball to make it livelier; attendance at major-league games skyrocketed. A record 300,000 people attended the six-game 1921 World Series between the New York Giants and New York Yankees. Millions more gathered regularly to watch local teams.

Sports, movies, and the news gave Americans a galaxy of heroes. As society became more anonymous and the individual less significant, people clung to heroic personalities as

Sports Heroes

a means of identifying with the unique. Names such as Tilden in tennis, Gertrude Ederle in swimming (in 1926 she became the first woman to swim across the English Channel), and Bobby Jones in golf became household words. But it was the power and action of boxing, football, and baseball that produced the most popular sports heroes.

This portrait shows the powerful hands, arms, and body of the famous baseball slugger, but more riveting is the complex sight of hard, penetrating, yet sad eyes set in a sensuous, boyish face.   Museum of Modern Art, Gift of Mrs. Nickolas Muray.

Heavyweight champion Jack Dempsey, a powerful brawler from Manassa, Colorado, attracted the first of many million-dollar gates in his fight with Georges Carpentier in 1921. Harold "Red" Grange, the running back for the University of Illinois football team, thrilled thousands and became the idol of sportswriters. During his senior year in 1925, Grange was offered huge contracts by real-estate and motion-picture companies, and collected $42,000 for his first two games as a professional with the Chicago Bears.

Baseball's foremost hero was George Herman "Babe" Ruth, who began his career as a pitcher but found he could use his prodigious strength to better advantage hitting home runs. Ruth hit 29 in 1919, 54 in 1920 (the year he moved from the Boston Red Sox to the New York Yankees), 59 in 1924, and 60 in 1927—each year a record. His exaggerated gestures on the field, defiant lifestyle, and boyish grin endeared him to millions. Ruth became a national legend. Known for overindulgence in food, drink, and women, he made fans forgive his excesses by appearing at public events and visiting hospitalized children.

While identifying with the physical exploits of sports stars, Americans fulfilled a yearning for romance and adventure through movie stars.

Movie Stars and Public Heroes

The films and personal lives of Douglas Fairbanks, Gloria Swanson, and Charlie Chaplin were discussed in parlors and pool halls across the country. The decade's most ballyhooed personality probably was Rudolph Valentino, whose smooth Latin seductiveness made women swoon and men imitate his pomaded hairdo and slick sideburns. Valentino's films exploited the era's newfound sexual liberalism and flirtation with evil. In his most famous film, Valentino played a passionate sheik who carried away beautiful women to his tent, combining the roles of seducer and abductor. When he died at thirty-one of complications from ulcers and appendicitis, the press turned his funeral into a public extravaganza. Mourners lined up for over a mile to file past his coffin.

The news media also created heroes. For two weeks in 1925 newspapers kept readers on edge with reports on Floyd Collins, a young explorer trapped in a Kentucky cave. By the time rescuers found Collins dead, the entire country had idolized him as a hero battling nature. Flagpole sitters, marathon dancers, and other record seekers regularly occupied the front pages. The most notable news hero was Charles A. Lindbergh, the pilot whose daring nonstop solo flight across the Atlantic in 1927 excited millions. A modest, independent midwesterner whom writers dubbed the Lone Eagle, Lindbergh accepted fame but did not try to profit from it. The stark contrast between his personality and the ballyhoo that surrounded him made Americans admire him even more fervently.

Americans' adulation of Lindbergh may have arisen in part from guilt at having abandoned the traditional virtues of restraint and moderation. In

Prohibition

their quest for fun and self-expression, Americans had become lawbreakers and supporters of crime. The Eighteenth Amendment (1919) and federal law (1920) that prohibited the manufacture, sale, and transportation of alcoholic beverages (see Chapter 21) worked well

Rudolph Valentino became the idol of men and women alike in The Sheik, *his most famous movie. With flashing eyes and wanton smile, Valentino carries a swooning woman to his tent. This immensely popular movie earned $1 million for Paramount Pictures.*   Museum of Modern Art Film Still Archive.

at first. Per capita consumption of liquor dropped, as did arrests for drunkenness, and the price of illegal booze rose higher than average workers could afford. But aside from passing supportive laws, legislators saw little need to enforce Prohibition. In 1922 Congress gave the Prohibition Bureau only three thousand employees and less than $7 million for nationwide enforcement.

Prohibition was especially effective in regions where temperance movements had historically been successful. If it had applied only to hard liquor and not to beer and wine it might have succeeded more widely. But after about 1925 the so-called noble experiment broke down in cities, where the desire for personal freedom overwhelmed weak enforcement. The law allowed manufacture of beer for dilution into near-beer (with half the alcoholic content of regular beer) and sale of alcohol for medicinal and sacramental purposes, but bootleggers cleverly obtained and sold such spirits for other purposes. Smuggling and home manufacture of liquor were rampant. Thou-

sands of people made their own wine and bathtub gin, and bootleg importers along the country's borders and shorelines easily evaded the few patrols that attempted to curb them.

Local officials realized that it was impractical to devote their scarce resources to strict enforcement of Prohibition. Drinking, like gambling and prostitution, was a business with willing customers, and criminal organizations quickly capitalized on public demand. The most notorious of such mobs belonged to Al Capone, a burly tough who seized control of illegal liquor and vice in Chicago and maintained his grip through intimidation, bribery, and violence. Capone and his armed force of gangsters influenced local politics as well as vice until 1931, when a federal court convicted and imprisoned him for income-tax evasion.

It is important to recognize that Prohibition and its weak enforcement did not create organized crime. Gangs like Capone's had provided illegal

Al Capone

goods and services long before the 1920s. As Capone put it, "Prohibition is a business. All I do is supply a public demand. I do it in the least harmful way I can." Americans wanted their liquor and their freedom; Capone and others like him took advantage of these desires.

Thus during the 1920s Americans were caught between two value systems. A Puritan tradition of hard work, sobriety, and restraint—"Waste not, want not"—still prevailed, especially in rural areas where new diversions were unavailable. Elsewhere, however, liberating opportunities to play beckoned. Never before in American history had so many types of commercial recreation existed. Not just mass entertainment such as nightclubs, movies, sports, and radio, but individual amusements such as stamp collecting, puzzle working, and playing and listening to music became commonplace. Few of these activities were illegal or immoral, but Americans were increasingly willing to ignore old behavioral restraints and break the law if such restrictions interfered with their personal quest for pleasure. As political columnist Walter Lippmann wrote in 1931, "The high level of lawlessness is maintained by the fact that Americans desire to do so many things which they also desire to prohibit."

CULTURAL CURRENTS

The tension between conflicting value systems pulled artists and intellectuals in new directions. In literature, art, and music, rejection of old beliefs prompted experimentation. Concern over materialism and conformity gave the era's artistic output a bitterly critical tinge. Yet artists seldom voiced a radical message; they wanted not so much to destroy modern society as to fend off the era's rampant vulgarity.

The disillusioned writers who found crass materialism at odds with art became know as the Lost Generation. A number of them, including novelist Ernest Hemingway and poets Ezra Pound and T. S. Eliot, moved to Europe. Others, such as novelists William Faulkner and Sinclair Lewis, remained in America but assailed the racism and irrationality they saw around them. Along with innovative forms of expression and realistic portrayals of emo-

Literature of Alienation

tion, these writers produced biting social commentary.

Indictments of materialism and the impersonality of modern society dominated literature. F. Scott Fitzgerald's *This Side of Paradise* (1920) and *The Great Gatsby* (1925); Lewis's *Babbitt* (1922), *Arrowsmith* (1925), and *Elmer Gantry* (1927); and Eugene O'Neill's plays exposed Americans' preoccupation with money. Edith Wharton explored the clash of old and new moralities in novels such as *The Age of Innocence* (1921). Ellen Glasgow, the South's leading literary figure, lamented the trend toward impersonality in *Barren Ground* (1925). Willa Cather looked to previous eras for moral strength in *My Antonia* (1918). John Dos Passos's *Three Soldiers* (1921) and Hemingway's *Farewell to Arms* (1929) skillfully interwove antiwar sentiment with passionate critiques of the impersonality of modern relationships.

A spiritual discontent quite different from that of white writers inspired a new generation of young African-American artists. Middle-class, well-educated, and proud of their African heritage, these writers rejected the amalgamation of black and white cultures and exalted the militantly assertive "New Negro." Most of them lived in Harlem, in upper Manhattan; in this "Negro Mecca," black intellectuals and artists, aided by a few white patrons, celebrated modern black culture during what became known as the Harlem Renaissance.

Harlem Renaissance

The popular black 1921 musical comedy "Shuffle Along" is often credited with initiating the Harlem Renaissance. The musical showcased talented African-American artists such as lyricist Noble Sissle and composer Eubie Blake. It also introduced catchy songs such as "Love Will Find a Way" and "I'm Just Wild About Harry," two of the first such songs to become "standards" among whites. More important, the show boosted the careers of such black performing artists as singers Florence Mills, Josephine Baker, and Mabel Mercer. Harlem in the 1920s also fostered a number of gifted writers, among them Langston Hughes, whose poems captured the mood and rhythm of blues and jazz; Countee Cullen, a poet of moving lyrical skill; and Claude McKay, whose militant verses urged rebellion against bigotry. Jean Toomer's poems and his novel *Cane* (1923) portrayed black life with passionate realism, and Alain

Locke's essays defined the spirit of the artistic renaissance. The movement also included visual artists such as Aaron Douglas, a painter who illustrated many of the books of Harlem Renaissance writers; James A. Porter, whose paintings were shown in every important exhibition of black artists; and Augusta Savage, who sculpted busts of many famous black personalities and who became an object of controversy in 1923 when the French government rejected her application to a summer art school because of her race.

Issues of identity troubled the Harlem Renaissance. Many white supporters were patronizers as well as patrons, attracted to what they called the "primitivism" of African-American culture. Although intellectuals and artists cherished their African cultural heritage, they realized that blacks had to come to terms with themselves as Americans. Thus Locke urged that the New Negro should "lay aside the status of beneficiary and ward for that of a collaborator and participant in American civilization." And Langston Hughes wrote, "We younger Negro artists who create now intend to express our individual dark-skinned selves without fear or shame. If white people are pleased we are glad. If they are not, it doesn't matter. We know we are beautiful."

The Jazz Age, as the decade of the 1920s is sometimes called, owed its name to music that developed from black urban experience. Evolving from African and black American folk music, early jazz communicated an exuberance, humor, and authority that African-Americans seldom expressed in their public, working, and political lives. With its emotional rhythms and emphasis on improvisation, jazz blurred the distinction between composer and performer and created intimacy between performer and audience.

Jazz

As African-Americans moved northward, jazz traveled with them. By the 1920s dance halls and bars in major cities throughout the country featured jazz, sometimes popularized by white musicians such as Paul Whiteman and Bix Beiderbecke. Gifted black performers like trumpeter Louis Armstrong, trombonist Kid Ory, and singer Bessie Smith enjoyed wide fame. Phonograph records and radio, better suited than sheet music to the spontaneity of jazz, helped to popularize it. In fact, jazz boosted the recording industry immensely, and

Florence Mills was a talented African-American performer whose singing career received a major boost from her appearance in the musical comedy "Shuffle Along," a show that heralded the beginning of the Harlem Renaissance.   James VanDer Zee.

music recorded by black artists and aimed at black consumers (sometimes called "race records") gave African-Americans a distinctive place in the new consumer culture. More important, jazz endowed America with its most distinctive art form.

In many ways the 1920s were the most creative years the nation had yet experienced. Influenced by jazz and experimental writing, painters such as Georgia O'Keeffe and John Marin tried to forge a unique American style of painting. European composers and performers still dominated classical music, but Americans such as Henry Cowell, who pioneered electronic music, and Aaron Copland, who built orchestral and vocal works around native folk motifs, began careers that later won wide acclaim. George Gershwin blended jazz rhythms, classical forms, and folk melodies in his serious compositions (*Rhapsody in Blue*, 1924, and *Concerto in F*, 1925), musical dramas (*Funny Face*, 1927), and numerous hit tunes such as "Summertime" and "Someone to Watch Over Me." In architecture the skyscraper boom drew worldwide attention, and Frank Lloyd Wright's "prairie-style" houses, churches, and schools celebrated the magnificence of the American landscape. At the beginning of the decade, essayist Harold Stearns had complained that "the most . . . pathetic fact in the social life of America today is emotional and aesthetic starvation." By 1929 that contention was hard to support.

THE ELECTION OF 1928 AND THE END OF THE NEW ERA

Intellectuals' uneasiness about the materialism of the 1920s had no place in the confident rhetoric of politics. Herbert Hoover epitomized that confidence in his speech accepting the Republican nomination for president in 1928. "We in America today," Hoover boasted, "are nearer to the final triumph over poverty than ever before in the history of any land. . . . We have not yet reached the goal, but, given a chance to go forward with the policies of the last eight years, we shall soon, with the help of God, be in sight of the day when poverty will be banished from this nation."

Hoover was a particularly apt Republican party candidate in 1928 (Coolidge had chosen not to run for re-election), because he fused old values of individual success through hard work with new emphasis on collective action. A Quaker from Iowa, orphaned at age ten, Hoover worked his way through Stanford University and became a wealthy mining engineer. During and after the First World War, he distinguished himself as U.S. food administrator and head of food relief for Europe. As secretary of commerce under Harding and Coolidge, Hoover had what has been called an "associational vision." Recognizing the extent to which large nationwide associations had come to dominate commerce and industry, Hoover tried to stimulate cooperation between business and government. He took every opportunity to make the Department of Commerce a center for the promotion of business,

Herbert Hoover

encouraging the formation of trade associations, holding conferences, sponsoring studies, and issuing reports, all aimed at improving production, marketing, and profitability. His active leadership prompted one observer to quip that Hoover was "Secretary of Commerce and assistant secretary of everything else."

As Hoover's opponent, Democrats chose Governor Alfred E. Smith of New York, whose background contrasted sharply with Hoover's. Hoover had rural, native, Protestant, business roots and had never run for public office. Smith was an urbane, gregarious politician of immigrant stock with a career rooted in New York City's Tammany Hall. His relish for the fast-paced give-and-take of city streets is apparent in his response during the campaign to a heckler who taunted Smith by shouting, "Tell them all you know, Al. It won't take long!" Smith unflinchingly retorted, "I'll tell them all we both know, and it won't take any longer!"

Al Smith

Smith was the first Roman Catholic to run for president on a major party ticket. His religion contributed to his considerable appeal among urban ethnic groups, who were voting in increasing numbers, but intense anti-Catholic sentiments lost him southern and rural votes. Smith had compiled a strong record as a promoter of progressive reforms and civil rights during his governorship, but his campaign failed to build a reform coalition of farmers and city dwellers because he stressed issues unlikely to unite these groups. He openly opposed Prohibition and struck back at charges that his Catholicism made him a puppet of the pope.

Smith waged a spirited campaign, but Hoover, who stressed the nation's prosperity under Republican administrations, won the popular vote by 21 million to 15 million, the electoral vote by 444 to 87. Smith's candidacy nevertheless had beneficial effects on the Democratic party. He carried the nation's twelve largest cities, which formerly had given majorities to Republican candidates, and he lured millions of foreign-stock voters to the polls for the first time. From 1928 onward, the Democratic party would solidify this urban base, which in conjunction with its traditional strength in the South made the party a formidable force in national elections.

Democrats and Republicans both had reason to be encouraged in 1928. In his inaugural address,

Hoover proclaimed a New Day, "bright with hope." His cabinet, composed mostly of businessmen committed to the existing order, included six millionaires. To the lower ranks of government Hoover appointed young professionals who agreed with him that scientific methods could be applied to solve national problems. In time, Hoover and his experts believed, they could establish a stable social order based on cooperation between government and various civic groups.

Hoover's Administration

If the Hoover administration was optimistic, so were most Americans. Reverence for what Hoover called "the American system"—which now offered such exciting products as radios and refrigerators—ran high. The belief was widespread that individuals were responsible for their own situations and that unemployment or poverty suggested personal failing. Prevailing opinion also held that the ups and downs of the business cycle were natural and therefore not to be tampered with by the government.

This confidence was jolted in the fall of 1929 when stock prices suddenly plunged. Analysts explained the drop as a temporary condition caused by a "lunatic fringe." But on October 24, "Black Thursday," panic selling set in. The prices of many stocks hit record lows; some sellers could find no buyers. Stunned crowds gathered outside the frantic New York Stock Exchange. At noon, leading bankers met at the headquarters of J. P. Morgan and Company. To restore faith, they put up $20 million and ceremoniously began buying stocks like U.S. Steel. The mood changed and some stocks rallied. The bankers, it seemed, had saved the day.

Stock Market Crash

But as news of Black Thursday spread across the country, fearful investors decided to sell their stocks rather than risk further losses. On "Black Tuesday," October 29, stock prices plummeted again. The market settled into a grim pattern of declines and weak rallies. Hoover, who had never approved of what he called "the fever of speculation," assured Americans that the economy was sound. He shared the popular assumptions that the stock market's ills could be quarantined and that the economy was strong enough to endure until the market righted itself.

But instead of reversing, the crash ultimately helped to unleash a devastating depression. The economic downturn did not arrive suddenly (see Chapter 25); it was more like a slow leak than a blowout. Had conditions been as sound as businesspeople maintained, the nation would have stood a better chance of weathering the Wall Street crash. In fact, however, some historians suggest that the stock market collapse merely moved an ongoing recession into depression.

The economic weakness that underlay the Great Depression had several interrelated causes. The first was declining demand. Some industries, like coal, railroads, and textiles were in distress long before 1929, but the major growth industries—automobiles, construction, and mechanized agriculture—had been able to expand as long as consumers bought their goods and services. But the frenzied expansion could not continue unabated. When demand leveled off, owners could not accumulate funds to build new plants and hire new workers. Instead, unsold inventories stacked up in warehouses, and laborers were laid off. The more that wages and purchasing power lagged behind industrial production, the more that workers who produced the consumer products could not afford to buy them in sufficient quantities to sustain the economy's momentum. Farmers, too, had to trim their purchases. Thus by 1929 a sizable population of under-consumers was causing serious repercussions.

Declining Demand

Underconsumption also resulted from the maldistribution of income. As the rich grew much richer in the 1920s, others made only modest gains. Though average per capita disposable income (income after taxes) rose about 9 percent between 1920 and 1929, the income of the wealthiest 1 percent rose 75 percent, accounting for most of the increase. Much of this increase was put into luxuries, savings, and stock market investments instead of being spent on consumer goods.

Furthermore, American businesses were overloaded with debt. In 1929 the top two hundred nonfinancial corporations controlled 49 percent of corporate wealth. Many corporations built pyramidlike empires supported by shady, though legal, manipulation of assets and weakly supported liabilities. The na-

Corporate Debt

tion's banking system also was on precarious footing. When one part of the edifice collapsed, the entire structure crumbled.

The depression also derived from largely unregulated pell-mell speculation on the stock market. Corporations and banks invested huge sums in stocks, and some even speculated in their own issues. Brokers sold stocks to buyers who borrowed in order to purchase them, putting up little or no cash, and then used the stocks they had bought but not fully paid for as collateral for more loans. When stock prices collapsed, brokers demanded that buyers repay their loans. Buyers tried to do so by withdrawing their savings from banks or selling their stocks at a loss for whatever they could get. Bankers in turn thus needed cash and put pressure on brokers to pay back their loans, tightening the vise further. The more obligations went unmet, the more the system crumbled; inevitably, banks and investment companies collapsed.

Speculation on the Stock Market

International economic troubles also contributed to the crash and depression. As the world's leading creditor and trader, the United States was deeply bound up with the world economy. Billions of dollars in loans had flowed to Europe during the First World War and during postwar reconstruction. By the late 1920s, however, American investors were beginning to keep their money at home, in order to invest it in the more lucrative U.S. stock market. Europeans, unable to borrow more funds and unable to sell their goods easily in the American market because of high tariffs, began to buy less from the United States and to default on the crippling debts left over from the First World War. Pinched at home, they raised their own tariffs, further disabling international commerce, and withdrew their investments from America. Reacting to the collapse of European economies, Hoover complained that "the European disease had contaminated the United States." He would have been more accurate had he said that the European and American illnesses were mutually infectious.

International Economic Troubles

Finally, government policies and practices contributed to the crash and depression. The federal government failed to regulate wild speculation, contenting itself with occasionally scolding bankers and businesspeople. The Federal Reserve Board pursued easy credit policies before the crash, charging low discount rates (interest rates on its loans to member banks) even though easy money was financing the speculative mania.

Failure of Federal Policies

Partly because of their optimism and partly because of the relatively undeveloped state of economic analysis and statistics gathering, neither the experts nor people on the street realized in 1929 what factors had brought on the depression. Conventional wisdom, based on the experience of previous depressions, held that little could be done to correct economic problems—that they simply had to run their course. So in 1929 people waited for the deflation to bottom out, never realizing that the era of expansion and frivolity had come to an end and that the nation's culture and politics, as well as its economy, would have to be rebuilt.

The onset of the Great Depression revealed with brutal clarity how many of the features and values of the 1920s had been consequences of prosperity. The decade's consumerism, preoccupation with leisure and entertainment, tendency toward free-wheeling behavior, celebration of the automobile, and suburbanization all resulted from higher incomes and shorter work hours. And when the bubble of prosperity broke, these new habits were all the more difficult to modify.

Beneath the "era of excess," as some historians have labeled it, lurked two other important phenomena. One was the continued resurfacing of prejudice and intolerance that had long tainted the American dream. As disaffected prohibitionists, Klansmen, and immigration restrictionists made their voices heard, they encouraged an environment in which discrimination against racial minorities and slurs against supposed "inferior" ethnic groups remained acceptable. Meanwhile, however, the distinguishing forces of twentieth-century life—technological change, bureaucratization, and the growth of the middle class—accelerated, making the decade truly a "new era." Both phenomena would recur as major themes in the nation's history for the rest of the twentieth century.

SUGGESTIONS FOR FURTHER READING

Overviews of the 1920s

William E. Akin, *Technocracy and the American Dream* (1977); Frederick Lewis Allen, *Only Yesterday* (1931); John Braeman et al., eds., *Change and Continuity in Twentieth Century America: The 1920s* (1968); Paul A. Carter, *Another Part of the Twenties* (1977); John D. Hicks, *Republican Ascendancy* (1960); William E. Leuchtenburg, *The Perils of Prosperity* (1958); Robert Lynd and Helen Lynd, *Middletown* (1929); Donald R. McCoy, *Coming of Age* (1973).

Business and the Economy

William W. Barber, *Herbert Hoover, the Economists, and American Economic Policy, 1921–1933* (1986); Irving L. Bernstein, *The Lean Years: A History of the American Worker, 1920–1933* (1960); Peter Fearon, *War, Prosperity, and Depression* (1987); John Kenneth Galbraith, *The Great Crash*, rev. ed. (1989); Morton Keller, *Regulating a New Economy* (1990); David Montgomery, *The Fall of the House of Labor* (1987); Allan Nevins, *Ford*, 2 vols. (1954–1957).

Politics and Law

Christine Bolt, *American Indian Policy and American Reform* (1987); David Burner, *The Politics of Provincialism* (1968); Paula Elder, *Governor Alfred E. Smith: The Politician as Reformer* (1983); J. Joseph Huthmacher, *Massachusetts People and Politics* (1959); Allan J. Lichtman, *Prejudice and the Old Politics: The Presidential Election of 1928* (1979); Richard Lowitt, *George W. Norris* (1971); Donald R. McCoy, *Calvin Coolidge* (1967); Alpheus Mason, *The Supreme Court from Taft to Warren* (1958); Robert K. Murray, *The Harding Era* (1969); Andrew Sinclair, *The Available Man* (1965); George Tindall, *The Emergence of the New South* (1967); James Weinstein, *The Decline of Socialism in America, 1912–1925* (1967); Joan Hoff Wilson, *Herbert Hoover: The Forgotten Progressive* (1975).

African-Americans and Hispanics

Rodolfo Acuna, *Occupied America: A History of Chicanos* (1980); Kenneth Kusmer, *A Ghetto Takes Shape* (1976); Matt S. Meier and Feliciano Rivera, *The Chicanos* (1972); Gilbert Osofsky, *Harlem: The Making of a Ghetto* (1965); Mark Reisler, *By the Sweat of Their Brows* (1976) (on Mexican-Americans); Ricardo Romo, *East Los Angeles: History of a Barrio* (1983); Virginia E. Sanchez, *From Colonia to Community: The History of Puerto Ricans in New York, 1917–1948* (1983); Alan Spear, *Black Chicago* (1967); Judith Stein, *The World of Marcus Garvey* (1986); Theodore Vincent, *Black Power and the Garvey Movement* (1971).

Women and the Family

W. Andrew Achenbaum, *Shades of Gray: Old Age, American Values, and Federal Policies Since 1920* (1983); William H. Chafe, *The American Woman: Her Changing Social, Economic, and Political Role* (1972); Howard P. Chudacoff, *How Old Are You? Age in Ameri-* *can Culture* (1989); Nancy F. Cott, *The Grounding of Modern Feminism* (1987); Ruth Schwartz Cowan, *More Work for Mother* (1983); David H. Fischer, *Growing Old in America* (1977); Linda Gordon, *Woman's Body, Woman's Right: A Social History of Birth Control in America* (1976); J. Stanley Lemons, *The Woman Citizen: Social Feminism in the 1920s* (1973); Sheila Rothman, *Woman's Proper Place* (1978); Lois Scharf, *To Work and to Wed* (1980); Susan Strasser, *Never Done: A History of American Housework* (1982); Winifred D. Wandersee, *Women's Work and Family Values, 1920–1940* (1981).

Lines of Defense

Paul Avrich, *Sacco and Vanzetti* (1991); David M. Chalmers, *Hooded Americanism: The History of the Ku Klux Klan* (1965); Norman F. Furnis, *The Fundamentalist Controversy* (1954); Joseph R. Gusfeld, *Symbolic Crusade* (1963); John Higham, *Strangers in the Land: Patterns of American Nativism* (1955); Kenneth T. Jackson, *The Ku Klux Klan and the City* (1967); William G. McLoughlin, *Modern Revivalism* (1959); Andrew Sinclair, *Prohibition: The Age of Excess* (1962).

Mass Culture

Stanley Coben, *Rebellion Against Victorianism* (1991); Robert Creamer, *Babe* (1974); Kenneth S. Davis, *The Hero, Charles A. Lindbergh* (1959); Susan J. Douglas, *Inventing American Broadcasting* (1987); Paula Fass, *The Damned and the Beautiful: American Youth in the 1920s* (1977); James J. Flink, *The Car Culture* (1975); Stephen Fox, *The Mirror Makers: A History of American Advertising and Its Creators* (1984); Harvey J. Levenstein, *Revolution at the Table: The Transformation of the American Diet* (1988); Roland Marchand, *Advertising the American Dream* (1985); John Rae, *The Road and the Car in American Life* (1971); Randy Roberts, *Jack Dempsey, The Manassa Mauler* (1979); Philip T. Rosen, *The Modern Stentors: Radio Broadcasting and the Federal Government, 1920–1933* (1980); Robert Sklar, *Movie-made America* (1976); Ronald A. Smith, *Sports and Freedom: The Rise of Big-Time College Athletics* (1988).

Literature and Thought

Mary Campbell, *Harlem Renaissance: Art of Black America* (1987); Robert Crunden, *From Self to Society: Transition in American Thought, 1919–1941* (1972); George H. Douglas, *H. L. Mencken* (1978); Nathan I. Huggins, *Harlem Renaissance* (1971); Gloria T. Hull, *Color, Sex and Poetry: Three Woman Writers of the Harlem Renaissance* (1987); David L. Lewis, *When Harlem Was in Vogue* (1981); Roderick Nash, *The Nervous Generation: American Thought, 1917–1930* (1969); Marvin K. Singleton, *H. L. Mencken and the American Mercury Adventure* (1962); Cecilia Tichi, *Shifting Gears: Technology, Literature and Culture in Modernist America* (1987); Kenneth M. Wheller and Virginia L. Lussier, eds., *Women and the Arts and the 1920s in Paris and New York* (1982).

Boom and Bust: The Crash

William W. Barber, *Herbert Hoover, the Economists, and American Economic Policy, 1921–1933* (1986); Peter Fearon, *War, Prosperity, and Depression* (1987); and John Kenneth Galbraith, *The Great Crash: 1929* (1989).

The Great Depression and the New Deal, 1929–1941

BUTCH BEUSCHER WAS fifty-six years old when he was laid off from the job he had held for twenty-nine years as a boilermaker in the Dubuque, Iowa, railroad shops. The year was 1931, and businesses and farms across the country were collapsing. Butch's wife Tessie was a part-time seamstress, but since her customers were also unemployed or irregularly employed, her earnings declined to three or four dollars a week. The Beuschers had a partially paid-up insurance policy, but they also had a mortgaged home and ten children, four of whom still lived at home. As their income plummeted, the family lived off loans against the insurance policy, Tessie's earnings, and credit from the grocery store. Their unpaid bills mounted, as did the overdue notices for mortgage and property-tax payments. Then, in the fall of 1933, Butch announced that the family would have to face facts and "try to get relief" from the government. Tessie recalled gasping at the suggestion that they ask for welfare, but there was no alternative.

For Butch Beuscher, as for countless other Americans, going down to the courthouse to apply for relief was the hardest thing he had ever had to

do; his hand was "on the door-knob five times" before he turned it. Two months later, the family finally received a $4.50 grocery order. Butch never felt comfortable asking for welfare. "You know," he said, "you went down to City Hall, and had to wait in line, and you saw all your friends; it was funny in a way, though it was pitiful, too." The government helped the Beuschers in a variety of ways. The city of Dubuque furnished a plot of land and seeds, so the family grew vegetables. And the federal government under President Franklin D. Roosevelt's New Deal served as the employer of last resort, providing a job for Butch as a laborer on a public works project and for his son Bob with the Civilian Conservation Corps.

Butch was one of the lucky Americans called back to work during the Great Depression, and because of his seniority he returned to the shops at his old rate of pay in late 1935. The Beuschers had suffered four years of deprivation and economic insecurity, but relief payments and public works jobs had helped tide them over. In the process, the family's skepticism about the role of government in their lives had turned to gratitude.

Tenements & Tracks, an oil painting by Harry Leith-Ross, shows a working-class neighborhood near Philadelphia during the Great Depression.

Statistics—the Beuschers' among them—suggest the magnitude of the Great Depression's human tragedy. The stock market crash in October 1929 had shocked investors and caused a financial panic (see Chapter 24). Between 1929 and 1933 a hundred thousand businesses failed; corporate profits fell from $10 billion to $1 billion; and the gross national product was cut in half. Banks failed by the thousands. Americans who believed that saving was a virtue, a path to material fulfillment, discovered that their deposits had disappeared with the banks.

Americans lost jobs as well as savings. Although most people remained employed, thousands of men and women received severance slips every day. At the beginning of 1930 the number of jobless reached at least 4 million; by November it had jumped to 6 million. When President Herbert Hoover left office in 1933, about one-fourth of the labor force was idle—13 million workers—and millions more were underemployed, working only part time. Unemployment strained relations within the family. African-Americans and other minorities sank deeper into destitution. Overall, the economic catastrophe aggravated old tensions: labor versus capital, white versus black, male versus female.

Elected amid prosperity and optimism, Herbert Hoover spent the years from late 1929 to his departure from office in early 1933 presiding over a gloomy and sometimes angry nation. Hoover appeared cold and indifferent to Americans' suffering: although he activated more of the federal government's resources than had any of his predecessors in an economic crisis, he opposed direct relief payments for the unemployed. When Hoover refused to take measures strong enough to relieve people's hardships, voters turned him out of office in 1932. His successor in the White House was Franklin D. Roosevelt, the governor of New York, who promised vigorous action and projected hope in a time of despair.

From the first days of his presidency, Roosevelt displayed a buoyancy and willingness to experiment that helped to restore public confidence in the government and the economy. He acted not only to reform the banks and securities exchanges, but also to provide central planning for industry and agriculture and direct government relief for the jobless. This sweeping emergency legislation was based on the concept of "pump-priming," or deficit financing, to stimulate consumer buying power, business and industrial activity, and, ultimately, employment by pouring billions of federal dollars into the economy.

Roosevelt's New Deal was opposed from both the left and the right. Businesspeople and economic conservatives found it fiscally irresponsible; demagogues and left-wing politicians thought it too conservative. Ultimately Roosevelt prevailed, revitalizing the progressive movement, vastly expanding the scope of the federal government and the popularity of the Democratic party, and in the process establishing America's welfare system.

During these years several million workers seized the chance to organize for better wages and working conditions. The new Congress of Industrial Organizations (CIO) established unions in the automobile, steel, meat-packing, and other major industries. Blacks registered political and economic gains, too, though they benefited less from the New Deal than did whites. Two-and-a-half million additional women workers joined the labor force during the 1930s. But female workers were segregated in low-income jobs, and New Deal legislation excluded many women from Social Security coverage and minimum-wage protection.

The New Deal was not a revolution, but it transformed the United States. Farmers still plant according to federal crop allotments. The elderly and disabled still collect Social Security payments. The Federal Deposit Insurance Corporation still insures bank deposits. The Securities and Exchange Commission still monitors the stock exchanges. But the New Deal did not accomplish one of its goals—putting back to work all the people who wanted jobs. That would await the nation's entry into the Second World War in 1941.

HOOVER AND HARD TIMES: AMERICA'S WORSENING DEPRESSION, 1929–1933

As the Great Depression deepened in the early 1930s, its underlying causes—principally overproduction and underconsumption grew in severity.

Causes of the Deepening Depression

So too did instability in the banking industry. What happened to America's banks illustrates the cascading nature of the depression. Banks tied into

• Important Events •

1931	Nine African-American men arrested in Scottsboro affair
	Hoover declares moratorium on First World War debts and reparations
1932	Reconstruction Finance Corporation established to make loans to businesses
	Bonus Expeditionary Force marches on Washington
	Franklin D. Roosevelt elected president
1933	13 million Americans unemployed
	National bank holiday suspends banking activities
	Agricultural Adjustment Act encourages decreased farm production
	Civilian Conservation Corps provides jobs to 300,000 people
	Tennessee Valley Authority established to aid economies of seven states
	Banking Act creates Federal Deposit Insurance Corporation (FDIC)
	National Industrial Recovery Act attempts to spur industrial growth
	Twentieth (Lame Duck) Amendment sets presidential inaugurations at January 20
	Twenty-first Amendment repeals Eighteenth (Prohibition) Amendment
1934	Townsend devises Old Age Revolving Pensions plan
	Huey Long starts Share Our Wealth Society
	Indian Reorganization (Wheeler-Howard) Act restores lands to tribal ownership
	Democrats win victories in congressional elections
	Coughlin creates National Union for Social Justice
1935	Emergency Relief Appropriation Act authorizes establishment of public works programs

	Works Progress Administration creates jobs in public works projects
	Schechter v. *U.S.* invalidates NIRA
	National Labor Relations (Wagner) Act grants workers right to unionize
	Social Security Act establishes insurance for aged and unemployed
	Huey Long assassinated
	Committee for Industrial Organization (CIO) established
	Revenue (Wealth Tax) Act raises taxes on business and the wealthy
1936	*U.S.* v. *Butler* invalidates AAA
	Roosevelt defeats Landon
1937	United Auto Workers hold sit-down strikes
	Roosevelt's court-packing plan fails
	NLRB v. *Jones & Laughlin* upholds Wagner Act
	Memorial Day Massacre leaves ten steel strikers dead in Chicago
	Farm Security Administration established to aid farm workers
1937–39	Business recession
1938	AFL expels CIO unions
	Fair Labor Standards Act establishes minimum wage
	10.4 million Americans unemployed
1939	Marian Anderson performs at the Lincoln Memorial
1940	Roosevelt defeats Willkie
1941	African-Americans threaten to march on Washington to protest unequal access to defense jobs
	Fair Employment Practices Committee (FEPC) prohibits discrimination in war industries and government

the stock market or foreign investments were badly weakened. When nervous Americans made runs on banks to salvage their threatened savings, a powerful momentum—panic—set in. In 1929, 659 banks folded; in 1930 the number of failures more than doubled to 1,350. The Federal Reserve Board blundered after the crash, drastically raising the discount rate and thus tightening the money market at a time when just the opposite was needed: loosening to spur borrowing and spending. In 1931, 2,293 banks shut their doors, and another 1,453 ceased to do business in 1932.

As unemployment soared in the early 1930s, people's fortunes hit bottom. In Detroit, auto workers roamed from plant to plant only to find padlocked gates. Western apple growers sent their surplus to the cities, where a new class of street-corner entrepreneurs peddled apples at 5 cents apiece. Both women and men suffered homelessness. Hundreds of women were sleeping nightly in Chicago's parks. "No fewer than 200 women are sleeping in Grant and Lincoln Parks, on the lake front," reported the city's commissioner of public welfare in 1931, "to say nothing of those in the other parks." In 1932, a squad of New York City police officers arrested twenty-five men in "Hoover Valley," the shantytown they had constructed in the bed of an old reservoir in Central Park. Twelve shacks made of everything from egg crates to discarded boards and bricks were built in a row called "Depression Street." Urban shanty-towns, bitterly called "Hoovervilles," sprouted up throughout the country. In Oakland, California, hundreds of people lived in leftover concrete waste ducts in "Sewer-Pipe City."

During these years people's diets deteriorated, malnutrition became common, and the under-nourished frequently fell victim to disease. Some

Deterioration of Health
———

people quietly lined up at Red Cross and Salvation Army soup kitchens or in breadlines. Others ate only potatoes, crackers, or dandelions, or scratched through garbage cans for bits of food. Milk consumption decreased to such an extent that Kentucky miners called it "medicine." Pregnant women went without essential foods like eggs and vegetables, and doctors reported increases in tuberculosis, typhoid, dysentery, and heart and stomach disorders. Millions of Americans were not only hungry and ill; they were cold. Unable to afford fuel, they huddled in unheated tenements and shacks. Families doubled up in crowded apartments, and those unable to pay the rent were evicted, furniture and all.

In the countryside, hobbled long before the depression struck, economic hardship deepened. Between 1929 and 1933 farm prices dropped 60

Plight of the Farmers
———

percent. At the same time, production decreased only 6 percent as individual farmers tried to make up for lower prices by producing more, thus creating an excess and depressing prices even further. The surplus could not be exported because foreign demand had shrunk. Drought, foreclosure, clouds of hungry grasshoppers, and bank failures further plagued American farmers. Some became transients in search of jobs or food. Dispossessed tenant farmers—husbands, wives, and children—wandered the roads of the South. Hundreds of thousands of other people jumped aboard freight trains or hitchhiked. The California Unemployment Commission reported in 1932 that an "army of homeless" had trooped into the state and was moving constantly from place to place, forced by one town after another to move on.

Economic woe also affected marriage patterns and family life. People postponed marriage, and married couples postponed having children. Divorces declined, but desertions rose as husbands unable to provide for their families simply took off. Families were beset in other ways as well. With less money available for outside recreation, families were forced to spend more time together, which further increased tension in those suffering unemployment and crowded living quarters. Out-of-work fathers felt ashamed of their diminished role. "A child who was playing irritated him," recalled the son of an unemployed tool-and-die maker. "It wasn't just my own father. They all got shook up."

Most Americans met the crisis not with protest or violence but with bewilderment and inability to fix the blame. They scorned businesspeople and

Farmers' Holiday Association
———

bankers, of course, but often blamed themselves as well, as the traditional ideology of the self-made man had taught them to do. Some people were angry, though, and scattered protests raised the specter of popular revolt. Farmers in the Midwest prevented evictions and slowed foreclosures on farm properties by harassing sheriffs, judges, and lawyers. In Nebraska, Iowa, and Minnesota, farmers protesting low prices put up barricades of spiked logs and telegraph poles. They stopped trucks, smashed headlights, and dumped milk and vegetables in roadside ditches. Some of these demonstrations were organized by the Farmers' Holiday Association, whose leader, Milo Reno, encouraged farmers to take a holiday—a farm strike that would keep their products off the market until they commanded a better price. In Nebraska, farmers stopped a freight train and stole an entire shipment of cattle, and dairy farmers in Wisconsin fought pitched battles with deputy sher-

Plagued by dust storms and evictions, thousands of tenant farmers and sharecroppers were forced to leave their land during the Great Depression. Known as "Okies" and "Arkies," they took off for California with their few belongings. These refugees from drought-stricken Oklahoma experienced car trouble and were stalled on a New Mexico highway. Library of Congress.

iffs. Soon the farmers' protests spread east to New York State and south to Georgia. And in 1932 one farm leader warned a congressional committee that "the biggest and finest crop of little revolutions I ever saw is ripe all over this country right now."

Isolated protests also sounded in cities and in mining regions. In Chicago, Los Angeles, and Philadelphia, the unemployed marched on city halls. **Bonus Expeditionary Force** In Harlan County, Kentucky, when miners struck against wage reductions, mine owners responded with strikebreakers, bombs, the National Guard, the closing of relief kitchens, and evictions from company-owned housing. The most spectacular confrontation shook Washington, D.C., in the summer of 1932. Congress was considering a bill to authorize immediate issuance of $2.4 billion in bonuses already allotted to First World War veterans but not due for payment until 1945. To lobby for the bill, fifteen thousand unemployed veterans and their families converged on the tense nation's capital, calling themselves the Bonus Expeditionary Force (BEF), or "Bonus Army," and camping on vacant lots and in empty government buildings. President Hoover threw his weight against the bonus bill, but the House passed it. The showdown came in the Senate, which, after much debate, voted no. One BEF member shouted: "We were heroes in 1917, but we're bums today." Many of the bonus marchers left Washington, but several thousand stayed on during the summer. Hoover grew impatient, carelessly labeled them "insurrectionists" and Communists, and refused to meet with them.

In July General Douglas MacArthur, assisted by Major Dwight D. Eisenhower and Major George S. Patton, confronted the veterans and their families with cavalry, tanks, and bayonet-bearing soldiers. The BEF hurled back stones and bricks. What followed shocked the nation. Men and women were chased down by horsemen; children were tear-gassed; shacks were set afire. Hoover's image as a humanitarian was further tarnished. When presidential hopeful Franklin D. Roosevelt heard about the attack on the Bonus Army, he turned to his friend Felix Frankfurter and remarked: "Well, Felix, this will elect me."

Herbert Hoover (1874–1964), the wealthy mining engineer and businessman, headed a relief program during the First World War and served as secretary of commerce in the 1920s. His reputation for compassion was tarnished when as president he faced the Great Depression and seemed heartless in his response to massive human suffering. Library of Congress.

With capitalism on its knees, American Communists in various parts of the nation organized "unemployment councils" to raise class consciousness and agitate for jobs and

Communist Party
———

food. In 1930 they led urban demonstrations, some of which ended in violent clashes with local police, and in 1931 they led a hunger march on Washington, D.C., under the slogan "Fight—Don't Starve." The Communists' tangles with authority publicized the human tragedy of the depression. Still, total party membership in 1932 remained small at twelve thousand. The Socialist party, which took issue with both capitalists and Communists, fared better. More reformist than radical, the Socialists ran well in

municipal elections after the stock-market crash but scored few victories. Indeed, few Americans looked to left-wing doctrines, protest marches, or violence for relief from their misery. Americans were frightened, and they were angry, but they were not revolutionaries. "Given the sordid conditions of the lengthy depression," historian Roger Biles has written, "Americans remained remarkably law-abiding and docile." For solutions, they turned not to the streets but to institutions of considerable longevity and stability: their local, state, and federal governments.

But when urgent daily appeals for government relief for the jobless reached the White House, Hoover at first became defensive, if not hostile, rejecting direct relief in the belief that it would undermine character and individualism. Based on his belief that the depression was international in origin, not domestic, Hoover replied, "We cannot legislate ourselves out of a world depression; we can and will work ourselves out." To a growing number of Americans, Hoover seemed heartless and inflexible at a time when humanitarianism and action were called for. True to his beliefs, the president urged people to help themselves and their neighbors. He applauded private voluntary relief through the Red Cross and other charitable agencies. Yet when the need was greatest, donations declined. State and urban officials found their treasuries drying up, too. Philadelphia, after hiring the unemployed to paint city buildings, exhausted its relief funds by 1931, leaving 57,000 families without assistance. These Philadelphians got no sympathy from Secretary of the Treasury Andrew Mellon, who believed that business cycles of boom and bust were not only inevitable but desirable. He advised Hoover to "let the slump liquidate itself. Liquidate labor, liquidate stocks, liquidate the farmers, liquidate real estate. . . . It will purge the rottenness out of the system."

As the depression intensified, Hoover's opposition to federal action gradually diminished. He rejected Mellon's insensitive counsel, hesitantly

Hoover's Antidepression Remedies
———

energizing the White House and federal agencies to take action—more action than the government had taken before. He won pledges from business and labor leaders to maintain wages and production and to avoid strikes. He urged state governors to increase their expenditures on public works. And he created the President's Organization on Unemployment Relief (POUR) to generate private contributions for relief of the destitute. Though POUR proved ineffective, Hoover's spurring of federal public works projects (including the Hoover and Grand Coulee dams) did provide some jobs. Help also came from the Federal Farm Board, created under the Agricultural Marketing Act of 1929. An outcome of Hoover's emphasis on cooperation among individuals, groups, and government, the Farm Board supported crop prices by lending money to cooperatives to buy products and keep them off the market. But the board soon found itself short of money, and unsold surplus commodities jammed warehouses. The federally sponsored and privately funded National Credit Corporation assisted faltering banks, but it barely slowed the number of bank failures. To retard the collapse of the international monetary system, Hoover announced a moratorium on the payment of First World War debts and reparations (1931).

The president also asked Congress to charter the Reconstruction Finance Corporation (RFC). Created in 1932 and eventually empowered with

Reconstruction Finance Corporation

$2 billion, the RFC was designed to make loans to banks, insurance companies, and railroads and later to state and local governments. In theory, the RFC would lend money to large entities at the top of the economic system, and benefits would filter down to people at the bottom. Liberal Republican Representative Fiorello La Guardia of New York labeled the plan a "millionaires' dole." It did not work; banks continued to collapse and small companies went into bankruptcy. Few Americans took comfort in Hoover's prediction that prosperity was "just around the corner."

Despite warnings from prominent economists, Hoover also signed the Hawley-Smoot Tariff (1930). A congressional compromise serving special interests, the tariff raised du-

Hawley-Smoot Tariff

ties by about one-third. Besides fulfilling a Republican party pledge, Hoover argued that the tariff would help farmers and manufacturers by keeping foreign goods off the market. Actually, the tariff further weakened the economy by making it even more difficult for foreign nations to sell their products and, thus, to earn dollars to buy American products and pay off their First World War debts.

Like most of his contemporaries, Hoover believed that a balanced budget was sacred and deficit spending sinful. In 1931 he therefore appealed for a decrease in federal expenditures and an increase in taxes. The following year he supported a sales tax on manufactured goods, which liberal Democrats charged was an attempt to avoid higher income and corporate taxes. The sales tax was defeated, but the Revenue Act of 1932 raised corporate, excise, and personal income taxes. Hoover seemed tangled in a contradiction: he urged people to spend to spur recovery, but his tax policies deprived them of spending money. Nor did he ever balance the budget.

Although Hoover expanded public works projects and approved loans to some institutions, he vetoed a variety of relief bills presented to him by the Democratic Congress. In

Hoover's Traditionalism

rejecting a public power project for the Tennessee River, he argued that its cheap electricity would compete with power from private companies. Hoover's traditionalism was also well demonstrated by his handling of Prohibition. Despite the Eighteenth Amendment, Americans were producing and drinking liquor with grand illegality and hypocrisy. Although the law was not and could not be enforced, Hoover resisted mounting public pressure for repeal. Opponents of Prohibition argued not only that it encouraged crime but also that its repeal would stimulate economic recovery by reviving the nation's breweries and distilleries. But the president refused to tamper with the Constitution; he declared that the liquor industry, having no socially redemptive value, was best left depressed. Even though it cost him votes during the presidential election of 1932, Hoover stood firm against repeal.

Still, President Hoover stretched governmental activism as far as he thought he could without violating his cherished principles. Because Hoover mobilized the resources of the federal government as never before, some historians have depicted him as a bridge to the New Deal of the 1930s. If nothing else, he prepared the way for massive federal activity by giving private enterprise the opportunity to solve the depression—and to fail in the attempt.

FRANKLIN D. ROOSEVELT AND THE ELECTION OF 1932

Herbert Hoover and the Republican party faced dreary prospects in 1932. The president kept blaming international events for the economic crisis, when Americans were less concerned with abstract explanations than with tomorrow's meal. He grumbled and grew impatient with his critics. But what soured public opinion most was that Hoover did not offer leadership at a time when innovative generalship was required. So unpopular had he become by 1932 that Republicans who did not want to be associated with a loser ran independent campaigns. The president made few major speeches and rarely left Washington, and when he did venture out he was frequently jeered.

Franklin D. Roosevelt enjoyed quite a different reputation. Though born into the upper class of old money and privilege, the smiling, ingratiating governor of New York appealed to people of all classes, races, and regions, and he shared the American penchant for optimism. He had served for eight years as assistant secretary of the navy under Woodrow Wilson and in 1920 had been the robust vice-presidential candidate of the Democratic party. The Democratic ticket went down to defeat, and the next year Roosevelt suffered a more devastating loss: he was stricken with polio and was left totally paralyzed in both legs.

Franklin D. Roosevelt

What should Roosevelt do next? Should he retire from public life, a rich invalid? His answer and his wife Eleanor's was no. Throughout the 1920s Franklin and Eleanor contended with his handicap. Rejecting self-pity, Roosevelt worked to rebuild his body. Friends commented that polio had made him a "twice-born man" and that his fight against the disease had given him new moral and physical strength. As Roosevelt explained it: "If you had spent two years in bed trying to wiggle your big toe, after that anything would seem easy."

For her part, Eleanor Roosevelt—who had grown up shy and sheltered in a distant branch of the Roosevelt family—launched her own career in public life. In her memoirs, she described having changed in the 1920s from a depressed, isolated person into an independent woman with significant political commitments and personal relationships in her life. Her depression lifted when she developed intimate and supportive friendships with several women who were activists in the feminist movement and the Democratic party. Eleanor Roosevelt worked hard to become an effective public speaker, and participated in the activities of the League of Women Voters, the Women's Trade Union League, and the Democratic party. In a short time, she became the leading figure in a network of feminist activists, and discovered, as the historian Blanche Wiesen Cook has written, that she was a "woman with power who enjoyed power." She became deeply committed to equal opportunity for women and for African-Americans, and wanted to alleviate the suffering of the poor. On these issues, she made fact-finding trips for her husband and served as his conscience.

Eleanor Roosevelt

Elected governor of New York in 1928, after the stock market crash Roosevelt launched relief programs and an unemployment commission. Roosevelt's governorship coincided with Hoover's presidency, and both coincided with the onset of the Great Depression. But whereas Hoover appeared hardhearted and unwilling to help the jobless, Roosevelt seemed quite the opposite. He endorsed unemployment insurance and direct relief payments for the jobless. Under his leadership, New York's Temporary Emergency Relief Administration (1931) became the first state agency to mobilize on behalf of the poor. Aid to the unemployed, Roosevelt declared, "must be extended by Government, not as a matter of charity, but as a matter of social duty."

Roosevelt as Governor of New York

Roosevelt was also more willing than Hoover to experiment. As governor of New York, he advocated creating jobs in publicly funded reforestation, land reclamation, and hydroelectric power projects. He endorsed old-age pensions and protective legislation for labor unions. Roosevelt warned people not to dismiss such experimentation "with the word *radical*. Remember the radical of yesterday is almost [always] the reactionary of today." When he was re-elected in 1930 by a record-setting plurality of 735,000 votes, politicians had to take a serious look at Roosevelt's vote-getting ability.

To prepare a national political platform, Roosevelt surrounded himself with a "Brain Trust" of lawyers and university professors. Tracing their

Roosevelt's "Brain Trust"

intellectual origins to the New Nationalism of Theodore Roosevelt and Herbert Croly (see Chapter 21), they reasoned that bigness was unavoidable in the modern American economy. It thus followed that the cure for the nation's ills was not to go on a rampage of trustbusting but to place large corporations, monopolies, and oligopolies under effective government regulation. "We are no longer afraid of bigness," declared Columbia University professor Rexford G. Tugwell, speaking in the tradition of Theodore Roosevelt's New Nationalism. "We are resolved to recognize openly that competition in most of its forms is wasteful and costly; that larger combinations in any modern society must prevail."

Roosevelt and his Brain Trust agreed that it was essential to restore purchasing power to farmers, blue-collar workers, and the middle classes, and that the way to do so was to cut production. If demand for a product remained constant and the supply were cut, they reasoned, the price would rise. Producers would make higher profits, and workers would earn more. This method of combating a depression has been called "the economics of scarcity," which the Brain Trust saw as the preferred alternative to deficit spending, or "pump-priming," in which the government borrowed money to prime the economic pump and thereby revive purchasing power. Indeed, Roosevelt and Hoover both campaigned as fiscal conservatives committed to a balanced budget. But unlike Hoover, Roosevelt also advocated immediate and direct relief to the unemployed. And Roosevelt and his advisers rejected Hoover's explanation that the depression was international in origin. They demanded that the federal government engage in centralized economic planning and experimentation to bring about recovery.

Upon accepting the Democratic nomination, Roosevelt called for a "new deal for the American people." The two party platforms differed little,

1932 Election Results

but the Democrats were willing to abandon Prohibition and to launch federal relief. More people went to the polls in 1932 than in any election since

In November 1930 Franklin D. Roosevelt (1882–1945) read the good news. Re-elected governor of New York by 735,000 votes, he immediately became a leading contender for the Democratic presidential nomination. Note Roosevelt's leg braces, rarely shown in photographs because of an unwritten agreement by photographers to shoot him from the waist up. UPI/Bettmann Archives.

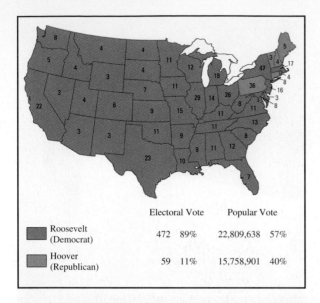

	Electoral Vote		Popular Vote	
Roosevelt (Democrat)	472	89%	22,809,638	57%
Hoover (Republican)	59	11%	15,758,901	40%

Presidential Election, 1932 *One factor above all decided the 1932 presidential election: the Great Depression. Roosevelt won 42 states, Hoover 6.*

the First World War. In a crisis-ridden moment, Americans followed their traditional pattern and exchanged one government for another. The presidential election of 1932 had never been much of a contest: Roosevelt's 22.8 million popular votes far outdistanced Hoover's 15.8 million; Hoover won only 59 electoral votes compared with Roosevelt's 472 (see map). Cities continued the trend, begun in 1928, of voting Democratic. Democrats also won overwhelming control of the Senate and the House.

Once elected, Roosevelt had to wait until his inauguration on March 4 to act. (To eliminate similar losses of time, the Twentieth Amendment to the Constitution—the Lame Duck Amendment, ratified in 1933—shifted all future inaugurations to January 20.) It was a troubled four months. Millions of jobless Americans walked the streets; prices for agricultural and manufactured goods continued to plummet; industrial production sank to new depths. While farmers in the Farmers' Holiday movement poured milk into ditches, another kind of holiday was observed in some states: the bank holiday. Throughout the United States, depositors lined up in front of banks to withdraw their savings. Banks with insufficient funds on hand to pay depositors had to close their doors and

declare themselves insolvent. In February, Michigan and Maryland suspended banking operations, and by March 4 thirty-six other states, including New York, had followed suit.

On March 2, 1933, President-elect Roosevelt and his family and friends boarded a train for Washington, D.C., and the inauguration ceremony. Roosevelt was carrying with him rough drafts of two presidential proclamations, one summoning a special session of Congress, the other declaring a national bank holiday, suspending banking transactions throughout the nation.

LAUNCHING THE NEW DEAL AND RESTORING CONFIDENCE

"First of all," declared the newly inaugurated president, "let me assert my firm belief that the only thing we have to fear is fear itself—nameless, unreasoning, unjustified terror." In his inaugural address Roosevelt scored his first triumph as president, instilling hope and courage in the rank and file. He invoked "the analogue of war," proclaiming that, as in the First World War, the American people must march forward "as a trained and loyal army willing to sacrifice for the good of a common discipline." If need be, Roosevelt asserted, "I shall ask the Congress for the one remaining instrument to meet the crisis—broad Executive power to wage a war against the emergency, as great as the power that would be given to me if we were in fact invaded by a foreign foe."

The next day, Roosevelt declared a four-day national bank holiday and summoned Congress to an emergency session. Congress convened on

Launching the First New Deal

March 9 to launch what observers would call the First Hundred Days. This was also the beginning of the vast legislative output of 1933–1934 that historians would call the First New Deal. Roosevelt's initial requests to Congress were cautious; portions had even been drafted by Hoover's advisers before he left office. The first measure, the Emergency Banking Relief Bill, was introduced on March 9, passed sight-unseen by unanimous House vote, approved 73 to 7 in the Senate, and signed by the president that evening. The act provided for the reopening, under Treasury Department license, of banks that were solvent and for the reorganization and management of those that were not. It also prohibited the hoarding and export of gold. It was, however, a fundamentally conservative law that upheld the status quo and left the same bankers in charge—a special disappointment to those who had taken seriously the anti-banker rhetoric of Roosevelt's inaugural address. As one representative complained, "The President drove the money-changers out of the Capitol on March 4th—and they were all back on the 9th."

On March 12, a Sunday evening, the president broadcast the first of his "fireside chats," and 60 million people heard his comforting voice on their

First Fireside Chat
———

radios. His message: banks were once again safe places for depositors' savings. On Monday morning the banks opened their doors, but instead of queuing up to withdraw their savings, people were waiting outside to deposit their money. The bank runs were over; Roosevelt had re-established people's confidence in their political leadership, their banks, even their economic system.

Roosevelt next pursued a measure, the Beer-Wine Revenue Bill, that was deflationary because it would actually take money out of people's pockets. The bill would generate revenues by legalizing the sale of low-alcohol wines and beers and levying a tax on them. (Congress had proposed repeal of Prohibition in February 1933 in the Twenty-first Amendment, and the states ratified it by December 1933.) To many, levying new taxes seemed a strange way to restore purchasing power to people who could not afford to buy what they needed. Roosevelt knew that. "I realize well," he wrote a friend, "that thus far we have actually given more of deflation than of inflation. . . . It is simply inevitable that we must inflate." He added that his "banker friends may be horrified" by the large-scale federal spending that was to come.

Roosevelt began to seek congressional authorization to spend in mid-March with the Agricultural Adjustment bill, designed to restore farmers' purchasing power. If overproduc-

Agricultural Adjustment Act
———

tion was the cause of farmers' problems—falling prices and mounting surpluses—then the government had to encourage farmers to grow less food. Under the domestic allotment plan, the government would pay farmers

A gloomy Hoover and a buoyant Roosevelt ride to the inauguration in 1933. This magazine cover was never published, apparently because the editors of the New Yorker *thought it inappropriate after an assassination attempt on the president-elect just three weeks before.*   Franklin D. Roosevelt Library.

to reduce their acreage or plow under crops already in the fields. Farmers would receive payments based on *parity*, a system of regulated prices for corn, cotton, wheat, rice, hogs, and dairy products that would provide them the same purchasing power they had had during the prosperous period of 1909 to 1914. For years, farmers had called for a "fair exchange value" for their crops, and *Wallace's Farmer*, an Iowa publication, had dubbed the concept "parity." In effect, the government was making up the difference between the actual market value of farm products and the income farmers needed to make a profit. The subsidies would be funded by taxes levied on the processors of agricultural commodities.

Roosevelt's farm plan immediately encountered vehement opposition. How could there be crop surpluses when some Americans were hungry and even starving? Underconsumption, people ar-

The Economy before and after the New Deal, 1929–1941

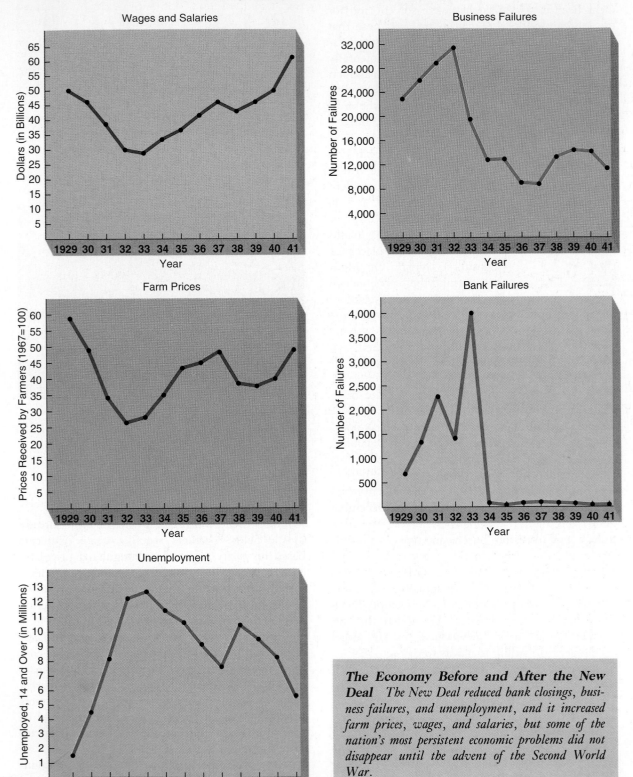

The Economy Before and After the New Deal *The New Deal reduced bank closings, business failures, and unemployment, and it increased farm prices, wages, and salaries, but some of the nation's most persistent economic problems did not disappear until the advent of the Second World War.*

gued, was the result of a maldistribution of wealth and power as well as of goods and services. Some politicians wanted to put more money into circulation by coining silver or printing greenbacks. Cheap money, they contended, would make it easier for farmers to repay their debts. On May 12, Congress finally overcame opposition to the domestic allotment plan and passed the Agricultural Adjustment Act (AAA). A month later the Farm Credit Act was passed, providing short- and medium-term loans that enabled many farmers to refinance their mortgages and hang onto their homes and land.

Meanwhile, other relief measures became law. On March 21 the president requested three kinds of massive relief: a job corps called the Civilian Conservation Corps (CCC), direct cash grants to the states for relief payments to needy citizens, and public works projects. Ten days later Congress approved the CCC. Within four months, 1,300 camps were in operation and 300,000 young men between the ages of eighteen and twenty-five were planting trees; clearing camping areas and beaches; and building bridges, dams, reservoirs, fish ponds, and fire towers. More than 2.5 million young men eventually lived and worked in CCC camps. On May 12, Congress passed the Federal Emergency Relief Act, which authorized $500 million in aid to state and local governments.

Civilian Conservation Corps

Roosevelt's proposed plan for public works became Title II of the National Industrial Recovery Act (NIRA). Passed on June 16, NIRA established the Public Works Administration (PWA) and appropriated $3.3 billion for hiring the unemployed to build roads, sewage and water systems, public buildings, ships, naval aircraft, and a host of other projects. The purpose of the PWA was to prime the economic pump to spur recovery. Roosevelt resorted to pump priming only as a last-ditch measure. He remained fiscally orthodox, anxious to return to a balanced budget at the earliest opportunity.

If the AAA was the agricultural cornerstone of the New Deal, the National Industrial Recovery Act was the industrial cornerstone. The NIRA was a testimony to the New Deal belief in national planning as opposed to an individualistic, intensely competitive, laissez-faire economy. It was essential,

Economic Planning under the NIRA

the planners argued, for businesses to end cutthroat competition and raise prices by limiting production. Like the War Industries Board (WIB) during the First World War, the NIRA exempted businesses from antitrust laws by establishing the National Recovery Administration (NRA). Under its auspices, competing businesses met with representatives of workers and consumers to draft codes of fair competition, which limited production and established prices. With businesses enjoying new concessions, workers wanted a share of the pie too. Congress responded with Section 7(a) of the NIRA, which guaranteed their right to unionize and to bargain collectively.

RESETTLEMENT ADMINISTRATION
Rescues Victims
Restores Land to Proper Use

Under the Agricultural Adjustment Act, farmers received government payments for not planting crops or for destroying crops that had already been planted. Some farmers, however, needed help of a different kind. The Resettlement Administration, established by executive order in 1935, was authorized to resettle destitute farm families from areas of soil erosion, flooding, and stream pollution to homestead communities. This poster was done by Ben Shahn. Library of Congress.

The New Deal also strengthened public confidence in the stock exchanges and banks. Roosevelt signed the Federal Securities Act, which compelled brokers to tell the truth about new securities issues, and the Banking Act of 1933, which set up the Federal Deposit Insurance Corporation for insuring bank deposits. During the First Hundred Days, Roosevelt also took the United States off the gold standard, no longer guaranteeing the gold value of the dollar abroad. Freed from the gold standard, the Federal Reserve System could expand the supply of currency in circulation, thus enabling monetary policy to become another weapon for economic recovery.

TVA

One of the boldest programs enacted by Congress addressed the badly depressed Tennessee River valley, which runs through Tennessee, North Carolina, Kentucky, Virginia, Mississippi, Georgia, and Alabama. For years progressives like Senator George

Norris had advocated government operation of the Muscle Shoals electric power and nitrogen facilities on the Tennessee River. Roosevelt's Tennessee Valley Authority (TVA), established in May, was a much broader program. Its dams (one of which was named for Norris) would not only control floods but also generate hydroelectric power. The TVA would produce and sell nitrogen fertilizers to private citizens and nitrate explosives to the government; dig a 650-mile navigation channel from Knoxville, Tennessee, to Paducah, Kentucky; and construct public power facilities as a yardstick for determining fair rates for privately produced electric power. The goal of the TVA was nothing less than enhancement of the economic well-being of the entire Tennessee River valley (see map).

The TVA achieved its goals, but it also became—largely in unforeseen ways—the most notorious polluter in the region, if not in the entire country. To power its coal-burning generators, the TVA engaged in massive strip mining that caused

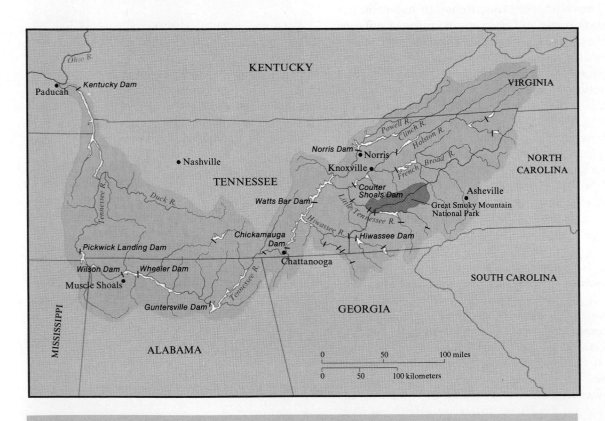

The Tennessee Valley Authority *For flood control and to generate electricity, the Tennessee Valley Authority constructed dams along the Tennessee River and its tributaries from Paducah, Kentucky, to Knoxville, Tennessee.*

TVA's Environmental Legacy

landslides and festering soil erosion. The generators also released sulfur oxides, which combined with water vapor to produce acid rain, a poison that not only killed aquatic life and destroyed forests in New England and Canada but also attacked human lungs and promoted heart disease. Above all, the TVA degraded the water by dumping untreated sewage, toxic chemicals, and metal pollutants from strip mining into streams and rivers. As this waste decayed, it seriously restricted the dissolved oxygen available for fish, mussels, and other aquatic life. Many creatures and plants died. In reservoirs created by TVA dams, certain kinds of water life, such as a fish called the snail darter, became extinct or endangered. The TVA would prove to be a monumental disaster in America's environmental history, but when it became law on May 18, 1933, it was heralded as a bold step forward.

End of the First Hundred Days

Congress finally adjourned on June 16. During the First Hundred Days, Roosevelt had delivered fifteen messages to Congress, and fifteen significant laws had been enacted (see table, page 766). Within a few months of Roosevelt's succession to office, the United States had rebounded from hysteria and near-collapse. As columnist Walter Lippmann wrote, at the time of the inauguration the country was a collection of "disorderly panic-stricken mobs and factions. In the hundred days from March to June we became again an organized nation confident of our power to provide for our own security and to control our own destiny."

Taylor Grazing Act

Throughout the remainder of 1933 and the spring and summer of 1934, more New Deal bills became law, benefiting farmers, the unemployed, investors, homeowners, workers, and the environment. The Commodity Credit Corporation, organized in 1933, bolstered crop prices by lending farmers money secured by their underpriced crops, thereby allowing them to withhold their crops from the market until prices rose. In 1934 additional hundreds of millions of federal dollars were appropriated for unemployment relief and public works. Legislation that year also established the Securities and Exchange Commission, the National Labor Relations Board, and the Federal Housing Administration. In 1934, too, the Taylor Grazing Act was passed. For years, use of the public lands had been largely unregulated, and cattle had caused soil erosion through overgrazing. The Taylor act, which created the Grazing Service (later the Bureau of Land Management), established federal supervision of most of the remaining public domain, and it also closed 80 million acres of grasslands to further settlement. "If unrestricted use of the public domain is crucial," historian Patricia Nelson Limerick has observed, "[then] the frontier ended in 1934, with the Taylor Grazing Act and the leasing of grazing rights on the public domain."

Interest-Group Democracy

The New Deal represented interest-group democracy at work. Its welter of legislation seemed to promise something for every group: industrial workers, urban dwellers, land-owning farmers, and the jobless, not to mention industrialists, bankers, stockbrokers, educators, and social workers. In the midst of this coalition of special interests was President Roosevelt, the artful broker, who pointed to the economy as proof that this approach was working. Following the passage of New Deal legislation, unemployment fell steadily from 13 million in 1933 to 9 million in 1936. Net farm income rose from just over $3 billion in 1933 to $5.85 billion in 1935. Manufacturing salaries and wages also increased, from $6.25 billion in 1933 to almost $13 billion in 1937.

There was no question about the popularity of either the New Deal or the president during those early years of Roosevelt's presidency. In the 1934 congressional elections, the Democrats gained ten seats in the House and ten in the Senate. The New Deal, according to Arthur Krock of the *New York Times*, had won "the most overwhelming victory in the history of American politics." As for Roosevelt, William Allen White wrote that "he has been all but crowned by the people."

OPPOSITION TO THE FIRST NEW DEAL

There was more than one way to read employment and income statistics and election returns. For example, while unemployment had dropped from a high of 25 percent in 1933 to 16.9 percent in 1936,

New Deal Achievements

	Labor	Agriculture	Business and Industrial Recovery	Relief	Reform
1933	Section 7(a) of NIRA	Agricultural Adjustment Act Farm Credit Act	Emergency Banking Act Beer and Wine Revenue Act Banking Act of 1933 (guaranteed deposits) National Industrial Recovery Act	Civilian Conservation Corps Federal Emergency Relief Act Home Owners Refinancing Act Public Works Administration Civil Works Administration	TVA Federal Securities Act
1934	National Labor Relations Board				Securities Exchange Act
1935	National Labor Relations (Wagner) Act	Resettlement Administration Rural Electrification Administration		Works Progress Administration and National Youth Administration	Banking Act of 1935 Social Security Act Public Utilities Holding Company Act Revenue Act (wealth tax)
1937		Farm Security Administration			
1938	Fair Labor Standards Act	Agricultural Adjustment Act of 1938			

Source: Adapted from Charles Sellers, Henry May, and Neil R. McMillen, *A Synopsis of American History*, 6th ed. Copyright © 1985 by Houghton Mifflin Company. Reprinted by permission.

it had been only 3.2 percent in 1929. And although manufacturing wages and salaries had reached almost $13 billion in 1937, that figure was almost $1.5 billion less than the total for 1929. Regardless of the New Deal's successes, in other words, it had a long way to go before reaching predepression standards.

With the arrival of partial economic recovery, many businesspeople and conservatives became vocal critics of the New Deal. Some charged that

Conservative Critics of the New Deal

there was too much taxation and government regulation. Others criticized the deficit financing of relief and public works. In 1934, the leaders of General Motors, U.S. Steel, Du Pont, and other corporations joined with Al Smith, John W. Davis, and disaffected conservative Democrats to establish the American Liberty League. Contending that the New Deal was sub-

The door of this farm shed in Cimarron County, Oklahoma, was blocked by wind-blown sand, which would pile up around the building one day and disappear the next. This photograph was taken by Arthur Rothstein of the Farm Security Administration.   Library of Congress.

verting individual initiative and self-reliance by providing welfare payments, the Liberty League announced that its goal was to slash government by abolishing welfare and "encouraging people to get rich."

While businesspeople considered the government their enemy, others thought the government favored business too much. Critics argued that business leaders had dominated the drafting of National Recovery Administration codes that favored industry's needs over those of workers and consumers. Criticism grew with time. Farmers, labor unions, and individual entrepreneurs complained that the NRA set prices too high and favored large producers over small businesses. The federal courts also began to scrutinize the constitutionality of the legislation in cases brought by critics.

The Agricultural Adjustment Act also came under attack for its encouragement of cutbacks in production. Farmers had plowed under 10.4 million acres of cotton and slaughtered 6 million pigs in 1933—a time when people were ill-clothed and ill-fed. Although for landowning farmers the pro-

gram was successful, the average person found such waste to be shocking. Tenant farmers and sharecroppers were also supposed to receive government payments for taking crops out of cultivation, but very few received what they were entitled to, especially if they were African-American. Furthermore, the AAA's hopes that landlords would keep their tenants on the land even while cutting production were not fulfilled. In the South the number of sharecropper farms dropped by 30 percent between 1930 and 1940. The result was a homeless population, dispossessed Americans heading to cities and towns in all parts of the country.

Joining the migration to the West Coast were "Okies" and "Arkies," many of whom were evicted from their tenant farms during the depression.

The Dust Bowl
——

They also took to the road to escape the drought that plagued the southern plains states of Kansas, Colorado, New Mexico, Oklahoma, Arkansas, and Texas, known in the mid-1930s as the Dust

Bowl. The Dust Bowl was the result of an environmental tragedy. Indeed, one expert has ranked it as one of the three worst ecological mistakes in history.

For fifteen years, farmers on the southern plains had bought tens of thousands of tractors and ploughed under millions of acres. In 1915 there were 3,000 tractors in Kansas; in 1930, there were 66,000. The historian Donald Worster has written that when "white men came to the plains, they talked expansively of 'busting' and 'breaking' the land. And that is exactly what they did." The result was not only overexpansion and falling crop prices but also soil exhaustion. Then, in the 1930s, the rain stopped. Soil that had been ploughed was particularly vulnerable to the drought that gripped the plains. Strong winds caused dust storms; there were 40 dust storms in 1935, 68 in 1936, 72 in 1937, and 61 in 1938. A storm in 1934 carried 300 million tons of dust from the plains and dropped it on East Coast cities and into the Atlantic Ocean. One of the worst storms, Black Sunday, struck the plains on April 14, 1935. Ed and Ada Phillips and their young daughter were driving home to Boise City, Oklahoma, when they saw an immense black wall heading toward them. They ran for shelter in an adobe hut by the road, but they were engulfed. After groping their way to the hut, they found ten people already inside, covered with dust.

Farmers shuttered their homes as tightly as possible, but, as a woman in western Kansas recounted in 1935, "those tiny particles seemed to seep through the very walls. It got into cupboards and clothes closets; our faces were as dirty as if we had rolled in the dirt; our hair was gray and stiff and we ground dirt between our teeth." Farm animals lacked all protection. The photographer Margaret Bourke-White observed that "cattle quickly become blinded. They run around in circles until they fall and breathe so much dust that they die."

Some farmers blamed the government for their woes, others blamed themselves. As dissatisfaction mounted in the countryside as well as the cities, so too did the appeal of various demagogues, who presented an analysis of American society that people understood: the wealthy and powerful were ruling people's lives from distant cities, eroding community morale, and ruining family farms and small businesses. Father Charles Coughlin, a Roman Catholic priest whose weekly radio sermons offered a curious combination of anticommunism and anticapitalism, was one of the best-known demagogues. For a while he supported the New Deal but opposed the AAA's plowing-under of crops and slaughtering of livestock. In late 1934, Coughlin organized the National Union for Social Justice and began to criticize the New Deal. He also became increasingly anti-Semitic, telling his listeners that the cause of their woes was an international conspiracy of Jewish bankers.

Demagogic Attacks on the New Deal

Another challenge to the New Deal came from Dr. Francis E. Townsend, a public health officer in Long Beach, California, who was thrown out of work at age sixty-seven with only $100 in savings. Disturbed by the plight of old people, Townsend devised the Old Age Revolving Pensions plan, under which the government would pay monthly pensions of $200 to all citizens over age sixty on condition that they spent the money in the same month they received it. Townsend claimed his plan would not only aid the aged but cure the depression by pumping enormous purchasing power into the economy. The plan was fiscally impossible, but it addressed the real needs of elderly Americans.

Then there was Huey Long, perhaps the most successful demagogue in American history. Long was elected governor of Louisiana in 1928 with the slogan "Every Man a King, But No One Wears a Crown." As a U.S. senator, Long at first supported the New Deal, but he found the NRA too conservative and began to believe that Roosevelt had fallen captive to big business. Long countered in 1934 with the Share Our Wealth Society, which advocated the seizure by taxation of all incomes over $1 million and all inheritances over $5 million. With the resulting funds, the government would furnish each family a homestead allowance of $5,000 and an annual income of $2,000. By mid-1935 Long's movement claimed 7 million members, and few doubted that Long aspired to the presidency. An assassin's bullet extinguished his ambition in September 1935. The Share Our Wealth movement persisted under a new leader, the vitriolic anti-Semite Gerald L. K. Smith, but it never regained its earlier following.

While not demagogues, some politicians who had lost faith in the capitalist system declared themselves socialists in the 1930s. Governor Floyd Olson of Minnesota sought a third party that would "preach the gospel of government and collective ownership of the means of produc-

Left-Wing Critics of the New Deal

tion and distribution." In neighboring Wisconsin the left-wing Progressive party re-elected Robert La Follette, Jr., to the Senate in 1934, sent seven of the state's ten representatives to Washington, and placed La Follette's brother Philip in the governorship. And the old muckraker and socialist Upton Sinclair won the Democratic gubernatorial nomination in California in 1934 with the slogan "End Poverty in California."

Perhaps the most controversial alternative to the New Deal was the Communist Party of the United States of America. Its membership remained small until 1935, when the party leadership changed its strategy. Proclaiming "Communism is Twentieth Century Americanism," the Communists disclaimed any intention of overthrowing the U.S. government and began to cooperate with left-wing labor unions, student groups, and writers' organizations. At its high point for the decade, in 1938, the party had 55,000 members.

In addition to challenges from the right and the left, the New Deal was also subject to challenge

Supreme Court Decisions Against the New Deal

by the Supreme Court. Many New Deal laws that had been hastily drafted and enacted were vulnerable, especially since the majority of the justices feared that this legislation had vested too much power in the presidency. In *Panama Refining Co.* v. *Ryan*, the Court struck down part of the NIRA in 1935. By granting the president power to prohibit interstate and foreign shipment of oil, the Court ruled, Congress had unconstitutionally delegated legislative power to the executive branch. Later the same year, the Court unanimously struck down the entire NIRA (*Schechter* v. *U.S.*) on the grounds that it granted the White House excessive legislative power and that the commerce clause of the Constitution did not give the federal government authority to regulate intrastate businesses. Roosevelt's industrial recovery program was dead. In early 1936 his farm program met a similar fate when the Court invalidated the AAA (*U.S.* v. *Butler*), deciding that

Senator Huey Long (center) had a mass following in the 1930s, and he had presidential ambitions. But he was assassinated in 1935, the same evening this photograph was taken. Long fell into the arms of James O'Connor (left), a political crony, while Louisiana Governor O. K. Allen (right) seized a pistol and dashed into the corridor after the murderer shouting, "If there's shooting, I want to be in on it." National Archives.

agriculture was a local problem and thus, under the Tenth Amendment, subject to state, not federal, action.

As Roosevelt looked ahead to the presidential election of 1936, he foresaw the danger of losing his capacity to lead and to govern. His coalition of all interests was breaking up; radicals and demagogues were offering Americans alternative programs; and the Supreme Court was dismantling the New Deal. In early 1935, Roosevelt took the initiative once more. So impressive was the spate of new legislation that historians have called it the Second New Deal.

THE SECOND NEW DEAL AND THE ELECTION OF 1936

The Second New Deal differed in important ways from the First New Deal. When the chief legislative goal had been economic recovery, Roosevelt had cooperated with business.

Works Progress Administration

Beginning in 1935, however, he denounced business leaders for placing their own selfish interests above the national welfare. The first triumph of the Second New Deal was an innocuous-sounding but momentous law called the Emergency Relief Appropriation Act, which authorized the president to establish massive public works programs for the jobless. The first such program was the Works Progress Administration (WPA), later renamed the Work Projects Administration. The WPA ultimately employed more than 8.5 million people and built over 650,000 miles of highways and roads, 125,000 public buildings, and 8,000 parks, as well as numerous bridges, airports, and other structures. But the WPA did more than lay bricks. Its Federal Theater Project brought plays, vaudeville, and circuses to cities and towns across the country, and its Federal Writers' Project hired talent like John Steinbeck and Richard Wright to write local guidebooks and regional and folk histories.

The Emergency Relief Appropriation Act also funded the Resettlement Administration, which resettled destitute families and organized rural homestead communities and suburban greenbelt towns for low-income workers. The Rural Electrification Administration (REA) brought electricity to isolated rural areas. And the National Youth Administration (NYA) sponsored work-relief programs for young adults and part-time jobs for students.

Roosevelt also wanted new legislation aimed at controlling the activities of big business. The Supreme Court had condemned the government-business cooperation that had been the foundation of the First Hundred Days. In addition, businesspeople had become increasingly critical of Roosevelt and the New Deal, complaining that they were overtaxed and overregulated. If big business would not cooperate with government, Roosevelt decided, government should "cut the giants down to size" through antitrust suits and heavy corporate taxes. In 1935 he asked Congress to enact several major bills, including a labor bill sponsored by Senator Robert Wagner of New York, a Social Security bill, and a "soak-the-rich" tax bill.

When the summer of 1935 that constituted the Second Hundred Days was over, the president had everything he had requested. The National Labor Relations (Wagner) Act granted workers the right to unionize and bargain collectively with management. When the Supreme Court had struck down the NIRA, labor unions had lost their federal protection. The Wagner Act, however, was even stronger than the previous legislation (Section 7(a) of the NIRA). The new act empowered the National Labor Relations Board to guarantee democratic union elections and to penalize unfair labor practices by employers, such as firing workers for union membership.

Roosevelt's Second Hundred Days

The Social Security Act established old-age insurance for workers who paid Social Security taxes out of their wages. Social Security was a conservative measure: the government did not pay for old-age benefits; workers and their bosses did. The tax was also regressive in that the more workers earned, the less they were taxed proportionally; and it was deflationary because it took out of people's pockets money that it did not repay for years. Finally, the law excluded from coverage farm workers, domestic servants, and many hospital and restaurant workers, occupations that included many women and people of color.

Social Security Act

Nevertheless, the Social Security Act was a milestone. With its passage, the federal government acknowledged its responsibility to establish a system of insurance not only for the aged but also for the temporarily jobless. To assist the unemployed, the act established a cooperative federal-state system of unemployment compensation funded by employers and the states. It also authorized grants to the states for relief of dependent children and disabled people, and it funded public health programs.

As summer neared its end, Congress also passed the Revenue (Wealth Tax) Act of 1935, as Roosevelt had requested. The act, which some critics saw as the president's attempt to "steal Huey Long's thunder," did not result in a redistribution of income, though it did raise the income taxes of the wealthy. It also imposed a new tax on excess business profits and increased taxes on inheritances, large gifts, and profits from the sale of property.

The Second Hundred Days made it unmistakably clear that the president was once again in charge and preparing to run for re-election. The

Election of 1936

campaign was less heated than might have been expected. The Republican nominee, Governor Alf Landon of Kansas, criticized Roosevelt but did not advocate wholesale repeal of the New Deal. Followers of Father Coughlin, Dr. Townsend, and the late Senator Long banded together in the Union party and nominated Representative William Lemke of North Dakota. The Socialists nominated Norman Thomas; the Communists, Earl Browder.

The president and the Democratic party swept to a landslide victory. Roosevelt polled 27.8 million votes to Landon's 16.7 million; Lemke, Thomas, and Browder together received slightly over 1 million. The Democrats carried every state but Maine and Vermont and won huge majorities in the House and Senate. Some observers even worried that the two-party system was about to collapse.

By 1936 Roosevelt and the Democrats had forged what observers have called "the New Deal coalition." In the 1920s and 1930s the sons and daughters of 13 million south-

New Deal Coalition

ern and eastern European immigrants were reaching voting age and swelling the ranks of their parents' traditional party.

The 6 million Americans who had migrated from farms to cities in the 1920s were looking to the government for help, and they too were gravitating to the Democratic party. The growing strength of the party in the cities and the New Deal's responsiveness to social distress combined to make Roosevelt the champion of the urban masses, many farmers, and members of labor unions. The Congress of Industrial Organizations fused the interests of millions of workers, native-born and foreign-born, black and white, male and female, skilled and unskilled (see page 773). Black voters in northern cities, most of whom had been Republicans prior to the 1930s, now also cast their lot with the Democratic party, as did many lifelong socialists. Finally, the party retained "the Solid South," the eleven states of the Confederacy that had voted Democratic since the end of Reconstruction. With the New Deal coalition, the Democratic party had become the dominant half of the two-party system and would occupy the White House for most of the next thirty years.

ROOSEVELT'S SECOND TERM: COURT PACKING AND OTHER FAILURES

Roosevelt faced a darkening horizon during his second term. The economy faltered again between 1937 and 1939, bringing renewed unemployment and suffering. And Europe drew closer to war, threatening to drag the United States into the conflict (see Chapter 26). To gain support for his foreign and military policies, Roosevelt began to court conservative opponents of his domestic reforms. The eventual result was the demise of the New Deal.

In several instances Roosevelt brought about his own defeat. The Supreme Court had invalidated much of the work of the First Hundred

Roosevelt's Court-packing Plan

Days; now Roosevelt feared it would do the same with the fruits of the Second Hundred Days. Four of the justices steadfastly opposed the New Deal; three generally approved of it; two were swing votes. What the federal judiciary needed, the president claimed, was a more

President Roosevelt's plan to expand the membership of the Supreme Court was met by angry opposition, not only from his Republican opponents but from within the Democratic party as well.   Library of Congress.

enlightened and progressive world view. His Judiciary Reorganization Bill requested the authority to add a federal judge whenever an incumbent failed to retire within six months of reaching age seventy; he also wanted the power to name up to fifty additional federal judges, including six to the Supreme Court. Roosevelt frankly envisioned using the bill to create a Supreme Court sympathetic to the New Deal. Opposition was widespread and vocal. Opponents thundered that the president's true aim was dictatorship. Liberals joined Republicans and conservative Democrats in resisting the bill, and Roosevelt had to concede defeat. The bill he signed into law provided pensions to retiring judges but denied him the power to increase the number of judges.

This episode had a final ironic twist. During the public debate over court packing, the two swing-vote justices on the Supreme Court began to vote in favor of liberal, pro–New Deal rulings. In short order the Court delivered a series of 5-to-4 decisions upholding a Washington state minimum-wage statute; the Wagner Act (*NLRB* v. *Jones & Laughlin Steel Corp.*, ruling that Congress's power to regulate interstate commerce also involved the power to regulate the production of goods for inter-

state commerce); and the Social Security Act. Moreover, the new pensions encouraged judges over age seventy to retire, and the president was able to appoint seven new associate justices in the next four years, including such notables as Hugo Black, Felix Frankfurter, and William O. Douglas.

Another New Deal setback was the renewed economic recession of 1937–1939. Roosevelt had never abandoned his commitment to a balanced budget. In 1937, confident that the depression had largely been cured, he began to order drastic cutbacks in government spending. At the same time the Federal Reserve Board, concerned about a 3.6 percent inflation rate, tightened credit. The two actions sent the economy into a tailspin: unemployment climbed from 7.7 million in 1937 to 10.4 million in 1938. Soon Roosevelt was forced to resume deficit financing. But even with sudden infusions of relief, unemployment still stood at 9.5 million in 1939.

Recession of 1937–1939

In the spring of 1938, with conflict over events in Europe commanding more and more of the nation's attention, the New Deal came to an end. Roosevelt sacrificed further domestic reforms in return for conservative support for his programs of military rearmament and preparedness. The last significant New Deal laws enacted were the National Housing Act (1937), which established the U.S. Housing Authority and built housing projects for low-income families; a new Agricultural Adjustment Act (1938); and the Fair Labor Standards Act (1938), which forbade labor by children under age sixteen and established a minimum wage and forty-hour workweek for many, but by no means all, workers.

INDUSTRIAL WORKERS AND THE RISE OF THE CIO

Working people gained from the New Deal the right to organize labor unions and bargain collectively with their bosses. Enactment of Section 7(a) of the NIRA had inspired vigorous recruitment of union members. Organizers for the United Mine Workers (UMW) told coal miners, "President Roosevelt wants you to join the union," and many thousands did so. With passage of the Wagner Act in mid-1935, union recruiting received another big boost; within three years, total membership surpassed 7 million.

These gains did not always come easily. Management resisted vigorously in the 1930s, relying on the police or hiring armed thugs to intimidate workers and break up strikes. Violence surfaced in the steel, automobile, and textile industries and among lumber workers in the Pacific Northwest and teamsters in the Midwest. In 1934 a strike of longshoremen was met with violence by police on the docks of San Francisco; two union members were killed, and workers' anger spread to other industries. Eventually 130,000 workers joined the general strike.

Labor confronted yet another obstacle in the American Federation of Labor (AFL) craft unions' traditional hostility toward industrial unions. Craft

Rivalry Between Craft and Industrial Unions

unions typically consisted of skilled workers in a particular trade, such as carpentry or plumbing. Industrial unions represented all the workers, skilled and unskilled, in a given industry; the UMW and the International Ladies' Garment Workers Union were both industrial unions. Ever since its establishment in 1886, the AFL had been dominated by craft unions. But far more impressive gains were made in industrial unions than in craft unions in the 1930s, as hundreds of thousands of workers organized in such industries as autos, garments, rubber, and steel.

The craft and industrial unions competed bitterly for control of the growing labor movement. Personifying this power struggle were John L. Lewis of the UMW and William Green of the AFL. Lewis, a fighter with a flair for the dramatic, was probably the most colorful and tenacious labor leader in the nation's history. But he presided over only one of the many unions within the AFL, whereas the lackluster Green was president of the entire federation. Attempts to reconcile the craft and industrial union movements failed, and in 1935 Lewis resigned as vice president of the AFL. He and other industrial unionists then formed the Committee for Industrial Organization (CIO). When the AFL demanded that the CIO disband, Lewis replied: "The American Federation of Labor is standing still, with its face toward the dead

past." The AFL expelled the CIO unions in 1938, and the CIO reorganized itself as the Congress of Industrial Organizations. By that time CIO membership had reached 3.7 million, more than the AFL's 3.4 million.

The CIO evolved during the 1930s into a pragmatic bread-and-butter labor organization that organized millions of workers, including women and

Sit-down Strikes

African-Americans, who had never before had an opportunity to join a union. One of these unions, the United Auto Workers (UAW), scored a major victory in late 1936. The UAW, thirty thousand strong, demanded recognition from General Motors, Chrysler, and Ford. When GM refused, workers at the Fisher Body plant in Flint, Michigan, launched a sit-down strike and refused to leave the building. To discourage the strikers, GM turned off the heat. When that tactic failed, they called in the police, who were met by a barrage of iron bolts, coffee mugs, and bottles. The police then resorted to tear gas, and the strikers turned the plant's water hoses on them.

The strike lasted for weeks. GM obtained a court order to evacuate the plant, but the strikers stood firm, risking imprisonment and fines. With the support of their families and neighborhoods, the workers maintained rigid discipline. Community women organized an "emergency brigade" to picket and deliver food and supplies to the strikers. The UAW prevailed: GM agreed to recognize the union. Chrysler signed a similar agreement, but Ford held out for four more years, which were marked by bloody encounters between the UAW and union-busting hoodlums hired by the Ford Service Department.

The sit-down strike as a tactic spread dramatically; it was used by workers in the textile, glass, and rubber industries; dime-store clerks; janitors; dressmakers; and bakers. Some people condemned the sit-down as a trespass on private property; others endorsed it, including muckraker Upton Sinclair, who wrote that "for 75 years big business has been sitting down on the American people, and now I am delighted to see the process reversed." Most important, participation in the sit-downs bestowed self-respect on the strikers. One man proudly compared his actions to those of Davy Crockett: "Yes sir, Chevy [Plant] No. 4 was my Alamo."

How do historians know

who was responsible for the 1937 Memorial Day Massacre in Chicago? There is both photographic and medical evidence of the police's culpability. Covering the story at the Republic Steel plant were a cameraman from Paramount News and photographers from Life magazine and Wide World Photos (see photograph). Paramount News suppressed its film footage, claiming that releasing it "might very well incite local riots," but an enterprising reporter alerted a congressional committee to its existence, and a private viewing was arranged. Spectators at this showing, the reporter noted, "were shocked and amazed by scenes showing scores of uniformed policemen firing their revolvers pointblank into a dense crowd of men, women, and children, and then pursuing the survivors unmercifully as they made frantic efforts to escape." Medical evidence also substantiated the picketers' version: none of the ten people killed by police had been shot from the front. Clearly, the picketers were trying to flee the police when they were shot or clubbed to the ground.   Photo: World Wide Photos.

In 1937, the Steel Workers Organizing Committee (SWOC) signed a contract with the nation's largest steelmaker, U.S. Steel, that guaranteed an eight-hour day and a forty-hour week. Other steel companies refused to go along. Confrontations between these so-called little steel companies and the SWOC soon led to violence. On Memorial Day, strikers and their families joined with sympa-

Memorial Day Massacre

thizers in a picket line in front of the Republic Steel plant in Chicago. Violence erupted, in which ten strikers were killed and forty suffered gunshot wounds. The police explained that the marchers had attacked them with clubs and bricks and that they had responded with reasonable force to defend themselves and disperse the mob. Some newspapers agreed, among them the Chicago *Tribune*, which described the attack as an invasion by "a trained military unit of a revolutionary body," and the *New York Times*, which carried the headline: "STEEL MOB HALTED." The strikers argued that the police, without provocation, had brutally attacked citizens who were peacefully asserting their constitutional rights.

Though senseless, the Memorial Day Massacre was not surprising. During the 1930s industries had hired private police agents and accumulated large stores of arms and ammunition for use in deterring workers from organizing and joining unions. Meanwhile the CIO continued to enroll new members. By 1938 industrial unions had enlisted 600,000 miners, 375,000 steelworkers, 400,000 auto workers, 300,000 textile workers, 250,000 ladies' garment workers, and 100,000 agricultural and packing-house workers. By the end of the decade the CIO had succeeded in organizing most of the nation's mass-production industries. And as these industries were converted for war production in the decade ahead, employment soared and the CIO registered even more impressive membership gains.

MIXED PROGRESS FOR PEOPLE OF COLOR

The depression plunged the vast majority of African-Americans deeper into fear, political disfranchisement, Jim Crow segregation, and privation.

African-Americans in the Depression

In 1930 about three-fourths of all blacks lived in the South. Almost all were prohibited from voting or serving on juries. They were routinely denied access to hospitals, universities, public parks, and swimming pools. And they were hired only for the least desirable, most menial jobs. Blacks living in rural areas in the South were propertyless sharecroppers, tenants, or wage hands. In many cases, white landowners failed to share with tenants and sharecroppers the government payments they received for taking land out of cultivation. They were often evicted and, in any case, were caught in a cycle of poverty, disease, and illiteracy. Their life expectancy was ten years lower than that of whites (47 years versus 57). And the specter of the lynch mob was a growing threat: in 1929, seven black men were lynched; in 1930, twenty; and in 1933, at the peak of the depression, twenty-four.

Racism also plagued African-Americans living in the North. Southern blacks who migrated to northern cities discovered that employers discriminated against them. Black unemployment rates ran high; in Pittsburgh 48 percent of black workers were jobless in 1933, compared with 31 percent of white laborers.

As African-Americans were aware, Herbert Hoover shared prevailing white racial attitudes. Hoover sought a lily-white GOP and attempted to push blacks out of the Republican party in order to attract white southern Democrats. He appointed few blacks to federal office, disbanded the Negro Division of the Republican National Committee, rejected appeals for a federal antilynching law, and perpetuated the segregation of the army and of facilities in federal buildings in the nation's capital. Hoover's philosophy of individualism, opportunity, and fair play was, like signs posted across the country, "For Whites Only."

In 1930, the president demonstrated his racial insensitivity by nominating Judge John J. Parker of North Carolina to the Supreme Court. Ten years earlier Parker had endorsed the disfranchisement of blacks; the NAACP remembered and protested his nomination. The AFL joined the protest, and the joint opposition plus liberal votes in the Senate defeated Parker's nomination, 41 to 39. Unmoved, Hoover stood by his nominee throughout.

Shortly thereafter, a celebrated civil rights case revealed the ugliness of race relations in the depression era. In March 1931, nine African-Americans who were riding a

Scottsboro Trials

freight train near Scottsboro, Alabama, were arrested by armed sheriff's deputies who charged them with roughing up some white hoboes and throwing them off the train. Two white women removed from the same train claimed the nine men had raped them. Medical evidence later showed that the women were lying (perhaps to save themselves from arrest as prostitutes). But within two weeks, eight of the so-called "Scottsboro boys" were convicted of rape by all-white juries and sentenced to death.

After several trials, the first defendant, Haywood Patterson, was condemned to die. A Supreme Court ruling intervened, however, on the grounds that African-Americans were systematically excluded from juries in Alabama. Patterson was found guilty again in 1936 and was given a seventy-five-year jail sentence. Four of the other youths were sentenced to life imprisonment. Not until 1950 were all five out of jail—four by parole and Patterson by escaping from his work gang.

African-Americans coped with their white-circumscribed environment and fought racism in a variety of ways. The NAACP, though internally divided, lobbied quietly against a long list of injustices, and the Brotherhood of Sleeping Car Porters, under the astute leadership of A. Philip Randolph, fought for the rights of black workers. In Harlem the militant Harlem Tenants League fought rent increases and evictions, and African-American consumers began to boycott white merchants who refused to hire blacks as clerks. Their slogan was, "Don't Buy Where You Can't Work." But America's white leaders made few concessions. Only the Supreme Court provided a measure of protection for African-Americans by attempting to correct the abuse in the Scottsboro trials, and by declaring the Texas "white primary" law unconstitutional. But

southern states circumvented this ruling by declaring that political parties were actually "private clubs" and could set their own membership requirements.

With the election of Franklin D. Roosevelt, blacks' attitudes toward government changed, as did their political affiliation. For African-Americans—an important component of the New Deal coalition—Franklin D. Roosevelt would become the most appealing president since Abraham Lincoln. Part of the reason was the courageous way he bore his physical disability. Blacks suffered from their own handicap—racism—and knew what courage was. Moreover, Roosevelt was a decided improvement over Hoover, and the personal magnetism and buoyancy he exhibited in his fireside chats spoke directly to them. Blacks were heartened by photographs of African-American visitors at the White House and by news stories about Roosevelt's Black Cabinet. Most important, through the WPA and other relief programs, the

Numerous African-American families were evicted from their farms during the Great Depression. White planters who received government payments for taking land out of cultivation were supposed to share these payments with their tenants and sharecroppers. Instead, many kicked these families off the land and kept the money for themselves. This family in Putnam County, Georgia, loaded all its possessions into a rickety truck for the trip north. National Archives.

Mary McLeod Bethune, pictured here with her friend and supporter Eleanor Roosevelt, became the first African-American woman to head a federal agency as director of the Division of Negro Affairs of the National Youth Administration. UPI/Bettmann Newsphotos.

New Deal aided black people in their struggle for economic survival.

The Black Cabinet, or black brain trust, was unique in U.S. history. Never before had there been so many African-American advisers at the White House, and never had

Black Cabinet
——

they been highly trained professionals. There were black lawyers, journalists, and Ph.D.s and black experts on housing, labor, and social welfare. William H. Hastie and Robert C. Weaver, holders of advanced degrees from Harvard, served in the Department of the Interior. Mary McLeod Bethune, educator and president of the National Council of Negro Women, was director of the Division of Negro Affairs of the National Youth Administration. There were also among the New Dealers some whites who had committed themselves to first-class citizenship for African-Americans. Foremost among these people was Eleanor Roosevelt. In 1939, when the acclaimed black contralto Marian Anderson was barred from performing in Washington's Constitution Hall by its owners, the Daughters of the American Revolution, Mrs. Roosevelt arranged for Anderson to sing on Easter Sunday at the Lincoln Memorial.

The president himself, however, remained uncommitted to African-American civil rights. Fearful of alienating southern whites, he never endorsed two key goals of the

**The
New Deal's
Racism**
——

civil rights struggle: a federal law against lynching and abolition of the poll tax. Furthermore, some New Deal programs functioned in ways that were definitely damaging to African-Americans. The AAA, rather than benefiting black tenant farmers and sharecroppers, had the effect of forcing many of them off the land. The Federal Housing Administration (FHA) refused to guarantee mortgages on houses purchased by blacks in white neighborhoods. The CCC was racially segregated, as was much of the TVA, which constructed all-white towns and handed out skilled jobs to whites first. Finally, Social Security coverage and the minimum-wage provisions of the Fair Labor Standards Act of 1938 excluded waiters, cooks, hospital orderlies, janitors, farm workers, and domestics, many of whom were African-Americans.

In short, though African-Americans benefited from the New Deal, they did not get their fair share. Even so, they overwhelmingly supported the New Deal for the benefits they did receive. And at election time, black voters showed their gratitude by giving Roosevelt large majorities.

But not all African-Americans trusted the mixed message of the New Deal. Some concluded that they could depend only on themselves and organized self-help and direct-action movements. In 1934, black tenant farmers and share-croppers joined with poor whites to form the Southern Tenant Farmers' Union. In the North, blacks organized tenants' unions, boycotted stores, and launched "Jobs for Negroes" campaigns. In 1935 when police in Harlem beat to death a black youth, a race riot erupted as mobs of poor and angry people smashed store windows and raided shelves. Working-class blacks criticized the NAACP for ignoring the economics of second-class citizenship and for being too middle class and legalistic in its war on racism. The NAACP was scoring notable victories in opening up graduate and professional schools to black students, but critics charged that these gains benefited only the middle class, not the masses who above all needed jobs.

Black Protest

Nowhere was the trend toward direct action more evident than in the March on Washington Movement in 1941. That year, billions of federal dollars flowed into American industry as the nation prepared for the possibility of another world war. Thousands of new jobs were created, but discrimination deprived blacks of their fair share. One executive notified black job applicants that "the Negro will be considered only as janitors and other similar capacities." A. Philip Randolph, president of the Brotherhood of Sleeping Car Porters, proposed that blacks march on the nation's capital to demand equal access to jobs in defense industries.

March on Washington Movement

By midsummer thousands were ready to march. Fearing that the march might provoke riots and that Communists might infiltrate the move-

ment, Roosevelt announced that he would issue an executive order prohibiting discrimination in war industries and in the government if the march was canceled. The result was Executive Order No. 8802, which established the Fair Employment Practices Committee (FEPC). The March on Washington Movement anticipated future trends in the civil rights movement: it was all-black; its tactic was direct action—a threat by the masses to take to the streets; and its beneficiaries were the urban working class.

Another group, American Indians, sank further into malnutrition and disease during the early 1930s. In Oklahoma, where the Choctaws, Cherokees, and Seminoles lived with over twenty other tribes on infertile soil, three-fourths of all Native American children were undernourished. Tuberculosis swept through the reservations. At the heart of the problem was a 1929 ruling by the U.S. comptroller general that landless tribes were ineligible for federal aid. Not until 1931 did the Bureau of Indian Affairs take steps to relieve the suffering. A federal relief program was launched to provide flour from the Red Cross, surplus clothing from the War Department, and seed from the Department of Agriculture. Yet when Congress substantially increased the bureau's budget that year, much of the money went to hire more bureaucrats.

The New Deal approach to Native Americans differed greatly from that of earlier administrations; as a result, Indians benefited more directly than blacks from the New Deal. As commissioner of Indian affairs, Roosevelt appointed John Collier, the founder of the American Indian Defense Association. Collier had crusaded for tribal landownership and an end to the allotment policy established by the Dawes Severalty Act of 1887 (see Chapter 17). "The allotment act," Collier wrote, "contemplates total landlessness for the Indians of the third generation of each allotted tribe." First, the Dawes Act sought to dissolve tribes by dividing landholdings among tribal members—160 acres to each head of family and 80 acres to each single adult. Many individuals then sold their allotments to white ranchers, miners, and farmers. Second, reservation land remaining after the distribution of allotments was opened for settlement to non-Indian homesteaders. The result was that, after 1887, Indian landholdings dropped from 138 million acres to 48

A New Deal for Native Americans

million acres, 20 million of which were arid or semiarid.

The Indian Reorganization (Wheeler-Howard) Act, passed by Congress in 1934, aimed to reverse this process by restoring lands to tribal ownership and forbidding future division of Indian lands into individual parcels. Other provisions of the act enabled tribes to obtain loans for economic development and to establish self-government. Under Collier, the Bureau of Indian Affairs also encouraged the perpetuation of Indian religions and cultures. One order stated: "No interference with Indian religious life or expression will hereafter be tolerated. The cultural history of Indians is in all respects to be considered equal to that of any nonIndian group." Collier's reforms would stand until 1953.

Mexican-Americans also suffered extreme hardship during the depression, but no government programs benefited them. During these years many Mexicans and Mexican-Americans packed up their belongings and moved south of the border, sometimes willingly and sometimes deported by immigration officials or forced out by California officials eager to purge them from the relief rolls. As an inducement, the government offered free one-

Depression Hardships for Mexican-Americans

way train tickets to Mexico. From 1929 through 1934, about 425,000 people, mostly from Texas, California, Indiana, and Illinois, returned to Mexico.

According to the federal census, the Mexican-born population in the United States dropped from 617,000 in 1930 to 377,000 in 1940. Many employers had changed their minds about the desirability of hiring Mexican-American farm workers. Before the 1930s farmers had boasted that Mexican-Americans were a cheap, docile labor supply and that they would not join unions. But in the 1930s Mexican-Americans overturned the stereotype by engaging in prolonged and sometimes bloody strikes. During one protest in the strawberry fields of El Monte, California, workers established their own union, which waged two dozen strikes from 1933 to 1936. In the San Joaquin valley, eighteen thousand cotton pickers walked off their jobs in 1933 and set up a "strike city" after being evicted from the growers' camps. Shortly thereafter, their union hall was riddled with bullets and two strikers died.

The New Deal offered Mexican-Americans little help. The AAA was created to assist property-owning farmers, not migratory farm workers. The Wagner Act did not cover farm workers' unions; nor did the Social Security Act or the Fair Labor

Violence erupted in October 1933 in California's San Joaquin Valley. When Mexican farm workers went on strike, the growers evicted them and their families. The growers also fired upon workers holding strike meetings at Pixley and Arvin, killing three. This group of Mexican women was bound for the picket line to protest for food relief for the hungry families.   Library of Congress.

Standards Act cover farm laborers. One New Deal agency, the Farm Security Administration (FSA), was established in 1937 to help farm workers, in part by setting up migratory labor camps. But the FSA came too late to help Mexican-Americans, most of whom had by then been replaced in the fields by dispossessed white farmers. Between 1935 and 1940 more than 350,000 Okies and Arkies fled to California from Oklahoma, Arkansas, Texas, and other drought-stricken Dust Bowl states. As early as 1936 they made up 85 to 90 percent of the state's migratory work force, compared with less than 20 percent before the depression. In just a few years, however, Mexican-Americans would be back. With the onset of the Second World War, the United States would again need Mexican-Americans to work in the fields and on the railroads.

WOMEN, WORK, AND THE DEPRESSION

During the depression women had to work overtime to maintain themselves and their families. In *It's Up to the Women* (1933), Eleanor Roosevelt wrote that wives and mothers

Mothers and Households Face the Depression

often bore a heavier burden than husbands and fathers during such periods. "The women know," she asserted, "that life must go on and that the needs of life must be met." Wives and mothers experiencing severe income reductions followed the maxim "Use it up, wear it out, make it do, or do without." Making do, Eleanor Roosevelt wrote, meant "endless little economies and constant anxiety for fear of some catastrophe such as accident or illness which may completely swamp the family budget." Women bought day-old bread and cheap cuts of meat; they relined old coats with blankets and saved string, rags, and broken crockery for possible future use. Many families were able to maintain their standard of living only because of astute spending and because women substituted their own labor for goods and services they used to purchase. Husbands shared these financial concerns, but it was usually women's responsibility to do the family budgeting; it was estimated that wives and mothers in the 1930s allocated over 80 percent of all family income.

While they were cutting corners to make ends meet, women were also seeking paid work outside the home. In 1930 approximately 10.5 million women were paid workers; ten years later, the female labor force exceeded 13 million. There were no "separate spheres" for women who were their families' sole providers; they had to do it all, at home and on the job. Despite these social realities, most Americans continued to believe that women should not take jobs outside the home, that they should strive instead to be good wives and mothers, and that women who worked were doing so for "pin money" to buy frivolous things. When a 1936 Gallup poll asked whether wives should work if their husbands had jobs, 82 percent of the respondents (including 75 percent of the women) answered no.

Severe job discrimination resulted from these attitudes. For example, of the 1,500 urban school systems surveyed by the National Education Association in 1930–1931, 77 percent refused to hire married women as teachers and 63 percent fired female teachers who married while employed. Most insurance companies, banks, railroads, and public utilities had similar policies against hiring married women. And from 1932 to 1937, federal law prohibited more than one family member from working for the civil service. Because wives usually earned less than their husbands, they were the ones who quit their government jobs.

Job Discrimination Against Married Women

In part, such thinking stemmed from the widely held belief that a woman who worked caused a man to be unemployed. That view missed the point, for two reasons. First, women were heavily concentrated in "women's jobs," including clerical positions (49 percent of all employees were women), teachers (81 percent), telephone operators (95 percent), and nurses (98 percent). Men rarely sought these jobs and probably would not have been hired had they applied. Second, most women workers (72 percent in 1930) were single and thus self-supporting. Since the economy had become segregated into "men's jobs" and "women's jobs," the problem for these women was that their wages lagged far behind those for men. Lagging furthest were women of color, some of whom lost their low-paying menial jobs to white women during the depression. For many African-American women there was only the "slave market," an informal hiring process that took place every morning on designated urban streetcorners, where women waited for potential employers for day work at pitiful wages.

Married women constituted 35 percent of the female work force in 1940, an increase from 29 percent in 1930 and 15 percent in 1900. They worked to keep their families from slipping into poverty, but their assistance with family expenses did not improve their status. As the sociologists Robert and Helen Lynd observed at the time: "The men, cut adrift from their usual routine, lost most of their sense of time and dawdled helplessly and dully about the streets; while in the homes the women's world remained largely intact and the round of cooking, housecleaning, and mending became if anything more absorbing." And even though women were making greater contributions to the family, their husbands, including those without jobs, still expected to rule the roost and to remain exempt from childcare and housework.

The New Deal did take women's needs into account, but only when forcefully reminded to do so by the activist women who advised the administration. These women, mainly government and Democratic party officials, formed a network united by their commitment to social reform and to the participation of women in politics and government. Many were long-time personal friends and professional allies who had worked together in the National Consumers' League, Women's Trade Union League, and other organizations during the Progressive era and the 1920s. Most believed that working women needed protective laws for their health and safety on the job. The network's most prominent member was Eleanor Roosevelt, who was her husband's valued adviser. Secretary of Labor Frances Perkins was the nation's first woman cabinet officer. Other historic New Deal appointments included the first woman federal appeals judge and the first women ambassadors. Molly Dewson, head of the Democratic party's Women's Division, noted with pride: "The change from women's status in government before Roosevelt is unbelievable."

Women in the New Deal

Even with increased participation by women, however, New Deal provisions for women were mixed. The maximum-hour and minimum-wage provisions mandated by the NRA won women's support. Women workers in the lowest-paying

Even while unemployment in heavy industry remained high throughout the 1930s, women increased their numbers in the work force during the decade. Many became clerical workers, or Office Girls, *which is the title of this 1936 oil painting by Raphael Soyer.* Collection of Whitney Museum of American Art.

jobs, many of whom labored under sweatshop conditions, had the most to gain from these standards. Some NRA codes mandated pay differentials based on gender, however, making women's minimum wages lower than men's. Federal relief agencies, such as the Civil Works Administration and the Federal Emergency Relief Administration, hired only one woman for every eight to ten men placed in relief jobs. A popular New Deal program, the Civilian Conservation Corps, was limited to young men. And women in agriculture and domestic service were not protected by the 1935 Social Security Act or the 1938 Fair Labor Standards Act.

Nevertheless, significant changes in women's lives were imminent. The reason for the changes, however, was not that the government would suddenly decide to stress women's equality with men, but that beginning in 1941 the country would be at war—a war it could not win without employing womanpower in the nation's aircraft factories, shipyards, and munitions works.

THE ELECTION OF 1940 AND THE LEGACY OF THE NEW DEAL

As the presidential election of 1940 approached, many Americans speculated about whether Roosevelt would run for a third term. (No president had ever served more than two terms.) Roosevelt himself seemed undecided until May 1940, when Adolf Hitler's military advances in Europe apparently convinced him to stay on. He confided his decision to no one, however, and even sent a message to the Democratic convention that he did not want to be renominated. But at a timely moment, loudspeakers broadcast the chant "We want Roosevelt!" throughout the convention hall, and delegates began to snake-dance up and down the aisles. Roosevelt wanted the nomination, but he also wanted the appearance of a draft. He was nominated on the first ballot and selected Henry A. Wallace, an Iowa farm-journal editor who was serving as Roosevelt's secretary of agriculture, as his running mate.

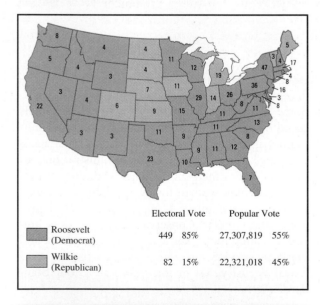

	Electoral Vote		Popular Vote	
Roosevelt (Democrat)	449	85%	27,307,819	55%
Wilkie (Republican)	82	15%	22,321,018	45%

Presidential Election, 1940   *Roosevelt won an unprecedented third term in the 1940 presidential election. He did not repeat his landslide 1936 victory, in which he won all but two states. But he did capture thirty-eight states in 1940 to Republican Wendell Willkie's ten.*

The Republican candidate was Wendell Willkie, an Indiana lawyer and utilities executive who was once a Democrat but had become a prominent business opponent of the New Deal. As a politician Willkie was an unknown, and as late as April 1940 he did not have a single delegate to the Republican convention two months away. In May, with the Nazi invasion of the Low Countries and France, Willkie's support mounted in public opinion polls. Other anti-New Deal Democrats joined with eastern Republicans to boost his candidacy, painting him as an internationalist who would halt the Nazi advance before it reached England. On the sixth ballot Willkie defeated New York's Governor Thomas E. Dewey.

Wendell Willkie

Willkie campaigned against the New Deal, contending that its meddling in business had failed to return the nation to prosperity. He also criticized the government's lack of military preparedness. But Roosevelt pre-empted the defense issue by beefing up military and naval contracts. As workers streamed into the factories to fill new orders, unemployment figures dropped as well. In his speeches Roosevelt reminded workers that it was his administration that had provided the defense jobs. When Willkie reversed his approach and accused Roosevelt of warmongering, the president promised, "Your boys are not going to be sent into any foreign wars."

Willkie never did come up with an effective campaign issue, and on election day Roosevelt received 27 million popular votes to Willkie's 22 million. In the electoral college Roosevelt buried Willkie 449 to 82. Willkie did manage to win the farm and small-town vote in the Midwest, but the New Deal coalition was triumphant. As in 1936, Roosevelt triumphed in the cities, primarily among blue-collar workers, ethnic Americans, and African-Americans. He also won every state in the South. Although the New Deal was over at home, Roosevelt was still riding a wave of public approval.

Any analysis of the New Deal must begin with Franklin Delano Roosevelt. Assessments of his career varied widely during his presidency. Most historians consider him a truly great president, citing his courage and buoyant self-confidence, his willingness to experiment, and his capacity to inspire the nation during the

Franklin D. Roosevelt Assessed

most somber days of the depression. Those who criticize him charge that he lacked vision and failed to formulate a bold and coherent strategy of economic recovery and political and economic reform. He was not a socialist, but a capitalist: he wanted to alleviate suffering, but not at the expense of private property and the profit motive. Essentially he was a pragmatist whose goal was to conserve the system.

Even scholars who criticize Roosevelt's performance agree that he transformed the presidency. "Only Washington, who made the office, and Jackson, who remade it, did more than Roosevelt," according to political scientist Clinton Rossiter, "to raise it to its present condition of strength, dignity, and independence." With his radio "fireside chats," Roosevelt became the first president to use that medium to appeal for the people's support for his programs. "In the 1930s," political scientist Theodore J. Lowi has observed, "we built strong national programs around a strong President who derived his strength from going directly to the people."

On the other hand, some scholars have charged that it was Roosevelt who initiated "the imperial presidency." Whether for good or ill, Roosevelt strengthened not only the presidency but the whole federal government. "For the first time for many Americans," the historian William Leuchtenburg has written, "the federal government became an institution that was directly experienced. More than state and local governments, it came to be *the* government."

In the past, the federal government had served primarily as an economic regulator; during the New Deal it became an economic guarantor and stimulator as well. For the first time the federal government acknowledged a responsibility to offer relief to the jobless and the needy, and for the first time it resorted to deficit spending to stimulate the economy. Millions of Americans benefited from government programs that are still operating today. The New Deal laid the foundation of the welfare system on which subsequent presidential administrations would build.

Origins of America's Welfare System

Although the government's role in the economy expanded under the New Deal, the economy itself remained basically capitalistic. The profit motive and private property remained fundamental to the system. Some redistribution of wealth did result from the New Deal, but the wealthy survived as a class. In 1929, for example, the most affluent 5 percent of the population received 30 percent of total family income. By 1941, their share had shrunk but was still a healthy 24 percent. Most of the income lost by the wealthy ended up in the pockets of the middle and upper-middle classes, not those of the poor (see figure, page 784).

The New Deal brought about limited change in the nation's power structure. Beginning in the 1930s, business interests had to share their political clout with others. Labor gained influence in Washington, and farmers got more of what they wanted from Congress and the White House. If people wanted their voices to be heard, they had to organize into labor unions, trade associations, or other special-interest lobbies. Not everybody's voice was heard, however. Because of the persistence of racism, there was no real increase in the power of African-Americans and other minorities.

The New Deal was a liberal, evolutionary reform program, not a revolutionary break with the past. Although the New Deal coalition emerged as a political force in the 1930s, New Deal ideas such as the TVA and Social Security had been around for decades. Moreover, prominent New Dealers had been active in reform movements since the Progressive era. Historians generally view the New Deal as a reform movement that benefited middle-class Americans. William Leuchtenburg has concluded that the New Deal "swelled the ranks of the bourgeoisie but left many Americans—sharecroppers, slum dwellers, most Negroes—outside of the new equilibrium."

The New Deal failed in its fundamental purpose: to put people back to work. As late as 1939, over 10 million men and women were still jobless. That year unemployment was 19 percent; over the next two years it fell no lower than 14 percent. What plagued the nation throughout the 1930s was underconsumption: people and businesses did not purchase enough goods to sustain high levels of employment. In the end it was not the New Deal but massive government spending during the Second World War that put people back to work. In 1941, as a result of mobilization for war, unemployment would drop to 10 percent, and in 1944, at the height of the war, only 1 percent of the labor force would be jobless.

The New Deal's most lasting accomplishments were its programs to ameliorate the suffering of unemployment. The United States has suffered

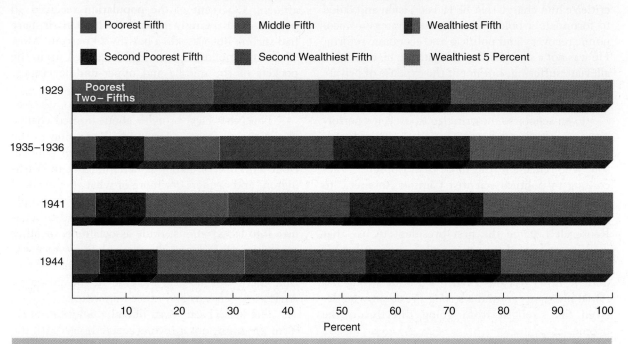

Distribution of Total Family Income Among the American Population, 1929–1944 (In Percentages)   Although the New Deal provided economic relief to the American people, it did not, as its critics so often charged, significantly redistribute income downward from the rich to the poor.   Source: Adapted from U.S. Bureau of the Census, *Historical Statistics of the United States, Colonial Times to 1970*, Bicentennial Edition (Washington, D.C.: U.S. Government Printing Office, 1975), p. 301.

several economic recessions since 1945, but even Republican presidents have "primed the pump" during these periods of slump. Prior to the New Deal, the United States had experienced a major depression every fifteen or twenty years. The Great Depression was the last of its kind. Since the New Deal, thanks to unemployment compensation, Social Security, and other measures, the United States has not re-experienced this national nightmare.

SUGGESTIONS FOR FURTHER READING

Hoover and the Worsening Depression

William W. Barber, *Herbert Hoover, the Economists, and American Economic Policy, 1921–1933* (1986); Michael A. Bernstein, *The Great Depression: Delayed Recovery and Economic Change in America,*

1929–1939 (1988); David Burner, *Herbert Hoover* (1979); Martin L. Fausold, *The Presidency of Herbert C. Hoover* (1985); Peter Fearon, *War, Prosperity, and Depression* (1987); John A. Garraty, *The Great Depression* (1986); David E. Hamilton, *From New Day to New Deal: American Farm Policy from Hoover to Roosevelt, 1928–1933* (1991); Donald J. Lisio, *The President and Protest: Hoover, Conspiracy, and the Bonus Riot* (1974); James S. Olson, *Herbert Hoover and the Reconstruction Finance Corporation, 1931–1933* (1977); Albert B. Romasco, *The Poverty of Abundance: Hoover, the Nation, the Depression* (1965); Jordan A. Schwarz, *Interregnum of Despair* (1970).

The New Deal

Anthony J. Badger, *The Deal: The Depression Years, 1933–1940* (1989); Barton J. Bernstein, "The New Deal: The Conservative Achievements of Liberal Reform," in Barton J. Bernstein, ed., *Towards a New Past* (1968), pp. 263–288; Gary Dean Best, *Pride, Prejudice, and Politics: Roosevelt Versus Recovery, 1933–1938* (1990); Roger Biles, *A New Deal for the American People* (1991); Steve Fraser and Gary Gerstle, eds., *The Rise and Fall of the New Deal Order, 1930–1980* (1989); William E. Leuchtenburg, *Franklin D. Roosevelt and the New Deal* (1963); Robert S. McElvaine, *The Great*

Depression (1984); Albert U. Romasco, *The Politics of Recovery: Roosevelt's New Deal* (1983); Harvard Stikoff, ed., *Fifty Years Later: The New Deal Evaluated* (1985).

Franklin and Eleanor Roosevelt

James MacGregor Burns, *Roosevelt: The Lion and the Fox* (1956); Blanche Wiesen Cook, *Eleanor Roosevelt: Volume One, 1884–1933* (1992); Kenneth S. Davis, *FDR: The New Deal Years, 1933–1937* (1986); Kenneth S. Davis, *FDR: Into the Storm, 1937–1940* (1993); Frank Freidel, *Franklin D. Roosevelt: A Rendezvous with Destiny* (1990); Joan Hoff-Wilson and Marjorie Lightman, eds., *Without Precedent: The Life and Career of Eleanor Roosevelt* (1984); Joseph P. Lash, *Eleanor and Franklin* (1971); William E. Leuchtenburg, *In the Shadow of FDR* (1983); Arthur M. Schlesinger, Jr., *The Age of Roosevelt*, 3 vols. (1957–1960).

Voices from the Depression

James Agee, *Let Us Now Praise Famous Men* (1941); Ann Banks, ed., *First-Person America* (1980); Federal Writers' Project, *These Are Our Lives* (1939); Gerald Markowitz and David Rosner, eds., *"Slaves of the Depression": Workers' Letters About Life on the Job* (1987); Robert S. McElvaine, ed., *Down and Out in the Great Depression: Letters from the Forgotten Man* (1983); Studs Terkel, *Hard Times: An Oral History of the Great Depression* (1970); Tom E. Terrill and Jerrold Hirsch, eds., *Such as Us: Southern Voices of the Thirties* (1978).

Alternatives to the New Deal

Alan Brinkley, *Voices of Protest: Huey Long, Father Coughlin, and the Great Depression* (1982); William Ivy Hair, *The Kingfish and His Realm: The Life and Times of Huey P. Long* (1992); Robin D. G. Kelley, *Hammer and Hoe: Alabama Communists During the Great Depression* (1991); R. Alan Lawson, *The Failure of Independent Liberalism, 1930–1941* (1971); Mark Naison, *Communists in Harlem During the Depression* (1983); Fraser M. Ottanelli, *The Communist Party of the United States from the Depression to World War II* (1991); Leo Ribuffo, *The Old Christian Right: The Protestant Far Right from the Great Depression to the Cold War* (1983); Frank A. Warren, *An Alternative Vision: The Socialist Party in the 1930s* (1976); T. Harry Williams, *Huey Long* (1969).

Labor

John Barnard, *Walter Reuther and the Rise of the Auto Workers* (1983); Irving Bernstein, *A Caring Society: The New Deal, the Worker, and the Great Depression* (1985); Irving Bernstein, *Turbulent Years: A History of the American Worker, 1933–1941* (1969); Lizabeth Cohen, *Making a New Deal: Industrial Workers in Chicago, 1919–1939* (1991); Melvin Dubofsky and Warren Van Tine, *John L. Lewis: A Biography* (1977); Sidney Fine, *Sit-Down: The General Motors Strike of 1936–1937* (1969); August Meier and Elliott Rudwick, *Black Detroit and the Rise of the UAW* (1979); David Milton, *The Politics of U.S. Labor: From the Great Depression to the New Deal* (1980).

Agriculture and the Environment

William U. Chandler, *The Myth of TVA: Conservation and Development in the Tennessee Valley, 1933–1983* (1984); David E. Conrad, *The Forgotten Farmers: The Story of Sharecroppers in the New Deal* (1965); Michael J. McDonald and John Muldowny, *TVA and the Dispossessed* (1982); Theodore M. Saloutos, *The American Farmer and the New Deal* (1982); John L. Shover, *Cornbelt Rebellion: The Farmers' Holiday Association* (1965); Walter J. Stein, *California and the Dust Bowl Migration* (1973); Donald Worster, *Dust Bowl: The Southern Plains in the 1930s* (1979).

People of Color

Francisco E. Balerman, *In Defense of LaRaza: The Los Angeles Mexican Consulate and the Mexican Community, 1929–1936* (1982); Dan T. Carter, *Scottsboro*, rev. ed. (1979); Laurence M. Hauptman, *The Iroquois and the New Deal* (1981); Abraham Hoffman, *Unwanted Mexican Americans in the Great Depression: Repatriation Pressures, 1929–1939* (1974); Laurence C. Kelly, *The Assault on Assimilation: John Collier and the Origins of Indian Policy Reform* (1983); John B. Kirby, *Black Americans in the Roosevelt Era: Liberalism and Race* (1980); Donald J. Lisio, *Hoover, Blacks, and Lily-Whites* (1985); Donald L. Parman, *The Navajos and the New Deal* (1975); Kenneth Philp, *John Collier's Crusade for Indian Reform, 1920–1954* (1977); Mark Reisler, *By the Sweat of Their Brow: Mexican Immigrant Labor in the United States, 1900–1940* (1976); Harvard Sitkoff, *A New Deal for Blacks* (1978); Nancy J. Weiss, *Farewell to the Party of Lincoln: Black Politics in the Age of FDR* (1983); Raymond Wolters, *Negroes and the Great Depression: The Problem of Economic Recovery* (1970).

Women

Julia Kirk Blackwelder, *Women of the Depression: Caste and Culture in San Antonio, 1929–1939* (1984); Glen H. Elder, Jr., *Children of the Great Depression: Social Change in Life Experience* (1974); Lois Scharf, *To Work and to Wed: Female Employment, Feminism, and the Great Depression* (1980); Winifred Wandersee, *Women's Work and Family Values, 1920–1940* (1981); Susan Ware, *Holding Their Own: American Women in the 1930s* (1982); Susan Ware, *Beyond Suffrage: Women in the New Deal* (1981); Jeane Westin, *Making Do: How Women Survived the '30s* (1976).

Cultural and Intellectual History

Daniel Aaron, *Writers on the Left: Episodes in American Literary Communism* (1961); Andrew Bergman, *We're in the Money: Depression America and Its Films* (1971); Jerre Mangione, *The Dream and the Deal: The Federal Writers' Project, 1935–1943* (1972); Alice Goldfarb Marquis, *Hopes and Ashes: The Birth of Modern Times, 1929–1939* (1986); David P. Peeler, *Hope Among Us Yet: Social Criticism and Social Solace in Depression America* (1987); Richard H. Pells, *Radical Visions and American Dreams: Culture and Social Thought in the Depression Years* (1973); Warren I. Susman, "The Culture of the Thirties," in Warren I. Susman, ed., *Culture as History* (1984), pp. 150–183; Edmund Wilson, *The American Earthquake* (1958).

Foreign Relations in a Broken World, 1920–1941

PRISONER 9653 STRODE OUT of Atlanta's federal penitentiary on December 24, 1921. After a train ride to Washington, D.C., he met the man who had just pardoned him. "I have heard so damned much about you, Mr. Debs," said the congenial President Warren G. Harding as Debs entered the White House, "that I am now very glad to meet you personally." They had a good talk, and Eugene V. Debs told reporters that Harding was a "gentleman" who "possesses human impulses." The First World War now over for him, Debs went home to Terre Haute, Indiana.

It seemed unusual for the conservative, probusiness Republican Harding, who had supported the American effort in the First World War, to pardon Eugene V. Debs, the anticapitalist Socialist party leader who, from his jail cell, had run against Harding in 1920 and had won nearly a million votes. Because of his strong antiwar views, Debs had received a ten-year sentence for violating the wartime Sedition Act. President Woodrow Wilson had snarled a firm no to the suggestion that he pardon the man he judged a "traitor." Harding was more compassionate. But he also believed that Debs's continued imprisonment re-

minded Americans of a troubled past they should try to forget.

Debs's release was one of Harding's ways of saying that the United States was returning to what he called "normalcy." "I thought the spirit of clemency was quite in harmony with the things we were trying to do here in Washington," he explained. What did he mean? A return to peacetime pursuits, free from missionary zeal, overseas crusades, huge military expenditures, and domestic divisiveness. Interpreting his 1920 victory as a repudiation of Wilson's League of Nations, Harding also wished to shelve that issue. The United States would not again, he vowed, become "entangled" in "Old World affairs."

In November 1921 the president took further steps to put the war behind the American people. To initiate "a new and lasting era of peace," he buried the Unknown Soldier in Arlington Cemetery. He then signed peace treaties with the defeated Central Powers, which had still been technically at war with the United States because of the Senate's rejection of the Treaty of Paris. Harding promoted these peace treaties "so that we may put aside the last remnant" of the war. The same month he opened an international con-

Herbert Hoover and Lou Henry Hoover on the U.S.S. *Maryland* during a goodwill trip to Latin America in 1929.

ference in Washington. His goal: a reduction in naval armaments to ensure a stable world order. Harding's pardon of Debs was thus only one component of a concerted effort to heal the nation's war wounds and to chart a new foreign policy for a warless future.

Harding's desire to shove the war into the past, and his emphasis on avoiding entanglements with Europe, did not mean that Americans cut themselves off from international affairs after the First World War. To be sure, many Americans had become disillusioned with their war experience. But the United States remained quite active in the world in the 1920s—from gunboats on Chinese rivers to negotiations in European financial centers to interventions in Latin America.

The most apt description of interwar U.S. foreign policy is *independent internationalism*. The United States was active on a global scale but retained its independence of action, its traditional unilateralism. Even if they had wanted to, Americans could not have escaped the tumult of international relations; their interests were too far-flung and too vast —colonies, client states, overseas naval bases, investments, trade, missionaries. At the same time, many Americans called themselves *isolationists*, by which they meant that they wanted to isolate themselves from Europe's political squabbles, from military alliances and interventions, and from commitments like the League of Nations that might restrict their freedom of choice. Americans, then, were isolationists in their desire to avoid war but independent internationalists in their behavior.

Independent Internationalism and Isolationism Defined

In the aftermath of the First World War, Americans had grown disenchanted with military methods of achieving order and protecting American prosperity and security. As Herbert Hoover said, "We can never herd the world into the paths of righteousness with the dogs of war." American diplomats thus increasingly sought to exercise the power of the United States through conferences, moral lectures and calls for peace, nonrecognition of disapproved regimes, arms control, and economic and financial ties in accord with the principle of the Open Door. They pulled the marines out of Caribbean and Central American nations and fashioned a Good Neighbor policy for Latin America.

The United States failed, however, to create a stable world order. Severe economic problems undercut it, and many other nations schemed to disrupt it. The debts and reparations bills left over from the First World War bedeviled the 1920s, and the Great Depression of the 1930s shattered world trade and finance. The depression threatened America's prominence in international markets; it also spawned revolutions in Latin America and political extremism, militarism, and war in Europe and Asia. As Nazi Germany marched toward world war, the United States tried to protect itself from the conflict by adopting a policy of neutrality. At the same time, the United States sought to defend its interests in Asia against Japanese aggression by invoking the venerable Open Door policy.

In the late 1930s, and especially after the outbreak of European war in September 1939, many Americans changed their minds. They came to agree with President Franklin D. Roosevelt that Germany and Japan had become menaces to the national interest because those nations were building exclusive, self-sufficient spheres of influence based on military power and economic domination. Roosevelt first pushed for American military preparedness and then for the abandonment of neutrality in favor of aiding Britain and France. A German victory in Europe, he reasoned, would imperil Western political principles, destroy traditional American economic ties, threaten U.S. influence in the Western Hemisphere, and place at the pinnacle of European power a fanatical man—Adolf Hitler—whose ambitions and barbarities seemed limitless.

At the same time, Japan seemed determined to dismember America's Asian friend China, to emasculate the Open Door principle by creating a closed economic sphere in Asia, and to endanger the U.S. colony of the Philippines. To deter Japanese expansion in the Pacific, the United States ultimately cut off supplies of vital American products like oil. But economic warfare had the effect not of containing Japan but rather of intensifying antagonisms. Japan's surprise attack on Pearl Harbor in December 1941 finally brought the United States into the Second World War. The interwar U.S. policies designed for a peaceful and prosperous world order went up in the smoke of the burning battleships in Hawaii.

• *Important Events* •

1921	Washington Conference opens to limit naval arms race
1922	Mussolini comes to power in Italy Fordney-McCumber Tariff Act raises duties
1924	Dawes Plan eases German reparations payments U.S. troops depart Dominican Republic
1926	American troops occupy Nicaragua
1927	Jiang Jieshi attacks Communists in China
1928	Kellogg-Briand Pact outlaws war
1929	Great Depression hits United States Young Plan reduces German reparations
1930	Hawley-Smoot Tariff raises duties
1931	Japan seizes Manchuria
1932	Stimson Doctrine protests Japanese control of Manchuria
1933	Hitler establishes Nazi government in Germany United States recognizes Soviet Union Good Neighbor policy announced for Latin America
1934	Batista comes to power in Cuba; United States abrogates Platt Amendment Reciprocal Trade Agreements Act attempts to spur foreign commerce by lowering tariffs U.S. troops withdraw from Haiti Export-Import Bank founded to expand foreign trade
1935	Italy invades and annexes Ethiopia Neutrality Act prohibits arms shipments
1936	United States votes for nonintervention at Pan American Conference Spanish Civil War breaks out between Loyalists and Franco's fascists Neutrality Act forbids loans to belligerents
1937	Neutrality Act creates cash-and-carry trade with warring nations Sino-Japanese War breaks out ("China incident") Roosevelt delivers quarantine speech against aggressors Ponce Massacre in Puerto Rico
1938	Mexico nationalizes American-owned oil companies Practicing appeasement, Munich Conference grants part of Czechoslovakia to Germany
1939	Nazi-Soviet Pact carves up Eastern Europe Germany invades Poland Second World War begins Unites States repeals arms embargo to help Allies
1940	Soviets invade Finland Committee to Defend America by Aiding the Allies formed Germany, Italy, and Japan join in Tripartite Pact Great Britain and the United States swap destroyers for bases Isolationists form America First Committee Selective Training and Service Act starts first peacetime draft
1941	Lend-Lease Act gives aid to Allies Germany attacks Soviet Union United States freezes Japanese assets; trade drops Atlantic Charter produced at Roosevelt-Churchill meeting Roosevelt exploits *Greer* incident to convoy British ships Japanese flotilla attacks Pearl Harbor, Hawaii United States enters Second World War

SEARCHING FOR PEACE AND ORDER IN THE 1920s

In the early 1920s U.S. Secretary of State Charles Evans Hughes predicted that "there will be no permanent peace unless economic satisfactions are enjoyed." Like the nation's business leaders, Hughes expected continued U.S. economic expansion to bring about international stability: out of economic prosperity would spring a world free from political extremes, revolution, arms races, aggression, and war. Despite valiant efforts, this never developed.

Europe lay in shambles at the end of the First World War. Between 1914 and 1921 Europe suffered 60 million casualties from world war, civil war, massacre, epidemic, and famine. Germany and France both lost 10 percent of their workers. Crops, livestock, factories, trains, forests, bridges —little was spared. Americans responded with humanitarian aid. The American Relief Administration delivered food to needy Europeans, including Russians wracked by famine in 1921 and 1922. All told, private charities and official relief programs sent Europeans foodstuffs worth more than half a billion dollars.

Distributed by the Women's Peace Union (WPU) in the 1920s, this flier recalled the human costs of the First World War and predicted worse to come. One of many peace societies active in the interwar years, the WPU lobbied for an amendment requiring a national referendum on a declaration of war. But the efforts of Representative Louis Ludlow of Indiana in the 1930s to pass such a measure in Congress always fell short. Schwimmer-Lloyd Collection, Freida Langer Lazarus Papers. The New York Public Library, Astor, Lenox, and Tilden Foundations.

American peace groups also worked to create international stability. During the 1920s and 1930s peace societies like the Fellowship of Reconciliation, the Women's International League for Peace and Freedom, and the National Council for Prevention of War gained unprecedented popularity. They advocated a variety of strategies to ensure world order. Some urged cooperation with the League of Nations, membership in the World Court, and arbitration of international disputes. Others stressed disarmament and arms reduction, curbs on exploitative business ventures, the outlawing of war, and strict neutrality in times of belligerency. The Women's Peace Union lobbied for a constitutional amendment to require a national referendum on a declaration of war. Most peace groups reminded Americans of the carnage of the First World War and the futility of war as a solution to international problems. Antiwar films like *What Price Glory?* (1926) and *Submarine* (1928) dramatized the cruelties of military combat.

American Peace Movement

The Washington Conference (November 1921–February 1922) seemed to mark a substantial step toward arms control. The United States and eight other nations (Britain, Japan, France, Italy, China, Portugal, Belgium, and The Netherlands) discussed limits on naval armaments. Britain, the United States, and Japan—the three major powers—were facing a costly naval arms race, and they welcomed the opportunity to deflect it. As Secretary Hughes argued, arms competition had to stop because huge military expenditures endangered economic rehabilitation.

Washington Conference

The conference produced three treaties. The Five-Power Treaty set a ten-year moratorium on the construction of capital ships (battleships and aircraft carriers) and established a total tonnage ratio of 5 (Britain):5 (United States):3 (Japan):1.75 (France):1.75 (Italy). The first three nations actually agreed to dismantle some existing vessels to satisfy the ratio. They also pledged not to build new fortifications in their Pacific possessions (such as the Philippines in the case of the United States). In the Nine-Power Treaty, the conferees reaffirmed the Open Door in China, recognizing Chinese sovereignty. In the Four-Power Treaty, the United States, Britain, Japan, and France agreed to respect each other's Pacific possessions. The three

The imposing figure of U.S. Secretary of State Charles Evans Hughes (1862–1948), fifth from right, stood at the center of this 1921 photograph of major participants at the Washington Conference. Hughes boldly opened the meeting on naval disarmament with a dramatic call for the scrapping of large numbers of ships. The conference treaties cooled but did not stop the naval arms race.   Brown Brothers.

treaties represented a rare example of mutual disarmament. But they did not limit submarines, destroyers, or cruisers; nor did they provide enforcement powers for the Open Door declaration. Subsequent conferences in the 1930s, moreover, produced meager results. Rearmament soon supplanted disarmament.

Peace advocates also welcomed the Locarno Pact of 1925, a series of agreements among European nations that sought to reduce tensions between Germany and France.

Kellogg-Briand Pact

——

The "spirit of Locarno" preceded the Kellogg-Briand Pact of 1928, a treaty eventually signed by sixty-two nations. The signatories agreed to "condemn recourse to war for the solution of international controversies, and renounce it as an instrument of national policy." The backers of this accord billed it as a first step in a long journey toward international cooperation and the outlawry of war. The document passed the Senate 85 to 1, but many senators considered it nothing more than a statement of moral

preference because it lacked provisions for enforcement. Although weak, the Kellogg-Briand Pact reflected popular sentiment that war was barbaric and wasteful; it also served to educate by prompting people to think about issues of peace and war.

The League of Nations, envisioned as a peacemaker, disappointed peace advocates. The new institution exhibited conspicuous feebleness, not because the United States refused to join but because its members themselves usually chose not to use it to settle disputes. Starting in the mid-1920s, American officials participated discreetly in League meetings on public health, prostitution, drug trafficking, and other questions. By 1930, American "observers" had sat in on more than forty League conferences. American jurists like Charles Evans Hughes served on the World Court in Geneva, though the United States also refused to join that international body. Ultimately neither the World Court, nor the League of Nations, nor the Kellogg-Briand Pact, nor the peace movement proved capable of muzzling the dogs of war, which fed on the economic troubles that upended world order.

of 1929, which reduced Germany's reparations, salvaged little as the international economy sputtered and collapsed. That year the British rejected an ingenious offer from President Hoover to trade their total debt for British Honduras (Belize), Bermuda, and Trinidad. By 1931, when Hoover declared a moratorium on payments, the Allies had paid back only $2.6 billion, approximately 20 percent of their debt. Staggered by the Great Depression, they defaulted on the rest. World trade, heavily dependent on an easy and safe exchange of currencies, also faltered: from 1929 to 1933, it declined in value by some 40 percent. American merchandise exports slumped from $5.2 billion to $1.7 billion.

By the early 1930s, U.S. economic power had failed to sustain a healthy world economy. As the depression accelerated, so did economic national-

Economic Nationalism
———

ism. By 1932 some twenty-five nations had retaliated against rising American tariffs (created in the Fordney-McCumber Act of 1922 and the Hawley-Smoot Act of 1930) by imposing higher rates on U.S. imports. Critics argued that much of the international economic disorder could have been avoided or at least ameliorated. Instead of raising their tariff rates, Americans might have lowered them so that Europeans could sell their goods in the United States and thus earn dollars to pay off their debts. Americans might have worked for a comprehensive, multinational settlement. Selfish, vengeful Europeans might have trimmed Germany's huge indemnity. The Germans might have borrowed less from abroad and taxed themselves more. The Soviets might have agreed to pay rather than repudiate Russia's $4 billion debt. Many nations, in short, shared responsibility for the economic cataclysm.

Mentioning the world economic emergency in his first inaugural address in 1933, President Franklin D. Roosevelt said that he favored a "practical policy of putting first things first." In other words, he would work to restore world trade, but he would attend first to the emergency at home. Roosevelt then barred American cooperation in international monetary stabilization at the London Conference (1933). Secretary of State Hull privately disagreed with the president, bemoaning Roosevelt's decision as yet another contribution to the world's nose-dive into economic nationalism and political disequilibrium.

A revival of world trade, Hull insisted, would not only help the United States pull itself out of the economic doldrums but also boost the chances for global peace. Call-

Reciprocal Trade Agreements Act
———

ing the protective tariff the "king of evils," Hull successfully pressed Congress to pass the Reciprocal Trade Agreements Act in 1934. This important legislation, which would guide American economic foreign policy long into the future, empowered the president to reduce American tariffs by as much as 50 percent through special agreements with foreign countries. The central feature of the act was the *most-favored-nation principle*, whereby the United States was entitled to the lowest tariff rate set by any nation with which it had an agreement. If, for example, Belgium and the United States granted each other most-favored-nation status, and Belgium then negotiated an agreement with Germany that reduced the Belgian tariff on German typewriters, American typewriters would receive the same low rate.

In 1934 Hull also created the Export-Import Bank, a government agency that provided loans to foreigners for the purchase of American goods. The bank not only stimulated trade but also became a formidable diplomatic weapon, allowing the United States to exact concessions through the approval or denial of loans. But in the short term, Hull's ambitious programs—examples of America's independent internationalism—brought only mixed results.

U.S. SPHERE OF INFLUENCE IN LATIN AMERICA

Before the First World War the United States had thrown an imperial net over much of Latin America. Its tools for doing so were the Platt Amendment, the Roosevelt Corollary, control of the Panama Canal, military intervention, and economic domination (see Chapter 22). A patronizing attitude permeated North American activities in the region. A leading State Department officer told the Foreign Service School that Latins were incapable of political progress because of their temperament, the tropical climate, and their "low racial quality." They were, however, "very easy people to deal with if properly managed." And managed they were. By the 1920s U.S.-built schools, roads, telephones, and irrigation systems dotted Caribbean and Central American nations. U.S. advisers supervised government budgets; U.S. soldiers were occupying Cuba, the Dominican Republic, Haiti, Panama, and Nicaragua; and U.S. authorities maintained Puerto Rico as a colony (see map on page 796).

A distinguished Argentine writer, Manuel Ugarte, asserted that the United States had become a new Rome: it annexed wealth rather than territory, enjoying the "essentials of domination" without the "dead-weight of areas to administrate and multitudes to govern." To such criticism, the U.S. ambassador to Chile replied that "American capital will be the controlling factor in public and private finance in these countries. . . . American civilization, material and cultural, is bound to impress itself upon, and I believe, benefit these peoples. If anti-American critics wish to describe this as our 'imperialism' let them make the most of it."

Imperialism was exactly what some U.S. critics saw and protested—especially the military interventions. Senator William Borah of Idaho urged that Latin Americans be granted the right of self-determination. Others charged that the president was usurping constitutional power by ordering troops abroad without a congressional declaration of war. Businesspeople feared that Latin American nationalists would direct their anti-Yankee feelings against American *gringos* and their property. Some North Americans also became troubled by the double standard that prevailed. Secretary of State Henry L. Stimson acknowledged the problem in 1932 when he was protesting Japanese incursions in China: "If we landed a single soldier among those South Americans now . . . it would put me absolutely in the wrong in China, where Japan has done all this monstrous work under the guise of protecting her nationals with a landing force."

Anti-Imperialism

Renouncing unpopular military intervention, the United States tried other methods to maintain its influence in Latin America: Pan-Americanism, support for strong local leaders, training of national guards, economic penetration, Export-Import Bank loans, and political subversion. Although this general approach predated his presidency, Franklin

Good Neighbor Policy

This government recruiting poster captured the postwar American mood of independent internationalism by offering overseas duty to prospective marines.   Library of Congress.

D. Roosevelt gave it a name in 1933: the Good Neighbor policy. It meant that the United States would be less blatant in its domination—less willing to defend exploitative business practices, less eager to launch military expeditions, and less reluctant to consult with Latin Americans. "Give them a share," FDR recommended. In 1936, for example, the United States restored some sovereignty to Panama and increased that nation's income from the canal. Such acts greatly enhanced Roosevelt's popularity in Latin America.

Meanwhile, U.S. interests in the hemisphere were growing. From 1914 to 1929, direct American investments in Latin America (excluding bonds and securities) jumped from almost $1.3 billion to $3.5 billion. In the same period American exports to the area tripled in value. In country after country Latin Americans felt and understood the repercussions of U.S. economic and political decisions. The price Americans set for Chilean copper determined the health of the Chilean economy. American oil executives bribed Venezuelan politicians for

The United States and Latin America Between the Wars *As this map shows, the United States repeatedly wielded its hegemonic power in Latin America. The many interventions and disputes demonstrated that U.S. hegemony faced recurrent challenges from nationalists who resented U.S. meddling in their sovereign affairs. The Good Neighbor Policy decreased U.S. military interventions, but U.S. economic interests remained strong.*

William E. Borah (1865–1940), chairman of the Senate Foreign Relations Committee (left), and Henry L. Stimson (1867–1950), secretary of state (right), were often at loggerheads. The Idaho senator became a passionate anti-imperialist and isolationist who protested U.S. interventions abroad. Because of critics like Borah, Stimson grew eager to find nonmilitary means to maintain U.S. hegemony in the Western Hemisphere. Library of Congress.

tax breaks. In Honduras, where United Fruit and Standard Fruit accounted for most of the nation's revenue, North American interests so manipulated and disrupted politics that U.S. troops were sent there in 1924 to restore calm and protect property. What was more, U.S. businesses were drawing substantially greater sums out of Latin America in profits than they were putting in as investments. Latin American nationalists complained that their resources were being drained away, leaving them in a state of dependency.

The training of national guards went hand in hand with support of dictators. Some Latin American dictators rose to power through the ranks of U.S.-trained national guards. For example, before the United States withdrew its troops from the Dominican Republic in 1924, U.S. personnel created a guard. One of its first officers was Rafael Leonidas Trujillo, who became head of the national army in 1928 and, through fraud and intimidation, became president two years later. Trujillo ruled the Do-

National Guard in the Dominican Republic

——

minican Republic with an iron fist until his assassination in 1961. "He may be an S.O.B.," Roosevelt supposedly remarked, "but he is our S.O.B."

Nicaraguans endured a similar experience. U.S. troops occupied Nicaragua from 1912 to 1925 and returned in late 1926 during a civil war. Washington claimed that it was only trying to stabilize Nicaragua's politics, but critics at home and abroad saw a case of U.S. imperialism. Nationalistic Nicaraguan opposition, led by César Augusto Sandino, who denounced the Monroe Doctrine as meaning "America for the Yankees," helped persuade Washington to end the occupation. In 1933 the U.S. Marines departed; but they left behind a powerful national guard headed by General Anastasio Somoza, who "always played the game fairly with us," according to the top-ranked American military officer there. With American backing, the Somoza family ruled Nicaragua from 1936 to 1979 through corruption, political suppression, and torture. The revolutionaries who overthrew the Somoza dictatorship in

Somoza and Sandino in Nicaragua

——

These children in Nicaragua seem amused by the comic strips U.S. marines are explaining to them in 1927, during the U.S. military occupation of that Central American nation. The marines actually spent most of their time chasing the troops of César Augusto Sandino, who fought the North American intruders until his death in 1934. National Archives.

1979 called themselves Sandinistas in honor of the patriot Sandino who, more than three decades earlier, had battled the U.S. Marines and been assassinated by Somoza henchmen (see Chapter 31).

Occupation of Haiti

The marine occupation of black French-speaking Haiti from 1915 to 1934 also left a very negative legacy, prompting one bitter Haitian leader to call Americans "exploiters" and to ask: "How can they teach us when they have so much to learn themselves?" U.S. officials censored the Haitian press, manipulated elections, wrote the constitution, jailed or killed thousands of protesters, managed government finances, and created a national guard. The National City Bank of New York became the owner of the Haitian Banque Nationale, and the United States became Haiti's largest trading partner. The American high commissioner, General John H. Russell of Georgia, boasted that the Haitian president "has never taken a step without first consulting me." African-American leaders were prominent among the critics of this blatant manipulation of foreigners. The

NAACP's James Weldon Johnson reported after a fact-finding trip that Haitians forced to build roads without pay (the *corvée* system) "were in the same category with the convicts in the negro chain gangs" of the American South. Indeed, Jim Crow became entrenched in Haiti.

In 1929 Haitians protested violently against U.S. rule. When an official U.S. investigative commission told President Hoover that the occupation had failed to bring benefits to the Haitian people, Washington decided to withdraw its soldiers. Haiti continued to suffer Latin America's highest illiteracy rate, lowest per capita income, and poorest health, as well as dictatorship and police-state repression.

Cuban Revolution of 1933

The Cubans, too, grew restless under North American domination. By 1929 American investments in the Caribbean nation totaled $1.5 billion, up from $220 million in 1913. North Americans came to own two-thirds of the Cuban sugar industry, and the U.S. military uniform remained conspicuous at the Guantánamo

Naval Base. Especially at the elite level, U.S. influences continued to permeate Cuban culture. In 1933, Cubans rebelled against the dictator and U.S. ally Gerardo Machado. In open defiance of U.S. warships cruising offshore, Professor Ramón Grau San Martín became president and declared the Platt Amendment (see Chapter 22) null and void. His government also seized some North American-owned mills, refused to repay North American bank loans, and talked of land reform. Unsettled by this bold display of nationalism, U.S. officials refused to recognize the Grau government and successfully plotted with army sergeant Fulgencio Batista to overthrow it in 1934. The United States, Cuban nationalists charged, had stolen their nation's revolution.

During the Batista era, which lasted until Fidel Castro's revolutionary forces overthrew Batista in 1959, Cuba attracted and protected U.S. investments while it aligned with U.S. foreign policy goals. The United States provided military aid and Export-Import Bank loans, abrogated the Platt Amendment, and gave Cuban sugar a favored position in the U.S. market. Cuba became further incorporated into the U.S. consumer culture and American tourists flocked to Havana's night life of rum, rhumba, prostitution, and gambling. Many Cubans grumbled that their nation had become a mere extension—a dependency—of the United States.

Elsewhere in the Caribbean, Puerto Ricans chafed under U.S. tutelage. Throughout the 1920s and 1930s, incompetent and often tactless American governors who could

Puerto Rico

not speak Spanish disparaged Puerto Ricans as people of color unfit to govern themselves. The Jones Act of 1917 granted Puerto Ricans U.S. citizenship, but the United States rejected calls for the colony's independence or statehood. (Not until 1947 did the United States permit Puerto Ricans to elect their own governor.) A few absentee American landowners and corporate barons made sugar the island's major economic activity. Under U.S. paternalism, schools and roads were improved, but 80 percent of the island's rural folk were landless and others crowded into urban slums. The per capita income of Puerto Rico in 1930 was $122 (one-fifth of the U.S. figure); it dropped to $85 when the depression struck. New Deal relief programs fell far short of need.

Students, professors, and graduates of the University of Puerto Rico formed the nucleus of islanders critical of U.S. tutelage. Some founded the Nationalist party under the leadership of the Harvard-trained lawyer Pedro Albizo Campos, who eventually advocated the violent overthrow of U.S. rule. Police fired on a Nationalist party march in 1937; nineteen people, including two policemen, died in the "Ponce Massacre." Other Puerto Ricans followed the socialist Luis Muñoz Marín, whose Popular Democratic party ultimately settled for the compromise of "commonwealth" status (officially conferred in 1952). In the 1950s, under Operation Bootstrap, the island received a huge infusion of U.S. capital and shifted to industrialization. At the same time, increasing numbers of Puerto Ricans journeyed to the United States, creating barrios in American cities—especially in New York. To this day, Puerto Ricans remain divided into statehood, commonwealth, and independence factions.

Mexico, torn by revolution and civil war, was a unique case in inter-American relations. Woodrow Wilson had sent troops to Mexico in 1914 and

U.S. Clash with Mexican Nationalism

1916 in an attempt to install a pro-U.S. government, but those military expeditions only united the Mexican people against the United States. In 1917 the Mexicans adopted a new constitution specifying that all "land and waters" and all subsoil raw materials (like oil) belonged to the Mexican nation. This nationalistic document represented a threat to U.S. landholdings and petroleum interests there. If Mexico succeeded, Washington officials worried, would not other Latin Americans attempt to follow the Mexican model of defying U.S. hegemonic power in the hemisphere?

Washington and Mexico City wrangled for years over the rights of U.S. economic interests. Then, in 1938, Mexico boldly expropriated the property of all foreign-owned petroleum companies. The United States countered by reducing purchases of Mexican silver and encouraging a business boycott against the nation. But President Roosevelt decided to compromise because he feared the Mexicans would sell their oil to Germany and Japan. In 1942 the United States conceded that Mexico owned its raw materials and could treat them as it saw fit, and Mexico compensated U.S. companies for their lost property. Although American investments and trade continued to claim an important share of Mexican business, U.S. power there had been diminished. Nationalists across Latin America, moreover, drew inspiration from Mexico's defiance of its giant neighbor.

Roosevelt's movement toward nonmilitary methods—the Good Neighbor policy—was also expressed in Pan-Americanism. Throughout the

Pan-Americanism
———

1920s the United States had refused to renounce its self-declared right of intervention in the hemisphere. In 1936, however, at the Pan American Conference in Buenos Aires, U.S. officials endorsed nonintervention. Although U.S. activities of a nonmilitary sort remained conspicuous in Latin America, the new policy marked a distinct change from the Roosevelt Corollary and marine expeditions. One payoff was the Declaration of Panama (1939), in which Latin American governments drew a security line around the hemisphere and warned aggressors away. In exchange for more

At the 1928 Pan American Conference in Havana, Cuba, many Latin American representatives wanted but could not obtain a resolution declaring that "no state has the right to intervene in the internal affairs of another." U.S. Secretary of State Charles Evans Hughes blocked the measure, as this cartoon by J. N. "Ding" Darling shows. Des Moines Register and Tribune Company.

U.S. trade and foreign aid, Latin Americans also reduced their sales of raw materials to Germany, Japan, and Italy and increased shipments to the United States. On the eve of the Second World War, then, the U.S. sphere of influence was virtually intact, and most Latin American regimes backed U.S. diplomatic objectives. For a long time, however, memories of strong-arm methods would fuel anti-Yankee nationalism throughout the region.

NAZI GERMANY AND APPEASEMENT IN EUROPE

In depression-wracked Germany, Adolf Hitler came to power in 1933. Like Benito Mussolini, who had gained control of Italy in 1922, Hitler was a fascist. Fascism (called Nazism, or National Socialism, in Germany) was a collection of ideas and prejudices that celebrated supremacy of the state over the individual; of dictatorship over democracy; of authoritarianism over freedom of speech; of a regulated, state-oriented economy over a free-market economy; and of militarism and war over peace. The Nazis vowed not only to revive German economic and military strength but also to cripple communism and "purify" the German "race" by destroying those people Hitler disparaged as inferior: Jews, homosexuals, and gypsies.

Hitler, resentful of the punitive terms of the 1919 Treaty of Paris, immediately pulled Germany out of the League of Nations, ended reparations payments, and began to rearm.

Hitler's Aggression
———

While secretly laying plans for the conquest of neighboring states, he watched admiringly as Mussolini's troops invaded the African nation of Ethiopia in 1935. The next year Hitler ordered his goose-stepping troopers into the Rhineland, an area that the Treaty of Paris had declared demilitarized. When Germany's timid neighbor France did not attempt to reverse this aggressive act, Hitler crowed: "The world belongs to the man with guts!"

Soon the aggressors joined hands. In 1936 Italy and Germany formed an alliance called the Rome-Berlin Axis. Shortly thereafter Germany and Japan united against the Soviet Union in the Anti-Comintern Pact. To these events Britain and France responded with a policy of appeasement, hoping to curb Hitler's expansionist appetite by permitting him a few nibbles. The policy of ap-

The German leader Adolf Hitler (1889–1945) often used mass rallies like this one in 1937, which a million people attended, to spew forth his hate. On one occasion, the anti-Semitic Hitler denounced the United States as a "Jewish rubbish heap" of "inferiority and decadence" that was "incapable of conducting war." Hugo Jaeger, LIFE Magazine © Time Warner, Inc.

peasing Hitler proved disastrous, for the hate-filled German leader continually raised his demands.

In those hair-trigger times, a civil war in Spain soon turned into an international struggle. From 1936 to 1939, the Loyalists defended Spain's elected republican government against Francisco Franco's fascist movement. Although the Soviet Union backed the Loyalist Republicans, Hitler and Mussolini sent far more military aid to Franco. France and Britain held to the fiction of a nonintervention pledge that even Italy and Germany had signed. About three thousand American volunteers known as the Lincoln Battalion joined the fight on the side of the Republicans. When Franco won in 1939, his victory tightened the grip of fascism on the European continent.

Spanish Civil War

Early in 1938 Hitler once again tested the limits of European tolerance when he sent soldiers into Austria to annex the nation of his birth. Then in September he seized the Sudeten region of Czechoslovakia. Appeasement reached its apex that month when France and Britain, without consulting the helpless Czechs, agreed at the Munich Conference to allow Hitler this one last territorial bite. British Prime Minister Neville Chamberlain returned home to proclaim "peace in our time," confident that Hitler was satiated. In March 1939 Hitler swallowed the rest of Czechoslovakia.

Poland was next on the German leader's list. Scuttling appeasement, London and Paris announced that they would stand by their ally Poland. Undaunted, Berlin signed the Nazi-Soviet Pact with Moscow in August. Soviet leader Josef Stalin believed that the West's appeasement of Hitler had left him no choice but to cut a deal with the Nazi ruler. But Stalin also coveted territory: a top-secret protocol attached to the pact carved Eastern Europe into German and Soviet zones, with the Soviets grabbing half of Poland and the three Baltic states of Lithuania, Estonia, and Latvia. On September 1 Hitler launched *blitzkrieg* attacks—highly mobile land forces and armor combined with tactical aircraft—against Poland. Britain and France declared war on Germany two days later. The Second World War had begun.

The Second World War Begins

As the world hurtled toward war, the Soviet Union posed a special problem for American foreign relations. Following Wilsonian precedent, the Republican administrations of the 1920s had not recognized the Soviet government, arguing that the Bolsheviks had failed to pay $600 million for con-

It seems odd that a supreme U.S. capitalist like Henry Ford would be active in Communist Russia, a nation the United States did not even officially recognize in the 1920s. Yet at that very time Ford began to market automobiles and tractors in the land of the Bolsheviks. Here some Fordson tractors are readied in Novorossick. Ford, of course, grasped an economic opportunity, and the industrializing Russians admired the mass-production techniques Ford used in his American factories. Ford Archives, Henry Ford Museum.

fiscated American-owned property and had repudiated pre-existing Russian debts. To Americans, the Communists were also godless, radical malcontents bent on destroying the American way of life through world revolution. U.S. businesses like General Electric and International Harvester nonetheless began to enter the Soviet marketplace, offering technology and machinery. "Fordson" tractors went into production, and Henry Ford signed a contract in 1929 to build a huge automobile plant using mass-production methods the Soviets called *Fordizatsia*. By 1930 the Soviet Union had become the largest buyer of American farm and industrial equipment.

In the early 1930s, when trade began to slump, some U.S. businesspeople began to lobby for diplomatic recognition of the Soviet Union to stimulate trade and help the United States pull out of the depression. "We would recognize the Devil with a false face if he would contract for some pitchforks," quipped the noted American humorist Will Rogers. President Roosevelt agreed that a change in policy was necessary, not only because it would improve commerce but also because nonrecogni-

tion had failed to alter the Soviet system and closer Soviet-American relations might deter Japan.

Practicing personal one-on-one diplomacy, Roosevelt negotiated in 1933 with Soviet Commissar for Foreign Affairs Maxim Litvinov. The two men hammered out agreements, some of them vaguely phrased: U.S. recognition of the Soviet Union, future discussion of the debts question, a Soviet promise to forgo subversive activities in the United States, and religious freedom and legal rights for Americans in the Soviet Union. The first U.S. embassy in Moscow opened in 1934. Within just a few years, however, Soviet-American relations once again became embittered. Americans expressed outrage against Josef Stalin's authoritarian rule, the Soviet pact with Nazi Germany, the Soviet invasion of Poland in September 1939, the Soviets' November attack on Finland, and the incorporation of the three Baltic states into the Union of Soviet Socialist Republics in 1940. These events in the expanding Soviet sphere persuaded many

U.S. Recognition of the Soviet Union

Americans that Europe had gone mad once again and that the United States had little chance of altering the destructive behavior.

ISOLATIONISM AND ROOSEVELT'S LEADERSHIP

As depression-induced authoritarianism, racial hatred, and military expansion descended on Europe and Asia in the 1930s, Americans affirmed their isolationist beliefs. They had learned powerful negative lessons from the First World War: that war wounds reform movements, undermines civil liberties, dangerously expands federal and presidential power, disrupts the economy, and accentuates racial and class tensions (see Chapter 23). A 1937 Gallup poll found that nearly two-thirds of the respondents thought U.S. participation in the First World War had been a mistake. Conservative isolationists feared higher taxes and increased executive power if the nation went to war again. Liberal isolationists worried that domestic problems might go unresolved as the nation spent more on the military. Senator Gerald P. Nye of North Dakota, for example, pointed out that the federal government appropriated more for the care of National Guard horses than for the Children's Bureau. Many isolationists predicted that in attempting to spread democracy abroad, Americans would lose it at home. One isolationist criticized America's "Roman Empire psychology" of wanting to "police the world." The vast majority of isolationists opposed fascism and condemned aggression, but they did not think the United States should have to do what Europeans themselves refused to do: block Hitler.

Isolationist sentiment was strongest in the Midwest and among anti-British ethnic groups, especially German- and Irish-Americans, but it was a nationwide phenomenon that cut across socioeconomic, ethnic, party, and sectional lines and attracted a majority of the American people. Prominent isolationists in the 1930s included Republicans like Congressman Hamilton Fish of New York, Senator William Borah of Idaho, and former president Herbert Hoover; Democrats like Congressman Maury Maverick of Texas; Socialists like Norman Thomas;

Isolationists

UNCOMFORTABLE GRANDSTAND   *(Copyright in All Countries.)*

This cartoon in a British newspaper on September 22, 1939, suggests how precarious was U.S. neutrality shortly after the outbreak of war in Europe. The cartoonist obviously feels some pique that the United States is watching rather than joining the war, and his message is clear: flying bombs will inevitably hit the United States. President Franklin D. Roosevelt turns a quizzical face to Secretary of State Cordell Hull. "Uncomfortable Grandstand" by David Low, Evening Standard, London, September 22, 1939.

Communists and Nazi sympathizers; and pacifists like Congresswoman Jeannette Rankin of Montana. They also included the publisher Robert R. McCormick of the *Chicago Tribune*, the historian Charles Beard, the physicist Albert Einstein, and the anti-Semitic radio priest Charles E. Coughlin. What united these dissimilar people was the opinion that there were alternatives to American participation in another European war that was certain to damage U.S. national interest.

Some liberal isolationists, critical of business practices at home, charged that corporate "merchants of death" were assisting the aggressors. From 1934 to 1936 a congressional committee chaired by Senator Nye held hearings on the role of business interests and financiers in the U.S. decision to enter the First World War. The hearings did not prove that American business had dragged a reluctant nation into that war, but they did uncover evidence that corporations had bribed foreign politicians to bolster arms sales in the 1920s and 1930s and had lobbied against arms control.

Records show that isolationists were correct to suspect American business ties with Nazi Germany and fascist Italy. Twenty-six of the top one

U.S. Business Ties with Germany and Italy

hundred U.S. corporations in 1937 had contractual agreements with German firms. And after Italy attacked Ethiopia in 1935, American petroleum, copper, and iron-and-steel scrap exports to Italy increased substantially, despite Roosevelt's call for a moral embargo on such commerce. Du Pont, Standard Oil, General Motors, and Union Carbide executives apparently agreed with the Dow Chemical Company officer who stated, "We do not inquire into the uses of the products. We are interested in selling them." Not all U.S. executives thought this way. The Wall Street firm of Sullivan and Cromwell, for example, severed lucrative ties with Germany to protest the Nazi persecution of Jews.

President Roosevelt shared isolationist views in the early 1930s. Like his older cousin Theodore, Franklin as a young man had believed that the United States should ensure American security and prosperity by exerting leadership in the world community and flexing its military muscle. FDR was an expansionist and interventionist who had thoroughly imbibed the belief that Americans knew what was best for other societies. Indeed, as assistant secretary of the navy under Wilson, he had helped write and impose on Haiti a new constitution. But during the interwar period, like most Americans, Roosevelt talked less about preparedness and more about disarmament and the horrors of war, less about managing the affairs of the world and more about handling U.S. problems at home.

Roosevelt acted on his and the nation's preference for avoiding European squabbles when he signed a series of neutrality acts. Congress sought

Neutrality Acts

to protect the nation by outlawing the kinds of contacts that had compromised U.S. neutrality two decades earlier. The Neutrality Act of 1935 prohibited arms shipments to either side in a war once the president had declared the existence of belligerency. Roosevelt had wanted the authority to name the aggressor and apply an arms embargo against it alone, but Congress was reluctant to grant the president such discretionary power. The Neutrality Act of 1936 forbade loans to belligerents. After a joint resolution in 1937 declared the United States neutral in the Spanish Civil War, Roosevelt embargoed

arms shipments to both sides. The Neutrality Act of 1937 introduced the cash-and-carry principle: warring nations wishing to trade with the United States would have to pay cash for their nonmilitary purchases and carry the goods away in their own ships. The act also forbade Americans from traveling on the ships of belligerent nations.

In a stirring speech in August 1936 at Chautauqua, New York, Roosevelt expressed prevailing isolationist opinion and made a pitch for the pacifist vote in the upcoming election: "I have seen war. . . . I have seen blood running from the wounded. I have seen men coughing out their gassed lungs. . . . I have seen the agony of mothers and wives. I hate war." The United States, he promised, would remain distant from European conflict. During the Czech crisis of 1938 Roosevelt actually endorsed appeasement. The United States, he wrote to Hitler, had "no political involvements in Europe." On another occasion, he commented that the results of the Munich Conference elicited a "universal sense of relief."

All the while, Roosevelt was becoming increasingly troubled by the arrogant behavior of Germany, Italy, and Japan, the aggressors he tagged

Roosevelt's Changing Views

the "three bandit nations." He condemned the Nazi persecution of the Jews and the Japanese slaughter of Chinese civilians. Privately he chastised the British and French for failing to collar Hitler in their own back yards, and he worried that the United States was militarily ill-prepared to confront the aggressors.

Roosevelt did not neglect the U.S. military. New Deal public works programs included millions for the construction of new ships. In 1935 the president requested the largest peacetime defense budget in American history; three years later, in the wake of Munich, he asked Congress for funds to build up the air force. "Had we had this summer 5,000 planes and the capacity immediately to produce 10,000 per year," he told advisers, "Hitler would not have dared to take the stand he did." (Whether Hitler would have been deterred by a militarily superior United States is debatable, given the Führer's view of Americans as a mongrel race incapable of playing an important role in foreign affairs.) The president also began to cast about for ways to encourage the British and French to show more backbone. One result was his agreement in January 1939 to sell bombers to France.

Early in 1939 the president lashed out at the international lawbreakers and urged Congress to repeal the arms embargo and permit the sale of munitions to belligerents on a cash-and-carry basis. Roosevelt knew that repeal would aid Britain, which dominated the seas. When the Senate Foreign Relations Committee voted down repeal, Roosevelt raged: "I think we ought to introduce a bill for statues of [Senators] Austin, Vandenberg, Lodge and Taft . . . to be erected in Berlin and put the swastika on them."

When Europe descended into the abyss of war in September 1939, Roosevelt declared neutrality. But unlike Woodrow Wilson, he did not ask

Repeal of the Arms Embargo
———

Americans to be neutral in thought, and he pressed again for repeal of the arms embargo. Senator Arthur Vandenberg, an isolationist from Michigan, roared back that the United States could not be "an arsenal for one belligerent without becoming a target for the other." After much debate, however, Congress in November lifted the embargo on contraband and approved cash-and-carry exports of arms. Short of going to war, Roosevelt was ready to aid the Allies.

JAPAN, CHINA, AND A NEW ORDER IN ASIA

If U.S. power and influence were massive in Latin America and limited in Europe, they were minuscule in Asia. Still, the United States had Asian interests that needed protection: the Philippines and Pacific islands, religious missions, trade and investments, and the Open Door in China. In traditional missionary fashion, Americans also believed that they were China's special friend, its protector and uplifter. "With God's help," Senator Kenneth Wherry of Nebraska once proclaimed, "we will lift Shanghai up and up, ever up, until it is just like Kansas City." Pearl Buck's best-selling novel *The Good Earth* (1931), made into a widely distributed film six years later, confirmed American opinion with its image of the noble, persevering Chinese peasant. By contrast, Japan loomed as a threat to American attitudes and interests. The Tokyo government seemed bent on subjugating China and unhinging the Open Door doctrine of equal trade and investment opportunity.

The Chinese themselves were uneasy about the U.S. presence in Asia. Like the Japanese, they wished to reduce the influence of white foreigners in the region. The highly nationalistic Chinese Revolution of 1911 still rumbled in the 1920s; antiforeign riots damaged American property and imperiled American missionaries, business representatives, and sailors. Chinese nationalists complained that Americans joined with other imperialists in the practice of extraterritoriality (the exemption of foreigners accused of crimes from Chinese legal jurisdiction), and they demanded an end to this affront to Chinese sovereignty.

In the late 1920s, civil war broke out in China when Jiang Jieshi (Chiang Kai-shek) ousted Mao Zedong and his Communist followers from the ruling Guomindang party. Amer-

Rise of Jiang Jieshi in China
———

icans applauded this display of anti-Bolshevism and Jiang's conversion to Christianity in 1930. Jiang's new wife, Soong Meiling, also won their hearts. The American-educated daughter of a Chinese businessman, Madame Jiang spoke flawless English, dressed in Western fashion, and cultivated social and political ties with prominent Americans. Warming to Jiang, U.S. officials abandoned one imperial vestige by signing a treaty in 1928 restoring control of tariffs to the Chinese. American gunboats and marines, however, remained in China.

The Japanese grew increasingly suspicious of U.S.-Chinese ties. Japanese-American relations were seldom cordial in the early twentieth century, as Japan intruded more and more into China and drove economic and political stakes into Manchuria, Shandong, and Korea. The Japanese were determined not only to oust Western imperialists from Asia but also to dominate Asian territories that produced the raw materials their island nation depended on. The Japanese also resented the discriminatory immigration law of 1924, which excluded them from entry into the United States. Despite the Washington Conference treaties of 1922, naval competition continued; in fact, American naval officers used Japan as the imaginary enemy in war games at the Naval War College. Finally, although the volume of Japanese-American trade was twice that of Chinese-American trade, commercial rivalry strained relations between Japan and the United States. American producers and workers whose profits and jobs were threatened by the importation of inexpensive Japanese

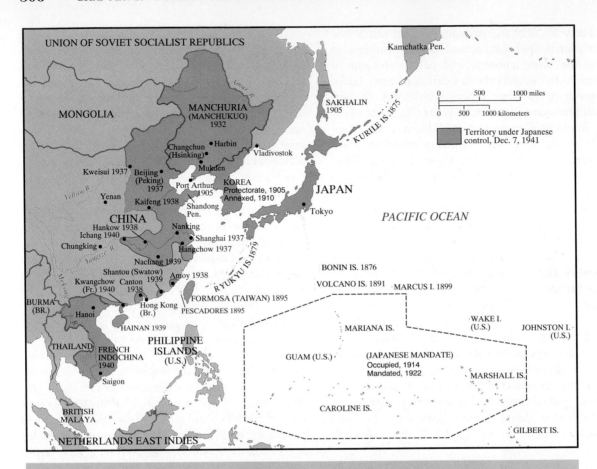

Japanese Expansion Before Pearl Harbor   *The Japanese quest for predominance began at the turn of the century and intensified in the 1930s, with China suffering the most at the hands of Tokyo's military. Vulnerable U.S. possessions in Asia and the Pacific proved no obstacle to Japan's ambitions for a Greater East Asia Co-Prosperity Sphere.*

goods, especially textiles, organized "Buy America" campaigns and boycotts.

Relations deteriorated further after the Japanese military seized Manchuria in 1931 (see map). Only nominally a Chinese region, Manchuria was

Japanese Seizure of Manchuria

important to the Japanese both as a buffer against the Soviets and as a vital source of coal, iron, timber, and food. More than half of Japan's foreign investments rested in Manchuria; the South Manchurian Railway, which the Chinese coveted, linked the extensive Japanese holdings. "We are seeking room that will let us breathe," said a Japanese politician, arguing that his tiny, heavily populated nation (65 million people in an area slightly smaller than California) needed to expand

in order to survive. Although the seizure of Manchuria violated the Nine-Power Treaty and the Kellogg-Briand Pact, the United States did not have the power to compel Japanese withdrawal. The American response therefore went no further than a moral lecture known as the Stimson Doctrine (1932): the United States would not recognize any impairment of China's sovereignty or of the Open Door policy, Secretary of State Henry L. Stimson declared.

Hardly cowed by protests from Western capitals, Japan continued to harry China. In mid-1937 full-scale Sino-Japanese war erupted, although Tokyo preferred to call it the "China incident" to maintain the fiction that it had not violated the Kellogg-Briand Pact. The Japanese seized cities and bombed innocent civilians. The gruesome bombing of Shanghai intensified anti-Japanese sentiment in the United States. Senator Norris, an isolationist who moved further away from isolationism with each new Japanese thrust, condemned the Japanese as "disgraceful, ignoble, barbarous, and cruel, even beyond the power of language to describe." In an effort to help China, Roosevelt refused to declare the existence of war, thus avoiding activation of the Neutrality Acts and allowing the Chinese to buy weapons in the United States.

In a stirring speech denouncing the aggressors in October 1937, he called for a "quarantine" to curb the "epidemic of world lawlessness." People
Roosevelt's Quarantine Speech
who thought Washington had been too gentle with Japan cheered. Confirmed isolationists warned that the president was edging toward war. Actually, Roosevelt had formulated no program to halt the Japanese. When in late 1937 Japanese aircraft sank the American gunboat *Panay*, an escort for Standard Oil Company tankers on the Yangtze River, Roosevelt demanded an apology but stopped short of retaliation. He was much relieved when Tokyo apologized and offered to pay for damages.

Japan's declaration of a "New Order" in Asia, in the words of one American official, "banged, barred, and bolted" the Open Door. Alarmed, the Roosevelt administration found small ways to assist China and thwart Japan in 1938 and 1939. Military equipment flowed to the Chinese, as did a $25 million loan. Secretary of State Hull declared a moral embargo on the shipment of airplanes to Japan. Meanwhile, the U.S. Navy continued to grow, aided by a billion-dollar congressional appropriation in 1938. In mid-1939 the United States abrogated the 1911 Japanese-American trade treaty; yet America continued to ship oil, cotton, and machinery to Japan. The administration hesitated to initiate economic sanctions because such economic pressure might spark a Japanese-American war at a time when Germany posed a more serious threat. When war broke out in Europe in 1939, Japanese-American relations were stalemated.

COLLISION COURSE, 1939–1941

"What worries me, especially," President Roosevelt told interventionist William Allen White in late 1939, "is that public opinion over here is patting itself on the back every morning and thanking God for the Atlantic Ocean [and the Pacific]." The European war, he went on, seriously jeopardized

H. S. Wong's widely circulated photograph of a child after the Japanese bombing of Shanghai, in 1937, helped galvanize world opinion against Tokyo's brutal subjugation of China. National Archives.

American security, and the American people had better recognize their precarious place in world affairs. Polls showed that Americans strongly favored the Allies and that most supported aid to Britain and France—but the great majority emphatically wanted the United States to remain at peace. Troubled by this conflicting advice—oppose Hitler, aid the Allies, but stay out of the war—the president gradually moved the nation from neutrality to undeclared war and then to full-scale war itself.

Because the stakes were so high, Americans vigorously debated the direction of their foreign policy in 1939–1941. Unprecedented numbers of Americans paid attention to foreign affairs, spoke out, and joined organizations that addressed the issues. Spine-chilling events and the widespread use of radio, the nation's chief source of news, helped stimulate this high level of public interest. So did ethnic affiliations with the various belligerents and victims of aggression. The American Legion, League of Women Voters, labor unions, and local chapters of the Committee to Defend America by Aiding the Allies and the America First Committee (both organized in 1940) provided outlets for citizen participation in the national debate. But the House of Representatives, pressed by Roosevelt, defeated a constitutional amendment proposed by Louis Ludlow (Democrat of Indiana) to require a majority vote in a national referendum before a congressional declaration of war could go into effect (unless the United States were attacked).

National Debate

The isolationist America First Committee published this bumper sticker in 1941 in a vain attempt to halt the U.S. descent into war. America Firsters organized in September 1940 and attracted many prominent members, including the famous aviator Charles Lindbergh. Herbert Hoover Presidential Library.

In September 1939 Poland succumbed to German stormtroopers, while the Red Army seized Poland's eastern district (see map). In spring 1940 Germany invaded Denmark, Norway, The Netherlands, and Belgium. By March 1940 the Soviets had also defeated Finland. "The small countries are smashed up, one by one, like matchwood," sighed the new British Prime Minister Winston Churchill. In May several German divisions attacked France. By early June they had pushed French and British forces back to the English Channel. At Dunkirk, more than 300,000 Allied soldiers, abandoning their equipment on the beaches, frantically escaped to Britain on a flotilla of small boats. France's collapse and the installation of a fascist regime there stunned Americans, who wondered if the Nazis would conquer Britain next.

Fall of France

In the United States, isolationist sentiment gradually declined. Alarmed by the swift defeat of one European nation after another, some liberals left the isolationist fold; it became more and more the province of conservatives. Emotions ran high. Roosevelt called the isolationists "ostriches" and charged that some were pro-Nazi subversives. The White House began to turn over to the Federal Bureau of Investigation letters that criticized Roosevelt's foreign policy. Isolationists retorted that he was a warmonger.

After Roosevelt tried futilely to draw the belligerents to the peace table, he told his advisers that he was "not willing to fire the first shot" but was waiting for some incident to bring the United States into the war. In the meantime, assuring Americans that New Deal reforms would not have to be sacrificed to achieve military preparedness, Roosevelt began to aid the beleaguered Allies to prevent the fall of Britain. In May 1940 he had ordered the sale of old surplus military equipment to Britain and France. In July he cultivated bipartisan support by naming Republicans Henry L. Stimson and Frank Knox, ardent backers of aid to the Allies, secretaries of war and the navy respectively. In September, by executive agreement, the president traded fifty old American destroyers for leases to eight British bases, including those in Newfoundland, Bermuda, and Jamaica.

Two weeks later Roosevelt signed into law the hotly debated and narrowly passed Selective Training and Service Act, the first peacetime mili-

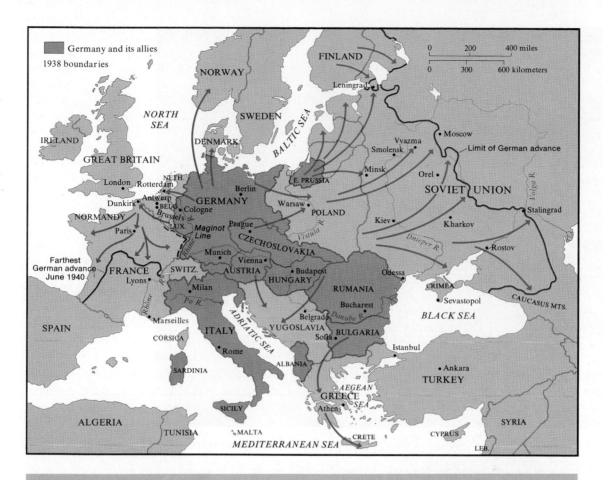

The German Advance, 1939–1942 *Hitler's drive to dominate Europe carried German troops deep into France and the Soviet Union. Great Britain took a beating but held on with the help of U.S. economic and military aid before the United States itself joined the Second World War.*

First Peacetime Military Draft

tary draft in U.S. history. The act called for the registration of all men between the ages of twenty-one and thirty-five. Soon more than 16 million men had been signed up, and draft notices began to be delivered. Ironically, Roosevelt won re-election that fall with promises of peace: "Your boys are not going to be sent into any foreign wars." Republican candidate Wendell Willkie, who in the emerging spirit of bipartisanship had not made an issue of foreign policy, snapped, "That hypocritical son of a bitch! This is going to beat me!" It did.

Roosevelt claimed that the United States could stay out of the war by enabling the British to win. The United States must, he said, become

Lend-Lease Act

the "great arsenal of democracy." As Britain suffered financial woes and heavy German bombing, Churchill frantically appealed to Roosevelt for help. In January 1941 the administration sent to Congress the controversial Lend-Lease bill. Because Britain was broke, the president explained, the United States should lend rather than sell weapons, much as a neighbor lends a garden hose to fight a fire. Roosevelt's analogy did not persuade strict isolationist Senator Burton K. Wheeler of Montana, who shouted out another comparison: Lend-Lease was "the New Deal's triple A foreign policy; it will plow under every fourth American boy." But in March 1941, with pro-British sentiment running

President Franklin D. Roosevelt (left) and British Prime Minister Winston Churchill (1874–1965) confer on board a ship near Newfoundland during their summit meeting of August 1941 when they signed the Atlantic Charter. Upon his return to England, Churchill told his advisers that Roosevelt had promised to "wage war" against Germany and do "everything" to "force an incident." Franklin D. Roosevelt Library, Hyde Park, New York.

high, the House passed the Lend-Lease Act 317 to 71; the Senate followed suit, 60 to 31. The initial appropriation was $7 billion, but by the end of the war the amount had reached $50 billion, more than $31 billion of it for England.

To ensure the safe delivery of Lend-Lease goods, Roosevelt ordered the navy to patrol halfway across the Atlantic and sent American troops to Greenland. In June 1941 Hitler attacked the Soviet Union. (Two months earlier, in anticipation of just such an attack, the Soviets had signed a neutrality treaty with Japan, thus reducing the chances that they would have to fight a two-front war.) In July, arguing that Iceland was essential to the defense of the Western Hemisphere, Roosevelt dispatched four thousand marines there. He also sent Lend-Lease aid to the Soviet Union. If the Soviets could hold off two hundred German divisions in the east, he calculated, Britain would gain some

breathing time. Churchill, who had thundered loudly against the Communists for years, now applauded aid to the Soviets: "If Hitler invaded Hell, I would make at least a favorable reference to the Devil in the House of Commons."

In August 1941 Churchill and Roosevelt met for four days on a British battleship off the coast of Newfoundland. They got along well, trading naval stories, deferring to each other, and taking pleasure in the fact that Churchill was half American. "It is fun to be in the same decade with you," Roosevelt later wrote to his new friend. At this conference the two leaders issued the Atlantic Charter, a set of war aims reminiscent of Wilsonianism (see Chapter 23): collective security, disarmament, self-determination, economic cooperation, and freedom of the seas. On

"Atlantic Charter" Conference

January 1, 1942, twenty-six nations signed the Declaration of the United Nations, pledging allegiance to the charter. According to Churchill, the president told him in Newfoundland that, although he could not ask Congress for a declaration of war against Germany, "he would wage war" and "become more and more provocative."

In September 1941 there occurred an incident Roosevelt could exploit when the U.S. destroyer *Greer* was fired on (but not hit) by a German submarine. In a special national radio broadcast the president protested German "piracy" and announced a policy he had already privately promised Churchill: American naval vessels would now convoy British merchant ships all the way to Iceland and would shoot German submarines, the "rattlesnakes of the Atlantic," on sight. Roosevelt practiced deliberate deception in the *Greer* case, for he did not mention that the *Greer* had been tailing a German U-boat for hours, signaling the submarine's location to British airplanes hunting the ship with depth charges. He and his advisers thought it necessary to manipulate public opinion in order to scare Americans into defending Britain.

The United States had entered into an undeclared war with Germany. When in early October a German submarine torpedoed the American destroyer *Kearny* off the coast of Iceland, the president announced that "the shooting has started. And history has recorded who fired the first shot." Later that month, when the destroyer *Reuben James* went down with the loss of more than one hundred American lives, Congress scrapped the cash-and-carry policy and further revised the Neutrality Acts to permit transport of munitions to England on armed American merchant ships. Many nervous Americans foresaw that the United States was not far from full-scale war in Europe.

WHY WAR CAME: PEARL HARBOR AND THE INTERWAR ERA

In retrospect, it seems ironic that the Second World War came to the United States by way of Asia. Roosevelt had wanted to avoid war with Japan in order to concentrate American resources on the defeat of Germany. In September 1940, after Germany,

Cutoff of Trade with Japan

Italy, and Japan had signed the Tripartite Pact, Roosevelt slapped an embargo on shipments of aviation fuel and scrap metal to Japan. Because the president believed the petroleum-thirsty Japanese would consider a cutoff of oil a life-or-death matter, he did not embargo that vital commodity. But after Japanese troops occupied French Indochina in July 1941, Washington froze Japanese assets in the United States, virtually ending trade (including oil) with Japan. "The oil gauge and the clock stood side by side," wrote one observer.

Tokyo recommended a summit meeting between President Roosevelt and Prime Minister Prince Konoye, but the United States rejected the idea. American officials insisted that the Japanese first agree to respect China's sovereignty and territorial integrity and to honor the Open Door policy—in short, to get out of China. According to polls in the fall of 1941, the American people seemed willing to risk war with Japan to thwart further aggression, but Roosevelt was not ready for an Asian war; Europe claimed first priority. Still, he would not back down in Asia, and he supported Secretary Hull's hard-line policy against Japan's pursuit of the Greater East Asia Co-Prosperity Sphere—the name Tokyo gave to the vast Asian region it intended to dominate.

Roosevelt told his advisers to string out ongoing Japanese-American talks to gain time—time to fortify the Philippines and check the fascists in Europe. "Let us do nothing to precipitate a crisis," he told the cabinet in November 1941. By breaking the Japanese code and deciphering intercepted messages through Operation MAGIC, American officials learned that Tokyo's patience with diplomacy was fast dissipating. In late November the Japanese rejected U.S. demands that they withdraw from Indochina. An intercepted message that U.S. experts decoded on December 3 instructed the Japanese embassy in Washington to burn codes and destroy cipher machines—a sure sign that war was coming. Why not attack first? asked aide Harry Hopkins. No, said Roosevelt. Secretary Stimson explained later that the United States let Japan fire the first shot so as "to have the full support of the American people" and "so that there should remain no doubt in anyone's mind as to who were the aggressors."

The Japanese plotted a daring raid on Pearl Harbor in Hawaii. An armada of 60 Japanese ships, with a core of 6 carriers bearing 360 airplanes, crossed 3,000 miles of the Pacific Ocean.

Surprise Attack on Pearl Harbor

To avoid detection, every ship maintained radio silence. In the early morning of December 7, some 230 miles northwest of Honolulu, the carriers unleashed their planes, each stamped with a red sun representing the Japanese flag. They swept down on the unsuspecting U.S. naval base and nearby airfields, dropping torpedoes and bombs and strafing buildings.

The battleship USS *Arizona*, resting at its berth on Ford Island, swallowed a Japanese bomb in its forward section. When the bomb ignited explosives below deck, more than 1,000 sailors died in the thundering blast. The USS *Nevada* tried to escape the inferno by heading to sea, but a second wave of aerial attackers struck that battlewagon. Altogether the invaders sunk or damaged 8 battleships and several smaller vessels and smashed more than 160 aircraft on the ground. Huddled in an air-raid shelter, sixteen-year-old Mary Ann Ramsey watched the injured come in "with filthy black oil covering shredded flesh. With the first sailor,

so horribly burned, personal fear left me; he brought me the full tragedy of the day." A total of 2,403 died; 1,178 were wounded. By chance, three aircraft carriers, at sea, escaped the disaster. The Pearl Harbor tragedy, from the perspective of the war's outcome, counted more as a military inconvenience than a disaster.

How could the stunning attack on Pearl Harbor have happened? After all, U.S. cryptanalysts had broken the Japanese diplomatic code. Although the intercepted Japanese messages told codebreakers and policymakers that war lay ahead because Japanese-American relations had so deteriorated, the intercepts never revealed naval or military plans and never specifically mentioned Pearl Harbor. Roosevelt did not, as some critics charged, conspire to leave the fleet vulnerable to attack so that the United States could enter the Second World War through the "back door" of Asia. The base was not ready—not on red alert—because a message sent from Washington warning

Explaining Pearl Harbor

The stricken USS California *was one of the eight battleships caught in the surprise Japanese attack at Pearl Harbor, Hawaii, on December 7, 1941. The* California *was sunk, but months later it was floated and moved to a drydock for modernization. The ship rejoined the U.S. fleet in 1943 and went on to win seven battle stars during the Second World War.* National Archives.

How do historians know

that American leaders knew in December 1941, before the attack on Pearl Harbor, that Japan intended to go to war with the United States? In September 1940, U.S. cryptanalysts, or codebreakers, of the Signal Intelligence Service cracked the most secret diplomatic cipher of the Japanese government, a machine they called PURPLE. The codebreakers discovered patterns in the incoherent letters of telegraphed messages, produced texts, and even duplicated the complicated PURPLE machine (shown above). Thereafter, under Operation MAGIC, they decoded thousands of intercepted messages sent by Japanese officials around the world. Important intercepts were delivered to a handful of top U.S. leaders, including the president. These dispatches made increasingly clear through 1941 that Tokyo expected all-out war with the United States. An intercept on December 3, just a few days before the surprise attack on Pearl Harbor, revealed that Tokyo had ordered the Japanese embassy in Washington to destroy all codes and machines, a sure sign that war was imminent. After the onslaught against Pearl Harbor, and after it became public knowledge that the United States had broken the Japanese diplomatic code, the cry sounded that President Roosevelt must have known what was coming and yet failed to prepare for the Japanese attack. The many intercepted messages of fall and winter 1941, however, never revealed Japan's military plans. Not one intercepted message mentioned an attack on Pearl Harbor; indeed, Japanese diplomats in Washington were themselves never told that Pearl Harbor would be hit. And few Americans expected the Japanese to attack Hawaii or the United States itself. Photo: National Archives.

of the imminence of war had been too casually transmitted by a slow method and had arrived too late. Base commanders were too relaxed, believing Hawaii too far from Japan to be a target for all-out attack. Like Roosevelt's advisers, they expected an assault at British Malaya, Thailand, or the Philippines. The Pearl Harbor calamity stemmed from mistakes and insufficient information, not from conspiracy.

On December 8, referring to the previous day as "a date which will live in infamy," Roosevelt asked Congress for a declaration of war against Japan. He noted that the Japanese had also attacked Malaya, Hong Kong, Guam, the Philippines,

Wake, and Midway, and he expressed the prevailing sense of revenge when he remarked that Americans would never forget "the character of the onslaught against us." A unanimous vote in the Senate and a 388 to 1 vote in the House thrust America into war. (Only Representative Jeannette Rankin of Montana voted no, matching her vote against entry into the First World War.) Three days later Germany and Italy, honoring the Tripartite Pact they had signed with Japan in September 1940, declared war against the United States. The war was now a global conflict. "Hitler's fate was sealed," Britain's Winston Churchill wrote. "Mussolini's fate was sealed. As for the Japanese, they would be ground to powder. . . . I went to bed and slept the sleep of the saved and thankful."

Americans, remembering the bitter experience of the First World War, had tried to stay out. Diplomacy and economic sanctions had not stopped the aggressors, who kept pushing on, threatening U.S. interests. A fundamental clash of systems explains why diplomacy failed and war came. Germany and Japan preferred a world divided into closed spheres of influence. The United States sought conditions that would ensure its continued international stature and domestic well-being: a liberal capitalist world order in which all nations enjoyed the freedom to trade with and invest in all other nations. U.S. principles manifested a respect for human rights; fascists in Europe and militarists in Asia defiantly trampled on the rights of individuals and groups. The United States prided itself on its democratic system; Germany and Japan embraced authoritarian regimes backed by the military.

Clash of Systems

When the United States protested against German and Japanese expansion, Berlin and Tokyo reminded Washington of the United States's sphere in Latin America. German, Italian, and Japanese leaders also charged that Americans were applying a double standard. Had not the United States itself built an empire through conquest, military occupation, and economic privilege, at times violating avowed American principles? Americans rejected such comparisons and claimed that their expansionism had benefited not just themselves but the rest of the world. So many incompatible objectives and outlooks made conflict inevitable. But the question historians still struggle to answer is this: could better diplomatic leadership from Roosevelt have prevented U.S. entry into a *two*-theater war?

By the late 1930s, the earlier U.S. emphasis on independent internationalism and economic and nonmilitary means to peace seemed increasingly archaic. The Great Depression, which had brought on so much international havoc, also faded in memory as the economy geared up for war. The Neutrality Acts, which had been designed to insulate the United States from European troubles, had been gradually revised and retired in the face of growing danger and receding isolationism. Roosevelt hesitantly moved the nation from neutrality, to aid for the Allies, to outright belligerency.

Looking back with sadness, Americans had to admit that their policies of the 1920s and 1930s had failed to create the peaceful and prosperous world order they intended. The Washington treaties failed to curb a naval arms race or to protect China; the Dawes Plan collapsed; the Kellogg-Briand Pact proved ineffective; Germany and the aggressors ignored repeated U.S. protests, from the Stimson Doctrine onward; recognition of the Soviet Union barely improved relations; trade policies did not liberate international commerce from protectionism; and the Neutrality Acts failed to prevent U.S. entanglements in Europe. Even where U.S. power and policies seemed to work to satisfy U.S. goals—in Latin America—nationalist resentments simmered and Mexico challenged U.S. hegemony.

The Second World War offered yet another opportunity for Americans to set things right in the world. As publisher Henry Luce put it in *American Century* (1941), the United States must "exert upon the world the full impact of our influence, for such purposes as we see fit and by such means as we see fit." As they had so many times before, Americans flocked to the colors. Isolationists now joined the president in spirited calls for victory. "We are going to win the war, and we are going to win the peace that follows," Roosevelt predicted.

SUGGESTIONS FOR FURTHER READING

Interwar Issues and the Road to War

Thomas H. Buckley, *The United States and the Washington Conference, 1921–1922* (1970); Warren I. Cohen, *Empire Without Tears*

(1987); Frank Costigliola, *Awkward Dominion* (1984) (on Europe); Justus D. Doenecke and John E. Wilz, *From Isolation to War, 1931–1941*, 2nd ed. (1991); Robert H. Ferrell, *American Diplomacy in the Great Depression* (1957); Peter G. Filene, *Americans and the Soviet Experiment, 1917–1933* (1967); Melvyn P. Leffler, *The Elusive Quest* (1979); Elting E. Morison, *Turmoil and Tradition* (1964) (on Stimson); Emily S. Rosenberg, *Spreading the American Dream* (1982); James C. Schneider, *Should America Go to War?: The Debate over Foreign Policy in Chicago, 1939–1941* (1989); Michael S. Sherry, *The Rise of American Airpower* (1987); Raymond Sontag, *A Broken World, 1919–1939* (1971); Joan Hoff Wilson, *Herbert Hoover* (1975).

The Peace Movement and Kellogg-Briand Pact

Charles Chatfield, *For Peace and Justice: Pacifism in America, 1914–1941* (1971); Charles DeBenedetti, *The Peace Reform in American History* (1980); Charles DeBenedetti, *Origins of the Modern American Peace Movement, 1915–1929* (1978); Robert H. Ferrell, *Peace in Their Time* (1952); Sybil Oldfield, *Women Against the Iron Fist* (1990); Lawrence Wittner, *Rebels Against War* (1984).

The United States in the World Economy

Frederick Adams, *Economic Diplomacy* (1976); Derek H. Aldcroft, *From Versailles to Wall Street, 1919–1929* (1977); Herbert Feis, *The Diplomacy of the Dollar, 1919–1932* (1950); Lloyd C. Gardner, *Economic Aspects of New Deal Diplomacy* (1964); Michael J. Hogan, *Informal Entente* (1977) (on Anglo-American relations); Charles Kindleberger, *The World in Depression* (1973); Stephen J. Randall, *United States Foreign Oil Policy, 1919–1948* (1986); Mira Wilkins, *The Maturing of Multinational Enterprise* (1974); Joan Hoff Wilson, *American Business and Foreign Policy, 1920–1933* (1971).

Latin America

Bruce J. Calder, *The Impact of Intervention* (1984) (on Dominican Republic); Arturo Morales Carrión, *Puerto Rico* (1983); Truman B. Clark, *Puerto Rico and the United States, 1917–23* (1975); Alton Frye, *Nazi Germany and the American Hemisphere, 1933–1941* (1967); Irwin F. Gellman, *Good Neighbor Diplomacy* (1979); David Green, *The Containment of Latin America* (1971); Walter LaFeber, *Inevitable Revolutions*, 2nd ed. rev. (1993) (on Central America); Lester D. Langley, *The United States and the Caribbean, 1900–1970* (1980); Neil Macaulay, *The Sandino Affair* (1967); Lorenzo Meyer, *Mexico and the United States in the Oil Controversy, 1917–1942* (1977); Richard Millett, *Guardians of the Dynasty* (1977) (on Nicaragua); Louis A. Pérez, *Cuba and the United States* (1990); Louis A. Pérez, *Cuba Under the Platt Amendment* (1986); Brenda G. Plummer, *Haiti and the United States* (1992); Stephen G. Rabe, *The Road to OPEC* (1982) (on Venezuela and oil); Robert F. Smith, *The United States and Revolutionary Nationalism in Mexico, 1916–1932* (1972); Bryce Wood, *The Making of the Good Neighbor Policy* (1961).

Isolationism and Isolationists

Warren I. Cohen, *The American Revisionists* (1967); Wayne S. Cole, *Roosevelt and the Isolationists, 1932–1945* (1983); Wayne S. Cole, *America First* (1953); Manfred Jonas, *Isolationism in America, 1935–1941* (1966); Thomas C. Kennedy, *Charles A. Beard and American Foreign Policy* (1975); Richard Lowitt, *George W. Norris*, 3 vols. (1963–1978); John Wiltz, *In Search of Peace: The Senate Munitions Inquiry, 1934–1936* (1963).

Europe, the Coming of World War II, and Roosevelt

Edward Bennett, *Recognition of Russia* (1970); J. Garry Clifford and Samuel R. Spencer, Jr., *The First Peacetime Draft* (1986); James V. Compton, *The Swastika and the Eagle* (1967); David H. Culbert, *News for Everyman: Radio and Foreign Affairs in Thirties America* (1976); Robert Dallek, *Franklin D. Roosevelt and American Foreign Policy, 1932–1945* (1979); Robert A. Divine, *The Reluctant Belligerent*, 2nd ed. (1979); Robert A. Divine, *Roosevelt and World War II* (1969); Manfred Jonas, *The United States and Germany* (1984); Warren F. Kimball, *The Most Unsordid Act* (1969) (on Lend-Lease); Douglas Little, *Malevolent Neutrality* (1985) (on Spanish Civil War); Thomas R. Maddux, *Years of Estrangement* (1980) (on U.S.-Soviet Union relations); Arnold A. Offner, *American Appeasement* (1969); Julius W. Pratt, *Cordell Hull*, 2 vols. (1964); David Reynolds, *The Creation of the Anglo-American Alliance, 1937–1941* (1982); David F. Schmitz, *The United States and Fascist Italy, 1922–1944* (1988); Richard Steele, *Propaganda in an Open Society* (1985); Donald C. Watt, *How War Came* (1989).

China, Japan, and the Coming of War in Asia

Charles A. Beard, *President Roosevelt and the Coming of the War, 1941* (1948); Dorothy Borg and Shumpei Okomoto, eds., *Pearl Harbor as History* (1973); R. J. C. Butow, *Tojo and the Coming of War* (1961); Warren I. Cohen, *America's Response to China*, 3rd ed. (1989); Hilary Conroy and Harry Wray, eds., *Pearl Harbor Reexamined: Prologue to the Pacific War* (1990); Roger Dingman, *Power in the Pacific* (1976); Herbert Feis, *The Road to Pearl Harbor* (1950); Waldo H. Heinrichs, Jr., *Threshold of War* (1988); Akira Iriye, *The Origins of the Second World War in Asia and the Pacific* (1987); Akira Iriye, *Across the Pacific* (1967); Akira Iriye, *After Imperialism* (1965); Charles Neu, *The Troubled Encounter* (1975); Paul W. Schroeder, *The Axis Alliance and Japanese-American Relations, 1941* (1958); Jonathan Utley, *Going to War with Japan* (1985).

Pearl Harbor

David Kahn, *The Codebreakers* (1967); Martin V. Melosi, *The Shadow of Pearl Harbor* (1977); Gordon W. Prange, *Pearl Harbor* (1986); Gordon W. Prange, *At Dawn We Slept* (1981); John Toland, *Infamy* (1982); Roberta Wohlstetter, *Pearl Harbor* (1962).

27

The Second World War at Home and Abroad, 1941–1945

THE SECOND WORLD WAR scarred many soldiers and sailors for life. It also devastated their families. Henrietta Bingham, who lived in western Montana, was nine when the Japanese attacked Pearl Harbor. In December 1941, she remembered later, "all the war meant to me . . . was excitement. By 1945 that excitement had turned our family to tragedy & sorrow & especially for a 13 year old." In 1942 her sixteen-year-old brother Gerald falsified his age to enlist in the U.S. Air Corps and became a top turret gunner on a bomber. The next year, he was killed on a mission in the Pacific. Her brother Gene enlisted in the Air Corps the day after his graduation from high school in 1943. He, too, became a gunner on a bomber, and the next year he was killed in a mid-air collision. In 1945, when Gerald's class graduated from high school, an empty chair was placed on the stage. Henrietta's parents had aged greatly; her "young pretty mother had turned almost white," and her father "appeared an old man." And Henrietta herself, watching the graduation ceremony, "remembered how excited I was at age 9 when the war began in

1941 & how I felt just a few short years later. I had lost my childhood."

Other children saw their fathers go to war. Ruth Wagner was born on a farm near Arapahoe, Nebraska, just a week after Pearl Harbor. The next spring, her father was inducted into the army and assigned to Corvallis, Oregon, for basic training. Ruth and her mother took the train to Oregon and lived off base for six months until her father was shipped to the South Pacific. She did not see him again for over two years. Like tens of thousands of other service families, Ruth and her mother returned home, as people phrased it, "for the duration."

Ruth's mother went to work, as a teacher in a Nebraska country school, for the first time in her married life; she loved teaching. Meanwhile Ruth was cared for by her grandmother, who adored her. Ruth was elated when the war ended and her father returned home from an island in the Pacific. But he was distant and "never talked about his job there, except that it was hot, primitive, and insect-infested." To put the army behind him, he threw himself into his work as the manager of a grocery store. Her mother stopped working and had two more babies, in 1946 and 1953. "I think the war did a lot for her too," Ruth wrote. "She was the sole provider and decision maker . . . but she had to take a far back seat to my Dad when he came home."

The Second World War was a turning point in Americans' lives and in the history of the United States. Most deeply affected were those who fought the war, on the battlefields and in the skies, on the beaches and at sea. For forty-five months Americans fought abroad to subdue the Nazi and Japanese aggressors. After military engagements against fascists in North Africa and Italy, American troops joined the dramatic crossing of the English Channel on D-Day in June 1944. The massive invasion forced the Germans to retreat through France to Germany. Battered by merciless bombing raids, leaderless after Adolf Hitler's suicide, and pressed by a Soviet advance from the east, the Nazis capitulated in May 1945. In the Pacific, Americans drove the Japanese from one island after another before turning to the just-tested atomic bombs that demolished Hiroshima and Nagasaki in August and helped spur a Japanese surrender.

Throughout the war the Allies—Britain, the Soviet Union, and the United States—were held together by their common goal of defeating Germany. But they squabbled over many issues: when to open a second front; how to structure a new international organization; how Eastern Europe, liberated from the Germans, would be reconstructed; how Germany itself would be governed after defeat. At the end of the war, Allied leaders seemed more intent on retaining and expanding their own nations' spheres of influence than on building a community of mutual interest. The United States and the Soviet Union emerged from the war as direct competitors. The prospects for post-war international cooperation seemed bleak, and the advent of the atomic age frightened everyone.

The war transformed America's soldiers and sailors. Horizons expanded for the 16.4 million men and women who served in the armed forces, seeing new parts of the world and acquiring new skills. But at war's end they were older than their years, both physically and emotionally, and many felt they had sacrificed the best years of their lives.

Also on the move during the Second World War were African-Americans, Mexican-Amer-

icans, whites, and women of all races who migrated to war-production centers in the North and the West. For numerous African-Americans, the war offered new economic and political opportunities, encouraging them to demand their full rights as citizens. But it also created the conditions for racial violence; in 1943, race riots erupted across the country.

American women experienced mixed progress during the war. Although prohibited from engaging in combat, 350,000 women joined the armed forces and worked at a wide range of noncombat jobs, including as transport pilots and as nurses directly behind the front lines. Furthermore, employers' negative attitudes toward women workers eased during the war, and millions of married middle-class women, many of them over thirty-five, took jobs in war industries. For some, work was an economic necessity; for others, it was a patriotic obligation. Whatever the motivation, paying jobs brought women benefits—financial independence and enhanced self-esteem—that many were reluctant to give up at war's end.

The United States underwent profound changes during the course of the war. The American people united behind the war effort, collecting scrap iron, rubber, and old newspapers and planting "victory gardens." But more than national unity and enthusiasm were required to win the war. Essential to victory was the successful mobilization of all sectors of the economy—industry, finance, agriculture, and labor. America's big businesses got even bigger, as did its central government, labor unions, and farms. The federal government had the monumental task of coordinating these spheres, as well as a couple of new ones: higher education and science. For this was a scientific and technological war, supported by the development of new weapons like radar and the atomic bomb. For all these reasons the Second World War was a watershed in American history.

WINNING THE SECOND WORLD WAR IN EUROPE

"We are now in the midst of a war, not for conquest, not for vengeance, but for a world in which this Nation, and all that this Nation represents, will be safe for our children." President Franklin D. Roosevelt was speaking just two days after the

• *Important Events* •

1941   Japan attacks Pearl Harbor; United States enters Second World War

1942   National War Labor Board created to deal with labor-management conflict
War Production Board begins to oversee conversion to military production
West Coast Japanese-Americans interned in prison camps
War Manpower Commission created to manage labor supply
Office of Price Administration created to control inflation
Bataan Death March intensifies anti-Japanese sentiment
U.S. defeats Japanese forces at battles of Coral Sea and Midway
Office of War Information created
Manhattan Project set up to produce atomic bomb
Allies invade North Africa
Republicans gain in Congress
Synthetic-rubber program begins

1943   Russian Red Army defeats German troops at Stalingrad
Soft-coal and anthracite miners strike
Office of War Mobilization established
Congress passes War Labor Disputes (Smith-Connally) Act
Race riots break out in Detroit, Harlem, and forty-five other cities

Allies invade Italy
Roosevelt, Churchill, and Stalin meet at Teheran Conference

1944   Roosevelt requests Economic Bill of Rights
War Refugee Board established
Supreme Court upholds Japanese-American internment
GI Bill of Rights provides educational benefits for veterans
Allied troops land at Normandy; D-Day
Dumbarton Oaks Conference approves charter for United Nations
Roosevelt re-elected
United States retakes the Philippines

1945   Roosevelt, Stalin, and Churchill meet at Yalta Conference
Battles of Iwo Jima and Okinawa result in heavy U.S. and Japanese losses
Roosevelt dies; Harry S Truman assumes the presidency
United Nations founded
Germany surrenders
Potsdam Conference calls for Japan's "unconditional surrender"
First atomic bomb exploded in test at Alamogordo, New Mexico
Atomic bombs devastate Hiroshima and Nagasaki
Japan surrenders

---

surprise attack on Pearl Harbor. Few Americans knew much about the principles of the Atlantic Charter (see Chapter 26) or about U.S. war aims. But practically without exception they agreed with Roosevelt that they were defending their homes and families against aggressive, even satanic, Japanese and Nazis. After all, had not Japan provoked the war with its bombing of Hawaii?

America's men and women responded eagerly to Roosevelt's call to arms. In 1941, though Selective Service had been functioning for a full year, only 1.8 million people were serving on active duty. In 1942 the number more than doubled to 3.9 million; in 1943 it more than doubled again to 9 million. In 1945 the number of women and men serving in the army, navy, and marines peaked at

12.1 million. Fighting a world war on two fronts required such a massive force.

Despite nearly unanimous support for the war effort, various government leaders worried that Americans would become suspicious of lofty rhetoric, remembering how Woodrow Wilson had promised so much and delivered too little during the First World War. Concerned that public morale would lag as the war dragged on, the army hired prominent Hollywood director Frank Capra to produce a series of propaganda films called *Why We Fight*. In these widely distributed films, and in the popular mind, the Allies were heroic partners in a common effort against evil.

In actuality, wartime relations among the United States, Great Britain, and the Soviet Union

Be with him at every mail call

V-MAIL IS PRIVATE, RELIABLE, PATRIOTIC

During the war Americans were urged to make every sacrifice possible for the fighting men at the front. Government posters like the one above exhorted people to buy war bonds, conserve gasoline, and (above) write daily to the soldiers and sailors. National Archives.

ran hot and cold. Although winning the war was the top priority, Allied leaders knew that military decisions also had political consequences. If one ally became desperate, for instance, it might destroy the alliance by pursuing a separate peace. Moreover, the positions of troops at the end of the war might determine the politics of the regions they occupied. Thus an undercurrent of mutual suspicion ran just beneath the surface of Allied cooperation.

Roosevelt, British Prime Minister Winston Churchill, and Soviet Premier Josef Stalin differed vigorously over the opening of a second, or west-

Second-Front Controversy
——

ern, front. After Germany conquered France in 1940 and invaded Russia in 1941, the Russians bore the brunt of the war until mid-1944, suffering heavy casualties. By late 1941, before the fierce Russian winter stalled their onslaught, German troops had nearly reached Moscow and Leningrad

and had slashed deeply into the Ukraine, taking Kiev. Stalin pressed for a British-American landing on the northern coast of Europe to draw German troops away from the eastern front, but Churchill would not agree. The Russians therefore did most of the fighting and dying on land, while the British and Americans concentrated on getting Lend-Lease supplies across the Atlantic and harassing the Germans from the air with attacks on factories and civilians alike. When Secretary of State Cordell Hull bemoaned the 200,000 American casualties suffered from 1941 to 1943, a Russian official replied, "We lose that many each day before lunch. You haven't got your teeth in the war yet."

Roosevelt was sensitive to the suggestion that Americans were shirking their responsibility by avoiding an invasion of Europe. He feared that Russia might be knocked out of the war, leaving Hitler free to invade England. In 1942 Roosevelt told the Russians that they could expect the Allies to cross the English Channel and invade France later that year. This was exactly what Stalin sought to take pressure off his wracked country. But Churchill balked. "To postpone that evil day, all his arts, all his eloquence, all his great experience was spent," the prime minister's chief military adviser later wrote. Churchill feared heavy losses in a premature cross-channel invasion. While American generals George C. Marshall and Dwight D. Eisenhower argued for a direct attack on the heart of German power, Churchill held out for a series of small jabs at the enemy's Mediterranean forces. American officials suspected that Churchill's strategy derived from his desire to reassert British imperial power in the Mediterranean.

Churchill won the debate. Instead of attacking France, the British and Americans invaded North Africa in November 1942 (see map). To minimize fascist French resistance to the invasion, the Americans agreed to recognize the pro-Nazi Vichy French regime in North Africa—a "deal" many critics denounced as unsavory. Roosevelt deemed the bargain justified in order to get Americans into combat. "We are striking back," the cheered president declared. The news from Russia also buoyed Roosevelt. In the battle for Stalingrad (September 1942–January 1943)—probably the turning point of the European war—the Red Army defeated the Germans in bloody block-by-block fighting, forcing Hitler's divisions to retreat. But shortly thereafter, the president once again angered the Russians by declaring another delay in launching the

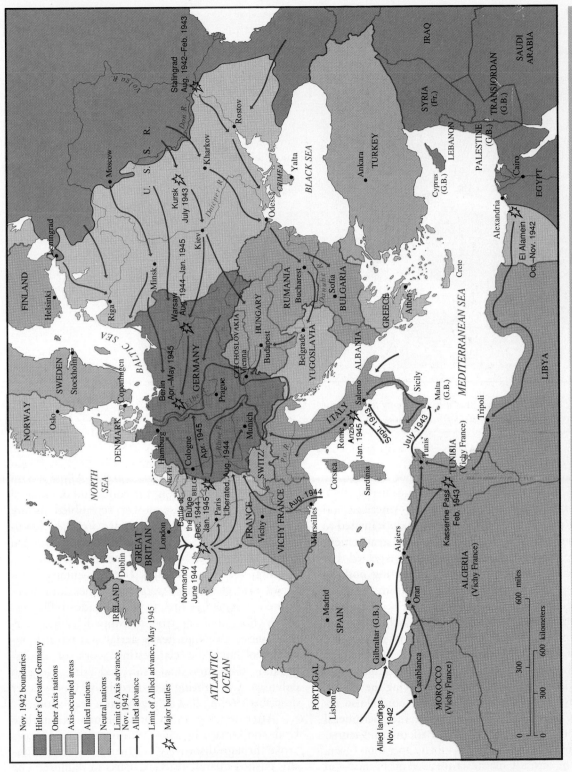

CHAPTER 27 THE SECOND WORLD WAR AT HOME AND ABROAD, 1941–1945

The Allies on the Offensive in Europe, 1942–1945 *The United States pursued a "Europe first" policy: first defeat Germany, then focus on Japan. American military efforts began in North Africa in late 1942 and ended in Germany in 1945 on V-E Day (May 8).*

Nov. 1942 boundaries
Hitler's Greater Germany
Other Axis nations
Axis-occupied areas
Allied nations
Neutral nations
Limit of Axis advance, Nov. 1942
Allied advance
Limit of Allied advance, May 1945
Major battles

NORWAY
Oslo
SWEDEN
Stockholm
FINLAND
Helsinki
Leningrad
DENMARK
Copenhagen
BALTIC SEA
Riga
Moscow
U. S. S. R.
Minsk
Volga R.
Don R.
Stalingrad
Aug. 1942–Feb. 1943
Rostov
Kharkov
Kursk
July 1943
Kiev
Dnieper R.
Warsaw
Aug. 1944–Jan. 1945
Odessa
CRIMEA
Yalta
BLACK SEA
Ankara
TURKEY
GERMANY
Berlin
Apr.–May 1945
Prague
CZECHOSLOVAKIA
Vienna
Budapest
HUNGARY
Danube R.
RUMANIA
Bucharest
Sofia
BULGARIA
YUGOSLAVIA
Belgrade
ALBANIA
GREECE
Athens
Crete
Cyprus (G.B.)
SYRIA (Fr.)
LEBANON
IRAQ
TRANSJORDAN (G.B.)
PALESTINE (G.B.)
SAUDI ARABIA
Cairo
EGYPT
Alexandria
El Alamein
Oct.–Nov. 1942
MEDITERRANEAN SEA
LIBYA
Tripoli
Malta (G.B.)
Sicily
July 1943
Salerno
Sept. 1943
Anzio
Jan. 1945
Rome
ITALY
Corsica
Sardinia
Tunis
TUNISIA
(Vichy France)
Kasserine Pass
Feb. 1943
Algiers
Oran
ALGERIA
(Vichy France)
Casablanca
MOROCCO
(Vichy France)
Allied landings
Nov. 1942
Gibraltar (G.B.)
SPAIN
Madrid
PORTUGAL
Lisbon
ATLANTIC OCEAN
IRELAND
Dublin
GREAT BRITAIN
London
Normandy
June 1944
Battle of the Bulge
Dec. 1944–Jan. 1945
NETH.
BELG.
Hamburg
Cologne
Apr. 1945
Munich
Paris
Liberated, Aug. 1944
Rhine R.
Elbe R.
Po R.
Rhône R.
SWITZ.
FRANCE
Vichy
VICHY FRANCE
Aug. 1944
Marseilles
NORTH SEA
BALTIC SEA

600 miles
600 kilometers
0   300
0   300   600

The B-17 "Flying Fortress" was a workhorse for the Army Air Corps. This bomber had just helped to destroy a German aircraft plant in East Prussia. National Archives.

second front. Marshal Stalin was not mollified by the Allied invasion of Italy in the summer of 1943. Italy surrendered in September to American and British officers; Russian officials were not invited to participate. Stalin grumbled that the arrangement smacked of a separate peace, and he suspected that the Anglo-American policy of accepting nothing less than unconditional surrender from the Axis had been violated.

With the alliance badly strained, Roosevelt sought reconciliation through personal diplomacy. The three Allied leaders met in Teheran, Iran, in December 1943. Stalin dismissed Churchill's repetitious justifications for further delaying the second front. Roosevelt had had enough, too; he also rejected Churchill's proposal for another peripheral attack, this time through the Balkans to Vienna. The three finally agreed to launch Operation Overlord—the cross-Channel invasion of France—in early 1944. And Russia promised to aid the Allies against Japan once Germany was defeated.

The second front opened in the dark morning hours of June 6, 1944—D-Day. In the largest am-

phibious landing in history, 200,000 Allied troops under the command of General Eisenhower scrambled ashore in Normandy, France. Thousands of ships ferried the men within a hundred yards of the sandy beaches. Landing craft and soldiers became entangled in sharp obstacles; they triggered mines and were pinned down by fire from cliffside pillboxes. Meanwhile, airborne troops dropped behind German lines. Although heavy aerial and naval bombardment and the clandestine work of underground saboteurs had softened the German defenses, the fighting was ferocious. One soldier described feeling like a "pigeon at a trap shoot."

D-Day

After digging in at now-famous places like Utah and Omaha beaches, reinforced Allied forces broke through disorderly German lines and gradually pushed inland, reaching Paris in August. The same month another force invaded southern France and threw the stunned Germans back. Allied troops soon spread across the countryside, liberating France and Belgium and entering Germany itself in September. In December, German armored divisions counterattacked in Belgium's Ardennes Forest, hoping to push on to Antwerp to halt the flow of Allied supplies through that Belgian port. After weeks of heavy fighting in what has come to be called the Battle of the Bulge—because of a noticeable bulge in the Allied line—the Allies pushed the enemy back once again. Meanwhile, battle-hardened Russian troops marched through Poland and cut a path to Berlin, the German capital. American forces crossed the Rhine in March 1945 and captured the heavily industrial Ruhr valley. Several units peeled off to enter Austria and Czechoslovakia, where they met up with Russian soldiers. As the Americans marched east, a new president took office in Washington: Franklin D. Roosevelt died on April 12, and Harry S Truman became commander-in-chief. Eighteen days later, in bomb-ravaged Berlin, defended largely by teenage boys and old men, Adolf Hitler killed himself. On May 8 Germany surrendered.

WINNING THE SECOND WORLD WAR IN THE PACIFIC

Allied strategists had devised a "Europe first" formula: knock out Germany and then concentrate on an isolated Japan. Nevertheless, the Pacific theater claimed headlines throughout the war, for the American people regarded Japan as the United States's chief enemy. The Japanese—called "monkeys" and "bastards" by Admiral William Halsey—had to be repaid for Pearl Harbor and later American losses. By mid-1942 Japan had seized the Philippines, Guam, Wake, Hong Kong, Singapore, Malaya, and the Netherlands East Indies. In the Philippines in 1942, Japanese soldiers forced American and Filipino prisoners weakened by insufficient rations to walk sixty-five miles, clubbing, shooting, or starving to death about 10,000 of

On June 6, 1944, an Allied invasion force opened the second front against Germany with an amphibious landing at Normandy Beach, France. Led by the United States, the D-Day invasion was met with ferocious resistance by the enemy.   UPI/Bettmann Archives.

them. The so-called Bataan Death March intensi-fied American hatred of the Japanese.

In April 1942, Americans began to hit back, initially by bombing Tokyo. In May, in the mo-mentous Battle of the Coral Sea, carrier-based

Battle of Midway

——

U.S. planes halted a Japanese advance toward Australia (see map). The next month Ameri-can forces defeated the Japa-nese at Midway, sinking four of the enemy's valuable aircraft carriers. Thanks to the success of Operation MAGIC—the work of American experts who deciphered the secret code used by the Japanese to transmit messages— American naval officers knew ahead of time the approximate date and direction of the Japanese as-sault. The Battle of Midway was a turning point in the Pacific war, breaking the Japanese momen-tum and relieving the threat to Hawaii. Thereafter

Japan was never able to match American man-power, sea power, air power, or economic power. Still, the war in Asia was contested until the very end, even after victory in Europe. "There are no breathers in this schedule," exclaimed General H. H. Arnold in the football jargon of the day. "You take on Notre Dame every time you play!"

American strategy was to "island-hop" toward Japan itself, skipping the most strongly fortified points whenever possible and taking the weaker ones. In an effort to strand the Japanese armies on their island outposts and to cut off raw materials from the home islands, Americans also set out to sink the Japanese merchant marine. The first American offensive—at Guadalcanal in the Solo-mon Islands in mid-1942—gave troops their first taste of jungle warfare: thick vegetation, mosqui-toes, scorpions, tropical heat, and rotting gear. From the Solomons the U.S. military pushed re-

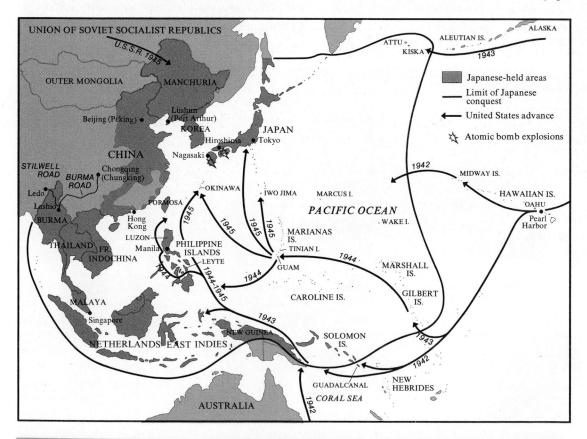

The Pacific War *U.S. strategy was to "island-hop" from Hawaii in 1942 to Iwo Jima and Okinawa in 1945. Naval battles were also decisive, notably the Battles of the Coral Sea and Midway in 1942. The war ended with Japan's surrender on V-J Day (August 15).* Source: From Paterson et al., *American Foreign Policy: A History*, vol. 2, 3rd ed. rev., copyright 1991, page 494. Reprinted by permission of D.C. Heath.

How *do historians know*

whether photographs tell the truth? On February 23, 1945, U.S. Marines planted the American flag atop Mount Suribachi on the island of Iwo Jima. This was trumpeted as the first American flag to fly over conquered Japanese territory. The Associated Press's Joe Rosenthal's famous photo (left) not only won a Pulitzer prize but also inspired the building of the Marine Corps monument in Arlington, Virginia. The truth is that three hours earlier, before Mount Suribachi had been secured, another group of marines had climbed to the summit and raised a smaller flag atop a fifteen-foot section of drainage pipe. Fearing that this historical flag might be stolen by other marines, the commander had ordered a replacement flag. The right-hand photograph shows the first flag coming down and the famous replacement going up.   Photos: National Archives.

lentlessly on, colliding with the entrenched enemy in the Gilberts, Marshalls, and Marianas in 1943 and 1944. In June 1944 the navy smashed Japanese forces in the Battle of the Philippine Sea. In October, General Douglas MacArthur landed at Leyte to reclaim the Philippines for the United States.

Despite these victories, tough fighting lay ahead in the Pacific. In February 1945 both sides took heavy losses at Iwo Jima, an island less than 5 miles long located 700 miles south of Tokyo. The Japanese put radar stations there to warn of American bombers headed to Japan, and fighter planes were ready to shoot down B-29s. Also stationed on the island were 21,000

Battles of Iwo Jima and Okinawa

———

troops living in pillboxes and miles of caves, trenches, and connecting tunnels. The American objective was Mount Suribachi, the highest point and most heavily fortified spot on Iwo Jima. American casualties were heavy from the outset, and the mountain had to be taken yard by yard. Victory finally came after twenty days of fighting, but it had been a bitter battle: 24,891 American casualties, including 6,821 killed. A month later, American troops landed on the island of Okinawa, 350 miles from Japan. Fighting raged on for two months; death was everywhere. Almost the entire Japanese garrison of 100,000 was killed, and there were 80,000 Okinawan civilian casualties. The American military lost 7,374 men killed and 31,807 wounded. At sea, the supporting fleet reported al-

This scorched watch, found in the rubble at Hiroshima, stopped at the time of the blast at 8:16. The shock waves and fires caused by the atomic bomb leveled great expanses of the city. Radiation released by the bomb caused lingering deaths for thousands who survived the explosion. Watch: Hiroshima: National Archives; John Launois/Black Star.

most 5,000 seamen killed or missing; most were the victims of *kamikaze* (suicide) attacks, in which Japanese pilots flew their planes directly into American ships.

Still, Japanese leaders refused to admit defeat. Hoping to avoid a humiliating unconditional surrender (and to preserve the emperor's sovereignty), they hung on even while American bombers leveled their cities. In one staggering attack on Tokyo on May 23, 1945, American planes dropped napalm-filled bombs that engulfed the city in a firestorm, killing 83,000 people. Observers described the ghastly scene as a mass burning.

Impatient for victory, American leaders began to plan a fall invasion of the Japanese islands, an expedition that was sure to incur high casualties.

The Atomic Bomb

But the successful development of an atomic bomb by American scientists provided another route to victory. The secret atomic program, known as the Manhattan Project, began in August 1942 and cost $2 billion. The first bomb was exploded in the desert near Alamogordo, New Mexico, on July 16, 1945. Only three weeks later, on August 6, the Japanese city of Hiroshima was destroyed by a bomb dropped from an American B-29 called the *Enola Gay*. A flash of dazzling light shot across the sky; then a huge purplish mushroom cloud boiled 40,000 feet into the atmosphere. Dense smoke, swirling fires, and suffocating dust soon engulfed the ground for miles. Much of the city was leveled almost instantly. Approximately 130,000 people were killed; tens of thousands more suffered severe burns and nuclear poisoning. As Hiroshima suffered its unique nightmare, Washington, D.C., celebrated its military and scientific triumph. "This is the greatest thing in history," exclaimed President Truman on hearing of the successful mission.

American planes continued their devastating conventional bombing and also scattered leaflets over other Japanese cities, warning that they, too, would face atomic terror unless the Japanese empire surrendered. On August 9 another atomic attack flattened Nagasaki, killing at least 60,000 people. The next day a sobered President Truman suspended further atomic bombing of Japan; he had belated qualms about killing "all those kids." Four days later the Japanese, who had been sending out peace feelers since June, surrendered. The victors promised that the Japanese emperor could remain as the nation's titular head. Formal surrender ceremonies were held September 2 aboard the battleship *Missouri*. The Second World War was over.

Most Americans agreed with President Truman that the atomic bombing of two Japanese cities had been necessary to end the war as quickly as possible and to save American lives. Use of the bomb to achieve victory had, in fact, been the primary goal of the Manhattan Project. At the highest government levels and among atomic scientists, alternatives had been discussed: detonate the bomb on an unpopulated Pacific island, with international observers as witnesses; blockade and bomb Japan conventionally; follow up Tokyo's peace feelers; encourage a Russian declaration of war on Japan. But Truman's aides had rejected these options because they would take too long and would not convince the tenacious Japanese that they had been beaten. Then, too, memories of Pearl Harbor played a part. "When you have to deal with a beast, you have to treat him as a beast," Truman said.

Why the Atomic Bomb Was Used

Diplomatic considerations also influenced the decision to use the bomb. U.S. leaders wanted to employ the real and psychological power the bomb would bestow on the United States. It might serve as a deterrent against aggression; it might intimidate Russia into making concessions in Eastern Europe; it might end the war in the Pacific before the Soviet Union could claim a role in the postwar management of Asia. "If it explodes, as I think it will," Truman remarked, "I'll certainly have a hammer on those boys [the Soviets]."

ECONOMIC EFFECTS OF THE WAR AT HOME

The Second World War was won at great cost, not only abroad but also on the American home front. While the guns boomed in Europe and Asia, the war was changing American lives and institutions. One month after Pearl Harbor, President Roosevelt established the War Production Board (WPB) and assigned to it the task of converting the economy from civilian to military production. Factories that had manufactured silk ribbons began to turn out silk parachutes; automobile companies switched to the production of tanks and airplanes; adding-machine companies started manufacturing automatic pistols. Factories had to be expanded and new ones built.

The WPB was so successful that the production of durable goods more than tripled. Since this was the world's first massive air war, the need for fighter planes and bombers was crucial. And America's factories responded: the manufacture of military aircraft, which had totaled 6,000 in 1940, jumped to over 47,000 in 1942 and 85,000 in 1943.

The wartime emergency also spurred the establishment of totally new industries, most notably synthetic rubber. The Japanese, in their conquest of the South Pacific following Pearl Harbor, had captured 90 percent of the world's supply of crude rubber. The American government resorted to conservation measures, including a national speed limit and gasoline rationing to save wear on tires, but neither conservation nor recycling could meet wartime needs. So, with an investment of $700 million, the government underwrote the creation of a synthetic-rubber industry. By war's end the nation that had been the world's largest importer of rubber had become the world's largest exporter of rubber—all of it synthetic.

New industries, however, brought with them new and hazardous pollutants. The production of

These are two views of a West Virginia valley near Morgantown. The first photograph was taken in 1941, the second in late 1942 when the Du Pont chemical company put into operation its massive new ordnance plant.   Courtesy, E.I. du Pont de Nemours and Company.

synthetic rubber, whether from petroleum or grain alcohol, spewed forth dangerous gases like sulfur dioxide and carbon monoxide. War industries fouled the water with both solid and petrochemical wastes. The dumping of radioactive waste began at Hanford, Washington, where plutonium was produced for the atomic bomb. Sulfur vapors from the Kaiser steel plant in Fontana, California, burned the leaves off trees and killed the grapefruit crop. And air pollution—smog—was first detected

in Los Angeles in 1943, the result of that city's rapid wartime industrialization combined with people's dependence on the automobile. Although these were ominous signs, few people worried during the war, or later, about human-made threats to America's seemingly endless supplies of fresh air, water, and soil.

This was a time to win the war and, in order to gain the cooperation of business, the WPB and other government agencies met business more

**Government
Incentives
to Business**

than halfway. The government guaranteed profits in the form of cost-plus-fixed-fee contracts, generous tax writeoffs, and exemptions from antitrust prosecution. It also allowed prime contractors to distribute subcontracts as they saw fit, including those involving scarce war-related materials. Such concessions made sense for a nation that wanted vast quantities of war goods manufactured in the shortest possible time.

From mid-1940 through September 1944 the government awarded contracts totaling $175 billion, no less than two-thirds of which went to the top one hundred corporations. General Motors alone received 8 percent of the total; big awards also went to other automobile companies and to aircraft, steel, electrical, and chemical companies. Almost all these industries had been dominated by big corporations at the beginning of the war; the billions of dollars they received in government contracts only accentuated their dominance. Although the expression "military-industrial complex" had not yet been coined—President Dwight Eisenhower would do so in 1961 (see Chapter 28)—the web of military-business interdependence had begun to be woven.

In science and higher education, too, the big got bigger as federal contracts mobilized science and technology for the war effort. The National Defense Research Committee and the Office of Scientific Research and Development—government agencies established by President Roosevelt in 1940 and 1941—administered these contracts. Massachusetts Institute of Technology received $117 million to develop radar and do other research. California Institute of Technology was in second place, with contracts totaling $83 million, followed by Harvard, Columbia, the University of California, Johns Hopkins, and the University of Chicago. Some wartime contracts accelerated medical progress. Indeed, because of the development of sulfa drugs, which greatly reduced deaths from infected war wounds, the survival rate among injured soldiers was 90 percent, compared with 10 percent in the First World War.

Most federal contracts, however, were for weapons. The most spectacular result of government contracts with universities was the atomic bomb. The Manhattan Project, run by the army, financed research at the University of Chicago, which in 1942 was the site of the world's first sus-

**Manhattan
Project**

tained nuclear chain reaction. Testing of the atomic bomb was run by the University of California at Berkeley, which under contract operated the Los Alamos Scientific Laboratory in New Mexico. American universities became valued participants in the military-industrial complex.

Labor also grew bigger during the war. Membership in unions ballooned from 8.5 million in 1940 to 14.75 million in 1945. Less than a week after Pearl Harbor, a White House labor-management conference agreed to a no-strike–no-lockout pledge to guarantee uninterrupted war production. "When the nation is attacked," declared John L. Lewis, the gruff president of the United Mine Workers, "every American must rally to its defense. All other considerations become insignificant." To minimize labor-management conflict, President Roosevelt created the National War Labor Board (NWLB), sometimes referred to as the Supreme Court for labor disputes. Unions were permitted to enroll as many new members as possible, but workers were not required to join a union. Thus the NWLB forged a temporary compromise between the unions' demand for a closed shop, in which only union members could be hired, and management's interest in open shops.

But when the NWLB attempted in 1943 to limit wage increases to cost-of-living pay increases, workers responded with wildcat strikes and other work stoppages that tripled the amount of lost production time over that of the previous year. "Strikes are spreading at an alarming rate," warned a member of the NWLB, "and unless they are checked immediately, the 'no strike-no lockout' agreement will become meaningless." The worst labor disruptions of 1943 occurred in the coal fields, where 450,000 soft-coal miners and 80,000 anthracite miners struck. "When the mine workers' children cry for bread, they cannot be satisfied [with words]," declared John L. Lewis, who seemed to have forgotten his earlier patriotic commitment to sacrifice. Public hostility grew toward organized labor in general and toward Lewis in particular.

To discourage further work stoppages, Congress passed the War Labor Disputes (Smith-Connally) Act in June 1943. The act conferred on the president the authority to seize and operate any strike-bound plant deemed necessary to the

**Wartime Labor
Strikes**

The Wartime Economic Boom, 1940–1945

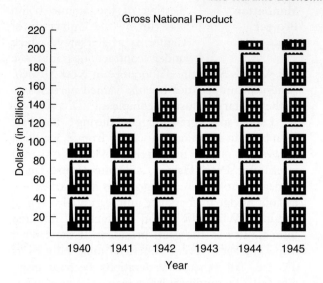

Gross National Product

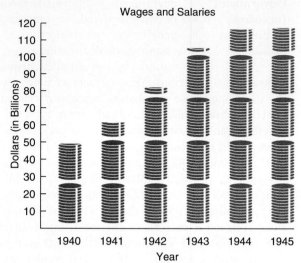

Wages and Salaries

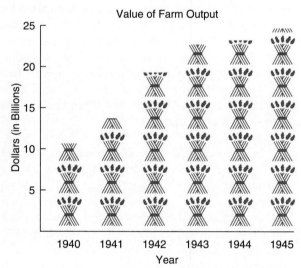

Value of Farm Output

The Wartime Economic Boom, 1940–1945
War production finally ended the Great Depression. This chart shows the wartime increases in key economic indicators: gross national product; wages and salaries; farm prices and value of farm output. At the same time, women's employment soared, as did federal military and civilian employment. So, too, did the national debt for financing the war.

national security, and it established a mandatory thirty-day cooling-off period before any new strike could be called. The Smith-Connally Act also gave the NWLB the legal authority to settle labor disputes for the duration of the war. Over the course of the war the NWLB handled close to eighteen thousand disputes, reducing time lost due to strikes to one-third the peacetime level.

Although the war demanded sacrifices from Americans, it also rewarded them with new highs in personal income (see figure). Savings deposits jumped from $32.4 billion in 1942 to $51.4 billion in 1945. Corporations doubled their net profits between 1939 and 1943, and employees' wages and salaries rose more than 135 percent from 1940 to

1945. The government did not tax this extra income as heavily as it might have. Instead it resorted to deficit financing and borrowed approximately 60 percent of the cost of waging the war, about half of it in the form of war bonds sold to patriotic citizens. The national debt skyrocketed from $49 billion in 1941 to $259 billion in 1945.

Agriculture also made an impressive contribution to the war effort, through hard work and the introduction of labor-saving machinery to replace

Wartime Changes in Agriculture

men and women who had gone to the front or migrated to war-production centers. Before the war, farming had been in the midst of a transition from the

The Wartime Economic Boom, 1940–1945

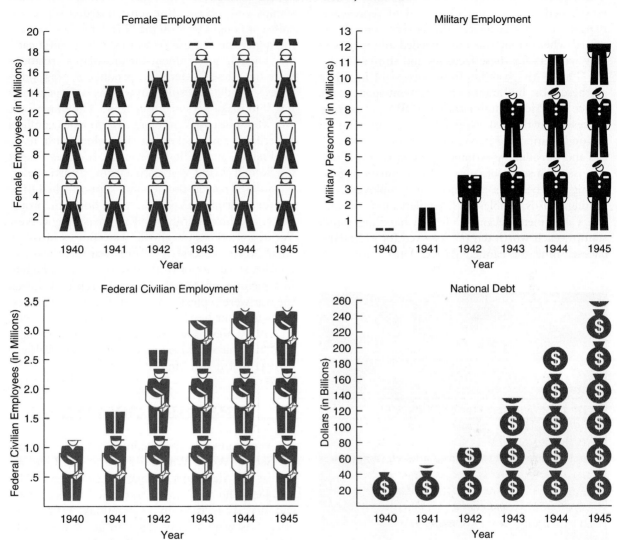

family-owned and -operated farm to the large-scale, mechanized agribusiness dominated by banks, insurance companies, and farm co-ops. The Second World War accelerated the trend, for wealthy financial institutions were better able than family farmers to pay for expensive new machinery. From 1940 to 1945 the value of American agricultural machinery rose from $3.1 billion to $6.5 billion, and average acreage per farm jumped from 175 to 195. The use of new machines and fertilizers boosted farm output per labor-hour by 25 percent. At the same time, the farm population fell from 30.5 million to 24.4 million. Like business and labor, agriculture was becoming more consolidated as it contributed to the war effort.

At the apex of the burgeoning national economy stood the federal government, whose size and importance, like that of business and labor, was mushrooming: from 1940 to 1945 the federal bureaucracy expanded from 1.1 million workers to 3.4 million. The executive branch—which included the Office of the Commander-in-Chief and bore responsibility for directing the war effort—grew most dramatically. Besides raising the armed forces, mobilizing industrial production, pacifying labor and management, and controlling inflation, the executive branch also had to manage the labor supply.

Growth in the Federal Government

Through the War Manpower Commission (WMC), established in 1942 and composed of representatives of various agencies, the government determined where labor was most needed and recruited new workers for these factories and shipyards.

The WMC was far from successful in filling all these jobs, but another government agency, the Office of Price Administration (OPA), was very successful at the task assigned to it: combating inflation by imposing maximum prices on commodities and introducing rationing programs. The OPA also issued a series of rules and proclamations governing the behavior of landlords, employers, rationing boards, wholesalers, retailers, and consumers. Consumers became skilled at handling ration stamps, each worth ten points—red for meats and cheese, blue for canned goods. Most Americans

The federal government used a variety of methods to exhort Americans to fulfill their patriotic obligation. This recruiting poster urged women to secure America's future by entering the armed forces.   National Archives.

abided by the rules, and many shared their ration stamps with others. But some hoarded sugar and coffee or bought beef on the "black market," meaning under the counter or from the trunk of a car.

Though government-business-labor relations were sometimes bitter, and production was sometimes slowed as a result, Americans were generally ready to make personal sacrifices. They knew the war would be costly and long. In previous conflicts Americans had flocked to the colors with flags, wild rallies, and militaristic songs, but they fought the Second World War with a grim, realistic determination. To elicit the people's support, the Office of War Information took charge of domestic propaganda and hired Hollywood filmmakers and New York copywriters to sell the war. But as historian Allan Nevins observed, "In this war there was . . . no such straw fire of frothy enthusiasm." The motion pictures produced and books released during the war were typically light, fluffy, sentimental escapes from the harsh realities of life. In 1861, 1898, and 1917, Nevins wrote, Americans had thought that "the war would be easy. They knew full well in 1941 that it wouldn't."

THE MILITARY LIFE

To American servicepeople in Asia and in Europe, the Second World War was a grimy job. Like cartoonist Bill Mauldin's popular GI characters Willy and Joe, who were more interested in tasty food and dry socks than in abstractions, millions of other GIs were simply eager to get it over with. The largest of the services was the army, in which a total of 11.3 million Americans served; 4.2 million were on active duty in the navy, and 670,000 in the Marine Corps. American troops served overseas for an average of sixteen months. Some never returned: total deaths exceeded 405,000. In terms of lost American lives, the cost of the war was second only to that of the Civil War.

Large numbers of women also served in America's armed forces during the war. The WACs (Women's Army Corps) enlisted 140,000 women, while 100,000 served in the navy's WAVES (Women Accepted for Volunteer Emergency Service) and 39,000 in the Marine Corps and Coast Guard. Another 75,000 women served in the U.S. Army and Navy's Nursing Corps, where they saw

Women in the Armed Forces

duty during the invasions of North Africa, Italy, and France. Women also served as pilots in the WASP (Women Air Service Pilots), where they taught basic flying, towed aerial targets for gunnery practice, and served as test pilots. They flew every kind of military aircraft, including the latest fighters, which they ferried across the country. WASP flying duty was often hazardous, and thirty-eight women lost their lives.

Military service demanded enormous personal adjustments. Soldiers and sailors who had never been more than a few miles from home became homesick; GIs joked, somewhat bitterly, about having found a home in the army. But loneliness was inconsequential compared with the intense fear that soldiers admitted to feeling in battle. Combat veterans told a group of psychologists that a man who burst out weeping was "not regarded as a coward unless he made no apparent effort to stick to his job."

Some Americans became looters. One veteran explained that when soldiers took a town, they "wanted something to drink. Then they wanted a woman. And then they wanted to go out and see what they could loot." In other ways, too, America's combat veterans were like those in other countries and in other wars. Although the American Psychiatric Association did not identify the illness known as post-traumatic stress disorder until 1980, it is clear in retrospect that many of America's Second World War veterans suffered from it after the war. The symptoms included nightmares and flashbacks to the battlefield, depression and anger, and widespread alcoholism.

While combat's cruelties robbed many GIs of their innocence, military service itself broadened the horizons of millions of men and women. "Take these kids from the hills," noted one GI, "the service opened their eyes some. . . . And some of these guys from Chicago, why they'd never been outside of Chicago. They talked about fellows 'from the sticks' and they'd never been out in the 'sticks'—they'd never even known what the 'sticks' were."

Broadening of GIs' Horizons

Among the millions of people who had left their homes and neighborhoods were men and women who had experienced homosexual attraction in peacetime. Freed of their familial environments and serving in sex-segregated units, many acted on their feelings. "When I first got

into the navy—in the recreation hall, for instance," recalled a chief petty officer, "there'd be eye contact. . . . All of a sudden you had a vast network of friends." The military court-martialed homosexuals, but gay relationships usually went unnoticed by the heterosexual world. For lesbians in the armed forces, the military environment offered friendships and a positive identity. "For many gay Americans," the historian John D'Emilio has written, "World War II created something of a nationwide coming out situation." Gay people took different directions after the war: some of them went back in the closet; others moved to cities in order to lay the foundations for a gay subculture.

Wartime service not only broadened horizons but also fostered soldiers' ambitions. A soldier from the Midwest, who found himself "living among fellows from all over the country," recalled that "I picked up a lot of ideas from them, not only [about] what the United States was really like—I mean the whole country—but about how to live my own life and to get more out of it. . . . I came out a lot more ambitious than I was before I went in." Finally, many GIs returned to civilian life with new skills they had learned in the military's technical schools. Some became fluent in foreign languages; others became medical technicians, electronics experts, and aircraft mechanics. Still others took advantage of the educational benefits provided by the GI Bill of Rights (1944) to study for a college degree (see Chapter 30).

Still, after two or three years abroad, men and women in the service returned to the United States not knowing what to expect from civilian life. Earlier in the war, troops had been given orientation lectures and booklets introducing them to the historical backgrounds and social customs of the foreign nations where they would serve. Now they were coming home, "to a surprising degree," as one observer wrote, "foreigners in their own land."

Most disturbing to many GIs was the feeling that life at home had passed them by. They were much older in experience and exposure to brutality; many came back to the United States convinced that they had sacrificed their youth. And they found that home had changed as well. "Our friends are gone," one GI lamented. "The family and the town naturally had to go on even if we weren't there, and somehow it seems things have sort of closed in and filled that space we used to occupy."

THE INTERNMENT OF JAPANESE-AMERICANS

After America entered the war, U.S. leaders had to consider whether enemy agents were operating within the nation's borders and threatening the war effort. It was clear that not all Americans were enthusiastic supporters of the nation's involvement. After Pearl Harbor, several thousand "enemy aliens" were arrested and taken into custody, some of them Nazi agents who had accumulated firearms, shortwave radios, and codes in the course of their work. Other people had conscientious objections to the war, particularly Quakers, Mennonites, and members of the Church of the Brethren. During the Second World War conscientious objectors (COs) had to have a religious (as opposed to moral or ethical) reason for refusing military service. About 25,000 qualified COs accepted noncombat service, most as medical corpsmen. An additional 12,000 were sent to civilian public service camps, where they worked at forestry or conservation or as orderlies in public health hospitals. Approximately 5,500, three-fourths of whom were Jehovah's Witnesses, refused to participate in any way; they were imprisoned.

The one enormous exception to the nation's generally creditable wartime civil liberties record was the internment in "relocation centers" of, ultimately, 120,000 Japanese-Americans. Of these people, 77,000 were Nisei, or native-born citizens of the United States. Their imprisonment was based not on suspicion or evidence of treason; their crime was solely their ethnic origin—the fact that they were of Japanese descent. As General John L. DeWitt, chief of the Western Defense Command, expressed it:

"An Enemy Race"

> The Japanese race is an enemy race and while many second and third generation Japanese born on United States soil, possessed of United States citizenship, have become "Americanized," the racial strains are undiluted. . . . It, therefore, follows that along the vital Pacific Coast over 112,000 potential enemies, of Japanese extraction, are at large today.

With strained illogic he declared: "The very fact that no sabotage [by Japanese-Americans] has taken place to date is a disturbing and confirming indica-

tion that such action will be taken." DeWitt was not alone in his paranoia.

Charges of criminal behavior were never brought against any Japanese-Americans; none was ever indicted or tried for espionage, treason, or sedition. Their alleged crime, disloyalty to the United States, was not even against the law. Nevertheless in 1942, all the 112,000 Japanese-Americans living in California, Oregon, and the state of Washington were rounded up and imprisoned. "It was really cruel and harsh," recalled Joseph Y. Kurihara, a citizen and a veteran of the First World War. "To pack and evacuate in forty-eight hours was an impossibility. Seeing mothers completely bewildered with children crying from want and peddlers taking advantage and offering prices next to robbery made me feel like murdering those responsible." After the war, Kurihara, along with 8,000 other Japanese-Americans, did the next best thing: he emigrated to Japan, a country he had never seen.

The internees were sent to flood-damaged lands at Relocation, Arkansas; to the intermountain terrain of Wyoming and the desert of western Arizona; and to other arid and desolate spots in the West. Although the names were evocative—Topaz, Utah; Rivers, Arizona; Heart Mountain, Wyoming; Tule Lake and Manzanar, California—the camps themselves were bleak and demoralizing. Behind barbed wire stood tar-papered wooden barracks where entire families lived in a single room furnished only with cots, blankets, and a bare light bulb. Toilets and dining and bathing facilities were communal; privacy was almost nonexistent. Japanese-Americans were forced to sell property valued at $500 million, and they lost their positions in the truck-garden, floral, and fishing industries. Indeed, their economic competitors were among the most vocal proponents of their relocation.

Life in the Internment Camps

The Supreme Court upheld the government's policy of internment. In wartime, the Court said in the *Hirabayashi* ruling (1943), "residents having ethnic affiliations with an invading enemy may be a greater source of danger than those of different ancestry." In the *Korematsu* case (1944), the Court, with three justices dissenting, approved the removal of the Nisei from the West Coast. One dissenter, Justice Frank Murphy, denounced the decision as the "legalization of racism," and Justice

Robert Jackson warned that the precedent established by the cases "lies about like a loaded weapon ready for the hand of any authority that can bring forward a plausible claim of an urgent need."

In 1983, forty-one years after he had been sent to a government camp, Fred Korematsu had the satisfaction of hearing a federal judge rule that he—and by implication all detainees—had been the victim of "unsubstantiated facts, distortions and misrepresentations of at least one military commander whose views were affected by racism." A year earlier, the government's special Commission on Wartime Relocation and Internment of Civilians had recommended compensating the victims of this policy. Because of "race prejudice, war hysteria and a failure of political leadership," the commission concluded, the government had committed "a grave injustice" to 120,000 people. Finally, in 1988, Congress voted to award $20,000 each and a public apology to the surviving 60,000 Japanese-American internees.

JOBS AND RACISM ON THE HOME FRONT

At peak enrollment the army had over 700,000 African-American troops. An additional 187,000 black men and women enlisted in the navy, the Coast Guard, and the once all-white Marine Corps. In response to the March on Washington Movement of 1941 (see Chapter 25), the Selective Service System and the War Department agreed to draft black Americans in proportion to their presence in the population: about 10 percent.

Although they served in segregated units, African-Americans made real advances toward racial equality during these years. For the first time the

African-American Troops

War Department sanctioned the training of blacks as pilots. After instruction at Tuskegee Institute in Alabama, pilots saw heroic service in such all-black units as the Ninety-ninth Pursuit Squadron, winner of eighty Distinguished Flying Crosses. In 1940 Colonel Benjamin O. Davis was the first African-American to be promoted to brigadier general. Wherever black people were offered opportunities to distinguish themselves, they proved that they could do the job. The performance of black marines in the Pacific theater

In February 1942 President Franklin D. Roosevelt ordered that all Japanese-Americans living on the West Coast be rounded up and placed in prison camps. These families were awaiting a train to take them to an assembly center in Merced, California; from there, they would be sent to relocation camps in remote inland areas.   National Archives.

was such that the corps commandant proclaimed: "Negro Marines are no longer on trial. They are Marines, period."

These accomplishments, however, were undercut by serious failures in race relations. Race riots instigated by whites broke out on military bases, and white civilians assaulted black soldiers and sailors throughout the South. In North Carolina a white bus driver who murdered a black soldier in full view of the passengers was found not guilty. When the War Department issued an order in mid-1944 forbidding racial segregation in military recreation and transportation, the *Montgomery Advertiser* replied, "Army orders, even armies, even bayonets, cannot force impossible and unnatural social relations upon us."

Experiences such as these caused black soldiers and sailors to wonder what, in fact, they were fighting for. They rankled at the remark of the governor of Tennessee, when blacks urged him to appoint African-Americans to local draft boards:

A leader of the Tuskegee airmen, Benjamin O. Davis, Jr., was the fourth African-American to be graduated from West Point. During the war, Colonel Davis commanded the 332nd Fighter Group, which destroyed over two hundred enemy planes in southern Europe. National Archives.

"This is a white man's country. . . . The Negro had nothing to do with the settling of America." They noted that the Red Cross separated blood according to the race of the donor, as if there were some difference. Many considered black participation in the First World War a mistake, for it had resulted not in social advances but in race riots and lynchings. Some even argued that the Second World War was a white man's war, and that American racism was little different from German racism.

But there were persuasive reasons for African-Americans to participate in the war effort. Perhaps, as the NAACP believed, this was an opportunity "to persuade, embarrass, compel and shame our government and our nation . . . into a more enlightened attitude toward a tenth of its people." Proclaiming that in the Second World War they were waging a "Double V" campaign (for victory at home and abroad), blacks were more militant than before and readier than ever to protest. Membership in civil rights organizations soared. The NAACP, 50,000 strong in 1940, had 450,000

members by 1946. In 1942 civil rights activists founded the Congress of Racial Equality (CORE), which stressed "nonviolent direct action" and staged sit-ins to desegregate restaurants and movies in northern cities.

The war also created opportunities in industry. Roosevelt's Executive Order 8802, issued in 1941 in response to the March on Washington Movement, required employers in defense industries to make jobs available "without discrimination because of race, creed, color or national origin."

African-American War Workers

To secure defense jobs, 1.2 million black Americans migrated from the South to the industrial cities of the North and West in the 1940s. Almost three-fourths settled in the urban-industrial states of California, Illinois, Michigan, New York, Ohio, and Pennsylvania. More than half a million became active members of CIO unions like the United Auto Workers, the United Steel Workers, and the United Rubber Workers. African-American voters in northern cities were beginning to constitute a vital swing vote, not only in local and state elections but also in presidential contests.

But the benefits of urban life came with a high price tag. The migrants had to make enormous emotional and cultural adjustments, and white hostility and ignorance made their task difficult. Southern whites who had migrated north brought with them the racial prejudices of the Deep South. Blacks competed with these whites for housing, jobs, and seats on buses; they rubbed elbows with them in city schools and parks and at the beaches. Equally hostile were the attitudes of northern whites, more than half of whom believed in 1942 that blacks should be segregated in separate schools and neighborhoods; that black people were receiving all the opportunities they deserved; and that if blacks suffered economically, politically, or socially, it was their own fault. Such attitudes encouraged racial violence.

Many people, black and white, feared that the summer of 1943 would be like 1919, another Red Summer. Indeed, in 1943 almost 250 racial conflicts exploded in forty-seven cities. Outright racial warfare bloodied the streets of Detroit in June. At the end of thirty hours of rioting, twenty-five blacks and nine whites lay dead. White mobs, un-

Race Riots of 1943

The bloodiest race riot of 1943 struck Detroit, where thirty-four people—twenty-five blacks and nine whites— were killed. At the peak of the rioting a white mob overturned an African-American's car, showering trolley passengers with burning gasoline.   UPI/Bettmann Archives.

deterred by police, had roamed the city attacking blacks and overturning cars. Blacks had hurled rocks at police and hauled white passengers off streetcars. A city councilman suggested that the city build a bigger ghetto and pen blacks up in it. Surveying the damage, an elderly black woman said, "There ain't no North any more. Everything now is South."

The federal government did practically nothing to prevent further racial violence. From President Roosevelt on down, most federal officials put the war first, domestic reform second. Unquestionably many government leaders were racists themselves; Secretary of War Henry L. Stimson claimed that the riots were "the deliberate effort . . . on the part of certain radical leaders of the colored race to use the war for obtaining . . . racial equality and interracial marriages." But this time government neglect could not discourage African- Americans and their century-old civil rights movement. By war's end they were ready— politically, economically, and emotionally—to

wage a struggle for voting rights and for equal access to public accommodations and institutions.

Racial violence was not directed exclusively against blacks. To some whites, people of Mexican origin were as undesirable as those whose roots were African. In 1942, American farms and war industries needed workers, and the United States and Mexico had agreed to the *bracero* program, whereby Mexicans were admitted to the United States on short-term work contracts. Although the newcomers suffered racial discrimination and segregation, they seized the economic opportunities that had thus become available. In Los Angeles, 17,000 people of Mexican descent found shipyard jobs where before the war none had been available to them. But ethnic and racial animosities intensified during the war.

In 1943 Los Angeles witnessed the "zoot-suit riot," in which whites, most of them sailors and soldiers, wantonly attacked Mexican-Americans. Mexican-American street gangs (*pachucos*) had adopted ducktail haircuts and "zoot suits": long coats ("drapes") with wide padded shoulders, pegged pants, wide-brimmed hats, and long watch chains. White racist anger at the presumed arrogance of the zoot-suiters boiled over in June, and for four days mobs invaded Mexican-American neighborhoods. According to one report: "Procedure was standard: grab a zooter. Take off his pants and frock coat and tear them up or burn them. Trim the '. . . ducktail' haircut that goes with the screwy costume." Not only did white policemen look the other way during these assaults, but the city of Los Angeles even passed an ordinance that made it a crime to wear a zoot suit within city limits. Although the war briefly provided economic opportunities for Mexican-Americans, these years were not the transformational experience that they were for African-Americans.

WOMEN WORKING: PARTICIPATION AND DISCRIMINATION ON THE HOME FRONT

For patriotic as well as economic reasons, over 6 million women entered the labor force during the war years. During the Great Depression, when millions of men were unemployed, public opinion had been hostile to the hiring of women, but the war brought about a rapid increase in employment. Just when men were going off to war, industry had to recruit millions of new workers to supply the rapidly expanding need for military equipment. Filling these new jobs were African-Americans, southern whites, teenagers, Mexicans and Mexican-Americans, and, above all, women.

Statistics, no matter how impressive, tell only part of the story. Attitudinal change was also important. Until early in the war, employers had insisted that women were not

Women in War Production

suited for industrial jobs: if women were allowed to work in factories, they would begin to wear overalls instead of dresses, their muscles would bulge, and they might even drink whiskey and swear like men. As labor shortages began to threaten the war effort, employers did an about-face. "Almost overnight," said Mary Anderson, head of the Women's Bureau of the Department of Labor, "women were reclassified by industrialists from a marginal to a basic

labor supply for munitions making." Women became lathe operators, riveters, lumberjacks ("lumberjills"), welders, crane operators, keel benders, tool makers, shell loaders, cowgirls, blast-furnace cleaners, locomotive greasers, police officers, taxi drivers, and football coaches.

During the war years, the number of working women increased by 57 percent. Two million women took clerical jobs; another 2.5 million worked in manufacturing. The significance of these figures lay not just in the numbers themselves but also in the kinds of women who were entering the work force. Economist Claudia Goldin has observed that labor force participation rates increased most for women over age 45, and that "married, rather than single women, were the primary means of bolstering the nation's labor force." Of the new women workers, 75 percent were married and 3.7 million were mothers. Before the war the average female wage earner had been young, single, and largely self-supporting; by 1945 more working women were married than single, and more were over age thirty-five than under.

New employment opportunities also increased women's geographic and occupational mobility. Especially noteworthy were the gains made by African-American women; over 400,000 quit work as domestic servants to enjoy the better working conditions, higher pay, and union benefits of industrial employment. Hundreds of thousands of other women, black and white, abandoned menial jobs in dime stores, restaurants, laundries, and hospitals for higher-status, higher-paying jobs. To take these jobs, they willingly uprooted themselves. Over 7 million moved from their original counties of residence to war-production areas, such as Willow Run, Michigan, site of a massive bomber plant, and southern California, home of both shipyards and aircraft factories. Indeed, many sought jobs in the rapidly expanding aircraft industry, whose female work force increased from 4,000 in December 1941 to 310,000 two years later.

As public opinion shifted to support women's war work, posters and billboards appeared urging women to "Do the Job HE Left Behind." Newspapers and magazines, radio and movies proclaimed Rosie the Riveter a war hero. But very few people asserted that women's war work should bring about a permanent shift in sex roles: this was merely a response to a national emergency. Once the victory was won, women should go back to nurturing their husbands and children, leaving their jobs to returning GIs. From "a humanitarian point of view," stated the president of the National Association of Manufacturers, "too many women should not stay in the labor force. The home is the basic American institution." Wartime surveys showed, however, that many of the women wanted to remain in their jobs—80 percent of New York's women workers felt that way, as did 75 percent in Detroit. "War jobs have uncovered unsuspected abilities in American women," explained one woman. "Why lose all these abilities because of a belief that 'a woman's place is in the home?' For some it is," she added, "for others not."

Although women's wages rose when they acquired better jobs, they still received lower pay than men. In 1945, women in manufacturing earned only 65 percent of what men were paid. An important reason for this inequality was the sex-segregated labor market. Although the wartime emergency caused some traditionally male jobs to be reclassified for women, most jobs were defined as either "women's work" or "men's work." Sociologist Ruth Milkman has written that the absence of a feminist movement in the 1940s was a major reason for the failure "to combat gender inequality in the workplace at that critical historical juncture." Even in factories, most women worked in all-female shops.

Discrimination Against Women

Working women, particularly working mothers, suffered in other ways as well. Even as mothers were being encouraged to work in the national defense, there was still opposition to their doing so. One form this campaign took was a series of exaggerated articles in mass-circulation magazines about the suffering of "eight-hour orphans" or "latchkey children," left alone or deposited in all-night movie theaters while their mothers worked eight-hour shifts in war plants. Childcare centers were in short supply in some war-boom areas; communal or neighborhood kitchens were almost nonexistent.

By and large, however, the home-front children of working women were not neglected or abused during the war. Families made their own arrangements, which often involved leaving children in the care of their grandmothers. Some mothers disapproved of public childcare as a form of welfare; others feared their children might contract

Childcare in Wartime

contagious diseases in childcare centers. Gradually, though, both the demand for and the supply of childcare facilities grew. In 1940 Congress passed the Lanham Act to provide federal aid to communities that had to absorb large war-related populations. Benefits included funds for childcare centers, hospitals, sewer systems, police and firefighting facilities, and recreation centers. In late 1943, fewer than 60,000 children were enrolled in Lanham Act childcare centers; six months later, the number had more than doubled to 130,000. Another government program, Extended School Services, offered care for children before and after school; at the program's peak in 1943, it was providing care for 60,000 preschoolers and 260,000 school-age children. Although working mothers and their children received less of such help than they needed, the Second World War was the only era in U.S. history when the federal government articulated and financed any sort of childcare policy.

Serious social problems affected the nation's youth during the war: there were increases in vene-

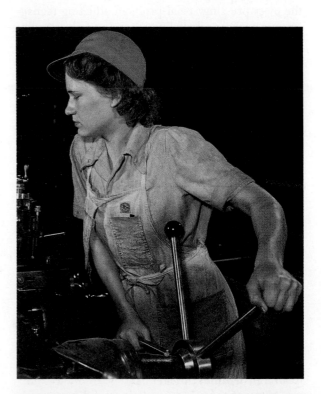

Women workers mastered numerous manufacturing skills during the war. Working for the Consolidated Aircraft Corporation in Fort Worth, Texas, in 1942, this lathe operator was machining parts for transport planes. Library of Congress.

real disease, teenage pregnancy, and juvenile delinquency—juvenile arrests jumped 20 percent nationwide in 1943. The increase was greater for girls than for boys; in San Diego, arrests increased 55 percent for boys and 355 percent for girls. Some of these girls became prostitutes: in 1943, arrests for that crime climbed 68 percent. Among boys the most common crime was theft, but vandalism and violence were also problems. And teenagers were dropping out of school in record numbers.

Perhaps because of such statistics, the massive contributions children and youth made to the war effort were often overlooked. Children contributed their own nickels and dimes to buy war stamps and bonds, and they pulled wagons from house to house collecting old newspapers and tin cans. The Boy Scouts collected 109 million pounds of rubber and 370 million pounds of scrap metal. More significant was that thousands of young people went to work during the war. In 1940, for example, 900,000 young people between the ages of fourteen and eighteen were employed. By the spring of 1944 their number had climbed to 3 million—one-third of their age group. Indeed, some observers felt that the most pressing social problem afflicting teenagers was not juvenile delinquency but failure to finish school. High-school enrollments hit new lows during the war, prompting a back-to-school drive in 1944.

While millions of women and youths were entering the work force, hundreds of thousands of women were also getting married. The number of

Increase in Marriage, Divorce, and Birth Rates

marriages rose from 73 per 1,000 unmarried women in 1939 to 93 in 1942. Some couples scrambled to get married so they could live together before the man was sent overseas; others doubtless married and had children to qualify for military deferments. But the rush to marry was also fueled by prosperity. A justice of the peace in Yuma, Arizona, explained that the marriage rate "began going up as soon as those boys were given employment in those plants at San Diego and Los Angeles and were taken off WPA." He was not exaggerating; 90 percent of the marriage licenses issued in Yuma went to aircraft workers.

Many of these hasty marriages did not survive long military separations, and divorces soared, too—from 25,000 in 1939, to 359,000 in 1943, and 485,000 in 1945. As might be expected, the birth rate also climbed: total births rose from about 2.4 million in 1939 to 3.1 million in 1943. Many of these births were "goodbye babies," conceived as a guarantee that the family would be perpetuated if the father died in battle overseas.

Ironically, women's efforts to hold their families together during the war posed problems for returning fathers. Women war workers had brought home the wages; they had taken over the budgeting of expenses and the writing of checks. In countless ways they had proved they could hold the reins in their husbands' absence. Many husbands returned home to find that the lives of their wives and children seemed complete without them.

What of the women who wanted to remain in the labor market? Many were forced, by employers or by their husbands, to quit. Others chose to leave their jobs for a year or two but then returned to work. And throughout the rest of the 1940s and 1950s, millions more who had never worked took jobs.

THE DECLINE OF LIBERALISM AND THE ELECTION OF 1944

Even before Pearl Harbor, political liberals had suffered major defeats. Some Democrats hoped to revive the reform movement during the war, but Republicans and conservative Democrats were on guard against such a move. New Dealers, warned Republican Senator Robert Taft of Ohio early in 1942, "are determined to make the country over under the cover of war if they can." Taft and his fellow conservatives not only successfully blocked such reform, they even dismantled significant New Deal programs like the Civilian Conservation Corps and the Work Projects Administration. The Republicans, in alliance with conservative southern Democrats, had become a formidable threat to the New Dealers.

Aided by a small turnout in November 1942, the Republicans scored impressive gains, winning forty-four new seats in the House and nine in the

Republican Gains in 1942

Senate and defeating Democratic governors in New York, California, and Michigan. Part of the Democrats' problem was that the war years, unlike the 1930s, were a time of full employment. Once people had acquired jobs and gained some economic security, they began to be more critical of New Deal policies. The New Deal coalition had always been a loose and fragile alliance: southern white farmers had little in common with northern blacks or white factory workers. In northern cities, blacks and whites who had voted for Roosevelt in 1940 were competing for jobs and housing and would soon collide in race riots.

But though Democratic liberalism was enfeebled, it was far from dead. At its head still stood Franklin D. Roosevelt, and it had a program to present to the American people. The liberal agenda began with a pledge to secure full employment. Roosevelt emphasized the concept in his Economic Bill of Rights, delivered as part of his 1944 State of the Union address. Every American had a right, the president declared, to a decent job; to sufficient food, shelter, and clothing; and to financial security in unemployment, illness, and old age. If to accomplish those goals the government had to operate at a deficit, Roosevelt was willing to do so. But first he had to be re-elected.

In 1944 Franklin D. Roosevelt looked like an exhausted old man. His eyes were tired and puffy; he was almost bald; and the loose flesh that hung on his large frame made him appear emaciated. The president's personal physician pronounced "nothing organically wrong with him at all—he's perfectly O.K.," but rumors of his ill health persisted. Whether or not Roosevelt expected to survive his fourth term, he selected a running mate who was inexperienced in international affairs: Senator Harry S Truman of Missouri. During the war Truman had gained favorable publicity for chairing a senatorial watchdog committee on favoritism and waste in the awarding of defense contracts. A representative of a border state and of a big-city machine (the Pendergast machine in Kansas City), Truman was acceptable both to southerners and to the bosses. An ardent and loyal New Dealer, the senator was also approved by liberals. There was little evidence, however, that he possessed the capacities for national and world leadership that he would need as president. Nor did Roosevelt take Truman into his confidence, failing even to inform his running mate about the atomic bomb project.

The Republicans were optimistic about their prospects for regaining the presidency. New York's Governor Thomas E. Dewey, who won the nomination on the first ballot, was moderate in his criticism of Roosevelt's foreign policy and did not advocate repeal of the essentials of the New Deal—Social Security, unemployment relief, collective bargaining, and price supports for farmers. But Dewey had one great liability—his public image. Stiff in manner and bland in personality, Dewey looked, as Theodore Roosevelt's daughter Alice Longworth described him, "like the bridegroom on a wedding cake."

Roosevelt won a fourth term, but with his narrowest-ever margin of victory in the popular vote; it was the closest presidential election since 1916.

A New President: Harry Truman
——

Nevertheless, he won 53.4 percent of the popular vote and 432 electoral votes to Dewey's 99. It was the urban vote that returned Roosevelt to the White House. Wartime population shifts had enhanced the cities' new political clout: southern whites who had been lifelong Democrats and southern blacks who had never before voted had migrated to the urban industrial centers (see map on page 842). Added to the urban vote was a less obvious factor. Many voters seemed to be exhibiting what has been called "depression psychosis." Fearful that hard times would return once war contracts were terminated, they remembered New Deal relief programs and voted for Roosevelt. Finally, as Senator Taft conceded, the Republicans had "underestimated the difficulty of changing a President at the very height of a victorious war." With victory within grasp, many Americans wanted Roosevelt's experienced hand to guide the nation, and the world, to a lasting international peace. But Roosevelt's death in April 1945 rendered that choice moot. The new president who would deal with the postwar world was Harry Truman.

WARTIME DIPLOMACY

The aftermath of the First World War weighed heavily on the minds of American diplomats throughout the war. Americans vowed to make a peace that would ensure a postwar world free from economic depression, totalitarianism, and war. The Atlantic Charter, so reminiscent of Woodrow Wilson's vision of an open world, was their general guide, tempered and compromised by the interests of the great powers. Thus American goals included the Open Door and lower tariffs; self-

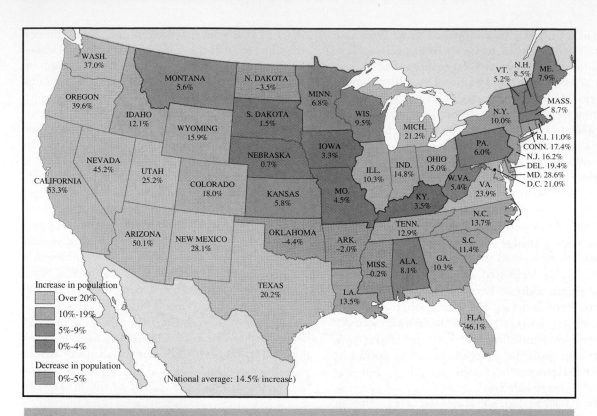

A Nation on the Move, 1940–1950 *American migration during the 1940s was the largest on record to that time. Men, women, and children moved to war-production areas and to army and navy bases, particularly on the West Coast. Note the increases in California, Oregon, and Washington, as well as in the Southwest.*

determination for liberated peoples; avoidance of the debts-reparations tangle that had plagued Europe after the First World War; expansion of the U.S. sphere of influence; and management of world affairs by what Roosevelt once called the Four Policemen: Russia, China, Great Britain, and the United States.

Although the Allies concentrated on defeating the aggressors, their suspicions of one another undermined cooperation. Eastern European questions proved the most difficult. The

Allied Disagreement over Eastern Europe

Soviet Union sought to fix its boundaries where they had stood before Hitler attacked in 1941. This meant that the part of Poland that the Soviets had invaded and captured in 1939 would become Soviet territory. The British and Americans hesitated, preferring to deal with Eastern Europe at the end of the war. But the Russian

armies' sustained drive through the region on the heels of the retreating Germans persuaded Churchill to act. In an October 1944 agreement, he and Stalin struck a bargain: the Soviet Union would gain Rumania and Bulgaria as a sphere of influence; Britain would have the upper hand in Greece; and the two countries would share authority in Yugoslavia and Hungary. The two leaders, however, did not agree on Poland.

Poland was a special case. In 1943, Moscow had broken off diplomatic relations with the conservative Polish government-in-exile in London. The Poles had angered Moscow by asking the International Red Cross to investigate German charges that the Soviets had massacred thousands of Polish army officers in the Katyn Forest in 1940. Then an uprising in Warsaw in July 1944 complicated matters still further. Encouraged by approaching Soviet troops to expect assistance, the Warsaw underground rose against the occupying

Germans. To the dismay of the world community, Soviet armies stood by as German troops slaughtered 166,000 people and devastated the city. The Soviets then set up a pro-Communist government in Lublin. Thus near the end of the war Poland had two competing governments, one in London, recognized by America and Britain, and another in Lublin.

Early in the war the Allies had begun talking about a new international peacekeeping organization. At Teheran in 1943 Roosevelt called for an

Creation of the United Nations Organization
———

institution controlled by the Four Policemen. The next year, at a Washington, D.C., mansion called Dumbarton Oaks, American, British, Russian, and Chinese representatives conferred on the details. Since American participation had been endorsed in public opinion polls and congressional resolutions, U.S. diplomats proceeded with some assurance that their handiwork would not meet the legislative fate of Wilson's League of Nations. The conferees approved a preliminary charter for a United Nations Organization, providing for a supreme Security Council dominated by the great powers and a weak General Assembly (Roosevelt called it "an investigatory body only"). The Security Council would have five permanent members, each with veto power.

Disagreement surfaced when the United States pushed China forward as a great power entitled to permanent membership on the council. Churchill complained that China was a captive vote on the side of the United States. To mollify him, the United States reluctantly agreed to elevate France to a permanent seat. Russia accepted both France and China, believing that its own veto power would protect its national interest against unfriendly decisions. But noting that the United States would have a group of sympathetic votes in the General Assembly among the Latin American states, and that Britain could muster support from members of its Commonwealth, the Soviets asked for separate membership in the General Assembly for each of the sixteen Soviet republics. This issue was not resolved at Dumbarton Oaks, but the meeting proved a success nevertheless. Pointing out that the conferees had achieved 90 percent of their goals, Roosevelt remarked, "that is what we used to call in the old days a darn good batting average."

Diplomatic action on behalf of the European

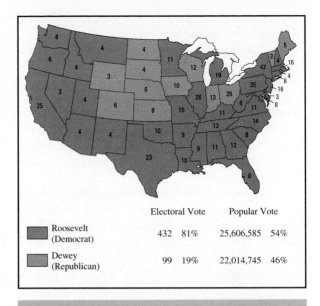

	Electoral Vote		Popular Vote	
Roosevelt (Democrat)	432	81%	25,606,585	54%
Dewey (Republican)	99	19%	22,014,745	46%

Presidential Election, 1944 *Franklin D. Roosevelt's fourth—and last—presidential election was his closest yet, but he still carried thirty-six of the country's forty-eight states.*

Jews, however, proved to be a tragic failure. Even before the war, Nazi officials had targeted Jews

Jewish Refugees from the Holocaust
———

throughout Europe for extermination. By war's end, about 6 million Jews had been forced into concentration camps and had been systematically killed by firing squads, unspeakable tortures, and gas chambers. The Nazis also exterminated as many as 250,000 gypsies and about 60,000 gay men. During the depression, the United States and other nations had refused to relax their immigration restrictions to save Jews fleeing persecution. The American Federation of Labor and Senator William Borah of Idaho, among others, argued that new immigrants would compete with American workers for scarce jobs, and public opinion polls supported their position. This fear of economic competition was fed by anti-Semitism. Bureaucrats applied the rules so strictly—requiring legal documents that fleeing Jews could not possibly provide—that otherwise-qualified refugees were kept out of the country. From 1933 to 1945, less than 40 percent of the German-Austrian immigration quota was filled.

Even the tragic voyage of the *St. Louis* did not change government policy. The vessel left Hamburg in mid-1939 carrying 930 desperate Jewish refugees who lacked proper immigration documents. Denied entry to Havana, the *St. Louis* headed for Miami, where Coast Guard cutters prevented it from docking. Outraged American citizens appealed to Washington, but the ship was forced to return to Europe. Some of those refugees took shelter in countries that were later overrun by Hitler's legions. "The cruise of the *St. Louis*," wrote the *New York Times*, "cries to high heaven of man's inhumanity to man."

As reports of the Nazi atrocities filled government files during the war years, American officials futilely attempted to persuade Latin American countries to accept refugees. They also approached the British, who proved unhelpful as well: they would not open Palestine. Some American leaders were themselves lax in their attention to the problem. The State Department officer in charge was Breckinridge Long, a nativist who in his hostility to European aliens actually hindered private citizens' efforts to save victims.

When evidence mounted that Hitler intended to exterminate the Jews, British and American representatives met in Bermuda (1943) but came up with no plans. Secretary Hull submitted a report to the president that emphasized "the unknown cost of moving an undetermined number of persons from an undisclosed place to an unknown destination." Appalled, Secretary of the Treasury Henry Morgenthau, Jr., charged that the State Department's foot-dragging made the United States an accessory to murder. "It takes months and months to grant the visa and then it usually applies to a corpse," he wrote bitterly. Early in 1944, stirred by Morgenthau's well-documented plea, Roosevelt created the War Refugee Board, which set up refugee camps in Europe and played a crucial role in saving 200,000 Jews from death. But, lamented one American official, "by that time it was too damned late to do too much."

American Inaction in the Face of the Holocaust

American officials had waited too long to act, and they also missed a chance to destroy the gas chambers and ovens at the extermination camp at Auschwitz in occupied Poland. They possessed aerial photographs and diagrams of the camp, but they argued that bombing it would detract from the war effort or prompt the Germans to step up the anti-Jewish terror. In 1944, American planes bombed factories in the industrial sector of Auschwitz, only five miles from the gas chambers and crematoria. "How could it be," the historian David S. Wyman has asked, "that Government officials knew that a place existed where 2,000 helpless human beings could be killed in less than an hour, knew that this occurred over and over again, and yet did not feel driven to search for some way to wipe such a scourge from the earth?"

THE YALTA CONFERENCE AND A FLAWED PEACE

With the war in Europe nearing an end, and a host of political questions—including what to do with Germany—yet to be settled, President Roosevelt called for another summit meeting. The three Allied leaders met at Yalta, in the Russian Crimea, in early February 1945. Controversy has surrounded the conference ever since. Roosevelt was obviously ill. "His appearance could change in a couple of hours from looking like a ghost to looking okay," remarked the new Secretary of State, Edward Stettinius, Jr. The sixty-two-year-old president suffered from hypertension, heart disease, and arteriosclerosis. His doctors prescribed rest, a reduction in cigarette smoking, and medication, but the president maintained a busy schedule. Critics of the Yalta agreements later charged that Roosevelt was too weak to resist Stalin's cunning, and that he struck a poor bargain. The evidence suggests, however, that Roosevelt was mentally alert and managed to sustain his strength during negotiations.

The Yalta meeting has also been criticized for keeping some of its agreements secret (suggesting that the Allies had something to hide) and for deciding the fates of weakened nations like Poland and China without their consent. Secrecy was necessary because some agreements contained military information that had to be kept from the still-undefeated Japanese and Germans. But the criticism that the Allies paid scant attention to small nations was well deserved. Wartime diplomacy simply assumed that the most powerful of the Allies would dominate international relations after the war.

Each of the Allies arrived at Yalta with definite goals. Britain sought to make France a partner in the postwar occupation of Germany, to curb Soviet

When the British liberated the Bergen-Belsen concentration camp near Hanover, Germany, in April 1945, they found this mass grave, which held the remains of thousands of Holocaust victims who had been starved, gassed, and machine-gunned by their Nazi jailers. This photograph and many others provide irrefutable proof of the Holocaust's savagery.   Imperial War Museum.

Allied Goals at Yalta

influence in Poland, and to ensure protection for the vulnerable British Empire. The Soviet Union wanted reparations from Germany to assist in the massive task of rebuilding at home, possessions in Asia, continued influence in Poland, and a permanently weakened Germany so that Russia would never again suffer a German attack. The United States lobbied for the United Nations Organization, where it believed it could exercise influence; for a Soviet declaration of war against Japan to aid in ending the Pacific war; for recognition of China as a major power; and for compromise between rival factions in Poland.

The various Allied armies' positions at the time of the conference helped to shape the final agreements. Soviet troops had occupied much of Eastern Europe, including Poland, while the Western Allies were still emerging from the Battle of the Bulge. In Asia, the Japanese were still resisting the American advance; millions of Japanese troops in

China, Manchuria, Korea, and the home islands seemed ready to die to the last man for the empire. Though victory was near, Britain and the United States still needed the Soviets to win the war.

The unsettled issue of Poland preoccupied the conferees. Stalin repeatedly pointed out that twice in the century German armies had marched through Poland into Russian territory, killing millions. He insisted on a government friendly to Moscow—the Lublin regime—in order to prevent another German onslaught. He also demanded boundaries that would give Poland part of Germany in the west and Russia part of Poland in the east. Churchill boiled over in protest; he wanted the London government-in-exile to return to Poland. With Roosevelt's help, a compromise was reached: a boundary favorable to the Soviet Union in the east, postponement of the western boundary issue, and the creation of a "more broadly based" coalition government that would include members

Compromise on Poland

The three Allied leaders—Winston Churchill, Franklin D. Roosevelt, and Josef Stalin—met at Yalta in February 1945. Having been president for twelve years, Roosevelt showed signs of age and fatigue. Two months later, he died of a massive cerebral hemorrhage.   Franklin D. Roosevelt Library.

of the London regime. Free elections would be held sometime in the future. The agreement was vague but, given Soviet occupation of Poland, Roosevelt considered it "the best I can do."

As for Germany, the Big Three agreed that it would be divided into four zones, the fourth to be administered by France. Berlin, within the Soviet zone, would also be divided among the four victors. On the question of reparations, Stalin wanted a precise figure, but Churchill and Roosevelt insisted on determining Germany's ability to pay. With Britain abstaining, the Americans and Russians agreed that an Allied committee would consider the sum of $20 billion as a basis for discussion in the future, with half the amount to go to the Soviet Union.

Other issues led to trade-offs. Stalin promised to declare war on Japan two or three months after Hitler's defeat. Since the atomic bomb was still on the drawing boards, American military leaders applauded the commitment. The Soviet premier also agreed to sign a treaty of friendship and alliance with Jiang Jieshi (Chiang Kai-shek), America's ally in China, rather than with the Communist Mao Zedong. In return, the United States agreed to Russia's recovery of holdings it had lost to Japan after the Russo-Japanese War in 1905: the southern part of Sakhalin Island and Lushun (Port Arthur). Regarding the new world organization, Roosevelt and Churchill granted the Soviets three votes in the General Assembly. (Fifty nations officially launched the United Nations Organization three months later.) Finally, the conferees issued the Declaration of Liberated Europe, a pledge to establish order and to rebuild economies by democratic methods.

Yalta marked the high point of the Grand Alliance; in the tradition of diplomatic give-and-take, each of the Allies came away with something it wanted. But as the great pow-

Potsdam Conference
———

ers jockeyed for influence at the close of the war, neither the spirit nor the letter of Yalta held firm. The crumbling of the alliance became evident almost immediately, at the Potsdam Conference, which began in mid-July. Roosevelt had died in April, and Truman—a novice at international diplomacy—was less patient with the Russians. Stalin "seems to like it when I hit him with a hammer," he bragged in a letter to his wife Bess. "I reared up on my hind legs and told 'em where to get off and they got off." Truman seemed further emboldened after learning during the conference that the atomic test in New Mexico was successful. "Now I know what happened to Truman," said Churchill. "When he got to the meeting after having read this report he was a changed man. He told the Russians just where they got off and generally bossed the whole meeting."

Despite the Potsdam "brawl," as Truman called it, the Big Three did agree on general policies toward Germany: complete disarmament, dismantling of industry used for military production, and dissolution of Nazi institutions and laws. In a compromise over reparations, they decided that each occupying nation should extract reparations from its own zone; but they could not agree on a total figure. To resolve other issues, such as peace treaties with Italy, Finland, and Hungary, the Big Three created the Council of Foreign Ministers.

Potsdam left much undone. As the war drew to a close, there was little that bound the Allies together. Roosevelt's cooperative style was gone; the spirit of Yalta was evaporating; the common enemy, Hitler, was defeated. And the United States, with the awesome atomic bomb in the offing to force defeat upon Japan, no longer needed or even wanted Russia in the Pacific war. Moreover, each of the victors was seeking to preserve and enlarge its sphere of influence. Britain claimed authority in Greece and parts of the Middle East; the Soviet Union already dominated much of Eastern Europe; and the United States retained its hegemony in Latin America. The United States also seized several Pacific islands as strategic outposts and laid plans to dominate a defeated Japan. Let the Americans have their Pacific bases, responded Churchill, "but 'Hands off the British Empire' is our maxim."

American interests also increased their stake in Middle Eastern oil during the war. By 1944, American petroleum companies controlled 42 percent of the proven oil reserves

Oil's Role in Victory
———

of the Middle East—a nineteenfold increase since 1936. Both the British and the Russians complained about this new evidence of American expansionism. But oil was crucial to victory. Japan and Germany had waged war to secure oil resources in the Dutch East Indies, Russia, and North Africa. Their failure to gain enough oil, while the Allies' supply continued flowing, led directly to their defeat on the battlefield and at sea. American officials, Daniel Yergin has written in *The Prize: The Epic Quest for Oil, Money, and Power* (1991), recognized that oil was "the critical stategic commodity for the war and was essential for national power and international predominance" both then and in the postwar world.

Hitler once said, "We may be destroyed, but if we are, we shall drag a world with us—a world in flames." Indeed, *rubble* was the word most often invoked to describe the European landscape at the end of the war. Hamburg, Stuttgart, and Dresden had been laid waste; three-quarters of Berlin was in ruins. In England, Coventry and parts of London were bombed out. Across the continent transportation systems had been disrupted and water supplies contaminated. Everywhere ghostlike people wandered about, searching desperately for food and mourning those who would never come home. Russia had lost more than 20 million people; Poland 5.8 million; Germany 4.5 million. In all, some 35 million Europeans died as a result of the war. In Asia untold millions of Chinese and 2 million Japanese died.

Only one major combatant escaped such grisly statistics: the United States. Its cities were not burned and its fields were not trampled. American deaths from the war—

Postwar Strength of the United States
———

405,399—were few compared with the losses of other nations. In fact, the United States emerged from the Second World War more powerful than it had ever been. It alone had the atomic bomb. The U.S. Air Force and Navy were the largest anywhere. And though the United States demobilized the bulk of its regular army after the war, it still had 2 million men in arms in 1946. What is more, only the United States had the capital and economic resources to spur international recovery. America, gloated Truman, was "a giant." In the coming struggle to fashion a new world out of the ashes of the old, soon to be called the Cold War (see Chapter 29), the United States held a commanding position.

Life for many Americans was fundamentally different in 1945 from what it had been before Pearl Harbor. For one thing, it was the war that finally ended the Great Depression, reducing unemployment practically to zero. But life differed in other ways. The Academy Award for 1946 went to *The Best Years of Our Lives*, a painful film about the postwar readjustments of three veterans and their families and friends. Many men returned home suffering deep emotional distress. One girl remembered that her father had flashbacks and nightmares. He even "seemed afraid to touch us," she said. "Dad came home a different man," recalled another girl; "he didn't laugh as much and he drank a lot."

The Second World War also stimulated the trend toward bigness, not only in business and labor but also in government, agriculture, higher education, and science. Over the next few years, government agencies that had been conceived as temporary would become permanent and grow in size and influence, resulting in the Department of Defense (consolidating the War and Navy Departments), the Central Intelligence Agency (succeeding the Office of Strategic Services), and the Atomic Energy Commission. The seeds of the military-industrial complex were sown in these years. Moreover, with the advent of the Cold War, millions of younger men would be inducted into the armed forces over the next thirty years. War and the expectation of war would become part of American life.

At the same time, the Second World War was a powerful engine of social change in the United States. The gains made during the war by African-Americans and women were overdue. And by blending New Deal ideology and wartime urgency, the government assumed the responsibility of ensuring prosperity and stepping in when

capitalism faltered. Finally, Americans emerged from the war fully confident that theirs was the greatest country in the world. The United States, they boasted, had preserved democracy and freedom around the globe. For better or worse—and clearly there were elements of both—the Second World War was a turning point in the nation's history.

SUGGESTIONS FOR FURTHER READING

Fighting the War

Robert H. Abzug, *Inside the Vicious Heart: Americans and the Liberation of Nazi Concentration Camps* (1985); Stephen A. Ambrose, *Eisenhower: Soldier, General of the Army, President-Elect* (1983); Hanson Baldwin, *Battles Lost and Won* (1966); A. Russell Buchanan, *The United States in World War II*, 2 vols. (1964); Peter Calvocoressi and Guy Wint, *Total War* (1972); John W. Dower, *War Without Mercy: Race and Power in the Pacific War* (1986); Richard B. Frank, *Guadalcanal* (1991); Paul Fussell, *Wartime* (1989); Kent R. Greenfield, *American Strategy in World War II* (1963); B. H. Liddell Hart, *History of the Second World War* (1970); Max Hastings, *OVERLORD: D-Day and the Battle of Normandy* (1984); D. Clayton James, *A Time for Giants: Politics of the American High Command in World War II* (1987); D. Clayton James, *The Years of MacArthur, 1941–1945* (1975); David Kahn, *The Codebreakers* (1967); John Keegan, *The Second World War* (1989); Eric Larabee, *Commander in Chief* (1987); Richard M. Leighton and Robert W. Coakley, *Global Logistics and Strategy, 1940–1945*, 2 vols. (1955–1968); Karal Ann Marling and John Wetenhall, *Iwo Jima* (1991); Samuel Eliot Morison, *The Two-Ocean War* (1963); Samuel Eliot Morison, *Strategy and Compromise* (1958); Forrest C. Pogue, *George C. Marshall*, 4 vols. (1963–1987); Bill D. Ross, *Iwo Jima* (1985); Ronald Schaffer, *Wings of Judgment: American Bombing in World War II* (1985); Bradley F. Smith, *The Shadow Warriors: O.S.S. and the Origins of the C.I.A.* (1983); Ronald H. Spector, *Eagle Against the Sun: The American War with Japan* (1984); Russell F. Weigley, *The American Way of War* (1973); Gordon Wright, *The Ordeal of Total War, 1939–1945* (1968).

Grand Alliance Diplomacy

Russell Buhite, *Decisions at Yalta* (1986); James MacGregor Burns, *Roosevelt: The Soldier of Freedom* (1970); Thomas Campbell, *Masquerade Peace: America's UN Policy, 1944–1945* (1973); Winston S. Churchill, *The Second World War*, 6 vols. (1948–1953); Diane Clemens, *Yalta* (1970); Robert Dallek, *Franklin D. Roosevelt and American Foreign Policy, 1932–1945* (1979); Robert A. Divine, *Roosevelt and World War II* (1969); Robert A. Divine, *Second Chance: The Triumph of Internationalism in America During World War II* (1967); Henry L. Feingold, *Politics of Rescue* (1970); Herbert Feis, *Churchill, Roosevelt, and Stalin* (1957); George C. Herring, *Aid to Russia, 1941–1946* (1973); Gary R. Hess, *The United States at War, 1941–1945* (1986); Akira Iriye, *Power and Culture: The Japanese-American War, 1941–1945* (1981); Gabriel Kolko, *The Politics of War* (1968); William R. Louis, *Imperialism at Bay: The United States and the Decolonization of the British Empire*

(1978); Vojtech Mastny, *Russia's Road to the Cold War* (1979); William H. McNeill, *America, Britain, and Russia* (1953); Keith Sainsbury, *The Turning Point* (1985); Gaddis Smith, *Diplomacy During the Second World War, 1941–1945*, 2nd ed. (1985); Michael Stoff, *Oil, War, and American Security* (1980); Mark Stoler, *The Politics of the Second Front* (1977); Christopher Thorne, *Allies of a Kind* (1977); David S. Wyman, *The Abandonment of the Jews* (1984).

The Home Front

Allan Berube, *Coming Out Under Fire: The History of Gay Men and Women in World War II* (1990); John Morton Blum, *V Was for Victory: Politics and American Culture During World War II* (1976); Alan Clive, *State of War: Michigan in World War II* (1979); John Costello, *Virtue Under Fire: How World War II Changed Our Social and Sexual Attitudes* (1985); John D'Emilio, *Sexual Politics, Sexual Communities: The Making of a Homosexual Minority in the United States, 1940–1970* (1983); Mark Jonathan Harris et al., *The Homefront* (1984); Richard R. Lingeman, *Don't You Know There's a War On?* (1970); Gerald D. Nash, *The American West Transformed* (1985); Geoffrey Perrett, *Days of Sadness, Years of Triumph: The American People, 1939–1945* (1973); Richard Polenberg, *War and Society* (1972); Studs Terkel, ed., *"The Good War": An Oral History of World War Two* (1984); William M. Tuttle, Jr., *"Daddy's Gone to War": The Second World War in the Lives of America's Children* (1993).

Mobilizing for War

David Brinkley, *Washington Goes to War* (1988); John Chambers, *To Raise an Army* (1980); George Q. Flynn, *The Draft, 1940–1973* (1993); Daniel J. Kevles, *The Physicists* (1977); Paul A. C. Koistinen, *The Hammer and the Sword: Labor, the Military, and Industrial Mobilization, 1920–1945* (1979); Clayton R. Koppes and Gregory D. Black, *Hollywood Goes to War* (1987); Harold G. Vatter, *The U.S. Economy in World War II* (1985); Gerald T. White, *Billions for Defense* (1980); Allen M. Winkler, *The Politics of Propaganda: The Office of War Information, 1942–1945* (1978).

Farmers and Workers, Soldiers and Sailors

John L. Blackman, Jr., *Presidential Seizure in Labor Disputes* (1967); Melvyn Dubofsky and Warren H. Van Tine, *John L. Lewis* (1977); Lee Kennett, *G.I.: The American Soldier in World War II* (1987); Nelson Lichtenstein, *Labor's War at Home: The CIO in World War II* (1983); Bill Mauldin, *Up Front*, rev. ed. (1968); Davis R. B. Ross, *Preparing for Ulysses: Politics and Veterans During World War II* (1969); Joel Seidman, *American Labor from Defense to Reconversion* (1953); Samuel A. Stouffer et al., *The American Soldier*, 2 vols. (1949); Walter W. Wilcox, *The Farmer in the Second World War* (1947).

Japanese-American Internment

Commission on Wartime Relocation and Internment of Civilians, *Personal Justice Denied* (1982); Roger Daniels, *Prisoners Without Trial* (1993); Bill Hosokawa, *Nisei: The Quiet Americans* (1969); Peter Irons, *Justice at War* (1983); Thomas James, *Exile Within: The Schooling of Japanese-Americans, 1942–1945* (1987); John Tateishi, ed., *And Justice for All: An Oral History of the Japanese-American Detention Camps* (1984); Jacobus tenBroek et al., *Prejudice, War and the Constitution* (1954); Michi Weglyn, *Years of Infamy* (1976).

Politics

Richard E. Darilek, *A Loyal Opposition in Time of War* (1976); James C. Foster, *The Union Politic: The CIO Political Action Committee* (1975); Maurice Isserman, *Which Side Were You On? The American Communist Party During the Second World War* (1982); Roland Young, *Congressional Politics in the Second World War* (1956).

African-Americans and Wartime Violence

A. Russell Buchanan, *Black Americans in World War II* (1977); Dominic J. Capeci, Jr., *Race Relations in Wartime Detroit* (1984); Dominic J. Capeci, Jr., *The Harlem Riot of 1943* (1977); Richard M. Dalfiume, *Desegregation of the U.S. Armed Forces* (1969); Lee Finkle, *Forum for Protest: The Black Press During World War II* (1975); Mauricio Mazon, *The Zoot-Suit Riots* (1984); Phillip McGuire, ed., *Taps for a Jim Crow Army: Letters from Black Soldiers in World War II* (1982); Patrick S. Washburn, *A Question of Sedition: The Federal Government's Investigation of the Black Press During World War II* (1986); Neil A. Wynn, *The Afro-American and the Second World War* (1976).

Women at War

Karen T. Anderson, *Wartime Women* (1981); D'Ann Campbell, *Women at War with America* (1984); William H. Chafe, *The Paradox of Change* (1991); Sherna Berger Gluck, *Rosie the Riveter Revisited* (1987); Claudia Goldin, *Understanding the Gender Gap: An Economic History of American Women* (1990); Susan M. Hartmann, *The Home Front and Beyond* (1982); Margaret Randolph Higgonet et al., eds., *Behind the Lines: Gender and the Two World Wars* (1987); Ruth Milkman, *Gender at Work: The Dynamics of Job Discrimination by Sex During World War II* (1987); Leila J. Rupp, *Mobilizing Women for War: German and American Propaganda, 1939–1945* (1978); Peter A. Soderbergh, *Women Marines: The World War II Era* (1992).

The Atomic Bomb and Japan's Surrender

Gar Alperovitz, *Atomic Diplomacy*, rev. ed. (1985); Barton J. Bernstein, ed., *The Atomic Bomb* (1976); Robert J. C. Butow, *Japan's Decision to Surrender* (1954); Committee for the Compilation of Materials on Damage Caused by the Atomic Bombs in Hiroshima and Nagasaki, *Hiroshima and Nagasaki* (1981); Herbert Feis, *The Atomic Bomb and the End of World War II* (1966); Gregg Herken, *The Winning Weapon* (1980); John Hersey, *Hiroshima*, rev. ed. (1985); Richard G. Hewlett and Oscar E. Anderson, *The New World* (1962); Richard Rhodes, *The Making of the Atomic Bomb* (1987); Martin J. Sherwin, *A World Destroyed* (1975); Leon V. Sigal, *Fighting to a Finish* (1988).

28

Cold War Politics, McCarthyism, and Civil Rights, 1945–1961

R AIN FELL ON CAPITOL HILL on the afternoon of April 12, 1945. The House of Representatives had adjourned for the day, and Speaker Sam Rayburn had invited the House parliamentarian to join him for a drink in his office. "Be there around five," the Speaker had said. "Harry Truman is coming over."

Rayburn's telephone rang as he sipped his first drink. The caller was the White House press secretary; would the vice president telephone the White House as soon as possible? Shortly Truman arrived. In his double-breasted gray suit, blue polka-dot tie, and steel-rimmed glasses, the sixty-year-old Truman resembled nothing so much as a tightlipped small-town businessman. At Rayburn's suggestion he picked up the phone and called the White House. Truman's face drained of color as the press secretary urged him to come to the White House immediately and enter by the side door. *Jesus Christ and General Jackson,* he exclaimed. "Something must have happened."

Truman rushed to the White House, where an usher announced that Mrs. Roosevelt was waiting for him. When he entered the second-floor sit-ting room, Eleanor Roosevelt walked toward him, touched his shoulder, and said, "Harry, the President is dead."

When Truman became president, the nation knew little about its new leader. Contrary to his "Give 'em hell, Harry" image of 1948 and later, Truman's initial response to the challenge of the presidency was a deep feeling of inadequacy. As vice president, more-over, Truman had been left in the dark by Roosevelt about crucial foreign and military initiatives; nevertheless, he would have to deal with the onset of the Cold War (see Chapter 29). In do-mestic matters, too, the new president would need a crash course in the intri-cacies of governing the United States.

The nation's reconversion from war to peace was not smooth, and Tru-man managed to anger liberals, con-servatives, farmers, consumers, and union members during his first year as president. In 1946, voters reacted to inflation and a wave of strikes by elect-ing a Republican majority to Congress. Truman's actions also heightened fears that a Communist conspiracy was operating within the federal govern-ment. He issued an executive order in 1947 establishing the Employee Loy-alty Program for the executive branch of the government. Henceforth, all agency directors had to ensure that each employee under their jurisdiction was a loyal American. In doubtful cases, the agency's chief had to appoint a loyalty board to hear evidence. For the first time, government officials were authorized to pass judgment on a job applicant's personal beliefs and past associations. People already on the payroll were presumed to be guilty, not innocent, if accused of disloyalty.

But in 1948, Truman confounded political experts by winning the presidency in his own right. He had continued to espouse the New Deal and remained loyal to the welfare system fashioned in the 1930s. Truman was also the first president ever to pledge federal support for racial equality. His upset victory in 1948 was proof that the New Deal coalition was alive and well.

Truman's victory also demonstrated the volatility of postwar politics. The key domestic issues of the period—civil rights for African-Americans and the anti-Communist witch hunt led by Senator Joseph R. McCarthy and called McCarthyism— were both highly charged issues. Later, the outbreak of the Korean War in 1950 intensified discontent. The military stalemate frustrated war-weary citizens, inflation began another upward climb, and evidence of corruption surfaced in the White House. Truman's popularity plummeted, and in 1952 Americans cast their presidential votes for a hero of the Second World War, General Dwight D. Eisenhower.

During the 1950s, an age of consensus, Americans generally shared a belief in anticommunism and the primacy of economic progress over social agendas. President Eisenhower—hardly the passive, ill-informed chief executive the Democrats tried to depict—actively articulated both beliefs and worked hard to put them into action. But he moved cautiously and hesitantly, particularly in dealing with civil rights and McCarthyism. Eisenhower was reluctant to confront Senator McCarthy even when his anti-Communist tactics proved reckless and unscrupulous. McCarthy eventually destroyed himself with his excesses, but not before he had harmed many individuals and the nation itself.

To promote economic growth, Eisenhower pursued staunchly Republican goals: a balanced budget, reduced government spending, lower taxes, low inflation, private enterprise, a return of power to the states, and modest federal efforts to stimulate economic development. But Eisenhower administration officials did not attempt to roll back

the New Deal. In fact, however reluctantly, they expanded the welfare state.

During Eisenhower's eight-year presidency, the nation was quiescent both politically and intellectually. White Americans celebrated their economic system for providing a high standard of living. Americans liked the president's traditionalism, caution, and moderation. "Ike" reassured them, and they trusted him. These years were comforting to Americans who longed for a respite from social turbulence.

It was the infant civil rights movement that most vigorously challenged the national consensus. Not only were most African-Americans at the bottom of the economic ladder, they also were being denied their constitutional rights. How would blacks be incorporated into the consensus? The president, Congress, southern whites, and black civil rights activists all gave different answers as they debated *Brown* v. *Board of Education of Topeka*, the Supreme Court's momentous decision on school desegregation.

Still, however fragile, the age of consensus remained basically intact. President Eisenhower was succeeded in 1961 by a much younger man and a Democrat, Senator John F. Kennedy of Massachusetts. Eisenhower's vice president, Richard M. Nixon, had lost the election to Kennedy, who criticized Eisenhower's domestic policies as inadequate to sustain economic progress for all Americans and who faulted Eisenhower's foreign policy for not winning the Cold War. Meanwhile, throughout the country, race relations and urban conditions continued to deteriorate. In the 1960s the nation would have to deal with problems it had postponed in the 1950s.

A ROUGH TRANSITION AT HOME

The atomic bombs that fell on Hiroshima and Nagasaki in 1945 had brought victory much sooner than wartime planners had anticipated. Mid-1946 had been the target date for victory, and administrators had planned a gradual conversion from a war footing to a peacetime economy. But in 1945 the war was over, and important questions remained unanswered. What would be the effect of reconversion—the cancellation of war contracts,

• *Important Events* •

1945	Roosevelt dies; Harry S Truman assumes presidency Germany surrenders Japan surrenders Truman sends twenty-one-point economic message to Congress
1946	Congress passes Employment Act of 1946 Coal miners strike Truman fires Secretary of Commerce Wallace Inflation reaches 18.2 percent Republicans win both houses of Congress
1947	Truman institutes Employee Loyalty Program Taft-Hartley Act limits power of unions *To Secure These Rights* issued by the President's Committee on Civil Rights
1948	Truman appoints President's Committee on Equality of Treatment and Opportunity in the Armed Services Truman elected president
1949	Russia explodes an atomic bomb Communists win revolution in China
1950	Klaus Fuchs arrested as an atomic spy Alger Hiss convicted of perjury Hydrogen bomb project announced McCarthy alleges Communists in government Korean War begins Julius and Ethel Rosenberg charged with conspiracy to commit treason Internal Security (McCarran) Act passed
1951	*Dennis et al.* v. *U.S.* upholds Smith Act
1952	Eisenhower elected president Republicans win both houses of Congress
1953	Korean War ends Rosenbergs executed J. Robert Oppenheimer's security clearance is revoked Congress adopts termination policy for Native Americans Recession hits United States
1954	*Brown* decision rules "separate but equal" is illegal Senate condemns Senator McCarthy
1955	Montgomery bus boycott begins
1956	Highway Act launches interstate highway project Eisenhower re-elected
1957	Little Rock has desegregation crisis Congress passes Civil Rights Act Recession recurs
1958	National Defense Education Act passed Sherman Adams resigns over scandal St. Lawrence Seaway opens for traffic
1960	Sit-in in Greensboro, North Carolina SNCC formed John F. Kennedy elected president Recession hits again
1961	Eisenhower warns against "military-industrial complex"

termination of wage and price controls, and expiration of wartime labor agreements? Would depression recur as the artificial stimulus of the war was withdrawn, throwing people out of work and sending prices downward? Or would Americans go on a buying spree, driving prices up? After all, during the Great Depression penny-pinched Americans could not afford to buy autos, houses, appliances, and other consumer durables. During the prosperity of the Second World War, such civilian items were not even manufactured. By 1945 Americans had bulging bank accounts, and they wanted to treat themselves.

Yet most Americans seemed pessimistic about the future. Even before the war's end, cutbacks in production had caused layoffs. At Ford Motor Company's massive Willow Run plant outside Detroit, where nine thousand Liberator bombers had been produced, most workers were let go in the spring of 1945. Ten days after the victory over Japan, 1.8 million people nationwide received pink slips and 640,000 filed for unemployment compensation. At the peak of postwar unemployment in March 1946, 2.7 million people searched for work.

Postwar Job Layoffs

Swelling the ranks of job seekers were the millions of GIs who were discharged from the armed services in 1945 and 1946. Like the cancellation of government contracts, demobilization of the armed

Military Personnel on Active Duty, 1945–1961

Military Personnel on Active Duty, 1945–1961
Demobilization of the armed forces came rapidly after the Second World War. Between 1946 and 1950, there was little change in the size of the national defense forces. But with the Korean War, the numbers rose again, peaking in the mid-1950s.   Source: U.S. Department of Commerce, *Historical Atlas of the United States. Colonial Times to 1970,* Part 2, p. 1141.

forces came rapidly. The army had expected to muster out 1.1 million people in an eighteen-month period between victories in Europe and Japan, but the bombings of Hiroshima and Nagasaki had cut that period to four months. With victory in hand, Americans clamored for the speedy return of their husbands and sons; they flooded Congress with letters, children's photographs, baby shoes, and even locks of hair. In response, the army's demobilization rate was increased fivefold, with a target of 5.5 million by July 1946. The navy hurriedly converted landing and cargo ships into troop carriers and brought home 4 million GIs in the first year of peace. In mid-1945 the nation's armed forces

were over 12 million strong. A year later, the total had fallen to just over 3 million; in 1947 it hit 1.5 million (see figure). "The program we were following," Truman recalled, "was no longer demobilization—it was disintegration of our armed forces."

Fearing that an economic depression might result from the cancellation of war contracts, Truman declared his determination not only to combat unemployment but also to expand on New Deal programs begun in the 1930s. In September 1945 he delivered to Congress a twenty-one-point message urging extension of

Truman's Reconversion Plan

unemployment compensation, an increase in the minimum wage, adoption of permanent farm-price supports, and new public works projects. Truman also revived Roosevelt's Economic Bill of Rights: the right of every able-bodied American to hold a job. If the economy failed to provide one, the government should create it. Congress responded to Truman's message with the Employment Act of 1946, which announced that the government would use its resources, including deficit spending if necessary, to achieve "maximum employment, production, and purchasing power." Nevertheless, the act fell short of Truman's hopes: Congress had deleted a commitment to absolute full employment.

Despite high unemployment immediately after the war, the United States was not teetering on the brink of depression. In fact, after a brief period of readjustment, the economy would soon blast off into a quarter-century of unprecedented boom (see Chapter 30). People had plenty of savings to spend in 1945 and 1946, and suddenly there were new houses and cars for them to buy. Easy credit and the availability of new products from such war-inspired industries as synthetic rubber and electronics promoted the buying spree. As a result, despite the winding-down of war production that began in 1944, the gross national product (GNP) continued to rise in 1945. Following a slight dip in economic activity in 1946, the GNP jumped 11 percent the next year.

The nation's postwar economic problem was not depression; it was inflation, fueled by maddening shortages of consumer goods like meat and housing. Throughout 1945 and 1946 prices skyrocketed; inflation exceeded 18 percent in 1946. Meanwhile, though prices were spiraling upward, many people were earning less in real income (actual purchasing power) than they had earned during the war. Industrial workers had complained during the war that the National War Labor Board limited them to cost-of-living pay increases; in fact, manufacturing wages had risen 27 percent, largely due to the wartime increase in the average workweek from forty-one hours to forty-five hours. But by 1945, workers were returning to the forty-hour paycheck. Although employers claimed they could not afford to guarantee workers the same take-home pay for fewer hours, most workers believed it was possible. The result was a management-labor

Postwar Inflation

impasse, followed by a spate of strikes. In late 1945, daily absences due to strikes ballooned to 28.4 million, more than double the 1943 figure. Although massive and frequent, such strikes were peaceful compared with the fiery confrontations that had followed the First World War.

Throughout the period of reconversion, the federal government hesitated to act in the face of competing special-interest groups. Big and small business, management and labor, farmers and consumers, liberals and conservatives offered conflicting prescriptions, and to serve one interest was to risk offending others. For all these groups, Truman was the perfect scapegoat. "Sherman was *wrong*," Truman told an audience of journalists in late 1945. "I'm telling you I find *peace* is hell."

However severe the discontent of farmers, factory workers, and consumers in 1945, in 1946 it got worse. Volatile labor-management relations exploded in 1946 as over 4.5 million men and women went on strike, more even than in 1919. Daily absences due to strikes were four times as high as in 1945. One reason for workers' discontent was that net profits had reached all-time highs, jumping more than 50 percent from 1945 to 1946. Meanwhile, wages and salaries declined slightly in 1946. Indignant that they were not sharing in the prosperity, workers forced nationwide shutdowns in the coal, automobile, steel, and electric industries and halted railroad and maritime transportation.

Upsurge in Labor Strikes

John L. Lewis's United Mine Workers was among the most powerful unions to walk off the job. Coal was the nation's primary source of energy in 1946. When soft-coal production stopped on April 1, steel and automobile output plummeted, railroad service was canceled, thousands of people were laid off, and twenty-two states reinstituted wartime "dim-outs" to conserve coal. The miners' demands were legitimate—higher wages, a federal safety code, and a royalty of 10 cents per ton to finance health services and welfare and pension funds. A two-week truce in May failed to produce a solution; with time running out and the country still desperate for coal, Truman ordered federal seizure of the mines, placing them under the control of the secretary of the interior. Lewis and the government reached an accord a week later, and the miners returned to work. But within six months the agreement collapsed, and once again the government took over operation of the mines.

By 1946 there was no doubt about the growing unpopularity of labor unions and their leadership. Many Americans blamed the unions for strikes, which not only restricted the output of consumer goods and inflated prices but also threatened the national security. In May, when a nationwide railroad strike was threatened, Truman hopped aboard the anti-union bandwagon. A mediation board had managed to satisfy eighteen of the disgruntled unions, but two held out for a better settlement. In exasperation, Truman made a dramatic appearance before a joint session of Congress. If the government seized a strike-bound industry, he said, and the workers in that industry refused to honor a presidential order to return to work, "I [would] request the Congress immediately to authorize the President to draft into the Armed Forces of the United States all workers who are on strike against their government." He also requested authority to strip strikers of seniority benefits, to take legal action against union leaders, and to fine and even imprison them for con-

Truman's Attack on the Unions

tempt. Truman's speech alienated not just the railroad workers but union members in general. Many vowed to defeat him in the upcoming 1948 presidential election.

Truman fared little better in his direction of the Office of Price Administration (OPA). Now that the war was over, powerful interests wanted OPA controls lifted. Consumers grew impatient with shortages and black-market prices, and manufacturers and farmers wanted to jack up prices legally. Yet when most controls expired in mid-1946, inflation rose further. When the OPA price ceilings on beef expired, for example, the cost of beef soared; cattle ranchers were delighted and consumers grumbled. When the OPA reimposed ceilings two months later, producers retaliated by withholding beef from the market. Soon consumers were standing in long lines at butcher shops and buying beef on the black market. They blamed the Democrats. "This is going to be a damn *beefsteak* election," groused Speaker of the House Sam Rayburn of Texas.

Consumer Discontent

In 1946, ex-servicemen picketed coal mines in Panther Valley, Pennsylvania, complaining that mine owners had hired outside help during the war and then had refused to lay off those workers in favor of the returning veterans, former coalminers themselves. Wide World Photos.

Truman's approval rating plunged from 87 percent in late 1945 to 32 percent in 1946. Even liberals were unhappy with the president's performance. Harold Ickes, one of the two New Dealers left in the cabinet, had resigned to protest Truman's appointment of a California oil and real-estate baron (who also happened to be a Democratic fund-raiser) as undersecretary of the navy. Fearing another Teapot Dome scandal, Ickes denounced Truman's policy of "government by crony." Seven months later Truman fired Henry A. Wallace, the only remaining New Dealer, for publicly criticizing U.S. foreign policy. By election time, the president was out of favor with labor, consumers, farmers, liberals, and—because of his advocacy of welfare programs—conservative Democrats as well.

Republicans made the most of public discontent. "Got enough meat?" asked Republican Congressman John M. Vorys of Ohio. "Got enough houses? Got enough OPA? . . . Got enough inflation? . . . Got enough debt? . . . Got enough strikes?" In 1946 the Republicans won a majority in both houses of Congress and captured twenty-five of the thirty-two nonsouthern governorships. The White House in 1948 seemed within their grasp.

THE EIGHTIETH CONGRESS AND THE ELECTION OF 1948

The politicians who dominated the Eightieth Congress, whether Republicans or southern Democrats, were committed conservatives. They supported Truman's foreign policy but perceived the Republican landslide as a mandate to reverse the New Deal—that is, to curb the power of government and of labor. Truman had had little success with the previous Congress; he would have even less success with this one. Ironically, however, the Eightieth Congress would ultimately help him win the presidency in 1948. For if Truman had alienated labor, farmers, and liberals, the Eightieth Congress made them livid.

Particularly unpopular was the Taft-Hartley Act, which Congress approved over Truman's veto in 1947. A revision of the Wagner Act of 1935, the bill prohibited the "closed shop," a workplace where membership in a particular union was a pre-

Taft-Hartley Act

requisite for being hired. It also permitted the states to enact "right-to-work" laws banning union-shop agreements, which required all workers to join if a majority voted in favor of a union shop. Workers could still organize, elect a union to represent them, enroll new union members, bargain collectively, and strike, but the Taft-Hartley Act mandated an eighty-day cooling-off period before carrying out strikes that imperiled the national security. Union contributions to political candidates in federal elections were forbidden, and union leaders were required to sign non-Communist affidavits. Although it was not the slave-labor act that unions said it was, the act quickly distinguished labor's supporters from its opponents. Truman's veto therefore vindicated him in the eyes of labor. Only a year earlier, labor leaders had pledged all-out war on the president; now they threw their resources behind him.

Throughout 1947 and into 1948 the conservative Eightieth Congress offended a raft of interest groups, which in turn swung back to Truman. The president asked Congress for continued price supports for farmers; the Eightieth Congress responded with weakened price supports. The president requested nationwide health insurance; the Eightieth Congress refused. The pattern was the same with federal funding of public housing and aid to public education; with unemployment compensation, old-age and survivors' benefits, and the minimum wage; with funds for land reclamation, irrigation, and public power; and with anti-lynching, anti-poll tax, and fair-employment legislation. Truman proposed; Congress rejected or ignored his requests.

Overconfident Republicans seemed oblivious to public opinion. Not since 1928 had they been so confident of capturing the presidency, and most political experts agreed. "Only a political miracle or extraordinary stupidity on the part of the Republicans," according to *Time*, "can save the Democratic party." At their national convention, Republicans strengthened their position by nominating the governors of two of the nation's most populous states: Thomas E. Dewey of New York for president and Earl Warren of California for vice president. Democrats revealed their fragmentation when an alliance of big-city bosses and liberals tried to dump

Campaign of 1948

So few pollsters predicted that President Harry S Truman (1884–1972) would win in 1948 that the Chicago Tribune *announced his defeat before all the returns were in. Here a victorious Truman pokes fun at the newspaper for its premature headline.*   UPI/Bettmann Archives.

Truman in favor of General Dwight D. Eisenhower. But Eisenhower declined the overtures of both Democrats and Republicans, declaring that "life-long professional soldiers should abstain from seeking high political office," and Truman ultimately received the nomination.

Democrats were up against more than Republicans in 1948. After his dismissal from the cabinet, Henry Wallace ran for president on the Progressive party ticket, which advocated **Third Parties** friendship and negotiation with the Soviet Union, condemned the Truman Doctrine as "a global Monroe Doctrine," supported desegregation, and advocated nationalization of oil companies, railroads, and other basic industries. Experts predicted that the Progressives would poll enough votes to dash the Democratic party's hopes for victory. A fourth party, the Dix-

iecrats (States Rights Democratic party), was organized by southerners who walked out of the 1948 Democratic convention when it adopted a pro-civil rights plank; they nominated Governor Strom Thurmond of South Carolina. If Wallace's candidacy did not destroy Truman's chances, experts said, the Dixiecrats certainly would.

But Truman had a few ideas of his own. He called the Eightieth Congress into special session and challenged it to enact all the planks in the Republican platform. If Republi- **Truman's Upset Victory** cans really wanted to transform their convictions into law, said Truman, this was the time to do it. After Congress had debated for two weeks and accomplished nothing of significance, Truman took to the road. Traveling more than thirty thousand miles by train, he delivered scores of whistle-stop speeches denouncing the "do-nothing" Eightieth Congress. Still, no amount of furious campaigning by Truman seemed likely to change the predicted outcome. On election eve, the odds on a Truman victory were eighteen to one, so high the *Chicago Tribune* declared Dewey the winner before all the results were in.

By early morning, it was clear that Truman had confounded the experts. The final tally was 24 million popular votes and 303 electoral votes for Truman; 22 million popular votes and 189 electoral votes for Dewey (see map). Not only had Truman won four more years in the White House, but the Democrats had also regained control of Congress— by a majority of 93 in the House and 12 in the Senate.

How and why did the upset occur? First, the United States was prosperous, at peace, and essentially united on foreign policy. Moreover, Roosevelt's legacy—the New Deal coalition—had endured; big cities, northern blacks, southern whites, ethnic Americans, and labor unions had rallied to Truman's support. Ironically, the extremist image of the Progressive and Dixiecrat parties helped Truman by making the Democratic party look moderate. The Democrats, for their part, did not hesitate to distort the facts by denouncing the Progressives as a pack of Communists. Rather than the predicted 5 million votes each, Wallace and Thurmond polled just over 1 million each.

But in the end it was farmers whose votes made the difference. Truman advocated continued high price supports for farmers; Republicans wanted to reduce supports. In the bumper-crop year of 1948, Republicans actually wanted to cut back on grain storage. As the harvest mounted, prices began to fall; corn dropped from $1.78 a bushel in September to $1.38 in mid-October. Truman told farmers that the Eightieth Congress had "stuck a pitchfork in the farmer's back." Every one of the border states and several important midwestern states went for Truman.

Truman began his new term brimming with confidence. It was time, he believed, for government to fulfill its responsibility to provide economic security for the poor and the elderly. As he worked on his 1949 State of the Union message, he penciled in an expression of his intentions: "I expect to give every segment of our population a fair deal." Little did Truman know that he had chosen the label that historians would hereafter associate with his presidency: Fair Deal.

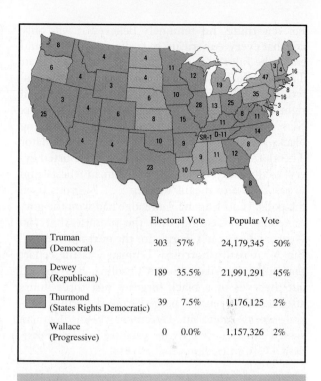

		Electoral Vote		Popular Vote	
Truman (Democrat)		303	57%	24,179,345	50%
Dewey (Republican)		189	35.5%	21,991,291	45%
Thurmond (States Rights Democratic)		39	7.5%	1,176,125	2%
Wallace (Progressive)		0	0.0%	1,157,326	2%

Presidential Election, 1948 *In 1948 Harry S Truman won perhaps the biggest upset in a presidential election, defeating not only the Republican candidate but also those of the States Rights Democratic and Progressive parties.*

PRESIDENTIAL AND JUDICIAL ACTIVISM IN CIVIL RIGHTS

Truman and other politicians knew they would have to compete for the growing African-American vote in urban-industrial states like California, Illinois, Michigan, Ohio, Pennsylvania, and New York. Many Republicans cultivated the black vote. Dewey, who as governor of New York had pushed successfully for a fair employment practices commission, was particularly popular with African-Americans. In Harlem, which had gone Democratic by a 4-to-1 margin in 1938, Dewey won by large margins in 1942 and 1946.

Clearly, then, Truman had compelling political reasons for supporting African-American civil rights. But he also felt a moral obligation to blacks.

For one thing, he genuinely believed it was only fair that every American, regardless of race, should enjoy the full rights of citizenship. More than that, Truman was disturbed by the resurgence of racial terrorism. To suppress black aspirations for civil rights unleashed by the war, a revived Ku Klux Klan was again burning crosses and murdering blacks who had had the audacity to vote. Senator Theodore G. Bilbo of Mississippi had exhorted every "redblooded Anglo-Saxon man in Mississippi to resort to any means to keep . . . Negroes from the polls," and Eugene Talmadge had won the governorship of Georgia with the promise that "no Negro will vote in Georgia for the next four years." But what really horrified Truman was the report that police in Aiken, South Carolina, had gouged out the eyes of a black sergeant just three hours after he had been discharged from the army. Several weeks later, in December 1946, Truman signed an executive order establishing the President's Committee on Civil Rights.

The committee's report, *To Secure These Rights*, would become the agenda for the civil rights movement for the next twenty years. Among its recom-

President's Committee on Civil Rights

mendations were the enactment of federal antilynching, antisegregation, and anti-poll tax laws. *To Secure These Rights* also called for laws guaranteeing voting rights and equal employment opportunity and for the establishment of both a permanent commission on civil rights and a civil rights division within the Department of Justice. Truman sent a special message to Congress calling the protection of citizens' rights "the duty of every government which derives its powers from the consent of the governed." Congress made no formal response. Some southerners warned Truman that, with such a civil rights program, "You won't be elected dogcatcher in 1948." There is evidence that the president did not expect congressional action, and that his real goal was the African-

Campaigning in Harlem on October 29, 1948, President Truman called for first-class citizenship for African-Americans. Truman recognized that black votes were crucial to his election effort in 1948. Cornell Capa, *Life* magazine © 1948 Time, Inc.

American vote in 1948. Whatever his motive, this was the first time since Reconstruction that a president had acknowledged the federal government's responsibility to protect blacks and strive for racial equality.

Truman took this responsibility seriously, and in 1948 he issued two executive orders declaring an end to racial discrimination in the federal government. One proclaimed a policy of "fair employment throughout the federal establishment" and created the Employment Board of the Civil Service Commission to hear charges of discrimination. The other ordered the racial desegregation of the armed forces and appointed the Committee on Equality of Treatment and Opportunity in the Armed Services to oversee this change. Despite strong, even fierce, opposition to desegregation within the military, segregated units were being phased out by the time the Korean War broke out.

African-Americans also benefited from a series of Supreme Court decisions. The trend toward judicial support of civil rights had begun in the late

Supreme Court Decisions on Civil Rights
———

1930s, when the NAACP established its Legal Defense Fund under Thurgood Marshall (who in 1967 would become the first African-American Supreme Court justice). Marshall and his colleagues set out to destroy the separate-but-equal doctrine established in *Plessy* v. *Ferguson* (1896) by insisting on a literal interpretation of its provisions. In higher education, the NAACP calculated, the cost of true equality in racially separate schools would be prohibitive. "You can't build a cyclotron for one student," as the president of the University of Oklahoma acknowledged. As a result of NAACP lawsuits in the 1930s and 1940s, African-American students won admission to professional and graduate schools at a number of state universities. In *Smith* v. *Allwright* (1944), the Supreme Court also outlawed the whites-only primaries held by the Democratic party in some southern states, branding them a violation of the Fifteenth Amendment's guarantee of the right to vote. Two years later the Court struck down segregation in interstate bus transportation (*Morgan* v. *Virginia*).

In 1947 the Department of Justice began to submit friend-of-the-court briefs on behalf of the civil rights movement, notably in cases involving higher education and restrictive covenants (private agreements among white homeowners not to sell

to blacks). In *Shelley* v. *Kraemer* (1948), the Court held that a racially restrictive covenant violated the equal protection clause of the Fourteenth Amendment and thus was not enforceable in a court of law. A Justice Department brief in *District of Columbia* v. *John R. Thompson Company* helped bring about the desegregation of restaurants and, eventually, hotels in the District of Columbia. But most momentous was the attorney general's brief supporting the NAACP's effort to desegregate the nation's public schools. Although the Supreme Court did not decide the landmark *Brown* v. *Board of Education of Topeka* until 1954 (see page 874), the Truman administration's legal efforts helped overturn the separate-but-equal doctrine that had been the law of the land since *Plessy* v. *Ferguson*.

A change in social attitudes accompanied these gains in black political and legal power. Books like Gunnar Myrdal's social science study *An American Dilemma* (1944) and Richard Wright's novels *Native Son* (1940) and *Black Boy* (1945) had increased white awareness of the social injustice that plagued African-Americans. A new black middle class had emerged, composed of college-educated activists, war veterans, and union workers. In their 1947 Journey of Reconciliation, black and white members of the Congress of Racial Equality rode buses into the South to test compliance with the *Morgan* v. *Virginia* bus desegregation decision. Blacks and whites also worked together in CIO unions and service organizations such as the National Council of Churches, the Anti-Defamation League, the National Urban League, and the American Friends Service Committee. In 1947 a black baseball player, Jackie Robinson, broke the major league color barrier and electrified Brooklyn Dodgers fans with his spectacular hitting and base running.

Cold War pressures also benefited blacks. As the Soviet Union was quick to point out, the United States could hardly pose as the leader of the free world or condemn the denial of human rights behind the Iron Curtain if it condoned racism at home. Nor could the United States convince new African and Asian nations of its dedication to human rights if African-Americans were subjected to segregation, disfranchisement, and racial violence. To win the support of nonaligned nations, the United States would have to live up to its own ideals. That the nation was not doing so was evident. Segregation was still standard practice in the 1950s, even if it was no longer the law of the land. Blacks continued to suffer job discrimina-

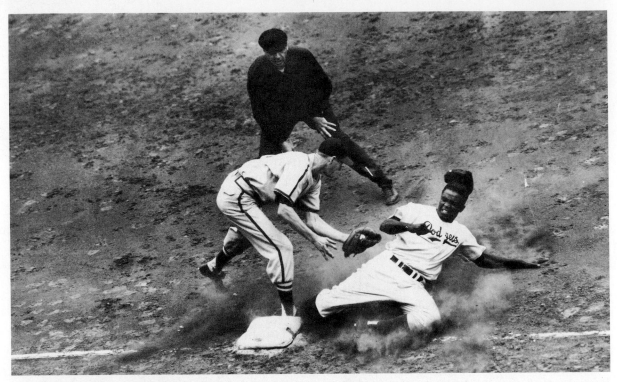

Jackie Robinson cracked the color line in major league baseball when he joined the Brooklyn Dodgers for the 1947 season. Sliding safely into third base, Robinson flashes the aggressive style that won him rookie-of-the-year honors. He was later elected to the Baseball Hall of Fame. Hy Peskin, LIFE Magazine © Time Warner Inc.

tion and disfranchisement. Even so, in the ten years following the Second World War, African-Americans made more progress than in any period since Reconstruction.

McCARTHYISM

It is a common misconception that anti-Communist hysteria began in 1950 with the furious speeches of Senator Joseph R. McCarthy. Actually, anti-communism had been a prominent strand in the American political fabric ever since the First World War and the Red Scare of 1919 and 1920. But the Cold War heightened anti-Communist fears, and by 1950 they reached hysterical proportions. Mc-Carthy did not create this hysteria; he manipulated it to his own advantage in order to become the most successful and frightening redbaiter the country had ever seen.

What reason was there to fear Communist influence in the 1940s and 1950s? The Communist party had never been strong in the United States,

Communist Party Membership

even during the hard times of the depression. When news of the trials and executions of thousands of soviet anti-Stalinists reached America in 1937 and 1938, followed shortly by the signing of the Nazi-Soviet Pact in August 1939, many party members had resigned in disgust. With the German invasion of Russia in 1941, however, American attitudes toward the Soviet Union became more favorable. Suddenly the United States and Russia were allies in the war against Hitler.

Meanwhile anticommunism persisted in the United States. In 1940 Congress enacted the Alien Registration (Smith) Act, which made it unlawful to advocate the overthrow of the U.S. government by force or violence or to join any organization that did so. Politicians began playing on anti-Communist paranoia again. In the 1944 presidential campaign Dewey charged that influential Communists within the Democratic party were about to take it over.

How do historians know

that public anxiety about communism was heightened by the media? This comic book, published in 1947 by the Catechetical Guild Educational Society, enjoyed several reprintings; 4 million copies were distributed free to church groups. Claiming that Communists had already "wormed their way into . . . government offices, trade unions, and other positions of trust," it warned Americans that, unless they were vigilant, they might be "living in Communist slavery." Films such as Invasion U.S.A. (1952) also featured Communist-takeover scenarios, as did newspaper and magazine articles and television specials, like Red Nightmare (1962).   Photo: The Michael Barson Collection, Glen Ridge, N.J.

Then in 1945 an incident occurred that tended to confirm anti-Communists' worst fears. In a raid on the offices of *Amerasia*, a little-known magazine whose editors sympathized with the Chinese Communists, the Office of Strategic Services confiscated classified government documents. Who had supplied the documents to the magazine, and why? Similar concern was mounting in Canada, where in 1946 a royal commission issued a report claiming that Soviet spies were operating there; among them, the report said, were a member of the Canadian Parliament and a scientist who had transmitted atomic secrets to a Soviet agent.

Spurred by these revelations, Truman in 1947 ordered investigations into the loyalty of the more than 3 million employees of the U.S. government.

Truman's Loyalty Probe
———

In 1950 the government began discharging people deemed "security risks," among them alcoholics, homosexuals, and debtors thought to be susceptible to blackmail. In most cases there was no evidence of disloyalty. Without the right to confront their accusers and demand such evidence, however, many were ruined for life. Still others became victims of guilt by association—their loyalty was considered questionable because they knew people thought to be subversive, disloyal, or dangerous.

The wellspring of this fear of communism was the Cold War: fear of internal subversion was intertwined with fear of external attack. It was no coincidence that Truman ordered the loyalty probe the same week he appeared before Congress to announce his containment policy (see Chapter 29). His alarmist rhetoric heightened public anxiety.

Truman was not alone in peddling fear; conservatives and liberal Democrats joined him. Republicans used the same methods to attack the Democratic candidates for president in 1948 and 1952; liberal Democrats used them to discredit the far-left, pro-Wallace wing of their party. The anti-Communist hysteria of the late 1940s, created by professional politicians, was embraced and promoted by labor union officials, religious leaders, Hollywood moguls, and other influential figures.

People began to point accusing fingers at each other. "Reds, phonies, and 'parlor pinks,'" in Truman's words, seemed to lurk everywhere. Holly-

Victims of Anti-Communist Hysteria

wood film personalities who had been ardent left-wingers such as Will Geer and Zero Mostel were blacklisted; and several prominent screenwriters and directors were sentenced to prison for contempt of Congress when they refused to provide names of alleged Communists. Schoolteachers and college professors were fired for expressing dissenting viewpoints, and in some communities "pro-Communist" magazines and books were removed from school libraries. The *Nation* was removed from school libraries in New York City, while the public library in Champaign, Illinois, banned the *New Republic*.

In labor union elections and even in local parent-teacher associations, redbaiting became a convenient tactic for discrediting the opposition. The hysteria was particularly damaging to the labor movement, which forsook its class-conscious militancy in favor of patriotism and anticommunism. Leaders of the United Auto Workers used redbaiting to discredit opposition within the union. Union bulletin boards, once bristling with strike notices and photographs of police clubbing strik-

ers, were now adorned with such slogans as "UAW Americanism for Us." At its 1949 convention, the CIO expelled eleven unions, with a combined membership of over 900,000, for alleged Communist domination. All this occurred at a time when membership in the Communist Party of the United States of America was rapidly declining, from a high of about 83,000 in 1947 to 55,000 in 1950 and 25,000 in 1954.

Despite the rampant false accusations, there was cause for alarm—especially in 1949, which dramatist Arthur Miller called "the year it came apart." Throughout that year,

Hiss Trial

a former State Department official, Alger Hiss, was on trial for perjury for swearing to a grand jury that he had never passed classified documents to his accuser, former American Communist spy Whittaker Chambers, and that he in fact had not seen Chambers since 1936. When Truman and Secretary of State Dean Acheson came to Hiss's defense, charging that the Republicans were publicizing the case to divert attention from their own legislative failures in Congress, some people began to suspect that the Democrats had something to hide. Republican Congressman Richard M. Nixon of California, a member of the House Committee on Un-American Activities that had led the investigation of the Hiss case, harped constantly on that theme. Then two events shoved the Hiss trial off the front page. In September the Russians exploded their first atomic bomb, and on October 1 the Chinese Communists, finally victorious in their civil war, proclaimed the People's Republic of China. A howl of indignation arose from alarmed Americans; Truman and Acheson were now on the defensive.

The new decade brought no end to the hysteria; indeed, 1950 saw more disquieting news. Hiss was convicted of perjury. A British court sentenced Klaus Fuchs, a nuclear scientist and Nazi refugee, to fourteen years in prison for turning over to Soviet agents secrets from the atomic-bomb project at Los Alamos, New Mexico. And President Truman announced that in response to the Russian atomic bomb, the United States would embark on a crash project to develop a hydrogen bomb. "Fuchs and Acheson and Hiss and hydrogen bombs threatening outside and New Dealism eating away at the vitals of the nation," exclaimed one right-wing Republican. "In the name of

Congressman Richard M. Nixon appeared to take little satisfaction in the newspaper headline proclaiming Alger Hiss's perjury conviction in early 1950. As a member of the House Un-American Activities Committee, Nixon had led the investigation into charges that Hiss had been a Communist party member and a spy in the 1930s. UPI/Bettmann Archives.

heaven, is this the best America can do?" Anti-Communists also exploited the hysteria to drive homosexuals from their jobs. "Sexual perverts have infiltrated our government in recent years," warned the Republican national chairman in 1950, declaring them "perhaps as dangerous as the actual Communists."

The circumstances were ripe for a demagogue: an irrational blurring of enemies, simplistic conspiracy theories, lies and half-truths, and an awareness that the Second World War had brought into being the new threat of nuclear holocaust. It was in this atmosphere that Senator Joseph McCarthy mounted a rostrum in Wheeling, West Virginia, in February 1950 and gave a name to the hysteria: McCarthyism.

That day in Wheeling, McCarthy proclaimed, "The reason we find ourselves in a position of impotency is . . . because of the traitorous actions of those who have been treated so well by this nation."

McCarthy's Attack on the State Department

The State Department, he asserted, was "thoroughly infested with Communists," and the most dangerous person in the State Department was Dean Acheson. The senator claimed to have a list of 205 Communists working in the department; McCarthy later lowered the figure to "57 card-carrying members," then raised it to 81. But the number did not matter. Tainted by scandal, McCarthy was in political trouble at home; what he needed was a winning campaign issue, and he had found it. Republicans, distraught over losing what had appeared to be a sure victory in 1948, were eager to support his attack. Here was a chance to discredit both Roosevelt's New Deal and Truman's Fair Deal. "A generation was on trial," as the journalist Alistair Cooke wrote.

McCarthy and McCarthyism gained momentum throughout 1950. Nothing seemed to slow the senator down, not even attacks by other Republicans. Seven Republican senators broke with their colleagues in 1950 and publicly condemned McCarthy for his "selfish political exploitation of fear, bigotry, ignorance, and intolerance"; a Senate committee reported that his charges against the State Department were "a fraud and a hoax." But McCarthy had much to sustain him, including Julius and Ethel Rosenberg's 1950 arrest for conspiracy to commit espionage; during the war, they allegedly had recruited and supervised a spy who worked at the Los Alamos atomic laboratory.

Widespread support for anti-Communist measures was also apparent in the adoption, over Truman's veto, of the Internal Security (McCarran) Act of 1950. The act made it unlawful to "contribute to the establishment . . . of a totalitarian dictatorship"; it also required members of "Communist-front" organizations to register with the government and prohibited them from holding defense jobs or traveling abroad. In a telling decision in 1951 (*Dennis et al.* v. *U.S.*), the Supreme Court upheld the Smith Act, under which eleven Communist party leaders had been convicted and imprisoned.

Meanwhile, McCarthy continued to display his unparalleled talent for demagoguery, making unsubstantiated charges, implying guilt by association, interpreting writings out of context, and telling outright lies. "It would seem easy to pin down the preposterous utterances," a reporter covering the Senate observed. "But no; McCarthy is as hard to catch as a mist—a mist that carries lethal contagion." And the outbreak of the Korean War in June 1950 made McCarthyism even more virulent.

THE ELECTION OF 1952 AND THE TRUMAN RECORD

As Senator McCarthy raged on and the nation mobilized for the war in Korea, Americans remembered the shortages of the last war and flocked to

Korean War on the Home Front

their grocery stores for sugar, shortening, razor blades, and canned goods. Fearing that Detroit would again have to convert to the manufacture of military vehicles, Americans bought cars in a hurry. Meanwhile orders for military supplies flooded factories. Ford built engines for B-36 bombers; the American Locomotive Company contracted for medium-size tanks; other companies filled requests for boots, sandbags, bandages, and jackets. By the end of 1950 U.S. Steel was enjoying its greatest profits since the First World War.

Fueled by panic buying and these huge federal expenditures, inflation (which had not been a problem since 1948) began to eat away at the economy again: prices rose 8 percent in the first eight months of the war. In January 1951, after six months of inflation, the government froze wages and prices. Administering the controls proved to be a nightmare—especially after Truman unconstitutionally seized the steel industry in 1952, when it rejected a government-recommended wage increase—but inflation was brought under control by mid-1951. Meanwhile factories hummed, the gross national product grew, disposable personal income increased, and unemployment fell. Reform-minded Democrats were not altogether pleased, however, for defense mobilization was taking precedence over Fair Deal programs. "Every liberal movement has been stopped cold at the time of national emergency," observed Senator Hubert Humphrey.

Draft boards began to call up men between the ages of eighteen and twenty-six, and national guardsmen and reservists were elevated to active duty. There was no rush to join. Husbands and fathers thought single men should go first; parents protested when the military began to draft eighteen-and-a-half-year-olds in 1951. "Everybody wants out; no one wants in," the director of the draft complained. When the government announced that college students would be granted deferments, young people enrolled in universities in hopes of the war's ending before their graduation. But the war did not end quickly, and by mid-1952 American military personnel numbered 3.6 million, up from 1.5 million two years earlier.

As the 1952 presidential election approached, the Democrats foundered. Frustration with the war and unrest over communism were exacerbated

Truman's Unpopularity

by the revelation of influence-peddling by some of Truman's cronies. Known as "five percenters," they had offered government contracts in return for 5 percent kickbacks. In exchange for expediting the import of perfume ingredients, Truman's military aide and friend Major General Harry Vaughn had accepted a freezer. Another presidential appointee admitted under oath, "I have only one thing to sell and that is influence." In 1951 Truman's public approval rating slumped to an all-time low of 23 percent and hovered at that level for a year. Joe Martin of Massachusetts, the House Republican minority leader, went so far as to call Truman "the worst president in history." Once again the Democratic party appeared doomed along with its leader—and this time appearances proved correct. Voters agreed with the 1952 Republican campaign slogan, "It's Time for a Change."

What sealed the fate of the Democratic party was the Republican candidacy of General Dwight D. Eisenhower, who had changed his mind about the appropriateness of a military man running for office. A bona fide war hero with a winning smile, "Ike" seemed to embody the virtues Americans most admired: humble origins, integrity, decency, lack of pretense, and native ability. His running mate, Senator Richard M. Nixon of California, was less likable. Accused during the campaign of having received money from a secret slush fund raised by wealthy Californians, Nixon went on television to deny the charge. The only gift his family had received, he said, was a puppy named Checkers. His daughters loved the little dog, and "we're gonna keep it."

Eisenhower's unlucky Democratic opponent was Adlai Stevenson, the thoughtful, cerebral, and witty governor of Illinois. Eisenhower's supporters derided him as an "egghead,"

Eisenhower's Victory

and from the outset it was never much of a contest. Eisenhower promised to end the Korean War. He remained cautiously silent on the subject of McCarthyism, but his running mate did not. Nixon scrambled for political points by referring to Stevenson as "Adlai the appeaser . . . who got a Ph.D. from Dean Acheson's College of Cowardly Communist Containment." The result was a landslide: Eisenhower won almost 34 million popular votes and 442 elec-

toral votes, to the Democrats' 27 million popular and 89 electoral votes.

Eisenhower's 1952 victory was a personal triumph. But several issues, notably the Korean War, also stirred the voters. By election day, armistice negotiations in Korea had been dragging on for almost a year and a half. There was still sporadic heavy fighting, and Eisenhower had promised to visit Korea and end the war. Americans were also upset by White House corruption and allegations that Communists still worked in the State Department. All these factors had coalesced to produce a record turnout of 61.5 million voters, 13 million more than in 1948. Many wanted to express their enthusiasm for Eisenhower, war hero and trusted statesman, who won the support of diverse socioeconomic groups, educational levels, and religious faiths. He even captured four states in the once-solid Democratic South. Moreover, Eisenhower's coattails were long enough to carry other Republicans to victory; the party gained control of both houses of Congress, though with only a one-seat margin in the Senate.

Although Truman was highly unpopular when he left office in 1953, historians now rate him among the nation's ten best presidents. Having

Truman's Presidential Legacy

come to office suddenly and with little experience, in eight years he strengthened the powers of the presidency. During the Truman administration, agencies that had been established for temporary duty during the Second World War were made permanent. The Atomic Energy Act of 1946 established the Atomic Energy Commission. Legislation in 1947 created a unified Department of Defense, the National Security Council, and a permanent intelligence service, the Central Intelligence Agency (CIA). Truman's main shortcomings stemmed from his overreaction to the alleged threat of Communist subversion in government. His loyalty program ruined innocent people's lives and careers, and his rhetoric helped pave the way for McCarthyism. He also sent American troops to fight in Korea without a declaration of war from Congress.

At the same time, Truman was a New Dealer who fought for social-welfare programs and legislation to benefit farmers, workers, homeowners, retired persons, and people in need of health care. Above all, his Fair Deal—most of which was en-

During the 1952 presidential campaign, Dwight D. Eisenhower received a delegation of Republican national committeewomen at his New York City headquarters. As the women chanted "I Like Ike," the Republican candidate opened his arms to welcome them.   UPI/Bettmann Archives.

This compact was given to Republican women who had used the telephones to get out the Eisenhower vote in 1952.   Smithsonian Institution, Division of Political History, Washington, D.C.

acted during subsequent presidential administrations—represented a commitment to first-class citizenship for African-Americans. Although he did suffer from a quick temper, he was personally honest and a devoted family man. And he showed his spunk and courage in 1948, when he pulled off the biggest upset in American political history. When Truman left office in 1953, he had set the United States on a course from which it would not veer, and he had cast a long shadow across the country's twentieth-century history.

CONSENSUS AND THE POLITICS OF THE EISENHOWER PRESIDENCY

Smiling Ike, with his folksy style, garbled syntax, and frequent escapes to the golf course, provoked Democrats to charge that he failed to lead. But it was not that simple. Dwight D. Eisenhower was no stranger to hard work. His low-key, hidden-hand style was a way of playing down his role as politician and highlighting his role as chief of state. He was also timid about tangling directly with the Republican party's vocal right wing. Eisenhower relied heavily on staff work, delegated authority to departments, and shied away from close involvement in the legislative process. This approach sometimes meant that he was not well informed on details, and it gave the impression that he was out of touch with his own government. In fact, he was not, and he remained a very popular president.

During Eisenhower's presidency most Americans clung to the status quo. It was an era of both self-congratulation and constant anxiety. The British journalist Godfrey Hodgson, describing the "consensus mood," has written that Americans were "confident to the verge of complacency about the perfectibility of American society, anxious to the point of paranoia about the threat of communism." Much as they might bicker about how the Cold War should be waged or how the economy should be managed, they were one when it came to anticommunism and faith in economic progress. Most white Americans believed that the United States was the greatest nation in the world and that its potential was boundless. For middle-class Americans who surrounded themselves with the symbols of economic success—automobiles, televisions, houses in suburbia—the American dream seemed a reality (see Chapter 30). Most would have agreed with the liberal economist and Harvard University professor John Kenneth Galbraith, who wrote in his influential *The Affluent Society* (1958) that since the Second World War capitalism had worked "quite brilliantly" in creating material comfort for the bulk of the American people.

The Consensus Mood

Demand for reform at such a time seemed to most Americans not only unnecessary but downright unpatriotic. The country was engaged in a moral struggle with communism, people believed, and during such a crusade one should support, not criticize, the government. The historian Henry Steele Commager saw conformity everywhere— "the uncritical and unquestioning acceptance of America as it is." Some intellectuals who had flirted with radicalism in the 1930s, like Sidney Hook and Irving Kristol, became impassioned

This smiling family, about to have its picture taken, symbolizes the optimism of the consensus mood in postwar America. Such confidence contrasted vividly with the American paranoia about communism. This scene by John Falter appeared on the cover of the Fourth of July 1952 issue of the Saturday Evening Post. © Curtis Publishing Company.

Cold War ideologues who believed that criticizing America gave comfort to the enemy. They even accepted CIA subsidies for their anti-Communist Congress for Cultural Freedom. College students shunned passionate political convictions. A weak minority on the left advocated checks on the political power of corporations, and a noisy minority on the right accused the government of a wishy-washy campaign against communism. But both liberal Democrats and moderate Republicans avoided extremism, satisfied to be occupying what historian Arthur M. Schlesinger, Jr., called "the vital center."

During the 1950s, scholars who subscribed to the prevailing consensus proclaimed "the end of ideology" in America. Many of the country's most distinguished historians articulated the view that gradual and peaceful social change, not conflict, explained America's success as a nation. History books themselves are the best evidence of the extent to which the consensus perspective shaped historical scholarship in the 1950s. Since the early twentieth century, historians had told the Ameri-

Consensus Historiography

can story as one of conflict—rich against poor, North against South, farmer against industrialist and banker. They focused on rebellions, strikes, moral crusades, and wars. The historians of the 1950s, on the other hand, wrote about stability, continuity, and cultural unity; they spoke of *the* American experience and *the* national character; they emphasized that commonly held values were were more important than conflicting ideologies.

Highly regarded books were published on these themes, among them Louis Hartz's *The Liberal Tradition in America* (1955), Richard Hofstadter's *The Age of Reform* (1955), and David Potter's *People of Plenty* (1954). Historians did not deny the existence of conflict in the American past, but they ascribed it less to flaws in society than to disturbed personalities. Among the groups historians identified as maladjusted were abolitionists, feminists, Populists, and progressive reformers. The consensus perspective thus shifted the focus away from society's faults—slavery, sexism, political corruption—and placed it on those who demanded reform. After analyzing his colleagues' consensus writings, the historian John Higham observed that "a psychological approach to conflict enables historians to substitute a schism in the soul for a schism in society."

In this age of consensus, President Eisenhower approached his duties with a philosophy he called "dynamic conservatism," by which he meant being "conservative when it comes to money and liberal when it comes to human beings." Eisenhower's was unabashedly "an Administration representing business and industry," as Interior Secretary Douglas McKay admitted. The president and his appointees gave priority to reducing the federal budget, but they did not always succeed. They recognized that dismantling New Deal and Fair Deal programs was politically impossible. And most government expenditures consisted of fixed, built-in costs such as veterans' pensions, Social Security benefits, and interest payments on the national debt. Soon the Republican right wing branded Ike a "fifth-column Democrat" for not slashing the budget and moving more forthrightly against the welfare state. In turn, Eisenhower grew impatient with those he privately scorned as "hidebound reactionaries." The president considered "progressive moderates" more sensible.

"Dynamic Conservatism"

——

True to the tenets of the free marketplace and a balanced budget, Eisenhower tried during his first term to extricate the federal government from agriculture. Since the 1930s the government had made price-support payments to farmers, based on the difference between the prevailing market price for farm goods and the higher parity price (see Chapter 25). After making parity payments to the farmers, the government stored their surplus products. Some farmers received large payments, and government bins bulged with surplus wheat and other commodities. Meanwhile, accelerated use of chemical fertilizers and machinery further increased farm production. Prices therefore fell, and farmers' purchasing power declined. Millions of farmers—most of them small landowners—abandoned farming altogether. Eisenhower officials concluded that lower, flexible price supports would discourage production. But the Agricultural Act of 1954 lowered price supports to only 75 to 90 percent of parity. Two years later the Soil Bank Act allocated federal payments for farmers who agreed to take cropland out of production. Another farm bill in 1958 reduced the price support for some crops to 65 percent of parity. None of these measures worked; the government spent more and the surpluses grew, causing President Eisenhower to remark later that the federal farm program was "a national disgrace."

Farm Parity Payments and Surpluses

——

Eisenhower made more headway in other spheres. In 1954 Congress passed legislation to construct a canal, the St. Lawrence Seaway, between Montreal and Lake Erie. This inland waterway was intended to spur the economic development of the Midwest by linking the Great Lakes to the Atlantic Ocean. The president also made a Cold War–inspired case for the joint Canadian-American project: it would strengthen the security of both nations. The same year Eisenhower revealed that he would not attempt to roll back New Deal programs when he signed into law amendments to the Social Security Act that raised benefits and added 7.5 million workers, mostly self-employed farmers, to the program's coverage. The Housing Act of 1954, the first of many such measures during the decade, provided federal funds to construct houses for low-income families displaced by urban renewal's destruction of their neighborhoods. Congress also obliged the president with tax reform that increased deductions and raised business depreciation allowances and with the Atomic Energy Act of 1954, which granted private companies the right to own reactors and nuclear materials for the production of electric power.

The Eisenhower administration's devotion to privatization also brought about a dramatic change in the lives of Native Americans. During the 1940s, sentiment had grown in Washington that the federal government should turn Native American affairs over to the states. In 1953, Congress adopted a policy of *termination:* the liquidation of Indian reservations and an end to federal services. Another act of the same year made Indians subject to state laws. Native Americans were not asked their opinions of these departures from policies established a century before. Administration officials applauded the changes because they would reduce federal costs and serve states' rights. Critics—including most Indians—denounced termination as one more attempt to grab Indian lands and further exploit Native Americans.

Termination Policy for Native Americans

Between 1954 and 1960, the federal government withdrew its benefits from sixty-one tribes. About one in eight Indians abandoned their reservations, many to join the ranks of the urban poor in low-paying jobs. The government's efforts to provide assistance and vocational training—at relocation centers in Chicago, Denver, Los Angeles, and elsewhere—faltered. Like the Dawes Severalty Act of 1887, termination and relocation were motivated largely by land greed. The Klamaths of Oregon, for example, lived on a reservation rich in ponderosa pine, which lumber interests coveted. Enticed by cash payments, almost four-fifths of the Klamaths accepted termination and voted to sell their shares of the forest land. A Senate committee reported later that, since termination, the Klamaths had suffered "extreme social disorganization" and that "many of them can be found in state mental and penal institutions." By the time termination was halted in the 1960s, observers compared the havoc it had wreaked on Native Americans to the devastation their forebears had endured in the late nineteenth century.

Another form of devastation was caused by McCarthyism. During Eisenhower's first term, the conduct of Senator Joseph R. McCarthy was one of the most vexing problems facing the administration. The Wisconsin senator's no-holds-barred search for subversives in government turned up none but it was an affront to political fair play, decency, and civil liberties. Eisenhower avoided confronting McCarthy, saying privately that he would not "get into the gutter with that guy"; the president also feared that a showdown would splinter the Republican party. Instead, he denounced unnamed "demagogues thirsty for personal power" and hoped the media and Congress would bring McCarthy down.

Eisenhower on McCarthy

While Eisenhower pursued this indirect strategy to undermine the senator, his administration practiced its own brand of anticommunism. A new executive order in 1953 expanded the criteria under which federal workers could be dismissed as "security risks." Vice President Nixon boasted that the administration was "kicking the communists and fellow travelers and security risks out of the government . . . by the thousands." In its first three years in office, the Eisenhower administration dismissed fifteen hundred people, more than Truman had fired in twice the time. One of Eisenhower's most controversial decisions was his denial of clemency to Julius and Ethel Rosenberg, who had been convicted of conspiracy to commit espionage and sentenced to death. As picketers marched outside the White House demanding their death, the Rosenbergs were executed at Sing Sing Prison in 1953, while others around the world listened to radio reports of this quintessential Cold War event. Later that year, at the urging of the chairman of the Atomic Energy Commission, the president suspended the security clearance of J. Robert Oppenheimer, the celebrated physicist who had directed the Manhattan atomic-bomb project at Los Alamos during the Second World War. Oppenheimer's "crimes" were not that he was either disloyal to his nation or a risk to its security, but rather that he lied about the details of a 1943 conversation with a friend on Soviet interest in atomic secrets and that he had later opposed the government's crash program to develop the hydrogen bomb.

In 1954 the Communist Control Act demonstrated that both liberals and conservatives shared in the consensus on anticommunism. The measure, which in effect made membership in the Communist party illegal, passed the Senate unanimously

These anti-Communist protesters marched outside the White House in 1953. They wanted to be sure that President Eisenhower would deny clemency to Julius and Ethel Rosenberg, who had been convicted of espionage. He did, and they were executed in June.   Elliott Erwitt/Magnum Photos.

McCarthy hearings, held by a Senate subcommittee in 1954, became a showcase for the senator's abusive treatment of witnesses. McCarthy, apparently drunk, alternately ranted and slurred his words. Finally, after he maligned a young lawyer who was not even involved in the hearings, Joseph Welch, counsel for the army, protested, "Have you no sense of decency, sir?" The gallery erupted in applause, and McCarthy's career as a witch-hunter plummeted. Republican Senator Ralph Flanders of Vermont, who had courageously challenged McCarthy in the Senate, remarked that "were the junior Senator from Wisconsin in the pay of Communists, he could not have done a better job for them." The Senate finally condemned McCarthy, in a 67-to-22 vote in December 1954, not for defiling the Bill of Rights but for sullying the dignity of the Senate. He remained a senator, but exhaustion and alcohol took their toll. McCarthy died in 1957 at the age of forty-eight.

President Eisenhower's reluctance to discredit McCarthy publicly had given the senator, other right-wing members of Congress, and some private and public institutions enough rein to divide the nation and destroy the careers of many innocent people. The City University of New York, for example, fired eighteen professors—and did not apologize to them until 1980. McCarthyism demoralized and frightened federal workers, some of whom were driven from public service. The anti-Communist campaigns of the 1950s also discouraged people from freely expressing themselves and hence from debating critical issues. Fear and a contempt for the Bill of Rights, in short, helped sustain consensus.

McCarthyism disgusted many voters, and the 1954 congressional elections revealed that, though they still liked Ike, they remained loyal to the

Interstate Highway System

Democratic party. With a recession just winding down and the controversy over McCarthy as a backdrop, the voters gave the Democrats control of both houses of Congress. Lyndon B. Johnson of Texas became the Senate's new majority leader. An energetic, pragmatic politician, Johnson tried to work with the Republican White House to pass legislation. A notable accomplishment was the Highway Act of 1956, which launched the largest public works program in American history. This law authorized the spending of $31 billion over the next thirteen years to

and the House 265 to 2. Its chief sponsor, liberal Democratic Senator Hubert H. Humphrey of Minnesota, told his colleagues just before he cast his vote: "We have closed all of the doors. These rats will not get out of the trap." Years later Humphrey said of his role in passing this legislation, "It's not one of the things I'm proudest of."

As for Senator McCarthy, he finally transgressed the limits of what the Senate and the public would tolerate. His crucial mistake was not merely

Army-McCarthy Hearings

taking on the U.S. Army, but doing so in front of millions of television viewers. At issue was the senator's wild accusation that the army was shielding and promoting Communists; he cited the case of one army dentist. The so-called Army-

build a 41,000-mile interstate highway system, intended to facilitate commerce and enable the military to move around the nation more easily. The Highway Trust Fund, fed by new taxes on gasoline, would finance much of the construction. The interstate highways invigorated the tourist industry, further weakened the already ailing railroads, and spurred the growth of suburbs farther and farther from the central cities (see Chapter 30).

Eisenhower suffered a heart attack in 1955 but regained his strength and declared his intention to run again. The president wanted to dump Richard

Election of 1956
———

M. Nixon as vice president, but after Nixon refused to take a cabinet post, Eisenhower reluctantly kept him on to avoid disrupting party unity. The Democrats nominated Adlai E. Stevenson once more. The campaign lacked spirit, and the parties' platforms differed little. With recent crises over Hungary and Suez much on their minds (see pages 901 and 956–958), Americans decided to stick with an experienced military man and statesman at a time of world unrest. Eisenhower won a landslide

victory in 1956: 36 million votes and 457 electoral votes to Stevenson's 26 million and 73. Still, his personal victory did not aid the Republicans in Congress, where the Democrats continued to dominate.

Eisenhower faced rising federal expenditures in his second term, in part because of the tremendous expense of America's global activities. In the first three years of his presidency he had managed to trim the budget, largely by controlling defense spending. But the president discovered that he had to tolerate deficit spending to achieve his goals. In 1959 federal expenditures climbed to $92 billion, about half of which went to the military; this budget produced the largest peacetime deficit to that point in American history. In fact, Eisenhower balanced only three of his eight budgets. The administration's resort to deficit spending was also fueled by the need to cushion the impact of three recessions—in 1953–1954, 1957–1958, and 1960–1961. A sluggish economy and unemployment, which peaked in 1958 at close to 8 percent, also reduced the tax dollars collected by the federal government. But most Americans remained employed,

The downfall of Senator Joseph R. McCarthy came in 1954, during the Army-McCarthy hearings, when the army's attorney, Joseph Welch (left), turned to the senator and asked, "Have you no sense of decency, sir?"   Robert Phillips, LIFE Magazine © Time Warner Inc.

and the administration succeeded in keeping inflation at about 1 percent per year through the 1950s.

A series of setbacks in 1958 made that year the low point for the administration. Besides a lingering recession, scandal unsettled the White House when the president's chief aide, Sherman Adams, resigned under suspicion of influence-peddling for accepting a vicuna coat and an oriental rug from a Boston industrialist in exchange for special treatment before federal regulatory agencies. Then came large Republican losses in the 1958 congressional elections. The Democrats—boosted by the Adams affair, the economic slump, discontent among farmers, and their own exaggerated claims that the administration had let the United States fall behind in the arms race—took the Senate 64 to 34 and the House 282 to 154. Some Republicans grumbled that Eisenhower had not given his party enough leadership; others realized that the Democrats were just too numerous to be beaten in the best of times. For the last two years of his presidency, then, Eisenhower had to confront what he called congressional "spenders," who proposed "every sort of foolish proposal" in the name of "national security and the 'poor' fellow."

Setbacks of 1958

AN AWAKENED CIVIL RIGHTS MOVEMENT

Eisenhower was pleased to be rid of McCarthy, but he did not welcome the invigorated civil rights movement. The president completed the desegregation of the armed forces, begun under Truman, and advanced the desegregation of the District of Columbia. Nonetheless, he favored gradual and voluntary change in race relations. Meanwhile black leaders became increasingly outspoken, insisting on significant federal action, and black people became less patient with their poverty and second-class citizenship. The NAACP challenged segregation vigorously in the courts, and young blacks took direct action by means of boycotts, sit-ins, and demonstrations.

In May 1954 the NAACP won a historic victory that stunned the white South and energized African-Americans to challenge segregation on

several fronts. *Brown* v. *Board of Education of Topeka* incorporated cases from several states, all involving segregated schools. Written by Earl Warren, whom Eisenhower had named chief justice in 1953, the Court's unanimous decision concluded that "in the field of public education the doctrine of 'separate but equal' has no place. Separate educational facilities are inherently unequal." Such facilities, Warren wrote, produced in black children "a feeling of inferiority . . . that may affect their hearts and minds in a way unlikely ever to be undone." Because of segregation, the Court said, blacks were being "deprived of the equal protection of the laws guaranteed by the Fourteenth Amendment." But the ruling did not demand immediate compliance. A year later the Court finally ordered school desegregation, but only "with all deliberate speed." This vague timetable encouraged the southern states to resist.

Brown v. Board of Education of Topeka

Some border states quietly implemented the order, and many southern moderates, recognizing that, in the words of the North Carolina school superintendent, "integration is as inevitable as the sunrise," advocated a gradual rollback of segregation. But the forces of resistance soon came to dominate, urging southern communities to defy the Court. Business and professional people created White Citizens' Councils for the express purpose of resisting the order. Known familiarly as "uptown Ku Klux Klans," the councils brought their economic power to bear against black civil rights activists, foreclosing on their mortgages and arranging to have them fired from their jobs or denied credit at local stores. Merchants withdrew their advertising from white-owned newspapers that did not editorialize on behalf of resistance. Exploiting the anticommunism of the era, the councils charged that integrationists had joined "a strategic campaign of the world communist movement." The Klan experienced another resurgence, and defiant whites formed new resistance groups, such as the so-called National Association for the Advancement of White People. One of the most effective resistance tactics was enactment of state laws that paid the private-school tuition of white children who had left public schools to avoid integration. In some cases, desegregated public schools were ordered closed.

Eisenhower came to regret his appointment of Earl Warren as "the biggest damn fool mistake I

In 1954 these students at the Fort Myers elementary school, in Virginia, joined in the Pledge of Allegiance. What is historic about this photograph is that this was the first racially integrated class in the formerly Confederate state of Virginia.   UPI/Bettmann Archives.

ever made." Although the president disapproved of segregation, he objected to

Eisenhower on Civil Rights

"punitive or compulsory federal law" in the belief that improved race relations would develop "only if it starts locally." He also feared that the ugly public confrontations likely to follow rapid desegregation would jeopardize Republican inroads in the South. Eisenhower had even remarked to the chief justice before the *Brown* decision that white Southerners "are not bad people. All they are concerned about is . . . that their sweet little girls are not required to sit in school alongside some big overgrown Negroes." Instead of stating forthrightly that the federal government would enforce the Court's decision as the nation's law—in short, instead of leading—Eisenhower spoke ambiguously and thereby tacitly encouraged massive resistance.

Events in Little Rock, Arkansas, forced the president to stop sidestepping the issue. In Sep-

tember 1957 Governor Orval E. Faubus intervened

Crisis in Little Rock, Arkansas

to halt a local plan for the gradual desegregation of Little Rock's Central High School. Faubus mobilized the Arkansas National Guard to block the entry of black students. Eisenhower made no effort to impede Faubus's actions, and he appeared to endorse the sentiment behind them when he told a press conference, "You cannot change people's hearts merely by laws." Late that month, bowing to a federal judge's order, Faubus withdrew the guardsmen. As hundreds of jeering whites threatened to storm the school, eight black children entered Central High. The next day, fearing violence, Eisenhower federalized the Arkansas National Guard and dispatched paratroopers to Little Rock to ensure the children's safety. Troops patrolled the school for the rest of the year; in response, Little Rock officials closed all public high schools in 1958 and 1959 rather than desegregate them.

In 1957, paratroopers of the 101st Airborne Division stand at the ready as African-American students enter Central High School in Little Rock, Arkansas, thus desegregating public education in the state.   Ed Clarke, LIFE Magazine © 1957 Time Warner, Inc.

Elsewhere, African-Americans did not wait for Supreme Court or White House decisions to claim equal rights. In 1955 Rosa Parks, a department-store seamstress and active member of the NAACP, was arrested for refusing to give up her seat to a white man on a public bus in Montgomery, Alabama. (Jim Crow practices required blacks to sit at the back of the bus and, when asked, to surrender their seats to whites.) Local black leaders decided to boycott the city's bus system, and they elected Martin Luther King, Jr., a local minister, as their leader. At an overflow mass meeting held in a Baptist church, King launched the boycott with a moving speech that preached both militancy and restraint. Although blacks would no longer accept "oppression," King declared, they would con-

Montgomery Bus Boycott

front their "white brothers" not with intimidation and violence but with "the deepest principles of our Christian faith." There could be no question of who was right, King went on. "If we are wrong, the Constitution is wrong. If we are wrong, God Almighty is wrong. If we are wrong, Jesus of Nazareth was merely a utopian dreamer. . . . If we are wrong, justice is a lie."

Martin Luther King, Jr., was an Atlanta-born, twenty-six-year-old Baptist minister who had recently earned a Ph.D. at Boston University. Disciplined and analytical, he was committed to nonviolent peaceful protest in the spirit of India's leader Mahatma Gandhi. During the boycott, he received hate letters and obscene telephone calls; he was also found guilty of violating the state's anti-boycott law and ordered to pay a fine or go to jail. A bomb blew the front off his house while his wife and child were inside. But King persisted. "Absence of fear," according to civil rights leader Bayard Rustin, was what the young minister-scholar's example and exhortation gave to black Americans. In 1957, King became president of the Southern Christian Leadership Conference, organized to coordinate civil rights activities. For years, African-American ministers in the South had led struggles for civil rights. Now they had a new organization and leader; as Ella Baker, another black leader, put it, "the movement made Martin rather than Martin making the movement."

Martin Luther King, Jr.

During the year-long Montgomery bus boycott, blacks young and old walked or carpooled. "My feets is tired," remarked an elderly black woman, "but my soul is rested." With the bus company near bankruptcy and downtown merchants hurt by declining sales, city officials adopted harassment tactics to frighten blacks into abandoning the boycott. King urged perseverance. "This is not a war between the white and the Negro," he said, "but a conflict between justice and injustice." Bolstered by a 1956 Supreme Court decision that declared unconstitutional Alabama's Jim Crow laws, Montgomery blacks triumphed. They and others across the nation were further heartened when Congress passed the Civil Rights Act of 1957, which created the U.S. Commission on Civil Rights to investigate systematic discrimination, such as voting discrimination. But this measure, like a voting-rights act passed three years later, proved ineffective. Critics charged that the Eisenhower administration was more interested in quelling the civil rights question than in addressing it.

African-Americans responded by adopting more aggressive tactics. In February 1960, four black students from North Carolina Agricultural and Technical College in Greensboro ordered coffee at a department-store lunch counter. Told that "we do not serve Negroes," the students refused to budge. "I felt better that day than I had ever felt in my life," recalled one of the young men. "I felt as though I had gained my manhood." Thus began the sit-in movement, which quickly spread northward. Inspired by the sit-ins, southern black college and high school students met on Easter weekend in 1960 and organized the Student Nonviolent Coordinating Committee (SNCC). In the face of angry white mobs, SNCC members challenged the status quo, all the while singing the anthem of the civil rights movement, "We Shall Overcome," which includes the words, "We are not afraid."

The Sit-Ins

Martin Luther King, Jr., personally joined the sit-in movement, and in October 1960 he was arrested in a sit-in to desegregate an Atlanta snack bar. Sent to a cold, cockroach-infested state penitentiary where he faced four months at hard labor, he became ill. As an apathetic Eisenhower White House looked on, King was rescued when Senator John F. Kennedy, running for the presidency, persuaded the sentencing judge to release King on bond. In November, grateful African-Americans cast their ballots for Kennedy in the expectation that, as president, he would provide federal protection of their civil rights movement.

For leading the movement to gain equality for blacks riding Montgomery, Alabama, buses, Martin Luther King, Jr. (1929–1968) and other African-Americans, including twenty-three other ministers, were indicted by an all-white jury for violating an old law banning boycotts. In late March 1956 King was convicted and fined $500. A crowd of well-wishers cheered a smiling King (here with his wife Coretta) outside the courthouse, where King proudly declared, "The protest goes on!" King's arrest and conviction made the bus boycott front-page news across America. UPI/ Bettmann Archives.

THE ELECTION OF 1960 AND THE EISENHOWER RECORD

The election of 1960 was one of the closest and most hard-fought in the twentieth century. The forty-three-year-old Democratic candidate, Senator Kennedy, was handsome

John F. Kennedy

and intelligent, and he injected new vigor and glamour into presidential politics. Kennedy had been born to wealth, had graduated from Harvard, and had served as a congressman before joining the Senate in 1953. His running mate in 1960 was Senator Lyndon B. Johnson of Texas, added to the ticket to keep white southerners loyal to the Democratic party as the

A turning point in the 1960 presidential election was the series of televised debates between John F. Kennedy and Richard M. Nixon. Kennedy came across as self-assured, Nixon as surly. Here they relax at the end of one of their debates. Ed Clarke, LIFE Magazine © Time Warner Inc.

civil rights issue heated up. The Republican candidate was Richard M. Nixon, the forty-seven-year-old vice president from California. He and his running mate, Ambassador Henry Cabot Lodge of Massachusetts, expected a rugged campaign.

Kennedy, exploiting the media to great advantage, ran a risky but ultimately brilliant race. Aware that his major liability with voters was his

How and Why Kennedy Beat Nixon

Roman Catholicism, he addressed the issue head-on: he went to the Bible Belt to tell a group of Houston ministers that he respected the separation of church and state and would take his orders from the American people, not the pope. Seeing opportunity in the African-American vote and calculating that Johnson could keep the white South loyal to the Democrats, Kennedy courted black voters. He promised to sign an executive order forbidding segregation in federally subsidized housing.

Foreign policy became a major issue. Nixon claimed that he alone knew how to deal with Communists, and he charged that Kennedy lacked experience in foreign affairs and could not stand up to Khrushchev. Kennedy shot back, "I was not the Vice President of the United States who presided over the Communization of Cuba" (see Chapter 29). The Democratic nominee hit hard on Cuba, but his most effective theme was that Eisenhower and Nixon had let American prestige and power erode. Kennedy offered voters victory instead of stalemate in the Cold War, and he vowed to win over Third World countries as allies of the United States. Kennedy subscribed to the two fundamental tenets of the 1950s consensus—economic growth and anticommunism—and asserted that he could expand the benefits of economic progress and win foreign disputes through more vigorous leadership.

As Kennedy gained momentum, Nixon was saddled with the handicaps of incumbency: he had to answer for the recession of 1960 and the Russian downing of a U-2 spy plane (see page 901). Nixon also looked unsavory on TV; in televised debates with Kennedy, he came across as heavy-jowled and surly. Perhaps worse, Eisenhower gave him only a tepid endorsement. Asked to list Nixon's significant decisions as vice president, Eisenhower replied: "If you give me a week, I might think of one."

In an election characterized by the highest voter participation (63 percent) in half a century, Kennedy defeated Nixon by the razor-slim margin of 118,000 votes. Kennedy's electoral college margin, 303 to 219, was much closer than the numbers suggest (see map). Slight shifts in the popular vote in Illinois and Texas—two states where electoral fraud helped produce narrow Democratic majorities—would have made Nixon president. Kennedy carried most of the large industrial states and most of the South. Black votes were decisive in his victories in North Carolina, South Carolina, and Texas, and blacks in the inner cities turned out for him in large numbers. Although his Catholicism lost him votes, especially in the Midwest, he won about 80 percent of Catholic voters. Religious bigotry did not decide the election, and Kennedy became the first Roman Catholic president.

Assessments of the Eisenhower administration used to emphasize its conservatism, passive style, limited achievements, and reluctance to confront difficult issues. In recent years, however, interpretations have been changing as scholars have begun examining the now-declassified documents of the consensus era. Many now stress Eisenhower's command of policymaking, sensibly moderate approach to most problems, political savvy, and great popularity. Many historians now argue that Eisenhower was not an aging bystander in the 1950s but a competent, pragmatic, compassionate leader who gave most Americans what they wanted at the time—a grandfatherly figure in the White House, economic comfort, and unrelenting anticommunism.

Eisenhower Presidency Assessed

The record of Eisenhower's presidency is nonetheless mixed. At home he failed to deal with racism, poverty, and urban decay—problems that would wrack the country in the next decade. He dragged his feet on civil rights. He exacerbated McCarthyism by refusing to come down hard on the reckless senator, and his own loyalty program was excessive. On the other hand, in comparison with his successors in the 1960s, Eisenhower was measured and cautious. He kept military budgets under control and managed crises adroitly so that the United States avoided major military ventures abroad. At home he curbed inflation and kept the nation prosperous. (The GNP rose 38 percent, from $365 billion to $504 billion, between 1953

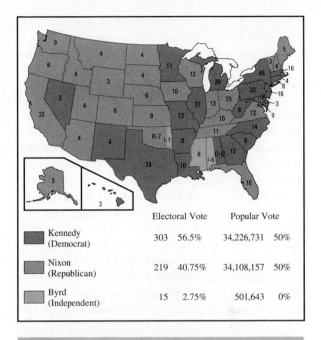

	Electoral Vote		Popular Vote	
Kennedy (Democrat)	303	56.5%	34,226,731	50%
Nixon (Republican)	219	40.75%	34,108,157	50%
Byrd (Independent)	15	2.75%	501,643	0%

Presidential Election, 1960   *In 1960 John F. Kennedy won the closest presidential election in twentieth-century American history. In fact, Richard M. Nixon won the popular votes of twenty-six states to Kennedy's twenty-four. In the electoral college, 15 southerners voted for neither Kennedy nor Nixon, but cast protest votes for Harry F. Byrd, a conservative senator from Virginia.*

and 1961.) He strengthened the infrastructure by building an interstate highway system, and he expanded Social Security coverage. Eisenhower brought dignity to the presidency, and the American people respected him.

Just before leaving office in early 1961, Eisenhower went on national radio and television to deliver his farewell address to the nation. Because of the Cold War, he observed, the United States had been "compelled to create a permanent industry of vast proportions," as well as a standing army of 3.5 million. "This conjunction of an immense military establishment and a large arms industry is new in the American experience," Eisenhower noted. "The total influence—economic, political, even spiritual—is felt in every city, every statehouse, every office of the federal

The "Military-Industrial Complex"

government." So powerful was this influence that it threatened the nation's "democratic processes." Then Eisenhower issued a direct warning, urging Americans to "guard against . . . the military-industrial complex." They did not.

President Eisenhower left office in 1961, to be succeeded by a much younger man and a Democrat. Senator Kennedy had criticized Eisenhower's domestic policies as inadequate to sustain economic progress for all Americans. And he had faulted Eisenhower's foreign policy for not winning the Cold War. Meanwhile, race relations and urban conditions continued to deteriorate throughout the country.

The postwar era had begun with the turbulence of demobilization and the growing criticism of President Truman. Politics was volatile after the war, and in 1948 Truman won a major upset, defeating not only the Republican candidate but also those of the Dixiecrat and Progressive parties. Political turbulence subsided after 1948, and with Eisenhower's election in 1952, the country became relatively passive. The unrest stimulated by McCarthyism proved the exception to this rule, but Senator McCarthy was silenced by the Senate in 1954.

Truman and Eisenhower, though both ranked as excellent presidents, presided over an era in which serious social problems—racism, poverty, and urban decay—were allowed to fester. It was a time of consensus and conformity, which went hand in hand with trust in and respect for established authority. In government, business, labor, the military, religion, and education, Americans were content to let those at the top decide on their behalf. They chose to pursue economic goals more than moral ones, seeming to believe that the latter were divisive and, in any case, seldom attainable.

Like their leaders, Americans were suspicious of mass movements, viewing even those with democratic goals like the civil rights movement as threats to stability. Rather than

An Age of Consensus

working for idealistic causes, people preferred to focus on earning a living, raising a family, and contributing their tax dollars to strengthen America. On the surface, the age of consensus remained intact throughout the 1950s, reinforced not only by economic development but also by the baby boom, the growth of suburbs, and an emphasis on patriotism, fads, and family togetherness (see Chapter 30).

During the 1960s, the nation would finally have to deal with the daunting social, economic, and political problems postponed since the end of the Second World War. Meanwhile the liberal consensus prevailed. "The fifties under Ike," Richard Lingeman of the *New York Times* observed, "represented a sort of national prefrontal lobotomy: tailfinned, we Sunday-drove down the superhighways of life while tensions that later bubbled up in the sixties seethed beneath the placid surface."

SUGGESTIONS FOR FURTHER READING

The Truman-Eisenhower Era

John Patrick Diggins, *The Proud Decades* (1988); Marty Jezer, *The Dark Ages* (1982); William L. O'Neill, *American High: The Years of Confidence, 1945–1960* (1986); Gary W. Reichard, *Politics as Usual* (1988).

Politics of the Truman Administration

Robert J. Donovan, *Tumultuous Years: The Presidency of Harry S Truman, 1949–1953* (1982); Robert J. Donovan, *Conflict and Crisis: The Presidency of Harry S Truman, 1945–1948* (1977); Andrew J. Dunar, *The Truman Scandals and the Politics of Morality* (1984); Alonzo L. Hamby, *Beyond the New Deal: Harry S Truman and American Liberalism* (1973); Susan Hartmann, *Truman and the 80th Congress* (1971); Michael J. Lacey, ed., *The Truman Presidency* (1989); Donald R. McCoy, *The Presidency of Harry S Truman* (1984); David McCullough, *Truman* (1992); William E. Pemberton, *Harry S Truman* (1989).

The Truman Administration and the Economy

Jack Stokes Ballard, *The Shock of Peace: Military and Economic Demobilization After World War II* (1983); Richard O. Davies, *Housing Reform During the Truman Administration* (1966); R. Alton Lee, *Truman and Taft-Hartley* (1966); Maeva Marcus, *Truman and the Steel Seizure Case* (1977); Allen J. Matusow, *Farm Policies and Politics in the Truman Years* (1967); Arthur F. McClure, *The Truman Administration and the Problems of Postwar Labor* (1969).

The Election of 1948

Norman D. Markowitz, *The Rise and Fall of the People's Century: Henry A. Wallace and American Liberalism, 1941–1948* (1973); Richard Norton-Smith, *Thomas E. Dewey and His Times* (1982); Irwin Ross, *The Loneliest Campaign: The Truman Victory of 1948* (1968); Allen Yarnell, *Democrats and Progressives: The 1948 Presidential Election as a Test of Postwar Liberalism* (1974).

Truman and Civil Rights

William C. Berman, *The Politics of Civil Rights in the Truman Administration* (1970); Richard M. Dalfiume, *Desegregation of the U.S. Armed Forces* (1969); Richard Kluger, *Simple Justice: The History of* Brown v. Board of Education *and Black America's Struggle for Equality* (1975); Donald R. McCoy and Richard T. Ruetten, *Quest and Response: Minority Rights and the Truman Administration* (1973); Mark V. Tushnet, *The NAACP's Legal Strategy Against Segregated Education* (1987); Jules Tygiel, *Baseball's Great Experiment: Jackie Robinson and His Legacy* (1983).

McCarthyism

David Caute, *The Great Fear* (1978); Larry Ceplair and Steven Englund, *The Inquisition in Hollywood* (1983); Richard M. Fried, *Nightmare in Red* (1990); Robert Griffith, *The Politics of Fear: Joseph R. McCarthy and the Senate*, rev. ed. (1987); Robert Griffith and Athan Theoharis, eds., *The Specter* (1974); Maurice Isserman, *If I Had a Hammer . . . : The Death of the Old Left and the Birth of the New Left* (1987); Stanley I. Kutler, *The American Inquisition* (1982); Victor Navasky, *Naming Names* (1980); David M. Oshinsky, *A Conspiracy So Immense: The World of Joe McCarthy* (1983); Ronald Radosh and Joyce Milton, *The Rosenberg File* (1983); Thomas C. Reeves, *The Life and Times of Joe McCarthy* (1982); Walter and Miriam Schneir, *Invitation to an Inquest*, rev. ed. (1983); Ellen W. Schrecker, *No Ivory Tower: McCarthyism in the Universities* (1986); Athan Theoharis, *Seeds of Repression: Harry S Truman and the Origins of McCarthyism* (1971); Athan Theoharis and John Stuart Cox, *The Boss: J. Edgar Hoover and the Great American Inquisition* (1988); Allen Weinstein, *Perjury: The Hiss-Chambers Case* (1978).

An Age of Consensus

Paul A. Carter, *Another Part of the Fifties* (1983); Howard Brick, *Daniel Bell and the Decline of Intellectual Radicalism* (1986); David Halberstam, *The Fifties* (1993) ; Douglas T. Miller and Marion Novak, *The Fifties* (1977); George H. Nash, *The Conservative Intellectual Movement in America* (1976); Richard H. Pells, *The Liberal Mind in a Conservative Age* (1985); Stephen J. Whitfield, *The Culture of the Cold War* (1987).

Eisenhower and the Politics of the 1950s

Charles C. Alexander, *Holding the Line* (1975); Stephen E. Ambrose, *Eisenhower: The President* (1984); Piers Brendon, *Ike* (1986); Robert F. Burk, *Dwight D. Eisenhower* (1986); Larry W. Burt, *Tribalism in Crisis: Federal Indian Policy, 1953–1961* (1982); Donald L. Fixico, *Termination and Relocation: Federal Indian Policy, 1945–1970* (1986); David A. Frier, *Conflict of Interest in the Eisenhower Administration* (1969); Fred I. Greenstein, *The Hidden-Hand Presidency* (1982); Chester J. Pach, Jr., and Elmo Richardson, *The Presidency of Dwight D. Eisenhower* (1991); Herbert Parmet, *Eisenhower and the American Crusades* (1972); Nicol C. Rae, *The Decline and Fall of the Liberal Republicans* (1989); Gary W. Reichard, *The Reaffirmation of Republicanism* (1975); Mark H. Rose, *Interstate: Express Highway Politics, 1941–1956* (1979).

The Civil Rights Movement and Martin Luther King, Jr.

Taylor Branch, *Parting the Waters: America in the King Years, 1954–1963* (1988); Robert F. Burk, *The Eisenhower Administration and Black Civil Rights* (1984); William H. Chafe, *Civilities and Civil Rights: Greensboro, North Carolina, and the Black Struggle for Freedom* (1980); David J. Garrow, *Bearing the Cross: Martin Luther King, Jr., and the Southern Christian Leadership Conference* (1986); Elizabeth Huckaby, *Crisis at Central High, Little Rock, 1957–1958* (1980); Stephen B. Oates, *Let the Trumpet Sound: The Life of Martin Luther King, Jr.* (1982); Harvard Sitkoff, *The Struggle for Black Equality, 1954–1980* (1981); Stephen J. Whitfield, *A Death in the Delta: The Story of Emmett Till* (1991).

WAR HEAD ASSEMBLY

LIQUID OXYGEN

DANGER

ALCOHOL

MASTER COMPUTER CONTROL

MISSILE TRACKING ROOM

The Cold War Era, 1945–1991

PRESIDENT HARRY S TRUMAN'S speech-writers considered his March 12, 1947, speech to a joint session of Congress as important as any since Pearl Harbor. Yet they were worried. Truman had a selling job to do if he wanted this Congress to approve his request for $400 million in aid to Greece and Turkey. Many members of the Republican 80th Congress wanted less, not more, spending, and many of them had little respect for the Democratic president whose administration the voters had repudiated in the 1946 congressional elections.

Already known for outspokenness, Truman on this occasion used alarmist language to persuade. Communism, he claimed, imperiled the world. "If Greece should fall under the control of an armed minority," he gravely concluded in an early version of the "domino theory," "the effect upon its neighbor, Turkey, would be immediate and serious. Confusion and disorder might well spread throughout the entire Middle East." Civil war, in which Communists played a prominent role, rocked Greece, and Turkey bordered the hostile Soviet Union. Events in these faraway places, Truman argued, threatened the United States.

Especially momentous in the dramatic speech were the words that would guide U.S. policymakers for almost a half century: "I believe that it must be the policy of the United States to support free peoples who are resisting attempted subjugation by armed minorities or by outside pressures." Two young members of the House of Representatives, John F. Kennedy and Richard M. Nixon, heard Truman's message that day, and when they assumed the presidency years later the doctrine still guided their policies.

Having thus announced the "Truman Doctrine," the exhausted president flew off to his vacation spot in Key West, Florida. The next day Truman wrote his daughter Margaret that he was relieved to have the speech behind him. Yet he felt confident that he had taken the right step, for "there is no difference in totalitarian or police states, call them what you will, Nazi, Fascist, Communist." As during the Second World War, he insisted, the United States had to block the expansion of such states—in this case, the Soviet Union.

The Truman Doctrine helped launch the *containment doctrine:* the United States had to draw the line against Communism everywhere. American presidents from Truman to George Bush have believed that a

Sketch of intercontinental ballistic missile (ICBM) in 1956.

• **I** *m p o r t a n t*   **E** *v e n t s* •

1945	Yalta Conference accords chart postwar order	**1950**	U.S. hydrogen bomb project announced

1945 Yalta Conference accords chart postwar order

Roosevelt dies; Truman assumes presidency

Germany surrenders

Potsdam Conference attempts to settle European issues and set terms for postwar control of Germany

Japan surrenders and U.S. occupation begins

1946 Soviets and Americans compete for influence in Iran

Kennan's "long telegram" depicts Soviet Union as uncompromising foe

Churchill gives "iron curtain" speech

Baruch Plan for control of atomic weapons fails

Truman fires Wallace for criticizing hard-line Cold War policy

1947 Truman Doctrine establishes containment doctrine against communism

Lippmann's critique of containment, *The Cold War*, is published

Communists take over in Hungary

Kennan's "Mr. X" article articulates containment doctrine

Marshall Plan announced to reconstruct Europe

National Security Act creates Defense Department and Central Intelligence Agency

Rio Pact organizes alliance in Latin America

1948 Organization of American States founded

Communist coup takes place in Czechoslovakia

Truman recognizes new nation of Israel

United States organizes airlift to break Berlin blockade

1949 North Atlantic Treaty Organization founded

Soviet Union explodes an atomic bomb

Communist victory occurs in China

1950 U.S. hydrogen bomb project announced

McCarthy alleges Communists in government

Secret NSC-68 document calls for huge military build-up

Korean War begins; China enters in fall

1951 Armistice talks begin in Korea

1952 U.S. hydrogen bomb exploded

1953 Dwight D. Eisenhower becomes president

Stalin dies

Eisenhower speaks of "atoms for peace"

United States Information Agency founded as propaganda instrument

Korean War ends

1954 Sino-American crisis occurs over Quemoy and Matsu

1955 Geneva summit meeting is first since 1945

Occupation of Austria ends

Soviets organize Warsaw Pact as defensive alliance in Eastern Europe

1956 Soviets crush Hungarian revolt

Suez crisis occurs in Middle East

1957 Soviets launch *Sputnik* into outer space

Committee for a Sane Nuclear Policy (SANE) is founded

1958 National Aeronautics and Space Administration (NASA) established

Quemoy-Matsu crisis recurs

Berlin crisis erupts

1959 Castro ousts Batista in Cuba

1960 Cuba and the United States feud; Castro looks to Soviet Union for help

U-2 incident occurs

---

ruthless Soviet Union was masterminding a worldwide Communist conspiracy against peace, free-market capitalism, and political democracy. Soviet leaders from Josef Stalin to Mikhail Gorbachev have protested that a militarized, economically aggressive United States sought nothing less than domination of the globe. This contest between the United States and the Soviet Union soon acquired the name *Cold War*.

The primary feature of world affairs for more than four decades, the Cold War was fundamentally a bipolar contest between the United States and the Soviet Union over spheres of influence. The two nations never fought one another directly on the battlefield. Instead, they waged the Cold War through competing alliances (the capitalist "West" versus the Communist "East"), regional wars between client states, rival ideologies, foreign

• *Important Events* •

1961	John F. Kennedy becomes president CIA-sponsored Bay of Pigs invasion fails in Cuba Berlin crisis recurs
1962	Cuban missile crisis brings world to brink of nuclear war
1963	Limited Test-Ban Treaty prohibits atmospheric testing of nuclear weapons Lyndon B. Johnson becomes president
1965	U.S. escalates Vietnam War
1967	Glassboro summit meeting
1968	Nuclear nonproliferation treaty signed Soviets invade Czechoslovakia
1969	Richard M. Nixon becomes president and, with Kissinger, launches détente policy
1972	Nixon visits China and ends years of Sino-American isolation SALT-I Treaty limits ABMs and strategic nuclear weapons
1977	Jimmy Carter becomes president and presses human rights policy
1979	American hostages seized in Iran (not released until early 1981) SALT-II treaty acknowledges Soviet-American nuclear parity Soviets invade Afghanistan
1980	Carter Doctrine declares U.S. will defend Persian Gulf area Grain embargo and boycott of Olympic Games imposed against Soviets
1981	Ronald Reagan becomes president Soviet crackdown in Poland prompts U.S. trade restrictions on Soviet Union
1982	START negotiations begin on reducing strategic nuclear forces
1983	Strategic Defense Initiative ("Star Wars") announced Nuclear freeze movement grows around the world U.S. Roman Catholic bishops' pastoral letter criticizes nuclear weapons Soviets shoot down Korean airliner U.S. Pershing missiles deployed in Western Europe
1985	Reagan Doctrine promises aid to anti-Soviet "freedom fighters" Gorbachev initiates *glasnost* and *perestroika* reforms in the Soviet Union United States and Soviet Union disagree over SDI at Geneva summit
1987	Gorbachev, Reagan sign INF treaty at Washington summit meeting
1989	George Bush becomes president Poland holds elections Berlin Wall opens and East German Communist regime collapses
1990	Communist regimes in Eastern Europe fall Germany reunified
1991	Soviet Union dissolves into independent states; Gorbachev retires Cold War ends

Note: For events in the Third World, see Chapter 31.

aid and economic sanctions, and the stockpiling of nuclear weapons. Like a glacier, the Cold War began in the 1940s to cut across the global terrain, changing the topography of international relations. The contest took the lives of more than 20 million people, emptied the treasuries of the combatants, spawned fears of doomsday, and destabilized politics in one nation after another, dragging localized conflicts into its path. Sometimes the two superpowers negotiated at summit conferences and signed agreements to temper the arms race; at other times they went to the brink of war and armed allies to fight vicious wars in the Third World (see Chapter 31). Decisions made in Moscow and Washington dominated world politics.

Throughout the Cold War era, critics in the United States challenged the architects of the Cold War, questioning their exaggerations of threats from abroad and the expensive militarization of U.S. foreign policy. But when leaders like Truman described the Cold War in extremist terms as a life-and-death struggle against a monstrous enemy, legitimate criticism became suspect and dissenters discredited. The critics' searching questions about the necessity and consequences of a global, interventionist foreign policy and a nuclear strategy based on the doctrine of "mutual assured destruction" (MAD) were drowned out by redbaiting charges that they were "soft on communism," if not un-American. U.S. decision makers successfully cultivated a Cold War consensus that dampened debate.

Ultimately the two great powers, weakened by the huge costs of their competition and challenged by other nations and blocs, faced an international system in which power had become diffused. In an effort to stem their relative decline, the two adversaries began in the late 1980s to take steps to end the Cold War. Its end finally came in 1991 with the disintegration of the Soviet Union, the collapse of other Communist regimes in Eastern Europe, and the reunification of Germany. Gloating Americans claimed victory in the Cold War, but slumping U.S. competitiveness in world markets, the faltering U.S. infrastructure, and the failure of many U.S. foreign interventions suggested that the Cold War had no winners. Like a retreating glacier, the Cold War left behind a scarred landscape and debris that complicated the shaping of a new world order.

THE SOURCES OF THE COLD WAR

After the Second World War, the international system was so unsettled that conflict became virtually inevitable. Economic chaos rocked Europe and Asia. Factories, transportation and communications links, and whole districts had been reduced to rubble. Agricultural production plummeted, and displaced persons wandered around in search of food and family. How would the devastated economic world be pieced back together? America and the Soviet Union offered very different answers and models. The collapse of Germany and Japan had also created power vacuums that drew the two major powers into collision as they both sought influence in countries where the Axis had once held sway. And the political turmoil that some nations experienced after the war also spurred Soviet-American competition. For example, in Greece and China, where civil wars raged between leftists and conservative regimes, the two powers supported different sides.

Unsettled International System

The international system was also unstable because empires were disintegrating. Financial constraints and nationalist rebellions forced the European imperial states to set their colonies free. As new nations were born in the Middle East and Asia, America and Russia vied to win these Third World states as friends that might provide military bases, resources, and markets. The shrinkage of the globe also ensured conflict. With the advent of the airplane, the world had become more compact. Faster travel brought nations closer at the same time that it made them more vulnerable to surprise attack from the air. The Americans and the Soviets collided as they strove to establish defensive positions, sometimes far from home.

Driven by different ideologies and different economic and strategic needs in this volatile international climate, the United States and the Soviet Union shelved diplomacy to build what Secretary of State Dean Acheson (1949–1953) called "situations of strength." Both nations marched into the Cold War with convictions of righteousness that gave the contest an almost religious character. Each saw the other as the world's bully. While Americans feared "Communist aggression," Soviets feared "capitalist encirclement."

"We are in this thing all over the world to the extent few people realize," Acheson's predecessor James F. Byrnes (1945–1947) told Truman's cabinet. Why was the United States "all over the world"? One reason was a determination never to repeat the experience of the 1930s: Americans vowed to accept no more Munichs, no more appeasement, and no more depressions that might spawn political extremism and war. To Americans after the Second World War, it seemed that Soviet Russia had simply replaced Nazi Germany, that communism was simply the flip side of the totalitarian coin. The popular term "Red fascism" captured this sentiment.

U.S. Economic Needs

American officials also knew that the nation's economic well-being depended on an activist foreign policy. In the postwar years the United States was the largest supplier of goods to world markets, but that trade was jeopardized by the postwar economic paralysis of Europe—traditionally America's major customer—and by discriminatory trade practices that violated the Open Door doctrine. "Any serious failure to maintain this flow," declared an assistant secretary of state, "would put millions of American businessmen, farmers, and workers out of business." The automobile, steel, and machine-tool industries, as well as wheat, cotton, and tobacco farmers, relied heavily on foreign trade. Indeed, exports constituted about 10 percent of the gross national product. And the United States also needed to import essential minerals such as zinc, tin, and manganese. Thus economic expansionism, so much a part of pre-Cold War history, remained a central feature of postwar foreign relations.

New strategic theory also propelled the United States toward an expansionist, globalist diplomacy. "As top dog, America becomes target No. 1,"

American Strategic Thinking
——

warned Air Force General Carl Spaatz. To be ready for a military challenge in the postwar "air age," American strategists believed that the nation's defenses had to extend far beyond its own borders. Thus the United States sought overseas bases to guard the approaches to the Western Hemisphere. These bases would also permit the United States to launch offensive attacks with might and speed. When asked where the U.S. Navy would float, Navy Secretary James Forrestal declared: "Wherever there is a sea."

President Truman, who shared all these assumptions, also had a personality that tended to increase international tensions. Whereas Franklin

Truman's "Get-Tough" Style
——

D. Roosevelt had been ingratiating, patient, and evasive, Truman was brash, impatient, and direct. He seldom displayed the appreciation of subtleties so essential to successful diplomacy; for him issues were simple either-or matters. As Winston Churchill said of him, Truman "takes no notice of delicate ground, he just plants his foot firmly on it." Shortly after Roosevelt's death, Truman met the Soviet Commissar of Foreign Affairs, V. M. Molotov, at the White House. The president sharply berated the Soviet Union for violating the Yalta agreement on Poland. Molotov denied the charge. When Truman shot back that the Soviets should honor their agreements, Molotov stormed out of the room. The president was pleased with what he called his "tough method": "I gave it to him straight 'one-two to the jaw.'" But the Yalta agreements were vague; although Soviet actions in Poland had been heavy-handed, whether they were in violation of the ac-

MAR. 4, 45.   THE SHAPE OF THINGS NOW.   ST. LOUIS POST-DISPATCH

Europe may have been liberated from Nazi Germany's grasp in 1945, but the survivors faced a bleak future. The Second World War left factories mangled and fields cropless. Millions of people grew weak and sick from hunger, crying out for relief supplies from one of the few belligerents to escape the war's devastation at home—the United States. Cold War tensions soon sprang from the massive task of postwar reconstruction. Daniel Robert Fitzpatrick, St. Louis Post-Dispatch. Victoria Schuck Collection, John F. Kennedy Library.

cord was open to interpretation. Truman's simplistic display of toughness would become a trademark of American Cold War diplomacy.

As for the Soviets, they were not easy to get along with either. Dean Acheson found them rude and abusive. A graduate of Yale and Harvard Law School and a conservative who once said he could talk with "everybody who was housebroken," Acheson asserted that the Soviets were not: "I think it is a mistake to believe that you can, at any time, sit down with the Russians and solve problems." But more than the Soviets' style bothered Americans. Soviet territorial acquisitions included a portion of eastern Poland; the Baltic states of Lithuania, Latvia, and Estonia; and parts of Finland and Rumania. In Eastern Europe Soviet officials began to suppress non-Communists and install Communist clients.

Under official postwar relief and recovery programs, including the Marshall Plan, the United States shipped billions of dollars worth of food and equipment to Western European nations struggling to overcome the destruction of the Second World War. Private efforts also succeeded, such as this one in 1950. The people of Jersey City, New Jersey, sent this snowplow to the mountainous Italian village of Capracotta. UPI/Bettmann Archives.

still reeling economically and politically unstable,

Marshall Plan
━━

lacked the dollars to buy vital U.S. goods. Americans, who already had spent billions of dollars on European relief and recovery by 1947, remembered all too well the troubles of the 1930s: global depression, political extremism, and war born of economic discontent. Such cataclysms could not be allowed to happen again. Western Europe, Dean Acheson declared, was "the keystone in the arch which supports the kind of a world which we have to have in order to conduct our lives."

In June 1947, Secretary of State George C. Marshall (1947–1949) announced that the United States would finance a massive European recovery program. Although Marshall did not exclude the Soviet Union or Eastern Europe, few American leaders believed that the Soviets and their allies would want to join a U.S.-dominated project that would surely loosen the Soviet grip on Eastern Europe. Indeed, the Soviet Union and Eastern Europe refused to participate in the Marshall Plan, blasting it as the enslavement of Europe. Launched in 1948, the Marshall Plan sent $12.4 billion to Western Europe before the program ended in 1951 (see map, page 891). To stimulate business at home, the legislation provided that the foreign aid dollars must be spent in the United States on U.S. products. The Marshall Plan proved a mixed success; some scholars today even argue that Europe could have revived without it. The program caused inflation, failed to solve a balance-of-payments problem, and took only tentative steps toward economic integration. But it sparked impressive Western European industrial production and investment and started the region toward self-sustaining economic growth.

To streamline the administration of U.S. defense, Truman worked with Congress on the National Security Act (July 1947). The act created

National Security Act
———

the Department of Defense (replacing the Department of War), the National Security Council (NSC) to advise the president, and the Central Intelligence Agency (CIA) to conduct spying and information gathering. By the early 1950s the CIA had expanded its functions to include covert (secret) operations aimed at overthrowing unfriendly foreign leaders and, as a high-ranking American official put it, a "Department of Dirty Tricks" to stir up economic trouble in "the camp of the enemy." In 1953 the United States Information Agency was created to counter Soviet propaganda.

American officials also reached out to cultivate new foreign friends and build new bases. The United States granted the Philippines independence in 1946 but retained military and economic hegemony. The following year, U.S. diplomats created the Rio Pact in Latin America. To enforce this military alliance, the United States helped found the Organization of American States (OAS) in 1948. Under this and other agreements the Truman administration sent several military missions to Latin America and to Greece, Turkey, Iran, China, and Saudi Arabia to improve the armed forces of those nations. In May 1948, Truman quickly recognized the newly proclaimed state of Israel, which had been carved out of British-held Palestine after years of Arab-Jewish dispute. Despite State Department objection that recognition would alienate oil-rich Arab nations, Truman made the decision for three reasons: he believed that, after the Holocaust, Jews deserved a homeland; he desired Jewish-American votes in the upcoming election; and he sought another international ally.

One of the most electric moments in the Cold War came in June 1948 after the Americans, French, and British had agreed to fuse their German zones, including their

Berlin Blockade and Airlift
———

three sectors of Berlin. They sought to integrate West Germany (the Federal Republic of Germany) into the Western European economy, complete with a reformed German currency. Fearing a resurgent Germany tied to the American Cold War

camp, the Soviets cut off Western access to the jointly occupied city of Berlin, located well inside the Soviet zone. In response to this bold move, President Truman ordered a massive airlift of food, fuel, and other supplies to Berlin. To Great Britain he dispatched B-29 bombers—the planes designated to drop atomic bombs. These bombers did not in fact carry atomic weapons, but the Soviets did not know that. Their spoiling effort blunted, the Soviets finally lifted the blockade in May 1949 and founded the German Democratic Republic, or East Germany.

The Berlin crisis also accelerated the movement toward a security pact. Convinced that a military shield should join the economic shield provided by the Marshall

Creation of NATO
———

Plan, the United States, Canada, and many western European nations founded the North Atlantic Treaty Organization (NATO) in April 1949 (see map, p. 891). The treaty aroused considerable domestic debate, for not since 1778 had the United States entered a formal European military alliance. Republican Senator Robert A. Taft of Ohio protested that NATO would provoke an accelerated arms race or war with the Soviet Union. Others complained that the scheme would cost too much and that it empowered the president to send troops into combat without a congressional declaration of war. Some critics argued that the Soviets did not pose a military threat. Administration officials themselves did not anticipate a Soviet military thrust against Western Europe, but they responded that, should the Soviets ever probe westward, NATO would function as a "tripwire," bringing the full force of the United States to bear on the Soviet Union. Truman officials also hoped that NATO would give Western Europeans the confidence to thwart communism in their midst and to resist any temptation to adopt neutralism in the Cold War. The Senate ratified the treaty 82 to 13, and the United States soon began to spend billions of dollars under the Mutual Defense Assistance Act.

In September 1949 an American reconnaissance aircraft detected unusually high radioactivity in the atmosphere. The news stunned U.S. officials: the Soviets had exploded an atomic bomb. With the American nuclear monopoly erased, Western Europe seemed more vulnerable. At the same time, the Communists were winning the civil war in China and Moscow was scoring propaganda points by advocating "peaceful coexistence" with the West. American leaders could have responded to this changed state of affairs with a call for high-level negotiations. But Secretary Acheson announced that there would be no "appeasement." Instead, in early 1950, Truman ordered development of the hydrogen bomb.

Worried about Mao's victory in China and the Soviet acquisition of the atomic bomb, Truman asked his advisers to give him a comprehensive study of world affairs. The National Security Council delivered to the president in April 1950 a significant top-secret document tagged NSC-68. Predicting continued tension with the Communists and describing "a shrinking world of polarized power," the report appealed for an enlarged military budget to counter an alleged Soviet ambition for global domination: The United States must more vigorously wage the Cold War. The authors of NSC-68 urged that public opinion be mobilized behind huge defense expenditures. Officials worried about how to sell this strong prescription to voters and budget-conscious members of Congress. "We were sweating over it, and then—with regard to NSC-68—thank God Korea came along," recalled one of Dean Acheson's aides.

NSC-68

CONFRONTATIONS IN ASIA: JAPAN, CHINA, AND THE KOREAN WAR

Asia, too, became ensnared in the Cold War. The victors in the Second World War dismantled Japan's empire. The United States and the Soviet Union divided Korea into competing spheres of influence. Pacific islands (the Marshalls, Marianas, and Carolines) came under American control and Formosa (Taiwan) was returned to the Chinese. As for Japan itself, the United States monopolized its reconstruction. Stalin wondered what the difference was between American domination of Japan and Soviet domination of Rumania. But General Douglas MacArthur, who envisioned turning the

Reconstruction of Japan

Pacific Ocean into "an Anglo-Saxon lake," had the last word in Japan. As director of the U.S. occupation, MacArthur wrote a democratic constitution for Japan, revitalized its economy, and destroyed the nation's weapons. In 1951, despite Soviet protests, the United States and Japan signed a separate peace formally ending their belligerency. The treaty restored Japan's sovereignty, ended the occupation, and granted the United States a military base on Okinawa and the right to station troops in Japan. Further expanding its global military network, Washington also initialed a defense pact with Tokyo.

Meanwhile, America's Chinese ally was faltering. The United States had long backed the Nationalists of Jiang Jieshi (Chiang Kai-shek) against Mao Zedong's and Zhou Enlai's Communists. But after the Second World War, Generalissimo Jiang became an unreliable partner who rejected U.S. advice. His government was corrupt, inefficient, and out of touch with the rebellious peasants, whom the Communists enlisted with promises of land redistribution. Jiang also subverted U.S. efforts to negotiate a cease-fire and a coalition government. "We picked a bad horse," Truman admitted, privately denouncing the Nationalists as "grafters and crooks." Still, seeing Jiang as the only alternative to Mao, Truman backed him to the end.

Chinese Civil War

On the question of whether Mao was a puppet of the Soviet Union, American officials were divided. Some considered him an Asian Tito—Communist but independent—but most believed him to be part of an international Communist movement that would give the Soviets a springboard into Asia. Acheson went so far as to claim that China's "Communist leaders have foresworn their Chinese heritage and have publicly announced their subservience to a foreign power." Thus, when the Chinese Communists made secret overtures to the United States to begin diplomatic talks in 1945 and again in 1949, American officials rebuffed them. Mao soon decided that he was "leaning to one side" in the Cold War—the Soviet side. But China always maintained a fierce independence that rankled the Soviets, gradually widening the Sino-Soviet split.

In fall 1949, Jiang fled to the island of Formosa and Mao proclaimed the People's Republic of China (PRC). Would the United States ex-

Nonrecognition of the People's Republic of China

tend diplomatic recognition to the new government? Truman hesitated and tried unsuccessfully to persuade the British to wait as well. "Are we to refuse to recognize facts, however unpleasant they may be?" the British prime minister replied. "Are we to cut ourselves off from all contact with one-sixth of the inhabitants of the world?" Washington did precisely that. American officials became alarmed by a Sino-Soviet treaty of friendship signed in early 1950, and Mao's followers had harassed Americans and seized American-owned property in China. Mao also antagonized the United States by blaming it for prolonging the bloody civil war. Wanting to "wait until the dust settles," Acheson predicted that Mao would conquer Formosa, eliminating Jiang, and that Sino-Soviet friction ultimately would persuade Mao to sever his ties with the Soviets.

Truman also chose nonrecognition because a vocal group of Republican critics, the so-called China lobby, were winning headlines by charging that the United States had "lost" China. The publisher Henry Luce, Senator William Knowland of California, and Representative Walter Judd of Minnesota pinned Jiang's defeat on Truman. Senator Joseph McCarthy of Wisconsin snorted that "egg-sucking liberals" and "queers" in the State Department had sold China into "atheistic slavery." Under such attack, Truman was reluctant to recognize a Communist government. He and Acheson answered that Jiang was not willing to help himself and that a U.S. military intervention to save him would have drained valuable resources from Europe, the primary front in the Cold War. The United States "cannot furnish the loyalty of a people to its government," Acheson insisted, adding that "China lost itself." Truman's policy hardened into decades of nonrecognition; not until 1979 did official Sino-American relations resume.

In the early morning hours of June 25, 1950, thousands of troops under the banner of the Democratic People's Republic of Korea (North Korea)

Outbreak of Korean War

moved across the 38th parallel into the Republic of Korea (South Korea). They "struck like a cobra," recalled General Douglas MacArthur. Since 1945, when the great powers divided Korea, the two halves had skirmished along the supposedly

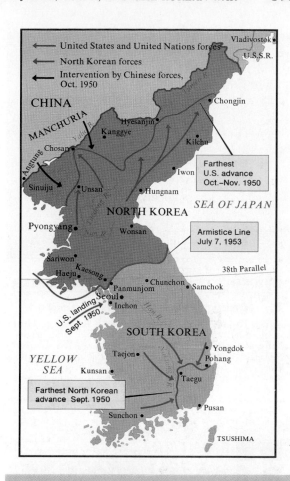

The Korean War, 1950–1953 *Beginning as a civil war between North and South, this war became international when the United States, under the auspices of the United Nations, and the Peoples Republic of China intervened.* Source: Adapted from Paterson et al., *American Foreign Policy: A History*, vol 2, 3rd ed. rev., © 1991, page 474. Reprinted by permission of D.C. Heath and Company.

temporary border. Both regimes sought reunification of their nation, but each on its own terms. Now it appeared that the North Koreans, heavily armed by the Soviets, would realize their goal by force, for the South Koreans, armed by the Americans, soon fell back. When the news reached Washington, people braced for a third world war.

For Truman, it was the 1930s all over again. "Communism was acting in Korea just as Hitler, Mussolini, and the Japanese had acted," he said. The president first ordered General MacArthur to send arms and troops to South Korea. Worried that

CHILDREN'S CRUSADE AGAINST COMMUNISM

2. MacArthur Heads UN Forces

North Korean Reds attacked South Korea in what is believed to be part of a communist plan gradually to conquer the whole world. The United Nations pitched in to help the South Koreans, like your dad would help the folks next door if some bad men were beating them up. The troops sent to Korea for the UN were put under command of General Douglas MacArthur. "Mac" has a long military record. But you know him best as the general who led the Allied forces to victory in the Pacific during the second world war.

 FIGHT THE RED MENACE

Intensely anti-Communist groups thrived in the United States during the Cold War. The "Children's Crusade Against Communism" distributed its exaggerated message in the early 1950s through bubble-gum cards like this one. The Michael Barson Collection, Glen Ridge, N.J.

Mao might attempt to take Formosa, Truman also directed the Seventh Fleet to patrol the waters between the Chinese mainland and Jiang's sanctuary on Formosa, thus inserting the United States once again into Chinese politics. "If Washington only will not hobble me," boasted MacArthur, "I can handle it with one arm tied behind my back." After the U.N. Security Council voted to assist South Korea, MacArthur became commander of U.N. forces in Korea (90 percent of them American).

Truman acted decisively for war because, in the Cold War mentality of the time, he believed that the Soviets had masterminded the North Ko-

Who Started the War?

rean attack. As an assistant secretary of state put it, the relationship between the Soviet Union and North Korea was "the same as that between Walt Disney and Donald Duck." There is scant evidence that the Soviets began the Korean War, but at the time there was reason to believe that the Soviets were exploiting an opportunity to expand their influence. When most American troops had been withdrawn from Korea in mid-1949, the Joint Chiefs of Staff had secretly declared South Korea nonvital to American security. In a public speech in early 1950, Secretary Acheson had drawn the American defense line in Asia through the Aleutians, Japan, and Okinawa to the Philippines. Although Formosa and Korea clearly lay beyond that line, Acheson did say that those areas could expect United Nations (and hence American) assistance in the event of attack. Stalin nonetheless could have read Acheson's speech as an abandonment of South Korea. The Soviet Union may also have been willing to risk war to challenge China for leadership of the Communist world or to disrupt American peace negotiations with Japan.

But unanswered questions dog the thesis that Moscow started the Korean War. When the Security Council voted to defend South Korea, the Soviet representative was not present to veto the resolution because the Soviets were then boycotting the United Nations to protest its refusal to seat the People's Republic of China as a member. Were the Soviets surprised by the North Korean attack? Were they caught off guard? And why did the Soviets give so little aid to the North Koreans once the war broke out? Why, when the Soviets were scoring important propaganda points by advocating peaceful coexistence, would they destroy their gains by igniting a war? Some scholars, emphasizing the Korean rather than international origins of the conflict, believe that the North Koreans began the war for their own nationalistic reasons. These historians focus on the civil war between the North Koreans led by Kim Il-sung and the South Koreans ruled by Syngman Rhee.

The war (Truman called it a "police action") went badly at first. North Korean tanks and superior firepower sent the South Korean army into chaotic retreat. The first American soldiers, taking heavy casualties, slowed but could not stop the North Korean advance. Within weeks after the initial North Korean attack, the South Koreans and

Americans found themselves pushed into the tiny Pusan perimeter at the base of South Korea, where they dug in (see map, page 895).

MacArthur began to plan a daring operation: an amphibious landing at Inchon, several hundred miles behind North Korean lines. Inchon seemed
Inchon Landing
an inhospitable place for such an attack, with narrow approach channels and heavy enemy fortifications. The Joint Chiefs of Staff balked, but MacArthur insisted. After U.S. naval guns and bombs pounded Inchon, marines sprinted ashore on September 15, 1950; by nightfall, 18,000 American troops had moved inland. They soon liberated the South Korean capital of Seoul and pushed the North Koreans back to the 38th parallel.

Even before the landing at Inchon, Truman had activated the rollback component of the containment doctrine by redefining the American war goal. That goal shifted from the containment of North Korea to the reunification of Korea by force. Communism would not only be stopped; it would be pushed back. In September Truman authorized United Nations forces to cross the 38th parallel.

Within several weeks U.S. troops had driven deeply into North Korea, and American aircraft soon began strikes against bridges on the Yalu
Chinese Entry into the Korean War
River, the border between North Korea and China. The Chinese watched warily, fearing that the Americans would now stab at the People's Republic. Mao warned that China could not permit the bombing of its transportation links with Korea or the annihilation of North Korea itself. MacArthur shrugged off the warnings, assuring Truman that the Chinese would face the "greatest slaughter" if they entered the war. Officials in Washington agreed with the strong-willed general. They were dead wrong.

In late October American troops had tangled with some Chinese soldiers, who pulled back quickly after the encounter. This may have been one of many Chinese signals to the United States that American advances to the Sino-Korean border should halt. Undeterred, the U.S. Eighth Army marched northward in a new offensive. On November 26, tens of thousands of Chinese troops counterattacked, surprising American forces and driving them pell-mell southward. Embarrassed, MacArthur demanded that Washington order a

Often in rugged terrain, U.S. troops fought in Korea for three years (1950–1953). The war became a stalemate. The combatants—the North Koreans and Chinese on one side and the South Koreans and Americans on the other—gained little from their warmaking, yet nearly 2 million people were either killed or wounded in a war President Truman never asked Congress to declare. Michael Rougier, LIFE Magazine © Time Warner Inc.

massive air attack on China. Truman hesitated, reflecting on the costs and consequences of a wider war. He hinted that he might use the atomic bomb. But he seemed chastened, reluctant to pursue a war that might drag on for years.

By early 1951 the military lines had stabilized around the 38th parallel. Both Washington and Moscow welcomed negotiations, but MacArthur had other ideas. The theatrical
Truman Fires MacArthur
general was making reckless public statements, calling for an attack on China and for Jiang's return to the mainland. Now was the time, he insisted, to smash communism by destroying its Asian flank. Denouncing the concept of limited war (war without nuclear weapons, confined to one place), he told one member of Congress: "There is no substitute for victory." MacArthur also hinted that the president was practicing appeasement. Fed up with the general's challenges to his authority, Truman fired MacArthur for insubordination in April. The general, who had not set foot in the United States for more than a decade, returned home to ticker-tape parades and the lecture circuit, but he soon faded from the American political scene.

Truman's popularity sagged because of the MacArthur episode and the stalemated war, but he weathered demands that he be impeached. The chairman of the Joint Chiefs of Staff, General Omar Bradley, backed Truman and defended the firing of MacArthur by disparaging the general's provocative ideas. Bradley pointed out that escalation could bring the Soviet Union into battle. After all, American bombs had already fallen close to the Siberian port of Vladivostok. And it was unwise to exhaust America's resources in an Asian war that promised no victory when there were allies in Europe to be protected. A showdown with Asian Communists, Bradley told a Senate committee, would be "the wrong war, at the wrong place, at the wrong time, and with the wrong enemy."

Armistice talks began in July 1951, but the fighting and dying went on for two more years. Dwight D. Eisenhower, elected president in 1952, went to Korea before his inauguration to fulfill a campaign pledge, but his visit brought no settlement. As president, Eisenhower let it be known that he was considering using atomic weapons in Korea. The most contentious point in the negotiations was the fate of prisoners of war (POWs): thousands of North Korean and Chinese captives did not want to return home, and some American and South Korean prisoners opted to stay in North Korea. Snubbing international custom, U.S. officials refused to ship their captives back.

The POW Question

An armistice was finally signed in July 1953. The combatants agreed to hand over the POW question to a special panel of neutral nations (which later gave prisoners their choice of staying or leaving). The North Korean–South Korean line was set near the 38th parallel, the prewar boundary. Thus ended a frustrating war—a limited war that Americans, accustomed to victory, had not won. American casualties reached 34,000 dead in battle and another 103,000 wounded. Total killed and wounded for all combatants was 1.9 million.

The Korean War carried major political consequences. The failure to achieve victory and the public's impatience with a limited war undoubtedly helped to elect Eisenhower (see Chapter 28). The powers of the presidency grew as Congress repeatedly deferred to Truman. The president had never asked Congress for a declaration of war, believing that as commander-in-chief he had the authority to send troops wherever he wished. A few dissenters like Senator Taft disagreed, but Truman saw no need to consult Congress—except when he wanted the $69.5 billion Korean War bill paid.

The Korean War set off a great national debate. Conservative critics of globalism—notably Taft, former ambassador to England Joseph P. Kennedy, and former president Herbert Hoover—suggested that America should reduce its overseas commitments and draw its defense line in the Western Hemisphere. If foreign nations were unwilling to commit their own resources to defending themselves, the United States had no obligation to help them. But Eisenhower's future secretary of state, John Foster Dulles, countered that "a defense that accepts encirclement quickly decomposes." Truman himself joined the debate with bloated rhetoric exaggerating the Communist threat: "We are fighting in Korea so we won't have to fight in Wichita, or in Chicago, or in New Orleans, or on San Francisco Bay."

Debate over Globalist Policy

The advocates of global defense won the debate, and the implementation of containment worldwide became entrenched as U.S. policy. Increased U.S. aid flowed to the French for their die-hard stand in Indochina against nationalist insurgents (see Chapter 31). South Korea and Formosa also became major recipients of American foreign aid. Australia and New Zealand joined the United States in a mutual defense agreement, the ANZUS Treaty (1951). The U.S. Army sent six divisions to Europe, and the administration initiated plans to rearm West Germany. The Korean War, Acheson cheerfully noted, removed "the recommendations of NSC-68 from the realm of theory and made them immediate budget issues." Indeed, the military budget shot up from $14 billion in 1949 to $44 billion in 1953; it remained between $35 billion and $44 billion a year throughout the 1950s. In sum, Truman's legacy was a highly militarized U.S. foreign policy active on a global scale.

EISENHOWER AND THE NUCLEAR ARMS RACE

As President, Dwight D. Eisenhower essentially perpetuated Truman's Cold War policies, applying the containment doctrine worldwide. He brought considerable experience in foreign affairs to his presidency. He had lived and traveled in Europe, Asia, and Latin America and, as a general during the Second World War, had negotiated with world leaders and made tough decisions of international consequence. After the war, as Army Chief of Staff and NATO Supreme Commander, he learned the essentials of nuclear weapons development and secret intelligence operations. Like most Americans, Eisenhower accepted the Cold War consensus about the threat of communism and the need for global vigilance. Partisan Democrats promoted an image of Eisenhower as a bumbling, aging hero, but as president he controlled the making of foreign policy and enjoyed comfortable vote margins in Congress on key resolutions and programs.

Eisenhower relied heavily on his trusted secretary of state, the strong-willed John Foster Dulles. A graduate of Princeton and George Washington universities, Dulles, at age thirty, had assisted Woodrow Wilson at Versailles. As a senior partner in a prestigious Wall Street law firm, Dulles had handled international cases, and as an officer of the Federal Council of Churches he had worked for world peace. He had also helped the Truman administration negotiate the peace treaty with Japan. Though polished and articulate, Dulles impressed people as arrogant, stubborn, and preachy—the "conscience and straightjacket of the free world," as one European newspaper put it. Few Cold Warriors rivaled Dulles's impassioned, uncompromising anti-Communist declarations.

John Foster Dulles

Like the president, Dulles conceded much to the anti-Communist McCarthyites of the early 1950s (see Chapter 28). Dulles appointed one of McCarthy's henchmen, Scott McLeod, as chief security officer of the State Department. McLeod went about trying to prove McCarthy's charge that the department was infested with Communists. Making few distinctions between New Dealers and Communists, he and Dulles forced many innocent, talented officers out of the Foreign Service. Among them were Asian specialists whose expertise was thus denied to the American decision makers who later sent the United States to war in Vietnam.

State Department Purge

Dulles considered containment too defensive a stance toward communism. He called instead for *liberation*, although he never explained precisely how the countries of Eastern Europe could be freed from Soviet control. *Massive retaliation* was the administration's phrase for the nuclear obliteration of the Soviet state or its assumed client, the People's Republic of China, if they took aggressive actions. Eisenhower said it "simply means the ability to blow hell out of them in a hurry if they start anything." The ability of the United States to make such a threat was thought to provide *deterrence*, or the prevention of hostile Soviet behavior.

In their "New Look" for the American military, Eisenhower and Dulles emphasized air power and nuclear weaponry. The president's preference for heavy weapons stemmed in part from his desire to trim the federal budget ("more bang for the buck," in the words of the time). With its huge military arsenal, the United States in the 1950s practiced *brinkmanship:* not backing down in a crisis, even if it meant taking the nation to the brink of war. Eisenhower also popularized the *domino theory,* according to which small, weak nations would fall to communism like a row of dominoes if they were not propped up by the United States. Eisenhower increasingly ordered CIA covert operations against governments in the Third World, where new states were emerging from colonialism to nationhood. Americans feared that revolutionary nationalism and unrest in Third World countries would threaten U.S. economic interests and also be exploited by Communists linked to a Soviet-led international conspiracy (see Chapter 31).

After Stalin's death in 1953, hopes ran high for a relaxation of Soviet-American relations. Instead, the nuclear arms race accelerated as the two superpowers developed new military technology and nuclear delivery systems. In November 1952 the United States detonated the first hydrogen bomb. Then, in early 1954, the largest bomb the United States has ever tested destroyed the Pacific island of Bikini. This H-bomb, packing the power of 15 million tons of TNT (750 times as powerful as the atomic bomb that leveled Hiroshima), produced a fallout of radioactive dust that showered a Japanese fishing boat in the area. The crew of the *Lucky Dragon* suffered severe nausea, fever, and blisters. When one of the sailors died, becoming the world's first victim of a hydrogen bomb, international protest bombarded the United States.

Hydrogen Bomb

Precariously balanced on the nuclear warhead of a menacing missile, Soviet Premier Nikita Khrushchev (1894–1971) and President Dwight D. Eisenhower (1890–1969) make their points in the dangerous Cold War setting of the late 1950s. Eisenhower invited Khrushchev to the United States to "melt the ice" of the Cold War. Although the list of outstanding Soviet-American issues was lengthy—including the nuclear arms race and Berlin—Khrushchev's visit of September 1959 did little to ease superpower tensions. © 1959 Newsweek Inc. All rights reserved. Reprinted by permission.

Development of Missiles

The Soviets tested their first H-bomb in 1953. Four years later they shocked Americans by firing the world's first intercontinental ballistic missile (ICBM) and then propelling the world's first man-made satellite, *Sputnik*, into outer space. Americans now felt more vulnerable to air attack and inferior to the Russians in rocket technology. The United States soon tested its own ICBMs. It also enlarged its fleet of long-range bombers (B-52s) and deployed intermediate-range missiles in Europe, targeted against the Soviet Union. By the end of 1960 the United States had added Polaris missile-bearing submarines to its navy. To foster future technological advancement, the National Aeronautics and Space Administration (NASA) was created in 1958.

The CIA's U-2 spy planes collected information demonstrating that the Soviets had deployed very few ICBMs. Yet critics charged that Eisenhower had allowed the United States to fall behind in the missile race. The much-publicized "missile gap" was actually a false notion inspired in part by political partisanship. "Everyone knows," Air Force General Nathan Twining privately told the president, "we already have a [nuclear] stockpile large enough to obliterate the Soviet Union." As the 1950s closed, the United States enjoyed overwhelming strategic dominance because of its air-sea-land "triad" of long-range bombers, submarine-launched ballistic missiles (SLBMs), and ICBMs.

President Eisenhower had long been uneasy about the arms race. He feared nuclear war, and the cost of the new weapons made it difficult to balance the budget. In a

Eisenhower's Critique of the Nuclear Arms Race

1953 speech, the president noted that "every gun that is made, every warship launched, every rocket fired signifies, in the final sense, a theft from those who hunger and are not fed. . . . The cost of one modern heavy bomber is this: a modern brick school in more than 30 cities." He also doubted the need for more and bigger nuclear weapons. How many times, he once asked, "could [you] kill the same man?" Spurred by such thoughts, by citizens' groups like the Committee for a Sane Nuclear Policy (SANE), founded in 1957, and by neutralist and Soviet appeals, the president cautiously initiated arms-control proposals.

Eisenhower's 1953 "atoms for peace" initiative recommended that fissionable materials be contributed to a United Nations agency for use in industrial projects. Two years later he issued his "open skies" proposal: aerial surveillance of both Soviet and American military sites to reduce the chances of surprise attacks. In response to worldwide criticism of radioactive fallout, the two powers unilaterally suspended atmospheric testing from 1958 until 1961, when the Soviets resumed it. The United States also began testing again at the same time, but underground. Despite a series of disarmament talks in Geneva, Switzerland, and Eisenhower's meeting there in 1955 with Stalin's successor Nikita Khrushchev (the first summit meeting in ten years), neither side could agree on suitable inspection systems to ensure compliance with arms control treaties or bans on nuclear testing. Because Eisenhower did not trust the Soviets, arms control talks never became a top priority for him. Indeed, he fully intended to preserve the American advantage.

In 1956 Khrushchev called for "peaceful coexistence" between capitalists and Communists, denounced Stalin, and suggested that Moscow would tolerate different brands of communism. Soon, however, events in Eastern Europe revived the customary acrimony of the Cold War. Revolts against Soviet power erupted in Poland and Hungary, testing Khrushchev's new permissiveness. After a new Hungarian government announced its withdrawal from the Warsaw Pact that the Soviets had formed in 1955, Soviet troops and tanks battled students and workers in the streets of Budapest and crushed the rebellion. The Eisenhower administration, on record as favoring the liberation of Eastern Europe, found itself unable to aid the rebels without igniting a world war. The United States could only welcome Hungarian immigrants in greater numbers than American quota laws allowed. The West could have reaped some propaganda advantage from this display of Soviet brute force had not British, French, and Israeli troops— U.S. allies—invaded Egypt just before the Soviets smashed the Hungarian Revolution (see page 956).

Hungarian Uprising

Hardly had the turmoil subsided in Eastern Europe when the divided city of Berlin once again became a Cold War flashpoint. The Soviets railed against the placement in West Germany of U.S. bombers capable of carrying nuclear warheads, and they complained that West Berlin had become an escape route for disaffected East Germans. In 1958, Khrushchev announced that the Soviet Union would recognize East German control of all of Berlin unless the United States and its allies began talks on German reunification and rearmament. The United States refused to give up its hold on West Berlin or to break West German ties with NATO. The two sides talked of war; finally Khrushchev backed away from his ultimatum, promising to raise the issue at future conferences.

Berlin and Germany were on the agenda of a summit meeting planned for Paris in 1960. Shortly before the conference, a U-2 spy plane carrying high-powered cameras crashed 1,200 miles inside the Soviet Union. Moscow claimed credit for shooting down the aircraft and displayed the captured CIA pilot, Francis

U-2 Incident

Gary Powers, and the pictures he had been snapping of Soviet military installations. Moscow demanded an apology, Washington refused, and the Soviets walked out of the Paris summit. Once again diplomacy fell victim to great-power antagonisms.

While sparring over Europe, both sides kept a wary eye on the People's Republic of China. Despite growing evidence of a Sino-Soviet split, most American officials still treated communism as a unified world movement. Washington continued to prop up Jiang on Formosa, which the Chinese claimed as part of the People's Republic, and to fret about China's encouragement of anti-imperialist rebellions in the Third World.

Dispute over two tiny islands off the Chinese coast brought the United States and the People's Republic to the brink of war. Jiang's forces used Jinmen (Quemoy) and Mazu (Matsu) as bases for commando raids against the mainland. China bombarded the islands in 1954. Eisenhower decided to defend the outposts and let it be known that he was considering the use of nuclear weapons. Why massive retaliation over such an insignificant issue? "Let's keep the Reds guessing," advised John Foster Dulles. But what if they guessed wrong? critics replied. Congress passed the Formosa Resolution (1955), authorizing the president to deploy U.S. forces to defend Formosa and adjoining islands, and two years later the United States installed on Formosa missiles capable of carrying nuclear warheads. Though Chinese and American diplomats held secret meetings in Geneva and Warsaw, war loomed again in 1958 over Jinmen and Mazu. Neither Beijing nor Washington, however, judged the controversy serious enough to risk full-scale war. The crisis passed, but one consequence accelerated the arms race: Eisenhower's nuclear threats persuaded the Chinese that they, too, needed nuclear arms. In 1964 China exploded its first nuclear bomb.

Quemoy and Matsu

In eight years of adopting a globalist perspective and applying the containment doctrine worldwide, Eisenhower held the line—against the Soviet Union, Communist China, neutralism, communism, nationalism, and revolution everywhere. Eisenhower found no way to relax Cold War tensions, and ultimately he accelerated the nuclear arms race he so disliked. Even U.S. friends seemed antagonistic; anti-American riots in Japan forced

When the East Germans first put up the Berlin Wall in 1961, they hastily constructed it of barbed wire. Later they added concrete blocks to the twenty-eight-mile barricade that divided East Berlin (left) and West Berlin (right). The large building with the chariot on top is the Brandenburg Gate. The ugly wall—symbol of the Cold War—came down in 1989, when the long Soviet-American conflict finally waned.   UPI/Bettmann Archives.

Eisenhower to cancel a goodwill trip to that island ally in 1960. That year, too, during the presidential election, the young Democratic candidate, Senator John F. Kennedy of Massachusetts, went so far as to charge that under Eisenhower's leadership the United States was losing the Cold War.

KENNEDY, JOHNSON, AND THE CRISES OF THE 1960s

John F. Kennedy's diplomacy owed much to the past. He often invoked the tragedy of appeasement in the 1930s and the triumph of containment after the Second World War. He vowed to rout communism in the 1960s with a more vigorous prosecution of the Cold War. An eloquent speaker and fierce competitor, Kennedy had "enormous confidence in his own luck," remarked his assistant, the historian Arthur M. Schlesinger, Jr. "Everyone around him thought he had the Midas touch and could not lose." Preparing for his first meeting with Khrushchev, Kennedy seemed poised for a contest rather

than a talk: "I have to show him that we can be as tough as he is. I'll have to sit down with him and let him see who he's dealing with."

Kennedy appointed a staff of bright, often arrogant "action intellectuals," as the journalist Theodore White called them. In their quest for

Kennedy as Cold War Activist

Cold War victories, Under Secretary of State Chester Bowles noted with alarm, they were "full of belligerence." And U.S. Ambassador to the United Nations Adlai Stevenson told a friend that "they've got the damnedest bunch of boy commandos running around down there [in Washington] you ever saw." That there would be no halfway measures was apparent in Kennedy's inaugural address: "Let every nation know that we shall pay any price, bear any burden, meet any hardship, support any friend, oppose any foe to assure the survival and the success of liberty."

Khrushchev took up the challenge. He endorsed "wars of national liberation" in the Third World. In fall 1961 the Soviet Union ended its moratorium on above-ground nuclear testing by exploding a giant 50-megaton bomb; Khrushchev also bragged about Soviet ICBMs, raising American anxiety over Soviet capabilities. Intelligence data soon demonstrated that there was no "missile gap"—except the one in America's favor. Kennedy nonetheless sought to fulfill his campaign commitment to a military build-up based on the principle of *flexible response.* Junking Eisenhower's concept of massive retaliation, Kennedy sought ways to meet any kind of warfare, from guerrilla combat to nuclear showdown. Thus the United States could contain both the Soviet Union and Third World revolutionary movements. In 1961 the military budget shot up 15 percent and ICBM arsenals swelled further. By mid-1964, strategists measured a 150 percent increase in the number of American nuclear weapons. The government even encouraged citizens to build fallout shelters in their backyards. Kennedy could claim credit for the Arms Control and Disarmament Agency and the Limited Test Ban Treaty with the Soviet Union (1963), which banned nuclear testing in the atmosphere, in outer space, and under water, but his real legacy was an accelerated arms race.

Once again, in 1961, the Soviets demanded negotiations to end Western occupation of West Ber-

The leader of the Cuban Revolution, Fidel Castro (1927–   ) (left), visited the United States in April 1959, just a few months after his victory over the dictatorial and corrupt Fulgencio Batista, a U.S. ally. In Washington, D.C., Vice President Richard Nixon met with Castro, who proudly wore the symbols of the revolution: beard and green fatigues. Their two-hour meeting was cordial, but Cuba and the United States were already on a collision course. UPI/Bettmann Archives.

lin. Calling the city "the great testing place of Western courage and will,"

Berlin Wall

Kennedy rejected negotiations and asked Congress for an additional $3.2 billion for defense and the authority to call up reservists. Events took an ugly turn in August 1961 when the Soviets, upon the urging of the East German regime, erected a concrete-and-barbed-wire barricade designed to halt the exodus of East Germans into the more prosperous and politically free West Berlin. The Berlin Wall inspired protests throughout the non-Communist world. The crisis passed but the wall remained.

U.S. hostilities with Cuba provoked Kennedy's most serious confrontation with the Soviet Union. Cold War and Third World issues dramatically intersected in Cuba. In

The Cuban Revolution

early 1959 Fidel Castro's rebels, driven by virulently anti-American nationalism, had ousted Fulgencio Batista, a long-time U.S. ally who had welcomed North American investors, U.S. military advisers, and tourists to the Caribbean island. Batista's corrupt and dictatorial regime had helped turn Havana into a haven for gambling and prostitution run by organized crime.

Cubans had resented U.S. domination ever since the early twentieth century, when the Platt Amendment was imposed on them (see Chapter 22). Reducing U.S. influence became a rallying cry of the Cuban Revolution. Castro sought from the start to break the economic power of U.S. business, which had invested some $1 billion on the island, and to end U.S. domination of Cuban trade. His increasing authoritarianism and anti-Yankee declarations alarmed Washington. In early 1960, after Cuba signed a trade treaty with the Soviet Union, Eisenhower ordered the CIA to organize an invasion force of Cuban exiles to overthrow the Castro government. The president also drastically cut U.S. purchases of Cuban sugar. Castro responded by seizing all North American-owned companies that had not yet been nationalized. Threatened by U.S. decisions designed to bring him and his revolution down, Castro appealed to the Soviet Union, which offered loans and expanded trade.

Just before leaving office, Eisenhower broke diplomatic relations with Cuba and advised Kennedy to advance plans for the invasion. The scenario sketched by the CIA appealed to Kennedy: Cuban exiles would land at the Bay of Pigs and secure a beachhead; the Cuban people would rise up against Castro and welcome a new government brought in from the United States. Kennedy was nonetheless uneasy over such a blatant attempt to topple a sovereign government; he ordered that no Americans be directly involved in the invasion so that the United States could claim that the operation was solely a Cuban affair. The president never attempted to negotiate with Castro over Cuban-American troubles; Kennedy preferred victory over compromise.

Directed by the CIA and escorted by U.S. warships, fourteen hundred commandos scrambled ashore at the Bay of Pigs in April 1961. Despite Kennedy's order, the first man to hit the beaches was an American—a CIA operative. The Cuban people did not rise up against Castro. On the contrary, the revolutionary leader remained popular because of his spellbinding oratory and zealous pursuit of nationalism, land reform, and improvements in health care and education. Within two days most of the invaders had been captured. Many of them later blamed Kennedy for the disaster, citing his refusal to permit an air strike at the time of the landing. But the operation, with or without more air support, had had little chance of success. Boats went aground on coral reefs that the CIA had dismissed as seaweed.

Bay of Pigs

Equipment malfunctioned. If the exiles had managed to move inland, they would have faced Castro's large armed militia, and the mountains that might have served as a sanctuary were eighty miles away. Before it was over, four Americans had died. "How could I have been so stupid to let them go ahead?" Kennedy reproached himself. Critics posed the problem differently. Conservatives charged that Kennedy had lost his courage, failing to see the operation through to victory. Liberals protested that Kennedy's endorsement of the invasion revealed the ruthless, dark side of the Cold War that was corrupting the United States itself.

Kennedy did not suffer defeat easily. He vowed to bring Castro down. His brother, Attorney General Robert Kennedy, promised "to stir things up on the island with espionage, sabotage, [and] general disorder." Let "no time, money, effort—or manpower—be spared," he instructed the CIA, which soon came up with Operation Mongoose. In this project, government agents disrupted the island's trade, supported raids on Cuba from Miami, and plotted with organized-crime bosses to assassinate Castro. The United States also tightened its economic blockade, engineered Cuba's eviction from the Organization of American States, and undertook military maneuvers that Castro read as preparations for another invasion.

Had there been no Bay of Pigs invasion, no Operation Mongoose, no assassination plots, and no program of diplomatic and economic isolation, there probably would have been no Cuban missile crisis because Cuba would have had no urgent need for Soviet military assistance. For Castro, the relentless U.S. hostility represented a real threat to Cuba's independence. For the Soviets, American actions challenged the only pro-Communist regime in Latin America. Premier Khrushchev also saw an opportunity to improve the Soviet position in the nuclear arms race. So Castro and Khrushchev devised a daring plan to deter any new U.S. intervention, especially an invasion: they agreed to install in Cuba nuclear-armed missiles capable of hitting the United States. The world soon faced a frightening episode of brinkmanship.

Cuban Missile Crisis

Although the Kennedy administration was aware of a military build-up on the island, it was not until October 1962 that a U-2 plane photo-

How do historians know

that at the outset of the Cuban missile crisis President John F. Kennedy insisted that the Soviet missiles had to be forced from Cuba, even at the risk of nuclear war? Long before the 1962 crisis, Kennedy had ordered the Secret Service to install a taping system throughout the White House. Listening devices were placed in meeting rooms and on telephones. Neither Secretary of State Dean Rusk (with the window behind him to Kennedy's right) nor Secretary of Defense Robert McNamara (with the flag behind him to Kennedy's left) knew that their remarks were being taped. Only a few members of the presidential staff knew about the secret system. Whether Kennedy wanted the tapes because he sought an accurate record for the memoirs he intended one day to write or because he hoped to

protect himself against public misrepresentations of what he said to others in private, he left historians a rich source. During the missile crisis of October 1962, he regularly convened and taped meetings of an advisory Executive Committee, shown gathered here. The John F. Kennedy presidential library in Boston has declassified and transcribed several tapes of that time and others, although many more remain to be opened to researchers. Because of such tapes (some of Kennedy's predecessors and successors also made recordings), historians can study the minute-by-minute, hour-by-hour handling of a crisis that brought the Soviet Union and the United States to the nuclear brink.   Photo: John F. Kennedy Presidential Library.

Executive Committee Debate
———

graphed sites for medium-range missiles. Whether the Soviets had acted to protect Cuba, to improve their own nuclear capability, to trigger negotiations over Berlin, or to force the United States to pull its missiles out of Turkey remains debatable. In any case, the presi-

dent immediately organized the "Executive Committee" to find a way to force the removal of the missiles from Cuba. Some members advised a surprise air strike, likely to kill both Soviet technicians and Cubans. Robert Kennedy scotched that idea; he wanted no Pearl Harbors on his brother's record. The Joint Chiefs of Staff recommended a full-scale military invasion, an option that risked a prolonged war with Cuba, a Soviet attack against West Berlin, or even nuclear holocaust. The Soviet expert Charles Bohlen unsuccessfully urged quiet, direct negotiations with Soviet officials. Secretary of Defense Robert S. McNamara proposed the formula that the president found most acceptable: a naval quarantine of Cuba to prevent further military shipments. Halfway between armed warfare and doing nothing, McNamara's proposal left the administration free to attack or negotiate, depending on the Soviet response.

Kennedy addressed the nation on television on October 22 to demand that the Soviets retreat. U.S. warships began criss-crossing the Caribbean, while B-52s loaded with nuclear bombs took to the skies and U.S. military forces around the globe went on alert. Khrushchev replied that the missiles would be withdrawn if Washington pledged never to attack Cuba. He then added that American Jupiter missiles, aimed at the Soviet Union, must be removed from Turkey. Kennedy accepted the first condition but rejected the second. Edgy and exhausted advisers predicted war. But on October 28 Khrushchev finally accepted the U.S. pledge to respect Cuban sovereignty. Soviet technicians began to dismantle the missiles for shipment back to the Soviet Union. Kennedy informally and privately promised to withdraw the Jupiters from Turkey and did so. Forcing the Soviets to back down and out, many said, was Kennedy's finest hour.

But critics then and now have raised questions. Would such a frightening crisis have occurred at all if Kennedy had not been hell-bent on overthrowing the Castro regime and expunging the Cuban Revolution from the hemisphere? Was the crisis really necessary? Why did the president attempt to solve the crisis with brinkmanship instead of private negotiations? Television addresses are the stuff of politics, not statesmanship—and the congressional elections were just weeks away. Critics have also noted that Kennedy passed up a chance to protest the presence of the missiles and defuse the crisis when he met privately on October 18 with Foreign Minister Andrei Gromyko.

Questions About Kennedy's Handling of the Crisis

Hardly an exemplary model of crisis management, Kennedy's handling of the crisis courted disaster. His sleepless advisers made decisions under tremendous stress, and military commanders had to make hurried choices. At the height of the crisis, a U.S. jet mistakenly crossed into Soviet territory, nearly setting off an air war. National Security Affairs Adviser McGeorge Bundy remembered that the crisis was in danger of "spinning out of control." Each day the chances for error grew greater. The missiles were armed with warheads, and the Soviet commander in Cuba had the authority to fire them. And what if Castro, whom Khrushchev considered "an impetuous hothead," had decided to provoke war on his own? Finally, critics have argued that the strategic balance of power was not seriously altered by the placement of Soviet missiles in Cuba; the United States still enjoyed a tremendous advantage over the Soviets in the nuclear arms race. Did Kennedy risk doomsday unnecessarily?

The Cuban missile crisis did produce some relaxation in Soviet-American relations. The adversaries signed a treaty banning nuclear tests in the atmosphere, and Washington and Moscow installed a teletype "hot line" staffed around the clock by translators and technicians. They also refrained from further confrontation in Berlin. In June 1963 Kennedy spoke at American University in conciliatory terms about Soviet-American relations, urging cautious steps toward disarmament. Some analysts predicted a thaw in the Cold War, but the assassination of President Kennedy left unresolved the question of whether he was shedding his Cold Warriorism.

President Lyndon B. Johnson shared the Cold War traditions of his predecessors. He saw the world in simple terms—them against us—and privately disparaged both his enemies and his allies. Johnson dismissed Vietnam as a "raggedy-ass fourth-rate country" and his critics at home as "rattlebrains" and "nervous nellies." He often exaggerated and sometimes lied, creating what became known as a credibility gap. His public speeches, larded with trite metaphors and delivered in a belabored drawl, led some to conclude that he was unintelligent. In fact, Johnson had a quick mind; his limitation was that he held firmly to fixed ideas about American superiority, the menace of communism, and the necessity of global intervention in the Cold War. The problem, said Senator J. William Fulbright of Arkansas, chairman of the Foreign Relations Committee, was that both John-

Johnson and the Cold War

son and the American people suffered from an "arrogance of power."

Although Johnson improved Soviet-American relations somewhat by meeting with Soviet Premier Alexei Kosygin at Glassboro State College in New Jersey in 1967 and by pushing for a nonproliferation treaty to curb the spread of nuclear weapons (signed in 1968), the Cold War hardly relented. The Soviets—having vowed to catch up with the United States after the Cuban missile crisis—reached numerical parity with the United States by the end of the decade. The Soviets' invasion of Czechoslovakia in 1968 caused Johnson to shelve further arms control talks. Meanwhile, Johnson had become preoccupied by the war in Southeast Asia. With the Soviet Union and the United States backing opposing forces in the Vietnam War, opportunities for relaxing the Cold War seemed to diminish (see Chapter 31).

NIXON, KISSINGER, AND DÉTENTE

Richard M. Nixon had been an ardent Cold Warrior as a congressman, senator, and vice president, and few observers expected him to produce a thaw in the Cold War during his presidency. Nixon's chief foreign policy aide was Henry A. Kissinger, a German-born political scientist teaching at Harvard. Kissinger served as Nixon's national security adviser until 1973, when he became secretary of state. Ambitious, witty, and knowledgeable, Kissinger became a formidable negotiator. Critics, however, distrusted him for adhering to the principle that the end justifies the means. They cited his willingness to unseat foreign governments through secret operations, as in Chile (see page 976), and to sell arms to dictators like the shah of Iran (see page 975). Kissinger even had his own staff wiretapped.

Together Nixon and Kissinger pursued a grand strategy designed to promote a global balance of power, which they called "equilibrium."

The Pursuit of Détente

The first part of the strategy was *détente:* measured cooperation with the Soviets through negotiations within a general environment of rivalry. Détente's primary purpose, like that of the containment doctrine it resembled, was to check Soviet expansion and limit the Soviet arms build-up. The second part of the strategy was curbing revolution and radicalism in the Third World so as to quash threats to U.S. interests. The grand design seemed attractive to its architects: the Cold War and limited wars like Vietnam were costing too much, and more trade with a friendlier Soviet Union might reduce the huge U.S. balance-of-payments deficit.

Critics faulted the Nixon-Kissinger posture for its arrogant assumption that the United States had the ability and the right to manipulate a disorderly world. But Nixon and Kissinger pursued détente with extraordinary energy and fanfare. They expanded trade relations with the Soviet Union; a 1972 deal sent $1 billion worth of American grain to the Soviets at bargain prices. To slow the costly arms race, they initiated the Strategic Arms Limitations Talks (SALT). In 1972 Soviet and American negotiators produced a SALT Treaty that limited antiballistic missile (ABM) systems. (By making offensive missiles less vulnerable to attack, these defensive systems had accelerated the arms race because both sides built more missiles to overcome the ABM protection.) A second agreement imposed a five-year freeze on the number of offensive nuclear missiles each side could possess. At the time of the agreement the Soviets held an advantage in total strategic forces (ICBMs, SLBMs, and long-range bombers)—2,547 to 2,160. But the United States had more warheads per missile because it could outfit each missile with MIRVs (multiple independently targeted re-entry vehicles) that could send warheads to several different targets. In short, the United States had a 2-to-1 advantage in deliverable warheads (5,700 to 2,500). Because SALT did not restrict MIRVs, the nuclear arms build-up continued.

SALT Talks

Nixon and Kissinger also cultivated détente with the People's Republic of China, ending almost three decades of Sino-American hostility. In 1972 the president made a historic trip to what he had long called "Red China." The Chinese welcomed him because they sought to improve trade and hoped that friendlier Sino-American relations would make their enemy, the Soviet Union, more cautious. Nixon reasoned the same way. The president and the venerable Chinese leaders Mao Zedong and Zhou Enlai agreed to disagree on a num-

Opening to China

During his dramatic trip to the People's Republic of China in February 1972, President Richard M. Nixon (left) and his wife Patricia toured the Great Wall, a 1,500-mile structure first built about 210 B.C.E. as a defensive barrier against invaders. Rebuilt in later centuries, the wall also served as a communications link for the vast country. Nixon's visit to China ended more than two decades of Sino-American hostility and opened an era of détente.   Tashi/Black Star.

ber of issues, except one: the Soviet Union should not be permitted to make gains in Asia. The opening of a Sino-American dialogue ended one of the postwar era's longest and most bitter contests. Official diplomatic recognition and the exchange of ambassadors came in 1979.

Like disputes in the Middle East, Latin America, and Africa (see Chapter 31), global economic issues bedeviled the Nixon-Kissinger grand
design for world order. Kissinger explained that "international political stability requires international economic stability." But in the 1970s there was little economic stability. The worldwide recession early in the decade was the worst since the 1930s. Inflation and high oil prices pinched rich and poor nations alike. Pro-

International Economic Instability

tectionist tendencies raised tariffs and impeded world trade. And the debt-ridden developing nations of the Third World—sometimes called the "South"—insisted that the wealthier, industrial "North" share economic resources. The gulf between rich and poor nations threatened world peace.

The United States could not escape these problems. It began to suffer a trade deficit—importing more goods than it exported (see figure). America's economic standing had declined since the Olympian days of the 1940s and 1950s as other nations, notably Japan and West Germany, recovered from wartime devastation and as Third World countries gained more control over their raw materials. Americans nonetheless remained the richest people in the world. The United States produced about one-third of the world's goods and services. Many American companies, like Coca-Cola and Exxon, earned over half their profits abroad. One-fourth of agricultural sales came from exports; one out of every nine manufacturing jobs depended on exports. The U.S. economy also depended on imports of strategic raw materials: three-fourths of the tin consumed in the United States, more than 95 percent of the manganese, and over half of the zinc came from abroad. Such ties, as well as American investments abroad totaling more than $133 billion in the mid-1970s, explain in part why the United States welcomed détente as a means to calm international relations and protect the U.S. stake in the world economy.

CARTER AND A REINVIGORATED COLD WAR

President Jimmy Carter promised fresh initiatives and diplomatic activism when he took office in 1977. He asked Americans to put their "inordinate fear of Communism" behind them. The old Cold War consensus had appeared fractured two years earlier when the Vietnam War finally ended, and Americans seemed uncertain about their nation's place in the world. Some wanted Carter to spare no expense to expand the military to face down U.S. adversaries. Others wanted an end to bluster, reductions in the military, and less interventionism.

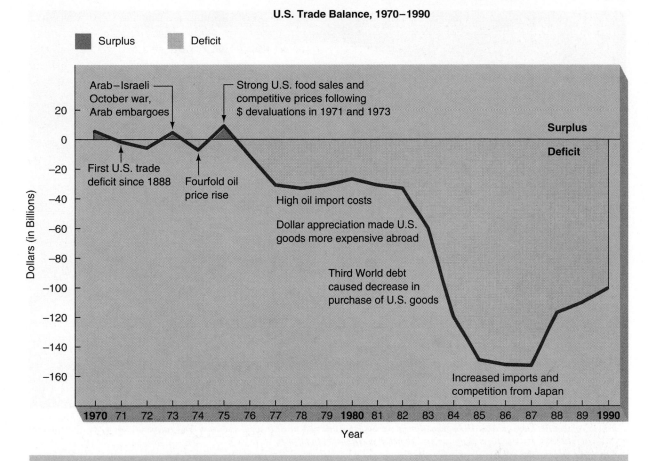

U.S. Trade Balance, 1970–1990

■ Surplus   ■ Deficit

Arab–Israeli
October war,
Arab embargoes

Strong U.S. food sales and
competitive prices following
$ devaluations in 1971 and 1973

First U.S. trade
deficit since 1888

Fourfold oil
price rise

Surplus

Deficit

High oil import costs

Dollar appreciation made U.S.
goods more expensive abroad

Third World debt
caused decrease in
purchase of U.S. goods

Increased imports and
competition from Japan

Dollars (in Billions)

Year

U.S. Trade Balance, 1970–1990 *Importing more than it exports, the United States has suffered trade deficits for years. Foreign political and economic crises and growing competition from Japanese products in the U.S. marketplace weakened the U.S. position in the world economy. Trade deficits must be financed by borrowing. One result has been a mounting U.S. external debt ($650 billion by 1989).* Source: U.S. Department of State.

With reformist zeal, Carter set out to address long-range issues so as not to become trapped by a reactive foreign policy controlled by day-to-day crises. The new president pledged to devote as much attention to North-South as to East-West issues, to reduce the American military presence overseas, to cut back arms sales (which had reached unprecedented heights under Nixon), and to slow the nuclear arms race. He also promised preventive diplomacy: advancing the peace process in the Middle East, mediating conflict in the Third World, and creating worldwide economic stability through agreements on the law of the sea, energy, and clean air and water. A

Carter's Foreign Policy Goals

deeply religious man, Carter said he intended to infuse international relations with moral force. "The soul of our foreign policy," he declared, would be the championing of individual human rights abroad—the freedom to vote, worship, travel, speak out, and get a fair trial. Human-rights groups like Amnesty International, founded in the 1960s, welcomed this attention to a long-ignored issue.

Almost from the start, Carter spoke and acted inconsistently, in part because he himself seemed uncertain about the direction of his foreign policy and in part because his advisers squabbled among themselves. One source of the problem was Zbigniew Brzezinski, a Polish-born political scientist who became Carter's national security adviser. The

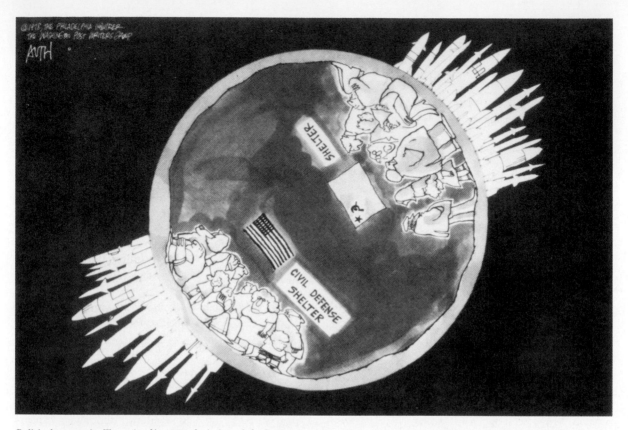

Political cartoonist Tony Auth's 1978 depiction of the Soviet-American nuclear arms race said that, although the Cold War powers had signed the SALT accord six years earlier, the race continued. Huddled in their shelters, people in both nations continued to live in fear of attack as the nuclear-tipped missiles grew in number and destructive power. "Long Distance View of the Arms Race" by Tony Auth, in the Philadelphia Inquirer, November 5, 1978. Universal Press.

stern-faced Brzezinski was an old-fashioned Cold Warrior who viewed foreign crises in globalist terms—that is, he blamed them on the Soviet Union. Carter gradually listened more to Brzezinski than to Secretary of State Cyrus Vance, an experienced, widely respected public servant who had served in the Defense Department in the 1960s and who advocated quiet diplomacy to find avenues toward Soviet-American cooperation.

Under Carter, détente deteriorated and the Cold War deepened. The president first angered the Soviets by demanding that they respect their citizens' human rights and tolerate dissent. Moscow told him to mind his own business. American officials then denounced the Soviets for sponsoring Cuban troops in Angola, where a leftist government was struggling against U.S.-backed rebels. Soviet leaders worried, too, that the United States was playing its "China card"—building up China in order to threaten the Soviet Union.

Despite this rocky start, a new treaty, SALT-II, codified Soviet-American nuclear parity in 1979. The agreement placed a ceiling of 2,250 delivery vehicles (long-range bombers, ICBMs, and SLBMs) on each side. The Soviet Union had to dismantle more than 250 existing delivery vehicles, whereas the United States was permitted to expand from its existing 2,060 to the new ceiling. The treaty did not affect nuclear warheads, which stood at 9,200 for the United States and 5,000 for the Soviet Union. Critics on the right charged that verification of compliance was difficult; critics on the left protested that the treaty did not go far enough to quell the arms race. Carter tried to win votes from skeptical conservatives by announcing an expensive military expansion program and deployment of Pershing II missiles and cruise missiles in the NATO nations of Western Europe.

SALT-II

As Senate ratification of SALT-II stalled and Moscow fumed over the Pershings, events in Afghanistan led to Soviet-American confrontation. In late 1979 the Red Army bludgeoned its way into Afghanistan to shore up a faltering Communist government under siege by Muslim rebels. An embittered Carter shelved SALT-II (the two powers nonetheless unilaterally honored its terms later), suspended shipments of grain and high-technology equipment to the Soviet Union, and initiated an international boycott of the 1980 Summer Olympics in Moscow. The CIA began to aid the Afghan insurgents. But all of Carter's efforts proved fruitless: the Soviets refused to withdraw their forces from Afghanistan.

The president also announced the Carter Doctrine: the United States would intervene, unilaterally and militarily if necessary, against Soviet aggression in the petroleum-rich Persian Gulf. Prominent critics spoke out against the declaration. Senator Edward Kennedy declared that Americans would rather ration gas than spill the blood of their children for Middle Eastern oil. George F. Kennan, the father of containment, called Carter's reaction exaggerated, alarmist, and wrongheaded in assuming that the Soviets would attack elsewhere in the Middle East. Kennan noted that in Afghanistan the Soviet Union was dealing with a local crisis in a strategically important client state on its southern border, not with the entire Gulf region. He faulted Carter for not trying diplomacy first and for playing all his nonmilitary cards prematurely. "Was this really mature statesmanship on our part?" Kennan asked.

Carter lost the 1980 presidential election to Ronald Reagan, not because the Cold War had become more frigid but because the Iranian hostage crisis had paralyzed the administration and because Carter seemed to have contradicted many of his own goals (see page 977). As Chapter 31 will show, Carter enjoyed some diplomatic successes in the Middle East, Africa, and Latin America. But his legacy also included a revived Cold War.

REAGAN, DEVIL THEORY, AND MILITARY EXPANSION

President Ronald Reagan assumed the presidency in 1981 with no experience in foreign relations and no firm grasp of international issues, history, or geography. Simplistic, often mistaken about elementary facts, and prone to joking when the issues demanded sophisticated analysis, Reagan acted more on instinct than on patient reasoning. Reagan and the conservatives around him, including Secretary of State George P. Shultz, believed in a devil theory: that a malevolent Soviet Union—Reagan branded it an "evil empire"—was the source of the world's troubles. Reagan buried détente in an avalanche of strident anti-Soviet rhetoric, charging that the Soviets were prepared "to commit any crime, to lie, to cheat" to achieve a Communist world. He attributed Third World disorders to Soviet intrigue as well, rejecting arguments that the civil wars in Central America and elsewhere derived not from Soviet meddling but from deep-seated economic instability, poverty, and class oppression.

Reagan asserted that a substantial military build-up would thwart the Soviet threat and intimidate Moscow into negotiating on terms favorable to the United States. The new president launched the largest peacetime arms build-up in American history, driving up the federal debt with multi-trillion-dollar defense spending. In 1985 the Pentagon was spending an average of $28 million an hour, twenty-four hours a day, seven days a week. Assigning low priority to arms control talks, Reagan advanced development of the B-1 bomber, the MX missile, and an antimissile defense system in space he called the Strategic Defense Initiative (SDI), which critics soon dubbed "Star Wars." As the veteran diplomat George Ball observed when U.S. forces overthrew a leftist, pro-Cuban government on the tiny Caribbean island of Grenada in 1983, once again "we shiver in the icy winds of the Cold War."

Reagan Emphasis on Military Expansion

To gain public support for a more interventionist, militarized foreign policy, Reagan used his exceptional communicating skills to stimulate emotional patriotism. Most Americans shared Reagan's feeling that the nation had been ignobly retreating from global leadership. "America is back, standing tall," bragged the president, pronouncing the end of post-Vietnam "self-doubt." He made Americans feel good about themselves and their place in the world. Reagan also argued that the United States could win the Cold War by pressing other nations to embrace capitalism. At eight economic summit

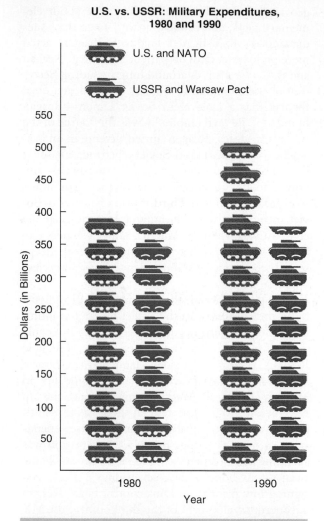

U.S. vs. USSR: Military Expenditures, 1980 and 1990

U.S. and NATO

USSR and Warsaw Pact

Year

U.S. vs. USSR: Military Expenditures, 1980 and 1990 *Despite détente in the 1970s, the United States and the Soviet Union and their allies continued to spend heavily on their militaries. The Reagan administration especially engorged U.S. military expenditures, which grew from $233 billion in 1980 to $312 billion in 1990. Such spending undercut the domestic economies of both nations.* Source: U.S. Department of Defense, U.S. Arms Control and Disarmament Agency, and other U.S. government sources.

The *Reagan Doctrine* also drove U.S. foreign policy. The term derived from the president's declaration in 1985 that the United States would openly support anti-Communist movements—he called them "freedom fighters"—wherever they were battling the Soviets or Soviet-backed governments. Under this doctrine, the CIA funneled aid to insurgents in Afghanistan, Nicaragua, Angola, and Ethiopia. In open defiance of the sovereignty of these nations, Reagan vowed the overthrow of governments deemed hostile to the interests of the United States.

Reagan Doctrine

In this atmosphere, Soviet-American relations became "white hot, thoroughly white hot," in the words of a Soviet leader. Actually, Reagan's first decision affecting the Soviets was friendly: fulfilling a campaign pledge to help American farmers, he lifted the grain embargo that Carter had imposed after the invasion of Afghanistan. The United States then sold the Soviet Union grain worth $3 billion. But this decision was followed by hostility when the Soviets cracked down on the Solidarity labor movement in Poland. In response, Washington placed restrictions on Soviet-American trade and hurled angry words at Moscow. In 1983, Reagan restricted commercial flights to the Soviet Union after a Soviet fighter pilot mistakenly shot down a South Korean commercial jet that had strayed some 300 miles off-course into Soviet air space. The world was shocked by the death of 269 passengers, and Reagan exploited the event to score Cold War points.

Reagan's expansion of the military, his careless utterances about winning a limited nuclear war, and his quest for nuclear supremacy stimulated worldwide debate. In 1981 hundreds of thousands of marchers in London, Rome, Bonn, and other European cities demanded Soviet-American negotiations to prevent a nuclear holocaust. The evangelist Billy Graham joined peace groups and politicians in appeals for a freeze in the nuclear arms race. In the largest peaceful protest in American history, a million people marched through New York City in June 1982 to support a freeze. Towns across the nation and the House of Representatives passed resolutions to freeze the development, production, and

Debate over Nuclear Weapons

meetings during his presidency, Reagan preached his private enterprise philosophy, while the U.S.-Canada Free Trade Agreement of 1988 put his message into practice.

*In one of several summit meetings, top Soviet leader Mikhail Gorbachev (1932–   ) and President Ronald Reagan (1911–   )
met in Moscow in May 1988 in hopes of signing a Strategic Arms Reduction Talks agreement. Yet the "chemistry" of warm
friendship that Reagan later claimed characterized his personal relationship with Gorbachev fell short of producing cuts in dangerous
strategic weapons. Their cordial interaction, however, encouraged the diplomatic dialogue that helped end the Cold War.*   Bill
Fitz-Patrick, Ronald Reagan Presidential Library.

deployment of new weapons. U.S. Roman Catholic bishops issued a pastoral letter in 1983 declaring that "we are the first generation since Genesis with the power to virtually destroy God's creation." The manifesto condemned nuclear weapons as "immoral" and urged an end to the arms race, "which robs the poor and the vulnerable." Meanwhile, scientists described the "nuclear winter" that would follow a nuclear war: the earth, cut off from the sun's rays, would turn cold, and food sources would disappear. An ABC television movie, *The Day After* (1983), riveted Americans with its vivid depiction of the human costs of nuclear war.

Responding to public opinion and pressure from NATO allies, and believing that reinvigorated military power had created a strong U.S. bargaining position, Reagan officials in 1981 began talks with the Soviets on limiting intermediate-range nuclear forces (INF) based in Europe. The Soviets had SS-20 missiles targeted at Western Europe, and the United States had cruise missiles and Pershing-IIs aimed at the Soviet Union. A year later, Reagan substituted the Strategic Arms Reduction Talks (START) for the inactive SALT talks. At a 1985 Geneva summit meeting, Reagan and the new Soviet leader Mikhail S. Gorbachev agreed in principle that strategic weapons should be substantially reduced. But summit meetings in subsequent years failed to produce a treaty. The sticking points were two: Gorbachev's insistence that no progress could be made unless the United States shelved SDI, and Reagan's determination to press on with it despite widespread scientific opinion that it would cost billions of dollars and never work.

Near the end of Reagan's presidency, as the Iran-contra scandal rocked his administration and

U.S. intervention in Central America faltered (see Chapter 31), Soviet-American relations markedly improved. The turnaround stemmed more from changes abroad than from Reagan's decisions. As Reagan said after returning from the 1988 Moscow summit, he had been "dropped into a grand historical moment." Under Gorbachev, a younger generation of Soviet leaders came to power in 1985. They were determined to restructure and modernize the highly bureaucratized, decaying economy (a program called *perestroika*) and to liberalize the suffocatingly authoritarian political system (a program called *glasnost*). These new Soviet officials understood that a reduction in military spending made possible by reduced international tensions would free up resources for their reform efforts. Gorbachev and Reagan visited each other's countries and in 1987 signed a treaty banning all land-based intermediate-range nuclear forces in Europe. Soon began the destruction of 2,800 missiles.

Mikhail S. Gorbachev

To the wonderment of Americans who could not believe that the Soviet bear was being tamed, Gorbachev unilaterally reduced his nation's armed forces. He also helped settle regional conflicts. In 1989 all remaining Soviet troops departed Afghanistan. Gorbachev also pressed Vietnam to pull out of Cambodia, and he promoted an accord to withdraw Cuban troops from Angola. To reduce the chances that nuclear war could start by accident, Soviet and American officials established in their capitals Nuclear Risk Reduction Centers with direct hookups operated around the clock. "We are beginning to break down the barriers of the postwar era," a cheerful Reagan remarked.

Reagan had at first judged Gorbachev to be another tough and untrustworthy Kremlin ideologue, but the president warmed to "Gorby" and toned down his strident anti-Soviet rhetoric in the late 1980s. Other American conservatives remained suspicious that a wily, smiling Gorbachev, adept at public relations, might be hoodwinking Americans. Vice President George Bush warned that "the Cold War isn't over." Dramatic events in the Soviet Union, Germany, and Eastern Europe, however, soon persuaded most Americans that the Cold War was winding down. "Who would have thought that the warmth of that fireplace in Geneva [at the summit] would melt the ice of the Cold War?" Reagan once remarked to Gorbachev. The U.S. president seemed as surprised as anybody.

THE END OF THE COLD WAR

George Bush entered the White House in 1989 with solid Cold War credentials, including experience as director of the CIA and ambassador to China (see Chapter 34). Cautious and conservative, Bush seemed to have few long-range foreign policy goals. His was a reactive diplomacy. Bush and Secretary of State James Baker often seemed mere bystanders at the exciting events sweeping the world. Shaped for so long by the Cold War, some American leaders found it difficult to imagine a world without communism and a Soviet threat. The stunning ferment in Europe forced them to think afresh.

Mikhail Gorbachev had set loose cascading changes in his own country, but he had also encouraged the people of East Germany and Eastern Europe to go their own ways. No longer would Moscow prop up unpopular Communist regimes. In 1989 East Germans startled the world by repudiating their Communist government, and in November joyful Germans scaled the Berlin Wall to dance atop it and then tear it down, opening East to West. The next year the two Germanies reunited and veteran Communist oligarchs fell—in Poland, Hungary, Czechoslovakia, and Rumania. Bulgaria and Albania soon held elections.

Collapse of Communism in Eastern Europe

Meanwhile, the Union of Soviet Socialist Republics itself was unraveling. In 1990 the Baltic states of Lithuania, Latvia, and Estonia declared independence. The following year, after Gorbachev himself denounced communism, the Soviet Union disintegrated into independent successor states—Russia, Ukraine, Tajikistan, and many others. With no government to lead, and muscled aside by reformers who thought he was moving too slowly toward democracy and free-market economics, Gorbachev himself lost power. Trying to understand these sudden changes, commented one observer, was like trying to paint a speeding train.

One conclusion became clear. The break-up of the Soviet empire, the dismantling of the Warsaw Pact, the repudiation of communism by its own leaders, the shattering of the myth of monolithic communism, the reunification of Germany, and the significant reduction in the risk of nuclear war signaled the end of the Cold War. The mammoth glacier had receded, leaving an unsettled world in search of a new order.

The Cold War ended because of the relative decline of the United States and the Soviet Union in the international system from the 1950s through the 1980s. The Cold War

Why the Cold War Ended
——

ended because the contest had undermined the power of its two major protagonists. They moved gradually toward a cautious cooperation whose urgent goals were the restoration of their economic well-being and the preservation of their diminishing global positions.

Four influential trends explain this gradual decline and the resulting attractions of détente. First was the burgeoning economic cost of the Cold War—trillions of dollars spent on weapons and interventions, rather than on improving domestic infrastructures. Foreign ventures starved domestic programs and strained budgets. As early as the 1950s President Eisenhower had pointed out that the expense of the Cold War was undermining sound economic policy at home. In the 1960s Americans debated "guns versus butter." In the 1970s, President Nixon, aware that Americans had grown weary of paying the costs of the Cold War, appealed to allies for "burden-sharing." In the 1980s, as the Cold War began to wane, Americans looked eagerly to a "peace dividend" to solve a host of domestic woes.

Challenges to the two major powers from within their own spheres of influence also help explain why the United States and the Soviet Union welcomed détente. Cuba's revolution and France's withdrawal from NATO in the 1960s are but two pieces of evidence that the United States was losing power. The Hungarian and Czech revolutions and the Sino-Soviet rift undercut the Soviet Union's hegemony within its network of allies. Détente seemed to offer a means to restore great-power management of unruly states.

Third, the Cold War ended because of the emergence of the Third World, which introduced new players into the international game, further diffused power, and eroded bipolarism (see Chapter 31). Soviet-American détente represented a means to deal with the volatile Third World, a fulcrum by which to apply leverage to Third World nations. As Secretary Baker once said, "When the United States and the Soviet Union

In November 1989, a new East German government ordered the opening of the Berlin Wall—a symbol of Cold War division since 1961. West Berliners climbed atop the wall, cheering and dancing, and East Berliners rushed through once heavily guarded check-points. Some revelers scratched graffiti on the breached wall: "Freiheit" (freedom). In this photograph, an East Berlin border guard hands a flower back to West Berliners who had come to celebrate the end of an era. The following year the two Berlins and the two Germanies reunited. UPI/ Bettmann Archives.

lead, others are likely to follow." Finally, the worldwide antinuclear movement of the 1980s pressed leaders, especially in Western Europe, to seek détente—to persuade Washington and Moscow to stop the arms race.

These four elements—economic burden, challenges from sphere members, the rise of the Third World, and the antinuclear movement—combined to weaken the standing of the two adversaries and ultimately to persuade Soviet and American leaders to halt their nations' decline by ending the Cold War. The Soviet Union fell much harder than the United States, but the implications of decline be-

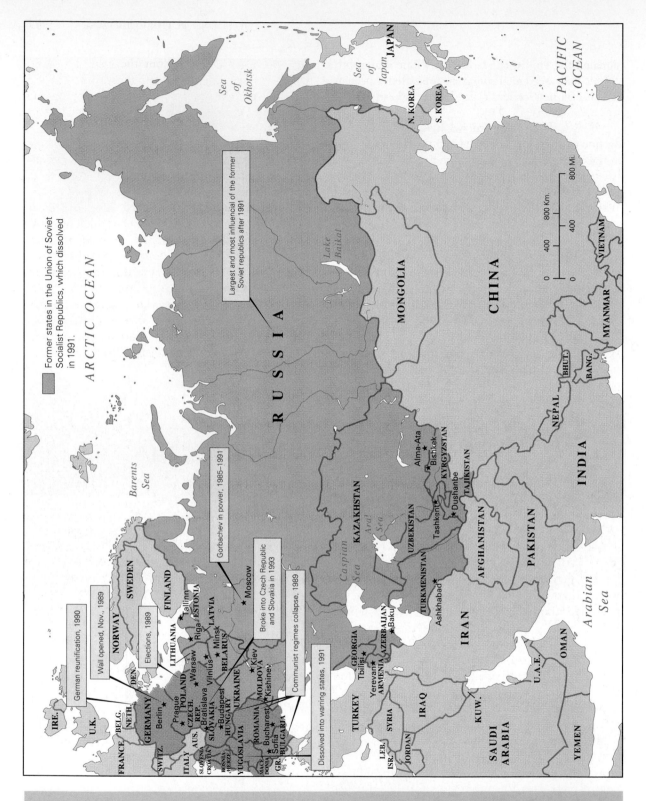

The End of the Cold War in Europe *When Mikhail Gorbachev came to power in the Soviet Union in 1985, he initiated reforms that ultimately undermined the Communist regimes in Eastern Europe and East Germany and led to the break-up of the Soviet Union itself, ensuring an end to the Cold War.*

came unmistakable for both: the Cold War they had made in the 1940s had to be unmade if the two nations were to remain prominent international superintendents.

By the early 1990s, the world had experienced the functional equivalent of a third world war: the two major Cold War combatants had not fought to the death, but the international system had been fundamentally transformed. An empire collapsed, boundaries were redrawn, and the Communist ideology was discredited. All three worlds were breaking up. The First World, or capitalist world, was subdividing into trading blocs and rivals— North America, Japan, and Europe's Economic Community. The Second World of Communism was disintegrating. The Third World, too, was fragmenting into newly industrializing countries, oil-rich nations, and yet a Fourth World—the poorest of nations. Americans crowed that they

had won the Cold War, but the contest had no winners. Both sides—and all the peoples of the world—paid an enormous price for waging the Cold War. At best, the United States had merely outlasted the Soviet Union.

The legacy of the Cold War cast a long shadow. For the United States, long-neglected domestic needs begged for attention and resources. A large arms industry had secured a firm hold on the American economy, and hundreds of thousands of workers continued to owe their jobs to defense contracts. A massive military establishment using an expansive definition of national security had tenaciously built a base of power within the American system, which struggled to adjust to the new international realities. Americans seemed better equipped to fight wars than to improve their declining economy or meet the intense competition of other nations, especially Japan and Germany.

"CONGRATULATIONS.....YOU WON THE COLD WAR!"

The veteran cartoonist Pat Oliphant captured the complexity of what many interpreted as a simple matter: U.S. victory in the Cold War. Oliphant reminded his readers that the Cold War had cost the United States itself a great deal—neglect of its domestic problems, including economic malaise, deteriorating infrastructure, unemployment, and millions of people defined by the U.S. government as poor and homeless. Given the domestic crisis, some analysts argue, it is difficult to claim that either side won the Cold War. Jim Borgmann for the Cincinnati Enquirer. Reprinted with special permission of King Features Syndicate.

During the Cold War era, the power of the presidency had expanded greatly at the expense of the checks-and-balances system; presidents launched covert operations, dispatched troops, and ordered invasions while barely consulting Congress. Government seemed less accountable because citizens found it difficult to peel away the layers of secrecy that enshrouded decision making. The Cold War also bequeathed a record of political extremism, cover-ups, lies, and scandals that made many Americans feel either cynical about their government and the political process or helpless to influence their leaders.

Throughout the world, the two great powers had intervened in civil wars, transforming local class, racial, religious, and economic conflicts into Cold War contests. Given these conflicts, millions would probably have died whether or not there had been a Cold War, but millions more surely died because of it. While they waged the Cold War, moreover, the superpowers had paid little attention to a burgeoning international environmental crisis. After some forty years, though the world had been spared nuclear war, nuclear proliferation still loomed as a danger. The list of nuclear nations grew. The Cold War had ended, but its consequences ensured continued international disorder.

SUGGESTIONS FOR FURTHER READING

For U.S. relations with the Third World since 1945, see Chapters 31 and 34. For George Bush's foreign policy, see Chapter 34.

The Cold War: General and Origins

Stephen Ambrose, *Rise to Globalism*, 5th ed. (1988); Frank Costigliola, *France and the United States* (1992); John L. Gaddis, *Russia, the Soviet Union, and the United States*, 2nd ed. (1990); John L. Gaddis, *The Long Peace* (1987); John L. Gaddis, *Strategies of Containment* (1982); Alexander George et al., eds., *U.S.-Soviet Security Cooperation* (1988); Francis Harbutt, *The Iron Curtain* (1986); Robert C. Hilderbrand, *Dumbarton Oaks* (1990) (on United Nations); Walter Isaacson and Evan Thomas, *The Wise Men* (1986); Robert C. Johansen, *The National Interest and the Human Interest* (1980); Charles W. Kegley, ed., *The Long Post War Peace* (1991); Paul Kennedy, *The Rise and Fall of the Great Powers* (1988); Gabriel Kolko and Joyce Kolko, *The Limits of Power* (1972); Walter LaFeber, *America, Russia, and the Cold War, 1945–1990*, 6th ed. (1991); Melvyn Leffler, *A Preponderance of Power* (1992); Thomas McCormick, *America's Half-Century* (1989); Thomas G. Paterson, *On Every Front: The Making and Unmaking of the Cold War* (1992); Thomas G. Paterson, *Meeting the Communist Threat* (1988); Thomas G. Paterson, *Soviet-American Confrontation* (1973); Michael Schaller, *The American Occupation of Japan* (1985); William Taubman, *Stalin's American Policy* (1982); Adam Ulam, *The Rivals* (1971); Daniel Yergin, *Shattered Peace* (1977).

Early Containment in Europe: Truman Doctrine, Marshall Plan, and NATO

Walter Hixson, *George F. Kennan* (1990); Michael Hogan, *The Marshall Plan* (1987); Lawrence S. Kaplan, *The United States and NATO* (1984); Bruce R. Kuniholm, *The Origins of the Cold War in the Near East* (1980); Alan Milward, *The Reconstruction of Western Europe* (1984); Wilson D. Miscamble, *George F. Kennan and the Making of American Foreign Policy, 1947–1950* (1992); Mark A. Stoler, *George C. Marshall* (1989); Imanuel Wexler, *The Marshall Plan Revisited* (1983); Lawrence S. Wittner, *American Intervention in Greece, 1943–1949* (1982).

Nuclear Arms Race

Desmond Ball, *Politics and Force Levels* (1980); Howard Ball, *Justice Downwind: America's Nuclear Testing Program in the 1950s* (1986); Paul Boyer, *By the Bomb's Early Light* (1986); McGeorge Bundy, *Danger and Survival* (1988); Robert A. Divine, *Blowing in the Wind: The Nuclear Test Ban Debate, 1954–1960* (1978); Lawrence Freedman, *The Evolution of Nuclear Strategy* (1981); Gregg Herken, *Counsels of War* (1985); Gregg Herken, *The Winning Weapon* (1981); Richard G. Hewlett and Jack M. Hall, *Atoms for Peace and War, 1953–1961* (1989); David Holloway, *The Soviet Union and the Arms Race* (1983); Robert Jervis, *The Meaning of the Nuclear Revolution* (1989); Jerome Kahan, *Security in the Nuclear Age* (1975); Fred Kaplan, *The Wizards of Armageddon* (1983); Michael Mandelbaum, *The Nuclear Question* (1979); Charles Morris, *Iron Destinies, Lost Opportunities* (1988); National Academy of Sciences, *Nuclear Arms Control* (1985); John Newhouse, *War and Peace in the Nuclear Age* (1989); John Newhouse, *Cold Dawn: The Story of SALT* (1973); David N. Schwartz, *NATO's Nuclear Dilemmas* (1983); Glenn Seaborg and Benjamin Loeb, *Stemming the Tide* (1987) (on Johnson years); Glenn Seaborg and Benjamin Loeb, *Kennedy, Khrushchev, and the Test Ban* (1981); Martin Sherwin, *A World Destroyed* (1975); Strobe Talbott, *The Master of the Game: Paul Nitze and the Nuclear Peace* (1988); Strobe Talbott, *Deadly Gambit* (1984) (on Reagan); Strobe Talbott, *Endgame* (1979) (SALT-II); Marc Trachtenberg, *History and Strategy* (1991); Spencer Weart, *Nuclear Fear* (1988).

America and the People's Republic of China

Dorothy Borg and Waldo Heinrichs, eds., *Uncertain Years* (1980); Gordon Chang, *Friends and Enemies* (1990); Warren I. Cohen, *America's Response to China*, 3rd ed. (1989); Harry Harding, *A Fragile Relationship* (1972); Akira Iriye, *The Cold War in Asia* (1974); E. J. Kahn, Jr., *The China Hands* (1975); Robert P. Newman, *Owen Lattimore and the "Loss" of China* (1992); David Shambaugh, *Beautiful Imperialist: China Perceives America, 1972–1990* (1991); William W. Stueck, Jr., *The Road to Confrontation: American Policy Toward China and Korea, 1947–1950* (1981); Christopher Thorne, *Allies of a Kind* (1978); Nancy B. Tucker, *Patterns in the Dust* (1983) (on 1949–1950); Shu Guang Zhang, *Deterrence and Strategic Culture: Chinese-American Confrontations, 1949–1958* (1993).

The Korean War

Roy E. Appleman, *Disaster in Korea* (1992); Roy E. Appleman, *Escaping the Trap* (1990); Roy E. Appleman, *Ridgeway Duels for Korea* (1990); Clay Blair, *The Forgotten War* (1988); Ronald J. Caridi, *The Korean War and American Politics* (1969); Bruce Cumings, *The Origins of the Korean War*, 2 vols. (1980, 1991); Rosemary Foot, *A Substitute for Victory* (1990); Rosemary Foot, *The Wrong War* (1985); John Halliday and Bruce Cumings, *Korea: The Unknown War* (1989); Burton I. Kaufman, *The Korean War* (1986); Peter Lowe, *The Origins of the Korean War* (1986); Callum A. MacDonald, *Korea* (1987); Glenn D. Paige, *The Korean Decision* (1968); Michael Schaller, *Douglas MacArthur* (1989); John W. Spanier, *The Truman-MacArthur Controversy and the Korean War* (1959); Allen Whiting, *China Crosses the Yalu* (1960).

Eisenhower-Dulles Foreign Policy

Stephen E. Ambrose, *Eisenhower*, 2 vols. (1982, 1984); Stephen E. Ambrose, *Ike's Spies* (1981); Michael Beschloss, *MAYDAY* (1986) (on the U-2 crisis); Robert A. Divine, *Eisenhower and the Cold War* (1981); Fred Greenstein, *The Hidden-Hand Presidency* (1982); Michael Guhin, *John Foster Dulles* (1972); Townsend Hoopes, *The Devil and John Foster Dulles* (1973); Richard Immerman, ed., *John Foster Dulles* (1990); Burton I. Kaufman, *Trade and Aid* (1982); Richard A. Melanson and David A. Mayers, eds., *Reevaluating Eisenhower* (1986); Jack M. Schick, *The Berlin Crisis* (1971).

Foreign Relations Under Kennedy and Johnson

Michael Beschloss, *The Crisis Years: Kennedy and Khrushchev, 1960–1963* (1991); Warren I. Cohen, *Dean Rusk* (1980); Philip Geyelin, *Lyndon B. Johnson and the World* (1966); James N. Giglio, *The Presidency of John F. Kennedy* (1991); David Halberstam, *The Best and the Brightest* (1972); Doris Kearns, *Lyndon Johnson and the American Dream* (1976); Montague Kern et al., *The Kennedy Crises* (1984); Herbert S. Parmet, *JFK* (1983); Thomas G. Paterson, ed., *Kennedy's Quest for Victory* (1989); Arthur M. Schlesinger, Jr., *Robert Kennedy and His Times* (1978); Arthur M. Schlesinger, Jr., *A Thousand Days* (1965); Thomas J. Schoenbaum, *Waging Peace and War* (1988).

Cuba and the Missile Crisis

Graham Allison, *Essence of Decision: Explaining the Cuban Missile Crisis* (1971); James G. Blight, *The Shattered Crystal Ball* (1990); James G. Blight and David A. Welch, *On the Brink* (1989); Dino Brugioni, *Eyeball to Eyeball* (1991); Raymond Garthoff, *Reflections on the Cuban Missile Crisis*, rev. ed. (1989); Trumbull Higgins, *The Perfect Failure* (1987) (on the Bay of Pigs); Morris Morley, *Imperial State and Revolution* (1987); James Nathan, ed., *The Cuban Missile Crisis Revisited* (1992); Louis A. Pérez, Jr., *Cuba and the United States* (1990); Tad Szulc, *Fidel* (1986).

Nixon, Kissinger, and Détente

Stephen Ambrose, *Nixon* (1987); Richard J. Barnet, *The Giants* (1977); Michael B. Froman, *The Development of the Idea of Détente* (1992); Raymond L. Garthoff, *Détente and Confrontation* (1985);

John R. Greene, *The Limits of Power* (1992); Seymour Hersh, *The Price of Power* (1983); Walter Isaacson, *Kissinger* (1992); Roger Morris, *Uncertain Greatness* (1977); Herbert S. Parmet, *Richard Nixon and His America* (1990); Andrew J. Pierre, *The Global Politics of Arms Sales* (1982); Robert D. Schulzinger, *Henry Kissinger* (1989); Tad Szulc, *The Illusion of Peace* (1978); Adam B. Ulam, *Dangerous Relations* (1983).

The United States in the World Economy and Environment

Richard J. Barnet, *The Lean Years* (1980); Richard J. Barnet and Ronald Müller, *Global Reach: The Power of the Multinational Corporations* (1974); David P. Calleo, *The Imperious Economy* (1982); Alfred E. Eckes, *The U.S. and Global Struggle for Minerals* (1979); Anne G. Keatley, ed., *Technological Frontiers and Foreign Relations* (1985); Stephen D. Krasner, *Defending the National Interest* (1978); John McCormick, *Reclaiming Paradise: The Global Environmental Movement* (1989); Robert K. Olson, *U.S. Foreign Policy and the New International Economic Order* (1981); Robert A. Pastor, *Congress and the Politics of U.S. Foreign Economic Policy, 1929–1976* (1980); Joan E. Spero, *The Politics of International Economic Relations*, 2nd ed. (1981); Herman Van Der Wee, *The Search for Prosperity: The World Economy, 1945–1980* (1986).

Carter Foreign Policy and Human Rights

Betty Glad, *Jimmy Carter* (1980); Erwin C. Hargrove, *Jimmy Carter as President* (1988); Ole R. Holsti and James N. Rosenau, *American Leadership in World Affairs: Vietnam and the Breakdown of Consensus* (1984); Charles O. Jones, *The Trusteeship Presidency: Jimmy Carter and the United States Congress* (1988); David S. McLellan, *Cyrus Vance* (1985); Richard A. Melanson, *Reconstructing Consensus: American Foreign Policy Since the Vietnam War* (1990); A. Glenn Mower, Jr., *Human Rights and American Foreign Policy* (1987); Kenneth A. Oye et al., *Eagle Entangled* (1979); Gaddis Smith, *Morality, Reason, and Power* (1986); Sandy Vogelgesang, *American Dream, Global Nightmare* (1980).

Reagan, Bush, and the End of the Cold War

Michael R. Beschloss and Strobe Talbott, *At the Highest Levels* (1993); Seweryn Bialer and Michael Mandelbaum, eds., *Gorbachev's Russia and American Foreign Policy* (1988); Lou Cannon, *President Reagan* (1991); Robert Dallek, *Ronald Reagan* (1984); John L. Gaddis, *The United States and the End of the Cold War* (1992); Bernard Gwertzman and Michael Kaufman, eds., *The Collapse of Communism* (1990); Seymour Hersh, *"The Target Is Destroyed"* (1987) (on Korean airliner); Michael Hogan, ed., *The End of the Cold War* (1992); Haynes Johnson, *Sleepwalking Through History* (1991); Robert G. Kaiser, *Why Gorbachev Happened* (1991); David E. Kyvig, ed., *Reagan and the World* (1990); Don Oberdorfer, *The Turn* (1991); Kenneth A. Oye et al., eds., *Eagle Resurgent?* (1987); Nicholas X. Rizopoulos, ed., *Sea-Changes* (1990); Michael Schaller, *The Reagan Years* (1992); Steven K. Smith and Douglas A. Wertman, *U.S.-West European Relations During the Reagan Years* (1992). For other works on the Bush foreign policy, see Chapter 34.

30

American Society During the Postwar Boom, 1945–1970

O NE OF THE FIRST THINGS Staff Sergeant Samuel Goldenberg did when he returned from the Second World War was to make love to his wife Eve. One of her first questions was whether he had been unfaithful. "Okay, Sammy, I don't want a list of names," she said. "I just want to know the name of the country." Sam told her that only one man in his entire unit "didn't fool around." When Sam came home to Eve and the daughter who had been born during his absence, he had one overriding goal: to build a happy life for his family.

Two more daughters and a son were born to Sam and Eve over the next few years, contributing to the postwar baby boom. Sam worked hard as an electrician, commuting daily from the Bronx to Manhattan. He was determined to succeed, so his children could grow up in grassy suburban yards and attend good public schools. In 1950 he shortened his name to Gordon, explaining that it was "the kind of name a person could remember" and thus was good for his business, which was prospering. In 1952 Sam and Eve bought a car and moved to Harbor Isle, a new suburb on the south shore of Long Island. Sam was the first

member of his family to own either a house or a car. Life in the suburbs "will be heaven . . . heaven on earth," he assured Eve. For the Gordons, the American Dream was coming true.

An attractive woman who had sung professionally, Eve Gordon devoted herself to her family and did volunteer work for a theater group and the Jewish Center Sisterhood. She and Sam liked to go dancing, and he continued to find her a sexy partner. As a mother, she fed aphorisms to her daughters along with their meals: "Clean while you cook," she told them, and "a marriage is a compromise."

The Gordons' lives were not perfect. Sam lost his temper at times, and Eve smashed dishes when she became agitated. But theirs seemed to be a success story, characterized by family togetherness and material success. Throughout the 1940s and 1950s, they consistently surpassed the goals they had set for themselves at war's end.

Ensconced in their suburban home, Sam and Eve Gordon were unprepared for the cultural turmoil of the 1960s. In 1964, their seventeen-year-old daughter Lorraine told them she was pregnant and was leaving home to marry her boyfriend and live in a squalid walkup on

One of the most popular fads of the 1950s was the Hula-Hoop.

the Lower East Side of New York City. Lorraine's choice of poverty seemed to mock their own aspirations for middle-class comfort and respectability. All four Gordon children joined the "hippie" counterculture and participated in sit-ins opposing the Vietnam War. And their son told them he was gay. The Gordon children were consumers like their parents, but their favorite products were drugs and rock 'n' roll (see Chapter 32).

Material comfort was the hallmark of the postwar middle classes. In terms of both income level and lifestyle, more Americans were better off than ever before—and most expected their good fortune to continue. The most obvious expression of this postwar optimism was the baby boom. From 1946 through 1964 births hit record highs. During this period 76 million babies were born in the United States, compared with only 44 million during the period of depression and war from 1929 through 1945.

Beginning with its size, this generation of newborns was different. During their childhoods, "family togetherness" took on almost religious significance. And as this vast age group grew older, it had successive impacts on housing, elementary and secondary education, fads and popular music, higher education, and the adult job market.

Though the baby boom began to decline in 1964, the economic boom lasted until 1970. The cornerstones of the twenty-five-year economic boom that began in 1946 were the automobile, construction, and defense industries. As the gross national product grew, income levels rose and property ownership spread. Automobiles rolled off the assembly lines; new houses and schools sprang up throughout the country. More and more Americans, including many unionized blue-collar workers, bought homes in the suburbs.

Indeed, most Americans enjoyed an increasingly comfortable standard of living even though the nation's economic progress was disrupted four times by recessions (1950, 1953–1954, 1957–1958, 1960–1961). Whatever the nation's shortcomings, economic and otherwise, Americans heralded it as the world's foremost land of opportunity. They boasted of their political self-determination and social mobility. And public education guaranteed a better life to all who were willing to study and work hard.

The exceptions to the American Dream went unnoticed by most Americans. An emphasis on femininity, piety, and family togetherness concealed the lack of equal opportunities for women. The affluent ignored evidence of poverty. Yet it became clear by the early 1960s that the American poor were much more numerous than people in the complacent 1950s had imagined: one in every four Americans was poor in the early 1960s.

The number of poor people fluctuated with the economy, but their declining numbers reflected the strength of the postwar boom. Poverty was most widespread during the 1950 recession, when 36 percent of Americans were classified as poor. Twenty years later, however, the figure had fallen to 13 percent. Although hard-core poverty was difficult to alleviate, this was an all-time low in American history; economic growth was reducing the ranks of the poor. So too were governmental programs, notably President Lyndon B. Johnson's war on poverty (see Chapter 32).

During the late 1960s the twenty-five year economic boom slowed, and by 1970 it was over. But between 1945 and 1970, booms in business and babies had transformed the economic, social, and cultural life of the American people.

THE POSTWAR BOOMS: BUSINESS AND BABIES

When the postwar era began, many Americans wondered whether it would resemble the most recent postwar epoch, the 1920s. In early 1946 a *New York Times* writer predicted a return of the Roaring Twenties. Not everyone agreed. Reminding readers that the 1920s had culminated in economic depression and world war, another writer responded that "there are too many people who, knowing the results which flowed from the attitudes of 1920, are going to see to it that history does not repeat itself." Indeed, most Americans expected a replay of the 1930s. After all, it was the war that had created jobs and prosperity; surely the end of war would bring a slump.

As it turned out, neither prediction was correct: in 1945 the United States entered one of its longest, steadiest periods of growth and prosperity, the keys to which were increasing output and increasing demand. The United States was not alone in establishing new standards for economic growth and stability. Beginning in the 1950s, Japan and the nations of Western Europe were also booming. "In the 'Golden Age' of the 1950's and 1960's," according to British economist Angus Maddison, "economic growth in the advanced capitalist countries surpassed virtually all historical records." For twenty-five years the American economy grew at an average annual rate of 3.5 percent. Despite occasional recessions the gross national product seldom faltered, rising from just under $210 billion in 1946 to $285 billion in 1950, $504 billion in 1960, and close to $1 trillion in 1970 (see figure on page 924).

When the economy produced more, Americans generally brought home bigger paychecks and had more money to spend. Between 1946 and 1950 per capita real income (based on actual purchasing power) rose 6 percent—but that was only the beginning. In the 1950s it jumped another 15 percent; in the 1960s the increase was even greater—32 percent. Suddenly

Increased Purchasing Power

many Americans could afford goods and services that previously had been beyond their means. The result was a noticeable increase in the standard of living. To the vast majority of Americans, such prosperity was a vindication of the American system of free enterprise. Sociologist Seymour Martin Lipset went so far as to announce that "the fundamental problems of the industrial revolution have been solved."

The end of the war also touched off a debate over whether the postwar population would grow, flatten out, or even decline. As late as 1948, the University of Chicago sociologist William F. Ogburn wrote that the United States would have "a totally new experience" during the postwar era: "a cessation of population growth." Since there would be no baby boom, the "children of the next generation . . . should have room to move around and will not have to go hungry because of population pressures." Schools would not suffer from overcrowding, according to Ogburn, and there would be little pressure for the construction of homes in the suburbs. Events proved Ogburn very wrong.

GNP and Per Capita Income, 1946–1970

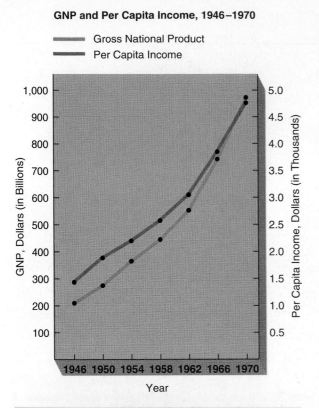

Gross National Product and Per Capita Income, 1946–1970 Both gross national product and per capita income soared during the economic boom from 1946 to 1970. Source: Adapted from U.S. Bureau of the Census, *Historical Statistics of the United States, Colonial Times to 1970*, Bicentennial Edition (Washington, D.C.: U.S. Government Printing Office), p. 224.

Baby Boom

The baby boom was both a cause and an effect of prosperity. It was natural for the birthrate to soar immediately following a war; what was unusual was that it continued to do so throughout the 1950s (see figure, page 925). During the 1950s the annual total exceeded 4 million, reversing the downward trend in birthrates that had prevailed for 150 years. Births began to decline after 1961, but continued to exceed 4 million per year through 1964. The baby-boom generation was the largest by far in the nation's history. One writer has compared "the baby-boom bulge" to "a pig in a python."

Many women who gave birth to a first child in 1946 or 1947 had second, third, fourth, and even fifth children in the years ahead. According to the U.S. Bureau of the Census, 83 percent of the increase in births between 1940 and 1950 was accounted for by first children. Of the increased births between 1950 and 1954, however, 84 percent occurred in families that already had at least one child. The popular belief that an only child was likely to grow up poorly adjusted had something to do with the continued increase. But *Business Week* was closer to the mark in crediting the boom to confidence in America's economic future. Professionals, white-collar workers, and college graduates contributed disproportionately to the baby boom. These were people who knew how to practice birth control and whose counterparts had done so in the past—during the depression the birthrate had declined most sharply among the urban middle class—but who were now having children by choice.

The baby boom meant business for builders, manufacturers, and school systems. "Take the 3,548,000 babies born in 1950," wrote Sylvia F. Porter in her syndicated newspaper column. "Bundle them into a batch, bounce them all over the bountiful land that is America. What do you get?" Porter's answer: "Boom. The biggest, boomiest boom ever known in history. Just imagine how much these extra people, these new markets, will absorb—in food, clothing, in gadgets, in housing, in services. Our factories must expand just to keep pace."

Of the three cornerstones of the postwar economic boom (construction, automobiles, and defense), two were directly related to the upsurge in births. Demand for housing and schools for all these children generated a building boom, furthered by construction of office buildings, shopping centers, factories, airports, and stadiums. Much of this construction took place in suburbs (see pages 930–932). The postwar suburbanization of America would in turn have been impossible without automobile manufacturing, for in these sprawling new communities a car was a necessity. Auto sales had plummeted during the Second World War, when manufacturers shifted to producing tanks and bombers, but in 1946 sales began to climb as Americans seized the chance to get back on the road again. The number of registered automobiles climbed from 26 million in 1945 to 89 million in 1970. Total automobile mileage more than

Housing and Auto Sales

Birthrate, 1940–1970

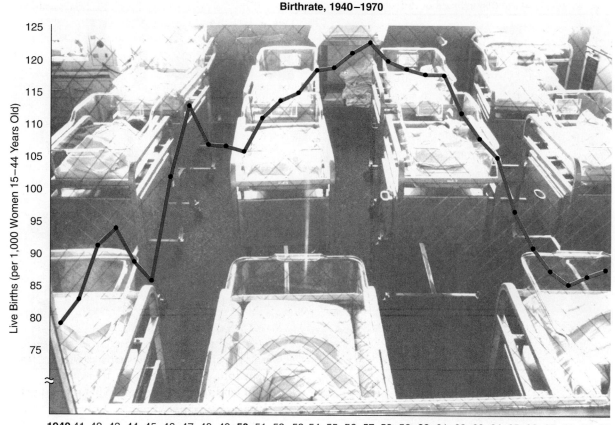

125
120
115
110
105
100
95
90
85
80
75

Live Births (per 1,000 Women 15–44 Years Old)

1940 41 42 43 44 45 46 47 48 49 **50** 51 52 53 54 55 56 57 58 59 **60** 61 62 63 64 65 66 67 68 69 **70**

Year

Birthrate, 1940–1970 *The birthrate began to rise in 1942 and 1943, but it skyrocketed during the postwar years beginning in 1946. Reaching its peak in 1957, the birthrate thereafter subsided throughout the 1960s.* Source: Adapted from U.S. Bureau of the Census, *Historical Statistics of the United States, Colonial Times to 1970,* Bicentennial Edition (Washington, D.C.: U.S. Government Printing Office, p. 49).

quadrupled, from 250 billion in 1945 to over 1 trillion in 1970.

The third cornerstone of the postwar economic boom was military spending. When the Defense Department was established in 1947, the nation

Military Spending

was spending just over $10 billion a year on defense. Beginning with the Korean War in the early 1950s, defense spending skyrocketed. It stood at $22 billion in 1951; two years later it was over $50 billion; in 1970, it exceeded $80 billion. Defense contracts also went to industries and universities to develop weapons. In 1947, the Department of Defense awarded contracts worth $470 million for

research and development; in 1970, these contracts totaled $7.4 billion. The government also supported space research; funds spent on this research alone zoomed from $76 million in 1957 to almost $6 billion in 1966.

Defense spending helped stimulate rapid advances in the electronics industry. The ENIAC computer, completed at the University of Pennsylvania in 1946, weighed thirty tons, required 18,000 vacuum tubes, and worked 1,000 times as quickly as its wartime predecessor, the Mark I. The introduction of the transistor in the 1950s accelerated the computer revolution; the silicon microchip—a "computer on a chip"—in the 1960s inaugurated even more stunning advances in electronics. Busi-

Babies meant big business for companies that produced baby foods, toys, and clothing. "In its first year as a consumer," read the caption for this 1958 Life *photo, "baby is a potential market for $800 worth of products."*   Yale Joel, LIFE Magazine © Time Warner, Inc.

nesses and governments were so eager to buy electronic computing equipment that their purchases catapulted from $25 million in 1953 to $1 billion in 1960.

The microchip facilitated the shift from heavy manufacturing to "high tech" industries in fiber optics, lasers, video equipment, robotics, and genetic engineering. Sales of office and business equipment reflected the growth in technology-based production. In 1965, almost $3 billion worth of computing equipment was sold; by 1970, the figure had almost doubled to $5.7 billion. And this was just the beginning. In the succeeding decades, the numbers of new computer users in America would continue to skyrocket (see Chapter 33), marking what the economist Herbert A. Simon called "an advance in

The Computer Revolution

man's thinking processes as radical as the invention of writing."

The evolution of electronics meant a large-scale trade-off for the American people. As industries automated, computerized processes replaced slower mechanical ones, generating a rapid rise in productivity. But in doing so they brought about technological unemployment: fewer workers were needed to accomplish the same amount of work. In the tool-and-die industry, for instance, computerized technology caused a decline in the demand for machinists; from 1950 to 1970 their numbers dropped from 535,000 to 390,000.

Electronic technology also promoted concentration of ownership in industry. Sophisticated technology was expensive. Typically, only large corporations could afford it; small corporations were shut out of the market. People who believed that competition was the lifeblood of the American economy saw this tendency toward bigness as a dangerous development.

As industry became more capital-intensive, established firms in high-technology fields expanded into related industries. General Electric, which during and after the war had manufactured electrical products, diversified during this period. It began producing computers, industrial automation systems, jet engines, and nuclear-powered generators. Other companies had similar experiences.

Another kind of corporate expansion also marked the early 1950s as the third great wave of mergers swept across American business. Unlike the first two such movements in the 1890s and 1920s, which had tended toward vertical and horizontal integration respectively this era was distinguished by conglomerate mergers. A *conglomerate* merges companies in unrelated industries as a hedge against instability in a particular market. International Telephone and Telegraph, for instance, bought up companies in the fields of car rental (Avis), baking (Continental Baking), suburban development and home construction (Levitt and Sons), food sales (Canteen Corporation), hotels and motels (Sheraton Corporation), and insurance (Hartford Fire Insurance).

Conglomerate Mergers

Such mergers resulted in unprecedented concentration of industry: the two hundred largest manufacturing corporations held the same proportion of total manufacturing assets in 1968 as had the thousand largest in 1941. In keeping with the thrust of America's postwar boom, the country's ten largest corporations at the time were in automobiles (GM, Ford, Chrysler), oil (Exxon, Mobil, Texaco), and electronics and communications (GE, IBM, IT&T, AT&T).

The labor movement also experienced a postwar merger. In 1955 the American Federation of Labor and the Congress of Industrial Organizations finally put aside their differences and formed the AFL-CIO. Union membership remained fairly constant, increasing from just around 18 million at the time of the merger to only 20.7 million in 1970. Some observers charged that union leaders had become smug and lost the zeal that had won over so many workers in the 1930s and 1940s. And revelations of corrupt union practices also tainted the labor movement. The nation's biggest union, the

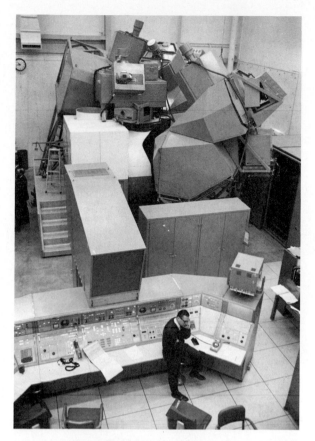

Prior to the advent of transistors and then microchip-based integrated circuits, computers were very large machines. The first postwar computer, powered by ten thousand vacuum tubes, weighed thirty tons and was as large as a railroad box car. Cartier Bresson/Magnum Photos.

International Brotherhood of Teamsters, had ties to organized crime. When the Teamsters failed to clean their house, the AFL-CIO expelled the union in 1957. Two Teamsters presidents, Dave Beck and James R. Hoffa, served federal prison sentences for offenses ranging from tax evasion to jury tampering. (Hoffa vanished without a trace in 1975.) But the main reason for the slow growth of union membership was a shift in employment patterns. Most new jobs were being created not in the heavy industries that hired blue-collar workers but in the union-resistant white-collar service trades.

The postwar economic boom was good for unionized blue-collar workers, many of whom won real increases in wages, sufficient to enjoy a

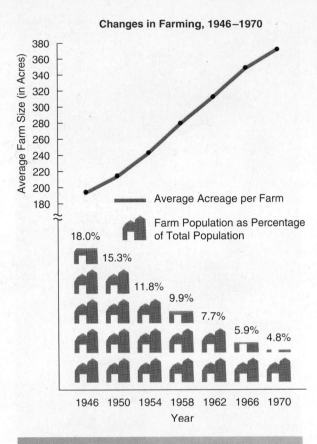

Changes in Farming, 1946–1970

Average Acreage per Farm

Farm Population as Percentage of Total Population

Changes in Farming, 1946–1970 *America's farm population plummeted from 18 percent of the total population in 1946 to 5 percent in 1970. At the same time, the size of the average farm nearly doubled.* Source: Adapted from U.S. Bureau of the Census, *Historical Statistics of the United States, Colonial Times to 1970*, Bicentennial Edition (Washington, D.C.: U.S. Government Printing Office), p. 457.

Union Workers' Benefits

middle-class lifestyle that previously had been the exclusive province of white-collar workers, businesspeople, and professionals. Union workers could qualify for mortgages for suburban homes, especially if their spouses also worked. Through collective bargaining, many now enjoyed job security, including a paid two-week vacation. Union and company pension plans, in addition to Social Security, meant that union workers could look forward to a secure retirement. They could aspire to college educations for their

children. And they were more protected against inflation: in 1948 General Motors and the United Auto Workers agreed on automatic cost-of-living adjustments (COLAs) in workers' wages, a practice that spread to other industries.

The trend toward economic consolidation also changed agriculture. New machines, such as mechanical cotton-, tobacco-, and grape-pickers and crop-dusting planes revolutionized farming methods, and the increased use of fertilizers and pesticides raised the total value of farm output from $29 billion in 1946 to (in constant dollars) $54 billion in 1970. Meanwhile labor productivity tripled. The resulting improvement in profitability drew large investors into agriculture, and average acreage per farm almost doubled, from 193 in 1946 to 374 in 1970. Simultaneously the value of farmland skyrocketed from $69 billion in 1945 to $266 billion in 1970. By the 1960s it took money—sometimes big money—to become a farmer. In many regions only banks, insurance companies, and large businesses could afford the necessary land, machinery, and fertilizer. The Gates Rubber Company of Cleveland entered farming in 1968, explaining that its purpose was to diversify and make money. In developing its 10,400-acre Big Creek Farms, including a 4,000-head cattle feedlot, it bought up numerous small farms in northeastern Colorado and purchased expensive tractors and sprinkler irrigation equipment.

The movement toward consolidation threatened the survival of the family farm. From 1946 to 1970 the nation's farm population declined from

Decline of the Family Farm

around 24 million to just under 10 million—from 18 percent of the population to just 5 percent. When the harvesting of cotton in the South was mechanized in the 1940s and 1950s, more than 4 million people were displaced. In southern tobacco farming, growers dismissed their tenant farmers, bought tractors to plow the land, and hired migratory workers to harvest the crop. Many of these displaced farmers traded southern rural poverty for northern urban poverty. Farm families that grew wheat on the plains were also displaced by machinery and farm consolidation. "We lost country life when we moved to tractors," one of these farmers lamented. Those who stayed behind did so not because they could still make a good living but because they were simply too old to leave their lifelong homes and follow their children and grand-children to the cities. Living in relative isolation on limited incomes, the rural aged were hidden victims of mechanization.

Economic growth also exacted environmental costs, to which most Americans were oblivious. All aspects of the environment—air, water, soil, wildlife—suffered degradation.

Environmental Costs of Economic Growth

Steel mills, coal-powered generators, and internal-combustion car engines polluted the air and imperiled people's health. In 1948, for example, twenty people in the steeltown of Donora, Pennsylvania, died of respiratory failure caused by air pollution. The smoke and sulfur gases pouring from the zinc smelter in Donora became so thick that people could not see or breathe. The poisonous smog also killed hundreds of sheep and chickens on neighboring farms.

America's water supplies also suffered. Human and industrial waste befouled many rivers and lakes, making them unfit for consumption or recreation. Municipalities were at fault as well as industries. Vast quantities of water were diverted from lakes and rivers to meet the needs of America's burgeoning Sunbelt cities, including the swimming pools that dotted Arizona and southern California. Arid lands bloomed for the first time, but once-fertile areas—such as Owens Valley on the eastern slope of the Sierras, which was pumped dry to supply water to Los Angeles—became dust bowls. The extraction of natural resources—strip-mining of coal, for example—also scarred the landscape, and toxic waste from chemical plants seeped deep into the soil. America was becoming a dumping ground as never before.

Among the country's worst polluters were defense contractors and farmers. Nuclear-processing plants that produced plutonium for atomic bombs also produced radioactive waste with a half-life of two thousand years. Refuse from nuclear weapons facilities at Hanford, Washington, and at Colorado's Rocky Flats arsenal polluted soil and water resources for years. Agriculture began employing massive amounts of pesticides and other chemicals and draining aquifers of water for nonstop irrigation of arid lands. A chemical called DDT, for example, which had been used on Pacific islands during the

DDT

The costs of the postwar economic boom included bumper-to-bumper traffic and air pollution. These cars snarled the Pasadena Freeway during rush hour in 1958. Courtesy EPA.

war to kill mosquitoes and lice that carried malaria and typhus, was released for public use in 1945. Over the next fifteen years, farmers eliminated chronic pests with DDT. In 1962, however, *Silent Spring* by Rachel Carson, a wildlife biologist, alerted Americans to the dangers of massive and indiscriminate use of farm chemicals; Carson specifically indicted DDT for the deaths of mammals, birds, and fish. DDT accumulates in the fatty tissues of eagles, trout, and other animals, causing cancer and leukemia. Where birds had once sung, Carson wrote, there was now "a strange stillness." Within six months of publication, *Silent Spring* had sold half a million copies. For the first time, many Americans realized that there were costs to human conquest of the environment. The federal government banned the sale of DDT in 1972.

Much of America's continued economic growth, however, was based on encouraging habits that would make the country a throwaway society. Under the auto industry's policy of "planned obsolescence," for example, cars were produced to be less durable. Massive advertising campaigns urged

Geographic Distribution of U.S. Population, 1930–1970 (in Percentages)

Year	Central Cities	Suburbs	Rural Areas and Small Towns
1930	31.8	18.0	50.2
1940	31.6	19.5	48.9
1950	32.3	23.8	43.9
1960	32.6	30.7	36.7
1970	31.4	37.6	31.0

Source: Adapted from U.S. Bureau of the Census, *Decennial Censuses, 1930–1970* (Washington, D.C.: U.S. Government Printing Office).

consumers to buy a new car every year or two; and according to the director of the Center for Auto Safety, the strategy of planned obsolescence was "implemented by purposeful proliferation of model types, which totaled 370 in 1967, to induce owners to trade up to something a little more glamorous." Cars were but one example of mass consumption in postwar America; disposable versions of consumer goods ranging from cigarette lighters to plastic cups to paper diapers were also marketed as conveniences.

THE GROWTH OF SUBURBS

Almost as many Americans resided in the suburbs as in the cities by 1960, and by 1970 suburbs had surpassed cities in total population (see table). A combination of motives drew people to the suburbs. One was racism, as white families fled from urban neighborhoods where African-American families had just settled. Others wanted to leave behind the noise and smells of the city and live closer to nature and further from their neighbors. They also wanted homes with yards so that, as one suburbanite put it, "every kid [would have] an opportunity to grow up with grass stains on his pants." They wanted family rooms, extra closets, and utility rooms. Many were also looking for a place where they could have a measure of political influence. Big-city government was dense and impenetrable; in the suburbs, citizens could become

involved in government and have an impact, particularly on the education their children received. "The American suburb," mused a Pittsburgh building executive in 1960, "is the last outpost of democracy, the only level on which the individual citizen can make his wishes felt, directly and immediately."

As the massive number of three- and four-bedroom houses built in the suburbs makes clear, the focus of suburbanites' lives was their children. "This is a paradise for children," observed a newspaper writer in 1950 about the new suburb where he lived. "There are so many babies here," commented one of his neighbors, "you would think everybody would be blasé about them. Still, when a new one is coming, all the neighbors make a fuss over you."

Another attraction of the suburbs was closeness in age and shared experience, which made for a community of like-minded people. Typically, suburban adults were young parents between the ages of twenty-five and thirty-five, and almost all the children were toddlers. In one suburb of nine thousand homes there were eight thousand children, only about one hundred of whom were old enough for high school; most of the rest were still in playpens. "People could not outdo each other," one resident of this community reported, "because they almost all have the same income. . . . Nobody talks about the [Second World] war much, because they've all been in it. And most of the men have the same . . . commuting problem—which many have solved by car pools. All this helps to cement neighbors into friends."

Men and women of their generation had grown up during the economic deprivation of the 1930s. In young adulthood during the Second World War, many had been physically separated from their families and friends. The sociologist Glen H. Elder, Jr., has written that men and women who had grown up in the 1930s "in Depression-marked homes were most likely to anchor their lives around family and children, perhaps reflecting the notion of home as a refuge in an unpredictable world." These men and women became ardent believers in and exponents of "family togetherness."

Family Togetherness

Government funding helped these new families to settle in the suburbs. Low-interest GI mortgages and Federal Housing Administration (FHA)

How do historians know

that the suburbs stimulated the postwar American economy? For one thing, they can point to census data that document the spiraling sales of houses and automobiles. There is also anecdotal evidence. In 1953 Leo Ferguson and his family moved into Los Angeles's fastest-growing suburb, Lakewood. During the first week in their new home, they were visited by over seventy-five representatives selling everything from Venetian blinds to hot water heaters, and from Fuller Brush products to weather stripping. Photo: J.R. Eyerman, LIFE Magazine @ Time Warner Inc.

Housing Boom

mortgage insurance made the difference for people who otherwise would have been unable to afford a home. It was this easy credit, combined with postwar prosperity, that produced a construction boom. In 1944 there had been only 142,000 housing starts, many of which represented temporary housing for soldiers and war workers. In a single year, from 1945 to 1946, housing starts climbed from 326,000 to over

1 million; they approached 2 million in 1950, and remained close to 1.5 million as late as 1970. Never before had new starts exceeded 1 million; not until the early 1980s would they again dip below that level.

To produce so much new housing so fast, contractors had to operate on a massive scale. In 1947 Arthur Levitt and Sons, a firm that built planned communities (Levittowns) in New York, New Jersey, and Pennsylvania, developed a method,

Examples of vernacular architecture dotted America's highways in the 1940s and 1950s. Along U.S. Route 66, the main route from Chicago to Los Angeles, there were teepee-shape motels and iceberg-shape gas stations. This motel accommodated weary travelers in Holbrook, Arizona. Mike Stoklos/TIME Magazine.

adopted by other companies, of using interchangeable materials and designs. Levitt erected rows of nearly identical houses on uniform treeless lots. As suburbia spread, pasture lands yielded to near-instant neighborhoods with astounding rapidity. To supply the new communities, supermarkets and shopping centers—surrounded by vast parking lots—soon dotted the countryside.

Highway construction opened up previously remote rural lands for transformation into suburbs. In 1947 Congress authorized construction of a 37,000-mile chain of highways.

Highway Construction

In 1956, President Eisenhower signed the Highway Act, which launched a 41,000-mile nationwide network. Federal expenditures on highways swelled from $79 million in 1946 to $429 million in 1950, $2.9 billion in 1960, and $4.6 billion in 1970. State and local spending on highways also mushroomed. Highways not only hastened suburbanization; they also promoted more uniformity in lifestyles and homogenized the landscape. The high-speed trucking that highways made possible also accelerated the integration of the South into the national economy.

The interstate system had been largely completed by the mid-1960s, and some towns along the way had prospered. Route I-70, for example, gave Junction City, Kansas, six new motels, several restaurants, and an economic boost. But the new road also siphoned traffic away from older roads. Small towns along two-lane highways withered as their residents left to seek a better living in the city. The towns "didn't dry up and blow away," observed the editor of Junction City's daily newspaper, "but they are much like the towns left off the railroad [lines] 100 years ago."

Highway construction in combination with the growth of suburbia produced a new phenomenon, the *megalopolis,* a term coined by urban experts in the early 1960s to refer to the almost uninterrupted metropolitan complex stretching along the northeastern seaboard from Boston six hundred miles south through New York, Philadelphia, and Baltimore all the way to Washington, D.C. "Boswash" encompassed parts of eleven states and a population of 49 million people, all linked by interstate highways. Although the suburbs within the megalopolis were politically independent, they were economically dependent on the cities and connecting highways. Other megalopolises that took shape following the Second World War were "Milipitts," a band of heavy industry and dense population stretching from Milwaukee to Pittsburgh, and "San-San," the area between San Francisco and San Diego.

Socially, the suburbs' emphasis on family togetherness tended to isolate families. Sociologist David Riesman, writing in 1957, criticized "the decentralization of leisure in the

Critics of Suburban Life

suburbs . . . as the home itself, rather than the neighborhood, becomes the chief gathering place for the family—either in the 'family room' with its games, its TV, its informality, or outdoors around the barbecue." The floor plan of the ranch-style home, whose centerpiece was the TV set enthroned on a swivel, was suited to the stay-at-home lifestyle. Even when families traveled, they were isolated in the family car.

Other observers denounced the suburbs for breeding conformity and status seeking. Some writers criticized suburbanites for trying to keep up with the Joneses by buying new cars and appliances. William H. Whyte's *The Organization Man*

The thrill is pure Thunderbird…

The Galaxie Club Victoria. Hold on to your heart!

Automobiles in postwar America were viewed as status symbols. According to this advertisement, the owner of the 1959 Ford Galaxie gets not only a low-priced car, but also "a sleek silhouette that says very, very Thunderbird."   Collection of Picture Research Consultants.

(1956), a study of Park Forest, Illinois, pronounced these suburbanites mindless conservatives and extreme conformists. Their value system featured a belief in the group as "the source of creativity" and "in 'belongingness' as the ultimate need of the individual." In Sloan Wilson's novel *The Man in the Gray Flannel Suit* (1955), the protagonist led a treadmill existence commuting to his white-collar job in the city. And C. Wright Mills, a sociologist, castigated white-collar suburbanites who "sell not only their time and energy but their personalities as well. They sell . . . their smiles and their kindly gestures."

Nonetheless, most residents of suburbia preferred family togetherness to any other lifestyle of which they were aware. Of the college students interviewed by Riesman in the 1950s, the vast majority looked forward to settling in the suburbs.

IDEALS OF MOTHERHOOD AND THE FAMILY

Earlier in the twentieth century, Sunday dinner had been exasperating for the youngest child in a large family, because the youngest was traditionally served last. If chicken was served, the little one typically got the back or the neck. "I was the youngest of five children, and by the time I was served, all the white meat was gone. . . . I swore to myself that when I grew up I would eat all the white meat I could," recalled one young father shortly after the Second World War. "So I'm grown up and a father—and my children get the first choice!" Times had changed, and so had the values of the American family; this generation, ex-

Dr. Benjamin Spock's Baby and Child Care *(1946) encouraged the mothers of the baby boom to consider their children's needs first and foremost. Although many mothers retained old-fashioned methods of discipline, in the postwar period there was a shift to more permissive approaches.* Curtis Publishing Company.

pected to defer to their parents, now catered to their children.

Much of the change was due to the publication in 1946 of Dr. Benjamin Spock's *Baby and Child Care*, which quickly became a perennial best seller.

Dr. Spock on Child Rearing

Unlike earlier manuals, *Baby and Child Care* urged mothers always to think of their children first. (Spock assigned fathers little formal role in child rearing.) He based his advice on new findings about the importance of responding to a baby's needs. Spock's predecessors had advised mothers to consider their own needs as well as their children's; they had recommended early and strict toilet training, "putting away your children at six o'clock" in order to enjoy the evening, and ignoring a baby's cries except at feeding time. Spock urged the mother to be constantly available to her baby and to encourage the baby's "self-realization" and "self-motivated behavior."

Guilt was the inevitable outcome of the effort to be not only mother but teacher, psychologist, and playmate. The mother of an epileptic son wrote to Dr. Spock: "I try to give him a great deal of affection, although I am a working woman. . . . Sometimes it is so difficult to maintain my control that my hands shake. . . . Does he need the help or do I?" Another mother wrote, "We like to read and listen to music. Maybe we have neglected some aspects of [our child's] development in our own selfishness."

Meanwhile the social critic Philip Wylie denounced such selfless behavior as "Momism." In the guise of sacrificing for her children, Wylie wrote in *Generation of Vipers* (1942, revised 1955), Mom was pursuing "love of herself." She smothered her children with affection to make them emotionally dependent on her and reluctant to leave home. Some medical experts agreed. Army psychiatrists blamed recruits' nervous disorders on mothers who, in the words of a psychiatric adviser to the secretary of war, had "failed in the elementary mother function of weaning [their] offspring emotionally as well as physically."

But women faced a double bind, for if they pursued a life outside the home they were accused of being "imitation men" or "neurotic" feminists. Echoing the psychoanalyst Sigmund Freud, critics of working mothers contended that a woman could be happy and fulfilled only through domesticity. "Anatomy is destiny" was their watchword; a woman's gender, in other words, determined her role in life, which was to provide her husband and children a cozy and stimulating haven from the outside world. But many women aspired to careers outside the home; they were dissatisfied with sex-role stereotypes. In a 1946 poll, when asked whether they would prefer to be born again as women or men, 25 percent of the women said they would choose to be men; of the men polled, only 3.3 percent preferred to be women. Reflecting on society's contradictory expectations of women, anthropologist Margaret Mead wrote in 1946, "Choose any set of criteria you like, and the answer is the same: women—and men—are confused, uncertain, and discontented with the present definition of women's place in America."

Women's Conflicting Roles

Meanwhile, however, women continued the wartime trend toward work outside the home. The

Although women moved into once all-male domains, such as police work, gender-based notions persisted. These policewomen in Richmond, Virginia, in 1955 were issued shoulder purses instead of holsters for carrying their revolvers.   Valentine Museum, courtesy of Grace Howerton.

Working Women
———

female labor force rose from 17 million in 1946 to 32 million in 1970. Most of these new women workers found themselves segregated in low-paying jobs as clerks, secretaries, and nurses. These women had entered the labor force without the support of an organized women's movement, which was in decline between the 1930s and the rebirth of feminism in the late 1960s. Most thus refrained from challenging sex-role stereotypes.

Many women were their families' sole source of income; they had to work. Others took jobs to supplement their husbands' income, to enjoy adult company, or to bolster their self-esteem. Despite the cult of motherhood, most new entrants to the job market were married—a trend that began during the Second World War—and most were mothers (see figure, page 937).

The GI Bill
———

Immediately after the Second World War, many former GIs had enrolled in college and set up housekeeping with their wives and babies in abandoned military barracks on college campuses. The legislation that made this possible was the Servicemen's Readjustment Act of 1944, popularly known as the GI Bill of Rights, which provided living allowances and tuition payments to college-bound veterans. Over 1 million veterans enrolled in 1946—accounting for one out of every two students. Despite pessimistic predictions, the veterans succeeded as students. Benjamin Fine, education editor of the *New York Times*, called it "the most astonishing fact in the history of American higher education. . . . The G.I.'s are hogging the honor rolls and the Deans' lists. . . . Far from being an educational problem, the veteran has become an asset to higher education." But there was nothing astonishing about it: veterans saw higher education as the key to upward mobility. (The downside of this success story was that colleges made places for male veterans by turning away qualified women.)

These veterans were asserting their determination to provide economic security for their families. Popular periodicals reinforced their convictions. "Ed and His Family Live Together and Love It" was the title of a typical article in a 1954 *McCall's*. "Caring for three lively children makes tremendous demands on Carol. . . . But Ed is a cheerful working partner to her, helps with the children and housework whenever he can, gives everything he has to make his family happy." In return, Ed's wife and children gave him "all the love and affection a husband and father could hope for." Carol even shared some household tasks traditionally performed by men: "Paneling that extra room in the cellar used to be the man's job. But Ed and Carol do it together." The magazine stopped short, however, of advocating complete equality: "For the sake of every member of the family, the family needs a head. This means Father, not Mother."

As the baby boom became a grade-school boom, American families became preoccupied with education. Convinced that their children's success in school was a prerequisite for economic and social success in adult life, parents joined the parent-teacher association so they would have a voice in the educational process. They worried that schools were overcrowded, understaffed, and aimless and that teachers were using obsolete methods. Critics of the schools encouraged parents' participation. "Just as war is 'too serious a matter to be left to the generals,' so, I think, the teaching of reading is too important to be left to the educators," wrote Dr. Rudolf Flesch in 1955 in his best-selling critique of public education, *Why Johnny Can't Read*.

When the Soviets launched *Sputnik*, the first earth-orbiting satellite, two years later, Americans were shocked and sobered by the Soviet feat (see Chapter 29). Almost overnight, education became a matter of national security. The Russian triumph threw into question American military and technological superiority, based ultimately on the nation's school system. Former Harvard president James B. Conant, Admiral Hyman G. Rickover, and others

Education of the Baby-Boom Generation

argued that what the United States needed to regain its technological leadership was a new emphasis on mathematics, foreign languages, and the sciences. Congress responded in 1958 with the National Defense Education Act (NDEA), which funded enrichment of elementary and high-school programs in those disciplines and offered fellowships and loans to college students. Public education was characterized as "the engine of democracy," crucial to both upward social mobility and military superiority. One of the clearest indications of this belief was the surge in college enrollments, which jumped from 1.5 million in 1940 to 2.3 million in 1950, 3.6 million in 1960, and 7.4 million in 1970.

But even as college enrollments swelled, women lost ground. In an era in which wives tended to subordinate their career goals to those of their husbands, the percentage of women earning college degrees declined. The proportion of women among college graduates dropped from 40 percent in 1940 to 25 percent in 1950. At the postgraduate level, only 11 percent of doctorates earned in the United States went to women, compared with 16 percent in 1920. The 1960s reversed this trend; by 1970 the figure had again reached the 1920 level.

As education became intertwined with national security, religion became a matter of patriotism. As President Eisenhower put it, "Recognition of the Supreme Being is the first, the most basic expression of Americanism." After all, the United States was locked in mortal combat with an atheistic enemy. Religious leaders also emphasized traditional values like family togetherness. "The family that prays together stays together" was a familiar refrain in the 1950s and 1960s. The Bible topped the best-seller lists, and books with religious themes, such as Reverend Norman Vincent Peale's *The Power of Positive Thinking* (1952), told people how to apply religious precepts to the pursuit of wordly success. Evangelist Billy Graham exhorted television viewers and stadium audiences throughout the country. Membership in religious congregations nearly doubled in the twenty-five years after the Second World War, increasing from 74 million in 1946 to 131 million in 1970.

Although Americans were eager to improve their minds and souls, they were not ready until

Religion in Postwar America

Marital Distribution of the Female Labor Force, 1944–1970

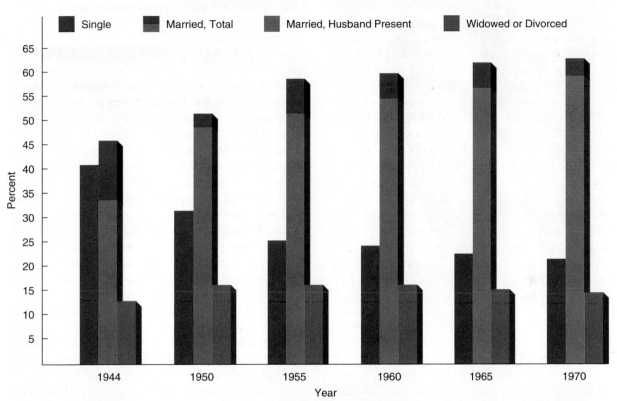

Marital Distribution of the Female Labor Force, 1944–1970 *In 1944 the percentage of women in the labor force who were single was 41; in 1970, only 22 percent was single. During the same years, the percentage of the female labor force that had a husband in the home jumped from 34 to 59. The percentage who were widowed or divorced remained about the same from 1944 to 1970.* Source: Adapted from U.S. Bureau of the Census, *Historical Statistics of the United States, Colonial Times to 1970,* Bicentennial Edition (Washington, D.C.: U.S. Government Printing Office, 1975), p. 133.

the 1960s to acknowledge their sexuality (see Chapter 32). In the 1940s and 1950s, there was a wide gap between sexual behavior and public discourse on the subject. When Dr. Alfred Kinsey, director of the Institute for Sex Research at Indiana University, published his pioneering study *Sexual Behavior in the Human Male* (1948), the American public was shocked. On the basis of interviews with 12,000 men, Kinsey estimated that 95 percent of all American men had engaged in masturbation, premarital or extramarital intercourse, or homosexual behavior. Princeton's President Harold Dodds denounced the volume as "the work of small boys

writing dirty words on fences." Five years later Kinsey caused an uproar with *Sexual Behavior in the Human Female,* which revealed that 62 percent of women masturbated and 50 percent had had intercourse before marriage. Some angry Americans condemned the report as a slanderous attack on motherhood and the family. A congressman from New York, who tried to bar the report from the mails, charged Kinsey with "hurling the insult of the century against our mothers, wives, daughters and sisters."

Movies and magazines reinforced the prevailing notion that sex was wrong and dangerous out-

One of the most dreaded epidemics of the 1940s and early 1950s was infantile paralysis. But in 1955 the Salk polio vaccine was approved by the government for general use. By 1962 the incidence of polio had dropped 97 percent. Library of Congress.

Momism to promiscuity, American women were the victims of male-inspired stereotypes.

THE AFFLUENT SOCIETY

The Harvard economist John Kenneth Galbraith gave a name to the United States during the postwar economic boom; he called it the affluent society. As U.S. productivity grew by leaps and bounds in the postwar years, so did Americans' appetite for goods and services. During the depression and the Second World War, many Americans had dreamed of buying a home or a car. In the affluent postwar years they could finally satisfy those deferred desires. Some families bought two cars and equipped their new homes with the latest appliances and amusements—dishwashers, television sets, and stereophonic sound systems. When they lacked cash to buy what they wanted, they borrowed money. Consumer credit to support the nation's shopping spree grew from around $8 billion in 1946 to $56 billion in 1960 and $127 billion in 1970. Easy credit was the economic basis of the consumer culture.

As Americans consumed goods and services, they were using up the world's resources. Consumption of crude petroleum soared 118 percent from 1946 to 1970, but domestic production increased only 97 percent; the extra oil had to be imported. Whether generated by coal, water, or nuclear energy, electricity use jumped too, from 270 billion kilowatt-hours to 1.6 trillion. By the mid-1960s the United States, with only 5 percent of the world's population, produced and consumed over one-third of the world's goods and services.

By contrast, advances in public health were a particularly happy effect of postwar prosperity. The average life span increased from 67 years in 1946 to 71 in 1970, due largely

Improvements in Public Health to a dramatic decline in the infant mortality rate. (Racial differences, however, continued to be significant. In 1970, white men lived 6.5 years longer than black men, and white women lived 6 years longer than black women.) Affluent Americans who could afford regular prenatal and pediatric care benefited from increased federal funding for medical research. As a result the infant mortality rate dropped from 34 deaths per 1,000 live births in 1945 to 20 per 1,000 in 1970. (Here, too,

side of marriage, while advice columns and marriage manuals with a scientific-

Sexual Taboos hygienic flavor treated it as something for wives to work at, in the interests of a healthy marriage. The historian Elaine Tyler May has written that, in postwar America, "containment was the key to security," not only in Cold War foreign policy but also in controlling sexual impulses. Promulgated by family, church, state, and media alike, "sexual containment" warned that premarital, extramarital, and homosexual behavior would bring "familial chaos and weaken the country's moral fiber," and it blamed women for the impending disaster. Despite any evidence of significant increases in women's sexual activity from the 1920s to the 1960s, female lust, according to May, was perceived to pose the greatest sexual threat to the future of the family. From

race was decisive: infant mortality in 1970 was about 18 per 1,000 live births for whites, but almost 31 per 1,000 blacks.) Penicillin had been introduced to the United States during the war, and the postwar discovery of wonder drugs such as streptomycin (1945) and aureomycin (1948) reduced deaths from influenza and postsurgical infection. The Salk polio vaccine, approved for public use in 1955, reduced reported cases of polio 97 percent by 1962. Diseases like tuberculosis, whooping cough, and diphtheria became little more than bad memories.

Millions of Americans began their search for affluence by migrating to the Sunbelt—roughly, the southern third of the United States, running

Growth of the Sunbelt

from southern California across the Southwest and South all the way to the Atlantic Coast. Between 1940 and 1950 Houston's population jumped from 385,000 to 596,000. Other Sunbelt cities that boomed in the 1940s were Baton Rouge, Long

Beach, Miami, Mobile, and Phoenix. This mass migration had started during the war, when GIs and their families were ordered to new duty stations and war workers moved to the shipyards and aircraft factories of San Diego and other cities of the West and South. Soon the Sunbelt encompassed most of America's southern rim.

The economic bases of the Sunbelt's spectacular growth were agribusiness, the aerospace industry, the oil industry, real-estate development, recreation, and defense spending. Government policies—generous tax breaks for oil companies, siting of military bases, and awarding of defense and aerospace contracts—were crucial to the Sunbelt's development. Industry was also drawn to the southern rim by right-to-work laws, which outlawed closed shops, and by low taxes and low heating bills.

The pattern of southward and westward migration continued in the 1950s and 1960s (see map). Houston became a center not only of the aerospace industry but also of oil and petrochemical produc-

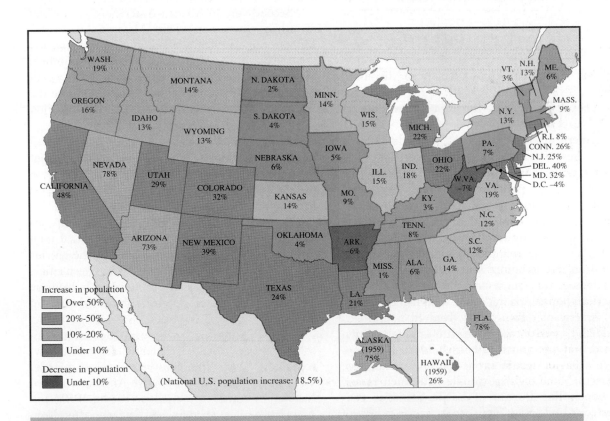

Rise of the Sunbelt, 1950–1960 *The years after the Second World War saw a continuation of the migration of Americans to the Sunbelt states of the Southwest and the West Coast.*

tion. Tucson, which had been scarcely more than a watering hole in the desert in 1950, had a population of 263,000 twenty years later. And California absorbed no less than one-fifth of the nation's entire population increase in the 1950s—enough by 1963 to make it the most populous state in the union.

The millions of people who left the chilly industrial cities of the North and East in the 1940s and 1950s strengthened the political clout of the Sunbelt. In 1969 Kevin Phillips, a conservative Republican political analyst, predicted an emerging Republican majority based on the conservatism of the South and West. Richard Nixon's triumph in the presidential election of 1968 seemed to support Phillips's thesis. So does the tendency of political parties to nominate Sunbelt candidates for national office. (All six of the nation's most recently elected presidents have hailed from the West or South— two from Texas, two from California, one from Georgia, and one from Arkansas.) And in 1980 the Census Bureau announced that, for the first time in the nation's history, the South and West accounted for a majority of eligible voters.

THE OTHER AMERICA

In an age of abundance, most Americans dismissed poverty, if they noticed it at all, as the fault of the poor people themselves. But in 1962—even after fifteen years of economic boom—about 42.5 million Americans (nearly one of every four) were poor. These were people who earned less than $4,000 per year for a family of four, or $2,000 per year for a single person living alone. Age, race, sex, education, and marital status were all factors in their poverty. One-fourth of the poor were over age sixty-five; many of them lived alone on fixed incomes, their meager purchasing power continually shrunk by inflation. One-fifth were people of color, including almost half the nation's African-American population and more than half of all Native Americans. Two-thirds lived in households headed by a person with an eighth-grade education or less, and one-fourth in households headed by a single woman. More than one-third were under age eighteen. None of these people had much reason for hope. The Bureau of Labor Statistics constructed a budget to show what a poor family of four could afford: one book a year, no telephone, a movie once every three weeks, a new car every twelve to eighteen years. It is clear from this meager budget that, no matter how much the economy might boom, there was a limit to the spending power that would trickle down to the poor.

While millions of Americans (most of them white) were settling in the suburbs, the poor were congregating in the inner cities. Almost 4.5 million

Poor People in the Inner Cities

African-Americans migrated to the cities from the South between the war years and the end of the 1960s. The black population, which had been 49 percent urban in 1940, was 81 percent urban by 1970. Joining African-Americans in the exodus to the cities were poor whites from the southern Appalachians, many of whom moved to Cincinnati, Baltimore, St. Louis, Columbus, Detroit, and Chicago. Meanwhile Latin Americans were arriving in growing numbers from Mexico, the Dominican Republic, Colombia, Ecuador, and Cuba. And New York City's Puerto Rican population exploded from 70,000 to over 600,000 in just twenty years.

Second only to African-Americans in numbers of urban newcomers were Mexican-Americans. Millions came as farm workers during and after the

Mexican-Americans

war, and increasing numbers remained to make their lives in the United States. Despite the initiation in 1953 of Operation Wetback, a federal program to find and deport illegal aliens, Mexicans continued to enter the country in large numbers, many of them illegally. Most settled in cities. According to the 1960 census, over 500,000 Mexican-Americans had migrated to the barrios of the Los Angeles– Long Beach area since 1940. Estimates of uncounted illegal aliens suggest that the actual total was far higher. The same was true of the barrios of El Paso, Phoenix, and other southwestern cities, and of Mexican-American communities in Denver, Kansas City, Chicago, Detroit, and other cities in the North.

Native Americans, whose average annual income was barely half the amount designated poverty level, were the country's poorest people.

Native Americans

Many Native Americans moved to the cities in the 1950s and 1960s, particularly after Congress in 1953 adopted a policy called "termination," which

The Moreira family gathered for an Easter celebration in Los Angeles in 1960. By the end of the 1950s many Mexican-American families had established businesses, bought homes, and entered the middle class. The photograph shows three generations of the Moreira family.   Security Pacific National Bank Collection, Los Angeles Public Library.

abolished the status of certain tribes as wards of the United States. Accustomed to semicommunal rural life on the reservation, many had difficulty adjusting to the urban environment. Like other groups who migrated to the cities in hope of finding a place to prosper, they found only a dumping-ground for the poor.

Not all of the poor, however, lived in cities. In 1960, 30 percent lived in small towns and 15 percent on farms. Tenant farmers and sharecroppers, both black and white, continued to suffer severe economic hardship. Migratory farm workers lived in abject poverty. Elderly people tended to be poor regardless of where they lived.

Poor Americans were poor in part because they had been shortchanged by federal legislation. Government-sponsored housing and highways were largely intended to improve life for middle-class whites; disadvantaged Americans did not share much in their benefits. In 1948, for example, the government cut mortgage subsidies for rental-unit construction and increased subsidies for privately owned single-family houses, a policy that worked against the poorest Americans. Moreover,

the FHA refused to guarantee suburban home loans to the poor, people of color, Jews, and other "inharmonious racial and ethnic groups." Additionally, the Wagner Act and federal farm programs established during the New Deal essentially ignored nonunion workers and farmers who owned no land (see Chapter 25). Neither Social Security nor the minimum wage covered hospital janitors and orderlies, dishwashers and other restaurant employees, or migratory farm workers. The programs available to the poor generally offered them cash outlays, not opportunities to earn an independent income.

Some federal programs actually worsened conditions for the poor. The National Housing Act of 1949, passed to make available "a decent home and a suitable living environment for every American family," failed in several respects. The primary features of the act were "urban redevelopment" (slum clearance), construction of public housing for low-income people, and FHA mortgages for home buyers. Slums were replaced, however, not with low-income housing but with parking lots, shopping centers, luxury high-rise buildings, highways,

Television covered the news in postwar America, but its methods were primitive. In 1952 Walter Cronkite and two technicians covered remote events from the back of a convertible. The camera produced a black-and-white image, which was transmitted by the microwave dish to a pickup point.   Photofest.

and factories. The planned 810,000 housing units for the poor were constructed not in four years but in twenty.

A disproportionate share of the poor were women. Occupational segregation was still pervasive, and the better-paying positions were reserved for men. In 1945 many women who wanted to remain in the factories and shipyards were pushed out to make way for returning veterans. Those who tried later to return to high-paying industrial work were discouraged, and many were forced into low-paying jobs in restaurants and laundries. "Rosie [the Riveter] feels something like Typhoid Mary when she applies for a factory job," stated the *Detroit Free Press*. Median annual earnings for full-time women workers stood at 60 percent of men's earnings in 1960. Ten years later women's earnings had dropped to 59 percent of men's. Moreover, many women's jobs were not covered by either the minimum wage or Social Security. Finally, if divorce, desertion, or death did break up a family, the woman was usually left with responsibility for the children. Many divorced fathers did not keep up their regular child-support payments. Single mothers and their children, dependent on welfare

Women in Poverty

or low wages, more often than not slipped into poverty.

One of the least-acknowledged effects of economic hardship was physical and emotional illness. A study in New Haven, Connecticut, in the late 1950s found that the rate of treated psychiatric illness was three times as high among the lowest-paid fifth of the population as it was among the upper-middle and upper classes. Psychiatrists at Cornell University's Medical School described the "low social economic status individual" as rigid, suspicious, with "a fatalistic outlook on life. . . . They are prone to depression, have feelings of futility, lack of belongingness . . . and a lack of trust in others."

Poverty and Emotional Distress

Graphic evidence of the emotional costs of poverty surfaced in 1960, when the National Federation of Settlements and Neighborhood Centers assembled reports from around the country on the effects of the economic recession. A social worker from Rochester, New York, reported a direct correlation between loss of jobs and sharp rises in "marital discord and desertions of families by the father, increased welfare dependency, increased crime, especially robberies, burglaries and muggings, and alcoholism." Ironically, all of this suffering and violence was occurring in a nation that was being heralded as the affluent society.

With the publication of Michael Harrington's *The Other America* in 1962, people became aware of this contradiction in their midst. America's poor, wrote Harrington, were "the strangest poor in the history of mankind." As Harrington put it, they "exist within the most powerful and rich society the world has ever known. Their misery has continued while the majority of the nation talked of itself as being 'affluent.'" Whether living in urban obscurity or rural isolation, the poor had "dropped out of sight and out of mind," particularly the minds of comfortable suburbanites.

MIDDLE-CLASS AMERICA AT PLAY

Having satisfied their basic needs for food, clothing, and shelter, many Americans began turning their attention to conveniences and luxury items. "More appliances make mom's work easier," read a typical 1950s advertisement. As families strove to acquire the latest conveniences, shopping became a form of recreation.

Of the new luxuries, television was the most revolutionary in its effects. "And so the monumental change began in our lives and those of millions of other Americans," recalled a

TV Enters the American Home

man whose parents bought their first TV set in 1950. "More than a year passed before we again visited a movie theater. Money which previously would have been spent for books was saved for the TV payments. Social evenings with friends became fewer and fewer still because we discovered we did not share the same TV program interests." By 1950 television had loosened radio's grip on the American public. The number of households with TVs climbed from 8,000 in 1946 to 4 million in 1950, 46 million in 1960 (a 920 percent increase), and 61 million in 1970.

Entertainment was TV's number-one product, and situation comedies and action series were among the most popular shows. Topping these categories in the 1950s were "I Love Lucy," starring Lucille Ball, and "Dragnet," a detective series. "Father Knows Best" and "Leave It to Beaver" celebrated family life. There were programs for all age groups, ranging from "Ding Dong School," quiz shows, and westerns to the roller derby. As average TV-viewing time reached five hours a day in 1956 and continued to increase, concern mounted that television was becoming more than just entertainment. Some critics worried that TV's distorted presentation of the world, including whitewashed images of how other people live, would significantly define people's sense of reality.

Advertising bankrolled the television industry, as it had also radio. The first TV commercial, made by the Bulova Watch Company in 1941, was a one-minute effort that cost nine dollars. By the end of the decade, the bargain rates had vanished; annual expenditures for TV advertising totaled $171 million in 1950 and $1.6 billion in 1960. By 1970 the figure had soared to $3.6 billion.

Critics of the television industry have often questioned why American viewers tolerate advertising. The answer appears to be that, far from being an intrusion, television advertising was a valuable service to consumers: if keeping up with or emulating the Joneses was a new version of the American Dream, television advertising provided

In this Mad *magazine cartoon, in which Alfred E. Neuman ("What, me worry?") joined the presidential pantheon on Mount Rushmore, the magazine parodied a venerable icon. Started in 1952,* Mad *was second in popularity only to* Life *magazine among teenagers by the early 1960s.* Mad *mocked suburbia, President Eisenhower, and the smugness of the American middle class.* Mad Magazine Mt. Rushmore cover used with permission © 1956, 1984 by E.C. Publications, Inc.

visual evidence of what the Joneses were buying. In the comfort of their living rooms, Americans could study how to elevate their status through the purchase of a particular automobile, cigarette, or electric appliance. Indeed, not just the commercials but the programs themselves tantalized viewers with glimpses of the sumptuous life. Situation comedies and dramas were nearly always set in well-furnished suburban homes; the characters dressed in the latest styles and drove the newest cars.

The more television brought the world into their living rooms, the less attentively Americans read newspapers and news magazines and listened to the radio. Nevertheless, book readership went up, in part because of the mass marketing of inexpensive paperbound books. Pocket Books hit the

One of the biggest Broadway hits of the 1950s was the musical West Side Story (1957), *Leonard Bernstein's recasting of* Romeo and Juliet *in which the warring families were the Jets and the Sharks, two New York street gangs.*   Collection of Picture Research Consultants.

market in 1939; soon westerns, detective stories, and science fiction appeared at newsstands, supermarkets, and drugstores. "The paperback democratized reading in America," Kenneth C. Davis has written in his history of "the paperbacking of America." The comic book, which had become popular in 1939 with the introduction of Superman, became another drugstore standard. Reprints of hardcover books and condensed books also sold well. Spending on books increased 220 percent between 1946 and 1960, and another 265 percent between 1960 and 1970.

An obvious casualty of the stay-at-home suburban culture was the motion picture. Americans continued to buy paperbacks and comic books, but

Rise of the Youth Subculture

——

many of them stopped visiting movie theaters. Why fight traffic if you could watch TV in the comfort of your living room? Why pay a babysitter? From 1946 to 1948 Americans had attended movies at the rate of nearly 90 million a week. By 1950 that figure had dropped to 60 million a week; by 1960, to 40 million. The post-

war years saw the steady closing of movie theaters—with the notable exception of the drive-in, which appealed to car-oriented suburban families and teenagers. In fact, teenagers were the one exception to the downturn in moviegoing. By the late 1950s the first wave of the postwar baby boom had reached adolescence, and they were flocking to the theaters. No less than 72 percent of moviegoers during the 1950s were under age thirty. Hollywood catered to this new audience with films portraying young people as sensitive and insightful, adults as boorish and hostile. *Rebel Without a Cause* (1955), starring James Dean, was one such movie. Its teenage heroes find in the youth culture qualities lacking in their own families, namely love and courage. The movie was a box office smash; the cult of youth had been born.

Soon the music industry began catering to teens with cheap 45-rpm records. Bored with the era's syrupy music, young Americans were electrified by the driving energy and hard beat of Bill Haley and the Comets, Chuck Berry, the Everly Brothers, Jerry Lee Lewis, Little Richard, and Buddy Holly. The release of Elvis Presley's first single, "Heartbreak Hotel," in 1956, and his appearance on Ed Sullivan's Sunday-night TV show, touched off a frenzy of adoration and hero worship; so much the better that parents were scandalized by his suggestive gyrations. Rebellious teens adopted Presley's ducktail haircut, black leather jacket, and sleepy sneer.

Parents feared that their children might become juvenile delinquents, even though there was little actual increase in juvenile crime during this period. Parental concern reached panic proportions in 1955 when the Senate Subcommittee to Study Juvenile Delinquency in the United States heard expert testimony about the evil influence of rock 'n' roll, comic books, television, and the new youth films. The staff read into the record thousands of letters from angry fathers and mothers blaming the popular culture that their children so eagerly consumed. "Not even the Communist conspiracy," intoned one senator, "could devise a more effective way to demoralize, disrupt, confuse, and destroy our future citizens than apathy on the part of adult Americans to the scourge known as Juvenile Delinquency."

Although the roots of rock 'n' roll lay in African-American rhythm-and-blues, few white musicians acknowledged the debt. Presley's "Hound

African-American Roots of Rock 'n' Roll

Dog," for example, had originally been performed by the black singer Big Mama Thornton, but she received little credit for her contribution.

Meanwhile serious black jazz artists like Charlie Parker and Dizzy Gillespie were experimenting with "bebop." In the 1950s jazz became increasingly fused with classical themes, compositions, and instrumentation. American and European intellectuals began to appreciate jazz, once considered vulgar, as a uniquely American art form.

In other arts, too, America's cultural influence grew worldwide in the 1950s and 1960s. In dance Martha Graham was lauded in international circles, and in painting Jackson Pollock became the pivotal figure of the abstract expressionist movement. Based on a belief that art should be intensely personal and reflect the artist's inner state of mind, abstract expressionism established New York City as the center of the art world in the 1950s. Rather than work with the traditional painter's easel, Pollock spread his canvas on the floor, where he was free to walk around it, "work from the four sides and literally be in the painting." He and other "action painters" worked with sticks, trowels, and knives, and they experimented with new materials like heavy impasto with "sand, broken glass and other foreign matter added." In the 1960s artists of the Pop Art movement rejected abstract expressionism and satirized the consumer society, using commercial techniques to depict everyday objects. Andy Warhol painted Campbell's soup cans; other artists did blowups of ice-cream sundaes, hamburgers, and comic-strip panels.

Consumerism was also evident in Americans' postwar play and in the era's fads. Slinky, selling for a dollar, began loping down people's stairs in 1947; Silly Putty was introduced in 1950. The 1950s and 1960s also had 3-D movies and Hula-Hoops. Within months of the Hula-Hoop's introduction in 1958, over 30 million had been sold. Although most crazes were short-lived, they created multimillion-dollar industries and effectively promoted dozens of movies and TV shows. Another postwar fad was the family vacation. With more money and leisure time and a much-improved highway system, middle-class families took vacations that formerly had been restricted to the rich. They visited national monuments and

While Elvis Presley's performances upset parents, they thrilled the young people who cheered the gyrations of "Elvis the Pelvis." In this 1956 photo, Presley rocked wildly as he reached the climax of the song "Hillbilly Heartbreak." UPI/Bettmann Archives.

parks and even ventured abroad. The destination of many family vacations was Disneyland, which opened in Anaheim, California, in 1955.

The consumer society was unreceptive to social criticism. The filmgoing public preferred noncontroversial doses of Doris Day and Rock Hudson and Dean Martin and Jerry Lewis. Readers of fiction escaped into the criminal underworld, the wild West, or science-fiction fantasy. Even serious artists tended to ignore the country's social problems.

There were exceptions. Ralph Ellison's *Invisible Man* (1952) gave white Americans a glimpse of the psychic costs to black Americans of exclusion from the American Dream.

Beat Generation

Two films—*Gentleman's Agreement* (1947) and *Home of the Brave* (1949)—examined anti-Semitism and white racism. And one group of writers noisily repudiated the materialistic and self-congratulatory world of the

In the 1960s Andy Warhol satirized the American consumer culture through his Pop Art. By the end of the decade, Pop Art was dead and Warhol was being satirized, as in this Esquire *magazine cover.* © Esquire Magazine 1969.

middle class and the suburbs. The Beat (for "beatific") writers rejected both social niceties and literary conventions, and they flaunted their free-wheeling sexuality and consumption of drugs. The Beats produced some memorable prose and poetry, including Allen Ginsberg's angry incantational poem *Howl* (1956) and Jack Kerouac's novel *On the Road* (1957). "I saw the best minds of my generation," *Howl* begins, "destroyed by madness, starving hysterical naked." Ginsberg's poem attributed Americans' alienation to sexual repression and the quest for materialism. Similarly, Kerouac's novel dismissed white middle-class conformity for offering "not enough ecstacy for me, not enough life, joy, kicks, darkness, music, not enough night." The Beats were largely ignored during the 1950s, but millions of young Americans discovered their writings and imitated their lifestyle in the 1960s.

Between 1945 and 1970, the baby boom and the economic boom transformed the United States economically, socially, and culturally. As the economy expanded, so too did the size of the American middle classes. Prosperity was evident in the proliferation not only of suburbs, cars, and household appliances but also of family activities. During the Great Depression and the Second World War, many Americans had delayed marrying and having children. But they enjoyed unprecedented material comforts during the postwar era; part of their enjoyment was family togetherness, which included evening TV-watching, Little League games, and outings to parks and beaches.

During the self-congratulatory 1950s, Americans were generally oblivious to pressing social needs. One of the period's most influential books was the best-selling *The Affluent Society* (1958), by John Kenneth Galbraith. Galbraith's thesis dovetailed with the prevalent belief that economic growth would bring prosperity to everyone. Some would have more than others, of course, but in time everybody would have enough. "Production has eliminated the more acute tensions associated with [economic] inequality," Galbraith wrote. He dismissed poverty as by no means "a universal or massive affliction" but "more nearly an afterthought."

Only a few years later, however, comfortable middle-class Americans discovered that millions of poor people lived in their midst, and that most of them had been deprived of the civil rights the rest of the nation took for granted. Politically and culturally, the 1960s were to prove vastly different from the years that immediately preceded them (see Chapter 32). Ironically, it would be the children of suburbia—the generation of the baby boom—who would form the vanguard of the assault on racism, poverty, and the whole value system of the postwar American middle class.

SUGGESTIONS FOR FURTHER READING

The Baby Boom

Richard A. Easterlin, *Birth and Fortune* (1980); Landon Y. Jones, *Great Expectations: America and the Baby Boom Generation* (1980); Donald Katz, *Home Fires: An Intimate Portrait of One Middle-Class Family in Postwar America* (1992); Paul C. Light, *Baby Boomers* (1988); Elaine Tyler May, *Homeward Bound: American Families in the Cold War Era* (1988); John Modell, *Into One's Own: From Youth to Adulthood in the United States, 1920–1975* (1989); Michael P. Nichols, *Turning Forty in the '80s* (1986).

Suburbia

Bennett M. Berger, *Working-Class Suburb* (1960); Robert Fishman, *Bourgeois Utopias* (1987); Herbert J. Gans, *The Levittowners* (1967); Mark I. Gelfand, *A Nation of Cities* (1975); Dolores Hayden, *Redesigning the American Dream* (1984); Kenneth T. Jackson, *Crabgrass Frontier: The Suburbanization of the United States* (1985); Zane L. Miller, *Suburb* (1982); John B. Rae, *The American Automobile* (1965); William H. Whyte, *The Organization Man* (1956); Gwendolyn Wright, *Building the Dream: A Social History of Housing in America* (1981).

The Spread of Education

Barbara B. Clowse, *Brainpower for the Cold War: The Sputnik Crisis and the National Defense Education Act of 1958* (1981); Keith W. Olson, *The GI Bill, the Veterans, and the Colleges* (1974); Diane Ravitch, *The Troubled Crusade: American Education, 1945–1980* (1983); Joel Spring, *The Sorting Machine: National Educational Policy Since 1945* (1976).

Women, Work, and Family Togetherness

Wini Breines, *Young, White, and Miserable: Growing Up Female in the Fifties* (1992); William H. Chafe, *The Paradox of Change: American Woman in the 20th Century* (1991); Ruth Schwartz Cowan, *More Work for Mother* (1983); Myra Dinnerstein, *Women Between Two Worlds* (1992); Barbara Ehrenreich, *The Hearts of Men: American Dreams and the Flight from Commitment* (1983); Betty Friedan, *The Feminine Mystique* (1963); Cynthia Harrison, *On Account of Sex: The Politics of Women's Issues, 1945–1968* (1988); Susan M. Hartmann, *The Homefront and Beyond: American Women in the 1940s* (1982); Eugenia Kaledin, *Mothers and More: American Women in the 1950s* (1984); Susan Estabrook Kennedy, *If All We Did Was to Weep at Home: A History of White Working-Class Women in America* (1979); Glenna Matthews, *"Just a Housewife"* (1987); Leila J. Rupp and Verta Taylor, *Survival in the Doldrums: The American Women's Rights Movement, 1945 to the 1960s* (1987); Susan Strasser, *Never Done: A History of American Housework* (1982); Susan Householder Van Horn, *Women, Work, and Fertility, 1900–1986* (1988).

The Affluent Society

Loren Baritz, *The Good Life: The Meaning of Success for the American Middle Class* (1982); Richard M. Bernard and Bradley R. Rice, eds., *Sunbelt Cities* (1983); David P. Calleo, *The Imperious Economy* (1982); Paul D. Escott and David R. Goldfield, eds., *The South for New Southerners* (1991); John Kenneth Galbraith, *The Affluent Society* (1958); John Kenneth Galbraith, *American Capitalism* (1952); David F. Noble, *Forces of Production: A Social History of Industrial Automation* (1988); David M. Potter, *People of Plenty* (1954); Kirkpatrick Sale, *Power Shift: The Rise of the Southern Rim and Its Challenge to the Eastern Establishment* (1975); Bruce J. Schulman, *From Cotton Belt to Sunbelt: Federal Policy, Economic Development, and the Transformation of the South, 1938–1980*

(1991); Jane S. Smith, *Patenting the Sun: Polio and the Salk Vaccine* (1990); Robert Sobel, *The Last Bull Market* (1980); Harold G. Vatter, *The U.S. Economy in the 1950s* (1963).

Farmers and Workers

Willard W. Cochrane and Mary E. Ryan, *American Farm Policy, 1948–1973* (1976); Gilbert C. Fite, *American Farmers* (1981); James R. Green, *The World of the Worker* (1980); John L. Shover, *First Majority—Last Minority: The Transforming of Rural Life in America* (1976); Philip Taft, *The A.F. of L. from the Death of Gompers to the Merger* (1959).

The Other America

Joseph H. Cash and Herbert T. Hoover, eds., *To Be an Indian: An Oral History* (1971); Harry M. Caudill, *Night Comes to the Cumberland* (1963); Richard B. Craig, *The Bracero Program* (1971); J. Wayne Flint, *Dixie's Forgotten People: The South's Poor Whites* (1979); Leo Grebler et al., *Mexican-American People* (1970); Michael Harrington, *The Other America*, rev. ed. (1981); August B. Hollingshead and Frederick C. Redlich, *Social Class and Mental Illness* (1958); Oscar Lewis, *La Vida* (1966); Herman P. Miller, *Rich Man, Poor Man* (1971); Dorothy K. Newman et al., *Politics and Prosperity: Black Americans and White Institutions, 1940–75* (1978); James T. Patterson, *America's Struggle Against Poverty, 1900–1985* (1986); David S. Walls and John B. Stephenson, eds., *Appalachia in the Sixties* (1972).

Postwar Culture

Peter Biskind, *Seeing Is Believing: How Hollywood Taught Us to Stop Worrying and Love the Fifties* (1983); Paul Boyer, *By the Bomb's Early Light: American Thought and Culture at the Dawn of the Atomic Age* (1985); Paul A. Carter, *Another Part of the Fifties* (1983); James Gilbert, *A Cycle of Outrage: America's Reaction to the Juvenile Delinquent* (1986); Charlie Gillett, *The Sound of the City: The Rise of Rock and Roll*, rev. ed. (1983); William S. Graebner, *The Age of Doubt: American Thought and Culture in the 1940s* (1991); Serge Guilbaut, *How New York Stole the Idea of Modern Art* (1982); David Halberstam, *The Fifties* (1993); Christin J. Mamiya, *Pop Art and Consumer Culture* (1991); Douglas T. Miller and Marion Novak, *The Fifties* (1977); Nora Sayre, *Running Time: Films of the Cold War* (1982); Jane and Michael Stern, *Elvis World* (1987); John Tytell, *Naked Angels: The Lives and Literature of the Beat Generation* (1976).

Television

Michael Arlen, *The Camera Age* (1981); Erik Barnouw, *Tube of Plenty*, rev. ed. (1982); Todd Gitlin, *Inside Prime Time* (1983); Frank Mankiewicz and Joel Swerdlow, *Remote Control: Television and the Manipulation of American Life* (1978); Joshua Meyrowitz, *No Sense of Place: The Impact of Electronic Media on Social Behavior* (1985); Ella Taylor, *Prime-Time Families: Television Culture in Postwar America* (1989).

31

Contesting Nationalism and Revolution: The Third World and the Vietnam War, 1945–1989

THE JOINT CHIEFS OF Staff memorandum lay on the table. Its recommendation: add another 100,000 to the 80,000 American troops already in Vietnam, because the war was not going well. "Is there anyone here of the opinion we should not do what the memorandum says?" President Lyndon B. Johnson asked his advisers in a tense meeting on July 21, 1965. Only Under Secretary of State George Ball spoke up: "Mr. President, I can foresee a perilous voyage, very dangerous." Johnson responded, "What other road can I go?" Ball answered, "Take our losses, let their government fall apart, negotiate, discuss, knowing full well there will be a probable takeover by the Communists." The president, already committed to an escalation of the U.S. intervention in Vietnam, did not like Ball's answer. The hard-driving Texan recoiled from thoughts of losing. He simply could not accept that a small, primitive country like Vietnam could deny the United States victory.

At an afternoon session, Ball again forthrightly argued a case he knew few of his colleagues endorsed. "The war will be long and protracted. The most

we can hope for is a messy conclusion." Not only did dangers arise from possible Chinese intervention, negative world opinion, and domestic political dissent, but "the enemy cannot be seen in Vietnam. He is indigenous to the country." Ball seriously doubted that "an army of Westerners can successfully fight Orientals in an Asian jungle." In the long run, he went on, the war "will disclose our weakness, not our strength." Worried about U.S. credibility, Johnson jumped in: "But George, wouldn't all these countries say that Uncle Sam was a paper tiger?" "No sir," Ball retorted. "The worse blow would be that the mightiest power on earth is unable to defeat a handful of guerrillas."

The next day Johnson met with the military brass. The generals told him that more men, more bombings, and more money were needed to save America's South Vietnamese ally from defeat at the hands of North Vietnamese and Vietcong forces. The president asked tough questions. "But if we put in 100,000 men, won't they put in an equal number, and then where will we be?" When an admiral claimed that if

Helicopter landing U.S. combat troops in Vietnam.

• *Important Events* •

1861–87	French consolidate colonial rule in Indochina			Bandung Conference organizes Nonaligned Movement
1940	Japan occupies Indochina and weakens French influence		**1956**	Suez crisis pits Nasser's Egypt against Israel, France, and Britain
1941	Vietminh organized as anti-French, anti-Japanese movement in Vietnam OSS cooperates with Vietminh		**1957**	Eisenhower Doctrine declares containment of communism in Middle East
1945	Ho Chi Minh declares independence for Democratic Republic of Vietnam		**1958**	U.S. troops land in Lebanon
1946	Anticolonial war against France begins in Vietnam United States backs shah during crisis in Iran		**1959**	Castro launches Cuban Revolution North Vietnam begins sending aid to Communists in the South
1947	Truman Doctrine declares policy of containment National Security Act creates Central Intelligence Agency		**1960**	Eighteen African colonies become independent nations National Liberation Front (Vietcong) organized in South Vietnam John F. Kennedy elected president
1948	State of Israel founded amid Arab-Jewish hostilities Harry S Truman elected president		**1961**	CIA-directed Bay of Pigs invasion fails to overthrow Castro Peace Corps founded Alliance for Progress announced to spur Latin American economies Kennedy increases aid and military "advisers" to Vietnam
1949	Communists win in China			
1950	Korean War begins Point Four Program of technical assistance to developing nations begins United States recognizes government of Bao Dai; sends military aid to French for war in Vietnam		**1962**	Agreement reached on neutralizing Laos Cuban missile crisis leads to nuclear brinkmanship
1952	Dwight D. Eisenhower elected president		**1963**	Strategic Hamlet Program established in South Vietnam Diem assassinated Kennedy assassinated; Lyndon B. Johnson assumes presidency
1953	Korean War ends United States helps restore shah to power in Iran			
1954	Seige of Dienbienphu in Vietnam persuades France to negotiate CIA intervenes in Guatemala Geneva Accords partition Vietnam SEATO created		**1964**	Tonkin Gulf resolution authorizes Johnson to handle the war his way
			1965	United States invades Dominican Republic Johnson Americanizes Vietnam War by sending large numbers of troops Operation Rolling Thunder bombs North Vietnam
1955	United States backs government of Ngo Dinh Diem			

the United States did not back the faltering South Vietnamese regime allies around the world would lose faith in America's word, Johnson knew better: "We have few allies really helping us now." And have the bombing raids hurt the enemy? Not really, the generals answered, but they would if more

sites were added to the target list. Johnson wondered, "Isn't this going off the diving board?" To the defense secretary's argument that the United States had a commitment to South Vietnam, the president shot back: "But, if you make a commitment to jump off a building and you find out how

• *Important Events* •

1965–66	Teach-ins at universities oppose U.S. intervention in Vietnam	**1976**	Jimmy Carter elected president
1967	Peace rallies staged across the nation Six-Day War in the Middle East	**1977**	Human rights policy announced
		1978	Panama Canal treaties approved by Congress Carter negotiates Egyptian-Israeli peace accord at Camp David
1968	Tet offensive in Vietnam sets back U.S. objectives Dollar/gold crisis threatens U.S. economy My Lai massacre leaves many women and children dead Vietnam peace talks open in Paris Richard M. Nixon elected president	**1979**	Egyptian-Israeli Peace Treaty signed Shah of Iran overthrown; American hostages seized
		1980	Carter Doctrine announced for Persian Gulf region Ronald Reagan elected president
1969	543,400 U.S. troops in Vietnam Nixon begins withdrawal of troops from Vietnam Nixon Doctrine declares United States will help nations that help themselves	**1981**	American hostages in Iran released after 444 days United States steps up role in El Salvador's civil war CIA begins to train contras for attacks against Nicaragua
1970	Invasion of Cambodia sets off U.S. demonstrations	**1982**	U.S. troops ordered to Lebanon
1971	*Pentagon Papers* indicate that administrations had lied about Vietnam	**1983**	Terrorists kill U.S. Marines in Lebanon Reagan orders invasion of Grenada
1972	In Christmas bombing, U.S. Air Force pounds North Vietnam	**1984**	Reagan administration aids contras, despite congressional ban
1973	Vietnam cease-fire agreement reached Allende ousted in Chile after U.S. subversive efforts Outbreak of Arab-Israeli war and imposition of Arab oil embargo War Powers Resolution restricts presidential warmaking authority	**1985**	Reagan Doctrine declares U.S. aid to "freedom fighters"
		1986	U.S. bombers attack Libya Iran-contra scandal breaks
		1987	Third World debt reaches $1.2 trillion
1974	Nixon resigns; Gerald Ford becomes president New International Economic Order proposed by Third World	**1988**	Palestinian uprising occurs in West Bank (*intifada*) George Bush elected president Terrorist bombing of Pan American flight
1975	Egyptian-Israeli accord authorizes U.N. peacekeeping force in Sinai Vietnam War ends Civil war breaks out in Angola after Portugal grants independence	**1989**	Cold War winds down

Note: See also "Important Events" in Chapter 29 for related events in the history of the Cold War.

high it is, you may want to withdraw that commitment."

President Johnson nonetheless decided in July to give the Joint Chiefs of Staff what they wanted. A turning point in the Vietnam War, this decision meant that the United States was for the first time assuming primary responsibility for fighting the war. Fearing that he would spark a national debate about deepening U.S. participation in a Southeast Asian war, Johnson underplayed the decision's importance when he announced it. By the end of 1965 nearly 200,000 American combat troops were at war in Vietnam. Yet Congress had not passed a declaration of war, and most of the American people remained ignorant of the venture. Ball later called Johnson's July decision "the greatest single error that America had made in its national history." Measured by the wrenching impact of the war on the United States, Ball was probably correct.

Vietnam bedeviled the United States from 1945, the year Vietnamese nationalists declared independence from France, to well beyond 1975, the year the last Americans withdrew from Vietnam. President Truman backed the futile efforts of France, America's ally in the emerging Cold War, to save its Indochinese empire. After the French pulled out in defeat and Vietnam was divided, Eisenhower sent U.S. military advisers and foreign aid to shore up the anti-Communist South Vietnamese government, which became dependent upon the United States. Kennedy, fearing that Communist China was expanding into Vietnam, greatly enlarged the U.S. presence to block Vietcong advances against the U.S.-backed regime. Johnson Americanized the war, increasing U.S. troops to more than half a million. Nixon struggled to pull American soldiers out of the war without losing it. His successors had to deal with defeat and the anguished aftermath of America's longest war.

Vietnam was part of the *Third World*, a general term for those nations that during the Cold War belonged neither to the capitalist "West" (the United States and its allies) nor to the Communist "East" (the Soviet Union and its allies). Sometimes called developing countries, Third World nations on the whole were nonwhite, nonindustrialized, and located in the southern half of the globe—in Asia, Africa, the Middle East, and Latin America. After the Second World War, when the United States and the Soviet Union coveted allies, the Third World became entangled in the Cold War. Even though the highly diverse Third World peoples had their own histories, cultures, and aspirations, they often found that they could not escape the pervasive effects of the great-power rivalry. Vietnam thus became one among many sites where the Cold War and the Third World intersected. American leaders thought of Vietnam as an Asian Berlin, a place to draw the line against Communism and to implement the containment doctrine (see Chapter 29).

Americans often interpreted Third World anti-imperialism, political instability, and restrictions on foreign-owned property as Soviet or Communist-inspired—as Cold War matters rather than as expressions of profound nationalism or consequences of indigenous developments. American leaders sometimes labeled radicals, nationalists, reformers, and neutralists as Communists, or assumed they were susceptible to Communist influence. Although the Soviets supported guerrilla wars and revolution, they seldom if ever initiated them. Had there been no Soviet Union or Cold War, in other words, the Third World would still have challenged U.S. strategic and economic interests. Interventionism, U.S. leaders came to believe, was necessary for two reasons: it would impress Moscow with American might and resolve, and it would counter nationalist strivings for independence and radical social change that threatened U.S. interests worldwide.

To thwart nationalist, radical, and Communist challenges, the United States directed its massive resources toward the Third World. In the 1950s technical assistance under the Point Four Program and development loans and grants flowed to developing nations. By 1961 more than 90 percent of American foreign aid went to the Third World. Washington also forged alliances with undemocratic but friendly regimes, meddled in civil wars, and unleashed CIA covert operations and propaganda campaigns against unfriendly governments. The stormy U.S. interaction with the Third World frequently violated American principles. It also diverted billions of dollars from domestic needs. Bitter resentments built up in the Third World, where millions of lives were lost in conflicts aggravated by U.S. intervention.

The emergence of the Third World in the 1950s began to undermine the bipolar Cold War international system the United States and the Soviet Union had constructed at the end of the Second World War. By the 1980s, power had become diffused: great-power management of world affairs had diminished, and international relations had become more fluid and less predictable as more and more nations demanded a voice and a vote. Secretary of State Henry Kissinger observed in the 1970s that the international order was coming "apart politically, economically, and morally." The world, he feared, was "tilting against us."

THE RISE OF THE THIRD WORLD

Decolonization

The process of decolonization began during the First World War but accelerated after the end of the Second World War, when the economically wracked imperial countries proved incapable of resisting their colonies' demands for freedom. A cavalcade of new nations earned independence. The United States granted independence to the Philippines in 1946. Britain freed India and Pakistan and present-day Bangladesh in 1947, Burma and Ceylon (Sri Lanka) in 1948. The Dutch reluctantly let go of Indonesia in 1949. The French fought on in Indochina but finally gave up in 1954. In 1960 alone, eighteen new African nations became independent. From 1943 to 1989 a total of ninety-six countries cast off their colonial bonds (see map on page 954). As George Ball recalled, the United States necessarily had to address "problems involving the bits and pieces of disintegrating empires." At the same time, the long-independent Third World nations of Latin America unsettled the world order by repeatedly challenging the hegemony of the United States.

By the early 1950s, when Cold War lines were drawn fairly tightly in Europe, Soviet-American rivalry shifted increasingly to the Third World. Much was at stake. Third World nations possessed such strategic raw materials as manganese, oil, and tin. They also attracted foreign investment—more than one-third of America's private foreign investments were in Third World countries in 1959. And Third World nations became markets for American manufactured products and technology. The great powers looked to these new states for votes in the United Nations and sought sites for military and intelligence bases. Many of the Third World states were poor and unstable: civil wars, dictatorial rulers, and tribal, ethnic, and class rivalries plagued their politics; their economies became dependent on the sale of only one commodity. They also became intensely nationalistic, proud of their self-determination. To the alarm of Washington, some Third World nations launched social revolutions and embraced socialist models of economic development.

The Nonaligned Movement

Many Third World states—notably India, Ghana, Egypt, and Indonesia—did not wish to take sides in the Cold War. To the dismay of both Washington and Moscow, they declared themselves nonaligned, or neutral. Nonalignment became an organized movement in 1955 when twenty-nine Asian and African nations met in 1955 at the Bandung Conference in Indonesia. "We will not be subjected," declared Egypt's Gamal Abdul Nasser, "either by West or East." Secretary of State John Foster Dulles, alarmed that neutralist tendencies would deprive the United States of potential allies, declared his opposition to neutralism—which he considered a first step on the road to communism. Both he and President Eisenhower argued that every nation should take a side in the life-and-death Cold War struggle. Neutralism had to be contained.

If this negative view of neutralism inhibited U.S. efforts to strengthen relations with the Third World, so did America's domestic race relations.

American Racism as Handicap

In 1955, G. L. Mehta, the Indian ambassador to the United States, was refused service in the whites-only section of a restaurant at Houston International Airport. The insult stung deeply and was not soon forgotten, either by him or by the millions of people in the Third World who heard about such incidents. Fearing injured relations with a nation whose allegiance the United States was seeking in the Cold War, Secretary Dulles telegraphed his apologies to the Indian diplomat.

Such embarrassments were not uncommon. Burma's minister of education was denied service at a Columbus, Ohio, restaurant, and the finance minister of Ghana was turned away from a Howard Johnson's just outside the nation's capital. Dulles complained that U.S. segregation was becoming a "major international hazard," spoiling U.S. efforts to gain the friendship of Third World countries. Americans stood publicly condemned as a people who did not honor their own ideal of equality. Thus when the U.S. attorney general appealed to the Supreme Court to strike down segregation in public schools, he underlined the international implications. "It is in the context of the present world struggle between freedom and tyranny that

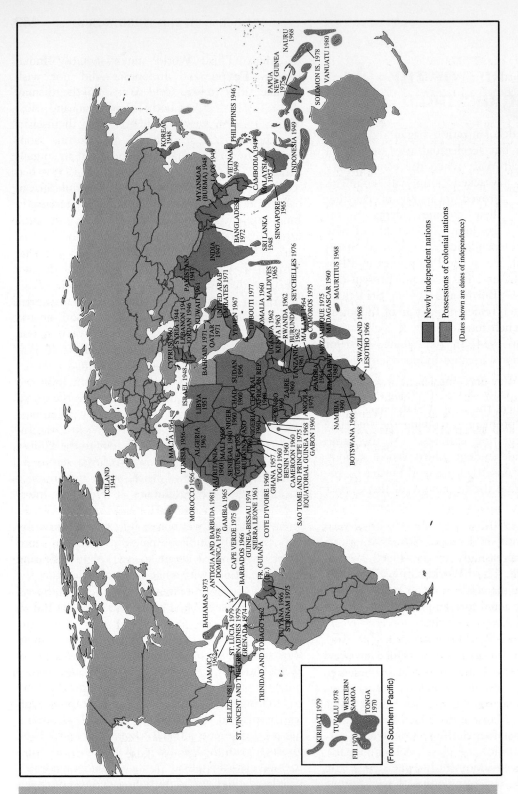

KOREA 1948

MYANMAR (BURMA) 1948
LAOS 1949
VIETNAM 1949
CAMBODIA 1949
PHILIPPINES 1946
INDONESIA 1949
PAPUA NEW GUINEA 1975
SOLOMON IS. 1978
NAURU 1968
VANUATU 1980

BANGLADESH 1972
SRI LANKA 1948
SINGAPORE 1965
MALAYSIA 1957

INDIA 1947
PAKISTAN 1947
MALDIVES 1965
SEYCHELLES 1976
MAURITIUS 1968

CYPRUS 1960
SYRIA 1944
LEBANON 1943
JORDAN 1946
KUWAIT 1961
UNITED ARAB EMIRATES 1971
QATAR 1971
BAHRAIN 1971
YEMEN 1967
DJIBOUTI 1977
SOMALIA 1960
UGANDA 1962
KENYA 1963
RWANDA 1962
BURUNDI 1962
TANZANIA 1961
MALAWI 1964
COMOROS 1975
MADAGASCAR 1960
SWAZILAND 1968
LESOTHO 1966

ISRAEL 1948
MALTA 1964
LIBYA 1951
SUDAN 1956
CHAD 1960
CENTRAL AFRICAN REP. 1960
ZAIRE 1960
CONGO 1960
ZAMBIA 1964
MOZAMBIQUE 1975
ZIMBABWE 1980

TUNISIA 1956
ALGERIA 1962
NIGER 1960
MALI 1960
NIGERIA 1960
GABON 1960
ANGOLA 1975
NAMIBIA 1990
BOTSWANA 1966

ICELAND 1944
MOROCCO 1956
MAURITANIA 1960
SENEGAL 1960
GUINEA 1958
BURKINA FASO
GHANA 1957
TOGO 1960
BENIN 1960
CAMEROON 1960
EQUATORIAL GUINEA 1968
SAO TOME AND PRINCIPE 1975
COTE D'IVOIRE 1960
GAMBIA 1965

ANTIGUA AND BARBUDA 1981
DOMINICA 1978
CAPE VERDE 1975
GUINEA-BISSAU 1974
SIERRA LEONE 1961
BARBADOS 1966
FR. GUIANA (Fr.)

BAHAMAS 1973
ST. LUCIA 1979
ST. VINCENT AND THE GRENADINES 1979
GRENADA 1974
TRINIDAD AND TOBAGO 1962
GUYANA 1966
SURINAM 1975

BELIZE 1981
JAMAICA 1962

KIRIBATI 1979
TUVALU 1978
WESTERN SAMOA
FIJI 1970
TONGA 1970

(From Southern Pacific)

Newly independent nations

Possessions of colonial nations

(Dates shown are dates of independence)

The Rise of the Third World: Newly Independent Nations Since 1943   *The influx of new nations into the international system challenged the United States and Soviet Union. Often voting as a bloc, they pitted one superpower against the other and, suffering economic and political disorder, became targets of great-power intrigue, but they resisted efforts to control them and their assets.*

the problem of racial discrimination must be viewed," he warned. The humiliation of dark-skinned diplomats in Washington, D.C., "the window through which the world looks into our house," was damaging to American interests. U.S. discrimination "furnished grist for the Communist propaganda mills." When the Court announced its *Brown* decision (see page 861), the U.S. Information Agency's Voice of America quickly broadcast news of the desegregation order around the world in thirty-five different languages.

U.S. hostility toward revolution also obstructed the American quest for influence in the Third World. Despite its own history, the United

American Intolerance of Revolution
———

States has openly opposed most twentieth-century revolutions— in Mexico, China, Russia, Cuba, Vietnam, Nicaragua, and Iran, among other nations. Though Americans celebrated the Spirit of '76, they grew intolerant of revolutionary disorder because Third World revolutions were often directed against America's Cold War allies. Such upheavals also threatened American investments, markets, and military bases. Indeed, the United States had become an established power in world affairs, eager for stability and order to protect American prosperity and security. During revolutionary crises, therefore, the United States usually supported its European allies or the conservative propertied classes in the Third World. In 1960, for example, when forty-three African and Asian states sponsored a United Nations resolution endorsing decolonization, the United States abstained from the vote, signaling that it stood with the white imperialists.

Another obstacle in America's relations with the rising Third World was the country's great wealth. Foreigners both envied and resented

U.S. Wealth as Obstacle
———

Americans who had so much and wasted so much while poorer peoples went without. American movies offered enticing glimpses of middle-class materialism; American products drew attention at international trade fairs and native marketplaces. And Americans stationed overseas often flaunted their higher standard of living. The popular novel *The Ugly American* (1958) spotlighted the "golden ghettoes" where American diplomats lived in compounds separated by high walls from their poorer surroundings. Finally, the people of many coun-

tries resented the ample profits that American corporations extracted from them.

For all these reasons, the United States often found itself the target of revolutionary nationalism rather than the model for Third World development. Americans often were blamed for the persistent poverty of the Third World, even though the leaders of those nations made decisions that hindered their progress. Underfed India, for example, poured millions of dollars into the production of a nuclear bomb when it might have spent those funds improving agricultural production.

The Soviet Union enjoyed only a slight edge, if any, in the great-power competition to win friends in the Third World. It was true that Com-

Obstacles to Soviet Influence
———

munist ideology encouraged anticolonialism and that the Soviet Union was free of association with the long years of Western European imperialism. But though Moscow kept up a heavy drumbeat of anti-imperialist propaganda, it could not easily explain away its subjugation of Eastern European countries. The Soviet invasion of Hungary in 1956 earned the Soviets international condemnation. Khrushchev toured India and Burma in the mid-1950s, but those nations refused to become Soviet clients. They were not about to replace one imperial master with another. Like Americans, the Soviets suspected that neutralist nations were playing off the two superpowers against one another in order to garner more aid and arms.

The Central Intelligence Agency became a major instrument of U.S. policy in the Third World. Though espionage and the gathering of informa-

CIA Covert Activities
———

tion had been defined as the CIA's primary functions at its birth in 1947, covert actions soon joined them. The CIA bribed foreign politicians, subsidized foreign newspapers, hired mercenaries, conducted sabotage, sponsored labor unions, dispensed "disinformation" (false information), plotted the assassination of foreign leaders, and staged coups—all in an effort to influence foreign governments toward pro-American positions. The CIA helped overthrow the governments of Iran (1953) and Guatemala (1954) but failed in attempts to topple regimes in Indonesia (1958) and Cuba (1961).

The CIA and other components of the American intelligence community followed the principle of "plausible deniability": covert operations should be conducted in such a way, and the decisions that launched them concealed so well, that the president could deny any knowledge of them. Thus President Eisenhower denied the U.S. role in Guatemala, even though he had ordered the operation; he also denied that he had instructed the CIA to assassinate Cuba's Fidel Castro, whose regime after 1959 became stridently anti-American.

THE EISENHOWER INTERVENTIONS

Anti-Yankee feelings grew in Latin America, long a U.S. sphere of influence, where poverty, class warfare, overpopulation, illiteracy, economic sluggishness, and foreign exploitation fed discontent (see map, page 981). In 1951 the leftist Jacobo Arbenz Guzmán was elected president of Guatemala, a poor country whose largest landowner was the American-owned United Fruit Company. United Fruit was an economic power throughout Latin America, where it owned three million acres of land and operated railroads, ports, ships, and telecommunications facilities. To fulfill his promise of land reform, Arbenz expropriated United Fruit's uncultivated land and offered compensation. United Fruit dismissed the offer and began an aggressive public relations campaign to rally Washington officials against what the company called a Communist threat to Guatemala.

Though lacking evidence of Communist control of Arbenz's government, U.S. officials cut off aid to Guatemala, and the CIA began a secret plot to subvert its government. When Arbenz learned that the CIA was working against him, he turned to Moscow for military aid, thus reinforcing American suspicions. The CIA airlifted arms into Guatemala, dropping them at United Fruit facilities, and in mid-1954 CIA-supported Guatemalans struck from Honduras. American planes bombed the capital city, and the invaders drove Arbenz from power. The new pro-American regime returned United Fruit's land.

CIA in Guatemala

Latin Americans wondered what had happened to the Good Neighbor policy (see page 795). Their accelerating hostility toward the United States surfaced in 1958, when rioters in Venezuela and elsewhere interrupted Vice President Richard M. Nixon's goodwill trip to South America and threatened his life. President Eisenhower ordered Operation Poor Richard as a military contingency should Nixon have to be rescued. The following year Panamanians rioted after U.S. officials denied them permission to raise the Panamanian flag in the Canal Zone.

In the volatile Middle East the Eisenhower administration confronted challenges to U.S. influence from Arab nationalists (see map). American interests were conspicuous: survival of the Jewish state of Israel and extensive oil holdings. (American companies produced about half the region's petroleum in the 1950s.) Oil-rich Iran was a special friend; its ruling shah had granted U.S. oil companies a 40 percent interest in a new petroleum consortium in return for CIA help in the successful overthrow of his rival, Mohammed Mossadegh, who had attempted to nationalize foreign oil interests.

U.S. Interests in the Middle East

Egypt's Gamal Abdul Nasser became a towering figure in a pan-Arabic movement to reduce Western interests in the Middle East. Nasser vowed to expel the British from the Suez Canal Zone and the Israelis from Palestine. The United States wished neither to anger the Arabs, for fear of losing valuable oil supplies, nor to alienate its ally Israel, which was supported at home by politically active American Jews. But when Nasser declared neutrality in the Cold War, Dulles lost patience. "Do nations which play both sides get better treatment than nations which are stalwart and work with us?" he asked. Eisenhower doubted that Nasser was really neutral. "If he was not a Communist," the president wrote later, "he certainly succeeded in making us suspicious of him."

In 1956 the United States abruptly reneged on its offer to Egypt to help finance the Aswan Dam, a project to provide inexpensive electricity and water for thirsty farmlands. "You fellows are out to kill me," Nasser angrily accused the American ambassador. Secretary Dulles's blunt economic pressure backfired, for Nasser responded by nationalizing the British-owned Suez Canal, intending to use its profits to build the dam. At a mass rally in Alexandria, Nas-

Suez Crisis

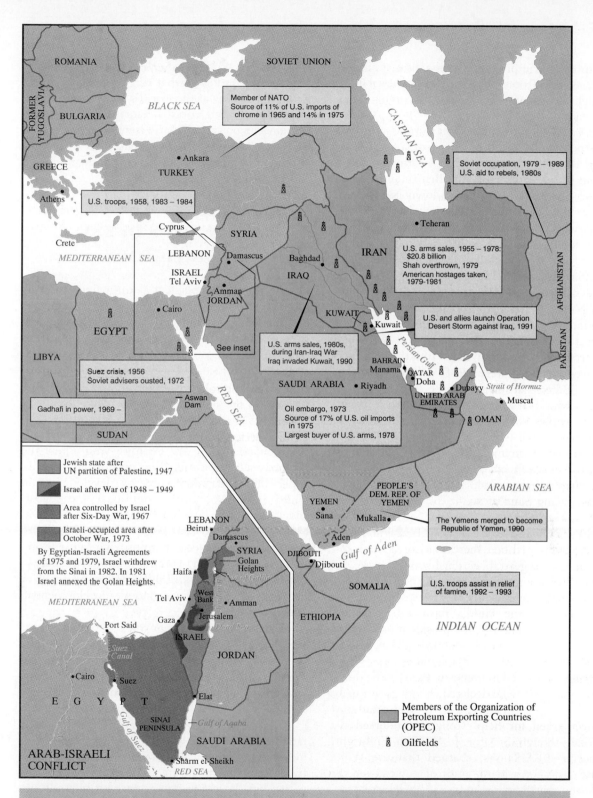

ROMANIA

SOVIET UNION

FORMER YUGOSLAVIA

BULGARIA

BLACK SEA

CASPIAN SEA

Member of NATO
Source of 11% of U.S. imports of
chrome in 1965 and 14% in 1975

Soviet occupation, 1979 – 1989
U.S. aid to rebels, 1980s

GREECE

• Ankara

TURKEY

Athens •

U.S. troops, 1958, 1983 – 1984

• Teheran

Crete

Cyprus

SYRIA

IRAN

AFGHANISTAN

MEDITERRANEAN SEA

LEBANON

• Damascus

Baghdad •

U.S. arms sales, 1955 – 1978:
$20.8 billion
Shah overthrown, 1979
American hostages taken,
1979-1981

ISRAEL
Tel Aviv •

IRAQ

PAKISTAN

• Amman
JORDAN

• Cairo

KUWAIT

U.S. and allies launch Operation
Desert Storm against Iraq, 1991

EGYPT

See inset

• Kuwait

U.S. arms sales, 1980s,
during Iran-Iraq War
Iraq invaded Kuwait, 1990

Persian Gulf

LIBYA

Suez crisis, 1956
Soviet advisers ousted, 1972

BAHRAIN
Manama •

QATAR
• Doha

Strait of Hormuz

Gadhafi in power, 1969 –

Aswan
Dam

SAUDI ARABIA

• Riyadh

Dubayy •

UNITED ARAB
EMIRATES

• Muscat

RED SEA

OMAN

SUDAN

Oil embargo, 1973
Source of 17% of U.S. oil imports
in 1975
Largest buyer of U.S. arms, 1978

PEOPLE'S
DEM. REP. OF
YEMEN

ARABIAN SEA

YEMEN
• Sana

Mukalla •

The Yemens merged to become
Republic of Yemen, 1990

Jewish state after
UN partition of Palestine, 1947

Israel after War of 1948 – 1949

LEBANON
Beirut •

• Aden

Gulf of Aden

DJIBOUTI
• Djibouti

Area controlled by Israel
after Six-Day War, 1967

Israeli-occupied area after
October War, 1973

• Damascus

SYRIA
Golan
Heights

Sea of Galilee

SOMALIA

U.S. troops assist in relief
of famine, 1992 – 1993

By Egyptian-Israeli Agreements
of 1975 and 1979, Israel withdrew
from the Sinai in 1982. In 1981
Israel annexed the Golan Heights.

Haifa •

ETHIOPIA

INDIAN OCEAN

MEDITERRANEAN SEA

Tel Aviv •

West
Bank

• Amman

Gaza •

Jerusalem
•

Dead Sea

Port Said •

ISRAEL

JORDAN

Suez
Canal

• Cairo

• Suez

• Elat

Members of the Organization of
Petroleum Exporting Countries
(OPEC)

E G Y P T

SINAI
PENINSULA

Gulf of Aqaba

Oilfields

Gulf of Suez

SAUDI ARABIA

ARAB-ISRAELI
CONFLICT

• Sharm el-Sheikh
RED SEA

The Middle East *Extremely volatile and often at war, the nations of the Middle East maintained precarious relations with the United States. To protect its interests, the United States extended large amounts of economic and military aid and sold huge quantities of weapons to the area. At times, Washington ordered U.S. troops to the region. The Arab-Israeli dispute particularly upended order.*

ser expressed the profound nationalism typical of Third World peoples shedding an imperial past: "Tonight our Egyptian canal will be run by Egyptians. *Egyptians!*"

Fully 75 percent of Western Europe's oil came from the Middle East, and most of it was transported through the Suez Canal. Fearing an interruption in this vital trade, the British and French conspired with Israel to bring down Nasser. On October 29, 1956, the Israelis invaded the Suez, joined two days later by Britain and France. Eisenhower fumed that U.S. allies had not consulted him and that the attack had shifted attention from Soviet intervention in Hungary (see page 901). The president also speculated that the invasion would cause Nasser to seek help from the Soviets, inviting them into the Middle East. Eisenhower sternly demanded that London, Paris, and Tel Aviv pull their troops out, and they did. From the U.S. perspective, the results were negative: Egypt took possession of the canal and the Soviets built the Aswan Dam. As for Nasser, he became a hero to Third World peoples, who applauded his resistance to Western imperialists. He advocated neutralism and Pan-Arabism even more vigorously. To counter Nasser's "evil influence," as Eisenhower called it, the United States pursued alignment with the conservative King Saud of Saudi Arabia. Washington officials worried that a "vacuum" existed in the Middle East—and that the Soviets might fill it. Nasserites insisted that there was no vacuum, but rather a growing Arab nationalism that provided the best defense against communism.

In an effort to improve the deteriorating Western position in the Middle East and to protect American interests there, the president proclaimed
Eisenhower Doctrine the Eisenhower Doctrine in 1957. The United States would intervene in the Middle East, he declared, if any government threatened by a Communist takeover asked for help. Congress endorsed the doctrine, though Senator J. William Fulbright, Democrat of Arkansas, charged that the White House "asks for a blank grant of power over our funds and armed forces, to be used in a blank way, for a blank length of time, under blank conditions with respect to blank nations in a blank area. . . . Who will fill in all these blanks?" One answer came in 1958 when fourteen thousand American troops scrambled ashore in Lebanon to quell an internal political dispute that Washington feared might be exploited by pro-Nasser groups or Communists. Some critics protested that the United States was wrongfully acting as the world's policeman. Others observed that such a drastic resort to military intervention demonstrated that Eisenhower had failed miserably at thwarting challenges to American power and winning Cold War allies in the Third World.

KENNEDY'S QUEST FOR VICTORY

During the 1960 presidential campaign, John F. Kennedy hammered the Eisenhower administration for failing to align the Third World with the U.S. side in the Cold War. Kennedy vowed to win the race for influence in the Third World, as well as the missile race, the arms race, and the space race. After Khrushchev endorsed "wars of national liberation" such as that in Vietnam, Kennedy called for "peaceful revolution" based on the concept of *nation building*. Drawing on the ideas of the economist Walt W. Rostow, who joined the Kennedy administration, the president set out to apply the American model of development in Third World countries: evolutionary, capitalist, and democratic. The United States would help them through the infant stages of nationhood with aid programs aimed at improving agriculture, transportation, and communications. Kennedy thus initiated the multibillion-dollar Alliance for Progress (1961) to spur economic development in Latin America.

Created for the same purpose, the Peace Corps sent American teachers, agricultural specialists, and health workers into developing nations. Within
Peace Corps three years, 10,000 idealistic young men and women had volunteered for service abroad. But the Peace Corps's humanitarian purpose sometimes competed with the administration's political agenda. Conflicts arose between corps members in the field, who identified with Third World peoples' desire for neutrality in the Cold War, and headquarters in Washington, where the goal was aligning those peoples with U.S. foreign policy.

Kennedy also relied on *counterinsurgency*—an organized effort to defeat revolutionaries who challenged Third World governments friendly with the

United States. American military and technical advisers trained native troops and police forces to quell unrest. And U.S. soldiers—especially the Special Forces units, or Green Berets—were deployed to provide a protective shield against insurgents while American civilian personnel worked on economic projects.

The CIA continued its covert operations, including the training of the exile brigade and the launching of Operation Mongoose in Cuba (see pages 903–906). The agency also plotted in the Congo (now Zaire) in 1960–1961 to poison Premier Patrice Lumumba with a lethal injection of a virus. A CIA-backed Congolese political faction finally murdered Lumumba, who had turned to the Soviet Union for help during a civil war. In Brazil, the CIA spent $20 million to influence the 1962 elections against President João Goulart, who had expropriated the property of the U.S. firm International Telephone and Telegraph and had refused

How do historians know

that the Central Intelligence Agency tried to assassinate foreign leaders? During the 1970s, Senator Frank Church (1924–1984), Democrat of Idaho, chaired a special investigating committee that looked into the activities of the CIA and other intelligence agencies. Although there had long been speculation that Washington headquarters ordered CIA agents to kill certain foreign leaders, incontrovertible evidence did not come to public light until Church's probe forced the CIA to declassify secret documents. Here, on November 20, 1975, Church holds a copy of his committee's report on assassination plots. Among other findings in this report, the committee detailed several bungled attempts on the life of Fidel Castro, the revolutionary leader of Cuba. In this case, the CIA actually hired Mafia crime bosses to help with the unsuccessful schemes. In other cases,

the Church committee discovered that the CIA tried to kill Patrice Lumumba of the Congo and either promoted or associated with plots against Rafael Trujillo of the Dominican Republic and Ngo Dinh Diem of South Vietnam. Most of the assassination plots, the committee concluded, failed. The committee could not confirm whether Presidents Eisenhower, Kennedy, and others personally ordered assassinations, although the report hinted that they gave orders that could only have been interpreted by underlings as licenses to kill. Because of such revelations, the CIA was later prohibited from conducting assassinations. But until another committee like Church's opens classified documents, the secrecy that enshrouds CIA operations makes it difficult for historians to know whether the ban has been observed.   Photo: UPI/Bettmann Archives.

to vote to oust Cuba from the Organization of American States. When Goulart's supporters won, the CIA helped organize opposition groups. In 1964, with U.S. complicity, the Brazilian military overthrew Goulart.

Nation building and counterinsurgency did not work. Americans assumed, as they had for much of the twentieth century in the Caribbean, that the U.S. model of capitalism and government could be transferred successfully to foreign cultures. But as much as they craved U.S. economic assistance and praised America's wealth, many foreign peoples resented meddling by outsiders in their affairs. And because aid was usually funneled through a self-interested elite, it often failed to reach the very poor. To people who preferred the relatively quick solutions of a managed economy, moreover, the American emphasis on private enterprise seemed inappropriate.

DESCENT INTO THE LONGEST WAR: VIETNAM

In Southeast Asia the belief that the United States could influence the internal affairs of Third World countries led to outright disaster. How Vietnam became the site of America's longest war (a quarter-century, from 1950 to 1975), and how the world's most powerful nation failed to subdue a peasant people who suffered enormous losses, is one of the most remarkable and tragic stories of modern history.

For decades after the French takeover of Indochina (Vietnam, Cambodia, and Laos) in the late nineteenth century, France exploited Vietnam for its rice, rubber, tin, and tungsten. Although the French beat back recurrent peasant rebellions, Vietnamese nationalists dedicated to independence grew in strength. Their leader Ho Chi Minh, born in 1890, lived in France before the First World War, and at the close of the war he joined the French Communist party to use it as a vehicle for Vietnamese independence. For the next two decades, living in China, the Soviet Union, and elsewhere, Ho patiently planned and fought to free his nation from French colonialism.

French Imperialism in Vietnam

Not until the Second World War, when the Japanese moved into Indochina, did French authority collapse. Seizing their chance, the Vietminh, an anti-imperialist coalition organized by Ho and other patriots, teamed up with agents of the American Office of Strategic Services (OSS) to harass the Japanese and their French collaborators. OSS officers who worked with Ho in Vietnam were impressed by his determination to win independence and by his frequent references to the United States as a revolutionary model. "Your statesmen make eloquent speeches about helping those with self-determination," Ho remarked to an OSS officer. "We are self-determined. Why not help us? Am I any different from . . . even your George Washington?" When Ho declared Vietnam's independence in September 1945, his words sounded familiar: "We hold these truths to be self-evident. That all men are created equal."

Yet the Truman administration never answered Ho's appeals for support; instead it endorsed the restoration of French rule. The United States did not recognize Vietnamese independence—in fact, attempted to undermine it—for several reasons. First, Americans wanted France's cooperation in the Cold War. Second, Southeast Asia was an economic asset; its rice could feed America's soon-to-be ally Japan, and it was the world's largest producer of natural rubber and a rich source of other commodities. Third, the area seemed strategically vital to the defense of Japan and the Philippines. Finally, Ho Chi Minh was a Communist, who, it was assumed, would assist Soviet expansionism. Thus Vietnam became another test for the containment of communism. Overlooking the native roots of the nationalist rebellion against France, and the long, tenacious Vietnamese resistance to foreign intruders, American presidents from Truman through Ford took a globalist view of Vietnam, interpreting events through a Cold War lens.

U.S. Rejection of Vietnamese Independence

In the 1940s Vietnam was a French problem that few Americans followed with keen interest. More dramatic crises in Europe commanded their attention, even after the Vietminh and the French went to war in 1946. But when Jiang Jieshi (Chiang Kai-shek) went down to defeat in China less

U.S. Support for the French

Ho Chi Minh (1890–1969) had already been working for Vietnamese independence for a quarter-century before this 1945 picture was snapped. Here Ho (seated fourth from left) sits with several agents of the U.S. Office of Strategic Services (OSS). These Americans had been parachuted into northern Vietnam in July to team up with Ho's anti-Japanese guerrillas near the close of the Second World War. The OSS officers departed soon after the war ended in August, but they expressed great respect for the lean Vietnamese nationalist and leader of rebel Vietminh forces who declared his country independent from France.   Alan Squires.

than three years later, the Truman administration made two crucial decisions—both in early 1950, before the Korean War. First, it recognized the French puppet government of Bao Dai, a playboy and former emperor who had collaborated with the French and Japanese. In Vietnamese eyes the United States thus became in essence a colonial power, an ally of the hated French. Second, the administration agreed to send weapons, and ultimately military advisers, to the French. Eisenhower continued these policies, and by 1954 the United States had provided more than $2 billion in military assistance and was bearing three-fourths of the cost of the war.

Despite American aid, the French lost steadily to the Vietminh. Finally, in early 1954, Ho's forces surrounded the French fortress at Dienbienphu in northwest Vietnam. What would the United States do? Could the French be saved? President Eisenhower huddled with his advisers. Some suggested a massive American air strike against Vietminh positions, perhaps even using tactical atomic weapons. Eisenhower moved deliberately. Although the United States had been advising and

Dienbienphu Crisis

bankrolling the French, it had not committed its own forces to the war. If American air power did not save the French, would ground troops be required next, and in hostile terrain? As one high-level doubter remarked, "One cannot go over Niagara Falls in a barrel only slightly." Some presidential advisers feared that American units might have to be moved from elsewhere in Asia and Europe, a shift that could leave other regions vulnerable.

Worrying aloud about a Communist victory, Eisenhower compared the weak nations of the world to a row of dominoes, all of which would topple if just one fell (a concept later known as the domino theory). He decided to press the British to help form a coalition to address the Indochinese crisis, but they refused. At home, influential members of Congress told the president they wanted "no more Koreas" and warned him to avoid any American military commitment, especially in the absence of allied cooperation. Some also felt uneasy about supporting colonialism. The issue became moot on May 7, when the weary French defenders at Dienbienphu surrendered.

To compound the administration's problems, the French wanted out of the war. In April they

Geneva Accords
——

had entered into peace talks at Geneva with the United States, the Soviet Union, Britain, the People's Republic of China, Laos, Cambodia, and the two competing Vietnamese regimes of Bao Dai and Ho Chi Minh. Dulles found the job of negotiating with Communists unpleasant; he conducted himself, according to one biographer, like a "puritan in a house of ill repute." Asked at a press conference if he would meet with Chinese delegates, Dulles replied: "Not unless our automobiles collide." The 1954 Geneva Accords, signed by France and Ho's Democratic Republic of Vietnam, temporarily divided Vietnam at the 17th parallel, with Ho's government confined to the North and Bao Dai's to the South. This parallel was meant to serve as a military truce line, not a national boundary; the country was scheduled to be unified after national elections in 1956. In the meantime, neither North nor South was to join a military alliance or permit foreign military bases on its soil.

Certain that the Geneva agreements would ultimately mean Communist victory, the United States and Bao Dai refused to accept the accords and set about to sabotage them. Soon after the conference, a CIA team entered Vietnam and undertook secret operations against the North, including commando raids across the 17th parallel. In fall 1954 the United States also joined Britain, France, Australia, New Zealand, the Philippines, Thailand, and Pakistan in the anti-Communist Southeast Asia Treaty Organization (SEATO), one purpose of which was to protect the southern part of Vietnam.

In the South, the United States helped Ngo Dinh Diem push Bao Dai aside. A Catholic in a Buddhist nation, Diem had many enemies and no mass support. But he was a nationalist and an anti-Communist, and with American aid he staged a fraudulent election that gave him a remarkable 98 percent of the vote. When Ho called for national elections in keeping with the Geneva agreements, Diem and Eisenhower refused, fearing the charismatic Vietminh leader would win. From 1955 to 1961 the Diem government received more than $1 billion in American aid, most of it military. American advisers organized and trained the South Vietnamese army. Michigan State University police experts helped build a national guard. American agriculturalists worked to improve crops. American consumer products flowed into Vietnamese

This presidential refrain during the Vietnam War, from Eisenhower to Kennedy to Johnson to Nixon and, finally, to Ford, declared eventual U.S. victory. But in the end, the United States failed to satisfy its goals and had to leave Southeast Asia under fire. Each president underestimated the determination of the nationalistic North Vietnamese and Vietcong to unite Vietnam under a truly independent government. At the same time, each president overestimated the capability of American power to deliver a U.S. victory. Reprinted by permission of Tribune Media Services.

In early 1966 Buddhist monks demonstrated in Saigon (shown here) and elsewhere in Vietnam. Buddhist protests had destabilized the Diem government three years earlier; this time the Buddhists sought to bring down a U.S.-backed military regime. Nationalistic Buddhists appealed for peace talks with the Vietcong, for an end to American interference in Vietnam's politics, and for free elections. The regime answered by arresting Buddhist leaders and crushing their movement—one of many signs that the political stability the United States so needed to win the war was lacking. Wide World Photos.

cities. Diem's Saigon regime became dependent on the United States for its very existence, and the culture of southern Vietnam became increasingly Americanized.

Diem proved a difficult ally. He became bent on dictatorial leadership, abolishing village elections and appointing to public office people beholden to him. He threw dissenters in jail and shut down newspapers that criticized his regime. Non-Communists and Communists alike began to strike back at Diem's corrupt and repressive government in the South. Encouraged by Ho's regime in the northern capital of Hanoi, southern insurgents embarked on a program of terror, assassinating hundreds of Diem's village officials. Then in 1960, southern Communists organized the National Liberation Front, known as the Vietcong. The Vietcong in turn attracted other anti-Diem groups in the South. The war against imperialism had become a two-part civil war: Ho's North versus Diem's South, and Vietcong guerrillas versus the Diem government.

President Kennedy, having suffered the humiliations of the Bay of Pigs and the Berlin Wall, de-

Kennedy's Escalation

cided to stand firm in Vietnam. He feared further criticism if the United States backed down in Asia (where he was already seeking to negotiate an end to the civil war in Laos). But, more important, he sought a Cold War victory. "How do we get moving?" he asked his advisers. Soon he ordered more U.S. military personnel to South Vietnam. By late 1963, Project Beef-up had sent more than 16,000 American "advisers." That year, 489 Americans were killed in Vietnam.

Kennedy also increased the flow of aid dollars, but Diem showed no signs of using the assistance effectively. Meanwhile, Diem's opponents in Vietnam grew in number. Fearing Diem would drag the United States down to defeat, the Kennedy administration urged him to reform, to no avail. An American project called the Strategic Hamlet Program actually strengthened resistance to Diem: the program, which aimed to isolate peasants from the Vietcong by uprooting them into barbed-wire compounds, simply alienated villagers. Buddhist priests began protests, charging Diem with religious persecution. In the streets of Saigon, protesting monks poured gasoline over their robes and ignited themselves.

American officials concluded that if Diem could not be reformed, he should be removed. American leaders also grew alarmed that Diem,

Removal of Diem

who knew that the United States was preparing to dump him, was apparently trying to make peace with the North— "a possible basic incompatibility with U.S. objectives," as General Maxwell Taylor put it. Through the CIA, the United States quietly encouraged disaffected South Vietnamese generals to stage a coup. With the ill-concealed backing of Ambassador Henry Cabot Lodge, the generals struck in November 1963. Diem was captured and murdered—only a few weeks before Kennedy himself met death by an assassin's bullet.

JOHNSON AND THE WAR WITHOUT VICTORY

With new governments in Saigon and Washington, some analysts thought it an appropriate time for reassessment. United Nations, Vietcong, and French leaders called for a coalition government in South Vietnam. But the new American president, Lyndon Johnson, would have none of it. America's purpose was victory, he declared, for anything less "would only be another name for a Communist take-over."

Johnson was a Texan who liked to say that he lived by the lesson of the Alamo: fight to the end. An old New Dealer, he talked about building Tennessee Valley Authorities around the world. "I want to leave the footprints of America there [in Vietnam]. I want them to say, 'This is what Americans left—schools and hospitals and dams.'" The footprints America eventually left were those of soldiers, bombs, and chemical defoliants.

On August 2, 1964, the USS *Maddox*, in the Gulf of Tonkin to assist South Vietnamese commando raids against North Vietnam, came under

Tonkin Gulf Incident

attack from northern patrol boats (see map). The small craft suffered heavy damage while the unharmed *Maddox* sailed away. "If they do it

again," remarked Secretary of State Dean Rusk, "they'll get another sting." Two days later, the *Maddox*, now joined by another destroyer, moved toward the North Vietnamese shore once again as if to bait the Communists. In bad weather, sonar technicians reported what they thought were enemy torpedoes; the two destroyers began firing ferociously. Yet when the captain of the *Maddox* asked his crew what had happened, not one had seen or heard hostile gunfire.

President Johnson, aware that the evidence was questionable but unwilling to acknowledge publicly that American ships were participating in covert raids against North Vietnam, announced on television that the United States would retaliate against the "unprovoked" attack in the Tonkin Gulf by bombing North Vietnam. Congress promptly passed the Tonkin Gulf Resolution, 466 to 0 in the House and 88 to 2 in the Senate, after brief debate. Only Wayne Morse of Oregon and Ernest Gruening of Alaska dissented from the resolution's sweeping language, which authorized the president to "take all necessary measures to repel any armed attack against the forces of the United States and to prevent further aggression." By passing the Tonkin Gulf Resolution—which Johnson later argued amounted to a declaration of war— Congress essentially surrendered its powers in the foreign policy process by giving the president wide latitude to conduct the war as he saw fit.

In neighboring Laos, meanwhile, American bombers hit the "Ho Chi Minh Trail" (supply routes) connecting the Vietcong with the North Vietnamese. The bombings were kept secret from the American Congress and public. The CIA had long manipulated politics in Laos, where in 1962 non-Communists and Communists had agreed to a neutralist government. As Ambassador William H. Sullivan admitted, "We ran Laos." After winning the presidency in his own right in fall 1964, Johnson directed the military to map plans for stepped-up bombing of both Laos and North Vietnam. Under Secretary George Ball urged caution: "Once on the tiger's back we cannot be sure of picking the place to dismount."

When the Vietcong, who controlled nearly half of South Vietnam, attacked the American airfield at Pleiku in February 1965, killing nine Americans, Johnson ordered carrier-based jets to ravage the North. Soon Operation Rolling Thunder—a sustained bombing program above the 17th

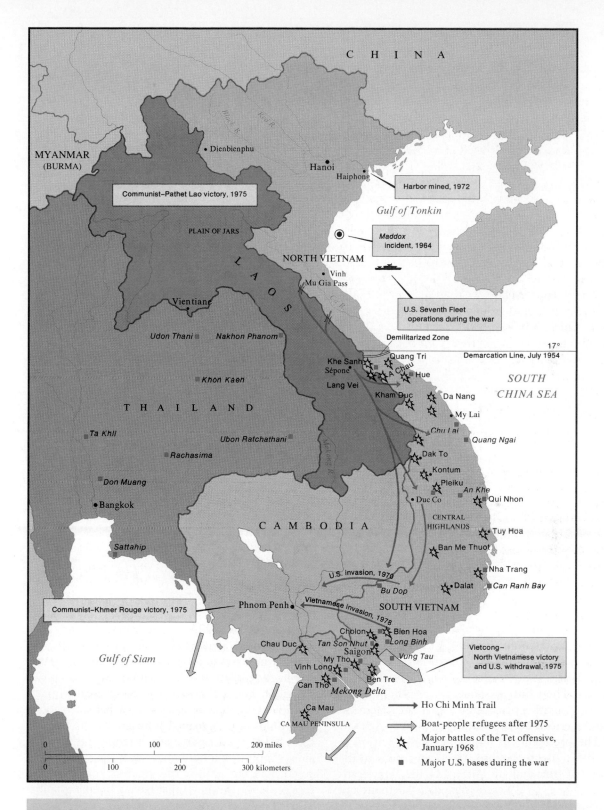

Southeast Asia and the Vietnam War To prevent Communists from coming to power in Vietnam, Cambodia, and Laos in the 1960s, the United States intervened massively in Southeast Asia. The interventions failed, and the remaining U.S. troops made a hasty exit from Vietnam in 1975, when the victorious Vietcong and North Vietnamese took Saigon and renamed it Ho Chi Minh City.

U.S. Troops in Vietnam, 1960–1972

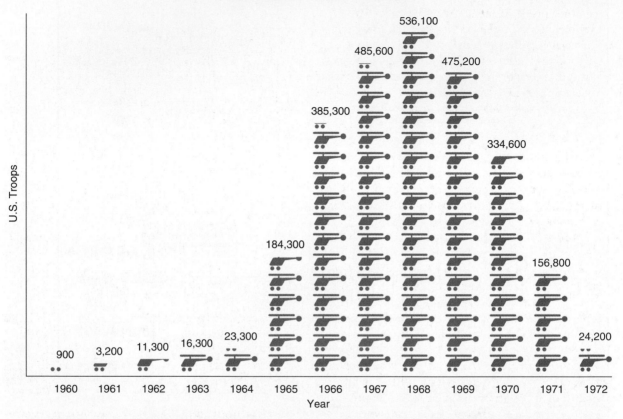

U.S. Troops in Vietnam *These numbers show the Americanization of the Vietnam War under President Lyndon B. Johnson, who ordered vast increases in troop levels. President Richard M. Nixon reversed the escalation, so that by the time of the cease-fire in early 1973 fewer than 25,000 American troops remained in Vietnam. Data for December 31 of each year.*   Source: U.S. Department of Defense.

parallel—was under way. Before the longest war was over, more bombs would fall on Vietnam than American aircraft had dropped in the Second World War. The North Vietnamese would not give up. They hid in shelters and rebuilt roads and bridges with a perseverance that frustrated and awed American decision makers.

The president, in his momentous decision of July 1965, also sent more American troops to the South. By the end of 1965, 184,300 Americans were assigned to Vietnam and in 1968, 536,100 (see figure). At one point in 1969, the number of U.S. troops peaked at 543,400 before falling by the end of the year to 475,200. In 1967 the secret CIA-run Phoenix Program began to kill Vietcong lead-

Americanization of the War

ers; probably 60,000 were assassinated, some after being tortured. Undeterred, Ho increased the flow of arms and men to the rebels in the South. In this seemingly endless war of attrition, each American escalation begot a new Vietnamese escalation. "I feel like a hitchhiker caught in a hailstorm on a Texas highway," groaned Johnson. "I can't run, I can't hide, and I can't make it stop." He and his aides simply could not believe that the Vietnamese could hold out against the greatest power on the face of the earth; they must have a breaking point. "What does he want?" Johnson kept saying about Ho, as if Ho could be bought off like a corrupt American politician.

The Americanization of the war under Johnson troubled growing numbers of Americans, especially as television coverage brought the war into their homes every night. The pictures and stories were not pretty. Innocent civilians were caught in the line of fire; refugees straggled into "pacification" camps; villages considered friendly to the enemy were burned to the ground. One private wrote home that he had just piled up 79 bodies of dead Vietcong: "Some of the Charlies were just kids, 14 or 15 years old. They must be crazy or something." To expose and destroy Vietcong hiding places, pilots sprayed chemical defoliants like Agent Orange over the landscape to denude it; their swaggering motto was "Only You Can Prevent Forests." The Vietcong and North Vietnamese contributed to the carnage, but American guns, bombs, and chemicals took by far the greatest toll, and the Vietnamese people knew it. Indeed, America's search-and-destroy missions were counterproductive; rather than winning the war, they were molding an ever-growing population of anti-American peasants who gave secret aid to the Vietcong. An American official later admitted, "It was as if we were trying to build a house with a bulldozer and wrecking crane."

Stories of atrocities made their way home. Most gruesome was the My Lai massacre of March 1968 (not made public until twenty months later because of a military cover-up).

My Lai Massacre

An American unit, frustrated by its inability to pin down an elusive enemy and eager to revenge the loss of some buddies, shot to death more than 200 unarmed Vietnamese civilians, most of them women and children. Private Paul Meadlo, himself the father of two children, was there. "We huddled them up. We made them squat down. . . . I poured about four clips into the group. . . . The mothers was hugging their children. . . . Well, we kept right on firing. They was waving their arms and begging. . . . I still dream about it. About the women and children in my sleep. Some days . . . some nights, I can't even sleep."

Many incidents of deliberate shooting of civilians, torturing and killing of prisoners, taking of Vietnamese ears as trophies, and burning of villages have been recorded, but most American soldiers were not committing atrocities. They were trying instead to save their own young lives (their average age was only nineteen) and to serve the U.S. mission by killing

American Soldiers in Vietnam

Civilian casualties in the Vietnam War became everyday occurrences, and sometimes "friendly fire" took its toll. In this 1968 incident in Saigon, a father carries his wounded child away after American troops fired on a horse they mistook for a Vietcong soldier.   Philip Jones Griffith/Magnum Photos.

enemy troops, whom they usually referred to with the racist term "gooks." Many of these Americans made up the rear-echelon forces that supported the "grunts" or "boonierats" in the field. But wherever they were, the environment was inhospitable, for no place in Vietnam was secure. Well-hidden booby traps blasted away body parts. And the enemy was everywhere yet nowhere, often burrowed into elaborate underground tunnels or melded into the population, where any Vietnamese might be a Vietcong terrorist.

Infantrymen on maneuvers humped heavy rucksacks into thick jungle growth, where every step was precarious. "In places the bamboo was over fifteen feet high," wrote the veteran John M. DelVecchio in his novel *The 13th Valley* (1982). "The point man felt as if he were breaking trail through knife blades of spring steel. His arms were soon slashed and bloody and his face had multiple

Wounded American soldiers after a battle in Vietnam.   Larry Burrows, LIFE Magazine © 1971 Time Warner, Inc.

tiny lacerations." Leeches sucked at weary bodies. Boots and human skin rotted from the rains, which alternated with withering suns. "It was as if the sun and the land itself were in league with the Vietcong," recalled the marine officer Philip Caputo in *A Rumor of War* (1977), "wearing us down, driving us mad, killing us." Wounded GIs shouted for a medic, who in turn might call in a "medevac" (medical evacuation helicopter), praying that it would not be shot down. A medevac could carry the wounded within minutes to operating tables in MASH (Mobile Army Surgical Hospital) units or hospital ships like the USS *Sanctuary*. "What I saw were young men coming in, eighteen or nineteen years old . . . and they would be without a leg," remembered Gayle Smith, a nurse at the 3rd Surgical Hospital. "Vietnam was not John Wayne," remarked Ruth Sidisin of the Air Force Nurse Corps. "In Vietnam every day was disaster day."

As the war ground on to no discernible conclusion and became increasingly unpopular at home,

the brutality of war heightened the belief among growing numbers of GIs that the United States had no business being in Vietnam. Morale in the U.S. armed forces sagged and discipline sometimes lapsed. The generals grew alarmed by reports of disobedience—and by peace symbols scratched on helmets. Desertions and absent-without-official-leave (AWOL) cases increased, especially near the end of the war in the 1970s, when no GI wanted to be the last man killed. Racial tensions between whites and blacks intensified. Drug abuse became serious. Many soldiers smoked plentiful, cheap marijuana; 10 percent of the troops took heroin. "Fragging"—murder of officers by enlisted men, usually using hand grenades—took at least 1,000 lives between 1969 and 1972. "Grenades leave no fingerprints. Nobody's going to jail," said a helicopter pilot.

At home, thousands of young men were expressing their opposition to the war by fleeing the draft. By the end of 1972 more than 30,000 draft resisters were living in Canada; thousands more had gone into exile in Sweden or Mexico or were living under false identities in the United States. In the course of the war more than a half-million men committed draft violations, including a quarter-million who never registered and thousands who burned their draft cards.

As American military engagements in Vietnam escalated, so did protest at home. Teach-ins at universities began in 1965, and in April of that year 25,000 people marched on **Antiwar Protest** the White House. In October the National Committee to End the War in Vietnam mobilized more than 80,000 in nationwide demonstrations. Early the following year, Senator J. William Fulbright held public hearings on whether the national interest was being served by pursuing the war in Asia. What exactly was the threat? senators asked. To the surprise of some, the father of the containment doctrine, George F. Kennan, testified before television cameras that his theory was meant for Europe, not the volatile environment of Southeast Asia. In October 1967, 100,000 people marched on Washington to protest the war. Disenchantment also rose in the administration itself. Secretary of Defense Robert McNamara worked quietly to scale back the American military presence in Vietnam and resigned when he failed to persuade President Johnson. "Ho Chi Minh is a tough old S.O.B.," McNamara told his aides. "And he won't quit no matter how much bombing we do." In a direct challenge to Johnson's policies, antiwar Senator Eugene McCarthy of Minnesota announced his candidacy for the Democratic presidential nomination.

Johnson dug in, dismissing his critics as "those little shits on the campuses." Cheered by opinion polls that showed Americans favored escalation over withdrawal, the president vowed to continue the battle. Though on occasion he halted the bombing to encourage Ho Chi Minh to negotiate, such pauses were often accompanied by increases in American troop strength. And the United States sometimes resumed or accelerated the bombing just when a diplomatic breakthrough seemed imminent—as in 1966, when a Polish diplomat's efforts were cut short by a resumption of bombing. The North demanded a complete suspension of bombing raids before sitting down at the conference table. And Ho could not accept American terms: nonrecognition of the Vietcong as a legitimate po-

litical organization, withdrawal of northern soldiers from the South, and an end to North Vietnamese military aid to the Vietcong—in short, abandonment of his lifelong dream of an independent, unified Vietnam.

In January 1968, a shocking event forced Johnson to reappraise his position. During Tet, the Vietnamese holiday of the lunar new year, Vietcong and North Vietnamese **Tet Offensive** forces struck all across South Vietnam, hitting and capturing provincial capitals. Vietcong raiders even penetrated the American embassy compound in Saigon. U.S. and South Vietnamese units eventually regained much of the ground they lost, inflicting heavy casualties on the enemy and devastating numerous villages. As one sober-faced American officer explained about the leveling of Ben Tre to drive the Vietcong out, "It became necessary to destroy the town to save it."

The Tet offensive jolted Americans. Although Tet ultimately counted as an American military victory—the Vietcong took heavy losses and South Vietnamese and U.S. forces recaptured most of the cities—it was also a psychological defeat for Americans. Hadn't the Vietcong and North Vietnamese demonstrated that they could strike when and where they wished? Didn't they have the advantage of fighting on home territory? Why did "their Vietnamese" fight harder than "our Vietnamese"? If all of America's airpower and dollars and half a million troops couldn't defeat the Vietcong once and for all, could anything do so? Had the American public been lied to? When the highly respected television anchorman Walter Cronkite somberly raised questions about the war on "CBS Evening News," President Johnson sensed political trouble: "If I've lost Cronkite, I've lost middle America."

The Tet offensive and its impact on public opinion hit the White House like a thunderclap. The new secretary of defense, Clark Clifford, told Johnson the war could not be won, even if the 206,000 more soldiers now requested by the army were sent to Vietnam. The ultimate Cold Warrior, Dean Acheson—one of the "wise men" Johnson brought in to advise him—bluntly told the surprised president that the military brass did not know what they were talking about.

The wise men were aware that the nation was suffering a financial crisis prompted by rampant

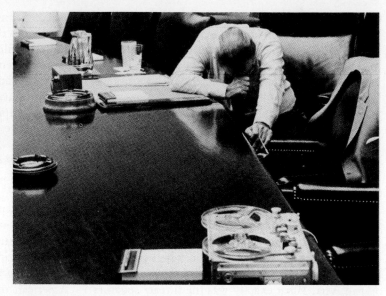

The agony of war pained many. On the left is Marine Lance Corporal James Farley in Danang after a Vietcong ambush that took the lives of American troops. On the right is President Lyndon B. Johnson after the Tet offensive and his decision to end his political career by not running again for the presidency.   Left: Larry Burrows, *Life* magazine © 1965 Time, Inc.; right: Lyndon B. Johnson Library.

Dollar/Gold Crisis ———

deficit spending, largely due to heavy U.S. expenditures abroad to sustain the war and other global commitments. Nervous foreigners were exchanging their U.S. dollars for gold at an alarming rate. On March 14 alone, foreigners—especially Europeans—redeemed $372 million for gold. A post-Tet effort to take the initiative in Vietnam would surely cost billions more, and thus further derange the budget, panic foreign owners of dollars, and wreck the economy. Clifford heard from his associates in the business community: "These men now feel we are in a hopeless bog," he told the president. To "maintain public support for the war without the support of these men" was impossible, Clifford concluded.

Strained by exhausting sessions with advisers, troubled by the economic implications of escalation, sensing that more soldiers and firepower would not bring victory, and faced with serious opposition within his own party and protesters wherever he went, Johnson changed course. On March 31 he announced on television that he had stopped the bombing of most of North Vietnam and asked Hanoi to begin negotiations. Then he stunned the nation by dropping out of the presidential race.

U.S. leaders, having come reluctantly to the view that they could not win the war, would at least try not to lose it. Peace talks began in May in Paris, but the war ground on. Johnson demanded North Vietnamese concessions before completely halting the bombing, but Hanoi rejected reciprocity. Later in the year President-elect Richard M. Nixon met with Johnson and his key advisers to discuss the war. "The travail of the long war was etched on the faces around me," Nixon recalled. "They had no new approaches to recommend to me. I sensed that, despite the disappointment of defeat, they were relieved to be able to turn this morass over to someone else."

———

DEFEAT AND EXIT: NIXON AND THE LEGACY OF VIETNAM

In July 1969, a few months after his inauguration, the new president announced the Nixon Doctrine: the United States would help those nations that helped themselves. This doctrine reflected official Washington's realizations that it could no longer afford to sustain its

Nixon Doctrine ———

many overseas commitments and that the United States would have to rely more on regional allies to maintain an anti-Communist world order. In Southeast Asia this doctrine was implemented as "Vietnamization"—building up South Vietnamese forces to replace American troops. Nixon began a gradual withdrawal of U.S. troops from Vietnam, decreasing their number to 156,800 by the end of 1971. But he also increased the bombing of the North, hoping to pound Hanoi into concessions: "jugular diplomacy," in the words of Nixon's national security adviser, Henry Kissinger. In October 1969, hundreds of thousands of Americans marched peacefully in cities across the nation to call for a moratorium on the war. On November 15, more than a quarter-million marchers protested in Washington, D.C., alone. "Don't get rattled—don't waver—don't react," Nixon told himself.

In April 1970, Nixon announced that South Vietnamese and American forces were invading Cambodia in search of arms depots and enemy forces that used the neutral nation as a sanctuary. This escalation of the war provoked angry demonstrations on college campuses. At Kent State University in Ohio, National Guardsmen ordered to suppress protest killed four people. Across the nation, students went "on strike" to protest the killing in Indochina and America. A belligerent Nixon publicly called them "bums." In June the Senate joined the protest against Nixon's broadening of the war by terminating the Tonkin Gulf Resolution of 1964.

Cambodia and Antiwar Protest

Nixon's troubles at home mounted in June 1971 when the *New York Times* began to publish the *Pentagon Papers*, a top-secret official study of U.S. decisions in the Vietnam War. Secretary McNamara had ordered preparation of the study in 1967 to preserve a documentary record. Daniel Ellsberg, a former Defense Department official working at the RAND Corporation (a think tank for analyzing defense policy), had leaked the report to the *Times*. Nixon secured an injunction to prevent publication, but the Supreme Court overturned the order. The *Pentagon Papers* revealed that U.S. leaders had frequently lied to the American people. President Johnson, for example, had repeatedly claimed in public that the United States increased its forces in South Vietnam only to respond to escalating North Vietnamese infiltration. The Pentagon study, on the other hand, revealed that after mid-1967 the United States itself escalated the war because American officials believed that more troops would deliver victory.

Nixon and Kissinger continued to expand the war, ordering "protective reaction strikes" against the North, bombing of Cambodia, and mining of Haiphong harbor in North Vietnam. In December 1972, they launched a massive air strike on the North called "the Christmas bombing." One of Kissinger's aides characterized it as "calculated barbarism." The air terror of 20,000 tons of bombs punished the Vietnamese. At the same time, the United States lost twenty-six planes, including fifteen B-52 bombers.

In Paris, meanwhile, the peace talks begun in 1968 seemed to be going nowhere. The South Vietnamese delegate, who saw defeat coming, purposely stalled the negotiations. But Kissinger was also meeting privately with Le Duc Tho, the chief delegate from North Vietnam. Nixon instructed Kissinger to make concessions because the president was eager to improve relations with the Soviet Union and China (see Chapter 29), to win back the allegiance of America's allies, and to restore stability at home. On January 27, 1973, Kissinger and Le Duc Tho signed a cease-fire agreement. The United States promised to withdraw all of its troops within sixty days. Vietnamese troops would stay in place, and a coalition government that included the Vietcong would eventually be formed in the South. Critics of the war, pleased that peace had been made, nonetheless noted that if the same terms had been accepted in 1969, more than 20,000 American lives would have been spared. To prevent a future Vietnam, Congress passed the War Powers Resolution in late 1973: the president could commit American troops abroad for no more than sixty days without obtaining congressional approval.

Cease-Fire Agreement

The United States pulled its troops out of Vietnam, leaving behind some advisers, and reduced but did not end its aid program. Both North and South soon violated the cease-fire, and full-scale war erupted once more. As many had predicted, the feeble South Vietnamese government—for so long an American puppet—could not hold out. Just before its surrender, hundreds of Americans, and Vietnamese who had worked for them, were hastily evacuated by helicopter from the roof of the U.S. embassy in Saigon. On April

29, 1975, the South Vietnamese government collapsed. Shortly thereafter Saigon was renamed Ho Chi Minh City for the persevering patriot who had died in 1969.

The overall costs of the war were immense. More than 58,000 Americans and about 1.5 million Vietnamese had died. The war cost the United

Costs of the Vietnam War
———

States more than $170 billion, and billions more would be paid out in veterans' benefits. The vast sums spent on the war became unavailable for investment at home to improve the infrastructure and quality of life. Instead, the nation suffered inflation and retreat from reform programs (see Chapters 32 and 33), as well as political schism, violations of civil liberties, and abuses of executive power. The war also had extremely negative consequences internationally: delay in improved relations with the Soviet Union and the People's Republic of China, friction with allies, and the alienation of Third World nations.

In 1975 Communists assumed control and instituted repressive governments in South Vietnam, Cambodia, and Laos, but the domino effect once predicted by pro-war U.S. officials never occurred. Acute hunger afflicted the people of those devastated lands. Soon refugees were crowding aboard unsafe vessels in an attempt to escape their battered homelands. Many of these "boat people" eventually emigrated to the United States, where they were received with mixed feelings by Americans reluctant to be reminded of their defeat in Asia. But many Americans faced the fact that the United States, which had relentlessly bombed, burned, and defoliated once-rich agricultural lands, bore considerable responsibility for the plight of the Southeast Asian peoples.

This sad conclusion prompted an American ambassador to pose a central question about the U.S. defeat: how was it that "so many with so much could achieve so little for so long against so few"? General Maxwell Taylor, summarizing the reasons Americans could not win the Vietnam War, said that "we didn't know our ally. Secondly, we knew even less about the enemy. And, the last, most inexcusable of our mistakes, was not knowing our own people."

When it was over, many Americans preferred to put the disaster out of mind. "Coming back to America," recalled a Vietnam veteran, "I was

shocked . . . that no one even talked about it." But the veterans were—and are—unable to forget. As one wrote,

> But I can still hear the gunfire
> The longest war is over
> Or so they say
> Again
> But I can still hear the gunfire
> Every night
> From
> My bed.
>
> The longest nightmare
> Never seems to
> Ever
> Quite come
> To
> An end.[1]

Americans seemed both angry and confused about the nation's war experience. For the first time in their history, the historian William Appleman

The Lessons of Vietnam
———

Williams observed, Americans were suffering from a serious case of "empire shock"—that is, shock over having had their overseas sphere of influence violently pushed back. Hawkish leaders claimed that America's failure in Vietnam undermined the nation's credibility and tempted enemies to exploit opportunities at the expense of U.S. interests. They pointed to a "Vietnam syndrome"—a suspicion of foreign entanglements—that they feared would inhibit the United States from exercising its power. Next time, they said, the military should be permitted to do its job, free from the constraints of whimsical public opinion, stab-in-the-back journalists, and meddlesome politicians. America lost in Vietnam, they asserted, because Americans lost their guts and will at home. "Remember," asserted a former battalion commander, "we're watchdogs you unchain to eat up the burglar. Don't ask us to be mayors or sociologists worrying about hearts and minds. Let us eat up the burglar our own way and then put us back on the chain."

Doveish leaders drew different lessons, denying that the military had suffered undue restraints. Some blamed the war on an imperial presidency that had permitted strong-willed men like Johnson

———
[1] From Jan Barry, "The Longest War." Reprinted by permission of the author.

In Washington, D.C., the solemn walls of the Vietnam Memorial include the etched names of more than 58,000 Americans who died in the war. Designed by Yale University student Maya Ying Lin and opened in 1982, the memorial became a stopping place for the many Americans whose lives were touched in some way by the long war. Department of Defense clerical errors placed on the black granite the names of at least fourteen living veterans. "The last mistakes," New Yorker magazine sadly wrote, "of a mistaken war."   Susan Meiselas/Magnum Photos.

to act without limits, and on pusillanimous Congresses that had conceded too much power to the executive branch, as with the Tonkin Gulf Resolution. Make the president adhere to the checks-and-balances system of the Constitution—make him go to Congress for a declaration of war—these critics counseled, and America would become less interventionist. Others took a more hard-headed, even fatalistic, view: as long as the United States remained a major power with compelling ideological, strategic, economic, and political needs that could be satisfied only through activism abroad, the nation would continue to be expansionist and interventionist. The United States was destined to intervene abroad, they argued, to sustain its role as the world's policeman, teacher, social worker, banker, and merchant. Still others blamed the containment doctrine for failing to make distinctions

between areas vital and peripheral to the national security and for relying too heavily on military means. Containment could not work, they believed, if there were no political stability and no effective popular government in the country where it was being applied. The journalist Walter Lippmann endorsed "neo-isolationism": "Compared to people who thought they could run the universe," he wrote, "I *am* a neo-isolationist and proud of it."

Public discussion of the lessons of the Vietnam War was also stimulated by veterans' calls for help in dealing with post-traumatic stress disorder, which afflicted thousands of

Post-traumatic Stress Disorder
_____

the 2.8 million Vietnam veterans after returning home. They suffered nightmares and extreme nervousness. Doctors reported that the disorder stemmed primarily from the soldiers' having seen so many children, women, and elderly people killed. Some GIs inadvertently killed these people, unable to distinguish the innocent from the enemy; some killed them vengefully and later felt guilt. As one troubled veteran admitted, "They were [Vietnamese] kids who did not know what Communism was any more than I did." By the early 1990s, some 60,000 veterans of the Vietnam War had committed suicide—more deaths than Americans had suffered during the war itself.

Many returning veterans were deeply stung by the unsympathetic glances of Americans who did not want to be reminded of the war or who blamed them for losing a war that could not be won. The veterans began to organize and demonstrate to demand respect, arguing that the leaders who ordered them to Southeast Asia, not the GIs, should be held responsible for the negative results of the long war. Other veterans heightened public awareness of the war by publicizing the effects of Agent Orange and other chemicals they had handled or were accidentally sprayed with in Vietnam. Films like *Coming Home* (1978), *The Deer Hunter* (1978), and *Apocalypse Now* (1979), personal accounts like Philip Caputo's *A Rumor of War* (1977), and novels like

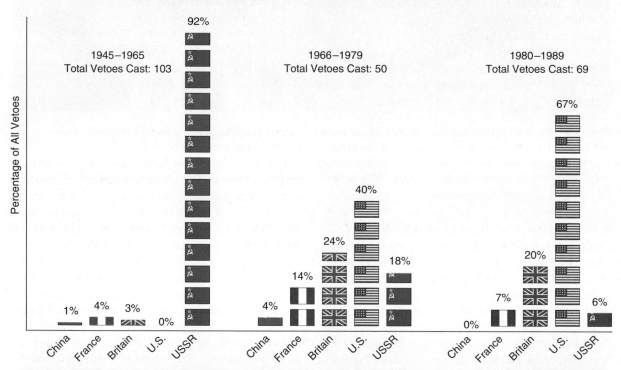

Vetoes in the Security Council of the United Nations, 1945–1989

Vetoes in the Security Council of the United Nations, 1945–1989   *Because the United States and its allies dominated the United Nations, the United States did not have to cast its first veto in the Security Council until 1970. But the rise of the Third World brought many new states into the United Nations, diminishing U.S. influence. By the late 1980s, the United States resembled the Soviet Union of the earlier period—casting the largest number of vetoes, often against Third World-initiated resolutions. Percentages are rounded. The five nations are the Permanent Members of the Security Council; under the United Nations charter only they can kill—by veto—resolutions they disapprove.*   Source: U.S. Department of State.

James Webb's *Fields of Fire* (1978), all of which depicted the soldier's Vietnam, raised questions about whether defeat had been inevitable, given the inhospitable environment and elusive enemy. The Vietnam Veterans Memorial, erected in Washington, D.C., in 1982, kept such questions alive.

CONTENDING WITH THE THIRD WORLD IN THE 1970s

President Nixon called Vietnam a "short-term problem," and Henry Kissinger declared the war a mere historical "footnote"; both considered Soviet-American relations the central question of international affairs. They nonetheless valued the Third World for its resources and markets, and they repeatedly exerted U.S. power against it to preserve the administration's grand strategy to achieve a stable world order through détente. Revolutions and radicalism in the Third World had to be contained. The Third World challenge to U.S. influence in international organizations like the United Nations had to be thwarted (see figure). Limited wars like Vietnam cost too much, and they risked drawing the two superpowers into direct conflict. Critics charged that the Nixon administration too often blamed Third World instability on Soviet or Communist intrigue, when in fact it derived from indigenous economic, political, religious, and ethnic differences.

Events in the Middle East revealed how fragile the Nixon-Kissinger grand strategy was. When Nixon took office in 1969 the Middle East was, in the president's words, a "powder keg." Israel, using American weapons, had scored victories against Egypt and Syria in the Six-Day War (1967), seizing the West Bank and the ancient city of Jerusalem from Jordan, the Golan Heights from Syria, and the Sinai peninsula from Egypt (see map, page 957). Israel's Arab adversaries had used Soviet arms. To further complicate matters, Palestinians, many of them expelled from their homes in 1948 when the nation of Israel was created, had organized the Palestine Liberation Organization (PLO) and pledged to destroy Israel. PLO sympathizers made hit-and-run raids on Jewish settlements, hijacked jetliners, and murdered Israeli athletes at the 1972 Olympic Games in Munich, West

Secretary of State Henry Kissinger (1923–   ) on one leg of his "shuttle diplomacy" between Cairo, Egypt, and Tel Aviv, Israel. In the aftermath of the Arab-Israeli War of 1973 and the oil embargo, Kissinger patiently worked to quiet tempers. Shortly after this 1975 photograph, Egypt and Israel initialed a historic Kissinger-designed agreement that placed a United Nations peacekeeping force in the Sinai region between the two nations.   Gerald Ford Presidential Library.

Germany. The Israelis retaliated by assassinating PLO figures abroad.

In October 1973, Egypt and Syria attacked Israel. In spite of détente, Moscow, backing Egypt, and Washington, backing Israel, put their armed forces—including nuclear forces—on alert. In an attempt to pressure Americans into a pro-Arab stance, the Organization of Petroleum Exporting Countries (OPEC) imposed an embargo on shipments of oil to the United States.

The 1973 War in the Middle East

Faced with an energy crisis at home due to dramatically higher oil prices, the Nixon administration had to find a way to end Mideast hostilities. Kissinger arranged a cease-fire and undertook "shuttle diplomacy," flying repeatedly between Middle Eastern capitals in search of a settlement. In March 1974, OPEC lifted the oil embargo. The next year Kissinger persuaded Egypt and Israel to accept a United Nations peacekeeping force in the Sinai. But many problems remained: the homeless Palestinian Arabs, Israeli occupation of Jerusalem and the West Bank, Israel's insistence on building Jewish settlements in occupied lands, and Arab threats to destroy the Jewish state. Soviet-American rivalry also remained very much alive in the Middle East, especially after Egypt moved closer to the United States, snubbing the Soviets.

In Latin America, Nixon continued President Johnson's interventionist policies (see map, page 981). Johnson had dispatched 20,000 American troops to the Dominican Republic in 1965 to prevent a leftist government from coming to power there. In the Johnson Doctrine, Johnson had declared that the United States would prevent Communists from coming to power in Western Hemispheric nations. Five years later, Nixon perceived a Communist threat in Chile, when the Chileans elected a Marxist president, Salvador Allende. The CIA began secret operations to disrupt the Chilean economy and apparently encouraged military officers to stage a coup. In 1973 a military junta ousted and killed Allende and installed an authoritarian regime in his place. Nixon and Kissinger privately pronounced their policy of "destabilization" successful, while publicly denying any role in the affair.

In Africa, the maneuvers of Nixon and Kissinger proved less successful. During the 1960s and early 1970s, while Washington publicly supported

Angola
———

Portugal, the CIA hedged its bets by channeling funds to groups fighting to liberate Angola from Portuguese colonial rule. After Angola won its independence in 1975, civil war erupted. The United States and South Africa covertly backed one faction while the Soviets helped another. When Congress learned about the secret U.S. aid, it voted to cut off all funds. While Kissinger claimed that the Soviets would gain a foothold in Africa, many members of Congress argued that Americans could not decide the outcome of an African civil war, that the United States should not be aligned with the white racist regime of South Africa, and that diplomacy should have been tried. After a leftist government came to power in Angola, Washington took a keener interest in the rest of Africa, building economic ties, sending arms to friendly black nations, and distancing the United States from the white minority governments of Rhodesia (now Zimbabwe) and South Africa. America had to "prevent the radicalization of Africa," said Kissinger.

The United States was interventionist in part because the American economy depended on imports of strategic raw materials like tin, zinc, and manganese. Furthermore,

U.S. Economic Interests Abroad
———

American investments abroad totaled more than $133 billion by the mid-1970s. American leaders thus read threats to markets, investments, and raw materials as deadly stabs at the high U.S. standard of living. American economic holdings did in fact become targets. Venezuela nationalized American oil properties in 1976, and terrorists around the world destroyed American facilities and kidnaped and sometimes murdered American business executives.

By the 1970s multinational corporations had become a symbol of America's conspicuous economic position overseas. U.S.-based multinationals like Exxon and General Mo-

Multinational Corporations
———

tors actually enjoyed budgets and incomes larger than those of most countries. These giant firms brought home profits and exported American culture, but they also provoked criticism at home and abroad. American workers protested that global oligopolies stole their jobs when they moved factories abroad in search of cheaper labor. Third World critics protested that multinationals robbed them of their natural resources and corrupted politics, as when International Telephone and Telegraph tried to undermine President Allende in Chile and Lockheed Aircraft bribed foreign leaders to promote sales. They also accused multinationals of providing "cover" for CIA agents and evading taxes by clever manipulations of their books.

Multinational executives and U.S. government officials defended these enterprises, pointing out that they invested in risky ventures that promised economic progress, including the transfer of technology. Multinationals helped rationalize a chaotic world economy, they insisted, and privately owned multinationals made more rational economic choices—hence benefiting the consumer—than did government-owned companies. Many nations nonetheless passed laws requiring a certain percentage of native ownership; India, for example, legislated that its nationals own a majority of voting shares in industrial firms. Other countries simply nationalized multinational properties.

Besides imposing restraints on multinationals, the South—as the Third World has sometimes been called—demanded low-interest loans, lower prices for the technology and manufactured goods they bought abroad, and higher prices for the raw materials they sold. In 1974 the United Nations called for a "New International Economic Order" in order to encompass many of these points, but the industrial North made few concessions. Food was another divisive issue in the North-South debate. Droughts, meager harvests, high birthrates, and swelling populations condemned millions to hunger. In Africa in the early 1970s famine killed thousands every day. The United States sent food aid—especially to nations considered political friends—but it preferred to sell its surplus food for profit, as evidenced by large-scale grain sales to the dollar-paying Soviets. Although total American foreign aid rose from $6.6 billion in 1970 to $7.8 billion in 1977, the dollars actually bought less because of rampant inflation.

CARTER AND DIPLOMATIC INTERVENTION

When President Jimmy Carter took office in 1977, he promised no more Vietnams. Instead he vowed new departures, including an emphasis on human rights and advancement of the North-South dialogue. Carter promised to be an interventionist, too, but through diplomacy instead of armed forces. The United States, he pledged, would respect Third World nations as never before. Like his predecessors, however, he frowned on radicalism and nationalism because they threatened America's prominent global position. At the time, more than 400,000 U.S. military personnel were stationed abroad, the United States had military links with ninety-two nations, American arms sales overseas had reached $10 billion per year, and the CIA was active on every continent.

Carter worked to improve relations with the Third World, where the opinion prevailed that the United States was a selfish imperial power. His appointment of Andrew Young, a black civil rights activist and member of Congress, as ambassador to the United Nations earned goodwill among developing nations. Young believed that the United States should stay out of local disputes, even if Communists were involved. When warfare broke out in 1979 between Zaire and Angola, where Cuban troops and Soviet advisers were stationed, Young persuaded the president to stand back until the fighting subsided, and no American interests were sacrificed. Third World leaders were shocked, however, when Carter forced Young to resign in 1979 after the ambassador had met privately with representatives of the PLO. (The United States refused to recognize the PLO as a legitimate entity because it did not recognize Israel's right to exist.)

In the Middle East, Carter markedly advanced the peace process. Through tenacious personal diplomacy at a Camp David meeting in 1978 with Egyptian and Israeli leaders, the president gained Israel's promise to withdraw from the Sinai. The agreement was finalized the following year. Other Arab states denounced the agreement for not requiring Israel to relinquish additional occupied territories—namely, the West Bank and Golan Heights—and for not guaranteeing a Palestinian homeland. But the treaty at least ended warfare along one frontier in that troubled area of the world.

Camp David Agreements

In Latin America, Carter sought compromise with nationalists (see map, page 981). Panamanians longed for restoration of the Canal Zone, which they believed had been wrongfully severed from their nation in 1903 (see Chapter 22). Some conservative Americans, like former California governor Ronald Reagan, who was running hard for the presidency, went so far as to claim that the Canal Zone was sovereign U.S. territory from which the United States should not retreat. Carter, however, feared that Panamanians might try to seize the canal by force or might damage the vulnerable waterway. Recognizing also that the canal's value had dwindled because many new ships were too large to squeeze through its locks, he concluded negotiations that had begun after the 1964 anti-American riots in Panama. The United States signed two treaties with Panama in 1977. One provided for the return of the Canal Zone to Panama in 2000, and the other guaranteed the United States the

Panama Canal Treaties

On March 26, 1979, Egypt's President Anwar el-Sadat (1918–1981) on the left, Israel's Prime Minister Menachem Begin (1913–1992) on the right, and U.S. President Jimmy Carter (1924–   ) signed a peace treaty known as the Camp David Accords. Studiously negotiated by Carter, the Egyptian-Israeli peace has held to this day—despite conflict in much of the rest of the Middle East.   Jimmy Carter Presidential Library.

right to defend the canal after that time. The Senate narrowly endorsed both agreements in 1978.

A year later in Nicaragua, leftist insurgents overthrew Anastasio Somoza, a long-time ally of the United States and member of the dictatorial family that had ruled the Central American nation since the mid-1930s. The revolutionaries called themselves Sandinistas in honor of the Nicaraguan who had fought U.S. Marines then (see Chapter 26). Carter welcomed Somoza's departure and recognized the new government, but he recoiled from the Sandinistas' radicalism. In early 1981, he halted aid to Nicaragua to express U.S. disapproval of the Sandinistas' curbing of civil liberties, ties with Castro's Cuba, and assistance to radical rebels in El Salvador.

Carter met his toughest test in Iran. Many Iranians had not forgotten that the United States had meddled in Iranian affairs by backing the shah in

Iranian Hostage Crisis

the 1946 crisis and restoring him to his throne in 1953. Iranian revolutionaries led by the Ayatollah Ruhollah Khomeini, a bitterly anti-American Moslem cleric, also resented the CIA's training of the shah's ruthless secret police and the huge infusion of U.S. arms into their country—$19 billion worth between 1973 and 1978 alone. When the shah was overthrown in 1979 and then admitted to the United States for medical treatment, mobs stormed the American embassy in Teheran. They took hostages, demanding the return of the shah to stand trial, along with his vast wealth. The Iranians eventually released a few of the American prisoners, but fifty-two others languished more than a year under Iranian guard. They suffered solitary confinement, beatings, and terrifying mock executions.

President Carter would not return the shah to Iran or apologize for past U.S. aid to his regime. Unable to gain the hostages' freedom through diplomatic intermediaries, Carter felt "the same kind of impotence that a powerful person feels when his child is kidnapped." He next took steps to isolate Iran economically, freezing Iranian assets in the United States and urging allies to sever trade links with the renegade state. The hostage takers continued to grab headlines, often parading their blindfolded and bound captives before television cameras to taunt the United States. Americans seethed in anger.

In April 1980, frustrated and at low ebb in public opinion polls, Carter broke diplomatic relations with Iran and ordered a daring rescue mission. But the rescue effort miscarried after equipment failure in the sandy Iranian desert, and during the hasty withdrawal two aircraft collided, killing eight American soldiers. Critics chided Carter for undertaking a risky operation that surely would have cost the lives of many hostages. "Thank God for the sandstorm," one hostage later remarked. Secretary of State Cyrus Vance, already upset over the growing militancy of Carter's foreign policy and the president's acceptance of Zbigniew Brzezinski's "visceral anti-Sovietism," resigned in protest. The hostages were not freed until January 1981, after the United States unfroze Iranian assets and promised not to intervene again in Iran's internal affairs.

Carter's diplomatic record failed to meet his aspirations. More American military personnel were stationed overseas in 1980 than in 1976; the

Carter's Mixed Record

defense budget climbed and foreign arms sales grew from $8.3 billion in 1977 to $15.3 billion in 1980. Carter's human rights policy also proved inconsistent. The president did persuade other nations to release hundreds of political prisoners, but he left himself vulnerable to the charge of a double standard by applying the human rights test to some nations (the Soviet Union, Argentina, and Chile) but not to American allies (South Korea, the shah's Iran, and the Philippines). Carter's successes in the Third World, moreover, were ultimately overshadowed by the shrillness of an invigorated Cold War (see Chapter 29).

Carter's performance did not satisfy Americans who wanted a post-Vietnam reinstatement of the economic hegemony and military edge the United States once enjoyed. As one Tennessee woman mused, "Growing up we learned in history that America was the best in everything. We had the respect of the whole world. But where can you go today and be respected for being American?" A broad segment of American public opinion agreed with her. An Oklahoma couple urged Carter to take up Teddy Roosevelt's big stick once again. "And club the hell out of them if you need to," urged the blunt husband. During the 1980 presidential election, this nostalgia for old-fashioned American militancy and supremacy found a ringing voice in Ronald Reagan.

REAGAN CONFRONTS THE THIRD WORLD

The facts and nuances of international relations often eluded Ronald Reagan. After returning from his first trip to South America, he commented, "Well, I've learned a lot. . . . You'd be surprised. They're all individual countries." Reagan blamed most Third World troubles on the Soviet Union and thought revolutionary movements took their orders from Communists. Invoking the Reagan Doctrine (see Chapter 29), the United States intervened both covertly and openly in civil wars in several Third World countries. The Reagan administration also preferred military solutions to negotiations with Third World states. In 1983, for example, the president ordered U.S. troops to invade the tiny Caribbean nation of Grenada to oust a leftist government that had developed ties with Castro's Cuba, and in 1986 U.S. warplanes bombed Libya to punish it for supporting terrorism.

Under the banner of private enterprise, Reagan pressed Third World nations to open their economies to competition and reduce the role of

Law of the Sea Treaty

the state in managing economic affairs. The Law of the Sea Treaty, patiently composed in the 1970s through extended negotiations and compromise, became a test case. Developing nations argued that rich sea-bed resources of petroleum and minerals should be shared under international supervision among all nations as a "common heritage of mankind." The First World industrial states, which alone had the capital and equipment to conduct the excavating and drilling, preferred private exploitation with minimal international management. The treaty represented a compromise, but the Reagan administration rejected the treaty on the grounds that it did not adequately protect private American companies. Angry Third World nations denounced the U.S. decision as selfish economic imperialism, whereas many American allies who supported the compromise predicted a chaotic future of competing claims of ownership, territorial disputes, and threats to freedom of navigation.

The United States even cast the only "no" vote against a United Nations resolution to restrict the marketing of baby formula in developing nations. Medical authorities had reported that American baby-formula companies were marketing their product so aggressively that many mothers abandoned healthy breast-feeding in favor of formula, which they diluted with polluted water (all that was available to them). Diseases spread and infant mortality rates remained high. Regardless, Reagan officials would tolerate no interference with private business. Overall, the Reagan administration stiff-armed the Third World.

In Central America, Reagan officials believed that the Soviets (and their Cuban allies) were fomenting disorder (see map). Throughout the twentieth century, the United States had established hegemony over this region consisting of Guatemala, Honduras, El Salvador, Nicaragua, and Costa Rica through large economic holdings, political influence, and repeated interventions. North Americans had long called Central America their "backyard," a phrase that rankled nationalists.

For Reagan officials, El Salvador appeared to be a textbook case of Communist aggression. In that small, very poor country, revolutionaries challenged the government, which was dominated by the military and a small landed elite. The regime used (or could not control) right-wing "death squads" that killed thousands of dissidents and other citizens, as well as some American missionaries who worked with landless peasants. Persuaded that a U.S.-funded counterinsurgency war could be won in a short time, Reagan eschewed negotiations and instead increased military assistance to the Salvadoran regime. The controversial U.S. intervention in the

El Salvador

Salvadoran civil war sparked a debate much like that which had erupted over Vietnam years before. Those who urged negotiations thought Reagan wrong to interpret the conflict as a Cold War contest. Oppression and poverty, not Communist plots, caused people to pick up guns to fight the regime, they argued. Resurrecting the discredited domino theory, Reagan retorted that the "Communists" would soon be at the Mexican-American border if they were not stopped in El Salvador. Reagan also made a strategic argument: Central America hugs the Caribbean Sea, "our lifeline to the outside world"; in time of war, the Soviets could cripple American shipping from Caribbean bases. After consistently intense debate, Congress repeatedly gave Reagan the funds he wanted for El Salvador. The civil war only continued, more bloody than before.

Reagan also intervened in Nicaragua, where the Sandinista leader Daniel Ortega defiantly explained that his people "have broken with their past history of servility to imperialist politics." When the Sandinistas bought Soviet weapons and invited Cubans to work in Nicaragua's hospitals and schools and to help reorganize their army, Reagan charged that Nicaragua was becoming a Soviet client. Washington also claimed that the Sandinistas were sending arms to the rebels in El Salvador. Reagan therefore decided to topple the Nicaraguan regime. In 1981 the CIA began to train, arm, and direct more than ten thousand counterrevolutionaries, called *contras*. Many of these anti-Sandinista rebels were former supporters of the Somoza dictatorship. From CIA-managed bases in Honduras and Costa Rica, the contras crossed into Nicaragua to kill officials and destroy oil refineries, transportation facilities, medical clinics, and day-care centers. Innocent people were killed. As the contra attacks multiplied, the Nicaraguan government curbed civil liberties and shifted scarce money to the military.

Undeclared War Against Nicaragua

It became known in 1984 that the CIA had mined the harbors of Nicaragua, blowing up merchant ships. The World Court ruled that Nicaragua had the right to sue the United States for damages. At the same time Congress voted to stop U.S. military aid to the contras. ("Humanitarian" aid was soon sent in its place.) Secretly the Reagan administration lined up other countries, including

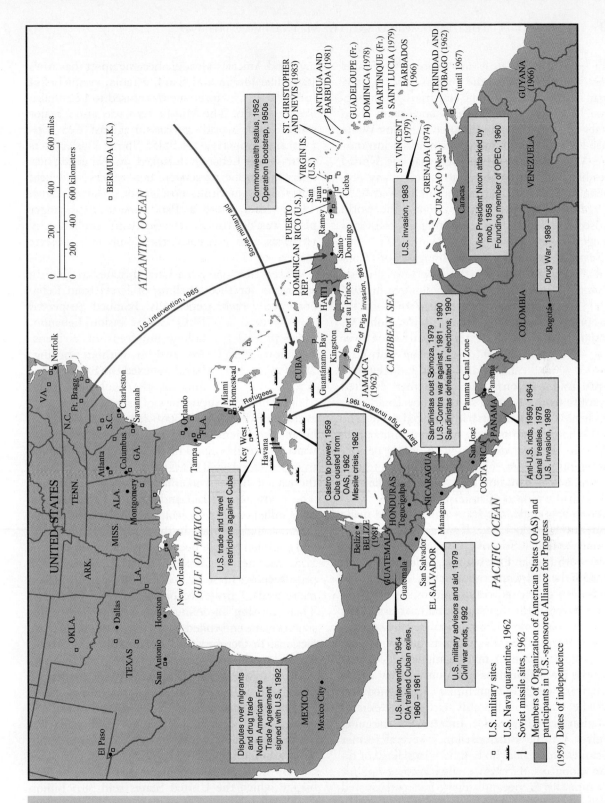

The United States in the Caribbean and Central America *The United States often has intervened in the Caribbean and Central America. Geographical proximity, economic stakes, political disputes, security links, trade in illicit drugs, and especially Cuba's defiance of the United States and alliance with the Soviet Union have kept North American eyes fixed on events to the south.*

Saudi Arabia, Panama, and Korea, to funnel money and weapons to the contras, and in 1985 Reagan imposed an economic embargo against Nicaragua. The next year, Congress once again voted military aid for the contras after vigorous White House lobbying and apparent Sandinista intransigence. (The Sandinistas insisted that the United States halt support for the contras before any permanent settlement.) During the undeclared U.S. war against Nicaragua, critics around the world chastised U.S. leaders for rejecting opportunities for negotiations.

Scandal, popularly called "Irangate" or "Contragate," tainted the North American crusade against the Sandinistas. It became known in 1986 that the president's national security affairs adviser, John M. Poindexter, and an aide, Oliver North, in collusion with CIA Director William J. Casey, had covertly sold weapons to Iran and then diverted the profits to the contras so that they could purchase arms. The diversion had occurred during the period when Congress had prohibited military assistance to the contras. During the same period, Washington had been condemning Iran as a terrorist nation and demanding that America's allies not trade with the radical Islamic state.

Iran-contra Scandal

From any angle, the Iran-contra scandal made President Reagan look bad. If Reagan did not know that the National Security Council was running guns to both Iran and the contras, he looked incompetent. If he did know about arms deliveries to Iran, he was guilty of breaking his own pledge not to aid a government that supported terrorists. And if he knew that Colonel North was illegally supplying the contras, the president was guilty of lying during the Iran-contra investigations and of violating the law—Congress's ban on military aid to the contras, which Reagan himself had signed into law. The scandal irreparably tarnished Reagan's reputation (see Chapter 33). In late 1992, outgoing President George Bush pardoned several former government officials who had been convicted of lying to Congress. Critics smelled a cover-up, for Bush himself, as vice president, had participated in high-level meetings on Iran-contra deals.

In the 1980s, as before, the deeply divided Middle East continued to defy American solutions (see map, page 957). An Iraqi-Iranian war, in which the United States aided Iraq, threatened Persian Gulf shipping. Lebanon was disintegrat-

ing. And American leaders became upset that Arab states like Jordan and Saudi Arabia, recipients of substantial U.S. foreign aid, refused to help stabilize the region. The Middle East was also a major source of the world's terrorism against U.S. citizens and property. In 1985, Shiite Moslem terrorists from Lebanon hijacked an American jetliner, killed one passenger, beat others, and held thirty-nine Americans hostage for seventeen days. Three years later, a Pan American passenger plane was destroyed over Scotland, probably by terrorists who concealed the bomb in a cassette player.

Even Israel gave the United States trouble. In retaliation for PLO shelling of Israel from Lebanon, the Israelis repeatedly bombed suspected PLO camps inside Lebanon, killing hundreds of civilians. And in 1981, without warning, Israel annexed the Syrian territory of the Golan Heights. Many American supporters of Israel, though well aware that the Jewish state faced hostile Arabs, became impatient with Israel's provocative acts toward its neighbors. The following year, Israeli troops invaded civil war–torn Lebanon, reaching the capital Beirut and inflicting massive damage. The beleaguered PLO and various Lebanese factions called on Syria to contain the Israelis. Thousands of civilians died in the multifaceted conflict, and a million people became refugees. Reagan sent U.S. Marines to Lebanon to serve as part of a peacekeeping force. "Too few to fight and too many to die," protested one member of Congress. Their mission ill-defined, the American troops soon became embroiled in a war between Lebanese factions. In October 1983, terrorist bombs demolished a marine barracks, killing 240 American servicemen. Four months later, Reagan recognized failure and pulled the remaining marines out.

Crisis in Lebanon

Mideast problems remained high on the U.S. foreign policy agenda. The United States had commitments (Israel, which in 1985 received more American foreign aid—$3 billion—than any other country in the world), political friends (Saudi Arabia, to which the United States sold $8.5 billion worth of military equipment in 1981), and enemies (the crusading Islamic states of Iran and Libya). Mideast oil supplies fueled Western economies—this was such a critical concern that in 1988 American warships escorted both American and foreign commercial ships through the Persian Gulf and even "reflagged" some foreign vessels to deter Iraqi or Iranian attack. One U.S. warship outfitted with high-technology equipment, its captain eager to be tested in battle, erred tragically when it shot down an Iranian commercial airliner, killing hundreds of civilians.

Washington, which openly sided with Israel, continued to propose peace plans designed to persuade the Israelis to give back occupied territories and the Arabs to give up attempts to push the Jews out of the Middle East (the "land-for-peace" formula). As the peace process stalled in 1987, Palestinians living in the West Bank began an uprising called *intifada* against Israeli forces that had occupied the area since 1967. The Israelis used brute force to quell rock-throwing youths, and sent bulldozers to knock down the houses of families whose sons or daughters were known to be active in the *intifada*. The unrest became more embittered. The PLO, meanwhile, declared the West Bank and Gaza Strip an independent Palestinian state. Israel refused to negotiate, but the United States decided to reverse its policy and talk with PLO leaders after PLO chief Yasser Arafat renounced terrorism and accepted Israel's right to live in peace and security. Still, the divide between Arabs and Jews remained wide, and peace elusive.

In Africa the Reagan administration struggled to define a policy toward South Africa, where a blatantly racist white minority imposed a rigidly segregationist system called *apartheid*

South Africa on the predominantly black population (85 percent). Blacks were kept poor, disfranchised, and geographically segregated in townships that resembled prisons. At first the Reagan administration pursued a patient policy it called "constructive engagement"—asking the South African government to reform its repressive system. But many Americans demanded economic sanctions: cutting off imports from South Africa and pressing some 350 American companies—led by Texaco, General Motors, Ford, and Goodyear—to cease operations there. By 1985 eleven American cities and five states had passed divestment laws, withdrawing dollars (such as pension funds used to buy stock) from U.S. companies active in South Africa. Public protest and congressional legislation forced the Reagan administration in 1986 to impose economic restrictions against South Africa. Within two years, about half of the American companies in South Africa pulled out.

Elsewhere in Africa, hunger and famine exacerbated by drought and wars took a ghastly human toll and contributed to political instability as governments failed to satisfy their people's basic needs.

Famine in Africa In the early 1980s experts estimated that annual hunger-related deaths numbered between 13 million and 18 million people—twenty-four people per minute, many of them in Africa. In Ethiopia and Sudan, both wracked by civil war, hundreds of thousands starved to death; competing armies in both nations sometimes callously seized international relief supplies for themselves. Almost the only good news to come out of Africa was the 1988 agreement, engineered by U.S. negotiators, among Angola, Cuba, and South Africa: withdrawal of Cuban troops from Angola and black majority rule in Namibia, the former German colony that had come under South Africa's rule after the First World War.

The Third World also presented the United States with economic problems that endangered American prosperity. Third World nations had sunk into staggering debt. Having borrowed heavily in the 1970s, they were unable to repay the loans when world prices for sugar, coffee, and other commodities slumped. By 1989 they owed creditors, including American banks, more than $1.2 trillion. Many Third World nations burdened with such debt—Mexico alone owed more than $100 billion—had to cut back on imports of U.S. goods. Hundreds of thousands of jobs in the United States were lost as a result, while economic instability spawned political unrest throughout the Third World.

From Truman to Reagan, the United States was at odds with the Third World. Foreign aid, trade and investment, CIA covert actions, USIA propaganda, military interventions, the cultural appeal of U.S. products like blue jeans—nothing seemed capable of closing the gap between the United States and the Third World. In fact, such activities widened the chasm. The clash was fundamentally a struggle for power, and it stemmed primarily from two sources: the Cold War and U.S. economic stakes.

Despite its own revolutionary past, the United States usually stood with its European Cold War allies to resist decolonization, slow the process toward independence, and preach evolution rather than revolution. Then the United States denounced the preference of many Third World nations for nonalignment in the Cold War. Take sides or else, became the American message. The U.S. globalist perspective also prompted Americans to interpret many Third World troubles as Cold War conflicts, inspired if not directed by Soviet-backed Communists. The intensity of the Cold War obscured for Americans the indigenous roots of most Third World troubles, as the Vietnam War attested.

Nor could the United States abide Third World nations' drive for economic independence—for gaining control of their own raw materials and economies. Deeply intertwined in the global economy as importer, exporter, and investor, the United States read Third World challenges as threats to an American standard of living and way of life characterized by private enterprise.

The Third World, in short, challenged U.S. strategic power by forming a third force in the Cold War, and it challenged U.S. economic power by demanding a new economic order of shared interests. Overall, the rise of the Third World introduced new actors into the international system, challenging its bipolarity. The developing nations contested great-power superintendancy of world affairs even as they often feuded among themselves. This destabilizing diffusion of power in turn made Moscow and Washington more eager for détente: through cooperation, they could team up to discipline the Third World (see Chapter 29). Even when the Cold War ended, Third World nations continued to challenge U.S. strategic and economic interests. Third World countries remained as resolute as ever about keeping their goals and problems high on the international agenda.

SUGGESTIONS FOR FURTHER READING

For Soviet-American relations, Sino-American relations, and the Cold War, see Chapter 29. Many works cited in Chapter 29 include discussion of issues related to the Third World.

The United States and the Third World: General

Richard J. Barnet, *Intervention and Revolution* (1972); Scott L. Bills, *Empire and Cold War* (1990); H. W. Brands, *The Specter of Neutralism: The United States and the Emergence of the Third World,*

1947–1960 (1989); Gabriel Kolko, *Confronting the Third World* (1988); Robert A. Packenham, *Liberal America and the Third World* (1973); David M. Reimers, *Still the Golden Door: The Third World Comes to America* (1992); Gerald T. Rice, *The Bold Experiment: JFK's Peace Corps* (1985); Alvin Z. Rubenstein and Donald E. Smith, eds., *Anti-Americanism in the Third World* (1985); L. S. Stavrianos, *Global Rift* (1981). For global economic issues, see works cited in Chapter 29.

The CIA and Counterinsurgency

Philip Agee, *Inside the Company* (1975); Douglas S. Blaufarb, *The Counterinsurgency Era* (1977); Ray Cline, *Secrets, Spies, and Scholars* (1976); Rhodi Jeffreys-Jones, *The CIA and American Democracy* (1989); Loch K. Johnson, *America's Secret Power* (1989); Mark Lowenthal, *U.S. Intelligence* (1984); Thomas Powers, *The Man Who Kept the Secrets* (1979); John Prados, *Presidents' Secret Wars* (1986); John Ranelagh, *The Agency* (1986); Harry H. Ransom, *The Intelligence Establishment* (1970); John Stockwell, *In Search of Enemies* (1978).

The Vietnam War and Southeast Asia: General

Loren Baritz, *Backfire* (1985); Eric M. Bergerud, *The Dynamics of Defeat* (1991); Frances FitzGerald, *Fire in the Lake* (1972); Leslie H. Gelb and Richard K. Betts, *The Irony of Vietnam* (1979); William C. Gibbons, *The U.S. Government and the Vietnam War* (1986–87); Daniel C. Hallin, *The "Uncensored War"* (1986); George C. Herring, *America's Longest War*, 2nd ed. (1986); Gary R. Hess, *Vietnam and the United States* (1990); Arnold R. Isaacs, *Without Honor: Defeat in Vietnam and Cambodia* (1983); Stanley Karnow, *Vietnam*, rev. ed. (1991); Gabriel Kolko, *Anatomy of a War* (1986); Guenter Lewy, *America in Vietnam* (1978); John C. Rowe and Rick Berg, eds., *The Vietnam War and American Culture* (1991); William Shawcross, *Sideshow* (1979) (on Cambodia); Anthony Short, *The Origins of the Vietnam War* (1989); Marilyn B. Young, *The Vietnam Wars* (1991). For works on the antiwar movement, see Chapter 32.

Truman, Eisenhower, and Vietnam

David L. Anderson, *Trapped by Success* (1991); James R. Arnold, *The First Domino* (1991); Melanie Billings-Yun, *Decision Against War: Eisenhower and Dien Bien Phu, 1954* (1988); Lloyd C. Gardner, *Approaching Vietnam* (1988); Gary Hess, *The United States' Emergence as a Southeast Asian Power* (1987); Lawrence S. Kaplan et al., eds., *Dien Bien Phu and the Crisis of Franco-American Relations* (1990); Andrew Rotter, *The Path to Vietnam* (1987).

Kennedy, Johnson, and Escalation in Vietnam

Larry Berman, *Lyndon Johnson's War* (1989); Larry Berman, *Planning a Tragedy* (1982); William C. Berman, *William Fulbright and the Vietnam War* (1988); Larry Cable, *Unholy Grail* (1991); Charles DeBenedetti and Charles Chatfield, *An American Ordeal: The Antiwar Movement of the Vietnam Era* (1990); David L. DiLeo, *George Ball, Vietnam, and the Rethinking of Containment* (1991); George McT. Kahin, *Intervention* (1986); Thomas G. Paterson, ed., *Kennedy's Quest for Victory* (1989); Deborah Shapley, *Promise and Power: The Life and Times of Robert McNamara* (1993); Melvin Small, *Johnson, Nixon and the Doves* (1988); Brian VanDerMark, *Into the Quagmire* (1991).

The Vietnam War: Military Aspects

Jeffrey J. Clarke, *United States Army in Vietnam* (1988); Mark Clodfelter, *The Limits of Power: The American Bombing of North Vietnam* (1989); Phillip B. Davidson, *Vietnam at War* (1988); Ronald H. Spector, *After Tet: The Bloodiest Year in Vietnam* (1992); Ronald H. Spector, *United States Army in Vietnam* (1983).

The Vietnam Legacy

Walter H. Capps, *The Unfinished War* (1982); John Hellman, *American Myth and the Legacy of Vietnam* (1986); Herbert Hendin and Ann P. Haas, *Wounds of War: The Psychological Aftermath of Combat in Vietnam* (1984); Ole R. Holsti and James Rosenau, *American Leadership in World Affairs: Vietnam and the Breakdown of Consensus* (1984); David Levy, *The Debate over Vietnam* (1991); Myra MacPherson, *Long Time Passing* (1984); Robert E. Osgood, *Limited War Revisited* (1979); Norman Podhoretz, *Why We Were in Vietnam* (1982); Earl C. Ravenal, *Never Again* (1978); Harrison E. Salisbury, ed., *Vietnam Reconsidered* (1984); Harry G. Summers, Jr., *On Strategy* (1982).

Latin America: General

Cole Blasier, *Hovering Giant* (1974); Thomas Carothers, *In the Name of Democracy* (1991) (on Reagan years); Richard Immerman, *The CIA in Guatemala* (1982); Lester Langley, *Mexico and the United States* (1991); Lester Langley, *America and the Americas* (1989); Abraham F. Lowenthal, ed., *Exporting Democracy* (1991); Abraham F. Lowenthal, *Partners in Conflict: The United States and Latin America* (1987); John D. Martz, ed., *United States Policy in Latin America* (1988); Stephen G. Rabe, *Eisenhower and Latin America* (1988); Stephen G. Rabe, *The Road to OPEC: United States Relations with Venezuela* (1982); William F. Sater, *Chile and the United States* (1990); Lars Schoultz, *National Security and United States Policy Toward Latin America* (1987). Books on Cuba and the missile crisis are cited in Chapter 29.

Central America and Panama

Cynthia J. Arnson, *Crossroads: Congress, the Reagan Administration, and Central America* (1989); Morris J. Blachman et al., eds., *Confronting Revolution* (1986); Raymond Bonner, *Weakness and Deceit: U.S. Policy and El Salvador* (1984); E. Bradford Burns, *At War in Nicaragua* (1987); Kenneth M. Coleman and George C. Herring, eds., *Understanding the Central American Crisis* (1991); Theodore Draper, *A Very Thin Line: The Iran-Contra Affairs* (1991); Roy Gutman, *Banana Diplomacy, 1981–1987* (1988) (on Nicaragua); J. Michael Hogan, *The Panama Canal in American Politics* (1986); Jane Hunter et al., *The Iran-Contra Connection* (1987); Stephen Kinzer, *Blood of Brothers* (1991) (on Nicaragua); Michael Klare and Peter Kornbluh, eds., *Low Intensity Warfare* (1988); Walter LaFeber, *The Panama Canal,* updated ed. (1989); Walter LaFeber, *Inevitable Revolutions* 2nd ed. rev. (1993); Anthony Lake, *Somoza Falling* (1989); Robert A. Pastor, *Condemned to Repetition: The United States and Nicaragua* (1987); Thomas W. Walker, ed., *Revolution and Counterrevolution in Nicaragua* (1991); Bob Woodward, *Veil: The Secret Wars of the CIA* (1987).

Middle East

James A. Bill, *The Eagle and the Lion* (1988) (Iran); William J. Burns, *Economic Aid and American Policy Toward Egypt, 1955–1981* (1985); Richard W. Cottam, *Iran and the United States* (1988); Mark Gasiorowski, *U.S. Foreign Policy and the Shah* (1991); Stephen Green, *Living by the Sword: America and Israel in the Middle East, 1968–87* (1988); Peter L. Hahn, *The United States, Great Britain, and Egypt, 1945–1956* (1991); Diane Kunz, *The Economic Diplomacy of the Suez Crisis* (1991); George Lenczowski, *The Middle East in World Affairs,* 4th ed. (1980); Aaron D. Miller, *Search for Security* (1980); Donald Neff, *Warriors at Suez* (1981); William B. Quandt, ed., *The Middle East Ten Years After Camp David* (1988); William B. Quandt, *Camp David* (1986); William B. Quandt, *Decade of Decision: American Policy Toward the Arab-Israeli Conflict, 1967–1976* (1977); Bernard Reich, *Quest for Peace* (1977) (Israel); Cheryl A. Rubenberg, *Israel and the American National Interest* (1986); Barry Rubin, *Paved with Good Intentions* (1980) (Iran); William Shawcross, *The Shah's Last Ride* (1988); Gary Sick, *October Surprise: America's Hostages in Iran and the Election of Ronald Reagan* (1991); Steven L. Spiegel, *The Other Arab-Israeli Conflict* (1985); William Stivers, *America's Confrontation with Revolutionary Change in the Middle East* (1986); Robert W. Stookey, *America and the Arab States* (1975); Daniel Yergin, *The Prize* (1991) (on oil).

Asia and Africa

Pauline H. Baker, *The United States and South Africa: The Reagan Years* (1989); H. W. Brands, *India and the United States* (1989); Christopher Coker, *The United States and South Africa, 1968–1985* (1986); Madeleine G. Kalb, *The Congo Cables* (1982); Stanley Karnow, *In Our Image* (1989) (on Philippines); Richard D. Mahoney, *JFK: Ordeal in Africa* (1983); Robert J. McMahon, *Colonialism and Cold War* (1981) (on Indonesia); Dennis Merrill, *Bread and the Ballot* (1990) (on India); Thomas J. Noer, *Cold War and Black Liberation* (1985).

32

Reform and Conflict: A Turbulent Era, 1961–1974

T HE FIRST DREADFUL FLASH from Dallas clattered over newsroom Teletype machines across the country at 1:34 p.m. Eastern Standard Time. Broadcast immediately on radio and television, the news was soon on the streets. People still remember precisely where they were and what they were doing when they heard that President John F. Kennedy had been assassinated. Time stopped for Americans, and they experienced what psychologists call flashbulb memory, the freeze-framing of an exceptionally emotional event down to the most incidental detail. For an earlier generation, the indelible memory was of December 7, 1941, when radio reports of the Japanese attack on Pearl Harbor stunned the nation into silence. Now it was November 22, 1963, the day John Kennedy's promise was snuffed out.

In New York City a driver stopped in the middle of a busy intersection and ran over to a sidewalk luncheonette. "Is it true?" he shouted. Without looking up, the counterman replied "Yes, he's dead." The man returned to his car and slumped over the wheel, oblivious to the impatient honking around him.

Ken Kesey's play *One Flew over the Cuckoo's Nest* had just opened on Broadway, and Kesey and a couple of friends were driving triumphantly back to the West Coast. They heard the news in Pennsylvania. As "we stopped in at service stations and Howard Johnson's and little fast-food places across the United States," Kesey later recalled, "a really profound thing happened to us. We felt like we were seeing the real soul of America with its shirt torn open in grief."

For four days Americans wept, prayed, and gazed at their television sets, numbed by the unbelievable. Throughout the afternoon and night before the funeral, 250,000 people trod silently past the president's coffin in the Capitol Rotunda. Jacqueline Kennedy and her daughter Caroline paid a last visit to pray and kiss the coffin. The next day a million people lined the streets of Washington and millions more watched on television as the president's body was borne by horse-drawn caisson to Arlington Cemetery.

Much of America's postwar confidence was riding on the caisson that carried Kennedy's body to the grave. "In retrospect," the journalist Godfrey Hodgson has written, "people looked back to Friday, November 22, 1963, as the end of a time of hope, the beginning of a time of troubles." The irony in America's outpouring of grief was that the Kennedy administration had

For this young African-American marcher in Selma, Alabama, in 1965, the goal of civil-rights protest was first-class citizenship through the vote.

failed to achieve many of its goals. In the final months of his presidency Kennedy had been criticized for being ineffectual in domestic affairs and reckless in foreign affairs. Nevertheless John Kennedy's assassination was a national tragedy. Grieving Americans remembered instead how handsome and eloquent he had been and how he had inspired them to hope for peace, prosperity, and social justice.

Hope had run especially high among the nation's poor. Kennedy's presidency coincided with and was energized by the modern African-American civil rights movement. His call for a New Frontier had inspired liberal Democrats, idealists, and brave young activists to work to eliminate poverty, segregation, and voting rights abuses. Americans also supported Kennedy's desire to court the Third World and prevail in the Cold War.

Lyndon Johnson, Kennedy's successor in the White House, presided over what he called the Great Society, an effort to eradicate deprivation in the United States and guarantee equal rights to all its citizens. Congress responded to Johnson's urgings with a flood of legislation. The 1960s witnessed more economic, political, and social reform than any period since the New Deal, including civil rights legislation, the War on Poverty, and Medicare. But even during these years of liberal triumph, anger and social tension intermittently flared into violence. Beginning with Kennedy's assassination in 1963, ten years of bloodshed—race riots, the murders of other political and civil rights leaders, and the war in Vietnam—shattered the optimism of the Kennedy and Johnson eras.

Many urban blacks were angry that poverty and segregation persisted despite the civil rights movement and the passage of landmark civil rights laws. Their discontent exploded during the 1960s' "long hot summers." This social turbulence, in conjunction with the growing movement opposing the Vietnam War, brought down the presidency of Lyndon Johnson. It also gave rise to the Black Power movement, the radical politics of the New Left, and a revived women's movement, as well as the "hippie" counterculture. The New Left and the counterculture first appeared in the early 1960s in Ann Arbor, Berkeley, and other university towns. By 1970, antiwar protests and alternative lifestyles based on drugs, rock music, and freely expressed sexuality had taken root in nearly every college community in the country.

Lyndon Johnson's departure from office did not produce calm. Richard Nixon, elected president in 1968, polarized the nation still further. The presidencies of Nixon's two immediate predecessors had ended tragically: Dallas and Vietnam were the sites of their undoings. A third location, the Watergate apartment complex in Washington, D.C., would prove to be Richard Nixon's downfall. In 1974 he resigned from office, the only American president to do so. Battered by over a decade of turmoil, many Americans ceased to believe in any version of the American Dream.

THE CIVIL RIGHTS MOVEMENT AND KENNEDY'S NEW FRONTIER

President John F. Kennedy was, as Norman Mailer wrote, "our leading man." Young, handsome, and vigorous, the new chief executive was the first president born in the twentieth century. Perceived by the public as an intellectual, he had a genuinely inquiring mind, and as a patron of the arts he brought wit and sophistication to the White House. Kennedy was born to wealth and politics: his Irish-American grandfather had been mayor of Boston, and his millionaire father, Joseph P. Kennedy, had served as ambassador to Great Britain. In 1946 the young Kennedy, having returned from the Second World War a hero, perpetuated the family tradition by campaigning to represent a Boston seat in the House of Representatives. He won easily.

As a Democrat, Kennedy inherited the New Deal commitment to America's social-welfare system. He generally cast liberal votes in line with the prolabor sentiments of his low-income, blue-collar constituents. But he avoided controversial issues such as civil rights and the censure of Joseph McCarthy, and he opposed liberal programs that were of no direct concern to his district—flood control, farm price supports, the Tennessee Valley Authority.

Kennedy won a Pulitzer Prize for *Profiles in Courage* (1956), a study of politicians who had acted on principle, but he shaded the truth when he claimed sole authorship of the book, which had been written largely by his staff. As one critic put

1960 Sit-ins begin at Greensboro, North Carolina
Birth control pill approved for use
John F. Kennedy elected president

1961 Freedom Rides protest segregation in transportation
First President's Commission on the Status of Women established

1962 John Glenn orbits the globe in space capsule
SDS makes Port Huron Statement
James Meredith enters University of Mississippi
Baker v. *Carr* establishes "one person, one vote" principle

1963 Friedan's *The Feminine Mystique* published
Civil rights advocates march on Washington
Birmingham, Alabama, Baptist church bombed
Kennedy assassinated; Lyndon B. Johnson assumes the presidency

1964 Beatles arrive in America
Economic Opportunity Act allocates funds to fight poverty
Civil Rights Act outlaws discrimination in jobs and public accommodations
Riots break out in first of the "long hot summers"
Free Speech Movement begins at Berkeley
Johnson elected president

1965 Malcolm X assassinated
Voting Rights Act allows federal supervision of voting registration
Medicare program established
Elementary and Secondary Education Act provides federal aid to education
Watts race riot leaves thirty-four dead

1966 National Organization for Women (NOW) founded
Miranda v. *Arizona* requires police to inform suspects of their rights

1967 Race riots erupt in Newark, Detroit, and other cities

1968 U.S.S. *Pueblo* captured by North Korea
Tet offensive causes fear of losing Vietnam War
Martin Luther King, Jr., assassinated
African-Americans riot in 168 cities and towns

Civil Rights Act bans discrimination in housing
Antiwar protests escalate
Robert F. Kennedy assassinated
Violence erupts at Democratic convention
Richard M. Nixon elected president

1969 Stonewall riot sparked by police harassment of homosexuals
400,000 gather at Woodstock festival
Moratorium Day calls for end to Vietnam War

1970 United States invades Cambodia
Students killed at Kent State and Jackson State universities
First Earth Day celebrated

1971 *Pentagon Papers* published
Twenty-sixth Amendment extends vote to eighteen-year-olds
Inmates revolt at Attica prison
Swann v. *Charlotte-Mecklenberg* upholds North Carolina desegregation plan

1972 Nixon visits China and Soviet Union
Equal Rights Amendment (ERA) approved by Congress
George Wallace shot and paralyzed
"Plumbers" break into Watergate
Revenue sharing distributes funds to states
Nixon re-elected

1973 Watergate burglars tried
Senator Sam Ervin chairs Watergate hearings
White House aides Ehrlichman and Haldeman resign
Roe v. *Wade* legalizes abortion
War Powers Act passed
Agnew resigns; Nixon appoints Ford vice president
Saturday Night Massacre provokes public outcry

1974 Supreme Court orders Nixon to release White House tapes
House Judiciary Committee votes to impeach Nixon
Nixon resigns; Ford becomes president
Nelson Rockefeller appointed vice president
Ford pardons Nixon

President John F. Kennedy, his wife Jacqueline, and their two young children John Jr. and Caroline, symbolized youthful energy and idealism. This photograph was taken at their vacation home at Hyannisport on Cape Cod in July 1963.   John F. Kennedy Presidential Library.

it, he himself showed "too much profile and not enough courage." Kennedy nevertheless enjoyed an enthusiastic following, especially after his landslide re-election to the Senate in 1958.

Although his margin of victory in the 1960 presidential election was razor-slim, Kennedy's vitality and style captured the imagination of many

"The Best and the Brightest"
——

Americans. In a departure from the Eisenhower administration's staid, conservative image, the new president surrounded himself with young men of intellectual verve who proclaimed that they had fresh ideas for invigorating the nation; the writer David Halberstam called them "the best and the brightest." (Kennedy appointed only one woman to a significant position; see page 1010.) Secretary of Defense Robert McNamara, age forty-four, had been an assistant professor at Harvard at twenty-four and later the whiz-kid president of the Ford Motor Company. Kennedy's special assistant for national security affairs, McGeorge Bundy, age forty-one, had become a Harvard dean at thirty-four with only a bachelor's degree. Kennedy himself was only forty-three, and his brother Robert, the attorney general, was thirty-five.

Kennedy's ambitious program, the New Frontier, promised more than Kennedy could deliver: an end to racial discrimination, federal aid to education, medical care for the elderly, and government action to halt the recession the country was suffering. Only eight months into his first year, it was evident that Kennedy lacked the ability to move Congress, which was dominated by a conservative coalition of Republicans and southern Democrats. Long-time members of Congress saw him and his administration as publicity hungry. Some feared the president would seek federal aid to parochial schools. The result was the defeat of federal aid to education and of a Kennedy-sponsored boost in the minimum wage.

Still struggling to appease conservative members of Congress, the new president pursued civil rights with a notable lack of vigor. Kennedy did establish the President's Committee on Equal Employment Opportunity to eliminate racial discrimination in government hiring. But he waited until late 1962 before honoring a 1960 campaign pledge to issue an executive order forbidding segregation in federally subsidized housing. Meanwhile he appointed five die-hard segregationists to the federal bench in the Deep South. The struggle for racial equality was the most important domestic issue of the time, and Kennedy's performance disheartened civil rights advocates.

Despite the White House's lack of commitment, African-American civil rights activists continued their struggle through the tactic of nonviolent civil disobedience.

The Civil Rights Movement
——

Volunteers organized by the Southern Christian Leadership Conference (SCLC), headed by the Reverend Martin Luther King, Jr., deliberately violated segregation laws by sitting in at whites-only lunch counters, libraries, and bus stations in the South. When arrested they went to jail as an act of conscience. Meanwhile the Congress of Racial Equality (CORE), originally organized in 1942, initiated the first Freedom Ride: in May 1961, an integrated group of thirteen people boarded a bus in Washington, D.C., and traveled into the South, where they braved attacks by white mobs for daring to desegregate interstate transportation. Unprotected by either federal or state authorities, the Freedom Riders were savagely beaten and their bus was burned outside of Anniston, Alabama. Six

A historic moment for the civil rights movement was the March on Washington of August 28, 1963. One-quarter million black people and white people stood together for racial equality. Waving to friends, the Reverend Martin Luther King, Jr., is about to begin delivering his "I Have a Dream" speech.   Francis Miller, *Life* magazine © 1963 Time, Inc.

days later, a second bus bearing Freedom Riders reached Montgomery, and again white vigilantes brutally attacked them.

Meanwhile, black high-school and college students in the South were banding together to organize the Student Non-Violent Coordinating Committee (SNCC). It was these young people who walked the dusty back roads of Mississippi and Georgia, encouraging African-Americans to resist segregation and register to vote. Some SNCC volunteers were white, and some were from the North, but most were black southerners and many were from low-income families. These volunteers understood from experience how racism, powerlessness, and poverty intersected in the lives of African-Americans.

As the civil rights movement gained momentum, President Kennedy gradually made a commitment to first-class citizenship for blacks. In 1962 he ordered U.S. marshals to protect James Meredith, the first African-American student to attend the University of Mississippi. A rioting mob confronted Meredith and his guards, who responded

with tear gas. In a single night of violence, 160 marshals were wounded—28 by gunfire—and two bystanders were killed by stray bullets. The next morning, President Kennedy ordered the first of 5,000 army troops onto the campus. Under court order the following spring, federal officials ignored the defiant governor of Alabama, George C. Wallace, and forced desegregation of the University of Alabama.

In mid-June 1963 Kennedy finally requested legislation to outlaw segregation in public accommodations. When more than 250,000 people, black and white, gathered at the Lincoln Memorial for a March on Washington that August, they did so with the knowledge that President Kennedy was at last on their side. "I have a dream," the civil rights movement's inspirational leader, Martin Luther King, Jr., told the crowd, "that my four little children will one day live in a nation where they will not be judged by the color of their skin but by the content of their character."

"I Have a Dream"

Meanwhile, television news programs brought the civil rights struggles into Americans' homes. The story was sometimes grisly. In 1963 Medgar Evers, director of the NAACP in Mississippi, was murdered in his own driveway. The same year police in Birmingham, Alabama, under the command of Sheriff "Bull" Connor attacked nonviolent civil rights demonstrators, including many children, with snarling dogs, fire hoses, and cattle prods. Then, while Kennedy's public accommodations bill was being held up by a southern filibuster in the Senate, two horrifying events helped to convince reluctant politicians that action on civil rights was long overdue. In September white terrorists exploded a bomb during Sunday-morning services at Birmingham's Sixteenth Street Baptist Church. Sunday school was in session, and four black girls were killed. A little more than two months later, John Kennedy was assassinated in Dallas. If ever the civil rights movement had the moral support of most of the American people, it was at this time of national tragedy and repugnance over violence.

Kennedy's murder still baffles many Americans. Was the accused assassin, Lee Harvey Oswald, acting alone or as part of a conspiracy? Was he the only gunman? What was his motive? Whatever the answers, Kennedy's death traumatized the entire nation. Then, two days later, in full view of millions of TV viewers, Oswald himself was shot dead by a nightclub owner and small-time Mafia figure named Jack Ruby. The same question was asked again: what was Ruby's motive? Was he silencing Oswald to prevent him from implicating others?

Who Killed President Kennedy?

Historians have wondered what John Kennedy would have accomplished had he lived. Although his legislative achievements were meager, he inspired genuine idealism in Americans. When Kennedy exhorted Americans in his inaugural address to "Ask not what your country can do for you. Ask what you can do for your country," tens of thousands volunteered to spend two years of their lives in the Peace Corps. "We had such faith in what Kennedy was doing," recalled one volunteer, "and we all wanted to be a part of it."

Kennedy also promoted a sense of national purpose through his vigorous support of the space program. America clearly lagged behind the Soviet Union, which sent a missile carrying cosmonaut Yuri Gagarin into orbit around the earth in April 1961. But Americans celebrated a month later when Alan Shephard, one of the seven original astronauts, rode the *Mercury 3* missile into space. After Marine Lieutenant Colonel John Glenn orbited the globe in a space capsule in February 1962, the United States accelerated its *Apollo* program, which developed more powerful rocket boosters and lunar landing vehicles for the first astronauts to set foot on the moon. And Americans embraced Kennedy's challenge to put a man on the moon before the Soviets did and by the end of the decade.

In recent years, writers have drawn attention to Kennedy's recklessness in world events, such as authorizing CIA attempts to assassinate Cuba's Premier Fidel Castro. They have also criticized his timidity in civil rights, and have pointed to his extramarital sex life as evidence of a serious character flaw. It is clear, however, that Kennedy had begun to grow as president during his last few months in office. He made a moving appeal for racial equality and called for reductions in Cold War tensions. And then there was the Kennedy aura. James Reston of the *New York Times* called Kennedy "a story-book president," handsome, graceful, "with poetry on his tongue and a radiant young woman at his side." Jacqueline Kennedy said after her husband's death that for her the Kennedy era had evoked the legendary kingdom of Camelot. Partly because of this aura of glamour and youth and hope, John Kennedy acquired a loftier reputation in death than he had enjoyed in life. And in a peculiar way he accomplished more in death than in life. In the post-assassination atmosphere of grief and remorse, Lyndon Johnson pushed through Congress practically the entire New Frontier agenda. Johnson accomplished, Walter Lippmann wrote, "what President Kennedy could not have done had he lived."

Kennedy in Retrospect

THE GREAT SOCIETY AND THE TRIUMPH OF LIBERALISM

The new president was a big man and a passionate one. As Senate majority leader from 1954 to 1960, Lyndon Johnson had learned how to manipulate people and power to achieve his ends. "This pon-

Surrounded by an illustrious group of civil rights leaders and members of Congress, President Lyndon B. Johnson signs the Civil Rights Act of 1964. Standing behind the president is the Reverend Martin Luther King, Jr.   Cecil Stoughton, Lyndon Baines Johnson Library.

derous . . . Texan knows more about the sources of power in the political world of Washington than any president in this century," wrote columnists Rowland Evans and Robert Novak. "He can be gentle and solicitous as a nurse, but as ruthless and deceptive as a riverboat gambler." In the aftermath of the assassination, Johnson resolved to unite the country behind the unfulfilled legislative program of the martyred president. More than that, he wanted to realize Roosevelt's and Truman's unmet goals. He called his new program the Great Society.

Johnson made civil rights his top legislative priority. "No memorial oration or eulogy," he told a joint session of Congress five days after the assassination, "could more elo-

Civil Rights Act of 1964

quently honor President Kennedy's memory than the earliest passage of the civil rights bill."

It was fortunate for the civil rights movement that Johnson, a southerner, had become president. According to Clarence Mitchell,

chief lobbyist for the NAACP, Johnson "made a greater contribution to giving a dignified and hopeful status to Negroes in the United States than any other president, including Lincoln, Roosevelt and Kennedy." Within months Johnson had signed into law the Civil Rights Act of 1964, which outlawed discrimination on the basis of race, color, religion, sex, or national origin, not only in public accommodations but also in employment. An Equal Employment Opportunity Commission was established the same year to investigate and judge complaints of job discrimination. The act also authorized the government to withhold funds from public agencies that discriminated on the basis of race, and it empowered the attorney general to guarantee voting rights and end school segregation.

Johnson enunciated another priority in his first State of the Union address: "The administration today, here and now, declares unconditional war on poverty." Eight months later, he signed into law the Economic Opportunity Act of 1964, which allocated almost $1 billion to fight poverty. The

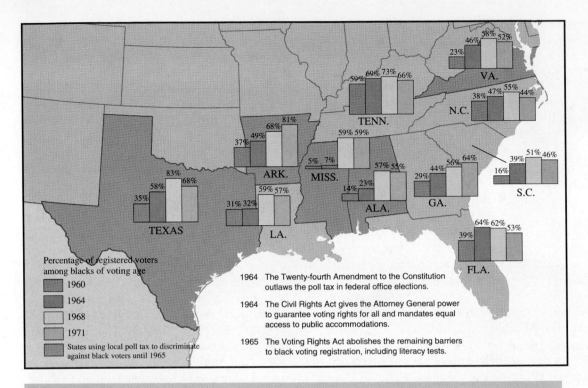

African-American Voting Rights, 1960–1971 Note the impact of the 1965 Voting Rights Act on African-American registration, which skyrocketed in Mississippi and Alabama and rose substantially in other southern states. Source: Harold W. Stanley, *Voter Mobilization and the Politics of Race: The South and Universal Suffrage, 1952–1984* (Praeger Publishers, an imprint of Greenwood Publishing Group, Westport, CT, 1987), p. 97. Copyright © 1987 by Harold W. Stanley. Used with permission.

act, which became the opening salvo in Johnson's War on Poverty, promised to eliminate poverty "by opening to everyone the opportunity to live in decency and dignity."

In the year following Kennedy's death, Johnson sought to govern by consensus, appealing to the shared values and aspirations of the majority of the nation for continued economic growth and social justice. Judging by his lopsided victory over his Republican opponent in 1964, Senator Barry Goldwater of Arizona, he succeeded. Johnson garnered 61 percent of the popular vote and the electoral votes of all but six states. Goldwater's narrowness certainly enhanced Johnson's appeal: the Republican candidate alienated voters by suggesting that Social Security be made voluntary and the Tennessee Valley Authority be abolished, and he appeared reckless and provocative when he ad-

Election of 1964

vocated using nuclear weapons in Vietnam. He also voted against the civil rights bill in 1964. Republican leaders from the moderate eastern wing of the party either refused to support Goldwater or gave him half-hearted endorsements. His support was solid in only a few states in the Southwest and South.

Riding on Johnson's coattails, the Democrats won large majorities in both the House (295 to 140) and the Senate (68 to 32). Johnson recognized that the opportunity to push through further reform had arrived. "Hurry, boys, hurry," he told his staff just after the election. "Get that legislation up to the Hill and out. Eighteen months from now ol' Landslide Lyndon will be Lame-Duck Lyndon." Congress responded in 1965 and 1966 with the most sweeping reform legislation since 1935. Skillfully guided by Johnson, the liberal Democratic majorities passed a remarkable 69 percent of the president's legislative proposals. The powerful conservative coalition of Republicans and southern Democrats, which had had its way on 74 percent of House roll-call votes in 1961 and 63 percent in 1963, was victorious on only 25 percent of the votes in 1965.

Three bills enacted in 1965 were legislative milestones: the Medicare program insured the elderly against medical and hospital bills; the Elementary and Secondary Education Act provided for general federal aid to education for the first time; and the Voting Rights Act of 1965 empowered the attorney general to supervise voter registration in areas where fewer than half the minority residents of voting age were registered (see map). In 1960 only 29 percent of the South's African-American population was registered to vote; when Johnson left office in 1969, the proportion was approaching two-thirds. Even in Mississippi, one of the most resistant states, black registration figures grew from 7 percent in 1964 to 60 percent in 1968.

Voting Rights Act of 1965

The flurry of legislation during Johnson's presidency was staggering: establishment of the Department of Housing and Urban Development and the National Endowments for the Arts and Humanities; water- and air-quality improvement acts; liberalization of immigration laws; and appropriations for the most ambitious federal housing program since 1949, including rent supplements to low-income families. In 1968 Johnson signed his third civil rights act, banning racial and religious discrimination in the sale and rental of housing. Another provision of this legislation, known as the Indian Bill of Rights, extended those constitutional protections to Native Americans living under tribal self-government on reservations.

By far the most ambitious of Johnson's initiatives was the War on Poverty. Because the gross national product (GNP) had increased in the mid-1960s, Johnson and his advisers reasoned that the government could expect a "fiscal dividend" of several billion dollars in additional tax revenues. They decided to spend the extra money to wipe out poverty through education and job-training programs. Beginning with the $1 billion appropriation in 1964, the War on Poverty evolved in 1965 and 1966 to include the Job Corps, a program to provide marketable skills, work experience, remedial education, and counseling for young people; Project Head Start, to prepare low-income preschoolers for grade school; and Upward Bound, for high-school students from low-income families who aspired to a college education. Other antipoverty programs were Legal Services for the Poor; Volunteers in Service to

War on Poverty

One of several programs established by the 1964 Economic Opportunity Act, VISTA (Volunteers in Service to America) helped poor people to help themselves. In promoting self-help, VISTA workers lived and worked on reservations, in barrios, and among the homeless. Some worked as advocates for migratory farm families. This VISTA volunteer, JoAnne Eggers, helps two migrant workers in Medford, Oregon. Paul Conklin.

Great Society Achievements

	1964	1965	1966	1968

CivilRights	Civil Rights Act
	Equal Employment
	   Opportunity
	   Commission
	24th Amendment
		Voting Rights Act		Civil Rights Act

War on Poverty	Economic
	   Opportunity Act
	Office of Economic
	   Opportunity
	Job Corps
	VISTA
			Model Cities	

Education		Elementary and
		   Secondary
		   Education Act
		Higher Education
		   Act
		Head Start
		Upward Bound		

Environment		Water Quality Act Air Quality Act	Clean Water Restoration Act	

New Government Agencies		Department of
		   Housing and
		   Urban Develop-
		   ment (HUD)
		National Endow-
		   ments for the
		   Arts and
		   Humanities
		   (NEA and NEH)
			Department of
			   Transportation	

Miscellaneous		Medicare Immigration Act		

The Great Society of the 1960s saw the biggest burst of reform legislation since the New Deal of the 1930s.

America (VISTA), a domestic Peace Corps to help the needy at home; and the Model Cities program, which channeled federal funds to upgrade employment, housing, education, and health in targeted neighborhoods.

The War on Poverty was a mixed success. For one thing, it was politically volatile because its "community-action programs" angered power-hungry mayors. It deliberately circumvented them and encouraged "maximum feasible participation" in decision making on the part of the poor, who served on antipoverty governing boards that allo-cated large sums of money. Furthermore, confusion abounded in the ambitious program. Not even R. Sargent Shriver, who administered the War on Poverty as head of the Office of Economic Opportunity (OEO), could deny this: "It's like we . . . launched a half-dozen rockets at once," he later conceded. Another failing was that the War on Poverty did little to reduce rural poverty or to discourage the South-to-North migration that worsened already overwhelming northern urban problems. "A good many of the urban poverty thinkers have written off the rural areas," noted

Poverty in America for Whites, African Americans, and All Races, 1959–1974

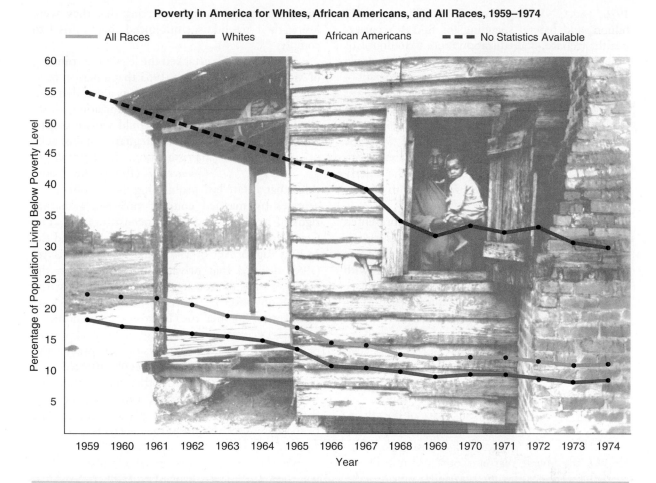

Poverty in America for Whites, Blacks, and All Races, 1959–1974 *Because of rising levels of economic prosperity, combined with the Great Society, the percentage of Americans living in poverty in 1974 was half that of 1959. African-Americans were still far more likely to be poor than white Americans. In 1959, more than half of all blacks (55.1 percent) were poor; in 1974, the figure remained high (30.3 percent). (The government did not record data on African-American poverty for the years 1960–1965.)*

James Sundquist of the Brookings Institution, "and have concluded that the only way to deal with rural poverty is to let the people move and then handle them in the cities."

Another large group that remained poor despite antipoverty initiatives consisted of women and children living in female-headed families, and they constituted 40 percent of the poor in the United States. The economic boom that lasted from 1963 to 1969 lifted 12 million people in male-headed families out of poverty. Left stranded in poverty were 11 million in families headed by women (the same number as in 1963), who earned pitiful wages and frequently did not receive child-support payments from ex-husbands.

Even so, in tandem with a rising GNP, the War on Poverty substantially alleviated hunger and suffering in the United States. Its legislation directly addressed the debilitating housing, health, and nutritional deficiencies from which the poor suffered. Also, the tax cut and fresh infusions of federal funds for defense fueled the economy, and beginning in the mid-1960s the social welfare budget soared. Between 1965 and

Successes in Reducing Poverty

1970, the GNP leapt from $685 billion to $977 billion, and federal spending for Social Security, health, welfare, and education more than doubled. Not only did some of this prosperity trickle down to the poor, but also—and more important— millions of new jobs were created. The result was a startling reduction in the number of poor people, from 25 percent of the population in 1962 to 11 percent in 1973. Particularly fortunate were the elderly, who benefited from large increases in Social Security benefits; poverty among the elderly dropped from about 40 percent in 1960 to 16 percent in 1974.

The period of liberal ascendancy represented by the War on Poverty was short-lived; its legislative achievements were limited to the years between from 1964 and 1966. Disillusioned with America's deepening involvement in Vietnam (see Chapter 31), many of Johnson's allies began to reject both him and his liberal consensus.

But one branch of government maintained the liberal tradition—the Supreme Court. In the volatile 1960s, the Court was disposed by political conviction and a belief in judicial activism to play a central role in the resurgence of liberalism. After the 1954 and 1955 school desegregation cases (see Chapter 28), the liberal Warren Court did not disturb the political waters for the remainder of the 1950s. The next decade was to be strikingly different. According to one constitutional historian, the United States "changed irrevocably in the 1960s," and the Warren Court was "midwife to that change—if not its sire." The intellectual and moral anchor of the Court was Chief Justice Earl Warren.

The Warren Court

The Court began handing down a series of important liberal decisions in 1962. *Baker* v. *Carr* (1962) and subsequent rulings established that the principle of "one person, one vote" must prevail at both the state and national levels. This decision required the reapportionment of state legislatures so that each representative would serve the same number of constituents. Previously, some legislators from sparsely settled rural areas represented only half as many people as their counterparts from populous urban areas. The Court also outlawed required prayers and Bible reading in public schools, explaining that such practices imposed an "indirect coercive pressure upon religious minorities." Some religious groups denounced these decisions, and a few towns, asserting that they were losing their freedoms, announced their refusal to comply.

The Court also attacked the legal underpinning of McCarthyism, ruling in 1965 that a person need not register with the government as a member of a subversive organization, since doing so would violate constitutional safeguards against self-incrimination. In *Griswold* v. *Connecticut* (1965), the Court ruled that a state law prohibiting the use of contraceptives by married couples violated "a marital right of privacy" and was unconstitutional. The Court upheld the Civil Rights Act of 1964 and the Voting Rights Act of 1965, and in *Jones* v. *Mayer* (1968) decided that private discrimination in the rental or sale of housing was prohibited by the Civil Rights Act of 1866. In ruling the 1866 act constitutional under the Thirteenth Amendment, the Court opened new avenues for the legal pursuit of equal rights. With its decisions on prayer and contraception, the Court had deeply affected people's personal lives. And in other rulings that particularly upset conservatives, the Court decreed that books, magazines, and films could not be banned as obscene unless they were found to be "utterly without redeeming social value."

Civil Rights Rulings

Perhaps most controversial of all, however, was the Court's transformation of the criminal justice system. Beginning with *Gideon* v. *Wainwright* (1963), the Court ruled that a poor person charged with a felony had the right to a state-appointed lawyer. In *Escobedo* v. *Illinois* (1964), it decreed that the accused had a right to counsel during interrogation and a right to remain silent. *Miranda* v. *Arizona* (1966) established that police had to inform criminal suspects that they had these rights and that any statements they made could be used against them. Critics denounced the decisions as victories for criminals, and the right-wing John Birch Society began a campaign to impeach Earl Warren.

Despite conservatives' demands for Warren's removal, constitutional historians consider him one of the two most influential chief justices in the nation's history. (The other was John Marshall.) Whether or not one approves of the decisions of the Warren Court (which ended with Warren's retirement in 1969), its impact on the American people is undeniable. Bernard Schwartz, a constitutional-law scholar, has made this appraisal: "In expanding civil liberties, broadening political freedom, extending the franchise, reinforcing freedoms of speech, assembly, and religion, limiting the power of the politicians in smoke-filled rooms, [and] defining the limits of police power, the Warren Court had no equal in American history."

CIVIL RIGHTS, RACE RIOTS, AND BLACK POWER

Even while the civil rights movement was winning legal and constitutional victories, some activists began to grumble that the federal government was not to be trusted. During the Mississippi Summer Project of 1964, hundreds of college-age volunteers from the North had joined SNCC and CORE field workers to establish "freedom schools," which taught African-American children their own history. Many of these volunteers believed that the Federal Bureau of Investigation was hostile to the civil rights movement. FBI Director J. Edgar Hoover was a racist, they charged, and they were disturbed by rumors (later confirmed) that Hoover had wiretapped and bugged Martin Luther King, Jr.'s hotel rooms and planted allegations in the newspapers about his sexual improprieties. Why, activists asked themselves, had Johnson allowed Hoover to remain in office?

Indeed, some FBI informants were not only members of the Ku Klux Klan but were even terrorists who instigated violence against civil rights volunteers. One informant had

Violent Attacks on Civil Rights Workers

organized several atrocities, including the bombing of Birmingham's Sixteenth Street Baptist Church in 1963. Small wonder that during the summer of 1964 there was an upsurge in racist violence in the South, particularly in Mississippi. White vigilantes bombed and burned two dozen black churches there, and three civil rights workers were murdered by a group that included sheriff's deputies in Philadelphia, Mississippi.

Amid the terror, SNCC volunteers joined with black activist Mississippians to establish the Mississippi Freedom Democratic party (MFDP), which sent an opposition delegation to the Democratic national convention. Arguing that the MFDP supported civil rights while the state's regular Democratic organization was vehemently segregationist, the MFDP demanded that the convention honor its credentials. Fannie Lou Hamer, a sharecropper and a leader of the MFDP, addressed the delegates and described her efforts to vote. "I was beaten until I was exhausted. I began to scream, and one white man . . . began to beat me on the head. . . . All of this on account we wanted to register, to become first-class citizens." If the MFDP were not seated, Hamer said, "I question America." But President Johnson, unwilling to alienate southern white politicians, resisted efforts to seat the delegation; he thus threw into question the Democratic commitment to racial equality. Despite Johnson's capitulation to Mississippi's regular Democratic party, the state's whites voted for Goldwater in 1964.

The year 1964 also witnessed the first of the "long hot summers" of race riots in northern cities. In Harlem and Rochester in New York, and in

Explosion of Black Anger

several cities in New Jersey, brutal actions by white police officers, including vicious unprovoked beatings in police stations, sparked riots in black neighborhoods. African-Americans deeply resented the unnecessary force that police sometimes used. As the black writer James Baldwin put it, the white officers patrolling black neighborhoods represented "the force of the white world."

Whites wondered why African-Americans were venting their frustration violently at a time when real progress was being made in the civil rights struggle. But the civil rights movement had been largely southern in focus, geared to abolishing Jim Crow and black disfranchisement. In the North, though African-Americans could vote, many were still living in deep poverty. The median income of blacks was little more than half that of whites: for every dollar the average white worker took home in 1964, the black worker earned 54 cents. Black unemployment in the mid-1960s was twice that of whites, and for black males between eighteen and twenty-five it was five times as high.

Many African-American families lived in perpetual poverty, particularly those headed by women, and their numbers were increasing rapidly. One reason was that eligibility for Aid to Families with Dependent Children (AFDC)—part of the 1935

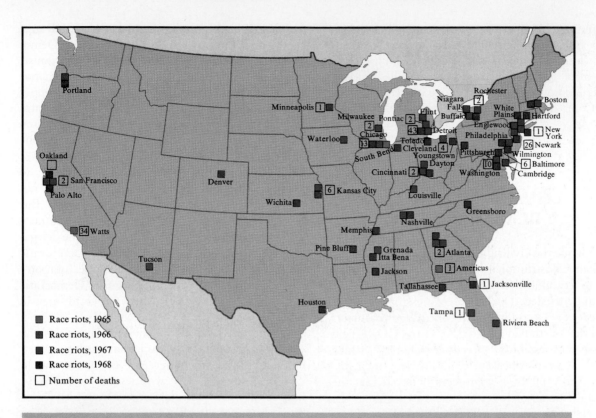

Race Riots, 1965–1968   *The first major race riot of the 1960s exploded in the Los Angeles neighborhood of Watts in 1965. The bloodiest riots of 1967 were in Newark, New Jersey, and Detroit; and scores of riots erupted in the aftermath of the Reverend Martin Luther King, Jr.'s assassination in 1968.*

Social Security Act, expanded in 1950 to provide payments to mothers as well as their dependent children—was withdrawn if there was an able-bodied man in the household. As a result, some unemployed men left home rather than make their families ineligible for AFDC. Furthermore, the payments themselves were inadequate to cover a family's rent, utilities, and household expenses, let alone its food. In 1970 it was estimated that more than 60 percent of African-American children were being raised in poverty.

Northern blacks, surveying the economic and civil rights gains of the 1960s, wondered when they, too, would benefit from the Great Society. Concentrated in the inner cities, they looked around the ghettos in which they lived and knew their circumstances were deteriorating. Their neighborhoods were more segregated than ever; in increasing numbers during the 1960s, whites had

responded to the continuing black migration from the South by fleeing to the suburbs. And as inner-city neighborhoods became all black, so did the neighborhood schools. "It doesn't cost anything to move a few feet along a hamburger counter to make room for a Negro," one writer observed. "But the cost—economic, social, psychological—of abolishing forever a Negro ghetto of half a million souls is only now becoming apparent."

If 1964 was fiery and violent, 1965 was even more so. In August, police brutality sparked rioting in the Los Angeles ghetto of Watts; thirty-four people were killed (see map).

The Watts Race Riot   Unlike earlier race riots in 1919 and 1943, white mobs did not initiate the violence; instead, blacks exploded in anger over their joblessness and lack of opportunity, as well as police brutality. They looted white-owned

Malcolm X, as chief spokesperson for the Black Muslims, espoused African-American pride and separatism from white society. After a pilgrimage to Mecca in 1964, Malcolm X softened his hostility to the white race. Here he is pictured in Egypt, on his way to Mecca. John Launois/Black Star.

stores, set fires, and threw rocks at police and fire fighters. "Get whitey!" they screamed. "Burn, baby, burn!"

Other cities exploded in riots between 1966 and 1968. In July 1967 twenty-six people were killed in street battles between blacks and police and army troops in Newark, New Jersey. A week later a race riot in Detroit led to the deaths of forty-three people. In 1968 the National Advisory Commission on Civil Disorders, chaired by Governor Otto Kerner of Illinois, released its report blaming white racism for the riots: "The nation is rapidly moving toward two increasingly separate Americas . . . a white society principally located in suburbs . . . and a Negro society largely concentrated within large central cities."

Clearly, many blacks, especially in the North, were beginning to question whether the nonviolent civil rights movement was serving their needs. In 1963 Martin Luther King, Jr., had appealed to whites' humanitarian instincts in his "I have a dream" speech. Now another voice was beginning to be heard, one that urged blacks to seize their freedom "by any means necessary." It was the voice of Malcolm X, a one-time pimp and street

hustler who had converted while in prison to the Nation of Islam faith, commonly known as the Black Muslims.

The Black Muslims, a small sect that espoused black pride and separatism from white society, condemned "the white devil" as the chief source of evil in the world. They dissoci-

Malcolm X

ated themselves from white society and exhorted blacks to lead sober lives and practice thrift. Unlike King, they sanctioned violence in self-defense. By the early 1960s Malcolm X had become the Black Muslims' chief spokesperson, and his advice was straightforward: "If someone puts a hand on you, send him to the cemetery."

Malcolm X was murdered in a hail of bullets in Harlem's Audubon Ballroom in early 1965; his assassins were Black Muslims who believed he had betrayed their cause. In fact, he had modified some of his positions just before his death. He had met whites who were not devils, he said, and he had expressed cautious support for the nonviolent civil rights movement. Still, for both blacks and whites, Malcolm X symbolized black defiance and self-respect. A compelling figure in life, in death he would become a hero to increasing numbers of black nationalists and proponents of Black Power.

Although Reverend King continued to be the most admired civil rights leader, many younger blacks questioned not only his tactic of nonviolence but also his dream of racial integration. In 1966 Stokely Carmichael, the intense and articulate chairman of SNCC, called on African-Americans to assert Black Power. To be truly free from white oppression, Carmichael believed, blacks had to control their own institutions. They had to elect black candidates and organize their own schools. Several influential organizations that had previously been committed to racial integration and nonviolence embraced Black Power. SNCC in 1966 and CORE in 1967 purged their white members and repudiated integration, arguing that black people needed power, not white friendship.

Black Power

The wellspring of this new militance was black nationalism, the concept that black peoples everywhere in the world share a unique history and cultural heritage that sets them apart from whites. College students pressed for black-studies programs, and activists adopted the terms *black* and *Afro-American* in preference to *Negro*. Once again, as in the 1920s, African-Americans saw themselves as a nation within a nation.

To white America, one of the most fearsome of the new groups was the Black Panther Party. Blending black nationalism and revolutionary Communism, the Panthers dedicated themselves to destroying both capitalism and "the military arm of our oppressors," the police in the ghettos. The Panthers defied authority. They wore leather jackets and carried rifles in homage to Mao Zedong's revolutionary slogan: "Power flows from the barrel of a gun." But they also instituted free breakfast and health-care programs for ghetto children, taught courses in African-American history, and demanded job opportunities for the unemployed and decent housing for the poor. What particularly worried white parents was that some of their own children agreed with the Panthers. This vocal subset of the baby-boom generation set out to "change the system." They began by denouncing the major political parties, big business and big labor, middle-class affluence, the suburban lifestyle, and the American Dream itself.

THE NEW LEFT AND THE COUNTERCULTURE

"I'm tired of reading history," a graduate student at the University of California's Berkeley campus complained in a letter to a friend in 1964. "I want to make it." Within a few months Mario Savio had realized his ambition as the leader of the campus Free Speech Movement, and Berkeley had become synonymous with campus unrest. After teaching in SNCC's Mississippi Summer Project, Savio and others returned to Berkeley convinced that the same power structure that dominated blacks' lives also controlled the bureaucratic machinery of the university. "Last summer I went to Mississippi to join the struggle there for civil rights," Savio wrote. "This fall I am engaged in another phase of the same struggle, this time in Berkeley. . . . The same rights are at stake in both places."

The University of California was in many respects a model university in 1964, with a worldwide reputation for excellence. Its chancellor, the economist Clark Kerr, had written in *The Uses of the University* (1963) that intellect had become "an instrument of national purpose, a component part of the 'military-industrial complex.'" He also likened the "multiversity" with its many separate colleges and research institutes to a big business, and himself to the chief executive officer. The largest single campus in the country, with tens of thousands of students, Berkeley had become hopelessly impersonal by the 1960s. Rather than learning from the famous professors listed in the time-table, undergraduates were herded into lecture classes taught by graduate students. Some students complained that they felt like cogs in a machine.

Free Speech Movement

The struggle at Berkeley began when the university administration yielded to pressure from political conservatives and banned recruitment by civil rights and antiwar organizations in Sproul Plaza, the students' traditional gathering place. Militant students defied Kerr's ban; the administration suspended them or had them arrested. On October 1 several thousand students surrounded a police car in which a militant was being held,

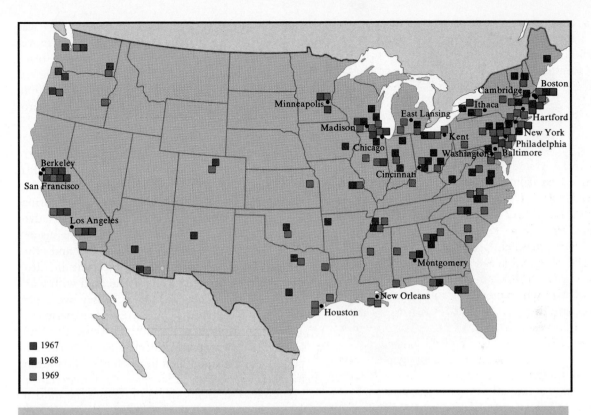

Berkeley
San Francisco
Los Angeles
Minneapolis
Madison
Chicago
East Lansing
Kent
Cincinnati
Washington
Baltimore
Cambridge
Boston
Ithaca
Hartford
New York
Philadelphia
Montgomery
New Orleans
Houston

■ 1967
■ 1968
■ 1969

Disturbances on College and University Campuses, 1967–1969 *Students on campuses from coast to coast protested against the Vietnam War. Some protests were peaceful, but others erupted into violent confrontations between protesters and police and army troops.*

immobilizing it for thirty-two hours. In December the Free Speech Movement seized and occupied the main administration building. Governor Pat Brown dispatched state police to Berkeley, and over eight hundred people were arrested. Angry students shut down classes for several days in protest.

The willingness of those in positions of authority to mobilize the police against unruly but not violent students was profoundly shocking and radicalizing to many young people. Having grown up comfortable and even indulged, they found themselves treated like criminals for questioning what they considered a criminal war in Vietnam and racial injustice in their country. By the end of the decade, the activism born at Berkeley would spread to hundreds of other campuses.

Two years before the confrontation in Berkeley, another group of students had met in Port Hu-

Students for a Democratic Society (SDS)
———

ron, Michigan, to found Students for a Democratic Society (SDS). Like their leaders Tom Hayden and Al Haber, most SDS members were white, middle-class college students. In their platform, the Port Huron Statement, they condemned racism, poverty in the midst of plenty, and "the enclosing fact of the Cold War," symbolized by the hydrogen bomb. SDS called on America to practice its democratic ideals, not merely pay them lip service. SDS sought nothing less than the revitalization of democracy by taking power from the corporations, the military, and the politicians and returning it to the people.

Inspired by the Free Speech Movement and SDS, a minority of students allied themselves with the New Left. United in their hatred of racism and the Vietnam War, the New Left was di-

Beginning in 1964 with the Beatles' sensational television appearance on the Ed Sullivan Show, *Beatlemania swept the nation. In addition to top-selling records, the Beatles made movies that delighted critics and audiences alike. These buttons, each depicting one of the Fab Four, promote the feature-length animated cartoon,* The Yellow Submarine *(1968), for which Paul McCartney and John Lennon wrote a number of songs.* The Nostalgia Factory.

vided in other ways. Indeed, the New Left was not a single organization or even a single movement. Some radicals were Marxists, others black nationalists, anarchists, or pacifists. Some believed in pursuing social change through negotiation; others were revolutionaries who regarded compromise as impossible.

By calling into question the basic foundations of American society, the New Left indirectly gave rise to a phenomenon that observers called the counterculture. Exhorted **Countercultural** by Timothy Leary—a former **Revolution** Harvard instructor and advocate of expanded consciousness through use of LSD and other mind-altering drugs—to "turn on, tune in, drop out," millions of students experimented with marijuana and hallucinogenic drugs. They were persuaded by their political outrage, drug experiences, and experiments with communal living that they lived in a new era unconnected to the past. The past in general and adults in particular had nothing to offer but moral bankruptcy and materialism. High-school students ranked history "the most irrelevant" in a list of twenty-one academic subjects.

It was music more than anything else that expressed the countercultural assault on the status quo. Bob Dylan promised revolutionary answers "blowin' in the wind," and **Rock 'n' Roll** young people cheered Jimi Hendrix, who sang of life in a drug-induced "purple haze," and Janis Joplin, who brought African-American blues to white Americans. Unlike their 1950s counterparts, the rock superstars of the 1960s acknowledged their roots in black rhythm-and-blues. Joplin, who moved crowds with her version of "Ball and Chain," was quick to credit its composer, Big Mama Thornton. Like sex and drugs, the music of the 1960s represented a quest to redefine reality and create a more just and joyful society. Rock festivals became cultural watersheds; in 1969 at Woodstock in upstate New York, 400,000 people ignored or reveled in days of rain and mud, without shelter and without violence. A number of them began to dream of a peaceful "Woodstock nation" based on love, drugs, and rock music.

Some young people tried to construct alternative ways of life. In the Haight-Ashbury section of San Francisco, "flower children" created an urban

Inspired by Ken Kesey and his Merry Pranksters who traveled in a 1939 International Harvester school bus, hippies seemed drawn to buses. This bus, named "The Road Hog," carries members of the New Buffalo Commune in the 1968 Fourth of July parade in El Rito, New Mexico. Lisa Law/Image Works.

subculture as distinctive as that of any Chinatown or Little Italy. "Hashbury" inspired numerous other communal-living experiments. Throughout the country, hitchhikers hit the road in search of communes, America, and themselves. The counterculture represented only a small proportion of American youth. But to disconcerted middle-class parents, hippies seemed to be everywhere. Parents were appalled by long hair, beards, and patched jeans. They complained that "acid rock" was loud, discordant, even savage. They feared their children would suffer lifelong damage from drugs.

The "generation gap" was yawning wide, but most disturbing to parents were the casual sexual mores that young people were adopting. In 1960 the government approved the birth-control pill, and use of the pill accelerated throughout the decade, especially among young people. Americans had formerly linked sexuality to romance and marriage and babies. In the 1960s many young people viewed sexuality as a

Sexuality
———

means of self-expression and as a gauge of personal happiness. For them, living together no longer equaled living in sin; and as attitudes toward premarital sex changed, so did notions about homosexuality and sex roles.

The militancy of blacks, feminists, and antiwar protesters also helped inspire the gay rights movement in the 1960s. Homosexuals had long feared that disclosing their sexual orientation would mean losing not only their jobs but even their friends and families. That attitude began to change in June 1969. In New York City's Greenwich Village, a riot erupted when police raided the Stonewall Inn, a gay bar on Christopher Street, and were greeted with a volley of beer bottles by patrons tired of police harassment. Rioting continued into the night, and graffiti calling for "Gay Power" appeared along Christopher Street. As John D'Emilio, the historian, has written, Stonewall "marked a critical divide in the politics and con-

**Gay Rights
Movement**
———

sciousness of homosexuals and lesbians. A small, thinly spread reform effort suddenly grew into a large, grass-roots movement for liberation. . . . as a furtive subculture moved aggressively into the open."

As the slogan "Make Love, Not War" suggests, the New Left and the counterculture discovered a common cause as the war in Vietnam escalated. Students held teach-ins—open forums for discussion of the war by students, professors, and guest speakers—and antiwar marches and demonstrations became a widespread protest tactic (see map, page 1003). Some young men fled the draft by moving abroad—mostly to Canada and Scandinavia—while others protested, violently and nonviolently, at local draft board offices. The Johnson administration charged that such acts threatened the nation's war-making powers.

By this time, however, growing numbers of Americans, young and old, had quit believing in the judgment and veracity of their elected leaders. President Johnson claimed the United States was fighting for honorable reasons, but people wondered what goal could justify the murder of Vietnamese women and children. As troop levels increased, many recalled ruefully that in 1964 they had voted for Johnson as the more cautious of the two presidential candidates. By 1968 almost half a million American soldiers were stationed in Vietnam, and Johnson's credibility had evaporated.

1968: A YEAR OF PROTEST, VIOLENCE, AND LOSS

As stormy and violent as the years from 1963 through 1967 had been, many Americans were still trying to downplay the nation's distress in the hope that it would go away. "We were in a kind of national sleepwalk," the novelist John Hersey has written, "aware, on a dream level, of black rage; of the undertow of Vietnam . . . of the way Lyndon Johnson's credibility gap was beginning to show." In 1968 the sleepers awoke to a series of violent quakes.

The first shock wave hit in January 1968, when the USS *Pueblo*, a navy intelligence ship, was captured by the North Koreans; not until Christmas of that year would the crew of eighty-two be re-

leased. On January 30 came the Tet offensive (see page 969), a surprise attack that caused many Americans to fear for the first time that they might lose the war. Meanwhile, American casualties had been climbing. In fact, more Americans died in the first six months of 1968 than in all of 1967; by July 4, 1968, total American fatalities had surpassed thirty thousand.

Controversy over the war deepened. Within the Democratic party two candidates rose to challenge Johnson for the 1968 presidential nomination. One of them, Senator Eugene McCarthy of Minnesota, entered the New Hampshire primary on March 12 solely to contest Johnson's war policies, and he won twenty of twenty-four convention delegates. Soon another Democrat, Senator Robert F. Kennedy of New York, the dead president's brother and former attorney general, entered the fray. Kennedy was a tough political in-fighter who in the wake of his brother's assassination had developed a deep empathy with the sufferings of the underprivileged and a strong opposition to the Vietnam War.

On March 31, President Johnson went on national television to announce a scaling-down of the bombing in North Vietnam. Then he hurled a political thunderbolt—he would not be a candidate for re-election. Prone to exaggeration and self-pity, Johnson told reporters: "The only difference between the Kennedy assassination and mine is that I am alive and it has been more torturous."

Less than a week later, a white man named James Earl Ray shot and killed Martin Luther King, Jr., in Memphis. It is still unclear whether

Assassination of Martin Luther King, Jr.

Ray was a deranged racist acting alone or a hireling in an organized conspiracy. Whatever his motive, the murder touched off massive grief and rage in the nation's ghettos. Many blacks blamed whites in general for King's murder. "When white America killed Dr. King last night, she declared war on us," charged Stokely Carmichael. Blacks rioted in 168 cities and towns, looting and burning white businesses and properties (see map, page 1000). Thirty-four blacks and five whites died in the violence. The terror provoked a white backlash. Tough talk was the response from Maryland Governor Spiro Agnew, who denounced Baltimore's black leaders for not controlling "your people," and from Chicago's Mayor Richard Daley, who ordered police to shoot to kill arsonists.

Gallup polls in April and May reported Robert Kennedy to be the front-running Democratic presidential candidate. In June he won the California primary with strong support from Hispanic- and African-Americans. After addressing his joyous supporters in a Los Angeles hotel, Kennedy took a short cut through the kitchen to a press conference. A young man stepped forward with a .22-caliber revolver and fired. The assassin was an Arab nationalist named Sirhan Sirhan who despised Kennedy for his unwavering support of Israel.

Assassination of Robert Kennedy

The cumulative effect of so many assassinations drove many Americans to the brink of despair. Whenever a charismatic, progressive leader with a vision of a more just and peace-loving nation rose to prominence, it seemed, he was mowed down. African-Americans and Hispanic-Americans were especially grief-stricken at the assassination of Robert Kennedy because he had befriended them. When Cesar Chavez had led the United Farm Workers' strike against growers in 1965, Kennedy had traveled to California to stand with them. Many antiwar liberals also felt they had lost a friend in Kennedy, but it was the poor of all races who most mourned his death. When Kennedy's body lay in state at St. Patrick's Cathedral in New York City, the poorest of the working class, blacks, Puerto Ricans, and old people waited in line for hours. "This endless line of people," wrote Norman Mailer, "had really loved him."

Violence erupted again in August at the Democratic national convention in Chicago. The Democrats were divided over the war, and thousands of antiwar protesters and members of the zany and anarchic Youth International Party ("Yippies") had traveled to Chicago to disrupt the convention and embarrass the Democrats. The Chicago police force was still in the psychological grip of Mayor Daley's shoot-to-kill directive. Twelve thousand police were assigned to twelve-hour shifts, and another twelve thousand army troops and National Guardsmen were on call with rifles, bazookas, and flame throwers. They attacked in front of the Hilton Hotel, wading into

Violence at the Democratic Convention

Cesar Chavez provided charismatic leadership for the United Farm Workers Union and in doing so attracted the support of celebrities and political leaders, most notably Robert F. Kennedy. This poster advertises a 1968 benefit performance for the union to be held at New York City's Carnegie Hall. Museum of American Political Life, University of Hartford. Photo by Sally Anderson-Bruce.

the ranks of demonstrators, reporters, and TV camera operators (see photo, page 1008). Throughout the nation, viewers watched as club-swinging police beat protesters to the ground. When onlookers rushed to shield the injured, they too were clubbed. Inside the convention hall, Senator Abraham Ribicoff of Connecticut put aside his prepared speech to denounce the "Gestapo tactics in the streets of Chicago."

The Democratic convention nominated Vice President Hubert Humphrey (Lyndon Johnson's hand-picked candidate) for president and Senator Edmund Muskie of Maine for vice president. Like Johnson and Kennedy before him, Humphrey was a political descendant of the New Deal, committed

Violence erupted in Chicago during the 1968 Democratic convention, as police and National Guardsmen used tear gas and clubs to stop twelve thousand protesters from marching to the convention hall. UPI/Bettmann Archives.

to the social welfare system and supported by a coalition of northern liberals, big-city bosses, African-Americans, and union members. First elected to the Senate from Minnesota in 1948, Humphrey was known not just as a champion of civil rights but as a supporter of the Cold War doctrine of containment that had led to Vietnam. Humphrey's unstinting public support of the war angered some and saddened others. Many Democrats repudiated him as the candidate of Johnson, Daley, and the war.

The Republicans selected Richard M. Nixon as their presidential nominee. After his defeat by John Kennedy in 1960 and his loss in the California gubernatorial race in 1962, Nixon's political career had seemed to be over. But he had spent much of the decade campaigning for fellow Republicans and had built up credits with party regulars and officeholders around the country. In 1968 Nixon cashed in his credits and defeated Governor Nelson Rockefeller of New York and Governor Ronald Reagan of California for the nomination. As his

running mate, Nixon chose the tough-talking Governor Spiro Agnew of Maryland.

Voter enthusiasm was minimal for both Humphrey and Nixon. The nation was deeply divided between "hawks" (who favored escalation of the war) and "doves" (who favored immediate withdrawal). A Gallup poll taken at the time of the conventions reported that 41 percent of the respondents described themselves as hawks and 41 percent as doves, with 18 percent holding no opinion. The same poll found that 66 percent of Americans believed the United States should turn over more of the fighting to the South Vietnamese and begin withdrawing American troops. Yet both major candidates endorsed the perpetuation of the war while negotiations stalled in Paris.

The candidate with the most appeal for conservatives was George C. Wallace, who in his inaugural address as governor of Alabama had declared, "Segregation now . . . segregation tomorrow . . .

Election of 1968

and segregation forever." As the nominee of the American Independent party, he exhorted citizens to "stand up for America," arguing that the United States should bomb North Vietnam to rubble with nuclear weapons. He also appealed to people concerned about "law and order," code words for the suppression of protest. If a civil rights protester ever lay down in front of his car, Wallace declared, he would not hesitate to step on the gas.

When the votes were tabulated, Nixon emerged the winner. Just four years after Goldwater's debacle, the Republicans had captured the White House by the slimmest of margins. Wallace collected nearly 10 million votes, or almost 14 percent of the total, the best performance by a third party since 1924. His strong showing made Nixon a minority president, elected with 43 percent of the popular vote (see map). Moreover, the Democrats maintained control of the House (243 to 192) and the Senate (58 to 42).

Still, the election had been a triumph for conservatism, in that the combined vote for Nixon and Wallace was 57 percent. The war had hurt the Democrats' appeal, but even more politically damaging was the party's identification with the cause of racial justice. In 1968, Humphrey received 97 percent of the black vote but only 35 percent of the white vote. Among the defectors from the New Deal coalition were northern blue-collar ethnic voters. "In city after city," one observer noted, "racial conflicts had destroyed the old alliance. The New Deal had unraveled block by block." Soon the nation would enter a new decade with a new president, but Americans doubted that he and they could heal the wounds of war, poverty, racism, sexism, black rage, youthful disaffection, and the shattered promise of the American Dream.

THE REBIRTH OF FEMINISM

Another liberation movement gained momentum during the turbulence of the 1960s, at first quietly and then on the picket line. The women's rights movement had languished following the adoption of the Nineteenth Amendment in 1920. But in the 1960s feminism was reborn. Many women were dissatisfied with their lives, and in 1963 they found a

The Feminine Mystique

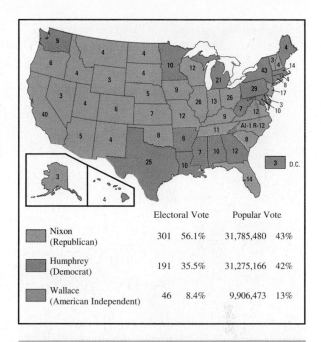

	Electoral Vote		Popular Vote	
Nixon (Republican)	301	56.1%	31,785,480	43%
Humphrey (Democrat)	191	35.5%	31,275,166	42%
Wallace (American Independent)	46	8.4%	9,906,473	13%

Presidential Election, 1968 *The popular vote was almost a dead heat between Richard M. Nixon and Hubert Humphrey, but Nixon won 31 states to Humphrey's 14, and triumphed easily in electoral votes. Note the success of George Wallace's American Independent candidacy, which won 5 states in the Deep South.*

voice with the publication of Betty Friedan's *The Feminine Mystique*. According to Friedan, women across the country were deeply troubled by "the problem that has no name." Most women had grown up believing that "all they had to do was devote their lives from earliest girlhood to finding a husband and bearing children." The problem was that this "mystique of feminine fulfillment" left many wives and mothers feeling empty and incomplete. Such feelings were at odds with the images conveyed by TV advertisers, magazine writers, beauticians, and psychiatrists, who conspired to create the image of a woman "gaily content in a world of bedroom, kitchen, sex, babies and home." Women who were dissatisfied with such limitations were considered neurotic. But, as Friedan pointed out, a woman who spent her life surrounded by children sacrificed her adult frame of reference and sometimes her very identity. Friedan quoted a young mother: "I've tried everything women are supposed to do—hobbies, gardening, pickling, canning, and being very social with my neigh-

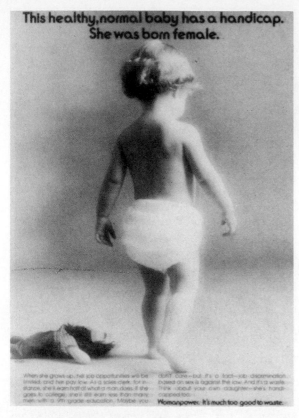

The National Organization for Women (NOW), founded in 1966, went from one thousand members in 1967 to forty thousand in 1974. NOW's advertisements about sexual inequality were simple and to the point.   NOW Legal Defense and Education Fund, Inc.

bors. . . . I love the kids and Bob and my home. . . . But I'm desperate. I begin to feel that I have no personality. . . . Who am I?"

President Kennedy had appointed only one woman to a policymaking post in his administration, but she was an effective advocate of equal rights. As assistant secretary of labor and director of the Women's Bureau, Esther Peterson, a former labor union official, urged Kennedy to establish the first President's Commission on the Status of Women in the nation's history. Eleanor Roosevelt served as the commission's first chairperson. Its report, *American Women* (1963), published only six months after *The Feminine Mystique*, argued that every obstacle to women's full participation in society must be removed. Interest in women's issues spread; by 1967, all fifty states had established

commissions to promote women's equality. Still, little federal action had resulted from the release of *American Women*, and the government was failing to enforce the gender-equality provisions of the Civil Rights Act of 1964. The need for action inspired the founding in 1966 of the National Organization for Women (NOW). In the reform tradition, NOW battled for "equal rights in partnership with men" by lobbying for legislation and testing laws in the courts.

Not long after NOW's formation, a new generation of radical feminists emerged. Once again, the baby boom was making its impact felt on American life. Most radical feminists

Radical Feminism were white and well educated; many were the daughters of working mothers. Most had been raised in the era of sexual liberation, taking for granted liberation from unwanted pregnancy. The intellectual ferment of their movement produced a new feminist literature. Radical feminists focused not only on legal barriers but also on cultural assumptions and traditions. In the process they introduced the term *sexism* to signify a phenomenon far more pervasive than lack of legal equality, and they challenged everything from women's economic and political inequality to sexual double standards and sex-role stereotypes. They were also practicing "personal politics." Charlotte Bunch, a feminist, explained, "There is no private domain of a person's life that is not political, and there is no political issue that is not ultimately personal."

Unlike NOW, the radical feminists practiced direct action, such as picketing the 1968 Miss America contest in Atlantic City. One woman auctioned off an effigy of Miss America: "Gentlemen, I offer you the 1969 model. . . . She walks. She talks. She smiles on cue. *And* she does the housework." Into the "freedom trash can" the pickets dumped false eyelashes, curlers, girdles, and *Playboy* to protest the prevailing view of women as domestic servants and sex objects.

Many radical feminists had joined the struggles for black civil rights and against the Vietnam War only to discover that they were second-class citizens, even in movements dedicated to equality. Instead of making policy, they were expected to make coffee, take minutes, and even provide sexual favors. Many of these feminists organized consciousness-raising groups to discuss such wide-ranging and sensitive matters as homosexuality, abortion, and power relationships in romance and marriage. The issue of homosexuality caused a split in the women's movement; in 1969 and 1970 NOW forced lesbians to resign from membership and offices in the organization. This rift was healed in 1971, largely because homosexuals had begun to fight back (see pages 1005–1006).

For working women in the 1960s, the most pressing problems were sex discrimination in employment, meager professional opportunities, unequal pay for equal work, lack

Occupational Segregation
_____

of adequate day care for children, and prohibitions against abortion. In 1963 the average woman earned 63 cents for every dollar a man earned. Ten years later the figure had fallen to 57 cents. What gender-based discrimination meant for many women was no health insurance, less food on the table, and no new shoes for the children. The main cause of this pay disparity was "occupational segregation": throughout the labor force, work was categorized into men's jobs and women's jobs, and women were concentrated in the low-paying positions. The situation became even more pronounced in the 1960s as baby boomers and mothers of baby boomers flooded entry-level jobs in female-dominated fields like secretarial and clerical work. The number of women workers jumped from 23 million in 1960 to 34 million in 1972, but "men's jobs" still paid higher wages. Women with college educations routinely earned less than men with eighth-grade educations.

It was thus natural that two feminist goals of the 1960s were equal job opportunity and equal pay for equal work. Another goal was child care, but here, too, opposition was widespread and intense. President Nixon vetoed a 1971 bill that would have set up a national system of day-care facilities for the children of working mothers. The bill, Nixon asserted, would have committed government to "communal approaches to child-rearing over against the family-centered approach," thus imperiling "the keystone of our civilization," the American family.

Despite such opposition, women made impressive gains. They entered professional schools in record numbers: from 1969 to 1973, the number of women law students almost quadrupled, and the number of women medical students more than doubled. Under Title IX of the Educational Amendments of 1972, female college athletes gained the right to the same financial support as male athletes. The same year, Congress approved the Equal Rights Amendment (ERA) and sent it to the states for ratification. (The ERA states that "Equality of rights under the law shall not be denied or abridged by the United States or by any State on account of sex.")

The Supreme Court also ruled on several issues essential to women. In 1973 the Court struck down state laws that made abortion a crime (_Roe_ v.

Roe v. Wade
_____

Wade). Ruling that such laws violated a woman's right of privacy, the justices held that the Constitution protected a woman's decision about whether to end her pregnancy. Only in the last three months of pregnancy could a state absolutely bar abortion; otherwise, the state's power to regulate abortion was either nonexistent or subordinate to the issue of maternal health. The Court also addressed sex discrimination. In a 1971 ruling (_Reed_ v. _Reed_), it held that legislation differentiating between the sexes "must be reasonable, not arbitrary," and in 1973 (_Frontiero_ v. _Richardson_), the justices went a step further in declaring that job-related classifications based on sex, like those based on race, were "inherently suspect." These victories gave the women's movement new confidence in the 1970s. "If the 1960s belonged to the blacks, the next ten years are ours," claimed one feminist. Well before the end of the 1970s, however, a full-fledged reaction against the women's movement would set in (see Chapter 33).

NIXON AND THE PERSISTENCE OF CHAOS

Richard Nixon's presidency was born in chaos. Bloody confrontations occurred at Berkeley, San Francisco State, Wisconsin, and scores of other colleges and universities in 1969. At Cornell, a hundred black students armed with rifles and shotguns occupied the student union for thirty-six hours. Harvard students took over the president's office before being evicted by police. In October three hundred Weathermen—an SDS splinter group—raced through Chicago's downtown district, smashing windows and attacking police officers in

In May 1970, at Kent State University in Ohio, National Guardsmen confronted student antiwar protesters with a tear gas barrage. Soon afterward, with no provocation, soldiers opened fire into a group of fleeing students. Four young people were killed, shot in the back, including two women who had been walking to class. There was outrage throughout the country; campuses closed down; and students by the thousands came to Washington to lobby against the war.   Gamma Liaison/Keza.

an attempt to incite armed class struggle. A month later half a million people assembled peacefully at the Washington Monument on Moratorium Day to call for an end to the Vietnam War.

If 1969 was bloody and turbulent, 1970 would prove to be even more so. President Nixon appeared on television on April 30 to announce that

Kent State and Jackson State

the United States had launched an "incursion" into Cambodia (see Chapter 31), a neutral country bordering Vietnam. Antiwar protest escalated. On May 4, National Guardsmen in Ohio fired into a crowd of fleeing students at Kent State University, killing four young people. Ten days later, police and state highway patrolmen armed with automatic weapons blasted a women's dormitory at Jackson State, an all-black university in Mississippi, killing two students and wounding nine others. The police claimed they had been shot at, but no evidence of sniping could be found; the police fired no tear gas or warning shots.

Many Americans, though disturbed by the increasing ferocity of campus confrontations, felt more personally endangered by street crime.

Fear of Crime

Newsweek entitled an article on crime "Fortress America: A Nation Behind Locked Doors." Sales of pistols, burglar alarms, and bulletproof vests soared, as did demand for private guards and special police. Crime was on the rise largely because many baby-boomers were eighteen to twenty-five years old, the age group that committed far more crime than any other. But conservatives accused liberals and the Supreme Court of causing the crime wave by coddling criminals. Government officials, responding to public calls for crackdowns, sometimes overreacted. Governor Nelson Rockefeller of New York did so in September 1971 when more than a thousand inmates of the state prison at Attica seized thirty-eight guards and took over a cellblock. Rather than give in to the prisoners' demand that he visit Attica to negotiate, Rockefeller ordered state troopers, sheriff's deputies, and guards to storm the prison. Under a pall of tear gas Rockefeller's army regained control, but at a horrifying cost: twenty-nine inmates and ten hostages were dead.

This new wave of riots, protests, and violent crime convinced Nixon that the nation was plunging into anarchy. Worried like Lyndon Johnson before him that the antiwar movement was Communist-inspired, he ordered the FBI, the CIA, the National Security Agency, and the Defense Intelligence Agency in mid-1970 to formulate a coordinated attack on "internal threats." Meanwhile the administration also worked to put the Democratic party on the defensive. Vice President Agnew took to the road in September to warn the country of threats to its internal security posed "by a disruptive, radical, and militant minority." The same month Jeb Stuart Magruder, a White House assistant, defined the theme of the upcoming congressional elections in a memorandum: "The Democrats should be portrayed as being on the fringes: radical liberals who . . . excuse disorder, tolerate crime, . . . and undercut the President's foreign policy." But Republican attempts to discredit the Democrats failed. The Democrats gained nine seats in the House and lost only two in the Senate. The Republicans lost eleven state governorships.

Politics of Divisiveness

Nixon's fortunes declined further in 1971. In June the *New York Times* began to publish the *Pentagon Papers*, a top-secret Defense Department study of the Vietnam War (see Chapter 31). Nixon also had to contend with inflation, a problem not entirely of his making; it was Lyndon Johnson's policy of "guns and butter"—massive deficit financing to support both the Vietnam War and the Great Society—that had fueled inflation. Not until 1967 had Johnson proposed tax increases to reduce the government deficit and dampen inflation, and not until mid-1968 had Congress responded with a 10 percent tax surcharge. Johnson also trimmed federal spending by $6 billion at this time, but the cut was too little, too late. Nixon's policies, including a $2.5 billion tax cut in late 1969, only boosted rising prices. By early 1971 the United States was suffering from a 5.3 percent inflation rate and a 6 percent unemployment rate. The word *stagflation* would shortly be coined to describe this coexistence of economic recession (stagnation) and inflation.

Stagflation

Nixon shocked both critics and allies by declaring in early 1971 that "I am now a Keynesian." (According to the British economist John Maynard Keynes, governments could stimulate economic growth in the private sector by means of "pump priming," or deficit financing.) Nixon's budget for fiscal 1971 would have a built-in deficit of $23 billion, just slightly under the all-time high of $25 billion (1968 to 1969). Then in August, in an effort to correct the nation's balance-of-payments deficit, Nixon suspended the convertibility of the dollar into gold, announcing that he would devalue the dollar and allow it to "float" in international money markets. Finally, to curb inflation, the president froze prices, wages, and rents for ninety days and set limits on subsequent increases. Nixon's commitment to these controversial wage-and-price controls buckled the next year under pressure from businesses and unions. Some economists, businesspeople, and politicians argued that the controls were bound to fail, whereas others contended that they would have been successful had they been allowed more time to work.

Wage and price controls were just one facet of what surprised observers called Nixon's "great turnabout" from outspoken conservative to pragmatic liberal. Another was his announcement in 1971 that he would travel to the People's Republic of China, a communist enemy Nixon had denounced for years. It was clear that the president was preparing for the 1972 presidential election.

NIXON'S SOUTHERN STRATEGY AND THE ELECTION OF 1972

Political observers believed that Nixon would have a hard time running for re-election on his first-term record. Having urged Americans to "lower our voices," he had ordered Vice President Agnew to denounce the press and student protesters. Having espoused unity, he had practiced the politics of polarization. Having campaigned as a fiscal conservative, he had authorized near-record budget deficits. And having promised peace, he had widened the war in Southeast Asia.

Moreover, Congress's accomplishments were more in spite of Nixon than because of him. The Democrats had dominated both houses during his first term, and they continued to pursue a liberal agenda. The Twenty-sixth Amendment extended the vote to eighteen-year-olds; Social Security payments and food-stamp funding were increased; and the Occupational Safety and

Liberal Legislative Victories

Americans, concerned about the pollution of the environment, celebrated the first Earth Day in 1970. This picture is from the Earth Day celebration in New York City.   Covello & Launois/Black Star.

Health Administration was established to reduce hazards in the work place.

Despite Nixon's opposition, the environmental movement also bore fruit during his first term. Alerted to ecological hazards by Rachel Carson's *Silent Spring*, growing numbers of Americans had begun to heed warnings of impending disaster due to unregulated population and economic growth, including Paul Ehrlich's *The Population Bomb* (1968) and Barry Commoner's *The Closing Circle* (1971). Commoner put the issue squarely: "The environment got here first, and it's up to the economic system to adjust to the environment. Any economic system must be compatible with the environment, or it will not survive."

Environmental Issues

Environmental tragedies such as the 1969 oil spill that fouled the beaches and killed wildlife in Santa Barbara, California, spurred citizen action. The Environmental Defense Fund, founded in 1967, successfully fought the use of DDT, and Greenpeace (1969) protested radioactive poisoning from nuclear-bomb testing. In 1970 Americans celebrated the first Earth Day (see photo). Gradually, too, the Congress responded, establishing the National Wilderness Preservation System (1964) and giving the federal government the power to set water-quality standards (1967). States also took action; Oregon, for example, passed the first bottle-recycling act in 1972. And although President Nixon was personally unsympathetic to the environmental movement, some of his subordinates were not. Nixon acknowledged the movement's political appeal by reluctantly agreeing to the establishment of the Environmental Protection Agency in 1970 and by signing into law the Clean Air Act (1970), Clean Water Act (1972), and Pesticide Control Act (1972).

One Nixon innovation that bore fruit in 1972 was revenue sharing, a program that distributed federal funds to the states to use as they saw fit. Invoking the federalism of the Founding Fathers, Nixon called this effort to shift responsibility back to state and local governments the New Federalism. The program also appealed, according to the historian Stephen E. Ambrose, to "the surburban, small-town, and rural homeowning Silent Majority," who expressed disgust that they had to pay "high taxes to support giveaway programs for the poor." They wanted to control their own tax dollars.

Less popular than the New Federalism was the Family Assistance Plan, under which a poor family of four would receive a guaranteed income of $1,600 per year plus $860 in food stamps. (Welfare payments were less than that in twenty states.) Michael Harrington, author of *The Other America*, called the plan "the most radical idea since the New Deal"; most conservatives denounced it, though a handful argued that simple cash payments to the poor would do away with the mammoth welfare bureaucracy. The program did not pass Congress, in part because Democrats considered the benefit payments too low.

In his campaign for re-election, Nixon employed a "southern strategy" of political conservatism. A product of the Sunbelt, he was acutely aware of the growing political power of that conservative region. He thus appealed to "the silent majority," the suburbanites, white ethnic groups, and blue-collar workers of "middle America." As in the 1970 congressional elections, Nixon equated the Republican party with law and order and the Democrats with permissiveness, crime, drugs, pornography, the hippie lifestyle, student radicalism, black militancy, feminism, homosexuality, and dissolution of the family.

Nixon's Southern Strategy

Actually, Nixon had been pursuing a southern strategy all along. A furor had arisen in 1970 when the press published a memorandum by Daniel Moynihan, Nixon's adviser on urban affairs and social welfare. While insisting that African-Americans should continue to make economic progress, Moynihan had recommended that "the issue of race could benefit from a period of benign neglect." Incensed, blacks and white liberals responded that this was another example of how uncaring the Nixon administration was. Moreover, Attorney General John Mitchell had courted southern white voters by trying to delay school desegregation in Mississippi and to prevent extension of the 1965 Voting Rights Act. Mitchell also sought vigorous prosecution of antiwar activists.

The southern strategy had also guided Nixon's nomination of Supreme Court justices. After appointing Warren Burger, a conservative federal judge, to succeed Earl Warren as chief justice, Nixon had selected two southerners to serve as associate justices. One was a segregationist. When the Senate declined to confirm either nominee,

Nixon protested angrily, "I understand the bitter feelings of millions of Americans who live in the South." By 1972, however, the president had managed to appoint three more conservatives to the Supreme Court. Ironically, the new appointees did not always vote as Nixon would have wished: the Court's decisions on abortion, publication of the *Pentagon Papers*, the death sentence, wiretapping, and busing for school desegregation all ran counter to Nixon's views.

The Court was at the center of one of the most emotional issues of the 1972 election: busing of schoolchildren for purposes of integration. In *Swann* v. *Charlotte-Mecklenberg* (1971), the justices had upheld a desegregation plan that required a school system in North Carolina to work toward racial integration through massive cross-town busing. The decision generated widespread protest. The next year Governor George Wallace of Alabama won the Democratic primary in Florida after taking a strong antibusing stand. Three days later Nixon proposed that Congress pass a busing moratorium, and he appeared on television to denounce busing as a reckless and extreme remedy for segregation. Nixon's opposition to busing was a well-planned aspect of his southern strategy, but it clearly appealed to many northern whites as well.

Besides Wallace, the Democratic candidates for the 1972 presidential nomination were Senators Hubert Humphrey, Edward Kennedy, George McGovern, and Edmund Muskie. After his defeat by Nixon in 1968, Humphrey inspired little enthusiasm. Kennedy had ceased to be a serious contender in 1969, when he left the scene of an accident at Chappaquiddick, off the Massachusetts coast near Martha's Vineyard, in which a woman passenger in his car drowned. Senator Muskie fell victim to a "dirty trick," a forged letter published during the New Hampshire primary that accused the senator of laughing at disparaging remarks about Canadian-Americans. Provoked to the point of tears by the letter and other slurs, Muskie also ceased to be a serious candidate. Governor Wallace was shot and paralyzed by a disturbed young man in Maryland and began a long convalescence. After his shooting, the right-wing law-and-order vote had no place to turn but to Nixon. Meanwhile, Senator McGovern of South Dakota won several primaries and arrived at the Democratic conven-

Election of 1972

tion with enough votes to secure the nomination of his party.

Nixon campaigned by assuming the elevated role of world statesman: in early 1972 he traveled to China and to the Soviet Union. Both trips were elaborately staged and televised for maximum political effect. But it was the inept campaign waged by George McGovern that handed victory to the Republicans. When McGovern endorsed a $30 billion cut in the defense budget, people began to fear that he was a neo-isolationist who would reduce the United States to a second-rate power. McGovern's proposals split the Democrats between his supporters—antiwar activists, blacks, feminists, young militants—and old-guard urban bosses, labor leaders, and white southerners.

Nixon benefited greatly from the rumor planted by his aides that the Vietnam War was near its end. Troops were being pulled out; by September 1972 the American death rate was almost zero. Then in late October, less than two weeks before the election, Henry Kissinger announced a breakthrough in the peace negotiations. "Peace is at hand," he proclaimed. The announcement proved inaccurate but helped persuade some people to vote for Nixon.

Nixon's victory in November was overwhelming: he polled 47 million votes, over 60 percent of the votes cast. McGovern received only 29 million and won just one state, Massa-

Nixon's Landslide Victory

chusetts, and the District of Columbia. Nixon's southern strategy had been supremely successful: he carried the entire Deep South, which had once been solidly Democratic. He also gained the suburbs and won over a majority of the urban vote, including such long-time Democrats as blue-collar workers, Catholics, and white ethnics. Only blacks, Jews, and low-income voters stuck by the Democratic candidate.

Yet the 1972 election had another significant result, one that would recur in subsequent elections. Despite Nixon's landslide victory, the Democrats retained control of both houses of Congress and won two additional seats in the Senate. Democratic voters were becoming independent, resorting to ticket-splitting to reject an unacceptable Democratic presidential candidate but support the party congressional candidates.

Little noticed during the campaign was a break-in at the Watergate apartment-office complex in Washington, D.C., on June 17, 1972. A watchman telephoned the police to

Watergate Break-in

report an illegal late-night entry into the building through an underground garage. At 2:30 a.m., police arrested five men who were attaching listening devices to telephones in the sixth-floor offices of the Democratic National Committee. The men had cameras and had been rifling through files.

One of those arrested was James W. McCord, a former CIA employee who had become security coordinator of the Committee to Re-Elect the President (CREEP). The other four were anti-Castro Cubans from Miami who had worked with the CIA before. Unknown to the police, two other men had been in the Watergate building at the time of the break-in. One was E. Howard Hunt, a one-time CIA agent who had become CREEP's security chief. The other was G. Gordon Liddy, a former FBI agent serving on the White House staff. What were these men trying to find in the Democrats' offices? What did they hope to overhear on the telephones? And most important, who had ordered the break-in? In the next twenty-two months the American people would learn the answers to some but not all of those questions.

WATERGATE AND NIXON'S RESIGNATION

The Watergate fiasco actually began in 1971, when the White House established not only CREEP but the Special Investigations Unit, known familiarly as "the Plumbers," to stop the leaking of secret government documents to the press. After publication of the *Pentagon Papers*, the Plumbers burglarized the office of Daniel Ellsberg's psychiatrist in an attempt to discredit Ellsberg, who had leaked the top-secret report to the press. It was the Plumbers who broke into the Democratic National Committee's headquarters to photograph documents and install wiretaps; CREEP raised money to pay the Plumbers' expenses both before and after the break-ins. CREEP's official duty was to solicit campaign contributions, and the committee managed to collect $60 million, much of it donated illegally by corporations, including big oil companies like Gulf Oil and Phillips Petroleum, as well as several defense contractors and airlines.

The arrest of the Watergate burglars generated furious activity in the White House. Incriminating documents were shredded; E. Howard Hunt's

White House Cover-up

name was expunged from the White House telephone directory; and President Nixon ordered his chief of staff, H. R. Haldeman, to discourage the FBI's investigation into the burglary on the pretext that it might compromise national security.

Soon after the break-in, the Democrats filed a damage suit against CREEP and the five burglars for invasion of privacy. John Mitchell, who had resigned as attorney general to chair Nixon's re-election campaign, called the suit "another example of sheer demagoguery." According to Mitchell, CREEP "did not authorize and does not condone the alleged actions of the five men apprehended there." Nixon announced to the press that his White House counsel, John Dean III, had conducted a "complete investigation" and that no one in the administration "was involved in this very bizarre incident." At the same time, Nixon privately authorized CREEP "hush-money" payments in excess of $460,000 to keep Hunt and others from implicating the White House in the crime.

Because of successful White House efforts to cover up the scandal, the break-in was almost unnoticed by the electorate. Had it not been for the

Watergate Hearings and Investigations

diligent efforts of reporters, government special prosecutors, federal judges, and members of Congress, President Nixon might have succeeded in disguising his involvement in Watergate. After his landslide re-election, however, the tangle of lies and distortions slowly began to unravel. In early 1973, U.S. District Court Judge John Sirica tried the burglars, one of whom implicated his superiors in CREEP and at the White House. From May until November, the Senate Select Committee on Campaign Practices, chaired by Senator Sam Ervin of North Carolina, heard testimony from White House aides. John Dean acknowledged not only that there had been a cover-up but that the president had directed it.

Another aide shocked the committee and the nation by disclosing that Nixon had had a taping system installed in his White House office and that conversations about Watergate had been recorded.

Nixon feigned innocence but feared that Dean's testimony would result in criminal indictments. He tried to distance himself from the cover-up by announcing the resignations of his two chief White House aides, John Ehrlichman and H. R. Haldeman. Speaking to a national television audience, the president pledged that he would find the facts and act on them. "There can be no whitewash at the White House," he declared.

As if to give substance to his words, the president appointed Elliot Richardson, the secretary of defense, to the post of attorney general. Richardson in turn selected Archibald

Saturday Night Massacre

Cox, a Harvard law professor with a reputation for uncompromising integrity, to fill the new position of special Watergate prosecutor. When Cox, supported by Richardson, sought in October to obtain the White House tapes by means of a court order, Nixon forced Richardson and his deputy to resign and ordered the next-ranking official in the Department of Justice to dismiss Cox. The public outcry provoked by this so-called "Saturday Night Massacre" compelled the president to agree to the appointment of a new special prosecutor, Leon Jaworski, a distinguished attorney from Texas and former president of the American Bar Association. When Nixon still refused to surrender the tapes, Jaworski took him to court.

In the same month as the Saturday Night Massacre, the Nixon administration was stung by another scandal. Vice President Spiro Agnew resigned after pleading no contest

Agnew's Resignation

to charges of income-tax evasion and acceptance of bribes. Under the provisions of the Twenty-fifth Amendment, ratified in 1964 after President Kennedy's assassination, Nixon nominated Gerald R. Ford, congressman from Michigan and the House minority leader, to replace Agnew. Ford's voting record was conservative—he had opposed most of the 1960s reform legislation—but he was congenial and popular on Capitol Hill. His nomination was confirmed promptly by Congress.

Throughout 1973 and 1974, enterprising reporters uncovered more details of the break-in, the hush money, and the various people from Nixon on down who had taken part in the cover-up. White House aides and CREEP subordinates began to go on trial, with Nixon cited as their "unindicted co-conspirator." *Washington Post* reporters Carl Bernstein and Bob Woodward found an informant in the White House, known as "Deep Throat," who provided damning evidence against Nixon and his aides. As Nixon's protestations of innocence became less credible, his hold on the tapes became more tenuous. In late April 1974 the president finally released an edited transcript of the tapes, which, he explained, would "at last, once and for all, show that what I knew and what I did with regard to the Watergate cover-up were just as I described them to you from the very beginning."

The edited tapes, however, were replete with gaps. They swayed neither the public nor the House Judiciary Committee, which had begun to draft articles of impeachment against the president. Nixon was still trying to hang onto the original tapes when the Supreme Court, in *U.S.* v. *Nixon*, unanimously ordered him in July to surrender the recordings to Judge Sirica. At about the same time, the Judiciary Committee began to conduct nationally televised hearings. After several days of testimony, the committee voted for impeachment on three of five counts: obstruction of justice through the payment of hush money to witnesses, lying, and withholding of evidence; defiance of a congressional subpoena of the tapes; and use of the CIA, the FBI, and the Internal Revenue Service to deprive Americans of their constitutional rights of privacy and free speech.

On August 5 the president finally handed over the complete tapes, which he knew would condemn him. Four days later he resigned the presidency.

Nixon's successor was Gerald R. Ford. His congressional colleagues hailed the new president as a decent and good man, respected by both Republicans and Democrats, who would bind up the wounds of Watergate. Ford's first substantive act, however, was to pardon Nixon, though he had said he would not do so. When the pardon was announced, some people concluded that Ford and Nixon had struck a deal.

The Watergate scandal prompted the reform of abuses that had predated the Nixon administration. The executive's usurpation of legislative prerogatives, which the historian Arthur M. Schlesinger, Jr., called "the imperial presidency," dated from Franklin D. Roosevelt's administration. Roosevelt had signed executive agreements that were in effect treaties with foreign nations, but he had never sent them to the Senate for its advice and consent. President Johnson had led the nation into the Vietnam War without securing a congressional declaration of war as required by the Constitution, and Nixon had authorized the secret bombing of Cambodia. Nixon had also refused to spend $15 billion in funds appropriated by Congress for social programs.

Post-Watergate Restrictions on Executive Power

To remedy many of these abuses, Congress in 1973 overrode Nixon's veto to pass the War Powers Act, which mandated that "in every possible instance" the president must consult with Congress before sending American troops into foreign wars. Under this law the president could commit American troops abroad for no more than sixty days, after which he had to obtain congressional approval. (The act did not specify what Congress could do if the president refused to comply.) The next year Congress approved the Congressional Budget and Impoundment Control Act, which prohibited the impounding of federal money.

In actions directly related to Watergate, Congress addressed campaign fund-raising abuses and the misuse of government agencies. The Federal Election Campaign Act of 1972 had restricted campaign spending to no more than 10 cents per constituent, and it required candidates to report individual contributions of more than $100. In 1974, Congress enacted additional legislation that set ceilings on campaign contributions and expenditures for congressional and presidential elections. Finally, to aid citizens who were victims of dirty-tricks campaigns, Congress strengthened the Freedom of Information Act, originally passed in 1966. The new legislation permitted access to government documents and provided penalties if the government "arbitrarily or capriciously" withheld such information.

The thirteen years coinciding with the presidencies of John Kennedy, Lyndon Johnson, and Richard Nixon were a period of increasing disillusionment in the United States. The period began

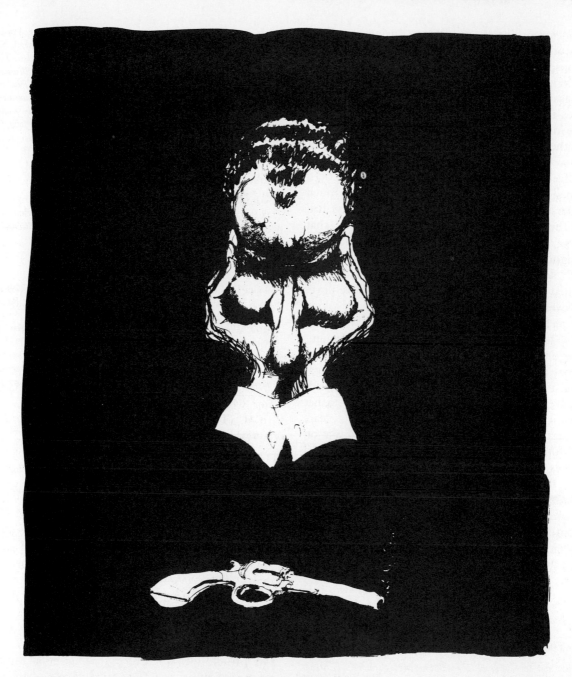

How do historians know

that President Richard M. Nixon was actually guilty of obstructing justice in the Watergate affair? What was the evidence—the "smoking gun"? The "smoking gun" referred to the tape recording of a June 23, 1972, White House conversation in which Nixon ordered his top aide to stop the Federal Bureau of Investigation's inquiry into the Watergate break-in. The Central Intelligence Agency, Nixon thundered, should call the FBI, claim that the break-in was a secret spy operation, and say, " 'Don't go further into this case[,] period'!" The June 23, 1972, tape proved that Nixon had instigated a cover-up and obstructed justice almost from the outset of the scandal. Photo: "The Smoking Gun" by Oliphant, 1984. Reprinted courtesy of Susan Corn Conway Gallery.

with extraordinary hopefulness during the Kennedy administration, and it was in part the dashing of those hopes that shattered Americans' illusions. Riots in cities, violence on campus, and white backlash in the suburbs had supplanted earlier hopes for peaceful social change. "Americans had gone into the age of Kennedy and Nixon convinced that their government's action . . . could make over the world, at home and abroad," the journalist Godfrey Hodgson explained. "Now they had been burned." They had learned that it was much harder to change the world than their leaders had told them it would be. They had learned, too, that "there was moral ambiguity where they had once thought the issues of right and wrong were clearest," according to Hodgson, and "that there seemed little that political action could achieve, however idealistic its intentions, without evoking unforeseen and unwanted reaction."

When John F. Kennedy delivered his inaugural address in 1961, he had challenged Americans to "pay any price, bear any burden, meet any hardship" to defend freedom and inspire the world. Twelve years later, Richard M. Nixon echoed that rhetoric: "Let us pledge to make these four years the best four years in America's history, so that on its 200th birthday America will be as young and vital as when it began, and as bright a beacon of hope for all the world." Largely because of the president's own actions, however, Nixon resigned the presidency before the nation could celebrate its bicentennial in 1976. Rather than young and vital, America seemed bruised and battered.

SUGGESTIONS FOR FURTHER READING

The 1960s

David Chalmers, *And the Crooked Places Made Straight: The Struggle for Social Change in the 1960s* (1991); Godfrey Hodgson, *America in Our Time* (1976); Allen J. Matusow, *The Unraveling of America: A History of Liberalism in the 1960s* (1984); Charles R. Morris, *A Time of Passion: America, 1960–1980* (1984); Geoffrey O'Brien, *Dream Time* (1988); Tom Shachtman, *Decade of Shocks: Dallas to Watergate, 1963–1974* (1983); Barbara L. Tischler, ed., *Sights on the Sixties* (1992); Theodore H. White, *America in Search of Itself: The Making of the President, 1954–1980* (1982).

The Kennedy Administration

Irving Bernstein, *Promises Kept: John F. Kennedy's New Frontier* (1991); Thomas Brown, *JFK: History of an Image* (1988); David Burner, *John F. Kennedy and a New Generation* (1988); James Giglio, *The Presidency of John F. Kennedy* (1991); Richard N. Goodwin, *Remembering America* (1988); David Halberstam, *The Best and the Brightest* (1972); Bruce Miroff, *Pragmatic Illusions* (1976); Herbert S. Parmet, *J.F.K.—The Presidency of John F. Kennedy* (1983); Thomas C. Reeves, *A Question of Character* (1991); Arthur M. Schlesinger, Jr., *Robert Kennedy and His Times* (1978); Arthur M. Schlesinger, Jr., *A Thousand Days: John F. Kennedy in the White House* (1965); Theodore C. Sorensen, *Kennedy* (1965); Gary Wills, *The Kennedy Imprisonment* (1982).

The Kennedy Assassination

Edward Jay Epstein, *Legend: The Secret World of Lee Harvey Oswald* (1978); Henry Hurt, *Reasonable Doubt* (1985); Michael L. Kurtz, *Crime of the Century* (1982); Anthony Summers, *Conspiracy* (1980).

The Johnson Administration

Vaughn D. Bornet, *The Presidency of Lyndon B. Johnson* (1983); Paul K. Conkin, *Big Daddy from the Pedernales: Lyndon Baines Johnson* (1986); Ronnie Dugger, *The Politician* (1982); Doris Kearns, *Lyndon Johnson and the American Dream* (1976); Sar A. Levitan and Robert Taggart, *The Promise of Greatness* (1976); Harry Middleton, *LBJ* (1990); Charles Murray, *Losing Ground: American Social Policy, 1950–1980* (1983); James T. Patterson, *America's Struggle Against Poverty, 1900–1985* (1986); John E. Schwarz, *America's Hidden Success: A Reassessment of Twenty Years of Public Policy* (1983).

Civil Rights and Black Power

Taylor Branch, *Parting the Waters: America in the King Years, 1954–1963* (1988); Clayborne Carson, *In Struggle: SNCC and the Black Awakening of the 1960s* (1981); William H. Chafe, *Civilities and Civil Rights: Greensboro, North Carolina, and the Black Struggle for Freedom* (1980); David J. Garrow, *Bearing the Cross: Martin Luther King, Jr., and the Southern Christian Leadership Conference* (1986); Hugh Davis Graham, *Civil Rights and the Presidency* (1992); Steven F. Lawson, *Running for Freedom* (1991); Doug McAdam, *Freedom Summer* (1988); Malcolm X and Alex Haley, *The Autobiography of Malcolm X* (1965); August Meier and Elliott Rudwick, *CORE* (1973); Harvard Sitkoff, *The Struggle for Black Equality, 1954–1980* (1981); Mark Stern, *Calculating Visions: Kennedy, Johnson, and Civil Rights* (1992); Robert Weisbrot, *Freedom Bound* (1991).

The Warren Court

Alexander M. Bickel, *The Supreme Court and the Idea of Progress* (1970); Gerald Dunne, *Hugo Black and the Judicial Revolution* (1977); G. Theodore Mitau, *Decade of Decision: The Supreme Court and the Constitutional Revolution, 1954–1964* (1967); Bernard Schwartz, *Super Chief: Earl Warren and His Supreme Court* (1983); G. Edward White, *Earl Warren* (1982).

The New Left and the Antiwar Movement

Judith Clavir Albert and Stewart Edward Albert, eds., *The Sixties Papers* (1984); Wini Breines, *Community and Organization in the New Left, 1962–1968*, rev. ed. (1989); Charles DeBenedetti, *An American Ordeal: The Antiwar Movement of the Vietnam Era*

(1990); Todd Gitlin, *The Sixties* (1987); Maurice Isserman, *If I Had a Hammer . . . : The Death of the Old Left and the Birth of the New Left* (1987); James Miller, *"Democracy Is in the Streets": From Port Huron to the Siege of Chicago* (1987); Thomas Powers, *Vietnam, the War at Home* (1984); W. J. Rorabaugh, *Berkeley at War* (1989); Sohnya Sayres et al., eds., *The 60s, Without Apology* (1984); Nancy Zaroulis and Gerald Sullivan, *Who Spoke Up? American Protest Against the War in Vietnam, 1963–1975* (1984).

The Counterculture

Stanley Booth, *Dance with the Devil: The Rolling Stones and Their Times* (1984); Morris Dickstein, *Gates of Eden: American Culture in the Sixties* (1977); Michael Medved and David Wallechinsky, *What Really Happened to the Class of '65?* (1976); Philip Norman, *Shout! The Beatles in Their Generation* (1981); Charles Perry, *The Haight-Ashbury* (1984); Charles Reich, *The Greening of America* (1970); Theodore Roszak, *The Making of a Counter Culture* (1969); Philip Slater, *The Pursuit of Loneliness*, rev. ed. (1976); Jay Stevens, *Storming Heaven: LSD and the American Dream* (1987); Jon Weiner, *Come Together: John Lennon in His Time* (1984); Tom Wolfe, *The Electric Kool-Aid Acid Test* (1968).

The Rebirth of Feminism

William H. Chafe, *The Paradox of Change: American Women in the Twentieth Century* (1991); Alice Echols, *Daring to Be Bad: Radical Feminism in America, 1965–1975* (1989); Sara Evans, *Born for Liberty* (1989); Sara Evans, *Personal Politics* (1978); Marian Faux, *Roe v. Wade* (1988); Jo Freeman, *The Politics of Women's Liberation* (1975); Betty Friedan, *The Feminine Mystique* (1963); Cynthia Harrison, *On Account of Sex: The Politics of Women's Issues, 1945–1968* (1988); Judith Hole and Ellen Levine, *Rebirth of Feminism* (1971); Robin Morgan, ed., *Sisterhood Is Powerful* (1970); Rosalind Rosenberg, *Divided Lives: American Women in the Twentieth Century* (1992); Gayle Graham Yates, *What Women Want: The Ideas of the Movement* (1975).

Year of Shocks: 1968

David Caute, *The Year of the Barricades* (1988); Lewis Chester et al., *An American Melodrama: The Presidential Campaign of 1968* (1969); David Farber, *Chicago '68* (1988); Ronald Fraser et al., *1968: A Student Generation in Revolt* (1988); Charles Kaiser, *1968 in America* (1988); George Katsiaficas, *The Imagination of the New Left: A Global Analysis of 1968* (1987); Hans Koning, *Nineteen-Sixty-Eight* (1987); Theodore H. White, *The Making of the President, 1968* (1969).

The Nixon Administration

Stephen E. Ambrose, *Nixon*, 3 vols. (1987–1991); Roger Morris, *Richard Milhous Nixon* (1990); Richard M. Nixon, *RN: The Memoirs of Richard Nixon* (1978); Herbert S. Parmet, *Richard Nixon and His America* (1990); Kevin Phillips, *The Emerging Republican Majority* (1969); James A. Reichley, *Conservatives in an Era of Change: The Nixon and Ford Administrations* (1981); Jonathan Schell, *Observing the Nixon Years* (1989); Jonathan Schell, *The Time of Illusion* (1975); Tom Wicker, *One of Us* (1991); Garry Wills, *Nixon Agonistes* (1970).

Watergate

Seymour M. Hersh, "The Pardon: Nixon, Ford, Haig, and the Transfer of Power," *Atlantic Monthly* 252 (1983): 55–78; Jim Hougan, *Secret Agenda: Watergate, Deep Throat and the CIA* (1984); Stanley I. Kutler, *The Wars of Watergate* (1990); J. Anthony Lukas, *Nightmare: The Underside of the Nixon Years* (1976); Kim McQuaid, *The Anxious Years: America in the Vietnam-Watergate Era* (1989); Arthur M. Schlesinger, Jr., *The Imperial Presidency* (1973); John J. Sirica, *To Set the Record Straight* (1979); Theodore H. White, *Breach of Faith* (1975); Bob Woodward and Carl Bernstein, *The Final Days* (1976); Bob Woodward and Carl Bernstein, *All the President's Men* (1974).

A Turn to the Right, 1974–1989

JANUARY 20, 1981, WAS a memorable day in American history. "It was Day 444 and Day One come together in historic symmetry," stated *Newsweek*, "—the end of the long ordeal of the hostages in Iran and the beginning of what [President Ronald] Reagan promised would be 'an era of national renewal.'" That morning Reagan took the oath of office and was sworn in as president of the United States. In his inaugural address, Reagan pledged to stamp out inflation and work for "a healthy, vigorous, growing economy that provides equal opportunities for all Americans." He also reminded the American people of one of the central themes of his campaign. "In this present crisis," the new president asserted, "government is not the solution to our problem; government *is* the problem." Finally, Reagan guaranteed that he would make America "the exemplar of freedom and a beacon of hope" for the entire world while maintaining sufficient military strength to keep the peace.

Just twenty-eight minutes after Reagan became president, the fifty-two American hostages—after 444 days in captivity—boarded a plane that flew them from Teheran to freedom. The hostage crisis had contributed to the nation's sense of impotence and frustration. Now the ordeal was over. On hearing the news, Bruce German's mother ran onto Main Street in Edwardsville, Pennsylvania, ringing a cowbell and shouting, "My Bruce is free! My Bruce is free!" Church bells rang, sirens wailed, people tied yellow ribbons everywhere, and the nation rejoiced. At the corner of 57th Street and Madison Avenue in New York City, a crowd of several thousand people erupted in cheers and shouting as adding-machine confetti was showered on them from the office windows above. Workmen on a nearby construction site replaced an enormous countdown sign, which vowed that day 444 would be the last, with a new motto: "Free at last! Free at last! Thank God they are free at last!" At the bottom, it read: "Never again."

Never had a presidential administration enjoyed a more auspicious beginning than that of Ronald Reagan. But the challenges facing the new administration were immense. Reagan's 1980 victory took place during a period of economic decline; Americans, reeling under the one-two punch of stagflation, were filled with uncertainty.

First, there was the economic stagnation known as a *recession*, which economists define as at least two consecutive quarters of no growth in the gross national product (GNP). Unemployment was on the upswing, particularly in heavy industry. Americans saw once-proud automobile and steel plants close. As a result of such "deindustrialization," many jobs were jeopardized while others disappeared forever. Second, there was inflation. As soaring prices eroded the purchasing power of workers' paychecks, people raided their savings, sacrificing future security to present needs.

America's economic dominance in the world had begun to decline in the 1970s. The 1973 Arab oil embargo led to the realization that the United States was not a fortress that could stand alone; it was dependent for its survival on imported oil. The postwar boom was over, but Presidents Gerald Ford and Jimmy Carter seemed unable to cope with the floundering economy.

Women and people of color were particularly hard-hit, for they were usually the last hired and the first to be laid off. Even when they had jobs, they were paid less than white men, and experts pointed to the growing "feminization" and "blackening" of poverty. Poverty became even more concentrated during the 1970s. Meanwhile opposition to the aspirations of both women and racial minorities was mounting.

By 1980, economic uncertainty was higher than at any time since the 1930s. The 1970s was the first decade since the Great Depression in which Americans' purchasing power declined. A decade of inflation and declining real wages, plus the changing nature of the labor market, the 1970s had shaken people's confidence that they could shape their personal destinies.

It was in this context that Ronald Reagan rode a wave of conservatism into office. Reagan promised a return to old-fashioned morality and a balanced budget, and he blamed government for fettering American economic creativity. Reagan's victory revealed what had already become obvious to numerous scholars and politicians: conservatism had become the dominant mood of the nation.

Ronald Reagan was successful during his first term. Although unemployment had risen between 1981 and 1983, the economy then rebounded, and by 1984 Reagan's policies had helped lower inflation and interest rates as well as unemployment. As the 1984 election approached, many Americans applauded Reagan's successes, including his foreign policy; they were proud that their nation was confronting the Russians not only with strong words but with military interventions and a large military build-up. Patriotism was back in style, and so were traditional values. A proponent of prayer in the public schools and an opponent of abortion, Reagan argued for a return to the morality that had dominated American culture prior to the 1960s.

Reagan also provoked severe criticism as president. Opponents lambasted his economic policies ("Reaganomics") as favoring the rich and penalizing the poor. Reagan seemed to escape personal blame. He was a master at distancing himself not only from scandals in the White House but even from problems in foreign and domestic policy. Representative Patricia Schroeder, a Colorado Democrat, gave this phenomenon a memorable label: Reagan, she said, was "perfecting a Teflon-coated presidency. . . . He sees to it that nothing sticks to him."

Reagan's victory in 1984 was never in doubt, but his forty-nine-state sweep convinced some observers that he had transformed American politics by forging a New Right coalition that could dominate national politics for years to come.

Because of Reagan's economic policies—most of which were solidly endorsed by Congress—wealth in the United States was being redistributed upward. While the rich got richer in the 1980s, poverty deepened for many people. The United States was polarizing racially and economically, and societal divisions were being exacerbated by new problems: AIDS (acquired immune deficiency syndrome) and the cocaine-derived drug known as "crack."

Reagan's influence collapsed during his final two years in office, due to the Republicans' loss of their Senate majority in 1986 combined with the Iran-contra scandal (see Chapter 31). Encouraged, a host of Democratic presidential hopefuls entered the 1988 primaries. But the voters went to the polls with the nation at peace and with unemployment and inflation at low levels. George Bush, President Reagan's vice president, was the beneficiary of the Reagan legacy, and as the Republican candidate he rode it to victory. Reagan, however, bequeathed to the new president and the American people a host of unsolved problems from the 1980s. The challenge of the 1990s would be to find solutions.

• *Important Events* •

1974 OPEC oil prices increase
Supreme Court orders Nixon to release
White House tapes
House Judiciary Committee votes to impeach
Nixon
Nixon resigns the presidency; Gerald Ford
becomes president
Nelson Rockefeller appointed as vice pres-
ident
Ford pardons Nixon
Ford creates WIN program to fight inflation
Equal Credit Opportunity Act equalizes loan
and credit card terms for men and women

1975 Nuclear accident occurs at Brown's Ferry
Antibusing agitation erupts in Louisville and
Boston
Economic recession hits nation

1976 Hyde Amendment cuts off Medicaid funds
for abortions
Jimmy Carter elected president

1978 *Bakke* v. *University of California* outlaws quotas but upholds affirmative action
California voters approve Proposition 13

1979 Three Mile Island nuclear accident raises
fears of meltdown
Moral Majority established
Federal Reserve Board tightens money
supply
American hostages seized in Iran

1980 Economic recession recurs
Government bails out Chrysler Corporation
Race riots break out in Miami and Chatta-
nooga
Ronald Reagan elected president

1981 American hostages released after 444 days
Prime interest rate reaches 21.5 percent

AIDS first observed in United States
Congress approves Reagan's budget cuts
Reagan breaks air traffic controllers strike
Economic Recovery Tax Act
Economic recession; unemployment hits 8
percent

1982 Prime interest rate at 14 percent
Unemployment reaches 10 percent
Voting Rights Act of 1965 renewed
Democrats gain twenty-six House seats

1983 Prime interest rate at 10.5 percent
More than half of adult women work outside
the home
ERA dies for lack of ratification

1984 Unemployment drops to 7.1 percent
Reagan re-elected
Inflation falls to 4 percent

1985 Gramm-Rudman bill calls for balanced
budget by 1991

1986 Tax Reform Act lowers personal income
taxes
Immigration Reform and Control Act provides amnesty to undocumented workers
Iran-contra scandal breaks
Republicans lose control of Senate in congressional elections

1987 Stock market prices drop 508 points in
one day

1988 *Understanding AIDS* mailed to 107 million
households
Reagan travels to the Soviet Union
George Bush elected president

1989 Bush inaugurated as president
Federal deficit rises to $206 billion

THE ENERGY CRISIS AND END OF THE ECONOMIC BOOM

It was already evident in the early 1970s that the United States was suffering serious economic de-cline. Any lingering doubts about this assessment disappeared during the Arab oil embargo of 1973 (see Chapter 31). Even before the embargo, the United States had suffered occasional shortages of natural gas, heating oil, and gasoline. But the American people, who had grown up on cheap, abundant energy, made no effort to conserve; they drove big cars and lived in poorly insulated homes. By late 1973 the country had to import one-third of its oil supplies.

Price increases ordered by the Organization of Petroleum Exporting Countries (OPEC) struck the United States another blow. Oil prices rose

OPEC Price Increases Fuel Inflation

350 percent in 1973. And even when the majority of OPEC members lifted the five-month-old oil embargo in early 1974, prices remained high. Federal officials began to fear not merely that the price of home air conditioning and heating would soar beyond the reach even of the middle class, but that runaway inflation would ensue.

As Americans grappled with the social and political costs of the price hikes, multinational oil companies prospered: their profits jumped 70 percent in 1973 and another 40 percent in 1974. Meanwhile the boost in the price of imported oil reverberated through the entire economy, driving up both inflation and unemployment and slowing economic growth considerably. Inflation jumped from 3 percent in 1972 to 6 percent in 1973 and a frightening 11 percent in 1974. At the same time recession hit the auto industry. In Detroit, General Motors laid off 38,000 workers indefinitely—6 percent of its domestic work force—and put another 48,000 on leave for up to ten days at a time. Sales of gas-guzzling American autos had plummeted as consumers rushed to purchase energy-efficient foreign subcompacts. Like Ford and Chrysler, GM was stuck with mostly large-car assembly plants.

For years the American automobile industry had based production on the tenet that large autos were more profitable to manufacture than small

Recession in the Auto Industry

ones. By late 1973, however, compact-car sales had exceeded standard-size sales, a turnaround that most auto makers had not expected before 1977. Moreover, the ailing American auto companies were not buying steel, glass, rubber, or tool-and-die products. Soon the recession in the auto industry had spread to other manufacturers, who quit hiring new workers and began laying off experienced employees with seniority.

Unlike earlier postwar recessions, this one did not fade away in a year or two. Part of the reason was inflation. In the earlier recessions, Republican as well as Democratic administrations had held to a policy of neo-Keynesianism. To minimize the swings in the business cycle, they had manipulated federal policies—both fiscal policies (taxes and government spending) and monetary policies (interest rates and the money supply). They hoped by so doing to keep employment up and inflation down.

Beginning in the 1970s, however, joblessness and prices both began to rise sharply. Policies designed to correct one problem only seemed to worsen the other.

Even in the best of times, the economy would have been hard-pressed to produce jobs for the millions of baby-boomers who joined the labor market

The Shifting Occupational Structure

in the 1970s. As it was, economic activity created 27 million additional jobs during the decade, a remarkable increase of 32 percent. (By contrast, during the 1960s, total jobs increased by 12 million, or 17 percent.) But deindustrialization was causing a shift in the occupational structure. In Youngstown and Pittsburgh, steel mills sat idle; in Detroit, weeds grew in empty parking lots next to abandoned automobile factories. As these heavy industries collapsed, laid-off workers took jobs in fast-food restaurants, all-night gas stations, and convenience stores—but at half their former wages. Workers who once had held high-paying blue-collar jobs saw their middle-class standard of living slipping away.

There were other economic problems, too. One was a slowing of growth in productivity—the average output of goods per hour of labor. Between 1947 and 1965 American

Decreased Productivity

industrial productivity had increased an average of 3.3 percent a year, raising manufacturers' profits and lowering the cost of products to consumers. From 1966 to 1970 annual productivity growth averaged only 1.5 percent; it fell further between 1971 and 1975 and reached a mere 0.2 percent between 1976 and 1980. Economists blamed lack of business investment in state-of-the-art technology, the shift from an industrial to a service economy, and an alleged erosion of the work ethic. Whatever the causes, American goods cost more than those of foreign competitors. The Joint Economic Committee of Congress warned, "The average American is likely to see his standard of living drastically decline in the 1980s unless the United States accelerates its rate of productivity growth."

The lag in productivity was not matched by a decrease in workers' expectations. Wage increases regularly exceeded production increases, and some economists blamed the raises for inflation. Indeed, wages that went up seldom came down again, regardless of market conditions. Managers of the

The Organization of Petroleum Exporting Countries (OPEC) raised oil prices several times in the 1970s. Each increase fueled the rise of inflation in the United States; and Americans, who had expected cheap energy to last forever, saw their expectations dashed. Long lines at the gas pumps were a reminder that an era of easy abundance had passed.   Don Wright in the Miami News, 1976, Tribune Media Services.

nation's basic industries—steel, autos, rubber—complained that the automatic cost-of-living adjustments in their labor contracts left them little margin to restrain price hikes.

Another spur to inflation was easy credit. Fearing scarcity, many people went on a buying spree; between 1975 and 1979, household and business borrowing more than tripled (from $94 billion to $328 billion). More people had credit cards; the number of MasterCard cardholders jumped from 32 million in 1974 to 57 million five years later. The credit explosion helped bid up the price of everything, from houses to gold. Farmers bought new farm land and expensive machinery and irrigation equipment. The nation's farm debt, $55 billion in 1971, had reached $123 billion by 1977 and $166 billion by 1980. Overburdened with debts, many farmers faced bankruptcy in the 1980s.

Easy Credit and Inflation

Every expert had a scapegoat to blame for the nation's economic doldrums. Labor leaders cited foreign competition and called for protective tariffs. Some businesspeople and economists blamed the cost of obeying federal health and safety laws and pollution controls. Such regulations not only discouraged business investments, they charged, but also burdened industries already hurt by recession with billions of dollars in extra costs. They urged officials to abolish the Environmental Protection Agency and the Occupational Safety and Health Administration. They also pressed for deregulation of the oil, airline, and trucking industries on the theory that competition would drive down prices.

Above all, critics attacked the federal government's massive spending programs; the mounting national debt, they said, was the sad result. Since the New Deal, both Republican and Democratic administrations had resorted to pump priming to cure recessions. But the Johnson administration's attempt to finance both the War on Poverty and the Vietnam War had backfired. To pay for those costly programs and to service interest on the growing national debt, the government had to compete with private businesses for investment funds. This competition forced up interest rates, making loans more expensive; thus it was more difficult for businesses to expand. Critics of neo-Keynesian pump priming pointed to stagflation as evidence of the failure of New Deal and Great Society economics.

Inflation was certainly getting out of hand. By the time Gerald Ford became president in 1974, OPEC price increases had pushed the inflation rate to 11 percent. Appalled, Ford created Whip Inflation Now (WIN), a voluntary program that encouraged businesses, consumers, and workers to save energy and organize grass-roots anti-inflation efforts. In the 1974 congressional elections, voters responded to WIN, Watergate, and Ford's pardon of Nixon by giving the Democrats forty-three additional seats in the House and four in the Senate.

Government Response to the Economic Crisis

Ford's response to inflation was to curb federal spending and encourage the Federal Reserve Board to raise its interest rates to banks, thus tightening credit. Ford was following the tenets of monetary theory, which held that the best way to reduce inflation was to keep the nation's money supply growing at a slow, consistent rate. With less money available to chase the supply of goods, monetarists contended, price increases would gently slow down. But these actions prompted a recession—this time the worst in forty years. Unemployment jumped to 8.5 percent in 1975 and, because the economy had stagnated, the federal deficit for the fiscal year 1976–1977 hit a record $60 billion.

Ford devised no lasting solutions to the energy crisis, but the crisis seemed to pass when OPEC ended the embargo—and the incentive to prevent future shortages dissolved as well. The energy crisis did, however, intensify public debate over nuclear power. For the sake of energy independence, advocates asserted, the United States had to rely more on nuclear energy. Environmental activists countered that the risk of nuclear accident was too great and that there was no safe way to store nuclear waste. In 1975 an accident in one of the world's largest nuclear reactors at Brown's Ferry, Alabama, gave credence to the opponents' argument. And in 1979,

Nuclear Power

in a plant at Three Mile Island, Pennsylvania, a stuck valve overheated the reactor core and raised fears of meltdown and radiation poisoning; a hundred thousand people were evacuated from the area. By that time ninety-six reactors were under construction throughout the nation, and thirty more were on order.

Meanwhile the combined effects of the energy crisis, stagflation, and the flight of industry and the middle class to the suburbs and the Sunbelt were producing fiscal disaster in the nation's cities. Not since 1933, when Detroit defaulted on its debts, had a major American city gone bankrupt. But New York City was near financial collapse by late 1975, unable to meet its payroll and make payments on bonds. President Ford vowed "to veto any bill that has as its purpose a federal bail-out of New York City," but he relented after the Senate and House Banking Committees approved loan guarantees, and the city was saved. New York was not alone in its financial problems; other Frostbelt cities were in trouble, saddled with growing welfare rolls, deindustrialization, and a declining tax base. In 1978 Cleveland became the first major city to default since the Great Depression.

Throughout Ford's term, Congress enjoyed new power. Although Ford almost routinely vetoed its bills, Congress often overrode his vetoes. Watergate and criticism of the imperial presidency accounted for Congress's new self-confidence. For the first time in the nation's history, furthermore, neither the president nor vice president had been popularly elected. One of Ford's first acts as president had been to select Nelson Rockefeller, former governor of New York, as his vice president. But Republican prospects for retaining the presidency in the 1976 election seemed gloomy.

THE FAILED PROMISE OF THE CARTER PRESIDENCY

While Ford struggled with a Democratic Congress, the Democratic party geared up for the presidential election of 1976. Against the background of Watergate secrecy and corruption, one candidate in particular promised honesty and openness. "I will never lie to you," pledged Jimmy Carter,

Election of 1976

On inauguration day, President Jimmy Carter (1924–   ) and his wife, Rosalyn, caught the public's fancy by walking from the Capitol to the White House. Despite this symbolic beginning, Carter became increasingly isolated both from the American people and from Congress.

an obscure former one-term governor of Georgia. A graduate of the U.S. Naval Academy, Carter had served aboard nuclear submarines before returning to Georgia to follow in his father's footsteps as a peanut farmer and politician. When this born-again Christian promised voters efficiency and decency in government, they believed him.

Carter was as ambitious as he was sincere. He also worked harder and longer than the other candidates, and he arrived at the convention with more than enough delegates to win the nomination. His choice of Senator Walter Mondale of Minnesota as his running mate cemented relations with northern liberals, African-Americans, union members, and political bosses.

Carter presented himself as a fiscal conservative who would restrain government spending, but also as a social liberal who would fight for the poor, the aged, people of color, workers, urban dwellers, and farmers. In foreign affairs, he asserted, the United States should work for human rights, arms control, and nonintervention. Above all, he emphasized his own credentials as a simple, down-home farmer and family man; a white southerner who had won the support of African-Americans and northern liberals; and an honest politician.

President Ford won his party's nomination after a bitter challenge by Ronald Reagan, former governor of California and champion of the party's growing conservative wing. Ford had grown in the public's estimation since his pardon of Nixon, and the economy had improved while he was in office: inflation had dropped to 6 percent. But neither Ford nor Carter inspired much interest, and on election day only 54 percent of the electorate bestirred itself to vote. Nevertheless, an analysis of the turnout was instructive. One political commentator concluded that the vote was "fractured to a marked degree along the fault line separating the haves and have-nots." Though Carter won nearly 90 percent of the African- and Mexican-American vote, he squeaked to victory by a slim 1.7 million votes out of 80 million cast. Ford's appeal was strongest among middle- and upper-middle-class white voters.

Carter's most noteworthy domestic accomplishments were in energy, transportation, and conservation policy. To encourage domestic production of oil, he phased in decontrol of oil prices. To moderate the social effects of the energy crisis, he called for a windfall-profits tax on excessive profits resulting from decontrol, and for grants

Carter's Accomplishments

to the poor and elderly for the purchase of heating fuel. Carter also deregulated the airline, trucking, and railroad industries and persuaded Congress to ease federal control of banks. His administration established a $1.6 billion "superfund" to clean up abandoned chemical-waste sites, and created two free-standing departments—those of energy and education. Finally, in what Carter called "the most important decision on conservation matters that the Congress will face in this century," he placed over 100 million acres of Alaskan land under the federal government's protection as national parks, national forests, and wildlife refuges.

Despite these accomplishments, Carter's popularity waned early. He seemed cold and uncommanding, and he lacked the ability to inspire Americans. Carter was the first

Carter's Flagging Popularity

president since Woodrow Wilson without prior experience in Washington. Despite his need for allies, he never established a close working relationship with congressional leaders, nor did he forge friendly relations with other power bases such as the AFL-CIO. Elected as an outsider, he remained one throughout his presidency.

Carter's conservative economic policies alienated Democrats who had grown up in the party's New Deal liberal tradition. His support of deregulation and his opposition to wage and price controls and gasoline rationing ran counter to liberal Democratic principles. Carter viewed inflation as a greater threat to the nation's economy than either recession or unemployment; his top priority, he announced, would thus be to cut federal spending, even though doing so would add to the jobless rolls. But inflation continued to rise. Liberals grumbled that Carter was a closet Republican, the most conservative Democratic president since Grover Cleveland. In late 1979, Senator Edward M. Kennedy of Massachusetts announced that he would contest the president's renomination.

Carter's problems were not entirely of his own making. The shah of Iran's government fell to revolutionary forces in 1979; the new government then cut off oil supplies to the United States (see Chapter 31). The same year OPEC raised its prices again, and the cost of crude oil nearly doubled. As Americans waited in long lines at gasoline pumps, public approval of the president reached a new low. The Carter administration did respond to the economic woes of the Chrysler Corporation, which

suffered losses of $466 million in the first six months of 1979. In the 1980 Chrysler "bail-out," Congress authorized loan guarantees of $1.5 billion on condition that Chrysler obtain wage reductions from employees, concessions from banks, and state and local aid.

Carter also inherited political problems. In the wake of Vietnam and Watergate, Congress had subjected the president to what Nixon's secretary of state William Rogers called

Decline of Presidential Authority

"a straitjacket of legislation": campaign laws, the impoundment act, and the War Powers Act (see Chapter 32). Power had temporarily shifted from the White House to Capitol Hill. Meanwhile Congress was filling up with political newcomers, men and women unaccustomed to reflex obedience to established leadership. Despite the large Democratic majorities in Congress following the Watergate scandal, party discipline seemed to be a thing of the past, and comparatively few legislative milestones were enacted during the 1970s.

To complicate matters, Capitol Hill was crawling with lobbyists from special-interest groups: trade associations, corporations, labor unions, and single-issue groups like the National Rifle Association. In 1980, there were 2,765 political-action committees (PACs), more than four times as many as in 1974. Carter complained that the nation had become "fragmented, Balkanized." With party discipline in tatters and each group clamoring for its own program, the president was forced to form what one White House aide called a "roll-your-own majority" for each proposal. The task called for skills that Carter did not possess—trading pork-barrel projects for votes, mobilizing public opinion, and massaging politicians' egos. Another obstacle was Carter's belief that since the people had elected him to make changes in Washington, he might violate their trust if he were to compromise too much.

By 1980 the economy was in a shambles. Inflation had jumped in 1979 to over 13 percent, and traders around the world had lost confidence in the dollar, causing unprecedented increases in the price of gold. To steady the dollar and curb inflation, the Federal Reserve Board had taken drastic measures in late 1979. Fully embracing the monetarist formula, the board had cut the money supply—partly by selling Treasury securities to take money out of circulation—thus forcing borrowers to bid up interest rates sufficiently to dampen the economy and reduce inflation. In early 1980 the Federal Reserve Board put on the brakes again, this time by increasing the reserves required of banks and raising the rate at which the Federal Reserve loaned money to banks. As a result, mortgage-interest rates leaped beyond 15 percent, and the prime lending rate (the rate charged to businesses) hit an all-time high of 20 percent. Inflation fell, but only to 12 percent.

Worse still, by 1980 the nation was in a full-fledged recession. The 1980 unemployment rate of 7.5 percent, combined with the 12 percent inflation rate, had produced a staggeringly high "discomfort index" of just under 20 percent (see figure). Yet the government was unable to control the causes of the discomfort. In 1976 Carter had gibed at the incumbent president, Gerald Ford, by saying, "Anything you don't like about Washington, I suggest you blame on him." In 1980 Carter was the incumbent, and many Americans blamed him for the problems that beset the country.

Economic Discomfort in 1980

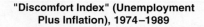

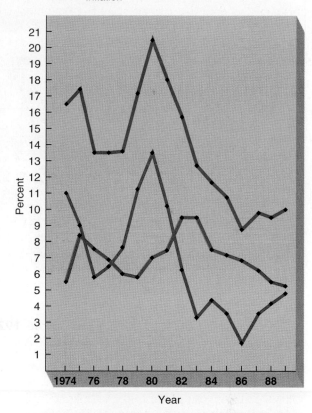

Discomfort Index (Unemployment Plus Inflation), 1974–1989 Americans' economic "discomfort" (unemployment plus inflation) directly determined their political behavior. When the "discomfort index" was high in 1976 and 1980, Americans voted for a change in presidents. When the economic discomfort declined in 1984 and 1988, Ronald Reagan and George Bush were the political beneficiaries. Source: Adapted from Economic Report of the President, 1992 (Washington, D.C.: U.S. Government Printing Office, 1992), pp. 340, 365.

RONALD REAGAN AND THE ELECTION OF 1980

The 1980 federal census revealed significant growth in the elderly population—24 percent—and a two-year rise in the median age. By 1980 there were as many Americans over thirty as under, and the number of retired people had increased by more than 50 percent since 1972. The census also documented the continuing shift of large numbers of people from the politically liberal Frostbelt states of the Northeast and Midwest to the more conservative Sunbelt states of the South and West (see map, page 1032). The census findings meant that seventeen seats in the House of Representatives would shift from the Frostbelt to the Sunbelt by the 1982 elections. Florida would gain four seats and New York would lose five; Texas would gain three, California two.

A Shifting Population

Besides growing political power, the Sunbelt enjoyed abundant energy resources and a wider tax base than the North. In 1980, Louisiana produced over four times its own energy needs, New Mexico over three, and Texas over two. By contrast, Michigan and New York had to import most of their energy, at a price jacked up by export taxes imposed by producing states. Taxes were lower in the Sunbelt too; Texas families paid less than half

The Continued Shift to the Sunbelt in the 1970s *Throughout the 1970s, Americans continued to leave economically-declining areas of the North and the East in pursuit of opportunity in the Sunbelt.*

as much of their incomes for state and local taxes as New York families did.

A consequence of the shift of population to the Sunbelt was the resurgence of conservatism in the 1970s and 1980s. At the heart of this political conservatism was doubt about government's capacity to serve the people. Senator Gary Hart, a Colorado Democrat, characterized this mood in 1977 as "a nonideological skepticism about the old, Rooseveltian solutions to social problems." Conservatives were hard at work trying to repeal the social welfare system. California voters approved a 1978 tax-cutting referendum called Proposition 13, which reduced property taxes and put stringent limits on state spending for social programs. Proposition 13 set off shock waves: nearly a score of other states imposed similar ceilings on taxes and expenditures. On the national level, conservatives lobbied for

Resurgence of Conservatism

a constitutional amendment to prohibit federal budget deficits.

A new political alignment was taking place. Economic conservatives were being joined by evangelical Christians, who believed they had a moral obligation to enter politics on the side of "a pro-life, pro-traditional family, pro-moral position." In 1979 the Reverend Jerry Falwell, a radio-TV minister from Lynchburg, Virginia, helped to found the Moral Majority, which quickly registered between two and three million new voters, started a newspaper, and bought daily time on 140 radio stations. Together with conservative think tanks like the Hoover Institution and conservative magazines like the *National Review*, these church groups formed a flourishing network of potential supporters for conservative candidates.

In 1980 several conservative Republican politicians ran for the White House. Foremost among them was Ronald Reagan, former movie star and

A former movie actor and host of television shows, Ronald Reagan made effective use of TV in arguing for "family values," an aggressive anti-Soviet foreign and military policy, and tax cuts. To numerous Americans, Reagan was "the great communicator." Ronald Reagan Presidential Library, TV courtesy of Zenith Electronics Corporation.

Ronald Reagan's Early Career

two-term governor of California. A small-town boy from Dixon, Illinois, Reagan had been a radio sportscaster before moving to Hollywood in the mid-1930s. As president of the Screen Actors Guild, his politics had been those of a New Deal Democrat. But touring the country in the 1950s as host of the television program "General Electric Theatre," Reagan became increasingly conservative. In 1964 he made a televised appeal for Senator Barry Goldwater, the conservative Republican presidential candidate. Reagan's persuasive speech not only catapulted him to the forefront of conservative politics, it became his personal platform for the presidency. America, Reagan said, had come to "a time for choosing" between free enterprise and big government, between individual liberty and "the ant heap of totalitarianism." Two years later he was elected governor of California.

During his two four-year terms as governor, Reagan had maintained his conservatism but had also displayed a pragmatic approach to governing. While denouncing welfare, he had presided over reform of the state's social welfare bureaucracy. While demanding that student radicals at the University of California either obey the rules or face the prospect of a "bloodbath," he had endorsed most of the university's budget requests. And he had signed one of the nation's most liberal abortion laws.

Election of 1980

In the Republican primaries, Reagan triumphed easily over Representative John Anderson and former CIA director George Bush. His appeal to the voters in the presidential campaign was much broader than experts had predicted. He promised economy in government and a balanced budget, and he committed himself to "supply-side" eco-

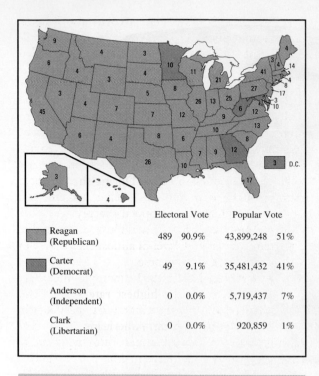

	Electoral Vote		Popular Vote	
Reagan (Republican)	489	90.9%	43,899,248	51%
Carter (Democrat)	49	9.1%	35,481,432	41%
Anderson (Independent)	0	0.0%	5,719,437	7%
Clark (Libertarian)	0	0.0%	920,859	1%

Presidential Election, 1980 *Ronald Reagan scored the first of two political landslides in 1980, when he won forty-four states to Jimmy Carter's six.*

nomics, or tax reductions to businesses to encourage capital investment. Although Reagan planned to slash federal spending, he also pledged to cut income taxes and boost the defense budget—a prescription that George Bush ridiculed as "voodoo economics." Reagan declared that he now opposed legalized abortion, and his stand against the Equal Rights Amendment (ERA) recommended him to the "profamily" movement.

Indeed, Reagan's candidacy united the old right wing with the new. The old right, explained one fund-raiser, had never been very interested in social issues. "But when political conservative leaders began to . . . strike an alliance with social conservatives—the pro-life people, the anti-ERA people, the evangelical and born-again Christians, the people concerned about gay rights, prayer in the schools, sex in the movies or whatever—that's when this whole movement began to come alive."

In the Democratic primaries, President Carter easily beat back Senator Edward Kennedy's challenge; Kennedy's New Deal liberalism seemed out of place in a conservative era, and memories of

Chappaquiddick lingered in voters' minds (see Chapter 32). But the president had more formidable problems. American hostages were still held captive in Iran, and stagflation beset the economy. Carter's major problem was his approval rating of 21 percent, even lower than Richard Nixon's 24 percent during the Watergate crisis.

On election day, voters gave Reagan and his running mate George Bush 51 percent of the vote to 41 percent for Carter and almost 7 percent for Anderson (see map). Reagan's sweep was nationwide; Carter carried only six states and the District of Columbia. The vote was not only an affirmation of Reagan's conservatism but also a signal of the nation's deep dissatisfaction with Jimmy Carter's management of both the economy and foreign policy. As startling as Reagan's sweep was the capture of eleven Senate seats by Republican candidates, giving the party a majority in that house. Republicans also gained thirty-three seats in the House and four state governorships.

The preceding fifteen years had been difficult ones for the Democratic party. Fragmented by the issues of race and war, the party had lost the support of many whites in the 1970s. With self-proclaimed "Reagan Democrats" supporting Republican candidates, it seemed clear that the Democrats would be running scared in the 1980s.

"REAGANOMICS"

Upon taking office, President Reagan wasted little time announcing what he called "a new beginning." He immediately launched a double-barreled attack on problems in the economy. First, he asked Congress to cut billions from domestic programs, including urban aid, Medicare and Medicaid, food stamps, welfare subsidies for the working poor, and school meals. Congress endorsed most of Reagan's demands. He soon initiated a second round of budget cuts, resulting among other things in the trimming of a million food-stamp recipients from government rolls.

Tax cuts were the second facet of Reagan's economic plan. A fervent believer in supply-side economics, he called for reductions in the income taxes **Tax Cuts** of the affluent and of corporations in order to stimulate savings and investments. New capital would be invested, the argument went, and would produce new plants, new jobs, and new products. As prosperity returned, the profits at the top would "trickle down" to the middle classes and even to the poor. Congress responded with a five-year, $750 billion tax cut, the largest ever in American history, featuring a 25 percent reduction in personal income taxes over three years. Other provisions increased business investment tax credits and depreciation allowances and lowered the maximum tax on income from 70 to 50 percent. The wealthy gained the most from these tax cuts. In an unguarded moment, budget director David Stockman acknowledged that Reagan's supply-side doctrines were a "Trojan horse" for tax relief to the rich. It was hard to sell a policy known as "trickle down," Stockman explained, so the administration had dignified it by calling it "supply-side economics."

A third item occupied Reagan's agenda: a vigorous assault on federal environmental, health, and safety regulations that, Reagan believed, excessively reduced business prof-

Weakened Environmental Enforcement

its and discouraged economic growth. The president appointed opponents of these regulations to enforce them. Some critics likened such appointments to hiring foxes to guard the chicken coops. Even the business-oriented *Wall Street Journal* observed that the president was "naming regulators who by virtue of attitude or inexperience are more likely to be nonregulators." Reagan officials explained that slackened enforcement was necessary to reduce business costs and make American goods competitive in world markets, but environmentalists countered that such policies invited disaster, such as toxic-waste poisoning or nuclear reactor accidents.

Reagan scored two notable economic successes during his first two years in office: the inflation rate plummeted, as did the cost of borrowing money. With the Federal Re-

Falling Inflation

serve Board leading the way by lowering its prime rate for bank loans, interest rates, which had stood at a record high of 21.5 percent in early 1981, dropped to 10.5 percent by early 1983. Inflation fell from 12 percent in 1980 to less than 7 percent in 1982. Oil led the way in price declines; after eight years OPEC had at last increased its oil output, thus lowering prices. In 1981 the United States was awash with oil, as world production exceeded demand by two million

barrels a day. Some Americans had also become conservation-minded. Homeowners by the millions turned down their thermostats and installed insulation.

But there was also a sobering explanation for the decline in inflation. "It wasn't just luck on food and oil," said an economist with a leading economic-forecasting firm. "It was . . . the stagnant economy that brought the prices down." By mid-1981 the nation was mired in a recession that not only persisted but deepened. During the last three months of the year, the GNP fell 5 percent, and sales of cars and houses dropped sharply. With declining economic activity, unemployment soared to 8 percent, the highest level in almost six years. But worse news was still to come.

A year later, in late 1982, unemployment had reached 10 percent, the highest rate since 1940. Most of the jobless were adult men, particularly African-Americans who suf-

Rising Unemployment

fered an unemployment rate of 20 percent. Many of the unemployed were blue-collar workers in such ailing "smokestack industries" as autos, steel, and rubber. Reagan and his advisers had promised that his supply-side economics would produce demand-side results and that, by spending their tax cuts, consumers would lift the economy out of the recession. But as late as April 1983, unemployment still stood at 10 percent and people were angry. Heavy industry was in a shambles. Jobless steelworkers paraded through McKeesport, Pennsylvania, carrying a coffin that bore the epitaph "American Dream." Facing a bleak future, people took to the road; most headed to the Sunbelt. Agriculture, too, was faltering and near collapse. Farmers suffered from floods and droughts and from burdensome debts they had incurred at high interest rates. Many lost their property through mortgage foreclosures and farm auctions. Others filed for bankruptcy.

As the recession deepened in 1982, poverty rose to its highest level since 1965. The Bureau of the Census reported that the number of Americans

Resurgence of Poverty

living in poverty increased from 26 million in 1979 to 34 million in 1982. Poverty increased most among African-Americans (36 percent of whom were poor) and Hispanic-Americans (30 percent). Predictably, the largest single category of poor families consisted of households headed by

Many farm families in the 1980s, like this couple in southern Illinois, were forced to sell their land, machinery, and personal possessions to pay off their debts. Burdened by low prices and, in some areas, by severe drought, few family farmers looked forward to the future. Roy Roper/ Gamma-Liaison.

women (36 percent). With one exception, poverty continued its rise in 1983, returning to the level that had prevailed before the enactment of President Johnson's Great Society. That exception was the elderly; politicians had begun paying attention to the needs of this vocal and rapidly growing group.

President Reagan had announced that his administration would halt the expansion of social and health programs but would retain a "safety net" for the "truly needy." But he reneged on this promise, and Congress, unwilling to buck the popular president, sustained most of his decisions. Facing a budget deficit in excess of $200 billion in mid-1982, Reagan had three choices, and in each case he made a conservative decision. First, he could cut back on his rearmament plans to spend $1.7 trillion over five years. This he refused to do; in fact, the budget he signed raised defense spending another 13 per-

cent. Second, he could suspend or reduce the second installment of his tax cut. This choice, too, he found unacceptable. Third, he could—and did— cut welfare and social programs, pushing through Congress further cuts in Medicare and Medicaid, food stamps, federal pensions, and government-guaranteed home mortgages. Nevertheless, in the absence of other budget cuts, the deficit continued to grow.

Democrats predicted victories for their party in the 1982 congressional elections. Just a week before the elections, however, a *New York Times/CBS News* poll reported that the American public was being tugged sharply in different directions: toward the Democrats by unemployment, toward the Republicans by declining inflation and the president's popularity. Nothing revealed Reagan's winning style better than his courageous response to an attempt on his life by a deranged young man in March 1981. John W. Hinckley, Jr. wounded the president, his press secretary, a Secret Service agent, and a police officer. Reagan's courage and grace caused his popularity ratings to soar.

In the 1982 elections, 26 House seats swung to the Democrats, giving them a lead of 267 to 166. The Senate remained pro-Reagan, with a continued Republican majority of 54 to 46. In another two years, there would be a presidential election. The president had to prove before then that he could restore prosperity to the nation.

1982 Elections

REAGAN TRIUMPHANT: THE ELECTION OF 1984

President Reagan prepared for his 1984 re-election campaign with the knowledge that, although most white men supported him, the majority of women and people of color opposed him. Joining them in the anti-Reagan camp were most of the nation's labor unions.

Even without Reagan in the White House, hard times would have hit the unions in the 1980s. Faced with recession and unemployment, union negotiators had to settle for less than they were accustomed to receiving. American workers who ratified contracts during the first three months of Reagan's term settled for pay increases averaging only 2.2 percent, the biggest drop in wage settlements since the government began collecting such data in 1954. Unions had suffered large membership losses when unemployment hit the "smokestack industries," and their efforts to unionize the high-growth electronics and service sectors of the economy were failing. The Supreme Court ruled in 1984 that companies declaring bankruptcy could unilaterally cancel union contracts without even a hearing.

Hard Times for Labor Unions

Reagan made the unions' hard times worse. He presided over the government's busting of the Professional Air Traffic Controllers Organization (PATCO) during the union's 1981 strike. His appointees to the National Labor Relations Board consistently voted against labor and for management. Although Reagan appeared to be an enemy

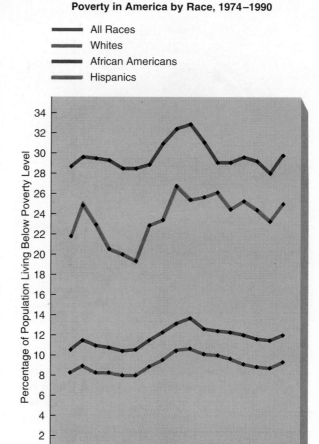

Poverty in America by Race, 1974–1990

- All Races
- Whites
- African Americans
- Hispanics

Percentage of Population Living Below Poverty Level vs. Year

Poverty in America by Race, 1974–1989
Poverty in America rose in the early 1980s, but subsided afterwards. Many people of color, however, experienced little relief during the decade. Note that the percentage of African-Americans living below the poverty level was three times higher than that for whites. It was also much higher for Hispanic-Americans.   Source: Adapted from U.S. Bureau of the Census, *Statistical Abstract of the United States* (Washington, D.C.: U.S. Government Printing Office, 1992), p. 461.

of labor, union leaders could not rally their members to oppose his re-election. An estimated 44 percent of union families had voted for Reagan in 1980; many still responded positively to his genial personality, espousal of old-fashioned values, and anticommunism.

In 1984 Geraldine Ferraro, Democratic congresswoman from New York, made history by being the first woman nominated to run for the vice presidency on a major party's ticket. Smithsonian Institution, Division of Political History, Washington, D.C.

Reagan's opponents denounced the "country club ethics" of his appointees, several of whom resigned after accusations of illegal or improper behavior. An example was Rita **Reagan Administration Scandals** Lavelle, an official with the Environmental Protection Agency (EPA), who was convicted of perjury and obstruction of justice for impeding a congressional investigation into her role in halting an EPA crackdown on her former employer, Aerojet-General Corporation. Meanwhile, the number two administrators of both the CIA and the Department of Defense left office after newspapers reported that they had taken part in illegal stock transactions. In ordinary political times, the Democrats would have profited from the issue of corruption in government ("the sleaze factor"). But voters were more concerned about the economy, which showed unmistakable signs of recovery.

In 1984 the GNP rose 7 percent, the sharpest increase since 1951, and midyear unemployment fell to a four-year low of 7 percent. The economy was heating up, but without sparking inflation. Indeed, inflation (4 percent in 1984) fell to its lowest level since 1967. A second factor in Reagan's favor was people's perception of him as a strong leader in foreign as well as national affairs. Reagan was the enthusiastic choice not only of political conservatives but also of social and religious conservatives across the country. He won the approval of millions of other Americans who agreed with his television ads that "America is back" after two decades of turmoil and self-doubt.

Aiding Reagan was the Democrats' failure to field a convincing alternative. The Democratic nominee—former Vice President Walter Mondale—did not inspire Americans; most people identified him with the ineffectuality of the Carter administration. Mondale, speaking for the New Deal tradition of the welfare system, received endorsements from the National Organization for Women, the AFL-CIO, and various civil rights organizations. What enthusiasm there was for the Democratic ticket arose from Mondale's historic selection of Congresswoman Geraldine Ferraro of New York as his vice-presidential running mate. Ferraro showed herself to be an intelligent, indefatigable campaigner.

The Democratic party, however, was in disarray; its policies seemed timeworn and out of step with the nation's conservatism. It was fragmented into separate caucuses of union members, blacks, women, Jews, homosexuals, Hispanics, and other groups. Each group had its own agenda, and at the 1984 Democratic National Convention each threatened to walk out if its demands were not met. Many Americans concluded that the Democratic party was concerned less with the national welfare than with dividing up the spoils among its special-interest groups.

During the 1930s the New Deal coalition had gained the allegiance of economic liberals who subscribed to the social welfare system. But in the 1980s a deep reaction set in against the liberalized moral standards of the 1960s. Many Democrats still held conservative views on abortion, homosexuality, and other social issues, and they switched their votes to Ronald Reagan. Reagan's personality seemed to fit the public mood. In 1984 the pollster Daniel Yankelovich reported that "defeatism is gone." Confidence had returned, and the political cycle had turned farther to the right, as it had in earlier epochs like the 1920s and 1950s.

Mondale attempted to debate the federal deficit and the nuclear arms race, but Reagan preferred to invoke the theme of leadership and rely on slogans. Mondale chastised Reagan for the deficit, which had reached $175 billion in fiscal year 1984. But when Mondale announced that he would raise

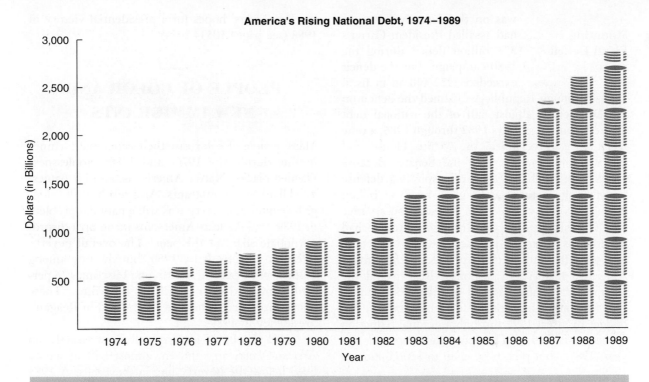

America's Rising National Debt, 1974–1989

America's Rising National Debt, 1974–1989 *America's national debt, which rose sporadically through-out the 1970s, soared to record heights during the 1980s. Under President Reagan, large defense expenditures and tax cuts caused the national debt to grow by $1.5 trillion. The years in this illustration are budget years, which begin in preceding calendar years (the 1989 budget year, for example, began October 1, 1988).* Source: Adapted from U.S. Bureau of the Census, *Statistical Abstract of the United States* (Washington, D.C.: U.S. Government Printing Office, 1992), p. 315.

taxes to cut the deficit, he lost votes. Mondale also attacked Reagan's foreign policy as militaristic, but Americans were attracted to Reagan's pledge to restore American global power.

Voters in 1984 had a clear choice, and in every state but Minnesota—Mondale's home state—they chose the Republican ticket. The election returns were the most convincing evidence yet that the nation had shifted to the right. The only groups still loyal to the Democratic ticket were African-Americans, Hispanics, Jews, the poor, and the unemployed. Reagan scored solid victories with all other voting groups, including young people, whites in both the North and the South, high-school and college graduates, Protestants and Catholics, and families with incomes exceeding $12,500.

Reagan's Victory

In his second inaugural address, Reagan announced that his "new American Emancipation" would eradicate the excesses of fifty years of Democratic liberalism and thus "tear down economic barriers to liberate the spirit of enterprise." Whether Reagan had forged a lasting conservative coalition—one that would eventually repeal the New Deal—remained to be seen. What was not debatable was that he had succeeded in his principal aims during his first term and had restored the presidency to its central role in politics and the government. Columnist David Broder wrote that "with the nation prosperous and at peace and his personal popularity high," Reagan could already lay claim to being "a historically significant president."

Broder also noted, however, that "Reagan's issue-free, feel-good 1984 campaign created no policy mandate," and for much of 1985 the president

Mounting Fiscal Deficit
was on the defensive. Reagan had assailed President Carter's $73 billion deficit during the 1980 campaign, but the deficit exceeded $222 billion in fiscal 1985. Although Republicans blamed the deficit on the Democrats, almost half of the national debt derived from fiscal years 1982 through 1986, a time when Reagan occupied the White House and the Republicans controlled the Senate. Because of tax reductions and upwardly spiraling defense budgets, the national debt grew by $954 billion during this five-year period. A fiscal conservative long committed to balanced budgets, Reagan had nonetheless overseen the accumulation of more new debt than all previous presidents throughout America's history. In response, Reagan and the Congress reluctantly agreed to the 1985 Gramm-Rudman bill, which called for a balanced federal budget by fiscal 1991 through a gradual reduction of the annual deficit. The deficit did drop—for one year, 1987—but then rose again to $206 billion in 1989.

Reagan was more successful in confronting other challenges. Following Warren Burger's decision to retire from the Supreme Court, he nominated William Rehnquist to serve as chief justice and Antonin Scalia to fill Rehnquist's seat; the Senate confirmed both choices. Another victory was the Tax Reform Act of 1986, which lowered personal income taxes while closing some flagrant loopholes and eliminating six million poor people from the tax rolls. The law represented a compromise between supply-side conservatives, who argued that lower tax rates would act as an incentive to savings, investment, and growth, and liberals whose focus was the inequity of the tax codes.

Meanwhile, economically and racially, American society became increasingly polarized. People of color and new immigrants found themselves battling not only rising poverty levels, but also white hostility. Large numbers of women and children also slipped into poverty in the 1980s, a decade of growing economic inequality and social problems. Hard drugs brought devastation to entire neighborhoods, while AIDS killed tens of thousands of Americans.

Until late 1986, Reagan's place in history was secure. But the Iran-contra disclosures would cause his aura to fade, sullying his last two years in office, endangering his historical reputation, and raising the Democrats' hopes for a presidential victory in 1988 (see pages 1051–1054).

PEOPLE OF COLOR AND NEW IMMIGRANTS

Many people of color saw their economic fortunes decline during the 1970s and 1980s. Joblessness plagued blacks, Native Americans, and Hispanics, as well as new immigrants. As a result of the sluggish economy, poverty was still a national problem in 1989, and African-Americans made up a disproportionate share of the poor. The overall poverty rate was 13 percent by 1980, but the rate among blacks was 33 percent and among Hispanics 26 percent, compared with 10 percent for whites. These figures had barely changed by the end of Reagan's presidency in 1989.

The weight of poverty fell most heavily on African-American children, almost half of whom lived below the poverty line in the 1980s. A 1981 Children's Defense Fund survey reported that black children in the United States were four times more likely than whites to be born into poverty, twice as likely to drop out of school before twelfth grade, five times as likely as white teenagers to be murdered, and three times as likely to be unemployed. "Millions of black children lack self-confidence, feel discouragement, despair, numbness or rage as they try to grow up on islands of poverty, ill health, inadequate education . . . crime and rampant unemployment in a nation of boastful affluence," the report concluded. Many black children lived in families headed by single women who were forced to rely on welfare or earned meager incomes as domestic servants, laundresses, and kitchen helpers.

Some whites and even other blacks grumbled that poor blacks were responsible for their own poverty. But the job market was far different
Declining Job Opportunities for African-Americans
in the 1970s and 1980s from that of twenty-five, fifty, or seventy-five years before. During periods of rapid industrialization, unskilled European immigrants and black migrants from the South had been able to find blue-collar jobs. Beginning in the 1970s, fewer such jobs were available; demand was great-

est for skilled workers such as computer operators, bank tellers, secretaries, and bookkeepers. Most jobless people could not qualify. Moreover, blue-collar jobs in the inner cities were disappearing or moving to the suburbs. New York City alone had 234,000 fewer blue-collar workers in 1980 than it had at the beginning of the decade. The situation was tragic for young African-American men and women who lacked marketable skills. As the black psychiatrist Alvin Poussaint has observed, "A lot of black kids simply feel they don't count. . . . In terms of what makes this society run, they're expendable."

African-American Middle Class

Even as the plight of the African-American poor worsened, the black middle class expanded. The number of black college students increased from 282,000 in 1966 to over 1 million in 1980; by 1980 about one-third of all black high-school graduates were going on to college, the same proportion as among white youths. And by 1990, the number of black college students had increased further to 1.3 million. At least at the upper levels of black society, the dream of equality was being realized.

White Backlash

As middle-class African-Americans made gains, however, resentful whites complained that they were being victimized by "reverse discrimination." To meet federal affirmative-action requirements, some schools and companies had established quotas for minorities and women; in some cases the requirements were lower than those for whites. When Allan Bakke, a white man, was denied admission to medical school, he sued on the grounds that less-qualified black applicants had been admitted. In a 5-to-4 ruling in 1978 the Supreme Court outlawed quotas and ordered that Bakke be admitted. But the Court also upheld the principle of affirmative action, explaining that race or ethnicity could be counted as "a 'plus' in a particular applicant's file" (*Bakke* v. *University of California*). In 1989, however, the Court chipped away at this ruling. It reasserted that "the sorry history" of discrimination in America did not "justify a rigid racial quota" and further decided that white workers could sue to reopen affirmative-action cases settled in federal courts years earlier (*Richmond* v. *Croson, Martin* v. *Wilks*).

White anger over affirmative action and busing combined with the effects of stagflation to produce an upsurge in racism. In Louisville in 1975, bumper stickers urged people to "honk if you oppose busing." The Ku Klux Klan stepped up its recruiting in Louisville, and violence soon erupted: one hundred people were injured and two hundred arrested. In Boston, where busing provoked numerous riots, a group of white students attacked a black passer-by outside city hall. "Get the nigger; kill him," one shouted, and they ran at him with the sharp end of a flagstaff flying an American flag. Tension rose all across the nation. There was also a rise in terrorism by neo-Nazi "skinheads," young men who brutally attacked people of African and Asian descent. At the same time, college campuses reported increased hate crimes against blacks, Jews, and homosexuals.

Black Anger

African-Americans were tense, and they showed it more openly than in the past. "After 350 years of fearing whites," Charles Silberman wrote in *Criminal Violence, Criminal Justice* (1978), "black Americans have discovered that fear runs the other way, that whites are intimidated by their very presence. . . . The taboo against expression of anti-white anger is breaking down, and 350 years of festering hatred has come spilling out." That hatred erupted several times in 1980, most notably in Miami and Chattanooga, after all-white juries acquitted whites of the murder of blacks. Miami's three days of rioting left eighteen dead, four hundred injured, and $100 million worth of property damage.

African-American civil rights leaders denounced not only the judicial system but also the executive branch headed by President Ronald Reagan. Appointments were one issue: whereas 12 percent of President Jimmy Carter's high-level appointees had been black and 12 percent women, Reagan's were 4 percent black and 8 percent women. (Reagan did appoint four women to his cabinet, and he made history by appointing Sandra Day O'Connor as the first woman associate justice of the Supreme Court.) Furthermore, Reagan's administration favored tax exemptions for fundamentalist Christian schools that cited the Bible to justify racial segregation and whites-only admissions policies. (In an 8-to-1 decision the Supreme Court ruled against such exemptions in 1983 and ordered the Internal Revenue Service to deny tax exemptions to two such schools.) Although Reagan denounced as "plain baloney" the allegation that his administration was taking a less active approach to protecting civil rights, his record proved otherwise. Reagan's civil rights chief in the Justice Department fought against renewing the Voting Rights Act of 1965, opposed busing and affirmative action, and was criticized for lax enforcement of fair-housing laws and laws banning sexual and racial discrimination in federally funded education programs.

"The Kerner report warning is coming true," asserted a group of scholars, politicians, and civil rights leaders who met in 1988 to assess race relations on the twentieth anniversary of the publication of the Kerner Commission report (see Chapter 32). "America is again becoming two separate societies," whites residing in the suburbs while African-Americans in inner cities lived amid poverty, segregation, and crime. "Even the most pessimistic observers of the social scene in the later 1960s," observed sociologist William Julius Wilson, a member of the group, "probably did not foresee or anticipate the sharp increases in the rates of social dislocation and massive breakdown of social institutions in ghetto areas."

Every bit as angry as African-Americans were Native Americans. Their new militancy burst into the headlines in late 1969, when a small group of Indians seized Alcatraz Island

Native American Militancy

in San Francisco Bay. Arguing that an 1868 Sioux treaty entitled them to possession of unused federal lands, the group occupied the island until mid-1971. More was at stake than an abandoned federal penitentiary. "Not just on Alcatraz," explained Richard Oakes, a spokesperson for the Indians, "but every place else, the Indian is in his last stand for cultural survival." Two years later, members of the militant American Indian Movement (AIM), demanding the rights guaranteed Indians in treaties with the United States, seized eleven hostages and a trading post on the Pine Ridge Reservation at Wounded Knee, South Dakota, where troops of the 7th Cavalry had massacred the Sioux in 1890. Their seventy-one-day confrontation with federal marshals ended with a government agreement to examine the treaty rights of the Oglala Sioux.

White society posed more than a cultural threat to Indians. Four out of ten Native Ameri-

cans were unemployed, and nine out of ten lived in substandard housing. Often, being an Indian also meant being unhealthy: Native Americans suffered the highest incidence of alcoholism, tuberculosis, and suicide of any ethnic group in the United States. Although their numbers had risen since the Second World War to 1.7 million in 1990—more than half of whom lived in California, Oklahoma, Arizona, New Mexico, and North Carolina—that was only a fraction of the Native American population when the first Europeans arrived in North America.

Since 1924, Indians have had dual legal status as U.S. citizens and as members of tribal nations subject to special treaty agreements with the United States. Their dual status has proved a curse, in large part because the government found it easier to breach its treaty commitments—especially when Indian lands contained valuable minerals. In 1946 Congress established the Indian Claims Commission to compensate Indians for lands stolen from them. Under the legislation, lawyers for the Native American Rights Fund and other groups scored notable victories, including protection of Indians' hunting and fishing rights and restitution of their land and water. In 1980, for example, the Supreme Court ordered the government to pay $106 million plus interest to the Sioux Indian Nation for the Black Hills of South Dakota, stolen when gold was discovered there in the 1870s. Nevertheless, corporations and government agencies continued to covet Indian lands and disregard Indian religious beliefs: a coal company strip-mined a portion of the Hopi Sacred Circle, which according to tribal religion is the source of all life. And the sacred Black Hills of South Dakota were also being mined, this time for uranium.

As Indians fought to regain old rights, Hispanic-Americans struggled to make a place for themselves. An influx of immigrants unequaled

Hispanic-Americans

since the turn of the century coupled with a high birthrate made Hispanic peoples America's fastest-growing minority by the 1970s. Of the more than 20 million Hispanics living in the United States in the 1970s, 8 million were Mexican-Americans concentrated in Arizona, California, Colorado, New Mexico, and Texas. Several million Puerto

For 110 years, an Arizona land dispute has divided the Hopi and Navajo Indian tribes. A law passed by Congress in 1974 called for the division of 1.8 million acres between the tribes, and ordered the relocation of tribal members who lived on land given to the other tribe. Hopi and Navajo traditionalists claimed that they had no dispute, but that powerful economic interests were using the issue as a cover for seizing the area's rich coal and water rights. In 1986 these Hopi and Navajo joined to protest another federal law, directing the Secretary of the Interior to "expedite" relocation "without regard to any law or regulation."   Lawrence Gus/Sygma.

Ricans and Cubans clustered principally on the East Coast.

These officially acknowledged Hispanics were joined by millions of undocumented workers, or illegal aliens. Beginning in the mid-1960s, large numbers of poverty-stricken Mexicans began to cross the poorly guarded two-thousand-mile border. The movement north continued in the 1970s; in the last eight years of that decade the Mexican-American population increased 60 percent. And from 1980 to 1987, the nation's Hispanic population increased five times as fast as the rest of the population. By 1990, one out of three Los Angelenos and Miamians was Hispanic, as well as 20 percent of the population of San Diego, 48 percent of San Antonio, and 70 percent of El Paso.

Poverty awaited these new immigrants, as it had previous groups of newcomers. Like many earlier groups, Hispanics faced a language barrier. Most inner-city schools did not provide bilingual education for Spanish-speaking students. Finally, the larger the Hispanic population has become, the more widespread has been the discrimination. "Anglos are afraid," said California Assemblyman Richard Alatorre. "They think they will get to be the minorities and we'll be opposing them."

Most of these new Americans preferred their family-centered culture to Anglo culture and, for that reason, resisted assimilation. "We want to be here," explained Daniel Villanueva, a TV executive, "but without losing our language and our culture. They are a richness, a treasure that we don't care to lose." A Puerto Rican woman in New York added, "We have been trying to become American for too long, and we are forgetting our roots, culture and the values of our nationality."

Hispanic Cultural Pride

Like other minorities, Hispanics wanted political power—"brown power." Cesar Chavez's

United Farm Workers was the first Hispanic interest group to gain national attention. The militant Brown Berets also attracted notice for their efforts to provide meals to preschoolers and courses in Chicano studies and consciousness raising to older students. And throughout the 1970s the Mexican-American political party La Raza Unida was a potent force in the Southwest and East Los Angeles.

Still, for the group that was becoming the nation's largest minority, Hispanics exercised a disproportionately small share of political power. One reason was that Latin America is tremendously diverse. Although they shared a language and a religion, Mexican-Americans, Puerto Ricans, Cubans, and other groups differed in countless ways. And differences were not only in country of origin: economic immigrants such as Mexican-Americans crowded into West Coast barrios side by side with political refugees from Central American wars. Poverty was most severe where the population was most concentrated. "If current poverty trends continue," proclaimed the Census Bureau, "by 1990 Hispanics will replace blacks as the ethnic group with the highest poverty rate in the United States." (The worst poverty of all, however, was suffered by reservation Indians.) "We need a Spanish Bobby Kennedy or Martin Luther King," observed Daniel Villanueva. "Right now he's just not there."

During the 1980s Hispanic and Native Americans joined African-Americans in denouncing the Reagan administration. The League of United Latin American Citizens censured Reagan for his "very, very dismal record" in dealing with their problems, and the National Tribal Chairmen's Association charged that under Reagan "the delivery of services by federal agencies to Indians was in a shambles."

During the 1970s and 1980s people of color immigrated to the United States in record numbers from Indochina, Mexico, Central and South America, and the Caribbean. Refugees of the Vietnam War arrived; other immigrants came from the Philippines, Korea, Taiwan, India, the Dominican Republic, and Jamaica; and boat people poured in from the islands of Cuba and Haiti. Between 1970 and 1980 the United States absorbed more than 4 million immigrants and refugees and perhaps twice that number of illegal aliens. High as these figures were, they doubled again during the next decade.

New Influx of Immigrants

With 9 million new arrivals, the 1980s surpassed the historic high mark set by the 8.7 million immigrants who had reached American shores between 1901 and 1910. The new immigrants consisted largely of families. By contrast to the traditional pattern of working-age men seeking economic opportunity, women and children accounted for two-thirds of all legal immigrants. Although well-wishers were on hand to greet some of these people, the history of the nation's treatment of people of color did not augur well for many of them. "Some people derive great benefit from the present situation," explained Leon Castillo, former commissioner of immigration, referring to the low wages paid to aliens.

Although the new residents faced a long struggle, most were willing to work hard to succeed. Among the newcomers, Asian-Americans seemed to be the most successful, whether they were Korean greengrocers on Manhattan's Upper West Side; Laotian or Vietnamese refugees drawn to Garden City, Kansas, to work in the world's largest meat-packing plant; or Chinese workers assembling integrated circuits in California's Silicon Valley.

The arrival of so many newcomers threw the immigration control system into such disarray that, as officials of the Immigration and Naturalization Service conceded, practically anyone who wished to could illegally enter the United States and stay for months or years, if not for good. Pressure mounted on Congress to curtail this flow and perhaps offer amnesty to aliens already living illegally in the United States.

In 1978 Congress authorized a comprehensive re-examination of America's immigration policy. The immigration commission completed its study in 1981, but legislative solutions were delayed until 1986, when Congress passed the Immigration Reform and Control (Simpson-Rodino) Act. The act provided amnesty to undocumented workers who had arrived before 1982. The act's purpose was to discourage illegal immigration by imposing sanctions on employers who hired undocumented workers, but it failed to stem the flow of people fleeing Mexico's economic woes. "It's harder to get across," explained a Mexican man, "but we do get across, if not on the first try, then on the second, third or fourth." In 1988 the number of new immi-

Immigration Reform

The decades of the 1970s and 1980s saw the mass immigration to the United States of people of color from numerous Asian and Latin American countries. As evidenced by these Boy Scouts, younger Asian-Americans took quickly to the ways of their new country. Leif Skoogfors/Woodfin Camp & Associates.

grants from Mexico approached the record numbers reached just before the reform law went into effect. "There is no sign the legislation has had any impact on the flows," explained a Mexican scholar. "The basic, underlying pattern has not changed in any significant way."

WOMEN AND CHILDREN LAST

Feminists scored some impressive legislative victories in the 1970s. In 1974, Congress passed the Equal Credit Opportunity Act, which enabled women to get bank loans and obtain credit cards on the same terms as men. Many states also revised their statutes on rape, prohibiting defense lawyers from discrediting rape victims by revealing their previous sexual experience.

Perhaps most significant were women's gains from affirmative action in hiring. As mandated by the Civil Rights Act of 1964 and the establishment of the Equal Employment Opportunity Commission, women and people of color applying for jobs had to receive the same consideration as white males. To take advantage of new opportunities, many women delayed having children until reaching their thirties and establishing themselves in their careers. The number of women enrolled in college rose 45 percent between 1970 and 1975, and numerous women were elected to political offices.

Still, women continued to encounter opposition in their quest for equality. Particularly formidable was the antifeminist or "profamily" move-

Antifeminist Movement

ment, which contended that men should lead and women should follow, especially within the family, and that women should stay home and raise children. The backlash against feminism became

The rebirth of feminism in the 1960s and 1970s saw joy and determination in the bonds of sisterhood that were forged. This 1971 women's liberation rally, held in Seneca Falls, New York, commemorated both the 1848 manifesto for women's equality and the 1920 woman suffrage amendment to the Constitution. Suzanne Szasz/Photo Researchers.

an increasingly powerful political force in the United States. In defense of the family—especially the patriarchal, or father-led, family—antifeminists campaigned against the Equal Rights Amendment, the gay rights movement, and abortion on demand.

Antifeminists blamed the women's movement for the country's spiraling divorce rate; they charged that feminists would jettison their husbands and even their children in their quests for job fulfillment and sexual equality. Although the number of divorces almost tripled from 1960 to 1976, the decision to divorce was often made by the husbands. According to Barbara Ehrenreich, a feminist scholar, men started walking out on their families in large numbers in the 1950s, well before the rebirth of feminism. Tired of fulfilling the role of husband, father, and financial provider, men responded to the image of carefree bachelorhood pre-

sented in the pages of men's magazines. *Playboy* attacked wives as parasites who gobbled up their husbands' salaries but were too sexually repressed to give much in return. Many men came to see their wives as the agent of their entrapment; in "flight from commitment," they chose divorce.

Antifeminists successfully stalled ratification of the Equal Rights Amendment, which after quickly passing thirty-five state legislatures fell three states short of success in the late 1970s. Phyllis Schlafly's "Stop ERA" campaign falsely claimed that the ERA would abolish alimony and legalize homosexual marriages. The debate was occasionally vicious. Refusing to acknowledge gender-based discrimination, Schlafly derided ERA advocates as "a bunch of bitter women seeking a constitutional cure for their personal problems." The ERA died in 1983 when the time limit expired for ratification by the states.

Equal Rights Amendment

Many antifeminists also participated in the anti-abortion or "prolife" movement, which sprang up almost overnight in the wake of the Supreme Court's 1973 decision in *Roe* v. *Wade* (see Chapter 32). People whose opposition to abortion was heartfelt and uncompromising denounced that ruling and called for an amendment to the Constitution defining human life as beginning at conception. Along with Catholics, Mormons, and other religious opponents of abortion, the prolife movement supported the successful legislative effort of Representative Henry Hyde of Illinois in 1976 to cut off most Medicaid funds for abortions. In 1980 the Supreme Court upheld the Hyde Amendment, deciding that the government had no obligation to make even medically necessary abortions available to the poor (*Harris* v. *McRae*).

Feminists fought back. Indeed, Ronald Reagan's most vocal critics were women who mobilized in opposition to the conservative agenda of the White House. The *New York Times* reported a "gender gap" between men's and women's opinions of Reagan's performance in 1983: far fewer women (38 percent) than men (53 percent) believed Reagan deserved re-election. What accounted most centrally for the gender gap were Reagan's social welfare, health, and education cuts. Many working mothers expressed shock at the Reagan administration's insen-

Women Opponents of Reagan's Conservatism

sitivity to children's welfare. One feminist critic quipped that for Reagan, "life begins at conception and ends at birth." Edwin Meese, then legal counsel to the president, lacked the facts when he said that he had seen no "authoritative evidence" that children in America went hungry. Such evidence appeared in 1984, when the House Select Committee on Children, Youth, and Families reported: "The number of poor children increased by two million between 1980 and 1982. Today, one out of five children and one out of two black children live in poverty." Poor children were three times more likely to die in their first year of life due to lack of prenatal care. Children's poverty continued its rise throughout the decade, increasing by 11 percent during the 1980s, compared with 6 percent in the 1970s. In 1989, children accounted for about 40 percent of America's poor people.

Reagan's critics assailed him for failing to reverse "the feminization of poverty" and for approving cuts in food stamps and school meals. The Reagan administration also opposed federally subsidized childcare and the feminist goal of "comparable worth." Because of persistent occupational segregation, 80 percent of all working women in 1985 were concentrated in such low-paying "female" occupations as clerking, selling, teaching, and waitressing. Recognizing this, feminists supplemented their earlier rallying cry of "equal pay for equal work" with a call for "equal pay for jobs of comparable worth." Why, women asked, should a grade-school teacher earn less than an electrician, if the two jobs require comparable training and skills and involve comparable responsibilities? By the end of the 1970s, female workers still took home only 60 cents to every male worker's dollar; a decade later, the figure had risen to 70 cents.

Activists in the women's struggle had to acknowledge certain harsh realities. One was the tight job market created by the impact of the economic recessions of the 1970s

Increased Burdens on Women

and 1980s. "Millions of women are a divorce away from destitution" wrote an observer in 1986; "millions of workers are a layoff away from poverty." Divorced women and their children in California, for example, suffered a decline of 73 percent in their standard of living after divorce. (Men, meanwhile, enjoyed an increase of 42 percent.) In the 1980s, with about one in every two marriages ending in divorce and with high pregnancy rates

among teenagers and unmarried women in their twenties, a progressively smaller proportion of America's children lived with two parents.

Many mothers in the 1980s thus had to work. Still others worked to preserve the living standard of two-parent households that otherwise would have experienced substantial declines. In 1983, for the first time in the nation's history, more than half of all adult American women (51 percent) held jobs. Another milestone was recorded in 1987: the share of women returning to work or actively seeking jobs within a year after the arrival of a baby exceeded 50 percent for the first time. (By contrast, in 1976 the figure was 31 percent.) The working mother had become the norm in America.

Such women had to contend with what came to be called "the Superwoman Squeeze." According to a report by the Worldwatch Institute, most working wives and mothers, even those with full-time jobs, "retained an unwilling monopoly on unpaid labor at home." Combining housework and outside employment, wives worked 71 hours a week; husbands worked 55 hours a week. Women traded stories of "couch-potato" husbands who watched television while their wives did chores. Soon only one in four wives would be a full-time housewife and mother. The remainder would be trying to balance the more-than-full-time demands of a family and a career without shortchanging either—or themselves—in the process.

A POLARIZED PEOPLE: AMERICAN SOCIETY IN THE 1980s

The United States became an increasingly polarized society in the 1980s. The rich got even richer, while the poor sank deeper into despair (see figure, page 1048). While the incomes of the bottom fifth of American families fell by 13 percent, the top fifth earned 27 percent more and the top 1 percent saw their incomes double. Indeed, by 1989 the top 1 percent (834,000 households with $5.7 trillion in net worth) was worth more than the bottom 90 percent (84 million households with $4.8 trillion in net worth).

By the end of the 1980s, as many Americans lived in poverty as in 1964, when 36 million were poor and President Johnson declared war on

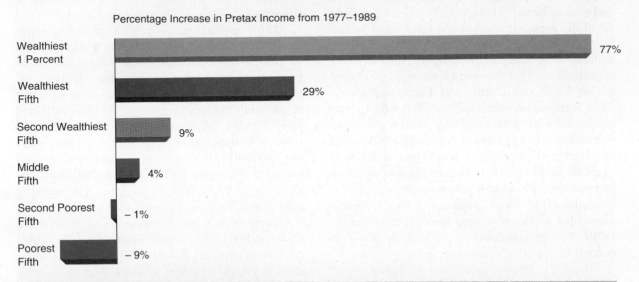

While the Rich Got Richer in the 1980's, the Poor Got Poorer

Percentage Increase in Pretax Income from 1977–1989

Wealthiest 1 Percent	77%
Wealthiest Fifth	29%
Second Wealthiest Fifth	9%
Middle Fifth	4%
Second Poorest Fifth	– 1%
Poorest Fifth	– 9%

While the Rich Got Richer in the 1980s, the Poor Got Poorer *Between 1977–1989, the richest 1 percent of American families reaped most of the gains from economic growth. In fact, the average pretax income of families in the top percent rose 77 percent. At the same time, the typical family saw its income edge up only 4 percent. And the bottom 40 percent of families had actual declines in income.* Source: Data from the New York Times, March 5, 1992. Copyright © 1992 by The New York Times Company. Reprinted by permission.

Increasing Inequality
——

poverty. Today's poverty, explained the authors of a 1988 report of the Social Science Research Council, "is found less among the elderly and people living in nonurban areas and more among children living with one parent—in households headed principally by young women." As inequality grew, the gap widened between affluent whites and poor blacks, Indians, and Hispanics; between the suburbs and the inner cities; between the country's social and defense needs; and culturally between liberal lifestyles and religious conservatism. And as inequality increased, so too did social pathology. Violent crime, particularly murders and gang warfare, grew alarmingly, as did school-dropout rates, crime rates, and child maltreatment. "The ghettos today," observed the 1988 report, "appear to be more mean-spirited, more isolated, and more damaging to their poor residents than those that arose in major urban areas after World War II."

Poverty stemmed from a variety of causes. Certainly it was the result of economic recessions. Race was another significant factor. African- and Hispanic-Americans were much more likely than whites to be poor. Similarly, women were more likely than men to be poor, with occupational segregation accounting for much of the disparity. By 1990, one women in six lived in poverty, compared with one man in eight.

Poverty also resulted from the changing structure of the labor market. As steel and textile mills and automobile and shoe factories shut down,

Changing Job Market
——

the job market shifted from high-paying unionized blue-collar jobs to low-paying service jobs. Minimum-wage employment burgeoned in fast-food restaurants, but such jobs meant a substantial drop in workers' standard of living. In 1974, blue-collar jobs accounted for half of the employment of African-American males between the ages of twenty and twenty-four. Just ten years later, such jobs accounted for only one-fourth of their employment. North Lawndale, a black neighborhood on Chicago's West Side, exemplified the problem. In prosperous days, the community's economy had depended on the 43,000 jobs at the Hawthorne

For this family, which includes a one-week-old baby, homelessness came suddenly. Home had been a squalid motor inn in North Bergen, New Jersey, but the board of health condemned the motel and the police put the family out on the street. In 1988, as many as a million people were homeless.   Eugene Richards/Magnum.

plant of Western Electric. But the Hawthorne plant closed in 1984. Soon, so did the banks and small stores that depended on the workers' wages.

According to the sociologist William Julius Wilson, the issue of "the truly disadvantaged" was "one of the most important social issues of the remainder of the 20th century." Life was becoming precarious not only for the underclass but also for "the working poor," whose numbers increased by more than one-third during the 1980s. By the end of the decade, 40 percent of the nation's poor were working, but few had full-time, year-round jobs. At the same time, social workers reported that more and more of the nation's homeless were families. Estimates of the number of homeless varied from 350,000 to more than 1 million in 1988.

About a third of the homeless were former psychiatric patients who found themselves living on the streets after psychiatric hospitals emptied their wards in a burst of enthusiasm for "deinstitu-tionalization." By 1985, 80 percent of the total number of beds in state mental hospitals had been eliminated on the premise that small neighborhood programs would be more responsive than large state hospitals to people's needs. The truth was that such programs failed to materialize, and former patients went to live in unsafe boarding houses and cheap hotels. Few provisions were made for medical treatment, and these troubled people increasingly found that they had nowhere to go except the street.

Drugs were the scourge of the urban underclass. Mired in hopelessness, poverty-stricken men and women tried to find forgetfulness in hard

Tragic Effects of Drugs

drugs, especially cocaine and its derivative "crack." Crack first struck New York City's poorest neighborhoods in 1985. Users included children eleven and twelve years old and young single mothers.

A stunned nation watched in 1986 as the space shuttle Challenger exploded a minute after lifting off. The Challenger explosion comprises a flashbulb memory for many of today's college students, some of whom saw the tragedy as a sign of America's decline in the world. NASA/Lyndon B. Johnson Space Center.

"The rising number of women involved with crack is striking, and the amount of child abuse and neglect is clear," commented the head of the addiction unit at a Brooklyn hospital. Another doctor in New York concurred that crack destroyed families. "It is such a devastating addiction," he said, "that these people are willing to abandon food and water and child to take care of their crack habit."

The crack epidemic had other pernicious results. Children and youths became drug dealers. Dealers too young for a driver's license had access to submachine guns and other state-of-the-art firearms. Gang shootouts were deadly: the toll in Los Angeles in 1987 was 387 deaths, and more than half of the victims were innocent bystanders. "Crack, guns, and youth are an extremely lethal mixture," observed a prosecutor in Detroit. After a bloody drug murder in New York City's Spanish Harlem, a sixteen-year-old girl moaned, "It's frightening. . . . It's crazy. There's no answer to it. And there's no end to it."

Another lethal by-product of the 1980s drug epidemic was the spread of AIDS. First observed in the United States in 1981, AIDS is a disease transmittable through the exchange of infected body fluids, often during sexual contact or sharing of intravenous needles by drug users. Caused by a virus that attacks cells in the immune system, AIDS makes its victims susceptible to deadly infections and cancers. In the United States, AIDS initially was linked to the sexual practices of male homosexuals, but the disease spread to heterosexuals. Between 1981 and 1988, of the 57,000 AIDS cases reported, nearly 32,000 resulted in death. But because it takes seven years or more for symptoms to appear, the worst has not yet revealed itself. A 1988 study reported that half of the gay men in San Francisco would develop AIDS and another 25 percent would develop the AIDS-related complex within about nine years of infection.

AIDS

AIDS—along with such other sexually transmitted diseases as genital herpes and chlamydia—affected Americans' sexual behavior. Caution replaced the mores of "the sexual revolution." "Safe sex" campaigns urged the use of condoms. Still, infection rates varied widely. In the South Bronx, a center of drug activity, the AIDS virus infected one in five sexually active men. "In this epidemic," said one doctor, "geography is destiny. . . . The risk of AIDS for a gay man in Manhattan, Kansas, is probably less than for a straight man in Manhattan, New York."

For several years Americans pretended the disease was limited to promiscuous homosexuals and drug addicts. But as writers, artists, athletes, actors, and relatives and friends died, people began to confront the horrifying epidemic. Nonetheless, AIDS divided communities. Conservative Protestant sects joined the Roman Catholic Church in warning that condom advertising implicitly sanctioned contraception and encouraged promiscuity. Sex education should not be offered in the schools, they contended, citing their deep belief that any sexual activity other than heterosexual, matrimonial monogamy was wrong. Some religious leaders and politicians heartlessly blamed the victims. "A man reaps what he sows," declared the Reverend Jerry Falwell of the Moral Majority. "If he sows seed in the field of his lower nature, he will reap from it a harvest of corruption." Gay men expected

In 1987 the San Francisco-based Names Project started to make quilts in remembrance of those who had died of AIDS. By 1992, when the AIDS quilt was unfolded near the Washington Monument, it contained 21,000 decorated panels and stretched over 15 acres of land. Jeff Tinsley/Smithsonian Institution.

little assistance from the conservative executive branch, but they were partly wrong. Under the leadership of Surgeon General Dr. C. Everett Koop, the federal government published a booklet entitled *Understanding AIDS*, which was mailed to 107 million households in 1988. Nevertheless, AIDS continued to be one of several unsolved social problems dividing the nation as the presidential election drew near in 1988.

REAGAN'S DECLINE AND THE ELECTION OF 1988

Ronald Reagan's political troubles began on election day 1986. From Lebanon came a bizarre story that the president's national security adviser had traveled to Iran with a Bible, a cake, and a planeload of weapons seeking the release of Americans held hostage in the Middle East. "No comment," Reagan told reporters, but details of the Iran-contra scandal soon began to surface. That day the Republicans also lost control of the Senate, stripping the president of a crucial power base.

"An irony of the Reagan era," wrote Senator Daniel Patrick Moynihan, Democrat of New York, in 1988, "is that having at midpoint reached a crescendo of triumphalism—morning in America—it is closing amid talk of decline." On a personal level, President Reagan had lost his mastery; the "great communicator" had taken on the appearance of a tired, bumbling old man. "Who's in Charge Here?" asked a *Time* magazine headline. The Iran-contra hearings focused attention on President Reagan's "hands-off" management style. Some observers, both outsiders and insiders, argued that Reagan was unengaged and uninformed. Donald T. Regan

Computing equipment, videocassette recorders, and other electronics technology became commonplace in American households in the 1980s. Here a father gives his son instruction on the family's home computer.   Laima Druskis/Stock Boston.

described his experience: "In the four years that I served as Secretary of the Treasury I never saw President Reagan alone and never discussed economic philosophy or fiscal and monetary policy with him one-on-one." The political satirists were in hot pursuit. The real question, went one gibe, was not "what did the President know and when did he know it?" but "what didn't the President know, and why didn't he know it?"

Half the people in the country believed that Reagan was lying about his uninvolvement in the Iran-contra scandal. Doubtless any lame-duck president would have suffered a loss of power in his second term, but the scandal encouraged Reagan's opponents. "No one is afraid of him anymore," said one political observer. In early 1987, Congress overrode Reagan's veto of a massive highway-construction bill.

Reagan's problems continued in 1987 and 1988. Not once but twice his nominees for the Supreme Court failed to win confirmation by the Senate. His first nominee, federal judge Robert Bork, failed to convince the Senate that he was not a right-wing ideologue; his second nominee, another federal judge, withdrew his name from consider-

Reagan's Political Woes

ation after revelations that he had smoked marijuana while a professor at Harvard Law School. Scandals continued to tarnish the White House as well. Then, on October 19, 1987, the stock market went into a nose-dive and fell 508 points.

According to polls conducted early in 1988, the nation's political mood was "drift and uncertainty." Aides reported that Reagan would spend his last year in office "summing up"; he planned no major initiatives. Yet the Democrats could not count on success in the 1988 elections. First, Reagan had moderated his anti-Soviet rhetoric and in 1988, to the applause of most Americans, had traveled to the Soviet Union—the first American president to visit Moscow since Richard Nixon in 1972. Second—and of greater importance to voters—following the economic recession of 1981 and 1982, the United States had embarked on a six-year business recovery. The "discomfort index," which had risen alarmingly in the 1970s and early 1980s, dropped to more comfortable levels in the later 1980s. And while unemployment dropped to a decade-low 5.4 percent in April 1988, it did so without refueling inflation.

The Reagan administration pointed to the economy as proof of the success of supply-side economics. Critics retorted that Reagan's policy

Continuing Economic Recovery
———

of pursuing massive tax cuts while greatly increasing the defense budget was just another form of Keynesianism—deficit financing to stimulate the economy. But the average American, caring little about this kind of debate, was content to enjoy the economic recovery. It was true that the poor had little to rejoice over and that Americans viewed the economic future with uncertainty. But it was also true that in the 1980s most Americans had jobs and lived very comfortably.

One measure of comfort was the spread of technology to the household. Sales of home computers, videocassette recorders (VCRs), microwave ovens, camcorders, and compact disc players soared throughout the 1980s. Companies raced to market with ever-speedier technology. In 1985, a new computer was introduced to the public at the Lawrence Livermore Laboratory in California. "What took a year in 1952," explained a scientist, "we can now do in a second." In 1981, the number of personal computers in use in America numbered 2 million; in 1988, the figure was 45 million. At-home comfort was an important reason for buying a VCR. In just four years, from 1980 to 1984, the number of videotapes rented by Americans for viewing movies at home jumped from 26 million to 304 million. But sales of VCRs began to fall off in 1987 and 1988; the middle classes had bought all they could use, and the poor could not afford them.

Had Reagan been allowed by the Constitution to run for a third term, he probably would have ridden the economic boom to victory. But this election was for his successor; and the competition in both parties was intense. The candidates on the Republican side included Vice President George Bush, Senate minority leader Bob Dole, and Pat Robertson, a television evangelist. Bush emerged with the nomination after bitter Republican infighting in state primaries. A native of Connecticut and a Yale graduate, Bush had served heroically as a navy pilot during the Second World War. He had moved to Texas to enter the oil business and had become involved in politics. Bush possessed broad governmental experience, including service as a congressman, ambassador to China, and director of the Central Intelligence Agency. In 1980 he had contested Reagan for the Republican nomination but

George Bush
———

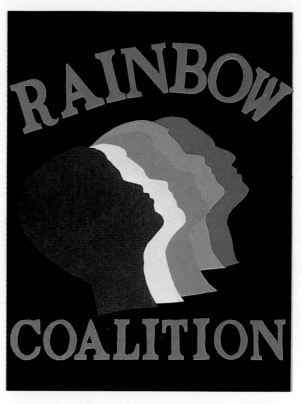

During the 1984 and 1988 campaigns, the Reverend Jesse Jackson won a large following as the first African-American to make a serious bid for the presidential nomination of a major party. His multi-ethnic political organization, the Rainbow Coalition, included people of all colors. Smithsonian Institution, Division of Political History, Washington, D.C.

had then served as Reagan's vice president for eight years. Bush appeared to be a team player without firm convictions.

On the Democratic side there was also a scramble for the presidential nomination. Beginning with a half-dozen campaigners, the race narrowed to a two-person contest between Michael Dukakis, under whose governorship Massachusetts had seemed a model of economic recovery and welfare reform, and Jesse Jackson, a former colleague of the Reverend Martin Luther King, Jr., who had moved to Chicago to organize economic and educational programs for the poor. An eloquent preacher, Jackson campaigned on his dream of forming a "Rainbow Coalition" of the "rejected"—African-Americans, women, and Hispanics. Jackson was the first African-American to win mass support in seeking the presidential nomination of a major political party.

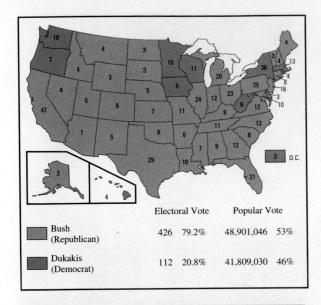

	Electoral Vote		Popular Vote	
Bush (Republican)	426	79.2%	48,901,046	53%
Dukakis (Democrat)	112	20.8%	41,809,030	46%

Presidential Election, 1988 *George Bush easily defeated Michael Dukakis in both the popular and electoral vote. The key to Bush's victory was his ability to retain the political support which Ronald Reagan had enjoyed in 1980 and 1984.*

Both Bush and Dukakis avoided serious debate of the issues: childcare, drugs, environmental collapse, corruption in government, poverty, rising medical and educational costs, and the fiscal and trade deficits. Despite the gravity of these problems, the candidates relied on clichés and negative campaigning. Television dominated the presidential election as never before. Bush aimed his appeals at the "Reagan Democrats" by pushing such emotional "hot buttons" as "patriotism" and the death penalty. A Republican advertisement for television appealed to racism and fear by accusing Dukakis of being soft on crime for furloughing Willie Horton, a black convict. As Bush's media adviser explained, "There are three things that get covered [on television]: visuals, attacks, and mistakes. You try to avoid mistakes and give them as many attacks and visuals as you can." Voters expressed their disgust at the 1988 race. Former President Richard Nixon, no stranger to political combat, called it "trivial, superficial and inane."

Presidential Campaign of 1988

But with America at peace and inflation and unemployment both low, Bush's victory was seldom in doubt. His margin over Dukakis was substantial: 53 percent of the popular vote to 46 percent (see map). Bush retained 85 percent of Reagan's supporters by promising to keep the nation on the course set by his predecessor. Significantly, "Reagan Democrats" crossed over and voted for Bush in sufficient numbers for him to carry key industrial states such as Michigan, Pennsylvania, and Ohio.

The 1988 election confirmed that the "Solid South," once a Democratic stronghold, had become solidly Republican. Bush won every state in the region. In both South and North, race was a key factor, as it had been in every presidential election since 1964: for twenty-five years, the Republican vote had been almost exclusively white and almost all blacks had voted Democratic. Another political constant was low voter turnout. Only 50 percent of Americans who were eligible to vote in 1988 voted, compared with 63 percent in 1960. Voter turnout had declined markedly after the 1968 election, but after turning slightly upward in 1984 (53 percent), it fell again in 1988.

Many Americans seemed unconcerned as they confronted the new decade. College students in the 1990s, unlike many of their predecessors in the 1960s, aspired to join the system. They yearned not to save the world but to scramble up the corporate ladder, and many educated young people worked long hours in pursuit of that goal. "If the 1970s were the Me Decade," *Newsweek* declared, "the 1980s have been the Work Decade." Baby-boomers and their younger sisters and brothers reported frustration in their efforts to replicate their parents' standard of living, particularly because of high housing costs. But polls in 1989 reported that the American people were generally happy with the direction in which their own lives and the life of their country was moving.

George Bush was inaugurated as the forty-first president of the United States on January 20, 1989. The American people prepared to greet not only a new presidency but also a new decade. "Ronald Reagan leaves no Vietnam War, no Watergate, no hostage crisis," reported the *New York Times*. "But he leaves huge question marks—and much to

Legacies of the 1980s

Southern States in Presidential Elections, 1960–1988

*Mississippi Voters elected Harry Byrd in 1960. In 1968, George Wallace carried Alabama, Arkansas, Georgia, Louisiana, and Mississippi.

How do historians know

that the South was a key factor in presidential elections? This figure illustrates that the once-solid Democratic South had become Republican by 1972, when Richard M. Nixon won every state in the region. In the aftermath of the Watergate scandal, a southern Democrat, Jimmy Carter of Georgia, did win all of the South but one state. But the Republicans' ascendancy returned in 1980, when Ronald Reagan won every southern state but Georgia. And in 1984 and 1988, the Republican ticket handily won all of the South. Note that in each of these presidential elections, whoever won the South won the general election as well. Data: *New York Times*, October 18, 1992. Copyright © 1992 by the New York Times Company. Reprinted by permission.

do." First, inequality had escalated in the 1980s, as the poor got poorer and the rich got richer. The poorest Americans of all were children, and economics and racism had conspired to widen the gap between the races. Second, the effects of mismanagement and deception were beginning to show in certain industries, forcing the federal government to consider massive bailouts and threatening greater fiscal deficits. In 1989 Congress debated putting up $157 billion to rescue insolvent savings-and-loan associations. Third, the country was losing control of its economic destiny. Between 1983 and 1989, foreigners invested $700 billion more in America than Americans invested abroad. It was clear that the American people and their leaders would have to make difficult economic, political, diplomatic, and social choices in the 1990s.

SUGGESTIONS FOR FURTHER READING

Deficits, Deindustrialization, and Other Economic Woes

Donald L. Bartlett and James B. Steele, *America: What Went Wrong?* (1992); Barry Bluestone and Bennett Harrison, *The Deindustrialization of America* (1982); David P. Calleo, *The Bankrupting of America* (1992); Richard Feldman and Michael Betzold, *End of the Line: Autoworkers and the American Dream* (1988); Robert Heilbroner and Peter Bernstein, *The Debt and the Deficit* (1989); John P. Hoerr, *And the Wolf Finally Came: The Decline of the American Steel Industry* (1988); Gregory Pappas, *The Magic City: Unemployment in a Working-Class Community* (1989).

The Ford and Carter Administrations

Betty Glad, *Jimmy Carter* (1980); John Robert Greene, *The Limits of Power: The Nixon and Ford Administrations* (1992); Erwin C. Hargrove, *Jimmy Carter as President* (1989); Haynes Johnson, *In the Absence of Power* (1980); Charles O. Jones, *The Trusteeship Presidency: Jimmy Carter and the United States Congress* (1988); Burton I. Kaufman, *The Presidency of James Earl Carter, Jr.* (1993); A. James Reichley, *Conservatives in an Age of Change: The Nixon and Ford Administrations* (1981); Laurence H. Shoup, *The Carter Presidency and Beyond* (1980); James L. Sundquist, *The Decline and Resurgence of Congress* (1981).

Women and Children's Struggles

Marian Wright Edelman, *Families in Peril* (1987); Barbara Ehrenreich, *The Hearts of Men: American Dreams and the Flight from Commitment* (1983); David T. Ellwood, *Poor Support: Poverty in the American Family* (1988); Sara M. Evans and Barbara J. Nelson, *Wage Justice: Comparable Worth and the Paradox of Technocratic Reform* (1989); Susan Faludi, *Backlash: The Undeclared War Against American Women* (1991); Judith Lewis Herman, *Trauma and Recovery* (1992); Sylvia Ann Hewlett, *When the Bough Breaks: The Cost of Neglecting Our Children* (1991); Arlie Russell Hochschild, *The Second Shift: Working Parents and the Revolution at Home* (1989); Rebecca E. Klatch, *Women of the New Right* (1987); Jonathan Kozol, *Rachel and Her Children: Homeless Families in America* (1988); Kristin Luker, *Abortion and the Politics of Motherhood* (1984); Harrell R. Rodgers, Jr., *Poor Women, Poor Families* (1986); Maggie Scarf, *Unfinished Business: Pressure Points in the Lives of Women* (1980); Ruth Sidel, *Women and Children Last* (1986); Winifred D. Wandersee, *On the Move: American Women in the 1970s* (1988); Lenore J. Weitzman, *The Divorce Revolution* (1985).

People of Color and New Immigrants

Nathan Caplan et al., *The Boat People and Achievement in America* (1989); James D. Cockcroft, *Outlaws in the Promised Land: Mexican Immigrant Workers and America's Future* (1986); John Crewdson, *The Tarnished Door: The New Immigrants and the Transformation of America* (1983); Roger Daniels, *Coming to America* (1990); Marilyn P. Davis, *Mexican Voices, American Dreams* (1990); Reynolds Farley and Walter R. Allen, *The Color Line and the Quality of Life in America* (1987); Ronald P. Formisano, *Boston Against Busing* (1991); Gil Loescher and John A. Scanlan, *Calculated Kindness: Refugees and America's Half-Open Door* (1986); J. Anthony Lukas, *Common Ground* (1985); Peter Matthiessen, *In the Spirit of Crazy Horse* (1983); David M. Reimers, *Still the Golden Door: The Third World Comes to America* (1985); Ronald Takaki, *Strangers from a Different Shore: A History of Asian Americans* (1989); William Julius Wilson, *The Truly Disadvantaged: The Inner City, the Underclass, and Public Policy* (1987).

The New Conservatism and the Election of 1980

Sidney Blumenthal, *The Rise of the Counter-Establishment* (1986); Alan Crawford, *Thunder on the Right* (1980); Thomas Byrne Edsall, *The New Politics of Inequality* (1984); Jack W. Germond and Jules Witcover, *Blue Smoke and Mirrors: How Reagan Won and Why Carter Lost the Election of 1980* (1981); Gillian Peele, *Revival and Reaction* (1984); David W. Reinhard, *The Republican Right Since 1945* (1983); Peter Steinfels, *The NeoConservatives* (1979).

Ronald Reagan and His Presidency

Sidney Blumenthal, *Our Long National Daydream* (1988); Lou Cannon, *President Reagan* (1991); Hodding Carter, *The Reagan Years* (1988); Paul D. Erickson, *Reagan Speaks: The Making of an American Myth* (1985); Mark Hertsgaard, *On Bended Knee: The Press and the Reagan Presidency* (1988); Haynes Johnson, *Sleepwalking Through History: America in the Reagan Years* (1991); Jane Mayer and Doyle McManus, *Landslide: The Unmaking of the President, 1984–1988* (1988); Michael Rogin, *Ronald Reagan, the Movie* (1987); Michael Schaller, *Reckoning with Reagan* (1992); Hedrick Smith, *The Power Game* (1988); John Kenneth White, *The New Politics of Old Values* (1988); Garry Wills, *Reagan's America* (1987).

"Reaganomics"

Joan Claybrook, *Retreat from Safety: Reagan's Attack on America's Health* (1984); Benjamin Friedman, *Day of Reckoning: The Consequences of American Economic Policy Under Reagan and After* (1988);

Jonathan Lash, *A Season of Spoils: The Story of the Reagan Administration's Attack on the Environment* (1984); Robert Lekachman, *Greed Is Not Enough: Reaganomics* (1982); Frank Levy, *Dollars and Dreams: The Changing American Income Distribution* (1987); William A. Niskanen, *Reaganomics* (1988); Charles Noble, *Liberalism at Work: The Rise and Fall of OSHA* (1986); Kevin Phillips, *The Politics of Rich and Poor* (1990); Frances Fox Piven and Richard Cloward, *The New Class War* (1982).

A Polarized Society in the 1980s

Chandler Davidson, *Race and Class in Texas Politics* (1990); Leslie W. Dunbar, ed., *Minority Report: What Has Happened to Blacks, Hispanics, American Indians, and Other Minorities in the Eighties* (1984); Michael Harrington, *The New American Poverty* (1984); John Langone, *AIDS: The Facts* (1988); Randy Shilts, *And the Band Played On: Politics, People and the AIDS Epidemic* (1987); Studs Terkel, *The Great Divide* (1988); E. Fuller Torrey, *Nowhere to Go: The Tragic Odyssey of the Homeless Mentally Ill* (1988).

The Presidential Elections of 1984 and 1988

Sidney Blumenthal, *Pledging Allegiance: The Last Campaign of the Cold War* (1990); Richard Ben Cramer, *What It Takes* (1992); Thomas Byrne Edsall and Mary D. Edsall, *Chain Reaction: The Impact of Race, Rights, and Taxes on American Politics* (1991); Thomas Ferguson and Joel Rogers, *Right Turn: The Decline of the Democrats and the Future of American Politics* (1986); Jack W. Germond and Jules Witcover, *Whose Broad Stripes and Bright Stars?* (1989); Jack W. Germond and Jules Witcover, *Wake Us When It's Over: Presidential Politics of 1984* (1985); Peter Goldman and Tony Fuller, *The Quest for the Presidency, 1984* (1985); Frances Fox Piven and Richard A. Cloward, *Why Americans Don't Vote* (1988); Adolph L. Reed, Jr., *The Jesse Jackson Phenomenon* (1986).

A New Century Beckons: America and the World in the 1990s

"I feel like they rob me without a gun," remarked Jo Harris, a seventy-nine-year-old Montana widow in early 1993. She had just paid $89.95 for a month's supply of the pills she needed to alleviate her severe arthritis pain. "When I paid the drugstore clerk, I told him, 'You know Bill Clinton's watching you, don't you?'" Indeed, the new president was watching. Shortly after taking office, he lambasted drug firms for "shocking" overcharges on prescriptions. Hillary Rodham Clinton echoed her husband's views. Makers of childhood vaccines, she protested, had shamefully raised prices 1,000 percent over the last decade.

Having promised health-care reform during the campaign, President Clinton set two goals for his new administration. He pledged to extend care to the thirty-seven million Americans who lacked medical insurance. Most were middle-class working people, for the poor received Medicaid and the rich could afford coverage. "How many of you are only one illness away from bankruptcy?" Clinton asked voters. He also vowed to control the soaring costs of medical care, which had reached more than $900 billion a year. One out of every seven dollars Americans spent went to medical care, and health care accounted for one seventh of the federal government's budget, driving up the deficit. Ford Motor Company reported that it was spending more on health care for its workers than on steel. Health insurance had become the leading labor issue in the country; in 1990, 55 percent of all strikes began over medical-insurance disputes.

The health-care system in the United States was in crisis. Insurance companies cut benefits to control their costs. Employers shifted a greater share of health-care expenses to their workers, many of whom could not afford the burden and had to drop insurance policies. The McDonnell Douglas Corporation slashed the health benefits its retirees had counted on and contributed to.

Critics pointed to waste and inefficiency (more than 1,500 different insurance forms were in use around the country) and to the expensive and sometimes unnecessary tests ordered by doctors who feared malpractice suits and thus practiced "defensive medicine." Analysts also noted that health-care costs were mounting because Americans were living longer with treatable illnesses. Many critics denounced price gouging by pharmaceutical companies. Some residents of the Sunbelt drove to Mexico to buy medicines at a fraction of U.S. prices. Others crossed into Canada, where Tylenol with Codeine 3 cost $3.32 for one hundred tablets, compared to $19.38 in the United States.

President Clinton named his talented wife Hillary, an attorney who had skillfully led the fight for education reform in Arkansas, to head a task force to reform the health-care system. Obstacles and acrimonious debate loomed. Skeptics doubted that the administration could generate enough savings through cost controls to pay for the expanded coverage. Would Americans accept higher taxes, including greater taxes on cancer-causing tobacco products, to make up the difference? Would health-care providers—doctors, hospitals, and insurance companies—and drug firms succeed in blocking federally imposed price controls? Could a new system stimulate competition among providers on the basis of price (the so-called managed competition approach) or were market forces inoperative in the health-care industry? "We're facing one of the biggest political and policy fights ever seen in this country," predicted Cathy Hurwit of Citizen Action, a health-care reform advocacy group.

The president whom Democrat Bill Clinton defeated in the 1992 election, Republican George Bush, had offered no solutions to the health-care crisis. Chronically worried that government action would undermine private business, Bush opted for inaction on this and so many other issues that observers called his administration a "status quo presidency." Bush certainly had his chances to lead. With the collapse of the Soviet empire and the end of the Cold War, there arose a need to redefine the international role of the United States. Many Americans also envisioned a "peace dividend"—a shift of federal resources from weaponry and interventionism to domestic needs, including improvements in education, long-term investment in productive capacity, and reduction of the federal debt. But Bush did not redefine the nation's priorities, insisting that trouble still stalked the world.

He also blamed America's domestic ills and sagging economy on an uncooperative and spendthrift Congress responsible for "Washington gridlock."

Nor did the president's interpretation of U.S. interests in the Third World change with the end of the Cold War. President Bush ordered military interventions in Panama and the Middle East, and he dispatched a military expedition to Africa to ensure the distribution of food to starving Somalis. Meanwhile, environmental ruin, political instability, massive debt, large-scale population growth and migration, and illicit drug trafficking in the Third World threatened the prosperity and health of the United States. Bush seldom took the initiative to help resolve these problems. He seemed more comfortable as commander-in-chief than as long-range planner, and the domestic political benefits of military victory abroad seemed rewarding. For example, after triumph in the Gulf War in 1991, Bush's popularity rating soared to eighty-nine percent despite rising unemployment, factory closings, massive federal debt, heightening racial tensions, drug abuse, decaying cities, collapse of real-estate markets, and the costly bailout of failed savings-and-loan institutions.

Bush's re-election seemed guaranteed, but it was not. The American people demanded leadership on the domestic front, especially on economic and medical-care questions. Bush wanted to be president, but did not seem to know what he wanted his presidency to do. His administration continued to drive up the federal debt through deficit spending, and its tax policies favored the wealthy. The economy continued to slump, and layoffs climbed. Bush pandered to the right wing of his party on issues like abortion and school prayer. He appointed highly conservative justices to the Supreme Court, one of whom, Clarence Thomas, became the source of controversy when a former employee charged him with sexual harassment, highlighting women's rights issues that President Bush had ignored.

In the topsy-turvy political year of 1992, many voters embraced an anti-incumbent mood and endorsed the third-party candidacy of H. Ross Perot. In the end, the electorate defeated George Bush and elected the young governor of Arkansas, Bill Clinton. The voters also changed Congress, electing more women, African-Americans, and Hispanics. People with fresh ideas, high optimism, and a mandate for change moved into Washington,

1989   George Bush inaugurated president
Best-selling car in United States is the
Honda Accord
Helsinki agreement outlines phase-out of
ozone-destroying chemicals
Berlin Wall is opened
U.S. troops invade Panama

1990   Sandinistas defeated in Nicaraguan elections
Clean Air Act requires reduction in emission
of pollutants
Communist regimes in Eastern Europe col-
lapse
Iraq invades Kuwait
Bush orders U.S. armed forces to Persian
Gulf region
Bush-Congress budget agreement raises taxes
Americans with Disabilities Act prohibits dis-
crimination
Reunification of Germany signals Cold War's
end

1991   Persian Gulf War
Antarctica agreement bans oil exploration
and mining
Military ousts elected government in Haiti;
more Haitians flee to the United States
START I treaty reduces nuclear warheads
in Soviet Union and United States
Soviet Union disintegrates; Yeltsin ousts
Gorbachev
Confirmation hearings of Clarence Thomas
to Supreme Court spotlight issue of sexual
harassment

1992   World population reaches 5.4 billion
Federal deficit hits $4 trillion
Perot third-party candidate
Los Angeles riots erupt
Twenty-seventh Amendment prohibits mid-
term congressional pay raises
Bill Clinton and Bush win nominations
United States opposes many resolutions at
Rio "Earth Summit"
California pays bills with IOUs
Clinton elected president
U.S. troops sent to Somalia to ensure deliv-
ery of relief supplies
North American Free Trade Agreement
signed by Canada, Mexico, and the
United States
Bush pardons Weinberger in Iran-contra
scandal
START II agreement calls for cuts in war-
heads and ICBMs

1993   Clinton and Gore inaugurated
Hillary Rodham Clinton heads task force on
health-care reform
Clinton lifts restrictions on abortions
President's proposal to lift ban on homosexu-
als in the military stirs controversy
Congress modifies and passes Clinton's eco-
nomic proposals
Yeltsin and Clinton meet at Vancouver sum-
mit to discuss U.S. foreign aid to Russia
Clinton appoints Ruth Bader Ginsburg to
the Supreme Court
Motor-voter and family-leave bills are signed

D.C., the center of a serious debate on how to stem America's decline and how to chart a more prosperous and secure future.

BUSH'S FOREIGN POLICY IN THE POST-COLD WAR ORDER

Unlike Ronald Reagan, George Bush preferred foreign policy to domestic affairs. Bush considered himself an expert on international relations, but he hardly anticipated the transformation of the Cold-War world he had come to know so well as an oil businessman, member of Congress, ambassador to the United Nations and to China, CIA director, and vice president (see Chapter 29). When the Cold War ended, Bush spoke vaguely of a "new world order," but he seemed hesitant to explain its dimensions or shape its agenda.

Bush was a cautious conservative. "People say I'm indecisive," Bush once joked. "Well, I don't know about that." Adaptable rather than ideologically zealous, yet eager to satisfy the right wing of the Republican party, Bush seldom innovated in foreign policy. The new president, moreover, liked to deal in facts, not in what he called "visions." But, as a *New York Times* editorial put it, "Why Not Prudence Plus Leadership?" Secretary of State James A. Baker III, a close friend from Texas who had directed Bush's political campaigns, seemed to thrive on managing day-to-day events rather than planning for the long term. Theirs was largely a reactive foreign policy, short on new ideas, wedded to the "truths" of the past.

This posture became particularly evident in the Bush administration's use of military force in Latin America, the Middle East, and Africa. Although the end of the Cold War eliminated a great-power threat to U.S. security for the first time in fifty years, Bush cut back only minimally on the large defense budget and discouraged hopes for a "peace dividend." Critics known as "declinists" spotlighted a fundamental legacy of the Cold War: the United States still spent heavily on its military while neglecting its domestic development. According to the historian Paul Kennedy's *The Rise and Fall of the Great Powers* (1987), one of the best-selling books in the United States in the late 1980s and early 1990s, the United States suffered from "imperial overstretch." Professor Kennedy argued that U.S. power, like that of Spain and Great Britain in earlier centuries, would continue to erode unless it restored its productive vitality and marketplace competitiveness to compete with Japan and Germany, reduced its huge federal debt, put more resources into long-term investment, and improved its educational system. One way to stem economic decline was to curb America's global interventionism.

Bush dismissed the declinists as "gloomsayers." He seemed to agree with those commentators who envisioned the United States as the supreme power in a unipolar world. But the list of world problems and domestic ills that Reagan had bequeathed to Bush was daunting. Reagan had paid little attention to global environmental issues, for example. Warming of the earth's climate due to the "greenhouse effect"—the build-up of carbon dioxide and other gases in the atmosphere—threatened a rise in ocean levels, flooding farm lands and dislocating millions of people. The United States produced five tons of carbon dioxide each year for every person in the nation. In addi-

Declinists

International Environmental Issues

tion, scientists discovered a growing hole in the earth's protective ozone layer over the South Pole. This expanding hole allowed deadly ultraviolet rays to reach the earth's surface. Methane, chlorofluorocarbons, and other harmful gases used in aerosol spray cans and air-conditioning units caused this depletion of the ozone layer, and Americans released about one third of all chlorofluorocarbons in the world.

In the early 1990s, the human costs of environmental damage mounted, and governments found themselves hard-pressed to feed and care for their people. At a time when the world's population was growing at a rate of more than eighty million a year, reaching 5.4 billion in 1992, soil erosion was reducing food production. Acid rain, overcutting of forests, and overgrazing of fields destroyed livelihoods and drove people into overcrowded cities. Food riots and migrations of refugees from environmentally damaged areas became common.

Meanwhile, the Bush administration withheld monies from the U.N. Fund for Population Activities and International Planned Parenthood, because, U.S. officials claimed, those agencies supported abortion. Washington also continued to oppose the Law of the Sea Treaty (see Chapter 31) because Bush believed that the provisions governing the marine environment would hamper American private business. He addressed the global-warming problem by warning against policies that would interfere with the free marketplace. Worried that environmental controls would slow economic growth, the administration dragged its feet so obstinately at the Rio de Janeiro "Earth Summit" in 1992 that the conference produced few agreements. Environmental specialists like Worldwatch Institute's Lester R. Brown pressed for urgent action: "We do not have generations. We only have years in which to turn things around." Some advances were achieved: in 1989 eighty-six nations, including the United States, agreed to phase out use of ozone-destroying chemicals by the year 2000, and Bush signed a tougher Clean Air Act in 1990 (see page 1072). The following year the United States and twenty-five other nations agreed to protect the fragile environment of Antarctica by banning oil exploration and mining there for fifty years.

As the world split into competing economic spheres—Europe's Economic Community, Japan's Asian trading community, and the U.S.-dominated Western Hemispheric community—the Bush administration negotiated the North American

The United States among the Economic Superpowers, 1980–1991

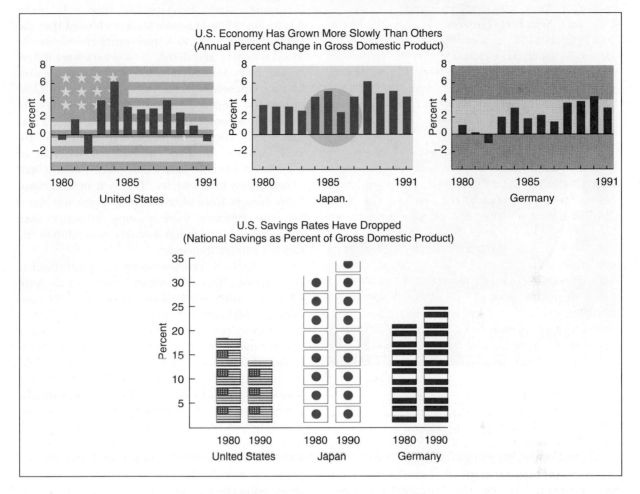

How do historians know

that the United States has suffered relative decline? Scholars who argue that the United States has declined use comparative statistics like the above. Handicapped by a falling savings rate, which meant that fewer dollars were available for long-term investment, *and unable to keep up a growth rate to match its economic rivals—Germany and Japan—the United States, some scholars have concluded, appeared to be slipping in the 1980s.* Data: U.S. government and U.N. publications.

Free Trade Agreement (NAFTA) with Canada and Mexico. Signed in late 1992, the pact envisioned tariff-free trade among the three nations. Critics claimed that the agreement would cost many U.S. workers their jobs because corporations would move south to exploit less expensive Mexican labor and minimal environmental controls. Bush called it "the first giant step" toward a free-trade zone encompassing the entire Western Hemisphere. NAFTA faced acrimonious debate.

Tense Japanese-American Relations
———

Trade issues lay at the heart of tense U.S.-Japanese relations. Most nettlesome was the huge trade deficit in Japan's favor (about $50 billion in 1989). Japanese products flooded American stores and won customers who appreciated their price and quality. The best-selling car in the United States in 1989 was the Honda Accord (many of which

In June 1992 the leaders of 178 nations gathered in Brazil to attend the United Nations "Earth Summit." President Bush traveled to this largest international conference ever, but he was a reluctant participant because he believed that strong environmental protection rules would interfere with private business and cost jobs. So he refused to sign the Biodiversity Treaty to slow the loss of endangered species. And only after the conferees watered down a climate-change treaty, designed to control emissions of gases that were heating up the earth, did the United States sign. Demonstrators in Rio de Janeiro held up a large sign: "Bush lead or get out of the way." Courtesy United Nations Conference on Environment and Development.

were assembled by American workers in the United States). American manufacturers complained that Japan's tariffs, cartels, and government subsidies made it difficult for American goods to penetrate Japanese markets. The Japanese countered that obsolete equipment, poor education, and inadequate spending on research and development undercut U.S. competitiveness.

In 1990 the world's ten largest banks were all in Japan, as were seven of the world's largest public companies (ranked by market value). "Some might say the Cold War had indeed ended," observed

Professor Chalmers Johnson of the University of California, "and the Japanese won." It stung Americans when Japanese leaders claimed that the United States was no longer number one in the world economy and that U.S. workers were illiterate and lazy. Many Americans feared that the dollar-rich Japanese were buying up too many U.S. businesses. Japanese and other foreign investors used their accumulating dollars to buy U.S. Treasury bonds, companies, stock, and real estate. By 1990 Japanese interests controlled 25 percent of California's banking assets and owned almost half of downtown Los Angeles. The year before, Sony Corp. bought Columbia Pictures, triggering alarm that the Japanese were gaining influence over American public opinion through ownership of the nation's culture industries.

As the U.S. economy slipped, protectionists championed "Buy American" campaigns. Auto workers in Michigan and others practiced "Japan-bashing," blaming U.S. woes on the Japanese. Was a damaging economic war in the offing? Some thought not, because the two economies were so interdependent that economic warfare would be mutually destructive. Furthermore, many American products did manage to penetrate the Japanese market. McDonald's fast food, Schick razor blades, and Coca-Cola became pre-eminent in their markets, suggesting a Japanese embrace of American culture. And Japan and the United States remained security partners. Still, as economic competitors, neither nation seemed willing to give much ground.

Elsewhere in Asia, Sino-American relations took a turn for the worse in June 1989, when Chinese armed forces stormed into Beijing's Tiananmen Square. They slaughtered hundreds—perhaps thousands—of unarmed students and other citizens who had for weeks been holding peaceful prodemocracy rallies. China's leader Deng Xiaoping, who had been moving his populous nation toward economic but not political liberalization, crushed the prodemocracy movement. Bush officials initially expressed revulsion, but their response gradually became muted. They believed that America's global security needs required friendly Sino-American ties. Critics charged that the United States was shortsightedly allying itself with China's elderly governing

Tiananmen Square Massacre

In the hard economic times of the early 1990s, many Americans blamed the Japanese for America's troubles. They worried that Japanese products were crowding out American products in the U.S. marketplace, and they protested that Japan was closing the door to American goods, thus creating a huge trade deficit in Japan's favor. Outside a Toyota car dealership in Michigan, these demonstrating auto workers recall the patriotism of 1945, when the United States defeated Japan in the Second World War.   Jim West/Impact Visuals.

clique while alienating the nation's progressive future leaders. Bush cheered such leaders in Bucharest, Prague, and Warsaw, but snubbed them in Beijing.

In European affairs, Bush was suspicious at first that Mikhail Gorbachev was attempting to lull Americans into powerlessness through appeals to reform, disarmament, and an end to great-power conflict. Circumscribed by the Cold War mentality and lacking contingency plans, the Bush administration seemed unready when Eastern Europeans disengaged from the Soviet empire and jettisoned communism (see Chapter 29). In 1991, when the Soviet Union itself disintegrated, and ethnic warfare, political upheaval, and economic recession staggered the successor states, Bush and other "orphans of containment," as one analyst called them, seemed lost and passive—spectators rather than shapers. From the president's perspective, prudence suited the rapidly changing course of world affairs. But critics chastised Washington for its

slowness in offering aid to ease the transition to non-Communist societies. When the United States finally joined other nations in granting assistance to Eastern Europe and Russia, the amounts fell far short of the needs.

The START talks on limiting strategic nuclear forces gradually produced substantive results. In mid-1991 Russia and the United States signed the

START
———

START I pact to reduce each's nuclear warheads to 6,000 and each's strategic delivery systems to 1,600. In late 1992, Bush signed a START II agreement with Russia's President Boris Yeltsin, who had ousted Gorbachev. This accord provided for the reduction of warheads to about three thousand each by the year 2003 and the elimination of land-based intercontinental ballistic missiles (ICBMs) with more than one warhead, leaving each side with about 500 ICBMs. Arms-control advocates welcomed START II, but they warned of dangers ahead.

First, it was not clear that the other Soviet successor states would go along; Ukraine, for example, balked at transferring long-range missiles on its territory to Russia. Second, dismantling the warheads, missiles, and missile silos was costly, and Russia lacked the necessary funds. Third, to earn hard currency, the Russians might be tempted to sell nuclear technology and weapons-grade fissionable materials. And, last, the proliferation of nuclear weapons promised a dangerous future. Iran, Iraq, North Korea, Pakistan, and Israel, for example, seemed close to acquiring them.

One of the many events that signaled an end to the Cold War was the reunification of Germany on October 2, 1990. U.S. officials grew wary that

German Reunification Germany would dominate the continent—that it could not be anchored in or controlled by NATO or the European Community and that its economic prowess would further diminish U.S. competitiveness in world markets.

INTERVENTIONS AND RECURRENT ISSUES IN THE THIRD WORLD

The Cold War may have ended, but America's stormy relations with Third World countries did not relent. In Latin America, the Bush administration tried to cool the zeal with which Reagan had intervened, for the interventions had largely failed. The costly U.S.-financed contra war had not forced the Sandinista National Liberation Front from power in Nicaragua (see pages 980–982). In 1989 the Central American presidents devised a workable plan for free elections in Nicaragua and the disbanding of the contras. In the elections that followed in 1990, the Sandinista Front lost to the U.S.-backed National Opposition Union (UNO). The United States claimed victory, but Nicaragua's economy lay in shambles and little U.S. foreign aid was forthcoming. Elsewhere in Central America, Bush's efforts to dampen crises came to fruition in 1992 when Salvadoran leftists agreed to lay down their arms in favor of pressing their agenda through the political process.

Poverty-wracked Haiti held its first free elections in decades in 1990. But the next year the army overthrew the newly elected government of Jean-Bertrand Aristide. Though

Haiti the United States imposed economic sanctions, the military regime refused to restore Aristide to the presidency. Thousands of Haitians fled in boats for the United States, but the U.S. government classified them as economic rather than political refugees, rejecting their pleas for asylum and sending many back. Some observers defined them as environmental refugees because deforestation in Haiti had caused such soil depletion that Haitians could no longer produce food from the barren land. Critics charged Washington with discriminating against the Haitians because they are black.

Debt joined political instability to burden Latin America. By 1990 Latin American nations owed more than $400 billion (total Third World

Debt Burdens debt stood at more than $1.2 trillion). Brazil, Mexico, and Argentina owed the most, much of it to U.S. banks. The debt crisis hurt the United States when debtors trimmed their imports as they struggled to meet debt-service payments. As a result, U.S. exports slumped by billions of dollars and North American jobs were lost. Required by the International Monetary Fund to restructure their economies in order to qualify for assistance, Latin American governments drastically cut budgets. As health services and educational outlays were reduced, political unrest increased. Migrants fleeing grinding poverty pressed against U.S. immigration gates, sometimes entering illegally by sneaking across the Mexican-American border.

The profitable trade in illicit drugs also troubled inter-American relations. By 1990 the U.S. drug market was probably worth $100 billion.

The "Drug War" "This is more serious than the Vietnam War," declared Maryland's governor. As the Cold War receded, the "Drug War" accelerated, and Washington used the U.S. military to quash drug producers and traffickers in Colombia, Bolivia, and Peru, sources of cocaine and crack, both of which are processed from coca leaves. Bush officials concentrated on interrupting *supply* through interdiction and eradication programs. Others stressed the need to halt *demand* inside the United States itself.

The drug issue became conspicuous as Panamanian-U.S. relations deteriorated. Soon after General Manuel Antonio Noriega took power in Panama in 1983, he cut deals with Colombia's cocaine barons and laundered drug money in Panamanian banks. By the late 1980s his dictatorial rule and drug running had angered North Americans eager to blame the swaggering Panamanian for U.S. drug problems. The American people were unaware—though Bush knew—that Noriega had long been on the CIA payroll and that he had helped the United States aid and train the contras. Grateful for this cooperation, Washington had long turned a blind eye to his links with drug traffickers. When exposés of Noriega's sordid record provoked protests in Panama, the United States decided to dump the dictator. But he would not leave. After a U.S.-encouraged coup failed, Noriega heated up his anti-Americanism. In the United States Bush suffered criticism for not acting.

Invasion of Panama
Operation Just Cause was launched in the early hours of December 20, 1989. The largest American military operation since the Vietnam War, the invasion of Panama by 22,500 troops proved a bloodsoaked success. At least 500 Panamanians died; 23 American soldiers perished. Property damage in Panama City amounted to $1 billion. Noriega was captured and taken to Miami. In 1992 he was convicted of drug trafficking and sentenced to prison. Devastated Panama, meanwhile, like war-torn Nicaragua, became all the more dependent on the United States, which offered little reconstruction aid.

Gulf War
President Bush also took the United States to war in the Middle East. In August 1990, Iraq's dictator Saddam Hussein—resentful that the feudal dynasty of Kuwait would not reduce the huge debt Iraq owed to it and eager to acquire Kuwait's vast petroleum industry—ordered his troops to invade his peaceful neighbor. Oil-rich Saudi Arabia, long a U.S. ally, felt threatened. President Bush dispatched more than 500,000 U.S. forces to the region to defend Saudi Arabia and to press Saddam to pull out of Kuwait. If Iraq gained control of Kuwaiti and Saudi oilfields, the world would become vulnerable

On Thanksgiving Day 1991, George and Barbara Bush visited American soldiers after the success of Operation Desert Storm. The president had skillfully organized a multinational force to expel Iraqi forces from the oil-rich Persian Gulf state. Bush's popularity soared at first. By fall 1991, however, polls showed that Americans wanted him to shift his attention from world to domestic affairs. Diana Walker/Gamma Liaison.

to Saddam's economic and military power, Bush argued. Likening Saddam to Hitler and declaring that this was the first post-Cold War "test of our mettle," Bush rallied to war a deeply divided Congress (the Senate vote was 52–47). The United Nations also voted for war and helped organize a coalition of forces. Many Americans believed that economic sanctions on Iraq should be given more time to persuade Saddam to retreat and that the Iraqi-Kuwaiti quarrel should be resolved by Arabs themselves. "This will not be another Vietnam," the president assured Americans, for this time military power would be applied swiftly and massively.

When Operation Desert Storm began on January 16, 1991, the greatest air armada in history began pummeling Iraq and Iraqi forces in Kuwait. U.S. missiles joined round-the-clock bombing raids on Baghdad, Iraq's capital. In late February,

An estimated 300,000 Somalis had already starved to death and another 30,000 had died from weapons fire from warlord and clan armies. Beginning in December 1992, in Operation Restore Hope, U.S. troops landed in Somalia, fought off looters of relief supplies, and convoyed food and medicine to the needy. One U.S. Navy veteran protested this new military mission: "When the first dead Marine is sent home, what do we say to his grieving family? That their son died defending a bag of rice? That his killer escaped with a carton of dried milk? It may hardly seem like a fair trade." But American and world opinion applauded this example of "humanitarian intervention." Benson, Tribune Media Services.

coalition forces launched a ground war that routed the Iraqis from Kuwait in just one hundred hours. The war's toll: an estimated 100,000 Iraqis dead; only 148 American service personnel dead, 35 of them killed inadvertently by their comrades in "friendly fire." "By God," Bush exclaimed, "we've kicked the Vietnam syndrome once and for all." The United States was not a declining power, he crowed, but a reborn superpower.

The celebratory mood was short-lived. Environmental disaster followed when the retreating Iraqis set fire to Kuwait's oil wells, polluting the air and releasing millions of barrels of the black riches into Persian Gulf waters. American bombs had so damaged Iraq's infrastructure that spreading disease and hunger took countless lives. Saddam

The Aftermath of War

Hussein remained in power and brutally suppressed revolts by Iraqi Shiites and Kurds; only after many people had been slaughtered did the United States declare certain areas of Iraq off-limits to Saddam's military. Some Americans felt betrayed. They had endorsed a war for the principle of beating back aggression. But, in the end, the principle had been sullied when the United States failed to defend people whom Washington itself had urged to revolt against dictatorship. The U.S. military, furthermore, had tightly controlled the press and heavily censored the news; among the casualties of the war, critics charged, were a free press and an informed citizenry. Evidence soon surfaced, too, that the United States, virtually up to the moment of the Iraqi onslaught against Kuwait, had actually been pursuing closer relations with the brutal Saddam as a counterweight to Iran.

The Bush administration itself had sent foreign aid that enabled Saddam to buy arms, and U.S. companies had sold high-tech equipment that advanced Iraq's project to develop nuclear weapons.

The United States had demonstrated that it possessed the most impressive high-technology military force in the world, but the war had cost the United States $1 billion a day at a time when U.S. education, health, and economic competitiveness languished. "If we can make the best smart bomb, why can't we make the best VCR?" asked one senator. A larger question reverberated: Was war the means the United States was going to use to create a new post-Cold War world order? The prospects of both perpetual interventionism and economic decline took the spirit out of the U.S. victory.

The Persian Gulf War had some impact on the conflict between Arabs and Jews. Secretary Baker now demanded that Israel back off from its stern control of the Palestin-

Arab-Israeli Peace Talks

ians: "Lay aside, once and for all, the unrealistic vision of a greater Israel," he implored. "Forswear annexation. Stop settlement activity. . . . Reach out to the Palestinians as neighbors who deserve political rights." Baker's patient efforts led to a breakthrough in October 1991, when the Israelis sat down to negotiate with their Arab neighbors. Israel, however, came to the bargaining table vowing to give up no occupied territory. The peace talks sputtered, and Great Britain, China, and the United States itself heightened prospects for continued warfare by making huge arms sales to the region.

Operation Restore Hope was a Bush military expedition of a very different kind. The people of the African nation of Somalia had long suffered from the effects of soil erosion

Humanitarian Role in Somalia

and famine. After Somalia jilted its Cold-War ally the Soviet Union in the late 1970s, the Indian Ocean nation became a recipient of U.S. aid, including large amounts of weapons. When Somalia's repressive dictator was driven from power in early 1991, rival clans led by "warlords" vied for power and public authority broke down. Gun-toting bandits regularly stole the relief supplies sent by international agencies. "He [Bush] would not want to leave office with 50,000 people starving

that he could have saved," a senior official remarked. After gaining United Nations approval, the president ordered more than 20,000 American troops to Somalia in December 1992 to ensure the delivery of relief aid. A soldier from Klamath Falls, Oregon, described the emaciated Somalis he saw as appearing to be "coming out of graves walking." A U.N. peacekeeping force replaced U.S. troops in mid-1993.

Many Americans cheered this humanitarian work as an appropriate post-Cold War mission for the United States. But because Bush had neither looked very far into the future nor given direction to the "new world order," America's role in the tumultuous world remained unclear when he left office in early 1993.

THE BUSH PRESIDENCY AT HOME

Concluding his multi-volume history of the United States in 1989, the political scientist James MacGregor Burns took a final look at the American experiment and was discouraged by what he saw. The American people seemed mired in "political immobility." Fewer and fewer Americans bothered to vote, and "it would take rare leadership . . . to attract them to the polls." Indeed, Burns wrote, what the United States needed above all was "creative and transforming leadership" to mobilize the country and "carry through great projects." Burns, a Democrat, did not think Bush was up to the task.

George Bush was a political chameleon. Once a supporter of family planning and a woman's right to abortion, he had switched positions and denounced abortion as murder.

George Bush

In 1980 he had dismissed Ronald Reagan's economic ideas as "voodoo economics," but as the vice-presidential candidate he quickly endorsed Reagan's policies. In his loyal support for Reagan's conservative agenda, Bush seemed to lack firm convictions of his own. In the 1988 presidential campaign he turned nasty. As the television commentator Barbara Walters remarked to Bush shortly before his inauguration, "It's as if Clark Kent became Superman."

Although Bush called for a "kinder, gentler nation" on inauguration day, expectations of a com-

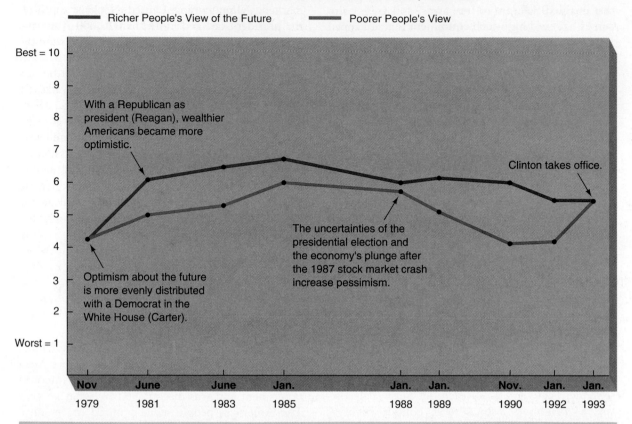

Rich and Poor Americans View the Future, 1979–1993

— Richer People's View of the Future　　— Poorer People's View

Best = 10

9

8　With a Republican as president (Reagan), wealthier Americans became more optimistic.

7

6

5

4　Optimism about the future is more evenly distributed with a Democrat in the White House (Carter).

3

2

Worst = 1

Clinton takes office.

The uncertainties of the presidential election and the economy's plunge after the 1987 stock market crash increase pessimism.

| Nov. | June | June | Jan. | | Jan. | Jan. | Nov. | Jan. | Jan. |
| 1979 | 1981 | 1983 | 1985 | | 1988 | 1989 | 1990 | 1992 | 1993 |

Rich and Poor Americans View the Future The New York Times/*CBS News Poll has periodically measured public attitudes about the future. People were asked to rate, on a scale of one to ten, how they felt about the nation's future. In 1979, richer people were defined as having a household income of more than $25,000; in 1993 the figure was more than $50,000. In 1979, poorer people were defined as having a household income of less than $10,000; in 1993 the figure was less than $15,000.* Source: New York Times, *January 31, 1993.*

passionate, vigorous presidency soon dimmed.

Economic Crisis

President Bush inherited an economy in which the discomfort index—a composite of inflation and unemployment—remained high. Over the next four years the economy took a nose dive. The gross national product increased on average only 0.7 percent a year, the slowest growth since the Great Depression of the 1930s. By 1992, several million Americans had joined the unemployment rolls and factory employment skidded. Even for Americans with jobs, personal income was stagnant. In 1991 median household income fell by 3.5 percent, the

most severe decline since the 1973 recession. In 1992, the number of poor people in America reached the highest level since 1964. Bush seemed uncaring when he defended tax breaks for the rich but opposed extending relief payments to the long-term unemployed. One reporter wrote that the administration was "leading a retreat from social responsibility."

Because of the ever-mounting federal deficit spending ($220 billion in 1990, $269 billion in 1991, and $290 billion in 1992) and federal debt ($4 trillion in 1992), which required huge interest payments, the president thought he could do little to stimulate the economy and create jobs. The total cost of the federal bailout of the failed savings-and-loan industry alone had reached $130 billion in 1992. Reduced federal aid to city and state governments and the ailing economy, among other factors, pushed these governments to the brink of bankruptcy. In mid-1992, for example, California had to pay its state employees and creditors in IOUs. A series of "tax revolts," beginning in 1978, had cut property taxes just when California's population boomed.

Businesses also became deeply burdened with debt; real-estate, home-building, and insurance firms had overextended themselves. Companies of all kinds laid off workers as the recession deepened. In efforts to cut costs and increase productivity, many businesses replaced workers with computers and other machines. Some businesses moved their plants to countries where wages were lower, environmental controls weaker, and benefits packages nonexistent. The Bush administration did not invest in programs to retrain the many workers let

go by the defense industry, whose contracts for weapons shrank at the end of the Cold War. "The recession," *Newsweek* claimed in fall 1991, "has average Americans spooked and politicians running scared."

The Bush administration seemed to have no solution to the economic crisis. The president's motto, "First, do no harm," expressed his long-standing aversion to governmental action to solve economic and social problems. Remembering the Republican president who had served at the onset of the Great Depression, punsters began to call him George Herbert Hoover Bush. His popularity declined. The conservative political analyst Kevin Phillips noted that Bush's "dithering" over domestic issues had prompted "Washington's vultures" to begin "another political death watch."

Bush's Passivity

The Persian Gulf War of early 1991 temporarily shored up Bush's floundering presidency. Just

The cartoonist Mike Luckovich seemed to know what Bush and his advisers were thinking inside the White House when signs of trouble were going up in 1991. Bush officials had hoped to turn victory in the Gulf War into votes for the president's re-election, but Americans wearied of Desert Storm celebrations when Bush seemed unwilling to take the lead in solving domestic problems.   © 1991 Mike Luckovich–Atlanta Constitution/Creators Syndicate.

as the president's domestic passivity was drawing the most severe criticism, he earned high praise for assembling the multinational force that drove Iraqi troops from Kuwait. Shortly after this victory, Bush's advisers told him that the stagnant economy was about to boom and that Americans distrusted government solutions to economic problems and wanted him to pursue further foreign-policy triumphs. "The idea," recalled a senior official, "was that he'd ride the wave from the war" to reelection. "Mr. President," Budget Director Richard Darman remarked, "you could go out there and tell them a depression is upon us and no one would even notice." Darman's advice was frequently wrong, as was that of John Sununu, the president's arrogant chief of staff. Bush's complacency and inactivity on unemployment, health care, and the environment, among many other issues, proved a serious miscalculation.

"Read my lips: no new taxes," Bush had proclaimed at the 1988 Republican convention. But during the 1990 budget negotiations with Congress, the White House agreed to a trade-off to reduce the federal deficit: Democratic leaders accepted budget cuts and the president endorsed a tax hike. Bush's press secretary was shocked when he heard about the deal: "That means we've broken the pledge." Soon television newscasts began running the videotape of Bush's "Read my lips" statement, raising anew doubts about his consistency. Democratic Representative Patricia Schroeder of Colorado, noting the bad advice that Bush had once again received from his chief of staff, remarked, "George Bush is in deep Sununu." As for John Sununu, he was soon forced to resign over revelations that he had used expensive government jets for dentist appointments in Boston and other personal trips.

Breaking the No-New-Taxes Pledge

In his 1988 campaign, Bush had promised to be both "the environmental president" and "the education president." He became neither. Bush won plaudits for signing the 1990 reauthorization of the Clean Air Act, which required businesses to control emissions of sulfur dioxide and nitrogen oxides, but he gutted enforcement of the act by creating the Council on Competitiveness. Headed by Vice President Dan Quayle, the council undercut environmental regulations on

Weakening of Environmental Regulations

the grounds that they slowed economic growth and cost jobs. In addition, the Justice Department overruled the Environmental Protection Agency when it sought to prosecute large corporate polluters.

As for education, President Bush had announced that by the year 2000 American students would rank second to none in science and mathematics. But other than argue for government vouchers that parents could use to pay tuition at public or private schools of their choice, Bush did little to improve education. The high-school dropout rate increased, urban schools became battlegrounds of gangs and drug dealers, and an increasing number of illiterates entered the work force. Some observers charged that right-wing ideologues in the Bush administration were waging cultural war against universities, the National Endowment for the Humanities, and the National Endowment for the Arts because these institutions tolerated dissenting and experimental views.

Bush provoked further controversy when he nominated Clarence Thomas to the Supreme Court in 1991 to replace the retiring Thurgood Marshall. Few people believed that Thomas, a young and inexperienced federal judge, was the best candidate. An African-American of extremely conservative views, he opposed affirmative action in hiring, believed in permitting prayer in the schools, and opposed abortion. Bush's nomination of a black conservative was a clever political move "calculated," in the words of Eleanor Holmes Norton, the congressional delegate from Washington, D.C., to "mute the expected reaction to yet another conservative nominee."

Clarence Thomas and Sexual Harassment

Thomas nonetheless seemed likely to win confirmation. Then in October, Anita Hill, a black law professor at the University of Oklahoma, electrified the nation. She charged that Thomas had sexually harassed her when she worked for him in the early 1980s. As shown in the photo on page 1073, she testified before the all-male Senate Judiciary Committee about her discomfort when Thomas insisted on describing pornographic movies and when he made sexual advances. Republican senators sought to discredit Hill, but her testimony elicited nationwide support. The Senate confirmed Thomas, but Hill's testimony and many senators' disregard of it angered women, especially those who had suffered similar experiences of sexual harassment in the workplace. Many vowed to oppose the Republican party in 1992.

The social ills that had plagued the United States in the 1980s persisted into the new decade: AIDS, homelessness, drug and alcohol addiction, racism and inequality, poverty among children, the day-to-day struggle of single-parent families, child abuse, teen suicide, the income gap between rich and poor, inadequate health-insurance coverage (see Chapter 33). In the 1990s, however, economic and social problems that had once afflicted only the poor now touched the lives of increasing numbers of middle-class people whose standard of living declined. Scholars tracking the nation's "social health" reported that it was at its lowest level since the data were first analyzed in 1970.

Social Problems

As unemployment and poverty rose, so did racial tensions. In April 1992, when a California jury acquitted four police officers charged with beating Rodney King, an African-American motorist, violence erupted in Los Angeles. In the bloodiest urban riot since the 1960s, forty-four

Los Angeles Riots

people died and two thousand were injured. Entire blocks of houses and stores went up in flames, leaving $1 billion in charred ruins. According to a California legislative committee, the 1965 Watts riot (see Chapter 32) had sprung from "poverty, segregation, lack of education and employment opportunities, [and] widespread perceptions of police abuse. . . . Little has changed in 1992 Los Angeles." Bush advocated emergency aid, but he passed up an opportunity to address the country's urban and racial problems. "So much for the Los Angeles riots," said a disgusted Jack Kemp, Bush's secretary of housing and urban development.

In contrast, Bush did push for the progressive change represented by the Americans with Disabilities Act of 1990. This act banned job discrimination against blind, deaf, mentally retarded, and physically impaired people, as well as those who were HIV-positive or had cancer. Applicable to companies with twenty-five or more employees, the act covered 87 percent of all jobs. The statute also required "reasonable accommodations," such as wheelchair ramps, for people with disabilities.

Americans with Disabilities Act

University of Oklahoma law professor Anita Hill testified in October 1991 at the confirmation hearings for Supreme Court nominee Clarence Thomas. She charged that he had sexually harassed her. In bitter countertestimony viewed by millions on television, Thomas denied the allegations. The Senate confirmed Thomas as a justice. Believing that the predominantly male political world preferred to dodge the issue of sexual harassment, Hill continued to focus attention on the problem through speeches across the nation. Dennis Brack/Black Star.

The U.S. Chamber of Commerce applauded the bill for opening up "a huge untapped resource of workers." Bush signed the bill, marking one of his presidency's few upbeat moments on domestic issues.

But the Republican president and the Democrat-controlled Congress seldom worked together. Instead of compromise and negotiated solutions, they produced stalemate. Beginning in 1989 with his rejection of a minimum-wage increase, Bush vetoed thirty-seven bills during his presidency, only one of which was overridden by the necessary two-thirds vote of both houses of Congress. Rarely in American history had legislative results been so meager.

Americans did not blame the gridlock solely on the president: they also grew impatient with a Congress that seemed mired in scandal and privilege. The most blatant example

**Scandals in
Congress**

was the mismanagement of the House bank, where representatives wrote thousands of bad checks that the bank covered at no fee. Some senators brought shame on themselves by badgering Anita Hill in the Thomas hearings. During the savings-and-loan scandal, evidence became public that still other senators had done favors for a money manipulator who had deceitfully misused the funds of unsuspecting small investors, costing them their savings. Many members of Congress received payments from corporate and other interest-group lobbyists who offered free jet flights and high honoraria for speeches. The public grew angrier when members of Congress voted themselves a pay raise. In 1992, the necessary number of states ratified the new Twenty-seventh Amendment to the Constitution to prohibit mid-term congressional pay raises.

THE ELECTION OF 1992

Bush watched the economic crisis deepen. "He lacks any fingertip feel," noted one political analyst, "for what it is to be a member of the wage-earning middle class in America." In a poll taken in January 1992, eight out of ten Americans rated the economy as "fairly bad" or "very bad." Most people—especially Democrats—blamed Bush. The

president also faced harsh criticism from within his own party. The tough-talking conservative neo-isolationist Patrick Buchanan entered the New Hampshire primary to contest Bush's renomination.

Beginning with Nixon's election in 1968, the Republican party had won the White House in five out of six elections by building a coalition of ideologically diverse constituencies. Economic conservatives

**Republican
Constituencies**

who had always voted Republican were joined by cultural conservatives, particularly fundamentalist and evangelical Christians who advocated "family values" and opposed abortion and homosexuality. The "Radical Right," people of extremely conservative views whom George Bush had once called "the nut fringe," also voted Republican. "Reagan Democrats"—blue-collar workers and one-time Democrats—had supported Bush in 1988 as Reagan's heir. White voters in the South who disliked the Democratic party's liberalism on civil rights issues could be counted on to vote Republican, as could young Americans between eighteen and thirty who had come of age politically during the "make-money" frenzy of the Reagan years. Finally, there were the residents of America's ever-growing suburbs, which in 1990 accounted for almost half of the nation's population. The sheer size of the suburban vote, which tended to be antitax and antigovernment, made this group the most significant of all. What had held these constituencies together in the 1980s were relative prosperity, anti-Communism, and Ronald Reagan. In 1992 these three factors had disappeared; in their place, an anti-incumbency mood—"throw the rascals out"—had grown.

Among the Democratic hopefuls in 1992 were William Jefferson "Bill" Clinton, governor of Arkansas; Paul Tsongas, former senator from Massachusetts; and Jerry Brown, former governor of California. By

Bill Clinton

July, when the Democrats convened to nominate their candidate, Clinton had become the clear victor in the primaries. Born in 1946—the first baby boomer nominated for president by a major party—Clinton had wanted to be president most of his life. When he attended college in the 1960s he had opposed the Vietnam War and pulled strings to avoid being drafted (as had Vice President Dan Quayle, also of the Vietnam generation). After studying in Britain as a Rhodes Scholar and graduating from Yale Law School, Clinton returned to Arkansas. He was elected state attorney general in 1976 and governor three years later—at the age of thirty-two. He failed to be re-elected, but in 1983 Arkansas voters once again chose him to lead the state.

Clinton sought to move the Democratic party to the right to make it more attractive to white suburbanites, Reagan Democrats, and members of the business community. He hoped, said an ally, "to modernize liberalism so it could sell again." To this end, Clinton applauded private business as the engine of economic progress and endorsed reform to move people off welfare and to put more police officers on the streets. But, in the liberal tradition, he also advocated greater public investment in the nation's infrastructure of roads, bridges, and communications; greater access to job-training projects and college educations; less costly and more inclusive health care; and a shift of funds from defense to civilian programs. He also took a "pro-choice" stand, declaring it a woman's right to choose abortion. His running mate, Tennessee Senator Albert Gore, was like Clinton a baby-boomer, a white southerner, a Baptist, and a moderate Democrat. But Gore had served in Vietnam. He had also gained a reputation as a specialist on environmental issues. His book, *Earth in the Balance: Healing the Global Environment* (1992), received a great deal of attention.

In 1992 the American people witnessed the most active third-party campaign since 1968, when George Wallace had run for president. H. Ross

H. Ross Perot
━━━

Perot, a Texas multibillionaire who had amassed his fortune in the computer industry, spoke in plain language about economic issues. His one-liners caught on with many people who thought a Washington outsider and successful businessman could fix the deficit and spark economic growth. "He doesn't have to answer to anybody but the people," explained one backer. The mercurial Perot entered the race in the spring, dropped out in the summer, and re-entered in October.

Meanwhile the Republicans renominated George Bush and Dan Quayle. The extremely conservative and error-prone vice president proved a liability for Bush: Quayle remained the subject of countless jokes about incompetence and mental lapses, and

the contrast with the bright, articulate Gore made his shortcomings even more conspicuous. As Bush campaigned, he failed to give Americans a sure sense of who he was or what remedies he prescribed for the nation's ills. "Nobody ever says, 'Let Bush be Bush,'" wrote the conservative columnist William Safire, "because nobody can be sure what that would be."

At the Republican convention in August, Bush assumed the identity of guardian of "family values." Cultural conservatism dominated the convention,

Republican Attacks on Clinton
━━━

where speaker after speaker championed the traditional two-parent family, denounced unconventional lifestyles, and disparaged homosexuals—all the while suggesting that the Clintons had strayed outside acceptable boundaries. Bush's acceptance speech offered little to voters who wanted solutions to the nation's economic crisis. As Bush himself admitted, the "vision thing" had always eluded him.

The Bush-Quayle campaign strategy featured negative campaigning, particularly attacks on Clinton's character. Clinton's Vietnam draft status and alleged extramarital affairs drew constant criticism. Republicans caricatured him as "Slick Willie." The issue, Bush insisted, was "trust."

Claiming that he had ended the Cold War and highlighting triumph in the Gulf War, Bush also asked Americans if they could trust the inexperienced Clinton to handle international affairs. Clinton rebutted that Bush's taking credit for the ending of the Cold War was like "the rooster who took credit for the dawn." Clinton also chastised Bush for befriending dictators, especially the "appeasement" of Saddam Hussein before the war. Debate on foreign relations was shallow, with neither candidate helping the American people to reorient themselves to the transformed world. Clinton often straddled issues and catered to defense hawks who sought to keep alive pet weapons programs like the Seawolf submarine. The Arkansas governor promised to curb the proliferation of weapons, but then endorsed Bush's sale of F-15 fighter jets to Saudi Arabia and F-16s to Taiwan. But domestic policy, not foreign policy, dominated the campaign.

With three candidates, the election had become a much closer race than political experts had predicted. One prediction proved sound: the

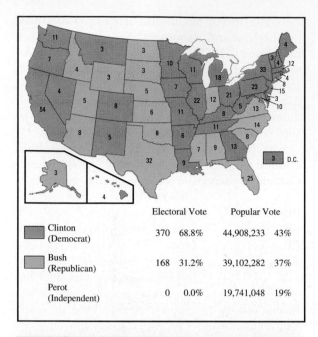

	Electoral Vote	Popular Vote
Clinton (Democrat)	370 68.8%	44,908,233 43%
Bush (Republican)	168 31.2%	39,102,282 37%
Perot (Independent)	0 0.0%	19,741,048 19%

Presidential Election, 1992 Although a minority of voters cast ballots for Bill Clinton, he won handily in the electoral college. Clinton's share of the popular vote was the lowest for anyone elected president since Woodrow Wilson won with a lower percentage in 1912. Clinton took a majority of votes only in the District of Columbia and Arkansas, but Bush and Perot failed to win a majority of votes in any state. Exit polls revealed that the votes for Perot would have divided about evenly between Clinton and Bush had Perot not been in the race.

Clinton's Victory

American people demanded change. On November 3, with the highest voter turnout (55 percent) since 1976, the Clinton-Gore ticket scored well in the Northeast, the Pacific Coast, and the industrial heartland of the Midwest, and made inroads into the South (see map). Clinton-Gore also ran well in normally Republican strongholds: suburbs, high-tech areas, retirement communities, and the Sunbelt. Overall, the Democrats won 43 percent of the popular vote and 370 electoral votes; Bush and Quayle tallied 37 percent and 168 electoral votes; and Perot earned 19 percent but no electoral votes. Perot polled the largest popular-vote percentage for

a third party since the Bull Moose party ran Theodore Roosevelt eighty years earlier.

Voters also changed their Congress. The party distribution remained about the same, with the Democrats in control of both houses, but four more women were sent to the Senate and nineteen more to the House. Voters also elected more African-American and Hispanic representatives. Many of the first-term members of Congress were—like Clinton—in their forties with advanced degrees, no military service, and considerable experience in politics at the state level. "The baby boomers' generation—or at least some of its most upwardly mobile members—is taking over," observed the respected *Washington Post* columnist David Broder. "It will be different."

One of Bush's last decisions, however, smacked of the discredited past: Just before leaving office, he pardoned former Secretary of Defense Caspar Weinberger and other Iran-contra figures who had been indicted on felony counts for lying to Congress and obstructing a congressional inquiry. Had nothing been learned from the Watergate scandal, asked Broder, especially "their duty to obey the law?" The veteran journalist added: "We have failed as a society to express our contempt and disgust for those who violate their oaths of office with such impunity."

Bush Pardon of Iran-contra Figures

THE CLINTON PRESIDENCY

President Clinton could not reverse Bush's pardon, but he could try to mobilize the nation to pull itself out of its economic, social, and political doldrums. Clinton named to his cabinet a mix of seasoned politicos, young politicians, intellectuals, women, and minorities. He called for a national mission of shared sacrifice. He appointed Hillary Rodham Clinton to draft a plan for health-care reform. The new president immediately overturned Bush's "gag rule," which had prohibited abortion counseling in clinics that received federal funds. When Clinton announced that he planned to lift the ban on homosexuals in the military, the military brass joined Republicans in harshly criticizing the move. Seeing that the American people were evenly di-

The night the 1992 election tallies poured in, Hillary Clinton (left), Bill Clinton, Al Gore, and Tipper Gore celebrated the Democratic triumph in Little Rock, Arkansas. Dancing to rock-'n'-roll music, they declared a generational shift to more youthful leadership, reminding some observers of the transition from Eisenhower to Kennedy more than thirty years earlier.   Sygma/Ira Wyman.

vided on the issue, and fearful of losing support for his economic proposals, Clinton delayed a decision for months; finally he accepted a compromise that prohibited discrimination against gays in the military but held them to a strict code of behavior.

The frail economy drew the president's closest scrutiny. When Clinton took office in early 1993 the unemployment rate stood at 7.2 percent and the federal debt had passed $4 trillion. IBM and other major corporations were laying off thousands of workers. The troubled economies of Europe and Japan portended lower U.S. exports and a bigger trade deficit; the trade deficit had already reached $84.3 billion in 1992, a 29-percent jump from 1991. Still reeling from losses on real-estate loans, banks were hesitant to lend to small businesses, although interest rates were dropping. Health-care costs continued to mount, driving up the federal deficit.

The economic plan sent to Congress in February 1993 called for higher taxes for the middle class, a 10-percent surtax on individuals with tax-

Clinton's Economic Proposals

able incomes over $250,000, an energy tax, and a higher corporate tax. Clinton promised to end business deductions for expense accounts, such as memberships in country clubs. He also proposed to cut government spending through a smaller defense budget and a downsized bureaucracy, and he offered an immediate stimulus to the economy through public projects.

Interest-group lobbyists wasted no time in attacking the comprehensive plan. Republicans protested that Clinton was not cutting back enough on spending, and other critics hammered him for reneging on his campaign pledge to provide tax relief for middle-class Americans. The president fought back, arguing that federal indebtedness was graver than anticipated, and that all Americans must pay to clean up the mess the deficit-spending Republicans had left them. Intent on avoiding the "trappings of Washington," he criss-crossed the na-

This Tony Auth cartoon captured two features of early 1993. First, that Bill Clinton intended to be a very active, get-the-job-done president. Second, that the American people had high hopes that their forty-six-year-old president would successfully tackle the economic problems besetting the nation.   Tony Auth for The Philadelphia Inquirer © 1993.

tion to speak directly to people. Congress killed his stimulus proposal but passed most of his requests by close votes.

Clinton's popularity dropped fast. People protested higher taxes and showed impatience with the slowness of his plan to revive the economy. Critics charged that Clinton was indecisive (backing down when pressed) and unwilling to take risks. Public-relations gaffes and late-hour White House abandonment of controversial appointees raised doubts about the president's management ability. "I try to adhere to Napoleon's old adage of never interfere with your enemy while he's in the process of destroying himself," remarked Republican National Committee Chairman Haley Barbour. Clinton admitted after a few months in office that he had gotten "out of focus." That was not the problem, wrote the liberal columnist Barbara Ehrenreich; the problem was Clinton's "inexorable stagger to the right." The president did move some of his agenda forward: he signed the "motor-voter" and family-leave bills; he persuaded Congress to pass a campaign finance reform bill; and he reversed a Bush policy and announced that the United States would sign the international agreement protecting rare and endangered species.

When Byron R. White stepped down from the Supreme Court, Clinton appointed as justice Ruth Bader Ginsburg, an experienced women's rights advocate and federal appeals court judge.

Although Clinton's first priority was domestic policy, he and his secretary of state, the veteran diplomat Warren Christopher, could not ignore the highly volatile, multipolar world of the post-Cold War era. The danger of nuclear proliferation heightened just as the superpowers were scaling back their nuclear-tipped missiles. Borderless issues continued to accelerate. The environment still suffered from acid rain and toxic waste, and the ozone layer continued to deteriorate. An AIDS pandemic threatened the lives of millions, and famine stalked Africa. Arab-Israeli tensions remained taut and peace talks were on-again, off-again. Iraq continued to cross Washington; in June 1993 Clinton ordered a Tomahawk cruise-missile attack against Baghdad in retaliation for an alleged Iraqi plot to assassinate former President Bush. Terrorism remained a constant danger; in early 1993 Islamic extremists bombed the World Trade Center in New York City. Ethnic hostilities

America and a Multipolar World

in the former Soviet states and Yugoslavia, where the Serbs were killing off Muslims in Bosnia, and racial strife in South Africa, where the transition from apartheid proved violent, bespoke a future of instability in which the nation-state seemed less able to maintain order. Russia needed vast amounts of foreign aid to stave off economic collapse and preserve steps toward democracy. At the Vancouver, Canada, summit meeting in April 1993 with Russian leader Boris Yeltsin, Clinton pledged American assistance.

The central questions in public debate on American foreign policy were simple, but the answers were not: Should or could the United States play the expensive role of global policeman while at the same time undertaking the expensive task of economic renewal at home? What mix of retrenchment and international activism, of unilateralism and multilateralism, lay ahead? Which foreign disturbances threatened vital U.S. interests, and which did not?

Throughout American history, the closing decade of a century has been a time of turbulence and transformation. In the 1690s, as the colonists struggled to adjust to the Navigation Acts that governed their membership in the far-flung British mercantile empire, King William's War pitted the French and their Indian allies against British-Americans. Accusations of witchcraft in Massachusetts revealed political disorder and a society in stress. In the 1790s, a new republic with a new constitution confronted the Whiskey Rebellion, the Alien and Sedition Acts, the rise of partisan political parties, and entanglement in Europe's wars. The 1890s witnessed devastating depression, agrarian revolt, burgeoning cities, bloody labor strikes, the emergence of corporate giants, the onset of a major reform movement, and a new empire abroad that anti-imperialists considered a violation of U.S. principles.

As the twenty-first century beckoned, the 1990s, too, promised turmoil and adjustment for Americans. In charting their nation's future in a turbulent present, their many different memories of the past would guide them. In his 1993 inaugural address, President Clinton invoked Thomas Jefferson's prediction that "to preserve the very foundations of our nation we would need dramatic change from time to time." In the poem she read at the inauguration, Maya Angelou also spoke of the tenacious link between past and future:

> History, despite its wrenching pain,
> Cannot be unlived, but if faced
> With courage, need not be lived again.

SUGGESTIONS FOR FURTHER READING

The Bush Administration

Donald L. Bartlett and James B. Steele, *America: What Went Wrong?* (1992); Colin Campbell and Bert A. Rockman, eds., *The Bush Presidency* (1991); Michael Duffy and Don Goodgame, *Marching in Place: The Status Quo Presidency of George Bush* (1992); Otis L. Graham, *Losing Time: The Industrial Policy Debate* (1992).

Bush and the World

See some works cited in Chapter 29; Graham Allison and Gregory F. Treverton, *Rethinking America's Security* (1992); Richard E. Benedick, *Ozone Diplomacy* (1991); James Chace, *The Consequences of Peace* (1992); David E. Fisher, *Fire & Ice: The Greenhouse Effect, Ozone Depletion, and Nuclear Winter* (1990); Edward M. Graham and Paul R. Krugman, *Foreign Direct Investment in the United States* (1989); Sheila K. Johnson, *The Japanese Through American Eyes* (1990); Paul Kennedy, *The Rise and Fall of the Great Powers* (1987); Jeffrey Lefebvre, *Arms for the Horn: U.S. Security Policy in Ethiopia and Somalia, 1953–1991* (1992); Sean Lynn-Jones, ed., *The Cold War and After* (1991); Joseph S. Nye, Jr., *Bound to Lead* (1990); Kenneth A. Oye et al., eds., *Eagle in a New World* (1992); Robert W. Tucker and David C. Hendrickson, *The Imperial Temptation* (1992).

To follow recent topics, see *Great Decisions* (annual) and *Headline Series*, both published by the Foreign Policy Association; the *America and the World* series, published annually by *Foreign Affairs* magazine; and Worldwatch Institute's *State of the World*, published annually on environmental issues.

Latin America and North America

Kevin Buckley, *Panama* (1991); John Dinges, *Our Man in Panama* (1990); Guy Gugliotta and Jeff Leen, *Kings of Cocaine* (1989); Gary Hufbauer and Jeffrey Schott, *North American Free Trade* (1992); Abraham F. Lowenthal, *Partners in Conflict*, rev. ed. (1990); Donald J. Mabry, ed., *The Latin American Narcotics Trade and U.S. National Security* (1989); Robert A. Pastor, *Whirlpool* (1992); Peter Dale Scott and Jonathan Marshall, *Cocaine Politics: Drugs, Armies, and the CIA in Central America* (1991).

Persian Gulf War

Deborah Amos, *Lines in the Sand* (1992); Lawrence Freedman and Efraim Karsh, *The Gulf Conflict 1990–1991* (1993); Stephen Graubard, *Mr. Bush's War* (1992); Roger Hilsman, *George Bush vs. Saddam Hussein* (1992); Alex Hybel, *Power over Rationality* (1993); John MacArthur, *Second Front: Censorship and Propaganda in the Gulf War* (1992); Joseph S. Nye, Jr., and Roger K. Smith, eds., *After the Storm* (1992); Michael Palmer, *Guardians of the Gulf* (1992); Jean Edward Smith, *George Bush's War* (1992); Philip M. Taylor, *War and the Media* (1992).

Politics and the Election of 1992

E. J. Dionne, *Why Americans Hate Politics* (1992); Alan Ehrenhalt, *The United States of Ambition* (1991); William Greider, *Who Will Tell the People* (1992); Jerry Hagstrom, *Beyond Reagan* (1988); Kathleen Hall Jamieson, *Dirty Politics* (1992); Kevin Phillips, *The Politics of Rich and Poor* (1990); Ruy A. Teixeira, *The Disappearing American Voter* (1992); George F. Will, *Restoration: Congress, Term Limits and the Recovery of Deliberative Democracy* (1992).

Historical Reference Books by Subject: Encyclopedias, Dictionaries, Atlases, Chronologies, and Statistics

American History: General

John D. Buenker and Edward R. Kantowicz, eds., *Historical Dictionary of the Progressive Era, 1890–1920* (1988); Gorton Carruth, ed., *The Encyclopedia of American Facts and Figures* (1987); John Drexel, ed., *The Facts on File Encyclopedia of the 20th Century* (1991); Robert H. Ferrell and John S. Bowman, eds., *The Twentieth Century: An Almanac* (1984); George H. Gallup, *The Gallup Poll: Public Opinion, 1935–1971* (1972), *1972–1977* (1978), and annual reports (1979–); Bernard Grun, *The Timetables of History* (1991); Stanley Hochman, *Yesterday and Today* (1979); *International Encyclopedia of the Social Sciences* (1968–); R. Alton Lee, ed., *Encyclopedia USA* (1983–); Michael Martin and Leonard Gelber, *Dictionary of American History* (1981); Richard B. Morris, *Encyclopedia of American History* (1982); James S. Olson, *Historical Dictionary of the 1920s* (1988); Thomas Parker and Douglas Nelson, *Day by Day: The Sixties* (1983); Harry Ritter, *Dictionary of Concepts in History* (1986); Arthur M. Schlesinger, Jr., ed., *The Almanac of American History* (1983); *Scribner Desk Dictionary of American History* (1984); U.S. Bureau of the Census, *Historical Statistics of the United States* (1975); Philip P. Wiener, ed., *Dictionary of the History of Ideas* (1973).

American History: General Atlases

Geoffrey Barraclough, ed., *The Times Concise Atlas of World History* (1982); Robert H. Ferrell and Richard Natkiel, *Atlas of American History* (1987); Edward W. Fox, *Atlas of American History* (1964); Kenneth T. Jackson and James T. Adams, *Atlas of American History* (1978); Catherine M. Mattson and Mark T. Mattson, *Contemporary Atlas of the United States* (1990); National Geographic Society, *Historical Atlas of the United States* (1988); Charles O. Paullin, *Atlas of the Historical Geography of the United States* (1932); U.S. Department of the Interior, *National Atlas of the United States* (1970). Other atlases are listed under specific categories.

American History: General Biographies

Lucian Boia, ed., *Great Historians of the Modern Age* (1991); *Dictionary of American Biography* (1928–); John A. Garraty, ed., *Encyclopedia of American Biography* (1974); *National Cyclopedia of American Biography* (1898–). Other biographical works appear under specific categories.

African-Americans

Molefi Asante and Mark T. Mattson, *Historical and Cultural Atlas of African-Americans* (1991); Bruce Kellner, *The Harlem Renaissance* (1984); Rayford W. Logan and Michael R. Winston, eds., *The Dictionary of American Negro Biography* (1983); W. A. Low and Virgil A. Clift, eds., *Encyclopedia of Black America* (1981); Charles D. Lowery and John F. Marszalek, eds., *Encyclopedia of African-American Civil Rights* (1992); Randall M. Miller and John D. Smith, eds., *Dictionary of Afro-American Slavery* (1988); Harry A. Ploski and James Williams, eds., *The Negro Almanac* (1989); Dorothy C. Salem, ed., *African American Women* (1993); Edgar A. Toppin, *A Biographical History of Blacks in America* (1971).

American Revolution

Richard Blanco, ed., *The American Revolution* (1993); Mark M. Boatner III, *Encyclopedia of the American Revolution* (1974); Lester J. Cappon, ed., *Atlas of Early American History: The Revolutionary Era, 1760–1790* (1976); John M. Faragher, ed., *The Encyclopedia of Colonial and Revolutionary America* (1990); Jack P. Greene and J. R. Pole, eds., *The Blackwell Encyclopedia of the American Revolution* (1991); Douglas W. Marshall and Howard H. Peckham,

Campaigns of the American Revolution (1976); Gregory Palmer, ed., *Biographical Sketches of Loyalists of the American Revolution* (1984); John W. Raimo, ed., *Biographical Directory of American Colonial and Revolutionary Governors, 1607–1789* (1980); *Rand-McNally Atlas of the American Revolution* (1974).

Architecture

William D. Hunt, Jr., ed., *Encyclopedia of American Architecture* (1980).

Business and the Economy

Christine Ammer and Dean S. Ammer, *Dictionary of Business and Economics* (1983); Douglas Auld and Graham Bannock, *The American Dictionary of Economics* (1983); Michael J. Freeman, *Atlas of World Economy* (1991); Douglas Greenwald, *Encyclopedia of Economics* (1982); John N. Ingham, *Biographical Dictionary of American Business Leaders* (1983); John N. Ingham and Lynne B. Feldman, *Contemporary American Business Leaders* (1990); William H. Mulligan, Jr., ed., *A Historical Dictionary of American Industrial Language* (1988); Glenn G. Munn, *Encyclopedia of Banking and Finance* (1973); Glenn Porter, *Encyclopedia of American Economic History* (1980); Richard Robinson, *United States Business History, 1602–1988* (1990). See also "Transportation."

Cities and Towns

Charles Abrams, *The Language of Cities: A Glossary of Terms* (1971); John L. Androit, ed., *Township Atlas of the United States* (1979); Melvin G. Holli and Peter d'A. Jones, eds., *Biographical Dictionary of American Mayors, 1820–1980: Big City Mayors* (1981); Ory M. Nergal, ed., *The Encyclopedia of American Cities* (1980); David D. Van Tassel and John J. Grabowski, eds., *The Encyclopedia of Cleveland History* (1987). See also "Politics and Government."

The Civil War and Reconstruction

Mark M. Boatner III, *The Civil War Dictionary* (1988); Richard N. Current, ed., *Encyclopedia of the Confederacy* (1993); Patricia L. Faust, *Historical Times Encyclopedia of the Civil War* (1986); Mark E. Neely, Jr., *The Abraham Lincoln Encyclopedia* (1982); Craig L. Symonds, *A Battlefield Atlas of the Civil War* (1983); Hans L. Trefousse, *Historical Dictionary of Reconstruction* (1991); U.S. War Department, *The Official Atlas of the Civil War* (1958); Jon L. Wakelyn, ed., *Biographical Dictionary of the Confederacy* (1977); Ezra J. Warner and W. Buck Yearns, *Biographical Register of the Confederate Congress* (1975). See also "The South" and "Politics and Government."

Constitution, Supreme Court, and Judiciary

Congressional Quarterly, *Guide to the Supreme Court* (1979); Leon Friedman and Fred I. Israel, eds., *The Justices of the United States Supreme Court, 1789–1978* (1980); Kermit L. Hall, ed., *The Oxford Companion to the Supreme Court of the United States* (1992); Richard F. Hixson, *Mass Media and the Constitution* (1989); Robert J. Janosik, ed., *Encyclopedia of the American Judicial System* (1987); John W. Johnson, ed., *Historical U.S. Court Cases, 1690–1990* (1992); Arthur S. Leonard, ed., *Sexuality and the Law* (1993); Leonard W. Levy et al., eds., *Encyclopedia of the American Constitution* (1986); Fred R. Shapiro, *The Oxford Dictionary of American Legal Quotations* (1993). See also "Politics and Government."

Crime, Violence, and Police

William G. Bailey, *Encyclopedia of Police Science* (1987); Sanford H. Kadish, ed., *Encyclopedia of Crime and Justice* (1983); Michael Newton and Judy Ann Newton, *The FBI Most Wanted: An Encyclopedia* (1989); Michael Newton and Judy Ann Newton, *Racial and Religious Violence in America* (1991); Michael Newton and Judy Newton, *The Ku Klux Klan* (1990); Carl Sifakis, *Encyclopedia of Assassinations* (1990); Carl Sifakis, *The Encyclopedia of American Crime* (1982).

Culture and Folklore

Hennig Cohen and Tristam Potter Coffin, eds., *The Folklore of American Holidays* (1987); Richard M. Dorson, ed., *Handbook of American Folklore* (1983); Robert L. Gale, *The Gay Nineties in America* (1992); M. Thomas Inge, ed., *Handbook of American Popular Culture* (1979–1981); Wolfgang Mieder et al., eds., *A Dictionary of American Proverbs* (1992); J. F. Rooney, Jr., et al., eds., *This Remarkable Continent: An Atlas of United States and Canadian Society and Cultures* (1982); Jane Stern and Michael Stern, *Encyclopedia of Pop Culture* (1992); Marjorie Tallman, *Dictionary of American Folklore* (1959); Justin Wintle, ed., *Makers of Nineteenth Century Culture, 1800–1914* (1982). See also "Entertainment," "Mass Media and Journalism," "Music," and "Sports."

Education

Lee C. Deighton, ed., *The Encyclopedia of Education* (1971); Joseph C. Kiger, ed., *Research Institutions and Learned Societies* (1982); John F. Ohles, ed., *Biographical Dictionary of American Educators* (1978).

Entertainment

Tim Brooks and Earle Marsh, *The Complete Directory to Prime Time Network TV Shows, 1946–Present* (1979); Barbara N. Cohen-Stratyner, *Biographical Dictionary of Dance* (1982); John Dunning, *Tune in Yesterday* (radio) (1967);

Stanley Green, *Encyclopedia of the Musical Film* (1981); Larry Langman and Edgar Borg, *Encyclopedia of American War Films* (1989); Larry Langman and David Ebner, *Encyclopedia of American Spy Films* (1990); *Notable Names in the American Theater* (1976); *New York Times Encyclopedia of Television* (1977); Andrew Sarris, *The American Cinema: Directors and Directions, 1929–1968* (1968); Anthony Slide, *The American Film Industry* (1986); Evelyn M. Truitt, *Who Was Who on Screen* (1977); Don B. Wilmeth and Tice L. Miller, eds., *The Cambridge Guide to American Theatre* (1993). See also "Culture and Folklore," "Mass Media and Journalism," "Music," and "Sports."

The Environment and Conservation

Forest History Society, *Encyclopedia of American Forest and Conservation History* (1983); Robert J. Mason and Mark T. Mattson, *Atlas of United States Environmental Issues* (1990); World Resources Institute, *Environmental Almanac* (1992).

Exploration: From Columbus to Space

Silvio A. Bedini, ed., *The Christopher Columbus Encyclopedia* (1992); Michael Cassutt, *Who's Who in Space* (1987); W. P. Cumming et al., *The Discovery of North America* (1972); William Goetzmann and Glyndwr Williams, *The Atlas of North American Exploration* (1992); Adrian Johnson, *America Explored* (1974); Kenneth Nebenzahl, *Atlas of Columbus and the Great Discoveries* (1990).

Foreign Relations

Gerard Chaliand and Jean-Pierre Rageau, *Strategic Atlas* (1990); Alexander DeConde, ed., *Encyclopedia of American Foreign Policy* (1978); Margaret B. Denning and J. K. Sweeney, *Handbook of American Diplomacy* (1992); Graham Evans and Jeffrey Newnham, eds., *The Dictionary of World Politics* (1990); John E. Findling, *Dictionary of American Diplomatic History* (1989); Stephen A. Flanders and Carl N. Flanders, *Dictionary of American Foreign Affairs* (1991); *Foreign Affairs Chronology, 1978–1989* (1990); Michael Kidron and Daniel Smith, *The New State of War and Peace: An International Atlas* (1991); Warren F. Kuehl, ed., *Biographical Dictionary of Internationalists* (1983); George T. Kurian, *Encyclopedia of the Third World* (1981); Edward Lawson, *Encyclopedia of Human Rights* (1991); Jack C. Plano and Roy Olton, eds., *The International Relations Dictionary* (1988); Bruce W. Watson et al., eds., *United States Intelligence: An Encyclopedia* (1990). See also "Peace Movements and Pacifism," "Politics and Government," "Wars and the Military," and specific wars.

Immigration and Ethnic Groups

James P. Allen and Eugene J. Turner, *We the People: An Atlas of America's Ethnic Diversity* (1988); Stephanie Bernardo, *The Ethnic Almanac* (1981); Francesco Cordasco, ed., *Dictionary of American Immigration History* (1990); Hyung-Chan Kim, ed., *Dictionary of Asian American History* (1986); Matt S. Meier, *Mexican American Biographies* (1988); Matt S. Meier and Feliciano Rivera, *Dictionary of Mexican American History* (1981); Sally M. Miller, ed., *The Ethnic Press in the United States* (1987); Stephan Thernstrom, ed., *Harvard Encyclopedia of American Ethnic Groups* (1980). See also "Jewish-Americans."

Jewish-Americans

American Jewish Yearbook (1899–); Jack Fischel and Sanford Pinsker, eds., *Jewish-American History and Culture* (1992); Geoffrey Wigoder, *Dictionary of Jewish Biography* (1991).

Labor

Ronald L. Filippelli, *Labor Conflict in the United States* (1990); Gary M. Fink, ed., *Biographical Dictionary of American Labor* (1984); Gary M. Fink, ed., *Labor Unions* (1977); Philip S. Foner, *First Facts of American Labor* (1984).

Literature

James T. Callow and Robert J. Reilly, *Guide to American Literature* (1976–1977); *Dictionary of Literary Biography* (1978–); Eugene Ehrlich and Gorton Carruth, *The Oxford Illustrated Literary Guide to the United States* (1982); Jon Tuska and Vicki Piekarski, *Encyclopedia of Frontier and Western Fiction* (1983). See also "Culture and Folklore," "The South," and "Women."

Mass Media and Journalism

Robert V. Hudson, *Mass Media* (1987); Joseph P. McKerns, ed., *Biographical Dictionary of American Journalism* (1989); William H. Taft, ed., *Encyclopedia of Twentieth-Century Journalists* (1986). See also "Constitution, Supreme Court, and Judiciary," "Entertainment," and "Immigration and Ethnic Groups."

Medicine and Nursing

Rima D. Apple, ed., *Women, Health, and Medicine in America* (1990); Vern L. Bullough et al., eds., *American Nursing: A Biographical Dictionary* (1988); Martin Kaufman et al., eds., *Dictionary of American Nursing Biography* (1988); Martin Kaufman et al., eds., *Dictionary of American Medical Biography* (1984); George L. Maddox, ed., *The Encyclopedia of Aging* (1987).

Music

John Chilton, *Who's Who of Jazz* (1972); Donald Clarke, ed., *The Penguin Encyclopedia of Popular Music* (1989);

Edward Jablonski, *The Encyclopedia of American Music* (1981); Roger Lax and Frederick Smith, *The Great Song Thesaurus* (1984); Philip D. Morehead, *The New International Dictionary of Music* (1993). See also "Culture and Folklore" and "Entertainment."

Native Americans and Indian Affairs

Gretchen M. Bataille, ed., *Native American Women* (1992); Michael Coe et al., *Atlas of Ancient America* (1986); Frederick J. Dockstader, *Great North American Indians* (1977); *Handbook of North American Indians* (1978–); J. Norman Heard et al., *Handbook of the American Frontier: Four Centuries of Indian-White Relationships* (1987–); Barry Klein, ed., *Reference Encyclopedia of the American Indian* (1993); Francis P. Prucha, *Atlas of American Indian Affairs* (1990); Paul Stuart, *Nation Within a Nation: Historical Statistics of American Indians* (1987); Helen H. Tanner, ed., *Atlas of Great Lakes Indian History* (1987); Carl Waldman, *Encyclopedia of Native American Tribes* (1988); Carl Waldman, *Atlas of the North American Indian* (1985).

The New Deal and Franklin D. Roosevelt

Otis L. Graham, Jr., and Meghan R. Wander, eds., *Franklin D. Roosevelt: His Life and Times* (1985); James S. Olson, ed., *Historical Dictionary of the New Deal* (1985). See also "Politics and Government."

Peace Movements and Pacifism

Harold Josephson et al., eds., *Biographical Dictionary of Modern Peace Leaders* (1985); Ervin Laszlo and Jong Y. Yoo, eds., *World Encyclopedia of Peace* (1986); Robert S. Meyer, *Peace Organizations Past and Present* (1988); Nancy L. Roberts, *American Peace Writers, Editors, and Periodicals* (1991). See also "Wars and the Military" and specific wars.

Politics and Government: General

Erik W. Austin, *Political Facts of the United States Since 1789* (1986); Mari Jo Buhle et al., eds., *Encyclopedia of the American Left* (1990); *The Columbia Dictionary of Political Biography* (1991); Jack P. Greene, ed., *Encyclopedia of American Political History* (1984); Leon Hurwitz, *Historical Dictionary of Censorship in the United States* (1985); Bernard K. Johnpoll and Harvey Klehr, eds., *Biographical Dictionary of the American Left* (1986); Earl R. Kruschke, *Encyclopedia of Third Parties in the United States* (1991); Edwin V. Mitchell, *An Encyclopedia of American Politics* (1968); Philip Rees, *Biographical Dictionary of the Extreme Right Since 1890* (1991); Charles R. Ritter et al., *American Legislative Leaders, 1850–1910* (1989); William Safire, *Safire's Political Dictionary* (1978); Edward L. Schapsmeier and Frederick H. Schapsmeier, eds., *Political Parties and Civic Action Groups* (1981); Arthur M. Schlesinger, Jr., and

Fred I. Israel, eds., *History of American Presidential Elections, 1789–1968* (1971); Robert Scruton, *A Dictionary of Political Thought* (1982); Jay M. Shafritz, *The HarperCollins Dictionary of American Government and Politics* (1992); Hans Sperber and Travis Trittschuh, *American Political Terms* (1962). See also "Cities and Towns," "Constitution, Supreme Court, and Judiciary," "States," and the following sections.

Politics and Government: Congress

Congressional Quarterly, *Congress and the Nation, 1945–1984* (1965–1985); Kenneth C. Martis, *Historical Atlas of Political Parties in the United States Congress, 1789–1989* (1989); Kenneth C. Martis, *Historical Atlas of United States Congressional Districts, 1789–1983* (1982); U.S. Congress, *Biographical Directory of the United States Congress, 1774–1989* (1989).

Politics and Government: Election Statistics

Erik W. Austin and Jerome C. Clubb, *Political Facts of the United States Since 1789* (1986); Congressional Quarterly, *Guide to U.S. Elections* (1975); L. Sandy Maisel, ed., *Political Parties and Elections in the United States* (1991); Richard M. Scammon et al., eds., *America Votes* (1956–); Harold W. Stanley and Richard G. Niemi, *Vital Statistics on American Politics* (1990); G. Scott Thomas, *The Pursuit of the White House: A Handbook of Presidential Election Statistics and History* (1987).

Politics and Government: Presidency and Executive Branch

Henry F. Graff, *The Presidents* (1984); Richard S. Kirkendall, ed., *The Harry S Truman Encyclopedia* (1989); Leonard W. Levy and Louis Fisher, eds., *Encyclopedia of the American Presidency* (1993); Merrill D. Peterson, ed., *Thomas Jefferson: A Reference Biography* (1986); Robert A. Rutland, ed., *The James Madison Encyclopedia* (1992); Robert Sobel, ed., *Biographical Directory of the United States Executive Branch, 1774–1977* (1977). See other categories for various presidents.

Religion and Cults

Henry Bowden, *Dictionary of American Religious Biography* (1993); John T. Ellis and Robert Trisco, *A Guide to American Catholic History* (1982); Edwin S. Gaustad, *Historical Atlas of Religion in America* (1976); Samuel S. Hill, Jr., ed., *Encyclopedia of Religion in the South* (1984); Charles H. Lippy and Peter W. Williams, eds., *Encyclopedia of the American Religious Experience* (1988); J. Gordon Melton, *The Encyclopedia of American Religions* (1987); J. Gordon Melton, *Biographical Dictionary of American Cult and Sect Leaders* (1986); J. Gordon Melton, *The Encyclopedic Handbook of Cults in America* (1992); Mark A. Noll and Nathan

O. Hatch, eds., *Eerdmans Handbook to Christianity in America* (1983); Arthur C. Piepkorn, *Profiles in Belief: The Religious Bodies of the United States and Canada* (1977–1979).

Science and Technology

James W. Cortada, *Historical Dictionary of Data Processing* (1987); Clark A. Elliott, *Biographical Index to American Science: The Seventeenth Century to 1920* (1990); Charles C. Gillispie, ed., *Dictionary of Scientific Biography* (1970–); National Academy of Sciences, *Biographical Memoirs* (1877–). See also "Exploration."

Social History and Reform

Mary K. Cayton et al., eds., *Encyclopedia of American Social History* (1993); Louis Filler, *Dictionary of American Social Change* (1982); Louis Filler, *A Dictionary of American Social Reform* (1963); Robert S. Fogarty, *Dictionary of American Communal and Utopian History* (1980); Joseph M. Hawes and Elizabeth I. Nybakken, eds., *American Families* (1991); Harold M. Keele and Joseph C. Kiger, eds., *Foundations* (1984); Mark E. Lender, *Dictionary of American Temperance Biography* (1984); Patricia M. Melvin, ed., *American Community Organizations* (1986); Alvin J. Schmidt, *Fraternal Organizations* (1980); Walter I. Trattner, *Biographical Dictionary of Social Welfare in America* (1986). See also "Crime, Violence, and Police."

The South

Robert Bain et al., eds., *Southern Writers: A Biographical Dictionary* (1979); Kenneth Coleman and Charles S. Gurr, eds., *Dictionary of Georgia Biography* (1983); William S. Powell, ed., *Dictionary of North Carolina Biography* (1979–); David C. Roller and Robert W. Twyman, eds., *The Encyclopedia of Southern History* (1979); Walter P. Webb et al., eds., *The Handbook of Texas* (1952, 1976); Charles R. Wilson and William Ferris, eds., *Encyclopedia of Southern Culture* (1986). See also "The Civil War," "Politics and Government," and "States."

Sports

Peter C. Bjarkman, ed., Encyclopedia of Major League Baseball Team Histories (1991); Ralph Hickok, *The Encyclopedia of North American Sports History* (1991); Zander Hollander, *The NBA's Official Encyclopedia of Pro Basketball* (1981); Frank G. Menke and Suzanne Treat, *The Encyclopedia of Sports* (1977); *The NFL's Official Encyclopedic History of Professional Football* (1977); David L. Porter, *Biographical Dictionary of American Sports: Baseball* (1987), *Basketball and Other Indoor Sports* (1989), *Football* (1987), and *Outdoor Sports* (1988); Paul Soderberg et al., *The Big Book of Halls of Fame in the United States and Canada* (1977); David Wallechinsky, *The Complete Book of the Olympics* (1984). See also "Culture and Folklore."

States

Roy R. Glashan, comp., *American Governors and Gubernatorial Elections, 1775–1978* (1979); John Hoffmann, ed., *A Guide to the History of Illinois* (1991); Joseph E. Kallenback and Jessamine S. Kallenback, *American State Governors, 1776–1976* (1977); Joseph N. Kane et al., eds., *Facts About the States* (1989); John E. Kleber et al., eds., *The Kentucky Encyclopedia* (1992); Thomas A. McMullin and David Walker, *Biographical Directory of American Territorial Governors* (1984); Marie Mullaney, *Biographical Directory of the Governors of the United States, 1983–1987* (1988); John W. Raimo, ed., *Biographical Directory of the Governors of the United States, 1978–1983* (1985); James W. Scott and Ronald L. De Lorme, *Historical Atlas of Washington* (1988); Robert Sobel and John W. Raimo, eds., *Biographical Directory of the Governors of the United States, 1789–1978* (1978); Richard W. Wilkie and Jack Tager, eds., *Historical Atlas of Massachusetts* (1991). See also "Politics and Government," "The South," and "The West and Frontier."

Transportation

Keith L. Bryant, ed., *Railroads in the Age of Regulation, 1900–1980* (1988); Robert L. Frey, ed., *Railroads in the Nineteenth Century* (1988). See also "Business and the Economy."

The Vietnam War

John S. Bowman, ed., *The Vietnam War: An Almanac* (1986); James S. Olson, ed., *Dictionary of the Vietnam War* (1988); Harry G. Summers, Jr., *Vietnam War Almanac* (1985). Also see "Peace Movements and Pacifism" and the next section.

Wars and the Military

William M. Arkin et al., *Encyclopedia of the U.S. Military* (1990); Charles D. Bright, ed., *Historical Dictionary of the U.S. Air Force* (1992); R. Ernest Dupuy and Trevor N. Dupuy, *The Harper Encyclopedia of Military History* (1993); Holger H. Herwig and Neil M. Heyman, *Biographical Dictionary of World War I* (1982); Michael Kidron and Dan Smith, *The State of War Atlas* (1983); Kenneth Macksey and William Woodhouse, *The Penguin Encyclopedia of Modern Warfare* (1992); James I. Matray, ed., *Historical Dictionary of the Korean War* (1991); Trevor Royle, *A Dictionary of Military Quotations* (1990); Roger J. Spiller and Joseph G. Dawson III, eds., *Dictionary of American Military Biography* (1984); Peter G. Tsouras et al., *The United States Army* (1991); U.S. Military Academy, *The West Point Atlas of American Wars, 1689–1953* (1959); Bruce W. Watson et al., eds., *United States Intelligence* (1990); *Webster's American Military Biographies* (1978); Bruce W. Watson and Susan M. Watson, *The United States Air Force*

(1992); Bruce W. Watson and Susan M. Watson, *The United States Navy* (1991). See also "American Revolution," "The Civil War and Reconstruction," "The Vietnam War," and "World War II."

The West and Frontier

William A. Beck and Ynez D. Haase, *Historical Atlas of the American West* (1989); Doris O. Dawdy, *Artists of the American West* (1974–1984); J. Norman Heard, *Handbook of the American Frontier* (1987); Howard R. Lamar, ed., *The Reader's Encyclopedia of the American West* (1977); Doyce B. Nunis, Jr., and Gloria R. Lothrop, eds., *A Guide to the History of California* (1989); Dan L. Thrapp, *The Encyclopedia of Frontier Biography* (1988). See also "Literature" and "Native Americans and Indian Affairs."

Women

Anne Gibson and Timothy Fast, *The Women's Atlas of the United States* (1986); Maggie Humm, *The Dictionary of Feminist Theory* (1990); Edward T. James et al., *Notable American Women, 1607–1950* (1971); Lina Mainiero, ed., *American Women Writers* (1979–1982); Barbara G. Shortridge, *Atlas of American Women* (1987); Barbara Sicherman and Carol H. Green, eds., *Notable American Women, The Modern Period* (1980); Helen Tierney, ed., *Women's Studies Encyclopedia* (1991); Angela H. Zophy and Frances M. Kavenik, eds., *Dictionary of American Women's History* (1990). See also "African-Americans," "Medicine and Nursing," and "Native Americans and Indian Affairs."

World War II

Marcel Baudot et al., eds., *The Historical Encyclopedia of World War II* (1980); David G. Chandler and James Lawton Collins, Jr., eds., *The D-Day Encyclopedia* (1983); Simon Goodenough, *War Maps: Great Land Battles of World War II* (1988); Robert Goralski, *World War II Almanac, 1931–1945* (1981); John Keegan, ed., *The Times Atlas of the Second World War* (1989); Thomas Parrish, ed., *The Simon and Schuster Encyclopedia of World War II* (1978); Norman Polmer and Thomas B. Allen, *World War II: America at War* (1991); Louis L. Snyder, *Louis L. Snyder's Historical Guide to World War II* (1982); U.S. Military Academy, *Campaign Atlas to the Second World War: Europe and the Mediterranean* (1980); Peter Young, ed., *The World Almanac Book of World War II* (1981). See also "Wars and the Military."

Documents

DECLARATION OF INDEPENDENCE IN CONGRESS, JULY 4, 1776

When, in the course of human events, it becomes necessary for one people to dissolve the political bonds which have connected them with another, and to assume, among the powers of the earth, the separate and equal station to which the laws of nature and of nature's God entitle them, a decent respect to the opinions of mankind requires that they should declare the causes which impel them to the separation.

We hold these truths to be self-evident: That all men are created equal; that they are endowed by their Creator with certain unalienable rights; that among these are life, liberty, and the pursuit of happiness; that, to secure these rights, governments are instituted among men, deriving their just powers from the consent of the governed; that whenever any form of government becomes destructive of these ends, it is the right of the people to alter or to abolish it, and to institute new government, laying its foundation on such principles, and organizing its powers in such form, as to them shall seem most likely to effect their safety and happiness. Prudence, indeed, will dictate that governments long established should not be changed for light and transient causes; and accordingly all experience hath shown that mankind are more disposed to suffer, while evils are sufferable, than to right themselves by abolishing the forms to which they are accustomed. But when a long train of abuses and usurpations, pursuing invariably the same object, evinces a design to reduce them under absolute despotism, it is their right, it is their duty, to throw off such government, and to provide new guards for their future security. Such has been the patient sufferance of these colonies; and such is now the necessity which constrains them to alter their former systems of government. The history of the present King of Great Britain is a history of repeated injuries and usurpations, all having in direct object the establishment of an absolute tyranny over these states. To prove this, let facts be submitted to a candid world.

He has refused his assent to laws, the most wholesome and necessary for the public good.

He has forbidden his governors to pass laws of immediate and pressing importance, unless suspended in their operation till his assent should be obtained; and, when so suspended, he has utterly neglected to attend to them.

He has refused to pass other laws for the accommodation of large districts of people, unless those people would relinquish the right of representation in the legislature, a right inestimable to them, and formidable to tyrants only.

He has called together legislative bodies at places unusual, uncomfortable, and distant from the depository of their public records, for the sole purpose of fatiguing them into compliance with his measures.

He has dissolved representative houses repeatedly, for opposing, with manly firmness, his invasions on the rights of the people.

He has refused for a long time, after such dissolutions, to cause others to be elected; whereby the legislative powers, incapable of annihilation, have returned to the people at large for their exercise; the state remaining, in the mean time, exposed to all the dangers of invasions from without and convulsions within.

He has endeavored to prevent the population of these states; for that purpose obstructing the laws for naturalization of foreigners; refusing to pass others to encourage their migration hither, and raising the conditions of new appropriations of lands.

He has obstructed the administration of justice, by refusing his assent to laws for establishing judiciary powers.

He has made judges dependent on his will alone, for the tenure of their offices, and the amount and payment of their salaries.

He has erected a multitude of new offices, and sent hither swarms of officers to harass our people and eat out their substance.

He has kept among us, in times of peace, standing armies, without the consent of our legislatures.

He has affected to render the military independent of, and superior to, the civil power.

He has combined with others to subject us to a jurisdiction foreign to our constitution, and unacknowledged by our laws, giving his assent to their acts of pretended legislation:

For quartering large bodies of armed troops among us;

For protecting them, by a mock trial, from punishment for any murders which they should commit on the inhabitants of these states;

For cutting off our trade with all parts of the world;

For imposing taxes on us without our consent;

For depriving us, in many cases, of the benefits of trial by jury;

For transporting us beyond seas, to be tried for pretended offenses;

For abolishing the free system of English laws in a neighboring province, establishing therein an arbitrary government, and enlarging its boundaries, so as to render it at once an example and fit instrument for introducing the same absolute rule into these colonies;

For taking away our charters, abolishing our most valuable laws, and altering fundamentally the forms of our governments;

For suspending our own legislatures, and declaring themselves invested with power to legislate for us in all cases whatsoever.

He has abdicated government here, by declaring us out of his protection and waging war against us.

He has plundered our seas, ravaged our coasts, burned our towns, and destroyed the lives of our people.

He is at this time transporting large armies of foreign mercenaries to complete the works of death, desolation, and tyranny already begun with circumstances of cruelty and perfidy scarcely paralleled in the most barbarous ages, and totally unworthy the head of a civilized nation.

He has constrained our fellow-citizens, taken captive on the high seas, to bear arms against their country, to become the executioners of their friends and brethren, or to fall themselves by their hands.

He has excited domestic insurrection among us, and has endeavored to bring on the inhabitants of our frontiers the merciless Indian savages, whose known rule of warfare is an undistinguished destruction of all ages, sexes, and conditions.

In every stage of these oppressions we have petitioned for redress in the most humble terms; our repeated petitions have been answered only by repeated injury. A prince, whose character is thus marked by every act which may define a tyrant, is unfit to be the ruler of a free people.

Nor have we been wanting in our attentions to our British brethren. We have warned them, from time to time, of attempts by their legislature to extend an unwarrantable jurisdiction over us. We have reminded them of the circumstances of our emigration and settlement here. We have appealed to their native justice and magnanimity; and we have conjured them, by the ties of our common kindred, to disavow these usurpations, which would inevitably interrupt our connections and correspondence. They, too, have been deaf to the voice of justice and of consanguinity. We must, therefore, acquiesce in the necessity which denounces our separation, and hold them, as we hold the rest of mankind, enemies in war, in peace friends.

We, therefore, the representatives of the United States of America, in General Congress assembled, appealing to the Supreme Judge of the world for the rectitude of our intentions, do, in the name and by the authority of the good people of these colonies, solemnly publish and declare, that these United Colonies are, and of right ought to be, FREE AND INDEPENDENT STATES; that they are absolved from all allegiance to the British crown, and that all political connection between them and the state of Great Britain is, and ought to be, totally dissolved; and that, as free and independent states, they have full power to levy war, conclude peace, contract alliances, establish commerce, and do all other acts and things which independent states may of right do. And for the support of this declaration, with a firm reliance on the protection of Divine Providence, we mutually pledge to each other our lives, our fortunes, and our sacred honor.

JOHN HANCOCK
and fifty-five others

ARTICLES OF CONFEDERATION

Whereas the Delegates of the United States of America in Congress assembled did on the fifteenth day of November in the Year of our Lord One Thousand Seven Hundred and Seventy seven, and in the Second Year of the Independence of America agree to certain articles of Confederation and perpetual Union between the States of Newhampshire, Massachusetts-bay, Rhodeisland and Providence Plantations, Connecticut, New York, New Jersey, Pennsylvania, Delaware, Maryland, Virginia, North-Carolina, South-Carolina and Georgia in the Words following, viz. "Articles of Confederation and perpetual Union between the states of Newhampshire,

Massachusetts-bay, Rhodeisland and Providence Plantations, Connecticut, New-York, New-Jersey, Pennsylvania, Delaware, Maryland, Virginia, North-Carolina, South-Carolina and Georgia.

Article I The Stile of this confederacy shall be "The United States of America."

Article II Each state retains its sovereignty, freedom and independence, and every Power, Jurisdiction and right, which is not by this confederation expressly delegated to the United States, in Congress assembled.

Article III The said states hereby severally enter into a firm league of friendship with each other, for their common defence, the security of their Liberties, and their mutual and general welfare, binding themselves to assist each other, against all force offered to, or attacks made upon them, or any of them, on account of religion, sovereignty, trade, or any other pretence whatever.

Article IV The better to secure and perpetuate mutual friendship and intercourse among the people of the different states in this union, the free inhabitants of each of these states, paupers, vagabonds and fugitives from Justice excepted, shall be entitled to all privileges and immunities of free citizens in the several states; and the people of each state shall have free ingress and regress to and from any other state, and shall enjoy therein all the privileges of trade and commerce, subject to the same duties, impositions and restrictions as the inhabitants thereof respectively, provided that such restriction shall not extend so far as to prevent the removal of property imported into any state, to any other state of which the Owner is an inhabitant; provided also that no imposition, duties or restriction shall be laid by any state, on the property of the united states, or either of them.

If any Person guilty of, or charged with treason, felony, or other high misdemeanor in any state, shall flee from Justice, and be found in any of the united states, he shall upon demand of the Governor or executive power, of the state from which he fled, be delivered up and removed to the state having jurisdiction of his offence.

Full faith and credit shall be given in each of these states to the records, acts and judicial proceedings of the courts and magistrates of every other state.

Article V For the more convenient management of the general interests of the united states, delegates shall be annually appointed in such manner as the legislature of each state shall direct, to meet in Congress on the first Monday in November, in every year, with a power reserved to each state, to recal its delegates, or any of them, at any time within the year, and to send others in their stead, for the remainder of the Year.

No state shall be represented in Congress by less than two, nor by more than seven Members; and no person shall be capable of being a delegate for more than three years in any term of six years; nor shall any person, being a delegate, be capable of holding any office under the united states, for which he, or another for his benefit receives any salary, fees or emolument of any kind.

Each state shall maintain its own delegates in a meeting of the states, and while they act as members of the committee of the states.

In determining questions in the united states, in Congress assembled, each state shall have one vote.

Freedom of speech and debate in Congress shall not be impeached or questioned in any Court, or place out of Congress, and the members of congress shall be protected in their persons from arrests and imprisonments, during the time of their going to and from, and attendance on congress, except for treason, felony, or breach of the peace.

Article VI No state without the Consent of the united states in congress assembled, shall send any embassy to, or receive any embassy from, or enter into any conference, agreement, or alliance or treaty with any King, prince or state; nor shall any person holding any office of profit or trust under the united states, or any of them, accept of any present, emolument, office or title of any kind whatever from any king, prince or foreign state; nor shall the united states in congress assembled, or any of them, grant any title of nobility.

No two or more states shall enter into any treaty, confederation or alliance whatever between them, without the consent of the united states in congress assembled, specifying accurately the purposes for which the same is to be entered into, and how long it shall continue.

No state shall lay any imposts or duties, which may interfere with any stipulations in treaties, entered into by the united states in congress assembled, with any king, prince or state, in pursuance of any treaties already proposed by congress, to the courts of France and Spain.

No vessels of war shall be kept up in time of peace by any state, except such number only, as shall be deemed necessary by the united states in congress assembled, for the defence of such state, or its trade; nor shall any body of forces be kept up by any state, in time of peace, except such number only, as in the judgment of the united states, in congress assembled, shall be deemed requisite to garrison the forts necessary for the defence of such state; but every state shall always keep up a well regulated and disciplined militia, sufficiently armed and accoutred, and shall provide and constantly have ready for use, in public stores, a due number of field pieces and tents, and a proper quantity of arms, ammunition and camp equipage.

No state shall engage in any war without the consent of the united states in congress assembled, unless such state be actually invaded by enemies, or shall have received certain advice of a resolution being formed by some nation of Indians to invade such state, and the danger is so imminent as not to admit of a delay, till the united states in congress assembled can be consulted: nor shall any state grant commissions to any ships or vessels of war, nor letters of marque or reprisal, except it be after a declaration of war by the united states in congress assembled, and then only against the kingdom or state and the subjects thereof, against which war has been so declared, and under such regulations as shall be established by the united states in congress assembled, unless such state be infested by pirates, in which case vessels of war may be fitted out for that occasion, and kept so long as the danger shall continue, or until the united states in congress assembled shall determine otherwise.

Article VII When land-forces are raised by any state for the common defence, all officers of or under the rank of colonel, shall be appointed by the legislature of each state respectively by whom such forces shall be raised, or in such manner as such state shall direct, and all vacancies shall be filled up by the state which first made the appointment.

Article VIII All charges of war, and all other expences that shall be incurred for the common defence or general welfare, and allowed by the united states in congress assembled, shall be defrayed out of a common treasury, which shall be supplied by the several states, in proportion to the value of all land within each state, granted to or surveyed for any Person, as such land and the buildings and improvements thereon shall be estimated according to such mode as the united states in congress assembled, shall from time to time direct and appoint. The taxes for paying that proportion shall be laid and levied by the authority and direction of the legislatures of the several states within the time agreed upon by the united states in congress assembled.

Article IX The united states in congress assembled, shall have the sole and exclusive right and power of determining on peace and war, except in the cases mentioned in the sixth article—of sending and receiving ambassadors—entering into treaties and alliances, provided that no treaty of commerce shall be made whereby the legislative power of the respective states shall be restrained from imposing such imposts and duties on foreigners, as their own people are subjected to, or from prohibiting the exportation or importation of any species

of goods or commodities whatsoever—of establishing rules for deciding in all cases, what captures on land or water shall be legal, and in what manner prizes taken by land or naval forces in the service of the united states shall be divided or appropriated.—of granting letters of marque and reprisal in times of peace—appointing courts for the trial of piracies and felonies committed on the high seas and establishing courts for receiving and determining finally appeals in all cases of captures, provided that no member of congress shall be appointed a judge of any of the said courts.

The united states in congress assembled shall also be the last resort on appeal in all disputes and differences now subsisting or that herafter may arise between two or more states concerning boundary, jurisdiction or any other cause whatever; which authority shall always be exercised in the manner following. Whenever the legislative or executive authority or lawful agent of any state in controversy with another shall present a petition to congress, stating the matter in question and praying for a hearing, notice thereof shall be given by order of congress to the legislative or executive authority of the other state in controversy, and a day assigned for the appearance of the parties by their lawful agents, who shall then be directed to appoint by joint consent, commissioners or judges to constitute a court for hearing and determining the matter in question: but if they cannot agree, congress shall name three persons out of each of the united states, and from the list of such persons each party shall alternately strike out one, the petitioners beginning, until the number shall be reduced to thirteen; and from that number not less than seven, nor more than nine names as congress shall direct, shall in the presence of congress be drawn out by lot, and the persons whose names shall be so drawn or any five of them, shall be commissioners or judges, to hear and finally determine the controversy, so always as a major part of the judges who shall hear the cause shall agree in the determination: and if either party shall neglect to attend at the day appointed, without shewing reasons, which congress shall judge sufficient, or being present shall refuse to strike, the congress shall proceed to nominate three persons out of each state, and the secretary of congress shall strike in behalf of such party absent or refusing; and the judgment and sentence of the court to be appointed, in the manner before prescribed, shall be final and conclusive; and if any of the parties shall refuse to submit to the authority of such court, or to appear to defend their claim or cause, the court shall nevertheless proceed to pronounce sentence, or judgment, which shall in like manner be final and decisive, the judgment or sentence and other proceedings being in either case transmitted to congress, and lodged among the acts of congress for the security of the parties concerned: provided that every commissioner, before he sits in judgment, shall take an oath to be administered by one of the judges of the supreme or superior court of the state, where the cause shall be tried, "well and truly to hear and determine the matter in question, according to the best of his judgment, without favour, affection or hope of reward:" provided also that no state shall be deprived of territory for the benefit of the united states.

All controversies concerning the private right of soil claimed under different grants of two or more states, whose jurisdictions as they may respect such lands, and the states which passed such grants are adjusted, the said grants or either of them being at the same time claimed to have originated antecedent to such settlement of jurisdiction, shall on the petition of either party to the congress of the united states, be finally determined as near as may be in the same manner as is before prescribed for deciding disputes respecting territorial jurisdiction between different states.

The united states in congress assembled shall also have the sole and exclusive right and power of regulating the alloy and value of coin struck by their own authority, or by that of the respective states—fixing the standard of weights and measures throughout the united states.—regulating the trade and managing all affairs with the Indians, not members of any of the states, provided that the legislative right of any state within its own limits be not infringed or violated—establishing and regulating post-offices from one state to another, throughout all the united states, and exacting such postage on the papers passing thro' the same as may be requisite to defray the expences of the said office—appointing all officers of the land forces, in the service of the united states, excepting regimental officers.—appointing all the officers of the naval forces, and commissioning all officers whatever in the service of the united states—making rules for the government and regulation of the said land and naval forces, and directing their operations.

The united states in congress assembled shall have authority to appoint a committee, to sit in the recess of congress, to be denominated "A Committee of the States," and to consist of one delegate from each state; and to appoint such other committees and civil officers as may be necessary for managing the general affairs of the united states under their direction—to appoint one of their number to preside, provided that no person be allowed to serve in the office of president more than one year in any term of three years; to ascertain the necessary sums of Money to be raised for the service of the united states, and to appropriate and apply the same for defraying the public expences—to borrow money, or emit bills on the credit of the united states, transmitting every half year to the respective states an account of the sums of money so borrowed or emitted,—to build and equip a navy—to agree upon the number of land forces, and to make requisitions from each state for its quota, in proportion to the number of white inhabitants in such state; which requisition shall be binding, and thereupon the legislature of each state shall appoint the regimental officers, raise the men and cloath, arm and equip them in a soldier like manner, at the expence of the united states, and the officers and men so cloathed, armed and equipped shall march to the place appointed, and within the time agreed on by the united states in congress assembled: But if the united states in congress assembled shall, on consideration of circumstances judge proper that any state should not raise men, or should raise a smaller number than its quota, and that any other state should raise a greater number of men than the quota thereof, such extra number shall be raised, officered, cloathed, armed and equipped in the same manner as the quota of such state, unless the legislature of such state shall judge that such extra number cannot be safely spared out of the same, in which case they shall raise, officer, cloath, arm and equip as many of such extra number as they judge can be safely spared. And the officers and men so cloathed, armed and equipped, shall march to the place appointed, and within the time agreed on by the united states in congress assembled.

The united states in congress assembled shall never engage in a war, nor grant letters of marque and reprisal in time of peace, nor enter into any treaties or alliances, nor coin money, nor regulate the value thereof, nor ascertain the sums and expences necessary for the defence and welfare of the united states, or any of them, nor emit bills, nor borrow money on the credit of the united states, nor appropriate money, nor agree upon the number of vessels of war, to be built or purchased, or the number of land or sea forces to be raised, nor appoint a commander in chief of the army or navy, unless nine states assent to the same: nor shall a question on any other point, except for adjourning from day to day be determined, unless by the votes of a majority of the united states in congress assembled.

The congress of the united states shall have power to adjourn to any time within the year, and to any place within the united states, so that no period of adjournment be for a longer duration than the space of six Months, and shall publish the Journal of their proceedings monthly, except such parts thereof relating to treaties, alliances or military operations as in their judgment require secresy; and the yeas and nays of the delegates of each state on any question shall be entered on the Journal, when it is desired by any delegate; and the delegates of a state, or any of them, at his or their request shall be furnished with a transcript of the said Journal, except such parts as are above excepted, to lay before the legislatures of the several states.

Article X The committee of the states, or any nine of them, shall be authorised to execute, in the recess of congress, such of the powers of congress as the united states in congress assembled, by the consent of nine states, shall from time to time think expedient to vest them with; provided that no power be delegated to the said committee, for the exercise of which, by the articles of confederation, the voice of nine states in the congress of the united states assembled is requisite.

Article XI Canada acceding to this confederation, and joining in the measures of the united states, shall be admitted into, and entitled to all the advantages of this union: but no other colony shall be admitted into the same, unless such admission be agreed to by nine states.

Article XII All bills of credit emitted, monies borrowed and debts contracted by, or under the authority of congress, before the assembling of the united states, in pursuance of the present confederation, shall be deemed and considered as a charge against the united states, for payment and satisfaction whereof the said united states, and the public faith are hereby solemnly pledged.

Article XIII Every state shall abide by the determinations of the united states in congress assembled, on all questions which by this confederation are submitted to them. And the Articles of this confederation shall be inviolably observed by every state, and the union shall be perpetual; nor shall any alteration at any time hereafter be made in any of them; unless such alteration be agreed to in a congress of the united states, and be afterwards confirmed by the legislatures of every state.

AND WHEREAS it hath pleased the Great Governor of the World to incline the hearts of the legislatures we respectively represent in congress, to approve of, and to authorize us to ratify the said articles of confederation and perpetual union. KNOW YE that we the under-signed delegates, by virtue of the power and authority to us given for that purpose, do by these presents, in the name and in behalf of our respective constituents, fully and entirely ratify and confirm each and every of the said articles of confederation and perpetual union, and all and singular the matters and things therein contained: And we do further solemnly plight and engage the faith of our respective constitutents, that they shall abide by the determinations of the united states in congress assembled, on all questions, which by the said confederation are submitted to them. And that the articles thereof shall be inviolably observed by the states we respectively represent, and that the union shall be perpetual. In Witness whereof we have hereunto set our hands in Congress. Done at Philadelphia in the state of Pennsylvania the ninth Day of July in the Year of our Lord one Thousand seven Hundred and Seventy-eight, and in the third year of the independence of America.

CONSTITUTION OF THE UNITED STATES OF AMERICA AND AMENDMENTS*

Preamble

We the people of the United States, in order to form a more perfect union, establish justice, insure domestic tranquillity, provide for the common defense, promote the general welfare, and secure the blessings of liberty to ourselves and our posterity, do ordain and establish this Constitution for the United States of America.

Article I

Section 1 All legislative powers herein granted shall be vested in a Congress of the United States, which shall consist of a Senate and a House of Representatives.

Section 2 The House of Representatives shall be composed of members chosen every second year by the people of the several States, and the electors in each State shall have the qualifications requisite for electors of the most numerous branch of the State Legislature.

No person shall be a Representative who shall not have attained to the age of twenty-five years, and been seven years a citizen of the United States, and who shall not, when elected, be an inhabitant of that State in which he shall be chosen.

Representatives and direct taxes shall be apportioned among the several States which may be included within this Union, according to their respective numbers, *which shall be determined by adding to the whole number of free persons, including those bound to service for a term of years and excluding Indians not taxed, three-fifths of all other persons.* The actual enumeration shall be made within three years after the first meeting of the Congress of the United States, and within every subsequent term of ten years, in such manner as they shall by law direct. The number of Representatives shall not exceed one for every thirty thousand, but each State shall have at least one Representative; *and until such enumeration shall be made, the State of New Hampshire shall be entitled to choose three, Massachusetts eight, Rhode Island and Providence Plantations one, Connecticut five, New York six, New Jersey four, Pennsylvania eight, Delaware one, Maryland six, Virginia ten, North Carolina five, South Carolina five, and Georgia three.*

*Passages no longer in effect are printed in italic type.

When vacancies happen in the representation from any State, the Executive authority thereof shall issue writs of election to fill such vacancies.

The House of Representatives shall choose their Speaker and other officers; and shall have the sole power of impeachment.

Section 3 The Senate of the United States shall be composed of two Senators from each State, *chosen by the legislature thereof,* for six years; and each Senator shall have one vote.

Immediately after they shall be assembled in consequence of the first election, they shall be divided as equally as may be into three classes. The seats of the Senators of the first class shall be vacated at the expiration of the second year, of the second class at the expiration of the fourth year, and of the third class at the expiration of the sixth year, so that one-third may be chosen every second year; *and if vacancies happen by resignation or otherwise, during the recess of the legislature of any State, the Executive thereof may make temporary appointments until the next meeting of the legislature, which shall then fill such vacancies.*

No person shall be a Senator who shall not have attained to the age of thirty years, and been nine years a citizen of the United States, and who shall not, when elected, be an inhabitant of that State for which he shall be chosen.

The Vice-President of the United States shall be President of the Senate, but shall have no vote, unless they be equally divided.

The Senate shall choose their other officers, and also a President *pro tempore,* in the absence of the Vice-President, or when he shall exercise the office of President of the United States.

The Senate shall have the sole power to try all impeachments. When sitting for that purpose, they shall be on oath or affirmation. When the President of the United States is tried, the Chief Justice shall preside: and no person shall be convicted without the concurrence of two-thirds of the members present.

Judgment in cases of impeachment shall not extend further than to removal from the office, and disqualification to hold and enjoy any office of honor, trust or profit under the United States: but the party convicted shall nevertheless be liable and subject to indictment, trial, judgment and punishment, according to law.

Section 4 The times, places and manner of holding elections for Senators and Representatives shall be prescribed in each State by the legislature thereof; but the Congress may at any time by law make or alter such regulations, except as to the places of choosing Senators.

The Congress shall assemble at least once in every year, and such meeting *shall be on the first Monday in December, unless they shall by law appoint a different day.*

Section 5 Each house shall be the judge of the elections, returns and qualifications of its own members, and a majority of each shall constitute a quorum to do business; but a smaller number may adjourn from day to day, and may be authorized to compel the attendance of absent members, in such manner, and under such penalties, as each house may provide.

Each house may determine the rules of its proceedings, punish its members for disorderly behavior, and with the concurrence of two-thirds, expel a member.

Each house shall keep a journal of its proceedings, and from time to time publish the same, excepting such parts as may in their judgment require secrecy; and the yeas and nays of the members of either house on any question shall, at the desire of one-fifth of those present, be entered on the journal.

Neither house, during the session of Congress, shall, without the consent of the other, adjourn for more than three days, nor to any other place than that in which the two houses shall be sitting.

Section 6 The Senators and Representatives shall receive a compensation for their services, to be ascertained by law and paid out of the treasury of the United States. They shall in all cases except treason, felony and breach of the peace, be privileged from arrest during their attendance at the session of their respective houses, and in going to and returning from the same; and for any speech or debate in either house, they shall not be questioned in any other place.

No Senator or Representative shall, during the time for which he was elected, be appointed to any civil office under the authority of the United States, which shall have been created, or the emoluments whereof shall have been increased, during such time; and no person holding any office under the United States shall be a member of either house during his continuance in office.

Section 7 All bills for raising revenue shall originate in the House of Representatives; but the Senate may propose or concur with amendments as on other bills.

Every bill which shall have passed the House of Representatives and the Senate, shall, before it become a law, be presented to the President of the United States; if he approve he shall sign it, but if not he shall return it with objections to that house in which it originated, who shall enter the objections at large on their journal, and proceed to reconsider it. If after such reconsideration two-thirds of that house shall agree to pass the bill, it shall be sent, together with the objections, to the other house, by which it shall likewise be reconsidered, and, if approved by two-thirds of that house, it shall become a law. But in all such cases the votes of both houses shall be determined by yeas and nays, and the names of the persons voting for and against the bill shall be entered on the journal of each house respectively. If any bill shall not be returned by the President within ten days (Sundays excepted) after it shall have been presented to him, the same shall be a law, in like manner as if he had signed it, unless the Congress by their adjournment prevent its return, in which case it shall not be a law.

Every order, resolution, or vote to which the concurrence of the Senate and House of Representatives may be necessary (except on a question of adjournment) shall be presented to the President of the United States; and before the same shall take effect, shall be approved by him, or being disapproved by him, shall be repassed by two-thirds of the Senate and House of Representatives, according to the rules and limitations prescribed in the case of a bill.

Section 8   The Congress shall have power

To lay and collect taxes, duties, imposts, and excises, to pay the debts and provide for the common defense and general welfare of the United States; but all duties, imposts and excises shall be uniform throughout the United States;

To borrow money on the credit of the United States;

To regulate commerce with foreign nations, and among the several States, and with the Indian tribes;

To establish an uniform rule of naturalization, and uniform laws on the subject of bankruptcies throughout the United States;

To coin money, regulate the value thereof, and of foreign coin, and fix the standard of weights and measures;

To provide for the punishment of counterfeiting the securities and current coin of the United States;

To establish post offices and post roads;

To promote the progress of science and useful arts by securing for limited times to authors and inventors the exclusive right to their respective writings and discoveries;

To constitute tribunals inferior to the Supreme Court;

To define and punish piracies and felonies committed on the high seas and offenses against the law of nations;

To declare war, grant letters of marque and reprisal, and make rules concerning captures on land and water;

To raise and support armies, but no appropriation of money to that use shall be for a longer term than two years;

To provide and maintain a navy;

To make rules for the government and regulation of the land and naval forces;

To provide for calling forth the militia to execute the laws of the Union, suppress insurrections, and repel invasions;

To provide for organizing, arming, and disciplining the militia, and for governing such part of them as may be employed in the service of the United States, reserving to the States respectively the appointment of the officers, and the authority of training the militia according to the discipline prescribed by Congress;

To exercise exclusive legislation in all cases whatsoever, over such district (not exceeding ten miles square) as may, by cession of particular States, and the acceptance of Congress, become the seat of government of the United States, and to exercise like authority over all places purchased by the consent of the legislature of the State, in which the same shall be, for erection of forts, magazines, arsenals, dockyards, and other needful buildings; — and

To make all laws which shall be necessary and proper for carrying into execution the foregoing powers, and all other powers vested by this Constitution in the government of the United States, or in any department or officer thereof.

Section 9   The migration or importation of such persons as any of the States now existing shall think proper to admit shall not be prohibited by the Congress prior to the year 1808; but a tax or duty may be imposed on such importation, not exceeding $10 for each person.

The privilege of the writ of habeas corpus shall not be suspended, unless when in cases of rebellion or invasion the public safety may require it.

No bill of attainder or ex post facto law shall be passed.

No capitation, or other direct, tax shall be laid, unless in proportion to the census or enumeration herein before directed to be taken.

No tax or duty shall be laid on articles exported from any State.

No preference shall be given by any regulation of commerce or revenue to the ports of one State over those of another; nor shall vessels bound to, or from, one State, be obliged to enter, clear, or pay duties in another.

No money shall be drawn from the treasury, but in consequence of appropriations made by law; and a regular statement and account of the receipts and expenditures of all public money shall be published from time to time.

No title of nobility shall be granted by the United States: and no person holding any office of profit or trust under them, shall, without the consent of the Congress, accept of any present, emolument, office, or title, of any kind whatever, from any king, prince, or foreign state.

Section 10   No State shall enter into any treaty, alliance, or confederation; grant letters of marque and reprisal; coin money; emit bills of credit; make anything but gold and silver coin a tender in payment of debts; pass any bill of attainder, ex post facto law, or law impairing the obligation of contracts, or grant any title of nobility.

No State shall, without the consent of Congress, lay any imposts or duties on imports or exports, except what may be absolutely necessary for executing its inspection laws: and the net produce of all duties and imposts, laid by any State on imports or exports, shall be for the use of the treasury of the United States; and all such laws shall be subject to the revision and control of the Congress.

No State shall, without the consent of Congress, lay any duty of tonnage, keep troops or ships of war in time of peace, enter into any agreement or compact with another State, or with a foreign power, or engage in war, unless actually invaded, or in such imminent danger as will not admit of delay.

Article II

Section 1   The executive power shall be vested in a President of the United States of America. He shall hold his office during the term of four years, and, together with the Vice-President, chosen for the same term, be elected as follows:

Each State shall appoint, in such manner as the legislature thereof may direct, a number of electors, equal to the whole number of Senators and Representatives to which the State may be entitled in the Congress; but no Senator or Representative, or person holding an office of trust or profit under the United States, shall be appointed an elector.

The electors shall meet in their respective States, and vote by ballot for two persons, of whom one at least shall not be an inhabitant of the same State with themselves. And they shall make a list of all the persons voted for, and of the number of votes for each; which list they shall sign and certify, and transmit sealed to the seat of government of the United States, directed to the President of the Senate. The President of the Senate shall, in the presence of the Senate and House of Representatives, open all the certificates, and the votes shall then be counted. The person having the greatest number of votes shall be the President, if such number be a majority of the whole number of electors appointed; and if there be more than one who have such majority, and have an equal number of votes, then the House of Representatives shall immediately choose by ballot one of them for President; and if no person have a majority, then from the five highest on the list said house shall in like manner choose the President. But in choosing the President the votes shall be taken by States, the representation from each State having one vote; a quorum for this purpose shall consist of a member or members from two-thirds of the States, and a majority of all the States shall be necessary to a choice. In every case, after the choice of the President, the person having the greatest number of votes of the electors shall be the Vice-President. But if there should remain two or more who have equal votes, the Senate shall choose from them by ballot the Vice-President.

The Congress may determine the time of choosing the electors and the day on which they shall give their votes; which day shall be the same throughout the United States.

No person except a natural-born citizen, *or a citizen of the United States at the time of the adoption of this Constitution,* shall be eligible to the office of President; neither shall any person be eligible to that office who shall not have attained to the age of thirty-five years, and been fourteen years a resident within the United States.

In cases of the removal of the President from office or of his death, resignation, or inability to discharge the powers and duties of the said office, the same shall devolve on the Vice-President, and the Congress may by law provide for the case of removal, death, resignation, or inability, both of the President and Vice-President, declaring what officer shall then act as President, and such officer shall act accordingly, until the disability be removed, or a President shall be elected.

The President shall, at stated times, receive for his services a compensation, which shall neither be increased nor diminished during the period for which he shall have been elected, and he shall not receive within that period any other emolument from the United States, or any of them.

Before he enter on the execution of his office, he shall take the following oath or affirmation:—"I do solemnly swear (or affirm) that I will faithfully execute the office of the President of the United States, and will to the best of my ability preserve, protect and defend the Constitution of the United States."

Section 2   The President shall be commander in chief of the army and navy of the United States, and of the militia of the several States, when called into the actual service of the United States; he may require the opinion, in writing, of the principal officer in each of the executive departments, upon any subject relating to the duties of their respective offices, and he shall have power to grant reprieves and pardons for offenses against the United States, except in cases of impeachment.

He shall have power, by and with the advice and consent of the Senate, to make treaties, provided two-thirds of the Senators present concur; and he shall nominate, and by and with the advice and consent of the Senate, shall appoint ambassadors, other public ministers and consuls, judges of the Supreme Court, and all other officers of the United States, whose appointments are not herein otherwise provided for, and which shall be established by law: but Congress may by law vest the appointment of such inferior officers, as they think proper, in the President alone, in the courts of law, or in the heads of departments.

The President shall have power to fill up all vacancies that may happen during the recess of the Senate, by granting commissions which shall expire at the end of their next session.

Section 3   He shall from time to time give to the Congress information of the state of the Union, and recommend to their consideration such measures as he shall judge necessary and expedient; he may, on extraordinary occasions, convene both houses, or either of them, and in case of disagreement between them, with respect to the time of adjournment, he may adjourn them to such time as he shall think proper; he shall receive ambassadors and other public ministers; he shall take care that the laws be faithfully executed, and shall commission all the officers of the United States.

Section 4   The President, Vice-President and all civil officers of the United States shall be removed from office on impeachment for, and on conviction of, treason, bribery, or other high crimes and misdemeanors.

Article III

Section 1   The judicial power of the United States shall be vested in one Supreme Court, and in such inferior courts as the Congress may from time to time ordain and establish. The judges, both of the Supreme and inferior courts, shall hold their offices during good behavior, and shall, at stated times, receive for their services a compensation which shall not be diminished during their continuance in office.

Section 2   The judicial power shall extend to all cases, in law and equity, arising under this Constitution, the laws of the United States, and treaties made, or which shall be made, under their authority;—to all cases affecting ambassadors, other public ministers and consuls;—to all cases of admiralty and maritime jurisdiction;—to controversies to which the United States shall be a party;—to controversies between two or more States;—*between a State and citizens of another State;*—between citizens of different States;—between citizens of the same State claiming lands under grants of different States, and between a State, or the citizens thereof, and foreign states, citizens or subjects.

In all cases affecting ambassadors, other public ministers and consuls, and those in which a State shall be party, the Supreme Court shall have original jurisdiction. In all the other cases before mentioned, the Supreme Court shall have appellate jurisdiction, both as to law and fact, with such exceptions, and under such regulations, as the Congress shall make.

The trial of all crimes, except in cases of impeachment, shall be by jury; and such trial shall be held in the State where said crimes shall have been committed; but when not committed within any State, the trial shall be at such place or places as the Congress may by law have directed.

Section 3   Treason against the United States shall consist only in levying war against them, or in adhering to their enemies, giving them aid and comfort. No person shall be convicted of treason unless on the testimony of two witnesses to the same overt act, or on confession in open court.

The Congress shall have power to declare the punishment of treason, but no attainder of treason shall work corruption of blood, or forfeiture except during the life of the person attainted.

Article IV

Section 1   Full faith and credit shall be given in each State to the public acts, records, and judicial proceedings of every other State. And the Congress may by general laws prescribe the manner in which such acts, records, and proceedings shall be proved, and the effect thereof.

Section 2   The citizens of each State shall be entitled to all privileges and immunities of citizens in the several States.

A person charged in any State with treason, felony, or other crime, who shall flee from justice, and be found in another State, shall on demand of the executive authority of the State from which he fled, be delivered up, to be removed to the State having jurisdiction of the crime.

No person held to service or labor in one State, under the laws thereof, escaping into another, shall, in consequence of any law or regulation therein, be discharged from such service or labor, but shall be delivered up on claim of the party to whom such service or labor may be due.

Section 3   New States may be admitted by the Congress into this Union; but no new State shall be formed or erected within the jurisdiction of any other State; nor any State be formed by the junction of two or more States, or parts of States, without the consent of the legislatures of the States concerned as well as of the Congress.

The Congress shall have power to dispose of and make all needful rules and regulations respecting the territory or other property belonging to the United States; and nothing in this Constitution shall be so construed as to prejudice any claims of the United States, or of any particular State.

Section 4   The United States shall guarantee to every State in this Union a republican form of government, and shall protect each of them against invasion; and on application of the legislature, or of the executive (when the legislature cannot be convened), against domestic violence.

Article V

The Congress, whenever two-thirds of both houses shall deem it necessary, shall propose amendments to this Constitution, or, on the application of the legislatures of two-thirds of the several States, shall call a convention for proposing amendments, which, in either case, shall be valid to all intents and purposes, as part of this Constitution, when ratified by the legislatures of three-fourths of the several States, or by conventions in three-fourths thereof, as the one or the other mode of ratification may be proposed by the Congress; provided *that no amendments which may be made prior to the year one thousand eight hundred and eight shall in any manner affect the first and fourth clauses in the ninth section of the first article;* and that no State, without its consent, shall be deprived of its equal suffrage in the Senate.

Article VI

All debts contracted and engagements entered into, before the adoption of this Constitution, shall be as valid against the United States under this Constitution, as under the Confederation.

This Constitution, and the laws of the United States which shall be made in pursuance thereof; and all treaties made, or which shall be made, under the authority of the United States, shall be the supreme law of the land; and the judges in every State shall be bound thereby, anything in the Constitution or laws of any State to the contrary notwithstanding.

The Senators and Representatives before mentioned, and the members of the several State legislatures, and all executive and judicial officers, both of the United States and of the several States, shall be bound by oath or affirmation to support this Constitution; but no religious test shall ever be required as a qualification to any office or public trust under the United States.

Article VII

The ratification of the conventions of nine States shall be sufficient for the establishment of this Constitution between the States so ratifying the same.

Done in Convention by the unanimous consent of the States present, the seventeenth day of September in the year of our Lord one thousand seven hundred and eighty-seven and of the Independence of the United States of America the twelfth. In witness whereof we have hereunto subscribed our names.

GEORGE WASHINGTON
and thirty-seven others

Amendments to the Constitution*

Amendment I

Congress shall make no law respecting an establishment of religion, or prohibiting the free exercise thereof; or

---

*The first ten Amendments (the Bill of Rights) were adopted in 1791.

abridging the freedom of speech, or of the press; or the right of the people peaceably to assemble, and to petition the government for a redress of grievances.

Amendment II

A well-regulated militia being necessary to the security of a free State, the right of the people to keep and bear arms shall not be infringed.

Amendment III

No soldier shall, in time of peace, be quartered in any house without the consent of the owner, nor in time of war, but in a manner to be prescribed by law.

Amendment IV

The right of the people to be secure in their persons, houses, papers, and effects, against unreasonable searches and seizures, shall not be violated, and no warrants shall issue but upon probable cause, supported by oath or affirmation, and particularly describing the place to be searched, and the persons or things to be seized.

Amendment V

No person shall be held to answer for a capital, or otherwise infamous crime, unless on a presentment or indictment of a grand jury, except in cases arising in the land or naval forces, or in the militia, when in actual service in time of war or public danger; nor shall any person be subject for the same offense to be twice put in jeopardy of life or limb; nor shall be compelled in any criminal case to be a witness against himself, nor be deprived of life, liberty, or property, without due process of law; nor shall private property be taken for public use without just compensation.

Amendment VI

In all criminal prosecutions, the accused shall enjoy the right to a speedy and public trial, by an impartial jury of the State and district wherein the crime shall have been committed, which district shall have been previously ascertained by law, and to be informed of the nature and cause of the accusation; to be confronted with the witnesses against him; to have compulsory process for obtaining witnesses in his favor, and to have the assistance of counsel for his defense.

Amendment VII

In suits at common law, where the value in controversy shall exceed twenty dollars, the right of trial by jury shall be preserved, and no fact tried by a jury shall be otherwise reexamined in any court of the United States, than according to the rules of the common law.

elect shall act as President until a President shall have qualified; and the Congress may by law provide for the case wherein neither a President-elect nor a Vice-President-elect shall have qualified, declaring who shall then act as President, or the manner in which one who is to act shall be selected, and such persons shall act accordingly until a President or Vice-President shall have qualified.

Section 4 The Congress may by law provide for the case of the death of any of the persons from whom the House of Representatives may choose a President whenever the right of choice shall have devolved upon them, and for the case of the death of any of the persons from whom the Senate may choose a Vice-President whenever the right of choice shall have devolved upon them.

Section 5 Sections 1 and 2 shall take effect on the 15th day of October following the ratification of this article.

Section 6 This article shall be inoperative unless it shall have been ratified as an amendment to the Constitution by the Legislatures of three-fourths of the several States within seven years from the date of its submission.

Amendment XXI

[Adopted 1933]

Section 1 The eighteenth article of amendment to the Constitution of the United States is hereby repealed.

Section 2 The transportation or importation into any State, Territory, or Possession of the United States for delivery or use therein of intoxicating liquors, in violation of the laws thereof, is hereby prohibited.

Section 3 This article shall be inoperative unless it shall have been ratified as an amendment to the Constitution by conventions in the several States, as provided in the Constitution, within seven years from the date of submission thereof to the States by the Congress.

Amendment XXII

[Adopted 1951]

Section 1 No person shall be elected to the office of President more than twice, and no person who has held the office of President, or acted as President, for more than two years of a term to which some other person was elected President shall be elected to the office of President more than once. But this article shall not apply to any person holding the office of President when this article was proposed by the Congress, and shall not prevent any person who may be holding the office of President, or acting as President, during the term within which this article becomes operative from holding the office of President or acting as President during the remainder of such term.

Section 2 This article shall be inoperative unless it shall have been ratified as an amendment to the Constitution by the legislatures of three-fourths of the several States within seven years from the date of its submission to the States by the Congress.

Amendment XXIII

[Adopted 1961]

Section 1 The District constituting the seat of Government of the United States shall appoint in such manner as the Congress may direct:

A number of electors of President and Vice-President equal to the whole number of Senators and Representatives in Congress to which the District would be entitled if it were a State, but in no event more than the least populous State; they shall be in addition to those appointed by the States, but they shall be considered for the purposes of the election of President and Vice-President, to be electors appointed by a State; and they shall meet in the District and perform such duties as provided by the twelfth article of amendment.

Section 2 The Congress shall have the power to enforce this article by appropriate legislation.

Amendment XXIV

[Adopted 1964]

Section 1 The right of citizens of the United States to vote in any primary or other election for President or Vice-President, for electors for President or Vice-President, or for Senator or Representative in Congress, shall not be denied or abridged by the United States or any State by reason of failure to pay any poll tax or other tax.

Section 2 The Congress shall have the power to enforce this article by appropriate legislation.

Amendment XXV

[Adopted 1967]

Section 1 In case of the removal of the President from office or of his death or resignation, the Vice-President shall become President.

Section 2 Whenever there is a vacancy in the office of the Vice-President, the President shall nominate a Vice-President who shall take office upon confirmation by a majority vote of both Houses of Congress.

Section 3 Whenever the President transmits to the President pro tempore of the Senate and the Speaker of the House of Representatives his written declaration that he is unable to discharge the powers and duties of his office, and until he transmits to them a written declaration to the contrary, such powers and duties shall be discharged by the Vice-President as Acting President.

Section 4 Whenever the Vice-President and a majority of either the principal officers of the executive departments or of such other body as Congress may by law provide, transmit to the President pro tempore of the Senate and the Speaker of the House of Representatives their written declaration that the President is unable to discharge the powers and duties of his office, the Vice-President shall immediately assume the powers and duties of the office as Acting President.

Thereafter, when the President transmits to the President pro tempore of the Senate and the Speaker of the House of Representatives his written declaration that no inability exists, he shall resume the powers and duties of his office unless the Vice-President and a majority of either the principal officers of the executive department[s] or of such other body as Congress may by law provide, transmit within four days to the President pro tempore of the Senate and the Speaker of the House of Representatives their written declaration that the President is unable to discharge the powers and duties of his office. Thereupon Congress shall decide the issue, assembling within forty-eight hours for that purpose if not in session. If the Congress, within twenty-one days

after receipt of the latter written declaration, or, if Congress is not in session, within twenty-one days after Congress is required to assemble, determines by two-thirds vote of both Houses that the President is unable to discharge the powers and duties of his office, the Vice-President shall continue to discharge the same as Acting President; otherwise, the President shall resume the powers and duties of his office.

Amendment XXVI

[Adopted 1971]

Section 1 The right of citizens of the United States, who are eighteen years of age or older, to vote shall not be denied or abridged by the United States or by any State on account of age.

Section 2 The Congress shall have power to enforce this article by appropriate legislation.

Amendment XXVII

[Adopted 1992]

No law, varying the compensation for the services of the Senators and Representatives, shall take effect, until an election of Representatives shall have intervened.

The American People and Nation: A Statistical Profile

Population of the United States

Year	Number of States	Population	Percent Increase	Population Per Square Mile	Percent Urban/ Rural	Percent Male/ Female	Percent White/ Non-white	Persons Per House-hold	Median Age
1790	13	3,929,214		4.5	5.1/94.9	NA/NA	80.7/19.3	5.79	NA
1800	16	5,308,483	35.1	6.1	6.1/93.9	NA/NA	81.1/18.9	NA	NA
1810	17	7,239,881	36.4	4.3	7.3/92.7	NA/NA	81.0/19.0	NA	NA
1820	23	9,638,453	33.1	5.5	7.2/92.8	50.8/49.2	81.6/18.4	NA	16.7
1830	24	12,866,020	33.5	7.4	8.8/91.2	50.8/49.2	81.9/18.1	NA	17.2
1840	26	17,069,453	32.7	9.8	10.8/89.2	50.9/49.1	83.2/16.8	NA	17.8
1850	31	23,191,876	35.9	7.9	15.3/84.7	51.0/49.0	84.3/15.7	5.55	18.9
1860	33	31,443,321	35.6	10.6	19.8/80.2	51.2/48.8	85.6/14.4	5.28	19.4
1870	37	39,818,449	26.6	13.4	25.7/74.3	50.6/49.4	86.2/13.8	5.09	20.2
1880	38	50,155,783	26.0	16.9	28.2/71.8	50.9/49.1	86.5/13.5	5.04	20.9
1890	44	62,947,714	25.5	21.2	35.1/64.9	51.2/48.8	87.5/12.5	4.93	22.0
1900	45	75,994,575	20.7	25.6	39.6/60.4	51.1/48.9	87.9/12.1	4.76	22.9
1910	46	91,972,266	21.0	31.0	45.6/54.4	51.5/48.5	88.9/11.1	4.54	24.1
1920	48	105,710,620	14.9	35.6	51.2/48.8	51.0/49.0	89.7/10.3	4.34	25.3
1930	48	122,775,046	16.1	41.2	56.1/43.9	50.6/49.4	89.8/10.2	4.11	26.4
1940	48	131,669,275	7.2	44.2	56.5/43.5	50.2/49.8	89.8/10.2	3.67	29.0
1950	48	150,697,361	14.5	50.7	64.0/36.0	49.7/50.3	89.5/10.5	3.37	30.2
1960	50	179,323,175	18.5	50.6	69.9/30.1	49.3/50.7	88.6/11.4	3.33	29.5
1970	50	203,302,031	13.4	57.4	73.5/26.5	48.7/51.3	87.6/12.4	3.14	28.0
1980	50	226,545,805	11.4	64.0	73.7/26.3	48.6/51.4	86.0/14.0	2.75	30.0
1990	50	248,709,873	9.8	70.3	75.2/24.8	48.7/51.3	80.3/19.7	2.63	32.8

NA = Not available.

Vital Statistics

Year	Birth Rate*	Death Rate*	Life Expectancy in Years					Marriage Rate	Divorce Rate
			Total Population	White Females	Nonwhite Females	White Males	Nonwhite Males		
1790	NA	NA	NA	NA	NA	NA	NA	NA	NA
1800	55.0	NA	NA	NA	NA	NA	NA	NA	NA
1810	54.3	NA	NA	NA	NA	NA	NA	NA	NA
1820	55.2	NA	NA	NA	NA	NA	NA	NA	NA
1830	51.4	NA	NA	NA	NA	NA	NA	NA	NA
1840	51.8	NA	NA	NA	NA	NA	NA	NA	NA
1850	43.3	NA	NA	NA	NA	NA	NA	NA	NA
1860	44.3	NA	NA	NA	NA	NA	NA	NA	NA
1870	38.3	NA	NA	NA	NA	NA	NA	NA	NA
1880	39.8	NA	NA	NA	NA	NA	NA	NA	NA
1890	31.5	NA	NA	NA	NA	NA	NA	NA	NA
1900	32.3	17.2	47.3	48.7	33.5	46.6	32.5	NA	NA
1910	30.1	14.7	50.0	52.0	37.5	48.6	33.8	NA	NA
1920	27.7	13.0	54.1	55.6	45.2	54.4	45.5	12.0	1.6
1930	21.3	11.3	59.7	63.5	49.2	59.7	47.3	9.2	1.6
1940	19.4	10.8	62.9	66.6	54.9	62.1	51.5	12.1	2.0
1950	24.1	9.6	68.2	72.2	62.9	66.5	59.1	11.1	2.6
1960	23.7	9.5	69.7	74.1	66.3	67.4	61.1	8.5	2.2
1970	18.4	9.5	70.9	75.6	69.4	68.0	61.3	10.6	3.5
1980	15.9	8.8	73.7	78.1	73.6	70.7	65.3	10.6	5.2
1990	16.7	8.6	75.4	79.3	76.3	72.6	68.4	9.8	4.7

Data per one thousand for Birth, Death, Marriage, and Divorce rates.

NA = Not available.

*Data for 1800, 1810, 1830, 1850, 1870, and 1890 for whites only.

Immigrants to the United States

Immigration Totals by Decade			
Years	**Number**	**Years**	**Number**
1820–1830	151,824	1911–1920	5,735,811
1831–1840	599,125	1921–1930	4,107,209
1841–1850	1,713,251	1931–1940	528,431
1851–1860	2,598,214	1941–1950	1,035,039
1861–1870	2,314,824	1951–1960	2,515,479
1871–1880	2,812,191	1961–1970	3,321,677
1881–1890	5,246,613	1971–1980	4,493,000
1891–1900	3,687,546	1981–1990	7,338,000
1901–1910	8,795,386	Total	56,993,620

Sources: U.S. Bureau of the Census, Historical Statistics of the United States, Colonial Times to 1970 *(1975); U.S. Bureau of the Census*, Statistical Abstract of the United States, 1993 *(1993)*.

Major Sources of Immigrants by Country or Region (in thousands)										
Period	Germany	Asia[a]	Italy	Britain (UK)	Ireland	Austria-Hungary	Canada	Mexico	Russia (USSR)[b]	Caribbean	Denmark, Norway, Sweden[c]
1820–1830	8	—	—	27	54	—	2	5	—	4	—
1831–1840	152	—	2	76	207	—	14	7	—	12	2
1841–1850	435	—	2	267	781	—	42	3	—	14	14
1851–1860	952	42	9	424	914	—	59	3	—	11	25
1861–1870	787	65	12	607	436	8	154	2	3	9	126
1871–1880	718	124	56	548	437	73	384	5	39	14	243
1881–1890	1,453	70	307	807	655	354	393	2[d]	213	29	656
1891–1900	505	75	652	272	388	593	3	1[e]	505	—	372
1901–1910	341	324	2,046	526	339	2,145	179	50	1,597	108	505
1911–1920	144	247	1,110	341	146	896	742	219	922	123	203
1921–1930	412	112	455	330	221	64	925	459	89	75	198
1931–1940	114	16	68	29	13	11	109	22	7	16	11
1941–1950	227	37	58	132	28	28	172	61	4	50	27
1951–1960	478	153	185	192	57	104	378	300	6	123	57
1961–1970	200	445	207	231	42	31	287	443	16	520	45
1971–1980	66	1,634	130	124	14	16	115	637	43	760	15
1981–1990	70	2,817	33	142	33	14	119	1,653	84	893	19
Total	7,062	6,161	5,332	5,075	4,765	4,337	4,077	3,872	3,528	2,761	2,518

Notes: Numbers are rounded. Dash indicates less than one thousand.

[a] Includes Middle East.

[b] Includes Finland, Latvia, Estonia, and Lithuania.

[c] Includes Iceland.

[d] Figure for 1881–1885 only.

[e] Figure for 1894–1900 only.

Sources: U.S. Bureau of the Census, Historical Statistics of the United States: Colonial Times to 1970 *(1975); U.S. Bureau of the Census,* Statistical Abstract of the United States, 1993 *(1993); U.S. Immigration and Naturalization Service.*

The American Farm

Year	Farm Population (in thousands)	Percent of Total Population	Number of Farms (in thousands)	Total Acres (in thousands)	Average Acreage Per Farm	Corn Production (millions of bushels)	Wheat Production (millions of bushels)
1850	NA	NA	1,449	293,561	203	592[a]	100[a]
1860	NA	NA	2,044	407,213	199	839[b]	173[b]
1870	NA	NA	2,660	407,735	153	1,125	254
1880	21,973	43.8	4,009	536,082	134	1,707	502
1890	24,771	42.3	4,565	623,219	137	1,650	449
1900	29,875	41.9	5,740	841,202	147	2,662	599
1910	32,077	34.9	6,366	881,431	139	2,853	625
1920	31,974	30.1	6,454	958,677	149	3,071	843
1930	30,529	24.9	6,295	990,112	157	2,080	887
1940	30,547	23.2	6,102	1,065,114	175	2,457	815
1950	23,048	15.3	5,388	1,161,420	216	3,075	1,019
1960	15,635	8.7	3,962	1,176,946	297	4,314	1,355
1970	9,712	4.8	2,949	1,102,769	374	4,200	1,370
1980	6,051	2.7	2,440	1,039,000	426	6,600	2,400
1990	4,591	1.9	2,140	987,000	461	7,933	2,739

[a] Figure for 1849.
[b] Figure for 1859.
NA = Not available.

The American Worker

Year	Total Number of Workers	Males as Percent of Total Workers	Females as Percent of Total Workers	Married Women as Percent of Female Workers	Female Workers as Percent of Female Population	Percent of Labor Force Unemployed	Percent of Workers in Labor Unions
1870	12,506,000	85	15	NA	NA	NA	NA
1880	17,392,000	85	15	NA	NA	NA	NA
1890	23,318,000	83	17	13.9	18.9	4 (1894 = 18)	NA
1900	29,073,000	82	18	15.4	20.6	5	3
1910	38,167,000	79	21	24.7	25.4	6	6
1920	41,614,000	79	21	23.0	23.7	5 (1921 = 12)	12
1930	48,830,000	78	22	28.9	24.8	9 (1933 = 25)	11.6
1940	53,011,000	76	24	36.4	27.4	15 (1944 = 1)	26.9
1950	59,643,000	72	28	52.1	31.4	5	31.5
1960	69,877,000	68	32	55.5	37.7	5.4	31.4
1970	82,049,000	63	37	58.6	43.3	4.8	27.3
1980	108,544,000	58	42	59.7	50.9	7.1	21.9
1990	124,787,000	55	45	58.4	54.8	5.5[a]	16.1

[a] Figure for 1991.
NA = Not available.

The American Economy

Year	Gross National Product (GNP) (in $ billions)	Steel Production (in tons)	Automobiles Registered	New Housing Starts	Foreign Trade (in millions of dollars)	
					Exports	Imports
1790	NA	NA	NA	NA	20	23
1800	NA	NA	NA	NA	71	91
1810	NA	NA	NA	NA	67	85
1820	NA	NA	NA	NA	70	74
1830	NA	NA	NA	NA	74	71
1840	NA	NA	NA	NA	132	107
1850	NA	NA	NA	NA	152	178
1860	NA	13,000	NA	NA	400	362
1870	7.4[a]	77,000	NA	NA	451	462
1880	11.2[b]	1,397,000	NA	NA	853	761
1890	13.1	4,779,000	NA	328,000	910	823
1900	18.7	11,227,000	8,000	189,000	1,499	930
1910	35.3	28,330,000	458,300	387,000 (1918 = 118,000)	1,919	1,646
1920	91.5	46,183,000	8,131,500	247,000 (1925 = 937,000)	8,664	5,784
1930	90.7	44,591,000	23,034,700	330,000 (1933 = 93,000)	4,013	3,500
1940	100.0	66,983,000	27,465,800	603,000 (1944 = 142,000)	4,030	7,433
1950	286.5	96,836,000	40,339,000	1,952,000	10,816	9,125
1960	506.5	99,282,000	61,682,300	1,365,000	19,600	15,046
1970	1,016.0	131,514,000	89,279,800	1,469,000	42,700	40,189
1980	2,732.0	111,835,000	121,600,000	1,313,000	220,783	244,871
1990	5,524.5	98,906,000	143,026,000	1,193,000	393,600	495,300

[a] Figure is average for 1869–1878.

[b] Figure is average for 1879–1888.

NA = Not available.

Federal Spending and Debt

Year	Defense[a]	Veterans Benefits and Services[a]	Income Security[ad]	Health[a]	Education and Manpower[a]	Interest on Public Debt[a]	Federal Debt (dollars)
1790	14.9	4.1[b]	NA	NA	NA	55.0	75,463,000[c]
1800	55.7	.6	NA	NA	NA	31.3	82,976,000
1810	48.4 (1814 = 79.7)	1.0	NA	NA	NA	34.9	53,173,000
1820	38.4	17.6	NA	NA	NA	28.1	91,016,000
1830	52.9	9.0	NA	NA	NA	12.6	48,565,000
1840	54.3 (1847 = 80.7)	10.7	NA	NA	NA	.7	3,573,000
1850	43.8	4.7	NA	NA	NA	1.0	63,453,000
1860	44.2 (1865 = 88.9)	1.7	NA	NA	NA	5.0	64,844,000
1870	25.7	9.2	NA	NA	NA	41.7	2,436,453,000
1880	19.3	21.2	NA	NA	NA	35.8	2,090,909,000
1890	20.9 (1899 = 48.6)	33.6	NA	NA	NA	11.4	1,222,397,000
1900	36.6	27.0	NA	NA	NA	7.7	1,263,417,000
1910	45.1 (1919 = 59.5)	23.2	NA	NA	NA	3.1	1,146,940,000
1920	37.1	3.4	NA	NA	NA	16.0	24,299,321,000
1930	25.3	6.6	NA	NA	NA	19.9	16,185,310,000
1940	15.7 (1945 = 85.7)	6.5	15.2	.5	.8	10.5	42,967,531,000
1950	30.4 (1953 = 59.4)	20.5	10.9	.6	.5	13.4	257,357,352,000
1960	49.0	5.9	20.6	.9	1.1	10.0	286,330,761,000
1970	41.8	4.4	8.0	3.0	4.4	9.9	370,918,707,000
1980	22.7	3.6	14.6	3.9	5.4	12.7	907,700,000,000
1990	23.9	2.3	11.8	4.6	3.0	21.2	3,233,300,000,000

[a] Figures represent percentage of total federal spending for each category.

[b] 1789–1791 figure.

[c] 1791 figure.

[d] Includes Social Security and Medicare.

NA = Not available.

Territorial Expansion
of the United States

Territory	Date Acquired	Square Miles	How Acquired
Original states and territories	1783	888,685	Treaty with Great Britain
Louisiana Purchase	1803	827,192	Purchase from France
Florida	1819	72,003	Treaty with Spain
Texas	1845	390,143	Annexation of independent nation
Oregon	1846	285,580	Treaty with Great Britain
Mexican Cession	1848	529,017	Conquest from Mexico
Gadsden Purchase	1853	29,640	Purchase from Mexico
Alaska	1867	589,757	Purchase from Russia
Hawaii	1898	6,450	Annexation of independent nation
The Philippines	1899	115,600	Conquest from Spain (granted independence in 1946)
Puerto Rico	1899	3,435	Conquest from Spain
Guam	1899	212	Conquest from Spain
American Samoa	1900	76	Treaty with Germany and Great Britain
Panama Canal Zone	1904	553	Treaty with Panama (returned to Panama by treaty in 1978)
Corn Islands	1914	4	Treaty with Nicaragua (returned to Nicaragua by treaty in 1971)
Virgin Islands	1917	133	Purchase from Denmark
Pacific Islands Trust (Micronesia)	1947	8,489	Trusteeship under United Nations (some granted independence)
All others (Midway, Wake, and other islands)		42	

Admission of States into the Union

State	Date of Admission	State	Date of Admission
1. Delaware	December 7, 1787	26. Michigan	January 26, 1837
2. Pennsylvania	December 12, 1787	27. Florida	March 3, 1845
3. New Jersey	December 18, 1787	28. Texas	December 29, 1845
4. Georgia	January 2, 1788	29. Iowa	December 28, 1846
5. Connecticut	January 9, 1788	30. Wisconsin	May 29, 1848
6. Massachusetts	February 6, 1788	31. California	September 9, 1850
7. Maryland	April 28, 1788	32. Minnesota	May 11, 1858
8. South Carolina	May 23, 1788	33. Oregon	February 14, 1859
9. New Hampshire	June 21, 1788	34. Kansas	January 29, 1861
10. Virginia	June 25, 1788	35. West Virginia	June 20, 1863
11. New York	July 26, 1788	36. Nevada	October 31, 1864
12. North Carolina	November 21, 1789	37. Nebraska	March 1, 1867
13. Rhode Island	May 29, 1790	38. Colorado	August 1, 1876
14. Vermont	March 4, 1791	39. North Dakota	November 2, 1889
15. Kentucky	June 1, 1792	40. South Dakota	November 2, 1889
16. Tennessee	June 1, 1796	41. Montana	November 8, 1889
17. Ohio	March 1, 1803	42. Washington	November 11, 1889
18. Louisiana	April 30, 1812	43. Idaho	July 3, 1890
19. Indiana	December 11, 1816	44. Wyoming	July 10, 1890
20. Mississippi	December 10, 1817	45. Utah	January 4, 1896
21. Illinois	December 3, 1818	46. Oklahoma	November 16, 1907
22. Alabama	December 14, 1819	47. New Mexico	January 6, 1912
23. Maine	March 15, 1820	48. Arizona	February 14, 1912
24. Missouri	August 10, 1821	49. Alaska	January 3, 1959
25. Arkansas	June 15, 1836	50. Hawaii	August 21, 1959

Presidential Elections

Year	Number of States	Candidates	Parties	Popular Vote	% of Popular Vote	Elec- toral Vote	% Voter Partici- pation[b]
1789	11	George Washington	No party			69	
		John Adams	designations			34	
		Other candidates				35	
1792	15	George Washington	No party			132	
		John Adams	designations			77	
		George Clinton				50	
		Other candidates				5	
1796	16	John Adams	Federalist			71	
		Thomas Jefferson	Democratic- Republican			68	
		Thomas Pinckney	Federalist			59	
		Aaron Burr	Democratic- Republican			30	
		Other candidates				48	
1800	16	Thomas Jefferson	Democratic- Republican			73	
		Aaron Burr	Democratic- Republican			73	
		John Adams	Federalist			65	
		Charles C. Pinckney	Federalist			64	
		John Jay	Federalist			1	
1804	17	Thomas Jefferson	Democratic- Republican			162	
		Charles C. Pinckney	Federalist			14	
1808	17	James Madison	Democratic- Republican			122	
		Charles C. Pinckney	Federalist			47	
		George Clinton	Democratic- Republican			6	
1812	18	James Madison	Democratic- Republican			128	
		DeWitt Clinton	Federalist			89	
1816	19	James Monroe	Democratic- Republican			183	
		Rufus King	Federalist			34	
1820	24	James Monroe	Democratic- Republican			231	

Presidential Elections, Continued

Year	Number of States	Candidates	Parties	Popular Vote	% of Popular Vote	Elec-toral Vote	% Voter Partici-pation[b]
		John Quincy Adams	Independent Republican			1	
1824	24	**John Quincy Adams**	Democratic-Republican	108,740	30.5	84	26.9
		Andrew Jackson	Democratic-Republican	153,544	43.1	99	
		Henry Clay	Democratic-Republican	47,136	13.2	37	
		William H. Crawford	Democratic-Republican	46,618	13.1	41	
1828	24	**Andrew Jackson**	Democratic	647,286	56.0	178	57.6
		John Quincy Adams	National Republican	508,064	44.0	83	
1832	24	**Andrew Jackson**	Democratic	688,242	54.5	219	55.4
		Henry Clay	National Republican	473,462	37.5	49	
		William Wirt	Anti-Masonic	101,051	8.0	7	
		John Floyd	Democratic			11	
1836	26	**Martin Van Buren**	Democratic	765,483	50.9	170	57.8
		William H. Harrison	Whig			73	
		Hugh L. White	Whig	739,795	49.1	26	
		Daniel Webster	Whig			14	
		W. P. Mangum	Whig			11	
1840	26	**William H. Harrison**	Whig	1,274,624	53.1	234	80.2
		Martin Van Buren	Democratic	1,127,781	46.9	60	
1844	26	**James K. Polk**	Democratic	1,338,464	49.6	170	78.9
		Henry Clay	Whig	1,300,097	48.1	105	
		James G. Birney	Liberty	62,300	2.3		
1848	30	**Zachary Taylor**	Whig	1,360,967	47.4	163	72.7
		Lewis Cass	Democratic	1,222,342	42.5	127	
		Martin Van Buren	Free Soil	291,263	10.1		
1852	31	**Franklin Pierce**	Democratic	1,601,117	50.9	254	69.6
		Winfield Scott	Whig	1,385,453	44.1	42	
		John P. Hale	Free Soil	155,825	5.0		
1856	31	**James Buchanan**	Democratic	1,832,955	45.3	174	78.9
		John C. Frémont	Republican	1,339,932	33.1	114	
		Millard Fillmore	American	871,731	21.6	8	
1860	33	**Abraham Lincoln**	Republican	1,865,593	39.8	180	81.2
		Stephen A. Douglas	Democratic	1,382,713	29.5	12	
		John C. Breckinridge	Democratic	848,356	18.1	72	
		John Bell	Constitutional Union	592,906	12.6	39	
1864	36	**Abraham Lincoln**	Republican	2,206,938	55.0	212	73.8
		George B. McClellan	Democratic	1,803,787	45.0	21	
1868	37	**Ulysses S. Grant**	Republican	3,013,421	52.7	214	78.1
		Horatio Seymour	Democratic	2,706,829	47.3	80	

Presidential Elections, Continued

Year	Number of States	Candidates	Parties	Popular Vote	% of Popular Vote	Electoral Vote	% Voter Participation[b]
1872	37	**Ulysses S. Grant**	Republican	3,596,745	55.6	286	71.3
		Horace Greeley	Democratic	2,843,446	43.9	[a]	
1876	38	**Rutherford B. Hayes**	Republican	4,036,572	48.0	185	81.8
		Samuel J. Tilden	Democratic	4,284,020	51.0	184	
1880	38	**James A. Garfield**	Republican	4,453,295	48.5	214	79.4
		Winfield S. Hancock	Democratic	4,414,082	48.1	155	
		James B. Weaver	Greenback-Labor	308,578	3.4		
1884	38	**Grover Cleveland**	Democratic	4,879,507	48.5	219	77.5
		James G. Blaine	Republican	4,850,293	48.2	182	
		Benjamin F. Butler	Greenback-Labor	175,370	1.8		
		John P. St. John	Prohibition	150,369	1.5		
1888	38	**Benjamin Harrison**	Republican	5,477,129	47.9	233	79.3
		Grover Cleveland	Democratic	5,537,857	48.6	168	
		Clinton B. Fisk	Prohibition	249,506	2.2		
		Anson J. Streeter	Union Labor	146,935	1.3		
1892	44	**Grover Cleveland**	Democratic	5,555,426	46.1	277	74.7
		Benjamin Harrison	Republican	5,182,690	43.0	145	
		James B. Weaver	People's	1,029,846	8.5	22	
		John Bidwell	Prohibition	264,133	2.2		
1896	45	**William McKinley**	Republican	7,102,246	51.1	271	79.3
		William J. Bryan	Democratic	6,492,559	47.7	176	
1900	45	**William McKinley**	Republican	7,218,491	51.7	292	73.2
		William J. Bryan	Democratic; Populist	6,356,734	45.5	155	
		John C. Wooley	Prohibition	208,914	1.5		
1904	45	**Theodore Roosevelt**	Republican	7,628,461	57.4	336	65.2
		Alton B. Parker	Democratic	5,084,223	37.6	140	
		Eugene V. Debs	Socialist	402,283	3.0		
		Silas C. Swallow	Prohibition	258,536	1.9		
1908	46	**William H. Taft**	Republican	7,675,320	51.6	321	65.4
		William J. Bryan	Democratic	6,412,294	43.1	162	
		Eugene V. Debs	Socialist	420,793	2.8		
		Eugene W. Chafin	Prohibition	253,840	1.7		
1912	48	**Woodrow Wilson**	Democratic	6,296,547	41.9	435	58.8
		Theodore Roosevelt	Progressive	4,118,571	27.4	88	
		William H. Taft	Republican	3,486,720	23.2	8	
		Eugene V. Debs	Socialist	900,672	6.0		
		Eugene W. Chafin	Prohibition	206,275	1.4		
1916	48	**Woodrow Wilson**	Democratic	9,127,695	49.4	277	61.6
		Charles E. Hughes	Republican	8,533,507	46.2	254	
		A. L. Benson	Socialist	585,113	3.2		
		J. Frank Hanly	Prohibition	220,506	1.2		

Presidential Elections, Continued

Year	Number of States	Candidates	Parties	Popular Vote	% of Popular Vote	Electoral Vote	% Voter Participation[b]
1920	48	Warren G. Harding	Republican	16,143,407	60.4	404	49.2
		James M. Cox	Democratic	9,130,328	34.2	127	
		Eugene V. Debs	Socialist	919,799	3.4		
		P. P. Christensen	Farmer-Labor	265,411	1.0		
1924	48	Calvin Coolidge	Republican	15,718,211	54.0	382	48.9
		John W. Davis	Democratic	8,385,283	28.8	136	
		Robert M. La Follette	Progressive	4,831,289	16.6	13	
1928	48	Herbert C. Hoover	Republican	21,391,993	58.2	444	56.9
		Alfred E. Smith	Democratic	15,016,169	40.9	87	
1932	48	Franklin D. Roosevelt	Democratic	22,809,638	57.4	472	56.9
		Herbert C. Hoover	Republican	15,758,901	39.7	59	
		Norman Thomas	Socialist	881,951	2.2		
1936	48	Franklin D. Roosevelt	Democratic	27,752,869	60.8	523	61.0
		Alfred M. Landon	Republican	16,674,665	36.5	8	
		William Lemke	Union	882,479	1.9		
1940	48	Franklin D. Roosevelt	Democratic	27,307,819	54.8	449	62.5
		Wendell L. Wilkie	Republican	22,321,018	44.8	82	
1944	48	Franklin D. Roosevelt	Democratic	25,606,585	53.5	432	55.9
		Thomas E. Dewey	Republican	22,014,745	46.0	99	
1948	48	Harry S Truman	Democratic	24,179,345	49.6	303	53.0
		Thomas E. Dewey	Republican	21,991,291	45.1	189	
		J. Strom Thurmond	States' Rights	1,176,125	2.4	39	
		Henry A. Wallace	Progressive	1,157,326	2.4		
1952	48	Dwight D. Eisenhower	Republican	33,936,234	55.1	442	63.3
		Adlai E. Stevenson	Democratic	27,314,992	44.4	89	
1956	48	Dwight D. Eisenhower	Republican	35,590,472	57.6	457	60.6
		Adlai E. Stevenson	Democratic	26,022,752	42.1	73	
1960	50	John F. Kennedy	Democratic	34,226,731	49.7	303	62.8
		Richard M. Nixon	Republican	34,108,157	49.5	219	
1964	50	Lyndon B. Johnson	Democratic	43,129,566	61.1	486	61.7
		Barry M. Goldwater	Republican	27,178,188	38.5	52	
1968	50	Richard M. Nixon	Republican	31,785,480	43.4	301	60.6
		Hubert H. Humphrey	Democratic	31,275,166	42.7	191	
		George C. Wallace	American Independent	9,906,473	13.5	46	
1972	50	Richard M. Nixon	Republican	47,169,911	60.7	520	55.2
		George S. McGovern	Democratic	29,170,383	37.5	17	
		John G. Schmitz	American	1,099,482	1.4		
1976	50	Jimmy Carter	Democratic	40,830,763	50.1	297	53.5
		Gerald R. Ford	Republican	39,147,793	48.0	240	
1980	50	Ronald Reagan	Republican	43,899,248	50.8	489	52.6
		Jimmy Carter	Democratic	35,481,432	41.0	49	
		John B. Anderson	Independent	5,719,437	6.6	0	
		Ed Clark	Libertarian	920,859	1.1	0	

Presidential Elections, Continued

Year	Number of States	Candidates	Parties	Popular Vote	% of Popular Vote	Electoral Vote	% Voter Participation[b]
1984	50	**Ronald Reagan**	Republican	54,455,075	58.8	525	53.1
		Walter Mondale	Democratic	37,577,185	40.6	13	
1988	50	**George Bush**	Republican	48,901,046	53.4	426	50.2
		Michael Dukakis	Democratic	41,809,030	45.6	111[c]	
1992	50	**Bill Clinton**	Democratic	44,908,233	43.0	370	55.0
		George Bush	Republican	39,102,282	37.4	168	
		Ross Perot	Independent	19,741,048	18.9	0	

Candidates receiving less than 1 percent of the popular vote have been omitted. Thus the percentage of popular vote given for any election year may not total 100 percent.

Before the passage of the Twelfth Amendment in 1804, the Electoral College voted for two presidential candidates; the runner-up became vice president.

Before 1824, most presidential electors were chosen by state legislatures, not by popular vote.

[a] Greeley died shortly after the election; the electors supporting him then divided their votes among minor candidates.

[b] Percent of voting-age population casting ballots.

[c] One elector from West Virginia cast her Electoral College presidential ballot for Lloyd Bentsen, the Democratic party's vice-presidential candidate.

Presidents, Vice Presidents, and Cabinet Members

The Washington Administration

President	George Washington	1789–1797
Vice President	John Adams	1789–1797
Secretary of State	Thomas Jefferson	1789–1793
	Edmund Randolph	1794–1795
	Timothy Pickering	1795–1797
Secretary of Treasury	Alexander Hamilton	1789–1795
	Oliver Wolcott	1795–1797
Secretary of War	Henry Knox	1789–1794
	Timothy Pickering	1795–1796
	James McHenry	1796–1797
Attorney General	Edmund Randolph	1789–1793
	William Bradford	1794–1795
	Charles Lee	1795–1797
Postmaster General	Samuel Osgood	1789–1791
	Timothy Pickering	1791–1794
	Joseph Habersham	1795–1797

The John Adams Administration

President	John Adams	1797–1801
Vice President	Thomas Jefferson	1797–1801
Secretary of State	Timothy Pickering	1797–1800
	John Marshall	1800–1801
Secretary of Treasury	Oliver Wolcott	1797–1800
	Samuel Dexter	1800–1801
Secretary of War	James McHenry	1797–1800
	Samuel Dexter	1800–1801
Attorney General	Charles Lee	1797–1801
Postmaster General	Joseph Habersham	1797–1801
Secretary of Navy	Benjamin Stoddert	1798–1801

The Jefferson Administration

President	Thomas Jefferson	1801–1809
Vice President	Aaron Burr	1801–1805
	George Clinton	1805–1809
Secretary of State	James Madison	1801–1809
Secretary of Treasury	Samuel Dexter	1801
	Albert Gallatin	1801–1809
Secretary of War	Henry Dearborn	1801–1809
Attorney General	Levi Lincoln	1801–1805
	Robert Smith	1805
	John Breckinridge	1805–1806
	Caesar Rodney	1807–1809
Postmaster General	Joseph Habersham	1801
	Gideon Granger	1801–1809
Secretary of Navy	Robert Smith	1801–1809

The Madison Administration

President	James Madison	1809–1817
Vice President	George Clinton	1809–1813
	Elbridge Gerry	1813–1817
Secretary of State	Robert Smith	1809–1811
	James Monroe	1811–1817
Secretary of Treasury	Albert Gallatin	1809–1813
	George Campbell	1814
	Alexander Dallas	1814–1816
	William Crawford	1816–1817
Secretary of War	William Eustis	1809–1812
	John Armstrong	1813–1814
	James Monroe	1814–1815
	William Crawford	1815–1817
Attorney General	Caesar Rodney	1809–1811
	William Pinkney	1811–1814
	Richard Rush	1814–1817
Postmaster General	Gideon Granger	1809–1814
	Return Meigs	1814–1817
Secretary of Navy	Paul Hamilton	1809–1813
	William Jones	1813–1814
	Benjamin Crowninshield	1814–1817

The Monroe Administration

President	James Monroe	1817–1825
Vice President	Daniel Tompkins	1817–1825
Secretary of State	John Quincy Adams	1817–1825
Secretary of Treasury	William Crawford	1817–1825

Presidents, Vice Presidents, and Cabinet Members, Continued

Secretary of War	George Graham	1817
	John C. Calhoun	1817–1825
Attorney General	Richard Rush	1817
	William Wirt	1817–1825
Postmaster General	Return Meigs	1817–1823
	John McLean	1823–1825
Secretary of Navy	Benjamin Crowninshield	1817–1818
	Smith Thompson	1818–1823
	Samuel Southard	1823–1825

The John Quincy Adams Administration

President	John Quincy Adams	1825–1829
Vice President	John C. Calhoun	1825–1829
Secretary of State	Henry Clay	1825–1829
Secretary of Treasury	Richard Rush	1825–1829
Secretary of War	James Barbour	1825–1828
	Peter Porter	1828–1829
Attorney General	William Wirt	1825–1829
Postmaster General	John McLean	1825–1829
Secretary of Navy	Samuel Southard	1825–1829

The Jackson Administration

President	Andrew Jackson	1829–1837
Vice President	John C. Calhoun	1829–1833
	Martin Van Buren	1833–1837
Secretary of State	Martin Van Buren	1829–1831
	Edward Livingston	1831–1833
	Louis McLane	1833–1834
	John Forsyth	1834–1837
Secretary of Treasury	Samuel Ingham	1829–1831
	Louis McLane	1831–1833
	William Duane	1833
	Roger B. Taney	1833–1834
	Levi Woodbury	1834–1837
Secretary of War	John H. Eaton	1829–1831
	Lewis Cass	1831–1837
	Benjamin Butler	1837
Attorney General	John M. Berrien	1829–1831
	Roger B. Taney	1831–1833
	Benjamin Butler	1833–1837
Postmaster General	William Barry	1829–1835
	Amos Kendall	1835–1837
Secretary of Navy	John Branch	1829–1831
	Levi Woodbury	1831–1834
	Mahlon Dickerson	1834–1837

The Van Buren Administration

President	Martin Van Buren	1837–1841
Vice President	Richard M. Johnson	1837–1841
Secretary of State	John Forsyth	1837–1841
Secretary of Treasury	Levi Woodbury	1837–1841
Secretary of War	Joel Poinsett	1837–1841
Attorney General	Benjamin Butler	1837–1838
	Felix Grundy	1838–1840
	Henry D. Gilpin	1840–1841
Postmaster General	Amos Kendall	1837–1840
	John M. Niles	1840–1841
Secretary of Navy	Mahlon Dickerson	1837–1838
	James Paulding	1838–1841

The William Harrison Administration

President	William H. Harrison	1841
Vice President	John Tyler	1841
Secretary of State	Daniel Webster	1841
Secretary of Treasury	Thomas Ewing	1841
Secretary of War	John Bell	1841
Attorney General	John J. Crittenden	1841
Postmaster General	Francis Granger	1841
Secretary of Navy	George Badger	1841

The Tyler Administration

President	John Tyler	1841–1845
Vice President	None	
Secretary of State	Daniel Webster	1841–1843
	Hugh S. Legaré	1843
	Abel P. Upshur	1843–1844
	John C. Calhoun	1844–1845
Secretary of Treasury	Thomas Ewing	1841
	Walter Forward	1841–1843
	John C. Spencer	1843–1844
	George Bibb	1844–1845
Secretary of War	John Bell	1841
	John C. Spencer	1841–1843
	James M. Porter	1843–1844
	William Wilkins	1844–1845
Attorney General	John J. Crittenden	1841
	Hugh S. Legaré	1841–1843
	John Nelson	1843–1845
Postmaster General	Francis Granger	1841
	Charles Wickliffe	1841
Secretary of Navy	George Badger	1841
	Abel P. Upshur	1841
	David Henshaw	1843–1844
	Thomas Gilmer	1844
	John Y. Mason	1844–1845

The Polk Administration

President	James K. Polk	1845–1849
Vice President	George M. Dallas	1845–1849
Secretary of State	James Buchanan	1845–1849

Presidents, Vice Presidents, and Cabinet Members, Continued

Secretary of Treasury	Robert J. Walker	1845–1849
Secretary of War	William L. Marcy	1845–1849
Attorney General	John Y. Mason	1845–1846
	Nathan Clifford	1846–1848
	Isaac Toucey	1848–1849
Postmaster General	Cave Johnson	1845–1849
Secretary of Navy	George Bancroft	1845–1846
	John Y. Mason	1846–1849

The Taylor Administration

President	Zachary Taylor	1849–1850
Vice President	Millard Fillmore	1849–1850
Secretary of State	John M. Clayton	1849–1850
Secretary of Treasury	William Meredith	1849–1850
Secretary of War	George Crawford	1849–1850
Attorney General	Reverdy Johnson	1849–1850
Postmaster General	Jacob Collamer	1849–1850
Secretary of Navy	William Preston	1849–1850
Secretary of Interior	Thomas Ewing	1849–1850

The Fillmore Administration

President	Millard Fillmore	1850–1853
Vice President	None	
Secretary of State	Daniel Webster	1850–1852
	Edward Everett	1852–1853
Secretary of Treasury	Thomas Corwin	1850–1853
Secretary of War	Charles Conrad	1850–1853
Attorney General	John J. Crittenden	1850–1853
Postmaster General	Nathan Hall	1850–1852
	Sam D. Hubbard	1852–1853
Secretary of Navy	William A. Graham	1850–1852
	John P. Kennedy	1852–1853
Secretary of Interior	Thomas McKennan	1850
	Alexander Stuart	1850–1853

The Pierce Administration

President	Franklin Pierce	1853–1857
Vice President	William R. King	1853–1857
Secretary of State	William L. Marcy	1853–1857
Secretary of Treasury	James Guthrie	1853–1857
Secretary of War	Jefferson Davis	1853–1857
Attorney General	Caleb Cushing	1853–1857
Postmaster General	James Campbell	1853–1857
Secretary of Navy	James C. Dobbin	1853–1857
Secretary of Interior	Robert McClelland	1853–1857

The Buchanan Administration

President	James Buchanan	1857–1861
Vice President	John C. Breckinridge	1857–1861
Secretary of State	Lewis Cass	1857–1860
	Jeremiah S. Black	1860–1861
Secretary of Treasury	Howell Cobb	1857–1860
	Philip Thomas	1860–1861
	John A. Dix	1861
Secretary of War	John B. Floyd	1857–1861
	Joseph Holt	1861
Attorney General	Jeremiah S. Black	1857–1860
	Edwin M. Stanton	1860–1861
Postmaster General	Aaron V. Brown	1857–1859
	Joseph Holt	1859–1861
	Horatio King	1861
Secretary of Navy	Isaac Toucey	1857–1861
Secretary of Interior	Jacob Thompson	1857–1861

The Lincoln Administration

President	Abraham Lincoln	1861–1865
Vice President	Hannibal Hamlin	1861–1865
	Andrew Johnson	1865
Secretary of State	William H. Seward	1861–1865
Secretary of Treasury	Samuel P. Chase	1861–1864
	William P. Fessenden	1864–1865
	Hugh McCulloch	1865
Secretary of War	Simon Cameron	1861–1862
	Edwin M. Stanton	1862–1865
Attorney General	Edward Bates	1861–1864
	James Speed	1864–1865
Postmaster General	Horatio King	1861
	Montgomery Blair	1861–1864
	William Dennison	1864–1865
Secretary of Navy	Gideon Welles	1861–1865
Secretary of Interior	Caleb B. Smith	1861–1863
	John P. Usher	1863–1865

The Andrew Johnson Administration

President	Andrew Johnson	1865–1869
Vice President	None	
Secretary of State	William H. Seward	1865–1869
Secretary of Treasury	Hugh McCulloch	1865–1869
Secretary of War	Edwin M. Stanton	1865–1867
	Ulysses S. Grant	1867–1868
	Lorenzo Thomas	1868
	John M. Schofield	1868–1869

Presidents, Vice Presidents, and Cabinet Members, Continued

Attorney General	James Speed	1865–1866
	Henry Stanbery	1866–1868
	William M. Evarts	1868–1869
Postmaster General	William Dennison	1865–1866
	Alexander Randall	1866–1869
Secretary of Navy	Gideon Welles	1865–1869
Secretary of Interior	John P. Usher	1865
	James Harlan	1865–1866
	Orville H. Browning	1866–1869

The Grant Administration

President	Ulysses S. Grant	1869–1877
Vice President	Schuyler Colfax	1869–1873
	Henry Wilson	1873–1877
Secretary of State	Elihu B. Washburne	1869
	Hamilton Fish	1869–1877
Secretary of Treasury	George S. Boutwell	1869–1873
	William Richardson	1873–1874
	Benjamin Bristow	1874–1876
	Lot M. Morrill	1876–1877
Secretary of War	John A. Rawlins	1869
	William T. Sherman	1869
	William W. Belknap	1869–1876
	Alphonso Taft	1876
	James D. Cameron	1876–1877
Attorney General	Ebenezer Hoar	1869–1870
	Amos T. Ackerman	1870–1871
	G. H. Williams	1871–1875
	Edwards Pierrepont	1875–1876
	Alphonso Taft	1876–1877
Postmaster General	John A. J. Creswell	1869–1874
	James W. Marshall	1874
	Marshall Jewell	1874–1876
	James N. Tyner	1876–1877
Secretary of Navy	Adolph E. Borie	1869
	George M. Robeson	1869–1877
Secretary of Interior	Jacob D. Cox	1869–1870
	Columbus Delano	1870–1875
	Zachariah Chandler	1875–1877

The Hayes Administration

President	Rutherford B. Hayes	1877–1881
Vice President	William A. Wheeler	1877–1881
Secretary of State	William B. Evarts	1877–1881
Secretary of Treasury	John Sherman	1877–1881
Secretary of War	George W. McCrary	1877–1879
	Alex Ramsey	1879–1881
Attorney General	Charles Devens	1877–1881
Postmaster General	David M. Key	1877–1880
	Horace Maynard	1880–1881

Secretary of Navy	Richard W. Thompson	1877–1880
	Nathan Goff, Jr.	1881
Secretary of Interior	Carl Schurz	1877–1881

The Garfield Administration

President	James A. Garfield	1881
Vice President	Chester A. Arthur	1881
Secretary of State	James G. Blaine	1881
Secretary of Treasury	William Windom	1881
Secretary of War	Robert T. Lincoln	1881
Attorney General	Wayne MacVeagh	1881
Postmaster General	Thomas L. James	1881
Secretary of Navy	William H. Hunt	1881
Secretary of Interior	Samuel J. Kirkwood	1881

The Arthur Administration

President	Chester A. Arthur	1881–1885
Vice President	None	
Secretary of State	F. T. Frelinghuysen	1881–1885
Secretary of Treasury	Charles J. Folger	1881–1884
	Walter Q. Gresham	1884
	Hugh McCulloch	1884–1885
Secretary of War	Robert T. Lincoln	1881–1885
Attorney General	Benjamin H. Brewster	1881–1885
Postmaster General	Timothy O. Howe	1881–1883
	Walter Q. Gresham	1883–1884
	Frank Hatton	1884–1885
Secretary of Navy	William H. Hunt	1881–1882
	William E. Chandler	1882–1885
Secretary of Interior	Samuel J. Kirkwood	1881–1882
	Henry M. Teller	1882–1885

The Cleveland Administration

President	Grover Cleveland	1885–1889
Vice President	Thomas A. Hendricks	1885–1889
Secretary of State	Thomas F. Bayard	1885–1889
Secretary of Treasury	Daniel Manning	1885–1887
	Charles S. Fairchild	1887–1889
Secretary of War	William C. Endicott	1885–1889
Attorney General	Augustus H. Garland	1885–1889
Postmaster General	William F. Vilas	1885–1888
	Don M. Dickinson	1888–1889
Secretary of Navy	William C. Whitney	1885–1889
Secretary of Interior	Lucius Q. C. Lamar	1885–1888
	William F. Vilas	1888–1889
Secretary of Agriculture	Norman J. Colman	1889

Presidents, Vice Presidents, and Cabinet Members, Continued

The Benjamin Harrison Administration

President	Benjamin Harrison	1889–1893
Vice President	Levi P. Morton	1889–1893
Secretary of State	James G. Blaine	1889–1892
	John W. Foster	1892–1893
Secretary of Treasury	William Windom	1889–1891
	Charles Foster	1891–1893
Secretary of War	Redfield Proctor	1889–1891
	Stephen B. Elkins	1891–1893
Attorney General	William H. H. Miller	1889–1891
Postmaster General	John Wanamaker	1889–1893
Secretary of Navy	Benjamin F. Tracy	1889–1893
Secretary of Interior	John W. Noble	1889–1893
Secretary of Agriculture	Jeremiah M. Rusk	1889–1893

The Cleveland Administration

President	Grover Cleveland	1893–1897
Vice President	Adlai E. Stevenson	1893–1897
Secretary of State	Walter Q. Gresham	1893–1895
	Richard Olney	1895–1897
Secretary of Treasury	John G. Carlisle	1893–1897
Secretary of War	Daniel S. Lamont	1893–1897
Attorney General	Richard Olney	1893–1895
	James Harmon	1895–1897
Postmaster General	Wilson S. Bissell	1893–1895
	William L. Wilson	1895–1897
Secretary of Navy	Hilary A. Herbert	1893–1897
Secretary of Interior	Hoke Smith	1893–1896
	David R. Francis	1896–1897
Secretary of Agriculture	Julius S. Morton	1893–1897

The McKinley Administration

President	William McKinley	1897–1901
Vice President	Garret A. Hobart	1897–1901
	Theodore Roosevelt	1901
Secretary of State	John Sherman	1897–1898
	William R. Day	1898
	John Hay	1898–1901
Secretary of Treasury	Lyman J. Gage	1897–1901
Secretary of War	Russell A. Alger	1897–1899
	Elihu Root	1899–1901
Attorney General	Joseph McKenna	1897–1898
	John W. Griggs	1898–1901
	Philander C. Knox	1901
Postmaster General	James A. Gary	1897–1898
	Charles E. Smith	1898–1901

Secretary of Navy	John D. Long	1897–1901
Secretary of Interior	Cornelius N. Bliss	1897–1899
	Ethan A. Hitchcock	1899–1901
Secretary of Agriculture	James Wilson	1897–1901

The Theodore Roosevelt Administration

President	Theodore Roosevelt	1901–1909
Vice President	Charles Fairbanks	1905–1909
Secretary of State	John Hay	1901–1905
	Elihu Root	1905–1909
	Robert Bacon	1909
Secretary of Treasury	Lyman J. Gage	1901–1902
	Leslie M. Shaw	1902–1907
	George B. Cortelyou	1907–1909
Secretary of War	Elihu Root	1901–1904
	William H. Taft	1904–1908
	Luke E. Wright	1908–1909
Attorney General	Philander C. Knox	1901–1904
	William H. Moody	1904–1906
	Charles J. Bonaparte	1906–1909
Postmaster General	Charles E. Smith	1901–1902
	Henry C. Payne	1902–1904
	Robert J. Wynne	1904–1905
	George B. Cortelyou	1905–1907
	George von L. Meyer	1907–1909
Secretary of Navy	John D. Long	1901–1902
	William H. Moody	1902–1904
	Paul Morton	1904–1905
	Charles J. Bonaparte	1905–1906
	Victor H. Metcalf	1906–1908
	Truman H. Newberry	1908–1909
Secretary of Interior	Ethan A. Hitchcock	1901–1907
	James R. Garfield	1907–1909
Secretary of Agriculture	James Wilson	1901–1909
Secretary of Labor and Commerce	George B. Cortelyou	1903–1904
	Victor H. Metcalf	1904–1906
	Oscar S. Straus	1906–1909
	Charles Nagel	1909

The Taft Administration

President	William H. Taft	1909–1913
Vice President	James S. Sherman	1909–1913
Secretary of State	Philander C. Knox	1909–1913
Secretary of Treasury	Franklin MacVeagh	1909–1913
Secretary of War	Jacob M. Dickinson	1909–1911
	Henry L. Stimson	1911–1913
Attorney General	George W. Wickersham	1909–1913
Postmaster General	Frank H. Hitchcock	1909–1913
Secretary of Navy	George von L. Meyer	1909–1913

Presidents, Vice Presidents, and Cabinet Members, Continued

Secretary of Interior	Richard A. Ballinger	1909–1911
	Walter L. Fisher	1911–1913
Secretary of Agriculture	James Wilson	1909–1913
Secretary of Labor and Commerce	Charles Nagel	1909–1913

The Wilson Administration

President	Woodrow Wilson	1913–1921
Vice President	Thomas R. Marshall	1913–1921
Secretary of State	William J. Bryan	1913–1915
	Robert Lansing	1915–1920
	Bainbridge Colby	1920–1921
Secretary of Treasury	William G. McAdoo	1913–1918
	Carter Glass	1918–1920
	David F. Houston	1920–1921
Secretary of War	Lindley M. Garrison	1913–1916
	Newton D. Baker	1916–1921
Attorney General	James C. McReynolds	1913–1914
	Thomas W. Gregory	1914–1919
	A. Mitchell Palmer	1919–1921
Postmaster General	Albert S. Burleson	1913–1921
Secretary of Navy	Josephus Daniels	1913–1921
Secretary of Interior	Franklin K. Lane	1913–1920
	John B. Payne	1920–1921
Secretary of Agriculture	David F. Houston	1913–1920
	Edwin T. Meredith	1920–1921
Secretary of Commerce	William C. Redfield	1913–1919
	Joshua W. Alexander	1919–1921
Secretary of Labor	William B. Wilson	1913–1921

The Harding Administration

President	Warren G. Harding	1921–1923
Vice President	Calvin Coolidge	1921–1923
Secretary of State	Charles E. Hughes	1921–1923
Secretary of Treasury	Andrew Mellon	1921–1923
Secretary of War	John W. Weeks	1921–1923
Attorney General	Harry M. Daugherty	1921–1923
Postmaster General	Will H. Hays	1921–1922
	Hubert Work	1922–1923
	Harry S. New	1923
Secretary of Navy	Edwin Denby	1921–1923
Secretary of Interior	Albert B. Fall	1921–1923
	Hubert Work	1923
Secretary of Agriculture	Henry C. Wallace	1921–1923
Secretary of Commerce	Herbert C. Hoover	1921–1923
Secretary of Labor	James J. Davis	1921–1923

The Coolidge Administration

President	Calvin Coolidge	1923–1929
Vice President	Charles G. Dawes	1925–1929
Secretary of State	Charles E. Hughes	1923–1925
	Frank B. Kellogg	1925–1929
Secretary of Treasury	Andrew Mellon	1923–1929
Secretary of War	John W. Weeks	1923–1925
	Dwight F. Davis	1925–1929
Attorney General	Henry M. Daugherty	1923–1924
	Harlan F. Stone	1924–1925
	John G. Sargent	1925–1929
Postmaster General	Harry S. New	1923–1929
Secretary of Navy	Edwin Derby	1923–1924
	Curtis D. Wilbur	1924–1929
Secretary of Interior	Hubert Work	1923–1928
	Roy O. West	1928–1929
Secretary of Agriculture	Henry C. Wallace	1923–1924
	Howard M. Gore	1924–1925
	William M. Jardine	1925–1929
Secretary of Commerce	Herbert C. Hoover	1923–1928
	William F. Whiting	1928–1929
Secretary of Labor	James J. Davis	1923–1929

The Hoover Administration

President	Herbert C. Hoover	1929–1933
Vice President	Charles Curtis	1929–1933
Secretary of State	Henry L. Stimson	1929–1933
Secretary of Treasury	Andrew Mellon	1929–1932
	Ogden L. Mills	1932–1933
Secretary of War	James W. Good	1929
	Patrick J. Hurley	1929–1933
Attorney General	William D. Mitchell	1929–1933
Postmaster General	Walter F. Brown	1929–1933
Secretary of Navy	Charles F. Adams	1929–1933
Secretary of Interior	Ray L. Wilbur	1929–1933
Secretary of Agriculture	Arthur M. Hyde	1929–1933
Secretary of Commerce	Robert P. Lamont	1929–1932
	Roy D. Chapin	1932–1933
Secretary of Labor	James J. Davis	1929–1930
	William N. Doak	1930–1933

The Franklin D. Roosevelt Administration

President	Franklin D. Roosevelt	1933–1945
Vice President	John Nance Garner	1933–1941
	Henry A. Wallace	1941–1945
	Harry S Truman	1945
Secretary of State	Cordell Hull	1933–1944
	Edward R. Stettinius, Jr.	1944–1945

Presidents, Vice Presidents, and Cabinet Members, Continued

Secretary of Treasury	William H. Woodin	1933–1934
	Henry Morgenthau, Jr.	1934–1945
Secretary of War	George H. Dern	1933–1936
	Henry A. Woodring	1936–1940
	Henry L. Stimson	1940–1945
Attorney General	Homer S. Cummings	1933–1939
	Frank Murphy	1939–1940
	Robert H. Jackson	1940–1941
	Francis Biddle	1941–1945
Postmaster General	James A. Farley	1933–1940
	Frank C. Walker	1940–1945
Secretary of Navy	Claude A. Swanson	1933–1940
	Charles Edison	1940
	Frank Knox	1940–1944
	James V. Forrestal	1944–1945
Secretary of Interior	Harold L. Ickes	1933–1945
Secretary of Agriculture	Henry A. Wallace	1933–1940
	Claude R. Wickard	1940–1945
Secretary of Commerce	Daniel C. Roper	1933–1939
	Harry L. Hopkins	1939–1940
	Jesse Jones	1940–1945
	Henry A. Wallace	1945
Secretary of Labor	Frances Perkins	1933–1945

The Truman Administration

President	Harry S Truman	1945–1953
Vice President	Alben W. Barkley	1949–1953
Secretary of State	Edward R. Stettinius, Jr.	1945
	James F. Byrnes	1945–1947
	George C. Marshall	1947–1949
	Dean G. Acheson	1949–1953
Secretary of Treasury	Fred M. Vinson	1945–1946
	John W. Snyder	1946–1953
Secretary of War	Robert P. Patterson	1945–1947
	Kenneth C. Royall	1947
Attorney General	Tom C. Clark	1945–1949
	J. Howard McGrath	1949–1952
	James P. McGranery	1952–1953
Postmaster General	Frank C. Walker	1945
	Robert E. Hannegan	1945–1947
	Jesse M. Donaldson	1947–1953
Secretary of Navy	James V. Forrestal	1945–1947
Secretary of Interior	Harold L. Ickes	1945–1946
	Julius A. Krug	1946–1949
	Oscar L. Chapman	1949–1953
Secretary of Agriculture	Clinton P. Anderson	1945–1948
	Charles F. Brannan	1948–1953
Secretary of Commerce	Henry A. Wallace	1945–1946
	W. Averell Harriman	1946–1948
	Charles W. Sawyer	1948–1953
Secretary of Labor	Lewis B. Schwellenbach	1945–1948
	Maurice J. Tobin	1948–1953

Secretary of Defense	James V. Forrestal	1947–1949
	Louis A. Johnson	1949–1950
	George C. Marshall	1950–1951
	Robert A. Lovett	1951–1953

The Eisenhower Administration

President	Dwight D. Eisenhower	1953–1961
Vice President	Richard M. Nixon	1953–1961
Secretary of State	John Foster Dulles	1953–1959
	Christian A. Herter	1959–1961
Secretary of Treasury	George M. Humphrey	1953–1957
	Robert B. Anderson	1957–1961
Attorney General	Herbert Brownell, Jr.	1953–1958
	William P. Rogers	1958–1961
Postmaster General	Arthur E. Summerfield	1953–1961
Secretary of Interior	Douglas McKay	1953–1956
	Fred A. Seaton	1956–1961
Secretary of Agriculture	Ezra T. Benson	1953–1961
Secretary of Commerce	Sinclair Weeks	1953–1958
	Lewis L. Strauss	1958–1959
	Frederick H. Mueller	1959–1961
Secretary of Labor	Martin P. Durkin	1953
	James P. Mitchell	1953–1961
Secretary of Defense	Charles E. Wilson	1953–1957
	Neil H. McElroy	1957–1959
	Thomas S. Gates, Jr.	1959–1961
Secretary of Health, Education, and Welfare	Oveta Culp Hobby	1953–1955
	Marion B. Folsom	1955–1958
	Arthur S. Flemming	1958–1961

The Kennedy Administration

President	John F. Kennedy	1961–1963
Vice President	Lyndon B. Johnson	1961–1963
Secretary of State	Dean Rusk	1961–1963
Secretary of Treasury	C. Douglas Dillon	1961–1963
Attorney General	Robert F. Kennedy	1961–1963
Postmaster General	J. Edward Day	1961–1963
	John A. Gronouski	1963
Secretary of Interior	Stewart L. Udall	1961–1963
Secretary of Agriculture	Orville L. Freeman	1961–1963
Secretary of Commerce	Luther H. Hodges	1961–1963
Secretary of Labor	Arthur J. Goldberg	1961–1962
	W. Willard Wirtz	1962–1963
Secretary of Defense	Robert S. McNamara	1961–1963
Secretary of Health, Education, and Welfare	Abraham A. Ribicoff	1961–1962
	Anthony J. Celebrezze	1962–1963

Presidents, Vice Presidents, and Cabinet Members, Continued

The Lyndon Johnson Administration

President	Lyndon B. Johnson	1963–1969
Vice President	Hubert H. Humphrey	1965–1969
Secretary of State	Dean Rusk	1963–1969
Secretary of Treasury	C. Douglas Dillon	1963–1965
	Henry H. Fowler	1965–1969
Attorney General	Robert F. Kennedy	1963–1964
	Nicholas Katzenbach	1965–1966
	Ramsey Clark	1967–1969
Postmaster General	John A. Gronouski	1963–1965
	Lawrence F. O'Brien	1965–1968
	Marvin Watson	1968–1969
Secretary of Interior	Stewart L. Udall	1963–1969
Secretary of Agriculture	Orville L. Freeman	1963–1969
Secretary of Commerce	Luther H. Hodges	1963–1964
	John T. Connor	1964–1967
	Alexander B. Trowbridge	1967–1968
	Cyrus R. Smith	1968–1969
Secretary of Labor	W. Willard Wirtz	1963–1969
Secretary of Defense	Robert F. McNamara	1963–1968
	Clark Clifford	1968–1969
Secretary of Health, Education, and Welfare	Anthony J. Celebrezze	1963–1965
	John W. Gardner	1965–1968
	Wilbur J. Cohen	1968–1969
Secretary of Housing and Urban Development	Robert C. Weaver	1966–1969
	Robert C. Wood	1969
Secretary of Transportation	Alan S. Boyd	1967–1969

The Nixon Administration

President	Richard M. Nixon	1969–1974
Vice President	Spiro T. Agnew	1969–1973
	Gerald R. Ford	1973–1974
Secretary of State	William P. Rogers	1969–1973
	Henry A. Kissinger	1973–1974
Secretary of Treasury	David M. Kennedy	1969–1970
	John B. Connally	1971–1972
	George P. Shultz	1972–1974
	William E. Simon	1974
Attorney General	John N. Mitchell	1969–1972
	Richard G. Kleindienst	1972–1973
	Elliot L. Richardson	1973
	William B. Saxbe	1973–1974
Postmaster General	Winton M. Blount	1969–1971
Secretary of Interior	Walter J. Hickel	1969–1970
	Rogers Morton	1971–1974
Secretary of Agriculture	Clifford M. Hardin	1969–1971
	Earl L. Butz	1971–1974

Secretary of Commerce	Maurice H. Stans	1969–1972
	Peter G. Peterson	1972–1973
	Frederick B. Dent	1973–1974
Secretary of Labor	George P. Shultz	1969–1970
	James D. Hodgson	1970–1973
	Peter J. Brennan	1973–1974
Secretary of Defense	Melvin R. Laird	1969–1973
	Elliot L. Richardson	1973
	James R. Schlesinger	1973–1974
Secretary of Health, Education, and Welfare	Robert H. Finch	1969–1970
	Elliot L. Richardson	1970–1973
	Casper W. Weinberger	1973–1974
Secretary of Housing and Urban Development	George Romney	1969–1973
	James T. Lynn	1973–1974
Secretary of Transportation	John A. Volpe	1969–1973
	Claude S. Brinegar	1973–1974

The Ford Administration

President	Gerald R. Ford	1974–1977
Vice President	Nelson A. Rockefeller	1974–1977
Secretary of State	Henry A. Kissinger	1974–1977
Secretary of Treasury	William E. Simon	1974–1977
Attorney General	William Saxbe	1974–1975
	Edward Levi	1975–1977
Secretary of Interior	Rogers Morton	1974–1975
	Stanley K. Hathaway	1975
	Thomas Kleppe	1975–1977
Secretary of Agriculture	Earl L. Butz	1974–1976
	John A. Knebel	1976–1977
Secretary of Commerce	Frederick B. Dent	1974–1975
	Rogers Morton	1975–1976
	Elliot L. Richardson	1976–1977
Secretary of Labor	Peter J. Brennan	1974–1975
	John T. Dunlop	1975–1976
	W. J. Usery	1976–1977
Secretary of Defense	James R. Schlesinger	1974–1975
	Donald Rumsfeld	1975–1977
Secretary of Health, Education, and Welfare	Casper Weinberger	1974–1975
	Forrest D. Mathews	1975–1977
Secretary of Housing and Urban Development	James T. Lynn	1974–1975
	Carla A. Hills	1975–1977
Secretary of Transportation	Claude Brinegar	1974–1975
	William T. Coleman	1975–1977

The Carter Administration

President	Jimmy Carter	1977–1981
Vice President	Walter F. Mondale	1977–1981

Presidents, Vice Presidents, and Cabinet Members, Continued

Secretary of State	Cyrus R. Vance	1977–1980
	Edmund Muskie	1980–1981
Secretary of Treasury	W. Michael Blumenthal	1977–1979
	G. William Miller	1979–1981
Attorney General	Griffin Bell	1977–1979
	Benjamin R. Civiletti	1979–1981
Secretary of Interior	Cecil D. Andrus	1977–1981
Secretary of Agriculture	Robert Bergland	1977–1981
Secretary of Commerce	Juanita M. Kreps	1977–1979
	Philip M. Klutznick	1979–1981
Secretary of Labor	F. Ray Marshall	1977–1981
Secretary of Defense	Harold Brown	1977–1981
Secretary of Health, Education, and Welfare	Joseph A. Califano	1977–1979
	Patricia R. Harris	1979
Secretary of Health and Human Services	Patricia R. Harris	1979–1981
Secretary of Education	Shirley M. Hufstedler	1979–1981
Secretary of Housing and Urban Development	Patricia R. Harris	1977–1979
	Moon Landrieu	1979–1981
Secretary of Transportation	Brock Adams	1977–1979
	Neil E. Goldschmidt	1979–1981
Secretary of Energy	James R. Schlesinger	1977–1979
	Charles W. Duncan	1979–1981

The Reagan Administration

President	Ronald Reagan	1981–1989
Vice President	George Bush	1981–1989
Secretary of State	Alexander M. Haig	1981–1982
	George P. Shultz	1982–1989
Secretary of Treasury	Donald Regan	1981–1985
	James A. Baker III	1985–1988
	Nicholas F. Brady	1988–1989
Attorney General	William F. Smith	1981–1985
	Edwin A. Meese III	1985–1988
	Richard L. Thornburgh	1988–1989
Secretary of Interior	James G. Watt	1981–1983
	William P. Clark, Jr.	1983–1985
	Donald P. Hodel	1985–1989
Secretary of Agriculture	John Block	1981–1986
	Richard E. Lyng	1986–1989
Secretary of Commerce	Malcolm Baldrige	1981–1987
	C. William Verity, Jr.	1987–1989
Secretary of Labor	Raymond J. Donovan	1981–1985
	William E. Brock	1985–1987
	Ann Dore McLaughlin	1987–1989
Secretary of Defense	Casper Weinberger	1981–1987
	Frank C. Carlucci	1987–1989

Secretary of Health and Human Services	Richard S. Schweiker	1981–1983
	Margaret Heckler	1983–1985
	Otis R. Bowen	1985–1989
Secretary of Education	Terrel H. Bell	1981–1984
	William J. Bennett	1985–1988
	Lauro F. Cavazos	1988–1989
Secretary of Housing and Urban Development	Samuel R. Pierce, Jr.	1981–1989
Secretary of Transportation	Drew Lewis	1981–1982
	Elizabeth Hanford Dole	1983–1987
	James H. Burnley IV	1987–1989
Secretary of Energy	James B. Edwards	1981–1982
	Donald P. Hodel	1982–1985
	John S. Herrington	1985–1989

The Bush Administration

President	George Bush	1989–1993
Vice President	Dan Quayle	1989–1993
Secretary of State	James A. Baker III	1989–1992
	Lawrence Eagleburger	1992–1993
Secretary of Treasury	Nicholas F. Brady	1989–1993
Attorney General	Richard L. Thornburgh	1989–1992
	William P. Barr	1992–1993
Secretary of Interior	Manuel Lujan, Jr.	1989–1993
Secretary of Agriculture	Clayton K. Yeutter	1989–1991
	Edward Madigan	1991–1993
Secretary of Commerce	Robert A. Mosbacher	1989–1992
	Barbara Hackman Franklin	1992–1993
Secretary of Labor	Elizabeth Hanford Dole	1989–1991
	Lynn Martin	1991–1993
Secretary of Defense	Richard B. Cheney	1989–1993
Secretary of Health and Human Services	Louis W. Sullivan	1989–1993
Secretary of Education	Lauro F. Cavazos	1989–1991
	Lamar Alexander	1991–1993
Secretary of Housing and Urban Development	Jack F. Kemp	1989–1993
Secretary of Transportation	Samuel K. Skinner	1989–1992
	Andrew H. Card	1992–1993
Secretary of Energy	James D. Watkins	1989–1993
Secretary of Veterans Affairs	Edward J. Derwinski	1989–1993

The Clinton Administration

President	Bill Clinton	1993–
Vice President	Albert Gore	1993–
Secretary of State	Warren M. Christopher	1993–

Presidents, Vice Presidents, and Cabinet Members, Continued

Secretary of Treasury	Lloyd Bentsen	1993–	Secretary of Education	Richard W. Riley	1993–
Attorney General	Janet Reno	1993–	Secretary of Housing and Urban Development	Henry G. Cisneros	1993–
Secretary of Interior	Bruce Babbitt	1993–			
Secretary of Agriculture	Mike Espy	1993–			
Secretary of Commerce	Ronald H. Brown	1993–	Secretary of Transportation	Federico F. Peña	1993–
Secretary of Labor	Robert B. Reich	1993–	Secretary of Energy	Hazel O'Leary	1993–
Secretary of Defense	Les Aspin	1993–	Secretary of Veterans Affairs	Jesse Brown	1993–
Secretary of Health and Human Services	Donna E. Shalala	1993–			

Party Strength in Congress

Period	Congress	House Majority Party		House Minority Party		Others	Senate Majority Party		Senate Minority Party		Others		Party of President
1789–91	1st	Ad	38	Op	26		Ad	17	Op	9		F	Washington
1791–93	2nd	F	37	DR	33		F	16	DR	13		F	Washington
1793–95	3rd	DR	57	F	48		F	17	DR	13		F	Washington
1795–97	4th	F	54	DR	52		F	19	DR	13		F	Washington
1797–99	5th	F	58	DR	48		F	20	DR	12		F	J. Adams
1799–1801	6th	F	64	DR	42		F	19	DR	13		F	J. Adams
1801–03	7th	DR	69	F	36		DR	18	F	13		DR	Jefferson
1803–05	8th	DR	102	F	39		DR	25	F	9		DR	Jefferson
1805–07	9th	DR	116	F	25		DR	27	F	7		DR	Jefferson
1807–09	10th	DR	118	F	24		DR	28	F	6		DR	Jefferson
1809–11	11th	DR	94	F	48		DR	28	F	6		DR	Madison
1811–13	12th	DR	108	F	36		DR	30	F	6		DR	Madison
1813–15	13th	DR	112	F	68		DR	27	F	9		DR	Madison
1815–17	14th	DR	117	F	65		DR	25	F	11		DR	Madison
1817–19	15th	DR	141	F	42		DR	34	F	10		DR	Monroe
1819–21	16th	DR	156	F	27		DR	35	F	7		DR	Monroe
1821–23	17th	DR	158	F	25		DR	44	F	4		DR	Monroe
1823–25	18th	DR	187	F	26		DR	44	F	4		DR	Monroe
1825–27	19th	Ad	105	J	97		Ad	26	J	20		C	J. Q. Adams
1827–29	20th	J	119	Ad	94		J	28	Ad	20		C	J. Q. Adams
1829–31	21st	D	139	NR	74		D	26	NR	22		D	Jackson
1831–33	22nd	D	141	NR	58	14	D	25	NR	21	2	D	Jackson
1833–35	23rd	D	147	AM	53	60	D	20	NR	20	8	D	Jackson
1835–37	24th	D	145	W	98		D	27	W	25		D	Jackson
1837–39	25th	D	108	W	107	24	D	30	W	18	4	D	Van Buren
1839–41	26th	D	124	W	118		D	28	W	22		D	Van Buren
1841–43	27th	W	133	D	102	6	W	28	D	22	2	W	W. Harrison
												W	Tyler
1843–45	28th	D	142	W	79	1	W	28	D	25	1	W	Tyler
1845–47	29th	D	143	W	77	6	D	31	W	25		D	Polk
1847–49	30th	W	115	D	108	4	D	36	W	21	1	D	Polk
1849–51	31st	D	112	W	109	9	D	35	W	25	2	W	Taylor
												W	Fillmore
1851–53	32nd	D	140	W	88	5	D	35	W	24	3	W	Fillmore
1853–55	33rd	D	159	W	71	4	D	38	W	22	2	D	Pierce
1855–57	34th	R	108	D	83	43	D	40	R	15	5	D	Pierce
1857–59	35th	D	118	R	92	26	D	36	R	20	8	D	Buchanan
1859–61	36th	R	114	D	92	31	D	36	R	26	4	D	Buchanan

Party Strength in Congress, Continued

Period	Congress	House Majority Party		House Minority Party		Others	Senate Majority Party		Senate Minority Party		Others	Party of President	
1861–63	37th	R	105	D	43	30	R	31	D	10	8	R	Lincoln
1863–65	38th	R	102	D	75	9	R	36	D	9	5	R	Lincoln
1865–67	39th	U	149	D	42		U	42	D	10		R	Lincoln
												R	Johnson
1867–69	40th	R	143	D	49		R	42	D	11		R	Johnson
1869–71	41st	R	149	D	63		R	56	D	11		R	Grant
1871–73	42nd	R	134	D	104	5	R	52	D	17	5	R	Grant
1873–75	43rd	R	194	D	92	14	R	49	D	19	5	R	Grant
1875–77	44th	D	169	R	109	14	R	45	D	29	2	R	Grant
1877–79	45th	D	153	R	140		R	39	D	36	1	R	Hayes
1879–81	46th	D	149	R	130	14	D	42	R	33	1	R	Hayes
1881–83	47th	D	147	R	135	11	R	37	D	37	1	R	Garfield
												R	Arthur
1883–85	48th	D	197	R	118	10	R	38	D	36	2	R	Arthur
1885–87	49th	D	183	R	140	2	R	43	D	34		D	Cleveland
1887–89	50th	D	169	R	152	4	R	39	D	37		D	Cleveland
1889–91	51st	R	166	D	159		R	39	D	37		R	B. Harrison
1891–93	52nd	D	235	R	88	9	R	47	D	39	2	R	B. Harrison
1893–95	53rd	D	218	R	127	11	D	44	R	38	3	D	Cleveland
1895–97	54th	R	244	D	105	7	R	43	D	39	6	D	Cleveland
1897–99	55th	R	204	D	113	40	R	47	D	34	7	R	McKinley
1899–1901	56th	R	185	D	163	9	R	53	D	26	8	R	McKinley
1901–03	57th	R	197	D	151	9	R	55	D	31	4	R	McKinley
												R	T. Roosevelt
1903–05	58th	R	208	D	178		R	57	D	33		R	T. Roosevelt
1905–07	59th	R	250	D	136		R	57	D	33		R	T. Roosevelt
1907–09	60th	R	222	D	164		R	61	D	31		R	T. Roosevelt
1909–11	61st	R	219	D	172		R	61	D	32		R	Taft
1911–13	62nd	D	228	R	161	1	R	51	D	41		R	Taft
1913–15	63rd	D	291	R	127	17	D	51	R	44	1	D	Wilson
1915–17	64th	D	230	R	196	9	D	56	R	40		D	Wilson
1917–19	65th	D	216	R	210	6	D	53	R	42		D	Wilson
1919–21	66th	R	240	D	190	3	R	49	D	47		D	Wilson
1921–23	67th	R	301	D	131	1	R	59	D	37		R	Harding
1923–25	68th	R	225	D	205	5	R	51	D	43	2	R	Coolidge
1925–27	69th	R	247	D	183	4	R	56	D	39	1	R	Coolidge
1927–29	70th	R	237	D	195	3	R	49	D	46	1	R	Coolidge
1929–31	71st	R	267	D	167	1	R	56	D	39	1	R	Hoover
1931–33	72nd	D	220	R	214	1	R	48	D	47	1	R	Hoover
1933–35	73rd	D	310	R	117	5	D	60	R	35	1	D	F. Roosevelt
1935–37	74th	D	319	R	103	10	D	69	R	25	2	D	F. Roosevelt
1937–39	75th	D	331	R	89	13	D	76	R	16	4	D	F. Roosevelt
1939–41	76th	D	261	R	164	4	D	69	R	23	4	D	F. Roosevelt
1941–43	77th	D	268	R	162	5	D	66	R	28	2	D	F. Roosevelt
1943–45	78th	D	218	R	208	4	D	58	R	37	1	D	F. Roosevelt
1945–47	79th	D	242	R	190	2	D	56	R	38	1	D	Truman
1947–49	80th	R	245	D	188	1	R	51	D	45		D	Truman

Party Strength in Congress, Continued

Period	Congress	House Majority Party		House Minority Party		Others	Senate Majority Party		Senate Minority Party		Others	Party of President	
1949–51	81st	D	263	R	171	1	D	54	R	42		D	Truman
1951–53	82nd	D	234	R	199	1	D	49	R	47		D	Truman
1953–55	83rd	R	221	D	211	1	R	48	D	47	1	R	Eisenhower
1955–57	84th	D	232	R	203		D	48	R	47	1	R	Eisenhower
1957–59	85th	D	233	R	200		D	49	R	47		R	Eisenhower
1959–61	86th	D	284	R	153		D	65	R	35		R	Eisenhower
1961–63	87th	D	263	R	174		D	65	R	35		D	Kennedy
1963–65	88th	D	258	R	117		D	67	R	33		D	Kennedy
												D	Johnson
1965–67	89th	D	295	R	140		D	68	R	32		D	Johnson
1967–69	90th	D	246	R	187		D	64	R	36		D	Johnson
1969–71	91st	D	245	R	189		D	57	R	43		R	Nixon
1971–73	92nd	D	254	R	180		D	54	R	44	2	R	Nixon
1973–75	93rd	D	239	R	192	1	D	56	R	42	2	R	Nixon
1975–77	94th	D	291	R	144		D	60	R	37	3	R	Ford
1977–79	95th	D	292	R	143		D	61	R	38	1	D	Carter
1979–81	96th	D	276	R	157		D	58	R	41	1	D	Carter
1981–83	97th	D	243	R	192		R	53	D	46	1	R	Reagan
1983–85	98th	D	267	R	168		R	55	D	45		R	Reagan
1985–87	99th	D	253	R	182		R	53	D	47		R	Reagan
1987–89	100th	D	258	R	177		D	55	R	45		R	Reagan
1989–91	101st	D	259	R	174		D	54	R	46		R	Bush
1991–93	102nd	D	267	R	167	1	D	56	R	44		R	Bush
1993–	103rd	D	255	R	176	4*	D	57	R	43		D	Clinton

*Three vacancies at start. AD = Administration; AM = Anti-Masonic; C = Coalition; D = Democratic; DR = Democratic-Republican; F = Federalist; J = Jacksonian; NR = National Republican; Op = Opposition; R = Republican; U = Unionist; W = Whig. Figures are for the beginning of first session of each Congress, except the 93rd, which are for the beginning of the second session.

Justices of the Supreme Court

	Term of Service	Years of Service	Life Span		Term of Service	Years of Service	Life Span
John Jay	1789–1795	5	1745–1829	William Strong	1870–1880	10	1808–1895
John Rutledge	1789–1791	1	1739–1800	Joseph P. Bradley	1870–1892	22	1813–1892
William Cushing	1789–1810	20	1732–1810	Ward Hunt	1873–1882	9	1810–1886
James Wilson	1789–1798	8	1742–1798	*Morrison R. Waite*	1874–1888	14	1816–1888
John Blair	1789–1796	6	1732–1800	John M. Harlan	1877–1911	34	1833–1911
Robert H. Harrison	1789–1790	—	1745–1790	William B. Woods	1880–1887	7	1824–1887
James Iredell	1790–1799	9	1751–1799	Stanley Matthews	1881–1889	7	1824–1889
Thomas Johnson	1791–1793	1	1732–1819	Horace Gray	1882–1902	20	1828–1902
William Paterson	1793–1806	13	1745–1806	Samuel Blatchford	1882–1893	11	1820–1893
*John Rutledge**	1795	—	1739–1800	Lucius Q. C. Lamar	1888–1893	5	1825–1893
Samuel Chase	1796–1811	15	1741–1811	*Melville W. Fuller*	1888–1910	21	1833–1910
Oliver Ellsworth	1796–1800	4	1745–1807	David J. Brewer	1890–1910	20	1837–1910
Bushrod Washington	1798–1829	31	1762–1829	Henry B. Brown	1890–1906	16	1836–1913
Alfred Moore	1799–1804	4	1755–1810	George Shiras, Jr.	1892–1903	10	1832–1924
John Marshall	1801–1835	34	1755–1835	Howell E. Jackson	1893–1895	2	1832–1895
William Johnson	1804–1834	30	1771–1834	Edward D. White	1894–1910	16	1845–1921
H. Brockholst Livingston	1806–1823	16	1757–1823	Rufus W. Peckham	1895–1909	14	1838–1909
Thomas Todd	1807–1826	18	1765–1826	Joseph McKenna	1898–1925	26	1843–1926
Joseph Story	1811–1845	33	1779–1845	Oliver W. Holmes	1902–1932	30	1841–1935
Gabriel Duval	1811–1835	24	1752–1844	William R. Day	1903–1922	19	1849–1923
Smith Thompson	1823–1843	20	1768–1843	William H. Moody	1906–1910	3	1853–1917
Robert Trimble	1826–1828	2	1777–1828	Horace H. Lurton	1910–1914	4	1844–1914
John McLean	1829–1861	32	1785–1861	Charles E. Hughes	1910–1916	5	1862–1948
Henry Baldwin	1830–1844	14	1780–1844	Willis Van Devanter	1911–1937	26	1859–1941
James M. Wayne	1835–1867	32	1790–1867	Joseph R. Lamar	1911–1916	5	1857–1916
Roger B. Taney	1836–1864	28	1777–1864	*Edward D. White*	1910–1921	11	1845–1921
Philip P. Barbour	1836–1841	4	1783–1841	Mahlon Pitney	1912–1922	10	1858–1924
John Catron	1837–1865	28	1786–1865	James C. McReynolds	1914–1941	26	1862–1946
John McKinley	1837–1852	15	1780–1852	Louis D. Brandeis	1916–1939	22	1856–1941
Peter V. Daniel	1841–1860	19	1784–1860	John H. Clarke	1916–1922	6	1857–1945
Samuel Nelson	1845–1872	27	1792–1873	*William H. Taft*	1921–1930	8	1857–1930
Levi Woodbury	1845–1851	5	1789–1851	George Sutherland	1922–1938	15	1862–1942
Robert C. Grier	1846–1870	23	1794–1870	Pierce Butler	1922–1939	16	1866–1939
Benjamin R. Curtis	1851–1857	6	1809–1874	Edward T. Sanford	1923–1930	7	1865–1930
John A. Campbell	1853–1861	8	1811–1889	Harlan F. Stone	1925–1941	16	1872–1946
Nathan Clifford	1858–1881	23	1803–1881	*Charles E. Hughes*	1930–1941	11	1862–1948
Noah H. Swayne	1862–1881	18	1804–1884	Owen J. Roberts	1930–1945	15	1875–1955
Samuel F. Miller	1862–1890	28	1816–1890	Benjamin N. Cardozo	1932–1938	6	1870–1938
David Davis	1862–1877	14	1815–1886	Hugo L. Black	1937–1971	34	1886–1971
Stephen J. Field	1863–1897	34	1816–1899	Stanley F. Reed	1938–1957	19	1884–1980
Salmon P. Chase	1864–1873	8	1808–1873	Felix Frankfurter	1939–1962	23	1882–1965

Justices of the Supreme Court, Continued

	Term of Service	Years of Service	Life Span		Term of Service	Years of Service	Life Span
William O. Douglas	1939–1975	36	1898–1980	Byron R. White	1962–1993	31	1917–
Frank Murphy	1940–1949	9	1890–1949	Arthur J. Goldberg	1962–1965	3	1908–1990
Harlan F. Stone	1941–1946	5	1872–1946	Abe Fortas	1965–1969	4	1910–1982
James F. Byrnes	1941–1942	1	1879–1972	Thurgood Marshall	1967–1991	24	1908–1993
Robert H. Jackson	1941–1954	13	1892–1954	*Warren C. Burger*	1969–1986	17	1907–
Wiley B. Rutledge	1943–1949	6	1894–1949	Harry A. Blackmun	1970–	—	1908–
Harold H. Burton	1945–1958	13	1888–1964	Lewis F. Powell, Jr.	1972–1987	15	1907–
Fred M. Vinson	1946–1953	7	1890–1953	*William H. Rehnquist*	1971–	—	1924–
Tom C. Clark	1949–1967	18	1899–1977	John P. Stevens III	1975–	—	1920–
Sherman Minton	1949–1956	7	1890–1965	Sandra Day O'Connor	1981–	—	1930–
Earl Warren	1953–1969	16	1891–1974	Antonin Scalia	1986–	—	1936–
John Marshall Harlan	1955–1971	16	1899–1971	Anthony M. Kennedy	1988–	—	1936–
William J. Brennan, Jr.	1956–	—	1906–	David H. Souter	1990–	—	1939–
Charles E. Whittaker	1957–1962	5	1901–1973	Clarence Thomas	1991–	—	1948–
Potter Stewart	1958–1981	23	1915–1985	Ruth Bader Ginsburg	1993–	—	1933–

*Appointed and served one term, but not confirmed by the Senate.

Note: Chief justices are in italics.

Index

Bakke v. *University of California* (1978), 1041
Balanced budget, 1040
Balance of payments, Europe and, 892
Balance of powers, 191, 203
Balboa, Vasco Núñez de, 26
Baldwin, James, 999
Baldwin, Roger, 707
Balkans, and First World War, 688
Ball, George, 911, 949, 953, 964
Ball, Lucille, 943
Baltic states, 802; Soviet Union and, 801
Baltimore, Lord (Cecilius Calvert), 48. *See also* Calvert family
Baltimore, Maryland, growth of, 337
Baltimore and Ohio Railroad, 270–271
Bands, of Native Americans, 5, 9–12
Bandung Conference (1955), 953
Bangladesh, 953
Banker, Newton, 698
Bank holiday, 760
Banking Act (1933), 764
Bank notes, 385
Bank of England, U.S. national bank and, 216
Bank of the United States: First, 216; Second, 259, 260, 384–385
Bank robberies, 575
Bankruptcy, 274; cities and, 1028
Banks and banking, 284; and *McCulloch* v. *Maryland*, 260; reform in, 284–285; credit and, 298; Second Bank of the United States and, 384–385; Jackson, Andrew, and, 384–386; Democrats and, 388; National Banking Acts and, 441; failures, 614; Federal Reserve Act and, 651; in Great Depression (1929–1941), 752–754, 760–761; New Deal and, 764; Edge Act and, 792; federal control and, 1030; Japan and, 1064
Banneker, Benjamin, 189
Bantu (language), 14
Bao Dai, 961, 962
Baptists, in Virginia, 119; and slavery, 329; Southern blacks and, 487. *See also* Christianity; Churches; Religion
Barbados, 40, 41; Charleston settlement and, 70
Barbary states, 248
Barbed wire, 522
Barnard, Eunice Fuller, 726
Barnard, S., 307 (illus.)
Barnum, P.T., 341
Barren Ground (1925), 744
Barrett, John, 659
Barrios, 588, 730, 731; Puerto Rican, 799; of Los Angeles-Long Beach, 940
Barrow, Bennet, 312–313, 418
Barry, Jan, 972n
Barton, Bruce, 728
Barton, Clara, 442
Bartram, John, 113
Bartram, William, 113
Baruch, Bernard, 889
Baruch Plan, 889

Baseball, 579, 581 (illus.), 741, 742; Knickerbocker Club rules and, 342; Black Sox scandal and, 719; Robinson, Jackie, in, 861, 862 (illus.)
Basketball, 580, 581 (illus.)
Bataan Death March, 823–824
Batangas, Philippine Islands, 674
Bathroom, lifestyle and, 550
Batista, Fulgencio, 799, 903 (illus.)
Baton Rouge, Louisiana, growth of, 939
Battle, *see* specific battles
Battle, William, 326
Battle of Antietam, 433
Battle of Bud Dajo, 676
Battle of the Bulge, 823
Battle of Bull Run, 429–430
Battle of Bunker Hill, 162
Battle of Chancellorsville, 448 (illus.), 449–450 and *map*
Battle of Chattanooga, 458
Battle of the Coral Sea (1942), 824 and *map*
Battle of Fallen Timbers, 197, 198 (illus.)
Battle of Fredericksburg, 448 (illus.)
Battle of Gettysburg, 432 (map), 451
Battle of Horseshoe Bend, 256
Battle of Midway (1942), 824 and *map*
Battle of New Orleans, 256–257
Battle of Oriskany, 169–170
Battle of the Philippine Sea (1944), 825
Battle of Put-in-Bay, 256
Battle of Queenstown, 255
Battle of Shiloh, 431
Battle of the Somme, 698
Battle of the Thomas (Canada), 256
Battle of Trafalgar, 248
Battle of Vicksburg, 450–451
Battle of the Wilderness, 460
"Battling Bob", *see* La Follette, Robert M.
Bay of Pigs invasion, 904
Bayonet Constitution, in Hawaii, 655
Beach, Moses Yale, 343–344
Beard, Charles A., 638, 707, 803
Beatles (musical group), 1004 (illus.)
Beat writers, 945–946
Beaumont, Gustave de, 343
Beauregard. P.G.T., 429
Beautification movement, 592
Beaver pelts, 37–38 and *illus.*, 39, 55 (illus.). *See also* Fur trade
Beaver Wars, 81
"Be-bop," 945
Beck, Dave, 927
Bedrock Tom, 510
Beecher, Henry Ward, 398
Beecher sisters, 347
Beef, *see* Cattle
Beekman family, 345
Beer-Wine Revenue Bill, 761
Bees (social-work gatherings), 334, 335 (illus.)
BEF, *see* Bonus Expeditionary Force
Begin, Menachem, 978 (illus.)

Behavior, in 1920s, 733–735. *See also* Lifestyles
Beiderbecke, Bix, 745
Beijing (Peking), 674
Beirut, Lebanon, 982
Belgium, 16, 808. *See also* First World War; Second World War
Belize, *see* British Honduras
Bell, John, 419
Bellamy, Edward, 556
Belleau Wood, 698
Bellomont (Earl of), 63–64
Bemis, Edward, 556
Benefits: Social Security Act and, 770–771; for union workers, 928; health care costs and, 1059
Benefits, workers', 724
Benevolent societies, for women and orphans, 371
Benin, 14
Bennehan, Rebecca, 312 (illus.)
Bennitt, James and Nancy, 311
Ben Tre, Vietnam, 969
Berbers, 12
Berenson, Senda, 580
Bergen-Belsen concentration camp, Holocaust and, 845 (illus.)
Berger, Victor, 630, 708
Beringia, 5
Bering Sea, fishing rights in, 664
Bering Strait, 5
Berkeley, California, counterculture at, 1002–1003
Berkeley, John, 68
Berkeley, William, Bacon's rebellion and, 82
Berlin, Germany: Soviet march to, 823; U-2 incident and, 901; reunification of, 915 (illus.). *See also* Germany
Berlin airlift, 893
Berlin Blockade, 893
Berlin Wall, 902 (illus.), 902–903, 915 (illus.)
Bermuda, 794
Bernard, Francis, 140
Bernstein, Carl, 1018
Bernstein, Leonard, 944 (illus.)
Berry, Chuck, 944
Best Years of Our Lives, The (movie), 848
Bethlehem Steel Company, 535
Bethune, Mary McLeod, 777 and *illus.*
Beuscher, Butch, 751
Beveridge, Albert, 670, 673
Bibb, Henry, 364
Bible, and colonial education, 112; public schools and, 637
Bicameral legislature, 201
Bicycling, 579–580
Biddle, Nicholas, 385
Bierce, Ambrose, 598
Big business: attitudes toward, 555–558, 557 (illus.); in 1920s, 720–722. *See also* Business; Corporations
Big Four, of First World War, 711
Big Three: at Yalta, 844–847; Poland and, 845–846; at Potsdam, 847

John Deere, 292
John I (Portugal), 19
"Johnny Get Your Gun" (song), 697
Johnson, Andrew, 456, 468, 472
(illus.); Reconstruction plan of, 471–
473; impeachment of, 476–477
Johnson, Chalmers, 1064
Johnson, Guy, 159 and *illus.*
Johnson, Hiram, 632
Johnson, James Weldon, 798
Johnson, Lyndon B., 872, 878, 988;
Cold War and, 906–907; war on pov-
erty of, 922; Vietnam War and,
949–952, 964–970; and Tet Offen-
sive (Vietnam), 969; withdrawal from
public life, 970 and *illus.*; and Tet
Offensive (Vietnam), 970 (illus.);
Great Society of, 992–999; 1968 and,
1006–1008
Johnson, Richard M., 388
Johnson, Tom, 591, 629
Johnson, William, 158, 159, 170
Johnson Act (1921), 738
Johnson Doctrine, 976
Johnson-Reid Act (1924), 738
Johnston, Albert Sidney, 431
Johnston, Joseph E., 451, 458
Johnston, William, 741
Joint Chiefs of Staff: Vietnam War
and, 949–951. *See also* Military
Joint Economic Committee, 1026
Joint-stock companies, 44
Jolliet, Louis, 81
Jones, Augustus, 362 (illus.)
Jones, Bobby, 741
Jones, Charles Colcock, Jr., 418
Jones, Mary "Mother," 544
Jones, Samuel "Golden Rule," 591
Jones Act (1917), 799
Jones v. *Mayer* (1968), 998
Joplin, Janis, 1004
Jordan, 975, 982
Journalism, *see* Newspapers
"Journey in the Seaboard Slave States,
A," 310 (illus.)
Journey of Reconciliation (1947),
861
Juan de Fuca Strait, 260
Judd, Walter, 895
Judicial activism, in civil rights,
859–862
Judicial review, principle of, 242
Judicial system, in Massachusetts Bay,
55; under Jefferson, 240–241; in Pro-
gressive era, 637; African-Americans
and, 1041
Judiciary Act (1789), 212–213
Judiciary Act (1801), 240–241
Judiciary Committee, House, 1018
Judiciary Reorganization Bill, 772
Julian, George, 444, 473
Junction City, Kansas, 932
Jungle, The (1906), 629, 646
Jupiter missiles, 906
Jury trials, and Seventh Amendment,
212
Justice Act (1774), 146

Justice Department: Hoover, J. Edgar,
and, 710; civil rights division in, 860;
higher education, restrictive covenants, and, 861
Juvenile Bible Society, 370
Juvenile delinquency, 944

Kaiser, 692 (illus.); and First World
War, 698
Kalakaua (King), 655, 656
Kansas: slavery and, 398; Lecompton
Constitution and, 417; Southern
migration to, 495
Kansas City, 729; political bosses in,
589
Kansas-Nebraska Act (1854), 408
(map), 409–410 and *illus.*; Whig
party and, 409–410; "Bleeding
Kansas" and, 413
Kaskaskia, 81
Katyn Forest, massacre of Poles in, 842
KDKA (Pittsburgh), 728
Kearny, Stephen, 402
Kearny (ship), 811
Keaton, Buster, 741
Kelley, Florence, 591, 625–626, 630,
638
Kelley, Oliver H., 609
Kellogg, John H., 550
Kellogg, Paul, 693
Kellogg, William K., 550
Kellogg-Briand Pact (1928), 791, 806
Kemp, Jack, 1073
Kennan, George F., 888, 889; "X"
article of, 890; Middle East and, 911;
and Vietnam War, 969
Kennedy, Caroline, 987, 990 (illus.)
Kennedy, Edward, 911, 1034; as presi-
dential candidate, 1015, 1030
Kennedy, Jacqueline, 987, 990 (illus.),
992
Kennedy, John, Jr., 990 (illus.)
Kennedy, John F., 877, 883; television
debates and, 878 (illus.); and election
of 1960, 878–879; foreign affairs
and, 902–906; Bay of Pigs invasion
and, 904; Cuban missile crisis and,
904–906, 905 (illus.); Vietnam and,
952; Third World and, 958–960;
Vietnam War and, 963–964; administration of, 987–988; assassination of
(1963), 987–988; background of, 988;
family and, 990 (illus.); assassination
of, 992; legacy of, 992; women's
movement and, 1010
Kennedy, Joseph P., 988; globalism
and, 898
Kennedy, Paul, 1062
Kennedy, Robert, 904, 990; Cuba and,
905; and 1968 election, 1006, 1007;
assassination of, 1007
Kent State University: antiwar protests
at, 971; violence at, 1012 and *illus.*
Kentucky, 227; and westward expansion, 227; and Second Great Awakening, 230; population of (1810), 253

(illus.); Clay (city), 259; as Union
state, 421
Kentucky resolution, 225–226
Kern, Jerome, 581
Kerner, Otto, 1001
Kerner Commission, 1001, 1042
Kerouac, Jack, 946
Kerr, Clark, 1002
Kesey, Ken, 987, 1005 (illus.)
Key, Francis Scott, 256
Keynes, John Maynard, Nixon and,
1013
Khomeini, Ayatollah Ruhollah, 978
Khrushchev, Nikita, 900 (illus.), 900–
901; summit meetings and, 900–901;
Hungarian uprising and (1956), 901;
nuclear testing and, 902
Kidd, William, 63–64
Kim II-sung, 896
King, Coretta Scott, 877 (illus.)
King, Martin Luther, Jr., 876–877,
990, 991, 993 (illus.); Montgomery
bus boycott and, 876; indictment of,
877 (illus.); FBI and, 999; nonvio-
lence and, 1001, 1002; assassination
of, 1006–1007. *See also* Civil rights
movement
King, Rodney, racial tensions and, 1073
King, Rufus, 245, 250
"King Cotton" diplomacy, 457
King George's War, 102–103, 117,
125, 127; impact of, 105
King of Kings, The (movie), 741
King Philip's War, 82
King's Mountain, battle at, 174
Kingston (New York), 337
King William's War, 89, 127
Kinsey, Alfred, 937
Kinship, of Native Americans, 12; fam-
ily life and, 578. *See also* Families
Kinship taboos, African, 321
Kipling, Rudyard, 562, 673
Kissinger, Henry, 907, 971, 1016; inter-
national order and, 952–953; shuttle
diplomacy of, 975 and *illus.*; Middle
East and, 975–976
Kitchen Cabinet, of Jackson, Andrew,
382
Kitchin, Claude, 695
Klamaths, termination and, 871
Klinger family, 331–332, 353
Knickerbocker Club, 342, 579
Knights of Labor, 541–542, 544, 611
Knights of the Golden Circle, 455
Knowland, William, 895
Know-Nothing party, 410–411; elec-
tion of 1856 and, 414
Knox, Frank, 808
Knox, Henry, 214
Knox College (Illinois), 486
Koale-xoa, 294
Konoye (of Japan), 811
Koop, C. Everett, 1051
Korea, 845; imperialism in, 674; Japan
in, 805; division of, 894; immigration
from, 1044. *See also* Korean War;
North Korea; South Korea

I-44   INDEX

Chapter Opening Photo Credits (Continued)

Page 266: Detail of *Progress of Cotton, No. 12 Printing* by Barfoot, ca. 1840. Copyright Yale University Art Gallery, Mabel Brady Garvan Collection.

Page 300: Detail of *St. John Plantation* by A. Persac, 1861. Courtesy Louisiana State University Museum of Art, Baton Rouge. Gift of the Friends of the Museum and Mrs. Ben Hamilton in memory of her mother, Mrs. Tela Meier Hamilton.

Page 330: Detail of *Moving Day in Philadelphia*, ca. 1829, artist unknown. Courtesy of Mr. and Mrs. Screven Lorillard, photo by Joshua Nefsky.

Page 366: Detail of *The County Election, Number Two* by George Caleb Bingham, 1854. Collection of Mr. and Mrs. Wilson Pile. Photo by Clive Russ.

Page 398: Detail of *Landing of the Troops at Veracruz*, artist unknown, 1848. Amon Carter Museum, Fort Worth, Texas.

Page 426: Detail of a Union encampment. Photo courtesy of the International Museum of Photography, George Eastman House.

Page 466: Detail of *The Shackle Broken by the Genius of Freedom*. Color lithograph published by E. Sachs & Company, Baltimore, 1874. Photo courtesy of the Chicago Historical Society.

Page 498: Detail of *Cliffs of Green River* by Thomas Moran, 1874. Amon Carter Museum, Fort Worth, Texas.

Page 528: Detail of *Topping the Furnace*, Harper's Weekly, November 1, 1873.

Page 560: *Jefferson Market* by John Sloan, 1922. Courtesy of the Pennsylvania Academy of the Fine Arts, Philadelphia, Henry D. Gilpin Fund.

Page 596: Detail of *Electioneering in a Country Town, 1913* by E. L. Henry. Private Collection.

Page 624: Hand-colored photograph of Theodore Roosevelt Campaigning, 1905. California Museum of Photography, University of California at Riverside.

Page 654: Detail of United States Fleet in the Straits of Magellan the morning of February 8, 1908. United States Naval Academy Museum.

Page 684: Detail of The Prisoners and the wounded, October 1918, by Harvey Dunn. Smithsonian Institution, Division of Political History.

Page 718: Detail of Commonwealth Edison Company Yearbook, 1927. Courtesy of Commonwealth Edison Company, Chicago.

Page 750: Detail of *Tenements and Tracks* by Harry Leith-Ross, Private Collection.

Page 786: Hand-colored photograph of Mr. and Mrs. Hoover on deck during their South American Tour, December 1928. Wide World Photos.

Page 816: Detail of antiaircraft crew in action by Dean Cornwell. U.S. Army Center of Military History, Washington, D.C.

Page 850: © Al Hirschfeld. Detail of drawing reproduced by special arrangement with Hirschfeld's exclusive representative, The Margo Feiden Galleries Ltd., New York.

Page 882: ICBMs, *Colliers Magazine*, March 16, 1956. The Michael Barson Collection, Glen Ridge, N.J.

Page 920: Teen with Hula-Hoop. Photo by Bill Ray, LIFE Magazine © Time Warner Inc.

Page 948: Soldiers and helicopter, Vietnam. Philip Jones Griffiths/Magnum Photos.

Page 986: Selma, 1965. Dan Budnik/Woodfin Camp & Associates.

Page 1022: People campaigning for Reagan, October 1980. Michael Evans/Sygma.

Page 1058: Hillary Clinton at Capitol Hill with Senator George Mitchell. Photo by Jerry Markowitz/Sygma.

An Invitation to Respond

We would like to find out a little about your background and about your reactions to the fourth edition of *A People and a Nation*. Your evaluation of the book will help us to meet the interests and needs of students in future editions. We invite you to share your reactions by completing the questionnaire below and returning it to *College Marketing, Houghton Mifflin Company, 222 Berkeley Street, Boston, MA 02116.*

1. How do you rate this textbook in the following areas?

	Excellent	*Good*	*Adequate*	*Poor*
a. Understandable style of writing	_____	____	_____	____
b. Physical appearance/readability	_____	____	_____	____
c. Fair coverage of topics	_____	____	_____	____
d. Comprehensiveness (covered major issues and time periods)	_____	____	_____	____
e. *How Do Historians Know?*	_____	____	_____	____
f. Presentation of maps and artwork	_____	____	_____	____

2. Can you comment on or illustrate your above ratings? _____

_____

_____

_____

3. What chapters or features did you particularly like? _____

_____

_____

_____

4. How interesting did you find the chapter-opening stories? _____

_____

_____

_____

5. What chapters or features did you dislike or think should be changed?

_____

_____

_____

6. What material would you suggest adding or deleting? _____

_____

_____

_____

7. Are you a student at a community college or a four-year school? _____

_____

8. Do you intend to major in history? _____

9. Did you use the *Study Guide* that accompanies this textbook?

_____ Yes _____ No

10. We would appreciate any other comments or reactions you are willing to share. _____

_____

_____